A SELECT LIBRARY

OF

NICENE AND POST-NICENE FATHERS

OF

THE CHRISTIAN CHURCH

Second Series.

TRANSLATED INTO ENGLISH WITH PROLEGOMENA AND EXPLANATORY NOTES

UNDER THE EDITORIAL SUPERVISION OF

PHILIP SCHAFF, D.D., LL.D., AND HENRY WACE, D.D.,

Professor of Church History in the Union Theological Seminary,   *Principal of King's College,*
New York.   *London.*

IN CONNECTION WITH A NUMBER OF PATRISTIC SCHOLARS OF EUROPE AND AMERICA.

VOLUME IV.

ST. ATHANASIUS:

SELECT WORKS AND LETTERS.

T&T CLARK
EDINBURGH

WM. B. EERDMANS PUBLISHING COMPANY
GRAND RAPIDS, MICHIGAN

British Library Cataloguing in Publication Data

Nicene & Post-Nicene Fathers. — 2nd series
1. Fathers of the church
I. Schaff, Philip   II. Mace, Henry
230′.11   BR60.A62

T&T Clark ISBN 0 567 09413 8

Eerdmans ISBN 0-8028-8118-1

Reprinted, June 1991

EDITORIAL PREFACE

It is with a sense of deep obligation to Mr. Robertson, the special editor, that this volume of the Post-Nicene series of the Fathers is presented to the subscribers and the public. It will furnish, as is believed, a more comprehensive and thorough introduction to the study of Athanasius than is elsewhere accessible, and the labour and devotion bestowed upon it are beyond all acknowledgment. Thanks must also be expressed to the publishers, by whose liberality the ordinary limits of the volumes of this series have been extended, in order that so important a Father as Athanasius might be represented with as much fulness as possible.

Mr. Robertson's Preface explains the care and respect with which the translation and notes of Cardinal Newman have been treated, in reprinting them for the purpose of this edition. But there appeared in some parts of the translation inaccuracies which could not be reproduced consistently with a faithful representation of the original; and so far, therefore, and so far only, it has been corrected. Where any correction has been made in the Cardinal's notes, it is of course distinctly specified.

I must add an expression of particular gratitude to my friend, the Rev. J. H. Lupton, Surmaster of St. Paul's School, for his generous help in reading the translations throughout, and for various valuable suggestions. The assistance of his scholarly learning gives me additional confidence in presenting this volume to the public.

I must take the opportunity of expressing my great regret that there has been so considerable an interruption in the issue of the series. But by the sudden failure, partly from illness, and partly from other unforeseen causes, of two important contributions at the very moment when they were needed, the editor and the publishers were exposed to difficulties which were for the time insuperable. But other volumes of the series are now steadily progressing, and it is believed there will be no further interruptions in the publication.

HENRY WACE.

King's College, London,
  21 *Nov.* 1891.

PREFACE

In preparing the present volume the Editor has aimed at providing the English reader with the most complete apparatus for the study of Athanasius, his life, and his theological influence, which could be brought within the compass of a single volume of the 'Nicene and Post-Nicene Library.' The volume contains all the most important treatises of Athanasius (in as nearly as possible their exact chronological order), with the exception of the *ad Serapionem*, the *contra Apollinarium*, the *ad Marcellinum*, and the exegetical remains. On these and other treatises omitted from the present collection the reader is referred to the Prolegomena, ch. iii.

A great part of the volume, including the bulk of the historical and anti-Arian works, and the Festal Letters, consists of a revision of translations and notes comprised in the Oxford Library of the Fathers. The notes to all, and the translation of most, of the works in question, excepting the Festal Letters, were prepared for that series by Mr. (since Cardinal) Newman. It was at first intended to incorporate his work without any change; but as the volume began to take shape this intention was inevitably to some extent modified; moreover, the limits of space demanded the sacrifice of some of the less important matter. The principles upon which the necessary changes have been made will be found stated on pp. 304, 305, 450. What is there said applies also to the *de Decretis* and *Letter of Eusebius*, as well as to the notes to the historical pieces; it may be added that the translation of the 'Fourth Discourse' has been very carefully revised, in order to secure the utmost closeness to the some what difficult original. In all the new translations, as well as in the revision of earlier work, the aim has been to secure the strictest fidelity compatible with clearness. The easy assumption that distinctions of tenses, constructions, &c., count for little or nothing in patristic Greek has been steadily resisted. Doubtless there are passages where the distinction, for example, of aorist and perfect, seems to fade away; but generally speaking, Athanasius is fully sensitive to this and other points of grammar.

The incorporation in this volume of so much of the ample patristic learning of Cardinal Newman has inevitably involved some sacrifice of uniformity. To provide the new matter with illustrative notes on anything like the same scale, even had it been within the present editor's power, would have involved the crowding out of many works which the reader will certainly prefer to have before him. Again, many opinions are expressed by Cardinal Newman which the present editor is unable to accept. It may not be invidious to specify as an example the many cases in which the notes enforce views of Church authority, especially of papal authority, or again of the justifiableness of religious persecution, which appear to be at any rate foreign to the mind of Athanasius; or the tacit assumption that the men of the fourth century can be divided by a broad and fast line into orthodox and heretical, and that while everything may be believed to the discredit of the latter, the former were at once uniform in their convictions and consistently right in practice. Such an assumption operates with special injustice against men like Eusebius, whose position does not fall in with so summary a classification. But it has been thought better to leave the notes in nearly all such cases as they stand, only very rarely inserting a reference or observation to call attention to another aspect of the case. And in no instance has the editor forgotten the respect due to the theological learning and personal greatness of Cardinal Newman, or to his peculiar eminence as a religious thinker.

But this has made it inevitable that many matters are regarded in one way in the notes of Newman, and in quite another where the present editor speaks for himself. What the great Cardinal says of his 'Historical Sketches' (Preface to vol. ii.) holds good to a large extent of his expositions of Athanasius. 'Though mainly historical, they are in their form and character polemical, as being directed against certain Protestant ideas and opinions.' The aim of the

SELECT WRITINGS AND LETTERS

OF

ATHANASIUS, BISHOP OF ALEXANDRIA.

EDITED, WITH PROLEGOMENA, INDICES, AND TABLES,

BY

ARCHIBALD ROBERTSON,

PRINCIPAL OF BISHOP HATFIELD'S HALL, DURHAM, LATE FELLOW OF TRINITY COLLEGE, OXFORD.

present editor has been throughout exclusively historical. He has regarded any polemical purpose as foreign to the spirit in which this series was undertaken, and moreover as fated in the long run to defeat its own aim. Whatever results may ultimately be reaped from the field of patristic studies, whether practical, dogmatic, or controversial, they must be resolutely postponed or rather ignored, pending the application of strict method to the criticism and interpretation of the texts, and to the reconstruction of the history whether of the life or of the doctrine of the Church. For the latter purpose, 'lucifera experimenta, non fructifera quærenda.' To follow this method, without concealing, but without obtruding, his personal convictions, has been the endeavour of the present editor. That he has succeeded, it is not for him to claim: but his work has been in this respect disinterested, and he ventures to hope that readers of all opinions will at least recognise in it 'un livre de bonne foy.'

The Prolegomena are not intended to be anything approaching to a complete treatise upon the history, writings, or theology of S. Athanasius. They are simply what their title implies, an attempt to furnish in a connected form a preliminary account of the matters comprised in the text of the volume, such as on the one hand to reduce the necessity for a running historical commentary, on the other hand to prepare the reader for the study of the text itself.

Full indices have been added for the same purpose. The general index comprises the leading theological and historical topics, and a complete register of all personal names. This latter seemed requisite in order to escape the arbitrariness of any line which might have been drawn between important and insignificant characters. The nobodies of history may occasionally be important witnesses. The index of Scripture texts has been made with painful attention to detail, and contains no unverified reference. To draw the line in each case between formal citation and mere reminiscence would have involved too great an expenditure of time and space; moreover there are many probable reminiscences of Scripture language which it would have been endless to include. But on the whole the index in question claims to be a complete synopsis of the use made of the Bible in the text of this volume. As such it is hoped that, with whatever occasional errors, it may be of use to the patristic and the biblical student alike.

For the original matter comprised in this volume the editor disclaims any credit of his own. He has aimed simply at consulting and comparing the best authorities, at sifting their conclusions, and at following those which seem best founded. That in doing so the original sources are ready to hand throughout is the peculiar good fortune of those who work at Athanasius. It remains, then, for the editor to express his principal obligations to modern writers. To mention those of earlier date, such as Montfaucon and Tillemont, is merely to say that he has not neglected the indispensable foundations of his task. But Athanasius has also attracted to the study of his works much of the best patristic scholarship of recent times. Among the names mentioned in the first chapter of the Prolegomena, that of Cardinal Newman speaks for itself. No English student will neglect his *Arians*, however much some of its views may require modification. Pre-eminent for accurate knowledge of the texts and for vivid presentment of the history is Dr. Bright, whose works have been constantly open before the present editor, and have secured him from many an oversight. His occasional divergence from Dr. Bright's views, especially on points of chronology, has gone along with grateful appreciation of this scholar's genuine historical interest, large theological grasp, and perhaps unequalled personal sympathy with Athanasius as a man and as a writer. (On the use made in this volume of his *Later Treatises of S. Athanasius*, the reader is referred to what is said, *infr.* p. 482.)

Last, but not least, the editor must acknowledge his obligations to Mr. Gwatkin. To say that that writer's *Studies of Arianism* have done more than any one work with which he is acquainted to place the intricate story of the period on a secure historical footing is saying a great deal, but by no means too much. To say that whatever historical accuracy has been attained in this volume has been rendered possible by Mr. Gwatkin's previous labours is to the present writer a matter of mere honest acknowledgment. Especially this is the case in chronological questions. Here Mr. Gwatkin has in no single instance been blindly followed, or without the attempt to interrogate the sources independently. But in nearly all cases Mr. Gwatkin's results, which, it should be added, are those accepted by the best continental students also, have held their own. It has been the editor's misfortune to differ from Mr. Gwatkin now and then, for example with regard to the Life of Antony: but even where he has differed as to conclusions, he has received help and instruction from Mr. Gwatkin's ample command of material, and genuinely scientific method.

In addition to the above writers, the manifold obligations of the editor are recorded in the introductions and notes: if any have been passed over, it has been due to inadvertence or to the necessity of condensation. For the suggestions and help of personal friends the editor's gratitude may be here expressed without the mention of names. But he may specially mention the Rev. H. Ellershaw and Miss Payne Smith, to the former of whom he owes the translation of the Life of Antony, while the latter has kindly revised the Oxford translation of the bulk of the Festal Letters. Lastly, the many kindnesses, and uniform consideration, shewn to him by the English editor of this series call for his warmest recognition: that they may prove not wholly thrown away is the utmost that their recipient can venture to hope.

The University, Durham, A. R.
 1891.

CONTENTS OF VOLUME IV.

*N.B. The Introductions are in every case by Rev. A. Robertson; the translations and the notes are by him except where otherwise stated. All additions made by him to Dr. Newman's notes are included in square brackets.

PROLEGOMENA

CHAPTER I

LITERATURE

§ 1. EDITIONS, &c. (A) Before 1601 only Latin translations. The first, at VICENZA, 1482, completed by Barnabas Celsanus after the death of the translator OMNIBONUS of Lonigo ; dedicated to Paul II. Contained a few works only, viz. the 'two books *c. Gentes*,' the letter to Serapion *de Morte Arii*, the *De Incarn. adv. Arian.* and *adv. Apollin.*, the 'Dispute with Arius at the Council of Nicæa.' (2) PARIS, 1520, pub. by Jean PETIT: two books *c. Gent.* fragment of the *ad Marcellin.* and some 'spuria.' (3) Second edition at STRASS-BURG, 1522. (4) BASEL, 1527, by ERASMUS : *Serap.* iii. and iv., *de Decr.*, *Apol. Fug.*, *Apol. c. Ar.* (part of), '*ad Monach.*,' and some 'spuria' (he rejected *Serap.* i. as unworthy of Athan. !). (5) LYONS, 1532, same contents as numbers (2) and (4), but with renderings by Politian, Reuchlin, Erasmus, &c. (6) COLOGNE, 1632, similar contents. (7) 1556, BASEL ('apud Frobenium'), by P. NANNIUS, in 4 volumes ; great advance on previous editions. 3 vols. contain the version by Nannius of the 'genuina,' the fourth 'spuria,' rendered by others. The Nannian version was ably tested, and found wanting, under the direction of the congregation of the Index (Migne xxv. pp. xviii. *sqq.*). (8) 1564 (or 1584?) BASEL (substantially the same). (9) 1570, PARIS, *Vita Antonii* and 'five dialogues *de Trin.*,' version of Beza. (10) 1572, PARIS, five volumes, combining Nos. 7 and 9. (11) 1574, PARIS, Letter *ad Amun*, *Letter* 39 (fragment), Letter *ad Rufinianum*. (12) 1581, PARIS, incorporating the latter with No. 10. (13) ROME, 1623, the spurious *de variis quæstionibus*.

(B) The first Greek Edition (14) 1601 at HEIDELBERG by COMMELINUS, with the Nannian Latin version (2 vols. fo. with a supplement of fragments, letters, &c., communicated by P. Felckmann). This edition was founded upon Felckmann's collation of numerous MSS., of which the chief were (α) that in the Public Library at Basel (sæc. xiv., *not* ix. as Felck. states ; formerly belonged to the Dominican Friary there). (β) The 'Codex Christophorsoni,' now at Trin. Coll., Camb., sæc. xvi. *ineunt*. (γ) A 'Codex Goblerianus' dated 1319, formerly τῆς μονῆς τοῦ κυρίζου, and principally used by Nannius. Neither this nor the remaining MSS. of Felckmann are as yet, I believe, identified. (Particulars, Migne, P.G. xxv. p. xliii.) (15) 1608, PARIS, pub. by C. Chappelet, edited by Fronton le Duc, S.J., Latin only. (17) 1612, PARIS, No. 15, with *Vit. Ant.* in Greek and Latin, from an edition (16) of 1611, AUGSBURG, by Höschel, 4°. (18) 1627, PARIS, Greek text of 1601 with version of Nannius from edition No. 17, both injudiciously revised by Jean le Pescheur, from the critical notes of Felckmann himself,[b] which however are omitted in this edition. (19) 'Cologne,' or rather LEIPZIG, 1686, poor reprint of No. 18 with the *Syntagma Doctrinæ* which Arnold had published in the previous year (see below, ch. ii. § 9). (Montf. wrongly dates this 1681.)

(c) All the above were entirely superseded by the great (20) **1698 Paris Benedictine** Edition by Bernard de MONTFAUCON, aided, for part of vol. 1, by Jacques Loppin, 3 volumes fol. (i.e. vol. 1, parts 1 and 2, 'genuina,' vol. 2 'dubia et spuria'), with a NEW Latin Version and ample prolegomena, &c. Montfaucon took over, apparently without revision, the critical data of Felckmann (including his mistake as to the age of the Basel MS.), but collated very many fresh MSS. (principally Parisian, full particulars in Migne xxvi. pp. 1449, *sqq.*), and for the first time put the text on a fairly satisfactory footing. The Works of Athanasius were freshly arranged with an attempt at chronological order, and a 'Monitum' or short introduction prefixed to each. Critical, and a few explanatory, notes throughout ; also an 'onomasticon' or glossary. This splendid edition was far more complete than its predecessors, and beautifully printed. After its completion, Montfaucon discovered fresh material, most of which he published in vol. 2 of his 'COLLECTIO NOVA PATRUM,' Paris, 1706, with some further supplementary matter to his Prolegomena, partly in reply to Tillemont upon various critical questions ; small additions in his *Biblioth. Coisliniana*, 1715. (The letters to Lucifer, included in Mont-faucon's edition, had already seen the light in vol. iv. of the Bibliotheca Maxima Patrum (Lyons, 1677, Greek fathers in Latin only), and the two notes to Orsisius were taken from the life of Pachomius in the Acta SS. for May.)

(21) 1746, ROME, the *de Titulis Psalmorum*, edited from Barberini and Vatican MSS. by Cardinal Niccolo ANTONELLI. (22) 1769, VENICE, part v. of the 'Bibliotheca Patrum' of the Oratorian Andrea GALLANDI. Contains the works omitted in No. 20, chiefly from Montf. *Coll. Nov.*, but with a few minor additions, and with the fragments and letters found by Maffei at Verona (see below, pp. 495, 554). (23) 1777, PADUA, by GIUSTINIANI, in four volumes, containing firstly Montfaucon's 'genuina' in two volumes, the 'dubia' and 'spuria' in the third, and the supplementary matter from (21) and (22) in the fourth. The printing of this standard edition is not equal to that of No. 20. (24) '1884' (1857), PARIS, vols. xxv.—xxviii. of MIGNE's Patrologia Græca, a reprint of No. 23, but in a new order (see vol. xxviii. p. 1650), and with the addition of the *Festal Letters* from Mai (see below, p. 501). The merits and demerits of this series are well known. Of the latter, the most serious are the misprints, with which every page literally teems.

(D) With Migne's edition the publication of a complete Athanasius (so far as his works are known to be extant) is attained, although there is still everything to be done towards the revision of the text on a critical basis. Among modern editions of large portions of Athanasius from the Benedictine text may be mentioned (25) THILO, *Athan. Opp. dogm. Selecta*, Leipz. 1853. (26) BRIGHT, *Orations against the Arians* (1873 2nd ed. 1883), and *Historical Writings* of Athanasius, 1881 (Oxf. Univ. Press), with Introductions ; both most convenient ; his *Lessons from the lives of three great Fathers* (Longmans, 1890) gives an interesting popular study of Athan. Editions of separate books will be noticed in the short Introductions prefixed in this volume.

§ 2. TRANSLATIONS. The principal Latin versions have been referred to in § 1. Of those in foreign languages it is not easy to procure adequate information. Fialon, in the work mentioned below, translates *Apol. Const.* and *Apol. Fug.* ; in German the 'Bibliothek der Kirchenväter,' vols. 13—18, *Ausgew. Schriften des h. Ath.*, contains translations of several works by FISCH, Kempten from 1872. The principal English Translations are those in the 'Library of the Fathers.' Of these, those edited or translated by NEWMAN are incorporated in this volume. Some letters included in this volume, as well as the work against Apollinarianism, are also comprised in the volume (*Lib. Fath.* 46, 1881) by BRIGHT, with excellent notes, &c., and with a preface by Dr. Pusey (see below, p. 482). Translations of single books will be noticed in the respective Introductions.

§ 3. BIOGRAPHIES. (a.) *Ancient.* The writings of Athanasius himself, while seldom furnishing precise chronological data, furnish almost all the primary information as to the facts of his eventful life. The earliest 'Life' is the panegyric of GREGORY of Nazianzus (Or. 21), delivered at CP. 379 or 380, rich in praises, but less so in historical material. More important in the latter respect is the *Historia Acephala* (probably earlier than 390) printed in this volume, pp. 496, *sqq.* (The Edition by SIEVERS in *Ztschr. für Hist. Theol.* for 1868 is referred to in this volume as 'Sievers' simply.) It is a priceless source of chronological information, especially where it coincides with and confirms the data of the *Festal Index* (pp. 503, *sqq.*), a document probably earlier than 400. A secondary place is occupied by the Church historians, especially Socrates, Sozomen, and Theodoret, who draw largely from Athanasius himself, and from Rufinus, also in part from the *Hist. Aceph.* (especially Sozomen), and from Arian sources, which are mainly used by Philostorgius. More scattered notices in later ecclesiastical writers of the fourth century, especially Epiphanius ; also Synesius, Jerome, Basil, &c., in the documents of the Councils, &c., and in the Life of Pachomius and other early documents relating to Egyptian Monasticism (see below, Introd. to *Vit. Anton.* and Appendix, pp 188, 487).

(b) *Medieval.* Under this head we may notice the Lives printed by Montfaucon among his Prolegomena. The first, 'Incerto Auctore,' is dependent on the fifth-century historians and of no value. A second, preserved by Photius (c. 840) is in the judgment of that scholar, which Montfaucon endorses, 'unparalleled rubbish.' That by the Metaphrast († 967) is a patchwork from earlier writers made with little skill, and not of use to the historian. An Arabic Life current in the Coptic Church, communicated to Montf. by Renandot, is given by Montf., as he says, that his readers may appreciate the 'stupendous ignorance and triviality' of that nation. Montf. mentions Latin 'Lives' compiled from Rufinus and from the *Hist. Tripartita*, 'of no value whatever.' Of the Life of Athanasius 'by Pachomius,' mentioned by Archd. Farrar (*infra*), I can obtain no particulars.

(c) *Modern.* The first was that by Tortelius prefixed to the edition of 1520 (§ 1 (2)), but compiled in the previous century and dedicated to Pope Eugenius IV. ('good for its time,' M.). Montf. mentions a valueless life by Lipomanus, and a worse one of unknown origin prefixed to other early editions. In 1671 HERMANT made the first attempt at a critical biography (Paris) ; in 1664 an English work, "History of the Life and Actions of St. Athanasius by N.B. *P.C.* Catholick," with the *imprimatur* of Abp. Sheldon, had been published at London, in 1677 the biography in Cave, *Lives of the Fathers*, and in 1686—1704 du Pin, *Nouvelle Bibliothèque*. About the same date appeared the first volume of the Acta SS. for May, which contains a careful life by PAPEBROCH (1685 ; ded. to Innocent XI.). But all previous (to say nothing of subsequent) labours were cast into the shade by the appearance of the 'Vita' of MONTFAUCON (Prolegg. to Tom. 1) in 1698, in which the chronology was reduced to order, and every particle of information lucidly digested ; and by the 'Memoires' of 'M. Lenain de TILLEMONT' (vol. viii. in 1702), which go over the ground with quite equal thoroughness, and on many points traverse the conclusions of Montfaucon, whose work came into Tillemont's hands only when the latter was on his death-bed (1698). The ground was once more traversed with some fulness and with special attention to the literary and doctrinal work of Athan. by Remy CEILLIER (*Aut. Sacrés*, vol. v. 1735). After this nothing remained to be done until the revival of interest in patristic studies during the present century. In 1827 appeared the monograph of MÖHLER 'Ath. der Grösse' (Mainz), a dogmatic (R.C.) rather than a historical study : in 1862 STANLEY ('Eastern Church,' Lect. vii.). BÖHRINGER's life (in vol. 6 of *Kirchengesch. in Biographien*, 1860—1879) is praised as 'thoroughly good and nearly exhaustive.' FIALON *St. Athanase*, Paris, 1877, is a most interesting and suggestive, though rather sketchy, treatment from an unusual point of view. P. BARBIER *Vie de St. A.* (Tours, 1888) I have not seen. The best English life is that of Dr. BRIGHT, first in the Introd. to the 'Orations' (*supra*, § 1, d. 26), but rewritten for the Dictionary of Christ. Biography. The same writer's Introd. to the *Hist. Writings* (*supra ib.*) is equally good and should also be consulted. A lucid and able sketch by Dr. REYNOLDS has been published by the Religious Tract Society, 1889, and Archd. FARRAR, *Lives of the Fathers*, I, pp. 445—571, is eloquent and sympathetic.

§ 4. HISTORY OF THE PERIOD, AND OF THE ARIAN CONTROVERSY. (a) Conflict of the Church with Heathenism. On the later persecutions AUBÉ, *Les Chrétiens dans l'Emp. romain*, Paris, 1881, id. '*L'église et l'état*,' ib. 1886, UHLHORN *Der Kampf des Christentums*, &c. (4th. ed.), 1886, BERNHARDT, *Gesch. Roms von Valerian bis Dioklet.*, 1876, GÖRRES, *Licinianische Christenverfolgung*, 1875. On Diocletian, MASON, *Persec. of Diocl.*, 1876, Monographs by VOGEL, 1857, PREUSS, 1869. On the general subject of the decline of paganism, LASAULX, *Untergang des Hellenismus*, 1854, Merivale's Boyle Lectures, 1864-5, CHASTEL, *Destruction du Paganisme*, 1850, SCHULTZE, *Gesch. des Untergangs des G.-R. Heidentums*, 1887 (not praised), DÖLLINGER, *Gentile and Jew* (E. Tr.), 1862. On the revival of paganism under Julian, RENDALL, *Julian*, 1879, Bp. J. WORDSWORTH in D.C.B., vol. iii., lives of Julian by NEANDER, 1813, RODE, 1877, MÜCKE, 1879, NAVILLE, 1877, STRAUSS, *der Romantiker, u.s.w.*, 1847, Julian's works, ed. HERTLEIN, 1875, and NEUMANN, 1880. Monographs by AUER, 1855, MANGOLD, 1862, SEMISCH, 1862, LÜBKER, 1864 ; CAPES, *University Life in Ancient Athens*, 1877, SIEVERS, *Leben des Libanius*, 1868.

(b) *The Christian Empire.* KEIM, *Uebertritt Konstantins*, 1862, BRIEGER, *Konst. der G.*, 1880, GIBBON's chapters on the subject should be carefully read. CHAWNER's *Legisl. of Constantine*, DE BROGLIE, *L'église et L'emp. romain*, iii., RANKE, *Weltgesch.* iv. pp. 1—100 (important), 1884, SCHILLER, *Gesch. der röm. Kaiserzeit* (ii.), 1887. See also the full bibliography in vol. 1 of this series, p. 445—465.

(c) *General History of the Church.* It is unnecessary to enumerate the well-known general histories, all of which devote special pains to Athanasius and the Arian controversy. This is especially the case with SCHAFF, *Nicene Christ.* ii. 616—678, 884—893, with full bibliography. See also supra § 3. BRIGHT'S *Notes on the Canons* (Oxf. 1882), and HEFELE, vol. 2 (E. Tra.), are most useful: also KAYE, *Council of Nicæa* (Works, vol. v. ed. 1888). Card. HERGENRÖTHER'S *Kirchengeschichte* (allowing for the natural bias of the writer) is fair and able, with good bibliographical references in the notes (ed. 1884). By far the best modern historical monograph on the Arian period is that of GWATKIN, *Studies of Arianism*, 1882, constantly referred to in this volume, and indispensable. His *Arian Controversy*, 1889, is an abridgement, but with supplementary discussions of importance on one or two points; very useful bibliography prefixed to both. (Cf. also below, Chap. v. § 1) KÖLLING'S *Geschichte der Arianischen Häresie* (1st vol., 1874, 2nd, 1883) is pretentious and uncritical.

§ 5. HISTORY OF DOCTRINE. For ancient sources see articles HERESIOLOGY and PERSON OF CHRIST in D.C.B., vols. iii., iv. The modern classics are the works of PETAVIUS, *de Trinitate* (in vols. ii. and iii. of his *De dogmat. Theol.*) of THOMASSINUS, *Dogmata Theologica*, and of BULL, *Defensio fidei Nicænæ* (maintaining against Petav. the fixity of pre-Nicene doctrine). Under this head we include NEWMAN'S *Arians of the Fourth Century*, an English classic, unrivalled as a dogmatic and religious study of Arianism, although unsatisfactory on its purely historical side. (Obsolete chronology retained in all editions.) The general histories of Doctrine are of course full on the subject of Arianism; for an enumeration of them, see Harnack, § 2 of his Prolegomena. In English we have SHEDD (N. Y., 1863, Edinb., 1884), HAGENBACH (Clark's *Foreign Theol. Lib.*), and the great work of DORNER (id.). The most important recent works are those of HARNACK, *Dogmengeschichte* (1886, third vol., 1890), a most able work and (allowing for the prepossessions of the Ritschl school) impartial and philosophical; and LOOFS, *Leitfaden zur Dogmengeschichte* (2 ed., 1890), on similar lines, but studiously temperate and fair. Both works are much used in this volume (quoted commonly as 'Harnack,' 'Loofs,' simply. Harnack, vol. i., is quoted from the *first* edition, but the later editions give comparative tables of the pages). For *Councils and Creeds*, in addition to the works of Hefele and Bright mentioned § 4 c., see HEURTLEY, *Harmonia Symbolica*; HAHN, *Bibliothek der Symbole*; HORT, *Two Dissertations* (1876), indispensable for history of the Nicene Creed; SWAINSON, *Nicene and Apostles' Creed*, 1875; CASPARI, *Ungedruckte u.s.w. Quellen zum Taufsymbol u.s.w.* (3 vols. in 2, Christiania, 1866—1875), and *Alte und Neue Quellen*, ib. 1879; one of the most important of modern pa'ristic works.

§ 6. PATRISTIC MONOGRAPHS. (a) Among the very numerous works of this kind, the most useful for our purpose are ZAHN, *Marcellus von Ancyra*, 1867, very important for doctrinal history; REINKENS, *Hilarius von Poitiers*, 1864; FIALON, *St. Basile*, 1868; ULLMANN, *Gregorius von Nazianz* (2 ed., 1867, part of earlier ed. trans. by Cox, 1855); KRÜGER, *Lucifer von Calaris* (excellent, especially for the Council of 362). Under this head may be mentioned the numerous excellent articles in *Dict. Chr. Biog.* referred to in their respective connexions.

(b) *On the doctrine of Athanasius.* In addition to the works of Ceillier and Möhler referred to above, ATZBERGER, *Die Logoslehre des h. Ath.* (Munich, 1880); VOIGT, *Die Lehre des Athan.* (Bremen, 1861); PELL, *Lehre des h. Ath. von der Sünde und Erlösung* (Passau, 1888, a careful and meritorious analysis, candidly in the interest of Roman Catholicism. Difficulties not always faced).

The above list of authorities, &c., does not pretend to completeness, nor to enumerate the sources for *general* secular or Church history. But in what relates specially to Athanasius it is hoped that an approximation to either requirement has been attained. Works bearing on more special points are referred to in their proper places. In particular, a special BRIEF BIBLIOGRAPHY is prefixed to the VITA ANTONII.

CHAPTER II.

LIFE OF ST. ATHANASIUS AND ACCOUNT OF ARIANISM.

Id primum scitu opus est in proposito nobis minime fuisse ut omnia ad Arium Arianos aliosque haereticos illius aetatis itidemque Alexandrum Alexandrinum Hosium Marcellum Serapionem aliosque Athanasii familiares aut synodos spectantia recensere sed solummodo ea quæ uel ad Athanasii Vitam pertinent uel ad eam proxime accedunt.—MONTFAUCON.

Athanasius was born between 296 and 298[1]. His parents, according to later writers, were of high rank and wealthy. At any rate, their son received a liberal education. In his most youthful work we find him repeatedly quoting Plato, and ready with a definition from the Organon of Aristotle. He is also familiar with the theories of various philosophical schools, and in particular with the developments of Neo-Platonism. In later works, he quotes Homer more than once (*Hist. Ar.* 68, *Orat.* iv. 29), he addresses to Constantius a defence bearing unmistakeable traces of a study of Demosthenes *de Corona* (Fialon, pp. 286 *sq.* 293). His education was that of a Greek: Egyptian antiquities and religion, the monuments and their history, have no special interest for him: he nowhere betrays any trace of Egyptian national feeling. But from early years another element had taken a first place in his training and in his interest. It was in the Holy Scriptures that his martyr teachers had instructed him, and in the Scriptures his mind and writings are saturated. Ignorant of Hebrew, and only rarely appealing to other Greek versions (to Aquila once in the Ecthesis, to other versions once or twice upon the Psalms), his knowledge of the Old Testament is limited to the Septuagint. But of it, as well as of the New Testament, he has an astonishing command, Ἀλεξανδρεὺς τῷ γένει, ἀνὴρ λόγιος, δυνατὸς ὢν ἐν ταῖς γραφαῖς. The combination of Scriptural study and of Greek learning was what one expects in a pupil of the famous Alexandrian School; and it was in this School, the School of Clement and Origen, of Dionysius and Theognostus, that young Athanasius learned, possibly at first from the lips of Peter the bishop and martyr of 311[2]. The influence of Origen still coloured the traditions of the theological school of Alexandria. It was from Alexander, Bishop of Alexandria 312—328, himself an Origenist 'of the right wing,' that Athanasius received his moulding at the critical period of his later teens.

Of his first introduction to Alexander a famous story is told by Rufinus (*Hist. Eccl.* I. xiv.). The Bishop, on the anniversary of the martyrdom of his predecessor, Peter, was expecting some clergy to dinner after service in a house by the sea. Out of the window, he saw some boys at play on the shore: as he watched, he saw that they were imitating the sacred rites of the Church. Thinking at last that they were going too far, he sent some of his clergy to bring them in. At first their enquiries of the little fellows produced an alarmed denial. But at length he elicited that one of them had acted the Bishop and had baptized some of the others in the character of catechumens. On ascertaining that all details had been duly observed, he consulted his clergy, and decided that the baptisms should be treated as valid, and that the boy-bishop and his clergy had given such plain proof of their vocation that their parents must be instructed to hand them over to be educated for the sacred profession. Young Athanasius accordingly, after a further course of elementary studies, was handed over to the bishop to be brought up, like Samuel, in the Temple of God. This, adds Sozomen (ii. 17), was the origin of his subsequent attachment to Alexander as deacon and secretary. The story is credited by some writers of weight (most recently by Archdeacon Farrar), but seems highly improbable. It depends on the single authority of a writer not famed for historical judgment, and on the very first anniversary of Peter's martyrdom, when Alexander had hardly ascended the episcopal throne, Athanasius was at least fourteen years old. The probability that the anniversary would have been other than the first, and the possibility that Athanasius was even older, coupled with the certainty that his theological study began before Peter's martyrdom, compel us to mark the story with at least a strong note of interrogation. But it may be allowed to confirm us in the belief that Alexander early singled out the promise of ability and devotion which marked Athanasius for his right-hand man long before the crisis which first proved his unique value.

His years of study and work in the bishop's household bore rich fruit in the two youthful works already alluded to. These works more than any later writings of Athanasius bear traces of the Alexandrian theology and of the influence of Origenism: but in them already we trace the independent grasp of Christian principles which mark Athanasius as the representative of something more than a school, however noble and many-sided. It was not as a theologian, but as a believing soul in need of a Saviour, that Athanasius approached the mystery of Christ. Throughout the mazes of the Arian controversy his tenacious hold upon this fundamental principle steered his course and balanced his theology. And it is this that above all else characterises the golden treatise on the Incarnation of the Word. There is, however, one

---

[1] He was unable to speak from memory of the events of the persecution of 303 (*Hist. Ar.* 64), but (*de Incarn.* 56. 2) had been instructed in religion by persons who had suffered as martyrs. This must have been before 311, the date of the last persecution in Egypt under Maximin. Before 319 he had written his first books 'against the Gentiles,' the latter of which, on the Incarnation, implies a full maturity of power in the writer, while the former is full of philosophical and mythological knowledge such as argues advanced education. But from several sources we learn that his election to the episcopate in 328 was impugned, at any rate in after years, on the ground of his not having attained the canonical age of thirty. There is no ground for supposing

that this was true: but such a charge would not be made without some ground at least of plausibility. We must therefore suppose that on June 8, 328, he was not much beyond his thirtieth year. His parents, moreover, were living after the year 358 (see below, p. 562, note 6); allowing them over fourscore years at that date, we find in 298 a reasonable date for the birth of their son. We must remember that in southern climates mind and body mature somewhat more rapidly than with ourselves, and the 'contra Gentes' and 'de Incarnatione' will scarcely appear precocious.

[2] The statements of Greg. Naz. that he frequented classes of grammar and rhetoric is probable enough; that of Sulpitius Severus that he was 'juris consultus' lacks corroboration.

element in the influence of Origen and and his successors which already comes out, and which never lost its hold upon Athanasius,—the principle of asceticism. Although the ascetic tendency was present in Christianity from the first, and had already burst forth into extravagance in such men as Tertullian, it was reserved for the school of Origen, influenced by Platonist ideas of the world and life, to give to it the rank of an acknowledged principle of Christian morals—to give the stimulus to monasticism (see below, p. 193). Among the acclamations which accompanied the election of Athanasius to the episcopate that of εἷς τῶν ἀσκητῶν was conspicuous (*Apol. Ar.* 6). In *de Incarn.* 51. 1, 48. 2, we seem to recognise the future biographer of Antony[3].

§ 2. *The Arian Controversy before Nicæa,* 319—325.

At the time when Athanasius first appeared as an author, the condition of Christian Egypt was not peaceful. Meletius, bishop of Lycopolis, was accused of having sacrificed during the persecution in 301 (pp. 131, 234); condemned by a synod under bishop Peter, he had carried on schismatical intrigues under Peter, Achillas, and Alexander, and by this time had a large following, especially in Upper Egypt. Many cities had Meletian bishops: many of the hermits, and even communities of monks (p. 135), were on his side.

The Meletian account of the matter (preserved by Epiphan. *Hær.* 58) was different from this. Meletius had been in prison along with Peter, and had differed from him on the question of the lapsed, taking the sterner view, in which most of the imprisoned clergy supported him. It would not be without a parallel (D.C.B. art. DONATISTS, NOVATIAN) in the history of the burning question of the *lapsi* to suppose that Meletius recoiled from a compromised position to the advocacy of impossible strictness. At any rate (*de Incarn.* 24. 4) the Egyptian Church was rent by a formidable schism. No doctrinal question, however, was involved. The alliance of Meletians and Arians belongs to a later date.

It is doubtful whether the outbreak of the Arian controversy at Alexandria was directly connected with the previous Christological controversies in the same Church. The great Dionysius some half-century before had been involved in controversy with members of his Church both in Alexandria and in the suffragan dioceses of Libya (*infr.* p. 173). Of the sequel of that controversy we have no direct knowledge : but we find several bishops and numerous clergy and laity in Alexandria and Libya[4] ready to side with Arius against his bishop.

The origin of the controversy is obscure. It certainly must be placed as early as 318 or 319, to leave sufficient time before the final deposition of Arius in the council of 321 (*infr.* p. 234). We are told that Arius, a native of Libya, had settled in Alexandria soon after the origin of the Meletian schism, and had from motives of ambition sided at first with Meletius, then with Peter, who ordained him deacon, but afterwards was compelled to depose him (Epiph. *Hær.* 69, Sozom. i. 15). He became reconciled to Achillas, who raised him to the presbyterate. Disappointed of the bishopric at the election of Alexander, he nurtured a private grudge (Thdt. *H. E.* i. 2), which eventually culminated in opposition to his teaching. These tales deserve little credit : they are unsupported by Athanasius, and bear every trace of invention *ex post facto*. That Arius was a vain person we see from his Thalia (*infr.* p. 308) : but he certainly possessed claims to personal respect, and we find him not only in charge of the urban parish of Baucalis, but entrusted with the duties of a professor of scriptural exegesis. There is in fact no necessity to seek for personal motives to explain the dispute. The Arian problem was one which the Church was unable to avoid. Not until every alternative had been tried and rejected was the final theological expression of her faith possible. Two great streams of theological influence had run their course in the third century : the subordinationist theology of Origen at Alexandria, the Monarchian theology of the West and of Asia which had found a logical expression in Paul of Samosata. Both streams had met in Lucian the martyr, at Antioch, and in Arius, the pupil of Lucian, produced a result which combined elements of both (see below, § 3 (2) a). According to some authorities Arius was the aggressor. He challenged some theological statements of Alexander as Sabellian, urging in opposition to them that if the Son were truly a Son He must have had a beginning, and that there had been therefore a time

---

3 The actual connection of Athanasius with Antony at this period is implied in the received text of 'Vit. Anton.' *Prolog.*, for it could scarcely fall at any later date. At the same time the youthful life of Athanasius seems fully accounted for in such a way as to leave little room for it (so Tillemont). But our ignorance of details leaves it just possible that he may for a time have visited the great hermit and ministered to him as Elisha did of old to Elijah. (Cf. p. 195, note 2.)

4 It is of interest to note the changed conditions. In 260 bishop Dionysius had to check the Monarchian tendency in Libya, and was accused by members of his own flock of separating the Son from the Being (οὐσία) of the Father. In 319 a Libyan, Arius, cries out upon the Sabellianism of his bishop, and formulates the very doctrine which Dionysius had been accused of maintaining.

when He did not exist. According to others (Constantine in Eus. *Vit.* ii. 69) Alexander had demanded of his presbyters an explanation of some passage of Scripture which had led Arius to broach his heresy. At any rate the attitude of Alexander was at first conciliatory. Himself an Origenist, he was willing to give Arius a fair hearing (Sozom. *ubi supra*). But the latter was impracticable. He began to canvass for support, and his doctrine was widely accepted. Among his first partisans were a number of lay people and virgins, five presbyters of Alexandria, six deacons, including Euzoius, afterwards Arian bishop at Antioch (A.D. 361), and the Libyan bishops Secundus of Ptolemais in Pentapolis (see p. 226) and Theonas of Marmarica (see p. 70). A letter was addressed to Arius and his friends by Alexander, and signed by the clergy of Alexandria, but without result. A synod was now called (*infr.* p. 70, *Socr.* i. 6) of the bishops of Egypt and Libya, and Arius a .d his allies deposed. Even this did not check the movement. In Egypt two presbyters and four deacons of the Mareotis, one of the former being Pistus, a later Arian bishop of Alexandria, declared for Arius ; while abroad he was in correspondence with influential bishops who cordially promised their support. Conspicuous among the latter was a man of whom we shall hear much in the earlier treatises of this volume, Eusebius, bishop of Berytus, who had recently, against the older custom of the Church (p. 103, note 6), but in accordance with what has ever since been general in the case of important sees, been translated to the imperial city of Nicomedia. High in the favour, perhaps related to the family, of Constantine, possessed of theological training and practical ability, this remarkable man was for nearly a quarter of a century the head and centre of the Arian cause. (For his character and history, see the excellent article in D.C.B. ii. 360—367.) He had been a fellow-pupil of Arius in the school of Lucian, and fully shared his opinions (his letter to Paulinus of Tyre, Thdt. *H. E.* i. 6). The letter addressed to him by Arius (ib. 5) is one of our most important Arian monuments. Arius claims the sympathy of Eusebius of Cæsarea and other leading bishops, in fact of all the East excepting Macarius of Jerusalem and two others, ' heretical and untutored persons.' Eusebius responded with zeal to the appeal of his ' fellow-Lucianist.' While Alexander was indefatigable in writing to warn the bishops everywhere against Arius (who had now left Alexandria to seek foreign support, first in Palestine, then at Nicomedia), and in particular addressed a long letter to Alexander, bishop of Byzantium (Thdt. *H. E.* i. 4), Eusebius called a council at Nicomedia, which issued letters in favour of Arius to many bishops, and urged Alexander himself to receive him to communion. Meanwhile a fresh complication had appeared in Egypt. Colluthus, whose name stands first among the signatures to the memorandum (to be mentioned presently) of the deposition of Arius, impatient it would seem at the moderation of Alexander, founded a schism of his own, and although merely a presbyter, took upon himself to ordain. In Egypt and abroad confusion reigned : parties formed in every city, bishops, to adopt the simile of Eusebius (*Vit. Const.*), collided like the fabled Symplegades, the most sacred of subjects were bandied about in the mouths of the populace, Christian and heathen.

In all this confusion Athanasius was ready with his convictions. His sure instinct and powerful grasp of the centre of the question made him the mainstay of his Bishop in the painful conflict. At a stage [1] of it difficult to determine with precision, Alexander sent out to the bishops of the Church at large a concise and carefully-worded memorandum of the decision of the Egyptian Synod of 321, fortified by the signatures of the clergy of Alexandria and the Mareotis (see *infra*, pp. 68—71).

This weighty document, so different in thought and style from the letter of Alexander preserved by Theodoret, bears the clear stamp of the mind and character of Athanasius : it contains the germ of which his whole series of anti-Arian writings are the expansion (see introd. and notes, pp. 68—71), and is a significant comment on the hint of the Egyptian bishops (*Apol. c. Ar.* 6 *ad init.*).

Early in 324 a new actor came upon the scene. Hosius, bishop of Cordova and confessor (he is referred to, not by name, *Vit. Const.* ii. 63, 73, cf. iii. 7, ὁ πάνυ βοώμενος ; by name, Socr. i. 7), arrived with a letter from the Emperor himself, intreating both parties to make peace,

---

[1] The chronology cannot be determined with precision. The Memorandum is signed by Colluthus and therefore precedes his schism. The letter to Alex. Byzant. was written after the Colluthian schism had begun. But the proceedings of Eusebius described above had at least begun when the Memorandum was circulated, which must, therefore, have been some time after the Synod of 321. The letter of Alexander to his clergy prefixed to the *depositio* was drawn up after it. and includes the names of the Mareotic seceders. We may, therefore, tentatively adopt the following series :—321 A.D. : Egyptian Synod de- | poses Arius. Arius in correspondence with Eusebius, &c. Leaves Alexandria for Palestine and Nicomedia. Letters sent abroad by Alexander. Eusebius holds council and writes to Alexander. 322 : Memorandum drawn up ; Alexandrian clergy assemble to sign it ; prefatory address to them by Alexar er with reference to the Mareotic defection which has just occurred ; circulation of Memorandum ; schism of Colluthus. 323 : Letter of Alexander to Alexander of Byzantium ; (Sept.) Constantine, master of the East, and ready to intervene in the controversy.

and treating the matter as one of trivial moment. The letter may have been written upon information furnished by Eusebius (D.C.B. *s.v.*) ; but the anxiety of the Emperor for the peace of his new dominions is its keynote. On the arrival of Hosius a council (p. 140) was held, which produced little effect as far as the main question was concerned : but the claims of Colluthus were absolutely disallowed, and his ordination of one Ischyras (*infr.* § 5) to the presbyterate pronounced null and void. Hosius apparently carried back with him a strong report in favour of Alexander ; at any rate the Emperor is credited (*Gelas. Cyz.* ii., Hard. *Conc.* i. 451—458) with a vehement letter of rebuke to Arius, possibly at this juncture. Such was the state of affairs which led to the imperial resolve, probably at the suggestion of Hosius, to summon a council of bishops from the whole world to decide the doctrinal question, as well as the relatively lesser matters in controversy.

§ 3 (1) *The Council of Nicæa.*

An ecumenical council was a new experiment. Local councils had long since grown to be a recognised organ of the Church both for legislation and for judicial proceedings. But no precedent as yet prescribed, no ecclesiastical law or theological principle had as yet enthroned, the 'General Council' as the supreme expression of the Church's mind. Constantine had already referred the case of the Donatists first to a select council at Rome under bishop Miltiades, then to what Augustine (*Ep.* 43) has been understood to call a 'plenarium ecclesiæ universæ concilium' at Arles in 314. This remedy for schism was now to be tried on a grander scale. That the heads of all the Churches of Christendom should meet in free and brotherly deliberation, and should testify to all the world their agreement in the Faith handed down independently but harmoniously from the earliest times in Churches widely remote in situation, and separated by differences of language race and civilisation, is a grand and impressive idea, an idea approximately realised at Nicæa as in no other assembly that has ever met. The testimony of such an assembly carries the strongest evidential weight ; and the almost unanimous horror of the Nicene Bishops at the novelty and profaneness of Arianism condemns it irrevocably as alien to the immemorial belief of the Churches. But it was one thing to perceive this, another to formulate the positive belief of the Church in such a way as to exclude the heresy ; one thing to agree in condemning Arian formulæ, another to agree upon an adequate test of orthodoxy. This was the problem which lay before the council, and with which only its more clearsighted members tenaciously grappled : this is the explanation of the reaction which followed, and which for more than a generation, for well nigh half a century after, placed its results in jeopardy. The number of bishops who met at Nicæa was over 250 [1]. They represented many nationalities (Euseb. *ubi supra.*), but only a handful came from the West, the chief being Hosius, Cæcilian of Carthage, and the presbyters sent by Silvester of Rome, whose age prevented his presence in person. The council lasted from the end of May till Aug. 25 (see D.C.A., 1389). With the many picturesque stories told of its incidents we have nothing to do (Stanley's *Eastern Church*, Socr. i. 10—12, Soz. i. 17, 18, Rufin. *H.E.* i. 3—5) ; but it may be well to note the division of parties. (1) Of thoroughgoing partisans of Arius, Secundus [2] and Theonas alone scorned all compromise. But Eusebius of Nicomedia, Theognis, Bishop of Nicæa itself, and Maris of Chalcedon, also belonged to the inner circle of Arians by conviction (Socr. i. 8 ; Soz. i. 21 makes up the same number, but wrongly). The three last-named were pupils of Lucian (Philost. ii. 15). Some twelve others (the chief names are Athanasius of Anazarbus and Narcissus of Neronias, in Cilicia ; Patrophilus of Scythopolis, Aetius of Lydda, Paulinus of Tyre, Theodotus of Laodicea, Gregory of Berytus, in Syria and Palestine ; Menophantus of Ephesus ; for a fuller discussion see Gwatk. p. 31, n. 3) completed the strength of the Arian party proper. (2) On the other hand a clearly formulated doctrinal position in contrast to Arianism was taken up by a minority only, although this minority carried the day. Alexander of Alexandria of course was the rallying point of this wing, but the choice of the formula proceeded from other minds. 'Υπόστασις and οὐσία are one in the Nicene formula : Alexander in 323 writes of τρεῖς ὑποστάσεις.

The test formula of Nicæa was the work of two concurrent influences, that of the anti-Origenists of the East, especially Marcellus of Ancyra, Eustathius of Antioch, supported by Macarius of 'Ælia,' Hellanicus of Tripolis, and Asclepas of Gaza, and that of the Western bishops, especially Hosius of Cordova. The latter fact explains the energetic intervention of

---

[1] So Eus. *Vit. Const.* iii. 8—over 270, Eustath. in Thdt. i. 8—in fact more than 300 (*de Decr.* 3), according to Athanasius, who again, toward the end of his life (*ad Afr.* 2) acquiesces in the precise figure 318 (Genesis xiv. 14 ; the Greek numeral τιη combines the Cross with the initial letters of the Sacred Name) which a later generation adopted (it first occurs in the alleged Coptic acts of the Council of Alexandria, 362, then in the Letter of Liberius to the bishops of Asia in 365, *infr.* § 9), on grounds perhaps symbolical rather than historical.

[2] The name of Secundus appears among the subscriptions (cf. Soz. i. 21), but this is contradicted by the primary evidence (Letter of the Council in Soc. i. 9, Thdt. i. 9) ; cf. Philost. i. 9, 10. But there is evidence that there were two Secundi.

Constantine at the critical moment on behalf of the test (see below, and *Ep. Eus.* p. 75) ; the word was commended to the Fathers by Constantine, but Constantine was 'prompted' by Hosius (Harnack, *Dogmg.* ii. 226) ; οὗτος τὴν ἐν Νικαίᾳ πίστιν ἐξέθετο (*infr.* p. 285, § 42). Alexander (the Origenist) had been prepared for this by Hosius beforehand (Soc. iii. 7 ; Philost. i. 7 ; cf. Zahn *Marcell.* p. 23, and Harnack's important note, p. 229). Least of all was Athanasius the author of the ὁμοούσιον ; his whole attitude toward the famous test (*infr.* p. 303) is that of loyal acceptance and assimilation rather than of native inward affinity. 'He was moulded by the Nicene Creed, did not mould it himself' (Loofs, p. 134). The theological keynote of the council was struck by a small minority ; Eustathius, Marcellus, perhaps Macarius, and the Westerns, above all Hosius ; the numbers were doubtless contributed by the Egyptian bishops who had condemned Arius in 321. The signatures, which seem partly incorrect, preserve a list of about 20. The party then which rallied round Alexander in formal opposition to the Arians may be put down at over thirty. 'The men who best understood Arianism were most decided on the necessity of its formal condemnation.' (Gwatkin.) To this compact and determined group the result of the council was due, and in their struggle they owed much—how much it is hard to determine— to the energy and eloquence of the deacon Athanasius, who had accompanied his bishop to the council as an indispensable companion (*infr.* p. 103 ; Soz. i. 17 *fin.*). (3) Between the convinced Arians and their reasoned opponents lay the great mass of the bishops, 200 and more, nearly all from Syria and Asia Minor, who wished for nothing more than that they might hand on to those who came after them the faith they had received at baptism, and had learned from their predecessors. These were the 'conservatives [3],' or middle party, composed of all those who, for whatever reason, while untainted with Arianism, yet either failed to feel its urgent danger to the Church, or else to hold steadily in view the necessity of an adequate test if it was to be banished. Simple shepherds like Spyridion of Cyprus ; men of the world who were more interested in their *libelli* than in the magnitude of the doctrinal issue ; theologians, a numerous class, 'who on the basis of half-understood Origenist ideas were prepared to recognise in Christ only the Mediator appointed (no doubt before all ages) between God and the World' (Zahn *Marc.* p. 30) ; men who in the best of faith yet failed from lack of intellectual clearsightedness to grasp the question for themselves ; a few, possibly, who were inclined to think that Arius was hardly used and might be right after all ; such were the main elements which made up the mass of the council, and upon whose indefiniteness, sympathy, or unwillingness to impose any effective test, the Arian party based their hopes at any rate of toleration. Spokesman and leader of the middle party was the most learned Churchman of the age, Eusebius of Cæsarea. A devoted admirer of Origen, but independent of the school of Lucian, he had, during the early stages of the controversy, thrown his weight on the side of toleration for Arius. He had himself used compromising language, and in his letter to the Cæsarean Church (*infra*, p. 76 *sq.*) does so again. But equally strong language can be cited from him on the other side, and belonging as he does properly to the pre-Nicene age, it is highly invidious to make the most of his Arianising passages, and, ignoring or explaining away those on the other side, and depreciating his splendid and lasting services to Christian learning, to class him summarily with his namesake of Nicomedia [4]. (See Prolegg. to vol. 1 of this series, and above all the article in D.C.B.) The fact however remains, that Eusebius gave something more than moral support to the Arians. He was 'neither a great man nor a clear thinker' (Gwatkin) ; his own theology was hazy and involved ; as an Origenist, his main dread was of Monarchianism, and his policy in the council was to stave off at least such a condemnation of Arianism as should open the door to 'confounding the Persons.' Eusebius apparently represents, therefore, the 'left wing,' or the last mentioned, of the 'conservative' elements in the council (*supra*, and Gwatkin, p. 38) ; but his learning, age, position, and the ascendency of Origenist Theology in the East, marked him out as the leader of the whole.

But the 'conservatism' of the great mass of bishops rejected Arianism more promptly than had been expected by its adherents or patrons.

The real work of the council did not begin at once. The way was blocked by innumerable applications to tne Christian Emperor from bishops and clergy, mainly for the redress of personal grievances. Commonplace men often fail to see the proportion of things, and to rise to the magnitude of the events in which they play their

---

[3] A term first brought into currency in this connection by Mr. Gwatkin (p. 38, note), and since adopted by many writers including Harnack : in spite of the obvious objection to the importations of political terms into the grave questions of this period, the term is too useful to be surrendered, and the 'conservatives' of the Post-Nicene reaction were in fact too often political in their methods and spirit. The *truly* conservative men,

here as in other instances, failed to enlist the sympathy of the conservative rank and file.

[4] The identity of name has certainly done Eusebius no good with posterity. But no one with a spark of generosity can fail to be moved by the appeal of Socrates (ii. 21) for common fairness toward the dead.

part. At last Constantine appointed a day for the formal and final reception of all personal complaints, and burnt the 'libelli' in the presence of the assembled fathers. He then named a day by which the bishops were to be ready for a formal decision of the matters in dispute. The way was now open for the leaders to set to work. Quasi-formal meetings were held, Arius and his supporters met the bishops, and the situation began to clear (Soz. i. 17). To their dismay (*de Decr.* 3) the Arian leaders realised that they could only count on some seventeen supporters out of the entire body of bishops. They would seem to have seriously and honestly under-rated the novelty of their own teaching (cf. the letter of Arius in Thdt. i. 5), and to have come to the council with the expectation of victory over the party of Alexander. But they discovered their mistake :—

> 'Sectamur ultro, quos opimus
> Fallere et effugere est triumphus.'

'Fallere et effugere' was in fact the problem which now confronted them. It seems to have been agreed at an early stage, perhaps it was understood from the first, that some formula of the unanimous belief of the Church must be fixed upon to make an end of controversy. The Alexandrians and 'Conservatives' confronted the Arians with the traditional Scriptural phrases (pp. 163, 491) which appeared to leave no doubt as to the eternal God-head of the Son. But to their surprise they were met with perfect acquiescence. Only as each test was propounded, it was observed that the suspected party whispered and gesticulated to one another, evidently hinting that each could be safely accepted, since it admitted of evasion. If their assent was asked to the formula 'like to the Father in all things,' it was given with the reservation that man as such is 'the image and glory of God.' The 'power of God' elicited the whispered explanation that the host of Israel was spoken of as δύναμις κυρίου, and that even the locust and caterpillar are called the 'power of God.' The 'eternity' of the Son was countered by the text, 'We that live are alway (2 Cor iv. 11)!' The fathers were baffled, and the test of ὁμοούσιον, with which the minority had been ready from the first, was being forced (p. 172) upon the majority by the evasions of the Arians. When the day for the decisive meeting arrived it was felt that the choice lay between the adoption of the word, cost what it might, and the admission of Arianism to a position of toleration and influ-ence in the Church. But then, was Arianism all that Alexander and Eustathius made it out to be ? was Arianism so very intolerable, that this novel test must be imposed on the Church ? The answer came (Newman *Ar.*[4] p. 252) from Eusebius of Nicomedia. Upon the assembling of the bishops for their momentous debate (ὡς δὲ ἐζητεῖτο τῆς πίστεως ὁ τρόπος, *Eustath.*) he presented them with a statement of his belief. The previous course of events may have convinced him that half-measures would defeat their own purpose, and that a challenge to the enemy, a forlorn hope, was the only resort left to him[4a]. At any rate the statement was an un-ambiguous assertion of the Arian formulæ, and it cleared the situation at once. An angry clamour silenced the innovator, and his document was publicly torn to shreds (ὑπ' ὄψει πάντων, says an eye-witness in Thdt. i. 8). Even the majority of the Arians were cowed, and the party were reduced to the inner circle of five (*supra*). It was now agreed on all hands that a stringent formula was needed. But Eusebius of Cæsarea came forward with a last effort to stave off the inevitable. He produced a formula, not of his own devising (Kölling, pp. 208 *sqq.*), but consisting of the creed of his own Church with an addition intended to guard against Sabellianism (Hort, *Two Diss.* pp. 56, *sq.* 138). The formula was unassailable on the basis of Scripture and of tradition. No one had a word to say against it, and the Emperor expressed his personal anxiety that it should be adopted, with the single improvement of the ὁμοούσιον. The suggestion thus quietly made was momentous in its result. We cannot but recognise the 'prompter' Hosius behind the Imperial recommendation : the friends of Alexander had patiently waited their time, and now their time was come : the two Eusebii had placed the result in their hands. But how and where was the necessary word to be inserted ? and if some change must be made in the Cæsarean formula, would it not be as well to set one or two other details right ? At any rate, the creed of Eusebius was carefully overhauled clause by clause, and eventually took a form materially different from that in which it was first pre-sented[4b], and with affinities to the creeds of Antioch and Jerusalem as well as Cæsarea.

All was now ready ; the creed, the result of minute and careful deliberations (we do not

---

[4a] Or possibly Theodoret, &c., drew a wrong inference from the words of Eustathius (in Thdt. i. 8), and the γράμμα was *not* submitted *by* Eusebius, but *produced* as evidence *against* him ; in this case it must have been, as Fleury observes, his letter to Paulinus of Tyre.

[4b] Hort, pp. 138, 139, and 59 : the changes well classified by Gwatkin, p. 41, cf. Harnack[2], vol. 2, p. 227. The main alterations were (1) The elimination of the word λόγος and substitution of υἱός in the principal place. This struck at the theology of Euse-bius even more directly than at that of Arius. (2) The addition

not only of ὁμοούσιον τῷ πατρί, but also of τούτεστιν ἐκ τῆς οὐσίας τοῦ πατρός between μονογενῆ and θεόν as a further qualification of γεννηθέντα (specially against Euseb. Nicom. : see his letter in Thdt. i. 6). (3) Further explanation of γεννηθέντα by γ. οὐ ποιη-θέντα, a glance at a favourite argument of Arius, as well as at Asterius. (4) ἐνανθρωπήσαντα added to explain σαρκωθέντα, and so to exclude the Christology which characterised Arianism from the first. (5) Addition of anathematisms directed against all the leading Arian doctrines.

know their history, nor even how long they occupied[5]), lay before the council. We are told 'the council paused.' The evidence fails us; but it may well have been so. All the bishops who were genuinely horrified at the naked Arianism of Eusebius of Nicomedia were yet far from sharing the clearsighted definiteness of the few: they knew that the test proposed was not in Scripture, that it had a suspicious history in the Church. The history of the subsequent generation shews that the mind of Eastern Christendom was not wholly ripe for its adoption. But the fathers were reminded of the previous discussions, of the futility of the Scriptural tests, of the locust and the caterpillar, of the whisperings, the nods, winks, and evasions. With a great revulsion of feeling the council closed its ranks and marched triumphantly to its conclusion. All signed,—all but two, Secundus and Theonas. Maris signed and Theognis, Menophantus and Patrophilus, and all the rest. Eusebius of Nicomedia signed; signed everything, even the condemnation of his own convictions and of his 'genuine fellow-Lucianist' Arius; not the last time that an Arian leader was found to turn against a friend in the hour of trial. Eusebius justified his signature by a 'mental reservation;' but we can sympathise with the bitter scorn of Secundus, who as he departed to his exile warned Eusebius that he would not long escape the same fate (Philost. i. 9).

The council broke up after being entertained by the Emperor at a sumptuous banquet in honour of his Vicennalia. The recalcitrant bishops with Arius and some others were sent into exile (an unhappy and fateful precedent), a fate which soon after overtook Eusebius of Nicomedia and Theognis (see the discussion in D.C.B. ii. 364 *sq.*). But in 329 'we find Eusebius once more in high favour with Constantine, discharging his episcopal functions, persuading Constantine that he and Arius held substantially the Creed of Nicæa.'

The council also dealt with the Paschal question (see *Vit. Const.* iii. 18; so far as the question bears on Athanasius see below, p. 500), and with the Meletian schism in Egypt. The latter was the main subject of a letter (Soc. i. 9; Thdt. i. 9) to the Alexandrian Church. Meletius himself was to retain the honorary title of bishop, to remain strictly at home, and to be in lay communion for the rest of his life. The bishops and clergy of his party were to receive a μυστικωτέρα χειροτονία (see Bright, *Notes on Canons*, pp. 25 *sqq.*; Gore, *The Church and the Ministry*, ed. 1, p. 192 note), and to be allowed to discharge their office, but in the strictest subordination to the Catholic Clergy of Alexander. But on vacancies occurring, the Meletian incumbents were to succeed subject to (1) their fitness, (2) the wishes of the people, (3) the approval of the Bishop of Alexandria. The terms were mild, and even the gentle nature of Alexander seems to have feared that immediate peace might have been purchased at the expense of future trouble (his successor openly blames the compromise, p. 131, and more strongly p. 137); accordingly, before carrying out the settlement he required Meletius to draw up an exact list of his clergy at the time of the council, so as to bar an indefinite multiplication of claims. Meletius, who must have been even less pleased with the settlement than his metropolitan, seems to have taken his time. At last nothing would satisfy both parties but the personal presentation of the Meletian bishops from all Egypt, and of their clergy

---

5 The events have been related in what seems to be their most likely order, but there is no real certainty in the matter. It is clear that there were at least two public sittings (Soz. i. 17, the language of Eus. *V.C.* iii. 10, is reconcileable with this) in the emperor's presence, at the first of which the *libelli* were burned and the bishops requested to examine the question of faith. This was probably on June 19. The tearing up of the creed of Eus. Nic. seems from the account of Eustathius to have come immediately before the final adoption of a creed. The creed of Eusebius of Cæsarea, which was the basis of that finally adopted, must therefore have been propounded after the failure of his namesake. (Montfaucon and others are clearly wrong in supposing 'that *this* was the 'blasphemy' which was torn to pieces!) The difficulty is, where to put the dramatic scene of whisperings, nods, winks, and evasions which compelled the bishops to apply a drastic test. I think (with Kölling, &c.) that it must have preceded the proposal of Eusebius, upon which the ὁμοούσιον was quietly insisted on by Constantine; for the latter was the only occasion (πρόφασις) of any modification in the Cæsarean Creed, which in itself does not correspond to the tests described *infr.* p. 163. But Montfaucon and others, followed by Gwatkin, place the scene in question *after* the proposal of Eus. Cæs. and the resolution to modify his creed by the insertion of a stringent test,—in fact at the 'pause' of the council before its final resolution. This conflicts with the clear statement of Eusebius that the ὁμοούσιον was the 'thin end of the wedge' which led to the entire recasting of his creed (see *infr.* p. 73. The idea of Kölling, p. 208, that the creed of Eusebius was drawn up by him for the occasion, and that the μάθημα of the council was ready beforehand as an alternative document, is refuted by the relation of the two documents; see Hort. pp. 138, 139). It follows, therefore, from the combined accounts of Ath., Euseb. and Eustathius (our only eye-witnesses)

that (1) the fathers were practically resolved upon the ὁμοούσιον before the final sitting. (2) That this resolve was clinched by the creed of Eusebius of Nicomedia. (3) That Eusebius of Cæsarea made his proposal when it was too late to think of half-measures. (4) That the creed of Eusebius was modified at the Emperor's direction (which presupposes the willingness of the Council). (5) That this revision was immediately followed by the signatures and the close of the council. The work of revision, however, shews such signs of attention to detail that we are almost compelled to assume at least one adjournment of the final sitting. When the other business of the council was transacted, including the settlement of the Easter question, the Meletian schism, and the Canons, it is impossible to say. Kölling *suo jure* puts them at the first public session. The question must be left open, as must that of the presidency of the council. The conduct of the proceedings was evidently in the hands of Constantine, so that the question of presidency reduces itself to that of identifying the bishop on Constantine's right who delivered the opening address to the Emperor: this was certainly not Hosius (see *Vit. C.* iii. 11, and vol. 1 of this series, p. 19), but may have been Eusebius of Cæsarea, who probably after a few words from Eustathius (Thdt.) or Alexander (Theod. Mops. and Philost.) was entrusted with so congenial a task. The name of Hosius stands first on the extant list of signatures, and he may have signed first, although the lists are bad witnesses. The words of Athanasius sometimes quoted in this connection (p. 256), 'over what synod did he not preside?' must be read in connection with the distinction made by Theodoret in quoting the passage in question (*H.E.* ii. 15), that Hosius 'was *very prominent* at the great synod of Nicæa, and *presided* over those who assembled at Sardica. This is the only evidence we possess to which any weight can be attached.

from Alexandria itself, to Alexander (p. 137, τούτους καὶ παρόντας παρέδωκεν τῷ ᾽Αλεξάνδρῳ), who was thus enabled to check the *Brevium* or schedule handed in by their chief[6]. All this must have taken a long time after Alexander's return, and the peace was soon broken by his death.

Five months after the conclusion of the negotiations, Alexander having now died, the flame of schism broke out afresh (*infr.* p. 131. Montfaucon, in Migne xxv. p. lvii., shews conclusively that the above is the meaning of the μῆνας πέντε.) On his death-bed, Alexander called for Athanasius. He was away from Alexandria, but the other deacon of that name (see signatures p. 71), stepped forward in answer to the call. But without noticing him, the Bishop repeated the name, adding, 'You think to escape, but it cannot be.' (Sozom. ii. 17.) Alexander had already written his Easter Letter for the year 328 (it was apparently still extant at the end of the century, p. 503). He died on April 17 of that year (Pharmuthi 22), and on the eighth of June Athanasius was chosen bishop in his stead.

§ 3 (2). *The situation after the Council of Nicæa.*

THE council (a) had testified, by its horrified and spontaneous rejection of it, that Arianism was a novelty subversive of the Christian faith as they had received it from their fathers. They had (b) banished it from the Church by an inexorable test, which even the leading supporters of Arius had been induced to subscribe. In the years immediately following, we find (c) a large majority of the Eastern bishops, especially of Syria and Asia Minor, the very regions whence the numerical strength of the council was drawn, in full reaction against the council; first against the leaders of the victorious party, eventually and for nearly a whole generation against the symbol itself; the final victory of the latter in the East being the result of the slow growth of conviction, a growth independent of the authority of the council which it eventually was led to recognise. To understand this paradox of history, which determines the whole story of the life of Athanasius as bishop, it is necessary to estimate at some length the theological and ecclesiastical situation at the close of the council: this will best be done by examining each point in turn (a) the novelty of Arianism, (b) the ὁμοούσιον as a theological formula, (c) the materials for reaction.

(a) 'Arianism was a new doctrine in the Church' (Harnack, p. 218); but it claimed to be no novelty. And it was successful for a long time in gaining 'conservative' patronage. Its novelty, as observed above, is sufficiently shewn by its reception at the Council of Nicæa. But no novelty springs into existence without antecedents. What were the antecedents of Arianism? How does it stand related to the history within the Church of the momentous question, 'What think ye of Christ?'

In examining such a question, two methods are possible. We may take as our point of departure the formulated dogma say of Nicæa, and examine in the light of it variations in theological statements in preceding periods, to shew that they do not warrant us in regarding the dogma as an innovation. That is the dogmatic method. Or we may take our start from the beginning, and trace the history of doctrine in the order of cause and effect, so as to detect the divergence and convergence of streams of influence, and arrive at an answer to the question, How came men to think and speak as they did? That is the historical method. Both methods have their recommendations, and either has been ably applied to the problem before us. In electing the latter I choose the more difficult road; but I do so with the conviction, firstly, that the former has tended (and especially in the ablest hands) to obscure our perception of the actual facts, secondly, that the saving faith of Christ has everything to gain from a method which appeals directly to our sense of historical truth, and satisfies, not merely overawes, the mind.

Let us then go back to 'the beginning of the Gospel.' Taking the synoptic gospels as our primary evidence, we ask, what did Christ our Lord teach about Himself? We do not find formal definitions of doctrine concerning His Person. Doubtless it may seem that such a definition on His part would have saved infinite dispute and searchings of heart in the history of the Church. But recognising in Him the unique and supreme Revealer of the Father, it is not for us to say what He should have taught; we must accept His method of teaching as that which Divine Wisdom chose as the best, and its sequel in history as the way in which God willed man to learn. We find then in the materials which we possess for the history of His Life and Teaching fully enough to explain the belief of His disciples (see below) in His Divinity. *Firstly*, there is no serious doubt as to His claim to be the Messiah. (The confession of Peter in all four Gospels, Matt. xvi. 16; Mark viii. 29; Luke ix. 27; John vi. 69; 'Son of Man,' Dan. vii. 13; ix. 24, &c.) In this character He is King in the kingdom of Heaven (Matt. xxv. 31—36, cf. Mk. viii. 38), and revises the Law with full authority (Matt. v. 21—44, cf. Luke v. 24; Matt. xii. 8). It may be added that whatever this claim conveyed to the Jews of His own time (see Stanton's *Jewish and Christian Messiah*) it is impossible to combine in one idea the Old Testament traits of the Coming One if we stop short of the identification of the Messiah with the God of Israel (see Delitzsch, *Psalms*, vol. i. pp. 94, 95, last English ed.). *Secondly*, Christ enjoys *and confers* the full authority of God (Matt. x. 40; Luke x. 16; cf. also Matt. xxiv. 35; Mk. xiii. 31; Luke xxi. 33), gives and promises the Holy Spirit ('the Spirit *of the Father*,' see Matt. x. 17, &c.; Luke xii. 12, and especially xxi. 15, ἐγὼ γὰρ δώσω, &c.), and apparently sends the prophets and holy men of old (cf Matt. xxiii. 34, ἐγὼ ἀποστέλλω with Luke xi. 49). *Thirdly*, the foundation of all this is laid in a passage preserved by the first and third gospels, in which He claims the unqualified possession of the mind of the Father (Luke x. 22;

---

[6] It is worth noting that the Nicene arrangement was successful in some few cases. See Index to this vol. *s.v.* Theon (of Nilopolis), &c.

Matt. xi. 27), 'No man knoweth [who] the Son [is], save the Father, neither knoweth any man [who] the Father [is] save the Son, and he to whomsoever the Son will (βούληται) reveal Him.' Observe the *reciprocity* of knowledge between the Son and the Father. This claim is a decisive *instantia fœderis* between the Synoptics and the Fourth Gospel, e.g. John xvi. 15; xiv. 9, &c. *Fourthly*, we observe the claim made by Him throughout the synoptic record to absolute confidence, absolute faith, obedience, self-surrender, such as no frail man is justified in claiming from another; the absence of any trace in the mind of the 'meek and lowly' one of that consciousness of sin, that need of reconciliation with God, which is to us an indispensable condition of the religious temper, and the starting-point of Christian faith (contrast Isa. vi. 5).

We now turn to the Apostles. Here a few brief remarks must suffice. (A suggestive summary in Sanday, 'What the first Christians thought about Christ,' *Oxford House Papers, First Series*.) That S. Paul's summary of the Gospel (1 Cor. xv. 3 *sqq.*) is given by him as common ground between himself and the older Apostles follows strictly from the fact that the verb used (παρέλαβον) links the facts of Redemption (v. 3, 4) with the personal experiences of the original disciples (5 *sqq.*). In fact it is not in dispute that the original Jewish nucleus of the Apostolic Church preached Jesus as the Messiah, and His death as the ground of forgiveness of sins (Pfleiderer, *Urchrist.* p. 20; Acts ii. 36, 38; iii. 26; iv. 12, &c.; the 'Hebraic colouring' of these early chapters is very characteristic and important). The question is, however, how much this implied as to the Divine Personality of the Saviour; how far the belief of the Apostles and their contemporaries was uniform and explicit on this point. Important light is thrown on this question by the controversy which divided S. Paul from the mass of Jewish Christians with respect to the observance of the Law. Our primary source of knowledge here is Galatians, ch. ii. We there learn that while S. Paul regarded this question as involving the whole essence of the Gospel, and resisted every attempt to impose circumcision on Gentile Christians, the older Apostles conceded the one point regarded as central, and, while reserving the obligation of the Law on those born under it (which S. Paul never directly assailed, 1 Cor. vii. 18) recognised the Gospel of the uncircumcision as legitimate. This concession, as the event proved, conceded everything; if the 'gospel of the uncircumcision' was sufficient for salvation, circumcision became a national, not a religious principle. Now this whole question was fundamentally a question about Christ. Men who believed, or were willing to grant, that the Law uttered from Sinai by the awful voice of the Most High Himself was no longer the supreme revelation of God, the one divinely ordained covenant of righteousness, certainly believed that some revelation of God different *in kind* (for no revelation of God *to* man could surpass the *degree* of Ex. xxxiii. 11) had taken place, a unique revelation of God *in* man. The revelation of God in Christ, not the revelation of God to Moses, was the one fact in the world's history; Sinai was dwarfed in comparison of Calvary. But it must be observed that while the older Apostles, by the very recognition of the gospel of the uncircumcision, went thus far with S. Paul, S. Paul realised as a central principle what to others lay at the circumference. What to the one was a *result* of their belief in Christ was to him the starting-point, from which logical conclusions were seen to follow, practical applications made in every direction. At the same time S. Paul taught nothing about Christ that was not *implied* in the belief of the older Apostles, or that they would not have felt impelled by their own religious position to accept. In fact it was **their fundamental union in the implicit belief of the divinity of the Lord** that made possible any **agreement between S. Paul and the Jewish Apostles as to the gospel of the uncircumcision.**

The apostles of the circumcision, however, stood between S. Paul and the zealot mass of Jewish Christians (Acts xxi. 20), many of whom were far from acquiescing in the recognition of S. Paul's Gospel. On the same principle that we have used to determine the belief of the Στῦλοι with regard to Christ, we must needs recognise that where the gospel of the uncircumcision was still assailed or disparaged, the Divinity of Christ was apprehended faintly, or not at all.

The name of the 'Ebionite' sect testifies to its continuity with a section of the Jerusalem Church (see Lightfoot's Galatians, *S. Paul and the Three*). It should be observed, however, firstly that between the clear-sighted Apostle of the Gentiles and the straitest of the zealots, there lay every conceivable gradation of intermediate positions (Loofs, *Leitf.* § 11. 2, 3); secondly, that while emancipation from legalism in the Apostolic Church implied what has been said above, a belief in the divinity of Jesus was in itself compatible with strict Jewish observance.

The divinity of Christ then was firmly held by S. Paul (the most remarkable passage is Rom. x. 9, 11, 13, where Κύριον 'Ιησοῦν = αὐτόν = Κύριον = יהוה Joel ii. 32), and his belief was held by him in common with the Jewish Apostles, although with a clearer illumination as to its consequences. That this belief was absolutely universal in the Church is not to be maintained, the elimination of Ebionism was only gradual (Justin, *Dial.* xlviii. *ad fin.*); but that it, and not Ebionism, represented the common belief of the Apostles and New Testament writers is not to be doubted.

But taking this as proved, we do not find an equally clear answer to the question *In what sense* is Christ God? The synoptic record makes no *explicit* reference to the pre-existence of Christ: but the witness of John and descent of the Spirit (Mark i. 7—11) at His baptism, coupled with the Virginal Birth (Mt., Lk.), *and with the traits of the synoptic portrait of Christ* as collected above, if they do not compel us to assert, yet forbid us to deny the presence of this doctrine to the minds of the Evangelists. In the Pauline (including Hebrews) and Johannine writings the doctrine is strongly marked, and in the latter (Joh. i. 1, 14, 18, μονογενὴς Θεός) Jesus Christ is expressly identified with the creative Word (Palestinian *Memra*, rather than Alexandrian or from Philo; see also Rev. xix. 13), and the Word with God. Moreover such passages as Philipp. ii. 6 *sqq.*, 2 Cor. xiii. 14 (the Apostolic benediction), &c., &c., are significant of the impression left upon the mind of the infant Churches as they started upon their history no longer under the personal guidance of the Apostles of the Lord.

Jesus Christ was God, was one with the Father and with the Spirit: that was enough for the faith, the love, the conduct of the primitive Church. The Church was nothing so little as a society of theologians; monotheists and worshippers of Christ by the same instinct, to analyse their faith as an intellectual problem was far from their thoughts: God Himself (and there is but one God) had suffered for them (Ign. *Rom.* vi.; Tat. *Gr.* 13; Melito *Fr.* 7), God's sufferings were before their eyes (Clem. R. I. ii. 1), they desired the drink of God, even His blood (Ign. *Rom.* vii., cf. Acts xx. 28); if enthusiastic devotion gave way for a moment to reflexion 'we must think of Jesus Christ as of God' ('Clem. R.' II. 1).

The 'Apostolic fathers' are not theological in their aim or method. The earliest seat of theological reflexion in the primitive Church appears to have been Asia Minor, or rather Western Asia from Antioch to the Ægean. From this region proceed the Ignatian letters, which stand alone among the literature of their day in theological depth and reflexion. Their theology ' is wonderfully mature in spite of its immaturity, full of reflexions, and yet at the same time full of intuitive originality' (Loofs, p. 61). The central idea is that of the renovation of man (*Eph.* 20), now under the power of Satan and *Death* (ib. 3, 19), which are undone (κατάλυσις) in Christ, the risen Saviour (*Smyrn.* 3), who is ' our true Life,' and endows us with immortality (*Smyrn.* 4, *Magn.* 6, *Eph.* 17). This is by virtue of His Divinity (*Eph.* 19, *Smyrn.* 4) in union with His perfect Manhood. He is the only utterance of God (λόγος ἀπὸ σιγῆς προελθών, *Magn.* 8), the 'unlying mouth by which the Father spake' (*Rom.* 8.) 'God come (γενόμενος) in the flesh,' ' our God' (*Eph.* 7, 18). His flesh partaken mystically in the Eucharist unites our nature to His, is the 'medicine of incorruption' (*Eph.* 20, *Smyrn.* 7, cf. *Trall.* 1). Ignatius does not distinguish the relation of the divine to the human in Christ : he is content to insist on both : ' one Physician, of flesh and of spirit, begotten and unbegotten' (*Eph.* 7). Nor does he clearly conceive the relation of the Eternal Son to the Father. He is unbegotten (as God) and begotten (as man): from eternity with the Father (*Magn.* 6) : through Him the One God manifested himself. The theological depth of Ignatius was perhaps in part called forth by the danger to the churches from the Docetic heretics, representative of a Judaic (*Philad.* 5, *Magn.* 8—10) syncretism which had long had a hold in Asia Minor (1 John and Lightfoot *Coloss.*, p. 73, 81 *sqq.*). To this he opposes what is evidently a *creed* (*Trall.* 9), with emphasis on the reality (ἀληθῶς) of all the facts of Redemption comprised in it.

It was in fact the controversies of the second century that produced a theology in the Catholic Church,—that in a sense produced the Catholic Church itself. The idea of the Church as distinct from and embracing the Churches is a New Testament idea (Eph. v. 25, cf. 1 Cor. xv. 9, &c.), and the name 'Catholic' occurs at the beginning of the second century (Lightfoot's note on Ign. *Smyrn.* 8) ; but the Gnostic and Montanist controversies compelled the Churches which held fast to the παράδοσις of the Apostles to close their ranks (episcopal federation) and to reflect upon their creed. The Baptismal Creed (Rom. x. 9, Acts viii. 37, *Text. Rec.*, cf. 1 Cor. xv. 3—4) began to serve as a *tessera* or passport of right belief, and as a regulative standard, a ' rule of faith.' The 'limits of the Christian Church ' began to be more clearly defined (Stanton, *ubi supr.* p. 167).

Another influence which during the same period led to a gradual formation of theology was the necessity of defending the Church against heathenism. If the Gnostics were 'the first Christian theologians' (Harnack), the APOLOGISTS (120—200) are more directly important for our present enquiry. The usual title of Justin ' Philosopher and Martyr' is significant of his position and typical of the class of writers to which he belongs. On the one hand the Apologists are philosophers rather than theologians. Christianity is 'the only true philosophy' (Justin) ; its doctrines are found piecemeal among the philosophers (λόγος σπερματικός), who are so far Christians, just as the Christians are the true philosophers (Justin and Minuc. Felix). But the Logos, who is imparted fragmentarily to the philosophers, is revealed in His entire divine Personality in Christ (so Justin beyond the others, *Apol.* ii. 8, 10). In the doctrine of God, their thought is coloured by the eclectic Platonism of the age before Plotinus. God, the Father of all things, is Creator, Lord, Master, and *as such* known to man, but in Himself Unoriginate (ἀγένητος), ineffable, mysterious (ἄρρητος), without a name, One and alone, incapable of Incarnation (for references to Justin and to Plato, D.C.B. iii. 572). His 'goodness' is metaphysical perfection, or beneficence to man, His 'righteousness' that of Moral Governor of the Universe (contrast the deeper sense of St. Paul, Rom. iii. 21, &c.). But the abstractness of the conception of God gives way to personal vividness in the doctrine of the 'visible God' (Tert. *Prax.* 15 *sq.*), the Logos (the subject of the O. T. 'theophanies' according to the Apologists) who was 'with' the Father before all things (Just. *Dial.* 62), but was 'begotten' or projected (προβληθείς) by the will of the Father (ib. 128) as God from God, as a flame from fire. He is, like the Father, ineffable (Χριστός, Just. *Apol.* ii. 6), yet is the ἄγγελος, ὑπηρέτης of the Father. In particular He is the Father's minister *in Creation :* to create He proceeded from the Father, a doctrine expressly deduced from Prov. viii. 22 (*Dial.* 61, 129). Before this He was the λόγος ἐνδιάθετος, after it the λόγος προφορικός, the Word uttered (Ps. xlv. 1 LXX ; this distinction is not in Justin, but is found Theophil. *ad Autol.* ii. 10, 22 : it is the most marked trace of philosophic [Stoic] influence on the Apologists). The Apologists, then, conceive of Christian theology *as philosophers*. Especially the Person of the Saviour is regarded by them from the cosmological, not the soteriological view-point. From the latter, as we have seen, St. Paul starts ; and his view gradually embraces the distant horizon of the former (1 Cor. viii. 6, Coloss. i. 15) ; from the soteriological side also (*directly*) he reaches the divinity of Christ (Rom. v. 1—8 ; 1 Cor. i. 30 ; Rom. x. 13, *as above*). Here, as we shall see, Athanasius meets the Arians substantially by St. Paul's method. But the Apologists, under the influence of their philosophy rather than of their religion, start from the cosmological aspect of the problem. They engraft upon an Apostolic (Johannine) title of the Saviour an Alexandrine group of associations : they go far towards transmuting the Word of St. John to the Logos of Philo and the Eclectics. Hence their view of His Divinity and of his relation to the Father is embarrassed. His eternity and His generation are felt to be hardly compatible : His distinct Personality is maintained at the expense of His true Divinity. He is God, and not the One God ; He can manifest Himself (Theophanies) in a way the One God cannot ; He is an intermediary between God and the world. The question has become philosophical rather than directly religious, and philosophy cannot solve it. But on the other hand, Justin was no Arian. If he was Philosopher, he was also Martyr. The Apologists are deeply saturated with Christian piety and personal enthusiastic devotion to Christ. Justin in particular introduces us, as no other so early writer, into the life, the worship, the simple faith of the Primitive Church, and we can trace in him influences of the deeper theology of Asia Minor (Loofs, p. 72 *sq.* but see more fully the noble article on Justin in D.C.B. vol. iii.). But our concern is with their influence on the *analysis* of the object of faith ; and here we see that unconsciously they have severed the Incarnate Son from the Eternal Father : not God (ὁ ὄντως θεός) but a *subordinate* divine being is revealed in Christ : the Logos, to adopt the words of Ignatius, is no longer a true breach of the Divine Silence.

We must now glance at the important period of developed Catholicism marked especially by the names of IRENÆUS, TERTULLIAN, and CLEMENT, the period of a consolidated organisation, a (relatively) fixed Canon of the New Testament, and a catholic rule of faith (see above, and Lumby, *Creeds*, ch. i. ; Heurtley, *Harmonia Symbolica*, i.—viii.). The problem of the period which now begins (180—250) was that of MONARCHIANISM ; the Divinity of Christ must be reconciled with the Unity of God. Monarchianism is in itself the expression of the truth common to all monotheism, that the ἀρχή or Originative Principle is strictly and Personally One and one only (in contrast to the plurality of ἀρχικαὶ ὑποστάσεις, see Newman, *Arians*[4], p. 112 note). No Christian deliberately maintains the contrary. The Apologists, as we have seen, tended to emphasise the distinction of Father and Son ; but this tendency makes of necessity in the direction of ' subordination ;' and *any* distinction of ' Persons ' or Hypostases in the Godhead involves to a Monotheist *some* subordination, in order to save the principle of the Divine [6] Monarchia.' The Monarchian denied *any* subordination or distinction of hypostases within the Godhead. This tendency we have now to follow up. We do not meet with it as a problem in IRENÆUS. (He 'is said to have written against it,' Newman, *Ar.* [4], p. 117, citing Dodw. *in Iren.*) This scholar of pupils of Apostles stands in the lines of the Asiatic theology. He is the successor of Ignatius and Polycarp. We find him, in sharp contrast to the Apologists, giving full expression to the revelation of God in Jesus (the 'Son is the Measure of the Father, for He contains Him'), and the union of man with God in the Saviour, as the carrying out of the original destiny of man, by the destruction of sin, which had for the time frustrated it (III. xviii. p. 211, Deus antiquam hominis plasmationem in se recapitulans). Hence the 'deification' of man's nature by union with Christ (a remarkable point of contact with Athanasius, see note on *de Incar.* 54. 3) ; incorruption is attained to by the knowledge of God (cf. John xvii. 3) through faith (IV. xx.) ; we cannot comprehend God, but we learn to know Him by His Love (ib.). At the same time we trace the influence of the Apologists here and there in his Christology (III. 6, 19, and the explanation of the 'Theophanies,' iv. 20). But in his younger contemporary TERTULLIAN, the reaction of Monarchianism makes itself felt. He is himself one of the Apologists, and at the same time under *Asiatic* influences. The two trains of influence converge in the name *Trinitas*, which he is the first to use (τρίας first in the *Asiatic* Apologist Theophilus). In combating the Monarchian Praxeas (see below) he carries subordinationism very far (cf. *Hermcg.* 3. 'fuit tempus cum Ei filius non fuit'), he distinguishes the Word as 'rationalis deus' from eternity, and 'sermonalis' not from eternity (cf. again, Theophilus, *supra*). The Generation of the Son is a προβολή (also 'eructare' from Ps. xlv. 1), but the divine 'Substance' remains the same (river and fountain, sun and ray, *Prax.* 8, 9). He aims at reconciling 'subordination' with the 'Monarchia,' (ib. 4). In the Incarnate Christ he distinguishes the divine and human as accurately as Leo the Great (ib. 27, 29). In spite of inconsistencies such as were inevitable in his strange individuality (Stoic, philosopher, lawyer, Apologist, 'Asiatic' theologian, Catholic, Montanist) we see in Tertullian the starting-point of Latin Theology (but see also Harnack ii. 287 note).

We must now examine more closely the history of MONARCHIAN tendencies, and firstly in ROME. The sub-Apostolic Church, simply holding the Divinity of Christ and the Unity of God, used language (see above) which may be called 'naively Monarchian.' This holds good even of Asiatic theology, as we find it in its earlier stage. The baptismal creed (as we find it in the primitive basis of the Apostles' Creed) does not solve the problem thus presented to Christian reflexion. Monarchianism attempted the solution in two ways. *Either* the One God was simply identified with the Christ of the Gospels and the Creeds, the Incarnation being a *mode* of the Divine manifestation (Father as Creator, Son as Redeemer, Spirit as Sanctifier, or the like) : 'Modalism' or Modalistic Monarchianism (including Patripassianism, Sabellianism, and later on the theology of Marcellus) ; *or* (this being felt incompatible with the constant personal distinction of Christ from the Father) a special effluence, influence, or power of the one God was conceived of as residing in the man Jesus Christ, who was accordingly *Son* of God by *adoption*, God by assimilation : 'dynamic' Monarchianism or Adoptionism ('Son' and 'Spirit' not so much modes of the Divine self-realisation as of the Divine *Action*). This letter, the echo but not the direct survival of Ebionism, was later on the doctrine of Photinus ; we shall find it exemplified in Paul of Samosata ; but our present concern is with its introduction at Rome by the two Theodoti, the elder of whom (a tanner from Byzantium) was excommunicated by Bishop Victor, while the younger, a student of the Peripatetic philosophy and grammatical interpreter of Scripture, taught there in the time of Zephyrinus. A later representative of this school, Artemon, claimed that its opinions were those of the Roman bishops down to Victor (Eus. *H.E.* v. 28). This statement cannot be accepted seriously ; but it appears to be founded on a real reminiscence of an epoch in the action and teachings of the Roman bishops at the time. It must be remembered that the two forms of Monarchianism—modalism and adoptionism—are, while very subtly distinguished in their essential principle, violently opposed in their appearance to the popular apprehension. Their doctrine of God is one, at least in its strict unitarianism ; but while to the Modalist Christ is the one God, to the Adoptionist He is essentially and exclusively man [1]. In the one case His Personality is divine, in the other human. Now there is clear proof of a strong Modalist tendency [2] in the Roman Church at this time ; this would manifest itself in especial zeal against the doctrine of such men as Theodotus the younger, and give some colour to the tale of Artemon. Both Tertullian and Hippolytus complain bitterly of the ignorance of those responsible for the ascendancy which this teaching acquired in Rome (Ζεφυρῖνον ἄνδρα ἰδιώτην καὶ ἄπειρον τῶν ἐκκλησιαστικῶν ὅρων, Hipp. 'idiotes quisque aut perversus,' 'simplices, ne dicam *imprudentes et idiotæ*.' Tert.). The utterances of Zephyrinus support this : 'I believe in one God, Jesus Christ' (Hipp., see above on the language of the sub-Apost. Church). The Monarchian influences were strengthened by the arrival of fresh teachers from Asia (Cleomenes and Epigonus, see note 2) and began to arouse lively opposition. This was headed by Hippolytus, the most learned of the Roman presbytery, and eventually bishop [3] in opposition to Callistus, the successor of Zephyrinus. The theology of Hippolytus was not unlike that of Tertullian, and was hotly charged by Callistus with 'Ditheism.' The position of Callistus himself, like that of his predecessor, was one of compromise between the two forms of Monarchianism, but somewhat more developed. A distinction was made between 'Christ' (the divine) and Jesus (the human) ; the latter suffered actually, the former indirectly ('filius patitur, pater vero compatitur.' Tert.) τὸν Πατέρα συμπεπονθέναι τῷ υἱῷ, Hipp.; it is clear that under 'Praxeas ' Tertullian is combating also the modified Praxeanism of Callistus. See *adv. Prax.* 27, 29 ; Hipp. ix. 7) ; not without reason does Hippolytus charge Callistus with combining the errors of Sabellius with those of Theodotus. The compromise of Callistus was only partially successful. On the one hand the

---

[1] While yet the distinction between the 'presence' and 'existence' of God in Christ (Newman, *Ar.* [4]. p. 123) is very delicate : both ideas are covered by 'Dasein.' The two forms of Monarchianism are related exactly as the Catholic doctrine of the Trinity is to the Nestorian.

[2] Our authorities are Hippolytus *Philosophum.*, Tertullian *Against Praxeas*, and the early fragment 'against heresies' printed in Tertullian's works. The statements of Tertullian and Hippolytus agree remarkably, though obviously independent. The first (modalist) Monarchian teacher in Rome was Praxeas (Tert.) from Asia, who was followed by the pupils of Noetus, also an Asiatic (Hippol.), Epigonus (Renan *Marc-Aurèle* 230, note, identifies 'Praxeas' with Epigonus; I cannot undertake to pronounce upon the point, but see Harnack, *Dogmg.* i[1]. p. 608),

and Cleomenes. Praxeas arrived in Rome under Victor (or earlier, Harnack, p. 610), and combined strong opposition to Montanism, with equally strong modalism in his theology. In both respects his influence told upon the heads of the Church. Montanism was expelled, Modalism tolerated, Theodotus excommunicated; 'Duo negotia diaboli Praxeas Romæ procuravit: prophetiam expulit et hæresin intulit: Paracletum fugavit et Patrem crucifixit.' (Tert.) 'Praxeas hæresin introduxit quam Victor[inus] (perhaps a confusion with Zephyrinus) corroborare curavit' ('Tertullian' *adv. Hær.*)

[3] This point is still in debate. Against it, see Lightfoot, *S. Clement of Rome* (ed. 1890), for it, Döllinger *Hipp. and Call.*, and Neumann, *Der Röm. Staat u. d. Allg. Kirche* (Leipz. 1890).

strictly modalist SABELLIUS, who from about 215 takes the place of Cleomenes at the head of Roman Monarchianism (his doctrine of the υἱοπάτωρ, of the Trinity as successive πρόσωπα, 'aspects,' of the One God, pure modalism as defined above) scorned compromise (he constantly reproached Callistus with having changed his front, *Hipp.*) was excommunicated, and became the head of a sect. And the fierce opposition of Hippolytus failed to command the support of more than a limited circle of enthusiastic admirers, or to maintain itself after his death. On the other hand (the process is quite in obscurity : see Harnack I¹, p. 620) the theology of Hippolytus and Tertullian eventually gained the day. NOVATIAN, whose 'grande volumen' (Jer.) on the Trinity represents the theology of Rome about 250 A.D., simply 'epitomises Tertullian,' and that *in explanation of the Rule of Faith*. As to the Generation of the Son, he drops the 'quando Ipse [Pater] voluit' of Tertullian, but like him combines a (modified) 'subordination' with the '*communio* substantiæ'—in other words the ὁμοούσιον. Monarchianism was condemned in the West ; its further history belongs to the East (under the name of Sabellianism first in Libya : see pp. 173, *sqq.*). But the hold which it maintained upon the Roman Church for about a generation (190—220) left its mark. Rome condemned Origen, the ally of Hippolytus ; Rome was invoked against Dionysius of Alexandria ; (Rome and) the West formulated the ὁμοούσιον at Nicæa ; Rome received Marcellus ; Rome rejected the τρεῖς ὑποστάσεις and supported the Eustathians at Antioch ; it was with Rome rather than with the prevalent theology of the East that Athanasius felt himself one. (Cf. also Harnack, *Dg.* I¹, p. 622 *sqq.*) Monarchianism was too little in harmony with the New Testament, or with the traditional convictions of the Churches, to live as a formulated theology. The 'naive modalism' of the 'simplices quae major semper pars credentium est' (Tert.) was corrected as soon as the attempt was made to give it formal expression [3a]. But the attempt to do so was a valuable challenge to the *conception of God* involved in the system of the Apologists. To their abstract, transcendent, philosophical first Principle, Monarchianism opposed a living, self-revealing, redeeming God, made known in Christ. This was a great gain. But it was obtained at the expense of the divine immutability. A God who passed through phases or modes, now Father, now Son, now Spirit, a God who could suffer, was not the God of the Christians. There is some justice in Tertullian's scoff at their 'Deum versipellem.'

The third great name associated with the end of the second century, that of Clement, is important to us chiefly as that of the teacher of ORIGEN, whose influence we must now attempt to estimate. Origen (185—254) was the first theologian in the full sense of the term ; the first, that is, to erect upon the basis of the rule of faith (Preface to *de Princ.*) a complete theological system, synthesising revealed religion with a theory of the Universe, of God, of man, which should take into account the entire range of truth and knowledge, of faith and philosophy. And in this sense for the Eastern Church he was the last theologian as well. In the case of Origen the Vincentian epigram, *absolvuntur magistri condemnantur discipuli* (too often applicable in the history of doctrine) is reversed. In a modified form his theology from the first took possession of the Eastern Church ; in the Cappadocian fathers it took out a new lease of power, in spite of many vicissitudes it conquered opposing forces (the sixth general council crushed the party who had prevailed at the fifth) ; John of Damascus, in whom the Eastern Church says its last word, depends upon the Origenist theology of Basil and the Gregories. But this theology was Origenism *with a difference.* What was the Origenism *of Origen?* To condense into the compass of our present purpose the many-sidedness of Origen is a hopeless task. The reader will turn to the fifth and sixth of Bigg's *Bampton Lectures* for the best recent presentation ; to Newman's *Arians* (I. § 3), especially the 'apology' at the end) ; to Harnack (ed. 1, pp. 510—556) and Loofs (§ 28) ; Shedd (vol. i. 288—305, should be read before Bigg and corrected by him) and Dorner ; to the sections in Bull (*Defens.* ii. 9, iii. 3) and Petavius (who in *Trin.* I. iv. pursues with fluent malignity 'omnigenis errorum portentis infamem scriptorem') ; to the *Origeniana* of Huet and the dissertations of the standard editors ; to the article ORIGENIST CONTROVERSIES, and to the comprehensive, exact, and sympathetic article ORIGEN in the Dictionary of Christian Biography. The fundamental works of Origen for our purpose are the *de Principiis,* the *contra Celsum,* and the *de Oratione ;* but the exegetical works are necessary to fill out and correct first impressions.

The general position of Origen with regard to the Person of Christ is akin to that of Hippolytus and Tertullian. It is to some extent determined by opposition to Gnosticism and to Monarchianism. His visit to Rome (Eus. *H. E.,* vi. 14) coincided with the battle of Hippolytus against Zephyrinus and his destined successor : on practical as well as on doctrinal points he was at one with Hippolytus. His doctrine of God is reached by the soteriological rather than the cosmological method. God is known to us in the Incarnate Word ; 'his point of view is moral, not . . . pseudo-metaphysical.' The impassibility of the abstract philosophical idea of God is broken into by 'the passion of Love' (Bigg, p. 158). In opposition to the perfection of God lies the material world, conditioned by evil, the result of the exercise of will. This cause of evil is antecedent to the genesis of the material universe, the κ α τ α βολὴ κόσμου ; materiality is the penalty and measure of evil. (This part of Origen's doctrine is markedly Platonic. Plotinus, we read, refused to observe his own birthday ; in like manner Origen quaintly notes that only wicked men are recorded in Scripture to have kept their birthdays ; Bigg, 203, note ; cf. Harnack, p. 523, note.) The soul (ψυχή as if from ψύχεσθαι) has in a previous state 'waxed cold,' i.e. lost its original integrity, and in this condition enters the body, i.e. 'is subjected to vanity' in common with the rest of the creature, and needs redemption (qualify this by Bigg, pp. 202 *sqq.*, on Origen's belief in Original Sin.) To meet this need the Word takes a Soul (but one that has never swerved from Him in its pre-existent state : on this antinomy Bigg, 190, note, 199) and *mediante Anima,* or rather mediante *hac substantia animæ* (*Prin.* II. vi.) unites the nature of God and of Man in One. (On the union of the two natures in the θεάνθρωπος, *in Ezek.* iii. 3, he is as precise as Tertullian : we find the *Hypostatic Union* and *Communicatio Idiomatum* formally explicit ; Bigg, 190.) The Word 'deifies' Human Nature, first His Own, then in others as well (*Cels.* iii. 28, ἵνα γένηται θεία : he does not use θεοποιεῖσθαι ; the thought is subtly but really different from that which we found in Irenæus : see Harnack, p. 551), by that perfect apprehension of Him ὅπερ ἦν πρὶν γένηται σάρξ, of which faith in the Incarnate is the earliest but not the final stage (applying 2 Cor. v. 16 ; cf. the Commentary on the Song of Songs).

What account then does Origen give of the beginning and the end of the great Drama of existence? He starts from the end, which is the more clearly revealed ; 'God shall be all in all.' But 'the end must be like the beginning ;' One is the end of all, One is the beginning. From 1 Cor. xv. he works back to Romans viii. : the one is his key to the eternity after, the other, to the eternity before (Bigg pp. 193 *sq.*). Into this scheme he brings creation, evil, the history of Revelation, the Church and its life, the final consummation of all things.

[3a] But only at Aquileia was the *rule of faith* adapted by the insertion of *impassibilis.*

The Universe is eternal : God is prior to it in conception, yet He was never other than Creator. But in the history of the Universe the material world which we know is but a small episode. It began, and will end. It began with the estrangement of Will from God, will end with its reconciliation : God, from Whom is the beginning of all, 'will be all in all.' (For Origen's eschatology see Bigg, 228—234.) From this point of view we must approach the two-sided Christology of Origen. To him the two sides were aspects of the same thing : but if the subtle presupposition as to God and the Universe is withdrawn, they become alternative and inconsistent Christologies, as we shall see to have actually happened. As God is eternally Creator, so *He is eternally Father* (Bigg, 160, note). The Son proceeds from Him not as *a part* of His Essence, but as the Ray from the Light ; it cannot be rightly or piously said that He had a beginning, ἦν ὅτε οὐκ ἦν (cf. *De Princ.* i. 2, iv. 28, and *infr.* p. 168) ; He is begotten *from the Essence* of the Father, He is *of the same essence* (ὁμοούσιος) (*Fragm.* 3 *in Heb.*, but see Bigg, p. 179), there is *no unlikeness whatever* between the Son and the Father (*Princ.* i. 2, 12). He was begotten ἐκ τοῦ θελήματος τοῦ Πατρός (but to Origen the θέλημα was inherent in the Divine Nature, cf. Bigg, 161, Harnack, p. 534 against Shedd, p. 301, note) *not by* προβολή or emanation (*Princ.* iv. 28, i. 2. 4), as though the Son's generation were something that took place once for all, instead of existing continuously. The Father is in the Son, the Son in the Father : there is 'coinherence.' On the other hand, the Word is God *derivatively not absolutely*, Ὁ λόγος ἦν πρὸς τὸν Θεόν, καὶ Θεὸς ἦν ὁ Λόγος. The Son is Θεός, the Father alone ὁ Θεός. He is of one οὐσία with the Father as compared with the creatures ; but as contrasted with the Father, Who may be regarded as ἐπέκεινα οὐσίας[1], and Who alone is αὐτόθεος, αὐτοαγαθός, ἀληθινὸς θεός, the Son is ὁ δεύτερος θεός (*Cels.* v. 39, cf. Philo's δευτερεύων θεός). As the Son of God, He is contrasted with all γενητά ; as contrasted with the Ingenerate Father, He stands at the head of the series of γεννητά ; He is μεταξὺ τῆς τοῦ ἀγεν[ν]ήτου καὶ τῆς τῶν γεννητῶν φύσεως[2]. He even explains the Unity of the Father and the Son as *moral* (δύο τῇ ὑποστάσει πράγματα, ἓν δὲ τῇ ὁμονοίᾳ καὶ τῇ ταυτότητι τοῦ βουλήματος, *Cels.* viii. 12). The Son takes His place even in the cosmic process from Unity to Unity through Plurality, 'God is in every respect One and Simple, but the Saviour by reason of the Many becomes Many' (on John i. 22, cf. Index to this vol., *s.v. Christ*). The Spirit is subordinated to the Son, the Son to the Father (ἐλάττων παρὰ τὸν πατέρα ὁ υἱὸς ... ἔτι δὲ ἧττον τὸ πνεῦμα τὸ ἅγιον, *Princ.* I. 3, 5 Gk.), while to the Spirit are subordinated *created* spirits, whose goodness is relative in comparison with God, and the fall of some of whom led to the creation of matter (see above). Unlike the Son and the Spirit they are mutable in will, subject to προκοπή, capable of embodiment even if in themselves immaterial.

The above slender sketch of the leading thoughts of Origen will suffice to show how intimately his doctrine of the Person of Christ hangs together with his philosophy of Religion and Nature. That philosophy is the philosophy of his age, and must be judged relatively. His deeply religious, candid, piercing spirit embodies the highest effort of the Christian intellect conditioned by the categories of the best thought of his age. Everywhere, while evading no difficulty, his strenuous speculative search is steadied by ethical and religious instinct. As against Valentinian and the Platonists, with both of whom he is in close affinity, he inexorably insists on the self-consciousness and moral nature of God, on human freewill. As against all contemporary non-Christian thought his system is pure monism. Yet the problem of evil, in which he merges the antithesis of matter and spirit, brings with it a necessary dualism, a dualism, however, which belongs but to a moment in the limitless eternity of God's all-in-allness before and after. Is he then a pantheist? No, for to him God is Love (*in Ezek.* vi. 6), and the rational creature is to be made divine and united to God by the reconciliation of *Will* and by conscious apprehension of Him. The idea of Will is the pivot of Origen's system, the centripetal force which forbids it to follow the pantheistic line which it yet undoubtedly touches. The 'moral' unity of the Father and the Son (see above, ταυτότης βουλήματος and ἐκ τοῦ θελήματος) is Unity in that very respect in which the Creator stands over against the self-determining rational creature. Yet the immutability, the Oneness of God, must be reconciled with the plurality, the mutability of the creature ; here the Logos mediates, διὰ τὰ πολλὰ γίνεται πολλά : but this must be from eternity :—*accordingly creation is eternal too.* Here we see that the cosmological idea has prevailed over the religious, the Logos of Origen is still in important particulars the Logos of the Apologists, of Philo and the philosophers. The difference lies in His *co-eternity*, upon which Origen insists without wavering. The resemblance lies in the intermediate[3] position ascribed to Him between the ἀγέννητος, (ὁ Θεός), and the γενητά ; He is, as Hypostasis, subordinate to the Father.

Now it is evident that the mere intellectual apprehension of a system which combines so many opposite tendencies, which touches every variety of the theological thought of the age (even modalism, for to Origen *the Father* is the Μονάς, the αὐτόθεος, while yet He is no abstraction but a God who exists in moral activity, *supra*) and subtly harmonises them all, must have involved no ordinary philosophical power. When we add to this fact the further consideration that precisely the fundamental ideas of Origen were those which called forth the liveliest opposition and were gradually dropped by his followers, we can easily understand that in the next generation Origenism was no longer either the system of Origen, or a single system at all.

In one direction it could lend itself to no compromise ; in spite of the justice done by Origen to the fundamental ideas both of modalism and of emanative adoptionism (cf. Harnack, pp. 548, note, and 586), to Monarchianism in either form he is diametrically opposed. The hypostatic distinctness of Son and Spirit is once for all made good for the theology of Eastern Christendom. We see his disciples exterminate Monarchianism in the East. On the left wing Dionysius refutes the Sabellians of Libya, on the right Gregory Thaumaturgus, Firmilian, and their brethren, after a long struggle, oust the adoptionist Paul from the See of Antioch. But its influence on the existing Catholic theology, however great (and in the East it was very great), inevitably made its way in the face of opposition, and at the cost of its original subtle consistency. The principal opposition came from Asia Minor, where the traditions of theological thought (see above, on Ignatius and Irenæus, below on Marcellus) were not in sympathy[4] with Origen. We cannot demonstrate the existence of a continuous theological school in Asia ; but

---

[1] See Newman's note *Ar.* p. 186, where the additions in brackets seriously modify his statement in the text. Also cf. *infr.* ch. iv. § 3, and Bigg, p. 179, note 2.

[2] *Cels.* iii. 34, cf. Alexander's μεσιτεύουσα φύσις μονογενής. But observe that the passage insisted on by Shedd, 294, ἕτερος κατ᾽ οὐσίαν καὶ ὑποκειμένου ὁ υἱὸς τοῦ πατρός, does not bear the sense he extracts from it. οὐσία here is not 'essence' but 'hypostasis.'

[3] The formula κτίσμα ὁ υἱός is ascribed to Origen by the anti-Chalcedonists of the sixth century, but is probably a 'consequenzmacherei' from the above; see Caspari *Alte u. N. Quellen*, p. 60, note. But κτίσμα was sometimes applied to the Son in a vague sense, on the ground of Prov. viii. 22, a text not used in this way by Origen.

[4] Compare the strong Origenist rejection of Chiliasm, the spiritualism of Origen as contrasted with the realism of Asia Minor, the Asiatic origin of Roman Monarchianism, of Montanism.

METHODIUS (270—300) certainly speaks with the voice of Ignatius and Irenæus. He deals with Origen much as Irenæus dealt with the Gnostics, defending against him the current sense of the *regula fidei*, and especially the literal meaning of Scripture, the origination of the soul along with the body, the resurrection of the body in its material sense, and generally opposing *realism* to the spiritualism of Origen. But in thus opposing Origen, Methodius is not uninfluenced by him (see Socr. vi. 13). He, too, is a student of Plato (with 'little of his style or spirit'); his 'realism' is 'speculative.' He no longer defends the Asiatic Chiliasm, his doctrine of the Logos is as coloured by Origen as that of Irenæus was by the Apologists. *The legacy of Methodius and of his Origenist contemporaries to the Eastern Church was a modified Origenism*, that is a theology systematised on the intellectual basis of the Platonic philosophy, but expurgated by the standard of the *regula fidei*. This result was a compromise, and was at first attended with great confusion. Origen's immediate following seized some one side, some another of his system; some were more, some less influenced by the 'orthodox' reaction against his teaching. We may distinguish an Origenist 'right' and an Origenist 'left.' If the Origenist view of the Universe was given up, the coeternity of the Son and Spirit with the Father was less firmly grasped. Origen had, if we may use the expression, 'levelled up.' The Son was mediator between the Ingenerate God and the created, but eternal Universe. If the latter was not eternal, and if at the same time the Word stood in some essential correlation to the creative energy of God, Origen's system no longer implied the strict coeternity of the Word. Accordingly we find Dionysius (see below, p. 173 *sqq.*) uncertain on this point, and on the essential relation of the Son to the Father. More cautious in this respect, but tenacious of other startling features of Origen, were Pierius and Theognostus, who presided over the Catechetical School at the end of the century [5].

On the other hand, very many of Origen's pupils, especially among the bishops, started from the other side of Origen's teaching, and held tenaciously to the coeternity of the Son, while they abandoned the Origenist 'paradoxes' with regard to the Universe, matter, pre-existence, and restitution. Typical of this class is Gregory Thaumaturgus, also Peter the martyr bishop of Alexandria, who expressly opposed many of Origen's positions (though hardly with the violence ascribed to him in certain supposed fragments in Routh, *Rell.* iv. 81) and Alexander himself. It was this 'wing' of the Origenist following that, in combination with the opposition represented by Methodius, bequeathed to the generation contemporary with Nicæa its average theological tone. The coeternity of the Son with the Father was not (as a rule) questioned, but the essential relation of the Logos to the Creation involved a strong subordination of the Son to the Father, and by consequence of the Spirit to the Son. Monarchianism was the heresy most dreaded, the theology of the Church was based on the philosophical categories of Plato applied to the explanation and systematisation of the rule of faith. This was very far from Arianism. It lacked the logical definiteness of that system on the one hand, it rested on the other hand on a different conception of God; the hypostatic subordination of the Son was insisted upon, but His true Sonship as of one Nature with the Father, was held fast. In the slow process of time this neo-Asiatic theology found its way partly to the Nicene formula, partly to the illogical acceptance of it with regard to the Son, with refusal to apply it to the Spirit (Macedonius). To the men who thought thus, the blunt assertion that the Son was a creature, not coeternal, alien to the Essence of the Father, was a novelty, and wholly abhorrent. Arius drew a sharper line than they had been accustomed to draw between God and the creature; so did Athanasius. But Arius drew his line without flinching between the Father and the Son. This to the instinct of any Origenist was as revolting as it would have been to the clear mind and Biblical sympathy of Origen himself. In theological and philosophical principles alike Arius was opposed even to the tempered Origenism of the Nicene age. The latter was at the furthest remove from Monarchianism, Arianism was *in its essential core* Monarchian; the common theology borrowed its philosophical principles and method from the Platonists, Arius from Aristotle. To anticipate, Arianism and (so-called) semi-Arianism have in reality very little in common except the historical fact of common action for a time. Arianism guarded the transcendence of the divine nature (at the expense of revelation and redemption) in a way that 'semi-Arianism,' admitting as it did inherent inequality in the Godhead, did not. They therefore tended in opposite directions; Arianism to Anomœanism, 'semi-Arianism' to the Nicene faith; their source was different. 'Aristotle made men Arians,' says Newman with truth, 'Plato, semi-Arians' (*Arians*[4], p. 335, note): but to say this is to allow that if Arianism goes back to Lucian and so to Paul of Samosata, semi-Arianism is a fragment from the wreck of Origen.

The Origenist bishops of Syria and Asia Minor had in the years 269—272, after several efforts, succeeded in deposing PAUL of Samosata from the See of Antioch. This remarkable man was the ablest pre-Nicene representative of Adoptionist Monarchianism. The Man Jesus was inhabited by the 'Word,' i.e. by an *impersonal* power of God, distinct from the Λόγος or reason (wisdom) inherent in God as an attribute, which descended upon him at His Baptism. His union with God, a union *of Will*, was unswerving, and by virtue of it He overcame the sin of mankind, worked miracles, and entered on a condition of Deification. He is God ἐκ προκοπῆς (cf. Luke ii. 52) by virtue of progress in perfection. That is in brief the system of Paul, and we cannot wonder at his deposition. For the striking points of contact with Arianism (two 'Wisdoms,' two 'Words,' προκοπή : cf. *Orat. c. Ar.* i. 5, &c.) we have to account [6]. The theology of Arius is a compromise between the Origenist doctrine of the Person of Christ and the pure Monarchian Adoptionism of Paul of Samosata; or rather it engrafts the former upon the latter as the

---

[5] The position of EUSEBIUS of Cæsarea is at the 'extreme left' of the Origenist body. ('A reflex of the unsolved problems of the Church of that time,' Dorner.) It is as though Dionysius instead of withdrawing and modifying his incriminated statements, had involved them in a further series of explanations and biblical phrases which left them where they were. But this is not so much Arianism as confusion. 'All is hollow and empty, precarious and ambiguous. With a vast apparatus of biblical expressions and the use of every possible formula, Monotheism is indeed maintained, but practically a created subordinate God is inserted between God and mankind' (Harnack, p. 648). See also Dorner, *Lehre der Pers. Chr.* Pt. 1, pp. 793—798. The language quoted by Ath. below, p. 459, was doubtless meant by Eusebius in an Origenist sense.

[6] The theological genesis of Paul's system is obscure. The theory of Newman that he was under strong Jewish influences is largely based upon the late and apparently quite erroneous tradition that his patroness Zenobia was a Jewess; see p. 296, note 9[a], and Gwatkin, p. 57, and note 3. Harnack regards him as the representative of 'archaic' East-Syrian adoptionism such as pervades the 'Discussion of Archelaus with Manes;' see Routh, *Rell.* v. especially pp. 178—184. But Paul would not have spoken of Mary as 'Dei Genetrix,' p. 128; I cannot see more in these 'Acta' than a naive adoptionism homologous to the 'naive modalism' of much early Christian language, but like it not representative of the entire view of those who use it; we must also note that the statements of 'Archelaus' are coloured by reaction against the docetism of 'Manes;' but Paul may well have taken up this naive adoptionism, and, *by strict Aristotelian logic*, developed it as the exclusive basis of his system. Whether Paul's use of the idea of the Logos betrays the faintest influence of Origen is to me, at least, extremely uncertain.

foundation principle, seriously modifying each to suit the necessity of combining the two. This compromise was not due to Arius himself but to his teacher, LUCIAN the Martyr. A native himself of Samosata, he stood in some relation of attachment (not clearly defineable) to Paul. Under him, he was at the head of a critical, exegetical, and theological school at Antioch. Upon the deposition of Paul he appears not so much to have been formally excommunicated as to have refused to acquiesce in the new order of things. Under Domnus and his two successors, he was in a state of suspended communion [7]; but eventually was reconciled with the bishop (Cyril?) and died as a martyr at Nicomedia, Jan. 7, 312. The latter fact, his ascetic life, and his learning secured him widespread honour in the Church; his pupils formed a compact and enthusiastic brotherhood, and filled many of the most influential Sees after the persecution. That such a man should be involved in the reproach of having given birth to Arianism is an unwelcome result of history, but one not to be evaded [1]. The history of the Lucianic compromise and its result in the Lucianic type of theology, are both matters of inference rather than of direct knowledge. As to the first, whatever evidence there is connects Lucian's original position with Paul. His reconciliation with Bishop Cyril must have involved a reapproachment to the formula of the bishops who deposed Paul,—a thoroughly Origenist document. We may therefore suppose that the *identification* of Christ with the Logos, or cosmic divine principle, was adopted by him from Origenist sources. But he could not bring himself to admit that He was thus essentially identified with God the eternal; he held fast to the idea of προκοπή as the path by which the Lord attained to Divinity; he distinguished the Word or Son who was Christ from the immanent impersonal Reason or Wisdom of God, as an offspring of the Father's *Will*, an idea which he may have derived straight from Origen, with whom of course it had a different sense. For to Origen Will was the very essence of God; Lucian fell back upon an arid philosophical Monotheism, upon an abstract God fenced about with negations (Harnack 2², 195, note) and remote from the Universe. It was counted a departure from Lucian's principles if a pupil held that the Son was the 'perfect Image of the Father's Essence' (Philost. ii. 15); Origen's formula, 'distinct in hypostasis, but one in will,' was apparently exploited in a Samosatene sense to express the relation of the Son to the Father. *The only two points in fact in which Lucian appears to have modified the system of Paul* were, *firstly* in hypostatising the Logos, which to Paul was an impersonal divine power, *secondly* in abandoning Paul's purely human doctrine of the historical Christ. To Lucian, the Logos assumed a body (or rather 'Deus *sapientiam suam misit* in hunc mundum *carne* vestitam, *ubi infra*, p. 6), but itself took the place of a soul² [2]; hence all the ταπειναì λέξεις of the Gospels applied to the Logos *as such*, and the inferiority and essential difference of the Son from the Father rigidly followed. •

The above account of Lucian is based on that of Harnack, *Dogmg.* ii. 184, *sqq.* It is at once in harmony with all our somewhat scanty data (Alexander, Epiphanius, Philostorgius, and the fragment of his last confession of faith preserved by Rufin. in Eus. *H. E.* ix. 9, Routh, *Rell.* iv. pp. 5—7, from which Harnack rightly starts) and is the only one which accounts for the phenomena of the rise of Arianism. We find a number of leading Churchmen in agreement with Arius, but in no way dependent on him. They are Eusebius of Nicomedia, Maris, Theognis, Athanasius of Anazarba, Menophantus; all Lucianists. The first Arian writer, Asterius (see below), is a Lucianist. (The Egyptian bishops Secundus and Theonas cannot be put down to any school; we do not know their history; but they are distinguished from the Lucianists by Philost. ii. 3.) It has been urged that, although Arius brought away heresy from the school of Lucian, yet he was not the only one that did so. True; but then the heresy was *all of the same kind* (list of pupils of Lucian in Philost. ii. 14, iii. 15). Aetius, the founder of logical ultra-Arianism and teacher of Eunomius, was taught the exegesis of the New Testament by the Lucianists Athanasius of Anazarba and Antony of Tarsus, of the Old by the Lucianist Leontius. This fairly covers the area of Arianism proper. But it may be noted that some Origenists of the 'left wing,' whose theology emphasized the subordination, and vacillated as to the eternity of the Son, would find little to shock them in Arianism (Eusebius of Cæsarea, Paulinus of Tyre), while on the other hand there are traces of a Lucianist 'right wing,' men like ASTERIUS, who while essentially Arian, made concessions to the 'conservative' position chiefly by emphasising the cosmic mediation of the Word and His 'exact likeness' to the Father [3]. The Theology of the Eastern Church was suffering from the effort to assimilate the Origenist theology: it could not do so without eliminating the underlying and unifying idea of Origenism; this done, the overwhelming influence of the great teacher remained, while dissonant fragments of his system, vaguely comprehended in many cases, permeated some here, some there [4]. Meanwhile the school of Lucian had a method and a system; they knew their own minds, and relied on reason and exegesis. This was the secret of their power. Had Arius never existed, Arianism must have tried its strength under such conditions. But the age was ready for Arius; and Arius was ready. The system of ARIUS was in effect that of Lucian: its formulation appears to have been as much the work of Asterius as of Arius himself. (Cf. p. 155, § 8, ὁ δὲ Ἀρ. μεταγράψας δέδωκε τοῖς ἰδίοις. The extant writings of Arius are his letters to Eus. Nic. and to Alexander, preserved by Theodoret and Epiph. *Hær.* 69, and the extracts from the 'Thalia' in Ath., pp. 308—311, 457, 458; also the 'confession' in Socr. i. 26, Soz. ii. 27. Cf. also references to his dicta in Ath. pp. 185, 229, &c.) Arius started from the *idea of God* and the *predicate* 'Son.' God is above all things uncreated, or unoriginate, ἀγέν[ν]ητος, (the ambiguity of the derivatives of γεννᾶσθαι and

---

[7] ἀποσυνάγωγος ἔμεινεν, Alex. Alexand. in Thdt.; the objections of Gwatkin, p. 18, note, are generously meant rather than convincing: the 'creed of Lucian' is not usable without discrimination for Lucian's position: see discussion by Caspari *A.u.N.Q.* p. 42, note.

[1] It was pointed out clearly by Newman, *Arians*, pp. 8, 403, but with an eagerly drawn inference to the discredit of the later Antiochene School and of the genuine principles of exegesis as recognised at the present day by Protestants and Catholics alike (see Wetzer und Welte-Kaulen, *Kirchen-Lexicon*, i. 953 *sqq.*, iv. 1116, and Patrizzi as abridged in Cornel. a Lap. *in Apoc.* ed. Par. 1859, pp. xvi. *sqq.* The Lucianic origin of Arianism was denied by Gwatkin in his *Studies*, but the denial is tacitly withdrawn in his *Arian Controversy*. Harnack, *Dogmgesch.* i¹. 598, ii². 183 *sqq.* must, I think, convince any open mind of the fact. Consult his article on Lucian in Herzog². viii. 767 (the best investigation), also Neander *H.E.* ii. 198, iv. 108; Möller *K.G.* i. 226, D.C.B. iii. 748; Kölling, vol. i, pp. 27—31, who makes the mistake of taking the 'Lucianic creed' as his point of departure.

[2] This is ascribed to Lucian by Epiph. *Ancor.* 33, and there is no reason whatever to doubt it. The tenet was part of the Arian system from the first, and was attacked already by Eustathius, *Fragm. apud Thdt. Dial.* iii., but often overlooked, e.g. even by Athanasius in his writings before 362, but see p. 352, note 5. It came to the front in the system of Eunomius, and was much discussed in the last decade of the life of S. Athan. The system of Apollinaris was different. (See pp. 570, note 1, 575, note 1.)

[3] ἀπαράλλακτον εἰκόνα, which an Arian would be prepared to admit as the result of the προκοπή. (See below, § 6, on the Creeds of 341.) I cannot regard Asterius as a 'semi-Arian;' the only grounds for it are the above phrase and the statement (*Lib. Syn.*) that he attended the Council of 341 with the Conservative Dianius. But Asterius was as ready to compromise with conservatism as he had formerly been with heathenism, and his anxiety for a bishopric would carry him to even greater lengths in order to attend a council under influential patronage.

[4] The letter of Alexander to his namesake of Byzantium in Thdt. i. 4, cannot be exempted from this generalisation

γενέσθα; are a very important element in the controversy. See p. 475, note 5, and Lightfoot, *Ignat.* ii. p. 90 *sqq.*) Everything else is created, γενητόν. The name 'Son' implies an *act* of procreation. Therefore, before such act, there was no Son, nor was God properly speaking a Father. The Son is not coeternal with Him. He was originated by the Father's will, as indeed were all things. He is, then, τῶν γενητῶν, He came into being from non-existence (ἐξ οὐκ ὄντων), and before that did not exist (οὐκ ἦν πρὶν γένηται). But His relation to God differs from that of the Universe generally. Created nature cannot bear the awful touch of bare Deity. God therefore created the Son that He in turn might be the agent in the Creation of the Universe—'created Him as the beginning of His ways,' (Prov. viii. 22, LXX.). This being so, the nature of the Son was in the essential point of ἀγεννησία unlike that of the Father; (ξένος τοῦ υἱοῦ κατ' οὐσίαν ὁ Πατὴρ ὅτι ἄναρχος): their substances (ὑπο-στάσεις) are ἀνεπίμικτοι,—have nothing in common. The Son therefore does not possess the fundamental property of sonship, identity of nature with the Father. He is a Son by Adoption, not by Nature; He has advanced by moral probation to be Son, even to be μονογενὴς θεός (Joh. i. 14). He is not the eternal Λόγος, reason, of God, but *a* Word (and God has spoken many): but yet He is *the* Word by grace; is *no longer*, what He is *by nature*, subject to change. He cannot know the Father, much less make Him known to others. Lastly, He dwells in flesh, not in full human nature (see above, p. xxviii. and note 2). The doctrine of Arius as to the Holy Spirit is not recorded, but probably He was placed between the Son and the other κτίσματα (yet see Harnack ii. 199, note 2).

Arian Literature. Beside the above-mentioned letters and fragments of Arius, our early Arian documents are scanty. Very important is the letter of Eus. Nic. to Paulinus, referred to above, § 3 (1), pp. xvi., xviii., other fragments of letters, p. 458 *sq.* The writings[5] of ASTERIUS, if preserved, would have been an invaluable source of information[6]. Asterius seems to have written before the Nicene Council; he may have modified his language in later treatises. He was replied to by Marcellus in a work which brought him into controversy (336) with Eusebius of Cæsarea. With the creeds and Arian literature after the death of Constantine we are not at present concerned.

Arianism was a novelty. Yet it combines in an inconsistent whole elements of almost every previous attempt to formulate the doctrine of the Person of Christ. Its sharpest antithesis was Modalism: yet with the modalist Arius maintained the strict personal unity of the Godhead. With dynamic monarchianism it held the adoptionist principle in addition; but it personified the Word and sacrificed the entire humanity of Christ. In this latter respect it sided with the Docetæ, most Gnostics, and Manichæans, to all of whom it yet opposes a sharply-cut doctrine of creation and of the transcendence of God. With Origen and the Apologists before him it made much of the cosmic mediation of the Word in contrast to the redemptive work of Jesus; with the Apologists, though not with Origen, it enthroned in the highest place the God of the Philosophers: but against both alike it drew a sharp broad line between the Creator and the Universe, and drew it between the Father and the Son. Least of all is Arianism in sympathy with the theology of Asia,—that of Ignatius, Irenæus, Methodius, founded upon the Joannine tradition. The profound Ignatian idea of Christ as the Λόγος ἀπὸ σιγῆς προελθών is in impressive contrast with the shallow challenge of the *Thalia*, 'Many words hath God spoken, which of these was manifested in the flesh?'

Throughout the controversies of the pre-Nicene age the question felt rather than seen in the background is that of the IDEA OF GOD. The question of Monotheism and Polytheism which separated Christians from heathen was not so much a question of abstract theology as of religion, not one of speculative belief, but of worship. The Gentile was prepared to recognise in the background of his pantheon the shadowy form of one supreme God, Father of gods and men, from whom all the rest derived their being. But his religion required the pantheon as well; he could not worship a philosophic supreme abstraction. The Christian on the other hand was prepared in many cases to recognise the existence of beings corresponding to the gods of the heathen (whether 1 Cor. viii. 5 can be quoted here is open to question). But such beings he would not worship. To him, as an object of religion, there was one God. The one God of the heathen was no object of practical personal religion; the One God of the Christian was. He was the God of the Old Testament, the God who was known to His people not under philosophical categories, but in His dealings with them as a Father, Deliverer, He who would accomplish all things for them that waited on Him, the God of the Covenant. He was the God of the New Testament, God in Christ reconciling the world to Himself, manifesting His Righteousness in the Gospel of Christ to whosoever believed. In Christ the Christian learned that God is Love. Now this knowledge of God is essentially religious; it lies in a different plane from the speculative ἀπορίαι as to God's transcendence or immanence, while yet it steadies the religious mind in the face of speculations tending either way. A God who is Love, if immanent, must yet be personal, if transcendent, must yet manifest His Love in such a way that we can know it and not merely guess it. Now as Christian instinct began to be forced to reflexion, in other words, as faith began to strive for expression in a theology[7], it could not but be that men, however personally religious, seized hold of religious problems by their speculative side. We have seen this exemplified in the influence of Platonic philosophy on the Apologists and Alexandrine Fathers. But to Origen, with all his Platonism, belongs the honour of enthroning the God of Love at the head and centre of a systematic theology. Yet the theology of the end of the third century assimilated secondary results of Origen's system rather than his underlying idea. On the one hand was the rule of faith with the whole round of Christian life and worship, determining the religious instinct of the Church; on the other, the inability to formulate this instinct in a coherent system so long as the central problem was overlooked or inadequately dealt with. God is One, not more; yet how is the One God to be conceived of,

---

[5] They appear to have comprised the Arian appeal to Scripture of which (considering the Biblical learning of Lucian and what we hear of the training of Aetius, to say nothing of the exegetical chair held by Arius at Alxa.) their use must be pronounced meagre and superficial. In the O.T. they harped upon three texts, Deut. vi. 4 (*Monotheism*), Ps. xlv. 8 (*Adoptionism*), and Prov. viii. 22, LXX. (*the Word a Creature*). In the N.T. they appeal for Monotheism (in their sense) to Luke xviii. 19, John xvii. 3; *The Son a Creature*, Acts ii. 36, 1 Cor. i. 24, Col. i. 15, Heb. iii. 2; *Adoptionism*, Matt. xii. 28; προκοπή, Luke ii. 52; also Matt. xxvi. 41, Phil. ii. 6, *sq.*, Heb. i. 4; *The Son* τρεπτὸς, &c., Mark xiii. 32, John xiii. 31, xi. 34; *inferior to the Father*, John xiv. 48, Matt. xxvii. 46, also xi. 27 a, xxvi. 39,

xxviii. 18, John xii. 27, and 1 Cor. xv. 28 (cf. pp. **407, sq.**). In this respect Origen is immeasurably superior.

[6] They are regarded by Athan., a generation after they were written, as the representative statement of 'the case' for Arianism (pp. 459 *sq.*; 324 *sqq.*, 361, 363, 368, &c., from which passages and Eus. *c. Marcell.* a fragmentary restoration might be attempted). For what is known of his history (not in D.C.B.) see Gwatkin, p. 72, note; for his doctrinal position see above, p. xxviii.

[7] A theology which aims at consistency must borrow a method, a philosophy, from outside the sphere of religion. The most developed system of Catholic theology, that of S. Thomas Aquinas, borrows its method from the same source as did Arius,—Aristotle.

what is His relation to the Universe of γένεσις and φθόρα? and the Son is God, and the Spirit; how are they One, and if One how distinct? How do we avoid the relapse into a polytheism of secondary gods? What is—not the essential nature of Godhead, for all agreed that that is beyond our ken—but the πρῶτον ἡμῖν, the essential idea for *us* to begin from if we are to synthesise belief and theology, πίστις and γνῶσις?

Arianism stepped in with a summary answer. God is one, numerically and absolutely. He is beyond the ken of any created intelligence. Even creation is too close a relation for Him to enter into with the world. In order to create, he must create an instrument (pp. 360 *sqq.*), intermediate between Himself and all else. This instrument is called Son of God, i.e. He is not coeternal (for what son was ever as old as his parent?), but the result of an act of creative will. How then is He different from other creatures? This is the weak point of the system; He is not really different, but a difference is created by investing Him with every possible attribute of glory and divinity except the possession of the incommunicable nature of deity. He is merely 'anointed above His fellows.' His 'divinity' is acquired, not original; relative, not absolute; in His character, not in His Person. Accordingly He is, as a creature, immeasurably far from the Creator; He does not know God, cannot declare God to us. The One God remains in His inaccessible remoteness from the creature. But yet Arians worshipped Christ; although not very God, He is God to us. Here we have the exact difficulty with which the Church started in her conflict with heathenism presented again unsolved. The desperate struggle, the hardly earned triumph of the Christians, had been for the sake of the essential principle of heathenism! The One God was, after all, the God of the philosophers; the idea of pagan polytheism was realised and justified in Christ[8]! To this Athanasius returns again and again (see esp. p. 360); it is the doom of Arianism as a Christian theology.

If Arianism failed to assist the thought of the Church to a solution of the great problem of God, its failure was not less conspicuous with regard to revelation and redemption. The revelation of the Gospel stopped short in the person of Christ, did not go back to the Father. God was *not* in Christ reconciling the world to Himself, we have access in Christ to a created intelligence, not to the love of God to usward, not to the everlasting Arms, but to a being neither divine nor human. Sinners against heaven and before God, we must accept an assurance of reconciliation from one who does not know Him whom we have offended; the kiss of the Father has never been given to the prodigal. Men have asked how we are justified in ascribing to the infinite God the attributes which we men call good: mercy, justice, love. If Christ is God, the answer lies near; if He is the Christ of Arius, we are left in moral agnosticism. Apart from Christ, the philosophical arguments for a God have their force; they proffer to us an ennobling belief, a grand 'perhaps'; but the historical inability of Monotheism to retain a lasting hold among men apart from revelation is an impressive commentary on their compelling power. In Christ alone does God lay hold upon the soul with the assurance of His love (Rom. v. 5—8; Matt. xi. 28; John xvii. 3). The God of Arius has held out no hand toward us; he is a far-off abstraction, not a living nor a redeeming God.

The illogicality of Arianism has often been pointed out (Gwatkin, pp. 21 *sqq.* esp. p. 28); how, starting from the Sonship of Christ, it came round to a denial of His Sonship; how it started with an interest for Monotheism and landed in a vindication of polytheism; how it began from the incomprehensibility of God even to His Son, and ended (in its most pronounced form) with the assertion that the divine Nature is no mystery at all, even to us. It is an insult to the memory of Aristotle to call such shallow hasty syllogising from ill-selected and unsifted first principles by his name. Aristotle himself teaches a higher logic than this. But at this date Aristotelianism proper was extinct. It only survived in the form of 'pure' logic, adopted by the Platonists, but also studied for its own sake in connection with rhetoric and the art of arguing (cf. Socr. ii. 35). Such an instrument might well be a cause of confusion in the hands of men who used it without regard to the conditions of the subject-matter. An illogical compromise between the theology of Paul of Samosata and of Origen, the marvel is that Arianism satisfied any one even in the age of its birth. What has been said above with regard to the conception of God in the early Church may help to explain it; the germ of ethical insight which is latent in adoptionism, and which when neglected by the Church has always made itself felt by reaction, must also receive justice; once again, its inherent intellectualism was in harmony with the dominant theology of the Eastern Church, that is with one side of Origenism. Where analogous conditions have prevailed, as for example in the England of the early eighteenth century, Arianism has tended to reappear with no one of its attendant incongruities missing.

But for all that, the doom of Arianism was uttered at Nicæa and verified in the six decades which followed. Every possible alternative formula of belief as to the Person of Christ was forced upon the mind of the early Church, was fully tried, and was found wanting. Arianism above all was fully tried and above all found lacking. The Nicene formula alone has been found to render possible the life, to satisfy the instincts of the Church of Christ. The choice lies—nothing is clearer—between that and the doctrine of Paul of Samosata. The latter, it has been said, was misunderstood, was never fairly tried. As a claimant to represent the true sense of Christianity it was I think once for all rejected when the first Apostles gave the right hand of fellowship to S. Paul (see above, p. xxii.); its future trial must be in the form of naturalism, as a rival to Christianity, on the basis of a denial of the claim of Christ to be the One Saviour of the World, and of His Gospel to be the Absolute Religion. But Arianism, adding to all the difficulties of a supernatural Christology the spirit of the shallowest rationalism and the fundamental postulate of agnosticism, can surely count for nothing in the Armageddon of the latter days,

Spiacente a Dio ed a' nemici suoi.

(b) *The ὁμοούσιον as a theological formula*[1].

The distinction, which in the foregoing discussion we have frequently had under our notice, between the

---

[8] This illustrates the famous paradox of Cardinal Newman (*Development*, ed. 1878, pp. 142-4), that the condemnation of Arian Christology *left vacant* a throne in heaven which the medieval Church legitimately filled with the Blessed Virgin; that the Nicene condemnation of the Arian theology is the vindication of the medieval; that 'the votaries of Mary do not exceed the true faith, unless the blasphemers of her Son come up to it.' But the question here was one of *worship*, not of *theology*. The Arians *worshipped* Christ, whom they regarded as a created being: therefore, the Nicene fathers urge with one consent, they were idolaters. The idea of a created being *capable of being worshipped* was an Arian legacy to the Church, no doubt. But this very idea, to Athanasius and Hilary, marked them out as idolaters. It was reserved for later times 'to find a subject for an Arian predicate' (Mozley). The argument is an astonishing admission.
[1] The enormous literature of the subject is partly given by Harnack, ii. p. 182, Schaff, *Nicene Christ.* §§ 119, 120. The student will find great help from Bigg, *Bampt. Lect.* pp. 179, note

πίστις and γνῶσις of the early Church, the πίστις common to all, and formulated in the *tessera* or rule of faith, the γνῶσις the property of apologists and theologians aiming at the expression of faith in terms of the thought of their age, and at times, though for long only slightly, reacting upon the rule of faith itself (Aquileia, Cæsarea, Gregory Thaumaturgus), makes itself felt in the account of the Nicene Council. That the legacy of the first world-wide gathering of the Church's rulers is a Rule of Faith moulded by theological reflexion, one in which the γνῶσις of the Church supplements her πίστις, is a momentous fact; a fact for which we have to thank not Athanasius but Arius. The πίστις of the Fathers repudiated Arianism as a novelty; but to exclude it from the Church some test was indispensable; and to find a test was the task of theology, of γνῶσις. The Nicene Confession is the Rule of Faith explained as against Arianism. Arianism started with the Christian profession of belief in our Lord's *Sonship*. If the result was incompatible with such belief, it was inevitable that an explanation should be given, not indeed of the full meaning of divine Sonship, but of that element in the idea which was ignored or assailed by the misconception of Arius. Such an explanation is attempted in the words ἐκ τῆς οὐσίας τοῦ πατρός, ὁμοούσιαν τῷ Πατρί, and again in the condemnation of the formula ἐξ ἑτέρας ὑποστάσεως ἢ οὐσίας. This explanation was not adopted without hesitation, nor would it have been adopted had any other barrier against the heresy, which all but very few wished to exclude, appeared effective. We now have to examine firstly the grounds of this hesitation, secondly the justification of the formula itself.

The objections felt to the word ὁμοούσιον at the council were (1) philosophical, based on the identification of οὐσία with either εἶδος (i.e. as implying a 'formal essence' prior to Father and Son alike) or ὕλη; (2) dogmatic, based on the identification of οὐσία with τόδε τι, and on the consequent Sabellian sense of the ὁμοούσιον; (3) Scriptural, based on the non-occurrence of the word in the Bible; (4) Ecclesiastical, based on the condemnation of the word by the Synod which deposed Paul at Antioch in 269.

All these objections were made and felt *bona fide*, although Arians would of course make the most of them. The subsequent history will shew that their force was outweighed only for the moment with many of the fathers, and that to reconcile the 'conservatism' of the Asiatic bishops to the new formula must be a matter of time. The third or Scriptural objection need not now be discussed at length. Precedent could be pleaded for the introduction into creeds of words not expressly found in Scripture (e.g. the word 'catholic' applied to the Church in many ancient creeds, the creed of Gregory Thaumaturgus with τρίας τελεία, &c. &c.); the only question was, were the non-scriptural words expressive of a *Scriptural idea?* This was the pith of the question debated between Athanasius and his opponents for a generation after the council; the 'conservative' majority eventually came round to the conviction that Athanasius was right. But the question depends upon the meaning of the word itself.

The word means *sharing in a joint or common* essence, οὐσία (cf. ὁμώνυμος, sharing the same name, &c. &c.). What then is οὐσία? The word was introduced into philosophical use, so far as we know, by Plato, and its technical value was fixed for future ages by his pupil Aristotle. Setting aside its use to express 'existence' in the abstract, we take the more general use of the word as indicating that which exists in the concrete. In this sense it takes its place at the centre of his system of 'categories,' as the something to which all determinations of quality, quantity, relation and the rest attach, and which itself attaches to nothing; in Aristotle's words it alone is self-existent, χωριστόν, whereas all that comes under any of the other categories is ἀχώριστον, non-existent except as a property of some οὐσία. But here the difficulty begins. We may look at a concrete term as denoting either this or that individual simply (τόδε τι), or as expressing its nature, and so as *common* to more individuals than one. Now properly (πρώτως) οὐσία is only appropriate to the former purpose. But it may be employed in a secondary sense to designate the latter; in this sense species and genera are δεύτεραι οὐσίαι, the wider class being less truly οὐσίαι than the narrower. In fact we here detect the transition of the idea of οὐσία from the category of οὐσία proper to that of ποιόν (cf. Athan. p. 478 *sq.*; he uses οὐσία freely in the secondary sense for non-theological purposes in *contra Gentes*, where it is often best rendered 'nature'). Aristotle accordingly uses οὐσία freely to designate what we call substances, whether simple or compound, such as iron, gold, earth, the heavens, τὸ ἀκίνητον, &c., &c. Corresponding again, to the logical distinction of γένος and εἶδος is the metaphysical distinction (not exactly of matter and form, but) of matter simply, regarded as τὸ ὑποκείμενον, and matter regarded as existing in this or that form, τὸ ποιὸν τὸ ἐν τῇ οὐσίᾳ, τὸ τί ἦν εἶναι, the meeting-point of logic and metaphysics in Aristotle's system. Agreeably to this distinction, οὐσία is used sometimes of the latter—the concrete thing regarded in its essential nature, sometimes of the former ἡ ὑποκειμένη οὐσία ὡς ὕλη, ὕλη being in fact the *summum genus* of the material world.

Now the use of the word in Christian theology had exemplified nearly every one of the above senses. In the quasi-material sense ὁμοούσιον had been used in the school of Valentinian to express the homogeneity of the two factors in the fundamental dualism of the Universe of intelligent beings. In a somewhat similar sense it is used in the Clementine Homilies xx. 7. The Platonic phrase for the Divine Nature, ἐπέκεινα πάσης οὐσίας, adopted by Origen and by Athanasius *contra Gentes*, appears to retain something of the idea of οὐσία as implying *material* existence; and this train of associations had to be expressly disclaimed in defending the Nicene formula. In the sense of homogeneity the word ὁμοούσιον is expressly applied by Origen, as we have seen, to the Father and the Son: on the other hand, taking οὐσία in the 'primary' Aristotelian sense, he has ἕτερος κατ' οὐσίαν καὶ ὑποκειμένον. In the West (see above on Tertullian and Novatian) the Latin *substantia* (Cicero had in vain attempted to give currency to the less euphonious but more suitable *essentia*) had taken its place in the phrase *unius substantiæ* or *communio substantiæ*, intended to denote not only the homogeneity but the Unity of Father and Son. Accordingly we find Dionysius of Rome pressing the test upon his namesake of Alexandria and the latter not declining it (below, p. 183). But a few years later we find the Origenist bishops, who with the concurrence of Dionysius of Rome deposed Paul of Samosata, expressly repudiating the term. This fact, which is as certain as any fact in Church history (see Routh *Rell.* iii. 364 &c., Caspari *Alte u. Neue. Q.*, pp. 161 *sqq.*), was a powerful support to the Arians in their subsequent endeavours to unite the conservative East in reaction against the council. Scholars are fairly equally divided as to the explanation of the fact. Some hold, following Athanasius

---

163—165, Gwatkin, *Studies*, p. 42, *sqq.*; pp. 185 to 193, and his notes and excursus embodied in this volume, especially that appended to *Epist. Euseb.* p. 77; Zahn's *Marcellus*, pp. 11—27 (also p. 87), perhaps the best modern discussion; Harnack ii. pp. 228—230, and note 3; Loofs §§ 32—34;

Shedd i. 362—372; and the Introduction to the *Tomus* and *ad Afros* in this volume pp. 482, 488. The use of οὐσία in Aristotle is tabulated by Bonitz in the fifth volume (index) to the Berlin edition: its use in Plato is less frequent and less technical, but see the brief account in Liddell and Scott.

and Basil, that Paul imputed the ὁμοούσιον (in a materialising sense) to his opponents, as a consequence of the doctrine they opposed to his own, and that 'the 80' in repudiating the word, repudiated the idea that the divine nature could be divided by the emanation of a portion of it in the Logos. Hilary, on the other hand, tells us that the word was used by Paul himself ('male ὁμοούσιον Paulus confessus est, sed numquid melius Arii negaverunt?') If so, it must have been meant to deny the existence of the Logos as an οὐσία (i.e. Hypostasis) distinct from the Father. Unfortunately we have not the original documents to refer to. But in either case the word was repudiated at Antioch in one sense, enacted at Nicæa in another. The fact however remains that the term does not exclude ambiguity. Athanasius is therefore going beyond strict accuracy when he claims (p. 164) that no one who is not an Arian can fail to be in agreement with the Synod. Marcellus and Photinus alone prove the contrary. But he is right in regarding the word as rigidly excluding the heresy of Arius.

This brings us to the question in what sense οὐσία is used in the Nicene definition. We must remember the strong Western and anti-Origenist influence which prevailed in the council (above, p. xvii.), and the use of ὑπόστασις and οὐσία as convertible terms in the anathematism (see Excursus A, pp. 77, sqq. below). Now going back for a moment to the correspondence of the two Dionysii, we see that Dionysius of Rome had contended not so much against the *subordination* of the Son to the Father as against their undue *separation* (μεμερισμέναι ὑποστάσεις). In other words he had pressed the ὁμοούσιον upon his namesake in the interest rather of the *unity* than of the *equality* of the Persons in the Holy Trinity. At Nicæa, the problem was (as shewn above) to explain (at least negatively) how the Church understood the Generation of the Son. Accordingly we find Athanasius in later years explaining that the Council meant to place beyond doubt the *Essential Relation* of the Divine Persons to one another (τὸ ἴδιον τῆς οὐσίας, ταὐτότης, see *de Decr.* pp. 161, 163 sq., 165, 168, 319 ; of course including identity of Nature, pp. 396, 413, 232), and maintaining to the end (where he expresses his own view, p. 490, &c.) the convertibility of οὐσία and ὑπόστασις for this purpose. By the word ὁ θεός or θεός he understands οὐδὲν ἕτερον ἢ τὴν οὐσίαν τοῦ ὄντος (*de Decr.* 22). The conclusion is that in their original sense the definitions of Nicæa assert not merely the *specific* identity of the Son with the Father (as Peter *qua* man is of one οὐσία with Paul, or the Emperor's statue of one form with the Emperor himself, p. 396), but the full unbroken continuation of the Being of the Father in the Son, the inseparable unity of the Son with the Father in the Oneness of the Godhead. Here the phrase is 'balanced' by the ἐκ τῆς [ὑποστάσεως ἢ] οὐσίας τοῦ Πατρὸς, not as though merely one οὐσία had given existence to another, but in the sense that with such origination the οὐσία remained the same. This is a 'first approximation to the mysterious doctrine of the περιχώρησις,' coinherence, or 'circuminsessio,' which is necessary to guard the doctrine of the Trinity against tritheism, but which, it must be observed, lifts it out of the reach of the categories of any system of thought in which the workings of human intelligence have ever been able to organise themselves. The doctrine of the Holy Trinity vindicated by the Nicene formula on the one hand remains, after the exclusion of others, as the one direction in which the Christian intellect can travel without frustrating and limiting the movement of faith, without bringing to a halt the instinct of faith in Christ as Saviour, implanted in the Church by the teaching of S. Paul and of S. John, of the Lord Himself : on the other hand it is not a full solution of the intellectual difficulties with which the analysis of that faith and those instincts brings us face to face. That God is One, and that the Son is God, are truths of revelation which the category of 'substance' fails to synthesise. The Nicene Definition furnishes a basis of agreement for the purpose of Christian devotion, worship, and life, but leaves two theologies face to face, with mutual recognition as the condition of the healthy life of either. The theology of Athanasius and of the West is that of the Nicene formula in its original sense. The inseparable Unity of the God of Revelation is its pivot. The conception of *personality* in the Godhead is its difficulty. The distinctness of the Father, Son, and Spirit is felt (ἄλλος ὁ Πατὴρ ἄλλος ὁ υἱός), but cannot be formulated so as to satisfy our full idea of personality. *For this Athanasius had no word ;* πρόσωπον meant too little (implying as it did no more than an aspect possibly worn but for a special period or purpose), ὑπόστασις (implying such personality as separates Peter from Paul) too much. But he recognised the admissibility of the sense in which the Nicene formula eventually, in the theology of the Cappadocian fathers, won its way to supremacy in the East. To them ὑπόστασις was an appropriate term to express the distinction of Persons in the Godhead, while οὐσία expressed the divine *Nature* which they possessed in common (see Excursus A. p. 77 sqq.). This sense of οὐσία *approximated* to that of species, or εἶδος (Aristotle's 'secondary' οὐσία), while that of ὑπόστασις gravitated toward that of personality in the empirical sense. But in neither case did the approximation amount to complete identity. The idea of trine personality was limited by the consideration of the Unity ; the περιχώρησις was recognised, although in a somewhat different form, the prominent idea in Athanasius being that of *coinherence* or immanence, whereas the Cappadocians, while using, of course, the language of John xiv. 11, yet prefer the metaphor of *successive dependence* ὥσπερ ἐξ ἁλύσεω. (Bas. *Ep.* 38, p. 118 D). To Athanasius, the Godhead is complete not in the Father alone, still less in the Three Persons *as parts* of the one οὐσία, but in *each* Person as much as in *all*. The Cappadocian Fathers go back to the Origenist view that the Godhead is complete primarily in the Father alone, but *mediately* in the Son or Spirit, by virtue of their origination from the Father as πηγή or αἰτία τῆς θεότητος. To Athanasius the *distinct Personality* of Son and Spirit was the difficulty ; his difference from Origen was wide, from Marcellus subtle. To the Cappadocians the difficulty was the *Unity* of the Persons ; to Marcellus they were *toto cælo* opposed, they are the pupils of Origen[2]. Accordingly when Basil makes a distinction between οὐσία and ὑπόστασις in the Nicene anathematism, he is giving not historical exegesis but his own opinion.

The Nicene definition in this sense emphasized the UNITY of the Godhead in Three Persons, against the Arian *division* of the Son from the Father. How then did it escape the danger of lending countenance to Monarchianism? Athanasius feels the difficulty without solving it, for the distinction given by him, p. 84, between ὁμοούσιος and μονοούσιος is without real meaning (*we* say with Tertullian 'of *one* substance'). On the whole in mature years he held that the title 'Son' was sufficient to secure the Trinity of Persons. 'By the name Father we confute Arius, by the name of Son we overthrow Sabellius' (p.434; cf. p. 413) ; and we find that the council in its revision of the Cæsarean creed shifted υἱός to the principal position where it took the place of λόγος. Beyond this the Creed imposed no additional test in that direction (the ἐκ τῆς οὐσίας is important but not

---

[2] Gregory Thaumaturgus was the great Origenist influence in northern Asia Minor : the Cappadocian fathers were also influenced in the direction of the ὁμοούσιον by Apollinarius : see the correspondence between Basil and the latter, Bas. *Epp.* 8, 9, edited by Dräseke in *Ztschr. für K.G.* viii. 85 sqq. Apollinarius was of course equally opposed to Arianism and to Origen : see also p. 449 sq.

decisive in this respect). This was felt as an objection to the Creed, and the objection was pointed by the influence of Marcellus at the council. The historical position of Marcellus is in fact, as we shall see, the principal key to the 'conservative' reaction which followed. The insertion into the conservative creeds of a clause asserting the endlessness of Christ's Kingdom, which eventually received ecumenical authority, was an expression of this feeling. But a final explanation between the Nicene doctrine and Monarchianism could not come about until the idea of Personality had been tested in the light of the appearance of the Son in the Flesh. The solution, or rather definition, of the problem is to be sought in the history of the Christological questions which began with Apollinarius of Laodicea.

The above account of the anti-Arian test formulated at Nicæa will suffice to explain the motives for its adoption, the difficulties which made that adoption reluctant, and the fact of the reaction which followed. One thing is clear, namely that given the actual conditions, nothing short of the test adopted would have availed to exclude the Arian doctrine. It is also I think clear, that not only was the current theology of the Eastern Church unable to cope with Arianism, but that it was itself a danger to the Church and in need of the corrective check of the Nicene definition. Hellenic as was the system of Origen, it was in its spirit Christian, and saturated with the influence of Scripture. It could never have taken its place as the expression of the whole mind of the Church ; but it remains as the noblest monument of a Christian intellect resolutely in love with truth for its own sake, and bent upon claiming for Christ the whole range of the legitimate activity of the human spirit. But the age had inherited only the wreck of Origenism, and its partial victory in the Church had brought confusion in its train, the leaders of the Church were characterised by secular knowledge rather than grasp of first principles, by dogmatic intellectualism rather than central apprehension of God in Christ. Eusebius of Cæsarea is their typical representative. The Nicene definition and the work of Athanasius which followed were a summons back to the simple first principles of the Gospel and the Rule of Faith. What then is their value to ourselves ? Above all, this, that they have preserved to us what Arianism would have destroyed, that assurance of Knowledge of, and Reconciliation to, God in Christ of which the divinity of the Saviour is the indispensable condition ; if we are now Christians in the sense of S. Paul we owe it under God to the work of the great synod. Not that the synod explained all ; or did more than effectually 'block off false forms of thought or avenues of unbalanced inference' which 'challenged the acceptance of Christian people.' The decisions of councils are 'primarily not the Church saying "yes" to fresh truths or developments or forms of consciousness ; but rather saying "no" to untrue and misleading modes of shaping and stating her truth,' (*Lux Mundi*, ed. i. p. 240, cf. p. 334). It is objected that the Nicene Formula, especially as understood by Athanasius, is itself a 'false form of thought,' a flat contradiction in terms. That the latter is true we do not dispute (see Newman's notes *infra*, p. 336, note 1, &c.). But before pronouncing the form of thought for that reason a false one, we must consider what the 'terms' are, and to what they are applied. To myself it appears that a religion which brought the divine existence into the compass of the categories of any philosophy would by that very fact forfeit its claim to the character of revelation. The categories of human thought are the outcome of organised experience of a sensible world, and beyond the limits of that world they fail us. This is true quite apart from revelation. The ideas of essence and substance, personality and will, separateness and continuity, cause and effect, unity and plurality, are all in different degrees helps which the mind uses in order to arrange its knowledge, and valid within the range of experience, but which become a danger when invested with absolute validity as things in themselves. Even the mathematician reaches real results by operating with terms which contain a perfect contradiction (e. g. $\sqrt{-1}$, and to some extent the 'calculus of operations'). The idea of Will in man, of Personality in God, present difficulties which reason cannot reconcile.

The revelation of Christ is addressed primarily to the will not to the intellect, its appeal is to Faith not to Theology. Theology is the endeavour of the Christian intellect to frame for itself conceptions of matters belonging to the immediate consequences of our faith, matters about which we must believe something, but as to which the Lord and His Apostles have delivered nothing formally explicit. Theology has no doubt its certainties beyond the express teaching of our Lord and the New Testament writers ; but its work is subject to more than the usual limitations of human thought : we deal with things outside the range of experience, with celestial things ; but 'we have no celestial language.' To abandon all theology would be to acquiesce in a dumb faith : we are to teach, to explain, to defend ; the λόγος σοφίας and λόγος γνώσεως have from the first been gifts of the Spirit for the building up of the Body. But we know in part and prophesy in part, and our terms begin to fail us just in the region where the problem of guarding the faith of the simple ends and the inevitable metaphysic, into which all pure reflexion merges, begins. Εἴτε οὖν φιλοσοφητέον εἴτε μὴ φιλοσοφητέον, φιλοσοφητέον, 'man is metaphysical *nolens volens :*' only let us recollect that when we find ourselves in the region of antinomies we are crossing the frontier line between revelation and speculation, between the domain of theology and that of ontology. That this line is approached in the definition of the great council no one will deny. But it was reached by the council and by the subsequent consent of the Church reluctantly and under compulsion. The bold assumption that we can argue from the revelation of God in Christ to mysteries beyond our experience was made by the Gnostics, by Arius : the Church met them by a denial of what struck at the root of her belief, not by the claim to erect formulæ applied merely for the lack of better into a revealed ontology. In the terms Person, Hypostasis, Will, Essence, Nature, Generation, Procession, we have the embodiment of ideas extracted from experience, and, as applied to God, representing merely the best attempt we can make to explain what we mean when we speak of God as Father and of Christ as His Son. Even these last sacred names convey their full meaning to us only in view of the historical person of Christ and of our relation to God through Him. That this meaning is based upon an absolute relation of Christ to the Father is the rock of our faith. That relation is mirrored in the name Son of God : but what it is in itself, when the empirical connotations of Sonship are stripped away, we cannot possibly know. Ὁμοούσιος τῷ Πατρί, ἐκ τῆς οὐσίας τοῦ Πατρός· these words assert at once our faith that such relation exists and our ignorance of its nature. To the simplicity of faith it is enough to know (and this knowledge is what our formula secures) that in Christ we have not only the perfect Example of Human Love to God, but the direct expression and assurance of the Father's Love to us.

(c) *Materials for Reaction.*

'The victory of Nicæa was rather a surprise than a solid conquest. As it was not the spontaneous and deliberate purpose of the bishops present, but a revolution which a minority had forced through by sheer strength of clearer Christian thought, a reaction was inevitable as soon as the half-convinced conservatives returned home' (Gwatkin). The reaction, however, was not for a long time overtly doctrinal. The defeat, the moral humiliation of Arianism at the council was too signal, the prestige of the council itself too overpowering, the Emperor too resolute in supporting its definition, to permit of this. Not till after the death of Constantine in 337 does the policy become manifest of raising alternative symbols to a coordinate rank with that of Nicæa ; not till six years after the establishment of Constantius as sole Emperor,—i.e. not till 357,—did Arianism once again set its mouth to the trumpet. During the reign of Constantine the reaction, though doctrinal in its motive, was personal in its ostensible grounds. The leaders of the victorious minority at Nicæa are one by one attacked on this or that pretence and removed from their Sees, till at the time of Constantine's death the East is in the hands of their opponents. What were the forces at work which made this possible?

(1) *Persecuted Arians.* Foremost of all, the harsh measures adopted by Constantine with at least the tacit approval of the Nicene leaders furnished material for reaction. Arius and his principal friends were sent into exile, and as we have seen they went in bitterness of spirit. Arius himself was banished to Illyricum, and would seem to have remained there five or six years. (The chronology of his recall is obscure, but see D.C.B. ii. 364, and Gwatkin, p. 86, note 2). It would be antecedently very unlikely that a religious exile would spare exertions to gain sympathy for himself and converts to his opinions. As a matter of fact, Arianism had no more active supporters during the next half-century than two bishops of the neighbouring province of Pannonia, VALENS of Mursa (Mitrowitz), and URSACIUS[1] of Singidunum (Belgrade). Valens and Ursacius are described as pupils of Arius, and there is every reason to trace their personal relations with the heresiarch to his Illyrian exile. The seeds sown in Illyria at this time were still bearing fruit nearly 50 years later (pp. 489, 494, note). Secundus nursed his bitterness fully thirty years (p. 294 ; cf. 456). Theognis grasped at revenge at Tyre in 335 (pp. 104, 114). Eusebius of Nicomedia, recalled from exile with his friend and neighbour Theognis, not long after the election of Athanasius in 328, was ready to move heaven and earth to efface the results of the council. The harsh measures against the Arians then, if insufficient to account for the reaction, at any rate furnished it with the energy of personal bitterness and sense of wrong.

(2) *The Eusebians and the Court.* Until the council of Sardica (i.e. a short time after the death of Eusebius of Nicomedia), the motive power of the reaction proceeded from the environment of Eusebius, οἱ περὶ Εὐσέβιον. It should be observed once for all that the term 'EUSEBIANS' is the later and inexact equivalent of the last named Greek phrase, which (excepting perhaps p. 436) has reference to Eusebius of Nicomedia only, and not to his namesake of Cæsarea. The latter, no doubt, lent his support to the action of the party, but ought not to suffer in our estimation from the misfortune of his name. Again, the 'Eusebians' are not a heresy, nor a theological party or school ; they are the 'ring,' or personal *entourage*, of one man, a master of intrigue, who succeeded in combining a very large number of men of very different opinions in more or less close association for common ecclesiastical action. The 'Eusebians' *sensu latiori* are the majority of Asiatic bishops who were in reaction against the council and its leaders ; in the stricter sense the term denotes the pure Arians like Eusebius, Theognis, and the rest, and those 'political Arians' who without settled adherence to Arian principles, were, for all practical purposes, hand in glove with Eusebius and his fellows. To the former class emphatically belong Valens and Ursacius, whose recantation in 347 is the solitary and insufficient foundation for the sweeping generalisation of Socrates (ii. 37), that they 'always inclined to the party in power,' and George, the presbyter of Alexandria, afterwards bishop of the Syrian Laodicea, who, although he went through a phase of 'conservatism,' 357—359, began and ended (Gwatkin, pp. 181—183) as an Arian, pure and simple. Among 'political Arians' of this period Eusebius of Cæsarea is the chief. He was not, as we have said above, an Arian theologically, yet whatever allowances may be made for his conduct during this period (D.C.B., ii. 315, 316) it tended all in one direction. But on the whole, political Arianism is more abundantly exemplified in the Homœans of the next generation, whose activity begins about the time of the death of Constans. The Eusebians proper were political indeed εἴ τινες καὶ ἄλλοι, but their essential Arianism is the one element of principle about them[2]. Above all, the employment of the term 'SEMI-ARIANS' as a synonym for Eusebians, or indeed as a designation of any party at this period, is to be strongly deprecated. It is the (possibly somewhat misleading, but reasonable and accepted) term for the younger generation of *convinced* 'conservatives,' whom we find in the sixth decade of the century becoming conscious of their essential difference in principle from the Arians, whether political or pure, and feeling their way toward fusion with the Nicenes. These are a definite party, with a definite theological position, to which nothing in the earlier period exactly corresponds. The Eusebians proper were not *semi-*, but *real* Arians. Eusebius *of Cæsarea* and the Asiatic conservatives are the *predecessors* of the semi-Arians, but their position is not quite the same. Reserving them for a moment, we must complete our account of the Eusebians proper. Their nucleus consisted of the able and influential circle of 'Lucianists ;' it has been remarked by an unprejudiced observer that, so far as we know, not one of them was eminent as a *religious* character (Harnack, ii. 185) ; their strength was in fixity of policy and in ecclesiastical intrigue ; and their battery was the imperial court. Within three years of the Council, Constantine had begun to waver, not in his resolution to maintain the Nicene Creed, *that* he never relaxed, but in his sternness toward its known opponents. His policy was dictated by the desire for unity : he was made to feel the lurking dissatisfaction of the bishops of Asia, perhaps as his anger was softened by time he missed the ability and ready counsel of the extruded bishop of his residential city. An Arian presbyter ('Eustathius' or 'Eutokius'?), who was a kind of chaplain to Constantia, sister of Constantine and widow of Licinius, is said to have kept the subject before the Emperor's mind after her death (in 328, see Socr. i. 25). At last, as we have seen, first Eusebius and Theognis were recalled, then Arius himself was pardoned upon his general assurance of agreement with the faith of the Synod.

---

[1] They were probably not yet bishops at this time, as they were *young* bishops at Tyre in 335 ; evidently they are 'the fairest of God's youthful flock' (!) alluded to in Eus. *V.C.* iv. 43.

[2] At the same time Arius himself and all his fellow Lucianists (unlike the obscure Secundus and Theonas, and the later generation of Eunomians) are open to the charge of subserviency at a pinch.

The atmosphere of a court is seldom favourable to a high standard of moral or religious principle ; and the place-hunters and hangers-on of the imperial courts of these days were an exceptionally worthless crew (see Gwatkin, p. 60, 110, 234). It is a tribute to the Nicene cause that their influence was steadily on the other side, and to the character of Constantine that he was able throughout the greater part of the period to resist it, at any rate as far as Athanasius was concerned. But on the whole the court was the centre whence the webs of Eusebian intrigue extended to Egypt, Antioch, and many other obscurer centres of attack.

The influences outside the Church were less directly operative in the campaign, but such as they were they served the Eusebian plans. The expulsion of a powerful bishop from the midst of a loyal flock was greatly assisted by the co-operation of a friendly mob; and Jews (pp. 94, 296), and heathen alike were willing to aid the Arian cause. The army, the civil service, education, the life of society were still largely heathen ; the inevitable influx of heathen into the Church, now that the empire had become Christian, brought with it multitudes to whom Arianism was a more intelligible creed than that of Nicæa ; the influence of the philosophers was a serious factor, they might well welcome Arianism as a ' Selbstersetzung des Christentums.' This is not inconsistent with the instances of persecution of heathenism by Arian bishops, and of savage heathen reprisals, associated with the names of George of Alexandria, Patrophilus, Mark of Arethusa, and others. (For a fuller discussion, with references, see Gwatkin, pp. 53—59.)

(3.) *The Ecclesiastical Conservatives.* Something has already been said in more than one connection to explain how it came to pass that the very provinces whose bishops made up the large numerical majority at Nicæa, also furnished the numbers which swelled the ranks of the Eusebians at Tyre, Antioch, and Philippopolis. The actual men were, of course, in many cases[3] changed in the course of years, but the sees were the same, and there is ample evidence that the staunch Nicene party were in a hopeless minority in Asia Minor[4] and but little stronger in Syria. The indefiniteness of this mass of episcopal opinion justifies the title 'Conservative.' In adopting it freely, we must not forget, what the whole foregoing account has gone to shew, that their conservatism was of the empirical or short-sighted kind, prone to acquiesce in things as they are, hard to arouse to a sense of a great crisis, reluctant to step out of its groove. If by conservatism we mean action which really tends to preserve the vital strength of an institution, then Athanasius and the leaders of Nicæa were the only conservatives. But it is not an unknown thing for vulgar conservatism to take alarm at the clear grasp of principles and facts which alone can carry the State over a great crisis, and by wrapping itself up in its prejudices to play into the hands of anarchy. Common men do not easily rise to the level of mighty issues. Where Demosthenes saw the crisis of his nation's destiny, Æschines saw materials for a personal impeachment of his rival. In the anti-Nicene reaction the want of clearness of thought coincided with the fatal readiness to magnify personal issues. Here was the opportunity of the Arian leaders: a confused succession of personal skirmishes, in which the mass of men saw no religious principle, nor any combined purpose (Soc. i. 13, νυκτομαχίας τε οὐδὲν ἀπεῖχε τὰ γινόμενα), was conducted from headquarters with a fixed steady aim. But their machinations would have been fruitless had the mass of the bishops been really in sympathy with the council to which they were still by their own action committed. ' Arian hatred of the council would have been powerless if it had not rested on a formidable mass of conservative discontent : while the conservative discontent might have died away if the court had not supplied it with the means of action ' (Gwatkin, p. 61. He explains the policy of the court by the religious sympathies of Asia Minor[5] and its political importance, pp. 90-91.) But the authority of the council remained unchallenged during the lifetime of Constantine, and no Arian raised his voice against it. One doctrinal controversy there was, of subordinate importance, but of a kind to rivet the conservatives to their attitude of sullen reaction.

It follows from what has been said of the influence of Origen in moulding the current theology of the Eastern Church, that the one theological principle which was most vividly and generally grasped was the horror of Monarchian and especially of ' Sabellian ' teaching. Now in replying to Asterius the spokesman of early Arianism, no less a person than MARCELLUS, bishop of Ancyra (Angora) in Galatia, and one of the principal leaders of Nicæa, had laid himself open to this charge. It was brought with zeal and learning (in 336) in two successive works by Eusebius of Cæsarea, which, with Ath., *Orat.* iv. are our principal source of information as to the tenets of Marcellus (see D.C.B. ii. 341, *sq.*, Zahn *Marcellus* 99 *sqq.*, fragments collected by Rettberg *Marcelliana*). On the other hand he was uniformly supported by the Nicene party, and especially by Athanasius and the Roman Church. His book was examined at Sardica, and on somewhat *ex parte* grounds (p. 125) pronounced innocent : a personal estrangement from Athanasius shortly after (Hilar. *Fragm.* ii. 21, 23) on account of certain ' ambiguæ prædicationes eius, in quam Photinus erupit, doctrinæ,' did not amount to a formal breach of communion (he is mentioned 14 years later as an exiled Nicene bishop, pp. 256, 271), nor did the anxious questioning of Epiphanius (see *Hær.* 72. 4) succeed in extracting from the then aged Athanasius more than a significant smile. He refuses to condemn him, and in arguing against opinions which appear to be his, he refrains from mentioning the name

---

3 Alexander of Thessalonica had been at Nicæa, Dianius of Caes. Capp. had not. The two are typical of the better sort of conservatives.
4 For Asia besides Marcellus we have only Diodorus of Tenedos, not at Nicæa, but expelled soon after 330, p. 271; signs at Sardica, p. 147, banished again p. 276, not in D.C.B. ; for Syria the names p. 271, cf. p. 256.

5 Always an important factor in the stability of the Byzantine throne, see, on Justinian, D.C.B. iii. 545a, *sub fin.* Newman, *Arians*, Appendix v., brings no conclusive proof of strong Nicene feeling among the masses of the laity in this region. But ' the people' in Galatia, according to Basil, remained devoted to Marcellus.

even of Photinus[6]. It may be well therefore to sketch in a few touches what we know of the system of Marcellus, in order that we may appreciate the relative right of Eusebius in attacking, and of Athanasius and the Romans in supporting him. Marcellus is a representative of the traditional theology of Asia Minor, as we find it in Ignatius and Irenæus (see above, pp. xxii.—xxiv., xxvi. *fin.*), and is independent of any influence of, or rather in conscious reaction against, Origenism. We cannot prove that he had studied either Ignatius or Irenæus, but we find the doctrine of ἀνακεφαλαίωσις with reference to Creation and the Incarnation, and the Ignatian thought of the Divine Silence, and a general unmistakeable affinity (cf. Zahn 236—244). Marcellus 'appeals from Origen to S. John.' He begins with the idea of Sonship, as Arius and the Nicene Council had done. Perceiving that on the one hand Arians and Origenists alike were led by the idea of Sonship as dependent on paternal will to infer the inferiority of the Son to the Father, and in the more extreme case to deny His coeternity, feeling on the other hand (with Irenæus II. xxviii. 6) our inability to find an idea to correspond with the relation implied in the eternal Sonship, he turns to the first chapter of S. John as the classic passage for the pre-existent nature of Christ. He finds that *before the Incarnation* the Saviour is spoken of as Logos *only:* accordingly all other designations, even that of Son, must be reserved for the Incarnate. Moreover (Joh. i. 1) the Word is strictly coeternal, and no name implying an *act* (such as γέννησις) can express the relation of the Word to God. But in view of the Divine Purpose of Creation and Redemption (for the latter is involved in the former by the doctrine of ἀνακεφαλαίωσις) there is a process, a stirring within the divine Monad. The Word which is potentially (δυνάμει) eternally latent in God proceeds forth in Actuality (ἐνεργείᾳ), yet without ceasing to be potentially in God as well. In this ἐνέργεια δραστική, to which the word γέννησις may be applied, begins the great drama of the Universe which rises to the height of the Incarnation, and which, after the Economy is completed, and fallen man restored (and more than restored) to the Sonship of God which he had lost, ends in the return of the Logos to the Father, the handing over of His Kingdom by the Son, that God may be all in all.

What strikes one throughout the scheme is the intense difficulty caused to Marcellus by the unsolved problem which underlies the whole theology of the Nicene leaders, the problem of *personality.* The Manhood of Christ was to Marcellus *per se* non-personal. The seat of its personality was the indwelling Logos. But in what sense was the Logos itself personal? Here Marcellus loses his footing: in what sense can any idea of personality attach to a merely potential existence? Again, if it was only in the ἐνέργεια δραστική that the personality of the Word was realised, and this only reached its fulness in the Incarnation of Christ, was the transition difficult to the plain assertion that the personality of the Son, or of the Word, originated with the Incarnation? But if this were not so, and if the Person of the Word was to recede at the consummation of all things into the Unity of the Godhead, what was to become of the Nature He had assumed? That it too could merge into a potential existence within the Godhead was of course impossible; what then was its destiny? The answer of Marcellus was simple: he did not know (Zahn, 179); for Scripture taught nothing beyond 1 Cor. xv. 28.

We now perceive the subtle difference between Marcellus and Athanasius. Neither of them could formulate the idea of Personality in the Holy Trinity. But Athanasius, apparently on the basis of a more thorough intelligence of Scripture (for Marcellus, though a devout, was a partial and somewhat ignorant biblical theologian), felt what Marcellus did not, the steady inherent personal distinctness of the Father and the Son. Accordingly, while Athanasius laid down and adhered to the doctrine of eternal γέννησις, Marcellus involved himself in the mystical and confused idea of a divine πλατυσμὸς and συστολή. Moreover, while Athanasius was clearsighted in his apprehension of the problem of the day, Marcellus was after all merely conservative: he went behind the conservatism of the Origenists,—behind even that of the West, where Tertullian had left a sharper sense of personal distinction in the Godhead,—to an archaic conservatism akin to the 'naive modalism' of the early Church; upon this he engrafted reflexion, in part that of the later Asiatic theology, in part his own. As the result, his faith was such as Athanasius could not but recognise as sincere; but in his attempt to give it theological expression he split upon the rocks of Personality, of Eschatology, of the divine immutability. His theology was an honest and interesting but mistaken attempt to grapple with a problem before he understood another which lay at its base. In doing so he exposed himself justly to attack; but we may with Athanasius, while acknowledging this, retain a kindly sympathy for this veteran ally of many confessors and sturdy opponent of the alliance between science and theology.

The feeling against Marcellus might have been less strong, at any rate it would have had less show of reason, but for the fact that he was the teacher of PHOTINUS. This person became bishop of Sirmium between 330 and 340, gave great offence by his teaching, and was deposed by the Arian party ineffectually in 347, finally in 351. After his expulsion he occupied himself with writing books in Greek and in Latin, including a work 'against all heresies,' in which he expounded his own (Socr. ii. 30). None of his works have survived, and our information is very scanty (Zahn, *Marc.* 189—196 is the best account), but he seems to have solved the central difficulty of Marcellus by placing the seat of the Personality of Christ in His Human Soul. How much of the system of his master he retained is uncertain, but the result was in substance pure Unitarianism. It is instructive to observe that even Photinus was passively supported for a time by the Nicenes. He was apparently (Hil. *Fr.* ii. 19, *sqq.*) condemned at a council at Milan in 345, but not at Rome till 380. Athanasius (pp. 444—447) abstains from mentioning his name although he refutes his opinions; once only he mentions him as a heretic, and with apparent reluctance (*c. Apoll.* ii. 19, τοῦ λεγομένου Φωτεινοῦ). The first[7] condemnation of him on the Nicene side in the East is by Paulinus of Antioch in 362 (p. 486). On the other hand the Eusebians eagerly caught at so irresistible a weapon. Again and again they hurled anathemas at Photinus, at first simply identifying him with Marcellus, but afterwards with full appreciation of his position. And even to the last the new Nicene party in Asia were aggrieved at the refusal of the old Nicenes at Alexandria and Rome to anathematise the master of such a heretic. Photinus was the scandal of Marcellus, Marcellus of the Council of Nicæa.

§ 4. *Early years of his Episcopate. The Anti-Nicene reaction,* 328—335.

Athanasius was elected bishop by general consent. Alexander, as we have seen, had practically nominated him, and a large body of popular opinion clamoured for his election,

---

[6] At the same time he adopts a certain reserve in speaking of Marcellus, and his name is absent from the roll of the orthodox, p. 227.

[7] But he is condemned by name in the alleged Coptic Acts of the Council of 362; moreover Eustathius appears to have written against him, see Cowper, *Syr. Misc.* 60.

as "the good, the pious, a Christian, one of the ascetics, a genuine bishop." The actual election appears (p. 103) to have rested with the bishops of Egypt and Libya, who testify ten years later (ib.) that the majority [7] of their body elected him.

The see to which he succeeded was the second in Christendom; it had long enjoyed direct jurisdiction over the bishops of all Egypt and Libya (p. 178, Socr. i. 9), the bishops of Alexandria enjoyed the position and power of secular potentates, although in a less degree than those of Rome, or of Alexandria itself in later times (Socr. vii. 11, cf. 7). The bishop had command of large funds, which, however, were fully claimed for church purposes and alms (see p. 105). In particular, the 'pope' of Alexandria had practically in his hands the appointment to the sees in his province: accordingly, as years go on, we find Arianism disappear entirely from the Egyptian episcopate. The bishop of Alexandria, like many other influential bishops in antiquity, was commonly spoken of as Papa or Pope; he also was known as the Ἀρχιεπίσκοπος, as we learn from a contemporary inscription (see p. 564, note 2).

The earliest biographer of Athanasius (see Introduction to *Hist. Aceph.* p. 495, 496, below) divides the episcopate of Athanasius into periods of 'quiet' and of exile, marking the periods of each according to what appears to be the reckoning officially preserved in the episcopal archives. His first period of 'quiet' lasts from June 8, 328, to July 11, 335 (departure for Tyre), a period of seven years, one month and three days; it is thus the third longest period of undisturbed occupancy of his see, the next being the last from his final restoration under Valens till his death (seven years and three months), and the longest of all being the golden decade (346 356, really nine years and a quarter) preceding the Third Exile.

Of the internal events of this first septennium of quiet we know little that is definite. At the end of it, however, we find him supported by the solid body of the Egyptian episcopate: and at the beginning one of his first steps (autumn of 329) was to make a visitation of the province 'to strengthen the churches of God' (*Vit. Pach.*, cf. also Epiph. *Hær.* 68. 6). We learn from the life of Pachomius (on which see below, p. 189), that he penetrated as far as Syene on the Ethiopian frontier, and, as he passed Tabenne, was welcomed by Pachomius and his monks with great rejoicings. At the request of Saprion, bishop of Tentyra, in whose diocese the island was, he appears to have ordained Pachomius to the presbyterate, thus constituting his community a self-contained body (Acta SS. Mai. iii. 30, Appx.). The supposed consecration of Frumentius at this time must be reserved, in accordance with preponderating evidence, for § 7.

Meanwhile, the anti-Nicene reaction was being skilfully fostered by the strategy of Eusebius of Nicomedia. Within a year of the election of Athanasius we find him restored to imperial favour, and at once the assault upon the Nicene strongholds begins. The controversy between Marcellus and Eusebius of Cæsarea (*supra*, p. xxxv.), appears to have begun later, but the latter was already, in conjunction with his friend Paulinus of Tyre and with Patrophilus, at theological war with Eustathius of Antioch. A synod of Arian and reactionary bishops assembled at Antioch, and deposed the latter on the two charges (equally *de rigueur* in such cases) of Sabellianism and immorality. Backed by a complaint (possibly founded on fact) that he had indiscreetly repeated a current tale (p. 271, n. 2) concerning Helena, the Emperor's mother, the sentence of the council had the full support of the civil arm, and Eustathius lost his see for ever. Although he lived till about 358, no council ventured to 'restore' him (discussed by Gwatkin, pp. 73, 74, note), but the Christian public of Antioch violently resented his extrusion, and a compact body of the Church-people steadily refused to recognise any other bishop during, and even after, his lifetime (*infr.* p. 481). Asclepas of Gaza was next disposed of, then Eutropius of Hadrianople, and many others (names, p. 271). Meanwhile everything was done to foment disturbance in Egypt. The Meletians had been stirring ever since the death of Alexander, and Eusebius was not slow to use such an opportune lever. The object in view was two-fold, the restoration of Arius to communion in Alexandria, without which the moral triumph of the reaction would be unachieved, and the extrusion of Athanasius. Accordingly a fusion took place [1] between the

---

[7] Eager opposition, however, was not lacking. The accounts are confused, but the statement of the bishops leaves room for a strong minority of malcontents, who *may* have elected 'Theonas' (was he the exiled Arian bishop of Marmarica? the electors of 'Theonas' in Epiph. *Hær.* 68 are Meletians, but there is no Theonas in the Meletian catalogue of 327; the Arians and Meletians very likely combined; the latter properly had no votes, but they were not likely to regard this; see Gwatkin, p. 66, note, *Church Quarterly Review.* xvi. p. 393). The protests of the poposition were apparently disregarded and Athanasius conse-

crated before the other side considered the question as closed, (The statement of Epiph. *Hær.* 69, that the Arians chose one Achillas, is unsupported.) Athanasius was probably only just thirty years old, and his opponents did not fail to question whether he were not under the canonical age.

[1] Soz. ii. 21, 22: the account is not very clear; probably there was a gradual approximation, the first step being the Meletian support of the Arian Theonas against Athanasius in 328, if the view suggested above is correct.

Arians of Egypt and the Meletians, now under the leadership of John 'Arcaph,' whom Meletius on his death-bed had consecrated as his successor against the terms of the Nicene settlement. At any rate, the Meletians were attached to the cause by Eusebius by means of large promises. At the same time (330?) Eusebius, having obtained the recall of Arius from exile, wrote to Athanasius requesting him to admit Arius and his friends (Euzoius, Pistus, &c.) to communion ; the bearer of the letter conveyed the assurance of dire consequences in the event of his non-compliance (p. 131). Athanasius refused to admit persons convicted of heresy at the Ecumenical Council. This brought a letter from the Emperor himself, threatening deposition by an imperial mandate unless he would freely admit 'all who should desire it ;'—a somewhat sweeping demand. Athanasius replied firmly and, it would seem, with effect, that 'the Christ-opposing heresy had no fellowship with the Catholic Church.' Thereupon Eusebius played what proved to be the first card of a long suit. A deputation of three Meletian bishops arrived at the Palace with a complaint. Athanasius had, they said, levied a precept (κανών) upon Egypt for Church expenses : they had been among the first victims of the exaction. Luckily, two Presbyters of Alexandria were at court, and were able to disprove the charge, which accordingly drew a stern rebuke upon its authors. Constantine wrote to Athanasius summoning him to an audience, probably with the intention of satisfying himself as to other miscellaneous accusations which were busily ventilated at this date, e.g., that he was too young (cf. p. 133) when elected bishop, that he had governed with arrogance and violence, that he used magic (this charge was again made 30 years later, Ammian. xv. 7), and subsidised treasonable persons. Athanasius accordingly started for court, as it would seem, late in 330 (see *Letter* 3, p. 512 *sq.*). His visit was successful, but matters went slowly ; Athanasius himself had an illness, which lasted a long time, and upon his recovery the winter storms made communication impossible. Accordingly, his Easter letter for 332 (*Letter* 4) was sent unusually late—apparently in the first navigable weather of that year—and Athanasius reached home, after more than a year's absence [2], when Lent was already half over.

The principal matters investigated by Constantine during the visit of Athanasius were certain charges made by the three Meletian bishops, whom Eusebius had detained for the purpose ; one of these, the story of Macarius and the broken chalice, will be given at length presently. All alike were treated as frivolous, and Athanasius carried home with him a commendatory letter from Augustus himself. Defeated for the moment, the puppets of Eusebius matured their accusations, and in a year's time two highly damaging stories were ripe for an ecclesiastical investigation.

(a) *The case of Ischyras.* This person had been ordained presbyter by Colluthus, and his ordination had been, as we have seen (§ 2), pronounced null and void by the Alexandrian Council of 324. In spite of this he had persisted in carrying on his ministrations at the village where he lived (Irene Secontaruri, possibly the hamlet ' Irene ' belonged to the township of S., there was a presbyter for the township, pp. 133, 145, but none at Irene, p 106). His place of worship was a cottage inhabited only by an orphan child ; of the few inhabitants of the place, only seven, and those his own relations, would attend his services. During a visitation of his diocese, Athanasius had heard of this from the presbyter of the township, and had sent Macarius, one of the clergy who were attending him on his tour (cf. pp. 109, 139), to summon Ischyras for explanations. Macarius found the poor man ill in bed and unable to come, but urged his father to dissuade him from his irregular proceedings. But instead of desisting, Ischyras joined the Meletians. His first version of the matter appears to have been that Macarius had used violence, and broken his chalice. The Meletians communicate this to Eusebius, who eggs them on to get up the case. The story gradually improves. Ischyras, it now appeared, had been actually celebrating the Eucharist ; Macarius had burst in upon him, and not only broken the chalice but upset the Holy Table. In this form the tale had been carried to Constantine when Athanasius was at Nicomedia. The relations of Ischyras, however, prevailed upon him to recall his statements, and he presented the Bishop with a written statement that the whole story was false, and had been extorted from him by violence. Ischyras was forgiven, but placed under censure, which probably led to his eventually renewing the charge with increased bitterness. Athanasius now was accused of *personally* breaking the chalice, &c. In the letter of the council of Philippopolis the cottage of Ischyras becomes a ' basilica ' which Athanasius had caused to be thrown down.

(b) *The case of Arsenius.* Arsenius was Meletian bishop of Hypsele (not in the Meletian catalogue of 327). By a large bribe, as it is stated, he was induced by John Arcaph to go into hiding among the Meletian monks of the Thebaid ; rumours were quietly set in motion that Athanasius had had him murdered, and had procured one of his hands for magical purposes. A hand was circulated purporting to be the very hand in question. A report of the case, including the last version of the Ischyras scandal, was sent to Constantine, who, startled by the new accusation, sent orders to his half-brother, Dalmatius, a high official at Antioch, to enquire into the case. He appears to have suggested a council at Cæsarea under the presidency of Eusebius, which was to meet at some time in the year 334 (πέρυσιν, p. 141, cf. note 2 there, also Gwatkin, p. 84 note ; the ' 30 months' of Soz. ii. 25 is an exaggeration). Athanasius, however, obstinately declined a trial before a judge whom he regarded as biassed ; his refusal bitterly offended the aged historian. Accordingly the *venue* was fixed for Tyre in the succeeding year ; a Count Dionysius was to represent the Emperor, and see that all was conducted fairly, and Athanasius was stringently (p. 137) summoned to attend. Meanwhile a trusted deacon was on the tracks of the missing man. Arsenius was traced to a 'monastery' of Meletian brethren in the nome of Antæopolis in Upper Egypt. Pinnes, the presbyter of the community, got wind of the discovery, and smuggled Arsenius away down the Nile ; presently he was spirited away to Tyre. The deacon, however, very astutely made a sudden descent upon the monastery in force, seized Pinnes, carried him to Alexandria, brought him before the 'Duke,' confronted him with the monk who had escorted Arsenius away, and forced them to confess to the whole plot. As soon as he was able to do so, Pinnes wrote to John Arcaph, warning him of the exposure, and suggesting that the charge had better be dropped (p. 135 ; the letter is an amusingly naive exhibition of human rascality). Meanwhile (Socr. i. 29) Arsenius was heard of at an inn in Tyre by the servant of a magistrate ; the latter had him arrested, and informed Athanasius [3]. Arsenius stoutly denied his identity, but was recognised by the bishop of Tyre, and at last confessed. The Emperor was informed and wrote to Athanasius (p. 135), expressing his indignation at the plot, as also did Alexander, bishop of Thessalonica. Arsenius made his peace with Athanasius, and in due time succeeded (according to the Nicene rule) to the sole episcopate of Hypsele (p. 548). John Arcaph even admitted his guilt and renounced his schism, and was invited to Court (p. 136) ; but his submission was not permanent.

According to the *Apology* of Athanasius, all this took place some time before the council of Tyre ; we cannot fix the date, except that it must have come after the Easter of 332 (see above). It appears most natural, from the language of *Apol. Ar.* 71, to fix the exposure of Arsenius not very long before the summoning of the council of Tyre, but long enough to allow for the renewed intrigues which led to its being convened. But this pushes us back behind the intended council of Cæsarea in 334 ; we seem therefore compelled to keep Arsenius waiting at Tyre from about 333 to the summer of 335.

It must be remembered that the Council of Tyre was merely a πάρεργον to the great Dedication Meeting at Jerusalem, which was to celebrate the *Tricennalia* of Constantine's reign by consecrating his grand church on Mount Calvary. On their way to Jerusalem the bishops were to despatch at Tyre their business of quieting the Egyptian troubles [4] (Eus. *V.C.* iv. 41). To Tyre accordingly Athanasius repaired. He left Alexandria on July 11, 335, and was absent, as it proved (according to the reckoning of the *Hist. Aceph.*, below, p. 496), two years, four months and eleven days.

§ 5.   *The Council of Tyre and first exile of Athanasius*, 335—337.

Many of the bishops who were making their way to the great festival met at Tyre. The Arian element was very strong. Eusebius of Nicomedia, Narcissus, Maris, Theognis, Patrophilus, George, now bishop of Laodicea, are all familiar names. Ursacius and Valens, 'young[1] both in years and in mind,' make their first entrance on the stage of ecclesiastical intrigue ; Eusebius of Cæsarea headed a large body of 'conservative' malcontents : in the total number of perhaps 150, the friends of Athanasius were outnumbered by nearly two to one. (See Gwatkin's note, p. 85, Hefele ii. 17, *Eng. Tra.*) Eusebius of Cæsarea took the chair (yet see D.C.B. ii. 316[b]). The proceedings of the Council were heated and disorderly ; promiscuous accusations were flung from side to side ; the president himself was charged by an excited Egyptian Confessor with having sacrificed to idols (p. 104, n. 2), while against Athanasius every possible charge was raked up. The principal one was that of harshness and violence. Callinicus, bishop of Pelusium, according to a later story [3], had taken up the cause of Ischyras, and been deposed by Athanasius in consequence. A certain Mark had been appointed to supersede him, and he had been subjected to military force. Certain Meletian bishops who had refused to communicate with Athanasius on account of his irregular election, had been beaten and imprisoned. A document from Alexandria testified that the Churches were emptied on account of the strong popular feeling against these proceedings. The number of witnesses, and the evident readiness of the majority of bishops to believe the worst against him, inspired Athanasius with profound misgivings as to his chance of obtaining justice. He had in vain objected to certain bishops as biassed judges ; when it was decided to investigate the case of Ischyras on the spot, the commission of six was chosen from among the very persons challenged (p. 138). Equally unsuccessful was the protest of the Egyptian bishops against the credit of the Meletian witnesses (p. 140). But on one point the accusers walked into a trap. The 'hand of Arsenius' was produced, and naturally made a deep impression (Thdt. *H.E.* i. 30). But Athanasius was ready. 'Did you know Arsenius personally?' 'Yes' is the eager reply from many sides. Promptly Arsenius is ushered in alive, wrapped up in a cloak. The Synod expected an explanation of the way he had lost his hand. Athanasius

---

3 Who perhaps visited Tyre himself at this time, according to an allusion in *Hist. Aceph.* xii., see Sievers, *Einl.* p. 131.

4 The conduct of Constantine will appear fairly consistent if we suppose that after ordering the investigation at Antioch, *supr.* (332 ?) he received proofs (333) of the falsehood of the Arsenius story, but that, finding that the complaints were constantly renewed, and that Ath. refused to meet his accusers at Cæsarea, he yielded to the suggestion (Eus. Nic. ?) that the assembly of so many bishops at Jerusalem might be a valuable opportunity for

finally dealing with so troublesome a matter. He desired peace, and had not lost his faith in councils. Hefele follows Socrates i. 29, in his error as to the date of the discovery of Arsenius (E. Tr. ii. 21).

1 p. 107 : Euseb. *V.C.* iv. 43, calls them 'the fairest of God's youthful flock.' The Council of Sardica in 343 describes them as 'ungodly and foolish youths,' Hil. *Frag.* ii., cf. pp. 120, 122.

3 Soz. ii. 25. But Callinicus was a Meletian all along : pp. 132, 137, 517.

turned up his cloak and shewed that one hand at least was there. There was a mome it of suspense, artfully managed by Athanasius. Then the other hand was exposed, and the accusers were requested to point out whence the third had been cut off (Socr. i. 29). This was too much for John Arcaph, who precipitately fled (so Socr., he seems to have gone to Egypt with the couriers mentioned below, cf. p. 142). But the Eusebians were made of sterner stuff: the whole affair was a piece of magic; or there had been an attempt to murder Arsenius, who had hid himself from fear. At any rate Athanasius must not be allowed to clear himself so easily. Accordingly, in order partly to gain time and partly to get up a more satisfactory case, they prevailed on Count Dionysius, in the face of strong remonstrances from Athanasius (p. 138), to despatch a commission of enquiry to the Mareotis in order to ascertain the real facts about Ischyras. The nature of the commission may be inferred, firstly, from its composition, four strong Arians and two (Theodore of Heraclea, and Macedonius of Mopsuestia) reactionaries; secondly, from the fact that they took Ischyras with them, but left Macarius behind in custody; thirdly, from the fact that couriers were sent to Egypt with four days' start, and with an urgent message to the Meletians to collect at once in as large numbers as possible at Irene, so as to impress the commissioners with the importance of the Meletian community at that place. The Egyptian bishops present at Tyre handed in strongly-worded protests to the Council, and to Count Dionysius, who received also a weighty remonstrance from the respected Alexander, Bishop of Thessalonica. This drew forth from him an energetic protest to the Eusebians (p. 142 *sq.*) against the composition of the commission. His protest was not, however, enforced in any practical way, and the Egyptians thereupon appealed to the Emperor (*ib.*). Athanasius himself escaped in an open boat with four of his bishops, and found his way to Constantinople, where he arrived on October 30. The Emperor was out riding when he was accosted by one of a group of pedestrians. He could scarcely credit his eyes and the assurance of his attendants that the stranger was none other than the culprit of Tyre. Much annoyed at his appearance, he refused all communication; but the persistency of Athanasius and the reasonableness of his demand prevailed. The Emperor wrote to Jerusalem to summon to his presence all who had been at the Council of Tyre (pp. 105, 145).

Meanwhile the MAREOTIC COMMISSION had proceeded with its task. Their report was kept secret, but eventually sent to Julius of Rome, who handed it over to Athanasius in 339 (p. 143). Their enquiry was carried on with the aid of Philagrius the prefect, a strong Arian sympathiser, whose guard pricked the witnesses if they failed to respond to the hints of the commissioners and the threats of the prefect himself. The clergy of Alexandria and the Mareotis were excluded from the court, and catechumens, Jews and heathen, none of whom could properly have been present on the occasion, were examined as to the interruption of the eucharistic service by Macarius (p. 119). Even with these precautions the evidence was not all that could be wished. To begin with, it had all taken place on an ordinary week-day, when there would be no Communion (pp. 115, 125, 143); secondly, when Macarius came in Ischyras was in bed; thirdly, certain witnesses whom Athanasius had been accused of secreting came forward in evidence of the contrary (p. 107). The prefect consoled himself by letting loose the violence of the heathen mob (p. 108) against the 'virgins' of the Church. The catholic party were helpless; all they could do was to protest in writing to the commission, the council, and the prefect (pp. 138—140. The latter protest is dated 10th of Thoth, i.e. Sep. 8, 335, Diocletian leap-year).

The commission returned to Tyre, where the council passed a resolution (Soz. ii. 25) deposing Athanasius. They then proceeded to Jerusalem for the Dedication[2] of the Church of the Holy Sepulchre. Here Arius with certain others (probably including Euzoius) was received to communion on the strength of the confession of faith he had presented to Constantine a few years before, and the assembled bishops drew up a synodal letter announcing the fact to Egypt and the Church at large (pp. 144, 460). At this juncture the summons from Constantine arrived. The terms of it shewed that the Emperor was not disposed to hear more of the broken chalice or the murdered Arsenius: but the Eusebians were not at a loss. They advised the bishops to go quietly to their homes, while five of the inner circle, accompanied by Eusebius of Cæsarea, who had a panegyric to deliver in the imperial presence, responded to the summons of royalty. They made short work of Athanasius. The whole farrago of charges examined at Tyre was thrown aside. He had threatened to starve the πανευδαίμων πατρίς, the chosen capital of Constantine, by stopping the grain ships which regularly left Alexandria every autumn. It was in vain for Athanasius to protest that he had neither the means nor the power to do anything of the kind. 'You are a rich man,' replied Eusebius of Nicomedia, 'and can do whatever you like.' The Emperor was touched in a sore place[3]. He promptly ordered the banishment of Athanasius to Treveri, whither he started, as it would seem, on Feb. 5, 336 (pp. 105, 146, 503, note 11). The friends of Athanasius professed to regard the banishment as an act of imperial clemency, in view of what might have been treated as a capital matter, involving as it did the charge of treason (p. 105); and Constantine II., immediately after his father's death, stated (pp. 146, 272, 288) in a letter (written before he became Augustus in Sept. 337) that he had been sent to Treveri merely to keep him out of danger, and that Constantine had been prevented only by death from carrying out his intention of restoring him. These charitable constructions need not be rudely ignored; but in all probability the anxiety to be rid of a cause of disturbance was at least one motive with the peace-loving Emperor. At

---

[2] The Greek Church still commemorates this Festival on Sep. 13; the *Chron. Pasch.* gives Sep. 17 for the Dedication. But if the Mareotic Commissioners returned to Tyre, as they certainly did (Soz. l.c.), these dates are untrustworthy.

[3] The philosopher Sopater had been put to death on a similar charge a few years before, D.C.B. i. 631.

any rate the Eusebians could not obtain the imperial sanction to their proposed election of a successor (Pistus?) to Athanasius. On his return after the death of Constantine he found his see waiting for him unoccupied (*Apol. c. Ar.* 29, p. 115).

The close of the Tricennalia was made the occasion of a council at Constantinople (winter 335—336). Marcellus was deposed for heresy and Basil nominated to the see of Ancyra, Eusebius of Cæsarea undertaking to refute the 'new Samosatene.' Other minor depositions were apparently carried out at the same time, and several Western bishops, including Protogenes of Sardica, had reason later on to repent of their signatures to the proceedings (Hil. *Fragm.* iii.).

Death of Arius. From Jerusalem Arius had gone to Alexandria, but (Soz. ii. 29) had not succeeded in obtaining admission to the Communion of the Church there. Accordingly he repaired to the capital about the time of the Council just mentioned. The Eusebians resolved that here at any rate he should not be repelled. Arius appeared before the Emperor and satisfied him by a sworn profession of orthodoxy, and a day was fixed for his reception to communion. The story of the distress caused to the aged bishop Alexander is well known. He was heard to pray in the church that either Arius or himself might be taken away before such an outrage to the faith should be permitted. As a matter of fact Arius died suddenly the day before his intended reception. His friends ascribed his death to magic, those of Alexander to the judgment of God, the public generally to the effect of excitement on a diseased heart (Soz. l. c.). Athanasius, while taking the second view, describes the occurrence with becoming sobriety and reserve (pp. 233, 565). Alexander himself died very soon after, and Paul was elected in his place (D.C.B. art. MACEDONIUS (2)), but was soon banished on some unknown charge, whereupon Eusebius of Nicomedia was translated to the capital see (between 336 and 340; date uncertain. Cf. D.C.B. ii. 367 a).

Of the sojourn of Athanasius at Treveri, the noble home of the Emperors on the banks of the Mosel, we know few details, but his presence there appeals to the historic imagination. (See D.C.B. i. 186 a.) He cannot have been there much above a year. He kept the Easter festival, probably of 336, certainly of 337, in the still unfinished Church (p. 244: the present Cathedral is said to occupy the site of what was then an Imperial palace: but the main palace is apparently represented by the 'Roman baths).' He was not suffered to want (p. 146): he had certain Egyptian brethren with him; and found a sympathetic friend in the good Bishop Maximinus (cf. p. 239). The tenth festal letter, § 1, preserves a short extract from a letter written from Trier to his clergy.

Constantine died at Nicomedia, having previously received baptism from the hands of Eusebius, on Whit-Sunday, May 22, 337. None of his sons were present, and the will is said to have been entrusted to the Arian chaplain mentioned above (p. xxxiv). Couriers carried the news to the three Cæsars, and at a very moderate[4] rate of reckoning, it may have been known at Trier by about June 4. Constantine, as the eldest son, probably expected more from his father's will than he actually obtained. At any rate, on June 17 he wrote a letter to the people and clergy of Alexandria, announcing the restoration of their bishop in pursuance of an intention of his father's, which only death had cut short. Constantius meanwhile hastened (from the East, probably Antioch) to Constantinople (D.C.B. i. 651): he too had expectations, for he was his father's favourite. The brothers met at Sirmium, and agreed upon a division of the Empire, Constantius taking the East, Constans Italy and Illyricum, and Constantine the Gauls and Africa. On Sep. 9 they formally assumed the title Augustus[5]. Athanasius had apparently accompanied Constantine to Sirmium, and on his way eastward met Constantius at Viminacium (p. 240), his first interview with his future persecutor. He presently reached Constantinople (p. 272), and on his way southward, at Cæsarea in Cappadocia, again met Constantius, who was hurrying to the Persian frontier. On Nov. 23 he reached Alexandria amid great rejoicings (pp. 104, 503, *Fest. Ind.* x.), the clergy especially 'esteeming that the happiest day of their lives.' But the happiness was marred by tumults (Soz. ii. 2, 5, Hil. *Fragm.* iii. 8, *Fest. Ind.* xi., next year 'again'), which were, however, checked by the civil power, the prefect Theodorus being, apparently, favourable to Athanasius (pp. 102, 527, note 2). The festal letter for 338 would seem to have been finished at Alexandria, but the point is not absolutely clear. Here begins his second period of 'quiet,' of one year, four months and twenty-four days, i.e., from Athyr 27 (Nov. 23), 337, to Pharmuthi 21 (April 16), 339.

§ 6. *Renewal of Troubles. Second Exile. Pistus and Gregory, culmination of Eusebian intrigue. Rome and Sardica.* (337—346).

(1). The stay of Athanasius at Alexandria was brief and troubled. The city was still disturbed by Arian malcontents, who had the sympathy of Jews and Pagans, and it was reported that the monks, and especially the famous hermit Antony, were on their side. This

---

4 The courier Palladius, who was considered a marvel, could carry a message from Nisibis to CP. on horseback in three days, about 250 miles a day, Socr. vii. 19. At 100 miles a day, i.e. eight miles an hour for 12½ hours out of the 24, the 1,300 miles from Nicomedia to Treveri would be easily covered by a horseman in the time specified; see Gibbon quoted p. 115, note 1, and for other examples, Gwatkin, p. 137.

5 This date is certain (Gwatk., 108, note), but the meeting at Sirmium may possibly fall in the following summer.

impression, however, was dissipated by the appearance of the great Ascetic himself, who, at the urgent request of the orthodox (pp. 214 *sq.*, 503), consented to shew himself for two days in the uncongenial atmosphere of the city. The mystery and marvellous reputation, which even then surrounded this much-talked-of character, attracted Christians and heathen alike, in large numbers, to hear and see him, and, if possible, to derive some physical benefit from his touch. He denounced Arianism as the worst of heresies, and was solemnly escorted out of town by the bishop in person. As an annalist toward the close of the century tells us, 'Antony, the great leader, came to Alexandria, and though he remained there only two days, shewed himself wonderful in many things, and healed many. He departed on the third of Messori' (i.e., July 27, 338).

Meanwhile the Eusebians were busy. In the new Emperor Constantius, the Nicomedian found a willing patron : probably his translation to the See of Constantinople falls at this time. It was represented to the Emperor that the restoration of the exiled Bishops in 337, and especially that of Athanasius, was against all ecclesiastical order. Men deposed by a Synod of the Church had presumed to return to their sees under the sanction of the secular authority. This was technically true, but the proceedings at Tyre were regarded by Athan. as depriving that Synod of any title to ecclesiastical authority (pp. 104, 271). It is impossible to accept *au pied de la lettre* the protests on either side against state interference with the Church : both parties were willing to use it on their own side, and to protest against its use by their opponents. Constantine had summoned[1] the Council of Nicæa, had (Soz. i. 17) fixed the order of its proceedings, and had enforced its decisions by civil penalties. The indignant rhetoric of *Hist. Ar.* 52 (p. 289) might *mutatis nominibus* have been word for word the remonstrance of a Secundus or Theonas against the great Ecumenical Synod of Christendom. At Tyre, Jerusalem, and CP., the Eusebians had their turn, and again at Antioch, 338—341. The Council of Sardica relied on the protection of Constans, that of Philippopolis on Constantius. The reign of the latter was the period of Arian triumph ; that of Theodosius secured authority to the Catholics. The only consistent opponents of civil intervention in Church affairs were the Donatists in the West and the Eunomians or later Arians in the East (with the obscure exception of Secundus and Theonas, the original Arians cannot claim the compliment paid by Fialon, p. 115, to their independence). To the Donatists is due the classical protest against Erastianism, ' Quid Imperatori cum ecclesia' (D. C. B. i. 652). Believing, as the present writer does, that the Donatist protest expresses a true principle, and that the subjection of religion to the State is equally mischievous with that of the State to the Church, it is impossible not to regret these consequences of the conversion of Constantine. But allowance must be made for the sanguine expectations with which the astonishing novelty of a Christian Emperor filled men's minds. It was only as men came to realise that the civil sword might be drawn in support of heresy that they began to reflect on the impropriety of allowing to even a Christian Emperor a voice in Church councils. Athanasius was the first to grasp this clearly. The voice of protest[2] sounds in the letter of the Egyptian Synod of 338-9 ; throughout his exiles he steadily regarded himself, and was regarded by his flock, as the sole rightful Bishop of Alexandria, and continued to issue his Easter Letters from first to last. At the same time, it must be admitted that if he was right in returning to Alexandria in 337 without restoration by a Synod, he could not logically object to the return of Eusebius and Theognis (p. 104), who had not been deposed at Nicæa, but banished by the Emperor. The *technical* rights of Chrestus and Amphion (*l. c.*) were no better than those of Gregory or George. The spiritual elevation of Athanasius over the head and shoulders of his opponents is plain to ourselves ; we see clearly the moral contrast between the councils of Rome and Antioch (340-41), of Sardica and Philippopolis (343), of Alexandria (362) and Seleucia (359). But to men like the Eastern ' conservatives' the technical point of view necessarily presented itself with great force, and in judging of their conduct we must not assume that it was either ' meaningless diabolism' or deliberate sympathy with Arianism that led so many bishops of good character to see in Athanasius and the other exiles contumacious offenders against Church order. (I am quite unable to accept M. Fialon's sweeping verdict upon the *majority* of Oriental bishops as ' weak, vicious, more devoted to their own interests than to the Church,' &c., p. 116. He takes as literally exact the somewhat turgid rhetorical complaints of Greg. Naz.)

But the Eusebians were not limited to technical complaints. They had stirring accounts to give of the disorders which the return of Athanasius had excited, of the ruthless severity with which they had been put down by the prefect, who was, it was probably added, a mere tool in the hands of the bishop. Accordingly in the course of 338 the subservient Theodorus was recalled, and Philagrius the Cappadocian, who had governed with immense[3] popularity in 335—337 (*Fest. Ind.* and p. 107 *sq.*), was sent to fill the office a second time. This was regarded at Alexandria as an Arian triumph (see p. 527, note 2). His arrival did not tend to allay the disorders. Old charges against Athanasius were raked up, and a new one added, namely that of embezzlement of the corn appropriated to the support of widows by the imperial bounty. The Emperor appears to have sent a letter of complaint to Athanasius (p. 273), but to have paid little attention to his defence. The Eusebians now ventured to send a bishop of their own to Alexandria in the person of Pistus, one of the original Arian presbyters, who was consecrated by the implacable Secundus. The date of this proceeding is obscure, probably it was conducted in an irregular manner, so as to render it possible to ignore it altogether if, as proved to be the case, a stronger candidate should be necessary. First, however, it was necessary to try the temper of the West. A deputation consisting of a presbyter Macarius and two deacons, Martyrius and Hesychius, was sent to Julius, bishop of Rome, to lay before him the enormities of Athanasius, Marcellus, Paul, Asclepas and the rest, and to

---

[1] As he had previously referred the Donatist schism to the commission of Rome and the Council of Arles.
[2] But they complain, p. 104, § 8, of *coercion* not of Erastianism.
[3] The ordinary time for the entry of the Prefect upon his duties seems to have been about the end of the Egyptian Year (end of August). Accordingly the prefectures and years in *Fest. Ind.* roughly correspond : Philagrius was already Prefect when the Mareotic Commission arrived (Aug. 335). According to the headings to the Festal Letters vi., vii., he had superseded Paternus

in 334 : either the Index or the headings are mistaken. For the popularity of Philagrius, see Greg. Naz. *Orat.* xxi. 28, who mentions that his reappointment was due to the request of a deputation from Alex. (this must have come from the Arians !) and that the rejoicings which welcomed his return exceeded any that could have greeted the Emperor, and *nearly* equalled those which had welcomed the return of Athanasius himself. But Gregory is a rhetorician ; see p. 138, and Tillem. viii. 664.

urge the superior title of Pistus to the recognition of the Church. But upon hearing of this Athanasius summoned the Egyptian Episcopate together (winter 338—339), and composed a circular letter (pp. 101—110) dealing fully with the charges against him, especially with regard to the manner of his election and the irregularity of his return a year before. Two presbyters carried the letter in haste to Rome, and enlightened the Church there as to the antecedents of Pistus. Next day it was announced that Macarius, 'in spite of a bodily ailment,' had decamped in the night. The deacons however remained, and requested Julius to call a council, undertaking that if Athanasius and the Eusebians were confronted all the charges brought by the latter should be made good. This proposal seemed unobjectionable, and Julius wrote inviting all parties to a council at Rome, or some other place to be agreed upon (p. 272); his messengers to the Eusebians were the Roman presbyters Elpidius and Philoxenus[4], (p. 111). The council was fixed for the following summer (so it would seem); but no reply was received from the Eusebians, who kept the presbyters in the East until the following January, when they at length started for Rome bearing a querulous and somewhat shifty reply (answered by Julius, p. 111, *sqq.*). But before the invitation had reached the Eusebians they had assembled at Antioch, where Constantius was in residence for the winter (laws dated Dec. 27; the court there in January? p. 92), repeated the deposition of Athanasius, and appointed Gregory, a Cappadocian, to succeed him. It had become clear that Pistus was a bad candidate; perhaps no formal synod could be induced to commit themselves to a man excommunicated at Nicæa and consecrated by Secundus. At any rate they tried to find an unexceptionable nominee. But their first, Eusebius, afterwards bishop of Emesa, refused the post, and so they came to Gregory[5], a former student of Alexandria, and under personal obligations to its bishop (Greg. Naz. *Or.* xxi. 15).

All was now ready for the blow at Athanasius. It fell in Lent (pp. 94, 503). His position since the arrival of Philagrius had been one of unrest. 'In this year again,' says our annalist, 'there were many tumults. On the xxii Phamenoth (i.e. Sunday, Mar. 18, 339) he was sought after by his persecutors in the night. On the next morning he fled from the Church of Theonas after he had baptized many. Then on the fourth day (Mar. 22) Gregory the Cappadocian entered the city as bishop' (*Fest. Ind.* xi.). But Athanasius (p. 95), remained quietly in the town for about four weeks more[6]. He drew up for circulation 'throughout the tribes' (cf. Judges xix. 29) a memorandum and appeal, describing the intrusion of Gregory and the gross outrages which had accompanied it. This letter was written on or just after Easter Day (April 15), and immediately after this he escaped from Alexandria and made his way to Rome. The data as to the duration of the periods of 'quiet' and exile fix the date of his departure for Easter Monday, April 16. This absence from Alexandria was his longest, lasting 'ninety months and three days,' i.e. from Pharmuthi 21 (April 16) 339 to Paophi 24 (October 21), 346.

(2.) The SECOND EXILE of Athanasius falls into two sections, the first of four years (p. 239), to the council of Sardica (339—343), the second of three years, to his return in Oct. 346. The odd six months cannot be distributed with certainty unless we can arrive at a more exact result than at present appears attainable for the month and duration of the Sardican synod.

In May, 339, Athanasius, accompanied by a few of his clergy (story of the 'detachment' of his monk Ammonius in Socr. iv. 23, *sub fin.*), arrived at Rome. He was within three months followed by Marcellus, Paul of CP., Asclepas, and other exiles who had been restored at the end of 337 but had once more been ejected. Soon after, Carpones, an original Arian of Alexandria, appeared as envoy of Gregory. He confirmed all that had been alleged against Pistus, but failed to convince Julius that his own bishop was anything but an Arian. Meanwhile time wore on, and no reply came from the Eusebians. Athanasius gave himself up to enforced leisure and to the services of the Church. Instead of his usual Easter letter for the following spring, he sent a few lines to the clergy of Alexandria and a letter to his right-hand man, bishop Serapion of Thmuis, requesting him to make the necessary announcement of the season. Gregory made his first attempt (apparently also his last) to fix the Easter Festival, but in the middle of Lent, to the amusement of the public, discovered that a mistake had been made, the correction of which involved his adherents in an extra week of Lenten austerities. We can well imagine that the spectacle of the abstracted asceticism of Ammonius aroused the curiosity and veneration of the Roman Christians, and thus gave an impulse to the ascetic life in the West (see Jerome, cited below, p. 191). That is all we know of the life of Athanasius during the first eighteen months of his stay at Rome.

In the early spring of 340 the presbyters returned (see above) with a letter from a number of bishops, including the Eusebian leaders, who had assembled at Antioch in January. This letter is carefully dissected in the

---

[4] It is *possible*, however, that these carried a *second* letter, after the arrival of Ath. See pp. 110, 273.

[5] Gregory shewed his Arianism by employing Ammon as his secretary, see p. 96. The curious parallelism between Gregory and George (*infr.* § 8),—the names differing (in Latin) by a single letter only, both Arians, both Cappadocians, both intruded bishops of Alexandria, both arriving from court, both arriving in Lent, both exercising violence, both charged by Ath. with the storming of churches, with similar scenes of desecration, maltreatment of virgins, &c., in either case,—is one of the strangest examples of history repeating itself within a few years. What wonder that the fifth-century historians confuse the two still further together, and

that they still find followers? The most important point of confusion is the alleged murder of Gregory (due to Theodoret), who really died a natural death. It is none too soon for this time-honoured blunder to do the like. On the inveterate tendency of Georges and Gregories to coalesce, and exchange names in transcription (to say nothing of modern typography), see D.C.B. ii. pp. 640—650, 778 *sq.*, 798 *sq.*, *passim*.

[6] In some church other than 'Theonas,' probably 'Quirinus,' which latter, however, was stormed on Easter Day, pp. 273, 95, note 3. The statement, *Hist. Ar.* 10, that he *sailed* for Rome before Gregory's arrival is in any case verbally inexact, but it may refer to his flight from 'Theonas.'

reply of the Roman Council, and appears to have been highly acrimonious in its tone. Julius kept it secret for a time (p. 111), hoping against hope that after all some of the Orientals would come for the council; but at length he gave up all expectations of the kind, and convoked the bishops of Italy, who examined the cases of the various exiles (p. 114). All the old charges against Athanasius were gone into with the aid of the Mareotic report (the *ex parte* character of which Julius strongly emphasises) and of the account of the proceedings at Tyre. The council had no difficulty in pronouncing Athanasius completely innocent on all points. The charge of ignoring the proceedings of a council was disposed of by pointing out the uncanonical character of Gregory's appointment (p. 115), and the infraction by the complainants of the decrees of Nicæa. With regard to Marcellus, he responded to the request of the bishops by volunteering a written confession of his faith (p. 116, Epiph. *Hær.* 72), which was in fact the creed of the Roman Church itself (Caspari, *Quellen* iii. 28, note, argues that the creed must have been tendered at an earlier visit, 336—337, but without cogent reasons). Either Julius and his bishops were (like the fathers of Sardica) very easily satisfied, or Marcellus exercised extreme reserve as to his peculiar tenets (Zahn, p. 71, makes out the best case he can for his candour). The other exiles were also pronounced innocent, and the synod 'restored' them all. It remained to communicate the result to the Oriental bishops. This was done by Julius in a letter drawn up in the name of the council, and preserved by Athanasius in his Apology. Its subject matter has been sufficiently indicated, but its statesmanlike logic and grave severity must be appreciated by reference to the document itself. It has been truly called 'one of the ablest documents in the entire controversy.' It is worth observing that Julius makes no claim whatever to pass a final judgment *as successor of S. Peter*, although the Orientals had expressly asserted the equal authority of all bishops, however important the cities in which they ruled (p. 113); on the contrary he merely claims that without his own consent, proceedings against bishops would lack the weight of *universal* consent (p. 118). At the same time he claims to be in possession of the *traditions* of S. Paul and especially of S. Peter, and is careful to found *upon precedent* (that of Dionysius) a claim to be consulted in matters alleged against a bishop of Alexandria. This claim, by its modesty, is in striking contrast with that which Socrates (ii. 17) and Sozom. (iii. 8, 10) make for him,—that owing to the greatness of his see, the care of all the churches pertained to him: and this again, which represents what the Greek Church of the early *fifth* century was accustomed to hear from Rome, is very different from the claim to a jurisdiction of divine right which we find formulated in Leo the Great.

The letter of Julius was considered at the famous COUNCIL OF THE DEDICATION (of Constantine's 'Golden' Church at Antioch, see Eus. *V.C.* iii. 50), held in the summer of 341 (between May 22 and Sept. 1, see Gwatkin, p. 114, note). Eusebius of Constantinople was there (he had only a few months longer to live), and most of the Arian leaders. Cæsarea was represented by Acacius, who had succeeded Eusebius some two years before; a man of whom we shall hear more. But of the ninety-odd bishops who attended, the majority must have been conservative in feeling, such as Dianius of Cæsarea, who possibly presided. At any rate Hilary (*de Syn.* 32) calls it 'a synod of saints,' and its canons passed into the accepted body of Church Law. Their reply to Julius is not extant, but we gather from the historians that it was not conciliatory. (Socr. ii. 15, 17; Soz. iii. 8, 10; they are in such hopeless confusion as to dates and the order of events that it is difficult to use them here; Theodoret is more accurate but less full.)

But the council marks an epoch in a more important respect; with it begins the formal DOCTRINAL REACTION against the Nicene Formula. We have traces of previous confessions, such as that of Arius and Euzoius, 330—335, and an alleged creed drawn up at CP. in 336. But only now begins the long series of attempts to raise some other formula to a position of equality with the Nicene, so as to eventually depose the ὁμοούσιον from its position as an ecumenical test.

The first suggestion of a new creed came from the Arian bishops, who propounded a formula (p. 461, § 22), with a disavowal of any intention of disparaging that of Nicæa (Socr. ii. 10), but suspiciously akin to the evasive confession of Arius, and prefaced with a suicidally worded protest against being considered as followers of the latter. The fate of this creed in the council is obscure; but it would seem to have failed to commend itself to the majority, who put forward a creed alleged to have been composed by Lucian the martyr. This (see above, p. xxviii, and p. 461, notes 5—9), was hardly true of the creed as it stood, but it may have been signed by Lucian as a test when he made his peace with bishop Cyril. At any rate the creed is catholic in asserting the *exact* Likeness of the Son to the Father's Essence (yet the Arians could admit this as *de facto* true, though not originally so; only the word Essence would, if honestly taken, fairly exclude their sense), but anti-Nicene in omitting the ὁμοούσιον, and in the phrase τῇ μὲν ὑποστάσει τρία, τῇ δὲ συμφωνίᾳ ἕν, an artfully chosen point of contact between Origen on the one hand, and Asterius, Lucian, and Paul of Samosata on the other. The anathemas, also, let in an Arian interpretation. This creed is usually referred to as the 'Creed of the Dedication' or 'Lucianic' Creed, and represents, on the one hand the extreme limit of concession to which Arians were willing to go, on the other the theological rallying point of the gradually forming body of reasoned conservative opinion which under the nickname of 'semi-Arianism' (Epiph. *Hær.* 73; it was repudiated by Basil of Ancyra, &c.) gradually worked toward the recognition of the Nicene formula.

A third formula was presented by Theophronius, bishop of Tyana, as a personal statement of belief, and was widely signed by way of approval. It insists like the Lucianic creed on the pretemporal γέννησις, against Marcellus, adding two other points (hypostatic pre-existence and eternal kingdom of the Son) in the same direction, and closing with an anathema against Marcellus, Sabellius, Paul, and all who communicate with any of their supporters. This was of course a direct defiance of Julius and the Westerns (Mr. Gwatkin, by a slip, assigns this anathema to the 'fourth' creed).

Lastly, a few months after the council (late autumn of 341) a few bishops reassembled in order to send a deputation to Constans (since 340 sole Western Emperor). They decided to substitute for the genuine creeds of the council a fourth formulary, which accordingly the Arians Maris and Narcissus, and the neutrals Theodore of Heraclea and Mark of Arethusa, conveyed to the West. The assertion of the eternal reign of Christ was strengthened, and the name of Marcellus omitted, but the Nicene anathemas were skilfully adapted so as to strike at the Marcellian and admit the Arian doctrine of the divine Sonship. This creed became the basis on which the subsequent Arianising confessions of 343 (Philippopolis), 344 (Macrostich), and 351 (Sirmium) were moulded by additions to and modifications of the anathemas. This series of creeds mark 'the stationary period of Arianism,' i.e. between the close of the first generation (Arius, Asterius, Eusebius of Nicomedia) and the beginnings of the divergence of parties under the sole reign of Constantius. At present opposition to the school of Marcellus and to the impregnable strength of the West under a Catholic Emperor kept the reactionary party united.

It has been necessary to dwell upon the work of this famous Council in view of its subsequent importance. It is easy to see how the Eastern bishops were prevailed upon to take the bold step of putting forth a Creed to rival the Nicene formula. The formal approval of Marcellus at Rome shewed, so they felt, the inadequacy of that formula to exclude Sabellianism, or rather the direct support which that heresy could find in the word 'homoüsion.' This being so, provided they made it clear that they were not favouring Arianism, they would be doing no more than their duty in providing a more efficient test. But here the Arian group saw their opportunity. Conservative willingness to go behind Nicæa must be made to subserve the supreme end of revoking the condemnation of Arianism. Hence the confusion of counsels reflected in the multiplicity of creeds. The result pleased no one. The Lucianic Creed, with its anti-Arian clauses, tempered by equivocal qualifications, was a feeble and indirect weapon against Marcellus, who could admit in a sense the pre-æonian γέννησις and the 'true' sonship. On the other hand, the three creeds which only succeeded in gaining secondary ratification, while express against Marcellus, were worthless as against Arianism. On the whole, the fourth creed, in spite of its irregular sanction, was found the most useful for the time (341—351); but as their doctrinal position took definite form, the Conservative wing fell back on the 'Lucianic' Creed, and found in it a bridge to the Nicene (cf. pp. 470, 472, Hil. de Syn. 33, and Gwatkin, p. 119, note).

(3.) Athanasius remained in Rome more than three years after his departure from Alexandria (April, 339—May? 342, see p. 239). During the last of these years, the dispute connected with him had been referred by Julius to Constans, who had requested his brother to send some Oriental bishops with a statement of their case: this was the reason of the deputation (see above) of the winter of 341. They found Constans at Treveri, but owing to the warnings of good Bishop Maximinus[3], he refused to accept their assurances, and sent them ignominiously away. This probably falls in the summer of 342, the deputation on arriving in Italy having found that Constans had already left Milan for his campaign against the Franks (Gwatkin, p. 122, note 3). If this be so, Constans had already made up his mind that a General Council was the only remedy, and had written to Constantius to arrange for one. Before leaving Milan he had summoned Athanasius from Rome, and announced to him what he had done. The young Prince was evidently an admirer of Athanasius, who had received from him in reply to a letter of self-defence, written from Alexandria, an order for certain πύκτια, or bound volumes of the Scriptures (see Montfaucon, Animadv. xv., in Migne xxv., p. clxxvi.). The volumes had been delivered before this date. Constans hurried off to Gaul, while Athanasius remained at Milan, where he afterwards received a summons to follow the Emperor to Treveri[4]; here he met the venerable Hosius and others, and learned that the Emperors had fixed upon SARDICA (now Sophia in Bulgaria), on the frontier line of the dominions of Constans[5], as the venue for the great Council, which was to assemble in the ensuing summer. Athanasius must have kept the Easter of 343 at Treveri: he had written his usual Easter letter (now lost) most probably from Rome or Milan, in the previous spring. The date of assembly and duration of the Sardican synod are, unfortunately, obscure. But the proceedings must have been protracted by the negotiations which ended in the departure of the Easterns, and (p. 124, note 2) by the care with which the evidence against the incriminated bishops was afterwards gone into[6].

We shall probably be safe in supposing that the Council occupied the whole of August

---

[3] Bitter complaint in Hil. Fragm. iii. 27; cf. infr. p. 462, Soz. iii. 10, who wrongly gives 'Italy' as the place.
[4] This may have been in the autumn, after the close of the campaign, but see infr. ch. v. § 3, c, d
[5] Hefele i. 91, is singular in placing it in the empire of Constantius. The Ichtiman range between Sophia and Philippopolis was the natural boundary between Thrace and Mœsia, or 'Dacia. Media.'
[6] On the one hand the deputation after the council reached Constantius at Antioch about Easter (April 15), 344. They were, however sent not directly by the Council, but by Constans after its close (Thdt. ii. 8). We may be certain that their arrival at

Antioch was at the very least two months after the close of the council; but in all probability the interval was much longer. Again, the course of events described above forbids us to put the council earlier than the early summer of 343. But according to the Festal Index xv. the council at any rate began before the end of August in that year. If the bishops left their churches after Easter (a very natural and usual arrangement, compare Nicæa, the Dedication, &c.), they could easily assemble by the end of June. The Orientals came somewhat later. The beginning of July is accordingly our terminus a quo, the end of January our terminus ad quem. What exact part of the interval the council occupied we cannot decide.

and September, and that Constans sent Bishops Euphrates and Vincent to his brother at Antioch as soon as the worst weather of winter was over.

The Western bishops assembled at Sardica to the number of about 95 (see p. 147). Athanasius, Marcellus, and Asclepas arrived with Hosius from Treveri. Paul of Constantinople, for some unknown reason, was absent, but was represented by Asclepas[7]. The Orientals came in a body, and with suspicion. They had the Counts Musonianus and Hesychius, and (according to *Fest. Ind.*, cf. p. 276) the ex-Prefect Philagrius, as advisers and protectors: they were lodged in a body at the Palace of Sophia. The proceedings were blocked by a question of privilege. The Easterns demanded that the accused bishops should not be allowed to take their seats in the Council; the majority replied that, pending the present enquiry, all previous decisions against them must be in fairness considered suspended. There was something to be said on both sides (see Hefele, p. 99), but on the whole, the synod being convoked expressly to re-hear both sides, the majority were perhaps justified in refusing to exclude the accused. A long interchange (p. 119), of communications followed, and at last, alleging that they were summoned home by the news of the victory in the Persian war, the minority disappeared by night, sending their excuse by the Sardican Presbyter Eustathius (p. 275). At Philippopolis, within the dominions of Constantius, they halted and drew up a long and extremely wild and angry statement of what had occurred, deposing and condemning all concerned, from Hosius, Julius and Athanasius downward. They added the Antiochene Confession ('fourth' of 341), with the addition of some anathemas directed at the system of Marcellus. Among the signatures, which included most of the surviving Arian leaders, along with Basil of Ancyra, and other moderate men, we recognise that of Ischyras, 'bishop from the Mareotis,' who had enjoyed the dignity without the burdens of the Episcopate since the Council of Tyre (p. 144). The document was sent far and wide, among the rest to the Donatists of Africa (Hef., p. 171).

This rupture doomed the purpose of the council to failure: instead of leading to agreement it had made the difference a hopeless one. But the Westerns were still a respectable number, and might do much to forward the cause of justice and of the Nicene Faith. Two of the Easterns had joined them, Asterius of Petra and Arius, bishop of an unknown see in Palestine. The only other Oriental present, Diodorus of Tenedos, appears to have come, like Asclepas, &c., independently of the rest. The work of the council was partly judicial, partly legislative. The question was raised of issuing a supplement to, or formula explanatory of, the Nicene creed, and a draft (preserved Thdt. *H.E.* ii. 8) was actually made, but the council declined to sanction anything which should imply that the Nicene creed was insufficient (p. 484, correcting Thdt. *ubi supra*, and Soz. iii. 12).

The charges against all the exiles were carefully examined and dismissed. This was also the case with the complaints against the orthodoxy of Marcellus, who was allowed to evade the very point which gave most offence (p. 125). Probably the ocular evidence (p. 124) of the violence which many present had suffered, indisposed the fathers to believe any accusations from such a quarter. The synod next proceeded to legislate. Their canons were twenty in number, the most important being canons 3—5, which permit a deposed bishop to demand the reference of his case to 'Julius bishop of Rome,' 'honouring the memory of Peter the Apostle;' the deposition to be suspended pending such reference; the Roman bishop, if the appeal seem reasonable, to request the re-hearing of the case in its own province, and if at the request of the accused he sends a presbyter to represent him, such presbyter to rank as though he were his principal in person. The whole scheme appears to be novel and to have been suggested by the history of the case of the exiles. The canons are very important in their subsequent history, but need not be discussed here. (Elaborate discussions in Hefele, pp. 112—129; see also D.C.A. pp. 127 *sq.*, 1658, 1671, Greenwood, *Cath. Petr.* i. 204—208, D.C.B. iii. 662 a, and especially 529—531.) The only legislation, however, to which Athanasius alludes is that establishing a period of 50 years during which Rome and Alexandria should agree as to the period for Easter (*Fest. Ind.* xv., *infr.* p. 544, also Hefele pp. 157 *sqq.*). The arrangement averted a dispute in 346, but differences occurred in spite of it in 349, 350, 360, and 368.

The synod addressed an encyclical letter to all Christendom (p. 123), embodying their decisions and announcing their deposition of eight or nine Oriental bishops (including Theodore of Heraclea, Acacius, and several Arian leaders) for complicity with Arianism. They also wrote to the Church of Alexandria and to the bishops of Egypt with special reference to Athanasius and to the Alexandrian Church, to Julius announcing their decisions, and to the Mareotis (Migne xxvi. 1331 *sqq.* printed with *Letters* 46, 47. Hefele ii. 165 questions the genuineness of all three, but without reason; see p. 554, note 1).

The effect of the Council was not at first pacific. Constantius shared the indignation of the Eastern bishops, and began severe measures against all the Nicene-minded bishops in his dominions (pp. 275 *sqq*). Theodulus, Bishop of Trajanople, died of his injuries before the Sardican Bishops had completed their work. At Hadrianople savage cruelties were perpetrated (*ib.*); and a close watch was instituted in case Athanasius should attempt to return on the strength of his synodical acquittal. Accordingly, he passed the winter and spring at

---

[7] The statement in the synodal letter of Philippopolis that Asclepas had been deposed 'seventeen' years before is clearly corrupt. The true reading may be 'seven'(council of CP. in 336) or xiii, which might easily be changed to xvii. (Cf. Hefele, pp. 89, 90).

Naissus (now Nish, see *Fest. Ind.* xvi.), and during the summer, in obedience to an invitation from Constans, repaired to Aquileia, where he spent the Easter of 345.

Meanwhile, Constans had made the cause of the Sardican majority his own. At the beginning of the year 344 he sent two of its most respected members to urge upon Constantius the propriety of restoring the exiles. Either now or later he hinted that refusal would be regarded by him as a *casus belli.* His remonstrance gained unexpected moral support from an episode, strange even in that age of unprincipled intrigue. In rage and pain at the apparent success of the envoys, Stephen, Bishop of Antioch, sought to discredit them by a truly diabolical trick (see p. 276). Its discovery, just after Easter, 344, roused the moral sense of Constantius. A Council was summoned, and met during the summer[8] (p. 462, § 26, 'three years after' the Dedication at Midsummer, 341). Stephen was ignominiously deposed (see Gwatkin 125, note 1), and Leontius, an Arian, but a lover of quiet and a temporiser, appointed. The Council also re-issued the 'fourth' Antiochene Creed with a very long explanatory addition, mildly condemning certain Arian phrases, fiercely anathematising Marcellus and Photinus, and with a side-thrust at supposed implications of the Nicene formula. A deputation was sent to Italy, consisting of Eudoxius of Germanicia and three others. They reached Milan at the Synod of 345, and were able to procure a condemnation of Photinus (not Marcellus), but on being asked to anathematise Arianism refused, and retired in anger. At the same Synod of Milan, however, Valens and Ursacius, whose deposition at Sardica was in imminent danger of being enforced by Constans, followed the former example of Eusebius of Nicomedia, Maris, Theognis, and Arius himself, by making their submission, which was followed up two years later by a letter in abject terms addressed to Julius, and another in a tone of veiled insolence to Athanasius (p. 131). In return, they were able to beat up a Synod at Sirmium against Photinus (Hil. *Frag.* ii. 19), but without success in the attempt to dislodge him.

Meanwhile, Constantius had followed up the Council at Antioch by cancelling his severe measures against the Nicene party. He restored to Alexandria certain Presbyters whom he had expelled, and in the course of the summer wrote a public letter to forbid any further persecution of the Athanasians in that city. This must have been in August, 344, and 'about ten months later' (p. 277), i.e., on June 26, 345 (*F. I.* xviii.), Gregory, who had been in bad health for fully four years, died[9]. Constantius, according to his own statement (pp. 127, 277), had already before the death of Gregory written twice to Athanasius (from Edessa; he was at Nisibis on May 12, 345), and had sent a Presbyter to request him urgently to come and see him with a view to his eventual restoration. As Gregory was known to be in a dying state, this is quite intelligible, but the language of *Hist. Ar.* 21, which seems to put all *all three* letters *after* Gregory's death, cannot stand if we are to accept the assurance of Constantius. Athanasius, at any rate, hesitated to obey, and stayed on at Aquileia (344 till early in 346), where he received a third and still more pressing invitation, promising him immediate restoration. He at once went to Rome to bid farewell to Julius, who wrote (p. 128 *sq.*) a most cordial and nobly-worded letter of congratulation for Athanasius to take home to his Church. Thence he proceeded to Trier to take leave of Constans (p. 239), and rapidly travelled by way of Hadrianople (p. 276) to Antioch (p. 240), where he was cordially received[10] by Constantius. His visit was short but remarkable. Constantius gave him the strongest assurances (pp. 277, 285) of goodwill for the future, but begged that Athanasius would allow the Arians at Alexandria the use of a single Church. He replied that he would do so if the Eustathians of Antioch (with whom alone he communicated during this visit) might have the same privilege. But this Leontius would not sanction, so the proposal came to nothing (Soc. ii. 23, Soz. iii. 20), and Athanasius hastened on his way. At Jerusalem he was detained by the welcome of a Council, which Bishop Maximus had summoned to greet him (p. 130), but on the twenty-first of October his reception by his flock took place; 'the people, and those in authority, met him a hundred miles distant' (*Fest. Ind.* xviii.), and amid splendid rejoicings (cf. p. xlii., note 3), he entered Alexandria, to remain there in 'quiet' 'nine years, three months and nineteen days' (*Hist. Aceph.* iv., cf. p. 496), viz., from Paophi 24 (Oct. 21), 346, to Mechir 13 (Feb. 8), 356. This period was his longest undisturbed residence in his see; he entered upon it in the very

---

[8] The 'ten months' of *Hist. Ar.* 21, p. 277, are to be reckoned, not from *Easter* 344, but from the letters of Const. to Alexandria some months after.

[9] It must be observed that the Index is loose in its statement here: see Gwatkin, p. 105, Sievers, p. 108. The statement of

Thdt., &c., that he was murdered is simply due to the usual confusion of Gregory with George (cf. p. xliii. note 5).

[10] This visit cannot have been between May 7 and Aug. 27, when Const. was at CP. Nor can it well have been before May 7. We must, therefore, with Sievers, p. 110, put it in September. Yet see Gwatkin, p. 127, note.

prime of life (he was 48 years old), and its internal happiness earns it the title of a golden decade.

§ 7. *The Golden Decade, 346—356.*

(1). This period is divided into two by the death of Constans in 350, or perhaps more exactly by the final settlement of sole power in the hands of Constantius on the day of Mursa, Sept. 28, 351 [1]. The *internal* condition of the Church at Alexandria, however, was not seriously disturbed even in the second period. From this point of view the entire period may be treated as one. Its opening was auspicious. Egypt fully participated in the 'profound and wonderful peace' (p. 278) of the Churches. The Bishops of province after province were sending in their letters of adhesion to the Synod of Sardica (*ib.* and p. 127), and those of Egypt signed to a man.

The public rejoicing of the Alexandrian Church had something of the character of a 'mission' in modern Church life. A wave of religious enthusiasm passed over the whole community. 'How many widows and how many orphans, who were before hungry and naked, now through the great zeal of the people were no longer hungry, and went forth clothed;' 'in a word, so great was their emulation in virtue, that you would have thought every family and every house a Church, by reason of the goodness of its inmates and the prayers which were offered to God' (p. 278). Increased strictness of life, the santification of home, renewed application to prayer, and practical charity, these were a worthy welcome to their long-lost pastor. But most conspicuous was the impulse to asceticism. Marriages were renounced and even dissolved in favour of the monastic life; the same instincts were at work (but in greater intensity) as had asserted themselves at the close of the era of the pagan persecutions (p. 200, § 4, *fin.*). Our knowledge of the history of the Egyptian Church under the ten years' peaceful rule of Athanasius is confined to a few details and to what we can infer from results.

Strong as was the position of Athanasius in Egypt upon his return from exile, his hold upon the country grew with each year of the decade. When circumstances set Constantius free to resume the Arian campaign, it was against Athanasius that he worked; at first from the remote West, then by attempts to remove or coax him from Alexandria. But Athanasius was in an impregnable position, and when at last the city was seized by the *coup de main* of 356, from his hiding-places in Egypt he was more inaccessible still, more secure in his defence, more free to attack. Now the extraordinary development of Egyptian MONACHISM must be placed in the first rank of the causes which strengthened Athanasius in Egypt. The institution was already firmly rooted there (cf. p. 190), and Pachomius, a slightly older contemporary of Athanasius himself, had converted a sporadic manifestation of the ascetic impulse into an organised form of Community Life. Pachomius himself had died on May 9, 346 (*infr.* p. lx., note 3, and p. 569, note 3: cf. *Theolog. Literaturztg.* 1890, p. 622), but Athanasius was welcomed soon after his arrival by a deputation from the Society of Tabenne, who also conveyed a special message from the aged Antony. Athanasius placed himself at the head of the monastic movement, and we cannot doubt that while he won the enthusiastic devotion of these dogged and ardent Copts, his influence on the movement tended to restrain extravagances and to correct the morbid exaltation of the monastic ideal. It is remarkable that the only letters which survive from this decade (pp. 556—560) are to monks, and that they both support what has just been said. The army of Egyptian monks was destined to become a too powerful weapon, a scandal and a danger to the Church: but the monks were the main secret of the power and ubiquitous activity of Athanasius in his third exile, and that power was above all built up during the golden decade.

Coupled with the growth of monachism is the transformation of the episcopate. The great power enjoyed by the Archbishop of Alexandria made it a matter of course that in a prolonged episcopate discordant elements would gradually vanish and unanimity increase. This was the case under Athanasius: but the unanimity reflected in the letter *ad Afros* had practically already come about in the year of the return of Ath. from Aquileia, when nearly every bishop in Egypt signed the Sardican letter (p. 127; the names include the new bishops of 346-7 in *Letter* 19, with one or two exceptions). Athanasius not infrequently (pp. 559 *sq.* and *Vit. Pach.* 72) filled up vacancies in the episcopate from among the monks, and Serapion of Thmuis, his most trusted suffragan, remained after his elevation in very close relation with the monasteries.

Athanasius consecrated bishops not only for Egypt, but for the remote Abyssinian kingdom of Auxume as well. The visit of Frumentius to Alexandria, and his consecration as bishop for Auxume, are referred by Rufinus i. 9 (Socr. i. 19, &c.) to the beginning of the episcopate of Athanasius. But the chronology of the story (Gwatkin, pp. 93 *sqq.*, D.C.B. ii. 236 where the argument is faulty) forbids this altogether, while the letter of Constantius (p. 250) is most natural if the consecration of Frumentius were then a comparatively recent matter, scarcely intelligible if it had taken place before the 'deposition' of Athan. by the council of Tyre. Athanasius had found Egypt distracted by religious dissensions; but by the time of the third exile we hear very little of Arians excepting in Alexandria itself (see p. 564); the 'Arians' of the rest of Egypt were the remnant of the Meletians, whose monks are still mentioned by Theodoret (cf. p. 299 *sq.*). An incident which shews the growing numbers of the Alexandrian Church during this period is the necessity which arose at Easter in one year of using the unfinished Church of the Cæsareum (for its history cf. p. 243, note 6, and *Hist. Aceph.* vi., *Fest. Ind.* xxxvii., xxxviii., xl.) owing to the vast crowds of worshippers. The Church was a gift of Constantius, and had been begun by Gregory, and its use before completion and dedication was treated by the Arians as an act of presumption and disrespect on the part of Athanasius.

---

[1] See below.

(2.) But while all was so happy in Egypt, the 'profound peace' of the rest of the Church was more apparent than real. The temporary revulsion of feeling on the part of Constantius, the engrossing urgency of the Persian war, the readiness of Constans to use his formidable power to secure justice to the Nicene bishops in the East, all these were causes which compelled peace, while leaving the deeper elements of strife to smoulder untouched. The riva ldepositions and anathemas of the hostile Councils remained without effect. Valens was in possession at Mursa, Photinus at Sirmium. Marcellus was, probably, not at Ancyra (Zahn 82); but the Arians deposed at Sardica were all undisturbed, while Athanasius was more firmly established than ever at Alexandria. On the whole, the Episcopate of the East was entirely in the hands of the reaction—the Nicene element, often large, among the laity was in many cases conciliated with difficulty. This is conspicuously the case at Antioch, where the temporising policy of Leontius managed to retain in communion a powerful body of orthodox Christians, headed by Diodorus and Flavian, whose energy neutralised the effect of his own steadily Arian policy (particulars, Gwatkin, pp. 133, *sqq.*, Newman, *Arians* 4, p. 455—from Thdt. *H. E.* ii. 24). The Eustathian schism at Antioch was, apparently, paralleled by a Marcellian schism at Ancyra, but such cases were decidedly the exception.

Of the mass of instances where the bishops were not Arian but simply conservative, the Church of Jerusalem is the type. We have the instructions given to the Catechumens of this city between 348 and 350 by CYRIL, who in the latter year (Hort, p. 92) became bishop, and whose career is typical of the rise and development of so-called semi-Arianism. Cyril, like the conservatives generally, is strongly under the influence of Origen (see Caspari iv. 146-162, and cf. the *Catechesis* in Heurtley *de Fid. et Symb.* 62 with the Regula Fidei in Orig. *de Princ.* 1). The instructions insist strongly on the necessity of *scriptural* language, and while contradicting the doctrines of Arius (without mentioning his name; cf. Athanasius on Marcellus and Photinus in pp. 433– 447) Cyril tacitly protests against the ὁμοούσιον as of human contrivance (*Cat.* v. 12), and uses in preference the words 'like to the Father according to the Scriptures' or 'in all things.' This language is that of Athanasius also, especially in his earlier works (pp. 84 *sqq.*), but in the latter phase of the controversy, especially in the Dated Creed of 359, which presents striking resemblances to Cyril's Catecheses, it became the watchword of the party of reaction. The Church of Jerusalem then was orthodox substantially, but rejected the Nicene formula, and this was the case in the East generally, except where the bishops were positively Arian. All were aggrieved at the way in which the Eastern councils had been treated by the West, and smarted under a sense of defeat (cf. Bright, Introd. to *Hist. Tr.*, p. xviii.).

Accordingly the murder of Constans in 350 was the harbinger of renewed religious discord. For a time the political future was doubtful. Magnentius, knowing what Athanasius had to fear from Constantius, made a bid for the support of Egypt. Clementius and Valens, two members of a deputation to Constantius, came round by way of Egypt to ascertain the disposition of the country, and especially of its Bishop. Athanasius received them with bitter lamentations for Constans, and, fearing the possibility of an invasion by Magnentius, he called upon his congregation to pray for the Eastern Emperor. The response was immediate and unanimous: 'O Christ, send help to Constantius' (p. 242). The Emperor had, in fact, sought to secure the fidelity of Athanasius by a letter (pp. 247, 278), assuring him of his continued support. And until the defeat of Magnentius at Mursa, he kept his word. That victory, which was as decisive for Valens as it was for Constantius (Gibbon, ii. 381, iii. 66, ed. Smith), was followed up by a Council at Sirmium, which successfully ousted the too popular Photinus (cf. pp. 280, 298 ; on the appeal of Photinus, and the debate between him and Basil of Ancyra, apparently in 355, see Gwatkin, pp. 145 *sq.*, note 6). This was made the occasion for a new onslaught upon Marcellus in the anathemas appended to a reissue of the 'fourth Antiochene' or Philippopolitan Creed (p. 465 ; on the tentative character of these anathemas as a polemical move, cf. Gwatkin, p. 147, note 1). The Emperor was occupied for more than a year with the final suppression of Magnentius (Aug. 10, 353), but 'the first Winter after his victory, which he spent at Arles, was employed against an enemy more odious to him than the vanquished tyrant of Gaul' (Gibbon).

It is unnecessary to detail the tedious and unedifying story of the councils of Arles and Milan. The former was a provincial council of Gaul, attended by legates of the Roman see. All present submissively registered the imperial condemnation of Athanasius. The latter, delayed till 355 by the Rhenish campaign of Constantius, was due to the request of Liberius, who desired to undo the evil work of his legates, and to the desire of the Emperor to follow up the verdict of a provincial with that of a more representative Synod. The number of bishops present was probably very small (the numbers in Socrates ii. 36, Soz. iv. 9, may refer to those who afterwards signed under compulsion, p. 280, cf. the case of Sardica, p. 127, note 10). The proceedings were a drama in three acts, first, submission, the legates protesting; secondly, stormy protest, after the arrival of Eusebius of Vercellæ; thirdly, open coercion. The deposition of Athanasius was proffered to each bishop for signature, and, if he refused, a sentence of banishment was at once pronounced, the emperor sitting with the 'velum' drawn, much as though an English judge were to assume the black cap at the *beginning* of a capital trial. He cut short argument by announcing that 'he was for the prosecution,' and remonstrance by the sentence of exile (p. 299); the ὅπερ ἐγὼ βούλομαι τοῦτο κανών put into his mouth by Athanasius (p. 281) represents at any rate the spirit of his proceedings as justly as does 'la tradizione son' io' that of the autocrat of a more recent council. At this council no creed was put forth: until the enemy was dislodged from Alexandria the next step would be premature. But a band of exiles were sent in strict custody to the East, of some of whom we shall hear later on (pp. 561, 481, 281, cf. p. 256, and the excellent monograph of Krüger, *Lucifer von Calaris*, pp. 9—23).

Meanwhile, Athanasius had been peacefully pursuing his diocesan duties, but not without a careful outlook as the clouds gathered on the horizon. The prospect of a revival of the charges against him moved him to set in order an unanswerable array of documents, in proof, firstly of the unanimity, secondly of the good reason, with which he had been acquitted of them (see p. 97). He had also, in view of revived assertions of Arianism, drawn up the two letters or memoranda on the rationale of the Nicene formula and on the opinion ascribed to his famous predecessor, Dionysius (the *Apology* was probably written about 351, the date of the *de Decr.*, and *de Sent. Dion.*[2] falls a little later). In 353 he began to apprehend danger, from the hopes with which the establishment of Constantius in the sole possession of the Empire was inspiring his enemies, headed by Valens in the West, and Acacius of Cæsarea in the East. Accordingly, he despatched a powerful deputation to Constantius, who was then at Milan, headed by Serapion, his most trusted suffragan (cf. p. 560, note 3 a; p. 497, § 3, copied by Soz. iv. 9; *Fest. Ind.* xxv.). The legates sailed May 19, but on the 23rd Montanus, an officer of the Palace, arrived with an Imperial letter, declining to receive any legates, but granting an alleged request of Athanasius to be allowed to come to Italy (p. 245 *sq.*). As he had made no request of the kind, Athanasius naturally suspected a plot to entice him away from his stronghold. The letter of Constantius did not convey an absolute command, so Athanasius, protesting his willingness to come when ordered to do so, resolved to remain where he was for the present. 'All the people were exceedingly troubled,' according to our chroniclers. 'In this year Montanus was sent against the bishop, but a tumult having been excited, he retired without effect.' Two years and two months later, i.e., in July—Aug. 355 (p. 497), force was attempted instead of stratagem, which the proceedings of Arles had, of course, made useless. 'In this year Diogenes, the Secretary of the Emperor, came with the intention of seizing the bishop,' 'and Diogenes pressed hard upon all, trying to dislodge the bishop from the city, and he afflicted all pretty severely; but on Sept. 4[3] he pressed sharply, and stormed a Church, and this he did continually for four months... until Dec. 23. But as the people and magistrates vehemently withstood Diogenes, he returned back without effect on the 23rd of December aforesaid' (*Fest. Ind.* xxvii., *Hist. Aceph.* iii.). The fatal blow was clearly imminent. By this time the exiles had begun to arrive in the East, and rumours came[4] that not even the powerful and popular Liberius, not even 'Father' Hosius himself, had been spared. Athanasius might well point out to Dracontius (p. 558) that in declining the bishopric of the 'country district of Alexandria' he was avoiding the post of danger. On the sixth of January the 'Duke' Syrianus arrived in Alexandria, concentrating in the city drafts from all the legions stationed in Egypt and Libya. Rumour was active as to the intentions of the commandant, and Athanasius felt justified in asking him whether he came with any orders from the Court. Syrianus replied that he did not, and Athanasius then produced the letter of Constantius referred to above (written 350—351). The magistrates and people joined in the remonstrance, and at last Syrianus protested 'by the life of Cæsar' that he would remain quiet until the matter had been referred to the Emperor. This restored confidence, and on Thursday night, Feb. 8, Athanasius was presiding at a crowded service of preparation for a Communion on the following morning (Friday after Septuagesima) in the Church of Theonas, which with the exception of the unfinished Cæsareum was the largest in the city (p. 243). Suddenly the church was surrounded and the doors broken in, and just after midnight Syrianus and the 'notary' Hilary 'entered with an infinite force of soldiers.' Athanasius (his fullest account is p. 263) calmly took his seat upon the throne (in the recess of the apse), and ordered the deacon to begin the 136th psalm, the people responding at each verse 'for His mercy endureth for ever.' Meanwhile the soldiers crowded up to the chancel, and in spite of entreaties the bishop refused to escape until the congregation were in safety. He ordered the prayers to proceed, and only at the last moment a crowd of monks and clergy seized the Archbishop and managed to convey him in the confusion out of the church in a half-fainting state (protest of Alexandrians, p. 301),

---

[2] In *de Sent. Dion.* 23, 24, Arius is spoken of in a way consistent with his being still alive. But the phase of the Arian controversy to which the tract relates begins a decade after Arius' death, and we therefore follow the indications which class the *de Sent.* with the *de Decr.*

[3] All the following dates are affected by Leap-Year, 355-6, **see** Table C, p. 501, and correct p. 246, note 3, to Jan. 6.
[4] Definite information came only after Feb. 8, see p. 248.

but thankful that he had been able to secure the escape of his people before his own (p. 264). From that moment Athanasius was lost to public view for 'six years and fourteen days' (*Hist. Aceph.*, i.e., Mechir 13, 356—Mechir 27, 362), 'for he remembered that which was written, Hide thyself as it were for a little moment, until the indignation be overpast (pp. 288, 252, 262). Constantius and the Arians had planned their blow with skill and delivered it with decisive effect. But they had won a 'Cadmean Victory.'

§ 8. *The Third Exile*, 356—362.

The third exile of Athanasius marks the summit of his achievement. Its commencement is the triumph, its conclusion the collapse of Arianism. It is true that after the death of Constantius the battle went on with variations of fortune for twenty years, mostly under the reign of an ardently Arian Emperor (364—378). But by 362 the utter lack of inner coherence in the Arian ranks was manifest to all; the issue of the fight might be postponed by circumstances but could not be in doubt. The break-up of the Arian power was due to its own lack of reality: as soon as it had a free hand, it began to go to pieces. But the watchful eye of Athanasius followed each step in the process from his hiding-place, and the event was greatly due to his powerful personality and ready pen, knowing whom to overwhelm and whom to conciliate, where to strike and where to spare. This period then of forced abstention from affairs was the most stirring in spiritual and literary activity in the whole life of Athanasius. It produced more than half of the treatises which fill this volume, and more than half of his entire extant works. With this we shall have to deal presently; but let it be noted once for all how completely the amazing power wielded by the wandering fugitive was based upon the devoted fidelity of Egypt to its pastor. Towns and villages, deserts and monasteries, the very tombs were scoured by the Imperial inquisitors in the search for Athanasius; but all in vain; not once do we hear of any suspicion of betrayal. The work of the golden decade was bearing its fruit.

(1.) On leaving the church of Theonas, Athanasius appears to have made his escape from the city. If for once we may hazard a conjecture, the numerous cells of the Nitrian desert offered a not too distant but fairly inpenetrable refuge. He must at any rate have selected a place where he could gain time to reflect on the situation, and above all ensure that he should be kept well informed of events from time to time. For in Athanasius we never see the panic-stricken outlaw; he is always the general meditating his next movement and full of the prospects of his cause. He made up his mind to appeal to Constantius in person. He could not believe that an Emperor would go back upon his solemn pledges, especially such a voluntary assurance as he had received after the death of Constans. Accordingly he drew up a carefully elaborated defence (*Ap. Const.* 1—26) dealing with the four principal charges against him, and set off through the Libyan[10] desert with the intention of crossing to Italy and finding Constantius at Milan. But while he was on his way, he encountered rumours confirming the reports of the wholesale banishment not only of the recalcitrants of Milan, but of Liberius of Rome and the great Hosius of Spain. Next came the news of the severe measures against Egyptian bishops, and of the banishment of sixteen of their number, coupled with the violence practised by the troops at Alexandria on Easter Day (p. 248 *sq.*); however, his journey was continued, until he received copies of letters from the Emperor, one denouncing him to the Alexandrians and recommending a new bishop, one George, as their future guide, the other summoning the princes of Auxumis to send Frumentius (*supr.* p. xlviii.) to Egypt in order that he might unlearn what he had been taught by 'the most wicked Athanasius' and receive instruction from the 'venerable George.' These letters, which shew how completely the pursuers were off the scent (p. 249), convinced Athanasius that a personal interview was out of the question. He returned into the desert,' and at leisure completed his apology (pp. 249—253), with the view partly of possible future delivery, partly no doubt of literary circulation. Before turning back, however, he appears to have drawn up his letter to the bishops of Egypt and Libya, warning them against the formula (see p. 222) which was being tendered for their subscription, and encouraging them to endure persecution, which had already begun at least in Libya (*Ep. Æg.*); the designation of George (§ 7) was already known, but he had not arrived, nor had Secundus (19) reappeared in Egypt, at any rate not in Libya (he was there in Lent, 357, p. 294). The letter to the bishops, then, must have been written about Easter, 356; not long after,

---

[10] The envoys of Magnentius had come from Italy *through Libya* in 350—351. The 'desert' (*Apol. Const.* 27, 32) must be the region between Alxa. and *Cyrenaica*, not *Palestine* as Tillem. viii. 186, infers from *Ep. Æg.* 5. There is no evidence that Ath. left his province during this exile, and Palestine was a most dangerous territory to venture into. The cautious vagueness of his language, *Ep. Æg.* 5, while it baffles even our curiosity, yet favours the hypothesis that the events referred to belong to the *Egyptian* persecution.

because it contains no details of the persecution in Egypt; not before, for the persecution had already begun, and Athanasius was already in Cyrenaica, whence he turned back not earlier than April (to allow time for Constantius (1) to hear that Athanasius was thought to have fled to Ethiopia, (2) to write to Egypt, (3) for copies of the letter to overtake Athanasius on his way to Italy. Constantius was at Milan Jan.—April).

Meanwhile in Alexandria disorders had continued. The 'duke' appears to have been either unable for a time, or to have thought it needless, to take possession of the churches; but we hear of a violent dispersion of worshippers from the neighbourhood of the cemetery on Easter Day (p. 249, cf. the Virgins *after Syrianus but before Heraclius*, p. 288); while throughout Egypt subscription to an Arianising formula was being enforced on the bishops under pain of expulsion. After Easter, a change of governor took place, Maximus of Nicæa (pp. 301 *sqq.*, 247) being succeeded by Cataphronius, who reached Alexandria on the 10th of June (*Hist. Aceph.* iv.). He was accompanied by a Count Heraclius, who brought a letter from Constantius threatening the heathen with severe measures (pp. 288, 290), unless active hostilities against the Athanasian party were begun (this letter was not the one given p. 249; Ath. rightly remarks 'it reflected great discredit upon the writer'). Heraclius announced that by Imperial order the Churches were to be given up to the Arians, and compelled all the magistrates, including the functionaries of heathen temples, to sign an undertaking to execute the Imperial incitements to persecution, and to agree to receive as Bishop the Emperor's nominee. These incredible precautions shew the general esteem for Athanasius even outside the Church, and the misgivings felt at Court as to the reception of the new bishop. The Gentiles reluctantly agreed, and the next acts of violence were carried out with their aid, 'or rather with that of the more abandoned among them' (p. 291). On the fourth day from the arrival of Cataphronius, that is in the early hours of Thursday, June 13, after a service (which had begun overnight, pp. 290, 256 *fin.*, *Hist. Aceph.* v.), just as all the congregation except a few women had left, the church of Theonas was stormed and violences perpetrated which left far behind anything that Syrianus had done. Women were murdered, the church wrecked and polluted with the very worst orgies of heathenism, houses and even tombs were ransacked throughout the city and suburbs on pretence of 'seeking for Athanasius.' Sebastian the Manichee, who about this time succeeded to the military command of Syrianus, appears to have carried on these outrages with the utmost zest (yet see *Hist. Ar.* 60). Many more bishops were driven into exile (compare the twenty-six of p. 297 with the 'sixteen' p. 248, but some may belong to a still later period, see p. 257), and the Arian bishops and clergy installed, including the bitterly vindictive Secundus in Libya (p. 257). The formal transfer of churches at Alexandria took place on Saturday, June 15 (*infr.*, p. 290, note 9): the anniversary of Eutychius (p. 292) was kept at Alexandria on July 11, (*Martyrol. Vetust.* Ed. 1668). After a further delay of 'eight months and eleven days' George, the new bishop, made his appearance (Feb. 24, 357[11], third Friday in Lent). His previous career[12] and character[13] were strange qualifications for the second bishopric in Christendom. He had been a pork-contractor at Constantinople, and according to his many enemies a fraudulent one; he had amassed considerable wealth, and was a zealous Arian. His violent temper perhaps recommended him as a man likely to crush the opposition that was expected. The history of his episcopate may be briefly disposed of here. He entered upon his See in Lent, 357, with an armed force. At Easter he renewed the violent persecution of bishops, clergy, virgins, and lay people. In the week

---

[11] This date, coming from the common source of the *Historia Acephala* and *Festal Index* (i.e. from the accredited Alexandrian chronology of the period), must be accepted unless there is cogent proof of its incorrectness. No such proof is offered: we have *no positive statement to the contrary*, but only (1) the fact that the intrusion of George is related, *Apol. Fug.* 6, immediately after an attack on the great church, possibly the *coup de main* of Syrianus, but more probably that of p. 290, note 9, without any hint of a long interval. This is true, and *if there were no evidence the other way* might justify a *guess* that George came in Lent, 356; but no one would claim that the passage is conclusive by itself; (2) the 'improbability' of George delaying his arrival so long. Improbability is a relative term; we know too little of George's consecration or movements to justify its use in the present connection. All the evidence goes to shew that the court party were far from sanguine as to the nature of his reception, and that their misgivings were well-founded. The above considerations look very small when we compare them with the mass of positive evidence the other way. (1.) The civil Governor had changed: Maximus held the post on Feb. 8, 356 (*Hist. Ar.* 81, &c.), Cataphronius when the churches were transferred to the party of George, see below, 6. (2.) The military Commander had changed: Syrianus was replaced by Sebastian, who appears just after the transfer of churches, *Hist. Ar.* 55—60 (Dr. Bright in D.C.B. i. 194, *note*, seems to admit that Sebastian belongs to a later date than the Lent of 356). (3.) The Wednesday (and Thursday) of *Hist. Ar.* 55 were *not* 'in Lent.' They suit the data of *Hist. Aceph.* perfectly well. (4.) Had George arrived before Easter 356, Athan. would have heard of it 'in the Desert,' *Apol. Const.* 27; but he has only heard of his *nomination* ὠνομάσθη 28, probably from the letters given in §§ 30, 31). (5.) The Letter to the Egyptian bishops was written from Libya or Cyrenaica, when the coercion of the episcopate had begun: it postulates some time since his expulsion, but George was then (§ 7) only in contemplation. (6.) There is no evidence that the *coup de main* of Syrianus was other than unpopular in the city. This was reported to Const., who *after* the (Easter) outrages on the Virgins (*Ap. Const.* 27; *Hist. Ar.* 48), and *after* the expulsion of the sixteen bishops (*Hist. Ar.* 54, this was probably about Easter, *Ap. Const.* 27) sent Heraclius (with the 'discreditable' letter), *in whose company* (*Hist. Ar.* 55) the new Prefect Cataphronius *first appears.* This let loose the refuse of the heathen population as described, ib. 55—60. (7.) Here the precise statement of the *Hist. Aceph.*

fits in exactly. The Presbyters and people of Ath. remained in possession of the Churches until the arrival of the new Prefect, *with Count Heraclius*, on June 10. (8.) Heraclius is expressly called the *precursor* of George (p. 288), and is evidently sent to disarm the reported hostility of the (even heathen) public to the appointment. It may be added that if we are to take 'probabilities' into account, it is easier to imagine a reason for a court nominee like George having been slow to take up a dangerous post, than for the Alexandrian chronologists of the day having invented a year's interval when none had existed. Montfaucon had already noticed that 'a good deal must have happened' between the irruption of Syrianus and the entry of George. The data of Athanasius are for the first time clearly explained by the light thrown on them by the chroniclers. I should also have urged the fact that the commemoration of George's Pentecost Martyrs on May 21 in the Roman Martyrology *suits* 357 *and not* 356, had I succeeded in tracing the history of the entry, which has, however, so far eluded my efforts.

[12] We are quite in the dark as to when, and by whom, George was consecrated bishop. The statement of Sozomen iv. 8, that he was ordained by a council of thirty bishops at Antioch, including Theodore of Heraclea, who had died before the exile of Liberius in 355 (Thdt. *H.E.* ii. 16, p. 93. 13), is involved in too hopeless a tangle of anachronisms to be of any value for our enquiry. But that George was ordained in Antioch is in itself likely enough, and if so, his ordination would probably follow close upon the expulsion of Athanasius. But the repeated assurances of Ath. that George came *from court* would imply that after his ordination George went to Italy. That at once puts his arrival in Alxa. in Lent 356 out of the question.

[13] The statements of Ath. as to George are made at second-hand, and must be taken *cum grano*. He is 'notoriously wealthy,' yet 'hired' by the Arians. (Cf. p. 249; but apparently he combined wealth and avarice.) That he was 'a heathen' is certainly untrue. His 'ignorance' is equally so: we know that he was a well-read man and possessed a remarkably good library (D.C.B. ii. 638). That he had 'the temper of a hangman' (p. 227) is in keeping with all that we know of him, and as to his general character, the statements of Athanasius and other churchmen are not stronger than Amm. Marcell. XXII. xi. 4 (cf. Gibbon, iii. 171 *sqq.*, ed. Smith, but correct his *jeu d'esprit* on 'S. George and the Dragon' by Bright, in D.C.B. *ubi supra*; yet see Stanley, *Eastern Church*, Lect. vii. III.).

after Pentecost he let loose the cruel commandant Sebastian against a number of persons who were worshipping at the cemetery instead of communicating with himself; many were killed, and many more banished. The expulsion of bishops ('over thirty,' p. 257, cf. other reff. above) was continued (the various data of Ath. are not easy to reconcile, the first 16 of p. 257 may be the 'sixteen' of p. 248, before Easter, 356: we miss the name of Serapion in all the lists!) Theodore, Bishop of Oxyrynchus, the largest town of middle Egypt, upon submitting to George, was compelled by him to submit to reordination. The people refused to have anything more to do with him, and did without a bishop for a long time, until they obtained a pastor in one Heraclides, who is said to have become a 'Luciferian.' (Cf. *Lib. Prec.*, and Le Quien ii. p. 578.) George carried on his tyranny eighteen months, till Aug. 29, 358. His fierce insults against Pagan worship were accompanied by the meanest and most oppressive rapacity. At last the populace, exasperated by his 'adder's bites' (Ammian.), attacked him, and he was rescued with difficulty. On Oct. 2 he left the town, and the party of Athanasius expelled his followers from the churches on Oct. 11, but on Dec. 24, Sebastian came in from the country and restored the churches to the people of George. On June 23, 359, 'the notary Paul' ('in complicandis calumniarum nexibus artifex dirus, unde ei *Catenæ* inditum est cognomentum,' Ammian. Marc. XIV. v., XV. iii.), the Jeffreys of the day, held a commission of blood, and 'vindictively punished many[14].' George was at this time busy with the councils of Seleucia and Constantinople (he was not actually present at the latter, Thdt. *H. E.* ii. 28), and was in no hurry to return. At last, just after the death of Constantius, he ventured back, Nov. 26, 361, but on the proclamation of Julian on Nov. 30 was seized by the populace and thrown into chains; on Dec. 24, 'impatient of the tedious forms of judicial proceedings,' the people dragged him from prison and lynched him with the utmost ignominy.

Athanasius meanwhile eluded all search. During part of the year 357—358 he was in concealment in Alexandria itself, and he was supposed to be there two years later (*Fest. Ind.* xxx., xxxii.; the latter gives some colour to the tale of Palladius—cf. Soz. v. 6—of his having during part of this period remained concealed in the house of a Virgin of the church), but the greater part of his time was undoubtedly spent in the numberless cells of Upper and Lower Egypt, where he was secure of close concealment, and of loyal and efficient messengers to warn him of danger, keep him informed of events, and carry his letters and writings far and wide. The tale of Rufinus (i. 18) that he lay hid all the six years in a dry cistern is probably a confused version of this general fact. The tombs of kings and private persons were at this time the common abode of monks (cf. p. 564, note 1; also Socr. iv. 13, a similar mistake). Probably we must place the composition of the *Life of Antony*, the great classic of Monasticism, at some date during this exile, although the question is surrounded with difficulties (see pp. 188 *sqq.*). The importance of the period, however, lies in the march of events outside Egypt. (For a brilliant sketch of the desert life of Athanasius see D.C.B. i. 194 *sq.*; also Bright, *Hist. Treatises*, p. lxxiv. *sq.*)

(2.) With the accession of Constantius to sole power, the anti-Nicene reaction at last had a free hand throughout the Empire. Of what elements did it now consist? The original reaction was conservative in its numerical strength, Arian in its motive power. The stream was derived from the two fountain heads of Paul of Samosata, the ancestor of Arius, and of Origen the founder of the theology of the Eastern Church generally and especially of that of Eusebius of Cæsarea. Flowing from such heterogeneous sources, the two currents never thoroughly mingled. Common action, dictated on the one hand by dread of Sabellianism, manipulated on the other hand by wire-pullers in the interest of Arianism, united the East till after the death of Constantine in the campaign against the leaders of Nicæa. Then for the last ten years of the life of Constans, Arianism, or rather the Reaction, had its 'stationary period' (Newman). The chaos of creeds at the Council of Antioch (*supr.* p. xliv.) shewed the presence of discordant aims; but opposition to Western interference, and the urgent panic of Photinus and his master, kept them together: the lead was still taken by the Arianisers, as is shewn by the continued prominence of the fourth Antiochene Creed at Philippopolis (343), Antioch (344), and Sirmium (351). But the second or Lucianic Creed was on record as the protest of the conservative majority, and was not forgotten. Yet until after 351, when Photinus was finally got rid of and Constantius master of the world, the reaction was still embodied in a fairly compact and united party. But now the latent heterogeneity of the reaction began to make itself felt. Differing in source and motive, the two main currents made in different directions. The influence of Aristotle and Paul and Lucian set steadily toward a harder and more consistent Arianism, that of Plato and the Origenists toward an understanding with the Nicenes.

(*a.*) The original Arians, now gradually dying out, were all tainted with compromise and political subserviency. Arius, Asterius, Eusebius of Nicomedia, and the rest (Secundus and Theonas are the solitary exception), were all at one time or another, and in different degrees, willing to make concessions and veil their more objectionable tenets under some evasive confession. But in many cases temporary humiliation produced its natural result in subsequent uncompromising defiance. This is exemplified in the history of VALENS and

---

[14] p. 497. George was at Sirmium in the Spring of 359 (Soz. (v. 16). Paul *Catena* came to Alxa. from a similar commission at Scythopolis. He was apparently aided in both places by Modestus the Comes Orientis. From Liban. *Ep.* 205, we gather, to the credit of George, that he was the intermediary of requests for mitigation of some of the sentences. He was at this time at Antioch, from whence also 'Ex Comitatu Principis,' Amm. XXII. xi., he returned to Alxa. in 361, evidently before he had heard of the Emperor's death. (Sievers, pp. 138 *sq.*)

Ursacius after 351. Valens, especially, figures as the head of a new party of 'ANOMŒANS' or ultra-Arians. The rise of this party is associated with the name of AETIUS, its after-history with that of his pupil Eunomius, bishop of Cyzicus from 361. It was marked by a genuine scorn for the compromises of earlier Arianism, from which it differed in nothing except its more resolute sincerity. The career of Aetius (D.C.B. i. 50, *sqq.*) was that of a struggling, self-made, self-confident man. A pupil of the Lucianists (*supr.*, p. xxviii.), he shrunk from none of the irreverent conclusions of Arianism. His loud voice and clear-cut logic lost none of their effect by fear of offending the religious sensibilities of others. In 350 Leontius ordained him deacon, with a licence to preach, at Antioch ; but Flavian and Diodorus (see above, § 7) raised such a storm that the cautious bishop felt obliged to suspend him. On the appointment of George he was invited to Alexandria, whither Eunomius was attracted by his fame as a teacher. His influence gradually spread, and he found many kindred spirits among the bishops. The survivors of the original Arians were with him at heart, as also were men like Eudoxius, bishop of Germanicia (of Antioch, 358, of CP. 360), who fell as far behind Aetius in sincerity as he surpassed him in profanity ; the Anomœans (ἀνόμοιος) were numerically strong, and morally even more so ; they were the wedge which eventually broke up the reactionary mass, rousing the sincere horror of the Conservatives, commanding the sometimes dissembled but always real sympathy of the true Arians, and seriously embarrassing the political Arians, whose one aim was to keep their party together by disguising differences of principle under some convenient phrase.

(*b.*) This latter party were headed by Acacius in the East and in the West by VALENS, who while in reality, as stated above, making play for the Anomœan cause, was diplomatist enough to use the influential 'party of no principle' as his instrument for the purpose. Valens during the whole period of the sole reign of Constantius (and in fact until his own death about 375) was the heart and soul of the new and last phase of Arianism, namely of *the formal attempt to impose an Arian creed upon the Church* in lieu of that of Nicæa. But this could only be done by skilful use of less extreme men, and in the trickery and statecraft necessary for such a purpose Valens was *facile princeps.* His main supporter in the East was ACACIUS, who had succeeded to the bishoprick, the library, and the doctrinal position of his preceptor Eusebius of Cæsarea. The latter, as we saw (p. xxvii. note 5), represented 'the extreme left' of the conservative reaction, meeting the right wing, or rather the extreme concessions, of pure Arianism as represented by its official advocate Asterius, whom in fact Eusebius had defended against the onslaught of Marcellus. In so far then as the stream of pure Arianism could be mingled with the waters of Conservatism, Acacius was the channel in which they joined. Eusebius had not been an Arian, neither was Acacius ; Eusebius had theological convictions, but lacked clearness of perception, Acacius was a clear-headed man but without convictions ; Eusebius was substantially conservative in his theology, but tainted with political Arianism ; Acacius was a political Arian first, and anything you please afterwards. On the whole, his sympathies seem to have been conservative, but he manifests a rooted dislike of principle of any kind. He appoints orthodox bishops (Philost. v. 1), but quarrels with them as soon as he encounters their true mettle, Cyril in 358, Meletius in 361 ; he befriends Arians, but betrays the too honest Aetius in 360. His ecclesiastical career begins with the council of four creeds in 341 ; in controversy with Marcellus he developed the concessions of Asterius till he almost reached the Nicene standard ; he hailed effusively the Anomœan Creed of Valens in 358 (Soz. iv. 12), and in 359-60 forced that of Nike in its amended form upon the Eastern Church far and wide. He is next heard of, signing the Ὁμοούσιον, in 363, and lastly (Socr. iv. 2) under Valens is named again along with Eudoxius. The real opinions of a man with such a record are naturally not easy to determine, but we may be sure that he was in thorough sympathy with the policy of Constantius, namely the union of all parties in the Church on the basis of subserviency to the State.

The difficulty was to find a formula. The test of Nicæa could not be superseded without putting something in its place, which should *in*clude Arianism as effectually as the other had excluded it. Such a test was eventually (after 357) found in the word ὅμοιος [15]. It was a word with a good Catholic history. We find it used freely by Athanasius in his earlier anti-Arian writings, and it was thoroughly current in conservative theology, as for example in Cyril's Catecheses (he has ὅμοιον κατὰ τας γραφάς and ὅμοιον κατὰ πάντα). It would therefore permit even the full Nicene belief. On the other hand many of the more earnest conservative theologians had begun to reflect on what was involved in the 'likeness' of the Son to the Father, and had formulated the conviction that this likeness was *essential,* not, as the Arians held, acquired. This was in fact a fair inference from the οὐσίας ἀπαράλλακτον εἰκόνα of the Dedication Creed. This question made an agreement between men like Valens and Basil difficult, but it could be evaded by keeping to the simple ὅμοιον, and deprecating non-scriptural precision. Lastly, there were the Anomœans to be considered. Now the ὅμοιον had the specious appearance of flatly contradicting this repellent avowal of the extremists; but to Valens and his friends it had the substantial recommendation of admitting it in reality. 'Likeness' is a relative term. If two things are only 'like' they are *ipso facto* to some extent unlike ; the two words are not contradictories but correlatives, and if the likeness is not essential, the unlikeness is. So far then as the 'Homœan' party rested on any doctrinal principle at all, that principle was the principle of Arius ; and that is how Valens forwarded the Anomœan cause by putting himself at the head of the Homœans. His plan of campaign had steadily matured. The deposition of Photinus in 351 had sounded the note of war, Arles and Milan (353-5) and the expulsion of Athanasius (356) had cleared the field of opponents, George was now in possession at Alexandria, and in the summer of 357 the triumph of Arianism was proclaimed. A small council of bishops met at Sirmium and published a Latin Creed, insisting strongly (1) on the unique Godhead of the Father, (2) on the subjection of the Son 'along with all things subjected to Him by the Father,' and (3) strictly proscribing the terms ὁμοούσιον, ὁμοιούσιον, and all discussion of οὐσία, as unscriptural and inscrutable.

This manifesto was none the less Anomœan for not explicitly avowing the obnoxious phrase. It *forbids* the definition of the 'likeness' as essential, and does not even condescend to use the ὅμοιον at all. The Nicene definition is for the first time overtly and bluntly denounced, and the 'conservatives' are commanded to hold their peace. The 'Sirmium blasphemy' was indeed a trumpet-blast of defiance. The echo came back from the Homœans assembled at Antioch, whence Eudoxius the new bishop, Acacius, and their friends addressed the

---

[15] **We** cannot fix the date when this word was first adopted as a shibboleth. It occurs, but not conspicuously, in the 'Macrostich' of 344, but not in any other creed till the 'dated' symbol of 359. But if (as Krüger, *Lucif.*, p. 42, *note*, assumes) the ὁμοιού-σιον was adopted as a protest against the bald ὅμοιον, the latter must have been current *long before* 357, when the former was proscribed. I incline to regard the ὅμοιον (*as a test word*) as a *later* rival to the ὁμοιούσιον.

Pannonians with a letter of thanks. But the blast heralded the collapse of the Arian cause ; the Reaction 'fell to pieces the moment Arianism ventured to have a policy of its own' (Gwatkin, p. 158, the whole account should be consulted). Not only did orthodox Gaul, under Phœbadius of Agen, the most stalwart of the lesser men whom Milan had spared, meet in synod and condemn the blasphemy, but the conservative East was up in arms against Arianism, for the first time with thorough spontaneity. Times were changed indeed ; the East was at war with the West, but on the side of orthodoxy against Arianism.

(c) We must now take account of the party headed by BASIL of ANCYRA and usually (since Epiphanius), but with some injustice, designated as SEMI-ARIANS. Their theological ancestry and antecedents have been already sketched (pp. xxvii., xxxv.); they are the representatives of that conservatism, moulded by the neo-Asiatic, or modified Origenist tradition, which warmly condemned Arianism at Nicæa, but acquiesced with only half a heart in the test by which the Council resolved to exclude it. They furnished the numerical strength, the material basis so to call it, of the anti-Nicene reaction ; but the reaction on their part had not been Arian in principle, but in part anti-Sabellian, in part the empirical conservatism of men whose own principles are vague and ill-assorted, and who fail to follow the keener sight which distinguishes the higher conservatism from the lower. They lent themselves to the purposes of the Eusebians (a name which ought to be dropped after 342) on purely negative grounds and in view of questions of personal rights and accusations. A positive doctrinal formula they did not possess. But in the course of years reflexion did its work. A younger generation grew up who had not been taught to respect Nicæa, nor yet had imbibed Arian principles. Cyril at Jerusalem, Meletius at Antioch, are specimens of a large class. The Dedication Creed at Antioch represents an early stage in the growth of this body of conviction, conviction not absolutely uniform everywhere, as the result shews, but still with a distinct tendency to settle down to a formal position with regard to the great question of the age. There was nothing in the Nicene *doctrine* that men like this did not hold : but the *word* ὁμοούσιον opened the door to the dreaded Sabellian error : was not the history of Marcellus and Photinus a significant comment upon it ? But if οὐσία meant not individuality, but *specific* identity (*supr.*, p. xxxi. *sq.*) even this term might be innocently admitted. But to make that meaning plain, what was more effective than the insertion of an *iota* ? Ὁμοιούσιος, then, was the satisfactory test which would banish Arius and Marcellus alike. Who first used the word for the purpose, we do not know, but its first occurrence is its prohibition in the 'blasphemy' of Valens in 357. The leader of the 'semi-Arians' in 357 was Basil of Ancyra, a man of deep learning and high character. George of Laodicea, an original Arian, was in active but short-lived [16] alliance with the party, other prominent members of it were Eustathius, Bishop of Sebaste (Sivas), Eleusius of Cyzicus, Macedonius of Constantinople, Eusebius of Emesa, Cyril of Jerusalem, and Mark of Arethusa, a high-minded but violent man, who represents the 'left' wing of the party as Cyril and Basil represent the 'right.'

Now the 'trumpet-blast' of Valens gave birth to the 'Semi-Arians' as a formal party. An attempt was made to reunite the reaction on a Homœan basis in 359, but the events of that year made the breach more open than ever. The tendency towards the Nicene position which received its impulse in 357 continued unchecked until the Nicene cause triumphed in Asia in the hands of the 'conservatives' of the next generation.

Immediately after the Acacian Synod at Antioch early in 358, George of Laodicea, who had reasons of his own for indignation against Eudoxius, wrote off in hot haste to warn Basil of the fearful encouragement that was being given to the doctrines of Aetius in that city. Basil, who was in communication (through Hilary) with Phœbadius and his colleagues, had invited twelve neighbouring bishops to the dedication of a church in Ancyra at this time, and took the opportunity of drawing up a synodical letter insisting on the Essential Likeness of the Son to the Father (ὅμοιον κατ' οὐσίαν), and eighteen anathemas directed against Marcellus and the Anomœans. (The censure of ὁμοούσιον ἢ ταὐτοούσιον is against the Marcellian sense of the ὁμοούσιον). Basil, Eustathius, and Eleusius then proceeded to the Court at Sirmium and were successful in gaining the ear of the Emperor, who at this time had a high regard for Basil, and apparently obtained the ratification by a council, at which Valens, &c., were present, of a composite formula of their own (Newman's 'semi-Arian digest of three Confessions') which was also signed by Liberius, who was thereupon sent back to Rome. (Soz. iv. 15 is our only authority here, and his account of the formula is not very clear : he seems to mean that two, not three, confessions were combined. (Cf. p. 449, note 4.) On the whole, it is most probable that the 'fourth' Antiochene formula in its Sirmian recension of 351 is intended, perhaps with the addition of twelve of the Ancyrene anathemas. (The question of the signatures of Liberius need not detain us.) The party of Valens were involved in sudden and unlooked-for discomfiture. Basil even succeeded in obtaining a decree of banishment against Eudoxius, Aetius, and 'seventy' others (Philost. iv. 8). But an Arian deputation from Syria procured their recall, and all parties stood at bay in mutual bitterness.

Now was the opportunity of Valens. He saw the capabilities of the Homœan compromise, as yet embodied in no creed, and resolved to try it : and his experiment was not unsuccessful. All parties alike seem to have agreed

---

[16] Apparently it began with the quarrel over the election to the bishopric of Antioch, which Eudoxius managed to seize after the death of Leontius. George was aggrieved at his rights as an elector being ignored, and may have had hopes of the see for himself. See Soz. iv. 13 ; but Philost. iv. 5 with much less likelihood puts this down to Basil.

upon the necessity for a council of the whole Church (on the origin of the proposal, and for other details, see p. 448). But Valens was determined what the result of the council must be. Accordingly he prevailed on the Emperor to divide it, the Western Synod to meet at Ariminum, the Eastern at 'Rocky Seleucia,' a mountain fortress in Cilicia where there happened to be plenty of troops. The management of the latter was entrusted to Acacius ; at Rimini Valens would be present in person. In event of the two synods differing, a delegation of ten bishops from each was to meet at Court and settle the matter. The Creed to be adopted had also to be arranged beforehand, and for this purpose, to his great discredit, Basil of Ancyra entered into a conference (along with Mark of Arethusa and certain colleagues) with Valens, George of Alexandria, and others of like mind. The result was the 'Dated Creed' (May 22, 359) drawn by Mark, prohibiting the word οὐσία (in a gentler tone than that of the creed of Valens in 357), but containing the definition ὅμοιον κατὰ πάντα ('as also the Scriptures teach,' see above, on Cyril, p. xlix.), words which Valens and Ursacius sought to suppress. But Constantius insisted on their retention, and Basil emphasised his subscription by a strongly-worded addition. Moreover in conjunction with George of Laodicea he drew up a memorandum (Epiph. 72. 12—22) vindicating the term οὐσία as implied in Scripture, insisting on the absolute essential likeness of the Son to the Father, except in respect of the Incarnation, and repudiating the idea that ἀγεννησία is the essential notion of Godhead. Such a protest was highly significant as an approach to the Nicene position, but Basil must have felt its inefficiency for the purpose in hand. Had the creed been anything but a surrender of principle on his part, no explanatory memoranda would have been needed.

After the *fiasco* of the Dated Creed, the issue of the Councils was not doubtful. The details may be reserved for another place (pp. 448, 453 *sqq.*), but the general result is noteworthy. At both Councils the court party were in a minority, and in both alike they eventually had their way. (See Bright, *Hist. Tr.* lxxxiv.—xc., and Gwatkin, 170—180.) On the whole the Seleucian synod came out of the affair more honourably than the other, as their eventual surrender was confined to their delegates. Both Councils began bravely. The majorities deposed their opponents and affirmed their own faith, the Westerns that of Nicæa, the Easterns that of the Dedication. From both Councils deputations from each rival section went to the Emperor, who was now at Constantinople. The deputies from the majority at Ariminum, where the meeting had begun fully two months before the other, were not received, but detained first at Hadrianople, then at Niké in Thrace (chosen, says Socr. ii. 37, to impose on the world by the name), where they were induced to sign a recension of the Dated Creed (the Creed itself had been revoked and recast without the date and perhaps without the κατὰ πάντα before the preliminary meeting at Sirmium broke up, p. 466) of a more distinctly Homœan character. Armed with this document Valens brought them back to the Council, and 'by threats and cajolery' obtained the signatures of nearly all the bishops. Yet the stalwart Phœbadius, Claudius of Picenum, the venerable African Muzonius, father of the Council, and a few others, were undaunted. But Valens, by adroit dissimulation and by guiding into a manageable shape the successive anathematisms by which his orthodoxy was tested, managed to deceive these simple-minded Westerns, and with applause and exultation, 'plausu quodam et tripudio' (Jer.), amidst which 'Valens was lauded to the skies' (!), the bishops were released from their wearisome detention and suspense. But Valens 'cum recessisset tunc gloriabatur' (Prov. xx. 14). The Western bishops realised too late what they had done, 'Ingemuit totus orbis, et se Arianum esse miratus est.' Valens hurried with the creed and the anathemas of Phœbadius to Constantinople, where he found the Seleucian deputies in hot discussion at court. The Eastern bishops at Seleucia had held to the 'Lucianic' creed, and contemptuously set aside not only the Acacian alternative (p. 466), but the whole compromise of Basil and Mark at the Sirmian conference of the preceding May. The 'Conservatives' and Acacians were at open war. But the change of the seat of war to the court gave the latter the advantage, and Valens and Acacius were determined to secure their position at any cost. The first step was to compel the signature of the 'semi-Arian' deputies to the creed of Ariminum. This was facilitated by the renewal on the part of Acacius and Valens of their repudiation, already announced at Seleucia (p. 466), of the Ἀνόμοιον, (of course with the mental reservation that the repudiation referred only to *will*). Even so, tedious discussions [17], and the threats of Constantius, with whom Basil had now lost all his influence (Thdt. ii. 27), were needed to bring about the required compliance late at night on New Year's Eve, 359—360 (Soz. iv. 23). In January, at the dedication of the Great Church of Constantine, the second step was taken. The revised creed of Niké was reissued without the anathemas of Ariminum. Aetius was offered by his friend Eudoxius as a sacrifice to the Emperor's scruples (see the account of the previous debates in Thdt. *ubi supra*), much as Arius had been sacrificed by his fellow-Lucianists at Nicæa (§ 2 *supra:* nine bishops protested, but were allowed six months to reconsider their objection ; the six months lasted two years, and then a reconciliation with Aetius took place for a time, Philost. vii. 6). Next a clean sweep was made of the leading semi-Arians on miscellaneous charges (Soz. iv. 24, *sq.*), and Eudoxius was installed as bishop of the New Rome in the place of Macedonius. The sacrifice of Aetius gave the Homœans a free hand against their opponents, and was compensated by the appointment of numerous Anomœans to vacant sees. In particular Eunomius replaced Eleusius at Cyzicus. In the eastern half of the Empire Homœanism was supreme, and remained so politically for nearly twenty years. But not in the West. Before the Council of Constantinople met, the power of the West had passed away from Constantius. Gaul had acknowledged Julian as Augustus, and from Gaul came the voice of defiance for the Homœan leaders and sympathy for their deposed opponents (Hil. *Frag.* xi.). And even in the East, throughout their twenty years the Homœans retained their hold upon the Church by a dead hand. 'The moral strength of Christendom lay elsewhere ;' on the one hand the followers of Eunomius were breaking loose from Eudoxius and forming a definitely Arian sect, those of Macedonius crystallising their cruder conservatism into the illogical creed of the 'Pneumatomachi;' on the other hand the second generation of the 'semi-Arians' were, under the influence of Athanasius, working their way to the Greek Catholicism of the future, the Catholicism of the neo-Nicene school, of Basil and the two Gregories.

The lack of inner cohesion in the Homœan ranks was exemplified at the start in the election of a new bishop for Antioch. Eudoxius had vacated the see for that of New Rome ; Anianus, the nominee of the Homœusian

---

[17] The discussions, reported with every appearance of substantial accuracy by Thdt. ii. 27, may have taken place at this time, or at the council of the succeeding month (Thdt. fails to distinguish the two meetings). Gwatkin, p. 180, appears to be right in adopting the former alternative, viz. that the party of Basil prudently abstained from attending a council in which they would be overpowered : cf. Soz. iv. 24, who however contradicts himself in the next chapter, *sub fin.* But the case is not quite clear.

majority of Seleucia, was out of the question; accordingly at a Council in 361 the Acacians fixed upon Meletius, who had in the previous year accepted from the Homœans of CP. the See of Sebaste in the room of the exiled Eustathius. The new Bishop was requested by the Emperor to preach on the test passage Prov. viii. 22. This he did to a vast and eagerly expectant congregation. To the delight of the majority (headed by Diodorus and Flavian), although he avoided the ὁμοούσιον, he spoke with no uncertain sound on the essential likeness of the Son to the Father. Formally 'Nicene,' indeed, the sermon was not (text in Epiph. *Hær.* lxxiii. 29–33, see Hort, p. 96, note 1), but the dismay of the Homœan bishops equalled the joy of the Catholic laity. Meletius was 'deposed' in favour of the old Arian Euzoius (*infr.*, p. 70), and after his return under Jovian gave in his formal adhesion to the Nicene test.

(3.) The history of Athanasius during this period is the history of his writings. Hidden from all but devotedly loyal eyes, whether in the cells of Nitria and the Thebaid, or lost in the populous solitude of his own city, he followed with a keen and comprehensive glance the march of events outside. Two men in this age had skill to lay the physician's finger upon the pulse of religious conviction; Hilary, the Western who had learned to understand and sympathise with the East, Athanasius, the Oriental representative of the theological instincts of the West. First of all came the writings of which we have spoken, the circular to the bishops and the Apology to Constantius; then the dignified Apology for his flight, written not long before the expulsion of George late in 358, when he had begun to realise the merciless enmity and profound duplicity of the Emperor. We find him not long after this in correspondence with the exiled confessor, Lucifer of Calaris (pp. 561 *sq.*, 481 *sqq.*), and warning the Egyptian monks against compromising relations with Arian visitors (*Letter* 53, a document of high interest), narrating to the trusted Serapion the facts as to the death of Arius, and sending to the monks a concise refutation of Arian doctrine (*Letters* 52, 54). With the latter is associated a reissue of the Apology of 351, and, as a continuation of it, the solitary monument of a less noble spirit which Athanasius has left us, the one work which we would gladly believe to have come from any other pen[18]. But this supposition is untenable, and in the ferocious pamphlet against Constantius known as the *Arian History* we are reminded that noble as he was, our saint yet lived in an age of fierce passions and reckless personal violence. The *Arian History* has its noble features—no work of Athanasius could lack them—but it reveals not the man himself but his generation; his exasperation, and the meanness of his persecutors. (For details on all these tracts see the Introductions and notes to them.) None of the above books directly relate to the doctrinal developments sketched above. But these developments called forth the three greatest works of his exile, and indeed of his whole career. *Firstly*, the four Λόγοι or *Tracts against Arianism*, his most famous dogmatic work. Of these an account will be given in the proper place, but it may be noticed here that they are evidently written with a conciliatory as well as a controversial purpose, and in view of the position between 357 and 359. *Next*, the four dogmatic letters *to Serapion*, the second of which reproduces the substance of his position against the Arians, while the other three are devoted to a question overlooked in the earlier stages of the controversy, the Coessentiality of the Holy Spirit. This work may possibly have come after the *third*, and in some ways the most striking, of the series, the *de Synodis* written about the end of 359, and intended as a formal offer of peace to the Homœusian party. Following as it did closely upon the conciliatory work of Hilary, who was present at Seleucia on the side of the majority, this magnanimous Eirenicon produced an immediate effect, which we trace in the letters of the younger Basil written in the same or following year; but the full effect and justification of the book is found in the influence exerted by Athanasius upon the new orthodoxy which eventually restored the 'ten provinces' to 'the knowledge of God' (Hil. *de Syn.* 63. Further details in Introd. to *de Syn.*, *infra*, p. 448. It may be remarked that the romantic idea of his secret presence at Seleucia, and even at Ariminum, must be dismissed as a too rigid inference from an expression used by him in that work: see note 1 there).

This brings us to the close of the eventful period of the Third Exile, and of the long series of creeds which registers the variations of Arianism during thirty years. We may congratulate ourselves on 'having come at last to the end of the labyrinth of expositions' (Socr. ii. 41), and within sight of the emergence of conviction out of confusion, of order out of chaos. The work of setting in order opens our next period. Of the exile there is nothing more to tell except its close. Hurrying from Antioch on his way from the Persian frontier to oppose the eastward march of Julian, Constantius caught a fever, was baptised by Euzoius, and died at Mopsucrenæ under Mount Taurus, on Nov. 3, 361. Julian at once avowed the heathenism he had long cherished in secret, and by an edict, published in Alexandria on Feb. 9, recalled from exile all

---

[18] He always used amanuenses, but we have no evidence that he entrusted them with actual composition, p. 242.

bishops banished by Constantius. 'And twelve days after the posting of this edict Athanasius appeared at Alexandria and entered the Church on the twenty-seventh day of the same month, Mechir (Feb. 21). He remained in the Church until the twenty-sixth of Paophi (i.e., Oct. 23) ... eight whole months' (*Hist. Aceph.* vii. The murder of George has been referred to above, p. liii.).

§ 9. *Athanasius under Julian and his successors; Fourth and Fifth Exiles.* Feb. 21, 362, to Feb. 1, 366.

(a) *The Council of Alexandria in* 362. The eight months of undisturbed residence enjoyed by Athanasius under Julian were well employed. One of his first acts was to convoke a Synod at Alexandria to deal with the questions which stood in the way of the peace of the Church. The Synod was one 'of saints and confessors,' including as it did many of the Egyptian bishops who had suffered under George (p. 483, note 3, again we miss the name of the trusted Serapion), Asterius of Petra and Eusebius of Vercellae, with legates from Lucifer of Calaris, Apollinarius of Laodicea, and Paulinus the Presbyter who ruled the Eustathian community of Antioch. Our knowledge of the proceedings of the Synod (with an exception to be referred to later on) is derived entirely from its 'Tome' or Synodal letter addressed to the latter community and to the exiles who were its guests. Rufinus, from whom or from the Tome itself Socrates appears to derive his knowledge, follows the Tome closely, with perhaps a faint trace of knowledge from some other[1] source. Sozomen gives a short and inadequate report (v. 12). But the importance of the Council is out of all proportion either to the number of bishops who took part in it or to the scale of its documentary records. Jerome goes so far as to say that by its judicious conciliation it 'snatched the whole world from the jaws of Satan' (*Adv. Lucif.* 20). If this is in any measure true, if it undid both in East and West the humiliating results of the twin Synods of 359, the honour of the achievement is due to Athanasius alone. He saw that victory was not to be won by smiting men who were ready for peace, that the cause of Christ was not to be furthered by breaking the bruised reed and quenching the smoking flax. (Best accounts of the Council, Newman, *Arians* V. i., Krüger, *Lucif.* 41—52, Gwatkin, p. 205, *sqq.*) The details may be reserved for the Introduction to the Tome, p. 481. But in the strong calm moderation of that document we feel that Athanasius is no longer a combatant arduously contending for victory, but a conqueror surveying the field of his triumph and resolving upon the terms of peace. The Council is the ripe first-fruits of the *de Synodis*, the decisive step by which he placed himself at the head of the reuniting forces of Eastern Christendom; forces which under the recognised headship of the 'Father of Orthodoxy' were able successfully to withstand the revived political supremacy of Arianism under Valens, and after his death to cast it out of the Church. The Council then is justly recognised as the crown of the career of Athanasius, for its resolutions and its Letter unmistakably proceed from him alone, and none but he could have tempered the fiery zeal of the confessors and taught them to distinguish friend from foe.

It would have been well had Lucifer been there in person and not by deputy only. As it was he had gone to Antioch in fiery haste, with a promise extorted by Eusebius to do nothing rashly. Fanatical in his orthodoxy, quite unable to grasp the theological differences between the various parties (his remonstrances with Hilary upon the conciliatory efforts of the latter shew his total lack of theology: see also Krüger, pp. 36, *sq.*), and concentrating all his indignation upon persons rather than principles, Lucifer found Antioch without a bishop; for Euzoius was an Arian, and Meletius, whose return to the church of the Palæa was (so it seems) daily expected, was to Lucifer little better. What to such a man could seem a quicker way to the extinction of the schism than the immediate ordination of a bishop whom all would respect, and whose record was one of the most uncompromising resistance to heresy? Lucifer accordingly, with the aid we may suppose of Kymatius and Anatolius, ordained Paulinus, the widely-esteemed head of the irreconcileable or (to adopt Newman's word) protestant minority, who had never owned any Bishop of Antioch save the deposed and banished Eustathius. The act of Lucifer had momentous consequences (see D.C.B. on MELETIUS and FLAVIAN, &c.); it perpetuated the existing tendency to schism between East and West; and but for the forbearance of Athanasius it would perhaps have wrecked the alliance of Conservative Asia with Nicene orthodoxy which his later years cemented. Even as it was, the relations between Athanasius and Basil were sorely tried by the schism of Antioch. The Tome however was signed by Paulinus[2], who added a short statement of his own faith, which, by recognising the legitimacy of the theological language of the other catholic party at Antioch, implicitly conceded the falseness of his own position.

---

[1] He states (1) That a rigorist party in the council were at first opposed to all conciliatory measures; this is highly probable, see Hieron. *adv. Lucif.* 20; (2) that former active Arians were to be admitted to lay communion only; this is not unlikely; (3) by implication, that Eusebius and Lucifer went first to Antioch, and agreed to take no step till after the Council which Eus. was to attend in person, and Luc. by deputy, at Alxa., but that Luc. broke his promise. This may contain a grain of truth, i.e. that Lucifer promised to do nothing before he heard from Alxa., but Eusebius can scarcely have gone to Antioch. I owe these notices to the excellent analysis of our sources of information in Krüger, *Lucif.* p. 46 *sq.*; but he makes an odd slip, p. 48, in saying that Soz. 'schweigt von der Synode zu Alex. uberhaupt.'

[2] This is placed later in 363 by Dr. Bright, D.C.B. i. 190, on the ground of a statement of Epiphanius, *Hær.* 77. 20, which, however, is not quite decisive on the point.

Eusebius and Asterius of Petra carried the letter to Antioch, where they found the mischief already done. In deep pain at the headstrong action of his fellow-countryman, Eusebius gave practical assurance to both parties of his full sympathy and recognition, and made his way home through Asia and Illyria, doing his best in the cause of concord wherever he came. Lucifer renounced communion with all the parties to what he considered a guilty compromise, and journeyed home to Sardinia, making mischief everywhere (terribly so at Naples, according to the grotesque tale in the *Lib. Prec.* ; see D.C.B. iv. 1221 under Zosimus (2)), and ended his days in the twofold reputation of saint and schismatic (Krüger, pp. 55, 116 *sq.*).

It may be well to add a few words upon the supposed Coptic acts of this council, and upon their connection with the very ancient *Syntagma Doctrinæ*, wrongly so named, and wrongly ascribed to Athanasius. These 'acts' are in reality a series of documents consisting of (1) The Nicene Creed, Canons, and Signatures; (2) A Coptic recension of the *Syntagma Doctrinæ*; (3) the letter of Paulinus from *Tom. Ant.*, sub fin., a letter of Epiphanius, and a fragmentary letter of 'Rufinus,' i. e. Rufinianus (see *infr.* p. 566, note 1). Revillout, who published these texts from a Turin and a Roman (Borgia) manuscript in 1881 (*Le Concile de Nicée d'après les textes Coptes*) jumped (*Archives des missions scientifiques et littéraires*, 1879) at the conclusion that the whole series emanated from the council of 362, from whose labours all our copies of the Nicene canons and signatures are supposed by him to emanate. His theory cannot be discussed at length in this place. It is worked out with ingenuity, but with insufficient knowledge of general Church history. It appears to be adopted wholesale by Eichhorn in his otherwise critical and excellent *Athanasii de vita ascetica testimonia* (see below, p. 189); but even those whose scepticism has not been awaked by the hypothesis itself must I think be satisfied by the careful study of M. Batiffol (*Studia Patristica*, fasc. ii.) that Revillout has erected a castle in the air. Of any 'acts' of the Council of 362 the documents contain no trace at all. It is therefore out of place to do more than allude here to the great interest of the *Syntagma* in its three or four extant recensions in connection at once with the history of Egyptian Monasticism and with the literature of the Διδαχὴ τῶν ιβ´ ἀποστόλων (see Harnack in *Theol. Litzg.* 1887, pp. 32, *sqq.*, Eichhorn, *ib.* p. 569, Warfield in *Andover Review*, 1886, p. 81, *sqq.*, and other American literature referred to by Harnack a.a.O).

All over the Empire the exiles were returning, and councils were held (p. 489), repudiating the Homœan formula of union, and affirming that of Nicæa. In dealing with the question of those who had formerly compromised themselves with Arianism, these councils followed the lead of that of Alexandria, which accordingly is justly said by Jerome (*adv. Lucif.* 20) to have snatched the world from the jaws of Satan, by obviating countless schisms and attaching to the Church many who might otherwise have been driven back into Arianism.

Such were the more enduring results of the recall of the exiled bishops by Julian; results very different from what he contemplated in recalling them. Apparently before the date of the council he had written to the Alexandrians (*Ep.* 26), explaining that he had recalled the exiles to their countries, not to their sees, and directing that Athanasius, who ought after so many sentences against him to have asked special permission to return, should leave the City at once on pain of severer punishment. An appeal seems to have been made against this order by the people of Alexandria, but without effect. Pending the appeal Athanasius apparently felt safe in remaining in the town, and carrying out the measures described above. In October (it would seem) Julian wrote an indignant letter to the Prefect Ecdikius Olympus (Sievers, p. 124), threatening a heavy fine if Athanasius, 'the enemy of the gods,' did not leave not only Alexandria, but Egypt, at once. He adds an angry comment on his having dared to baptize 'in my reign' Greek ladies of rank (*Ep.* 6). Another letter (*Ep.* 51) to the people of Alexandria, along with arguments in favour of Serapis and the gods, and against Christ, reiterates the order for Athanasius to leave Egypt by Dec. 1. Julian's somewhat petulant reference to the bishop as a 'contemptible little fellow' ill conceals his evident feeling that Athanasius, who had 'coped with Constantius like a king battling with a king' (Greg. Naz.), was in Egypt a power greater than himself. But no man has ever wielded such political power as Athanasius with so little disposition to use it. He bowed his head to the storm and prepared to leave Alexandria once more (Oct. 23). His friends stood round lamenting their loss. 'Be of good heart,' he replied, 'it is only a cloud, and will soon pass away' (Soz. v. 14). He took a Nile boat, and set off toward Upper Egypt, but finding that he was tracked by the government officers he directed the boat's course to be reversed. Presently they met that of the pursuers, who suspecting nothing asked for news of Athanasius. 'He is not far off' was the answer, given according to one account by Athanasius himself (Thdt. iii. 9, Socr. iii. 14). He returned to Chæreu, the first station on the road eastward from Alexandria (as is inferred from the Thereu or Thereon of *Hist. Aceph.* vii., viii.; but the identification is merely conjectural; for Chæreu cf. *Itin.* and *Vit. Ant.* 86), and after danger of pursuit was over, 'ascended to the upper parts of Egypt as far as Upper Hermupolis in the Thebaid and as far as Antinoupolis; and while he abode in these places it was learned that Julian the Emperor was dead, and that Jovian, a Christian, was Emperor' (*Hist. Aceph.*). Of his stay in the Thebaid (cf. *Fest. Ind.* xxxv.) some picturesque details are preserved in the life of Pachomius and the letter of Ammon (on which see below, p. 487). As he approached Hermupolis, the bishops, clergy, and monks ('about 100 in number') of the Thebaid lined both banks of the river to welcome him. 'Who are these,' he exclaimed, 'that fly as a cloud and as doves with their young ones' (Isa. lx. 8, LXX). Then he saluted the Abbat Theodore, and asked after the brethren. ' By thy holy prayers, Father, we are well.' He was mounted on an ass and escorted to the monastery with burning torches (they ' almost set fire to him '), the abbat walking before him on foot. He inspected the monasteries, and expressed his high approval of all he heard and saw, and when Theodore, upon departing for his Easter (363) visitation [3] of the brethren, asked ' the Pope' to remember him in his prayers, the answer was characteristic : ' If we forget thee, O Jerusalem ' (*Vit. Pachom.* 92, see p. 569). About midsummer he was near Antinoupolis, and trusted messengers warned him that the pursuers were again upon his track. Theodore brought his covered boat to escort him up to Tabenne, and in company with an ' abbat' called Pammon they made their way slowly against wind and stream. Athanasius became much alarmed and prayed earnestly to himself, while Theodore's monks towed the boat from the shore. Athanasius, in reply to an encouraging remark of Pammon, spoke of the peace of mind he felt when under persecution, and of the consolation of suffering and even death for Christ's sake. Pammon looked at Theodore, and they smiled, barely restraining a laugh. 'You think me a coward,' said Athanasius. 'Tell him,' said Theodore to Pammon. ' No, *you* must tell him.' Theodore then announced to the astonished archbishop that at that very hour Julian had been killed in Persia, and that he should lose no time in making his way to the new Christian Emperor, who would restore him to the Church. The story (below, p. 487) implies rather than expressly states that the day and hour tallied exactly with the death of Julian, June 26, 363. This story is, on the whole, the best attested of the many legends of the kind which surround the mysterious end of the unfortunate prince. (Cf. Thdt. *H. E.* iii. 23, Soz. vi. 2. For the religious policy of Julian and his relation to Church history, see Rendall's *Julian* and the full and excellent article by Wordsworth in *D.C.B.* iii. 484—525.)

Athanasius entered Alexandria secretly and made his way by way of Hierapolis (Sept. 6, *Fest. Ind.*) to Jovian at Edessa, and returned with him (apparently) to Antioch. On Feb. 14 (or 20, *Fest. Index*) he returned to Alexandria with imperial letters and took possession of the churches, his fourth exile having lasted ' fifteen months and twenty-two days ' (*Hist. Aceph.*). The visit to Antioch was important.

Firstly, it is clear from the combined and circumstantial testimony of the *Festal Index*, the *Hist. Aceph.*, and the narrative of Ammon, that Athanasius hurried to meet Jovian on his march from Persia to Antioch, and visited Alexandria only in passing and in private. He appears to have taken the precaution (see below) of taking certain bishops and others, representing the majority (πλῆθος) of the Egyptian Church, along with him. Accordingly the tale of Theodoret (iv. 2), that he assembled a council (τοὺς λογιμωτέρους τῶν ἐπισκόπων ἐγείρας), and wrote a synodal letter to Jovian, in reply to a request from the latter to furnish him with an accurate statement of doctrine (followed by Montf., Hefele, &c.) must be set aside as a hasty conjecture from the heading of the *Letter to Jovian* (see below, ch. v. § 3 (h), and cf. Vales. on Thdt. iv. 3, who suspected the truth).

Athanasius, secondly, had good reason for hurrying. The Arians had also sent a large deputation to petition against the restoration of Athanasius, and to ask for a bishop. Lucius, their candidate for the post, accompanied the deputation. But the energy of Athanasius was a match for their schemes. He obtained a short but emphatic letter from Jovian, bidding him return to his see, and placed in the Emperor's hands a letter (below, *Letter* 56, p. 567), insisting on the integrity of the Nicene creed, which it recites, and especially on the Godhead of the Holy Spirit.

Meanwhile at Antioch, where the winter was spent (Jovian was mostly there till Dec. 21), there was much to be attended to. Least important of all were the efforts of the Arian deputation to secure a hearing for their demands. Jovian's replies to them on the repeated occasions on which they waylaid him are perhaps undignified (Gwatkin) but yet shew a rough soldier-like common sense. ' Any one you please except Athanasius' they urged. ' I told you, the case of Athanasius is settled already : ' then, to the body-guard ' Feri, feri ' (i.e. use your sticks !) Some of the πλῆθος of Antioch seized Lucius and brought him to Jovian, saying, ' Look, your Majesty, at the man they wanted to make a bishop ! ' (See p. 568 *sq.*)

Athanasius appears to have attempted to bring about some settlement of the disputes which distracted the Church of Antioch. The *Hist. Aceph.* makes him ' arrange the affairs ' of that Church, but Sozom. (vi. 5), who copies the phrase, significantly adds ὡς οἷόν τε ἦν—' as far as it was feasible.' The vacillations (Philost. viii. 2, 7, ix. 3, &c.) of Euzoius between Eudoxius on the one hand, and the consistent Anomœans on the other, and the formation of a definite Anomœan sect, represented in Egypt by Heliodorus, Stephen, and other nominees of the bitter Arian Secundus (who appears to be dead at last) probably concerned Athanasius but little. But the breach

---

3 Krüger, in *Theol. Litzg.* 1890, p. 620 *sqq.*, fixes the death of Theodore for Easter 363, on the ground, as I venture to think, of a date (345) for the death of Pachomius too early by one year. | The question is too intricate to discuss here, but with all deference to so competent a critic, I am confident that Theodore lived till at any rate the following Easter. See *infr.* p. 569, note 3.

among the Antiochene Catholics was more hopeless than ever. The action of Paulinus in ordaining a bishop for Tyre, Diodorus by name (p. 580 note), shews that he had caught something of the spirit of Lucifer, while on the other hand we can well imagine that it was with mixed feelings that Athanasius saw a number of bishops assemble under Meletius to sign the Nicene Creed. To begin with, they explained the ὁμοούσιον to be equivalent to ἐκ τῆς οὐσίας and ὅμοιον κατ᾽ οὐσίαν. Now this was no more than taking Athanasius literally at his word (de Syn. 41 exactly; the confession, Socr. iii. 25, appears to meet Ath. de Syn.: cf. the reference to Ἑλληνικὴ χρῆσις with de Syn. 51), and there is no reason to doubt that the majority[4] of those who signed did so in all sincerity, merely guarding the ὁμοούσιον against its Sabellian sense (which Hilary de Syn. 71, had admitted as possible), and in fact, meaning by the term exactly what Basil the Great and his school meant by it. This is confirmed by the express denunciation of Arianism and Anomœanism. But Athanasius may have suspected an intention on the part of some signatories to evade the full sense of the creed, especially as touching the Holy Spirit, and this suspicion would not be lessened by the fact that Acacius signed with the rest. It must remain possible, therefore, that a clause in the letter to Jovian referred to above, expresses his displeasure[5] at the wording of the document. (On the significance of the confession in question, see Gwatkin, pp. 226 sq., 244, note 1.) We gather from language used by St. Basil at a later date (Bas. Epp. 89, 258) that Athanasius endeavoured to conciliate Meletius, and to bring about some understanding between the two parties in the Church. Meletius appears to have considered such efforts premature: Basil writes to him that he understands that Athanasius is much disappointed that no renewal of friendly overtures has taken place, and that if Meletius desires the good offices of the Bishop of Alexandria the first word must come from him (probably seven or eight years later than this date). In justice to Meletius it must be allowed that Paulinus did his best to embitter the schism by ordaining bishops at Tyre and elsewhere, ordinations which Meletius naturally resented, and appears to have ignored (D.C.B. iv. ZENO (3),—where observe that the breach of canons began with the appointment of Paulinus himself). Athanasius returned to Alexandria on Feb. 14 (Hist. Aceph.) or 20 (Fest. Ind.), and Jovian died, by inhaling the fumes of a charcoal fire in the bedroom of a wayside inn, on Feb. 17.

Valentinian, an officer of Pannonian birth, was elected Emperor by the army, and shorty co-opted his brother Valens to a share in the Empire. Valens was allotted the Eastern, Valentinian choosing the Western half of the Empire. Valentinian was a convinced but tolerant Catholic, and under his reign Arianism practically died away in the Latin West (infra, p. 488). Valens, a weak, parsimonious, but respectable and well-intentioned ruler, at first took no decided line, but eventually (from the end of 364) fell more and more into the hands of Eudoxius (from whom he received baptism in 367) and the Arian hangers-on of the Court (a suggestive, if in some details disputable, sketch of the general condition of the Eastern Church under Valens in Gwatkin, pp. 228—236, 247 sq.). The semi-Arians of Asia were continuing their advance toward the Nicene position, but the question of the Holy Spirit was already beginning to cleave them into two sections. At their council of Lampsacus (autumn of 364) they reasserted their formula of 'essential likeness' against the Homœans, but appear to have left the other and more difficult question undecided. After Valens had declared strongly on the side of the enemy, they were driven to seek Western aid. They set out to seek Valentinian at Milan, but finding him departed on his Gallic campaign (Gwatkin, 236, note) they contented themselves with laying before Liberius, on behalf of the Synod of Lampsacus and other Asiatic Councils, a letter accepting the Nicene Creed. After some hesitation (Soc. iv. 12) they were cordially received by Liberius, who gave them a letter to take home with them, in which the controverted question of the Holy Spirit is passed over in silence. (Letter of the Asiatics in Socr. iv. 12, that of Liberius in Hard. Conc. i. 743-5, the names include Cyril of Jerusalem, Macedonius, Silvanus of Tarsus, Athanasius of Ancyra, &c., and the Pope's letter is addressed to them 'et universis orientalibus orthodoxis'). On their return, the disunion of the party manifested itself by the refusal of several bishops to attend the synod convoked to receive the deputies at Tyana, and by their assembling a rival meeting in Caria to reaffirm the 'Lucianic' Creed (Hefele. ii. 287 E. Tr.). Further efforts at reunion were frustrated by the Imperial prohibition of an intended Synod at Tarsus, possibly in 367.

Athanasius remained in peace in his see until the spring of 365, when on May 5 a rescript was published at Alexandria, ordering that all bishops expelled under Constantius who had returned to their sees under Julian should be at once expelled by the civil authorities under pain of a heavy fine. The announcement was received with great popular displeasure. The officials were anxious to escape the fine, but the Church-people argued that the order could not apply to Athanasius, who had been restored by Constantius, expelled by Julian in the interest of idolatry, and restored by order of Jovian. Their remonstrances were backed up by popular riots: when these had lasted a month, the Prefect quieted the people by the assurance that the matter was referred back to Augustus (Hist. Aceph. x., followed by Soz. vi. 12). But on Oct. 5 an imperative answer seems to have come. The Prefect and the Commandant broke into the Church of Dionysius at night and searched the apartments of the clergy to seize the bishop. But Athanasius, warned in time, had escaped from the town that very night and retired to a country house which belonged to him near the 'New River'[7]. This was the shortest and mildest of the five exiles of Athanasius. In the autumn the dangerous revolt of Procopius threw the Eastern Empire into a panic. It was no time to allow popular discontent to smoulder at Alexandria, and on Feb. 1, 366, the notary Brasidas publicly announced the recall of

---

[4] This is certainly true of men like Athanasius of Ancyra, Eusebius of Samosata, Pelagius of Laodicea, Titus of Bostra, &c.

[5] The tract de Hypocrisi Meletii et Eusebii printed among the 'dubious' works of Athanasius may well express the sentiments of some of his friends of the party of Paulinus on this occasion. (Tillem. viii. 708.)

[6] Tillem. vi. 789, follows Socrates (a bad leader in chronology)

in putting it in 365. But Mr. Gwatkin, p. 267, has carefully sifted the evidence with the above result.

[7] So Hist. Aceph., Fest. Ind. Socrates iv. 13 says he hid four months 'in his Father's tomb.' Soz. vi. 12, mentions the story, but finding it contradicted by the Hist. Aceph., adopts the vague compromise εἴς τι χωρίον ἐκρύπτετο. The 'New River' divided Alexandria from its Western suburbs.

Athanasius to Imperial order. The notary and 'curiales' went out to the suburb in person and escorted Athanasius in state to the Church of Dionysius.

§ 10. *Last Years*, Feb. 1, 366—May 2, 373.

Athanasius now entered upon the last septennium of his life, a well-earned Sabbath of honoured peace and influence for good. Little occurred to disturb his peace at home, and if the confusion and distress of the Eastern Church under Valens could not but cause him anxiety, in Egypt at any rate, so long as he lived, the Catholic Faith was secure from molestation.

In 367 Lucius, who had been ordained Bishop of Alexandria by the Arian party at Antioch, made an attempt to enter the city. He arrived by night on Sept. 24, but on the following day the public got wind of his presence in Alexandria, and a dangerous riot was imminent. A strong military force rescued him from the enraged mob, and on Sept. 26 he was escorted out of Egypt. In the previous year a heathen riot had taken place and the great Church in the Cæsareum had been burned. But in May, 368, the building was recommenced (the incendiaries having been punished) under an Imperial order.

On Sept. 22, 368, Athanasius began to build a Church in the quarter 'Mendidium' (perhaps in commemoration of his completion of the 40th year of his Episcopate, see *Hist. Aceph.* xii.), which was dedicated Aug. 7, 370, and called after his own name.

In 368 or the following year we place the Synod at which Athanasius drew up his letter to the bishops of Africa giving an account of the proceedings at Nicæa, and mentioning his dissatisfaction at the continued immunity enjoyed by Auxentius at Milan (see p. 488).

Our knowledge of the last years of the life of Athanasius is derived partly from his own letters (59—64), partly from the scanty data of his latest works, partly from the letters of Synesius and Basil. From Synesius (*Ep.* 77) we hear of the case of Siderius, a young officer from the army who was present in Libya on civil duty. The Bishop of Erythrum, Orion by name, was in his dotage, and the inhabitants of two large villages in the diocese, impatient of the lack of supervision, clamoured for a bishop of their own, and for the appointment of Siderius. Siderius was accordingly consecrated by a certain Bishop Philo alone, without the canonical two assistants, and without the cognisance of Athanasius. But in view of the immense utility of the appointment Athanasius overlooked its irregularity, and even promoted Siderius to the Metropolitan see of Ptolemais, merging the two villages upon Orion's death once more into their proper diocese. (Fuller details D.C.B. iv. 777, *sq.*) But if Athanasius was no slave to ecclesiastical discipline when the good of the church was in question, he enforced it unsparingly in the interest of morality. An immoral governor of Libya was sternly excommunicated and the fact announced far and wide. We have the reply of BASIL the Great, who in 370 had become Bishop of Cæsarea in Cappadocia, to this notification, and from this time frequent letters passed between the champions of the Old and of the New Nicene orthodoxy. Unhappily we have none of the letters of Athanasius: those of Basil shew us that the loss is one to be deplored. The correspondence bore partly on the continuance of the unhappy schism at Antioch. Basil asks for the mediation of Athanasius; if he could not bring himself to write a letter to the bishops in communion with Meletius, he might at least use his influence with Paulinus and prevail upon him to withdraw. He also presses Meletius to take the initiative in conciliation: possibly he did so, at least one of Basil's letters is sent by the hand of one of Meletius' deacons (Bas. *Epp.* 60, 66, 69, 80, 82, 89). But 'nothing came of the application:' Meletius probably felt injured at the strong support Athanasius had given to Paulinus, even in so questionable an affair as that of Diodorus of Tyre (*supra*, § 9, and cf. *Letter* 64); while Athanasius was too deeply committed to surrender Paulinus, who again was the last man to yield of his own accord (Thdt. *H.E.* v. 23).

Basil obtained the good offices of Athanasius in his attempt to induce the bishops of Rome and the West to give him some support in his efforts against heresy in the East; but the failure here was due to the selfishness and arrogance of the Westerns. (*Epp.* 61, 67).

Basil was also troubled with the continued refusal of Athanasius and the Westerns to repudiate Marcellus, who was still living in extreme old age, and to whom the mass of the people at Ancyra were attached (Bas. Ep. 266, *Legat. Eugen.* 1, ἀναρίθμητον πλῆθος). This state of things, he urged, kept alive the prejudice of many against the Nicene decrees (*Ep.* 69). But the Marcellians, perhaps aware of the efforts of Basil, sent a deputation, headed by the deacon Eugenius, and fortified by letters from 'the bishops' of Macedonia and Achaia, to Alexandria. A synod was apparently in readiness to receive them, and upon demand they produced a statement of their faith, emphatically adopting the Nicene creed, condemning Sabellius, but affirming an ἐν ὑποστάσει τριάδα. The distinction between Λόγος and the Son is rejected, and the idea that the Monad existed before the Son anathematised. Photinus is classed as a heretic with Paul of Samosata. Only the eternal duration of Christ's kingdom is not mentioned. (It may be noted that while this letter gives up many points of the theology of Marcellus, the process is quite completed in a letter submitted by the Marcellian community in 375 to some exiled Egyptian bishops at Diocæsarea [8]; Epiph. *Haer.* 72, 11). Athanasius accepted the confession, and the assembled bishops subscribed their names (only a few

---

[8] For the best treatment of the document, see Zahn, p. 95. | 812; least of all the writer's suggestion that Athanasius was I am quite unable to follow the theory advanced in D. C. B. iii. | 'egregiously duped' (!) by Marcellus.

signatures are preserved). While we understand Basil's regret at the refusal of Athanasius to condemn Marcellus, we can scarcely share it. If Athanasius shewed partiality toward his old ally, it was an error of generosity, or rather let us say a recognition of the truth, too often forgotten in religious controversy, that mistakes are not necessarily heresies, and that a man may go very far wrong in his opinions and yet be entitled to sympathy and respect.

Basil speaks of Athanasius in terms of unbounded veneration and praise, and Athanasius in turn rebukes those who attempted to disparage Basil's orthodoxy, calling him a bishop such as any church might desire to call its own (p. 579 *sq.*).

During the last decade of his life the attention of Athanasius was drawn to the questions raised by the Arian controversy as to the human nature of our Lord. The Arian doctrine on this subject was apparently as old as Lucian, but the whole subject received little or no attention in the earlier stages of the controversy, and it was only with the rise of the Anomœan school that the questions came into formal discussion. In the later letters of Athanasius we see the traces of wide-spread controversy on the matter (especially in that to Epictetus, No. 59), and Apollinarius, bishop of the Syrian Laodicea, and a former close friend of Athanasius, whose legates in 362 had joined in condemning the Arian Christology, broached a peculiar theory on the subject, viz., that while Christ took a human *soul* along with His Body, the Word took the place of the human *spirit*, πνεῦμα (1 Thess. v. 23). The details of the system do not belong to our subject (an excellent sketch in Gwatkin's *Arian Controversy*, pp. 136—141) ; in fact it was two years after the death of Athanasius when Apollinarius definitely founded a sect by consecrating a schismatic bishop for the already distracted Church of Antioch. But Athanasius marked with alarm the tendency of his friend, and in the very last years of his life wrote a tract against his tenet in two short books, in which, as in writing against Marcellus and Photinus 15 years before, he refrains from mentioning Apollinarius by name. It may be observed that at the close of the second book he brings himself for the first time to censure by name ' him they call Photinus,' classing him along with Paul of Samosata.

Athanasius was active to the last ; spiritually (we are not able to say physically) ' his eye was not dim, nor his natural force abated.' In his seventy-fifth year he entered (Ruf. ii. 3) upon the forty-sixth year of his episcopate. Feeling that his end was near, he followed the example of his revered predecessor Alexander, and named Peter as the man whom he judged fittest to succeed him ; then ' on the seventh of Pachon [6] (May 2, 373) he departed this life in a wonderful manner.'

CHAPTER III.
Writings and Personal Characteristics of S. Athanasius.

§ 1. It will be attempted to give a complete list of his writings in chronological order ; those included in this volume will be marked with an asterisk and enumerated in this place without remark. The figures prefixed indicate the probable date.

(1) 318 : * Two books ' contra Gentes,' viz. c. Gent. and de Incarn. (2) 321–2 : * Depositio Arii (on its authorship, see Introd.) (3) 328–373 : * Festal Letters. (4) 328–335 ? * Ecthesis or Expositio Fidei. (5) Id. ? * In illud Omnia, etc. (6) 339 : * Encyclica ad Episcopos ecclesiæ catholicæ. (7) 343 : * Sardican Letters (46, 47, in this vol.). (8) 351 ? * Apologia contra Arianos. (9) 352 ? * De Decretis Concilii Nicæni, with the * Epistola Eusebii (a.d. 325) as appendix. (10) Id. ? * De Sententia Dionysii. (11) 350–353 ? * Ad Amun, (Letter 48). (12) 354 : * Ad Dracontium (Letter 49 in this vol.). (13) 356–362 ? * Vita Antonii. (14) 356 : * Epistola ad Episc. Ægypti et Libyæ. (15) 356–7 : * Apol. ad Constantium. (16) 357 : * Apol. de Fuga. (17) 358 : * Epist. ad Serapionem de Morte Arii (Letter 54). (18) Id. * Two Letters to Monks (52, 53). (19) 358 ? * Historia Arianorum ' ad monachos.' (20) Id. * Orationes adversus Arianos IV. (21) 359 ? * Ad Luciferum (Letters 50, 51). (22) Id. ? Ad Serapionem Orationes IV. (Migne xxvi. 529, *sqq*.). These λόγοι or dogmatic letters are the most important work omitted in the present volume. Serapion of Thmuis, who appears from the silence respecting him in the lists of exiles to have escaped banishment in 356–7, reported to Athanasius the growth of the doctrine that, while the Son was co-essential with the Father, the Spirit was merely a creature superior to Angels. Athanasius replied in a long dogmatic letter, upon receiving which Serapion was begged to induce the author to abridge it for the benefit of the simple. After some hesitation Athanasius sent two more letters, the second drawing out the proofs of the Godhead of the Son, the third restating more concisely the argument of the first. The objections by which these letters were met were replied to in a fourth letter which Athanasius declared to be his last word. The persons combated are not the Macedonians, who only formed a party on this question at a later date, and whose position was not quite that combated in these letters. Athanasius calls them Τροπικοί, or ' Figurists,' from the sense in which they understood passages of Scripture which seemed to deify the Holy Spirit. It is not within our compass to summarise the treatises, but it may be noted that Ath. argues that where πνεῦμα is absolute or anarthrous in Scripture it never refers to the Holy Spirit unless the context already supplies such reference (i. 4, *sqq*.). He meets the objection that the Spirit, if God and of God, must needs be a Son, by falling back upon the language of Scripture as our guide where human analogies fail us. He also presses his opponents with the consequence that they substitute a Dyad for a Trinity.

---

6 *Fest. Ind.* xlv. The *Hist. Aceph.* give May 3 ; probably he died after midnight: but May 2 is kept as his feast by the Copts and by the Western Church.

In the fourth letter, at the request of Serapion, he gives an explanation of the words of Christ about SIN AGAINST THE SPIRIT. Rejecting the view (Origen, Theognostus) that post-baptismal sin is meant (§§ 9, sqq.), as favouring Novatianist rigour, he examines the circumstances under which our Lord uttered the warning. The Pharisees refused to regard the Lord as divine when they saw His miracles, but ascribed them to Beelzebub. They blasphemed 'the Spirit,' i.e. the Divine Personality of Christ (§ 19, cf. Lam. iv. 20, LXX.). So far as the words relate to the Holy Spirit, it is not because the Spirit worked through Him (as through a prophet) but because He worked through the Spirit (20). Blasphemy against the Spirit, then, is blasphemy against Christ in its worst form (see also below, ch. iv., § 6). It may be noted lastly that he refers to Origen in the same terms of somewhat measured praise (ὁ πολυμαθὴς καὶ φιλόπονος), as in the De Decretis.

(23) 359-60. *DE SYNODIS Arimini et Seleuciæ celebratis. (24) 362: *TOMUS AD ANTIOCHENOS. (25) Id. SYNTAGMA DOCTRINÆ (?) see chapter ii. § 9, above. (26) 362: *Letter to RUFINIANUS (Letter 55). (27) 363-4: *Letter to JOVIAN (Letter 56). (28) 364? *Two small Letters to ORSISIUS (57, 58). (29) 369? *Synodal Letter AD AFROS. (30) Id.? *Letter to EPICTETUS (59). (31) Id.? *Letters to ADELPHIUS and MAXIMUS (60, 61). (32) 363—372? *Letter to DIODORUS OF TYRE (fragment, Letter 64). (33) 372: *Letters to JOHN AND ANTIOCHUS and to PALLADIUS (62, 63). (34) 372? Two books against Apollinarianism (Migne xxvi. 1093, sqq. Translated with notes, &c., in Bright, Later Treatises of St. Athan.). The two books are also known under separate titles: Book I. as 'DE INCARNATIONE D.N.J.C. CONTRA APOLLINARIUM,' Book II. as 'DE SALUTARI ADVENTU D.N.J.C.' The Athanasian authorship has been doubted, chiefly on the ground of certain peculiar expressions in the opening of Book I.; a searching investigation of the question has not yet been made, but on the whole the favourable verdict of Montfaucon holds the field. He lays stress on the affinity of the work to letters 59—61. I would add that the studious omission of any personal reference to Apollinarius is highly characteristic.) In the first book Athanasius insists on the reality of the human nature of Christ in the Gospels, and that it cannot be co-essential with the Godhead. 'We do not worship a creature?' No; for we worship not the Flesh of Christ as such but the Person who wears it, viz. the Son of God. Lastly, he urges that the reality of redemption is destroyed if the Incarnation does not extend to the spirit of man, the seat of that sin which Christ came to atone for (§ 19), and seeks to fasten upon his opponents a renewal (§§ 20, 21) of the system of Paul of Samosata.

The second book is addressed to the question of the compatibility of the entire manhood with the entire sinlessness of Christ. This difficulty he meets by insisting that the Word took in our nature all that God had made, and nothing that is the work of the devil. This excludes sin, and includes the totality of our nature. This closes the list of the *dated* works which can be ascribed with fair probability to Athanasius.

The remainder of the writings of Athanasius may be enumerated under groups, to which the 'dated' works will also be assigned by their numbers as given above. Works falling into more than one class are given under each.

 a. LETTERS. (Numbers 3, 7, 11, 12, 17, 18, 21, 26—28, 30—33; spurious letters, see infr. p. 581.)
 b. DOGMATIC. (2, 4, 5, 9, 10, 14, 20, 22—24, 26, 27, 29—31, 34.)

 (35.) De Trinitate et Spiritu Sancto (Migne xxvi. 1191). Preserved in Latin only, but evidently from the Greek. Pronounced genuine by Montfaucon, and dated (?) 365.

 (36) De Incarnatione et Contra Arianos (ib. 984). The Athanasian authorship of this short tract is very questionable. It is quoted as genuine by Theodoret Dial. ii. and by Gelasius de duabus naturis. In some councils it is referred to as 'On the Trinity against Apollinarius;' by Facundus as 'On the Trinity.' The tract is in no sense directed against Apollinarius. In reality it is an argument, mainly from Scripture, for the divinity of Christ, with a digression (13—19) on that of the Holy Spirit. On the whole the evidence is against the favourable verdict of Montfaucon, Ceillier, &c. That Athanasius should, at any date possible for this tract, have referred to the Trinity as 'the three Hypostases' is out of the question (§ 10): his explanation of Prov. viii. 22 in Orat. ii. 44 sqq. is in sharp contrast with its reference to the Church in § 6; at a time when the ideas of Apollinarius were in the air and were combated by Athanasius (since 362) he would not have used language savouring of that system (§§ 2, 3, 5, 7, &c.). It has been thought that we have here one of the Apollinarian tracts which were so industriously and successfully circulated under celebrated names (infra, on No. 40): the express insistence on two wills in Christ (§ 21), if not in favour of Athanasian might seem decisive against Apollinarian authorship, but the peculiar turn of the passage, which correlates the one will with σάρξ the other with πνεῦμα and θεός, is not incompatible with the latter, which is, moreover, supported by the constant insistence on God having come, ἐν σαρκὶ and ἐν ὁμοιώματι ἀνθρώπου. The ἄνθρωπος τέλειος of § 8 and the ὡμοιώθη κατὰ πάντα of § 11 lose their edge in the context of those passages. The first part of § 7 could scarcely have been written by an earnest opponent of Apollinarianism. This evidence is not conclusive, but it is worth considering, and, at any rate, leaves it very difficult to meet the strong negative case against the genuineness of the Tract. (Best discussion of the latter in Bright, Later Treatises of St. A., p. 143; he is supported by Card. Newman in a private letter.)

 (37) The Sermo Maior de Fide. (Migne xxvi. 1263 sqq., with an additional fragment p. 1292 from Mai Bibl. nov.). This is a puzzling document in many ways. It has points of contact with the earliest works of Ath. (especially pieces nearly verbatim from the de Incarn., see notes there), also with the Expos. Fid. Card. Newman calls it with some truth, 'Hardly more than a set of small fragments from Ath.'s other works.' However this may be, it is quoted by Theodoret as Athanasian more than once. The peculiarity lies in the constant iteration of Ἄνθρωπος for the Lord's human nature (see note on Exp. Fid.), and in some places as though it were merely the equivalent to σῶμα or σάρξ, while in others the Ἄνθρωπος might be taken as the seat of Personality (26, 32). Accordingly the tract might be taken advantage of either by Nestorians, or still more by Apollinarians. The 'syllogistic method,' praised in the work by Montfaucon, was not unknown to the last-mentioned school. (Prov. viii. 22 is explained in the Athanasian way. For a fuller discussion, result unfavourable, see Bright, ubi supr. p. 145.)

 (38) FRAGMENTS against Paul of Samosata, Macedonians, Novatians (Migne xxvi. 1293, 1313—1317). The first of these may well be genuine. It repeats the (mistaken) statement of Hist. Ar. 71, that Zenobia was a Jewess. Of the second, all that can be said is that it attacks the Macedonians in language borrowed

from *Ep. Æg.* II. The third, consisting of a somewhat larger group of five fragments, comprise a short sentence comparing the instrumentality of the priest in absolving to his instrumentality in baptizing. It may be observed that fragments of this brevity rarely furnish a decisive criterion of genuineness.

(39) *Interpretatio Symboli* (ib. 1232, Hahn, § 66). Discussed fully by Caspari, *Ungedruckte u.s.w. Quellen* i. pp. 1—72, and proved to be an adaptation of a baptismal creed drawn up by Epiphanius (*Ancor. ad fin.*) in 374. It may be Alexandrian, and, if so, by Bishop Peter or Theophilus about 380. It is a Ἑρμηνεία, or rather an expansion, of the Nicene, not as Montf. says, of the Apostles' (!), Creed.

(40) *De Incarnatione Verbi Dei* (Migne xxviii. 25—29). Quoted as Athanasian by Cyril of Alex., &c., and famous as containing the phrase Μίαν φύσιν τοῦ Λόγου σεσαρκωμένην. Apollinarian; one of the many forgeries from this school circulated under the names of Athanasius, Gregory Thaumaturgus, Julius, &c. See Caspari, *ubi supra* 151, Loofs, *Leontius*, p. 82, *sqq.* Caspari's proof is full and conclusive. See also Hahn, § 120.

(41) Verona Creed (Hahn, § 41, *q.v.*), a Latin fragment of a Western creed; nothing Athanasian but the MS. title.

(42) 'Damasine' Creed (Opp. ed. Ben. ii. 626, Migne P.L. lxii. 237 in *Vig. Thaps.*) forms the 'eighth' of the *Libri de Trinitate* ascribed now to Athan. now to Damasus, &c., &c. : see Hahn, § 128 and note.

(43) '*de Incarnatione*' (Migne xxviii. 89), Anti-Nestorian: fifth century.

c. HISTORICAL, or historico-polemical (6, 8—10, 13—19, 23).

(44) FRAGMENT concerning Stephen and the Envoys at Antioch (Migne xxvi. 1293). Closely related (relative priority not clear) to the account in Thdt. *H.E.*, ii. 9.

d. APOLOGETIC. To this class belong only the works under No. (1).

e. EXEGETICAL (5). The other exegetical works attributed to Athan. are mainly in Migne, vol. xxvii.

(45) AD MARCELLINUM de Interpretatione Psalmorum. Certainly genuine. A thoughtful and devout tract on the devotional use of the Psalter. He lays stress on its universality, as summing up the spirit of all the other elements of Scripture, and as applying to the spiritual needs of every soul in all conditions. He remarks that the Psalms are sung not for musical effect, but that the worshippers may have longer time to dwell upon their meaning. The whole is presented as the discourse τινὸς φιλοπόνου γέροντος, possibly an ideal character.

(46) EXPOSITIONES IN PSALMOS, with an Argumentum (ὑπόθεσις) prefixed. The latter notices the arrangement of the Hebrew Psalter, the division into books, &c., and accounts for the absence of logical order by the supposition that during the Captivity some prophet collected as best he could the Scriptures which the carelessness of the Israelites had allowed to fall into disorder. The titles are to be followed as regards authorship. Imprecatory passages relate to our ghostly enemies. In the Expositions each Psalm is prefaced by a short statement of the general subject. He occasionally refers to the rendering of Aquila, Theodotion, and Symmachus.

(47) FRAGMENTA IN PSALMOS. Published by Felckmann from the Catena of Nicetas Heracleota, who has used his materials somewhat freely, often combining the comments of more than one Father into a single whole.

(48) DE TITULIS PSALMORUM. First published by Antonelli in 1746. This work, consisting of very brief notes on the Psalter verse by verse, is spoken of disparagingly by Alzog, *Patrol.*, p. 229, and regarded as spurious, on good *prima facie* grounds, by Gwatkin, p. 69, note. Eichhorn, *de Vit. Ascet.*, p. 43, note, threatens the latter (1886) with a refutation which, however, I have not seen.

(49) FRAGMENTUM IN CANTICA. (Photius mentions a Commentary on Eccles. and Cant.) From a Catena published by Meursius in 1617. Very brief (on Cant. i. 6, 7, iii. 1, 2, vi. 1). A spurious homily is printed (pp. 1349-1361) as an appendix to it.

(50) FRAGMENTA IN EVANG. MATTHÆI. Also from MS. catenæ. Contain a remarkable reference to the Eucharist (p. 1380, on Matt. vii. 6) and a somewhat disparaging reference to Origen (*infr.* p. 33) in reference to Matt. xii. 32, which passage is explained as in Serap. iv. (*vide supra* 22). The extracts purport in some cases to be taken from a homiletical or expository work of Athanasius divided into separate λόγοι. The passage 'on the nine incurable diseases of Herod' is grotesque (Migne xxvi. 1252), but taken from Joseph., *B. J.* I. xxiii. 5. Cf. Euseb. *H. E.* i. 8.

(51) FRAGMENTA IN LUCAM. Also from MS. catenæ. At the end, a remarkable passage on the extent to which prayers can help the departed.

(52) FRAGMENTA IN JOB. From Nicetas and MS. catenæ. Contains little remarkable. 'Behemoth' is Satan, as elsewhere in Athan.

(53) FRAGMENTUM IN 1 COR. A short paragraph on 1 Cor. vii. 1, or rather on vi. 18, somewhat inadequately explained.

f. MORAL AND ASCETIC, (11—13, [25], 28).

(54) SERMO DE PATIENTIA. (Migne xxvi. 1295.) Of doubtful genuineness (Montf., Gwatkin).

(55) DE VIRGINITATE. (Migne xxviii. 251). Pronounced dubious by Montf., spurious by Gwatkin, genuine by Eichhorn (*ubi supr.*, pp. 27, *sqq.*), who rightly lays stress on the early stage of feminine asceticism which is implied. But I incline to agree with Mr. Gwatkin as to its claims to come from Athanasius. 'Three hypostases' are laid down in a way incompatible with Athanasius' way of speaking in later life.

(56) MISCELLANEOUS FRAGMENTS. These are too slight and uncertain to be either classed or discussed here. *De Amuletis* (xxvi. 1319); *de Azymis*, (1327), very dubious; *In Ramos palmarum* (1319), also dubious; various small homiletical and controversial pieces (pp. 1224—1258) of various value and claims to genuineness. (See also Migne xxv. p. xiv. No. xx.)

Of (57) LOS WORKS (in addition to those of which fragments have been mentioned above) a Refutation of Arianism is referred to in *Letter* 52. We also hear of a treatise against heresies (a fragment above, No. 56). A 'Synodicon,' with the names of all Bishops present at Nicæa, is quoted by Socr. i. 13, but is referred by Revillout to his alleged Acts of the Synod of Alexandria in 362, which he supposes to have reissued the Acts of Nicæa. See above, p. lix. A consolatory address to the Virgins maltreated by George is mentioned by Theodoret, *H. E.* ii. 14; he quotes a few words, referring to the fact that the Arians would not even allow them peaceable burial, but 'sit about the tombs like demons' to prevent it. The *Oratio de defunctis* (*infra*, ch. iv. § 6, fragment above, 56) is ascribed to him by John Damasc., but by others to Cyril of Alexandria.

Many of his letters must have been lost. The Festal Letters are still very incomplete, and his letters to S. Basil would be a welcome discovery if they exist anywhere. A doctrinal letter against the Arians, not preserved to us, is mentioned *de Decr.* 5. (See also Montfaucon's *Præf.* ii. (Migne xxv. p. xxv., *sqq.*), and Jerome, *de Vir. illustr.* 87, a somewhat careless and scanty list.)

The above enumeration includes all the writings attributed with any probability to S. Athanasius. The fragmentary character of many of them is no great presumption against their genuineness. The Abbat Cosmas in the sixth century advised all who met with anything by Athanasius to copy it, and if they had no paper, to use their clothes for the purpose. This will readily explain (if explanation is needed) the transmission of such numerous scraps of writing under the name of the great bishop. It will also partly explain the large body of SPURIOUS WORKS which have sheltered themselves under his authority. To this class we have already assigned several writings (25, 36, 37 ? 39—43, 44 ? 48 ? 53 ? 55, 56 in part). Others whose claims are even less strong may be passed over, with only the mention of one or two of the more important. They are all printed in Migne, vol. xxviii., and parallels to some, especially the 'dubious' *In passionem et crucem Domini*, are marked in Williams' notes to the Festal Letters, partly incorporated in this volume. The *epistola catholica* and *Synopsis Scripturæ sacræ* are among the better known, and are classed with a few others as 'dubia' by Montfaucon, the fictitious *Disputatio habita in concilio Nicæno contra Arium*, among the 'spuria.' The silly tale *de Imagine Berytensi* seems to have enjoyed a wide circulation in the middle ages. Of the other undoubtedly 'spurious' works the most famous is the 'Athanasian Creed' or *Quicunque Vult.* It is needless to say that it is unconnected with Athanasius: its origin is still *sub judice.* The second part of it bears traces of the period *circa* 430 A.D., and the question which still awaits a last word is whether the Symbol is or is not a fusion of two originally independent documents. Messrs. Lumby, Swainson and others have ably maintained this, but the difficulties of their hypothesis that the fusion took place as late as about 800 A.D. are very great, and I incline to think will eventually prove fatal to it. But the discussion does not belong to our present subject.

§ 2. *Athanasius as an author. Style and characteristics.*

Athanasius was not an author by choice. With the exception of the early apologetic tracts all the writings that he has left were drawn from him by the stress of theological controversy or by the necessities of his work as a Christian pastor. We have no systematic doctrinal treatise, no historical monograph from his pen, although his writings are rich in materials for history and dogmatics alike. The exception to this is in the exegetical remains, especially those on the Psalms, which (*supra*, No. 45, *sqq.*) imply something more than occasional work, some intention of systematic composition. For this, a work congenial to one who was engaged in preaching, his long intervals of quiet at Alexandria (especially 328—335, 346—356, 365—373) may well have given him leisure. But on the whole, his writings are those of a man of powerful mind indeed and profound theological training, but still of a man of action   The style of Athanasius is accordingly distinguished from that of many older and younger contemporaries (Eusebius, Gregory Naz., &c.) by its inartificiality. This was already observed by Erasmus, who did not know many of his best works, but who notes his freedom from the harshness of Tertullian, the exaggeration of Jerome, the laboured style of Hilary, the overloaded manner of Augustine and Chrysostom, the imitation of the Attic orators so conspicuous in Gregory ; 'sed totus est in explicanda re.' That is true. Athanasius never writes for effect, but merely to make his meaning plain and impress it on others. This leads to his principal fault, namely his constant self-repetition (see p. 47, note 6) ; even in apologising for this he repeats the offence. The praise by Photius (quoted below, Introd. to *Orat.*) of his ἀπέριττον seems to apply to his freedom not from repetition but from extravagance, or studied brilliancy. This simplicity led Philostorgius, reflecting the false taste of his age, to pronounce Athanasius a child as compared with Basil, Gregory, or Apollinarius. To a modern reader the manliness of his character is reflected in the unaffected earnestness of his style. Some will admire him most when, in addressing a carefully calculated appeal to an emperor, he models his periods on Demosthenes *de Corona* (see p. 237). To others the unrestrained utterance of the real man, in such a gem of feeling and character as the Letter (p. 557) to Dracontius, will be worth more than any studied apology. With all his occasional repetition, with all the feebleness of the Greek language of that day as an instrument of expression, if we compare it with the Greek of Thucydides or Plato, Athanasius writes with nerve and keenness, even with a silent but constant underflow of humour. His style is not free from Latinisms; πρέδα (= præda) in the *Encycl.*, βετερᾶνος (= veteranus), βῆλον (= velum), μάγιστρος, &c., are barbarisms belonging to the later decadence of Greek, but not without analogy even in the earliest Christian Literature. ξυνωρίς is used in an unusual sense, p. 447. Ἀρειομανῖται seems to be coined by himself ; ἀκαθήκων, ἀποξενίζειν, ἐπακούειν (= answer), ἐγκυκλεῖν, &c., are Alexandrinisms (see Fialon, p. 289). On the whole, no man was ever less of a stylist, while at the same time making the fullest use of the resources furnished by the language at his command. When he wrote, seven centuries of decay had passed over the language of Thucydides, the tragedians, Plato and the Orators. The Latin Fathers of the day had at their disposal a language only two centuries or so past its prime. The heritage of Thucydides had passed through Tacitus to the Latin prose writers of the silver age.   The Latin of Tertullian, Cyprian, Jerome, Augustin, Leo, with all its mannerisms and often false antithesis and laboured epigram, was yet a terse incisive weapon compared with the patristic Greek. But among the Greek Fathers Athanasius is the most readable, simply because his style is natural and direct, because it reflects the man rather than the age.

§ 3. *Personal characteristics* (see Stanley's *Eastern Church*, Lect. vii.). To write an

elaborate character of Athanasius is superfluous. The full account of his life (chap. ii.), and the specimens of his writings in this volume, may be trusted to convey the right impression without the aid of analysis. But it may be well to emphasise one or two salient points [1].

In Athanasius we feel ourselves in contact with a commanding personality. His early rise to decisive epoch-making influence,—he was scarcely more than 27 at the council of Nicæa,—his election as bishop when barely of canonical age, the speedy ascendancy which he gained over all Egypt and Libya, the rapid consolidation of the distracted province under his rule, the enthusiastic personal loyalty of his clergy and monks, the extraordinary popularity

---

[1] Of his personal appearance little is known. Gregory Naz. praises his beauty of expression, Julian sneers at his small stature. Later tradition adds a slight stoop, a hooked nose and small mouth, short beard spreading into large whiskers, and light auburn hair. (See Stanley *ubi supr.*)

enjoyed by him at Alexandria even among the heathen (excepting, perhaps, 'the more abandoned among them,' *Hist. Ar.* 58), the evident feeling of the Arians that as long as he was intact their cause could not prosper, the jealously of his influence shewn by Constantius and Julian, all this is a combined and impressive tribute to his personal greatness. In what then did this consist?

Principally, no doubt, in his moral and mental vigour; resolute ability characterises his writings and life throughout. He had the not too common gift of seeing the proportions of things. A great crisis was fully appreciated by him; he always saw at once where principles separated or united men, where the bond or the divergence was merely accidental. With Arius and Arianism no compromise was to be thought of; but he did not fail to distinguish men really at one with him on essentials, even where their conduct toward himself had been indefensible (*de Syn.*). So long as the cause was advanced, personal questions were insignificant. So far Athanasius was a partisan. It may be admitted that he saw little good in his opponents; but unless the evidence is singularly misleading there was little good to see. The leaders of the Arian interest were unscrupulous men, either bitter and unreasoning fanatics like Secundus and Maris, or more often political theologians, like Eusebius of Nicomedia, Valens, Acacius, who lacked religious earnestness. It may be admitted that he refused to admit error in his friends. His long alliance with Marcellus, his unvarying refusal to utter a syllable of condemnation of him by name; his refusal to name even Photinus, while yet (*Orat.* iv.) exposing the error associated with his name; his suppression of the name of Apollinarius, even when writing directly against him; all this was inconsistent with strict impartiality, and, no doubt, placed his adversaries partly in the right. But it was the partiality of a generous and loyal spirit, and he could be generous to personal enemies if he saw in them an approximation to himself in principle. When men were dead, unlike too many theologians of his own and later times, he restrained himself in speaking of them, even if the dead man were Arius himself.

In the whole of our minute knowledge of his life there is a total lack of self-interest. The glory of God and the welfare of the Church absorbed him fully at all times. We see the immense power he exercised in Egypt; the Emperors recognised him as a political force of the first order; Magnentius bid for his support, Constantius first cajoled, then made war upon him; but on no occasion does he yield to the temptation of using the arm of flesh. Almost unconscious of his own power, he treats Serapion and the monks as equals or superiors, degging them to correct and alter anything amiss in his writings. His humility is the more real for never being conspicuously paraded.

Like most men of great power, he had a real sense of humour (Stanley, p. 231, *sq.*, ed. 1883). Even in his youthful works we trace it (*infr.* p. 2), and it is always present, though very rarely employed with purpose. But the exposure of the Arsenius calumny at Tyre, the smile with which he answered the importunate catechising of an Epiphanius about 'old' Marcellus, the oracular interpretation of the crow's 'cras' in answer to the heathen (Sozom. iv. 10), the grave irony with which he often confronts his opponents with some surprising application of Scripture, his reply to the pursuers from the Nile boat in 362, allow us to see the twinkle of his keen, searching eye. Courage, self-sacrifice, steadiness of purpose, versatility and resourcefulness, width of ready sympathy, were all harmonised by deep reverence and the discipline of a single-minded lover of Christ. The Arian controversy was to him no battle for ecclesiastical power, nor for theological triumph. It was a religious crisis involving the reality of revelation and redemption. He felt about it as he wrote to the bishops of Egypt, 'we are contending for our all' (p. 234).

'A certain cloud of romance encircled him' (Reynolds). His escapes from Philagrius, Syrianus, Julian, his secret presence in Alexandria, his life among the monasteries of Egypt in his third exile, his reputed visits to distant councils, all impress the imagination and lend themselves to legend and fable. Later ages even claimed that he had fled in disguise to Spain and served as cook in a monastery near Calahorra (Act. SS. 2 Maii)! But he is also surrounded by an atmosphere of truth. Not a single miracle of any kind is related of him To invest him with the halo of miracle the Bollandists have to come down to the 'translation' of his body, not to Constantinople (an event surrounded with no little uncertainty), but to Venice, whither a thievish sea-captain, who had stolen it from a church in Stamboul, brought a body, which decisively proved its identity by prodigies which left no room for doubt. But the Athanasius of history is not the subject of any such tales. It has been said that no saint outside the New Testament has ever claimed the gift of miracles for himself. At any rate (though he displays credulity with regard to Antony), the saintly reputation of Athanasius rested on his life and character alone, without the aid of any reputation for miraculous power.

And resting upon this firm foundation, it has won the respect and admiration even of those who do not feel that they owe to him the vindication of all that is sacred and precious. Not only a Gregory or an Epiphanius, an Augustine or a Cyril, a Luther or a Hooker, not only Montfaucon and Tillemont, Newman and Stanley pay tribute to him as a Christian hero. Secular as well as Church historians fall under the spell of his personality, and even Gibbon lays aside his 'solemn sneer' to do homage to Athanasius the great.

CHAPTER IV.
The Theology of S. Athanasius.

§ 1. General considerations.
§ 2. Fundamental ideas; Anthropology, Soteriology.
§ 3. Fundamental ideas; God and Nature.
§ 4. Organs of Revelation. Bible, Church, Authority, &c.
§ 5. Content of Revelation. The Trinity, Incarnation, &c..
§ 6. Derivative truths, Grace, means of grace, Ethics, Eschatology.

§ 1. *General considerations.*

THE theological training of Athanasius was in the school of Alexandria, and under the still predominant although modified influence of Origen (see above, pp. xiv., xxvii.). The resistance which the theology of that famous man had everywhere encountered had not availed, in the Greek-speaking churches of the East, to stem its influence; at the same time it had made its way at the cost of much of its distinctive character. Its principal opponent, Methodius, who represented the ancient Asiatic tradition, was himself not uninfluenced by the theology he opposed. The legacy of his generation to the Nicene age was an Origenism tempered in various degrees by the Asiatic theology and by accommodations to the traditional canon of ecclesiastical teaching. The degrees of this modification were various, and the variety was reflected in the indeterminate body of theological conviction which we find at the time of the outbreak of Arianism, and which, as already explained, lies at the basis of the reaction against the definition of Nicæa. The theology of Alexandria remained Origenist, and the Origenist character is purest and most marked in Pierius, Theognostus, and in the non-episcopal heads of the Alexandrian School. The bishops of Alexandria after Dionysius represent a more tempered Origenism. Especially this holds good of the martyred Peter, whom we find expressly correcting distinctive parts of the system of his spiritual ancestor. In Alexander of Alexandria, the theological sponsor of the young Athanasius, the combination of a fundamentally Origenist theology with ideas traceable to the Asiatic tradition is conspicuous[1].

Athanasius, then, received his first theological ideas from Origenist sources, and in so far as he eventually diverged from Origen we must seek the explanation partly in his own theological or religious idiosyncrasy and in the influences which he encountered as time went on, partly in the extent to which the Origenism of his masters was already modified by different currents of theological influence.

To work out this problem satisfactorily would involve a separate treatise and a searching study, not only of Athanasius[2] but on the one hand of Origen and his school, on the other of Methodius and the earlier pre-Nicene theologians. What is here attempted is the more modest task of briefly drawing attention to some of the more conspicuous evidences of the process and to some of its results in the developed theology of the saintly bishop.

It has been said by Harnack that the theology of Athanasius underwent no development, but was the same from first to last. The truth of this verdict is I think limited by the fact that the Origenism of Athanasius distinctly undergoes a change, or rather fades away, in his later works. A non-Origenist element is present from the first, and after the contest with Arianism begins, Origen's ideas recede more and more from view. Athanasius was influenced *negatively* by the stress of the Arian controversy: while the vague and loose Origenism of the current Greek theology inclined the majority of bishops to dread Sabellianism rather than Arianism, and to underrate the danger of the latter (pp. xviii., xxxv.), Athanasius, deeply

---

[1] To begin with, we have the interesting fact that Alexander studied the writings of Melito of Sardis, and even worked up his tract περὶ ψυχῆς καὶ σώματος καὶ εἰς τὸ πάθος into a homiletical discourse of his own, omitting such passages as seemed to savour of 'modalism,' (see Krüger in *Zeitschr. f. wiss. Theol.* 1888, p. 434, *sqq.*: his grounds are convincing). Secondly, the expressions attributed to him by Arius (in his letter to Euseb.

Nic.), and his letter to his namesake of Byzantium, bear out the above statement.

[2] The reader is requested to supplement the necessarily very slender treatment of the Athanasian theology in this chapter by referring to the General Index to this volume, as well as to the Index of Texts, for guidance to the passages of Athanasius which are needed to check, fill out, and qualify what is here presented only in broad outline.

impressed, from personal experience, with the negation of the first principles of redemption which Arianism involved, stood apart from the first from the theology of his Asiatic contemporaries and went back to the authority of Scripture and the Rule of Faith.   He was influenced *positively* by the Nicene formula, which represents the combination of Western with anti-Origenist Eastern traditions in opposition to the dominant Eastern theology.   The Nicene formula found in Athanasius a mind predisposed to enter into its spirit, to employ in its defence the richest resources of theological and biblical training, of spiritual depth and vigour, of self-sacrificing but sober and tactful enthusiasm ; its victory in the East is due under God to him alone.

Athanasius was not a systematic theologian : that is he produced no many-sided theology like that of Origen or Augustine.   He had no interest in theological speculation, none of the instincts of a schoolman or philosopher.   His theological greatness lies in his firm grasp of *soteriological* principles, in his resolute subordination of everything else, even the formula ὁμοούσιος, to the central fact of Redemption, and to what that fact implied as to the Person of the Redeemer.   He goes back from the Logos of the philosophers to the Logos of S. John, from the God of the philosophers to God in Christ reconciling the world to Himself.   His legacy to later ages has been felicitously compared (Harnack, *Dg.* ii. 26, note) to that of the Christian spirit of his age in the realm of architecture.   ' To the many forms of architectural conception which lived in Rome and Alexandria in the fourth century, the Christian spirit added nothing fresh.   Its achievement was of a different kind.   Out of the many it selected and consecrated one ; the multiplicity of forms it carried back to a single dominant idea, not so much by a change in the spirit of the art as by the restoration of Religion to its place as the central motive.   It bequeathed to the art of the middle ages the Basilica, and rendered possible the birth of Gothic, a style, like that of the old Greek Temple, truly organic.   What the Basilica was in the history of the material, the central idea of Athanasius has been in that of the spiritual fabric ; an auspicious reduction, full of promise for the future, of the exuberant speculation of Greek theology to the one idea in which the power of religion then resided' (*ib.* and pp. 22 *sqq.*, freely reproduced).

§ 2.   *Fundamental ideas of man and his redemption.*

To Athanasius the Incarnation of the Son of God, and especially his Death on the Cross, is the centre of faith and theology (*Incar.* 19, κεφάλαιον τῆς πίστεως, cf. 9. 1 and 2, 20. 2, &c.). 'For our salvation' (*Incar.* 1) the Word became Man and died.   But how did Athanasius conceive of 'salvation'? *from* what are we saved, *to* what destiny does salvation bring us, and what idea does he form of the efficacy of the Saviour's death?   Now it is not too much to say that no one age of the Church's existence has done full justice to the profundity and manysidedness of the Christian idea of Redemption as effected in Christ and as unfolded by S. Paul.   The kingdom of God and His Righteousness ; the forgiveness of sins and the adoption of sons as a present gift ; the consummation of all at the great judgment ;—Christian men of different ages, countries, characters and mental antecedents, while united in personal devotion to the Saviour and in the sanctifying Power of His Grace, have interpreted these central ideas of the Gospel in terms of their own respective categories, and have succeeded in bringing out now one, now another aspect of the mystery of Redemption rather than in preserving the balance of the whole.   Who will claim that the last word has yet been said on S. Paul's deep conception of God's (not mercy but) Righteousness as the new and peculiar element (Rom. i. 17, iii. 22, 26) of the Gospel Revelation? to search out the unsearchable riches of Christ is the prerogative of Christian faith, but is denied, save to the most limited extent, to Christian knowledge (1 Cor. xiii. 9).   The onesidedness of any given age in apprehending the work of Christ is to be recognised by us not in a censorious spirit of self-complacency, but with reverent sympathy, and with the necessity in view of correcting our own : πάντα δοκιμάζετε, τὸ καλὸν κατέχετε.

Different ages and classes have necessarily thought under different categories.   The categories of the post-apostolic age were mainly ethical ; the Gospel is the new law, and the promise of eternal life, founded on true knowledge of God, and accepted by faith.   Those of the Asiatic fathers from Ignatius downwards were largely physical or realistic.   Mankind is brought in Christ (the physician) from death to life, from φθόρα to ἀφθαρσία (Ign. *passim*) ; τὸ εὐαγγέλιον . . . ἀπάρτισμα ἀφθαρσίας (Ign., Melit.) ; human nature is changed by the Incarnation, man made God.   Tertullian introduced into Western theology forensic categories.   He applied them to the Person, not yet to the Work, of Christ : but the latter application, pushed to a repellent length in the middle ages, and still more so since the Reformation, may without fancifulness be traced back to the fact that the first Latin Father was a lawyer. Again, Redemption was viewed by Origen and others under cosmological categories, as the turning point in the great conflict of good with evil, of demons with God, as the inauguration of the deliverance of the creation and its reunion with God. The many-sidedness of Origen combined, indeed, almost every representation of Redemption then current, from the propitiatory and mediatorial, which most nearly approached the thought of S. Paul, to the grotesque but widely-spread view of a ransom due to the devil which he was induced to accept by a stratagem. It may be said that with the exception of the last-named every one cf the above conceptions finds some point of contact in the New Testament; even the forensic idea, thoroughly unbiblical in its extremer forms, would not have influenced Christian thought as it has done had it not corresponded to something in the language of S. Paul.

Now Athanasius does not totally ignore any one of these conceptions, unless it be that of a transaction with the devil, which he scarcely touches even in *Orat.* ii. 52 (see note there). Of the forensic view he is indeed almost clear. His reference to the ' debt' (τὸ ὀφειλόμενον, *Incar.* 20, *Orat.* ii. 66) which had to be paid is connected not so much with the Anselmic idea of a satisfaction due, as with the fact that death was by the divine word (Gen. iii.), attached to sin as its penalty.

The aspect of the death of Christ as a vicarious sacrifice (ἀντὶ πάντων, *de Incar.* 9 ; προσφορὰ and θυσία, 10) is not passed over. But on the whole another aspect predominates. The categories under which Athanasius again and again states the soteriological problem are those of ζωή and θάνατος, φθόρα and ἀφθαρσία. So far as he works the problem out in detail it is under physical categories, without doing full justice to the ideas of guilt and reconciliation, of the reunion of *will* between man and God. The numberless passages which bear this out cannot be quoted in full, but the point is of sufficient importance to demand the production of a few details.

(*a*) The original state of man was not one of ' nature,' for man's nature is φθόρα ; (τὴν ἐν θανάτῳ κατὰ φύσιν φθόραν, *Incar.* 3, cf. 8, 10, 44) the Word was imparted to them in that they were made κατὰ τὴν τοῦ θεοῦ εἰκόνα (*ib*). Hence what later theology marks off as an exclusively supernatural gift is according to Athanasius inalienable from human nature, i.e. it can be impaired but not absolutely lost (*Incar.* 14, and apparently *Orat.* iii. 10 *fin.* ; the question of the teaching of Athan. upon the natural endowments of man belongs specially to the Introd. to *de Incarnatione*, where it will be briefly discussed). Accordingly their infraction of the divine command (by turning their minds, c. *Gent.* 3, to lower things instead of to the θεωρία τῶν θείων), *logically* involved them in non-existence (*de Incar.* 4), but actually, inasmuch as the likeness of God was *only gradually* lost, in φθόρα, regarded as a *process toward* non-existence. This again involved men in increasing *ignorance* of God, by the gradual obliteration of the εἰκών, the indwelling Logos, by virtue of which alone men could read the open book (c. *Gent.* 34 *fin.*) of God's manifestation of Himself in the Universe. It is evident that the pathological point of view here prevails over the purely ethical : the perversion of man's will merges in the general idea of φθόρα, the first need of man is a change in his *nature ;* or rather the renewed infusion of that higher and divine nature which he has gradually lost. (Cf. *de Incar.* 44, χρῃζόντων τῆς αὐτοῦ θεότητος διὰ τοῦ ὁμοίου).

(*b*) Accordingly the mere presence of the Word in a human body, the mere fact of the Incarnation, is the essential factor in our restoration (simile of the city and the king, *ib.* 9. 3, &c., cf. *Orat.* ii. 67, 70). But if so, what was the special need of the Cross? Athanasius felt, as we have already mentioned, the supremacy of the Cross as the purpose of the Saviour's coming, but he does not in fact give to it the central place in his system of thought which it occupies in his instincts. Man had involved himself in the sentence of death ; death must therefore take place to satisfy this sentence (*Orat.* ii. 69 ; *de Incar.* 20. 2, 5) ; the Saviour's death, then, put an end to death regarded as penal and as symptomatic of man's φθόρα (cf. *ib.* 21. 1, &c.). It must be confessed that Athanasius does not penetrate to the full meaning of S. Paul. The latter also ascribed a central import to the mere fact of the Incarnation (Rom. viii. 3, πέμψας), but primarily in relation to sin (yet see Athan. c. *Apoll.* ii. 6) ; and the destruction of the practical power of sin stands indissolubly correlated (Rom. viii. 1) with the removal of guilt and so with the Righteousness of God realising itself in the propitiation of the blood of Christ (*ib.* iii. 21—26).

To Athanasius nature is the central, will a secondary or implied factor in the problem. The aspect of the death of Christ most repeatedly dwelt upon is that in it death spent its force (πληρωθείσης τῆς ἐξουσίας ἐν τῷ κυριακῷ σώματι, *ib.* 8) against human nature, that the ' corruption ' of mankind might run its full course and be spent in the Lord's body, and so cease for the future. Of this Victory over death and the demons the Resurrection is the trophy. His death is therefore to us (*ib.* 10) the ἀρχὴ ζωῆς, we are henceforth ἄφθαρτοὶ διὰ τῆς ἀναστάσεως (27. 2, 32. 6, cf. 34. 1, &c.), and have a portion in the divine nature, are in fact deified (cf. *de Incarn.* 54, and note there). This last thought, which became (Harnack, vol. ii. p. 46) the common property of Eastern theology, goes back through Origen and Hippolytus to Irenæus. On the whole, its presentation in Athanasius is more akin to the Asiatic than to the Origenist form of the conception. To Origen, man's highest destiny could only be the return to his original source and condition: to Irenæus and the Asiatics, man had been created for a destiny which he had never realised; the interruption in the history of our race introduced by sin was repaired by the Incarnation, which carried back the race to a new head, and so carried it forward to a destiny of which under its original head it was incapable. To Origen the Incarnation was a *restoration to*, to Irenæus and to Athanasius (*Or.* ii. 67), an *advance upon*, the original state of man. (Pell, pp. 167—177, labours to prove the contrary, but he does not convince.)

(*c*) This leads us to the important observation that momentous as are to Athanasius the consequences of the introduction of sin into the world, he yet makes no such vast difference between the condition of fallen and unfallen men as has commonly been assumed to exist. The latter state was inferior to that of the members of Christ (*Orat.* ii. 67, 68), while the immense (*c. Gent.* 8, *de Incar.* 5) consequences of its forfeiture came about only by a gradual course of deterioration (*de Incar.* 6. 1, ἠφανίζετο; observe the tense), and in different degrees in different cases. The only difference of kind between the two conditions is in the universal reign of Death since the (partial) forfeiture of the τοῦ κατ᾽ εἰκόνα χάρις: and even this difference is a subtle one; for man's existence in Paradise was not one of ἀφθαρσία except prospectively (*de Incar.* 3. 4). He enjoyed present happiness, ἄλυπος ἀνώδυνος ἀμέριμνος ζωή, with promise of ἀφθαρσία *in heaven*. That is, death would have taken place, but not death as unredeemed mankind know it (cf. *de Incar.* 21. 1). In other words, man was created not so much in a state of perfection (τέλειος κτισθείς, p. 384) as with a capacity for perfection (and for even more than perfection, p. 385 *sq.*) and with a destiny to correspond with such capacity. This destination remains in force even after man has failed to correspond to it, and is in fact assigned by Athanasius as the reason why the Incarnation was a necessity on God's part (*de Incar.* 6. 4—7, 10. 3, 13. 2—4, *Orat.* ii. 66, &c., &c.). Accordingly, while man was *created* (*Orat.* ii. 59) through the Word, the Word became Flesh that man might receive the yet higher dignity of Sonship[3]; and while even before the Incarnation some men were *de facto* pure from sin (*Orat.* iii. 33) by virtue of the χάρις τῆς κλήσεως involved in 'τὸ κατ᾽ εἰκόνα' (see *ib.* 10, *fin.*; *Orat.* i. 39 is even stronger, cf. iv. 22), they were yet θνητοί and φθαρτοί; whereas those in Christ die, no longer κατὰ τὴν προτέραν γένεσιν ἐν τῷ Ἀδάμ, but to live again λογωθείσης τῆς σαρκός (*Orat.* iii. 33, *fin.*, cf. *de Incar.* 21. 1).

(*d*) The above slight sketch of the Athanasian doctrine of man's need of redemption and of the satisfaction of that need brings to light a system free from much that causes many modern thinkers to stumble at the current doctrine of the original state and the religious history of mankind. That mankind did not start upon their development with a perfect nature, but have fought their way up from an undeveloped stage through many lower phases of development; that this development has been infinitely varied and complex, and that sin and its attendant consequences have a pathological aspect which practically is as important as the forensic aspect, are commonplaces of modern thought, resting upon the wider knowledge of our age, and hard to reconcile with the (to us) traditional theological account of these things. The Athanasian account of them leaves room for the results of modern knowledge, or at least does not rudely clash with the instincts of the modern anthropologist. The recovery of the Athanasian point of view is *prima facie* a gain. 'At what cost is it obtained? Does its recognition involve us in mere naturalism veiled under religious forms of speech? That was certainly not the mind of Athanasius, nor does his system really lend itself to such a result. To begin with, the divine destiny of man from the first is an essential principle with our writer. Man was made and is still exclusively destined for knowledge of and fellowship with his Creator. Secondly the means, and the only means, to this end is Christ the Incarnate Son of God. In Him the religious

---

3 The above is strikingly illustrated by the discussion (pp. 381—383) of πρωτότοκος πάσης κτίσεως (Col. i. 15). At first sight Ath. appears to contradict himself, explaining πρωτότοκος as he does first solely of the Saviour as *Incarnate*, and then of the *cosmic* and *creative* function of the Word. But closer examination brings out his view of creation itself (p. 383) as an act of Grace, demanding not (as the current Eastern theology held, in common with Arius) the mediation of a subordinate Creator, but an act of absolutely Divine condescension analogous to, and anticipatory of, the Incarnation. The apparently disturbing persistence in the argument of the cosmological explanation of πρωτότοκος is really therefore due to a subtle change in it, by virtue of which it comes into relation with the Soteriological idea,—which is the pivot of the entire anti-Arian position of Athanasius on this question,—and with the ultimate scheme in which (cf. Rom. viii.) the effects of the Incarnation are to embrace the whole creation. Because creation as such involves the promise of adoption, and tends to deification as its goal, the Son is πρωτότοκος in the region of Grace and of Creation alike.

history of mankind has its centre, and from Him it proceeds upon its new course, or rather is enabled once more to run the course designed for it from the first. How far Athanasius exhausted the significance of this fact may be a question; that he placed the fact itself in the centre is his lasting service to Christian thought.

(e) The categories of Athanasius in dealing with the question before us are primarily physical, i.e., on the one hand cosmological, on the other pathological. But it is well before leaving the subject to insist that this was not exclusively the case. The purpose of the Incarnation was at once to renew us, and to make known the Father (de Incarn. 16); or as he elsewhere puts it (ib. 7 fin.), ἀνακτίσαι τὰ ὅλα, ὑπὲρ πάντων παθεῖν, and περὶ πάντων πρεσβεῦσαι πρὸς τὸν Πατέρα. The idea of ἀφθαρσία which so often stands with him for the summum bonum [4] imparted to us in Christ, involves a moral and spiritual restoration of our nature, not merely the physical supersession of φθόρα by ἀθανασία (de Incarn. 47, 51, 52, &c., &c.).

§ 3. Fundamental ideas of God, the World, and Creation.

The Athanasian idea of God has been singled out for special recognition in recent times; he has been claimed, and on the whole with justice, as a witness for the immanence of God in the universe in contrast to the insistence in many Christian systems on God's transcendence or remoteness from all created things. (Fiske, Idea of God, discussed by Moore in Lux Mundi (ed. 1) pp. 95—102.) The problem was one which Christian thought was decisively compelled to face by the Arian controversy (supra, p. xxix. sq.). The Apologists and Alexandrians had partially succeeded in the problem expressed in the dying words of Plotinus, 'to bring the God which is within into harmony with the God which is in the universe,' or rather to reconcile the transcendence with the immanence of God. But their success was only partial: the immanence of the Word had been emphasised, but in contrast with the transcendence of the Father. This could not be more than a temporary resting-place for the Christian mind, and Arius forced a solution. That solution was found by Athanasius. The mediatorial work of the Logos is not necessary as though nature could not bear the untempered hand of the Father. The Divine Will is the direct and sole source of all things, and the idea of a mediatorial nature is inconsistent with the true idea of God (pp. 87, 155, 362, comparing carefully p. 383). 'All things created are capable of sustaining God's absolute hand. The hand which fashioned Adam now also and ever is fashioning and giving entire consistence to those who come after him.' The immanence, or intimate presence and unceasing agency of God in nature, does not belong to the Word as distinct from the Father, but to the Father in and through the Word, in a word to God as God (cf. de Decr. 11, where the language of de Incarn. 17 about the Word is applied to God as such). This is a point which marks an advance upon anything that we find in the earliest writings of Athanasius, and upon the theology of his preceptor Alexander, to whom, amongst other not very clear formulæ, the Word is a μεσιτεύουσα φύσις μονογενής (Thdt. H. E. ii. 4; Alexander cannot distinguish φύσις from ὑπόστασις or οὐσία; Father and Son are δύο ἀχώριστα πράγματα, but yet τῇ ὑποστάσει δύο φύσεις). This is indeed the principal particular in which Athanasius left the modified Origenism of his age, and of his own school, behind. If on the other hand he resembled Arius in drawing a sharper line than had been drawn previously between the one God and the World, it must also be remembered that his God was not the far-off purely transcendent God of Arius, but a God not far from every one of us (Orat. ii. p. 361 sq.).

That God is beyond all essence ὑπερέκεινα πάσης οὐσίας (c. Gent. 2. 2, 40. 2, 35. 1 γενητῆς οὐσίας) is a thought common to Origen and the Platonists, but adopted by Athanasius with a difference, marked by the addition of γενητῆς. That God created all things out of pure bounty of being (c. Gent. § 2. 2, § 41. 2, de Incarn. § 3. 3, and note there) is common to Origen and Philo, being taken by the latter from Plato's Timæus. The Universe, and especially the human soul, reflects the being of its Author (c. Gent. passim). Hence there are two main paths by which man can arrive at the knowledge of God, the book of the Universe (c. Gent. 34 fin.), and the contemplation or self-knowledge of the soul itself (ib. 33, 34). So far Athanasius is on common ground with the Platonists (cf. Fialon, pp. 270, sqq.); but he takes up distinctively Christian ground, firstly, in emphasising the insufficiency of these proofs after sin has clouded the soul's vision, and, above all, in insisting on the divine Incarnation as the sole remedy for this inability, as the sole means by which man as he is can reach a true knowledge of God. Religion not philosophy is the sphere in which the God of Athanasius is manifest to man.

---

4 On the subject of § 2, see also Pell. Lehre des h. Athan. and Shedd ii. pp. 37, sqq., 237, sqq. The former demonstrates his full accord with modern Roman Catholic teaching, the latter, his exact harmony with the modern Protestant view of the doctrine. It is, at least, a tribute to the greatness of Athan. that advocates of all sides are so eager to claim him.

Here, again, Athanasius is 'Christo-centric.' With Origen, Athanasius refuses to allow evil any substantive existence (c. Gent. §§ 2, 6, de Incarn. § 4. 5); evil resides in the will only, and is the result of the abuse of its power of free choice (c. Gent. 5 and 7). The evil in the Universe is mainly the work of demons, who have aggravated the consequences of human sin also (de Incarn. 52. 4). On the other hand, the evil does not extend beyond the sphere of personal agency, and the Providence of God (upon which Athanasius insists with remarkable frequency, especially in the de Fuga and c. Gent. and de Incarn., also in Vit. Anton.) exercises untiring care over the whole. The problem of suffering and death in the animal creation is not discussed by him; he touches very incidentally, Orat. ii. 63, on the deliverance of creation in connection with Rom. viii. 19 —21.

§. 4. Vehicles of revelation; Scripture, the Church, Tradition.

(a) The supreme and unique revelation of God to man is in the Person of the Incarnate Son. But though unique the Incarnation is not solitary. Before it there was the divine institution of the Law and the Prophets, the former a typical anticipation (de Incarn. 40. 2) of the destined reality, and along with the latter (ib. 12. 2 and 5) 'for all the world a holy school of the knowledge of God and the conduct of the soul.' After it there is the history of the life and teaching of Christ and the writings of His first Disciples, left on record for the instruction of all ages. Athanasius again and again applies to the Scriptures the terms θεία and θεόπνευστα (e.g. de Decr. 15, de Incarn. 33. 3, &c.; the latter word, which he also applies to his own martyr teachers, is, of course, from 2 Tim. iii. 16). The implications of this as bearing on the literal exactness of Scripture he nowhere draws out. His strongest language (de Decr. ubi supra) is incidental to a controversial point: on Ps. lii. (liii.) 2, he maintains that 'there is no hyperbola in Scripture; all is strictly true,' but he proceeds on the strength of that principle to allegorise the verse he is discussing. In c. Gent. 2, 3, he treats the account of Eden and the Fall as figurative. But in his later writings there is, so far as I know, nothing to match this. In fact, although he always employs the allegorical method, sometimes rather strangely (e.g. Deut. xxviii. 66, in de Incarn. 35, Orat. ii. 19, after Irenæus, Origen, &c.), we discern, especially in his later writings, a tendency toward a more literal exegesis than was usual in the Alexandrian school. His discussion, e.g., of the sinlessness of Christ (c. Apol. i. 7, 17, ii. 9, 10) contrasts in this respect with that of his master Alexander, who appeals, following Origen's somewhat startling allegorical application, to Prov. xxx. 19, a text nowhere used by Ath. in this way (Thdt. H.E. i. 4). This is doubtless largely due to the pressure of the controversy with the Arians, who certainly had more to gain than their opponents from the prevalent unhistorical methods of exegesis, as we see from the use made by them of 2 Cor. iv. 11 at Nicæa, and of Prov. viii. 22 throughout[5]. Accordingly Athanasius complains loudly of their exegesis (Ep. Æg. 3—4, cf. Orat. i. 8, 52), and insists (id. i. 54, cf. already de Decr. 14) on the primary necessity of always conscientiously studying the circumstances of time and place, the person addressed, the subject matter, and purpose of the writer, in order not to miss the true sense. This rule is the same as applies (de Sent. Dion. 4) to the interpretation of any writings whatever, and carries with it the strict subordination of the allegorical to the historical sense, contended for by the later school of Antioch, and now accepted by all reasonable Christians (see Kihn in Wetzer-Hergenröther's Kirchen-Lex. vol. i. pp. 955—959, who calls the Antiochene exegesis 'certainly a providential phenomenon;' also supra, p. xxviii., note 1).

(b) The Canon of Scripture accepted by Athanasius has long been known from the fragments of the thirty-ninth Festal Letter (Easter, 367). The New Testament Canon comprises all the books received at the present day, but in the older order, viz., Gospels, Acts, Catholic Epistles, Pauline Epistles (Hebrews expressly included as S. Paul's between Thess. and Tim.), Apocalypse. The Old Testament canon is remarkable in several ways. The number of books is 22, corresponding to the Alexandrian Jewish reckoning, not to the (probably) older Jewish or Talmudic reckoning of 24 (the rolls of Ruth and Lam. counted separately, and with the Hagiographa). This at once excludes from the Canon proper the so-called 'Apocrypha,' with the exception of the additions to Daniel, and of Baruch and 'the Epistle,' which are counted as one book with Jeremiah. The latter is also the case with Lamentations, while on the other hand the number of 22 is preserved by the reckoning of Ruth as a separate book from Judges to make up for the exclusion of Esther. This last point is archaic, and brings Athanasius into connection with Melito (171 A.D.), who gives (Eus. H.E. iv. 26. 14, see also vol. 1, p. 144, note 1, in this series) a Canon which he has obtained by careful enquiry in Palestine. This Canon agrees with that of Athanasius except with regard to the order assigned to 'Esdras' (i.e. Ezra and Nehemiah,

---

5 Athanasius is not always innocent of the method of which he complains; e.g. when he uses Isa. i. 11, πλήρης εἰμί, as a proof of the Divine Perfection.

placed by M. at the end), to 'the twelve in one book' (placed by M. after Jer.), and Daniel (placed by M. before Ezekiel). Now, Esther is nowhere mentioned in the N.T., and the Rabbinical discussions as to whether Esther 'defiled the hands' (*i.e.* was 'canonical') went on to the time of R. Akiba (†135), an older, and even of R. Juda 'the holy' (150—210), a younger, contemporary of Melito (see Wildeboer, *Ontstaan van den Kanon*, pp. 58, *sq.*, 65, &c.). The latter, therefore, may represent the penultimate stage in the history of the Hebrew canon before its close in the second century, (doubted by Bleek, *Einl.* 5, § 242, but not unlikely). Here, then, Ath. represents an earlier stage of opinion than Origen (Eus. *H.E.* vi. 25), who gives the finally fixed Hebrew Canon of his own time, but puts Esther at the end. As to the *number* of books, Athan. agrees with Josephus, Melito, Origen, and with Jerome, who, however, knows of the other reckoning of 24 ('nonnulli' in *Prol. Gal.*). Athanasius enumerates, as 'outside the Canon, but appointed by the Fathers to be read by those who newly join us,' Wisdom, Ecclesiasticus, Esther, Judith, and Tobit, as well as what is called the Teaching of the Apostles and the Shepherd. In practice, however, he quotes several of the latter as 'Scripture' (Wisdom repeatedly so, see index to this vol.) ; 'The Shepherd' is 'most profitable,' and quoted for the Unity of the Creator (and cf. *de Decr.* 4), but not as 'Scripture ;' the 'Didache' is not used by him unless the *Syntagma* (*vide supra*, p. lix.) be his genuine work. He also quotes 1 Esdras for the praise of Truth, and 2 Esdras once, as a 'prophet.' 'Daniel' includes Susanna and Bel and the Dragon.

(*c*) On the sufficiency of Scripture for the establishment of all necessary doctrine Athanasius insists repeatedly and emphatically (*c. Gent.* 1, *de Incarn.* 5, *de Decr.* 32, *Vit. Ant.* 16, &c., &c.) ; and he follows up precept by example. 'His works are a continuous appeal to Scripture.' There is no passage in his writings which recognises tradition as *supplementing* Scripture, i.e., as sanctioning articles of faith not contained in Scripture. Tradition is recognised as authoritative in two ways : (1) Negatively, in the sense that doctrines which are novel are *prima acie* condemned by the very fact (*de Decr.* 7, note 2, *ib.* 18, *Orat.* i. 8, 10, ii. 34, 40, *de Syn.* 3, 6, 7, and *Letter* 59, § 3) ; and (2) positively, as furnishing a guide to the sense of Scripture (see references in note on *Orat.* iii. 58, end of ch. xxix.). In other words, tradition with Athanasius is a formal, not a material, source of doctrine. His language exemplifies the necessity of distinguishing, in the case of strong patristic utterances on the authority of tradition, between different senses of the word. Often it means simply truth conveyed *in Scripture*, and in that sense 'handed down' from the first, as for example *c. Apol.* i. 22, 'the Gospel tradition,' and *Letter* 60. 6 (cf. Cypr. *Ep.* 74. 10, where Scripture is 'divinæ traditionis caput et origo.'). Moreover, tradition as distinct from Scripture is with Athanasius not a secret unwritten body of teaching handed down orally [1], but is to be found in the *documents* of antiquity and the writings of the Fathers, such as those to whom he appeals in *de Decr.*, &c. That 'the appeal of Athanasius was to Scripture, that of the Arians to tradition' (Gwatkin) is an overstatement, in part supported by the pre-Nicene history of the word ὁμοούσιον (*supra*, p. xxxi. *sq.*). The rejection of this word by the Antiochene Council (in 268-9) is met by Athanasius, *de Synod.* 43, *sqq.*, partly by an appeal to still older witnesses in its favour, parly by the observation (§ 45) that 'writing in simplicity [the Fathers] arrived not at accuracy concerning the ὁμοούσιον, but spoke of the word as they understood it,' an argument strangely like that of the Homœans (Creed of Niké, *ib.* § 30) that the Fathers [of *Nicæa*] *adopted* the word 'in simplicity.'

(*d*) Connected with the function and authority of tradition is that of the Church. On the essential idea of the Church there is little or nothing of definite statement. The term 'Catholic Church' is of course commonly used, both of the Church as a whole, and of the orthodox body in this or that place. The unity of the Church is emphatically dwelt on in the opening of the encyclical written in the name of Alexander (*infr.*, p. 69 and *supr.*, p. xvi.) as the reason for communicating the deposition of Arius at Alexandria to the Church at large. 'The joyful mother of children' (*Exp. in Ps.* cxiii. 9) is interpreted of the Gentile Church, 'made to keep house,' ἅτε τὸν Κύριον ἔνοικον ἔχουσα, joyful 'because her children are saved through faith in Christ,' whereas those of the 'synagogue' are ἀπωλείᾳ παραδεδομένα : the 'strong city' πόλις περιοχῆς and 'Edom' of Ps. lx. 11 are likewise interpreted of the Church as gathered from all nations ; similarly the Ethiopians of Ps. lxxxvii. 4 (where the *de Tit. pss.* gives a quite different and more allegorical sense, referring the verse to baptism). The full perfection of the Church is referred by Athanasius not to the (even ideal) Church on earth but to the Church in heaven. The kingdom of God' (Matt. vi. 33) is explained as 'the enjoyment of the good things of the

---

[1] The idea of a mysterious unwritten tradition is a legacy of Gnosticism to the Church. Irenæus, in order to meet the Gnostic appeal to a supposed unwritten Apostolic tradition, confronts it with the consistency of the public and normal teaching of the Churches everywhere, of which the Roman Church is a convenient microcosm or compendium. The idea of a παράδοσις ἄγραφος is adopted by Clement and Origen, and passes from the latter to Eusebius, and to the Cappadocian Fathers (Basil *de Sp. S.* 27), applies it only to *practical* details), Epiphanius, and later writers. Details in Harnack ii. 90, note, cf. Salmon, *Infallibility*, Lect. ix. On the somewhat different subject of the 'Disciplina Arcani,' see Herzog-Plitt, *s.v.* 'Arkan-Disciplin.'

future, namely the contemplation and knowledge of God so far as man's soul is capable of it,' while the city of Ps. lxxxvii. 1—3 is ἡ ἄνω Ἱερουσαλήμ in the *de Titulis*, but in the *Expositio* the Church glorified by 'the indwelling of the Only-begotten.' In all this we miss any decisive utterance as to the *doctrinal authority* of the Church except in so far as the recognition of such authority is involved in what has been cited above in favour of tradition. It may be said that the conditions which lead the mind to throw upon the Church the weight of responsibility for what is believed were absent in the case of Athanasius as indeed in the earlier Greek Church generally.

But Athanasius was far from undervaluing the evidence of the Church's tradition. The organ by which the tradition of the Church does its work is the teaching function of her officers, especially of the Episcopate (*de Syn.* 3, &c.). But to provide against erroneous teaching on the part of bishops, as well as to provide for the due administration of matters affecting the Church generally, and for ecclesiastical legislation, some authority beyond that of the individual bishop is necessary. This necessity is met, in the Church as conceived by Athanasius, in two ways, firstly by Councils, secondly in the pre-eminent authority of certain sees which exercise some sort of jurisdiction over their neighbours. Neither of these resources of Church organisation meets us, in Athanasius, in a completely organised shape. A word must be said about each separately, then about their correlation.

(*a*) *Synods.* Synods as a part of the machinery of the Church grew up spontaneously. The meeting of the 'Apostles and Elders' at Jerusalem (Acts xv.) exemplifies the only way in which a practical resolution on a matter affecting a number of persons with independent rights can possibly be arrived at, viz., by mutual discussion and agreement. Long before the age of Athanasius it had been recognised in the Church that the bishops were the persons exclusively entitled to represent their flocks for such a purpose ; in other words, Councils of bishops had come to constitute the legislative and judicial body in the Church (Eus. *V.C.* i. 51). Both of these functions, and especially the latter, involved the further prerogative of judging of doctrine, as in the case of Paul of Samosata. But the whole system had grown up out of occasional emergencies, and no recognised laws existed to define the extent of conciliar authority, or the relations between one Council and another should their decisions conflict. Not even the area covered by the jurisdiction of a given Council was defined (*Can. Nic.* 5). We see a Synod at Arles deciding a case affecting Africa, and reviewing the decision of a previous Synod at Rome ; a Council at Tyre trying the case of a bishop of Alexandria ; a Council at Sardica in the West deposing bishops in the East, and restoring those whom Eastern Synods had deposed ; we find Acacius and his fellows deposed at Seleucia, then in a few weeks deposing their deposers at Constantinople ; Meletius appointed and deposed by the same Synod at Antioch in 361, and in the following year resuming his see without question. All is chaos. The extent to which a Synod succeeds in enforcing its decisions depends on the extent to which it obtains *de facto* recognition. The canons of the Council of Antioch (341) are accepted as Church law, while its creeds are condemned as Arian (*de Syn.* 22—25).

We look in vain for any statement of principle on the part of Athanasius to reduce this confusion to order. The classical passage in his writings is the letter he has preserved from Julius of Rome to the Eastern bishops (*Apol. c. Ar.* 20—35). The Easterns insist strongly on the authority of Councils, in the interests of their deposition of Athanasius, &c., at Tyre. Julius can only reply by invoking an old-established custom of the Church, ratified, he says, at Nicæa (*Can.* 5 ?), that the decisions of one Council may be revised by another; a process which leads to no finality. The Sardican canons of three years later drew up, for judicial purposes only, a system of procedure, devolving on Julius (or possibly on the Roman bishop for the time being) the duty of deciding, upon the initiative of the parties concerned, whether in the case of a deposed bishop a new trial of the case was desirable, and permitting him to take part in such new trial by his deputies. But Athanasius never alludes to any such procedure, nor to the canons in question. (Compare above, pp. xlii., xlvi.).

The absence of any *a priori* law relating to the authority of Synods applies to general as well as to local Councils. The conception of a general Council did not give rise to Nicæa, but *vice versa* (see above, p. xvii.). The precedent for great Councils had already been set at Antioch (268-9) and Arles (314); the latter in fact seems to be indirectly called by S. Augustine *plenarium universæ ecclesiæ concilium ;* but the widely representative character of the Nicene Council, and the impressive circumstances under which it met, stamped upon it from the first a recognised character of its own. Again and again (*de Decr.* 4, 27, *Orat.* i. 7, *Ep. Æg.* 5, &c., &c.) Athanasius presses the Arians with their rejection of the decision of a 'world-wide' Council, contrasting it (e.g. *de Syn.* 21) with the numerous and indecisive Councils held by them. He protests (*Ep. Æg.* 5, *Tom. ad Ant.*, &c.) against the idea that any new creed is necessary or to be desired in addition to the Nicene. But in doing so, he does not suggest by a syllable that the Council was formally and *a priori* infallible, independently of the character of its decision as faithfully corresponding to the tradition of the Apostles. Its authority is secondary to that of Scripture (*de Syn.* 6, *sub. fin.*), and its scriptural character is its justification (*ib.*). In short, Mr. Gwatkin speaks within the mark when he disclaims for Athan. any mechanical theory[2] of conciliar infallibility. To admit this candidly is not to depreciate, but to acknowledge, the value of the great Synod of Nicæa ; and to acknowledge it, not on the technical grounds of later ecclesiastical law, but on grounds which are those of Athanasius himself. (On the general subject see D.C.A. 475—484, and Hatch, *B.L.* vii.)

(β) *Jurisdiction of bishops over bishops.* The fully-developed and organised 'patriarchal' system does not meet us in the Nicene age. The bishops of important towns, however, exercise a very real, though not definable authority over their neighbours. This is especially true of Imperial residences. The migration of Eusebius to Nicomedia and afterwards to Constantinople broke through the time-honoured rule of the Church, but set the precedent commonly followed ever afterwards. In Egypt, although the name 'patriarch' was as yet unheard, the authority of the Bishop of Alexandria was almost absolute. The name 'archbishop' is here used for the first time. It is first applied apparently to Meletius (*Apol. Ar.* 71) in his list of clergy, but at a later date (about 358) to Athanasius in a contemporary inscription (see p. 564*, note 1). At the beginning of his episcopate (*supra,* p. xxxvii.) we find him requested to ordain in a diocese of Upper Egypt by its bishop. He sends bishops on deputations (*Fest. Ind.* xxv., &c.), and exercises ordinary jurisdiction over bishops and people of Libya and Pentapolis (cf. reference to Synesius, *supr.,* p. lxii.). This was a condition of things dating at least from the time of Dionysius (p. 178, note 2). In particular he had practically the appointment of bishops for all Egypt, so that in the course of his long episcopate all the Egyptian sees were manned by his faithful adherents (cf. p. 493). The mention of Dionysius suggests the question of the relation of the see of Alexandria to that of Rome, and of the latter to the Church generally. On the former point, what is necessary will be said in the Introd. to the *de Sent. Dion.* With regard to the wider question, Athanasius expresses reverence for that bishopric 'because it is *an* Apostolic throne,' and 'for Rome, because it is the metropolis of Romania' (p. 282). That is his only utterance on the subject. Such reverence ought, he says, to have secured Liberius from the treatment to which he had been subjected. The language cited excludes the idea of any divinely-given headship of the Church vested in the Roman bishop, for his object is to magnify the outrageous conduct of Constantius and the Arians. Still less can anything be elicited from the account given by Ath. of the case of the Dionysii, or of his own relations to successive Roman bishops. He speaks of them as his beloved brothers and fellow-ministers (e.g., p. 489) and cordially welcomes their sympathy and powerful support, without any thought of jurisdiction. But he furnishes us with materials, in the letter of Julius, for estimating not his own view of the Roman see, but that held by its occupant. The origin of the proceedings was the endeavour of the Easterns to procure recognition at Rome and in the West for their own nominee to the bishopric of Alexandria. They had requested Julius to hold a Council, 'and to be himself the judge if he so pleased' (*Apol. c. Ar.* 20). This was intended to frighten Athanasius, but not in the least, as the sequel shews, to submit the decisions of a Council to revision by a single bishop. Julius summoned a Council as described above (p. xliii.), and at the end of a long period of delay and controversy sent a letter expressing his view of the case to the Orientals. This document has been already discussed (p. xliv.). It forms an important landmark in the history of papal claims, standing at least as significantly in contrast with those of the successors of Julius, as with those of his predecessors.

(γ) *Bishops and Councils.* The superiority of councils to single bishops (including those

---

[2] What is conspicuously true of the Second General Council is in reality not less true of the First. Its high authority to later ages is due not to its formal character as a council, but to the character of its work ; the consent of the Church, and that not readily given, but as the result of a long process of searching and sifting, has given to it its 'irreformable' authority. Its authority *is expressly put on a par with that of the Antiochene Synod* of c. 269, by Ath. *de Syn.* 43 (consult the whole discussion, pp. 473, 475, &c.). Short of a council which should include every bishop of the entire Church, in unanimous agreement,—an impossible contingency,— the claim of any given council to be truly ecumenical are relative, not absolute ; and no consistent theory is possible of the conditions under which a council could *by virtue of its constitution* claim infallibility for its decisions. The supposed infallibility of general councils lies in reality outside them, in the authority which sanctions and consecrates their decisions. According to the precedent of Nicæa this is the Church 'diffusive' (cf. p. 489, and Pusey, *Councils,* p. 225, *sq.*), and such consent, again, must necessarily be partial and relative. If a more tangible and expeditious theory is wanted, we have it in the Roman system, according to which a council is infallible if ratified by the Pope. This at once puts all such councils, whether local or general, on one level, and affords a ready criterion. In other words, the only consistent (mechanical) theory of the infallibility of councils is one which makes councils superfluous. If such a theory had been known to the Church in the age of councils, the councils would not have been held.

of Rome, Alexandria, and Antioch) was questioned by no one in this age.   Julius claims the support, not of authority inherent in his see, but of *canons*, and on the basis of them claims a voice in matters affecting the Church at large, not in his own name, but in that of 'us all, that so a just sentence might proceed from *all*' (*Apol. c. Ar.* 35).   Again, just as the judgment of his predecessor Melchiades and his council was revised at Arles in 314 (Augustin. *Ep.* 105. 8), so the case of Athanasius and Marcellus was reheard at the Council of Sardica three years after the decision of Julius and his council.   The council was the supreme organ of the Church for legislative, judicial, and doctrinal purposes; had any other of superior or even equal rank been recognised, or had the authority of councils themselves been defined *a priori* by a system of Church law, the confusion of the fourth century would not have arisen.   Whether or no the age would have gained, we at least should have been the losers.

§ 5. *Content of Revelation.   God Three in One and the Incarnation.*

To dwell at length on the theology of Athanasius under this head is unnecessary here, not because there is little to say, but partly because what there is to say has been to some extent anticipated above, §§ 2, 3, and ch. ii. pp. xxxii., xxxvi., partly because the history of his life and work is the best exposition of what he believed and taught.   That his theology on these central subjects was profoundly moulded by the Nicene formula is (to the present writer at least) the primary fact (see ch. ii. § 3 (1), and (2) b).   This of course presupposes that the Nicene faith found in him a character and mind prepared to become its interpreter and embodiment; and that this was so his pre-Nicene writings sufficiently shew.

For instance, his progressive stress on the Unity of the Godhead in Father, Son, and Spirit is but the following up of the thought expressed *de Incarn.* 17. 1 ἐν μόνῳ τῷ ἑαυτοῦ Πατρὶ ὅλος ὢν κατὰ πάντα.   It may be noted that he argues also from the idea of the Trinity to the coessential Godhead of the Spirit, *ad Serap.* i. 28, *sq.*, Τριὰς δέ ἐστιν οὐχ ἕως ὀνομάτος μόνον ... ἀλλὰ ἀληθείᾳ καὶ ὑπάρξει τριάς· ... εἰπάτωσαν πάλιν ... τριάς ἐστιν ἢ δυάς; and that he meets the difficulty (see *infra*, p. 438, ten lines from end, also Petav. *Trin.* VII. xiv.) of differentiating the relation of the Spirit to the Father from the γέννησις of the Son by a confession of ignorance and a censure upon those who assume that they can search out the deep things of God (*ib.* 17—19).   The principle might be applied to this point which is laid down *de Decr.* 11, that 'an act' belonging to the essence of God, cannot, by virtue of the simplicity of the Divine Nature, be more than one: the 'act' therefore of divine γέννησις (the nature of which we do not know) cannot apply to the Spirit but only to the Son.   But I do not recollect any passage in which Athanasius draws this conclusion from his own premises.   The language of Athanasius on the procession of the Spirit is unstudied.   In *Exp. Fid.* 4, he appears to adopt the 'procession' of the Spirit from the Father *through* the Son (after Dionysius, see *Sent. Dion.* 17).   In *Serap.* i. 2, 20, 32, iii. 1, he speaks of the Spirit as ἴδιον τοῦ Λόγου, just as the Word is ἴδιος τοῦ Πατρός.   His language on the subject, expressing the *idea* common to East and West (under the cloud of logomachies which envelop the subject) might possibly furnish the basis of an ' eirenicon ' between the two separated portions of Christendom.   In explaining the 'theophanies' of the Old Testament, Athanasius takes a position intermediate between that of the Apologists, &c. (*supr.*, p. xxiii.) who referred them to the Word, and that of Augustine who referred them to Angels only.   According to Athanasius the 'Angel' was and was not the Word : regarded as visible he was an Angel simply, but the Voice was the Divine utterance through the Word (see *Orat.* iii. 12, 14 ; *de Syn* 27, Anath 15, note; also *Serap.* i. 14).

Lastly, it must again be insisted that in his polemic against Arianism Athanasius is centrally soteriological.   It is unnecessary to collect passages in support of what will be fully appreciated only after a thorough study of the controversial treatises.   The essence of his position is comprised in his paraphrase of St. Peter's address to the Jews, *Orat.* ii. 16, *sq.*, or in the argument, *ib.* 67, *sqq.*, i. 43, and iii. 13.   With regard to the Incarnation, it may be admitted that Athanasius uses language which might have been modified had he had later controversies in view.   His common use of ἄνθρωπος for the Manhood of Christ (see below, p. 83) might be alleged by the Nestorian, his comparison of it to the vesture of the High Priest (*Orat.* i. 47, ii. 8, see note there) by the Apollinarian or Monophysite partisan.   But at least his use of either class of expressions shews that he did not hold the doctrine associated in later times with the other.   Moreover, while from first to last he is explicitly clear as to the seat of personality in Christ, which is uniformly assigned to the Divine Logos (p. 40, note 2 and reff.), the integrity of the manhood of Christ is no less distinctly asserted (cf. *de Incarn.* 18. 1, 21. 7). He uses σῶμα and ἄνθρωπος indifferently during the earlier stages of the conflict, ignoring or failing to notice the peculiarity of the Luciano-Arian Christology. But from 362 onward the full integrity of the Saviour's humanity, σὰρξ and ψυχὴ λογικὴ or πνεῦμα, is energetically asserted against the theory of Apollinarius and those akin to it[3] (cf. *Letters* 59 and 60, and *c. Apoll.*). Some corollaries of this doctrine must now be mentioned.

The question of the *sinlessness* of Christ is not discussed by Athanasius *ex professo* until the controversy with Apollinarianism. In the earlier Arian controversy the question was in reality involved, partly by the Arian theory of the τρεπτότης of the Word, partly by the correlated theory of προκοπή (cf. *Orat.* ii. 6, *sqq.*), and Athanasius instinctively falls back on the consideration that the *Personality* of the Son, if Divine, is necessarily sinless. In *c. Apoll.* i. 7, 17, ii. 10 the question is more thoroughly analysed. The complete *psychological* identity of Christ's human nature with our own is maintained along with the absolute *moral* identity of His will (θέλησις, the determination of will, not the θέλημα οὐσιῶδες or volitional faculty) with the Divine will.

With regard to the *human knowledge* of Christ, the texts Mark xiii. 32, Luke ii. 52, lie at the foundation of his discussion *Orat.* iii. 42—53. The Arians appealed to these passages to support the contention that the *Word*, or Son of God in His Divine nature, was ignorant of 'the Day,' and advanced in knowledge. The whole argument of Athan. in reply is directed to shewing that these passages apply not to the Word or Son in Himself, but to the Son *Incarnate.* He knows as God, is ignorant as man. Omniscience is the attribute of Godhead, ignorance is proper to man. The Incarnation was not the sphere of advancement to the Word, but of humiliation and condescension; but the Manhood advanced in wisdom *as it did in stature* also, for advance belongs to man. That is the decisive and clear-cut position of Athanasius on this subject (which the notes there vainly seek to accommodate to the rash dogmatism of the schools). Athanasius appeals to the utterances of Christ which imply knowledge transcending human limitations in order to shew that such knowledge, or rather all knowledge, was possessed *by the Word;* in other words such utterances belong to the class of 'divine' not to that of 'human' phenomena in the life of Christ. So far as His human nature was concerned, He assumed its limitations of knowledge equally with all else that belongs to the physical and mental endowments of man. Why then was not Divine Omniscience exerted by Him at all times? This question is answered as all questions must be which arise out of any limitation of the Omnipotence of God in the Manhood of Christ. It was 'for our profit, as I at least think' (*ib.* 48). The very idea of the Incarnation is that of a *limiting* of the Divine under human conditions, the Divine being manifested in Christ only so far as the Wisdom of God has judged it necessary in order to carry out the purpose of His coming. In other words, Athanasius regarded the ignorance of Christ as 'economical' only in so far as the Incarnation is itself an οἰκονομία, a measured revelation, at once a veiling and a manifestation, of all that is in God. That the divine Omniscience wielded in the man Christ Jesus an adequate instrument for its own manifestation Athanasius firmly holds: the exact extent to which such manifestation was carried, the reserve of miraculous power or knowledge with which that Instrument was used, must be explained not by reference to the human mind, will, or character of Christ, but to the Divine Will and Wisdom which alone has both effected our redemption and knows the secrets of its bringing about. With Athanasius, we may quote St. Paul, τίς ἔγνω νοῦν Κυρίου.

It may be observed before leaving this point that Athanasius takes occasion (§ 43, *fin.*, cf. 45) to distinguish two senses of the words 'the Son,' as referring on the one hand to the eternal, on the other to the human existence of Christ. To the latter he limits Mark xiii. 32: the point is of importance in view of his relation to Marcellus (*supra*, p. xxxvi.).

As a further corollary of the Incarnation we may notice his frequent use (*Orat.* iii. 14, 29, 33, iv. 32, *c. Apoll.* i. 4, 12, 21) of the word θεοτόκος as an epithet or as a name for the Virgin Mary. The translation 'Mother of God' is of course erroneous. 'God-bearer' (Gottes-bärerin), the literal equivalent, is scarcely idiomatic English. The perpetual virginity of Mary is maintained incidentally (*c. Apoll.* i. 4), but there is an entire absence in his writings not only of worship of the Virgin, but of 'Mariology,' *i.e.*, of the tendency to assign to her

---

[3] The doctrine of Athanasius is, not formally but none the less really, the doctrine of Chalcedon, which again stands or falls together with that of Nicæa. Like the latter, it transcends the power of human thought to do more than state it in terms which exclude the (Nestorian and Monophysite) alternatives. The Man Jesus Christ is held to have *lacked* nothing that constitutes personality in man; the human personality which therefore belongs to it *ideally*, being *in fact* merged in the Divine personality of the Son. The 'impersonality,' as it is sometimes called, of Christ quâ man is therefore better spoken of as His *Divine* Personality. Personality and will are correlated but not identical ideas.

a personal agency, or any peculiar place, in the work of Redemption (Gen. iii. 15, *Vulg.*). Further, the argument of *Orat.* i. 51 *fin.*, that the sending of Christ in the flesh *for the first time* (λοιπόν) liberated human nature from sin, and enabled the requirement of God's law to be fulfilled in man (an argument strictly within the lines of Rom. viii. 3), would be absolutely wrecked by the doctrine of the freedom of Mary from original sin ('immaculate conception'). If that doctrine be held, sin was ' condemned in the flesh' (*i.e.*, first deposed from its place in human nature, see Gifford or Meyer-Weiss *in loc.*), not by the sending of Christ, but by the congenital sinlessness of Mary. If the Arians had only known of the latter doctrine, they would have had an easy reply to that powerful passage.

§ 6. *Derivative doctrines. Grace and the Means of Grace ; the Christian Life ; the last things.*

The idea of Grace is important to the theological system of Athanasius, in view of the central place occupied in that system by the idea of restoration and new creation as the specific work of Christ upon His fellow-men (*supra*, § 2, cf. *Orat.* ii. 56, *Exp. in Pss.* xxxiii. 2, cxviii. 5, LXX.). But, in common with the Greek Fathers generally, he does not analyse its operation, nor endeavour to fix its relation to free will (cf. *Orat.* i. 37 *fin.*, iii. 25 *sub fin.*). The divine predestination relates (for anything that Ath. says) not to individuals so much as to the Purpose of God, before all ages, to repair the foreseen evil of man's fall by the Incarnation (*Orat.* ii. 75, *sq.*). On the general subject of Sacraments and their efficacy, he says little or nothing. The initiatory rite of Baptism makes us sons of God (*de Decr.* 31, cf. *Orat.* i. 37 *ut supra*), and is the only complete renewal to be looked for in this life, *Serap.* iv. 13). It is accompanied (*de Trin. et Sp. S.* 7) by confession of faith in the Trinity, and the baptism administered by Arians who do not really hold this faith is therefore in peril of losing its value (*Orat.* ii. 42, *fin.*). The grace of the Spirit conferred at baptism will be finally withdrawn from the wicked at the last judgment (*Exp. in Ps.* lxxv. 13, LXX.). In the *de Trin. et Sp. S.* 21 baptism is coupled with the imposition of hands as one rite. On the Eucharist there is an important passage (*ad Serap.* iv. 19), which must be given in full. He has been speaking of sin against the Holy Spirit, which latter name he applies [see above, ch. iii. § 1 (22)] to the Saviour's Divine Personality. He proceeds to illustrate this by John vi. 62—64.

' For here also He has used both terms of Himself, flesh and spirit ; and He distinguished the spirit from what is of the flesh in order that they might believe not only in what was visible in Him, but in what was invisible, and so understand that what He says is not fleshly, but spiritual. For for how many would the body suffice as food, for it to become meat even for the whole world? But this is why He mentioned the ascending of the Son of Man into heaven ; namely, to draw them off from their corporeal idea, and that from thenceforth they might understand that the aforesaid flesh was heavenly from above, and spiritual meat, to be given at His hands. For 'what I have said unto you,' says He, ' is spirit and life ;' as much as to say, ' what is manifested, and to be given for the salvation of the world, is the flesh which I wear. But this, and the blood from it, shall be given to you spiritually at My hands as meat, so as to be imparted spiritually in each one, and to become for all a preservative to resurrection of life eternal.'

Beyond this he does not define the relation of the outward and visible in the Eucharist to the spiritual and inward. The *reality* of the Eucharistic gift is insisted on as strongly as its spirituality in such passages as *ad Max.* (*Letter* 61) 2 *sub fin.*, and the comment on Matt. vii. 6 (Migne xxvii. 1380), 'See to it, therefore, Deacon, that thou do not administer to the unworthy the purple of the sinless body,' and the protest of the Egyptian bishops (*Apol. c. Ar.* 5) that their churches 'are adorned only by the blood of Christ and by the pious worship of Him.' The Holy Table is expressly stated to have been made of wood (*Hist. Ar.* 56), and was situated (*Apol. Fug.*) in a space called the ἱερατεῖον. The Eucharist was celebrated in most places every Sunday, but not on week-days (*Apol. c. Ar.* 11). But in Alexandria we hear of it being celebrated on a Friday on one occasion, and this was apparently a normal one (*Apol. Fug.* 24, *Apol. Const.* 25). To celebrate the Eucharist was the office of the bishop or presbyter (*Apol. c. Ar.* 11). Ischyras (*supr.* p. xxxviii.) was held by Athanasius to be a layman only, and therefore incapable of offering the Eucharist. The sacrificial aspect of the Eucharist is not touched upon, except in the somewhat strange fragment (Migne xxvi. 1259) from an *Oratio de defunctis*, which contains the words ἡ δέ γε ἀναίμακτος θυσία ἐξιλασμός. He insists on the finality of the sacrifice of the Cross, *Orat.* ii. 9, αἱ μὲν γὰρ κατὰ νόμον . . . οὐκ εἶχον τὸ πιστόν, καθ' ἡμέραν παρερχόμεναι· ἡ δὲ τοῦ Σωτῆρος θυσία ἅπαξ γενομένη τετελείωκε τὸ πᾶν. On repentance and the confession of sins there is little to quote. He strongly asserts the efficacy of repentance, and explains Heb. vi. 4, of the *unique* cleansing and restoring power of baptism (*Serap.* iv. 13, as cited above.) A catena on Jeremiah preserves a fragment [*supra*, ch. iii. § 1 (38)], which compares the ministry of the priest in baptism to that in confession : οὕτως καὶ ὁ ἐξομολογούμενος ἐν μετανοίᾳ διὰ τοῦ ἱερέως λαμβάνει τὴν ἄφεσιν χάριτι Χριστοῦ. Of compulsory confession, or even of this ordinance as an ordinary element of the Christian life, we read nothing.

On the Christian ministry again there is little direct teaching. The ordinations by the presbyter Colluthus (*Apol. Ar.* 11, 12) are treated as null. The letter (49) to Dracontius contains vigorous and beautiful passages on the responsibility of the Ministry. On the principles of Christian conduct there is much to be gathered from *obiter dicta* in the writings of Athanasius. His description (cf. *supra*, p. xlviii.) of the revival of religious life at Alexandria in 346, and the exhortations in the Easter letters, are the most conspicuous passages for this purpose. In particular, he insists (e.g., p. 67) on the necessity of a holy life and pure mind for the apprehension of divine things, and especially for the study of the Scriptures. He strongly recommends the discipline of fasting, in which, as compared with other churches (Rome especially), the Alexandrian Christians were lax (*Letter* 12), but he warns them in his first Easter letter to fast 'not only with the body, but also with the soul.' He also dwells (*Letter* 6) on the essential difference of spirit between Christian festivals and Jewish observance of days. Christ is the true Festival, embracing the whole of the Christian life (*Letters* 5, 14). He lays stress on love to our neighbour, and especially on kindness to the poor (*Letter* i. 11, *Hist. Ar.* 61, *Vit. Ant.* 17, 30). On one important practical point he is very emphatic: 'Persecution is a device of the devil' (*Hist. Ar.* 33). This summary judgment was unfortunately less in accordance with the spirit of the times than with the Spirit of Christ.

The ascetic teaching of Athanasius must be reserved for the introduction to the *Vita Antoni* (cf. *Letters* 48, 49, also above, p. xlviii.). His eschatology calls for discussion in connection with the language of the *de Incarnatione*, and will be briefly noticed in the introduction to that tract. With regard to prayers for the departed, he distinguishes (on Luke xiii. 21, &c., Migne xxvii. 1404) the careless, whose friends God will move to assist them with their prayers, from the utterly wicked who are beyond the help of prayer.

CHAPTER V.

CHRONOLOGY AND TABLES.

§ 1. SOURCES. (1) The *Festal Letters* of Athanasius with their *Index* and the *Historia Acephala* constitute our primary source for chronological details (see below, § 2). (2) Along with these come the chronological notices scattered up and down the other writings of Athanasius. These are of course of the utmost importance, but too often lack definiteness. (3) The chronological data in the fifth-century historians, headed by Socrates, are a mass of confusion, and have been a source of confusion ever since, until the discovery of the primary sources, No. (1) mentioned above. They must, therefore, be used only in strict subordination to the latter. (4) More valuable but less abundant secondary notices are to be derived from the Life of Pachomius, from the letter of Ammon (*infra*, p. 487), and from other writers of the day. (5) For the movements of the Emperors the laws in the *Codex Theodosianus* (ed. Hänel in *Corpus Juris Ante-Justiniani*) give many dates, but the text is not in a satisfactory condition.

(6) *Modern discussions.* The conflicting attempts at an Athanasian chronology prior to the discovery of the Festal Letters are tabulated in the Appendix to Newman's *Arians*, and discussed by him in his introduction to the *Historical Tracts* (Oxf. Lib. Fathers). The notes to Dr. Bright's article ATHANASIUS in D.C.B., and his introduction to the *Hist. Writings of S. Ath.*, may be profitably consulted, as also may Larsow's *Fest-briefe* (Leipz., 1852), with useful calendar information by Dr. J. G. Galle, the veteran professor of Astronomy at Breslau, and Sievers on the *Hist. Aceph.* (*Supr.* ch. i. § 3.)

But by far the most valuable chronological discussions are those of Prof. Gwatkin in his *Studies of Arianism*. He has been the first to make full use of the best data, and moreover gives very useful lists of the great officials of the Empire and of the movements of the Eastern Emperors. Mr. Gwatkin's results were criticised in the *Church Quarterly Review*, vol. xvi. pp. 392—398, 1883, by an evidently highly-qualified hand [1]. The criticisms of the Reviewer have been most carefully weighed by the present writer, although they quite fail to shake him in his general agreement with Mr. Gwatkin's results.

---

[1] The candid, but friendly, and often just, criticisms on Mr. Gwatkin's book do not concern us here. But the Reviewer's chronological strictures are his weakest point: he uses his texts without criticism, and falls far short of Mr. Gwatkin's standard of searching historical method.

For the general chronology of the period we may mention Weingarten's *Zeit-tafeln* (ed. 3, 1888) as useful, though not especially so for our purpose, and above all Clinton's *Fasti Romani*, which, however, were drawn up in the dark ages before the discovery of the *Festal Letters*, and are therefore antiquated so far as the life of Athanasius is concerned.

§ 2. PRINCIPLES AND METHOD. The determination of the leading Athanasian dates depends mainly on the value to be assigned to the primary sources, § 1 (1). Reserving the fuller discussion of these texts for the Introduction to the *Letters* (pp. 495 *sq.*, 500 *sq.*), it will suffice to state here what seem to be the results of an investigation of their value. (1) The *Historia Acephala* and *Festal Index* are independent of each other (cf. Sievers, p. 95, misunderstood, I think, by Mr. Gwatkin, p. 221). (2) They both belong to the generation after the death of Athanasius, the *H.A.* being apparently the earlier. (3) The data as to which they agree must, therefore, come from a source prior to either, i.e., contemporary with Athanasius. (4) In several important particulars they are confirmed by our secondary Egyptian sources, such as the *Letter of Ammon* and *Life of Pachomius*. (5) They verify most of the best results arrived at independently of them (of this below), and (6) In no case do they agree in fixing a date which can be proved to be wrong, or which there are sound reasons for distrusting. On these grounds I have classed the *Historia* and *Index* as primary sources, and maintain that the dates as to which the two documents agree must be accepted as certain. This principle at once brings the doubtful points in the chronology within very moderate limits. The general chronological table, in which the dates fixed by the agreement of these sources are printed in black type, will make this plain enough. It remains to shew that the principle adopted works out well in detail, or in other words, that the old Alexandrian chronology, transmitted to us through the twofold channel of the *Historia* and the *Index*, harmonises the apparent discrepancies, and solves the difficulties, of the chronological statements of Athanasius, and tallies with the most trustworthy information derived from other sources. In some cases it has been found desirable to discuss points of chronology where they occur in the Life of Athanasius; what will be attempted here is to complete what is there passed over without thorough discussion, in justification of the scheme adopted in our general chronological table.

§ 3. APPLICATIONS. (a) *Death of Alexander and Election of Athanasius.* That the latter took place on June 8, 328, is established by the agreement of our sources, together with the numbering of the Festal Letters. Theodoret (*H.E.* i. 26) and others, misled by some words of Athanasius (*Apol. c. Ar.* 59), handed down to later ages the statement that Alexander died five months after the Council of Nicæa. It had long been seen that this must be a mistake (Tillemont, vi. 736, Montfaucon, *Monit. in Vit. S. Athan.*) and various suggestions[2] were made as to the *terminus a quo* for the 'five months' mentioned by Athanasius; that of Montfaucon remains the most probable (see ch. ii. § 3 (1), p. xxi.). But the field was left absolutely clear for the precise and concordant statement of our chroniclers, which, therefore, takes undisputed possession. (Further details, *supr.* p. xx. *sq.*; Introd. to *Letters*, pp. 495, 303).

(b) *The first exile of Athanasius.* The duration is fixed by the *Hist. Aceph.* (see Introd. p. 495, *sq.*) as two years, four months, and eleven days, and this exactly coincides with the dates given by the *Index* for his departure for Tyre, July 11, 335, and his return from exile Nov. 23, 337 (not 338; for the Diocletian year began at the end of August). Although, therefore, the *Hist. Aceph.* is not available for the date, the constructive agreement between it and the *Index* is complete. But it has been contended that the year of the return from this exile must still be placed in 338, in spite of the new evidence to the contrary. The reasons alleged are very weak. (1) The letter of Constantine II., dated Treveri, June 17, so far from making against the year 337, clinches the argument in its favour. Constantine is still only 'Cæsar' when he writes it (pp. 146, 272); he was proclaimed Augustus on Sep. 9, 337 (Montf. *in ann.* 338 tries in vain to parry this decisive objection to the later date. He appeals to Maximin in Eus. *H.E.* ix. 10, but overlooks the word σεβαστός there. Is it conceivable that a disappointed eldest son, as sensitive about his claims as Constantine was, would within so short a time of becoming 'Augustus' be content to call himself merely 'Cæsar'?) The objection as to the distance of Treveri from Nicomedia has no weight, as we show elsewhere (p. xli., note 4); Constantine might have heard of his father's death a fortnight before the date of this letter. (2) The law (*Cod. Th.* X. x. 4) dated Viminacium, June 12, 338, if correctly ascribed to Constantius, would certainly lend plausibility to the view that it was at that time that Athanasius met Constantius at Viminacium (p. 240). But the names are so often con-

---

[2] E.g. that he died five months after *his return home* from the council (Tillem.), or after the *reconciliation of Meletius* (Montf.). | As neither event is dated, both hypotheses render the 'five months' useless for chronology.

fused in MSS., and the text of the Theodosian Code requires such frequent correction, that there is no solid objection to set against the extremely cogent proofs (Gwatkin, p. 138) that the law belongs to Constantine, who in that case cannot have been at Trier on June 17, 338. As to Constantius, there is no reason against his having been in Pannonia at some time in the summer of 337.   (3) The statement of Theodoret (*H.E.* ii. 1) that Ath. 'stayed at Treveri two years and four months' seems to reproduce that of the *Hist. Aceph.* as to the length of the exile, and is only verbally inexact in applying it to the period actually spent in Trier.   (4) The language of *Letter* 10, the Festal letter for 338, is not absolutely decisive, but §§ 3, 11 certainly imply that when it was written, whether at Alexandria or elsewhere, the durance of Athanasius was at an end.   There can, we submit, be no reasonable doubt that the first exile of Athanasius began with his departure from Alexandria on July 11, 335, and ended with his return thither on Nov. 23, 337.

(c) *Commencement of the second exile.*   Here again the agreement of our chronicles is constructive only, owing to the loss of the earlier part of the *Hist. Aceph.*; but it is none the less certain.   The exile ended, as everyone now admits and as both chronicles tell us, on Paoph. 24 (Oct. 21), 346: it lasted, according to the *H.A.*, seven years, six months, and three days.   This carries us back to Phar. 21 (April 16), 339.   Now we learn from the *Index* that he left the Church of Theonas on the night of Mar. 18–19, and from the *Encyclical*, 4, 5, that he took refuge first in another church, then in some secret place till over Easter Sunday (Apr. 15). This fits exactly with Apr. 16 as the date of his flight to Rome.   To this there is only one serious objection, viz., that Ath. was summoned (p. 239) to Milan by Constantius after the end of three years from his leaving Alexandria.   It has been assumed (without any proof) that this took place 'just before' the council of Sardica.   As a matter of fact, Constans left Athan. in Milan, and (apparently after his summer campaign) ordered him to follow him to Trier, in order to travel thence to the Council.   Athanasius does not state either how long he remained at Milan, or when he was ordered to Trier; for a chronological inference, in opposition to explicit evidence, he furnishes no basis whatever.   I agree with Mr. Gwatkin (whom his Reviewer quite misunderstands) in placing the Milan interview about May, 342, and the journey from Trier to Sardica after Easter (probably later still) in 343 (Constans was in Britain in the spring of 343, and had returned to Trier before June 30, *Cod. Th.* XII. i. 36, see also *supr.* p. xlv.). A more reasonable objection to the statement of the *Index* is that of Dr. Bright (p. xv. note 5), who sets against its information that Athan. fled from 'Theonas' four days *before* Gregory's arrival, the statement of the *Encyclical* that he left a certain church *after* Gregory's outrages at Eastertide.   But clearly Athan. first escaped from the church of Theonas, afterwards (between Good Friday and Easter) from some other church (ἄλλη ἐκκλησία), not named by him ('Quirinus,' cf. p. 95, note 1), and finally from the City itself.   (Dr. Bright's arguments in favour of 340 are vitiated in part by his placing Easter on April 9, i.e. on a Wednesday, instead of the proper day, Sunday, Mar. 30).   The date, April 16, 339, is, therefore, well established as the beginning of the second exile, and there is no tangible evidence against it.   It is, moreover, supported by the subscription to the letter to Serapion, which stands in the stead of the Easter letter for 340, and which states that the letter was written from Rome.

(d) *Council of Sardica and death of Gregory.*   The confusion into which the whole chronology of the surrounding events was thrown by the supposition (which was naturally taken without question upon the authority of Socrates and Sozomen) that the Sardican council met in 347, is reflected in the careful digest of opinions made by Newman (*Arians*, Appendix, or better, Introduction to *Hist. Treatises of S. Ath.* p. xxvi.; cf. also Hefele, Eng. Tra., vol. 2, p. 188, *sq.*, notes), and especially in the difficulties caused by the necessity of placing the Council of Milan in 345 before Sardica, and the mission of Euphrates of Cologne to Antioch as late as 348.   Now the *Hist. Aceph.*, by giving October, 346, as the date of the return of Athanasius from his second exile, at once challenged the received date for Sardica, and J. D. Mansi, the learned editor of the 'Collectio Amplissima' of the Councils, used this fact as the key to unlock the chronological tangle of the period.   He argued that the Council of Sardica must be put back at least as early as 344; but the natural conservatism of learning resisted his conclusions until the year 1852, when the *Festal Letters*, discovered ten years earlier, were made available for the theological public of Europe.   The date 347 was then finally condemned.   Not only did *Letter* 18, written at Easter, 345, refer to the Council's decision about Easter, and *Letter* 19 refer to his restoration as an accomplished fact; the Index most positively dated the synod in the year 343, which year has now taken its place as the accepted date, although the month and duration of the assembly are still open to doubt (*Supr.* p. xlv., note 6).   In any case it is certain that the Easter at which the deputies from Constans and the Council reached Antioch was Easter, 344. This brings us to the question of the date of Gregory's death. Mr. Gwatkin rightly connects the Council which deposed Stephen for his behaviour to the Western deputies, and elected Leontius, with the issue of the 'Macrostich' creed 'three years' (*de Syn.* 26) after the Council of the Dedication, i.e., in the summer of 344. This is our only notice of time for the Council in question, and it is not very precise ; but the Council may fairly be placed in the early summer, which would allow time for the necessary preliminaries after Easter, and for the meeting of the fathers at reasonable notice. (Perhaps Stephen was *promptly and informally* deposed (Thdt.) after Easter, but a regular council would be required to ratify this act and to elect his successor.) After the Council (we are again not told how long after) Constantius writes a public letter to Alexandria forbidding further persecution of the orthodox (p. 277, note 3). This may well have been in the later summer of 344. Then 'about ten months later' (*ib.*) Gregory dies. This would bring us 'about' to the early summer of 345 ; and this rough calculation [3] is curiously confirmed by the precise statement of the *Index* xviii., that Gregory died on June 26 (345, although the *Index*, in accordance with its principle of arrangement, which will be explained in the proper place, puts the notice under the following year). Of course the date of the letter of Constantius, which Athanasius gives as the *terminus a quo* of the 'ten months,' cannot be fixed except by conjecture, and the date given by the *Index* is (1) the only precise statement we have, (2) is likely enough in itself, and (3) agrees perfectly with the datum of *de Synod* 26. That is to say, as far as our evidence goes it appears to be correct.

(e) *Return of Athanasius in* 346. Here the precise statements of the *Index* and *Hist. Aceph.* agree, and are confirmed by *Letter* 19, which was written after his return. The date therefore requires no discussion. But it is important as a signal example of the high value to be assigned to the *united* witness of our two chronicles. For this is the pivot date which, in the face of all previously accepted calculations, has taken its place as unassailably correct, and has been the centre from which the recovery of the true chronology of the period has proceeded. The difficulty in dating the interview with Constantius at Antioch is briefly discussed p. xlvii. note 10.

(f) *Irruption of Syrianus and Intrusion of George.* The former event is dated without any room for doubt on the night of Thursday, Feb. 8 (Mechir 13), 356 (see p. 301, also *Index* and *Hist. Aceph.*). Here again the accuracy of our chronicles *on points where they agree* comes out strongly. It should be noted that an ill-informed writer could hardly have avoided a blunder here ; for 356 was a leap-year : and in consequence of this (1) all the months from Thoth to Phamenoth, inclusive, began a day later, owing to the additional *Epagomenon* before the first day of Thoth : the 13th Mechir would, therefore, in these years correspond to Feb. 8, not as usual to Feb. 7. (2) Owing to the Roman calendar inserting its intercalary day at the end of February, Feb. 8 would fall on the Thursday, not on the Friday (reckoning back from Easter on Apr. 7 : see Tables C, D., pp. 501 *sq.*). This date, then, may rank as one of the absolutely fixed points of our chronology. After the above examples of the value of the *concordant* testimony of the two chronicles, we must demand positive and circumstantial proof to the contrary before rejecting their united testimony that George made his entry into Alexandria in the Lent of 357, not 356. As a matter of fact all the *positive* evidence (*supr.*, p. lii., note 11) is the other way, and when weighed against it, the feather-weight of an inference from *a priori* probability, and from the assumed silence of Athanasius (*Ap. Fug.* 6), kicks the beam.

(g) *Athanasius in* 362. The difficulty here is that Athanasius clearly returned *after* the murder of George, which, according to Amm. Marc. XXII. xi., took place upon the receipt at Alexandria of the news of the execution of Artemius at Antioch, which latter event must be placed in July. Therefore Athanasius would not have returned till August, 362. On the other hand the *Hist. Aceph.* makes George *arrested four days after his return* to Alexandria, and immediately upon the proclamation of the new Emperor, Nov. 30, 361. On Dec. 24 George is murdered, on Feb. 9 the edict for the return of the exiles is promulged, and on Feb. 21 Athanasius returns, to take flight again 'eight months' later, on Oct. 24. The difficulty is so admirably sifted by Mr. Gwatkin (pp. 220, 221) that I refer to his discussion instead of giving one here. His conclusion is clearly right, viz., that Ammianus here, as occasionally elsewhere, has missed the right order of events, and that George was really murdered at the time stated in *Hist. Aceph.* The only addition to be made to Mr. Gwatkin's decisive argument is that

---

[1] The above *resumé* of the details of the evidence makes it clear that Mr. Gwatkin's alleged oversights are in reality those of his | critic. The proposal of the latter to correct 'Epiph.' in *Fest. Ind.* to 'Pharmuthi' is especially gratuitous.

Ammianus is inconsistent with himself, and in agreement with the *Hist. Aceph.*, in dating the arrest of George *shortly after his return from court*. As George would not have been at *Julian's* court, this notice implies that the arrest took place only shortly after the death of Constantius. Moreover, George, who even under Constantius was not over-ready to visit his see, and who knew well enough the state of heathen feeling against him, would not be likely to return to Alexandria after Julian had been six months on the throne. We have then not so much to balance Ammianus against the *Hist. Aceph.*, as to balance one of his statements, not otherwise confirmed, against another which is supported by the *Hist. Aceph.*, and by other authorities as well, especially Epiph. *Hær.* 76. 1. (The *Festal Index* gives no precise date here, except Oct. 24, for the flight of Athanasius, which so far as it goes confirms the *Hist. Aceph.*) Moreover, "on the side of Ammianus there is at worst an oversight; whereas the *Hist. Aceph.* would need to be re-written." The murder of George, Dec. 24, 361, return of Athanasius, Feb. 21, and his flight, Oct. 24, 362, may therefore be taken as firmly-established dates.

(h) *Supposed Council at Alexandria in* 363. This Synod assumed by Baronius, Montfaucon (*Vit. in Ann.* 363. 3) and others, after Theodoret (*H.E.* iv. 2) must be pronounced fictitious (so already Vales. in Thdt. *l.c.*). (1) The letter of Ammon (extract printed in this volume, p. 487) tells us on the authority of Athanasius that when Pammon and Theodore miraculously announced the death of Julian, they informed Athan. that the new Emperor was to be a Christian, but that his reign would be short; that Athanasius must go at once and secretly to the Emperor, whom he would meet on his journey before the army reached Antioch, that he would be favourably received by him, and that he would obtain an order for his restoration. Now (apart from the possibility of a grain of truth in the φήμη of the death of Julian) all these details bear the unmistakeable character of a *vaticinium post eventum*, in other words, we have the story as it was current when Ammon drew up the document in question at the request of Archbishop Theophilus (see also p. 567, note 1). At that time, then, the received account was that Athan. hastened secretly to meet Jovian as soon as he knew of his accession, and that he met him between Antioch and Nisibis. Now this native Egyptian account is transmitted independently by two other channels. (2) The *Hist. Aceph.* viii. tells us that the bishop entered Alexandria secretly 'adventu eius non pluribus cognito,' went by ship to Jovian, and returned with letters from him. (3) The *Festal Index* tells us that eight months (i.e., Oct. 24— June 26) after the flight of Ath. Julian died. On his death *being published*, Athan. returned secretly by night to Alexandria. Then on Sept. 6 he crossed the Euphrates (this seems to be the meaning of 'embarked at the Eastern Hierapolis,' the celebrated city, perhaps the ancient Karkhemish, which commanded the passage of the river, though some miles from its W. bank) and met the Emperor Jovian, by whom he was eventually dismissed with honour, returning to Alexandria Feb. 20, 364. Jovian was at Edessa Sept. 27, at Antioch Oct. 23.

The agreement of the three documents is most striking, and the more so since the chronicles are clearly independent both of one another and especially of the letter of Ammon, as is clear from the fact that neither mentions the φήμη, while the *Festal Index* implicitly contradicts it. This appears to be a crucial case in many ways. *Firstly*, the three narratives are all consistent in excluding the possibility of any such council as is supposed to have been summoned (see above, p. lx.). Against this there is nothing but the hasty inference of Thdt. (corrected by Valois, see above, *ib.*); the valueless testimony of the *Libellus Synodicus* (9th cent.); the marvellous tale of Sozom. v. 7 (referred to this time by Tillem. viii. 219, but by Soz. to the death of George: probably an amplification of *Hist. Aceph.* 'visus est') that Athanasius suddenly to the delight of his people was found enthroned in his Church; and the more vague statement of Socr. (iii. 24) that he regained his church 'at once after Julian's death.' As the three fifth-century writers are implicitly contradicted by three writers of Alexandria at the end of the previous century, the latter must be believed against the former. *Secondly*, the *Index*, the later as it appears, of the two chronicles, would seem to represent a form of the story less marvellous and therefore earlier than that of the *Narratio*. Now the latter certainly belongs to the Episcopate of Theophilus. The *Index* therefore can scarcely be placed later, and the *Hist. Aceph.* would fall, as Sievers, *Einl.* 2, had indpendently placed it at the *beginning* of the Episcopate of Theophilus. *Thirdly*, we have here an excellent example not only of the value of the *combined* evidence of the two chronicles, but also of their character as representing in many important respects the Alexandrian tradition of the last third of the fourth century. Before leaving this question it will be well to consider the dates a little more closely. Hierapolis was counted eight days' journey from Antioch. From Alexandria to Antioch by sea was about 500 miles, i.e. with a fair wind scarcely more than four days' sail (it might be less, cf. Conybeare and Howson, *St. Paul*, vol. 2, p. 376, *sq.* ed. 1877). This allows about twelve days for Athan. to reach the Euphrates from Alexandria, remembering that southerly winds prevail in the Eastern Mediterranean at this season (Sievers, *Einl.* 28). Now Athan. reached Hierapolis on Sept. 6 (Thoth 8, Egyptian leap-year).   But according to the *Index*, he reached Alex. after Julian's death was published, and this according to *Hist. Aceph.* was on Mesori 26, i.e. Aug. 19.   From that day to Sept. 6 are eighteen days, leaving about a week's margin for Ath. to hear the news, reach Alexandria, and perhaps for delay in finding a vessel, &c.   But a far wider margin is really available, for the official announcement must have been preceded by many rumours, and was probably not despatched till more than a fortnight after Julian's death (as is observed by Mr. Gwatkin, p. 221).   If we remember that Athanasius, according to the Letter of Ammon, was making all possible haste (*supra*, § 9) we shall again realise the subtle cohesion of these three sources, and the impossibility of the ' large Synod ' imagined by some historians for the year 363.

(k) *Exile under Valens.*   The date of this is discussed by Tillem. (*note* 96) and Montf. *Vit.* who, on the unstable basis of a computation of Theophanes (about 800 A.D.) and of the vague and loose sequences of events in Socr. and Sozom., tentatively refer the exile to the year 367.   The only show of solid support for this date was that Tatianus (of later and unfortunate celebrity), whom the Photian Life and that by the Metaphrast connected with the expulsion, was known from *Cod. Theod.* to have been Prefect of Egypt in 367.   But this airy fabric now gives place to the precise and accurate data of the Theophilan chronicles. Both *Index* and *Hist. Aceph.* place the occurrence not under Tatian but under Flavian, governor of Egypt 364—366.   Both fix the year 365.   The *Hist. Aceph.* (used by Soz. vi. 12, who however makes no use of the dates) gives May 5, 365, for the Imperial order against bishops restored by Julian, June 8 for the reference to the Emperor (*supra*, ch. ii. § 9), Oct. 5 for the retreat of Athan. and search for him by Flavian and *Duke Victorinus*, Feb. 1 for the return of Athanasius.   This detailed chronology is corroborated in two ways ; first by a letter of Libanius (*Ep.* 569) to Flavian, thanking him for a present of [Egyptian] doves, and congratulating him on his ' victory ' (a play on the name *Victorinus* is added), but with a satirical hint that if only Victorinus had any prisoners to shew for his pains (a clear allusion to the escape of Ath.) he (Libanius) would think him a finer fellow even than Cleon (Siev. *Einl.* 31).   Secondly, the restoration of Ath. by Valens becomes historically intelligible, in view of the danger from Procopius, as pointed out *supr.* p. lxi., *fin.*   We cannot then doubt that the chronicles are here once more the channels of the genuine chronological tradition.

(l) *Death of Athanasius.*   It is superfluous to discuss this date at the present day, but it may be worth while to point out for the last time how admirably the combined testimony of our chronicles confirms the judgment of the best critics (Montfaucon, Tillemont, &c.) antecedent to their discovery, and how clearly the secondary value to be assigned to the chronological statements of Socrates and Sozomen once more comes out (Socr. iv. 21 puts the date at 371, and was followed by Papebroke, Petavius and others (fuller details and discussion of the question on its ancient footing in Newman's preface to *Hist. Tracts of St. Athan.*, pp. xx., *sqq.*).   But no one any longer questions the date of May 2-3, 373.   The fact that the *Hist. Aceph.* gives May 3 and the *Index* May 2 (the date observed in the later calendars) vouches for the independence of the two documents and for the very early date of the former : probably, as Sievers and others suggest, the true date is the night between May 2 and May 3.

I. GENERAL CHRONOLOGICAL TABLE OF THE LIFE OF S. ATHANASIUS.

N.B.—Dates upon which the *Historia Acephala* and *Festal Index* coincide are printed in **Thick Type.** Where the agreement, though certain, is constructive and not explicit, an asterisk is added.   Where the month, or day, is in ordinary type, the agreement does not extend to the details in question.   The more doubtful points of chronology are marked by *italics*.

284.	Aug. 29.	Beginning of ' Diocletian era.'
298.		BIRTH OF S. ATHANASIUS about this year.
301.		Death of Bishop Theonas. Peter, bishop of Alexandria.
303.	Feb. 23.	First edict of persecution by Diocletian and Galerius.
	December.	Vicennalia of Diocletian at Rome.
304.		' Fourth Edict ' of Persecution.
305.		Retirement of Diocletian (Constantine and Maximin ' Cæsars ').
306.		Constantine proclaimed ' Augustus ' at York.
307.		Maximin assumes title of ' Augustus ' (holds Syria and Egypt).
311.		First edict of Toleration, and death of Galerius.

311.		Renewed persecution by Maximin in Syria and Egypt. Martyrdom of Peter, &c., at Alexandria.
312.		*Edict of Toleration by Constantine at Milan.*
	Oct. 26.	Constantine defeats Maxentius at the Milvian Bridge.
		Achillas, bishop of Alexandria.
313.		EDICT OF MILAN (third Edict of Toleration), by Constantine and Licinius.
		ALEXANDER, bishop of Alexandria.
		Maximin defeated by Licinius. His Edict of Toleration, and death.
		Earliest possible date for the ' *boy-baptism* ' of Athanasius.
318.		Probable date of the *contra Gentes*, his first book.
319.		Commencement of Arian controversy.
321.		Deposition of Arius by an Egyptian Synod.
322		*Mareotic defection to Arius.*
		Memorandum of deposition signed by Clergy of Alexandria.
		Schism of Colluthus.
323.		*Letter of Alexander of Alexandria to his namesake of Byzantium.*
	Sept. 18.	Final defeat of Licinius. CONSTANTINE SOLE EMPEROR.
324.		First intervention of Constantine in Arian question.
		HOSIUS at Alexandria. Council there.
325.	Summer.	COUNCIL OF NICÆA.
327.	*November.*	Entire Meletian Episcopate collected at Alexandria, and reconciled to the Church (p. 137).
328.	April 17.	Death of Alexander.
	June 8.	**Athanasius, bishop of Alexandria.**
329, 330.		*Visitation of the Thebaid : ordains Pachomius presbyter.*
330.		Council at Antioch deposes Eustathius.
331.		Athanasius defends himself before Constantine.
334.		*Council at Cæsarea.* Athan. refuses to attend.
335.	**July 11 *.**	**Athanasius leaves Alex. for Council of Tyre** (beginning of first exile, Epiphi 17).
	Aug.—Sept.	Mareotic commission in Egypt.
	End of Sept. ?	Council at Jerusalem. Arius received to communion.
	Oct. 30.	Athanasius at CP.
336.	Feb. 8.	Athanasius starts for 'Treveri in Gaul.'
		Council at CP., Marcellus (*Asclepas*), &c., deposed.
		Basil, bishop of Ancyra.
		Death of Arius at CP.
337.	May 22.	Death of Constantine at Nicomedia.
	June 17.	Letter of 'Constantius Cæsar' ordering return of Athanasius (p. lxxxii.).
	Nov. 23 *.	*** Return of Athanasius to Alexandria.**
338.	July 25—27.	Visit of Antony to Alexandria.
		PISTUS intrusive bishop of Alexandria.
	Winter.	Council of Egyptian bishops at Alexandria.
		Envoys of both parties in Rome.
339.	*January.*	Synod at Antioch appoint GREGORY bishop of Alexandria.
339.	Mar. 19.	Flight of Athanasius from 'Theonas.'
	Mar. 22.	Arrival of Gregory at Alexandria.
	April 16.	*** Departure of Athanasius for Rome** (p. lxxxii., *the authorities agree as to the year, and their data combine readily as to the exact days*).
340.	*January.*	Eusebian bishops meet at Antioch and reply to Julius. Their letter reaches Rome in spring.
	Autumn.	Roman council and reply of Julius to Eusebians (eighteen months from arrival of Ath. in Rome).
341.	Midsummer.	COUNCIL OF THE DEDICATION at Antioch. Four creeds.
342.	May.	Athanasius leaves Rome (after three years' stay) for Milan.
		Constans leaves him there (Frankish Campaign).
	Summer.	Constans repels Eusebian deputies at Treveri (p. xlv.).
	Late autumn.	Death of Eusebius of Nicomedia or CP.
343.	Easter.	*Athanasius at Treveri.*
	July.	Assembly of COUNCIL OF SARDICA.
344.	Easter.	Athanasius at Naissus.
	After Easter.	Deposition of Stephen : Council at Antioch appoint Leontius and issue ' Macrostich.'
	August.	Constantius writes forbidding persecution of orthodox at Alexandria.
345.	Easter, April 7	Athanasius at Aquileia.
		Council at Milan. Photinus condemned.
	June 26.	Death of Gregory at Alexandria (about ten months after letter of Constantius).
346.	*September.*	Interview of Ath. with Constantius at Antioch.
	Oct. 21.	**Return to Alexandria.**
	End of year.	Earliest possible date for *consecration of Frumentius by Athanasius.*
347.		First council at Sirmium against Photinus.
349.		Controversy with Rome concerning Easter.
350.	Jan. 18.	Murder of Constans.
351.	Mar. 15.	Gallus proclaimed as ' Constantius Cæsar.'
	Sep. 28.	Battle of Mursa.
		Second council of Sirmium. Photinus deposed.
353.	May 19.	**Legation of Serapion, &c., to Constantius. Montanus at Alexandria.**

353.	Autumn.	Council at Arles against Athanasius.
354.		Execution of Gallus.
355.		Council at Milan against Athanasius.
	July—Dec.	**Diogenes at Alexandria.**
	November.	Julian 'Cæsar.'
356.	Jan. 6.	Syrianus at Alexandria.
	Feb. 8.	**Church of Theonas stormed by Syrianus.**
		Beginning of third exile.
	June 10.	Cataphronius becomes Prefect of Egypt.
357.	Feb. 24.	**George enters Alexandria as Bishop.**
	Summer.	Third council, and second creed ('blasphemy') of Sirmium.
358.	Lent.	Council of Ancyra.
	Oct. 2.	Expulsion of George from Alexandria.
359.	May 22.	Conference of Sirmium. The dated Creed.
	May—Dec.	Councils of Ariminum and Seleucia.
	Dec. 31.	Creed of Niké accepted by delegates at CP.
360.	Jan.	Julian proclaimed 'Augustus' at Paris.
		Dedication council at CP. (Homœan ; deposition of 'Semi-Arian' leaders and excommunication of Aetius).
361.		Meletius elected bishop of Antioch and deposed. Euzoius, **Arian bishop.**
	Nov. 3.	Death of Constantius.
362.	Feb. 9.	Julian's edict (for recall of bishops) posted at Alexandria.
	Feb. 21.	Return of Athanasius.
	Summer.	Council of the confessors at Alexandria.
		Lucifer founds the schism at Antioch.
	October 4.	**Renewed order of Julian against Athanasius.**
		Retirement of Athanasius.
363.	June 26.	Death of Julian. Athan. in Upper Egypt.
	August ?	**Athanasius secretly in Alexandria.**
	Sep. 6.	Athan. crosses the Euphrates.
	Sep.	Meets Jovian at Edessa.
	Winter.	**At Antioch.**
364.	**Feb. 14 (or 20).**	**Returns to Alexandria.**
	Feb. 17.	Death of Jovian.
	Mar. 29.	Valens appointed 'Augustus' by Valentinian.
	Autumn.	Council of Lampsacus.
365.	Spring.	Valens at Antioch. Renewal of Arian persecutions.
	May 5.	Rescript arrives at Alexandria for expulsion of **Athanasius.**
	Oct. 5.	**Athanasius retires to his country house.**
	Sep. 28.	Revolt of Procopius at CP.
366.	Feb. 1.	Athanasius officially restored.
	May 21.	Defeat of Procopius.
	July 21.	Cæsareum burnt at Alexandria.
367.	**Sep. 24.**	**Attempt of Lucius to enter Alexandria.**
368.	Sep. 22.	Athanasius begins his Memorial Church.
370.	Aug. 7.	Memorial Church dedicated.
		Correspondence between Athan. and **Basil begins.**
371.		*Deputation of the Marcellians of Ancyra to Athanasius.*
372.		*Two books against Apollinarianism.*
373.	**May 2—3.**	**Death of Athanasius.**

A table of the Egyptian months, and a table of the date of Easter, &c., **in each year of** the episcopate of Athanasius, will be given at the end of the introduction to the collection of Letters at the close of this volume (p. 501 *sq.*). A list of the consuls of each year is given in the *Festal Index.*

II. SYNOPTICAL TABLE OF THE BISHOPS OF THE CHIEF SEES,

AND OF THE PRINCIPAL COUNCILS HELD, DURING THE LIFETIME OF ATHANASIUS.

N.B.—The names *of bishops* in italics are open to doubt regarding their date.

An asterisk prefixed to a bishop's name means that he was elected when the see was not *de facto* vacant (the case of Ursinus of Rome in 366 is not free from doubt).

† after the name of a synod indicates that although not formally Arian it was held under the influence of Eusebius of Nicomedia.

* denotes a synod more or less implicated in Arianism by its creeds (N.B. no creed at Arles or Milan, 353—355).

** denote a formally Arian synod.

'Semi-Arian' synods are printed in italics.

W.	EMPEROR. E.	ROME.	ALEXANDRIA.	ANTIOCH.	CONSTANTINOPLE.	SYNODS.
	305. Gale_ius		301. Peter ...			
306. Constantine						305. Illiberis.
	307. Licinius.........					
	308—313. Maximin	309. Eusebius				
		310. Melchiades				
			312. Achillas.			
			313. Alexander. ...			
		314. Silvester (d. 335).				313. Rome.
						314. ARLES.
						314? Ancyra.
						315? Neo-Cæsarea.
				319. Philogonius. *Paulinus.*		
					320? Alexander.	
323. Constantine, sole Augustus						321. Alexandria.
				c. 324. Eustathius.		324. Alexandria.
						325. NICÆA.
		328. Athanasius.				
				330. '*Paulinus?*'	[330. 'Constantinople' made the new Rome].	330. Antioch†.
				Eulalius.		
				332. *Euphronius.*		
				333. Flacillus (or Placitus)		
						334. Cæsarea†.
						335. Tyre† and Jerusalem†.
		336. Mark ...			336. Paul (d. 350?).	336. CP. †
337. { Constantine II. (d. 340). Constans (d. 350). Constantius		337. Julius ...				
			338. *Pistus.*		337? *Eusebius (d. 341-2).	
			339. *Gregory			339&40. Antioch†
						340. Rome.
						340. Gangra†.
						341. Antioch†*
				342. Stephen.	342. *Macedonius.	
						343. SARDICA. Philippopolis*. }
				344. Leontius.		344. Antioch*.
						345. Milan.
						347. Sirmium I*.

EMPEROR.	ROME.	ALEXANDRIA.	ANTIOCH.	CONSTANTINOPLE.	SYNODS.
W.　　　　　　　　E.					
350. Constantius, sole Augustus.	....	....	....	....	
					351. Sirmium II *.
	352. Liberius.	....	....	....	
					353. Arles*.
					355. Milan*.
	357. *Felix...	357. *George.	357. Eudoxius.	....	357. Sirmium III**
					358. *Ancyra.*
			359. *Anianus.	....	359. Sirmium IV*.
					{ Ariminum*.
					{ Seleucia*.
				360. *Eudoxius. ...	360. CP**.
361. Julian.			361. Meletius.		
			*Euzoius.		
			362. *Paulinus.	....	362. Alexandria.
			(schism).		362. *Laodicea??*
363. Jovian.					363. Antioch.
364. Valentinian.　Valens.					364. *Lampsacus.*
	366. Damasus (d. 384).				
	366-7. *Ursi-nus.	367. *Lucius.			367. *Tyana.*
				370. Demophilus [Evagrius.]	
	373. Peter.				
375. { Gratian (d. 383). { Valentinian II. (d. 392).					
379. Theodosius.					

APPENDIX

The Civil and Military Government of Egypt in the Lifetime of Athanasius.

The name Egypt in the fourth century was applied firstly to the 'diocese' or group of provinces governed by the Præfectus Ægypti or 'Præfectus Augustalis,' secondly to the Delta or Ægyptus Propria, one of the provinces of which the diocese was made up. These provinces (Ammian. Marc. XXII. xvi.) were originally three in number: Egypt proper, Libya, and the Thebais. During our period they became five, firstly by the separation of the Eastern Delta from Egypt proper under the name of Augustamnica in 341 (*infr.* pp. 130, 504, note 17 a) ; secondly by the subdivision of Libya (at an uncertain date) into Hither Libya (Libya 'Inferior,' or 'Siccior'), and the Pentapolis or Libya Superior of which Ptolemais was the capital. At a later date still the Heptanomis was separated from 'Ægyptus' under the name of Arcadia, given in honour of the Emperor Arcadius. These then are the six provinces which make up 'Egypt' in the *Notitia* (shortly after A.D. 400). Each province, with the exception of Augustamnica, whose governor enjoyed the title of 'corrector,' was under a præses (ἡγούμενος): not one of the six was of consular rank. This regulation was due to the peculiar constitution of the diocese or province of Egypt in the wider sense. At the head of this latter, and subordinate in rank, though scarcely second in dignity, to the Comes Orientis, was the Prefect of Egypt, who enjoyed an exceptional position among the greater provincial officers. He appears to have been, at least in practice, directly under the Præfectus Prætorio per Orientem, the supreme civil representative of 'Augustus' throughout the Eastern Empire. The title Præfectus had in fact a different history as applied to the Prefect of the East and the Prefect of Egypt respectively. As applied to the latter, it was as old as Augustus. The importance of Egypt, mainly but not solely as a granary of Rome, had led the politic heir of Julius Cæsar to ensure its complete and peculiar dependence on the emperor. For this object, its government was committed to a nominee of the emperor, who must be not a Senator but an Eques only; i.e. he must never have held one of the great offices of state from Consul to quæstor. No one of senatorial rank was to be permitted to set foot in Egypt. (For the prerogatives of the præfectus Ægypti under Augustus see Tacitus *Ann.* xii. 60, also Ulp. *Digest.* I. xvii.). This arrangement survived the various vicissitudes of Egypt in the third century, and even the reorganisation of the Empire by Diocletian. Egypt was severed off between 365 and 386 from the Eastern 'Diocese' (Sievers, p. 117, appealing to Mommsen in *Abhandl. der Berliner Akad.* 1862). Upon the above facts was founded the (perhaps merely popular) title 'Augustalis' which we find already applied to the Prefect of Egypt about A.D. 350 (*infr.* p. 143, cf. p. 93 note). But Sievers (*ubi supr.*), following Mommsen, contends that there is reason to think that the dignity of 'Augustal' Prefect was officially created about A.D. 367. This view cannot be adequately discussed here, but it rests only in part upon the series of governors furnished by the *Festal Index.*

From that document we learn that the prefect of 'Egypt' in the wider sense in almost every case held also the office of 'governor' of Egypt in the narrower sense. The exceptions noted by Sievers (§ 14) are in most cases based on the errors of Larsow. But in 365 Flavianus is 'governor' only, next year 'Prefect' also: his successors Proclianus and Tatianus are each 'governor' only (366-7), but the latter is Prefect in 368, and 'governor' only in 369-70, as also is Palladius, 370—371, who is yet succeeded by Olympius as 'Prefect.' These variations may be due merely to careless use of language, or possibly to some change about the time referred to.

The list of prefects of Egypt is fuller than any that exists for a Roman province over so long a period, and on the whole it is in the highest degree trustworthy. But there are one or two drawbacks to take account of. Firstly, there are the discrepancies between the *Index* iii., vi., vii., and the headings to the corresponding letters (see notes). Also, the heading to Letter x. presupposes a change of governor in the previous year of which the Index tells us nothing. Again, a letter of Julian's (No. 23) is addressed to a 'Hermogenes, governor of Egypt,' for whom it is difficult to find room in the following list at the date required (end of 361, when Gerontius was prefect). Julianus, uncle of the Emperor, if not disguised under the name Italicianus (see below), possibly ruled Egypt (Jul. *Ep.* 11), as Comes Orientis, which office he held in 362. On the other hand the Olympus of *Index* xxxiv., and the Ecdikius of Julian, *Epp.* 6, 50, and *Cod. Theod.* xv. i. 8, are probably one and the same (Sievers, p. 124).

The Military command of Egypt was now in the hand of the ' dux,' who had the disposal of the troops in Egypt proper ; those of Libya and of the Thebais were, at any rate later on, entrusted to separate ' duces.' In the *Notitia*, while the two latter ' duces ' remain, the Dux Ægypti is replaced by a higher official, entitled the ' Comes Rei Militaris per Ægyptum.' But this belongs to a later date. In the time of Athanasius ' Counts ' appear in Egypt only as extraordinary or special commissioners whose authority is exercised concurrently with that of the Dux, as, e.g., Count Heraclianus or Heraclius (*infr.* pp. 290, 292), whose commission runs parallel with the command of the new 'dux' Sebastianus ; and Count Asterius (p. 289), who was in Egypt when Felicissimus was ' Duke.'

We now give a list of the governors and dukes of Egypt, with references to the *Festal Index :* these must also be supplemented by the general index to this volume :—

(1) *Prefect and Governor.*

328, 329.	Septimius Zenius (*Index* i., Heading i.).
330.	Magninianus (*Index* ii., Heading ii.).
331.	Hyginus (or ' Eugenius,' *Index* iii.), but Florentius (Heading iii.).
332.	Hyginus (Heading iv. and *Index* iv.).
333.	Paternus (Heading v. and *Index* v.).
334, 335.	Paternus (*Index*), but Philagrius (Heading iv., v.).
336-7.	Philagrius (*Index* viii., ix.).
338.	Theodorus (*Index* x.), superseded by Philagrius (Heading x.).
339, 340.	Philagrius (*Index* xi., xii., Heading xi.).
341—343.	Longinus (*Index* xiii.—xv., Headings xiii., xiv., and cf. *Cod. Th.* XVI. ii. 10, 11, correcting date by Sievers, p. 114).
344.	Palladius of Italy (*Index* xvi.).
345—352.	Nestorius of Gaza (*Index* xvii.—xxiv., Headings xvii.—xx., also *infr.* pp. 218, 219, notes, &c.).
353, 354.	Sebastianus of Thrace (*Index* xxv., xxvi.).
355, 356.	Maximus ' the elder' of Nicæa (*Index* xxvii., xxviii., and see pp. 246, 301).
356, 7.	Cataphronius (*Index* xxviii., xxix. ; he arrived on June 10, 356, see p. 290, note 9 ; also cf. Liban. *Epp.* 434, 435).
357—359.	Parnassius (*Index* xxix., xxxi., cf. for the latter year Amm. Marc. XIX., xii.).
359.	(For 3 months only) 'Italicianus of Italy,' perhaps for Julianus (so Siev., p. 121, cf. *Index* xxxi.).
359—361.	Faustinus (*Index* xxxi.—xxxiii., cf. p. 291 ?).
361, 362.	Gerontius (*Index* xxxiii., xxxiv., Liban. *Epp.* 294, 295, 547, 548).
362, 363.	Ecdikius Olympus (*Index* xxxiv., xxxv., cf. remarks above).
364.	Hierius or Aerius (*Index* xxxvi., Sievers, *Leben des Libanius*, Appendix A).
364.	Maximus (*Index ib.*, Liban. *Ep.* 1050, written in July or Aug.), for a short time only.
364—366.	Flavianus (*Index* xxxvi., xxxviii., Liban. *Ep.* 569, *supr.* ch. v. § 3, k).
366, 367.	Proclianus (*Index* xxxviii., xxxix.).
367—370.	Tatianus (*Index* xxxix., xlii., see Gibbon ch. xxix. and notes 6-8, for references).
370, 371.	Olympius Palladius (*Index* xlii., xliii.).
371—373.	Aelius Palladius (*Index* xliii.—xlv., Socr. iv. 21, &c.).

(2) *Dux Ægypti.*

Our materials for this list are very scanty, but we can verify the following :—

340 and 345.	Balacius or Valacius (pp. 219, 273, &c.).
350.	Felicissimus (p. 289).
356.	(Jan. and Feb.) Syrianus (*Index* xxviii., &c.).
356.	(Apparently after Midsummer, cf. p. 292 with 290.) Sebastianus ('successor of Syrianus,' *Ep. Ammon.* 21) ; he remains till after 358 (cf. Siev. p. 125 for references to letters of Libanius).
360.	Artemius ('succ. of Sebastianus,' *ib.*, *Index* xxxii., Letter 53. note 1).
365, 366.	Victorinus (ch. v. § 3, k).
367, 368.	Traianus (*Index* xxxix., Sievers, pp. 146, *sq.*).

On the matters dealt with in this appendix, consult Mommsen, *Provinces* (Eng. Tra.), . ii., pp. 233, 246 ; the *Notitia* (ed. Panciroli, Genev., 1623, Böcking, Bonn, 1839—1853, Seeck, Berlin, 1876) ; Gibbon, ch. xvii. ; Marquardt, *Röm. Staats-verwaltung*, vol. i. ; and Kuhn, *Die städtische, &c., Verfassung des R. Reiches*, vol. ii. ; also Sievers on the *Hist. Aceph.* (*supr.* ch. i., § 3).

On the Egyptian bishoprics, see, in addition to Le Quien, a Coptic list of sees in De Rougé, *Géographie de la Basse-Egypte*, Paris, 1891, which came out too late to be used for this volume.

INTRODUCTION TO THE TREATISE

CONTRA GENTES

THIS treatise and that which follows it form in reality two parts of a single work. Jerome (*De Script. Eccl.*) refers to them as 'Adversus Gentes Libri Duo.' They are, however, more commonly distinguished by the titles given them in the present volume. Both books, indeed, are mainly directed against the Gentiles, but in the present treatise the refutation is carried out with more special reference to the beliefs and worship of the heathen. The two books belong to the earlier years of Athanasius. The Arian controversy which broke out (319 A.D.) probably before his twenty-second year has left no trace upon them (not even *c. Gent.* 46. 8, see note there). How long before the limit thus fixed the work was composed it is impossible to say with certainty. The hint (*c. Gent.* 9. 5) that the time for the deification of emperors by decree of the Senate might have come to an end points to the conversion of Constantine as a *terminus a quo.* And the full maturity of power which marks out the *de Incarnatione* as a master-piece of Christian theology inclines us to put the composition as late as we can. Hence the date usually adopted, viz. in or shortly before 318 B.C., the twenty-first year (probably) of Athanasius' age.

The position of the book in relation to the general history of the theology of Athanasius and of the Church has been pointed out in the Prolegomena. It remains to sketch its argument, and tabulate its arrangement: a somewhat more extended summary is prefixed to each section.

His aim is to vindicate (§ 1) the Dignity and reasonableness of the Christian Faith. The main vindication of the Faith is seen in its practical results. But, that these may produce their proper effect, a removal of error from the mind is needed. Hence the necessity of refuting idolatry, which is deduced from the same cause as evil in general, namely, the departure of man from his original exemplar, the Logos (§§ 2—5). By the misuse of his power of conscious choice, man fell (6—8) into the degradation and illusions (9—15) of idolatry. He then examines the popular and learned pleas on behalf of idolatry (16—26), and thus arrives at the central problem of the conception of God. That God is not Nature is shewn (27—29) by the mutual dependence of the various constituents of the Universe: no one of these, therefore, can be God: nor can their totality; for God is not compounded of parts on which He depends, but is Himself the cause of existence to all. Such a God as this, the soul of man (30—33) can and, if purified from sin, will (34) recognise; if her imperfections hinder this, the spectacle of Reason and Order in the Universe (35—46) will assist her to recognise the handiwork of God, and the presence of the Logos, and through him the Father. The reclamation and restoration of sinful and degraded man can only be effected (47) by a return to the Logos. This opens the question dealt with in the second book, *de Incarnatione.*

Such is the general drift of the *c. Gentes,* and its high interest is beyond question. At the same time it may be admitted that to modern readers much of it fails to commend itself. In the two-fold work before us Athanasius 'looks before and after.' The second portion, on the Incarnation, waxes rather than wanes in its significance for modern theology.

B

It is more modern to us than the theology of any generation since then. But the *c. Gentes*, with its retrospect upon a past utterly dead[1] to the human spirit, its arguments addressed to a range of ideas widely remote from our own, its inadequate view of the genesis and history of heathen religions, its antiquated physics (36, 44, and the φυσικὸς λόγος of 39), its occasional glaring fallacies of argument (16 *sub fin.*, 33. 1), is apt to disappoint the modern student who reads it for the first time. This may explain its not having been translated before now. But while the defects of the book are evident at a glance, it grows upon the reader with repeated study. The moral elevation of its tone,—the firm grasp of central Christian truths,—the sure insight in dealing with such problems as evil and sin,—the relation of God to Nature,—the ethical contrast of Christian theism and heathen polytheism,—the grave humour of such passages as 16. 5; 10. 4 *fin.*; 11. 2 *fin.*, &c.,—and beyond all this a certain largeness of mind and simple unostentatious fervour of conviction, stamp the book as a great one, and as the worthy complement of its more renowned companion.

The two together 'are, next to Origen's *de Principiis*, the first attempt to construct a scientific system of the Christian religion upon certain fundamental ideas of God and world, sin and redemption; and they form the ripe fruit of the positive apology in the Greek Church.' (Schaff, Nicene Christianity, p. 82.) The polemic against idolatry and heathen mythology is common to the general class of Christian apologists, and is to be found in heathen writers like Lucian and even Porphyry (letter to Anebo). But what distinguishes Athanasius from previous apologists (excepting Origen) is the novel nature of his problem. The alliance between philosophy and gross popular idolatry had given Christian apology a new task. From Porphyry downwards (Porphyry himself was not consistent in this respect) the Neo-platonist school, in alarm at the progress of Christianity, had taken up the defence of popular paganism, endeavouring to subsume its grosser manifestations, its images, sacrifices, &c., under philosophico-religious principles (*infra* § 19, &c.). The idea of 'theurgy' as the necessary initiation into the higher life colours the teaching of Porphyry, but more strongly that of his pupil Iamblichus, who died early in the fourth century, and whose pupils (Ædesius, &c.) were contemporaries of Athanasius. This degeneration of Platonism, however, went along with the continued study of Plato, whose dialogues are to some extent common ground between Athanasius and his opponents (Phædrus, § 5, 33, Laws, 33, Timæus, 41, &c., &c.; but it is not in every case easy to say whether Athan. quotes Plato merely at second hand, or directly, as he certainly does 10. 4).

It may be remarked finally that in these early treatises the influence of Origen and his school is more distinct than in the later works of Athanasius. Not to lay too much stress on his proof of God's existence and unity from the Cosmos (cf. Orig. *c. Cels.* I. 23), the prominence of the philosophic doctrine of the Logos as a cosmic mediatorial Principle (compare Alexander's μεσιτεύουσα φύσις μονογενής) stands in contrast with his later insistence (cf. *Orat.* ii. 24, *sq.*) on the directness of the personal agency of God (see also below, note on '*In Illud*' 2). The Platonist idea of the Logos is utilised (*de Incarn.* 41) without sufficient explanation of its fundamental difference from the Christian doctrine. The influence of Origenism is traceable in his theory of the nature of evil as purely negative (cf. § 5 with Orig. *c. Cels.* iv. 66), in the explanation (to which I recall nothing parallel in his later works) of the garden of Eden as figurative (2. 4, cf. 3. 3), the stress laid on the restoration of *knowledge* of God through the Logos, and perhaps in the deification of man through Christ (Orig. *c. Cels.* iii. 28 *sub. fin.*), a thought which Athanasius brings forward in his later at least as often as in his earlier writings (see note on *de Incarn.* 54. 3). On the whole, however, the tendency of Athanasius in the course of the Arian controversy is to move away from Origen and toward the Western habit of thought: this is especially exemplified in the history of the term

---

[1] In heathen countries the case is different. An English translation was made a few years since for dissemination in India by the members of the Oxford Mission at Calcutta.

Hypostasis (see above, Prolegg. chap. II. § 3 (2) b, and below Introd. to *Tom. ad Ant.*; cf. also Introductions to *de Sent. Dionys.* and *ad Afros*). Some of the more characteristic speculations of Origen have left no trace even on the earliest works of Athanasius (see Introd. to the next Treatise). The translation (here as elsewhere, except where it is otherwise stated) is from the Benedictine text.

The contents of the *contra Gentes* fall into the following scheme :—

AGAINST THE HEATHEN

§ 1. *Introduction:—The purpose of the book a vindication of Christian doctrine, and especially of the Cross, against the scoffing objection of Gentiles. The effects of this doctrine its main vindication.*

THE knowledge of our religion and of the truth of things is independently manifest rather than in need of human teachers, for almost day by day it asserts itself by facts, and manifests itself brighter than the sun by the doctrine of Christ. 2. Still, as you nevertheless desire to hear about it, Macarius [1], come let us as we may be able set forth a few points of the faith of Christ: able though you are to find it out from the divine oracles, but yet generously desiring to hear from others as well. 3. For although the sacred and inspired Scriptures are sufficient [2] to declare the truth,—while there are other works of our blessed teachers [3] compiled for this purpose, if he meet with which a man will gain some knowledge of the interpretation of the Scriptures, and be able to learn what he wishes to know,—still, as we have not at present in our hands the compositions of our teachers, we must communicate in writing to you what we learned from them,—the faith, namely, of Christ the Saviour ; lest any should hold cheap the doctrine taught among us, or think faith in Christ unreasonable. For this is what the Gentiles traduce and scoff at, and laugh loudly at us, insisting on the one fact of the Cross of Christ ; and it is just here that one must pity their want of sense, because when they traduce the Cross of Christ they do not see that its power has filled all the world, and that by it the effects of the knowledge of God are made manifest to all. 4. For they would not have scoffed at such a fact, had they, too, been men who genuinely gave

heed to His divine Nature. On the contrary, they in their turn would have recognised this man as Saviour of the world, and that the Cross has been not a disaster, but a healing of Creation. 5. For if after the Cross all idolatry was overthrown, while every manifestation of demons is driven away by this Sign [4], and Christ alone is worshipped and the Father known through Him, and, while gainsayers are put to shame, He daily invisibly wins over the souls of these gainsayers [5],—how, one might fairly ask them, is it still open to us to regard the matter as human, instead of confessing that He Who ascended the Cross is Word of God and Saviour of the World? But these men seem to me quite as bad as one who should traduce the sun when covered by clouds, while yet wondering at his light, seeing how the whole of creation is illu mined by him. 6. For as the light is noble, and the sun, the chief cause of light, is nobler still, so, as it is a divine thing for the whole world to be filled with his knowledge, it follows that the orderer and chief cause of such an achievement is God and the Word of God. 7. We speak then as lies within our power, first refuting the ignorance of the unbelieving ; so that what is false being refuted, the truth may then shine forth of itself, and that you yourself, friend, may be reassured that you have believed what is true, and in coming to know Christ have not been deceived. Moreover, I think it becoming to discourse to you, as a lover of Christ, about Christ, since I am sure that you rate faith in and knowledge of Him above anything else whatsoever.

§ 2. *Evil no part of the essential nature of things. The original creation and constitution of man in grace and in the knowledge of God.*

In the beginning wickedness did not exist. Nor indeed does it exist even now in those who are holy, nor does it in any way belong to their

---

[1] See *de Incarn.* 1 and note there.
[2] Constantly insisted on by Athan. Cf. *de Incarn.* 5, and note on *de Decr.* 32.
[3] *De Incarn.* 56. 2 ; he may also be referring to works from the Alex. school, such as Orig. *de Princ.*

[4] Cf. *de Incarn.* 47. 2, 48. 3, *Vit. Ant.* passim.
[5] Cf. *de Incarn.* 50. 3, 51. 3, &c.

nature. But men later on began to contrive it, and to elaborate it to their own hurt. Whence also they devised the invention of idols, treating what was not as though it were. 2. For God, Maker of all and King of all, that has His Being beyond[6] all substance and human discovery, inasmuch as He is good and exceeding noble, made, through His own Word our Saviour Jesus Christ, the human race after His own image, and constituted man able to see and know realities by means of this assimilation to Himself, giving him also a conception[7] and knowledge even of His own eternity, in order that, preserving his nature intact, he might not ever either depart from his idea of God, nor recoil from the communion of the holy ones; but having the grace of Him that gave it, having also God's own power from the Word of the Father, he might rejoice and have fellowship with the Deity, living the life of immortality unharmed and truly blessed. For having nothing to hinder his knowledge of the Deity, he ever beholds, by his purity, the Image of the Father, God the Word, after Whose image he himself is made. He is awestruck as he contemplates that Providence[8] which through the Word extends to the universe, being raised above the things of sense and every bodily appearance, but cleaving to the divine and thought-perceived things in the heavens by the power of his mind. 3. For when the mind of men does not hold converse with bodies, nor has mingled with it from without aught of their lust, but is wholly above them, dwelling with itself as it was made to begin with, then, transcending the things of sense and all things human, it is raised up on high; and seeing the Word, it sees in Him also the Father of the Word, taking pleasure in contemplating Him, and gaining renewal by its desire toward Him; 4. exactly as the first of men created, the one who was named Adam in Hebrew, is described in the Holy Scriptures as having at the beginning had his mind to God-ward in a freedom unembarrassed by shame, and as associating with the holy ones in that contemplation of things perceived by the mind which he enjoyed in the place where he was—the place which the holy Moses called in figure a Garden. So purity of soul is sufficient of itself to reflect God, as the Lord also says, "Blessed are the pure in heart, for they shall see God."

§ 3. *The decline of man from the above condition, owing to his absorption in material things.*

Thus then, as we have said, the Creator fashioned the race of men, and thus meant it to remain. But men, making light of better things, and holding back from apprehending them, began to seek in preference things nearer to themselves. 2. But nearer to themselves were the body and its senses; so that while removing their mind from the things perceived by thought, they began to regard themselves; and so doing, and holding to the body and the other things of sense, and deceived as it were in their own surroundings, they fell into lust of themselves, preferring what was their own to the contemplation of what belonged to God. Having then made themselves at home in these things, and not being willing to leave what was so near to them, they entangled their soul with bodily pleasures, vexed and turbid with all kind of lusts, while they wholly forgot the power they originally had from God. 3. But the truth of this one may see from the man who was first made, according to what the holy Scriptures tell us of him. For he also, as long as he kept his mind to God, and the contemplation of God, turned away from the contemplation of the body. But when, by counsel of the serpent, he departed from the consideration of God, and began to regard himself, then they not only fell to bodily lust, but knew that they were naked, and knowing, were ashamed. But they knew that they were naked, not so much of clothing as that they were become stripped of the contemplation of divine things, and had transferred their understanding to the contraries. For having departed from the consideration of the one and the true, namely, God, and from desire of Him, they had thenceforward embarked in divers lusts and in those of the several bodily senses. 4. Next, as is apt to happen, having formed a desire for each and sundry, they began to be habituated to these desires, so that they were even afraid to leave them: whence the soul became subject to cowardice and alarms, and pleasures and thoughts of mortality. For not being willing to leave her lusts, she fears death and her separation from the body. But again, from lusting, and not meeting with gratification, she learned to commit murder and wrong. We are then led naturally to shew, as best we can, how she does this.

§ 4. *The gradual abasement of the Soul from Truth to Falsehood by the abuse of her freedom of Choice.*

Having departed from the contemplation of the things of thought, and using to the full the several activities of the body, and being pleased with the contemplation of the body, and seeing that pleasure is good for her, she was misled and abused the name of good, and thought that pleasure was the very es-

---

6 See Orig. *c. Cels.* vii. 42 *sqq. de Princ.* I. i.
7 Restored in Christ, see § 34.
8 Cf. *Ep. Æg.* 15, *Apol. Fug.* passim, *Orat.* iii. 37.

sence of good : just as though a man out of his mind and asking for a sword to use against all he met, were to think that soundness of mind. 2. But having fallen in love with pleasure, she began to work it out in various ways. For being by nature mobile, even though she have turned away from what is good, yet she does not lose her mobility. She moves then, no longer according to virtue or so as to see God, but imagining false things, she makes a novel use of her power, abusing it as a means to the pleasures she has devised, since she is after all made with power over herself. 3. For she is able, as on the one hand to incline to what is good, so on the other to reject it ; but in rejecting the good she of course entertains the thought of what is opposed to it, for she cannot at all cease from movement, being, as I said before, mobile by nature. And knowing her own power over herself, she sees that she is able to use the members of her body in either direction, both toward what is, or toward what is not. 4. But good is, while evil is not ; by what is, then, I mean what is good, inasmuch as it has its pattern in God Who is. But by what is not I mean what is evil, in so far as it consists in a false imagination in the thoughts of men. For though the body has eyes so as to see Creation, and by its entirely harmonious construction to recognise the Creator ; and ears to listen to the divine oracles and the laws of God ; and hands both to perform works of necessity and to raise to God in prayer ; yet the soul, departing from the contemplation of what is good and from moving in its sphere, wanders away and moves toward its contraries. 5. Then seeing, as I said before, and abusing her power, she has perceived that she can move the members of the body also in an opposite way : and so, instead of beholding the Creation, she turns the eye to lusts, shewing that she has this power too ; and thinking that by the mere fact of moving she is maintaining her own dignity, and is doing no sin in doing as she pleases ; not knowing that she is made not merely to move, but to move in the right direction. For this is why an apostolic utterance assures us " All things are lawful, but not all things are expedient 9."

§ 5. *Evil, then, consists essentially in the choice of what is lower in preference to what is higher.*

But the audacity of men, having regard not to what is expedient and becoming, but to what is possible for it, began to do the contrary ; whence, moving their hands to the contrary, it made them commit murder, and led away their hearing to disobedience, and their other members to adultery instead of to lawful pro-

creation ; and the tongue, instead of right speaking, to slander and insult and perjury ; the hands again, to stealing and striking fellow-men ; and the sense of smell to many sorts of lascivious odours ; the feet, to be swift to shed blood, and the belly to drunkenness and insatiable gluttony [1]. 2. All of which things are a vice and sin of the soul : neither is there any cause of them at all, but only the rejection of better things. For just as if a charioteer [2], having mounted his chariot on the race-course, were to pay no attention to the goal, toward which he should be driving, but, ignoring this, simply were to drive the horse as he could, or in other words as he would, and often drive against those he met, and often down steep places, rushing wherever he impelled himself by the speed of the team, thinking that thus running he has not missed the goal,—for he regards the running only, and does not see that he has passed wide of the goal ;—so the soul too, turning from the way toward God, and driving the members of the body beyond what is proper, or rather, driven herself along with them by her own doing, sins and makes mischief for herself, not seeing that she has strayed from the way, and has swerved from the goal of truth, to which the Christ-bearing man, the blessed Paul, was looking when he said, " I press on toward the goal unto the prize of the high calling of Christ Jesus [3] : " so that the holy man, making the good his mark, never did what was evil.

§ 6. *False views of the nature of evil : viz., that evil is something in the nature of things, and has substantive existence. (a) Heathen thinkers : (evil resides in matter). Their refutation. (b) Heretical teachers : (Dualism). Refutation from Scripture.*

Now certain of the Greeks, having erred from the right way, and not having known Christ, have ascribed to evil a substantive and independent existence. In this they make a double mistake : either in denying the Creator to be maker of all things, if evil had an independent subsistence and being of its own ; or again, if they mean that He is maker of all things, they will of necessity admit Him to be maker of evil also. For evil, according to them, is included among existing things. 2. But this must appear paradoxical and impossible. For evil does not come from good, nor is it in, or the result of, good, since in that case it would not be good, being mixed in its nature or a cause of evil. 3. But the sectaries, who have fallen away from the teaching of the

---

9 1 Cor. x. 23.

1 Rom. iii. 10 foll.   2 Cf. Plato *Phædrus* 246 C, 248 A, 253 E, 254.   3 Phil. iii. 14.

Church, and made shipwreck concerning the Faith[4], they also wrongly think that evil has a substantive existence. But they arbitrarily imagine another god besides the true One, the Father of our Lord Jesus Christ, and that he is the unmade producer of evil and the head of wickedness, who is also artificer of Creation. But these men one can easily refute, not only from the divine Scriptures, but also from the human understanding itself, the very source of these their insane imaginations. 4. To begin with, our Lord and Saviour Jesus Christ says in His own gospels confirming the words of Moses: "The Lord God is one;" and "I thank thee, Father, Lord of heaven and earth[5]." But if God is one, and at the same time Lord of heaven and earth, how could there be another God beside Him? or what room will there be for the God whom they suppose, if the one true God fills all things in the compass of heaven and earth? or how could there be another creator of that, whereof, according to the Saviour's utterance, the God and Father of Christ is Himself Lord. 5. Unless indeed they would say that it were, so to speak, in an equipoise, and the evil god capable of getting the better of the good God. But if they say this, see to what a pitch of impiety they descend. For when powers are equal, the superior and better cannot be discovered. For if the one exist even if the other will it not, both are equally strong and equally weak: equally, because the very existence of either is a defeat of the other's will: weak, because what happens is counter to their wills: for while the good God exists in spite of the evil one, the evil god exists equally in spite of the good.

§ 7. *Refutation of dualism from reason. Impossibility of two Gods. The truth as to evil is that which the Church teaches: that it originates, and resides, in the perverted choice of the darkened soul.*

More especially, they are exposed to the following reply. If visible things are the work of the evil god, what is the work of the good God? for nothing is to be seen except the work of the Artificer. Or what evidence is there that the good God exists at all, if there are no works of His by which He may be known? for by his works the artificer is known. 2. Or how could two principles exist, contrary one to another: or what is it that divides them, for them to exist apart? For it is impossible for them to exist together, because they are mutually destructive. But neither can the one be included in the other, their nature being unmixed and

unlike. Accordingly that which divides them will evidently be of a third nature, and itself God. But of what nature could this third something be? good or evil? It will be impossible to determine, for it cannot be of the nature of both. 3. This conceit of theirs, then, being evidently rotten, the truth of the Church's theology must be manifest: that evil has not from the beginning been with God or in God, nor has any substantive existence; but that men, in default of the vision of good, began to devise and imagine for themselves what was not, after their own pleasure. 4. For as if a man, when the sun is shining, and the whole earth illumined by his light, were to shut fast his eyes and imagine darkness where no darkness exists, and then walk wandering as if in darkness, often falling and going down steep places, thinking it was dark and not light,—for, imagining that he sees, he does not see at all; —so, too, the soul of man, shutting fast her eyes, by which she is able to see God, has imagined evil for herself, and moving therein, knows not that, thinking she is doing something, she is doing nothing. For she is imagining what is not, nor is she abiding in her original nature; but what she is is evidently the product of her own disorder. 5. For she is made to see God, and to be enlightened by Him; but of her own accord in God's stead she has sought corruptible things and darkness, as the Spirit says somewhere in writing, "God made man upright, but they have sought out many inventions[6]." Thus it has been then that men from the first discovered and contrived and imagined evil for themselves. But it is now time to say how they came down to the madness of idolatry, that you may know that the invention of idols is wholly due, not to good but to evil. But what has its origin in evil can never be pronounced good in any point,—being evil altogether.

§ 8. *The origin of idolatry is similar. The soul, materialised by forgetting God, and engrossed in earthly things, makes them into gods. The race of men descends into a hopeless depth of delusion and superstition.*

Now the soul of mankind, not satisfied with the devising of evil, began by degrees to venture upon what is worse still. For having experience of diversities of pleasures, and girt about with oblivion of things divine; being pleased moreover and having in view the passions of the body, and nothing but things present and opinions about them, ceased to think that anything existed beyond what is seen, or that anything was good save things temporal and bodily;

---

[4] 1 Tim. i. 19.   [5] Mark xii. 29; Matt. xi. 25.   [6] Eccl. vii. 29.

so turning away and forgetting that she was in the image of the good God, she no longer, by the power which is in her, sees God the Word after whose likeness she is made; but having departed from herself, imagines and feigns what is not. 2. For hiding, by the complications of bodily lusts, the mirror which, as it were, is in her, by which alone she had the power of seeing the Image of the Father, she no longer sees what a soul ought to behold, but is carried about by everything, and only sees the things which come under the senses. Hence, weighted with all fleshly desire, and distracted among the impressions of these things, she imagines that the God Whom her understanding has forgotten is to be found in bodily and sensible things, giving to things seen the name of God, and glorifying only those things which she desires and which are pleasant to her eyes. 3. Accordingly, evil is the cause which brings idolatry in its train; for men, having learned to contrive evil, which is no reality in itself, in like manner feigned for themselves as gods beings that had no real existence. Just, then, as though a man had plunged into the deep, and no longer saw the light, nor what appears by light, because his eyes are turned downwards, and the water is all above him; and, perceiving only the things in the deep, thinks that nothing exists beside them, but that the things he sees are the only true realities; so the men of former time, having lost their reason, and plunged into the lusts and imaginations of carnal things, and forgotten the knowledge and glory of God, their reasoning being dull, or rather following unreason, made gods for themselves of things seen, glorifying the creature rather than the Creator[7], and deifying the works rather than the Master, God, their Cause and Artificer. 4. But just as, according to the above simile, men who plunge into the deep, the deeper they go down, advance into darker and deeper places, so it is with mankind. For they did not keep to idolatry in a simple form, nor did they abide in that with which they began; but the longer they went on in their first condition, the more new superstitions they invented: and, not satiated with the first evils, they again filled themselves with others, advancing further in utter shamefulness, and surpassing themselves in impiety. But to this the divine Scripture testifies when it says, "When the wicked cometh unto the depth of evils, he despiseth[8]."

§ 9. *The various developments of idolatry: worship of the heavenly bodies, the elements, natural objects, fabulous creatures, personified lusts, men living and dead. The case of Antinous, and of the deified Emperors.*

For now the understanding of mankind

leaped asunder from God; and going lower in their ideas and imaginations, they gave the honour due to God first to the heaven and the sun and moon and the stars, thinking them to be not only gods, but also the causes of the other gods lower than themselves[9]. Then, going yet lower in their dark imaginations, they gave the name of gods to the upper æther and the air and the things in the air. Next, advancing further in evil, they came to celebrate as gods the elements and the principles of which bodies are composed, heat and cold and dryness and wetness. 2. But just as they who have fallen flat creep in the slime like land-snails, so the most impious of mankind, having fallen lower and lower from the idea of God, then set up as gods men, and the forms of men, some still living, others even after their death. Moreover, counselling and imagining worse things still, they transferred the divine and supernatural name of God at last even to stones and stocks, and creeping things both of land and water, and irrational wild beasts, awarding to them every divine honour, and turning from the true and only real God, the Father of Christ. 3. But would that even there the audacity of these foolish men had stopped short, and that they had not gone further yet in impious self-confusion. For to such a depth have some fallen in their understanding, to such darkness of mind, that they have even devised for themselves, and made gods of things that have no existence at all, nor any place among things created. For mixing up the rational with the irrational, and combining things unlike in nature, they worship the result as gods, such as the dog-headed and snake-headed and ass-headed gods among the Egyptians, and the ram-headed Ammon among the Libyans. While others, dividing apart the portions of men's bodies, head, shoulder, hand, and foot, have set up each as gods and deified them, as though their religion were not satisfied with the whole body in its integrity. 4. But others, straining impiety to the utmost, have deified the motive of the invention of these things and of their own wickedness, namely, pleasure and lust, and worship them, such as their Eros, and the Aphrodite at Paphos. While some of them, as if vying with them in depravation, have ventured to erect into gods their rulers or even their sons, either out of honour for their princes, or from fear of their tyranny, such as the Cretan Zeus, of such renown among them, and the Arcadian Hermes; and among the Indians Dionysus, among the Egyptians Isis and Osiris and Horus, and in our own

---

[7] Rom. i. 25. [8] Prov. xviii. 3.

[9] For the following chapters Döllinger, 'The Gentile and the Jew,' is a rich mine of illustration. The recently published 'Manual of the History of Religions,' by Prof. Chantepie de la Saussaye (Eng. Tra. pub. by Longmans), summarises the best results of recent research.

time Antinous, favourite of Hadrian, Emperor of the Romans, whom, although men know he was a mere man, and not a respectable man, but on the contrary, full of licentiousness, yet they worship for fear of him that enjoined it. For Hadrian having come to sojourn in the land of Egypt, when Antinous the minister of his pleasure died, ordered him to be worshipped; being indeed himself in love with the youth even after his death, but for all that offering a convincing exposure of himself, and a proof against all idolatry, that it was discovered among men for no other reason than by reason of the lust of them that imagined it. According as the wisdom of God testifies beforehand when it says, " The devising of idols was the beginning of fornication [1]." 5. And do not wonder, nor think what we are saying hard to believe, inasmuch as it is not long since, even if it be not still the case, that the Roman Senate vote to those emperors who have ever ruled them from the beginning, either all of them, or such as they wish and decide, a place among the gods, and decree them to be worshipped [2]. For those to whom they are hostile, they treat as enemies and call men, admitting their real nature, while those who are popular with them they order to be worshipped on account of their virtue, as though they had it in their own power to make gods, though they are themselves men, and do not profess to be other than mortal. 6. Whereas if they are to make gods, they ought to be themselves gods; for that which makes must needs be better than that which it makes, and he that judges is of necessity in authority over him that is judged, while he that gives, at any rate that which he has, confers a favour, just as, of course, every king, in giving as a favour what he has to give, is greater and in a higher position than those who receive. If then they decree whomsoever they please to be gods, they ought first to be gods themselves. But the strange thing is this, that they themselves, by dying as men, expose the falsehood of their own vote concerning those deified by them.

§ 10. *Similar human origin of the Greek gods, by decree of Theseus. The process by which mortals become deified.*

But this custom is not a new one, nor did it begin from the Roman Senate : on the contrary, it had existed previously from of old, and was formerly practised for the devising of idols. For the gods renowned from of old among the Greeks, Zeus, Poseidon, Apollo, Hephæstus, Hermes, and, among females, Hera and Demeter and Athena and Artemis, were decreed the title of gods by the order of Theseus,

of whom Greek history tells us [3]; and so the men who pass such decrees die like men and are mourned for, while those in whose favour they are passed are worshipped as gods. What a height of inconsistency and madness! knowing who passed the decree, they pay greater honour to those who are the subjects of it. 2. And would that their idolatrous madness had stopped short at males, and that they had not brought down the title of deity to females. For even women, whom it is not safe to admit to deliberation about public affairs, they worship and serve with the honour due to God, such as those enjoined by Theseus as above stated, and among the Egyptians [4] Isis and the Maid and the Younger one [5], and among others Aphrodite. For the names of the others I do not consider it modest even to mention, full as they are of all kind of grotesqueness. 3. For many, not only in ancient times but in our own also, having lost their beloved ones, brothers and kinsfolk and wives; and many women who had lost their husbands, all of whom nature proved to be mortal men, made representations of them and devised sacrifices, and consecrated them; while later ages, moved by the figure and the brilliancy of the artist, worshipped them as gods, thus falling into inconsistency with nature [6]. For whereas their parents had mourned for them, not regarding them as gods (for had they known them to be gods they would not have lamented them as if they had perished; for this was why they represented them in an image, namely, because they not only did not think them gods, but did not believe them to exist at all, and in order that the sight of their form in the image might console them for their being no more), yet the foolish people pray to them as gods and invest them with the honour of the true God. 4. For example, in Egypt, even to this day, the death-dirge is celebrated for Osiris and Horus and Typho and the others. And the caldrons [7] at Dodona, and the Corybantes in Crete, prove that Zeus is no god but a man, and a man born of a cannibal father. And, strange to say, even Plato, the sage admired among the Greeks, with all his vaunted understanding about God, goes down with Socrates to

[1] Wisd. xiv. 12.
[2] Constantine was the last Emperor officially deified (D.C.B., I. 649), but even Theodosius is raised to heaven by the courtly Claudian *Carm. de* iii *Cons. Honor.* 163 *sqq.*; cf. Gwatkin, p. 54, note.

[3] This is probably a reference to the ἱερὰ ἀναγραφὴ of Euhemerus, which Christian apologists commonly took as genuine history: see § 12, note 1.
[4] Cf. de la Saussaye, § 51. Isis, as goddess of the earth, corresponded to Demeter; as goddess of the dead, to the Κόρη (Persephone).
[5] The Νεωτέρα is a puzzle. The most likely suggestion is that of Montfaucon, who refers it to Cleopatra, who νέα Ἶσις ἐχρημάτιζε (Plut. *Vit. Anton.*). He cites also a coin of M. Antony, on which Cleopatra is figured as θέα νεωτέρα. Several such are given by Vaillant, *de Numism. Cleopatr.* 189. She was not the first of her name to adopt this style, see Head *Hist. Num.* pp. 716, 717. The text might be rendered 'Isis, *both* the Maid and the Younger.' [6] Cf. Wisd. xiv. 12 sqq., quoted below.
[7] Cf. Greg. Naz. Or. v. 32, p. 168 c, and Dict. G. and R. Geog. I. p. 783 a.

Peiræus[8] to worship Artemis, a figment of man's art.

§ 11. The deeds of heathen deities, and particularly of Zeus.

But of these and such like inventions of idolatrous madness, Scripture taught us beforehand long ago, when it said[9], " The devising of idols was the beginning of fornication, and the invention of them, the corruption of life. For neither were they from the beginning, neither shall they be for ever. For the vainglory of men they entered into the world, and therefore shall they come shortly to an end. For a father afflicted with untimely mourning when he hath made an image of his child soon taken away, now honoured him as a god which was then a dead man, and delivered to those that were under him ceremonies and sacrifices. Thus in process of time an ungodly custom grown strong was kept as a law. And graven images were worshipped by the commands of kings. Whom men could not honour in presence because they dwelt afar off, they took the counterfeit of his visage from afar, and made an express image of the king whom they honoured, to the end that by this their forwardness they might flatter him that was absent as if he were present. Also the singular diligence of the artificer did help to set forward the ignorant to more superstition : for he, peradventure, willing to please one in authority, forced all his skill to make the resemblance of the best fashion : and so the multitude, allured by the grace of the work, took him now for a god, which a little before was but honoured as a man : and this was an occasion to deceive the world, for men serving either calamity or tyranny, did ascribe unto stones and stocks the incommunicable Name." 2. The beginning and devising of the invention of idols having been, as Scripture witnesses, of such sort, it is now time to shew thee the refutation of it by proofs derived not so much from without as from these men's own opinions about the idols. For to begin at the lowest point, if one were to take the actions of them they call gods, one would find that they were not only no gods, but had been even of men the most contemptible. For what a thing it is to see the loves and licentious actions of Zeus in the poets ! What a thing to hear of him, on the one hand carrying off Ganymede and committing stealthy adulteries, on the other in panic and alarm lest the walls of the Trojans should be destroyed against his intentions ! What a thing to see him in grief at the death of his son

Sarpedon, and wishing to succour him without being able to do so, and, when plotted against by the other so-called gods, namely, Athena and Hera and Poseidon, succoured by Thetis, a woman, and by Ægaeon of the hundred hands, and overcome by pleasures, a slave to women, and for their sakes running adventures in disguises consisting of brute beasts and creeping things and birds ; and again, in hiding on account of his father's designs upon him, or Cronos bound by him, or him again mutilating his father ! Why, is it fitting to regard as a god one who has perpetrated such deeds, and who stands accused of things which not even the public laws of the Romans allow those to do who are merely men ?

§ 12. Other shameful actions ascribed to heathen deities. All prove that they are but men of former times, and not even good men.

For, to mention a few instances out of many to avoid prolixity, who that saw his lawless and corrupt conduct toward Semele, Leda, Alcmene, Artemis, Leto, Maia, Europe, Danae, and Antiope, or that saw what he ventured to take in hand with regard to his own sister, in having the same woman as wife and sister, would not scorn him and pronounce him worthy of death ? For not only did he commit adultery, but he deified and raised to heaven those born of his adulteries, contriving the deification as a veil for his lawlessness : such as Dionysus, Heracles, the Dioscuri, Hermes, Perseus, and Soteira. 2. Who, that sees the so-called gods at irreconcileable strife among themselves at Troy on account of the Greeks and Trojans, will fail to recognise their feebleness, in that because of their mutual jealousies they egged on even mortals to strife? Who, that sees Ares and Aphrodite wounded by Diomed, or Hera and Aïdoneus from below the earth, whom they call a god, wounded by Heracles, Dionysus by Perseus, Athena by Arcas, and Hephæstus hurled down and going lame, will not recognise their real nature, and, while refusing to call them gods, be assured (when he hears that they are corruptible and passible) that they are nothing but men[1], and feeble men too, and admire those that inflicted the wounds rather than the wounded? 3. Or who that sees the adultery of Ares with Aphrodite, and Hephæstus contriving a snare for the two, and the other so-called gods called by He-

---

[1] This explanation of gods as deified men is known as Euhemerism, from Euhemerus, who broached the theory in the third century, B.C. (*supra*, 10, note 1) ; but ' there were Euhemerists in Greece before Euhemerus' (Jowett's Plato, 2. 101). The Fathers very commonly adopt the theory, for which, however, there are very slight grounds. Such cases as those of Antinous and the Emperors, as well as the legends of heroes and demigods, gave it some plausibility (see Döllinger, *Gentile and Jew*, vol. i. p. 344, Eng. Tr.).

phæstus to view the adultery, and coming and seeing their licentiousness, would not laugh and recognise their worthless character? Or who would not laugh at beholding the drunken folly and misconduct of Heracles toward Omphale? For their deeds of pleasure, and their unconscionable loves, and their divine images in gold, silver, bronze, iron, stone, and wood, we need not seriously expose by argument, since the facts are abominable in themselves, and are enough taken alone to furnish proof of the deception; so that one's principal feeling is pity for those deceived about them. 4. For, hating the adulterer who tampers with a wife of their own, they are not ashamed to deify the teachers of adultery; and refraining from incest themselves they worship those who practise it; and admitting that the corrupting of children is an evil, they serve those who stand accused of it; and do not blush to ascribe to those they call gods things which the laws forbid to exist even among men.

§ 13. The folly of image worship and its dishonour to art.

Again, in worshipping things of wood and stone, they do not see that, while they tread under foot and burn what is in no way different, they call portions of these materials gods. And what they made use of a little while ago, they carve and worship in their folly, not seeing, nor at all considering that they are worshipping, not gods, but the carver's art. 2. For so long as the stone is uncut and the wood unworked, they walk upon the one and make frequent use of the other for their own purposes, even for those which are less honourable. But when the artist has invested them with the proportions of his own skill, and impressed upon the material the form of man or woman, then, thanking the artist, they proceed to worship them as gods, having bought them from the carver at a price. Often, moreover, the image-maker, as though forgetting the work he has done himself, prays to his own productions, and calls gods what just before he was paring and chipping. 3. But it were better, if need were to admire these things, to ascribe it to the art of the skilled workman, and not to honour the productions in preference to their producer. For it is not the material that has adorned the art, but the art that has adorned and deified the material. Much juster were it, then, for them to worship the artist than his productions, both because his existence was prior to that of the gods produced by art, and because they have come into being in the form he pleased to give them. But as it is, setting justice aside, and dishonouring skill and art, they worship the products of skill and art, and when the man is dead that made them, they honour his works as immortal, whereas if they did not receive daily attention they would certainly in time come to a natural end. 4. Or how could one fail to pity them in this also, in that seeing, they worship them that cannot see, and hearing, pray to them that cannot hear, and born with life and reason, men as they are, call gods things which do not move at all, but have not even life, and, strangest of all, in that they serve as their masters beings whom they themselves keep under their own power? Nor imagine that this is a mere statement of mine, nor that I am maligning them; for the verification of all this meets the eyes, and whoever wishes to do so may see the like.

§ 14. Image worship condemned by Scripture.

But better testimony about all this is furnished by Holy Scripture, which tells us beforehand when it says [2], " Their idols are silver and gold, the work of men's hands. Eyes have they and will not see; a mouth have they and will not speak; ears have they and will not hear; noses have they and will not smell; hands have they and will not handle; feet have they and will not walk; they will not speak through their throat. Like unto them be they that make them." Nor have they escaped prophetic censure; for there also is their refutation, where the Spirit says [3], " they shall be ashamed that have formed a god, and carved all of them that which is vain: and all by whom they were made are dried up: and let the deaf ones among men all assemble and stand up together, and let them be confounded and put to shame together; for the carpenter sharpened iron, and worked it with an adze, and fashioned it with an auger, and set it up with the arm of his strength: and he shall hunger and be faint, and drink no water. For the carpenter chose out wood, and set it by a rule, and fashioned it with glue, and made it as the form of a man and as the beauty of man, and set it up in his house, wood which he had cut from the grove and which the Lord planted, and the rain gave it growth that it might be for men to burn, and that he might take thereof and warm himself, and kindle, and bake bread upon it, but the residue they made into gods, and worshipped them, the half whereof they had burned in the fire. And upon the half thereof he roasted flesh and ate and was filled, and was warmed and said: ' It is pleasant to me, because I am warmed and have seen the fire.' But the residue thereof he worshipped, saying, ' Deliver me for thou art my god.' They

---

[2] Ps. cxv. 5 sqq.   [3] Isa. xliv. 9 sqq. (LXX.).

knew not nor understood, because their eyes were dimmed that they could not see, nor perceive with their heart ; nor did he consider in his heart nor know in his understanding that he had burned half thereof in the fire, and baked bread upon the coals thereof, and roasted flesh and eaten it, and made the residue thereof · an abomination, and they worship it. Know that their heart is dust and they are deceived, and none can deliver his soul. Behold and will ye not say, ' There is a lie in my right hand ? ' " 2. How then can they fail to be judged godless by all, who even by the divine Scripture are accused of impiety ? or how can they be anything but miserable, who are thus openly convicted of worshipping dead things instead of the truth ? or what kind of hope have they ? or what kind of excuse could be made for them, trusting in things without sense or movement, which they reverence in place of the true God ?

§ 15. *The details about the gods conveyed in the representations of them by poets and artists shew that they are without life, and that they are not gods, nor even decent men and women.*

For would that the artist would fashion the gods even without shape, so that they might not be open to so manifest an exposure of their lack of sense. For they might have cajoled the perception of simple folk to think the idols had senses, were it not that they possess the symbols of the senses, eyes for example and noses and ears and hands and mouth, without any gesture of actual perception and grasp of the objects of sense. But as a matter of fact they have these things and have them not, stand and stand not, sit and sit not. For they have not the real action of these things, but as their fashioner pleased, so they remain stationary, giving no sign of a god, but evidently mere inanimate objects, set there by man's art. 2. Or would that the heralds and prophets of these false gods, poets I mean and writers, had simply written that they were gods, and not also recounted their actions as an exposure of their godlessness and scandalous life. For by the mere name of godhead they might have filched away the truth, or rather caused the mass of men to err from the truth. But as it is, by narrating the loves and immoralities of Zeus, and the corruptions of youths by the other gods, and the voluptuous jealousies of the females, and the fears and acts of cowardice and other wickednesses, they merely convict themselves of narrating not merely about no gods, but not even about respectable men, but on the contrary, of telling tales about shameful persons far removed from what is honourable.

§ 16. *Heathen arguments in palliation of the above: and* (1) ' *the poets are responsible for these unedifying tales.' But are the names and existence of the gods any better authenticated ? Both stand or fall together. Either the actions must be defended or the deity of the gods given up. And the heroes are not credited with acts inconsistent with their nature, as, on this plea, the gods are.*

But perhaps, as to all this, the impious will appeal to the peculiar style of poets, saying that it is the peculiarity of poets to feign what is not, and, for the pleasure of their hearers, to tell fictitious tales ; and that for this reason they have composed the stories about gods. But this pretext of theirs, even more than any other, will appear to be superficial from what they themselves think and profess about these matters. 2. For if what is said in the poets is fictitious and false, even the nomenclature of Zeus, Cronos, Hera, Ares and the rest must be false. For perhaps, as they say, even the names are fictitious, and, while no such being exists as Zeus, Cronos, or Ares, the poets feign their existence to deceive their hearers. But if the poets feign the existence of unreal beings, how is it that they worship them as though they existed ? 3. Or perhaps, once again, they will say that while the names are not fictitious, they ascribe to them fictitious actions. But even this is equally precarious as a defence. For if they made up the actions, doubtless also they made up the names, to which they attributed the actions. Or if they tell the truth about the names, it follows that they tell the truth about the actions too. In particular, they who have said in their tales that these are gods certainly know how gods ought to act, and would never ascribe. to gods the ideas of men, any more than one would ascribe to water the properties of fire ; for fire burns, whereas the nature of water on the contrary is cold. 4. If then the actions are worthy of gods, they that do them must be gods ; but if they are actions of men, and of disreputable men, such as adultery and the acts mentioned above, they that act in such ways must be men and not gods. For their deeds must correspond to their natures, so that at once the actor may be made known by his act, and the action may be ascertainable from his nature. So that just as a man discussing about water and fire, and declaring their action, would not say that water burned and fire cooled, nor, if a man were discoursing about the sun and the earth, would he say the earth gave light, while the sun was sown with herbs and fruits, but if he were to say so would exceed the utmost height of madness, so neither would their writers, and especially the most eminent poet of all, if they really knew that Zeus and the others were gods, invest them with such actions as shew them to be not gods, but rather men, and not sober men. 5. Or if, as poets, they told falsehoods, and you are maligning them, why did they not also tell falsehoods about the courage of the heroes, and feign feebleness in the place of courage, and courage in that of feebleness? For they ought in that case, as with Zeus and Hera, so also to slanderously accuse Achilles of want of courage, and to celebrate the might of Thersites, and, while charging Odysseus with dulness, to make out Nestor a reckless person, and to narrate effeminate actions of Diomed and Hector, and manly deeds of Hecuba. For the fiction and falsehood they ascribe to the poets ought to extend to all cases. But in fact, they kept the truth for their men, while not ashamed to tell falsehoods about their so-called gods. 6. And as some of them might argue, that they are telling falsehoods about their licentious actions, but that in their praises, when they speak of Zeus as father of gods, and as the highest, and the Olympian, and as reigning in heaven, they are not inventing but speaking truthfully ; this is a plea which not only myself, but anybody can refute. For the truth will be clear, in opposition to them, if we recall our previous proofs. For while their actions prove them to be men, the panegyrics upon them go beyond the nature of men. The two things then are mutually inconsistent ; for neither is it the nature of heavenly beings to act in such ways, nor can any one suppose that persons so acting are gods.

§ 17. *The truth probably is, that the scandalous tales are true, while the divine attributes ascribed to them are due to the flattery of the poets.*

What inference then is left to us, save that while the panegyrics are false and flattering, the actions told of them are true? And the truth of this one can ascertain by common practice. For nobody who pronounces a panegyric upon anyone accuses his conduct at the same time, but rather, if men's actions are disgraceful, they praise them up with panegyrics, on account of the scandal they cause, so that by extravagant praise they may impose upon their hearers, and hide the misconduct of the others. 2. Just as if a man who has to pronounce a panegyric upon someone cannot find material for it in their conduct or in any personal qualities, on account of the scandal attaching to these, he praises them up in another manner, flattering them with what does not belong to them, so have their marvellous poets, put out of countenance by the scandalous ac-

tions of their so-called gods, attached to them the superhuman title, not knowing that they cannot by their superhuman fancies veil their human actions, but that they will rather succeed in shewing, by their human shortcomings, that the attributes of God do not fit them. 3. And I am disposed to think that they have recounted the passions and the actions of the gods even in spite of themselves. For since they were endeavouring to invest with what Scripture calls the incommunicable name and honour of [4] God them that are no gods but mortal men, and since this venture of theirs was great and impious, for this reason even against their will they were forced by truth to set forth the passions of these persons, so that their passions recorded in the writings concerning them might be in evidence for all posterity as a proof that they were no gods.

§ 18. *Heathen defence continued.* (2) '*The gods are worshipped for having invented the Arts of Life.' But this is a human and natural, not a divine, achievement. And why, on this principle, are not all inventors deified?*

What defence, then, what proof that these are real gods, can they offer who hold this superstition? For, by what has been said just above, our argument has demonstrated them to be men, and not respectable men. But perhaps they will turn to another argument, and proudly appeal to the things useful to life discovered by them, saying that the reason why they regard them as gods is their having been of use to mankind. For Zeus is said to have possessed the plastic art, Poseidon that of the pilot, Hephæstus the smith's, Athena that of weaving, Apollo that of music, Artemis that of hunting, Hera dressmaking, Demeter agriculture, and others other arts, as those who inform us about them have related. 2. But men ought to ascribe them and such like arts not to the gods alone but to the common nature of mankind, for by observing nature [5] men discover the arts. For even common parlance calls art an imitation of nature. If then they have been skilled in the arts they pursued, that is no reason for thinking them gods, but rather for thinking them men ; for the arts were not their creation, but in them they, like others, imitated nature. 3. For men having a natural capacity for knowledge according to the definition laid down [6] concerning them, there is nothing to surprise us if by human intelligence, and by looking of themselves at their own nature and coming to know it, they have hit upon the arts. Or if they say

4 Wisd. xiv. 21. Cf. Isa. xlii. 8, and xlviii. 11.
5 φύσις is here used in a double sense.
6 By Aristotle, *Top.* V. ii.—iv. where man is defined as ζῶον ἐπιστήμης δεκτικόν: compare *Metaph.* I. i. 'All men by nature desire to know.'

that the discovery of the arts entitles them to be proclaimed as gods, it is high time to proclaim as gods the discoverers of the other arts, on the same grounds as the former were thought worthy of such a title. For the Phœnicians invented letters, Homer epic poetry, Zeno of Elea dialectic, Corax of Syracuse rhetoric, Aristæus bee-keeping, Triptolemus the sowing of corn, Lycurgus of Sparta and Solon of Athens laws; while Palamedes discovered the arrangement of letters, and numbers, and measures and weights. And others imparted various other things useful for the life of mankind, according to the testimony of our historians. 4. If then the arts make gods, and because of them carved gods exist, it follows, on their shewing, that those who at a later date discovered the other arts must be gods. Or if they do not deem these worthy of divine honour, but recognise that they are men, it were but consistent not to give even the name of gods to Zeus, Hera, and the others, but to believe that they too have been human beings, and all the more so, inasmuch as they were not even respectable in their day; just as by the very fact of sculpturing their form in statues they shew that they are nothing else but men.

§ 19. *The inconsistency of image worship. Arguments in palliation.* (1) *The divine nature must be expressed in a visible sign.* (2) *The image a means of supernatural communications to men through Angels.*

For what other form do they give them by sculpture but that of men and women, and of creatures lower yet and of irrational nature, all manner of birds, beasts both tame and wild, and creeping things, whatsoever land and sea and the whole realm of the waters produce? For men having fallen into the unreasonableness of their passions and pleasures, and unable to see anything beyond pleasures and lusts of the flesh, inasmuch as they keep their mind in the midst of these irrational things, they imagined the divine principle to be in irrational things, and carved a number of gods to match the variety of their passions. 2. For there are with them images of beasts and creeping things and birds, as the interpreter of the divine and true religion says, "They became vain in their reasonings, and their senseless heart was darkened. Professing themselves to be wise, they became fools, and changed the glory of the incorruptible God for the likeness of an image of corruptible man, and of birds and four-footed beasts and creeping things, wherefore God gave them up unto vile passions." For having previously infected their soul, as I said above, with the irrationalities of pleasures, they then came down to this

making of gods; and, once fallen, thenceforward as though abandoned in their rejection of God, thus they wallow[7] in them, and portray God, the Father of the Word, in irrational shapes. 3. As to which those who pass for philosophers and men of knowledge[8] among the Greeks, while driven to admit that their visible gods are the forms and figures of men and of irrational objects, say in defence that they have such things to the end that by their means the deity may answer them and be made manifest; because otherwise they could not know the invisible God, save by such statues and rites. 4. While those[9] who profess to give still deeper and more philosophical reasons than these say, that the reason of idols being prepared and fashioned is for the invocation and manifestation of divine angels and powers, that appearing by these means they may teach men concerning the knowledge of God; and that they serve as letters for men, by referring to which they may learn to apprehend God, from the manifestation of the divine angels effected by their means. Such then is their mythology,—for far be it from us to call it a theology. But if one examine the argument with care, he will find that the opinion of these persons also, not less than that of those previously spoken of, is false.

§ 20. *But where does this supposed virtue of the image reside? in the material, or in the form, or in the maker's skill? Untenability of all these views.*

For one might reply to them, bringing the case before the tribunal of truth, How does God make answer or become known by such objects? Is it due to the matter of which they consist, or to the form which they possess? For if it be due to the matter, what need is there of the form, instead of God manifesting Himself through all matter without exception before these things were fashioned? And in vain have they built their temples to shut in a single stone, or stock, or piece of gold, when all the world is full of these substances. 2. But if the superadded form be the cause of the divine manifestation, what is the need of the material, gold and the rest, instead of God manifesting Himself by the actual natural animals of which the images are the figures? For the opinion held about God would on the same principle have been a nobler one, were He to manifest

---

7 Cf. Orat. iii. 16.
8 This may refer to Maximus of Tyre (Saussaye, § 11), or to the lost treatise of 'the divine Iamblichus' Περὶ ἀγαλμάτων, which was considered worth answering by Christian writers as late as the seventh century (Philoponus in Phot. Bibl. *Cod.* 215).
9 This is in effect the defence of the 'Scriptor de Mysteriis' (possibly Iamblichus, see Bernays '2 Abhandlungen' 1880, p. 37): material means of worship are a means of access directly to the lower (or quasi-material) gods, and so indirectly to the higher. Few men can reach the latter without the aid of their manifestation in the lower; πάρεστιν αὔλως τοῖς ἐνύλοις τὰ ἄϋλα (v. 23, cf. 14).

Himself by means of living animals, whether rational or irrational, instead of being looked for in things without life or motion. 3. Wherein they commit the most signal impiety against themselves. For while they abominate and turn from the real animals, beasts, birds, and creeping things, either because of their ferocity or because of their dirtiness, yet they carve their forms in stone, wood, or gold, and make them gods. But it would be better for them to worship the living things themselves, rather than to worship their figures in stone. 4. But perhaps neither is the case, nor is either the material or the form the cause of the divine presence, but it is only skilful art that summons the deity, inasmuch as it is an imitation of nature. But if the deity communicates with the images on account of the art, what need, once more, of the material, since the art resides in the men? For if God manifests Himself solely because of the art, and if for this reason the images are worshipped as gods, it would be right to worship and serve the men who are masters of the art, inasmuch as they are rational also, and have the skill in themselves.

§ 21. *The idea of communications through angels involves yet wilder inconsistency, nor does it, even if true, justify the worship of the image.*

But as to their second and as they say profounder defence, one might reasonably add as follows. If these things are made by you, ye Greeks, not for the sake of a self-manifestation of God Himself, but for the sake of a presence there of angels, why do you rank the images by which ye invoke the powers as superior and above the powers invoked? For ye carve the figures for the sake of the apprehension of God, as ye say, but invest the actual images with the honour and title of God, thus placing yourselves in a profane position. 2. For while confessing that the power of God transcends the littleness of the images, and for that reason not venturing to invoke God through them, but only the lesser powers, ye yourselves leap over these latter, and have bestowed on stocks and stones the title of Him, whose presence ye feared, and call them gods instead of stones and men's workmanship, and worship them. For even supposing them to serve you, as ye falsely say, as letters for the contemplation of God, it is not right to give the signs greater honour than that which they signify. For neither if a man were to write the emperor's name would it be without risk to give to the writing more honour than to the emperor; on the contrary, such a man incurs the penalty of death; while the writing is fashioned by the skill of the writer. 3. So also yourselves, had ye your reasoning power in full strength, would not reduce to matter so great a revelation of the Godhead: but neither would ye have given to the image greater honour than to the man that carved it. For if there be any truth in the plea that, as letters, they indicate the manifestation of God, and are therefore, as indications of God, worthy to be deified, yet far more would it be right to deify the artist who carved and engraved them, as being far more powerful and divine than they, inasmuch as they were cut and fashioned according to his will. If then the letters are worthy of admiration, much more does the writer exceed them in wonder, by reason of his art and the skill of his mind. If then it be not fitting to think that they are gods for this reason, one must again interrogate them about the madness concerning the idols, demanding from them the justification for their being in such a form.

§ 22. *The image cannot represent the true form of God, else God would be corruptible.*

For if the reason of their being thus fashioned is, that the Deity is of human form, why do they invest it also with the forms of irrational creatures? Or if the form of it is that of the latter, why do they embody it also in the images of rational creatures? Or if it be both at once, and they conceive God to be of the two combined, namely, that He has the forms both of rational and of irrational, why do they separate what is joined together, and separate the images of brutes and of men, instead of always carving it of both kinds, such as are the fictions in the myths, Scylla, Charybdis, the Hippocentaur, and the dog-headed Anubis of the Egyptians? For they ought either to represent them solely of two natures in this way, or, if they have a single form, not to falsely represent them in the other as well. 2. And again, if their forms are male, why do they also invest them with female shapes? Or if they are of the latter, why do they also falsify their forms as though they were males? Or if again they are a mixture of both, they ought not to be divided, but both ought to be combined, and follow the type of the so-called hermaphrodites, so that their superstition should furnish beholders with a spectacle not only of impiety and calumny, but of ridicule as well. 2. And generally, if they conceive the Deity to be corporeal, so that they contrive for it and represent belly and hands and feet, and neck also, and breasts and the other organs that go to make man, see to what impiety and godlessness their mind has come down, to have such ideas of the Deity. For it follows that it must be capable of all other bodily casualties as well, of being cut and divided, and even of perishing altogether. But these and like things are not properties of God, but rather of earthly bodies. 3. For while God is incorporeal and incorruptible, and immortal, needing nothing for any purpose, these are both corruptible, and are shapes of bodies, and need bodily ministrations, as we said before [1]. For often we see images which have grown old renewed, and those which time, or rain, or some or other of the animals of the earth have spoiled, restored. In which connexion one must condemn their folly, in that they proclaim as gods things of which they themselves are the makers, and themselves ask salvation of objects which they themselves adorn with their arts to preserve them from corruption, and beg that their own wants may be supplied by beings which they well know need attention from themselves, and are not ashamed to call lords of heaven and all the earth creatures whom they shut up in small chambers.

§ 23. *The variety of idolatrous cults proves that they are false.*

But not only from these considerations may one appreciate their godlessness, but also from their discordant opinions about the idols themselves. For if they be gods according to their assertion and their speculations, to which of them is one to give allegiance, and which of them is one to judge to be the higher, so as either to worship God with confidence, or as they say to recognise the Deity by them without ambiguity? For not the same beings are called gods among all; on the contrary, for every nation almost there is a separate god imagined. And there are cases of a single district and a single town being at internal discord about the superstition of their idols. 2. The Phœnicians, for example, do not know those who are called gods among the Egyptians, nor do the Egyptians worship the same idols as the Phœnicians have. And while the Scythians reject the gods of the Persians, the Persians reject those of the Syrians. But the Pelasgians also repudiate the gods in Thrace, while the Thracians know not those of Thebes. The Indians moreover differ from the Arabs, the Arabs from the Ethiopians, and the Ethiopians from the Arabs in their idols. And the Syrians worship not the idols of the Cilicians, while the Cappadocian nation call gods beings different from these. And while the Bithynians have adopted others, the Armenians have imagined others again. And what need is there for me to multiply examples? The men on the continent worship other gods than the islanders, while these latter serve other gods than those of the main lands. 3. And, in general, every city and village, not knowing the gods of its

neighbours, prefers its own, and deems that these alone are gods. For concerning the abominations in Egypt there is no need even to speak, as they are before the eyes of all: how the cities have religions which are opposite and incompatible, and neighbours always make a point of worshipping the opposite of those next to them [2]: so much so that the crocodile, prayed to by some, is held in abomination by their neighbours, while the lion, worshipped as a god by others, their neighbours, so far from worshipping, slay, if they find it, as a wild beast; and the fish, consecrated by some people, is used as food in another place. And thus arise fights and riots and frequent occasions of bloodshed, and every indulgence of the passions among them. 4. And strange to say, according to the statement of historians, the very Pelasgians, who learned from the Egyptians the names of the gods, do not know the gods of Egypt, but worship others instead. And, speaking generally, all the nations that are infatuated with idols have different opinions and religions, and consistency is not to be met with in any one case. Nor is this surprising. 5. For having fallen from the contemplation of the one God, they have come down to many and diverse objects; and having turned from the Word of the Father, Christ the Saviour of all, they naturally have their understanding wandering in many directions. And just as men who have turned from the sun and are come into dark places go round by many pathless ways, and see not those who are present, while they imagine those to be there who are not, and seeing see not; so they that have turned from God and whose soul is darkened, have their mind in a roving state, and like men who are drunk and cannot see, imagine what is not true.

§ 24. *The so-called gods of one place are used as victims in another.*

This, then, is no slight proof of their real godlessness. For, the gods for every city and country being many and various, and the one destroying the god of the other, the whole of them are destroyed by all. For those who are considered gods by some are offered as sacrifices and drink-offerings to the so-called gods of others, and the victims of some are conversely the gods of others. So the Egyptians serve the ox, and Apis, a calf, and others sacri-

---

[1] Supra xiii. 3.

[2] Hdt. ii. 69; cf. Juv. Sat. xv. 36,
    ' numina vicinorum
      Odit uterque locus.'
This is one of the few places where Athanasius has any Egyptian 'local colour' (cf. supra 9 and 10). M. Fialon is certainly too imaginative (p. 86, contradicted p. 283), when he sees in the *contra Gentes* an appreciation of the higher religious principles which the modern science ('toute Française') of Egyptology has enabled us to read behind the grotesque features of popular Egyptian polytheism.

fice these animals to Zeus. For even if they do not sacrifice the very animals the others have consecrated, yet by sacrificing their fellows they seem to offer the same. The Libyans have for god a sheep which they call Ammon, and in other nations this animal is slain as a victim to many gods. 2. The Indians worship Diony-sus, using the name as a symbol for wine, and others pour out wine as an offering to the other gods. Others honour rivers and springs, and above all the Egyptians pay especial honour to water, calling them gods. And yet others, and even the Egyptians who worship the waters, use them to wash off the dirt from others and from themselves, and ignominiously throw away what is used. While nearly the whole of the Egyptian system of idols consists of what are victims to the gods of other nations, so that they are scorned even by those others for deifying what are not gods, but, both with others and even among themselves, propitiatory offerings and victims.

§ 25. *Human sacrifice. Its absurdity. Its prevalence. Its calamitous results.*

But some have been led by this time to such a pitch of irreligion and folly as to slay and to offer in sacrifice to their false gods even actual men, whose figures and forms the gods are. Nor do they see, wretched men, that the victims they are slaying are the patterns of the gods they make and worship, and to whom they are offering the men. For they are offering, one may say, equals to equals, or rather, the higher to the lower; for they are offering living creatures to dead, and rational beings to things without motion. 2. For the Scythians who are called Taurians offer in sacrifice to their Virgin, as they call her, survivors from wrecks, and such Greeks as they catch, going thus far in impiety against men of their own race, and thus exposing the savagery of their gods, in that those whom Providence has rescued from danger and from the sea, they slay, almost fighting against Providence; because they frustrate the kindness of Providence by their own brutal character. But others, when they are returned victorious from war, thereupon dividing their prisoners into hundreds, and taking a man from each, sacrifice to Ares the man they have picked out from each hundred. 3. Nor is it only Scythians who commit these abominations on account of the ferocity natural to them as barbarians: on the contrary, this deed is a special result of the wickedness connected with idols and false gods. For the Egyptians used formerly to offer victims of this kind to Hera, and the Phœnicians and Cretans used to propitiate Cronos in their sacrifices of children. And even the ancient Romans used to worship Jupiter Latiarius, as he was

called, with human sacrifices, and some in one way, some in another, but all [1] without exception committed and incurred the pollution : they incurred it by the mere perpetration of the murderous deeds, while they polluted their own temples by filling them with the smoke of such sacrifices. 4. This then was the ready source of numerous evils to mankind. For seeing that their false gods were pleased with these things, they forthwith imitated their gods with like misdoings, thinking that the imitation of superior beings, as they considered them, was a credit to themselves. Hence mankind was thinned by murders of grown men and children, and by licence of all kinds. For nearly every city is full of licentiousness of all kinds, the result of the savage character of its gods ; nor is there one of sober life in the idols' temples [2] save only he whose licentiousness is witnessed to by them all [3].

§ 26. *The moral corruptions of Paganism all admittedly originated with the gods.*

Women, for example, used to sit out in old days in the temples of Phœnicia, consecrating to the gods there the hire of their bodies, thinking they propitiated their goddess by fornication, and that they would procure her favour by this. While men, denying their nature, and no longer wishing to be males, put on the guise of women, under the idea that they are thus gratifying and honouring the Mother of their so-called gods. But all live along with the basest, and vie with the worst among themselves, and as Paul said, the holy minister of Christ [4]: "For their women changed the natural use into that which is against nature : and likewise also the men, leaving the natural use of the woman, burned in their lust one toward another, men with men working unseemliness." 2. But acting in this and in like ways, they admit and prove that the life of their so-called gods was of the same kind. For from Zeus they have learned corruption of youth and adultery, from Aphrodite fornication, from Rhea licentiousness, from Ares murders, and from other gods other like things, which the laws punish and from which every sober man turns away. Does it then remain fit to consider them gods who do such things, instead of reckoning them, for the licentiousness of their ways, more irrational than the brutes? Is it fit to consider their worshippers human beings, in-

---

[1] On human sacrifice see Saussaye, § 17, and Robertson Smith, *Religion of the Semites*, pp. 343 *sqq.*, especially p. 347, note 1, for references to examples near the time of this treatise.
[2] Reading εἰδωλείοις e conj. Marr.
[3] i.e. among the licentious worshippers the lifeless image is the only one free from vice, although the worshippers credit him with divine attributes, and therefore, according to their superstition, with a licentious life.
[4] Rom. i. 26.

stead of pitying them as more irrational than the brutes, and more soul-less than inanimate things? For had they considered the intellectual part of their soul they would not have plunged headlong into these things, nor have denied the true God, the Father of Christ.

§ 27. *The refutation of popular Paganism being taken as conclusive, we come to the higher form of nature-worship. How Nature witnesses to God by the mutual dependence of all her parts, which forbid us to think of any one of them as the supreme God. This shewn at length.*

But perhaps those who have advanced beyond these things, and who stand in awe of Creation, being put to shame by these exposures of abominations, will join in repudiating what is readily condemned and refuted on all hands, but will think that they have a well-grounded and unanswerable opinion, namely, the worship of the universe and of the parts of the universe. 2. For they will boast that they worship and serve, not mere stocks and stones and forms of men and irrational birds and creeping things and beasts, but the sun and moon and all the heavenly universe, and the earth again, and the entire realm of water: and they will say that none can shew that these at any rate are not of divine nature, since it is evident to all, that they lack neither life nor reason, but transcend even the nature of mankind, inasmuch as the one inhabit the heavens, the other the earth. 3. It is worth while then to look into and examine these points also; for here, too, our argument will find that its proof against them holds true. But before we look, or begin our demonstration, it suffices that Creation almost raises its voice against them, and points to God as its Maker and Artificer, Who reigns over Creation and over all things, even the Father of our Lord Jesus Christ; Whom the would-be philosophers turn from to worship and deify the Creation which proceeded from Him, which yet itself worships and confesses the Lord Whom they deny on its account. 4. For if men are thus awestruck at the parts of Creation and think that they are gods, they might well be rebuked by the mutual dependence of those parts; which moreover makes known, and witnesses to, the Father of the Word, Who is the Lord and Maker of these parts also, by the unbroken law of their obedience to Him, as the divine law also says: "The heavens declare the glory of God, and the firmament sheweth His handiwork [5]." 5. But the proof of all this is not obscure, but is clear enough in all conscience to those the eyes of whose understanding are not wholly disabled.

For if a man take the parts of Creation separately, and consider each by itself,—as for example the sun by itself alone, and the moon apart, and again earth and air, and heat and cold, and the essence of wet and of dry, separating them from their mutual conjunction,—he will certainly find that not one is sufficient for itself, but all are in need of one another's assistance, and subsist by their mutual help. For the Sun is carried round along with, and is contained in, the whole heaven, and can never go beyond his own orbit, while the moon and other stars testify to the assistance given them by the Sun: while the earth again evidently does not yield her crops without rains, which in their turn would not descend to earth without the assistance of the clouds; but not even would the clouds ever appear of themselves and subsist, without the air. And the air is warmed by the upper air, but illuminated and made bright by the sun, not by itself. 6. And wells, again, and rivers will never exist without the earth; but the earth is not supported upon itself, but is set upon the realm of the waters, while this again is kept in its place, being bound fast at the centre of the universe. And the sea, and the great ocean that flows outside round the whole earth, is moved and borne by winds wherever the force of the winds dashes it. And the winds in their turn originate, not in themselves, but according to those who have written on the subject, in the air, from the burning heat and high temperature of the upper as compared with the lower air, and blow everywhere through the latter. 7. For as to the four elements of which the nature of bodies is composed, heat, that is, and cold, wet and dry, who is so perverted in his understanding as not to know that these things exist indeed in combination, but if separated and taken alone they tend to destroy even one another according to the prevailing power of the more abundant element? For heat is destroyed by cold if it be present in greater quantity, and cold again is put away by the power of heat, and what is dry, again, is moistened by wet, and the latter dried by the former.

§ 28. *But neither can the cosmic organism be God. For that would make God consist of dissimilar parts, and subject Him to possible dissolution.*

How then can these things be gods, seeing that they need one another's assistance? Or how is it proper to ask anything of them when they too ask help for themselves one from another? For if it is an admitted truth about God that He stands in need of nothing, but is self-sufficient and self-contained, and that in Him all things have their being, and that He ministers to all rather than they to Him, how is it right to proclaim as gods the sun and moon and other parts of creation, which are of no such kind, but which even stand in need of one another's help? 2. But, perhaps, if divided and taken by themselves, our opponents themselves will admit that they are dependent, the demonstration being an ocular one. But they will combine all together, as constituting a single body, and will say that the whole is God. For the whole once put together, they will no longer need external help, but the whole will be sufficient for itself and independent in all respects; so at least the would-be philosophers will tell us, only to be refuted here once more. 3. Now this argument, not one whit less than those previously dealt with, will demonstrate their impiety coupled with great ignorance. For if the combination of the parts makes up the whole, and the whole is combined out of the parts, then the whole consists of the parts, and each of them is a portion of the whole. But this is very far removed from the conception of God. For God is a whole and not a number of parts, and does not consist of diverse elements, but is Himself the Maker of the system of the universe. For see what impiety they utter against the Deity when they say this. For if He consists of parts, certainly it will follow that He is unlike Himself, and made up of unlike parts. For if He is sun, He is not moon, and if He is moon, He is not earth, and if He is earth, He cannot be sea : and so on, taking the parts one by one, one may discover the absurdity of this theory of theirs. 4. But the following point, drawn from the observation of our human body, is enough to refute them. For just as the eye is not the sense of hearing, nor is the latter a hand : nor is the belly the breast, nor again is the neck a foot, but each of these has its own function, and a single body is composed of these distinct parts,— having its parts combined for use, but destined to be divided in course of time when nature, that brought them together, shall divide them at the will of God, Who so ordered it;—thus (but may He that is above pardon the argument[6]), if they combine the parts of creation into one body and proclaim it God, it follows, firstly, that He is unlike Himself, as shewn above ; secondly, that He is destined to be divided again, in accordance with the natural tendency of the parts to separation.

§ 29. *The balance of powers in Nature shews that it is not God, either collectively, or in parts.*

And in yet another way one may refute their godlessness by the light of truth. For if God is incorporeal and invisible and intangible by nature, how do they imagine God to be a body,

and worship with divine honour things which we both see with our eyes and touch with our hands ? 2. And again, if what is said of God hold true, namely, that He is almighty, and that while nothing has power over Him, He has power and rule over all, how can they who deify creation fail to see that it does not satisfy this definition of God ? For when the sun is under the earth, the earth's shadow makes his light invisible, while by day the sun hides the moon by the brilliancy of his light. And hail ofttimes injures the fruits of the earth, while fire is put out if an overflow of water take place. And spring makes winter give place, while summer will not suffer spring to outstay its proper limits, and it in its turn is forbidden by autumn to outstep its own season. 3. If then they were gods, they ought not to be defeated and obscured by one another, but always to co-exist, and to discharge their respective functions simultaneously. Both by night and by day the sun and the moon and the rest of the band of stars ought to shine equally together, and give their light to all, so that all things might be illumined by them. Spring and summer and autumn and winter ought to go on without alteration, and together. The sea ought to mingle with the springs, and furnish their drink to man in common. Calms and windy blasts ought to take place at the same time. Fire and water together ought to furnish the same service to man. For no one would take any hurt from them, if they are gods, as our opponents say, and do nothing for hurt, but rather all things for good. 4. But if none of these things are possible, because of their mutual incompatibility, how does it remain possible to give to these things, mutually incompatible and at strife, and unable to combine, the name of gods, or to worship them with the honours due to God ? How could things naturally discordant give peace to others for their prayers, and become to them authors of concord ? It is not then likely that the sun or the moon, or any other part of creation, still less statues in stone, gold, or other material, or the Zeus, Apollo, and the rest, who are the subject of the poet's fables, are true gods : this our argument has shewn. But some of these are parts of creation, others have no life, others have been mere mortal men. Therefore their worship and deification is no part of religion, but the bringing in of godlessness and of all impiety, and a sign of a wide departure from the knowledge of the one true God, namely the Father of Christ. 5. Since then this is thus proved, and the idolatry of the Greeks is shewn to be full of all ungodliness, and that its introduction has been not for the good, but for the ruin, of human life ;—come now, as our argu-

---

ment promised at the outset, let us, after having confuted error, travel the way of truth, and behold the Leader and Artificer of the Universe, the Word of the Father, in order that through Him we may apprehend the Father, and that the Greeks may know how far they have separated themselves from the truth.

PART II.

§ 30. *The soul of man, being intellectual, can know God of itself, if it be true to its own nature.*

The tenets we have been speaking of have been proved to be nothing more than a false guide for life ; but the way of truth will aim at reaching the real and true God. But for its knowledge and accurate comprehension, there is need of none other save of ourselves. Neither, as God Himself is above all, is the road to Him afar off or outside ourselves, but it is in us, and it is possible to find it from ourselves, in the first instance, as Moses also taught, when he said[7] : "The word" of faith "is within thy heart." Which very thing the Saviour declared and confirmed, when He said: "The kingdom of God is within you[8]." 2. For having in ourselves faith, and the kingdom of God, we shall be able quickly to see and perceive the King of the Universe, the saving Word of the Father. And let not the Greeks, who worship idols, make excuses, nor let any one else simply deceive himself, professing to have no such road, and therefore finding a pretext for his godlessness. 3. For we all have set foot upon it, and have it, even if not all are willing to travel by it, but rather to swerve from it and go wrong, because of the pleasures of life which attract them from without. And if one were to ask, what road is this ? I say that it is the soul of each one of us, and the intelligence which resides there. For by it alone can God be contemplated and perceived. 4. Unless, as they have denied God, the impious men will repudiate having a soul ; which indeed is more plausible than the rest of what they say, for it is unlike men possessed of an intellect to deny God, its Maker and Artificer. It is necessary then, for the sake of the simple, to shew briefly that each one of mankind has a soul, and that soul rational ; especially as certain of the sectaries deny this also, thinking that man is nothing more than the visible form of the body. This point once proved, they will be furnished in their own persons with a clearer proof against the idols.

§ 31. *Proof of the existence of the rational soul. (1) Difference of man from the brutes. (2) Man's power of objective thought. Thought is to sense as the musician to his instrument. The phenomena of dreams bear this out.*

Firstly, then, the rational nature of the soul is strongly confirmed by its difference from irrational creatures. For this is why common use gives them that name, because, namely, the race of mankind is rational. 2. Secondly, it is no ordinary proof, that man alone thinks of things external to himself, and reasons about things not actually present, and exercises reflection, and chooses by judgment the better of alternative reasonings. For the irrational animals see only what is present, and are impelled solely by what meets their eye, even if the consequences to them are injurious, while man is not impelled toward what he sees merely, but judges by thought what he sees with his eyes. Often for example his impulses are mastered by reasoning ; and his reasoning is subject to after-reflection. And every one, if he be a friend of truth, perceives that the intelligence of mankind is distinct from the bodily senses. 3. Hence, because it is distinct, it acts as judge of the senses, and while they apprehend their objects, the intelligence distinguishes, recollects, and shews them what is best. For the sole function of the eye is to see, of the ears to hear, of the mouth to taste, of the nostrils to apprehend smells, and of the hands to touch. But what one ought to see and hear, what one ought to touch, taste and smell, is a question beyond the senses, and belonging to the soul and to the intelligence which resides in it. Why, the hand is able to take hold of a sword-blade, and the mouth to taste poison, but neither knows that these are injurious, unless the intellect decide. 4. And the case, to look at it by aid of a simile, is like that of a well-fashioned lyre in the hands of a skilled musician. For as the strings of the lyre have each its proper note, high, low, or intermediate, sharp or otherwise, yet their scale is indistinguishable and their time not to be recognized, without the artist. For then only is the scale manifest and the time right, when he that is holding the lyre strikes the strings and touches each in tune. In like manner, the senses being disposed in the body like a lyre, when the skilled intelligence presides over them, then too the soul distinguishes and knows what it is doing and how it is acting. 5. But this alone is peculiar to mankind, and this is what is rational in the soul of mankind, by means of which it differs from the brutes, and shews that it is truly distinct from what is to be seen in the body. Often, for example, when the body

---

[7] Deut. xxx. 14. [8] Luc. xvii. 12.

is lying on the earth, man imagines and contemplates what is in the heavens. Often when the body is quiet [9], and at rest and asleep, man moves inwardly, and beholds what is outside himself, travelling to other countries, walking about, meeting his acquaintances, and often by these means divining and forecasting the actions of the day. But to what can this be due save to the rational soul, in which man thinks of and perceives things beyond himself?

§ 32. (3) *The body cannot originate such phenomena ; and in fact the action of the rational soul is seen in its over-ruling the instincts of the bodily organs.*

We add a further point to complete our demonstration for the benefit of those [1] who shamelessly take refuge in denial of reason. How is it, that whereas the body is mortal by nature, man reasons on the things of immortality, and often, where virtue demands it, courts death? Or how, since the body lasts but for a time, does man imagine of things eternal, so as to despise what lies before him, and desire what is beyond? The body could not have spontaneously such thoughts about itself, nor could it think upon what is external to itself. For it is mortal and lasts but for a time. And it follows that that which thinks what is opposed to the body and against its nature must be distinct in kind. What then can this be, save a rational and immortal soul? For it introduces the echo of higher things, not outside, but within the body, as the musician does in his lyre. 2. Or how again, the eye being naturally constituted to see and the ear to hear, do they turn from some objects and choose others? For who is it that turns away the eye from seeing? Or who shuts off the ear from hearing, its natural function? Or who often hinders the palate, to which it is natural to taste things, from its natural impulse? Or who withholds the hand from its natural activity of touching something, or turns aside the sense of smell from its normal exercise [2]? Who is it that thus acts against the natural instincts of the body? Or how does the body, turned from its natural course, turn to the counsels of another and suffer itself to be guided at the beck of that other? Why, these things prove simply this, that the rational soul presides over the body. 3. For the body is not even constituted to drive itself, but it is carried at the will of another, just as a horse does not yoke himself, but is driven by his master. Hence laws for human beings to practise what is good and to abstain from evil-doing, while

to the brutes evil remains unthought of and undiscerned, because they lie outside rationality and the process of understanding. I think then that the existence of a rational soul in man is proved by what we have said.

§ 33. *The soul immortal. Proved by (1) its being distinct from the body, (2) its being the source of motion, (3) its power to go beyond the body in imagination and thought.*

But that the soul is made immortal is a further point in the Church's teaching which you must know, to shew how the idols are to be overthrown. But we shall more directly arrive at a knowledge of this from what we know of the body, and from the difference between the body and the soul. For if our argument has proved it to be distinct from the body, while the body is by nature mortal, it follows that the soul is immortal, because it is not like the body. 2. And again, if as we have shewn, the soul moves the body and is not moved by other things, it follows that the movement of the soul is spontaneous, and that this spontaneous movement goes on after the body is laid aside in the earth. If then the soul were moved by the body, it would follow that the severance of its motor would involve its death. But if the soul moves the body also, it follows all the more that it moves itself. But if moved by itself [3], it follows that it outlives the body. 3. For the movement of the soul is the same thing as its life, just as, of course, we call the body alive when it moves, and say that its death takes place when it ceases moving. But this can be made clearer once for all from the action of the soul in the body. For if even when united and coupled with the body it is not shut in or commensurate with the small dimensions of the body, but often [4], when the body lies in bed, not moving, but in death-like sleep, the soul keeps awake by virtue of its own power, and transcends the natural power of the body, and as though travelling away from the body while remaining in it, imagines and beholds things above the earth, and often even holds converse with the saints and angels who are above earthly and bodily existence, and approaches them in the confidence of the purity of its intelligence ; shall it not all the more, when separated from the body at the time appointed by God Who coupled them together, have its knowledge of immortality more clear? For if even when coupled with the body it lived a life outside the body, much more shall its life continue after the death of the body,

---

9 Cf. *Vit. Ant.* 34.   [1] Supra xxx.
[2] Compare the somewhat analogous argument in Butler, *Serm.* ii.

3 Cf. Plato *Phædr.* 245 C—E., *Legg.* 896, A, B. The former passage is more likely to be referred to here, as it is, like the text, an argument for immortality. Athan. has also referred to *Phædrus* above, § 5. (Against Gwatkin, *Studies,* p. 101.
4 Cp. xxxi. 5, and ref.

and live without ceasing by reason of God Who made it thus by His own Word, our Lord Jesus Christ. 4. For this is the reason why the soul thinks of and bears in mind things immortal and eternal, namely, because it is itself immortal. And just as, the body being mortal, its senses also have mortal things as their objects, so, since the soul contemplates and beholds immortal things, it follows that it is immortal and lives for ever. For ideas and thoughts about immortality never desert the soul, but abide in it, and are as it were the fuel in it which ensures its immortality. This then is why the soul has the capacity for beholding God, and is its own way thereto, receiving not from without but from herself the knowledge and apprehension of the Word of God.

§ 34. *The soul, then, if only it get rid of the stains of sin is able to know God directly, its own rational nature imaging back the Word of God, after whose image it was created. But even if it cannot pierce the cloud which sin draws over its vision, it is confronted by the witness of creation to God.*

We repeat then what we said before, that just as men denied God, and worship things without soul, so also in thinking they have not a rational soul, they receive at once the punishment of their folly, namely, to be reckoned among irrational creatures : and so, since as though from lack of a soul of their own they superstitiously worship soulless gods, they are worthy of pity and guidance. 2. But if they claim to have a soul, and pride themselves on the rational principle, and that rightly, why do they, as though they had no soul, venture to go against reason, and think not as they ought, but make themselves out higher even than the Deity ? For having a soul that is immortal and invisible to them, they make a likeness of God in things visible and mortal. Or why, in like manner as they have departed from God, do they not betake themselves to Him again ? For they are able, as they turned away their understanding from God, and feigned as gods things that were not, in like manner to ascend with the intelligence of their soul, and turn back to God again. 3. But turn back they can, if they lay aside the filth of all lust which they have put on, and wash it away persistently, until they have got rid of all the foreign matter that has affected their soul, and can shew it in its simplicity as it was made, that so they may be able by it to behold the Word of the Father, after Whose likeness they were originally made. For the soul is made after the image and likeness of God, as divine Scripture also shews, when it says in the person of God[5] : " Let us

make man after our Image and likeness." Whence also when it gets rid of all the filth of sin which covers it and retains only the likeness of the Image in its purity, then surely this latter being thoroughly brightened, the soul beholds as in a mirror the Image of the Father, even the Word, and by His means reaches the idea of the Father, Whose Image the Saviour is. 4. Or, if the soul's own teaching is insufficient, by reason of the external things which cloud its intelligence, and prevent its seeing what is higher, yet it is further possible to attain to the knowledge of God from the things which are seen, since Creation, as though in written characters, declares in a loud voice, by its order and harmony, its own Lord and Creator.

PART III.

§ 35. *Creation a revelation of God ; especially in the order and harmony pervading the whole.*

For God, being good and loving to mankind, and caring for the souls made by Him,—since He is by nature invisible and incomprehensible, having His being beyond all created existence[6], for which reason the race of mankind was likely to miss the way to the knowledge of Him, since they are made out of nothing while He is unmade,—for this cause God by His own Word gave the Universe the Order it has, in order that since He is by nature invisible, men might be enabled to know Him at any rate by His works[7]. For often the artist even when not seen is known by his works. 2. And as they tell of Phidias the Sculptor that his works of art by their symmetry and by the proportion of their parts betray Phidias to those who see them although he is not there, so by the order of the Universe one ought to perceive God its maker and artificer, even though He be not seen with the bodily eyes. For God did not take His stand upon His invisible nature (let none plead that as an excuse) and leave Himself utterly unknown to men ; but as I said above, He so ordered Creation that although He is by nature invisible He may yet be known by His works. 3. And I say this not on my own authority, but on the strength of what I learned from men who have spoken of God, among them Paul, who thus writes to the Romans[8] : " for the invisible things of Him since the creation of the world are clearly seen, being understood by the things that are made ;" while to the Lycaonians he speaks out and says[9] : " We also are men of like passions with you, and bring you good tidings, to turn from these

---

5 Gen. i. 26.

6 Cf. below, 40. 2.   7 Cf. *Orat.* ii. 32.
8 Rom. i. 20.   9 Acts xiv. 15.

vain things unto a Living God, Who made the heaven and the earth and the sea, and all that in them is, Who in the generations gone by suffered all nations to walk in their own ways. And yet He left not Himself without witness, in that He did good, and gave you [1] from heaven rains and fruitful seasons, filling your hearts with food and gladness." 4. For who that sees the circle of heaven and the course of the sun and the moon, and the positions and movements of the other stars, as they take place in opposite and different directions, while yet in their difference all with one accord observe a consistent order, can resist the conclusion that these are not ordered by themselves, but have a maker distinct from themselves who orders them? or who that sees the sun rising by day and the moon shining by night, and waning and waxing without variation exactly according to the same number of days, and some of the stars running their courses and with orbits various and manifold, while others move [2] without wandering, can fail to perceive that they certainly have a creator to guide them?

§ 36. *This the more striking, if we consider the opposing forces out of which this order is produced.*

Who that sees things of opposite nature combined, and in concordant harmony, as for example fire mingled with cold, and dry with wet, and that not in mutual conflict, but making up a single body, as it were homogeneous, can resist the inference that there is One external to these things that has united them? Who that sees winter giving place to spring and spring to summer and summer to autumn, and that these things contrary by nature (for the one chills, the other burns, the one nourishes the other destroys), yet all make up a balanced result beneficial to mankind,—can fail to perceive that there is One higher than they, Who balances and guides them all, even if he see Him not? 2. Who that sees the clouds supported in air, and the weight of the waters bound up in the clouds, can but perceive Him that binds them up and has ordered these things so? Or who that sees the earth, heaviest of all things by nature, fixed upon the waters, and remaining unmoved upon what is by nature mobile, will fail to understand that there is One that has made and ordered it, even God? Who that sees the earth bringing forth fruits in due season, and the rains from heaven, and the flow of

rivers, and springing up of wells, and the birth of animals from unlike parents, and that these things take place not at all times but at determinate seasons,—and in general, among things mutually unlike and contrary, the balanced and uniform order to which they conform,—can resist the inference that there is one Power which orders and administers them, ordaining things well as it thinks fit? 4. For left to themselves they could not subsist or ever be able to appear, on account of their mutual contrariety of nature. For water is by nature heavy, and tends to flow downwards, while the clouds are light and belong to the class of things which tend to soar and mount upwards. And yet we see water, heavy as it is, borne aloft in the clouds. And again, earth is very heavy, while water on the other hand is relatively light; and yet the heavier is supported upon the lighter, and the earth does not sink, but remains immoveable. And male and female are not the same, while yet they unite in one, and the result is the generation from both of an animal like them. And to cut the matter short, cold is opposite to heat, and wet fights with dry, and yet they come together and are not at variance, but they agree, and produce as their result a single body, and the birth of everything.

§ 37. *The same subject continued.*

Things then of conflicting and opposite nature would not have reconciled themselves, were there not One higher and Lord over them to unite them, to Whom the elements themselves yield obedience as slaves that obey a master. And instead of each having regard to its own nature and fighting with its neighbour, they recognise the Lord Who has united them, and are at concord one with another, being by nature opposed, but at amity by the will of Him that guides them. 2. For if their mingling into one were not due to a higher authority, how could the heavy mingle and combine with the light, the wet with the dry, the round with the straight, fire with cold, or sea with earth, or the sun with the moon, or the stars with the heaven, and the air with the clouds, the nature of each being dissimilar to that of the other? For there would be great strife among them, the one burning, the other giving cold; the heavy dragging downwards, the light in the contrary direction and upwards; the sun giving light while the air diffused darkness: yes, even the stars would have been at discord with one another, since some have their position above, others beneath, and night would have refused to make way for day, but would have persisted in remaining to fight and strive against it. 3. But if this were so, we should consequently see not

---

[1] ὑμῖν and ὑμῶν below are read by several MSS., and are probably correct as in the original passage.
[2] The 'fixed' stars as distinct from the planets. For the argument, cf. Plato, *Legg.* 966 E.

an ordered universe, but disorder, not arrangement but anarchy, not a system, but everything out of system, not proportion but disproportion. For in the general strife and conflict either all things would be destroyed, or the prevailing principle alone would appear. And even the latter would shew the disorder of the whole, for left alone, and deprived of the help of the others, it would throw the whole out of gear, just as, if a single hand and foot were left alone, that would not preserve the body in its integrity. 4. For what sort of an universe would it be, if only the sun appeared, or only the moon went her course, or there were only night, or always day? Or what sort of harmony would it be, again, if the heaven existed alone without the stars, or the stars without the heaven? Or what benefit would there be, if there were only sea, or if the earth were there alone without waters and without the other parts of creation? Or how could man, or any animal, have appeared upon earth, if the elements were mutually at strife, or if there were one that prevailed, and that one insufficient for the composition of bodies? For nothing in the world could have been composed of heat, or cold, or wet, or dry, alone, but all would have been without arrangement or combination. But not even the one element which appeared to prevail would have been able to subsist without the assistance of the rest: for that is how each subsists now.

§ 38. *The Unity of God shewn by the Harmony of the order of Nature.*

Since then, there is everywhere not disorder, but order, proportion and not disproportion, not disarray but arrangement, and that in an order perfectly harmonious, we needs must infer and be led to perceive the Master that put together and compacted all things, and produced harmony in them. For though He be not seen with the eyes, yet from the order and harmony of things contrary it is possible to perceive their Ruler, Arranger, and King. 2. For in like manner as if we saw a city, consisting of many and diverse people, great and small, rich and poor, old and young, male and female, in an orderly condition, and its inhabitants, while different from one another, yet at unity among themselves, and not the rich set against the poor, the great against the small, nor the young against the old, but all at peace in the enjoyment of equal rights,—if we saw this, the inference surely follows that the presence of a ruler enforces concord, even if we do not see him; (for disorder is a sign of absence of rule, while order shews the governing authority: for when we see the mutual harmony of the members in the body, that the

eye does not strive with the hearing, nor is the hand at variance with the foot, but that each accomplishes its service without variance, we perceive from this that certainly there is a soul in the body that governs these members, though we see it not); so in the order and harmony of the Universe, we needs must perceive God the governor of it all, and that He is one and not many. 3. So then this order of its arrangement, and the concordant harmony of all things, shews that the Word, its Ruler and Governor, is not many, but One. For if there were more than one Ruler of Creation, such an universal order would not be maintained, but all things would fall into confusion because of their plurality, each one biasing the whole to his own will, and striving with the other. For just as we said that polytheism was atheism, so it follows that the rule of more than one is the rule of none. For each one would cancel the rule of the other, and none would appear ruler, but there would be anarchy everywhere. But where no ruler is, there disorder follows of course. 4. And conversely, the single order and concord of the many and diverse shews that the ruler too is one. For just as though one were to hear from a distance a lyre, composed of many diverse strings, and marvel at the concord of its symphony, in that its sound is composed neither of low notes exclusively, nor high nor intermediate only, but all combine their sounds in equal balance,— and would not fail to perceive from this that the lyre was not playing itself, nor even being struck by more persons than one, but that there was one musician, even if he did not see him, who by his skill combined the sound of each string into the tuneful symphony; so, the order of the whole universe being perfectly harmonious, and there being no strife of the higher against the lower or the lower against the higher, and all things making up one order, it is consistent to think that the Ruler and King of all Creation is one and not many, Who by His own light illumines and gives movement to all.

§ 39. *Impossibility of a plurality of Gods.*

For we must not think there is more than one ruler and maker of Creation: but it belongs to correct and true religion to believe that its Artificer is one, while Creation herself clearly points to this. For the fact that there is one Universe only and not more is a conclusive proof that its Maker is one. For if there were a plurality of gods, there would necessarily be also more universes than one. For neither were it reasonable for more than one God to make a single universe, nor for the one universe to be made by more than one, because of the absurdities which would result from this. 2. Firstly, if the one universe were made by a plurality of gods, that would mean weakness on the part of those who made it, because many contributed to a single result; which would be a strong proof of the imperfect creative skill of each. For if one were sufficient, the many would not supplement each other's deficiency. But to say that there is any deficiency in God is not only impious, but even beyond all sacrilege. For even among men one would not call a workman perfect if he were unable to finish his work, a single piece, by himself and without the aid of several others. 3. But if, although each one was able to accomplish the whole, yet all worked at it in order to claim a share in the result, we have the laughable conclusion that each worked for reputation, lest he should be suspected of inability. But, once more, it is most grotesque to ascribe vainglory to gods. 4. Again, if each one were sufficient for the creation of the whole, what need of more than one, one being self-sufficient for the universe? Moreover it would be evidently impious and grotesque, to make the thing created one, while the creators were many and different, it being a maxim of science [3] that what is one and complete is higher than things that are diverse. 5. And this you must know, that if the universe had been made by a plurality of gods, its movements would be diverse and inconsistent. For having regard to each one of its makers, its movements would be correspondingly different. But such difference again, as was said before, would involve disarray and general disorder; for not even a ship will sail aright if she be steered by many, unless one pilot hold the tiller [4], nor will a lyre struck by many produce a tuneful sound, unless there be one artist who strikes it. 6. Creation, then, being one, and the Universe one, and its order one, we must perceive that its King and Artificer also is one. For this is why the Artificer Himself made the whole universe one, lest by the coexistence of more than one a plurality of makers should be supposed; but that as the work is one, its Maker also may be believed to be One. Nor does it follow from the unity of the Maker that the Universe must be one, for God might have made others as well. But because the Universe that has been made is one, it is necessary to believe that its Maker also is one.

§ 40. *The rationality and order of the Universe proves that it is the work of the Reason or Word of God.*

Who then might this Maker be? for this is a point most necessary to make plain, lest, from ignorance with regard to him, a man should suppose the wrong maker, and fall once more into the same old godless error, but I think no one is really in doubt about it. For if our argument has proved that the gods of the poets are no gods, and has convicted of error those that deify creation, and in general has shewn that the idolatry of the heathen is godlessness and impiety, it strictly follows from the elimination of these that the true religion is with us, and that the God we worship and preach is the only true One, Who is Lord of Creation and Maker of all existence. 2. Who then is this, save the Father of Christ, most holy and above all created existence [5], Who like an excellent pilot, by His own Wisdom and His own Word, our Lord and Saviour Christ, steers and preserves and orders all things, and does as seems to Him best? But that is best which has been done, and which we see taking place, since that is what He wills; and this a man can hardly refuse to believe. 3. For if the movement of creation were irrational, and the universe were borne along without plan, a man might fairly disbelieve what we say. But if it subsist in reason and wisdom and skill, and is perfectly ordered throughout, it follows that He that is over it and has ordered it is none other than the [reason or] Word of God. 4. But by Word I mean, not that which is involved and inherent in all things created, which some are wont to call the seminal [6] principle, which is without soul and has no power of reason or thought, but only works by external art, according to the skill of him that applies it,—nor such a word as belongs to rational beings and which consists of syllables, and has the air as its vehicle of expression,—but I mean the living and powerful Word of the good God, the God of the Universe, the very Word which is God [7], Who while different from things that are made, and from all Creation, is the One own Word of the good Father, Who by His own providence ordered and illumines this Universe. 5. For being the good Word of the Good Father He produced the order of all things, combining one with another things contrary, and reducing them to one harmonious order. He being the Power of God and Wisdom of God causes the heaven to revolve, and has suspended the earth, and made it fast, though resting upon nothing, by His own nod [8]. Illumined by Him, the sun gives light to the world, and the moon has her measured period of shining. By reason of Him the water is suspended in the clouds, the rains shower upon the earth, and the sea is

---

3 Or, perhaps, "innate, self-evident maxim" (λόγος φυσικός).
4 lit. "the steering-paddles."

5 Cf. above 2. 2 and note, also 35. 1.   6 σπερματικός.
7 Joh. i. 1.   8 νεῦμα, i.e. act of will, or fiat.

kept within bounds, while the earth bears grasses and is clothed with all manner of plants. 6. And if a man were incredulously to ask, as regards what we are saying, if there be a Word of God at all [9], such an one would indeed be mad to doubt concerning the Word of God, but yet demonstration is possible from what is seen, because all things subsist by the Word and Wisdom of God, nor would any created thing have had a fixed existence had it not been made by reason, and that reason the Word of God, as we have said.

§ 41. *The Presence of the Word in nature necessary, not only for its original Creation, but also for its permanence.*

But though He is Word, He is not, as we said, after the likeness of human words, composed of syllables ; but He is the unchanging Image of His own Father. For men, composed of parts and made out of nothing, have their discourse composite and divisible. But God possesses true existence and is not composite, wherefore His Word also has true Existence and is not composite, but is the one and only-begotten God [1], Who proceeds in His goodness from the Father as from a good Fountain, and orders all things and holds them together. 2. But the reason why the Word, the Word of God, has united Himself [2] with created things is truly wonderful, and teaches us that the present order of things is none otherwise than is fitting. For the nature of created things, inasmuch as it is brought into being out of nothing, is of a fleeting sort, and weak and mortal, if composed of itself only. But the God of all is good and exceeding noble by nature,—and therefore is kind. For one that is good can grudge nothing [3] : for which reason he does not grudge even existence, but desires all to exist, as objects for His loving-kindness. 3. Seeing then all created nature, as far as its own laws were concerned, to be fleeting and subject to dissolution, lest it should come to this and lest the Universe should be broken up again into nothingness, for this cause He made all things by His own eternal Word, and gave substantive existence to Creation, and moreover did not leave it to be tossed in a tempest in the course of its own nature, lest it should run the risk of once more dropping out of existence [4] ; but, because He is good He guides and settles the whole Creation by His own Word, Who is Himself also God, that by the govern-

ance and providence and ordering action of the Word, Creation may have light, and be enabled to abide alway securely. For it partakes of the Word Who derives true existence from the Father, and is helped by Him so as to exist, lest that should come to it which would have come but for the maintenance of it by the Word,—namely, dissolution,—"for He is the Image of the invisible God, the first-born of all Creation, for through Him and in Him all things consist, things visible and things invisible, and He is the Head of the Church," as the ministers of truth teach in their holy writings [5].

§ 42. *This function of the Word described at length.*

The holy Word of the Father, then, almighty and all-perfect, uniting with the universe and having everywhere unfolded His own powers, and having illumined all, both things seen and things invisible, holds them together and binds them to Himself, having left nothing void of His own power, but on the contrary quickening and sustaining all things everywhere, each severally and all collectively ; while He mingles in one the principles of all sensible existence, heat namely and cold and wet and dry, and causes them not to conflict, but to make up one concordant harmony. 2. By reason of Him and His power, fire does not fight with cold nor wet with dry, but principles mutually opposed, as if friendly and brotherly combine together, and give life to the things we see, and form the principles by which bodies exist. Obeying Him, even God the Word, things on earth have life and things in the heaven have their order. By reason of Him all the sea, and the great ocean, move within their proper bounds, while, as we said above, the dry land grows grasses and is clothed with all manner of diverse plants. And, not to spend time in the enumeration of particulars, where the truth is obvious, there is nothing that is and takes place but has been made and stands by Him and through Him, as also the Divine [6] says, "In the beginning was the Word, and the Word was with God, and the Word was God ; all things were made by Him, and without Him was not anything made." 3. For just as though some musician, having tuned a lyre, and by his art adjusted the high notes to the low, and the intermediate notes to the rest, were to produce a single tune as the result, so also the Wisdom of God, handling the Universe as a lyre, and adjusting things in the air to things on the

---

9 *De Incarn.* 41. 3.   1 Joh. i. 18, R. V. Marg.
2 ἐπιβέβηκεν, see for the sense *Incarn.* 43. 4, &c.
3 Plato *Timaeus* 29 E, quoted also *de Incarn.* 3. 3. This explanation of Divine Creation is also adopted by Philo *de Migratione Abrah.* 32 (and see Drummond's *Philo*, vol. 2, pp. 56, sqq.).
4 Plato *Politic.* (see *de Incarn.* 43. 7, note).

5 Col. i. 15—18.   6 Joh. i. 1.

earth, and things in the heaven to things in the air, and combining parts into wholes and moving them all by His beck and will, produces well and fittingly, as the result, the unity of the universe and of its order, Himself remaining unmoved with the Father while He moves all things by His organising action, as seems good for each to His own Father. 4. For what is surprising in His godhead is this, that by one and the same act of will He moves all things simultaneously, and not at intervals, but all collectively, both straight and curved, things above and beneath and intermediate, wet, cold, warm, seen and invisible, and orders them according to their several nature. For simultaneously at His single nod what is straight moves as straight, what is curved also, and what is intermediate, follows its own movement; what is warm receives warmth, what is dry dryness, and all things according to their several nature are quickened and organised by Him, and He produces as the result a marvellous and truly divine harmony.

§ 43. *Three similes to illustrate the Word's relation to the Universe.*

And for so great a matter to be understood by an example, let what we are describing be compared to a great chorus. As then the chorus is composed of different people, children, women again, and old men, and those who are still young, and, when one, namely the conductor, gives the sign, each utters sound according to his nature and power, the man as a man, the child as a child, the old man as an old man, and the young man as a young man, while all make up a single harmony; 2. or as our soul at one time moves our several senses according to the proper function of each, so that when some one object is present all alike are put in motion, and the eye sees, the ear hears, the hand touches, the smell takes in odour, and the palate tastes,—and often the other parts of the body act too, as for instance if the feet walk; 3. or, to make our meaning plain by yet a third example, it is as though a very great city were built, and administered under the presence of the ruler and king who has built it; for when he is present and gives orders, and has his eye upon everything, all obey; some busy themselves with agriculture, others hasten for water to the aqueducts, another goes forth to procure provisions,—one goes to senate, another enters the assembly, the judge goes to the bench, and the magistrate to his court. The workman likewise settles to his craft, the sailor goes down to the sea, the carpenter to his workshop, the physician to his treatment, the architect to his building; and

while one is going to the country, another is returning from the country, and while some walk about the town others are going out of the town and returning to it again: but all this is going on and is organised by the presence of the one Ruler, and by his management: 4. in like manner then we must conceive of the whole of Creation, even though the example be inadequate, yet with an enlarged idea. For with the single impulse of a nod as it were of the Word of God, all things simultaneously fall into order, and each discharge their proper functions, and a single order is made up by them all together.

§ 44. *The similes applied to the whole Universe, seen and unseen.*

For by a nod and by the power of the Divine Word of the Father that governs and presides over all, the heaven revolves, the stars move, the sun shines, the moon goes her circuit, and the air receives the sun's light and the æther his heat, and the winds blow: the mountains are reared on high, the sea is rough with waves, and the living things in it grow, the earth abides fixed, and bears fruit, and man is formed and lives and dies again, and all things whatever have their life and movement; fire burns, water cools, fountains spring forth, rivers flow, seasons and hours come round, rains descend, clouds are filled, hail is formed, snow and ice congeal, birds fly, creeping things go along, water-animals swim, the sea is navigated, the earth is sown and grows crops in due season, plants grow, and some are young, some ripening, others in their growth become old and decay, and while some things are vanishing others are being engendered and are coming to light. 2. But all these things, and more, which for their number we cannot mention, the worker of wonders and marvels, the Word of God, giving light and life, moves and orders by His own nod, making the universe one. Nor does He leave out of Himself even the invisible powers; for including these also in the universe inasmuch as he is their maker also, He holds them together and quickens them by His nod and by His providence. And there can be no excuse for disbelieving this. 3. For as by His own providence bodies grow and the rational soul moves, and possesses life and thought, and this requires little proof, for we see what takes place,—so again the same Word of God with one simple nod by His own power moves and holds together both the visible universe and the invisible powers, allotting to each its proper function, so that the divine powers move in a diviner way, while visible things move as they are seen to do. But Himself being over all, both Governor and King and organising power, He does all for the glory and knowledge of His own Father, so that almost by the very works that He brings to pass He teaches us and says, " By the greatness and beauty of the creatures proportionably the maker of them is seen 7."

§ 45. CONCLUSION. *Doctrine of Scripture on the subject of Part 1.*

For just as by looking up to the heaven and seeing its order and the light of the stars, it is possible to infer the Word Who ordered these things, so by beholding the Word of God, one needs must behold also God His Father, proceeding from Whom He is rightly called His Father's Interpreter and Messenger. 2. And this one may see from our own experience ; for if when a word proceeds from men 8 we infer that the mind is its source, and, by thinking about the word, see with our reason the mind which it reveals, by far greater evidence and incomparably more, seeing the power of the Word, we receive a knowledge also of His good Father, as the Saviour Himself says, " He that hath seen Me hath seen the Father 9." But this all inspired Scripture also teaches more plainly and with more authority, so that we in our turn write boldly to you as we do, and you, if you refer to them, will be able to verify what we say. 3. For an argument when confirmed by higher authority is irresistibly proved. From the first then the divine Word firmly taught the Jewish people about the abolition of idols when it said 1 : " Thou shalt not make to thyself a graven image, nor the likeness of anything that is in the heaven above or in the earth beneath." But the cause of their abolition another writer declares 2, saying : " The idols of the heathen are silver and gold, the works of men's hands : a mouth have they and will not speak, eyes have they and will not see, ears have they and will not hear, noses have they and will not smell, hands have they and will not handle, feet have they and will not walk." Nor has it passed over in silence the doctrine of creation ; but, knowing well its beauty, lest any attending solely to this beauty should worship things as if they were gods, instead of God's works, it teaches men firmly beforehand when it says 3 : " And do not when thou lookest up with thine eyes and seest the sun and moon and all the host of heaven, go astray and worship them, which the Lord thy God hath given to all nations under heaven." But He gave them, not to be their gods, but that by their agency

the Gentiles should know, as we have said, God the Maker of them all. 4. For the people of the Jews of old had abundant teaching, in that they had the knowledge of God not only from the works of Creation, but also from the divine Scriptures. And in general to draw men away from the error and irrational imagination of idols, He saith 4 : " Thou shalt have none other gods but Me." Not as if there were other gods does He forbid them to have them, but lest any, turning from the true God, should begin to make himself gods of what were not, such as those who in the poets and writers are called gods, though they are none. And the language itself shews that they are no Gods, when it says, " Thou shalt have none other gods," which refers only to the future. But what is referred to the future does not exist at the time of speaking.

§ 46. *Doctrine of Scripture on the subject of Part 3.*

Has then the divine teaching, which abolished the godlessness of the heathen or the idols, passed over in silence, and left the race of mankind to go entirely unprovided with the knowledge of God ? Not so : rather it anticipates their understanding when it says 5 : " Hear, O Israel, the Lord thy God is one God ; " and again, " Thou shalt love the Lord thy God with all thy heart and with all thy strength ; " and again, " Thou shalt worship the Lord thy God, and Him only shalt thou serve, and shalt cleave to Him." 2. But that the providence and ordering power of the Word also, over all and toward all, is attested by all inspired Scripture, this passage suffices to confirm our argument, where men who speak of God say 6 : " Thou hast laid the foundation of the earth and it abideth. The day continueth according to Thine ordinance." And again 7 : " Sing to our God upon the harp, that covereth the heaven with clouds, that prepareth rain for the earth, that bringeth forth grass upon the mountains, and green herb for the service of man, and giveth food to the cattle." 3. But by whom does He give it, save by Him through Whom all things were made ? For the providence over all things belongs naturally to Him by Whom they were made ; and who is this save the Word of God, concerning Whom in another psalm 8 he says : " By the Word of the Lord were the heavens made, and all the host of them by the Breath of His mouth." For He tells us that all things were made in Him and through Him. 4. Wherefore He also persuades us and says 9,

---

7 Wisd. xiii. 5.　　8 Cf. *de Sent. Dionys.* 23.　　9 Joh. xiv. 9.
　1 Ex. xx. 4.　　2 Ps. cxv. 4—7.　　3 Deut. iv. 19.

4 Ex. xx. 3.　　5 Deut. vi. 4, 5, 13.　　6 Ps. cxix. 90.
7 Ps. cxlvii. 7—9.　　Ps. xxxiii. 6.　　9 Ps. cxlviii. 5.

He spake and they were made, He commanded and they were created;" as the illustrious Moses also at the beginning of his account of Creation confirms what we say by his narrative[1], saying: and God said, "let us make man in our image and after our likeness:" for also when He was carrying out the creation of the heaven and earth and all things, the Father said to Him[2], "Let the heaven be made," and "let the waters be gathered together and let the dry land appear," and "let the earth bring forth herb" and "every green thing:" so that one must convict Jews also of not genuinely attending to the Scriptures. 5. For one might ask them to whom was God speaking, to use the imperative mood? If He were commanding and addressing the things He was creating, the utterance would be redundant, for they were not yet in being, but were about to be made; but no one speaks to what does not exist, nor addresses to what is not yet made a command to be made. For if God were giving a command to the things that were to be, He must have said, "Be made, heaven, and be made, earth, and come forth, green herb, and be created, O man." But in fact He did not do so; but He gives the command thus: Let us make man," and "let the green herb come forth." By which God is proved to be speaking about them to some one at hand: it follows then that some one was with Him to Whom He spoke when He made all things. 6. Who then could it be, save His Word? For to whom could God be said to speak, except His Word? Or who was with Him when He made all created Existence, except His Wisdom, which says[3]: "When He was making the heaven and the earth I was present with Him?" But in the mention of heaven and earth, all created things in heaven and earth are included as well. 7. But being present with Him as His Wisdom and His Word, looking at the Father He fashioned the Universe, and organised it and gave it order; and, as He is the power of the Father, He gave all things strength to be, as the Saviour says[4]: "What things soever I see the Father doing, I also do in like manner." And His holy disciples teach that all things were made "through Him and unto Him;" 8. and, being the good Offspring of Him that is good, and true Son, He is the Father's Power and Wisdom and Word, not being so by participation[5], nor as if these qualities were imparted to Him from without, as they are to those who partake of Him and are made wise by Him, and receive power and reason in Him; but He is the very Wisdom, very Word, and very own Power of the Father, very Light, very Truth, very Righteousness, very Virtue, and in truth His express Image, and Brightness, and Resemblance. And to sum all up, He is the wholly perfect Fruit of the Father, and is alone the Son, and unchanging Image of the Father.

§ 47. *Necessity of a return to the Word if our corrupt nature is to be restored.*

Who then, who can declare the Father by number, so as to discover the powers of His Word? For like as He is the Father's Word and Wisdom, so too condescending to created things, He becomes, to impart the knowledge and apprehension of Him that begat Him, His very Brightness and very Life, and the Door, and the Shepherd, and the Way, and King and Governor, and Saviour over all, and Light, and Giver of Life, and Providence over all. Having then such a Son begotten of Himself, good, and Creator, the Father did not hide Him out of the sight of His creatures, but even day by day reveals Him to all by means of the organisation and life of all things, which is His work. 2. But in and through Him He reveals Himself also, as the Saviour says[6]: "I in the Father and the Father in Me:" so that it follows that the Word is in Him that begat Him, and that He that is begotten lives eternally with the Father. But this being so, and nothing being outside Him, but both heaven and earth and all that in them is being dependent on Him, yet men in their folly have set aside the knowledge and service of Him, and honoured things that are not instead of things that are: and instead of the real and true God deified things that were not, "serving the creature rather than the Creator[7]," thus involving themselves in foolishness and impiety. 3. For it is just as if one were to admire the works more than the workman, and being awestruck at the public works in the city, were to make light of their builder, or as if one were to praise a musical instrument but to despise the man who made and tuned it. Foolish and sadly disabled in eyesight! For how else had they known the building, or ship, or lyre, had not the ship-builder made it, the architect built it, or the musician fashioned it? 4. As then he that reasons in such a way is mad, and beyond all madness, even so affected in mind, I think, are those who do not recognise God or worship His Word, our Lord Jesus Christ the Saviour of all, through Whom the Father orders, and

---

[1] Gen. i. 20.   [2] Gen. i. 6—11.
[3] Prov. viii. 27.   [4] Joh. v. 19; Col. i. 16.
[5] μετοχή, cf. *de Syn.* 48, 51, 53. This was held by Arians, but in common with Paul Samos. and many of the Monarchian heretics. The same principle in Orig. on Ps. 135 (Lomm. xiii. 134) οὐ κατὰ μετουσίαν ἀλλὰ κατ᾽ οὐσίαν θεός.

[6] Joh. xiv. 10.   [7] Rom. i. 25.

holds together all things, and exercises providence over the Universe; having faith and piety towards Whom, my Christ-loving friend, be of good cheer and of good hope, because immortality and the kingdom of heaven is the fruit of faith and devotion towards Him, if only the soul be adorned according to His laws. For just as for them who walk after His example, the prize is life everlasting, so for those who walk the opposite way, and not that of virtue, there is great shame, and peril without pardon in the day of judgment, because although they knew the way of truth their acts were contrary to their knowledge.

INTRODUCTION TO THE TREATISE

ON THE

INCARNATION OF THE WORD

THE tract 'against the Gentiles' leaves the reader face to face with the necessity of restoration by the Divine Word as the remedy for corrupt human nature. How this necessity is met in the Incarnation is shewn in the pages which follow. The general design of the second tract is to illustrate and confirm the doctrine of the Incarnation by shewing (1) its necessity and end, (2) the congruity of its details, (3) its truth, as against the objections of Jews and Gentiles, (4) its result. He begins by a review (recapitulating *c. Gent.* 2—7) of the doctrine of creation and of man's place therein. The abuse by man of his special Privilege had resulted in its loss. By foregoing the Divine Life, man had entered upon a course of endless undoing, of progressive decay, from which none could rescue him but the original bestower of his life (2—7). Then follows a description in glowing words of the Incarnation of the Divine Word and of its efficacy against the plague of corruption (8—10). With the *Divine Life*, man had also received, in the *knowledge of God*, the conscious reflex of the Divine Likeness, the faculty of reason in its highest exercise. This knowledge their moral fall dimmed and perverted. Heeding not even the means by which God sought to remind them of Himself, they fell deeper and deeper into materialism and superstition. To restore the effaced likeness the presence of the Original was requisite. Accordingly, condescending to man's sense-bound intelligence—lest men should have been created in vain in the Image of God—the Word took Flesh and became an object of Sense, that through the Seen He might reveal the Invisible (11—16).

Having dwelt (17—19) upon the meaning and purpose of the Incarnation, he proceeds to speak of the Death and Resurrection of the Incarnate Word. He, Who alone could renew the handiwork and restore the likeness and give afresh the knowledge of God, must needs, in order to pay the debt which all had incurred (τὸ παρὰ πάντων ὀφειλόμενον), die in our stead, offering the sacrifice on behalf of all, so as to rise again, as our first-fruits, from the grave (20—32, note especially § 20). After speaking of the especial fitness of the Cross, once the instrument of shame, now the trophy of victory, and after meeting some difficulties connected with the manner of the Lord's Death, he passes to the Resurrection. He shews how Christ by His triumph over the grave changed (27) the relative ascendancy of Death and Life: and how the Resurrection with its momentous train of consequences, follows of necessity (31) from the Incarnation of Him in Whom was Life.

The two main divisions of contemporary unbelief are next combated. In either case the root of the difficulty is moral; with the Greeks it is a frivolous cynicism, with the Jews, inveterate obstinacy. The latter (33—40) are confuted, firstly, by their own Scriptures, which predict both in general and in detail the coming of Jesus Christ. Also, the old Jewish polity, both civil and religious, has passed away, giving place to the Church of Christ.

Turning to the Greeks (41—45), and assuming that they allow the existence of a pervading Spirit, whose presence is the sustaining principle of all things, he challenges them to reject, without inconsistency, the Union of that Spirit, the Logos (compare St. Augustine *Conf.* VII. ix.), with one in particular of the many constituents of that Universe wherein he already dwells. And since man alone (43. 3) of the creatures had departed from the order of his creation, it was man's nature that the Word united to Himself, thus repairing the breach between the creature and the Creator at the very point where it had occurred.

God did not restore man by a mere fiat (44) because, just as repentance on man's part (7) could not eradicate his disease, so such a fiat on God's part would have amounted to the annihilation of human nature as it was, and the creation of a fresh race. Man's definite disorder God met with a specific remedy, overcoming death with life. Thus man has been enabled once more to shew forth, in common with the rest of Creation, the handiwork and glory of his Maker.

Athanasius then confronts the Greeks, as he had the Jews, with facts. Since the coming of Christ, paganism, popular and philosophic, had been falling into discredit and decay. The impotence and rivalries of the philosophic teachers, the local and heterogeneous character, the low moral ideals of the old worships, are contrasted with the oneness and inspiring power of the religion of the Crucified. Such are the two, the dying and the living systems; it remains for him who will to taste and see what that life is which is the gift of Christ to them that follow Him (46—end).

The purpose of the tract, in common with the *contra Gentes*, being to commend the religion of Christ to acceptance, the argument is concerned more with the Incarnation as a living fact, and with its place in the scheme of God's dealing with man, than with its analysis as a theological doctrine. He does not enter upon the question, fruitful of controversy in the previous century at Alexandria, but soon to burst forth into furious debate, of the Sonship of the Word and of His relation to God the Father. Still less does he touch the Christo-logical questions which arose with the decline of the Arian tempest, questions associated with the names of Apollinarius, Theodore, Cyril, Nestorius, Eutyches, Theodoret, and Dios-corus. But we feel already that firm grasp of soteriological principles which mark him out as the destined conqueror of Arianism, and which enabled him by a sure instinct to anticipate unconsciously the theological difficulties which troubled the Church for the century after his death. It is the broad comprehensive treatment of the subject in its relation to God, human nature, and sin, that gives the work its interest to readers of the present day. In strong reaction from modern or medieval theories of Redemption, which to the thoughtful Christian of to-day seem arbitrary, or worse, it is with relief that men find that from the beginning it was not so; that the theology of the early Church interpreted the great Mystery of godliness in terms which, if short of the fulness of the Pauline conception, are yet so free from arbitrary assumptions, so true to human nature as the wisest of men know it, so true to the worthiest and grandest ideas of God (see below, p. 33 *ad fin.*). The *de Incarnatione*, then, is perhaps more appreciated in our day than at any date since the days of its writer.

It may therefore be worth while to devote a word or two to some peculiarities incidental to its aim and method. We observe first of all how completely the power of the writer is absorbed in the subject under discussion. It is therefore highly precarious to infer anything from his silence even on points which might seem to require explanation in the course of his argument. Not a word is said of the doctrine of the Trinity, nor of the Holy Spirit; this directly follows from the purpose of the work, in accordance with the general truth that while the Church preaches Christ to the World, the Office and Personality of the Spirit belongs to her inner life. The teaching of the tract with regard to the constitution of man is another case in point. It might appear (§ 3, cf. 11. 2, 13. 2) that Athanasius ascribed the reasonable soul of man, and his immortality after death, not to the constitution of human nature as such, but to the grace superadded to it by the Creator (ἡ τοῦ κατ᾽ εἰκόνα χάρις), a grace which constituted men λογικοί (3. 4) by virtue of the power of the Logos, and which, *if not forfeited by sin*, involved the privilege of immortality. We have, then, to carefully consider whether Athanasius held, or meant to suggest, that man is by nature, and apart from union with God, (1) rational, or (2) immortal. If we confine our view to the treatise before us, there would be some show of reason in answering both questions in the negative; and with regard to immortality this has been recently done by an able correspondent of *The Times* (April 9, 1890).

But that Athanasius held the essential rationality *and immortality* of the soul is absolutely clear, if only from *c. Gent.* 32 and 33. We have, then, to find an explanation of his language in the present treatise. With regard to immortality, it should be observed (1) that the language employed (in 4. 5, where κενωθῆναι τοῦ εἶναι ἀεί is explained by τὸ διαλυθέντας μένειν ἐν τῷ θανάτῳ καὶ τῇ φθόρᾳ) suggests a *continued condition*, and therefore something short of annihilation, although not worthy of the name of existence or life,—(2) that even in the worst of men the image of God is defaced, but not effaced (14. 1, &c.), and that even when grace is lost (7. 4), man cannot be as though the contact with the divine had never taken place;—(3) that in this work, as by St. Paul in 1 Cor. xv., the final destiny of the wicked is passed over (but for the general reference 56. 3) in silence. It may be added (4) that Athanasius puts together *all* that separates man from irrational creatures without clearly drawing the line between what belongs to the natural man and what to the κατ᾽ εἰκόνα χάρις. The subject of eschatology is nowhere dealt with in full by Athanasius; while it is quite certain (*c. Gent.* 33) that he did not share the inclination of some earlier writers (see D.C.B. ii. p. 192) toward the idea of conditional immortality, there is also no reason to think that he held with the Universalism of Origen, Gregory of Nyssa and others (see Migne, Patr. Gr. xxvii. p. 1404 A, also 1384 C, where 'the unfortunate Origen's' opinions seem to be rejected, but with an implied deprecation of harsh judgment). As to his view of the essential rationality of man (see *c. Gent.* 32) the consideration (4) urged above once more applies (compare the discussion in Harnack, *Dg.* ii. 146 sqq.). Yet he says that man left to himself can have no idea of God at all (11. 1), and that this would deprive him of any claim to be considered a rational being (ib. 2). The apparent inconsistency is removed if we understand that man may be rational potentially (as all men are) and yet not rational in the sense of exercising reason (which is the case with very many). In other words, grace gives not the faculty itself, but its integrity, the latter being the result not of the mere psychological existence of the faculty, but of the reaction upon it of its highest and adequate object. (The same is true to a great extent of the doctrine of πνεῦμα in the New Testament.)

A somewhat similar caution is necessary with regard to the analogy drawn out (41, &c.) between the Incarnation and the Union of the Word with the Universe. The treatise itself (17. 1, ἐκτὸς κατ᾽ οὐσίαν, and see notes on 41) supplies the necessary corrective in this case. It may be pointed out here that the real difference between Athanasius and the neo-Platonists was not so much upon the Union of the Word with any created Substance, which they were prepared to allow, as upon the *exclusive* Union of the Word with Man, in Contrast to His essential distinctness from the Universe. This difference goes back to the doctrine of Creation, which was fixed as a great gulf between the Christian and the Platonist view of the Universe. The relation of the latter to the Word is fully discussed in the third part of the *contra Gentes*, the teaching of which must be borne in mind while reading the forty-first and following chapters of the present treatise.

Lastly, the close relation between the doctrine of Creation and that of Redemption marks off the Soteriology of this treatise from that of the middle ages and of the Reformation. Athanasius does not leave out of sight the idea of satisfaction for a debt. To him also the Cross was the central purpose (20. 2, cf. 9. 1, 2, &c.) of His Coming. But the idea of *Restoration* is most prominent in his determination of the necessity of the Incarnation.

God could have wiped out our guilt, had He so pleased, by a word (44): but human nature required to be healed, restored, recreated.   This (ἀνακτίσαι) is the foremost of the three ideas (7. 5) which sum up his account of the ' *dignus* tanto *Vindice nodus* [1].

The *translation* which follows is that printed in 1885 (D. Nutt, second edition, 1891) by the editor of this volume, with a very few changes (chiefly 2. 2, 8. 4, 34. 2, 44. 7, 8): it was originally made for the purpose of lectures at Oxford (1879—1882), and the *analytical headings* now prefixed to each chapter are extracted verbatim from notes made for the same course of lectures.   The *notes* have mostly appeared either in the former edition of the translation, or appended to the Greek text published (D. Nutt, 1882) by the translator. A few, however, have now been added, including some references to the *Sermo Major*, which borrows wholesale from the present treatise (Prolegg. ch. III. § 1. 37).   Two other English translations have appeared, the one (Parker, 1880) previous, the other (Religious Tract Society, n.d.) subsequent to that of the present translator.   The *text* followed is that of the Benedictine editors, with a few exceptions.   Of those that at all affect the sense, 43. 6 (καὶ τὸ σῶμα) and 51. 2 (κατὰ τῆς εἰδ·) are due to Mr. Marriott (*Analecta Christiana*, Oxf. 1844).   For the others (13. 2, omission of μή, 28. 3, κατὰ τοῦ πύρος rejecting conjectures of Montf. and Marriott, 42. 6, omission of πεποιηκέναι 57. 3, καὶ τὰ for τὰ καί) the present editor is alone responsible.

SYNOPSIS OF THE TREATISE.

[1] The Soteriology of Athanasius is well drawn out, and usefully compared with that of Anselm and of more modern theologians, in Norris' *Rudiments of Theology*, Appendix, ch. iii. (Rivington's, 1876).   See also the discussion above, Prolegomena, ch. iv. § 2.

ON THE INCARNATION OF THE WORD

§ 1. *Introductory.—The subject of this treatise: the humiliation and incarnation of the Word. Presupposes the doctrine of Creation, and that by the Word. The Father has saved the world by Him through Whom He first made it.*

WHEREAS in what precedes we have drawn out—choosing a few points from among many—a sufficient account of the error of the heathen concerning idols, and of the worship of idols, and how they originally came to be invented; how, namely, out of wickedness men devised for themselves the worshipping of idols: and whereas we have by God's grace noted somewhat also of the divinity of the Word of the Father, and of His universal Providence and power, and that the Good Father through Him orders all things, and all things are moved by Him, and in Him are quickened: come now, Macarius[1] (worthy of that name), and true lover of Christ, let us follow up the faith of our religion[2], and set forth also what relates to the Word's becoming Man, and to His divine Appearing amongst us, which Jews traduce and Greeks laugh to scorn, but we worship; in order that, all the more for the seeming low estate of the Word, your piety toward Him may be increased and multiplied. 2. For the more He is mocked among the unbelieving, the more witness does He give of His own Godhead; inasmuch as He not only Himself demonstrates as possible what men mistake, thinking impossible, but what men deride as unseemly, this by His own goodness He clothes with seemliness, and what men, in their conceit of wisdom, laugh at as merely human, He by His own power demonstrates to be divine, subduing the pretensions of idols by His

supposed humiliation—by the Cross—and those who mock and disbelieve invisibly winning over to recognise His divinity and power. 3. But to treat this subject it is necessary to recall what has been previously said; in order that you may neither fail to know the cause of the bodily appearing of the Word of the Father, so high and so great, nor think it a consequence of His own nature that the Saviour has worn a body; but that being incorporeal by nature, and Word from the beginning, He has yet of the loving-kindness and goodness of His own Father been manifested to us in a human body for our salvation. 4. It is, then, proper for us to begin the treatment of this subject by speaking of the creation of the universe, and of God its Artificer, that so it may be duly perceived that the renewal of creation has been the work of the self-same Word that made it at the beginning. For it will appear not inconsonant for the Father to have wrought its salvation in Him by Whose means He made it.

§ 2. *Erroneous views of Creation rejected. (1) Epicurean (fortuitous generation). But diversity of bodies and parts argues a creating intellect. (2.) Platonists (pre-existent matter.) But this subjects God to human limitations, making Him not a creator but a mechanic. (3) Gnostics (an alien Demiurge). Rejected from Scripture.*

Of the making of the universe and the creation of all things many have taken different views, and each man has laid down the law just as he pleased. For some say that all things have come into being of themselves, and in a chance fashion; as, for example, the Epicureans, who tell us in their self-contempt, that universal providence does not exist speaking right in the face of obvious fact and experience. 2. For if, as they say, everything

---

[1] See *Contra Gentes*, i. The word (Μακάριε) may be an adjective only, but its occurrence in *both* places seems decisive. The name was very common (*Apol. c. Ar.* passim). 'Macarius' was a Christian, as the present passage shews: he is presumed (*c. Gent.* i. 7) to have access to Scripture.

[2] τῆς εὐσεβείας. See 1 Tim. iii. 16, and note 1 on *De Decr.* 1.

has had its beginning of itself, and independently of purpose, it would follow that everything had come into [3] mere being, so as to be alike and not distinct. For it would follow in virtue of the unity of body that everything must be sun or moon, and in the case of men it would follow that the whole must be hand, or eye, or foot. But as it is this is not so. On the contrary, we see a distinction of sun, moon, and earth; and again, in the case of human bodies, of foot, hand, and head. Now, such separate arrangement as this tells us not of their having come into being of themselves, but shews that a cause preceded them; from which cause it is possible to apprehend God also as the Maker and Orderer of all. 3. But others, including Plato, who is in such repute among the Greeks, argue that God has made the world out of matter previously existing and without beginning. For God could have made nothing had not the material existed already; just as the wood must exist ready at hand for the carpenter, to enable him to work at all. 4. But in so saying they know not that they are investing God with weakness. For if He is not Himself the cause of the material, but makes things only of previously existing material, He proves to be weak, because unable to produce anything He makes without the material; just as it is without doubt a weakness of the carpenter not to be able to make anything required without his timber. For, *ex hypothesi*, had not the material existed, God would not have made anything. And how could He in that case be called Maker and Artificer, if He owes His ability to make to some other source—namely, to the material? So that if this be so, God will be on their theory a Mechanic only, and not a Creator out of nothing [4]; if, that is, He works at existing material, but is not Himself the cause of the material. For He could not in any sense be called Creator unless He is Creator of the material of which the things created have in their turn been made. 5. But the sectaries imagine to themselves a different artificer of all things, other than the Father of our Lord Jesus Christ, in deep blindness even as to the words they use. 6. For whereas the Lord says to the Jews [5]: "Have ye not read that from the beginning He which created them made them male and female, and said, For this cause shall a man leave his father and mother, and shall cleave to his wife, and they twain shall become one flesh?" and then,

referring to the Creator, says, "What, therefore, GOD hath joined together let not man put asunder:" how come these men to assert that the creation is independent of the Father? Or if, in the words of John, who says, making no exception, "All things [6] were made by Him, and "without Him was not anything made," how could the artificer be another, distinct from the Father of Christ?

§ 3. *The true doctrine. Creation out of nothing, of God's lavish bounty of being. Man created above the rest, but incapable of independent perseverance. Hence the exceptional and supranatural gift of being in God's Image, with the promise of bliss conditionally upon his perseverance in grace.*

Thus do they vainly speculate. But the godly teaching and the faith according to Christ brands their foolish language as godlessness. For it knows that it was not spontaneously, because forethought is not absent; nor of existing matter, because God is not weak; but that out of nothing, and without its having any previous existence, God made the universe to exist through His word, as He says firstly through Moses: "In [7] the beginning God created the heaven and the earth;" secondly, in the most edifying book of the Shepherd, "First [8] of all believe that God is one, which created and framed all things, and made them to exist out of nothing." 2. To which also Paul refers when he says, "By [9] faith we understand that the worlds have been framed by the Word of God, so that what is seen hath not been made out of things which do appear." 3. For God is good, or rather is essentially the source of goodness: nor [1] could one that is good be niggardly of anything: whence, grudging existence to none, He has made all things out of nothing by His own Word, Jesus Christ our Lord. And among these, having taken especial pity, above all things on earth, upon the race of men, and having perceived its inability, by virtue of the condition of its origin, to continue in one stay, He gave them a further gift, and He did not barely create man, as He did all the irrational creatures on the earth, but made them after His own image, giving them a portion even of the power of His own Word; so that having as it were a kind of reflexion of the Word, and being made rational, they might be able to abide ever in blessedness, living the true life which belongs to the saints in paradise. 4. But knowing once more how the will of man could

---

3 Or, "been made in one way only." In the next clause I formerly translated the difficult words ὡς ἐπὶ σώματος ἑνὸς 'as in the case of the universe;' but although the rendering has commended itself to others I now reluctantly admit that it puts too much into the Greek (in spite of § 41. 5).
4 εἰς τὸ εἶναι.
5 Matt. xix. 4, &c.

6 John i. 3.　　7 Gen. i. 1.　　8 Herm. *Mand.* 1.
9 Heb. xi. 3.　　1 *c. Gent.* xli. and Plato, *Timæus* 29 E.

sway to either side, in anticipation He secured the grace given them by a law and by the spot where He placed them. For He brought them into His own garden, and gave them a law: so that, if they kept the grace and remained good, they might still keep the life in paradise without sorrow or pain or care, besides having the promise of incorruption in heaven; but that if they transgressed and turned back, and became evil, they might know that they were incurring that corruption in death which was theirs by nature: no longer to live in paradise, but cast out of it from that time forth to die and to abide in death and in corruption. 5. Now this is that of which Holy Writ also gives warning, saying in the Person of God: "Of every tree[2] that is in the garden, eating thou shalt eat: but of the tree of the knowledge of good and evil, ye shall not eat of it, but on the day that ye eat, dying ye shall die." But by "dying ye shall die," what else could be meant than not dying merely, but also abiding ever in the corruption of death?

§§ 4, 5. *Our creation and God's Incarnation most intimately connected. As by the Word man was called from non-existence into being, and further received the grace of a divine life, so by the one fault which forfeited that life they again incurred corruption and untold sin and misery filled the world.*

You are wondering, perhaps, for what possible reason, having proposed to speak of the Incarnation of the Word, we are at present treating of the origin of mankind. But this, too, properly belongs to the aim of our treatise. 2. For in speaking of the appearance of the Saviour amongst us, we must needs speak also of the origin of men, that you may know that the reason of His coming down was because of us, and that our transgression[3] called forth the loving-kindness of the Word, that the Lord should both make haste to help us and appear among men. 3. For of His becoming Incarnate we were the object, and for our salvation He dealt so lovingly as to appear and be born even in a human body. 4. Thus, then, God has made man, and willed that he should abide in incorruption; but men, having despised and rejected the contemplation of God, and devised and contrived evil for themselves (as was said[4] in the former treatise), received the condemnation of death with which they had been threatened; and from thenceforth no longer remained as they were made, but[5] were being corrupted ac-

cording to their devices; and death had the mastery over them as king[6]. For transgression of the commandment was turning them back to their natural state, so that just as they have had their being out of nothing, so also, as might be expected, they might look for corruption into nothing in the course of time. 5. For if, out of a former normal state of non-existence, they were called into being by the Presence and loving-kindness of the Word, it followed naturally that when men were bereft of the knowledge of God and were turned back to what was not (for what is evil is not, but what is good is), they should, since they derive their being from God who IS, be everlastingly bereft even of being; in other words, that they should be disintegrated and abide in death and corruption. 6. For man is by nature mortal, inasmuch as he is made out of what is not; but by reason of his likeness to Him that is (and if he still preserved this likeness by keeping Him in his knowledge) he would stay his natural corruption, and remain incorrupt; as Wisdom[7] says: "The taking heed to His laws is the assurance of immortality;" but being incorrupt, he would live henceforth as God, to which I suppose the divine Scripture refers, when it says: "I have[8] said ye are gods, and ye are all sons of the most Highest; but ye die like men, and fall as one of the princes."

5. For God has not only made us out of nothing; but He gave us freely, by the Grace of the Word, a life in correspondence with God. But men, having rejected things eternal, and, by counsel of the devil, turned to the things of corruption, became the cause[9] of their own corruption in death, being, as I said before, by nature corruptible, but destined, by the grace following from partaking of the Word, to have escaped their natural state, had they remained good. 2. For because of the Word dwelling with them, even their natural corruption did not come near them, as Wisdom also says[1]: "God made man for incorruption, and as an image of His own eternity; but by envy of the devil death came into the world." But when this was come to pass, men began to die, while corruption thenceforward prevailed against them, gaining even more than its natural power over the whole race, inasmuch as it had, owing to the transgression of the commandment, the threat of the Deity as a further advantage against them. 3. For even in their misdeeds men had not stopped short at any set limits; but gradually

---

[2] Gen. ii. 16, *sq.*   [3] Cf. *Orat.* ii. 54, note 4.   [4] *c. Gent.* 3-5.
[5] Eccles. vii. 29; Rom. i. 21, 22.

[6] Rom. v. 14.   [7] Wisd. vi. 18.   [8] Ps. lxxxii. 6, *sq.*
[9] Cf. Concil. Araus. II. Can. 23. 'Suam voluntatem homines faciunt, non Dei, quando id agunt quod Deo displicet.'
[1] Wisd. ii. 23, *sq.*

pressing forward, have passed on beyond all measure : having to begin with been inventors of wickedness and called down upon themselves death and corruption ; while later on, having turned aside to wrong and exceeding all lawlessness, and stopping at no one evil but devising all manner of new evils in succession, they have become insatiable in sinning. 4. For there were adulteries everywhere and thefts, and the whole earth was full of murders and plunderings. And as to corruption and wrong, no heed was paid to law, but all crimes were being practised everywhere, both individually and jointly. Cities were at war with cities, and nations were rising up against nations ; and the whole earth was rent with civil commotions and battles ; each man vying with his fellows in lawless deeds. 8. Nor were even crimes against nature far from them, but, as the Apostle and witness of Christ says : " For their [2] women changed the natural use into that which is against nature : and likewise also the men, leaving the natural use of the women, burned in their lust one toward another, men with men working unseemliness, and receiving in themselves that recompense of their error which was meet."

§ 6. *The human race then was wasting, God's image was being effaced, and His work ruined. Either, then, God must forego His spoken word by which man had incurred ruin ; or that which had shared in the being of the Word must sink back again into destruction, in which case God's design would be defeated. What then ? was God's goodness to suffer this ? But if so, why had man been made ? It would have been weakness, not goodness on God's part.*

For this cause, then, death having gained upon men, and corruption abiding upon them, the race of man was perishing ; the rational man made in God's image was disappearing, and the handiwork of God was in process of dissolution. 2. For death, as I said above, gained from that time forth a legal [3] hold over us, and it was impossible to evade the law, since it had been laid down by God because [4] of the transgression, and the result was in truth at once monstrous and unseemly. 3. For it were monstrous, firstly, that God, having spoken, should prove false—that, when once He had ordained that man, if he transgressed the commandment, should die the death, after the transgression man should not die, but God's word should be broken. For God would

not be true, if, when He had said we should die, man died not. 4. Again, it were unseemly that creatures once made rational, and having partaken of the Word, should go to ruin, and turn again toward non-existence by the way of corruption [5]. 5. For it were not worthy of God's goodness that the things He had made should waste away, because of the deceit practised on men by the devil. 6. Especially it was unseemly to the last degree that God's handicraft among men should be done away, either because of their own carelessness, or because of the deceitfulness of evil spirits. 7. So, as the rational creatures were wasting and such works in course of ruin, what was God in His goodness to do ? Suffer corruption to prevail against them and death to hold them fast ? And where were the profit of their having been made, to begin with ? For better were they not made, than once made, left to neglect and ruin. 8. For neglect reveals weakness, and not goodness on God's part—if, that is, He allows His own work to be ruined when once He had made it—more so than if He had never made man at all. 9. For if He had not made them, none could impute weakness ; but once He had made them, and created them out of nothing, it were most monstrous for the work to be ruined, and that before the eyes of the Maker. 10. It was, then, out of the question to leave men to the current of corruption ; because this would be unseemly, and unworthy of God's goodness.

§ 7. *On the other hand there was the consistency of God's nature, not to be sacrificed for our profit. Were men, then, to be called upon to repent ? But repentance cannot avert the execution of a law ; still less can it remedy a fallen nature. We have incurred corruption and need to be restored to the Grace of God's Image. None could renew but He Who had created. He alone could (1) recreate all, (2) suffer for all, (3) represent all to the Father.*

But just as this consequence must needs hold, so, too, on the other side the just claims [6] of God lie against it : that God should appear true to the law He had laid down concerning death. For it were monstrous for God, the Father of truth, to appear a liar for our profit and preservation. 2. So here, once more, what possible course was God to take ? To demand repentance of men for their transgression ? For this one might pronounce worthy of God ; as

---

[2] Rom. i. 26, *sq.*   [3] Gen. ii. 15.
[4] Gal. iii. 19 (verbally only).

[5] Cf. Anselm *cur Deus Homo*, II. 4, 'Valde alienum est ab eo, ut ullam rationalem naturam penitus perire sinat.'
[6] Literally "what is reasonable with respect to God," i.e. what is involved in His attributes and in His relation to us, cf. Rom. iii. 26, cf. Anselm. *ib.* I. 12, who slightly narrows down the idea or Athan. 'Si peccatum sic dimittitur impunitum, similiter erit apud Deum peccanti et non peccanti, quod Deo *non convenit* . . . . *Inconvenientia autem iniustitia est.*'

though, just as from transgression men have become set towards corruption, so from repentance they may once more be set in the way of incorruption. 3. But repentance would, firstly, fail to guard the just claim [7] of God. For He would still be none the more true, if men did not remain in the grasp of death ; nor, secondly, does repentance call men back from what is their nature — it merely stays them from acts of sin. 4. Now, if there were merely a misdemeanour in question, and not a consequent corruption, repentance were well enough. But if, when transgression had once gained a start, men became involved in that corruption which was their nature, and were deprived of the grace which they had, being in the image of God, what further step was needed ? or what was required for such grace and such recall, but the Word of God, which had also at the beginning made everything out of nought ? 5. For His it was once more both to bring the corruptible to incorruption, and to maintain intact the just claim [7] of the Father upon all. For being Word of the Father, and above all, He alone of natural fitness was both able to recreate everything, and worthy to suffer on behalf of all and to be ambassador for all with the Father.

§ 8. *The Word, then, visited that earth in which He was yet always present ; and saw all these evils. He takes a body of our Nature, and that of a spotless Virgin, in whose womb He makes it His own, wherein to reveal Himself, conquer death, and restore life.*

For this purpose, then, the incorporeal and incorruptible and immaterial Word of God comes to our realm, howbeit he was not far from us [8] before. For no part of Creation is left void of Him : He has filled all things everywhere, remaining present with His own Father. But He comes in condescension to shew loving-kindness upon us, and to visit us. 2. And seeing the race of rational creatures in the way to perish, and death reigning over them by corruption ; seeing, too, that the threat against transgression gave a firm hold to the corruption which was upon us, and that it was monstrous that [9] before the law was fulfilled it should fall through : seeing, once more, the unseemliness of what was come to pass : that the things whereof He Himself was Artificer were passing away : seeing, further, the exceeding wickedness of men, and how by little and little they had increased it to an intolerable pitch against themselves : and seeing, lastly, how all men were under penalty of death : He

took pity on our race, and had mercy on our infirmity, and condescended to our corruption, and, unable to bear that death should have the mastery—lest the creature should perish, and His Father's handiwork in men be spent for nought—He takes unto Himself a body, and that of no different sort from ours. 3. For He did not simply will to become embodied, or will merely to appear [1]. For if He willed merely to appear, He was able to effect His divine appearance by some other and higher means as well. But He takes a body of our kind, and not merely so, but from a spotless and stainless virgin, knowing not a man, a body clean and in very truth pure from intercourse of men. For being Himself mighty, and Artificer of everything, He prepares the body in the Virgin as a temple unto Himself, and makes it His very own [2] as an instrument, in it manifested, and in it dwelling. 4. And thus taking from our bodies one of like nature, because all were under penalty of the corruption of death He gave it over to death in the stead of all, and offered it to the Father—doing this, moreover, of His loving-kindness, to the end that, firstly, all being held to have died in Him, the law involving the ruin of men might be undone (inasmuch as its power was fully spent in the Lord's body, and had no longer holding-ground against men, his peers), and that, secondly, whereas men had turned toward corruption, He might turn them again toward incorruption, and quicken them from death by the appropriation [2] of His body and by the grace of the Resurrection, banishing death from them like straw from the fire [3].

§ 9. *The Word, since death alone could stay the plague, took a mortal body which, united with Him, should avail for all, and by partaking of His immortality stay the corruption of the Race. By being above all, He made His Flesh an offering for our souls ; by being one with us all, He clothed us with immortality. Simile to illustrate this.*

For the Word, perceiving that no otherwise could the corruption of men be undone save by death as a necessary condition, while it was impossible for the Word to suffer death, being immortal, and Son of the Father; to this end He takes to Himself a body capable of death, that it, by partaking of the Word Who is above all, might be worthy to die in the stead of all, and might, because of the Word which was come

---

7 See previous note.   8 Acts xvii. 27.   9 Cf. vi. 3.

1 Cf. 43. 2.
2 Cf. *Orat.* iii. 33, note 5, also *ib.* 31, note 10.
3 The simile is inverted.   Men are the 'straw,' **death the 'fire.'** cf. xliv. 7.

to dwell in it, remain incorruptible, and that thenceforth corruption might be stayed from all by the Grace of the Resurrection. Whence, by offering unto death the body He Himself had taken, as an offering and sacrifice free from any stain, straightway He put away death from all His peers by the offering of an equivalent. 2. For being over all, the Word of God naturally by offering His own temple and corporeal instrument for the life [4] of all satisfied the debt by His death. And thus He, the incorruptible Son of God, being conjoined with all by a like nature, naturally clothed all with incorruption, by the promise of the resurrection. For the actual corruption in death has no longer holding-ground against men, by reason of the Word, which by His one body has come to dwell among them. 3. And like as [5] when a great king has entered into some large city and taken up his abode in one of the houses there, such city is at all events held worthy of high honour, nor does any enemy or bandit any longer descend upon it and subject it; but, on the contrary, it is thought entitled to all care, because of the king's having taken up his residence in a single house there: so, too, has it been with the Monarch of all. 4. For now that He has come to our realm, and taken up his abode in one body among His peers, henceforth the whole conspiracy of the enemy against mankind is checked, and the corruption of death which before was prevailing against them is done away. For the race of men had gone to ruin, had not the Lord and Saviour of all, the Son of God, come among us to meet the end of death [6].

§ 10. *By a like simile, the reasonableness of the work of redemption is shewn. How Christ wiped away our ruin, and provided its antidote by His own teaching. Scripture proofs of the Incarnation of the Word, and of the Sacrifice He wrought.*

Now in truth this great work was peculiarly suited to God's goodness. 1. For if a king, having founded a house or city, if it be beset by bandits from the carelessness of its inmates, does not by any means neglect it, but avenges and reclaims it as his own work, having regard not to the carelessness of the inhabitants, but to what beseems himself; much more did God the Word of the all-good Father not neglect the race of men, His work, going to corruption: but, while He blotted out the death which had

ensued by the offering of His own body, He corrected their neglect by His own teaching, restoring all that was man's by His own power. 2. And of this one may be assured at the hands of the Saviour's own inspired writers, if one happen upon their writings, where they say: "For the love of Christ [7] constraineth us; because we thus judge, that if one died for all, then all died, and He died for all that we should no longer live unto ourselves, but unto Him Who for our sakes died and rose again," our Lord Jesus Christ. And, again: "But [8] we behold Him, Who hath been made a little lower than the angels, even Jesus, because of the suffering of death crowned with glory and honour, that by the grace of God He should taste of death for every man." 3. Then He also points out the reason why it was necessary for none other than God the Word Himself to become incarnate; as follows: "For it became Him, for Whom are all things, and through Whom are all things, in bringing many sons unto glory, to make the Captain of their salvation perfect through suffering;" by which words He means, that it belonged to none other to bring man back from the corruption which had begun, than the Word of God, Who had also made them from the beginning. 4. And that it was in order to the sacrifice for bodies such as His own that the Word Himself also assumed a body, to this, also, they refer in these words [9]: "Forasmuch then as the children are the sharers in blood and flesh, He also Himself in like manner partook of the same, that through death He might bring to nought Him that had the power of death, that is, the devil; and might deliver them who, through fear of death, were all their lifetime subject to bondage." 5. For by the sacrifice of His own body, He both put an end to the law which was against us, and made a new beginning of life for us, by the hope of resurrection which He has given us. For since from man it was that death prevailed over men, for this cause conversely, by the Word of God being made man has come about the destruction of death and the resurrection of life; as the man which bore Christ [1] saith: For [2] since by man came death, by man came also the resurrection of the dead. For as in Adam all die, so also in Christ shall all be made alive:" and so forth. For no longer now do we die as subject to condemnation; but as men who rise from the dead we await the general resurrection of all, "which [3]

---

4 ἀντίψυχον.
5 Possibly suggested by the practice of the emperors. Constantinople was thus dignified a few years later (326). For this simile compare *Sermo Major de Fide*, c. 6.
6 Or, " to put an end to death."

7 2 Cor. v. 14.   8 Heb. ii. 9, *sq.*   9 Heb. ii. 14, *sq.*
1 Cf. Gal. vi. 17.   2 1 Cor. xv. 21, *sq.*   3 1 Tim. vi. 15.

in its own times He shall show," even God, Who has also wrought it, and bestowed it upon us. 6. This then is the first cause of the Saviour's being made man. But one might see from the following reasons also, that His gracious coming amongst us was fitting to have taken place.

§ 11. *Second reason for the Incarnation. God, knowing that man was not by nature sufficient to know Him, gave him, in order that he might have some profit in being, a knowledge of Himself. He made them in the Image of the Word, that thus they might know the Word, and through Him the Father. Yet man, despising this, fell into idolatry, leaving the unseen God for magic and astrology; and all this in spite of God's manifold revelation of Himself.*

God, Who has the power over all things, when He was making the race of men through His own Word, seeing the weakness of their nature, that it was not sufficient of itself to know its Maker, nor to get any idea at all of God; because while He was uncreate, the creatures had been made of nought, and while He was incorporeal, men had been fashioned in a lower way in the body, and because in every way the things made fell far short of being able to comprehend and know their Maker— taking pity, I say, on the race of men, inasmuch as He is good, He did not leave them destitute of the knowledge of Himself, lest they should find no profit in existing at all [4]. 2. For what profit to the creatures if they knew not their Maker? or how could they be rational without knowing the Word (and Reason) of the Father, in Whom they received their very being? For there would be nothing to distinguish them even from brute creatures if they had knowledge of nothing but earthly things. Nay, why did God make them at all, as He did not wish to be known by them? 3. Whence, lest this should be so, being good, He gives them a share in His own Image, our Lord Jesus Christ, and makes them after His own Image and after His likeness: so that by such grace perceiving the Image, that is, the Word of the Father, they may be able through Him to get an idea of the Father, and knowing their Maker, live the happy and truly blessed life. 4. But men once more in their perversity having set at nought, in spite of all this, the grace given them, so wholly rejected God, and so darkened their soul, as not merely to forget their idea of God, but also to fashion for themselves one invention after another.

For not only did they grave idols for themselves, instead of the truth, and honour things that were not before the living God, "and [5] serve the creature rather than the Creator," but, worst of all, they transferred the honour of God even to stocks and stones and to every material object and to men, and went even further than this, as we have said in the former treatise. 5. So far indeed did their impiety go, that they proceeded to worship devils, and proclaimed them as gods, fulfilling their own [6] lusts. For they performed, as was said above, offerings of brute animals, and sacrifices of men, as was meet for them [7], binding themselves down all the faster under their maddening inspirations. 6. For this reason it was also that magic arts were taught among them, and oracles in divers places led men astray, and all men ascribed the influences of their birth and existence to the stars and to all the heavenly bodies, having no thought of anything beyond what was visible. 7. And, in a word, everything was full of irreligion and lawlessness, and God alone, and His Word, was unknown, albeit He had not hidden Himself out of men's sight, nor given the knowledge of Himself in one way only; but had, on the contrary, unfolded it to them in many forms and by many ways.

§ 12. *For though man was created in grace, God, foreseeing his forgetfulness, provided also the works of creation to remind man of Him. Yet further, He ordained a Law and Prophets, whose ministry was meant for all the world. Yet men heeded only their own lusts.*

For whereas the grace of the Divine Image was in itself sufficient to make known God the Word, and through Him the Father; still God, knowing the weakness of men, made provision even for their carelessness: so that if they cared not to know God of themselves, they might be enabled through the works of creation to avoid ignorance of the Maker. 2. But since men's carelessness, by little and little, descends to lower things, God made provision, once more, even for this weakness of theirs, by sending a law, and prophets, men such as they knew, so that even if they were not ready to look up to heaven and know their Creator, they might have their instruction from those near at hand. For men are able to learn from men more directly about higher things. 3. So it was open to them, by looking into the height of heaven, and perceiving the

---

4 Cf. 13. 2.

5 Cf. Rom. i. 25.
6 αὐτῶν may refer to the δαίμονες, in which case compare c. Gent. 25. sub fin.
7 See c. Gent. 25. 1, τὰ ὅμοια τοῖς ὁμοίοις. Or the text may mean simply "as their due."

harmony of creation, to know its Ruler, the Word of the Father, Who, by His own providence over all things makes known the Father to all, and to this end moves all things, that through Him all may know God. 4. Or, if this were too much for them, it was possible for them to meet at least the holy men, and through them to learn of God, the Maker of all things, the Father of Christ; and that the worship of idols is godlessness, and full of all impiety. 5. Or it was open to them, by knowing the law even, to cease from all lawlessness and live a virtuous life. For neither was the law for the Jews alone, nor were the Prophets sent for them only, but, though sent to the Jews and persecuted by the Jews, they were for all the world a holy school of the knowledge of God and the conduct of the soul. 6. God's goodness then and loving-kindness being so great—men nevertheless, overcome by the pleasures of the moment and by the illusions and deceits sent by demons, did not raise their heads toward the truth, but loaded themselves the more with evils and sins, so as no longer to seem rational, but from their ways to be reckoned void of reason.

§ 13. *Here again, was God to keep silence ? to allow to false gods the worship He made us to render to Himself ? A king whose subjects had revolted would, after sending letters and messages, go to them in person. How much more shall God restore in us the grace of His image. This men, themselves but copies, could not do. Hence the Word Himself must come (1) to recreate, (2) to destroy death in the Body.*

So, then, men having thus become brutalized, and demoniacal deceit thus clouding every place, and hiding the knowledge of the true God, what was God to do? To keep still silence at so great a thing, and suffer men to be led astray by demons and not to know God? 2. And what was the use of man having been originally made in God's image? For it had been better for him to have been made simply like a brute animal, than, once made rational, for him to live[8] the life of the brutes. 3. Or where was any necessity at all for his receiving the idea of God to begin with? For if he be not fit to receive it even now, it were better it had not been given him at first. 4. Or what profit to God Who has made them, or what glory to Him could it be, if men, made by Him, do not worship Him, but think that others are their makers? For God thus proves to have made these for others instead of for Himself. 5. Once again, a merely human king does not let the lands he has colonized

pass to others to serve them, nor go over to other men; but he warns them by letters, and often sends to them by friends, or, if need be, he comes in person, to put them to rebuke in the last resort by his presence, only that they may not serve others and his own work be spent for nought. 6. Shall not God much more spare His own creatures, that they be not led astray from Him and serve things of nought? especially since such going astray proves the cause of their ruin and undoing, and since it was unfitting that they should perish which had once been partakers of God's image. 7. What then was God to do? or what was to be done save the renewing of that which was in God's image, so that by it men might once more be able to know Him? But how could this have come to pass save by the presence of the very Image of God, our Lord Jesus Christ? For by men's means it was impossible, since they are but made after an image; nor by angels either, for not even they are (God's) images. Whence the Word of God came in His own person, that, as He was the Image of the Father, He might be able to create afresh the man after the image. 8. But, again, it could not else have taken place had not death and corruption been done away. 9. Whence He took, in natural fitness, a mortal body, that while death might in it be once for all done away, men made after His Image might once more be renewed. None other then was sufficient for this need, save the Image of the Father.

§ 14. *A portrait once effaced must be restored from the original. Thus the Son of the Father came to seek, save, and regenerate. No other way was possible. Blinded himself, man could not see to heal. The witness of creation had failed to preserve Him, and could not bring Him back. The Word alone could do so. But how ? only by revealing Himself as man.*

For as, when the likeness painted on a panel has been effaced by stains from without, he whose likeness it is must needs come once more to enable the portrait to be renewed on the same wood: for, for the sake of his picture, even the mere wood on which it is painted is not thrown away, but the outline is renewed upon it; 2. in the same way also the most holy Son of the Father, being the Image of the Father, came to our region to renew man once made in His likeness, and find him, as one lost, by the remission of sins; as He says Himself in the Gospels: " I came[9] to find and to save the lost." Whence He said to the Jews also: " Except[1] a man be born again," not meaning,

---

[8] The Bened. text is corrected here on the ground (1) of MS. evidence, (2) of construction (for which see 6. 7, and c. Gent. 20, 3).

[9] Cf. Luc. xix. 10.   [1] See John iii. 3, 5.

as they thought, birth from woman, but speaking of the soul born and created anew in the likeness of God's image. 3. But since wild idolatry and godlessness occupied the world, and the knowledge of God was hid, whose part was it to teach the world concerning the Father? Man's, might one say? But it was not in man's power to penetrate everywhere beneath the sun; for neither had they the physical strength to run so far, nor would they be able to claim credence in this matter, nor were they sufficient by themselves to withstand the deceit and impositions of evil spirits. 4. For where all were smitten and confused in soul from demoniacal deceit, and the vanity of idols, how was it possible for them to win over man's soul and man's mind—whereas they cannot even see them? Or how can a man convert what he does not see? 5. But perhaps one might say creation was enough; but if creation were enough, these great evils would never have come to pass. For creation was there already, and all the same, men were grovelling in the same error concerning God. 6. Who, then, was needed, save the Word of God, that sees both soul and mind, and that gives movement to all things in creation, and by them makes known the Father? For He who by His own Providence and ordering of all things was teaching men concerning the Father, He it was that could renew this same teaching as well. 7. How, then, could this have been done? Perhaps one might say, that the same means were open as before, for Him to shew forth the truth about the Father once more by means of the work of creation. But this was no longer a sure means. Quite the contrary; for men missed seeing this before, and have turned their eyes no longer upward but downward. 8. Whence, naturally, willing to profit men, He sojourns here as man, taking to Himself a body like the others, and from things of earth, that is by the works of His body [He teaches them], so that they who would not know Him from His Providence and rule over all things, may even from the works done by His actual body know the Word of God which is in the body, and through Him the Father.

§ 15. *Thus the Word condescended to man's engrossment in corporeal things, by even taking a body. All man's superstitions He met halfway; whether men were inclined to worship Nature, Man, Demons, or the dead, He shewed Himself Lord of all these.*

For as a kind teacher who cares for His disciples, if some of them cannot profit by higher subjects, comes down to their level, and teaches them at any rate by simpler

courses; so also did the Word of God. As Paul also says: "For seeing[2] that in the wisdom of God the world through its wisdom knew not God, it was God's good pleasure through the foolishness of the word preached to save them that believe." 2. For seeing that men, having rejected the contemplation of God, and with their eyes downward, as though sunk in the deep, were seeking about for God in nature and in the world of sense, feigning gods for themselves of mortal men and demons; to this end the loving and general Saviour of all, the Word of God, takes to Himself a body, and as Man walks among men and meets the senses of all men half-way[3], to the end, I say, that they who think that God is corporeal may from what the Lord effects by His body perceive the truth, and through Him recognize[4] the Father. 3. So, men as they were, and human in all their thoughts, on whatever objects they fixed their senses, there they saw themselves met half-way[3], and taught the truth from every side. 4. For if they looked with awe upon the Creation, yet they saw how she confessed Christ as Lord; or if their mind was swayed toward men, so as to think them gods, yet from the Saviour's works, supposing they compared them, the Saviour alone among men appeared Son of God; for there were no such works done among the rest as have been done by the Word of God. 5. Or if they were biassed toward evil spirits, even, yet seeing them cast out by the Word, they were to know that He alone, the Word of God, was God, and that the spirits were none. 6. Or if their mind had already sunk even to the dead, so as to worship heroes, and the gods spoken of in the poets, yet, seeing the Saviour's resurrection, they were to confess them to be false gods, and that the Lord alone is true, the Word of the Father, that was Lord even of death. 7. For this cause He was both born and appeared as Man, and died, and rose again, dulling and casting into the shade the works of all former men by His own, that in whatever direction the bias of men might be, from thence He might recall them, and teach them of His own true Father, as He Himself says: "I came to save and to find that which was lost[5]."

§ 16. *He came then to attract man's sense-bound attention to Himself as man, and so to lead him on to know Him as God.*

For men's mind having finally fallen to things of sense, the Word disguised Himself

---

[2] 1 Cor. i. 21.   [3] Lit. "draws toward Himself."
[4] Lit. "infer."   [5] Cf. 14. 2.

by appearing in a body, that He might, as Man, transfer men to Himself, and centre their senses on Himself, and, men seeing Him thenceforth as Man, persuade them by the works He did that He is not Man only, but also God, and the Word and Wisdom of the true God. 2. This, too, is what Paul means to point out when he says: "That ye [6] being rooted and grounded in love, may be strong to apprehend with all the saints what is the breadth and length, and height and depth, and to know the love of Christ which passeth knowledge, that ye may be filled unto all the fulness of God." 3. For by the Word revealing Himself everywhere, both above and beneath, and in the depth and in the breadth— above, in the creation; beneath, in becoming man; in the depth, in Hades; and in the breadth, in the world—all things have been filled with the knowledge of God. 4. Now for this cause, also, He did not immediately upon His coming accomplish His sacrifice on behalf of all, by offering His body to death and raising it again, for by this [7] means He would have made Himself invisible. But He made Himself visible enough by what [7] He did, abiding in it, and doing such works, and shewing such signs, as made Him known no longer as Man, but as God the Word. 5. For by His becoming Man, the Saviour was to accomplish both works of love; first, in putting away death from us and renewing us again; secondly, being unseen and invisible, in manifesting and making Himself known by His works to be the Word of the Father, and the Ruler and King of the universe.

§ 17. *How the Incarnation did not limit the ubiquity of the Word, nor diminish His Purity.* (*Simile of the Sun.*)

For He was not, as might be imagined, circumscribed in the body, nor, while present in the body, was He absent elsewhere; nor, while He moved the body, was the universe left void of His working and Providence; but, thing most marvellous, Word as He was, so far from being contained by anything, He rather contained all things Himself; and just as while present in the whole of Creation, He is at once distinct in being from the universe, and present in all things by His own power,— giving order to all things, and over all and in all revealing His own providence, and giving life to each thing and all things, including the whole without being included, but being in His own Father alone wholly and in every respect,—2. thus, even while present in a human

body and Himself quickening it, He was, without inconsistency, quickening the universe as well, and was in every process of nature, and was outside the whole, and while known from the body by His works, He was none the less manifest from the working of the universe as well. 3. Now, it is the function of soul to behold even what is outside its own body, by acts of thought, without, however, working outside its own body, or moving by its presence things remote from the body. Never, that is, does a man, by thinking of things at a distance, by that fact either move or displace them; nor if a man were to sit in his own house and reason about the heavenly bodies, would he by that fact either move the sun or make the heavens revolve. But he sees that they move and have their being, without being actually able to influence them. 4. Now, the Word of God in His man's nature was not like that; for He was not bound to His body, but rather was Himself wielding it, so that He was not only in it, but was actually in everything, and while external to the universe, abode in His Father only. 5. And this was the wonderful thing that He was at once walking as man, and as the Word was quickening all things, and as the Son was dwelling with His Father. So that not even when the Virgin bore Him did He suffer any change, nor by being in the body was [His glory] dulled: but, on the contrary, He sanctified the body also. 6. For not even by being in the universe does He share in its nature, but all things, on the contrary, are quickened and sustained by Him. 7. For if the sun too, which was made by Him, and which we see, as it revolves in the heaven, is not defiled [8] by touching the bodies upon earth, nor is it put out by darkness, but on the contrary itself illuminates and cleanses them also, much less was the all-holy Word of God, Maker and Lord also of the sun, defiled by being made known in the body; on the contrary, being incorruptible, He quickened and cleansed the body also, which was in itself mortal: "who [9] did," for so it says, "no sin, neither was guile found in His mouth."

§ 18. *How the Word and Power of God works in His human actions: by casting out devils, by Miracles, by His Birth of the Virgin.*

Accordingly, when inspired writers on this matter speak of Him as eating and being born, understand [1] that the body, as body, was born, and sustained with food corresponding to its nature, while God, the Word Himself, Who

---

6 Eph. iii. 18, *sq.*
7 διὰ τούτου, perhaps, in both places—"by it," viz. His body.

8 Cf. St. Aug. *de Fid. et Symb.* 10, Rufin. *in Symb. Apost.* 12. So also Tertull. *adv. Marc.* 'Quodcunque induerit ipse dignum fecit.'
9 1 Pet. ii. 22.   1 Compare *Orat.* iii. 31, note 11.

was united with the body, while ordering all things, also by the works He did in the body shewed Himself to be not man, but God the Word. But these things are said of Him, because the actual body which ate, was born, and suffered, belonged to none other but to the Lord : and because, having become man, it was proper for these things to be predicated of Him as man, to shew Him to have a body in truth, and not in seeming. 2. But just as from these things He was known to be bodily present, so from the works He did in the body He made Himself known to be Son of God. Whence also He cried to the unbelieving Jews ; " If [2] I do not the works of My Father, believe Me not. But if I do them, though ye believe not Me, believe My works ; that ye may know and understand that the Father is in Me, and I in the Father." 3. For just as, though invisible, He is known through the works of creation ; so, having become man, and being in the body unseen, it may be known from His works that He Who can do these is not man, but the Power and Word of God. 4. For His charging evil spirits, and their being driven forth, this deed is not of man, but of God. Or who that saw Him healing the diseases to which the human race is subject, can still think Him man and not God? For He cleansed lepers, made lame men to walk, opened the hearing of deaf men, made blind men to see again, and in a word drove away from men all diseases and infirmities : from which acts it was possible even for the most ordinary observer to see His Godhead. For who that saw Him give back [3] what was deficient to men born lacking, and open the eyes of the man blind from his birth, would have failed to perceive that the nature of men was subject to Him, and that He was its Artificer and Maker? For He that gave back that which the man from his birth had not, must be, it is surely evident, the Lord also of men's natural birth. 5. Therefore, even to begin with, when He was descending to us, He fashioned His body for Himself from a Virgin, thus to afford to all no small proof of His Godhead, in that He Who formed this is also Maker of everything else as well. For who, seeing a body proceeding forth from a Virgin alone without man, can fail to infer that He Who appears in it is Maker and Lord of other bodies also ? 6. Or who, seeing the substance of water changed and transformed into wine, fails to perceive that He Who did this is Lord and Creator of the substance of all waters ? For to this end He went upon the sea also as its Master, and walked as on dry land, to afford evidence to them that saw it of His lordship

over all things. And in feeding so vast a multitude on little, and of His own self yielding abundance where none was, so that from five loaves five thousand had enough, and left so much again over, did He shew Himself to be any other than the very Lord Whose Providence is over all things ?

§ 19. *Man, unmoved by nature, was to be taught to know God by that sacred Manhood, Whose deity all nature confessed, especially in His Death.*

But all this it seemed well for the Saviour to do ; that since men had failed to know His Providence, revealed in the Universe, and had failed to perceive His Godhead shewn in creation, they might at any rate from the works of His body recover their sight, and through Him receive an idea of the knowledge of the Father, inferring, as I said before, from particular cases His Providence over the whole. 2. For who that saw His power over evil spirits, or who that saw the evil spirits confess that He was their Lord, will hold his mind any longer in doubt whether this be the Son and Wisdom and Power of God? 3. For He made even the creation break silence : in that even at His death, marvellous to relate, or rather at His actual trophy over death—the Cross I mean—all creation was confessing that He that was made manifest and suffered in the body was not man merely, but the Son of God and Saviour of all. For the sun hid His face, and the earth quaked and the mountains were rent : all men were awed. Now these things shewed that Christ on the Cross was God, while all creation was His slave, and was witnessing by its fear to its Master's presence. Thus, then, God the Word shewed Himself to men by His works. But our next step must be to recount and speak of the end of His bodily life and course, and of the nature of the death of His body ; especially as this is the sum of our faith, and all men without exception are full of it : so that you may know that no whit the less from this also Christ is known to be God and the Son of God.

§ 20. *None, then, could bestow incorruption, but He Who had made, none restore the likeness of God, save His Own Image, none quicken, but the Life, none teach, but the Word. And He, to pay our debt of death, must also die for us, and rise again as our first-fruits from the grave. Mortal therefore His body must be ; corruptible, His Body could not be.*

We have, then, now stated in part, as far as it was possible, and as ourselves had been able to understand, the reason of His bodily ap-

---

John x. 37, *sq.*　　　　3 Cf. 49. 2.

pearing; that it was in the power of none other to turn the corruptible to incorruption, except the Saviour Himself, that had at the beginning also made all things out of nought: and that none other could create anew the likeness of God's image for men, save the Image of the Father; and that none other could render the mortal immortal, save our Lord Jesus Christ, Who is the Very Life[4]; and that none other could teach men of the Father, and destroy the worship of idols, save the Word, that orders all things and is alone the true Only-begotten Son of the Father. 2. But since it was necessary also that the debt owing from all should be paid again: for, as I have already said[5], it was owing that all should die, for which especial cause, indeed, He came among us: to this intent, after the proofs of His Godhead from His works, He next offered up His sacrifice also on behalf of all, yielding His Temple to death in the stead of all, in order firstly to make men quit and free of their old trespass, and further to shew Himself more powerful even than death, displaying His own body incorruptible, as firstfruits of the resurrection of all. 3. And do not be surprised if we frequently[6] repeat the same words on the same subject. For since we are speaking of the counsel of God, therefore we expound the same sense in more than one form, lest we should seem to be leaving anything out, and incur the charge of inadequate treatment: for it is better to submit to the blame of repetition than to leave out anything that ought to be set down. 4. The body, then, as sharing the same nature with all, for it was a human body, though by an unparalleled miracle it was formed of a virgin only, yet being mortal, was to die also, conformably to its peers. But by virtue of the union of the Word with it, it was no longer subject to corruption according to its own nature, but by reason of the Word that was come to dwell[7] in it it was placed out of the reach of corruption. 5. And so it was that two marvels came to pass at once, that the death of all was accomplished in the Lord's body, and that death and corruption were wholly done away by reason of the Word that was united with it. For there was need of death, and death must needs be suffered on behalf of all, that the debt owing from all might be paid. 6. Whence, as I said before, the Word, since it was not possible for Him to die, as He was immortal, took to Himself a body such as could die, that He might offer it as His own in the stead of all, and as suffering, through His union[7] with it, on behalf of all, " Bring[8] to nought Him that had the power of death, that is the devil; and might deliver them who through fear of death were all their lifetime subject to bondage."

§ 21. *Death brought to nought by the death of Christ. Why then did not Christ die privately, or in a more honourable way? He was not subject to natural death, but had to die at the hands of others. Why then did He die? Nay but for that purpose He came, and but for that, He could not have risen.*

Why, now that the common Saviour of all has died on our behalf, we, the faithful in Christ, no longer die the death as before, agreeably to the warning of the law; for this condemnation has ceased; but, corruption ceasing and being put away by the grace of the Resurrection, henceforth we are only dissolved, agreeably to our bodies' mortal nature, at the time God has fixed for each, that we may be able to gain a better resurrection. 2. For like the seeds which are cast into the earth, we do not perish by dissolution, but sown in the earth, shall rise again, death having been brought to nought by the grace of the Saviour. Hence it is that blessed Paul, who was made a surety of the Resurrection to all, says: " This corruptible[9] must put on incorruption, and this mortal must put on immortality; but when this corruptible shall have put on incorruption, and this mortal shall have put on immortality, then shall be brought to pass the saying that is written, Death is swallowed up in victory. O death where is thy sting? O grave where is thy victory?" 3. Why, then, one might say, if it were necessary for Him to yield up His body to death in the stead of all, did He not lay it aside as man privately, instead of going as far as even to be crucified? For it were more fitting for Him to have laid His body aside honourably, than ignominiously to endure a death like this. 4. Now, see to it, I reply, whether such an objection be not merely human, whereas what the Saviour did is truly divine and for many reasons worthy of His Godhead. Firstly, be cause the death which befalls men comes to them agreeably to the weakness of their nature; for, unable to continue in one stay, they are dissolved with time. Hence, too, diseases befall them, and they fall sick and die. But the Lord is not weak, but is the Power of God and Word of God and Very Life. 5. If, then, He had laid aside His body somewhere in private,

---

4 αὐτοζωή, see c. Gent. 40, 46, and Orat. iv. 2, note 4.
5 See especially § 7.
6 e.g. viii. 4; x. 5, &c. 'It is quite a peculiarity of Ath. to repeat, and to apologise for doing so,' (Newman in Orat. ii. 80, note 1).
7 ἐπίβασις, compare ἐπιβαίνειν, 43. 4, &c.

7 ἐπίβασις, compare ἐπιβαίνειν, 43. 4, &c.
8 Cf. 10. 4, above.   9 1 Cor. xv. 53, sqq.

and upon a bed, after the manner of men, it would have been thought that He also did this agreeably to the weakness of His nature, and because there was nothing in him more than in other men. But since He was, firstly, the Life and the Word of God, and it was necessary, secondly, for the death on behalf of all to be accomplished, for this cause, on the one hand, because He was life and power, the body gained strength in Him ; 6. while on the other, as death must needs come to pass, He did not Himself take, but received at others' hands, the occasion of perfecting His sacrifice. Since it was not fit, either, that the Lord should fall sick, who healed the diseases of others ; nor again was it right for that body to lose its strength, in which He gives strength to the weaknesses of others also. 7. Why, then, did He not prevent death, as He did sickness? Because it was for this that He had the body, and it was unfitting to prevent it, lest the Resurrection also should be hindered, while yet it was equally unfitting for sickness to precede His death, lest it should be thought weakness on the part of Him that was in the body. Did He not then hunger? Yes ; He hungered, agreeably to the properties of His body. But He did not perish of hunger, because of the Lord that wore it. Hence, even if He died to ransom all, yet He saw not corruption. For [His body] rose again in perfect soundness, since the body belonged to none other, but to the very Life.

§ 22. *But why did He not withdraw His body from the Jews, and so guard its immortality?* (1) *It became Him not to inflict death on Himself, and yet not to shun it.* (2) *He came to receive death as the due of others, therefore it should come to Him from without.* (3) *His death must be certain, to guarantee the truth of His Resurrection. Also, He could not die from infirmity, lest He should be mocked in His healing of others.*

But it were better, one might say, to have hidden from the designs of the Jews, that He might guard His body altogether from death. Now let such an one be told that this too was unbefitting the Lord. For as it was not fitting for the Word of God, being the Life, to inflict death Himself on His own body, so neither was it suitable to fly from death offered by others, but rather to follow it up unto destruction, for which reason He naturally neither laid aside His body of His own accord, nor, again, fled from the Jews when they took counsel against Him. 2. But this did not shew weakness on the Word's part, but, on the contrary, shewed Him to be Saviour and Life ; in that He both awaited death to destroy it, and

hasted to accomplish the death offered Him for the salvation of all. 3. And besides, the Saviour came to accomplish not His own death, but the death of men ; whence He did not lay aside His body by a death of His own [1] —for He was Life and had none—but received that death which came from men, in order perfectly to do away with this when it met Him in His own body. 4. Again, from the following also one might see the reasonableness of the Lord's body meeting this end. The Lord was especially concerned for the resurrection of the body which He was set to accomplish. For what He was to do was to manifest it as a monument of victory over death, and to assure all of His having effected the blotting out of corruption, and of the incorruption of their bodies from thenceforward ; as a gage of which and a proof of the resurrection in store for all, He has preserved His own body incorrupt. 5. If, then, once more, His body had fallen sick, and the word had been sundered from it in the sight of all, it would have been unbecoming that He who healed the diseases of others should suffer His own instrument to waste in sickness. For how could His driving out the diseases of others have been believed [2] in if His own temple fell sick in Him [3]? For either He had been mocked as unable to drive away diseases, or if He could, but did not, He would be thought insensible toward others also.

§ 23. *Necessity of a public death for the doctrine of the Resurrection.*

But even if, without any disease and without any pain, He had hidden His body away privily and by Himself "in [4] a corner," or in a desert place, or in a house, or anywhere, and afterwards suddenly appeared and said that He had been raised from the dead, He would have seemed on all hands to be telling idle tales [5], and what He said about the Resurrection would have been all the more discredited, as there was no one at all to witness to His death. Now, death must precede resurrection, as it would be no resurrection did not death precede ; so that if the death of His body had taken place anywhere in secret, the death not being apparent nor taking place before witnesses, His Resurrection too had been hidden and without evidence. 2. Or why, while when He had risen He proclaimed the Resurrection, should He cause His death to take place in secret? or why, while He drove out evil spirits in the presence of all, and made the man blind from his birth recover his sight,

---

[1] Cf. Joh. x. 17, 18.   [2] Cf. Matt. xxvii. 42.
[3] *i.e.* when sustained by its union with Him.
[4] Acts xxvi. 26.   [5] Luke xxiv. 11.

and changed the water into wine, that by these means He might be believed to be the Word of God, should He not manifest His mortal nature as incorruptible in the presence of all, that He might be believed Himself to be the Life? 3. Or how were His disciples to have boldness in speaking of the Resurrection, were they not able to say that He first died? Or how could they be believed, saying that death had first taken place and then the Resurrection, had they not had as witnesses of His death the men before whom they spoke with boldness? For if, even as it was, when His death and Resurrection had taken place in the sight of all, the Pharisees of that day would not believe, but compelled even those who had seen the Resurrection to deny it, why, surely, if these things had happened in secret, how many pretexts for disbelief would they have devised? 4. Or how could the end of death, and the victory over it be proved, unless challenging it before the eyes of all He had shewn it to be dead, annulled for the future by the incorruption of His body?

§ 24. *Further objections anticipated. He did not choose His manner of death; for He was to prove Conqueror of death in all or any of its forms: (simile of a good wrestler). The death chosen to disgrace Him proved the Trophy against death: moreover it preserved His body undivided.*

But what others also might have said, we must anticipate in reply. For perhaps a man might say even as follows: If it was necessary for His death to take place before all, and with witnesses, that the story of His Resurrection also might be believed, it would have been better at any rate for Him to have devised for Himself a glorious death, if only to escape the ignominy of the Cross. 2. But had He done even this, He would give ground for suspicion against Himself, that He was not powerful against every death, but only against the death devised for[6] Him; and so again there would have been a pretext for disbelief about the Resurrection all the same. So death came to His body, not from Himself, but from hostile counsels, in order that whatever death they offered to the Saviour, this He might utterly do away. 3. And just as a noble wrestler, great in skill and courage, does not pick out his antagonists for himself, lest he should raise a suspicion of his being afraid of some of them, but puts it in the choice of the onlookers, and especially so if they happen to be his enemies, so that against whomsoever

they match him, him he may throw, and be believed superior to them all; so also the Life of all, our Lord and Saviour, even Christ, did not devise a death for His own body, so as not to appear to be fearing some other death; but He accepted on the Cross, and endured, a death inflicted by others, and above all by His enemies, which they thought dreadful and ignominious and not to be faced; so that this also being destroyed, both He Himself might be believed to be the Life, and the power of death be brought utterly to nought. 4. So something surprising and startling has happened; for the death, which they thought to inflict as a disgrace, was actually a monument of victory against death itself. Whence neither did He suffer the death of John, his head being severed, nor, as Esaias, was He sawn in sunder; in order that even in death He might still keep His body undivided and in perfect soundness, and no pretext be afforded to those that would divide the Church.

§ 25. *Why the Cross, of all deaths? (1) He had to bear the curse for us. (2) On it He held out His hands to unite all, Jews and Gentiles, in Himself. (3) He defeated the "Prince of the powers of the air" in his own region, clearing the way to heaven and opening for us the everlasting doors.*

And thus much in reply to those without who pile up arguments for themselves. But if any of our own people also inquire, not from love of debate, but from love of learning, why He suffered death in none other way save on the Cross, let him also be told that no other way than this was good for us, and that it was well that the Lord suffered this for our sakes. 2. For if He came Himself to bear the curse laid upon us, how else could He have "become[7] a curse," unless He received the death set for a curse? and that is the Cross. For this is exactly what is written: "Cursed[8] is he that hangeth on a tree." 3. Again, if the Lord's death is the ransom of all, and by His death "the middle[9] wall of partition" is broken down, and the calling of the nations is brought about, how would He have called us to Him, had He not been crucified? For it is only on the cross that a man dies with his hands spread out. Whence it was fitting for the Lord to bear this also and to spread out His hands, that with the one He might draw the ancient people, and with the other those from the Gentiles, and unite both in Himself. 4. For this is what He Himself has said, signifying by what manner of death

---

6 *i.e.* suggested as ἔνδοξον (*supra*, 1); a reading παρ' ἑαυτοῦ has been suggested: (devised) "by Himself."

7 Gal. iii. 13.　　8 Deut. xxi. 23.　　9 Eph. ii. 14.

He was to ransom all : "I, when[1] I am lifted up," He saith, "shall draw all men unto Me." 5. And once more, if the devil, the enemy of our race, having fallen from heaven, wanders about our lower atmosphere, and there bearing rule over his fellow-spirits, as his peers in disobedience, not only works illusions by their means in them that are deceived, but tries to hinder them that are going up (and about this[2] the Apostle says : "According to the prince of the power of the air, of the spirit that now worketh in the sons of disobedience"); while the Lord came to cast down the devil, and clear the air and prepare the way for us up into heaven, as said the Apostle : "Through[3] the veil, that is to say, His flesh"—and this must needs be by death—well, by what other kind of death could this have come to pass, than by one which took place in the air, I mean the cross? for only he that is perfected on the cross dies in the air. Whence it was quite fitting that the Lord suffered this death. 6. For thus being lifted up He cleared the air[4] of the malignity both of the devil and of demons of all kinds, as He says : "I beheld[5] Satan as lightning fall from heaven;" and made a new opening of the way up into heaven, as He says once more : "Lift[6] up your gates, O ye princes, and be ye lift up, ye everlasting doors." For it was not the Word Himself that needed an opening of the gates, being Lord of all; nor were any of His works closed to their Maker; but we it was that needed it, whom He carried up by His own body. For as He offered it to death on behalf of all, so by it He once more made ready the way up into the heavens.

§ 26. *Reasons for His rising on the Third Day.* (1) *Not sooner, for else His real death would be denied, nor* (2) *later; to (a) guard the identity of His body, (b) not to keep His disciples too long in suspense, nor (c) to wait till the witnesses of His death were dispersed, or its memory faded.*

The death on the Cross, then, for us has proved seemly and fitting, and its cause has been shewn to be reasonable in every respect; and it may justly be argued that in no other way than by the Cross was it right for the salvation of all to take place. For not even thus—not even on the Cross—did He leave Himself concealed; but far otherwise, while He made creation witness to the presence of its Maker, He suffered not the temple of His

body to remain long, but having merely shewn it to be dead, by the contact of death with it, He straightway raised it up on the third day, bearing away, as the mark of victory and the triumph over death, the incorruptibility and impassibility which resulted to His body. 2. For He could, even immediately on death, have raised His body and shewn it alive; but this also the Saviour, in wise foresight, did not do. For one might have said that He had not died at all, or that death had not come into perfect contact with Him, if He had manifested the Resurrection at once. 3. Perhaps, again, had the interval of His dying and rising again been one of two days[7] only, the glory of His incorruption would have been obscure. So in order that the body might be proved to be dead, the Word tarried yet one intermediate day, and on the third shewed it incorruptible to all. 4. So then, that the death on the Cross might be proved, He raised His body on the third day. 5. But lest, by raising it up when it had remained a long time and been completely corrupted, He should be disbelieved, as though He had exchanged it for some other body—for a man might also from lapse of time distrust what he saw, and forget what had taken place—for this cause He waited not more than three days; nor did He keep long in suspense those whom He had told about the Resurrection : 6. but while the word was still echoing in their ears and their eyes were still expectant and their mind in suspense, and while those who had slain Him were still living on earth, and were on the spot and could witness to the death of the Lord's body, the Son of God Himself, after an interval of three days, shewed His body, once dead, immortal and incorruptible; and it was made manifest to all that it was not from any natural weakness of the Word that dwelt in it that the body had died, but in order that in it death might be done away by the power of the Saviour.

§ 27. *The change wrought by the Cross in the relation of Death to Man.*

For that death is destroyed, and that the Cross is become the victory over it, and that it has no more power but is verily dead, this is no small proof, or rather an evident warrant, that it is despised by all Christ's disciples, and that they all take the aggressive against it and no longer fear it; but by the sign of the Cross and by faith in Christ tread

---

[1] John xii. 32.
[2] Eph. ii. 2, and see the curious visions of Antony, *Vit. Ant.,* 65, 66.   [3] Heb. x. 20.
[4] Cf. Lightfoot on Coloss. ii. 15, also the fragment of *Letter* 22. and *Letter* 60. 7.
[5] Luc. x. 18.   [6] Ps. xxiv. 7, LXX.

[7] Literally 'at an even' [distance], as contrasted with (a) the same day (2, above), (b) the third day (ἐν τριταίῳ διαστήματι (6, below). ἐν ἴσῳ must therefore be equivalent *in sense* to δευτεραίον. Possibly the literal sense is '[had the Resurrection taken place] at an equal interval between the Death and the [actual day of] the Resurrection.'

it down as dead. 2. For of old, before the divine sojourn of the Saviour took place, even to the saints death was terrible[8], and all wept for the dead as though they perished. But now that the Saviour has raised His body, death is no longer terrible; for all who believe in Christ tread him under as nought, and choose rather to die than to deny their faith in Christ. For they verily know that when they die they are not destroyed, but actually [begin to] live, and become incorruptible through the Resurrection. 3. And that devil that once maliciously exulted in death, now that its[9] pains were loosed, remained the only one truly dead. And a proof of this is, that before men believe Christ, they see in death an object of terror, and play the coward before him. But when they are gone over to Christ's faith and teaching, their contempt for death is so great that they even eagerly rush upon it, and become witnesses for the Resurrection the Saviour has accomplished against it. For while still tender in years they make haste to die, and not men only, but women also, exercise themselves by bodily discipline against it. So weak has he become, that even women who were formerly deceived by him, now mock at him as dead and paralyzed. 4. For as when a tyrant has been defeated by a real king, and bound hand and foot, then all that pass by laugh him to scorn, buffeting and reviling him, no longer fearing his fury and barbarity, because of the king who has conquered him; so also, death having been conquered and exposed by the Saviour on the Cross, and bound hand and foot, all they who are in Christ, as they pass by, trample on him, and witnessing to Christ scoff at death, jesting at him, and saying what has been written against him of old: "O death[1], where is thy victory? O grave, where is thy sting."

§ 28. *This exceptional fact must be tested by experience. Let those who doubt it become Christians."*

Is this, then, a slight proof of the weakness of death? or is it a slight demonstration of the victory won over him by the Saviour, when the youths and young maidens that are in Christ despise this life and practise to die? 2. For man is by nature afraid of death and of the dissolution of the body; but there is this most startling fact, that he who has put on the faith of the Cross despises even what is naturally fearful, and for Christ's sake is not afraid of death. 3. And just as, whereas fire has the natural property of burning, if some one said there was a substance which did not fear its burning, but on the contrary proved it weak—as the asbestos among the Indians is said to do—then one who did not believe the story, if he wished to put it to the test, is at any rate, after putting on the fireproof material and touching the fire, thereupon assured of the weakness attributed[2] to the fire: 4. or if any one wished to see the tyrant bound, at any rate by going into the country and domain of his conqueror he may see the man, a terror to others, reduced to weakness; so if a man is incredulous even still after so many proofs and after so many who have become martyrs in Christ, and after the scorn shewn for death every day by those who are illustrious in Christ, still, if his mind be even yet doubtful as to whether death has been brought to nought and had an end, he does well to wonder at so great a thing, only let him not prove obstinate in incredulity, nor case-hardened in the face of what is so plain. 5. But just as he who has got the asbestos knows that fire has no burning power over it, and as he who would see the tyrant bound goes over to the empire of his conqueror, so too let him who is incredulous about the victory over death receive the faith of Christ, and pass over to His teaching, and he shall see the weakness of death, and the triumph over it. For many who were formerly incredulous and scoffers have afterwards believed and so despised death as even to become martyrs for Christ Himself.

§ 29. *Here then are wonderful effects, and a sufficient cause, the Cross, to account for them, as sunrise accounts for daylight.*

Now if by the sign of the Cross, and by faith in Christ, death is trampled down, it must be evident before the tribunal of truth that it is none other than Christ Himself that has displayed trophies and triumphs over death, and made him lose all his strength. 2. And if, while previously death was strong, and for that reason terrible, now after the sojourn of the Saviour and the death and Resurrection of His body it is despised, it must be evident that death has been brought to nought and conquered by the very Christ that ascended the Cross. 3. For as, if after night-time the sun rises, and the whole region of earth is illumined by him, it is at any rate not open to doubt that it is the sun who has revealed his light everywhere, that has also driven away the dark and given light to all things; so, now that death has come into contempt, and been

---

[8] Cf. Ps. lv. 4, lxxxix. 47; Job. xviii. 14.   [9] Cf. Acts. ii. 24.
[1] Cf. above, 21. 2.

[2] κατὰ τοῦ πυρός. κατὰ appears to have the predicative force so common in Aristotle. The Bened. translation 'the weakness of fire against the asbestos' is based on a needless conjecture.

trodden under foot, from the time when the Saviour's saving manifestation in the flesh and His death on the Cross took place, it must be quite plain that it is the very Saviour that also appeared in the body, Who has brought death to nought, and Who displays the signs of victory over him day by day in His own disciples. 4. For when one sees men, weak by nature, leaping forward to death, and not fearing its corruption nor frightened of the descent into Hades, but with eager soul challenging it; and not flinching from torture, but on the contrary, for Christ's sake electing to rush upon death in preference to life upon earth, or even if one be an eye-witness of men and females and young children rushing and leaping upon death for the sake of Christ's religion; who is so silly, or who is so incredulous, or who so maimed in his mind, as not to see and infer that Christ, to Whom the people witness, Himself supplies and gives to each the victory over death, depriving him of all his power in each one of them that hold His faith and bear the sign of the Cross. 5. For he that sees the serpent trodden under foot, especially knowing his former fierceness, no longer doubts that he is dead and has quite lost his strength, unless he is perverted in mind and has not even his bodily senses sound.   For who that sees a lion, either, made sport of by children, fails to see that he is either dead or has lost all his power? 6. Just as, then, it is possible to see with the eyes the truth of all this, so, now that death is made sport of and despised by believers in Christ, let none any longer doubt, nor any prove incredulous, of death having been brought to nought by Christ, and the corruption of death destroyed and stayed.

§ 30. *The reality of the Resurrection proved by facts: (1) the victory over death described above: (2) the Wonders of Grace are the work of one Living, of One who is God: (3) if the gods be (as alleged) real and living, a fortiori He Who shatters their power is alive.*

What we have so far said, then, is no small proof that death has been brought to nought, and that the Cross of the Lord is a sign of victory over him.   But of the Resurrection of the body to immortality thereupon accomplished by Christ, the common Saviour and true Life of all, the demonstration by facts is clearer than arguments to those whose mental vision is sound.   2. For if, as our argument shewed, death has been brought to nought, and because of Christ all tread him under foot, much more did He Himself first tread him down with His own body, and bring him to nought.   But supposing death slain by Him, what could have happened save the rising again of His

body, and its being displayed as a monument of victory against death? or how could death have been shewn to be brought to nought unless the Lord's body had risen? But if this demonstration of the Resurrection seem to any one insufficient, let him be assured of what is said even from what takes place before his eyes.   3. For whereas on a man's decease he can put forth no power, but his influence lasts to the grave and thenceforth ceases; and actions, and power over men, belong to the living only; let him who will, see and be judge, confessing the truth from what appears to sight.   4. For now that the Saviour works so great things among men, and day by day is invisibly persuading so great a multitude from every side, both from them that dwell in Greece and in foreign lands, to come over to His faith, and all to obey His teaching, will any one still hold his mind in doubt whether a Resurrection has been accomplished by the Saviour, and whether Christ is alive, or rather is Himself the Life? 5. Or is it like a dead man to be pricking the consciences of men, so that they deny their hereditary laws and bow before the teaching of Christ?   Or how, if he is no longer active (for this is proper to one dead), does he stay from their activity those who are active and alive, so that the adulterer no longer commits adultery, and the murderer murders no more, nor is the inflicter of wrong any longer grasping, and the profane is henceforth religious?   Or how, if He be not risen but is dead, does He drive away, and pursue, and cast down those false gods said by the unbelievers to be alive, and the demons they worship? 6. For where Christ is named, and His faith, there all idolatry is deposed and all imposture of evil spirits is exposed, and any spirit is unable to endure even the name, nay even on barely hearing it flies and disappears. But this work is not that of one dead, but of one that lives—and especially of God.   7. In particular, it would be ridiculous to say that while the spirits cast out by Him and the idols brought to nought are alive, He who chases them away, and by His power prevents their even appearing, yea, and is being confessed by them all to be Son of God, is dead.

§ 31. *If Power is the sign of life, what do we learn from the impotence of idols, for good or evil, and the constraining power of Christ and of the Sign of the Cross? Death and the demons are by this proved to have lost their sovereignty. Coincidence of the above argument from facts with that from the Personality of Christ.*

But they who disbelieve in the Resurrection

afford a strong proof against themselves, if instead of all the spirits and the gods worshipped by them casting out Christ, Who, they say, is dead, Christ on the contrary proves them all to be dead. 2. For if it be true that one dead can exert no power, while the Saviour does daily so many works, drawing men to religion, persuading to virtue, teaching of immortality, leading on to a desire for heavenly things, revealing the knowledge of the Father, inspiring strength to meet death, shewing Himself to each one, and displacing the godlessness of idolatry, and the gods and spirits of the unbelievers can do none of these things, but rather shew themselves dead at the presence of Christ, their pomp being reduced to impotence and vanity ; whereas by the sign of the Cross all magic is stopped, and all witchcraft brought to nought, and all the idols are being deserted and left, and every unruly pleasure is checked, and every one is looking up from earth to heaven : Whom is one to pronounce dead ? Christ, that is doing so many works ? But to work is not proper to one dead. Or him that exerts no power at all, but lies as it were without life ? which is essentially proper to the idols and spirits, dead as they are. 3. For the Son of God is[3] "living and active," and works day by day, and brings about the salvation of all. But death is daily proved to have lost all his power, and idols and spirits are proved to be dead rather than Christ, so that henceforth no man can any longer doubt of the Resurrection of His body. 4. But he who is incredulous of the Resurrection of the Lord's body would seem to be ignorant of the power of the Word and Wisdom of God. For if He took a body to Himself at all, and—in reasonable consistency, as our argument shewed—appropriated it as His own, what was the Lord to do with it ? or what should be the end of the body when the Word had once descended upon it ? For it could not but die, inasmuch as it was mortal, and to be offered unto death on behalf of all : for which purpose it was that the Saviour fashioned it for Himself. But it was impossible for it to remain dead, because it had been made the temple of life. Whence, while it died as mortal, it came to life again by reason of the Life in it ; and of its Resurrection the works are a sign.

§ 32. *But who is to see Him risen, so as to believe ? Nay, God is ever invisible and known by His works only : and here the works cry out in proof. If you do not believe, look at those who do, and perceive the Godhead of Christ. The demons see this, though men be blind. Summary of the argument so far.*

But if, because He is not seen, His having risen at all is disbelieved, it is high time for those who refuse belief to deny the very course of Nature. For it is God's peculiar property at once to be invisible and yet to be known from His works, as has been already stated above. 2. If, then, the works are not there, they do well to disbelieve what does not appear. But if the works cry aloud and shew it clearly, why do they choose to deny the life so manifestly due to the Resurrection ? For even if they be maimed in their intelligence, yet even with the external senses men may see the unimpeachable power and Godhead of Christ. 3. For even a blind man, if he see not the sun, yet if he but take hold of the warmth the sun gives out, knows that there is a sun above the earth. Thus let our opponents also, even if they believe not as yet, being still blind to the truth, yet at least knowing His power by others who believe, not deny the Godhead of Christ and the Resurrection accomplished by Him. 4. For it is plain that if Christ be dead, He could not be expelling demons and spoiling idols ; for a dead man the spirits would not have obeyed. But if they be manifestly expelled by the naming of His name, it must be evident that He is not dead ; especially as spirits, seeing even what is unseen by men, could tell if Christ were dead and refuse Him any obedience at all. 5. But as it is, what irreligious men believe not, the spirits see—that He is God,—and hence they fly and fall at His feet, saying just what they uttered when He was in the body : "We[4] know Thee Who Thou art, the Holy One of God ;" and, "Ah, what have we to do with Thee, Thou Son of God ? I pray Thee, torment me not." 6. As then demons confess Him, and His works bear Him witness day by day, it must be evident, and let none brazen it out against the truth, both that the Saviour raised His own body, and that He is the true Son of God, being from Him, as from His Father, His own Word, and Wisdom, and Power, Who in ages later took a body for the salvation of all, and taught the world concerning the Father, and brought death to nought, and bestowed incorruption upon all by the promise of the Resurrection, having raised His own body as a first-fruits of this, and having displayed it by the sign of the Cross as a monument of victory over death and its corruption.

---

3 Heb. iv. 12.

4 Cf. Luc. iv. 34, and Marc. v. 7.

§ 33. *UNBELIEF OF JEWS AND SCOFFING OF GREEKS. THE FORMER confounded by their own Scriptures. Prophecies of His coming as God and as Man.*

These things being so, and the Resurrection of His body and the victory gained over death by the Saviour being clearly proved, come now, let us put to rebuke both the disbelief of the Jews and the scoffing of the Gentiles. 2. For these, perhaps, are the points where Jews express incredulity, while Gentiles laugh, finding fault with the unseemliness of the Cross, and of the Word of God becoming man. But our argument shall not delay to grapple with both, especially as the proofs at our command against them are clear as day. 3. For Jews in their incredulity may be refuted from the Scriptures, which even themselves read; for this text and that, and, in a word, the whole inspired Scripture, cries aloud concerning these things, as even its express words abundantly shew. For prophets proclaimed beforehand concerning the wonder of the Virgin and the birth from her, saying: "Lo, the [5] Virgin shall be with child, and shall bring forth a Son, and they shall call his name Emmanuel, which is, being interpreted, God with us." 4. But Moses, the truly great, and whom they believe to speak truth, with reference to the Saviour's becoming man, having estimated what was said as important, and assured of its truth, set it down in these words: "There [6] shall rise a star out of Jacob, and a man out of Israel, and he shall break in pieces the captains of Moab." And again: "How lovely are thy habitations O Jacob, thy tabernacles O Israel, as shadowing gardens, and as parks by the rivers, and as tabernacles which the Lord hath fixed, as cedars by the waters. A man shall come forth out of his seed, and shall be Lord over many peoples." And again, Esaias: "Before [7] the Child know how to call father or mother, he shall take the power of Damascus and the spoils of Samaria before the king of Assyria." 5. That a man, then, shall appear is foretold in those words. But that He that is to come is Lord of all, they predict once more as follows: "Behold [8] the Lord sitteth upon a light cloud, and shall come into Egypt, and the graven images of Egypt shall be shaken." For from thence also it is that the Father calls Him back, saying: "I called [9] My Son out of Egypt."

§ 34. *Prophecies of His passion and death in all its circumstances.*

Nor is even His death passed over in silence:

on the contrary, it is referred to in the divine Scriptures, even exceeding clearly. For to the end that none should err for want of instruction in the actual events, they feared not to mention even the cause of His death,—that He suffers it not for His own sake, but for the immortality and salvation of all, and the counsels of the Jews against Him and the indignities offered Him at their hands. 2. They say then: "A man [1] in stripes, and knowing how to bear weakness, for his face is turned away: he was dishonoured and held in no account. He beareth our sins, and is in pain on our account; and we reckoned him to be in labour, and in stripes, and in ill-usage; but he was wounded for our sins, and made weak for our wickedness. The chastisement of our peace was upon him, and by his stripes we were healed." O marvel at the loving-kindness of the Word, that for our sakes He is dishonoured, that we may be brought to honour. "For all we," it says, "like sheep were gone astray; man had erred in his way; and the Lord delivered him for our sins; and he openeth not his mouth, because he hath been evilly intreated. As a sheep was he brought to the slaughter, and as a lamb dumb before his shearer, so openeth he not his mouth: in his abasement his judgment was taken away [2]." 3. Then lest any should from His suffering conceive Him to be a common man, Holy Writ anticipates the surmises of man, and declares the power (which worked) for Him [3], and the difference of His nature compared with ourselves, saying: "But who shall declare his generation? For his life is taken away [2] from the earth. From the wickedness of the people was he brought to death. And I will give the wicked instead of his burial, and the rich instead of his death; for he did no wickedness, neither was guile found in his mouth. And the Lord will cleanse him from his stripes."

§ 35. *Prophecies of the Cross. How these prophecies are satisfied in Christ alone.*

But, perhaps, having heard the prophecy of His death, you ask to learn also what is set forth concerning the Cross. For not even this is passed over: it is displayed by the holy men with great plainness. 2. For first Moses predicts it, and that with a loud voice, when he

---

5 Matt. i. 23; Isa. vii. 14.   6 Num. xxiv. 5—17.
7 Isa. viii. 4.   8 Isa. xix. 1.   9 Hos. xi. 1.

[1] Isa. liii. 3, *sqq.*   [2] Or, "exalted."
[3] τὴν ὑπὲρ αὐτοῦ δύναμιν. The Ben. version simplifies this difficult expression by ignoring the ὑπέρ. Mr. E. N. Bennett has suggested to me that the true reading may be ὑπεράϋλον for ὑπὲρ αὐτοῦ (ἄϋλος supra 8. 1, ὑπεραϋλως in Philo). I would add the suggestion that αὐτοῦ stood after ὑπεράϋλον, and that the similarity of the five letters in MS. caused the second word to be dropped out. 'His exceeding immaterial power' would be the resulting sense. (See Class. Review, 1890, No. iv. p. 182.)

says: "Ye shall see [4] your Life hanging before your eyes, and shall not believe." 3. And next, the prophets after him witness of this, saying: "But [5] I as an innocent lamb brought to be slain, knew it not; they counselled an evil counsel against me, saying, Hither and let us cast a tree upon his [6] bread, and efface him from the land of the living." 4. And again: "They pierced [7] my hands and my feet, they numbered all my bones, they parted my garments among them, and for my vesture they cast lots." 5. Now a death raised aloft, and that takes place on a tree, could be none other than the Cross: and again, in no other death are the hands and feet pierced, save on the Cross only. 6. But since by the sojourn of the Saviour among men all nations also on every side began to know God; they did not leave this point, either, without a reference: but mention is made of this matter as well in the Holy Scriptures. For "there [8] shall be," he saith, "the root of Jesse, and he that riseth to rule the nations, on him shall the nations hope." This then is a little in proof of what has happened. 7. But all Scripture teems with refutations of the disbelief of the Jews. For which of the righteous men and holy prophets, and patriarchs, recorded in the divine Scriptures, ever had his corporal birth of a virgin only? Or what woman has sufficed without man for the conception of human kind? Was not Abel born of Adam, Enoch of Jared, Noe of Lamech, and Abraham of Tharra, Isaac of Abraham, Jacob of Isaac? Was not Judas born of Jacob, and Moses and Aaron of Ameram? Was not Samuel born of Elkana, was not David of Jesse, was not Solomon of David, was not Ezechias of Achaz, was not Josias of Amos, was not Esaias of Amos, was not Jeremy of Chelchias, was not Ezechiel of Buzi? Had not each a father as author of his existence? Who then is he that is born of a virgin only? For the prophet made exceeding much of this sign. 8. Or whose birth did a star in the skies forerun, to announce to the world him that was born? For when Moses was born, he was hid by his parents: David was not heard of, even by those of his neighbourhood, inasmuch as even the great Samuel knew him not, but asked, had Jesse yet another son? Abraham again became known to his neighbours as [9] a great man only subsequently to his birth. But of Christ's birth the witness was

not man, but a star in that heaven whence He was descending.

§ 36. *Prophecies of Christ's sovereignty, flight into Egypt, &c.*

But what king that ever was, before he had strength to call father or mother, reigned and gained triumphs over his enemies [10]? Did not David come to the throne at thirty years of age, and Solomon, when he had grown to be a young man? Did not Joas enter on the kingdom when seven years old, and Josias, a still later king, receive the government about the seventh year of his age? And yet they at that age had strength to call father or mother. 2. Who, then, is there that was reigning and spoiling his enemies almost before his birth? Or what king of this sort has ever been in Israel and in Juda—let the Jews, who have searched out the matter, tell us—in whom all the nations have placed their hopes and had peace, instead of being at enmity with them on every side? 3. For as long as Jerusalem stood there was war without respite betwixt them, and they all fought with Israel; the Assyrians oppressed them, the Egyptians persecuted them, the Babylonians fell upon them; and, strange to say, they had even the Syrians their neighbours at war against them. Or did not David war against them of Moab, and smite the Syrians, Josias guard against his neighbours, and Ezechias quail at the boasting of Senacherim, and Amalek make war against Moses, and the Amorites oppose him, and the inhabitants of Jericho array themselves against Jesus son of Naue? And, in a word, treaties of friendship had no place between the nations and Israel. Who, then, it is on whom the nations are to set their hope, it is worth while to see. For there must be such an one, as it is impossible for the prophet to have spoken falsely. 4. But which of the holy prophets or of the early patriarchs has died on the Cross for the salvation of all? Or who was wounded and destroyed for the healing of all? Or which of the righteous men, or kings, went down to Egypt, so that at his coming the idols of Egypt fell [1]? For Abraham went thither, but idolatry prevailed universally all the same. Moses was born there, and the deluded worship of the people was there none the less.

§ 37. *Psalm xxii. 16, &c. Majesty of His birth and death. Confusion of oracles and demons in Egypt.*

Or who among those recorded in Scripture was pierced in the hands and feet, or hung

---

4 Deut xxviii. 66, see *Orat.* ii. 16, note 1. 5 Jer. xi. 19.
6 Properly "let us destroy the tree with its bread" (*i.e.* fruit). The LXX. translate b^elaḥmō '*upon* his bread,' which is possible in itself; but they either mistook the verb, or followed some wrong reading. Their rendering is followed by all the Latin versions. For a comment on the latter see Tertull. *adv. Marc.* iii. 19, iv. 40.
7 Ps. xxii. 16, *sqq.*   8 Isa. xi. 10.
9 Or 'only after he had grown great,' i.e. to man's estate.

10 Isa. viii. 4, where note LXX.   1 Cf. *Letter* 61. 4.

at all upon a tree, and was sacrificed on a cross for the salvation of all? For Abraham died, ending his life on a bed; Isaac and Jacob also died with their feet raised on a bed; Moses and Aaron died on the mountain; David in his house, without being the object of any conspiracy at the hands of the people; true, he was pursued by Saul, but he was preserved unhurt. Esaias was sawn asunder, but not hung on a tree. Jeremy was shamefully treated, but did not die under condemnation; Ezechiel suffered, not however for the people, but to indicate what was to come upon the people. 2. Again, these, even where they suffered, were men resembling all in their common nature; but he that is declared in Scripture to suffer on behalf of all is called not merely man, but the Life of all, albeit He was in fact like men in nature. For "ye shall[2] see," it says, "your Life hanging before your eyes;" and "who shall declare his generation?" For one can ascertain the genealogy of all the saints, and declare it from the beginning, and of whom each was born; but the generation of Him that is the Life the Scriptures refer to as not to be declared. 3. Who then is he of whom the Divine Scriptures say this? Or who is so great that even the prophets predict of him such great things? None else, now, is found in the Scriptures but the common Saviour of all, the Word of God, our Lord Jesus Christ. For He it is that proceeded from a virgin and appeared as man on the earth, and whose generation after the flesh cannot be declared. For there is none that can tell His father after the flesh, His body not being of a man, but of a virgin alone; 4. so that no one can declare the corporal generation of the Saviour from a man, in the same way as one can draw up a genealogy of David and of Moses and of all the patriarchs. For He it is that caused the star also to mark the birth of His body; since it was fit that the Word, coming down from heaven, should have His constellation also from heaven, and it was fitting that the King of Creation when He came forth should be openly recognized by all creation. 5. Why, He was born in Judæa, and men from Persia came to worship Him. He it is that even before His appearing in the body won the victory over His demon adversaries and a triumph over idolatry. All heathen at any rate from every region, abjuring their hereditary tradition and the impiety of idols, are now placing their hope in Christ, and enrolling themselves under Him, the like of which you may see with your own eyes. 6. For at no other time has the impiety of the

Egyptians ceased, save when the Lord of all, riding as it were upon a cloud, came down there in the body and brought to nought the delusion of idols, and brought over all to Himself, and through Himself to the Father. 7. He it is that was crucified before the sun and all creation as witnesses, and before those who put Him to death: and by His death has salvation come to all, and all creation been ransomed. He is the Life of all, and He it is that as a sheep yielded His body to death as a substitute, for the salvation of all, even though the Jews believe it not.

§ 38. *Other clear prophecies of the coming of God in the flesh. Christ's miracles unprecedented.*

For if they do not think these proofs sufficient, let them be persuaded at any rate by other reasons, drawn from the oracles they themselves possess. For of whom do the prophets say: "I was[3] made manifest to them that sought me not, I was found of them that asked not for me: I said Behold, here am I, to the nation that had not called upon my name; I stretched out my hands to a disobedient and gainsaying people." 2. Who, then, one might say to the Jews, is he that was made manifest? For if it is the prophet, let them say when he was hid, afterward to appear again. And what manner of prophet is this, that was not only made manifest from obscurity, but also stretched out his hands on the Cross? None surely of the righteous, save the Word of God only, Who, incorporeal by nature, appeared for our sakes in the body and suffered for all. 3. Or if not even this is sufficient for them, let them at least be silenced by another proof, seeing how clear its demonstrative force is. For the Scripture says: "Be strong[4] ye hands that hang down, and feeble knees; comfort ye, ye of faint mind; be strong, fear not. Behold, our God recompenseth judgment; He shall come and save us. Then shall the eyes of the blind be opened, and the ears of the deaf shall hear; then shall the lame man leap as an hart, and the tongue of the stammerers shall be plain." 4. Now what can they say to this, or how can they dare to face this at all? For the prophecy not only indicates that God is to sojourn here, but it announces the signs and the time of His coming. For they connect the blind recovering their sight, and the lame walking, and the deaf hearing, and the tongue of the stammerers being made plain, with the Divine Coming which is to take place. Let them say, then, when such signs have come to pass in Israel, or where

---

2 Cf. 35. 2, and 34. 3.

3 Isa. lxv. 1, 2; cf. Rom. x. 20, *sq.* 4 Isa. xxxv. 3, *sqq.*

in Jewry anything of the sort has occurred.
5. Naaman, a leper, was cleansed, but no deaf
man heard nor lame walked. Elias raised a
dead man ; so did Eliseus ; but none blind
from birth regained his sight. For in good
truth, to raise a dead man is a great thing, but
it is not like the wonder wrought by the
Saviour. Only, if Scripture has not passed
over the case of the leper, and of the dead
son of the widow, certainly, had it come to
pass that a lame man also had walked and
a blind man recovered his sight, the narrative
would not have omitted to mention this also.
Since then nothing is said in the Scriptures,
it is evident that these things had never taken
place before. 6. When, then, have they taken
place, save when the Word of God Himself
came in the body? Or when did He come,
if not when lame men walked, and stammerers
were made to speak plain, and deaf men
heard, and men blind from birth regained
their sight? For this was the very thing the
Jews said who then witnessed it, because they
had not heard of these things having taken
place at any other time : " Since [5] the world
began it was never heard that any one opened
the eyes of a man born blind. If this man
were not from God, He could do nothing."

§ 39. *Do you look for another ? But Daniel
foretells the exact time. Objections to this
removed.*

But perhaps, being unable, even they, to
fight continually against plain facts, they will,
without denying what is written, maintain that
they are looking for these things, and that the
Word of God is not yet come. For this it is
on which they are for ever harping, not
blushing to brazen it out in the face of plain
facts. 2. But on this one point, above all,
they shall be all the more refuted, not at our
hands, but at those of the most wise Daniel,
who marks both the actual date, and the divine
sojourn of the Saviour, saying : " Seventy [6]
weeks are cut short upon thy people, and
upon the holy city, for a full end to be made
of sin, and for sins to be sealed up, and
to blot out iniquities, and to make atonement for iniquities, and to bring everlasting
righteousness, and to seal vision and prophet,
and to anoint a Holy of Holies ; and thou
shalt know and understand from the going
forth of the word to restore [7] and to build
Jerusalem unto Christ the Prince." 3. Perhaps with regard to the other (prophecies) they
may be able even to find excuses and to put
off what is written to a future time. But what

can they say to this, or can they face it at all?
Where not only is the Christ referred to, but
He that is to be anointed is declared to be
not man simply, but Holy of Holies ; and
Jerusalem is to stand till His coming, and
thenceforth, prophet and vision cease in Israel.
4. David was anointed of old, and Solomon
and Ezechias ; but then, nevertheless, Jerusalem
and the place stood, and prophets were prophesying : Gad and Asaph and Nathan ; and,
later, Esaias and Osee and Amos and others.
And again, the actual men that were anointed
were called holy, and not Holy of Holies.
5. But if they shield themselves with the captivity, and say that because of it Jerusalem was
not, what can they say about the prophets too?
For in fact when first' the people went down
to Babylon, Daniel and Jeremy were there,
and Ezechiel and Aggæus and Zachary were
prophesying.

§ 40. *Argument (1) from the withdrawal of prophecy and destruction of Jerusalem, (2) from
the conversion of the Gentiles, and that to the
God of Moses. What more remains for the
Messiah to do, that Christ has not done?*

So the Jews are trifling, and the time in question, which they refer to the future, is actually
come. For when did prophet and vision cease
from Israel, save when Christ came, the Holy
of Holies ? For it is a sign, and an important
proof, of the coming of the Word of God, that
Jerusalem no longer stands, nor is any prophet
raised up nor vision revealed to them,—and
that very naturally. 2. For when He that was
signified was come, what need was there any
longer of any to signify Him ? When the truth
was there, what need any more of the shadow?
For this was the reason of their prophesying at
all,—namely, till the true Righteousness should
come, and He that was to ransom the sins of all.
And this was why Jerusalem stood till then—
namely, that there they might be exercised in the
types as a preparation for the reality. 3. So
when the Holy of Holies was come, naturally
vision and prophecy were sealed and the kingdom of Jerusalem ceased. For kings were to
be anointed among them only until the Holy
of Holies should have been anointed ; and
Jacob prophesies that the kingdom of the Jews
should be established until Him, as follows :—
" The ruler [8] shall not fail from Juda, nor the
Prince from his loins, until that which is
laid up for him shall come ; and he is the
expectation of the nations." 4. Whence the
Saviour also Himself cried aloud and said :
" The [9] law and the prophets prophesied until
John." If then there is now among the Jews

---

5 John ix. 32, *sq.*   6 Dan. ix. 24, *sq.*
7 Lit. "answer," a misrendering of the Hebrew.

8 Gen. xlix. 10.   9 Matt. xi. 13 cf. Luc. xvi. 16.

king or prophet or vision, they do well to deny the Christ that is come. But if there is neither king nor vision, but from that time forth all prophecy is sealed and the city and temple taken, why are they so irreligious and so perverse as to see what has happened, and yet to deny Christ, Who has brought it all to pass? Or why, when they see even heathens deserting their idols, and placing their hope, through Christ, on the God of Israel, do they deny Christ, Who was born of the root of Jesse after the flesh and henceforth is King? For if the nations were worshipping some other God, and not confessing the God of Abraham and Isaac and Jacob and Moses, then, once more, they would be doing well in alleging that God had not come. 5. But if the Gentiles are honouring the same God that gave the law to Moses and made the promise to Abraham, and Whose word the Jews dishonoured,—why are they ignorant, or rather why do they choose to ignore, that the Lord foretold by the Scriptures has shone forth upon the world, and appeared to it in bodily form, as the Scripture said: "The[1] Lord God hath shined upon us;" and again: " He[2] sent His Word and healed them;" and again : "Not[3] a messenger, not an angel, but the Lord Himself saved them?" 6. Their state may be compared to that of one out of his right mind, who sees the earth illumined by the sun, but denies the sun that illumines it. For what more is there for him whom they expect to do, when he is come? To call the heathen? But they are called already. To make prophecy, and king, and vision to cease? This too has already come to pass. To expose the godlessness of idolatry? It is already exposed and condemned. Or to destroy death? He is already destroyed. 7. What then has not come to pass, that the Christ must do? What is left unfulfilled, that the Jews should now disbelieve with impunity? For if, I say,— which is just what we actually see,—there is no longer king nor prophet nor Jerusalem nor sacrifice nor vision among them, but even the whole earth is filled with the knowledge of God, and gentiles, leaving their godlessness, are now taking refuge with the God of Abraham, through the Word, even our Lord Jesus Christ, then it must be plain, even to those who are exceedingly obstinate, that the Christ is come, and that He has illumined absolutely all with His light, and given them the true and divine teaching concerning His Father.

8. So one can fairly refute the Jews by these and by other arguments from the Divine Scriptures.

§ 41. ANSWER TO THE GREEKS. *Do they recognise the Logos? If He manifests Himself in the organism of the Universe, why not in one Body? For a human body is a part of the same whole.*

But one cannot but be utterly astonished at the Gentiles, who, while they laugh at what is no matter for jesting, are themselves insensible to their own disgrace, which they do not see that they have set up in the shape of stocks and stones. 2. Only, as our argument is not lacking in demonstrative proof, come let us put them also to shame on reasonable grounds, —mainly from what we ourselves also see. For what is there on our side that is absurd, or worthy of derision? Is it merely our saying that the Word has been made manifest in the body? But this even they will join in owning to have happened without any absurdity, if they shew themselves friends of truth. 3. If then they deny that there is a Word of God at all, they do so gratuitously[4], jesting at what they know not. 4. But if they confess that there is a Word of God, and He ruler of the universe, and that in Him the Father has produced the creation, and that by His Providence the whole receives light and life and being, and that He reigns over all, so that from the works of His providence He is known, and through Him the Father,—consider, I pray you, whether they be not unwittingly raising the jest against themselves. 5. The philosophers of the Greeks say that the universe is a great body[5]; and rightly so. For we see it and its parts as objects of our senses. If, then, the Word of God is in the Universe, which is a body, and has united Himself with the whole and with all its parts, what is there surprising or absurd if we say that He has united Himself[6] with man also. 6. For if it were absurd for Him to have been in a body at all, it would be absurd for Him to be united with the whole either, and to be giving light and movement to all things by His providence. For the whole also is a body. 7. But if it beseems Him to unite Himself with the universe, and to be made known in the whole, it must beseem Him also to appear in a human body, and that by Him it should be illumined and work. For mankind is part of the whole as well as the rest. And if it be un-

---

[1] Cf. Ps. cxviii. 27, and for the literal sense, Num. vi. 25.
[2] Ps. cvii. 20.   [3] Isa. lxiii. 9 (LXX.), and the note in the (Queen's Printers') 'Variorum' Bible.

[4] Athan. here assumes, for the purpose of his argument, the principles of the Neo-platonist schools. They were influenced, in regard to the Logos, by Philo, but even on this subject the germ of their teaching may be traced in Plato, especially in the *Timæus*, (See Drummond's *Philo*, i. 65—88. Bigg's *Bamp. Lect.* 14, 18, 248—253, and St. Aug. *Confess.* in 'Nicene Fathers,' Series 1, vol. 1, p. 107 and notes.)   [5] Especially Plato, *Tim.* 30, &c.
[6] ἐπιβεβηκέναι, cf. above, 20. 4, 6. The Union of God and Man in Christ is of course 'hypostatic' or personal, and thus (*supra* 17. 1), different in kind from the union of the Word with Creation. His argument is *ad homines*. It was not for thinkers who identified the Universe with God to take exception to the idea of Incarnation.

seemly for a part to have been adopted as His instrument to teach men of His Godhead, it must be most absurd that He should be made known even by the whole universe.

§ 42. *His union with the body is based upon His relation to Creation as a whole. He used a human body, since to man it was that He wished to reveal Himself.*

For just as, while the whole body is quickened and illumined by man, supposing one said it were absurd that man's power should also be in the toe, he would be thought foolish ; because, while granting that he pervades and works in the whole, he demurs to his being in the part also ; thus he who grants and believes that the Word of God is in the whole Universe, and that the whole is illumined and moved by Him, should not think it absurd that a single human body also should receive movement and light from Him. 2. But if it is because the human race is a thing created and has been made out of nothing, that they regard that manifestation of the Saviour in man, which we speak of, as not seemly, it is high time for them to eject Him from creation also ; for it too has been brought into existence by the Word out of nothing. 3. But if, even though creation be a thing made, it is not absurd that the Word should be in it, then neither is it absurd that He should be in man. For whatever idea they form of the whole, they must necessarily apply the like idea to the part. For man also, as I said before, is a part of the whole. 4. Thus it is not at all unseemly that the Word should be in man, while all things are deriving from Him their light and movement and light, as also their authors say, " In [7] him we live and move and have our being." 5. So, then, what is there to scoff at in what we say, if the Word has used that, wherein He is, as an instrument to manifest Himself ? For were He not in it, neither could He have used it ; but if we have previously allowed that He is in the whole and in its parts, what is there incredible in His manifesting Himself in that wherein He is ? 6. For by His own power He is united [8] wholly with each and all, and orders all things without stint, so that no one could have called it out of place for Him to speak, and make known Himself and His Father, by means of sun, if He so willed, or moon, or heaven, or earth, or waters, or fire [9] ; inasmuch as He holds in one all things at once, and is in fact not only in all, but also in the part in question, and there invisibly manifests Himself. In like manner,

it cannot be absurd if, ordering as He does the whole, and giving life to all things, and having willed to make Himself known through men, He has used as His instrument a human body to manifest the truth and knowledge of the Father. For humanity, too, is an actual part of the whole. 7. And as Mind, pervading man all through, is interpreted by a part of the body, I mean the tongue, without any one saying, I suppose, that the essence of the mind is on that account lowered, so if the Word, pervading all things, has used a human instrument, this cannot appear unseemly. For, as I have said previously, if it be unseemly to have used a body as an instrument, it is unseemly also for Him to be in the Whole.

§ 43. *He came in human rather than in any nobler form, because* (1) *He came to save, not to impress ;* (2) *Man alone of creatures had sinned. As men would not recognise His works in the Universe, He came and worked among them as Man ; in the sphere to which they had limited themselves.*

Now, if they ask, Why then did He not appear by means of other and nobler parts of creation, and use some nobler instrument, as the sun, or moon, or stars, or fire, or air, instead of man merely ? let them know that the Lord came not to make a display, but to heal and teach those who were suffering. 2. For the way for one aiming at display would be, just to appear, and to dazzle the beholders ; but for one seeking to heal and teach the way is, not simply to sojourn here,. but to give himself to the aid of those in want, and to appear as they who need him can bear it ; that he may not, by exceeding the requirements of the sufferers, trouble the very persons that need him, rendering God's appearance useless to them. 3. Now, nothing in creation had gone astray with regard to their notions of God, save man only. Why, neither sun, nor moon, nor heaven, nor the stars, nor water, nor air had swerved from their order ; but knowing their Artificer and Sovereign, the Word, they remain as they were made [1]. But men alone, having rejected what was good, then devised things of nought instead of the truth, and have ascribed the honour due to God, and their knowledge of Him, to demons and men in the shape of stones. 4. With reason, then, since it were unworthy of the Divine Goodness to overlook so grave a matter, while yet men were not able to recognise Him

---

7 See Acts. xvii. 28.　　8 ἐπιβαίνων, see supra, note 3.
9 The superfluous πεποιηκέναι is ignored, being untranslateable as the text stands. For a less simple conjecture, see the Bened. note.

1 This thought is beautifully expressed by Keble :—
' All true, all faultless, all in tune, Creation's wondrous choir
Opened in mystic unison, to last till time expire.
And still it lasts : by day and night with one consenting voice
All hymn Thy glory, Lord, aright, all worship and rejoice :
Man only mars the sweet accord ' . . . .
　　　　　('Christian Year,' Fourth Sunday after Trinity.)

as ordering and guiding the whole, He takes to Himself as an instrument a part of the whole, His human body, and unites [2] Himself with that, in order that since men could not recognise Him in the whole, they should not fail to know Him in the part; and since they could not look up to His invisible power, might be able, at any rate, from what resembled themselves to reason to Him and to contemplate Him. 5. For, men as they are, they will be able to know His Father more quickly and directly by a body of like nature and by the divine works wrought through it, judging by comparison that they are not human, but the works of God, which are done by Him. 6. And if it were absurd, as they say, for the Word to be known through the works of the body, it would likewise be absurd for Him to be known through the works of the universe. For just as He is in creation, and yet does not partake of its nature in the least degree, but rather all things partake [3] of His power; so while He used the body as His instrument He partook of no corporeal property, but, on the contrary, Himself sanctified even the body. 7. For if even Plato, who is in such repute among the Greeks, says [4] that its author, beholding the universe tempest-tossed, and in peril of going down to the place of chaos, takes his seat at the helm of the soul and comes to the rescue and corrects all its calamities; what is there incredible in what we say, that, mankind being in error, the Word lighted down [5] upon it and appeared as man, that He might save it in its tempest by His guidance and goodness?

§ 44. *As God made man by a word, why not restore him by a word? But (1) creation out of nothing is different from reparation of what already exists. (2) Man was there with a definite need, calling for a definite remedy. Death was ingrained in man's nature: He then must wind life closely to human nature. Therefore the Word became Incarnate that He might meet and conquer death in His usurped territory. (Simile of straw and asbestos.)*

But perhaps, shamed into agreeing with this, they will choose to say that God, if He wished to reform and to save mankind, ought to have done so by a mere fiat [6], without His word taking a body, in just the same way as He did formerly, when He produced them out of nothing. 2. To this objection of theirs a reasonable answer would be: that formerly,

nothing being in existence at all, what was needed to make everything was a fiat and the bare will to do so. But when man had once been made, and necessity demanded a cure, not for things that were not, but for things that had come to be, it was naturally consequent that the Physician and Saviour should appear in what had come to be, in order also to cure the things that were. For this cause, then, He has become man, and used His body as a human instrument. 3. For if this were not the right way, how was the Word, choosing to use an instrument, to appear? or whence was He to take it, save from those already in being, and in need of His Godhead by means of one like themselves? For it was not things without being that needed salvation, so that a bare command should suffice, but man, already in existence, was going to corruption and ruin [7]. It was then natural and right that the Word should use a human instrument and reveal Himself everywhither. 4. Secondly, you must know this also, that the corruption which had set in was not external to the body, but had become attached to it; and it was required that, instead of corruption, life should cleave to it; so that, just as death has been engendered in the body, so life may be engendered in it also. 5. Now if death were external to the body, it would be proper for life also to have been engendered externally to it. But if death was wound closely to the body and was ruling over it as though united to it, it was required that life also should be wound closely to the body, that so the body, by putting on life in its stead, should cast off corruption. Besides, even supposing that the Word had come outside the body, and not in it, death would indeed have been defeated by Him, in perfect accordance with nature, inasmuch as death has no power against the Life; but the corruption attached to the body would have remained in it none the less [8]. 6. For this cause the Saviour reasonably put on Him a body, in order that the body, becoming wound closely to the Life, should no longer, as mortal, abide in death, but, as having put on immortality, should thenceforth rise again and remain immortal. For, once it had put on corruption, it could not have risen again unless it had put on life. And death likewise could not, from its very nature, appear, save in the body. Therefore He put on a body, that He might find death in the body, and blot it out. For how could the Lord have been proved at all to be the Life, had He not quickened what

[2] Cf. 41. 5, note 3.
[3] Cf. Orig. *c. Cels.* vi. 64, where there is the same contrast between μετέχειν and μετέχεσθαι.
[4] Ath. paraphrases loosely Plat. *Politic.* 273 D. See Jowett's Plato (ed. 2), vol. iv. pp. 515, 553.
[5] Lit. "sate down," as four lines above.
[6] With this discussion compare that upon 'repentance' above 7. (esp. 7. 4).

[7] Restoration by a mere fiat would have shewn God's *power*, the Incarnation shews His *Love*. See *Orat.* i. 52, note 1, ii. 68, note 1.
[8] Cf. *Orat.* i. 56, note 5, 65, no 3.

was mortal? 7. And just as, whereas stubble is naturally destructible by fire, supposing (firstly) a man keeps fire away from the stubble, though it is not burned, yet the stubble remains, for all that, merely stubble, fearing the threat of the fire—for fire has the natural property of consuming it; while if a man (secondly) encloses it with a quantity of asbestos, the substance said[9] to be an antidote to fire, the stubble no longer dreads the fire, being secured by its enclosure in incombustible matter; 8. in this very way one may say, with regard to the body and death, that if death had been kept from the body by a mere command on His part, it would none the less have been mortal and corruptible, according to the nature of bodies; but, that this should not be, it put on the incorporeal Word of God, and thus no longer fears either death or corruption, for it has life as a garment, and corruption is done away in it.

§ 45. *Thus once again every part of creation manifests the glory of God. Nature, the witness to her Creator, yields (by miracles) a second testimony to God Incarnate. The witness of Nature, perverted by man's sin, was thus forced back to truth. If these reasons suffice not, let the Greeks look at facts.*

Consistently, therefore, the Word of God took a body and has made use of a human instrument, in order to quicken the body also, and as He is known in creation by His works so to work in man as well, and to shew Himself everywhere, leaving nothing void of His own divinity, and of the knowledge of Him. 2. For I resume, and repeat what I said before, that the Saviour did this in order that, as He fills all things on all sides by His presence, so also He might fill all things with the knowledge of Him, as the divine Scripture also says[1]: "The whole earth was filled with the knowledge of the Lord." 3. For if a man will but look up to heaven, he sees its Order, or if he cannot raise his face to heaven, but only to man, he sees His power, beyond comparison with that of men, shewn by His works, and learns that He alone among men is God the Word. Or if a man is gone astray among demons, and is in fear of them, he may see this man drive them out, and make up his mind that He is their Master. Or if a man has sunk to the waters[2], and thinks that they are God,— as the Egyptians, for instance, reverence the water,—he may see its nature changed by Him, and learn that the Lord is Creator of the

waters. 4. But if a man is gone down even to Hades, and stands in awe of the heroes who have descended thither, regarding them as gods, yet he may see the fact of Christ's Resurrection and victory over death, and infer that among them also Christ alone is true God and Lord. 5. For the Lord touched all parts of creation, and freed and undeceived all of them from every illusion; as Paul says: "Having[3] put off from Himself the principalities and the powers, He triumphed on the Cross:" that no one might by any possibility be any longer deceived, but everywhere might find the true Word of God. 6. For thus man, shut in on every side[4], and beholding the divinity of the Word unfolded everywhere, that is, in heaven, in Hades, in man, upon earth, is no longer exposed to deceit concerning God, but is to worship Christ alone, and through Him come rightly to know the Father. 7. By these arguments, then, on grounds of reason, the Gentiles in their turn will fairly be put to shame by us. But if they deem the arguments insufficient to shame them, let them be assured of what we are saying at any rate by facts obvious to the sight of all.

§ 46. *Discredit, from the date of the Incarnation, of idol-cultus, oracles, mythologies, demoniacal energy, magic, and Gentile philosophy. And whereas the old cults were strictly local and independent, the worship of Christ is catholic and uniform.*

When did men begin to desert the worshipping of idols, save since God, the true Word of God, has come among men? Or when have the oracles among the Greeks, and everywhere, ceased and become empty, save when the Saviour has manifested Himself upon earth? 2. Or when did those who are called gods and heroes in the poets begin to be convicted of being merely mortal men[5], save since the Lord effected His conquest of death, and preserved incorruptible the body he had taken, raising it from the dead? 3. Or when did the deceitfulness and madness of demons fall into contempt, save when the power of God, the Word, the Master of all these as well, condescending because of man's weakness, appeared on earth? Or when[6] did the art and the schools of magic begin to be trodden down, save when the divine manifestation of the Word took place among men? 4. And, in a word, at what time has the wisdom of the Greeks become foolish, save when the true Wisdom of God manifested itself on earth? For formerly the whole world

---

3 Col. ii. 15.
4 The Incarnation completes the circle of God's self-witness and of man's responsibility.
5 Cf. notes on *c. Gent.* 10, and 12. 2.
6 On the following argument see Döllinger ii. 210 *sqq.*, and Bigg, *Bampt. Lect.* 248, note 1.

9 See above 28. 3. He appears not to have seen the substance.
1 Isa. xi. 9. For the argument, compare §§ 11—14.
2 See Döllinger, *Gentile and Jew*, i. 449.

and every place was led astray by the worshipping of idols, and men regarded nothing else but the idols as gods. But now, all the world over, men are deserting the superstition of the idols, and taking refuge with Christ; and, worshipping Him as God, are by His means coming to know that Father also Whom they knew not. 5. And, marvellous fact, whereas the objects of worship were various and of vast number, and each place had its own idol, and he who was accounted a god among them had no power to pass over to the neighbouring place, so as to persuade those of neighbouring peoples to worship him, but was barely served even among his own people; for no one else worshipped his neighbour's god—on the contrary, each man kept to his own idol [7], thinking it to be lord of all;—Christ alone is worshipped as one and the same among all peoples; and what the weakness of the idols could not do—to persuade, namely, even those dwelling close at hand,—this Christ has done, persuading not only those close at hand, but simply the entire world, to worship one and the same Lord, and through Him God, even His Father.

§ 47. *The numerous oracles,—fancied apparitions in sacred places, &c., dispelled by the sign of the Cross. The old gods prove to have been mere men. Magic is exposed. And whereas Philosophy could only persuade select and local cliques of Immortality and goodness,—men of little intellect have infused into the multitudes of the churches the principle of a supernatural life.*

And whereas formerly every place was full of the deceit of the oracles [8], and the oracles at Delphi and Dodona, and in Bœotia [9] and Lycia [1] and Libya [2] and Egypt and those of the Cabiri [3], and the Pythoness, were held in repute by men's imagination, now, since Christ has begun to be preached everywhere, their madness also has ceased and there is none among them to divine any more. 2. And whereas formerly demons used to deceive [4] men's fancy, occupying springs or rivers, trees or stones, and thus imposed upon the simple by their juggleries; now, after the divine visitation of the Word, their deception has ceased. For by the Sign of the Cross, though a man but use it, he drives out their deceits. 3. And while for-

merly men held to be gods the Zeus and Cronos and Apollo and the heroes mentioned in the poets, and went astray in honouring them; now that the Saviour has appeared among men, those others have been exposed as mortal men [5], and Christ alone has been recognised among men as the true God, the Word of God. 4. And what is one to say of the magic [6] esteemed among them? that before the Word sojourned among us this was strong and active among Egyptians, and Chaldees, and Indians, and inspired awe in those who saw it; but that by the presence of the Truth, and the Appearing of the Word, it also has been thoroughly confuted, and brought wholly to nought. 5. But as to Gentile wisdom, and the sounding pretensions of the philosophers, I think none can need our argument, since the wonder is before the eyes of all, that while the wise among the Greeks had written so much, and were unable to persuade even a few [7] from their own neighbourhood, concerning immortality and a virtuous life, Christ alone, by ordinary language, and by men not clever with the tongue, has throughout all the world persuaded whole churches full of men to despise death, and to mind the things of immortality; to overlook what is temporal and to turn their eyes to what is eternal; to think nothing of earthly glory and to strive only for the heavenly.

§ 48. *Further facts. Christian continence of virgins and ascetics. Martyrs. The power of the Cross against demons and magic. Christ by His Power shews Himself more than a man, more than a magician, more than a spirit. For all these are totally subject to Him. Therefore He is the Word of God.*

Now these arguments of ours do not amount merely to words, but have in actual experience a witness to their truth. 2. For let him that will, go up and behold the proof of virtue in the virgins of Christ and in the young men that practise holy chastity [8], and the assurance of immortality in so great a band of His martyrs. 3. And let him come who would test by experience what we have now said, and in the very presence of the deceit of demons and the imposture of oracles and the marvels of magic, let him use the Sign of that Cross which is laughed at among them, and he shall see how by its means demons fly, oracles cease, all magic and witchcraft is brought to nought. 4. Who, then, and how great is this Christ,

---

[7] On the local character of ancient religions, see Döllinger i. 109, &c., and Coulanges, *La Cité Antique*, Book III. ch. vi., and V. iii. (the substance in Barker's *Aryan Civilisation*).
[8] On these, see Döllinger, i. 216, &c., and Milton's *Ode on the Nativity*, stanza xix.
[9] i.e. that of Trophonius.   [1] Patara.   [2] Ammon.
[3] See Döllinger, i. 73, 164-70: the Cabiri were pre-Hellenic deities, worshipped in many ancient sanctuaries, but principally in Samothrace and Lemnos.
[4] Cf. *Vit. Ant.* xvi.—xliii., also Döllinger, ii. 212, and a curious catena of extracts from early Fathers, collected by Hurter in 'Opuscula SS. Patrum Selecta,' vol. 1, appendix.

[5] For this opinion, see note 1 on c. *Gent.* 12.
[6] See Döllinger, ii. 210, and (on Julian) 215.
[7] In Plato's ideal Republic, the notion of any direct influence of the highest ideals upon the masses is quite absent. Their happiness is to be in passive obedience to the few whom those ideals inspire. (Contrast Isa. liv. 13, Jer. xxxi. 34.)
[8] Cf. *Hist. Arian.* 25, *Apol. Const.* 33.

Who by His own Name and Presence casts into the shade and brings to nought all things on every side, and is alone strong against all, and has filled the whole world with His teaching? Let the Greeks tell us, who are pleased to laugh, and blush not. 5. For if He is a man, how then has one man exceeded the power of all whom even themselves hold to be gods, and convicted them by His own power of being nothing? But if they call Him a magician, how can it be that by a magician all magic is destroyed, instead of being confirmed? For if He conquered particular magicians, or prevailed over one only, it would be proper for them to hold that He excelled the rest by superior skill; 6. but if His Cross has won the victory over absolutely all magic, and over the very name of it, it must be plain that the Saviour is not a magician, seeing that even those demons who are invoked by the other magicians fly from Him as their Master. 7. Who He is, then, let the Greeks tell us, whose only serious pursuit is jesting. Perhaps they might say that He, too, was a demon, and hence His strength. But say this as they will, they will have the laugh against them, for they can once more be put to shame by our former proofs. For how is it possible that He should be a demon who drives the demons out? 8. For if He simply drove out particular demons, it might properly be held that by the chief of demons He prevailed against the lesser, just as the Jews said to Him when they wished to insult Him. But if, by His Name being named, all madness of the demons is uprooted and chased away, it must be evident that here, too, they are wrong, and that our Lord and Saviour Christ is not, as they think, some demoniacal power. 9. Then, if the Saviour is neither a man simply, nor a magician, nor some demon, but has by His own Godhead brought to nought and cast into the shade both the doctrine found in the poets and the delusion of the demons and the wisdom of the Gentiles, it must be plain and will be owned by all, that this is the true Son of God, even the Word and Wisdom and Power of the Father from the beginning. For this is why His works also are no works of man, but are recognised to be above man, and truly God's works, both from the facts in themselves, and from comparison with [the rest of] mankind.

§ 49. *His Birth and Miracles. You call Asclepius, Heracles, and Dionysus gods for their works. Contrast their works with His, and the wonders at His death, &c.*

For what man, that ever was born, formed a body for himself from a virgin alone? Or what man ever healed such diseases as the common Lord of all? Or who has restored what was wanting to man's nature, and made one blind from his birth to see? 2. Asclepius was deified among them, because he practised medicine and found out herbs for bodies that were sick; not forming them himself out of the earth, but discovering them by science drawn from nature. But what is this to what was done by the Saviour, in that, instead of healing a wound, He modified a man's original nature, and restored the body whole. 3. Heracles is worshipped as a god among the Greeks because he fought against men, his peers, and destroyed wild beasts by guile. What is this to what was done by the Word, in driving away from man diseases and demons and death itself? Dionysus is worshipped among them because he has taught man drunkenness; but the true Saviour and Lord of all, for teaching temperance, is mocked by these people. 4. But let these matters pass. What will they say to the other miracles of His Godhead? At what man's death was the sun darkened and the earth shaken? Lo even to this day men are dying, and they died also of old. When did any such-like wonder happen in their case? 5. Or, to pass over the deeds done through His body, and mention those after its rising again: what man's doctrine that ever was has prevailed everywhere, one and the same, from one end of the earth to the other, so that his worship has winged its way through every land? 6. Or why, if Christ is, as they say, a man, and not God the Word, is not His worship prevented by the gods they have from passing into the same land where they are? Or why on the contrary does the Word Himself, sojourning here, by His teaching stop their worship and put their deception to shame?

§ 50. *Impotence and rivalries of the Sophists put to shame by the Death of Christ. His Resurrection unparalleled even in Greek legend.*

Many before this Man have been kings and tyrants of the world, many are on record who have been wise men and magicians, among the Chaldæans and Egyptians and Indians; which of these, I say, not after death, but while still alive, was ever able so far to prevail as to fill the whole earth with his teaching and reform so great a multitude from the superstition of idols, as our Saviour has brought over from idols to Himself? 2. The philosophers of the Greeks have composed many works with plausibility and verbal skill; what result, then, have they exhibited so great as has the Cross of Christ? For the refinements they taught were plausible enough till they died; but even the influence they seemed to have while alive was subject to their mutual rivalries; and they were emulous, and declaimed against one another. 3. But the Word of God, most strange fact, teaching in meaner language, has cast into the shade the choice sophists; and while He has, by drawing all to Himself, brought their schools to nought, He has filled His own churches; and the marvellous thing is, that by going down as man to death, He has brought to nought the sounding utterances of the wise[9] concerning idols. 4. For whose death ever drove out demons? or whose death did demons ever fear, as they did that of Christ? For where the Saviour's name is named, there every demon is driven out. Or who has so rid men of the passions of the natural man, that whoremongers are chaste, and murderers no longer hold the sword, and those who were formerly mastered by cowardice play the man? 5. And, in short, who persuaded men of barbarous countries and heathen men in divers places to lay aside their madness, and to mind peace, if it be not the Faith of Christ and the Sign of the Cross? Or who else has given men such assurance of immortality, as has the Cross of Christ, and the Resurrection of His Body? 6. For although the Greeks have told all manner of false tales, yet they were not able to feign a Resurrection of their idols,—for it never crossed their mind, whether it be at all possible for the body again to exist after death. And here one would most especially accept their testimony, inasmuch as by this opinion they have exposed the weakness of their own idolatry, while leaving the possibility cpen to Christ, so that hence also He might be made known among all as Son of God.

§ 51. *The new virtue of continence. Revolution of Society, purified and pacified by Christianity.*

Which of mankind, again, after his death, or else while living, taught concerning virginity, and that this virtue was not impossible among men? But Christ, our Saviour and King of all, had such power in His teaching concerning it, that even children not yet arrived at the lawful age vow that virginity which lies beyond the law. 2. What man has ever yet been able to pass so far as to come among Scythians and Ethiopians, or Persians or Armenians or Goths, or those we hear of beyond the ocean or those beyond Hyrcania, or even the Egyptians and Chaldees, men that mind magic and are superstitious beyond nature and savage in their ways, and to preach at all about virtue and self-control, and against the worshipping of idols, as has the Lord of all, the Power of God, our Lord Jesus Christ? 3. Who not only preached by means of His own disciples, but also carried persuasion to men's mind, to lay aside the fierceness of their manners, and no longer to serve their ancestral gods, but to learn to know Him, and through Him to worship the Father. 4. For formerly, while in idolatry, Greeks and Barbarians used to war against each other, and were actually cruel to their own kin. For it was impossible for any one to cross sea or land at all, without arming the hand with swords[1], because of their implacable fighting among themselves. 5. For the whole course of their life was carried on by arms, and the sword with them took the place of a staff, and was their support in every emergency; and still, as I said before, they were serving idols, and offering sacrifices to demons, while for all their idolatrous superstition they could not be reclaimed from this spirit. 6. But when they have come over to the school of Christ, then, strangely enough, as men truly pricked in conscience, they have laid aside the savagery of their murders and no longer mind the things of war: but all is at peace with them, and from henceforth what makes for friendship is to their liking.

§ 52. *Wars, &c., roused by demons, lulled by Christianity.*

Who then is He that has done this, or who is He that has united in peace men that hated one another, save the beloved Son of the Father, the common Saviour of all, even Jesus Christ, Who by His own love underwent all things for our salvation? For even from of old it was prophesied of the peace He was to usher in, where the Scripture says: "They[2] shall beat their swords into ploughshares, and their pikes into sickles, and nation shall not take the sword against nation, neither shall they learn war any more." 2. And this is at least not incredible, inasmuch as even now those barbarians who have an innate savagery of manners, while they still sacrifice to the idols of their country, are mad against one another, and cannot endure to be a single hour without weapons: 3. but when they hear the teaching of Christ, straightway instead of fighting they turn to husbandry, and instead of arming their hands with weapons they raise them in prayer, and in a word, in place of fighting among themselves, henceforth they arm against the devil and against evil spirits, subduing these by self-restraint and virtue of soul. 4. Now this is at once a proof of the divinity of the Saviour, since what men could not

---

9 *e.g.* Iamblichus, &c., cf. Introd. to *c. Gent.*

1 Cf. Thucy. i. 5 6: '*πᾶσα γὰρ ἡ Ἑλλὰς ἐσιδηροφόρει,*' &c.
2 Isa. ii. 4.

learn among idols [3] they have learned from Him ; and no small exposure of the weakness and nothingness of demons and idols. For demons, knowing their own weakness, for this reason formerly set men to make war against one another, lest, if they ceased from mutual strife, they should turn to battle against demons. 5. Why, they who become disciples of Christ, instead of warring with each other, stand arrayed against demons by their habits and their virtuous actions : and they rout them, and mock at their captain the devil ; so that in youth they are self-restrained, in temptations endure, in labours persevere, when insulted are patient, when robbed make light of it : and, wonderful as it is, they despise even death and become martyrs of Christ.

§ 53. *The whole fabric of Gentilism levelled at a blow by Christ secretly addressing the conscience of man.*

And to mention one proof of the divinity of the Saviour, which is indeed utterly surprising, —what mere man or magician or tyrant or king was ever able by himself to engage with so many, and to fight the battle against all idolatry and the whole demoniacal host and all magic, and all the wisdom of the Greeks, while they were so strong and still flourishing and imposing upon all, and at one onset to check them all, as was our Lord, the true Word of God, Who, invisibly exposing each man's error, is by Himself bearing off all men from them all, so that while they who were worshipping idols now trample upon them, those in repute for magic burn their books, and the wise prefer to all studies the interpretation of the Gospels ? 2. For whom they used to worship, them they are deserting, and Whom they used to mock as one crucified, Him they worship as Christ, confessing Him to be God. And they that are called gods among them are routed by the Sign of the Cross, while the Crucified Saviour is proclaimed in all the world as God and the Son of God. And the gods worshipped among the Greeks are falling into ill repute at their hands, as scandalous beings ; while those who receive the teaching of Christ live a chaster life than they. 3. If, then, these and the like are human works, let him who will point out similar works on the part of men of former time, and so convince us. But if they prove to be, and are, not men's works, but God's, why are the unbelievers so irreligious as not to recognise the Master that wrought them ? 4. For their case is as though a man, from the works of creation,

failed to know God their Artificer. For if they knew His Godhead from His power over the universe, they would have known that the bodily works of Christ also are not human, but are the works of the Saviour of all, the Word of God. And did they thus know, "they would not," as Paul said [4], "have crucified the Lord of glory."

§ 54. *The Word Incarnate, as is the case with the Invisible God, is known to us by His works. By them we recognise His deifying mission. Let us be content to enumerate a few of them, leaving their dazzling plentitude to him who will behold.*

As, then, if a man should wish to see God, Who is invisible by nature and not seen at all, he may know and apprehend Him from His works : so let him who fails to see Christ with his understanding, at least apprehend Him by the works of His body, and test whether they be human works or God's works. 2. And if they be human, let him scoff ; but if they are not human, but of God, let him recognise it, and not laugh at what is no matter for scoffing ; but rather let him marvel that by so ordinary a means things divine have been manifested to us, and that by death immortality has reached to all, and that by the Word becoming man, the universal Providence has been known, and its Giver and Artificer the very Word of God. 3. For He was made man that we might be made God [5] ; and He manifested Himself by a body that we might receive the idea of the unseen Father ; and He endured the insolence of men that we might inherit immortality. For while He Himself was in no way injured, being impassible and incorruptible and very Word and God, men who were suffering, and for whose sakes He endured all this, He maintained and preserved in His own impassibility. 4. And, in a word, the achievements of the Saviour, resulting from His becoming man, are of such kind and number, that if one should wish to enumerate them, he may be compared to men who gaze at the expanse of the sea and wish to count its waves. For as one cannot take in the whole of the waves with his eyes, for those which are coming on baffle the sense of him

---

[3] St. Augustine, Civ. D. IV. xvi. commenting on the fact that the temple of 'Repose' (Quies) at Rome was not within the city walls, suggests 'qui illam turbam colere perseveraret . . . dœmoniorum, eum Quietem habere non posse.'

[4] 1 Cor. ii. 8.
[5] θεοποιηθῶμεν. See *Orat.* ii. 70, note 1, and many other passages in those Discourses, as well as *Letters* 60. 4, 61. 2. (Eucharistic reference), *de Synodis* 51, note 7. (Compare also Iren. IV. xxxviii. 4, 'non ab initio dii facti sumus, sed primo quidem homines, tunc demum dii,' cf. *ib.* praef. 4 *fin.* also V. ix. 2, 'sublevat in vitam Dei.' Origen *Cels.* iii. 28 *fin.* touches the same thought, but Ath. is here in closer affinity to the idea of Irenaeus than to that of Origen.) The New Test. reference is 2 Pet. i. 4, rather than Heb. ii. 9 sqq. ; the Old Test., Ps. lxxxii. 6, which seems to underlie *Orat.* iii. 25 (note 5). In spite of the last mentioned passage, 'God' is far preferable as a rendering, in most places, to 'gods,' which has heathenish associations. To us (1 Cor. viii. 6) there are no such things as 'gods.' (The best summary of patristic teaching on this subject is given by Harnack *Dg.* ii. p. 46 note.)

that attempts it; so for him that would take in all the achievements of Christ in the body, it is impossible to take in the whole, even by reckoning them up, as those which go beyond his thought are more than those he thinks he has taken in. 5. Better is it, then, not to aim at speaking of the whole, where one cannot do justice even to a part, but, after mentioning one more, to leave the whole for you to marvel at. For all alike are marvellous, and wherever a man turns his glance, he may behold on that side the divinity of the Word, and be struck with exceeding great awe.

§ 55. *Summary of foregoing. Cessation of pagan oracles, &c.: propagation of the faith. The true King has come forth and silenced all usurpers.*

This, then, after what we have so far said, it is right for you to realize, and to take as the sum of what we have already stated, and to marvel at exceedingly; namely, that since the Saviour has come among us, idolatry not only has no longer increased, but what there was is diminishing and gradually coming to an end: and not only does the wisdom of the Greeks no longer advance, but what there is is now fading away: and demons, so far from cheating any more by illusions and prophecies and magic arts, if they so much as dare to make the attempt, are put to shame by the sign of the Cross. 2. And to sum the matter up: behold how the Saviour's doctrine is everywhere increasing, while all idolatry and everything opposed to the faith of Christ is daily dwindling, and losing power, and falling. And thus beholding, worship the Saviour, "Who is above all" and mighty, even God the Word; and condemn those who are being worsted and done away by Him. 3. For as, when the sun is come, darkness no longer prevails, but if any be still left anywhere it is driven away; so, now that the divine Appearing of the Word of God is come, the darkness of the idols prevails no more, and all parts of the world in every direction are illumined by His teaching. 4. And as, when a king is reigning in some country without appearing but keeps at home in his own house, often some disorderly persons, abusing his retirement, proclaim themselves; and each of them, by assuming the character, imposes on the simple as king, and so men are led astray by the name, hearing that there is a king, but not seeing him, if for no other reason, because they cannot enter the house; but when the real king comes forth and appears, then the disorderly impostors are exposed by his presence, while men, seeing the real king, desert those who previously led them astray: 5. in like manner, the evil spirits formerly used to deceive men, investing themselves with God's honour; but when the Word of God appeared in a body, and made known to us His own Father, then at length the deceit of the evil spirits is done away and stopped, while men, turning their eyes to the true God, Word of the Father, are deserting the idols, and now coming to know the true God. 6. Now this is a proof that Christ is God the Word, and the Power of God. For whereas human things cease, and the Word of Christ abides, it is clear to all eyes that what ceases is temporary, but that He Who abides is God, and the true Son of God, His only-begotten Word.

§ 56. *Search then, the Scriptures, if you can, and so fill up this sketch. Learn to look for the Second Advent and Judgment.*

Let this, then, Christ-loving man, be our offering to you, just for a rudimentary sketch and outline, in a short compass, of the faith of Christ and of His Divine appearing to usward. But you, taking occasion by this, if you light upon the text of the Scriptures, by genuinely applying your mind to them, will learn from them more completely and clearly the exact detail of what we have said. 2. For they were spoken and written by God, through men who spoke of God. But we impart of what we have learned from inspired teachers who have been conversant with them, who have also become martyrs for the deity of Christ, to your zeal for learning, in turn. 3. And you will also learn about His second glorious and truly divine appearing to us, when no longer in lowliness, but in His own glory,—no longer in humble guise, but in His own magnificence,—He is to come, no more to suffer, but thenceforth to render to all the fruit of His own Cross, that is, the resurrection and incorruption; and no longer to be judged, but to judge all, by what each has done in the body, whether good or evil; where there is laid up for the good the kingdom of heaven, but for them that have done evil everlasting fire and outer darkness. 4. For thus the Lord Himself also says: "Henceforth [6] ye shall see the Son of Man sitting at the right hand of power, and coming on the clouds of heaven in the glory of the Father." 5. And for this very reason there is also a word of the Saviour to prepare us for that day, in these words: "Be [7] ye ready and watch, for He cometh at an hour ye know not." For, according to the blessed Paul: "We [8] must all stand before the judgment-seat of Christ, that each one

---

[6] Matt. xxvi. 64.   [7] Cf. Matt. xxiv. 42; Marc. xiii. 35.
[8] 2 Cor. v. 10; cf. Rom. xiv. 10.

may receive according as he hath done in the body, whether it be good or bad."

§ 57. *Above all, so live that you may have the right to eat of this tree of knowledge and life, and so come to eternal joys. Doxology.*

But for the searching of the Scriptures and true knowledge of them, an honourable life is needed, and a pure soul, and that virtue which is according to Christ; so that the intellect guiding its path by it, may be able to attain what it desires, and to comprehend it, in so far as it is accessible to human nature to learn concerning the Word of God. 2. For without a pure mind and a modelling of the life after the saints, a man could not possibly comprehend the words of the saints. 3. For just as, if a man wished to see the light of the sun, he would at any rate wipe and brighten his eye, purifying himself in some sort like what he desires, so that the eye, thus becoming light, may see the light of the sun; or as, if a man would see a city or country, he at any rate comes to the place to see it;—thus he that would comprehend the mind of those who speak of God must needs begin by washing and cleansing his soul, by his manner of living, and approach the saints themselves by imitating their works; so that, associated with them in the conduct of a common life, he may understand also what has been revealed to them by God, and thenceforth, as closely knit to them, may escape the peril of the sinners and their fire at the day of judgment, and receive what is laid up for the saints in the kingdom of heaven, which "Eye hath not seen [9], nor ear heard, neither have entered into the heart of man," whatsoever things are prepared for them that live a virtuous life, and love the God and Father, in Christ Jesus our Lord: through Whom and with Whom be to the Father Himself, with the Son Himself, in the Holy Spirit, honour and might and glory for ever and ever. Amen.

---

[9] 1 Cor. ii. 9.

DEPOSITIO ARII

INTRODUCTION TO THE 'DEPOSITION OF ARIUS' AND ENCYCLICAL LETTER
OF ALEXANDER.

THE following documents form the fittest opening to the series of Anti-Arian writings of Athanasius. They are included in the Benedictine edition of his works, and in the Oxford Collection of *Historical Tracts*, of which the present translation is a revision. The possibility that the Encyclical Letter was drawn up by Athanasius himself, now deacon and Secretary to Bishop Alexander (Prolegg. ch. ii. § 2), is a further reason for its inclusion. The Athanasian authorship is maintained by Newman on the following grounds, which his notes will be found to bear out. (1) Total dissimilarity of style as compared with Alexander's letter to his name-sake of Byzantium (given by Theodoret, *H. E.* i. 4). That piece is in an elaborate and involved style, full of compound words, with nothing of the Athanasian simplicity and vigour. (2) Re-markable identity of style with that of Athanasius, extending to his most characteristic expres-sions. (3) Distinctness of the 'theological view' and terminology of Alexander as compared with Athanasius; the Encyclical coinciding with the latter against the former. (4) Athanasian use of certain texts. These arguments are of great weight, and make out at least a *prima facie* case for Newman's view. The latter has the weight of Böhringer's opinion on its side, while the counter-arguments of Kölling (vol. i. p. 105) are trivial. Gwatkin, *Studies*, 29, note 4, misses the points (Nos. 1 and 3) of Newman's argument, which may fairly be said to hold the field. The deposition of Arius at Alexandria took place (Prolegg. *ubi supra*) in 320 or 321; more likely the latter. Whether the Encyclical was drawn up at the Synod which deposed Arius, as is generally supposed, or some two years later, as has been inferred from the references to Eusebius of Nicomedia (D. C. B. i. 80, cf. Prolegg. *ubi supra*, note 1), is a question that may for our present purpose be left open. In any case it is one of the earliest documents of the Arian controversy. It should be noted that the ὁμοούσιον does not occur in this document, a fact of importance in the history of the adoption of the word as a test at Nicæa, cf. Prolegg. ch. ii. § 3 (1) and (2) b. At this stage the Alexandrians were content with the formulæ ὅμοιος κατ᾽ οὐσίαν (Athan.), ἀπαράλλακτος εἰκών, ἀπηκριβωμένη ἐμφέρεια (Alex. in Thdt.), which were afterwards found inadequate.

The letter, after stating the circumstances which call it forth, and recording the doctrine propounded by Arius, and his deposition, points out some of the leading texts which condemn the doctrine (§§ 3, 4). The Arians are then (§ 5) compared to other heretics, and the bishops of the Church generally warned (§ 6) against the intrigues of Eusebius of Nicomedia. The letter is signed by the sixteen presbyters of Alexandria, and the twenty-four deacons (Athan-asius signs fourth), as well as by eighteen presbyters and twenty deacons of the Mareotis. The scriptural argument of the Epistle is the germ of the polemic developed in the successive Anti-Arian treatises which form the bulk of the present volume.

DEPOSITION OF ARIUS

S. Alexander's Deposition of Arius and his companions, and Encyclical Letter on the subject.

ALEXANDER, being assembled with his beloved brethren, the Presbyters and Deacons of Alexandria, and the Mareotis, greets them in the Lord.

Although you have already subscribed to the letter I addressed to Arius and his fellows, exhorting them to renounce his impiety, and to submit themselves to the sound Catholic Faith, and have shewn your right-mindedness and agreement in the doctrines of the Catholic Church: yet forasmuch as I have written also to our fellow-ministers in every place concerning Arius and his fellows, and especially since some of you, as the Presbyters Chares and Pistus[1], and the Deacons Serapion, Parammon, Zosimus, and Irenæus, have joined Arius and his fellows, and been content to suffer deposition with them, I thought it needful to assemble together you, the Clergy of the city, and to send for you the Clergy of the Mareotis, in order that you may learn what I am now writing, and may testify your agreement thereto, and give your concurrence in the deposition of Arius, Pistus, and their fellows. For it is desirable that you should be made acquainted with what I write, and that each of you should heartily embrace it, as though he had written it himself.

A Copy.

To his dearly beloved and most honoured fellow-ministers of the Catholic Church in every place, Alexander sends health in the Lord.

1. As there is one body[2] of the Catholic Church, and a command is given us in the sacred Scriptures to preserve the bond of unity and peace, it is agreeable thereto, that we should write and signify to one another whatever is done by each of us individually; so that whether one member suffer or rejoice, we may either suffer or rejoice with one another. Now there are gone forth in this diocese, at this time, certain lawless[3] men, enemies of Christ, teaching an apostasy, which one may justly suspect and designate as a forerunner[4] of Antichrist. I was desirous[5] to pass such a matter by without notice, in the hope that perhaps the evil would spend itself among its supporters, and not extend to other places to defile[6] the ears[7] of the simple[8]. But seeing that Eusebius, now of Nicomedia, who thinks that the government of the Church rests with him, because retribution has not come upon him for his desertion of Berytus, when he had cast an eye[9] of desire on the Church of the Nicomedians, begins to support these apostates, and has taken upon him to write letters every where in their behalf, if by any means he may draw in certain ignorant persons to this most base and antichristian heresy; I am therefore constrained, knowing what is written in the law, no longer to hold my peace, but to make it known to you all; that you may understand who the apostates are, and the cavils[10] which their heresy has adopted, and that, should Eusebius write to you, you may pay no attention to him, for he now desires by means of these men to exhibit anew his old malevolence[11], which has so long been concealed, pretending to write in their favour,

---

[1] Cf. *Apol. Ar.* § 24.
[2] (Eph. iv. 4.) St. Alexander in Theod. begins his Epistle to his namesake of Constantinople with some moral reflections, concerning ambition and avarice. Athan. indeed uses a similar introduction to his *Ep. Æg.*, but it is not addressed to an individual.

[3] παράνομοι. vid. *Hist. Ar.* § 71 init. 75 fin. 79.
[4] πρόδρομον 'Αντιχρίστου. vid. *Orat.* i. 7. *Vit. Ant.* 69. note on *de Syn.* 5.
[5] καὶ ἐβουλόμην μὲν σιωπῇ . . . . ἐπειδὴ δὲ . . . . ἀνάγκην ἔσχον. vid. *Apol. contra. Ar.* § 1 init. *de Decr.* § 2. *Orat.* i. 23 init. *Orat.* ii. init. *Orat.* iii. 1. *ad Serap.* i. 1. 16. ii. 1 init. iii. init. iv. 8 init. *Letters* 52. 2, 59. 3 fin. 61. 1. *contra Apollin.* i. 1 init.
[6] ῥυπώσῃ, and infr. ῥύπον. vid. *Hist. Ar.* § 3. § 80. *de Decr.* § 2. *Ep. Æg.* 11 fin. *Orat.* i. 10.
[7] ἀκοὰς, and infr. ἀκοὰς βύει. vid. *Ep. Æg.* § 13. *Orat.* i. § 7. *Hist. Ar.* § 56.
[8] ἀκεραίων. *Apol. contr.* Ar. § 1. *Ep. Æg.* § 18. *Letters* 59. 1, 60. 2 fin. *Orat.* i. 8.
[9] ἐποφθαλμίσας also used of Eusebius *Apol. contr.* Ar. § 6. *Hist. Ar.* § 7.
[10] ῥημάτια. vid. *de Decr.* § 8, 18. *Orat.* i. 10. *de Sent.* § 23 init S. Dionysius also uses it. Ibid. § 18.
[11] κακόνοιαν. vid *Hist. Ar.* § 75. *de Decr.* § 1. et al.

while in truth it clearly appears, that he does it to forward his own interests.

2. Now those who became apostates are these, Arius, Achilles, Aeithales, Carpones, another Arius, and Sarmates, sometime Presbyters: Euzoïus, Lucius, Julius, Menas, Helladius, and Gaius, sometime Deacons : and with them Secundus and Theonas, sometime called Bishops. And the novelties they have invented and put forth contrary to the Scriptures are these following :—God was not always a Father [12], but there was a time when God was not a Father. The Word of God was not always, but originated from things that were not; for God that is, has made him that was not, of that which was not; wherefore there was a time when He was not; for the Son is a creature and a work. Neither is He like in essence to the Father ; neither is He the true and natural Word of the Father ; neither is He His true Wisdom ; but He is one of the things made and created, and is called the Word and Wisdom by an abuse of terms, since He Himself originated by the proper Word of God, and by the Wisdom that is in God, by which God has made not only all other things but Him also. Wherefore He is by nature subject to change and variation, as are all rational creatures. And the Word is foreign from the essence [13] of the Father, and is alien and separated therefrom. And the Father cannot be described by the Son, for the Word does not know the Father perfectly and accurately, neither can He see Him perfectly. Moreover, the Son knows not His own essence as it really is ; for He is made for us, that God might create us by Him, as by an instrument ; and He would not have existed, had not God wished to create us. Accordingly, when some one asked them, whether the Word of God can possibly change as the devil changed, they were not afraid to say that He can ; for being something made and created, His nature is subject to change.

3. Now when Arius and his fellows made these assertions, and shamelessly avowed them, we being assembled with the Bishops of Egypt and Libya, nearly a hundred in number, anathematized both them and their followers. But Eusebius and his fellows admitted them to communion, being desirous to mingle falsehood with the truth, and impiety with piety. But they will not be able to do so, for the truth must prevail ; neither is there any "communion of light with darkness," nor any "concord of Christ with Belial [14]." For who ever heard such assertions before [15] ? or who that hears them now is not astonished and does not stop his ears lest they should be defiled with such language? Who that has heard the words of John, "In the beginning was the Word [16]," will not denounce the saying of these men, that "there was a time when He was not?" Or who that has heard in the Gospel, "the Only-begotten Son," and "by Him were all things made [17]," will not detest their declaration that He is "one of the things that were made." For how can He be one of those things which were made by Himself? or how can He be the Only-begotten, when, according to them, He is counted as one among the rest, since He is Himself a creature and a work? And how can He be "made of things that were not," when the Father saith, "My heart hath uttered a good Word," and "Out of the womb I have begotten Thee before the morning star [18] ?" Or again, how is He "unlike in substance to the Father," seeing He is the perfect "image" and "brightness [19]" of the Father, and that He saith, "He that hath seen Me hath seen the Father [20] ?" And if the Son is the "Word" and "Wisdom" of God, how was there "a time when He was not?" It is the same as if they should say that God was once without Word and without Wisdom [21]. And how is He "subject to change and variation," Who says, by Himself, "I am in the Father, and the Father in Me [20]," and "I and the Father are One [20] ;" and by the Prophet, "Behold Me, for I am, and I change not [22] ?" For although one may refer this expression to the Father, yet it may now be more aptly spoken of the Word, viz., that though He has been made man, He has not changed ; but as the Apostle has said, "Jesus Christ is the same yesterday, to-day, and for ever." And who can have persuaded them to say, that He was made for us, whereas Paul writes, "for Whom are all things, and by Whom are all things [23] ?"

---

[12] οὐκ ἀεὶ πατήρ. This enumeration of Arius's tenets, and particularly the mention of the first, corresponds to *de Decr.* § 6. *Ep. Æg.* § 12. as being taken from the *Thalia. Orat.* i. § 5. and far less with Alex. ap. Theod. p. 731, 2. vid. also *Sent. D.* § 16. καταχρηστικῶς, which is found here, occurs *de Decr.* § 6.

[13] οὐσίαν· οὐσία τοῦ λόγου or τοῦ υἱοῦ is a familiar expression with Athan. e.g. *Orat.* i. 45, ii. 7, 9, 11, 12, 13, 18 init. 22, 47 init. 56 init. &c., for which Alex. in Theod. uses the word ὑπόστασις e.g. τὴν ἰδιότροπον αὐτοῦ ὑπόστασιν· τῆς ὑποστάσεως αὐτοῦ ἀπεριεργαστοῦ· νεωτέραν τῆς ὑποστάσεως γένεσιν· ἢ τοῦ μονογενοῦς ἀνεκδιηγήτου ὑπόστασις· τὴν τοῦ λόγου ὑπόστασιν.

[14] (2 Cor. vi. 14.) κοινωνία φωτί. This is quoted Alex. ap. Theod. *H. E.* i. 3. p. 738; by S. Athan. in *Letter* 47. It seems to have been a received text in the controversy, as the Sardican Council uses it, *Apol. Ar.* 49, and S. Athan. seems to put it into the mouth of St. Anthony, *Vit. Ant.* 69.

[15] τίς γὰρ ἤκουσε. *Ep. Æg.* § 7 init. *Letter* 59. § 2 init. *Orat.* i. 8. *Apol. contr. Ar.* 85 init. *Hist. Ar.* § 46 init. § 73 init. § 74 init. *ad Serap.* iv. 2 init.   [16] John i. 1.

[17] John i. 3, 14.   [18] Ps. xlv. 1. and cx. 3.

[19] Heb. i. 3.

[20] (Joh. xiv. 9, 10, x. 29.) On the concurrence of these three texts in Athan. (though other writers use them too, and Alex. ap. Theod. has two of them), vid. note on *Orat.* i. 34.

[21] ἄλογον καὶ ἄσοφον τὸν θεόν. *de Decr.* § 15. *Orat.* i. § 19. *Ap. Fug.* 27. note, notes on *Or.* i. 19, *de. Decr.* 15, note 6.

[22] (Mal. iii. 6.) This text is thus applied by Athan. *Orat.* i. 30. ii. 10. In the first of these passages he uses the same apology, nearly in the same words, which is contained in the text.

[23] Heb. xiii. 8, ii. 10.

4. As to their blasphemous position that "the Son knows not the Father perfectly," we ought not to wonder at it ; for having once set themselves to fight against Christ, they contradict even His express words, since He says, "As the Father knoweth Me, even so know I the Father [24]." Now if the Father knows the Son but in part, then it is evident that the Son does not know the Father perfectly; but if it is not lawful to say this, but the Father does know the Son perfectly, then it is evident that as the Father knows His own Word, so also the Word knows His own Father Whose Word He is.

5. By these arguments and references to the sacred Scriptures we frequently overthrew them ; but they changed like chameleons [25], and again shifted their ground, striving to bring upon themselves that sentence, " when the wicked falleth into the depth of evils, he despiseth [26]." There have been many heresies before them, which, venturing further than they ought, have fallen into folly ; but these men by endeavouring in all their cavils to overthrow the Divinity of the Word, have justified the other in comparison of themselves, as approaching nearer to Antichrist. Wherefore they have been excommunicated and anathematized by the Church. We grieve for their destruction, and especially because, having once been instructed in the doctrines of the Church, they have now sprung away. Yet we are not greatly surprised, for Hymenaeus and Philetus [27] did the same, and before them Judas, who followed the Saviour, but afterwards became a traitor and an apostate. And concerning these same persons, we have not been left without instruction ; for our Lord has forewarned us ; " Take heed lest any man deceive you : for many shall come in My name, saying, I am Christ, and the time draweth near, and they shall deceive many : go ye not after them [28] ;" While Paul, who was taught these things by our Saviour, wrote, that " in the latter times some shall depart from the sound faith, giving heed to seducing spirits and doctrines of devils, which reject the truth [29]."

6. Since then our Lord and Saviour Jesus Christ has instructed us by His own mouth, and also hath signified to us by the Apostle concerning such men, we accordingly being personal witnesses of their impiety, have anathematized, as we said, all such, and declared them to be alien from the Catholic Faith and Church. And we have made this known to your piety, dearly beloved and most honoured fellow-ministers, in order that should any of them have the boldness [30] to come unto you, you may not receive them, nor comply with the desire of Eusebius, or any other person writing in their behalf. For it becomes us who are Christians to turn away from all who speak or think any thing against Christ, as being enemies of God, and destroyers [31] of souls; and not even to "bid such God speed [32]," lest we become partakers of their sins, as the blessed John hath charged us. Salute the brethren that are with you. They that are with me salute you.

Presbyters of Alexandria.

7. I, Colluthus, Presbyter, agree with what is here written, and give my assent to the deposition of Arius and his associates in impiety.

Alexander [33], Presbyter, likewise	Arpocration, Presbyter, likewise
Dioscorus [33], Presbyter, likewise	Agathus, Presbyter
	Nemesius, Presbyter
Dionysius [33], Presbyter, likewise	Longus [33], Presbyter
	Silvanus, Presbyter
Eusebius, Presbyter, likewise	Peroys, Presbyter
	Apis, Presbyter
Alexander, Presbyter, likewise	Proterius, Presbyter
	Paulus, Presbyter
Nilaras [33], Presbyter, likewise	Cyrus, Presbyter, likewise

Deacons.

Ammonius [34], Deacon, likewise	Ambytianus, Deacon
	Gaius [34], Deacon, likewise
Macarius, Deacon	Alexander, Deacon
Pistus [34], Deacon, likewise	Dionysius, Deacon
Athanasius, Deacon	Agathon, Deacon
Eumenes, Deacon	Polybius, Deacon, likewise
Apollonius [34], Deacon	
Olympius, Deacon	Theonas, Deacon
Aphthonius [34], Deacon	Marcus, Deacon
Athanasius [34], Deacon	Comodus, Deacon
Macarius, Deacon, likewise	Serapion [34], Deacon
	Nilon, Deacon
Paulus, Deacon	Romanus, Deacon, likewise
Petrus, Deacon	

---

[24] John x. 15.
[25] χαμαιλέοντες. vid. de Decr. § 1. Hist. Ar. § 79.
[26] Prov. xviii. 3 [cf. Orat. iii. 1, c. Gent. 8. 4, &c.]
[27] 2 Tim. ii. 17.   [28] Luke xxi. 8.
[29] (1 Tim. iv. 1.) Into this text which Athan. also applies to the Arians (cf. note on Or. i. 9.), Athan. also introduces, like Alexander here, the word ὑγιανούσης, e.g. Ep. Æg. § 20, Orat. i. 8 fin. de Decr. 3, Hist. Arian. § 78 init. &c. It is quoted without the word by Origen contr. Cels. v. 64, but with ὑγιοῦς in Matth. t. xiv. 16. Epiphan. has ὑγιαινούσης διδασκαλίας, Hær. 78. 2. ὑγιοῦς διδ. ibid. 23. p. 1055.

[30] προπετεύσαιντο. vid. de Decr. § 2.
[31] φθορέας τῶν ψυχῶν. but S. Alex. in Theod. uses the compound word φθοροποιός. p. 731. Other compound or recondite words (to say nothing of the construction of sentences) found in S. Alexander's Letter in Theod., and unlike the style of the Circular under review, are such as ἡ φίλαρχος καὶ φιλάργυρος πρόθεσις· χριστεμπορίαν· φρενοβλαβοῦς· ἰδιότροπον· ὁμοστοίχοις συλλαβαῖς· θεηγόρους ἀποστόλους· ἀντιδιαστολήν τῆς πατρικῆς μαιεύσεως· μελαγχολικήν· φιλόθεος σαφήνεια ἀνοσιουργίας· φληνάφων μύθων. Instances of theological language in S. Alex. to which the Letter in the text contains no resemblance are ἀχώριστα πράγματα δύο· ὁ υἱὸς τὴν κατὰ πάντα ὁμοιότητα αὐτοῦ ἐκ φύσεως ἀπομαξάμενος· δι' ἐσόπτρου ἀκηλιδώτου καὶ ἐμψύχου θείας εἰκόνος· μεσιτεύουσα φύσις μονογενής· τὰς τῇ ὑποστάσει δύο φύσεις.
[32] 2 John 10.   [33] Vid. Presbyters, Apol. Ar. 73.
[34] Vid. Presbyters, ib.

Presbyters of the Mareotis.

I, Apollonius, Presbyter, agree with what is here written, and give my assent to the deposition of Arius and his associates in impiety.

Ingenius [35], Presbyter, likewise	Serenus, Presbyter
Ammonius, Presbyter	Didymus, Presbyter
Dioscorus [35], Presbyter	Heracles [36], Presbyter
Sostras, Presbyter	Boccon [35], Presbyter
Theon [35], Presbyter	Agathus, Presbyter
Tyrannus, Presbyter	Achillas, Presbyter
Copres, Presbyter	Paulus, Presbyter
Ammonas [35], Presbyter	Thalelæus, Presbyter
Orion, Presbyter	Dionysius, Presbyter, likewise

[35] *Apol. Ar.* 75.   [36] Heraclius? ib.

Deacons.

Sarapion [37], Deacon, likewise	Didymus, Deacon
Justus, Deacon, likewise	Ptollarion [37], Deacon
Didymus, Deacon	Seras, Deacon
Demetrius [37], Deacon	Gaius [37], Deacon
Maurus [37], Deacon	Hierax [37], Deacon
Alexander, Deacon	Marcus, Deacon
Marcus [37], Deacon	Theonas, Deacon
Comon, Deacon	Sarmaton, Deacon
Tryphon [37], Deacon	Carpon, Deacon
Ammonius [37], Deacon	Zoilus, Deacon, likewise

3 Ib.

EPISTOLA EUSEBII

INTRODUCTION.

THE letter which follows, addressed by Eusebius of Cæsarea to his flock, upon the conclusion of the great Synod, is appended by Athanasius to his defence of the Definition of Nicæa (*de Decretis*), written about A.D. 350. It is, however, inserted here in the present edition, partly in accordance with the chronological principle of arrangement, but principally because it forms the fittest introduction to the series of treatises which follow. Along with the account of Eustathius in Theodoret *H. E.* i. 8, and that given by Eusebius, in his life of Constantine (vol. I. pp. 521—526 of this series), it forms one of our most important authorities for the proceedings at Nicæa, and the only account we have dating from the actual year of the Council. It is especially important as containing the draft Creed submitted to the Council by Eusebius, and the revised form of it eventually adopted. The former, which contained (in the *first paragraph* of § 3, from 'We believe' down to 'One Holy Ghost') the traditional Creed of the Church of Cæsarea, which Eusebius had professed at his baptism, was laid by him before the Council, and approved: but at the Emperor's suggestion the single word ὁμοούσιον was inserted (not by 'the majority' as distinct from the Emperor, as stated by Swainson, *Creeds*, p. 65). This modification opened the door for others, which eventually resulted in the Creed given in § 4. It is not altogether easy to reconcile this account with that given by Athanasius himself (below *de Decr.* 19, 20, *Ad Afr.* 5), according to which the Council were led to insist on the insertion of the ὁμοούσιον by the evasions with which the Arian bishops met every other test that was propounded, signalling to each other by nods winks and gestures, as each Scriptural attribute of the Son was enumerated, that this also could be accepted in an Arian sense. Probably (see Prolegg. ch. ii. § 3 (1) note 5) the discussions thus described came first (cp. Sozom. i. 17) : then Eusebius of Nicomedia presented the document which was indignantly torn up : then came the Confession of Eusebius of Cæsarea, which was adopted as the basis of the Creed finally issued. In any case, the Emperor's suggestion of the insertion of ὁμοούσιον must have been prompted by others, most likely by Hosius (*Hist. Ar.* 42, Cf. Hort, *Two Dissertations*, p. 58. Gwatkin, *Studies*, pp. 44, 45, puts the scene described by Athanasius during the debate upon the final adoption of the Creed).

The translation which follows, with the notes and Excursus A, is the unaltered work of Newman (Library of the Fathers, vol. 8, pp. 59-72), except that the word 'essence' (for οὐσία), as throughout this volume, has been substituted for 'substance,' and the translation of γενητός by 'generate' altered wherever it occurs, as explained in the preface. Additions by the editor of this volume are here as elsewhere included in square brackets.

COUNCIL OF NICÆA

Letter of Eusebius of Cæsarea to the people of his Diocese [1].

1. WHAT was transacted concerning ecclesiastical faith at the Great Council assembled at Nicæa, you have probably learned, Beloved, from other sources, rumour being wont to precede the accurate account of what is doing. But lest in such reports the circumstances of the case have been misrepresented, we have been obliged to transmit to you, first, the formula of faith presented by ourselves; and next, the second, which [the Fathers] put forth with some additions to our words. Our own paper, then, which was read in the presence of our most pious [2] Emperor, and declared to be good and unexceptionable, ran thus :—

2. "As we have received from the Bishops who preceded us, and in our first catechisings, and when we received the Holy Laver, and as we have learned from the divine Scriptures, and as we believed and taught in the presbytery, and in the Episcopate itself, so believing also at the time present, we report to you our faith, and it is this [3]:—

3. "We believe in One God, the Father Almighty, the Maker of all things visible and invisible. And in One Lord Jesus Christ, the Word of God, God from God, Light from Light, Life from Life, Son Only-begotten, first-born of every creature, before all the ages, begotten from the Father, by Whom also all things were made ; Who for our salvation was made flesh, and lived among men, and suffered, and rose again the third day, and ascended to the Father, and will come again in glory to judge the quick and dead. And we believe also in One Holy Ghost :

"believing each of these to be and to exist, the Father truly Father, and the Son truly Son, and the Holy Ghost truly Holy Ghost, as also our Lord, sending forth His disciples for the preaching, said, "Go teach all nations, baptizing them in the Name of the Father and of the Son, and of the Holy Ghost [4]." Concerning Whom we confidently affirm that so we hold, and so we think, and so we have held aforetime, and we maintain this faith unto the death, anathematizing every godless heresy. That this we have ever thought from our heart and soul, from the time we recollect ourselves, and now think and say in truth, before God Almighty and our Lord Jesus Christ do we witness, being able by proofs to shew and to convince you, that, even in times past, such has been our belief and preaching."

4. On this faith being publicly put forth by us, no room for contradiction appeared ; but our most pious Emperor, before any one else, testified that it comprised most orthodox state-

---

[1] This Letter is also found in Socr. *H. E.* i. 8. Theod. *H. E.* i. Gelas. *Hist. Nic.* ii. 34. p. 442. Niceph. *Hist.* viii. 22.

[2] And so infr. "most pious," § 4. "most wise and most religious," ibid. "most religious," § 8. § 10. Eusebius observes in his *Vit. Const.* the same tone concerning Constantine, and assigns to him the same office in determining the faith (being as yet unbaptized). E.g. "When there were differences between persons of different countries, as if some common bishop appointed by God, he convened Councils of God's ministers ; and not disdaining to be present and to sit amid their conferences," &c. i. 44. When he came into the Nicene Council, "it was," says Eusebius, "as some heavenly Angel of God," iii. 10. alluding to the brilliancy of the imperial purple. He confesses, however, he did not sit down until the Bishops bade him. Again at the same Council, "with pleasant eyes looking serenity itself into them all, collecting himself, and in a quiet and gentle voice" he made an oration to the Fathers upon peace. Constantine had been an instrument in conferring such vast benefits, humanly speaking, on the Christian Body, that it is not wonderful that other writers of the day besides Eusebius should praise him. Hilary speaks of him as "of sacred memory," *Fragm.* v. init. Athanasius calls him "most pious," *Apol. contr. Arian.* 9 ; "of blessed memory," *ad Ep. Æg.* 18. 19. Epiphanius "most religious and of ever-blessed memory," *Hær.* 70. 9. Posterity, as was natural, was still more grateful.

[3] "The children of the Church have received from their holy Fathers, that is, the holy Apostles, to guard the faith ; and withal to deliver and preach it to their own children. . . . Cease not, faithful aud orthodox men, thus to speak, and to teach the like from the divine Scriptures, and to walk, and to catechise, to the confirmation of yourselves and those who hear you ; namely, that holy faith of the Catholic Church, as the holy and only Virgin of God received its custody from the holy Apostles of the Lord ; and thus, in the case of each of those who are under catechising, who are to approach the Holy Laver, ye ought not only to preach faith to your children in the Lord, but also to teach them expressly, as your common mother teaches, to say : 'We believe in One God,'" &c. Epiph. *Ancor.* 119 fin., who thereupon proceeds to give at length the [so-called] Constantinopolitan Creed. And so Athan. speaks of the orthodox faith, as "issuing from Apostolical teaching and the Fathers' tradition, and confirmed by New and Old Testament." *Letter* 60. 6. init. Cyril Hier. too as "declared by the Church and established from all Scripture." *Cat.* v. 12. "Let us guard with vigilance what we have *received.* . . . What then have we received from the *Scriptures* but altogether this? that God made the world by the Word," &c., &c. Procl. *ad Armen.* p. 612. "That God, the Word, after the union remained such as He was, &c., so clearly hath divine Scripture, and moreover the doctors of the Churches, and the lights of the world taught us." Theodor. *Dial.* 3 init. "That it is the tradition of the Fathers is not the whole of our case ; for they too followed the meaning of Scripture, starting from the testimonies, which just now we laid before you from Scripture." Basil *de Sp.* § 16. vid. also a remarkable passage in *de Synod.* § 6 fin. infra.

[4] Matt. xxviii. 19.

ments. He confessed moreover that such were his own sentiments, and he advised all present to agree to it, and to subscribe its articles and to assent to them, with the insertion of the single word, One-in-essence, which moreover he interpreted as not in the sense of the affections of bodies, nor as if the Son subsisted from the Father in the way of division, or any severance; for that the immaterial, and intellectual, and incorporeal nature could not be the subject of any corporeal affection, but that it became us to conceive of such things in a divine and ineffable manner. And such were the theological remarks of our most wise and most religious Emperor; but they, with a view [4a] to the addition of One in essence, drew up the following formula:—

The Faith dictated in the Council.

"We believe in One God, the Father Almighty, Maker of all things visible and invisible:—

"And in One Lord Jesus Christ, the Son of God, begotten of the Father, Only-begotten, that is, from the essence of the Father; God from God, Light from Light, Very God from Very God, begotten not made, One in essence with the Father, by Whom all things were made, both things in heaven and things in earth; Who for us men and for our salvation came down and was made flesh, was made man, suffered, and rose again the third day, ascended into heaven, and cometh to judge quick and dead.

" And in the Holy Ghost.

" And those who say, 'Once He was not,' and 'Before His generation He was not,' and ' He came to be from nothing,' or those who pretend that the Son of God is 'Of other subsistence or essence [4b],' or 'created,' or 'alterable,' or 'mutable,' the Catholic Church anathematizes."

5. On their dictating this formula, we did not let it pass without inquiry in what sense they introduced " of the essence of the Father," and " one in essence with the Father." Accordingly questions and explanations took place, and the meaning of the words underwent the scrutiny of reason. And they professed, that the phrase " of the essence" was indicative of the Son's being indeed from the Father, yet without being as if a part of Him. And with this understanding we thought good to assent to the sense of such religious doctrine, teaching, as it did, that the Son was from

the Father, not however a part of His essence [5]. On this account we assented to the sense ourselves, without declining even the term " One in essence," peace being the object which we set before us, and stedfastness in the orthodox view.

6. In the same way we also admitted " begotten, not made;" since the Council alleged that " made" was an appellative common to the other creatures which came to be through the Son, to whom the Son had no likeness. Wherefore, say they, He was not a work resembling the things which through Him came to be [6], but was of an essence which is too high for the level of any work; and which the Divine oracles teach to have been generated from the Father [7], the mode of generation being inscrutable and incalculable to every originated nature.

7. And so too on examination there are

[4a] [Or, 'taking the addition as their pretext.']

[4b] The only clauses of the Creed which admit of any question in their explanation, are the " He was not before His generation," and " of other subsistence or essence.' Of these the former shall be reserved for a later part of the volume; the latter is treated of in a note at the end of this Treatise [see Excursus A.].

[5] Eusebius does not commit himself to any positive sense in which the formula " of the essence" is to be interpreted, but only says what it does not mean. His comment on it is " of the Father, but not as a part;" where, what is not negative, instead of being an explanation, is but a recurrence to the original words of Scripture, of which ἐξ οὐσίας itself is the explanation; a curious inversion. Indeed it is very doubtful whether he admitted the ἐξ οὐσίας at all. He says, that the Son is not like the radiance of light so far as this, that the radiance is an inseparable accident of substance, whereas the Son is by the Father's will, κατὰ γνώμην καὶ προαίρεσιν, *Demonstr. Ev.* iv. 3. And though he insists on our Lord being *alone*, ἐκ θεοῦ, yet he means in the sense which Athan. refutes, supr. § 6, viz. that He alone was created immediately from God, vid. next note [6]. It is true that he plainly condemns with the Nicene Creed the ἐξ οὐκ ὄντων of the Arians, " out of nothing," but an evasion was at hand here also; for he not only adds, according to Arian custom, " as others" (vid. note following) but he has a theory that no being whatever is out of nothing, for non-existence cannot be the cause of existence. God, he says, " proposed His own will and power as ' a sort of matter and substance' of the production and constitution of the universe, so that it is not reasonably said, that any thing is out of nothing. For what is from nothing cannot be at all. How indeed can nothing be to any thing a cause of being? but all that is, takes its being *from One* who only is, and was, who also said, 'I am that I am.'" *Demonstr. Ev.* iv. 1. Again, speaking of our Lord, " He who was from nothing would not truly be Son of God, 'as neither is any other of things generate.'" *Eccl. Theol.* i. 9 fin. [see, however, D.C.B. ii. p. 347].

[6] Eusebius distinctly asserts, *Dem. Ev.* iv. 2, that our Lord is a creature. " This offspring," he says, " did He first produce Himself from Himself as a foundation of those things which should succeed, the perfect handy-work, δημιούργημα, of the Perfect, and the wise structure, ἀρχιτεκτόνημα, of the Wise," &c. Accordingly his avowal in the text is but the ordinary Arian evasion of " an offspring, not as the offsprings." E.g. " It is not without peril to say recklessly that the Son is originate out of nothing ' similarly to the other originate.'" *Dem. Ev.* v. 1. vid. also *Eccl. Theol.* i. 9. iii. 2. And he considers our Lord the only Son by a divine provision similar to that by which there is only one sun in the firmament, as a *centre* of light and heat. " Such an Only-begotten Son, the excellent artificer of His will and operator, did the supreme God and Father of that operator Himself first of all beget, through Him and in Him giving subsistence to the operative works (ideas or causes) of things which were to be, and casting in Him the seeds of the constitution and governance of the universe; . . . Therefore the Father being One, it behoved the Son to be one also; but should any one object that He constituted not more, it is fitting for such a one to complain that He constituted not more suns, and moons, and worlds, and ten thousand other things." *Dem. Ev.* iv. 5 fin. vid. also iv. 6.

[7] Eusebius does not say that our Lord is " from the essence of" the Father, but has " an essence from" the Father. This is the Semi-arian doctrine, which, whether confessing the Son from the essence of the Father or not, implied that His essence was not the Father's essence, but a second essence. The same doctrine is found in the Semi-arians of Ancyra, though they seem to have confessed " of the essence. " And this is one object of the ὁμοούσιον, to hinder the confession " of the essence" from implying a second essence, which was not obviated or was even encouraged by the ὁμοιούσιον. The Council of Ancyra, quoting the text " As the Father hath life in Himself, so," &c., says, " since the life which is in the Father means essence, and the life of the Only-begotten which is begotten from the Father means essence, the

grounds for saying that the Son is "one in essence" with the Father; not in the way of bodies, nor like mortal beings, for He is not such by division of essence, or by severance, no nor by any affection, or alteration, or changing of the Father's essence and power [8] (since from all such the unoriginate nature of the Father is alien), but because "one in essence with the Father" suggests that the Son of God bears no resemblance to the originated creatures, but that to His Father alone Who begat Him is He in every way assimilated, and that He is not of any other subsistence and essence, but from the Father [9]. To which term also, thus interpreted, it appeared well to assent; since we were aware that even among the ancients, some learned and illustrious Bishops and writers [1] have used the term "one in essence," in their theological teaching concerning the Father and Son.

8. So much then be said concerning the faith which was published; to which all of us assented, not without inquiry, but according to the specified senses, mentioned before the most religious Emperor himself, and justified by the forementioned considerations. And as to the anathematism published by them at the end of the Faith, it did not pain us, because it forbade to use words not in Scripture, from which almost all the confusion and disorder of the Church have come. Since then no divinely inspired Scripture has used the phrases, "out of nothing," and "once He was not," and the rest which follow, there appeared no ground for using or teaching them; to which also we assented as a good decision, since it had not been our custom hitherto to use these terms.

9. Moreover to anathematize "Before His generation He was not," did not seem preposterous, in that it is confessed by all, that the Son of God was before the generation according to the flesh [2].

10. Nay, our most religious Emperor did at the time prove, in a speech, that He was in being even acccrding to His divine generation which is before all ages, since even before He was generated in energy, He was in virtue [3] with the Father ingenerately, the Father being always Father, as King always, and Saviour always, being all things in virtue, and being always in the same respects and in the same way.

11. This we have been forced to transmit to you, Beloved, as making clear to you the deliberation of our inquiry and assent, and how reasonably we resisted even to the last minute as long as we were offended at statements which differed from our own, but received without contention what no longer pained us, as soon as, on a candid examination of the sense of the words, they appeared to us to coincide with what we ourselves have professed in the faith which we have already published.

[word] 'so' implies a likeness of essence to essence." *Hær.* 73. 10 fin. Hence Eusebius does not scruple to speak of "two essences," and other writers of three essences, *contr. Marc.* i. 4. p. 25. He calls our Lord "a second essence." *Dem. Ev.* vi. *Præf. Præp. Ev.* vii. 12. p. 320, and the Holy Spirit a third essence, ibid. 15. p. 325. This it was that made the Latins so suspicious of three hypostases, because the Semi-arians, as well as they, understood ὑπόστασις to mean essence [but this is dubious]. Eusebius in like manner [after Origen] calls our Lord "another God," "a second God." *Dem. Ev.* v. 4. p. 226. v. fin. "second Lord." ibid. 3 init. 6. fin. "second cause." *Dem. Ev.* v. *Præf.* vid. also ἕτερον ἔχουσα τὸ κατ' οὐσίαν ὑποκείμενον, *Dem. Ev.* v. 1. p. 215. καθ' ἑαυτὸν οὐσιωμένος. ibid. iv. 3. And so ἕτερος παρὰ τὸν πατέρα. *Eccl. Theol.* i. 60. p. 90. and ζωὴν ἰδίαν ἔχων. ibid. and ζῶν καὶ ὑφεστὼς καὶ τοῦ πατρὸς ὑπάρχων ἐκτός. ibid. Hence Athan. insists so much, as in *de Decr.*, on our Lord *not* being external to the Father. Once admit that He is in the Father, and we may call the Father, the *only* God, for He is included. And so again as to the Ingenerate, the term does not exclude the Son, for He is generate in the Ingenerate.

[8] This was the point on which the Semi-arians made their principal stand against the "one in essence," though they also objected to it as being of a Sabellian character. E.g. Euseb. *Demonstr.* iv. 3. p. 148. d.p 149. a, b. v. 1. pp. 213—215. *contr. Marcell.* i. 4. p. 20. *Eccl. Theol.* i. 12. p. 73. *in laud. Const.* p. 525. *de Fide* i. ap. Sirmond. tom. i. p. 7. *de Fide* ii. p. 16, and apparently his *de Incorporali.* And so the Semi-arians at Ancyra, Epiph. *Hær.* 73. 11. p. 858. a, b. And so Meletius, ibid. p. 878 fin. and Cyril Hier. *Catech.* vii. 5. xi. 18. though of course Catholics would speak as strongly on this point as their opponents.

[9] Here again Eusebius does not say "from the Father's essence," but "not from other essence, but from the Father." According to note 5, supr. he considered the will of God a certain matter or substance. Montfaucon in loc. and *Collect. Nov. Præf.* p. xxvi. translates without warrant "ex Patris hypostasi et substantiâ." As to the Son's perfect likeness to the Father which he seems here to grant, it has-been already shewn, *de Decr.* 20, note 9, how the admission was evaded. The likeness was, but a likeness after its own kind, as a picture is of the original. "Though our Saviour Himself teaches," he says, "that the Father is the 'only true God,' still let me not be backward to confess Him also the true God, 'as in an image,' and that possessed; so that the addition of 'only' may belong to the Father alone as archetype of the image . . . . As, supposing one king held sway, and his image was carried about into every quarter, no one in his right mind would say that those who held sway were two, but one who was honoured through his image; in like manner," &c. *de Eccles. Theol.* ii. 23, vid. *ibid.* 7.

[1] Athanasius in like manner, *ad Afros.* 6. speaks of "testimony of ancient Bishops about 130 years back," and in *de Syn.* § 43. of "long before" the Council of Antioch, A.D. 269. viz. the Dionysii, &c. vid. note on *de Decr.* 20.

[2] Socrates, who advocates the orthodoxy of Eusebius, leaves out this heterodox paragraph [§§ 9, 10] altogether. Bull, however, *Defens. F. N.* iii. 9. n. 3. thinks it an interpolation. Athanasius alludes to the early part of the clause, supr. § 4. and *de Syn.* § 13. where he says, that Eusebius implied that the Arians denied even our Lord's existence before His incarnation. As to Constantine, he seems to have been used on these occasions by the court Bishops who were his instructors, and who made him the organ of their own heresy. Upon the first rise of the Arian controversy he addressed a sort of pastoral letter to Alexander and Arius, telling them that they were disputing about a question of words, and recommending them to drop it and live together peaceably. Euseb. *vit. C.* ii. 69. 72.

[3] [Rather 'potentially' both here and three lines below.] Theognis, [one] of the Nicene Arians, says the same, according to Philostorgius; viz. "that God even before He begat the Son was a Father, as having the power, δύναμις, of begetting." *Hist.* ii. 15. Though Bull pronounces such doctrine to be heretical, as of course it is, still he considers that it expresses what *otherwise* stated may be orthodox, viz. the doctrine that our Lord was called the Word from eternity, and the Son upon His descent to create the worlds. And he acutely and ingeniously interprets the Arian formula, "Before His generation He was not," to support this view. Another opportunity will occur of giving an opinion upon this question; meanwhile, the *parallel* on which the heretical doctrine is supported in the text is answered by many writers, on the ground that Father and Son are words of nature, but Creator, King, Saviour, are external, or what may be called accidental to Him. Thus Athanasius observes, that Father actually implies Son, but Creator only the power to create, as expressing a δύναμις; "a maker is before his works, but he who says Father, forthwith in Father implies the existence of the Son." *Orat.* iii. § 6. vid. Cyril too, *Dial.* ii. p. 459. Pseudo-Basil, *contr. Eun.* iv. 1. fin. On the other hand Origen argues the reverse way, that since God is eternally a Father, therefore eternally Creator also: "As one cannot be father without a son, nor lord without possession, so neither can God be called All-powerful, without subjects of His power;" *de Princ.* i. 2. n. 10. hence he argued for the eternity of matter.

EXCURSUS' A

On the meaning of the phrase ἐξ ἑτέρας ὑποστάσεως ἢ οὐσίας in the Nicene Anathema.

Bishop Bull has made it a question, whether these words in the Nicene Creed mean the same thing, or are to be considered distinct from each other, advocating himself the latter opinion against Petavius. The history of the word ὑπόστασις is of too intricate a character to enter upon here; but a few words may be in place in illustration of its sense as it occurs in the Creed, and with reference to the view taken of it by the great divine, who has commented on it.

Bishop Bull, as I understood him (*Defens. F. N.* ii. 9. § 11.), considers that two distinct ideas are intended by the words οὐσία and ὑπόστασις, in the clause ἐξ ἑτέρας ὑποστάσεως ἢ οὐσίας; as if the Creed condemned those who said that the Son was not from the Father's essence, and those also who said that He was not from the Father's hypostasis or subsistence; as if a man might hold at least one of the two without holding the other. And in matter of fact, he does profess to assign two parties of heretics, who denied this or that proposition respectively.

Petavius, on the other hand (*de Trin.* iv. 1.), considers that the word ὑπόστασις is but another term for οὐσία, and that not two but one proposition is contained in the clause in question; the word ὑπόστασις not being publicly recognised in its present meaning till the Council of Alexandria, in the year 362. Coustant. (*Epist. Pont. Rom.* pp. 274. 290. 462.) Tillemont (*Memoires* S. Denys. d'Alex. § 15.), Huet (*Origenian.* ii. 2. n. 3.), Thomassin (*de Incarn.* iii. 1.), and Morinus (*de Sacr. Ordin.* ii. 6.), take substantially the same view; while Maranus (*Præf. ad S. Basil.* § 1. tom. 3. ed. Bened.), Natalis Alexander, *Hist.* (Sæc. 1. *Diss.* 22. circ. fin.), Burton (*Testimonies to the Trinity*, No. 71), and [Routh] (*Reliqu. Sacr.* vol. iii. p. 189.), differ from Petavius, if they do not agree with Bull.

Bull's principal argument lies in the strong fact, that S. Basil expressly asserts, that the Council did mean the two terms to be distinct, and this when he is answering the Sabellians, who grounded their assertion that there was but one ὑπόστασις, on the alleged fact that the Council had used οὐσία and ὑπόστασις indifferently.

Bull refers also to Anastasius *Hodeg.* 21. (22. p. 343. ?) who says, that the Nicene Fathers defined that there are three hypostases or Persons in the Holy Trinity. Petavius considers that he derived this from Gelasius of Cyzicus, a writer of no great authority; but, as the passage occurs in Anastasius, they are the words of Andrew of Samosata. But what is more important, elsewhere Anastasius quotes a passage from Amphilochius to something of the same effect. c. 10. p. 164. He states it besides himself, c. 9. p. 150. and c. 24. p. 364. In addition, Bull quotes passages from S. Dionysius of Alexandria, S. Dionysius of Rome (vid. below, *de Decr.* 25—27 and notes), Eusebius of Cæsarea, and afterwards Origen; in all of which three hypostases being spoken of, whereas antiquity, early or late, never speaks in the same way of three οὐσίαι, it is plain that ὑπόστασις then conveyed an idea which οὐσία did not. To these may be added a passage in Athanasius, *in Illud, Omnia*, § 6.

---

4 [This excursus supports the view taken above, Prolegg. ch. ii. § 3 (2) b; the student should supplement Newman's discussion by Zahn *Marcellus* and Harnack *Dogmengesch.* as quoted at the head of that section of the Prolegg. The word 'Semi-arian' is used in a somewhat inexact sense in this excursus, see Prolegg. ch. ii. § 3 (2) c, and § 8 (2) c.]

Bishop Bull adds the following explanation of the two words as they occur in the Creed : he conceives that the one is intended to reach the Arians, and the other the Semi-arians ; that the Semi-arians did actually make a distinction between οὐσία and ὑπόστασις, admitting in a certain sense that the Son was from the ὑπόστασις of the Father, while they denied that He was from His οὐσία.   They then are anathematized in the words ἐξ ἑτέρας οὐσίας ; and, as he would seem to mean, the Arians in the ἐξ ἑτέρας ὑποστάσεως.

Now I hope it will not be considered any disrespect to so great an authority, if I differ from this view, and express my reasons for doing so.

1. First then, supposing his account of the Semi-arian doctrine ever so free from objection, granting that they denied the ἐξ οὐσίας, and admitted the ἐξ ὑποστάσεως, yet *who* are they who, according to his view, *denied* the ἐξ ὑποστάσεως, or said that the Son was ἐξ ἑτέρας ὑποστάσεως ? he does not assign any parties, though he implies the Arians.   Yet though, as is notorious, they denied the ἐξ οὐσίας, there is nothing to shew that they or any other party of Arians maintained specifically that the Son was not [from] the ὑπόστασις, or subsistence of the Father.   That is, the hypothesis supported by this eminent divine does not answer the very question which it raises. It professes that those who denied the ἐξ ὑποστάσεως, were not the same as those who denied the ἐξ οὐσίας ; yet it fails to tell us who did deny the ἐξ ὑποστάσεως, in a sense distinct from ἐξ οὐσίας.

2. Next, his only proof that the Semi-arians did hold the ἐξ ὑποστάσεως as distinct from the ἐξ οὐσίας, lies in the circumstance, that the three (commonly called) Semi-arian confessions of A.D. 341, 344, 351, known as Mark's of Arethusa [i.e. the 'fourth Antiochene'], the Macrostich, and the first Sirmian, anathematize those who say that the Son is ἐξ ἑτέρας ὑποστάσεως καὶ μὴ ἐκ τοῦ θεοῦ, not anathematizing the ἐξ ἑτέρας οὐσίας, which he thence infers was their own belief.   Another explanation of this passage will be offered presently ; meanwhile, it is well to observe, that Hilary, in speaking of the confession of Philippopolis which was taken from Mark's, far from suspecting that the clause involved an omission, defends it on the *ground of its retaining the Anathema* (*de Synod.* 35.), thus implying that ἐξ ἑτέρας ὑποστάσεως καὶ μὴ ἐκ τοῦ θεοῦ was equivalent to ἐξ ἑτέρας ὑποστάσεως ἢ οὐσίας.   And it may be added, that Athanasius in like manner, in his account of the Nicene Council (*de Decret.* § 20. fin.), when repeating its anathema, drops the ἐξ ὑποστάσεως altogether, and reads τοὺς δὲ λέγοντας ἐξ οὐκ ὄντων, ... ἢ ποίημα, ἢ ἐξ ἑτέρας οὐσίας, τούτους ἀναθεματίζει κ. τ. λ.

3. Further, Bull gives us no proof whatever that the Semi-arians *did* deny the ἐξ οὐσίας ; while it is very clear, if it is right to contradict so great a writer, that most of them did not deny it.   He says that it is " certissimum " that the heretics who wrote the three confessions above noticed, that is, the Semi-arians, " *nunquam fassos*, nunquam fassuros fuisse filium ἐξ οὐσίας, e substantia, Patris progenitum."   His reason for not offering any proof for this naturally is, that Petavius, with whom he is in controversy, maintains it also, and he makes use of Petavius's admission against himself.   Now it may seem bold in a writer of this day to differ not only with Bull, but with Petavius ; but the reason for doing so is simple ; it is because Athanasius asserts the very thing which Petavius and Bull deny, and Petavius admits that he does ; that is, he allows it by implication when he complains that Athanasius had not got to the bottom of the doctrine of the Semi-arians, and thought too favourably of them.   " Horum Semi-arianorum, quorum antesignanus fuit Basilius Ancyræ episcopus, prorsus obscura fuit hæresis . . . . . ut ne ipse quidem Athanasius satis illam exploratam habuerit." *de Trin.* i. x. § 7.

Now S. Athanasius's words are most distinct and express ; " As to those who receive all else that was defined at Nicæa, but dispute about the ' One in essence ' only, we must not feel as towards enemies . . . . for, as *confessing that the Son is from the essence of the Father* and not of other subsistence, ἐκ τῆς οὐσίας τοῦ πατρὸς εἶναι, καὶ μὴ ἐξ ἑτέρας ὑποστάσεως τὸν υἱὸν, . . . they are not far from receiving the phrase ' One in essence ' also.   Such is Basil of Ancyra, in what he has written about the faith " de Syn. § 41 ;—a passage, not only express for the matter in hand, but remarkable too, as apparently using ὑπόστασις and οὐσία as synonymous, which is the main point which Bull denies. What follows in Athanasius is equally to the purpose: he urges the Semi-arians to accept the ὁμοούσιον, in consistency, *because* they maintain the ἐξ οὐσίας and the ὁμοιούσιον would not sufficiently secure it.

Moreover Hilary, while defending the Semi-arian decrees of Ancyra or Sirmium, says expressly, that according to them, among other truths, "non creatura est Filius genitus, sed *a natura Patris* indiscreta substantia est." *de Syn.* 27.

Petavius, however, in the passage to which Bull appeals, refers in proof of this view of Semi-arianism, to those Ancyrene documents, which Epiphanius has preserved, *Hær.* 73. and which he considers to shew, that according to the Semi-arians the Son was not ἐξ οὐσίας τοῦ πατρός. He says, that it is plain from their own explanations that they considered our Lord to be, not ἐκ τῆς οὐσίας, but ἐκ τῆς ὁμοιότητος (he does not say ὑποστάσεως, as Bull wishes) τοῦ πατρὸς and that, ἐνεργείᾳ γεννητικῇ, which was one of the divine ἐνέργειαι, as creation, ἡ κτιστική, was another. Yet surely Epiphanius does not bear out this representation better than Athanasius; since the Semi-arians, whose words he reports, speak of "υἱὸν ὅμοιον καὶ κατ᾽ οὐσίαν ἐκ τοῦ πατρὸς, p. 825 b, ὡς ἡ σοφία τοῦ σοφοῦ υἱὸς, οὐσία οὐσίας, p. 853 c, κατ᾽ οὐσίαν υἱὸν τοῦ Θεοῦ καὶ πατρός, p. 854 c, ἐξουσίᾳ ὁμοῦ καὶ οὐσίᾳ πατρὸς μονογενοῦς υἱοῦ. p. 858 d, besides the strong word γνήσιος, ibid. and Athan. *de Syn.* § 41. not to insist on other of their statements.

The same fact is brought before us even in a more striking way in the conference at Constantinople, A.D. 360, before Constantius, between the Anomœans and Semi-arians, where the latter, according to Theodoret, shew no unwillingness to acknowledge even the ὁμοούσιον, *because* they acknowledge the ἐξ οὐσίας. When the Anomœans wished the former condemned, Silvanus of Tarsus said, "If God the Word be not out of nothing, nor a creature, *nor of other essence,* οὐσίας, therefore is He one in essence, ὁμοούσιος, with God who begot Him, as God from God, and Light from Light, and He has the same nature with His Father." *H. E.* ii. 23. Here again it is observable, as in the passage from Athanasius above, that, while apparently reciting the Nicene Anathema, he omits ἐξ ἑτέρας ὑποστάσεως, as if it were superfluous to mention a synonym.

At the same time there certainly is reason to suspect that the Semi-arians approximated towards orthodoxy as time went on; and perhaps it is hardly fair to determine what they held at Nicæa by their statements at Ancyra, though to the latter Petavius appeals. Several of the most eminent among them, as Meletius, Cyril, and Eusebius of Samosata conformed soon after; on the other hand in Eusebius, who is their representative at Nicæa, it will perhaps be difficult to find a clear admission of the ἐξ οὐσίας. But at any rate he does not maintain the ἐξ ὑποστάσεως, which Bull's theory requires.

On various grounds then, because the Semi-arians as a body did not deny the ἐξ οὐσίας, nor confess the ἐξ ὑποστάσεως, nor the Arians deny it, there is reason for declining Bishop Bull's explanation of these words as they occur in the Creed; and now let us turn to the consideration of the authorities on which that explanation rests.

As to Gelasius, Bull himself does not insist upon his testimony, and Anastasius [about 700 A.D.] is too late to be of authority. The passage indeed which he quotes from Amphilochius is important, but as he was a friend of S. Basil, perhaps it does not very much increase the weight of S. Basil's more distinct and detailed testimony to the same point, and no one can say that that weight is inconsiderable.

Yet there is evidence the other way which overbalances it. Bull, who complains of Petavius's rejection of S. Basil's testimony concerning a Council which was held before his birth, cannot maintain his own explanation of its Creed without rejecting Athanasius's testimony respecting the doctrine of his contemporaries, the Semi-arians; and moreover the more direct evidence, as we shall see, of the Council of Alexandria, A.D. 362, S. Jerome, Basil of Ancyra, and Socrates.

First, however, no better comment upon the sense of the Council can be required than the incidental language of Athanasius and others, who in a foregoing extract exchanges οὐσία for ὑπόστασις in a way which is natural only on the supposition that he used them as synonyms. Elsewhere, as we have seen, he omits the word ἢ ὑποστάσεως in the Nicene Anathema, while Hilary considers the Anathema sufficient *with* that omission.

In like manner Hilary expressly translates the clause in the Creed by ex altera substantia vel essentia. *Fragm.* ii. 27. And somewhat in the same way Eusebius says in his letter, ἐξ ἑτέρας τινὸς ὑποστάσεώς τε καὶ οὐσίας.

But further, Athanasius says expressly, *ad Afros*,—"Hypostasis is essence, οὐσία, and means nothing else than simply being, which Jeremiah calls existence when he says," &c. § 4. It is true, he elsewhere speaks of three Hypostases, but this only shews that he attached no fixed sense to the word. [Rather, he abandons the latter usage in his middle and later writings.] This is just what I would maintain ; its sense must be determined by the context ; and, whereas it always stands in all Catholic writers for the Una Res (as the 4th Lateran speaks), which οὐσία denotes, when Athanasius says, "three hypostases," he takes the word to mean οὐσία in that particular sense in which it is three, and when he makes it synonymous with οὐσία, he uses it to signify Almighty God in that sense in which He is one.

Leaving Athanasius, we have the following evidence concerning the history of the word ὑπόστασις. S. Jerome says, "The whole school of secular learning understanding nothing else by hypostasis than usia, essence," *Ep.* xv. 4, where, speaking of the Three Hypostases he uses the strong language, "If you desire it, then be a *new* faith framed *after* the Nicene, and let the orthodox confess in terms like the Arian."

In like manner, Basil of Ancyra, George, and the other Semi-arians, say distinctly, "This hypostasis our Fathers called essence," οὐσία. Epiph. *Hær.* 74. 12. fin. ; in accordance with which is the unauthorized addition to the Sardican Epistle, "ὑπόστασιν, ἣν αὐτοὶ οἱ αἱρετικοὶ οὐσίαν προσαγορεύουσι." Theod. *H. E.* ii. 6.

If it be said that Jerome from his Roman connection, and Basil and George as Semi-arians, would be led by their respective theologies for distinct reasons thus to speak, it is true, and may have led them to too broad a statement of the fact ; but then on the other hand it was in accordance also with the theology of S. Basil, so strenuous a defender of the formula of the Three Hypostases, to suppose that the Nicene Fathers meant to distinguish ὑπόστασις from οὐσία in their anathema.

Again, Socrates informs us that, though there was some dispute about hypostasis at Alexandria shortly before the Nicene Council, yet the Council itself "devoted not a word to the question," *H. E.* iii. 7. ; which hardly consists with its having intended to rule that ἐξ ἑτέρας ὑποστάσεως was distinct from ἐξ ἑτέρας οὐσίας.

And in like manner the Council of Alexandria, A.D. 362, in deciding that the sense of Hypostasis was an open question, not only from the very nature of the case goes on the supposition that the Nicene Council had not closed it, but says so in words again and again in its Synodal Letter. If the Nicene Council had already used "hypostasis" in its present sense, what remained to Athanasius at Alexandria but to submit to it ?

Indeed the history of this Council is perhaps the strongest argument against the supposed discrimination of the two terms by the Council of Nicæa. Bull can only meet it by considering that an innovation upon the "veterem vocabuli usum" began at the date of the Council of Sardica, though Socrates mentions the dispute as existing at Alexandria before the Nicene Council, *H. E.* iii. 4. 5. while the supposititious confession of Sardica professes to have received the doctrine of the one hypostasis by tradition as Catholic.

Nor is the use of the word in earlier times inconsistent with these testimonies ; though it occurs so seldom, in spite of its being a word of S. Paul [i.e. Heb. i. 3], that testimony is our principal evidence. Socrates' remarks deserve to be quoted ; "Those among the Greeks who have treated of the Greek philosophy, have defined essence, οὐσία, in many ways, but they had made no mention at all of hypostasis. Irenæus the Grammarian, in his alphabetical Atticist, even calls the term barbarous; because it is not used by any of the ancients, and if anywhere found, it does not mean what it is now taken for. Thus in the Phœnix of Sophocles it means an 'ambush;' but in Menander, 'preserves,' as if one were to call the wine-lees in a cask 'hypostasis.' However it must be observed, that, in spite of the old philosophers being silent about the term, the more modern continually use it for essence, οὐσίας," H. E. iii. 7. The word principally occurs in Origen among Ante-Nicene writers, and he, it must be confessed, uses it, as far as the context decides its sense, to mean subsistence or person. In other words, it was the word of a certain school in the Church, which afterwards was accepted by the Church; but this proves nothing about the sense in which it was used at Nicæa. The three Hypostases are spoken of by Origen, his pupil Dionysius, as afterwards by Eusebius of Cæsarea (though he may notwithstanding have considered hypostasis synonymous with essence), and Athanasius (Origen in Joan. ii. 6. Dionys. ap. Basil de Sp. S. n. 72. Euseb. ap. Socr. i. 23. Athan. in Illud Omnia, &c. 6); and the Two Hypostases of the Father and the Son, by Origen, Ammonius, and Alexander (Origen c. Cels. viii. 2. Ammon. ap. Caten. in Joan. x. 30. Alex. ap. Theod. i. 3. p. 740). As to the passage in which two hypostases are spoken of in Dionysius' letter to Paul of Samosata, that letter certainly is not genuine, as might be shewn on a fitting occasion, though it is acknowledged by very great authorities.

I confess that to my mind there is an antecedent probability that the view which has here been followed is correct. Judging by the general history of doctrine, one should not expect that the formal ecclesiastical meaning of the word should have obtained everywhere so early. Nothing is more certain than that the doctrines themselves of the Holy Trinity and the Incarnation were developed, or, to speak more definitely, that the propositions containing them were acknowledged, from the earliest times; but the particular terms which now belong to them are most uniformly of a later date. Ideas were brought out, but technical phrases did not obtain. Not that these phrases did not exist, but either not as technical, or in use in a particular School or Church, or with a particular writer, or as ἅπαξ λεγόμενα, as words discussed, nay resisted, perhaps used by some local Council, and then at length accepted generally from their obvious propriety. Thus the words of the Schools pass into the service of the Catholic Church. Instead then of the word ὑπόστασις being, as Maran says, received in the East " summo consensu," from the date of Noetus or at least Sabellius, or of Bull's opinion " apud Catholicos Dionysii ætate ratum et fixum illud fuisse, tres esse in divinis hypostases," I would consider that the present use of the word was in the first instance Alexandrian, and that it was little more than Alexandrian till the middle of the fourth century.

Lastly, it comes to be considered how the two words are to be accounted for in the Creed, if they have not distinct senses. Coustant supposes that ἐξ οὐσίας was added to explain ἐξ ὑποστάσεως, lest the latter should be taken in a Sabellian sense. On which we may perhaps remark besides, that the reason why ὑπόστασις was selected as the principal term was, that it was agreeable to the Westerns as well as admitted by the Orientals. Thus, by way of contrast, we find the Second General Council, at which there were no Latins, speaking of Three Hypostases, and Pope Damasus and the Roman Council speaking a few years sooner of the Holy Ghost as of the same hypostasis and usia with the Father and the Son. Theod. H. E. ii. 17. Many things go to make this probable. For instance, Coustant acutely points out, though Maran and the President of Magdalen [Routh, Rel. Sac. iii. 383] dissent, that this probably was a point of dispute between the two Dionysii; the Bishop of Alexandria asserting, as we know he did assert, Three Hypostases, the Bishop of Rome protesting in reply against "Three partitive Hypostases," as involving tritheism, and his namesake rejoining, "If because there are Three Hypostases, any say that they are partitive, three there are, though they like it not." Again, the influence of the West shews itself in the language of Athanasius, who, contrary to the custom of his Church, of Origen, Dionysius, and his own immediate patron and master Alexander, so varies his own use of the word, as to make his writings almost an example of that freedom which he vindicated in the Council of Alexandria. Again, when Hosius went to Alexandria before the Nicene Council, and a dispute arose with reference to Sabellianism about the words ὑπόστασις and οὐσία, what is this too, but the collision of East and West? It should be remembered moreover that Hosius presided at Nicæa, a Latin in an Eastern city; and again at Sardica, where, though the decree in favour of the One Hypostasis was not passed, it seems clear from the history that he was resisting persons with whom in great measure he agreed. Further, the same consideration accounts for the omission of the ἐξ οὐσίας from the Confession of Mark and the two which follow, on which Bull r(ies in proof that the Semi-arians rejected this formula. These three Semi-arian Creeds, and these only, were addressed to the Latins, and therefore their compilers naturally select that synonym which was most pleasing to them, as the means of securing a hearing; just as Athanasius on the other hand in his *de Decretis*, writing to the Greeks, omits ὑποστάσεως and writes οὐσίας.

EXPOSITIO FIDEI

THE date of this highly interesting document is quite uncertain, but there is every ground for placing it earlier than the explicitly anti-Arian treatises. Firstly, the absence of any express reference to the controversy against Arians, while yet it is clearly in view in §§ 3 and 4, which lay down the rule afterwards consistently adopted by Athanasius with regard to texts which speak of the Saviour as created. Secondly, the untroubled use of ὅμοιος (§ 1, note 4) to express the Son's relation to the Father. Thirdly, the close affinity of this Statement to the *Sermo Major de Fide* which in its turn has very close points of contact with the pre-Arian treatises. But see Prolegg. ch. iii. § 1 (37).

If we are to hazard a conjecture, we may see in this "ἔκθεσις" a statement of faith published by Athanasius upon his accession to the Episcopate, A.D. 328. The statement proper (Hahn § 119) consists of § 1. §§ 2—4 are an explanatory comment insisting on the distinct Existence of the Son, and on His essential uncreatedness.

The translation which follows has been carefully compared with one made by the late Prof. Swainson in his work on the Creeds, pp. 73—76. Dr. Swainson there refers to a former 'imperfect and misleading' translation (in Irons' *Athanasius contra Mundum*) which the present editor has not seen. Dr. Swainson expresses doubts as to the Athanasian authorship of the Ecthesis, but without any cogent reason. The only point of importance is one which acquaintance with the usual language of Athanasius shews to make distinctly in favour of, and not against, the genuineness of this little tract. Three times in the course of it the Human Body, or Humanity of the Lord is spoken of as ὁ Κυριακός ἄνθρωπος. Dr. Swainson exaggerates the strangeness of the expression by the barbarous rendering '*Lordly* man' (How would he translate κυριακὸν δεῖπνον?). But the phrase certainly requires explanation, although the explanation is not difficult. (1) It is quoted by Facundus of Hermiane from the present work (*Def. Tr. Cap.* xi. 5), and by Rufinus from an unnamed work of Athanasius ('libellus'), probably the present one. Moreover, Athanasius himself uses the phrase, frequently in the *Sermo Major de Fide,* and in his exposition of Psalm xl. (xli.). Epiphanius uses it at least twice (*Ancor.* 78 and 95); and from these Greek Fathers the phrase ('Dominicus Homo') passed on to Latin writers such as Cassian and Augustine (below, note 5), who, however, subsequently cancelled his adoption of the expression (*Retr.* I. xix. 8). The phrase, therefore, is not to be objected to as un-Athanasian. In fact (2) it is founded upon the profuse and characteristic use by Ath. of the word ἄνθρωπος to designate the manhood of our Lord (see *Orat. c. Ar.* i. 41, 45, ii. 45, note 2. Dr. Swainson appears unaware of this in his unsatisfactory paragraph p. 77, lines 14 and foll.). If the human nature of Christ may be called ἄνθρωπος (1 Tim. ii. 5) at all, there is no difficulty in its being called ὁ ἄνθρ. τοῦ σωτῆρος (*Serm. M. de F.* 24 and 30), or κυριακὸς ἄνθρωπος, a phrase equated with τὸ [κυριακὸν] σῶμα in *Serm. M. de F.* 19 and 28—31 (see also a discussion in Thilo *Athan. Opp. Dogm. select.* p. 2). This use of the word ἄνθρωπος, if carelessly employed, might lend itself to a Nestorian sense. But Athanasius does not employ it carelessly, nor in an ambiguous context; although of course he might have used different language had he foreseen the controversies of the fifth century. At any rate, enough has been said to shew that its use in the present treatise does not expose its genuineness to cavil.

STATEMENT OF FAITH

1. WE believe in one Unbegotten[9] God, Father Almighty, maker of all things both visible and invisible, that hath His being from Himself. And in one Only-begotten Word, Wisdom, Son, begotten of the Father without beginning and eternally; word not pronounced[1] nor mental, nor an effluence[2] of the Perfect, nor a dividing of the impassible Essence, nor an issue[3]; but absolutely perfect Son, living and powerful (Heb. iv. 12), the true Image of the Father, equal in honour and glory. For this, he says, 'is the will of the Father, that as they honour the Father, so they may honour the Son also' (Joh. v. 23): very God of very God, as John says in his general Epistles, 'And we are in Him that is true, even in His Son Jesus Christ: this is the true God and everlasting life' (1 Joh. v. 20): Almighty of Almighty. For all things which the Father rules and sways, the Son rules and sways likewise: wholly from the Whole, being like[4] the Father as the Lord says, 'he that hath seen Me hath seen the Father' (Joh. xiv. 9). But He was begotten ineffably and incomprehensibly, for 'who shall declare his generation?' (Isa. liii. 8), in other words, no one can. Who, when at the consummation of the ages (Heb. ix. 26), He had descended from the bosom of the Father, took from the undefiled Virgin Mary our humanity (ἄνθρωπον), Christ Jesus, whom He delivered of His own will to suffer for us, as the Lord saith: 'No man taketh My life from Me. I have power to lay it down, and have power to take it again' (Joh. x. 18). In which humanity He was crucified and died for us, and rose from the dead, and was taken up into the heavens, having been created as the beginning of ways for us (Prov. viii. 22), when on earth He shewed us light from out of darkness, salvation from error, life from the dead, an entrance to paradise, from which Adam was cast out, and into which he again entered by means of the thief, as the Lord said, 'This day shalt thou be with Me in paradise' (Luke xxiii. 43), into which Paul also once entered. [He shewed us] also a way up to the heavens, whither the humanity of the Lord[5], in which He will judge the quick and the dead, entered as precursor for us. We believe, likewise, also in the Holy Spirit that searcheth all things, even the deep things of God (1 Cor. ii. 10), and we anathematise doctrines contrary to this.

2. For neither do we hold a Son-Father, as do the Sabellians, calling Him of one but not of the same[6] essence, and thus destroying the existence of the Son. Neither do we ascribe the passible body which He bore for the salvation of the whole world to the Father. Neither can we imagine three Subsistences separated from each other, as results from their bodily nature in the case of men, lest we hold a plurality of gods like the heathen. But just as a river, produced from a well, is not separate, and yet there are in fact two visible objects and two names. For neither is the Father the Son, nor the Son the Father. For the Father is Father of the Son, and the Son, Son of the Father. For like as the well is not a river, nor the river a well, but both are one and the same water which is conveyed in a channel from the well to the river, so the Father's deity passes into the Son without flow and without division. For the Lord says, 'I came out from the Father and am come' (Joh. xvi. 28). But He is ever

---

9 See *de Syn.* §§ 3, 46, 47, and the **Excursus in Lightfoot's** Ignatius, vol. ii. pp. 90 and foll. (first ed.).

1 Cf. note by Newman on *de Synodis*, § 26 (5).

2 Cf. Newman's note (8) on *de Decr.* § 11.

3 Or 'development' (Gr. προβολή) a word with Gnostic and Sabellian antecedents, cf. Newman's note 8 on *de Synodis*, § 16.

4 This word, which became the watchword of the Acacian party, the successors of the Eusebians, marks the relatively early date of this treatise. At a later period Athanasius would not use it without qualification (see *Orat.* ii. § 22, note 4), and later still, rejected the Word entirely as misleading (*de Synodis*, § 53, note 9). Yet see *ad Afros.* 7, and *Orat.* ii. 34.

5 ὁ κυριακὸς ἄνθρωπος (see above, introductory remarks). The expression is quoted as used by Ath., apparently from this passage, by Rufinus (Hieron. Opp. ix. p. 131, ed. 1643), Theodoret, *Dial.* 3, and others. The expression 'Dominicus Homo' used by St. Augustine is rendered 'Divine Man' in *Nicene and P. N. Fathers*, Series i. vol. vi. p. 40 b.

6 μονοούσιον καὶ οὐχ ὁμοούσιον (see Prolegg. ch. ii. § 3 (2) b sub fin.). The distinction cannot (to those accustomed to use the 'Nicene' Creed in English) be rendered so as to imply a real difference. The real distinction lies, not in the prefixes μονο- and ὁμο-, but in the sense to be attached to the ambiguous term οὐσία.

with the Father, for He is in the bosom of the Father, nor was ever the bosom of the Father void of the deity of the Son. For He says, 'I was by Him as one setting in order' (Prov. viii. 30). But we do not regard God the Creator of all, the Son of God, as a creature, or thing made, or as made out of nothing, for He is truly existent from Him who exists, alone existing from Him who alone exists, in as much as the like glory and power was eternally and conjointly begotten of the Father. For 'He that hath seen' the Son 'hath seen the Father (Joh. xiv. 9). All things to wit were made through the Son; but He Himself is not a creature, as Paul says of the Lord: 'In Him were all things created, and He is before all' (Col. i. 16). Now He says not, 'was created' before all things, but 'is' before all things. To be created, namely, is applicable to all things, but 'is before all' applies to the Son only.

3. He is then by nature an Offspring, perfect from the Perfect, begotten before all the hills (Prov. viii. 25), that is before every rational and intelligent essence, as Paul also in another place calls Him 'first-born of all creation' (Col. i. 15). But by calling Him First-born, He shews that He is not a Creature, but Offspring of the Father. For it would be inconsistent with His deity for Him to be called a creature. For all things were created by the Father through the Son, but the Son alone was eternally begotten from the Father, whence God the Word is 'first-born of all creation,' unchangeable from unchangeable. However, the body which He wore for our sakes is a creature: concerning which Jeremiah says, according to the edition of the seventy translators [7] (Jer. xxxi. 22): 'The Lord created for us for a planting a new salvation, in which salvation men shall go about:' but according to Aquila the same text runs: 'The Lord created a new thing in woman.' Now the salvation created for us for a planting, which is new, not old, and for us, not before us, is Jesus, Who in respect of the Saviour [8] was made man, and whose name is translated in one place Salvation, in another Saviour. But

salvation proceeds from the Saviour, just as illumination does from the light. The salvation, then, which was from the Saviour, being created new, did, as Jeremiah says, 'create for us a new salvation,' and as Aquila renders: 'The Lord created a new thing in woman,' that is in Mary. For nothing new was created in woman, save the Lord's body, born of the Virgin Mary without intercourse, as also it says in the Proverbs in the person of Jesus: 'The Lord created me, a beginning of His ways for His works' (Prov. viii. 22). Now He does not say, 'created me before His works,' lest any should take the text of the deity of the Word.

4. Each text then which refers to the creature is written with reference to Jesus in a bodily sense. For the Lord's Humanity [9] was created as 'a beginning of ways,' and He manifested it to us for our salvation. For by it we have our access to the Father. For He is the way (Joh. xiv. 6) which leads us back to the Father. And a way is a corporeal visible thing, such as is the Lord's humanity. Well, then, the Word of God created all things, not being a creature, but an offspring. For He created none of the created things equal or like unto Himself. But it is the part of a Father to beget, while it is a workman's part to create. Accordingly, that body is a thing made and created, which the Lord bore for us, which was begotten for us [1], as Paul says, 'wisdom from God, and sanctification and righteousness, and redemption;' while yet the Word was before us and before all Creation, and is, the Wisdom of the Father. But the Holy Spirit, being that which proceeds from the Father, is ever in the hands [2] of the Father Who sends and of the Son Who conveys Him, by Whose means He filled all things. The Father, possessing His existence from Himself, begat the Son, as we said, and did not create Him, as a river from a well and as a branch from a root, and as brightness from a light, things which nature knows to be indivisible; through whom to the Father be glory and power and greatness before all ages, and unto all the ages of the ages. Amen.

---

7 Heb. For the Lord hath created a new thing in the earth, A woman shall encompass a man.' Cf. *Orat.* ii. 46, note 5.
8 The same phrase also in *Serm. M. de Fid.* 18.

9 κυριακὸς ἄνθρωπος, see above.
1 ἐγεννήθη (1 Cor. i. 30, ἐγενήθη). The two words are constantly confused in MSS., and I suspect that ἐγενήθη, which (*pace* Swainson p. 78, note) the context really requires, was what Ath. wrote
2 See also *de Sent. Dionys.* 17.

IN ILLUD 'OMNIA,' ETC.

THIS memorandum or short article was written, as its first sentence shews, during the lifetime of Eusebius of Nicomedia, and therefore not later than the summer of A.D. 342. The somewhat abrupt beginning, and the absence of any exposition of the latter portion of the text, have led to the inference that the work is a fragment: but its conclusion is evidently perfect, and the opening words probably refer to the text itself. The tract is a reply to the Arian argument founded upon Luke x. 22 (Matt. xi. 27). If 'all things' had been delivered to the Son by the Father, it would follow that once He was without them. Now 'all things' include His Divine Sonship. Therefore there was a time when the Son was not. Athanasius meets this argument by totally denying the minor premise. By 'all things,' he argues, Christ referred to His mediatorial work and its glories, not to His essential nature as Word of God. He then adduces Joh. xvi. 15, to shew at once the Son's distinctness from the Father, and that the Father's attributes must also be those of the Son.

The interpretation of the main text given in this tract was not subsequently maintained by Athanasius: in *Orat.* iii. 35, he explains it of the Son, as safeguarding His separate personality against the Sabellians. It should, however, be noted that this change of ground does not involve any concession to the Arian use of the passage: it merely transfers the denial of Athanasius from their minor to their major premise.

Beyond the fact that the tract was written before 342 there is no conclusive evidence as to its date. But it is generally placed (Montfaucon, Ceillier, Alzog) before the 'Encyclical,' which was written in 339, and in several particulars it differs from the later anti-Arian treatises: perhaps then we may conjecturally place it about 335, i.e. before the first exile of the 'Pope.'

ON LUKE X. 22 (MATT. XI. 27)

§ 1. *This text refers not to the eternal Word but to the Incarnate.*

" All things were delivered to Me by My Father. And none knoweth Who the Son is, save the Father ; and Who the Father is, save the Son, and he to whomsoever the Son willeth to reveal Him."

And from not perceiving this they of the sect of Arius, Eusebius and his fellows, indulge impiety against the Lord. For they say, if all things were delivered (meaning by ' all' the Lordship of Creation), there was once a time when He had them not. But if He had them not, He is not of the Father, for if He were, He would on that account have had them always, and would not have required to receive them. But this point will furnish all the clearer an exposure of their folly. For the expression in question does not refer to the Lordship over Creation, nor to presiding over the works of God, but is meant to reveal in part the intention of the Incarnation (τῆς οἰκονομίας). For if when He was speaking they ' were delivered' to Him, clearly before He received them, creation was void of the Word. What then becomes of the text " in Him all things consist " (Col. i. 17)? But if simultaneously with the origin of the Creation it was all ' delivered' to Him, such delivery were superfluous, for ' all things were made by Him' (Joh. i. 3), and it would be unnecessary for those things of which the Lord Himself was the artificer to be delivered over to Him. For in making them He was Lord of the things which were being originated. But even supposing they were ' delivered' to Him after they were originated, see the monstrosity. For if they ' were delivered,' and upon His receiving them the Father retired, then we are in peril of falling into the fabulous tales which some tell, that He gave over [His works] to the Son, and Himself departed. Or if, while the Son has them, the Father has them also, we ought to say, not ' were delivered,' but that He took Him as partner, as Paul did Silvanus. But this is even more monstrous ; for God is

not imperfect [1], nor did He summon the Son to help Him in His need ; but, being Father of the Word, He makes all things by His means, and without delivering creation over to Him, by His means and in Him exercises Providence over it, so that not even a sparrow falls to the ground without the Father (Matt. x. 29), nor is the grass clothed without God (ib. vi. 30), but at once the Father worketh, and the Son worketh hitherto (cf. Joh. v. 17). Vain, therefore, is the opinion of the impious. For the expression is not what they think, but designates the Incarnation.

§ 2. *Sense in which, and end for which all things were delivered to the Incarnate Son.*

For whereas man sinned, and is fallen, and by his fall all things are in confusion : death prevailed from Adam to Moses (cf. Rom. v. 14), the earth was cursed, Hades was opened, Paradise shut, Heaven offended, man, lastly, corrupted and brutalised (cf. Ps. xlix. 12), while the devil was exulting against us ;—then God, in His loving-kindness, not willing man made in His own image to perish, said, ' Whom shall I send, and who will go?' (Isa. vi. 8). But while all held their peace, the Son [2] said, ' Here am I, send Me.' And then it was that, saying ' Go Thou,' He ' delivered' to Him man, that the Word Himself might be made Flesh, and by taking the Flesh, restore it wholly. For to Him, as to a physician, man ' was delivered' to heal the bite of the serpent ; as to life, to raise what was dead ; as to light, to illumine the darkness ; and, because He was Word, to renew the rational nature (τὸ λογικόν). Since then all things ' were delivered' to Him, and He is made Man, straightway all things were set right and perfected. Earth receives

---

[1] See *Orat.* ii. § 24, 25, *De Decr.* § 8, and Harnack, *Dogmgesch.* (ed. 2) vol. 2. p. 208, note.

[2] This dramatic representation of the Mission of the Son stands alone in the writings of Athanasius, and, if pressed, lends itself to a conception of the relation of the Son to the Father which, if not Arian, is at least contrary to the more explicit and mature conception of Athanasius as formulated for example in *Orat.* ii. 31 (and see note 7 there). The same idea appears in Milton's Paradise Lost (e.g. Book X.). See Newman, *Arians* 4, p. 93, note.

blessing instead of a curse, Paradise was opened to the robber, Hades cowered, the tombs were opened and the dead raised, the gates of Heaven were lifted up to await Him that ' cometh from Edom' (Ps. xxiv. 7, Isa. lxiii. 1). Why, the Saviour Himself expressly signifies in what sense 'all things were delivered' to Him, when He continues, as Matthew tells us: 'Come unto Me all ye that labour and are heavy laden, and I will give you rest' (Matt. xi. 28). Yes, ye 'were delivered' to Me to give rest to those who had laboured, and life to the dead. And what is written in John's Gospel harmonises with this: 'The Father loveth the Son, and hath given all things into His hand' (Joh. iii. 35). Given, in order that, just as all things were made by Him, so in Him all things might be renewed. For they were not ' delivered' unto Him, that being poor, He might be made rich, nor did He receive all things that He might receive power which before He lacked: far be the thought: but in order that as Saviour He might rather set all things right. For it was fitting that while 'through Him' all things came into being at the beginning, 'in Him' (note the change of phrase) all things should be set right (cf. Joh. i. 3, Eph. i. 10). For at the beginning they came into being 'through' Him; but afterwards, all having fallen, the Word has been made Flesh, and put it on, in order that 'in Him' all should be set right. Suffering Himself, He gave us rest, hungering Himself, He nourished us, and going down into Hades He brought us back thence. For example, at the time of the creation of all things, their creation consisted in a fiat, such as 'let [the earth] bring forth,' 'let there be' (Gen. i. 3, 11), but at the restoration it was fitting that all things should be ' delivered' to Him, in order that He might be made man, and all things be renewed in Him. For man, being in Him, was quickened: for this was why the Word was united to man, namely, that against man the curse might no longer prevail. This is the reason why they record the request made on behalf of mankind in the seventy-first Psalm: 'Give the King Thy judgment, O God' (Ps. lxxii. 1): asking that both the judgment of death which hung over us may be delivered to the Son, and that He may then, by dying for us, abolish it for us in Himself. This was what He signified, saying Himself, in the eighty-seventh Psalm: 'Thine indignation lieth hard upon me' (Ps. lxxxviii. 7). For He bore the indignation which lay upon us, as also He says in the hundred and thirty-seventh: 'Lord, Thou shalt do vengeance for me' (Ps. cxxxviii. 8, LXX.).

§ 3. By ' all things' is meant the redemptive attributes and power of Christ.

Thus, then, we may understand all things to have been delivered to the Saviour, and, if it be necessary to follow up understanding by explanation, that hath been delivered unto Him which He did not previously possess. For He was not man previously, but became man for the sake of saving man. And the Word was not in the beginning flesh, but has been made flesh subsequently (cf. Joh. i. 1 sqq.), in which Flesh, as the Apostle says, He reconciled the enmity which was against us (Col. i. 20, ii. 14, Eph. ii. 15, 16) and destroyed the law of the commandments in ordinances, that He might make the two into one new man, making peace, and reconcile both in one body to the Father. That, however, which the Father has, belongs also to the Son, as also He says in John, 'All things whatsoever the Father hath are Mine' (Joh. xvi. 15), expressions which could not be improved. For when He became that which He was not, 'all things were delivered' to Him. But when He desires to declare His unity with the Father, He teaches it without any reserve, saying: 'All things whatsoever the Father hath are Mine.' And one cannot but admire the exactness of the language. For He has not said 'all things whatsoever the Father hath, He hath given to Me,' lest He should appear at one time not to have possessed these things; but 'are Mine.' For these things, being in the Father's power, are equally in that of the Son. But we must in turn examine what things 'the Father hath.' For if Creation is meant, the Father had nothing before creation, and proves to have received something additional from Creation; but far be it to think this. For just as He exists before creation, so before creation also He has what He has, which we also believe to belong to the Son (Joh. xvi. 15). For if the Son is in the Father, then all things that the Father has belong to the Son. So this expression is subversive of the perversity of the heterodox in saying that 'if all things have been delivered to the Son, then the Father has ceased to have power over what is delivered, having appointed the Son in His place. For, in fact, the Father judgeth none, but hath given all judgment to the Son' (Joh. v. 22). But 'let the mouth of them that speak wickedness be stopped' (Ps. lxiii. 11), (for although He has given all judgment to the Son, He is not, therefore, stripped of lordship: nor, because it is said that all things are delivered by the Father to the Son, is He any the less over all), separating as they clearly do the Only-begotten from God, Who is by nature inseparable from Him, even though in their madness they separate Him by their words, not perceiving, the impious men, that the Light can never be separated from the sun, in which it resides by nature. For one must use a poor simile drawn from tangible and familiar objects to put our idea into words, since it is over bold to intrude upon the incomprehensible nature [of God].

§ 4. *The text John xvi. 15, shews clearly the essential relation of the Son to the Father.*

As then the light from the Sun which illumines the world could never be supposed, by men of sound mind, to do so without the Sun, since the Sun's light is united to the Sun by nature ; and as, if the Light [1] were to say : I have received from the Sun the power of illumining all things, and of giving growth and strength to them by the heat that is in me, no one will be mad enough to think that the mention of the Sun is meant to separate him from what is his nature, namely the light; so piety would have us perceive that the Divine Essence of the Word is united by nature to His own Father. For the text before us will put our problem in the clearest possible light, seeing that the Saviour said, 'All things whatsoever the Father hath are Mine ;' which shews that He is ever with the Father. For 'whatsoever He hath' shews that the Father wields the Lordship, while 'are Mine' shews the inseparable union. It is necessary, then, that we should perceive that in the Father reside Everlastingness, Eternity, Immortality. Now these reside in Him not as adventitious attributes, but, as it were, in a well-spring they reside in Him, and in the Son. When then you wish to perceive what relates to the Son, learn what is in the Father, for this is what you must believe to be in the Son. If then the Father is a thing created or made, these qualities belong also to the Son. And if it is permissible to say of the Father 'there was once a time when He was not,' or 'made of nothing,' let these words be applied also to the Son. But if it is impious to ascribe these attributes to the Father, grant that it is impious also to ascribe them to the Son. For what belongs to the Father, belongs to the Son. For he that honoureth the Son, honoureth the Father that sent Him, and he that receiveth the Son, receiveth the Father with Him, because he that hath seen the Son hath seen the Father (Matt. x. 40 ; John xiv. 9). As then the Father is not a creature, so neither is the Son ; and as it is not possible to say of Him 'there was

a time when He was not,' nor 'made of nothing,' so it is not proper to say the like of the Son either. But rather, as the Father's attributes are Everlastingness, Immortality, Eternity, and the being no creature, it follows that thus also we must think of the Son. For as it is written (Joh. v. 26), 'As the Father hath life in Himself, so gave He to the Son also to have life in Himself.' But He uses the word 'gave' in order to point to the Father who gives. As, again, life is in the Father, so also is it in the Son, so as to shew Him to be inseparable and everlasting. For this is why He speaks with exactness, 'whatsoever the Father hath,' in order namely that by thus mentioning Father He may avoid being thought to be the Father Himself. For He does not say 'I am the Father,' but 'whatsoever the Father hath.'

§ 5. *The same text further explained.*

For His Only-begotten Son might, ye Arians, be called 'Father' by His Father, yet not in the sense in which you in your error might perhaps understand it, but (while Son of the Father that begat Him) 'Father of the coming age' (Isa. ix. 6, LXX.). For it is necessary not to leave any of your surmises open to you. Well then, He says by the prophet, 'A Son is born and given to us, whose government is upon his shoulder, and his name shall be called Angel of Great Counsel, mighty God, Ruler, Father of the coming age' (Isa. ix. 6). The Only-begotten Son of God, then, is at once Father of the coming age, and mighty God, and Ruler. And it is shewn clearly that all things whatsoever the Father hath are His, and that as the Father gives life, the Son likewise is able to quicken whom He will. For 'the dead,' He says, 'shall hear the voice of the Son, and shall live' (cf. John v. 25), and the will and desire of Father and Son is one, since their nature also is one and indivisible. And the Arians torture themselves to no purpose, from not understanding the saying of our Saviour, 'All things whatsoever the Father hath are Mine.' For from this passage at once the delusion of Sabellius can be upset, and it will expose the folly of our modern Jews. For this is why the Only-begotten, having life in Himself as the Father has, also knows alone Who the Father is, namely, because He is in the Father and the Father in Him. For He is His Image, and consequently, because He is His Image, all that belongs to the Father is in Him. He is an exact seal, shewing in Himself the Father; living Word and true, Power, Wisdom, our Sanctification and Redemption (1 Cor. i. 30). For 'in Him we both live and move and have

---

[1] Cf. *Orat.* iii. 36.

our being' (Acts xvii. 28), and 'no man know-eth Who is the Father, save the Son, and Who is the Son, save the Father' (Luke x. 22).

§ 6. The Trisagion wrongly explained by Arians. Its true significance.

And how do the impious men venture to speak folly, as they ought not, being men and unable to find out how to describe even what is on the earth? But why do I say 'what is on the earth?' Let them tell us their own nature, if they can discover how to investigate their own nature? Rash they are indeed, and self-willed, not trembling to form opinions of things which angels desire to look into (1 Pet. i. 12), who are so far above them, both in nature and in rank. For what is nearer [God] than the Cherubim or the Seraphim? And yet they, not even seeing Him, nor standing on their feet, nor even with bare, but as it were with veiled faces, offer their praises, with untiring lips doing nought else but glorify the divine and ineffable nature with the Trisagion. And nowhere has any one of the divinely speaking prophets, men specially selected for such vision, reported to us that in the first utterance of the word Holy the voice is raised aloud, while in the second it is lower, but in the third, quite low,—and that consequently the first utterance denotes lordship, the second subordination, and the third marks a yet lower degree. But away with the folly of these haters of God and senseless men. For the Triad, praised, reverenced, and adored, is one and indivisible and without degrees (ἀσχημάτιστος). It is united without confusion, just as the Monad also is distinguished without separation. For the fact of those venerable living creatures (Isa. vi. ; Rev. iv. 8) offering their praises three times, saying 'Holy, Holy, Holy,' proves that the Three Subsistences[2] are perfect, just as in saying 'Lord,' they declare the One Essence. They then that depreciate the Only-begotten Son of God blaspheme God, defaming His perfection and accusing Him of imperfection, and render themselves liable to the severest chastisement. For he that blasphemes any one of the Subsistences shall have remission neither in this world nor in that which is to come. But God is able to open the eyes of their heart to contemplate the Sun of Righteousness, in order that coming to know Him whom they formerly set at nought, they may with unswerving piety of mind together with us glorify Him, because to Him belongs the kingdom, even to the Father Son and Holy Spirit, now and for ever. Amen.

---

[2] τρεῖς ὑποστάσεις. This expression is a link between this tract and the *Expositio* (§ 2), and is one of the indications it bears of an early date. At this time we see that Athanasius speaks of Three 'Hypostases,' but qualifies his language by the caveat (*Expos.* 2) that they are not μεμερισμέναι. In this he follows his Origenist predecessor Dionysius, and the language of the present passage is that of Basil or the Gregories. But it is not the language of Athan. himself in his later years. See above, Prolegg. ch. ii. § 3 (2) b, and Introd. to *Tom. ad Ant.* and to *Ad Afr.*

ENCYCLICAL EPISTLE

TO THE

BISHOPS THROUGHOUT THE WORLD

ATHANASIUS wrote the following Epistle in the year 339. In the winter at the beginning of that year the Eusebians held a Council at Antioch. Here they appointed Gregory to the see of Alexandria in the place of Athanasius (see Prolegg. ch. ii. § 6). 'Gregory was by birth a Cappadocian, and (if Nazianzen speaks of the same Gregory, which some critics doubt) studied at Alexandria, where S. Athanasius had treated him with great kindness and familiarity, though Gregory afterwards took part in propagating the calumny against him of having murdered Arsenius. Gregory was on his appointment dispatched to Alexandria' (Newman). The proceedings on his arrival, Lent, 339, are related in the following Encyclical Epistle, which Athanasius forwarded immediately before his departure for Rome to all the Bishops of the Catholic Church. 'It is less correct in style, as Tillemont observes, than other of his works, as if composed in haste. In the Editions previous to the Benedictine, it was called an "Epistle to the Orthodox everywhere;" but Montfaucon has been able to restore the true title. He has been also able from his MSS. to make a far more important correction, which has cleared up some very perplexing difficulties in the history. All the Editions previous to the Benedictine read "George" throughout for "Gregory," and "Gregory" in the place where "Pistus" occurs. Baronius, Tillemont, &c., had already made the alterations from the necessity of the case' (Newman). After comparing the violence done to the Church with the outrage upon the Levite's wife in Judges, ch. xix., he appeals to the bishops of the universal Church to regard his cause as their own (§ 1). He then recounts the details of what has happened; the announcement by the Prefect Philagrius of the supersession of Ath. by Gregory, the popular indignation, and its grounds (§ 2); the instigation of the heathen mob by Philagrius to commit outrages upon the sacred persons and buildings (§ 3); the violent intrusion of Gregory (§ 4); the proceedings against himself (§ 5). He warns them against Gregory as an Arian, and asks their sympathy for himself (§ 6), and that they will refuse to receive any of Gregory's letters (§ 7). The 'Encyclical' was written just before his departure from Alexandria, where he must have been in retirement for three weeks (Index to Festal Letter, 339) previously, as he appears (§ 5) to have remained in the town till after Easter-day. Dr. Bright (p. xv. note) sees here a proof of the inaccuracy of the 'Index:' but there are other grounds for regarding it as correct (see Prolegg. ch. v. § 3, c, and Introd. to Letters): its chronology is therefore adopted by the present editor. The events which led up to the scenes described in the letter are more fully dealt with in Prolegg. ch. ii. § 6 (1), sub fin. and (2). It may be added that Sozomen, iii. 6 in describing this escape of Athan., inserts the scene in the Church which really took place in Feb. 356, while Socrates ii. 11 confuses the two occasions even more completely. Internal evidence shews that Soz. partially corrected Socr. by the aid of the Hist. Aceph. The confusion of Gregory with George (especially easy in Latin), to which almost every historian from Socrates and Theodoret to Neander and Newman has fallen an occasional victim, appears to have vitiated the transcription of this encyclical from very early times. But Sievers (p. 104) goes too far in ascribing to that cause the insertion of a great part of §§ 3—5.

CIRCULAR LETTER

To his fellow-ministers in every place, beloved lords, Athanasius sends health in the Lord.

§ 1. *The whole Church affected by what has occurred.*

Our sufferings have been dreadful beyond endurance, and it is impossible to describe them in suitable terms; but in order that the dreadful nature of the events which have taken place may be more readily apprehended, I have thought it good to remind you of a history out of the Scriptures. It happened that a certain Levite[1] was injured in the person of his wife; and, when he considered the exceeding greatness of the pollution (for the woman was a Hebrew, and of the tribe of Judah), being astounded at the outrage which had been committed against him, he divided his wife's body, as the Holy Scripture relates in the Book of Judges, and sent a part of it to every tribe in Israel, in order that it might be understood that an injury like this pertained not to himself only, but extended to all alike; and that, if the people sympathised with him in his sufferings, they might avenge him; or if they neglected to do so, might bear the disgrace of being considered thenceforth as themselves guilty of the wrong. The messengers whom he sent related what had happened; and they that heard and saw it, declared that such things had never been done from the day that the children of Israel came up out of Egypt. So every tribe of Israel was moved, and all came together against the offenders, as though they had themselves been the sufferers; and at last the perpetrators of this iniquity were destroyed in war, and became a curse in the mouths of all: for the assembled people considered not their kindred blood, but regarded only the crime they had committed. You know the history, brethren, and the particular account of the circumstances given in Scripture. I will not therefore describe them more in detail, since I write to persons acquainted with them, and as I am anxious to represent to your piety our present circumstances, which are even worse than those to which I have referred. For my object in reminding you of this history is this, that you may compare those ancient transactions with what has happened to us now, and perceiving how much these last exceed the other in cruelty, may be filled with greater indignation on account of them, than were the people of old against those offenders. For the treatment we have undergone surpasses the bitterness of any persecution; and the calamity of the Levite was but small, when compared with the enormities which have now been committed against the Church; or rather such deeds as these were never before heard of in the whole world, or the like experienced by any one. For in that case it was but a single woman that was injured, and one Levite who suffered wrong; now the whole Church is injured, the priesthood insulted, and worst of all, piety[2] is persecuted by impiety. On that occasion the tribes were astounded, each at the sight of part of the body of one woman; but now the members of the whole Church are seen divided from one another, and are sent abroad some to you, and some to others, bringing word of the insults and injustice which they have suffered. Be ye therefore also moved, I beseech you, considering that these wrongs are done unto you no less than unto us; and let every one lend his aid, as feeling that he is himself a sufferer, lest shortly ecclesiastical Canons, and the faith of the Church be corrupted. For both are in danger, unless God shall speedily by your hands amend what has been done amiss, and the Church be avenged on her enemies. For our Canons[3] and our forms were not given to the Churches at the present day, but were wisely and safely transmitted to us from our forefathers. Neither had our faith its beginning at this time, but

---

[1] Judg. xix 29.

[2] εὐσέβεια, orthodoxy, see *de Decr.* 1, note.
[3] Vid. Beveridg. *Cod. Can. Illustr.* i. 3. § 2. who comments ot this passage at length. Allusion is also made to the Canons in *Apol. contr. Arian.* § 69

it came down to us from the Lord through His disciples [4]. That therefore the ordinances which have been preserved in the Churches from old time until now, may not be lost in our days, and the trust which has been committed to us required at our hands; rouse yourselves, brethren, as being stewards of the mysteries of God [5], and seeing them now seized upon by others. Further particulars of our condition you will learn from the bearers of our letters; but I was anxious myself to write you a brief account thereof, that you may know for certain, that such things have never before been committed against the Church, from the day that our Saviour when He was taken up, gave command to His disciples, saying, 'Go ye and make disciples of all nations, baptizing them in the name of the Father, and of the Son, and of the Holy Ghost [6].'

§ 2. *Violent and uncanonical intrusion of Gregory.*

Now the outrages which have been committed against us and against the Church are these. While we were holding our assemblies in peace, as usual, and while the people were rejoicing in them, and advancing in godly conversation, and while our fellow-ministers in Egypt, and the Thebais, and Libya, were in love and peace both with one another and with us; on a sudden the Prefect of Egypt puts forth a public letter, bearing the form of an edict, and declaring that one Gregory from Cappadocia was coming to be my successor from the court. This announcement confounded every one, for such a proceeding was entirely novel, and now heard of for the first time. The people however assembled still more constantly in the churches [7], for they very well knew that neither they themselves, nor any Bishop or Presbyter, nor in short any one had ever complained against me; and they saw that Arians only were on his side, and were aware also that he was himself an Arian, and was sent by Eusebius and his fellows to the Arian party. For you know, brethren, that Eusebius and his fellows have always been the supporters and associates of the impious heresy of the Arian madmen [8], by whose means they have ever carried on their designs against me, and were the authors of my banishment into Gaul.

The people, therefore, were justly indignant and exclaimed against the proceeding, calling the rest of the magistrates and the whole city to witness, that this novel and iniquitous attempt was now made against the Church, not on the ground of any charge brought against me by ecclesiastical persons, but through the wanton assault of the Arian heretics. For even if there had been any complaint generally prevailing against me, it was not an Arian, or one professing Arian doctrines, that ought to have been chosen to supersede me; but according to the ecclesiastical Canons, and the direction of Paul, when the people were 'gathered together, and the spirit' of them that ordain, 'with the power of our Lord Jesus Christ [9]' all things ought to have been enquired into and transacted canonically, in the presence of those among the laity and clergy who demanded the change; and not that a person brought from a distance by Arians, as if making a traffic of the title of Bishop, should with the patronage and strong arm of heathen magistrates, thrust himself upon those who neither asked for nor desired his presence, nor indeed knew anything of what had been done. Such proceedings tend to the dissolution of all the ecclesiastical Canons, and compel the heathen to blaspheme, and to suspect that our appointments are not made according to a divine rule, but as a result of traffic and patronage [1].

§ 3. *Outrages which took place at the time of Gregory's arrival.*

Thus was this notable appointment of Gregory brought about by the Arians, and such was the beginning of it. And what outrages he committed on his entry into Alexandria, and of what great evils that event has been the cause, you may learn both from our letters, and by enquiry of those who are sojourning among you. While the people were offended at such an unusual proceeding, and in consequence assembled in the churches, in order to prevent the impiety of the Arians from mingling itself with the faith of the Church, Philagrius, who has long been a persecutor of the Church and her virgins, and is now Prefect [2] of Egypt, an apostate already, and a fellow-countryman of Gregory, a man too of no respectable character, and moreover supported by Eusebius and his fellows, and

---

4 Vid. *de Syn.* § 4. *Orat.* i. § 8. Tertull. *Præscr. Hær.* § 29.
5 1 Cor. iv. 1.　　　　　　6 Matt. xxviii. 19.
7 Assembling in the Churches seems to have been a sort of protest or demonstration, sometimes peaceably, but sometimes in a more exceptionable manner:—peaceably, during Justina's persecution at Milan, Ambros. Ep. i. 20. August. *Confess.* ix. 15, but at Ephesus after the third Ecumenical Council the Metropolitan shut up the Churches, took possession of the Cathedral, and succeeded in repelling the imperial troops. Churches were asylums, vid. Cod. Theodos. ix. 45: § 4. &c.; at the same time arms were prohibited.
8 ἀρειομανιτῶν, vid. note on *de Syn.* 13.

9 1 Cor. v. 4.　　　　　　1 *Orat.* i. 8, note.
2 The Prefect of Egypt was called [after 367, see Sievers, p. 119, and Prolegg. ch. v. Appendix, yet see *Apol. Ar.* § 83] Augustalis as having been first appointed by Augustus, after his victories over Antony. He was of the Equestrian, not, as other Prefects, of the Senatorian order. He was the imperial officer, as answering to Propraetors in the Imperial Provinces. vid. Hofman. in voc. [on Philagrius, see *Apol. c. Ari.* § 72, Prolegg. ch. ii. § 5 (1) note].

therefore full of zeal against the Church ; this person, by means of promises which he afterwards fulfilled, succeeded in gaining over the heathen multitude, with the Jews and disorderly persons, and having excited their passions, sent them in a body with swords and clubs into the churches to attack the people.

What followed upon this [3] it is by no means easy to describe : indeed it is not possible to set before you a just representation of the circumstances, nor even could one recount a small part of them without tears and lamentations. Have such deeds as these ever been made the subjects of tragedy among the ancients? or has the like ever happened before in time of persecution or of war? The church and the holy Baptistery were set on fire, and straightway groans, shrieks, and lamentations, were heard through the city ; while the citizens in their indignation at these enormities, cried shame upon the governor, and protested against the violence used to them. For holy and undefiled virgins [4] were being stripped naked, and suffering treatment which is not to be named, and if they resisted, they were in danger of their lives. Monks were being trampled under foot and perishing ; some were being hurled headlong ; others were being destroyed with swords and clubs ; others were being wounded and beaten. And oh ! what deeds of impiety and iniquity have been committed upon the Holy Table ! They were offering birds and pine cones [5] in sacrifice, singing the praises of their idols, and blaspheming even in the very churches our Lord and Saviour Jesus Christ, the Son of the living God. They were burning the books of Holy Scripture which they found in the church ; and the Jews, the murderers of our Lord, and the godless heathen entering irreverently (O strange boldness !) the holy Baptistery, were stripping themselves naked, and acting such a disgraceful part, both by word and deed, as one is ashamed even to relate. Certain impious men also, following the examples set them in the bitterest persecutions, were seizing upon the virgins and ascetics by the hands and dragging them along, and as they were haling them, endeavoured to make them blaspheme and deny the Lord ; and when they refused to do so, were beating them violently and trampling them under foot.

§ 4. *Outrages on Good Friday and Easter-day*, 339.

In addition to all this, after such a notable

and illustrious entry into the city, the Arian Gregory, taking pleasure in these calamities, and as if desirous to secure to the heathens and Jews, and those who had wrought these evils upon us, a prize and price of their iniquitous success, gave up the church to be plundered by them. Upon this licence of iniquity and disorder, their deeds were worse than in time of war, and more cruel than those of robbers. Some of them were plundering whatever fell in their way ; others dividing among themselves the sums which some had laid up there [6] ; the wine, of which there was a large quantity, they either drank or emptied out or carried away ; they plundered the store of oil, and every one took as his spoil the doors and chancel rails ; the candlesticks they forthwith laid aside in the wall [7], and lighted the candles of the Church before their idols : in a word, rapine and death pervaded the Church. And the impious Arians, so far from feeling shame that such things should be done, added yet further outrages and cruelty. Presbyters and laymen had their flesh torn, virgins were stript of their veils [7a], and led away to the tribunal of the governor, and then cast into prison ; others had their goods confiscated, and were scourged ; the bread of the ministers and virgins was intercepted. And these things were done even during the holy season of Lent [8], about the time of Easter ; a time when the brethren were keeping fast, while this notable Gregory exhibited the disposition of a Caiaphas, and, together with Pilate the Governor, furiously raged against the pious worshippers of Christ. Going into one of the churches on the Preparation [9], in company with the Governor and the heathen multitude, when he saw that the people regarded with abhorrence his forcible entry among them, he caused that most cruel person, the Governor, publicly to scourge in one hour, four and thirty virgins and married women, and men of rank, and to cast them into prison. Among them there was one virgin, who, being fond of study, had the Psalter in her hands, at the time when he caused her to be publicly scourged : the book was torn in pieces by the officers, and the virgin herself shut up in prison.

---

3 Cf. *Hist. Ar.* §§ 9 and 10. Apparently the great Church of 'Theonas' is meant, see *Fest. Index* xi.

4 The sister of S. Antony was one of the earliest known inmates of a nunnery, *vit. Ant.* § 2. 3. They were called by the Catholic Church by the title, "Spouse of Christ." *Apol. ad Const.* § 33.

5 The θύος or suffitus of Grecian sacrifices generally consisted of portions of odoriferous trees. vid. Potter. *Antiqu.* ii. 4. Some translate the word here used (στροβίλους), "shell-fish."

6 Churches, as heathen temples before them, were used for deposits. At the sack of Rome, Alaric spared the Churches and their possessions ; nay, he himself transported the costly vessels of St. Peter into his Church.

7 ἐν τῷ τοιχίῳ. [Reference uncertain.]

7a ἀπομαφορίζόμεναι ; see Sophocles' *Lexicon* under μαφόριον.

8 Lent and Passion Week was the season during which Justina's persecution of St. Ambrose took place, and the proceedings against St. Chrysostom at Constantinople. On the Paschal Vigils, vid. Tertull. *ad Uxor.* ii. 4. [*Ante-Nicene Fathers*, vol. iv. p. 46] p. 426, note n. Oxf. Tr.

9 παρασκευή, i.e., Good Friday. [Apr. 13, 339,] The word was used for Friday generally as early as S. Clem. Alex. *Strom.* vii. p. 877. ed. Pott. vid. Constit. Apostol. v. 13 Pseudo-Ign. *ad Philipp.* 13.

§ 5. *Retirement of Athanasius, and tyranny of Gregory and Philagrius.*

When all this was done, they did not stop even here ; but consulted how they might act the same part in the other church [1], where I was mostly living during those days ; and they were eager to extend their fury to this church also, in order that they might hunt out and dispatch me. And this would have been my fate, had not the grace of Christ assisted me, if it were only that I might escape to relate these few particulars concerning their conduct. For seeing that they were exceedingly mad against me, and being anxious that the church should not be injured, nor the virgins that were in it suffer, nor additional murders be committed, nor the people again outraged, I withdrew myself from among them, remembering the words of our Saviour, ' If they persecute you in this city, flee ye into another [2].' For I knew, from the evil they had done against the first-named church, that they would forbear no outrage against the other also. And there in fact they reverenced not even the Lord's day [3] of the holy Feast, but in that church also they imprisoned the persons who belonged to it, at a time when the Lord delivered all from the bonds of death, whereas Gregory and his associates, as if fighting against our Saviour, and depending upon the patronage of the Governor, have turned into mourning this day of liberty to the servants of Christ. The heathens were rejoicing to do this, for they abhor that day ; and Gregory perhaps did but fulfil the commands of Eusebius and his fellows in forcing the Christians to mourn under the infliction of bonds.

With these acts of violence has the Governor seized upon the churches, and has given them up to Gregory and the Arian madmen. Thus, those persons who were excommunicated by us for their impiety, now glory in the plunder of our churches ; while the people of God, and the Clergy of the Catholic Church are compelled either to have communion with the impiety of the Arian heretics, or else to forbear entering into them. Moreover, by means of the Governor, Gregory has exercised no small violence towards the captains of ships and others who pass over sea, torturing and scourging some, putting others in bonds, and casting them into prison, in order to oblige them not to resist his iniquities, and to take letters [4] from him. And not satisfied with all this, that he may glut himself with our blood, he has caused his savage associate, the Governor, to prefer an indictment against me, as in the name of the people, before the most religious Emperor Constantius, which contains odious charges, from which one may expect not only to be banished, but even ten thousand deaths. The person who drew it up is an apostate from Christianity, and a shameless worshipper of idols, and they who subscribed it are heathens, and keepers of idol temples, and others of them Arians. In short, not to make my letter tedious to you, a persecution rages here, and such a persecution as was never before raised against the Church. For in former instances a man at least might pray while he fled from his persecutors, and be baptized while he lay in concealment. But now their extreme cruelty has imitated the godless conduct of the Babylonians. For as they falsely accused Daniel [5], so does the notable Gregory now accuse before the Governor those who pray in their houses, and watches every opportunity to insult their ministers, so that through his violent conduct, many are endangered from missing baptism, and many who are in sickness and sorrow have no one to visit them, a calamity which they bitterly lament, accounting it worse than their sickness. For while the ministers of the Church are under persecution, the people who condemn the impiety of the Arian heretics choose rather thus to be sick and to run the risk, than that a hand of the Arians should come upon their heads.

§ 6. *All the above illegalities were carried or in the interest of Arianism.*

Gregory then is an Arian, and has been sent to the Arian party ; for none demanded him, but they only ; and accordingly as a hireling and a stranger, he makes use of the Governor to inflict these dreadful and cruel deeds upon the people of the Catholic Churches, as not being his own. For since Pistus, whom Eusebius and his fellows formerly appointed over the Arians, was justly anathematized [6] and excommunicated for his impiety by you the Bishops of the Catholic Church, as you all know, on our writing to you concerning him, they have now, therefore, in like manner sent this Gregory to them ; and lest they should a second time be put to shame, by our again writing against them, they have employed extraneous force against me, in order that, having obtained possession of the Churches, they may seem to have escaped all suspicion of being Arians. But in this too they have been mistaken, for none of the people of the Church are with them, except the heretics

---

[1] [On the difficulties of this part of the history, see Prolegg. ch. ii. § 6 (1) ad fin., and ch. v. § 3, c. It must be noted that according to the following passage Ath. had left the 'other church' before Easter Day. It was probably that of 'Quirinus,' *Hist. Ar.* 10.]   [2] Cf. *Ap. Fug.* 11, and Matt. x. 23.
[3] Easter Day [Apr. 15].   [4] i.e. letters of communion.

[5] Dan. vi. 13.   [6] *Apol. c. Ar.* §§ 19, 24.

only, and those who have been excommunicated on divers charges, and such as have been compelled by the Governor to dissemble. This then is the drama of Eusebius and his fellows, which they have long been rehearsing and composing; and now have succeeded in performing through the false charges which they have made against me before the Emperor[7]. Notwithstanding, they are not yet content to be quiet, but even now seek to kill me; and they make themselves so formidable to our friends, that they are all driven into banishment, and expect death at their hands. But you must not for this stand in awe of their iniquity, but on the contrary avenge: and shew your indignation at this their unprecedented conduct against us. For if when one member suffers all the members suffer with it, and, according to the blessed Apostle, we ought to weep with them that weep[8], let every one, now that so great a Church as this is suffering, avenge its wrongs, as though he were himself a sufferer. For we have a common Saviour, who is blasphemed by them, and Canons belonging to us all, which they are transgressing. If while any of you had been sitting in your Church, and while the people were assembled with you, without any blame, some one had suddenly come under plea of an edict as successor of one of you, and had acted the same part towards you, would you not have been indignant? would you not have demanded to be righted? If so, then it is right that you should be indignant now, lest if these things be passed over unnoticed, the same mischief shall by degrees extend itself to every Church, and so our schools of religion be turned into a market-house and an exchange.

§ 7. *Appeal to the bishops of the whole Church to unite against Gregory.*

You are acquainted with the history of the Arian madmen, beloved, for you have often, both individually and in a body, condemned their impiety; and you know also that Eusebius and his fellows, as I said before, are engaged in the same heresy; for the sake of which they have long been carrying on a conspiracy against me. And I have represented to you, what has now been done, both for them and by them, with greater cruelty than is usual even in time of war, in order that after the example set before you in the history which I related at the beginning, you may entertain a zealous hatred of their wickedness, and reject those who have committed such enormities against the Church. If the brethren at Rome[9] [last

year], before these things had happened, and on account of their former misdeeds, wrote letters to call a Council, that these evils might be set right (fearing which, Eusebius and his fellows took care previously to throw the Church into confusion, and desired to destroy me, in order that they might thenceforth be able to act as they pleased without fear, and might have no one to call them to account), how much more ought you now to be indignant at these outrages, and to condemn them, seeing they have added this to their former misconduct.

I beseech you, overlook not such proceedings, nor suffer the famous Church of the Alexandrians to be trodden down by heretics. In consequence of these things the people and their ministers are separated from one another, as one might expect, silenced by the violence of the Prefect, yet abhorring the impiety of the Arian madmen. If therefore Gregory shall write unto you, or any other in his behalf, receive not his letters, brethren, but tear them in pieces and put the bearers of them to shame, as the ministers of impiety and wickedness. And even if he presume to write to you after a friendly fashion, nevertheless receive them not. Those who bring his letters convey them only from fear of the Governor, and on account of his frequent acts of violence. And since it is probable that Eusebius and his fellows will write to you concerning him, I was anxious to admonish you beforehand, so that you may herein imitate God, Who is no respecter of persons, and may drive out from before you those that come from them; because for the sake of the Arian madmen they caused persecutions, rape of virgins, murders, plunder of the Church's property, burnings, and blasphemies in the Churches, to be committed by the heathens and Jews at such a season. The impious and mad Gregory cannot deny that he is an Arian, being proved to be so by the person who writes his letters. This is his secretary Ammon, who was cast out of the Church long ago by my predecessor the blessed Alexander for many misdeeds and for impiety.

For all these reasons, therefore, vouchsafe to send me a reply, and condemn these impious men; so that even now the ministers and people of this place, seeing your orthodoxy and hatred of wickedness, may rejoice in your concord in the Christian faith, and that those who have been guilty of these lawless deeds against the Church may be reformed by your letters, and brought at last, though late, to repentance. Salute the brotherhood that is among you. All the brethren that are with me salute you. Fare ye well, and remember me, and the Lord preserve you continually, most truly beloved lords.

---

[7] *Apol. c. Ar.* 3.   [8] 1 Cor. xii. 26; Rom. xii. 15.
[9] *Apol. Ar.* 22, 30, *Hist. Ar.* 9. [The word πέρυσιν, 'last year,' is absent from the best MS. used by Montfaucon.']

APOLOGIA CONTRA ARIANOS

"This Apology," says Montfaucon, "is the most authentic source of the history of the Church in the first half of the fourth century. Athanasius is far superior to any other historians of the period, both from his bearing for the most part a personal testimony to the facts he relates, and from his great accuracy and use of actual documents. On the other hand, Rufinus, Socrates, Sozomen, Theodoret, must not be used without extreme caution, unless they adduce documents, which is seldom the case." The 'Apology' is a personal defence by Athanasius against the charges laid against him by the Eusebian party, and does not directly concern matters of doctrine. After the Council of Nicæa, the Eusebian policy had been to oust the principal opponents from their sees on personal grounds, so as to pave the way for the abrogation of the Nicene formula. The attack upon Athanasius began in 331, but without success. It was renewed at Cæsarea and Tyre in 334—335, and resulted in the exile of Athanasius to Treveri, 336. His return in 337 was followed by a Synod at Antioch which 'deposed' him (close of 338), and by his expulsion in favour of Gregory (339). Then follow the intervention of Julius (339—340), and the Council of Sardica (343), which resulted in the eventual return of Athanasius in the autumn of 346. (The details are given more fully in the Prolegomena, ch. ii. §§ 4—6). After this latter date, and before the relapse of Valens and Ursacius which followed upon the death of Constans, Athanasius drew up a collection of documents in proof of his innocence, connecting them together by an explanatory narrative. (1) *The charges against him* related to events alleged to have occurred before the year 332 (extortion of money, subvention of the rebel Philumenus, the chalice of Ischyras, murder and mutilation of the bishop Arsenius): the principal evidence as to their falsehood was comprised in the proceedings of the Councils of Tyre and Jerusalem, and of the commission of enquiry sent by the assembled bishops to the Mareotis. (2) *The judicial investigations* which proved the innocence of Athanasius took place first at Rome under Julius, secondly at Sardica under Hosius; and were followed by the recognition of his innocence on the part of the Emperor Constantius, of bishops in various parts of the world, and lastly of some of his chief accusers.

The method of defence now adopted by Athanasius was *firstly* to show how complete that recognition had been: this he does by a series of documents from the eve of his departure to Rome down to the recantation of Ursacius and Valens soon after his return to Alexandria: these documents cover eight years (339—347) previous to the composition of the Apology (§§ 1—58). Having shewn the completeness of his acquittal, he next gives the evidence upon which it was based. Accordingly the *second part* (§§ 59—90) of the Apology deals with facts and documents earlier than those comprised in the first. Hence the inversion of chronological sequence (*praeposterus ordo*, Montf.) as between the two parts.

Referring the reader to the Prolegomena for a connected view of the history of which this Apology is the primary source, it will suffice for our present purpose to enumerate the documents quoted, with the briefest possible statement of their contents and bearing upon the general purpose of the work. It should be noted that while in the first part the documents follow one another in strict chronological order, those of the second part fall into groups *within which* the matters are arranged as best suits the argument, and not in order of time. In the following list the probable or approximate date of each document is given.

A. DOCUMENTS IN THE FIRST PART (general subject, the vindication of Athanasius before the bishops of the Christian world).

(i.) DOCUMENTS PRIOR TO THE COUNCIL OF SARDICA (§§ 1—35).

1. §§ 3—19 (end of 338 or beginning of 339). *Circular of Egyptian bishops* reciting the election of Athanasius, the plots and charges against him, the history of the Mareotic Commission, the testimony available in his defence, and requesting all bishops to join in vindicating him.

2. §§ 20—35 (340 A.D.). *Letter of Julius* to the Eusebian bishops (at the request of a Roman Council) remonstrating with their discourteous reply to a former letter, reciting the history of the intrigues against Athanasius, pressing them with their disrespect to the Synod of Nicæa, with their evasion of the invitation to the Council at Rome, vindicating Athanasius (on the ground of documentary proof of his innocence, and on that of the irregularity of the proceedings against him) and Marcellus (upon his own statement of belief), lastly, insisting on the propriety of a reference of the questions at issue to the whole Church, and upon the precedent giving the Roman Church a decisive voice in questions affecting that of Alexandria.

(ii.) COUNCIL OF SARDICA (§§ 36—50).

3. §§ 36—40 (A.D. 343) *Letter of the Council to the Church of Alexandria*, reciting the intrigues against Athanasius, and the confirmation by the council of his acquittal by Julius, encouraging the Alexandrine Church to patience, and announcing that they have requested the Emperors to give effect to their decisions.

4. §§ 41—43 (same date). *Letter of the Council to the bishops of Egypt and Libya*: identical with No. 3, except that it omits the reference to certain presbyters of Alexandria, and mentions several Arian leaders by name.

5. §§ 44—50 (same date). *Circular letter of the Council*, reciting the occasion of its assembling, the behaviour of the Eastern bishops, the violence inflicted by them upon orthodox bishops, the breakdown of the charges brought by them against Athanasius, and the purgation of Marcellus and Asclepas, who are pronounced innocent, while the Arian leaders are deposed and anathematised. The signatures follow of over 280 bishops, most of whom signed afterwards while the letter was in circulation.

(iii.) DOCUMENTS FORMING A SEQUEL TO THE COUNCIL OF SARDICA (§§ 51—58).

6—8. § 51. *Letters of Constantius to Athanasius* before and after death of Gregory.

6 (A.D. 345). Expressing sympathy with his sufferings, and inviting him to court; he has written to Constans to ask him to allow Athanasius to return.

7 (same year, later). Urging the same invitation.

8 (346, winter, or early spring). A similar summons, but more pressing.

9. § 52 (same year). *Letter of Julius to the Church of Alexandria*, eulogising Athanasius, complimenting them for their constancy, and congratulating them upon his return.

10. § 54 (same year). *Circular letter of Constantius to the Church at large*, announcing the restoration of Athanasius and the cassation of all decrees against him, with indemnity to all in his communion.

11. § 55 (same date). *Letter of Constantius to the Church of Alexandria*. Announcement of the restoration of Athanasius, with exhortation to peace, and warning against disturbances.

12. § 56 (same date). *To the Prefect of Egypt and other officials*. Revocation of decrees against those in communion with Athanasius, and restoration of their immunities.

13. § 57 (same year, autumn). *Letter of the bishops of Palestine to the Egyptian Church* congratulating them on the restoration of Athanasius.

14. § 58 (A.D. 347). *Letter of Valens and Ursacius to Julius* unreservedly withdrawing their allegations against Athanasius, anathematizing Arius and his heresy, and at the same time promising to take the consequences of their offence if required by Julius to do so.

15. ib. (same year). *Letter of the same to Athanasius*, with a greeting and assurance that they are in communion with him and with the Church.

B. DOCUMENTS IN THE SECOND PART.

(i.) LETTERS OF CONSTANTINE PREVIOUS TO THE COUNCIL OF TYRE (§§ 59—63).

16. § 59 (A.D. 331). *A fragment*, urging Athanasius with threats to admit to communion all (Arians) who wish it.

17. § 61 (same year). *Letter to the people of Alexandria*, remonstrating with them for their dissensions and stigmatising the calumnies against Athanasius (about the affair of Philumenus).

(ii.) **18.** § 64 (332). *Confession of Ischyras*, that he had been compelled by the violence of certain Meletians to fabricate false charges against Athanasius.

(iii.) THE AFFAIR OF ARSENIUS (§§ 65—70).

19. § 67 (probably 332). *Intercepted letter of the presbyter Pinnes to John Arcaph*, warning him of the discovery of the plot, and begging him to drop the matter.

20. § 68 (same year). *Letter of Constantine to Athanasius*, expressing indignation at the charges concerning Arsenius and Ischyras, and bidding him publish this letter in vindication of himself.

21. § 66 (same year). *Letter of Alexander, Bishop of Thessalonica*, praising Serapion, the son of an old friend, and congratulating Athanasius on the exposure of the plot about Arsenius.

22. § 69 (same year). *Letter of Arsenius to Athanasius*, offering submission and requesting communion with the Church.

23. § 70 (same year). *Letter of Constantine to John Arcaph* accepting his reconciliation to Athanasius, and summoning him to court.

(iv.) PROCEEDINGS AT TYRE IN 335 (§§ 71—83).

24. § 77. *Address to the Council by the Egyptian Bishops*, complaining of the presence of partizan judges, of the rejection of their evidence, and of the proposed constitution of the Mareotic Commission.

25. § 71. (Written A.D. 327, but put in as evidence at Tyre by Athanasius in the matter of Ischyras, after the exposure of the plot concerning Arsenius). *List of Meletian Bishops and Clergy* presented to Alexander of Alexandria shortly before his death, and *not containing the name of Ischyras*.

26. § 78. *Protest addressed by the Egptian Bishops to Count Dionysius*, repeating the above complaints (in No. 24), and requesting him to stop the irregularities.

27. § 80. *Alexander of Thessalonica to Dionysius*, warning him of the conspiracy against Athanasius, and of the character of the Mission to the Mareotis.

28. § 81. *Letter of Dionysius to the Council*, strongly remonstrating against their proceedings.

29. § 79. *Letter of the Egyptian Bishops to Dionysius appealing to the Emperor*.

30—32. *Protests made by Egyptian Clergy against the proceedings of the* MAREOTIC COMMISSION.

30. § 73. *Clergy of Alexandria to the Commissioners*, protesting against the exclusion of all independent persons from the proceedings.

31. §§ 74, 75. *Clergy of the Mareotis to the Council*, giving an account of the facts concerning Ischyras, and of the *ex-parte* character of the proceedings of the Commission.

32. § 76. *The same to the Prefect and other officials of Egypt* (dated Sep. 8, 335), denying upon oath the tale of Ischyras, and requesting them to forward their statement to the Emperor.

(v.) DOCUMENTS SUBSEQUENT TO THE COUNCIL OF TYRE (§§ 84—88).

33. § 86 (335). *Constantine to the Bishops assembled at Tyre*, summoning them to give an account of their proceedings.

34. § 84. *The Council of Jerusalem to the Church of Alexandria*, announcing that Arius has been received to communion.

35. § 87 (June 17, 337). *Constantine II. to the Church of Alexandria* (upon the death of Constantine, whose purpose he claims to be carrying out), announcing the restoration of Athanasius.

36. § 85 (perhaps in 337, but possibly as early as 335). *Order by Flavius Hemerius* for the erection of a church for Ischyras.

The two concluding sections (89, 90) of the Apology are a postscript added during the troubles under Constantius (about 358, see Introd. to *Hist. Ar.*). He points to the sufferings which many bishops, including Hosius and Liberius, had endured rather than surrender his cause, as fresh evidence of their belief in his innocence. He refuses to see any detraction from the force of this argument in the fall of the two bishops mentioned.

The importance to the historian of this collection of documents need not be dwelt upon. If the charges in dispute seem trivial and even grotesque, they none the less illustrate the temper of the parties concerned, and the character of the controversy during the very important twenty years which end with the death of Constans and the reign of Constantius over the undivided Empire.

DEFENCE AGAINST THE ARIANS

INTRODUCTION.

1. I supposed that, after so many proofs of my innocence had been given, my enemies would have shrunk from further enquiry, and would now have condemned themselves for their false accusations of others. But as they are not yet abashed, though they have been so clearly convicted, but, as insensible to shame, persist in their slanderous reports against me, professing to think that the whole matter ought to be tried over again (not that they may have judgment passed on them, for that they avoid, but in order to harass me, and to disturb the minds of the simple); I therefore thought it necessary to make my defence unto you, that you may listen to their murmurings no longer, but may denounce their wickedness and base calumnies. And it is only to you, who are men of sincere minds, that I offer a defence: as for the contentious, I appeal confidently to the decisive proofs which I have against them. For my cause needs no further judgment; for judgment has already been given, and not once or twice only, but many times. First of all, it was tried in my own country in an assembly of nearly one hundred of its Bishops [10]; a second time at Rome, when, in consequence of letters from Eusebius, both they and we were summoned, and more than fifty Bishops met [11]; and a third time in the great Council assembled at Sardica by order of the most religious Emperors Constantius and Constans, when my enemies were degraded as false accusers, and the sentence that was passed in my favour received the suffrages of more than three hundred Bishops, out of the provinces of Egypt, Libya, and Pentapolis, Palestine, Arabia, Isauria, Cyprus, Pamphylia, Lycia, Galatia, Dacia, Moesia, Thrace, Dardania, Macedonia, Epirus, Thessaly, Achaia, Crete, Dalmatia, Siscia, Pannonia, Noricum, Italy, Picenum, Tuscany, Campania, Calabria, Apulia, Bruttia, Sicily, the whole of Africa, Sardinia, Spain, Gaul, and Britain.

Added to these was the testimony [1] of Ursacius and Valens, who had formerly calumniated me, but afterwards changed their minds, and not only gave their assent to the sentence that was passed in my favour, but also confessed that they themselves and the rest of my enemies were false accusers; for men who make such a change and such a recantation of course reflect upon Eusebius and his fellows, for with them they had contrived the plot against me. Now after a matter has been examined and decided on such clear evidence by so many eminent Bishops, every one will confess that further discussion is unnecessary; else, if an investigation be instituted at this time, it may be again discussed and again investigated, and there will be no end to such trifling.

2. Now the decision of so many Bishops was sufficient to confound those who would still fain pretend some charge against me. But when my enemies also bear testimony in my favour and against themselves, declaring that the proceedings against me were a conspiracy, who is there that would not be ashamed to doubt any longer? The law requires that in the mouth of two or three witnesses [2] judgments shall be settled, and we have here this great multitude of witnesses in my favour, with the addition of the proofs afforded by my enemies; so much so that those who still continue opposed to me no longer attach any importance to their own arbitrary [3] judgment, but now have recourse to violence, and in the place of fair reasoning seek to injure [4] those by whom they were

---

[10] The Council of Sardica says eighty; which is a usual number in Egyptian Councils. (vid. Tillemont, vol. 8. p. 74.) There were about ninety Bishops in Egypt, the Thebais, and Libya. The present Council was held [at the end of 338 or possibly at the beginning of 339]. Its synodal Epistle is contained below, § 3, and is particularly addressed to Pope Julius, § 20.

[11] This was held in 340. Julius's Letter is found below, § 21.

[1] Vid. infr. § 58. This was A.D. 347.

[2] Deut. xvii. 6.

[3] ὡς ἠθέλησαν. vid. infr. § 14. de Decr. § 3. de Syn. § 13. Ep. Æg. § 5.

[4] This implies that Valens and Ursacius were subjected to some kind of persecution, which is natural [most improbable]. They relapsed in 351, when Constantius on the death of Constans came into possession of his brother's dominions; and professed to have been forced to their former recantation by the latter Emperor.

exposed. For this is the chief cause of vexation to them, that the measures they carried on in secret, contrived by themselves in a corner, have been brought to light and disclosed by Valens and Ursacius; for they are well aware that their recantation while it clears those whom they have injured, condemns themselves.

Indeed this led to their degradation in the Council of Sardica, as mentioned before; and with good reason; for, as the Pharisees of old, when they undertook the defence of Paul [5], fully exposed the conspiracy which they and the Jews had formed against him; and as the blessed David was proved to be persecuted unjustly when the persecutor confessed, 'I have sinned, my son David [6];' so it was with these men; being overcome by the truth they made a request, and delivered it in writing to Julius, Bishop of Rome. They wrote also to me requesting to be on terms of peace with me, though they have spread such reports concerning me; and probably even now they are covered with shame, on seeing that those whom they sought to destroy by the grace of the Lord are still alive. Consistently also with this conduct they anathematized Arius and his heresy; for knowing that Eusebius and his fellows had conspired against me in behalf of their own misbelief, and of nothing else, as soon as they had determined to confess their calumnies against me, they immediately renounced also that antichristian heresy for the sake of which they had falsely asserted them.

The following are the letters written in my favour by the Bishops in the several Councils; and first the letter of the Egyptian Bishops.

Encyclical Letter of the Council of Egypt.

The holy Council assembled at Alexandria, out of Egypt, the Thebais, Libya, and Pentapolis, to the Bishops of the Catholic Church everywhere, brethren beloved and greatly longed for in the Lord, greeting.

3. Dearly beloved brethren, we might have put forth a defence of our brother Athanasius, as respects the conspiracy of Eusebius and his fellows against him, and complained of his sufferings at their hands, and have exposed all their false charges, either at the beginning of their conspiracy or upon his arrival at Alexandria. But circumstances did not permit it then, as you also know; and lately, after the return of the Bishop Athanasius, we thought that they would be confounded and covered with shame at their manifest injustice: in consequence we prevailed with ourselves to remain silent. Since, however, after all his severe sufferings, after his retirement into Gaul, after his sojourn in a foreign and far distant country in the place of his own, after his narrow escape from death through their calumnies, but thanks to the clemency of the Emperor,—distress which would have satisfied even the most cruel enemy,—they are still insensible to shame, are again acting insolently against the Church and Athanasius; and from indignation at his deliverance venture on still more atrocious schemes against him, and are ready with an accusation, fearless of the words in holy Scripture [7], 'A false witness shall not be unpunished;' and, 'The mouth that belieth slayeth the soul;' we therefore are unable longer to hold our peace, being amazed at their wickedness and at the insatiable love of contention displayed in their intrigues.

For see, they cease not to disturb the ear of royalty with fresh reports against us; they cease not to write letters of deadly import, for the destruction of the Bishop who is the enemy of their impiety. For again have they written to the Emperors against him; again they wish to conspire against him, charging him with a butchery which has never taken place; again they wish to shed his blood, accusing him of a murder that never was committed (for at that former time would they have murdered him by their calumnies, had we not had a kind Emperor); again they are urgent, to say the least, that he should be sent into banishment, while they pretend to lament the miseries of those alleged to have been exiled by him. They lament before us things that have never been done, and, not satisfied with what has been done to him, desire to add thereto other and more cruel treatment.

So mild are they and merciful, and of so just a disposition; or rather (for the truth shall be spoken) so wicked are they and malicious; obtaining respect through fear and by threats, rather than by their piety and justice, as becomes Bishops. They have dared in their letters to the Emperors to pour forth language such as no contentious person would employ even among those that are without; they have charged him with a number of murders and butcheries, and that not before a Governor, or any other superior officer, but before the three Augusti; nor shrink they from any journey however long, provided only all greater courts may be filled with their accusations. For indeed, dearly beloved, their business consists in accusations, and that of the most solemn character, forasmuch as the

---

[5] Acts xxiii. 9.   [6] 1 Sam. xxvi. 21.   [7] Prov. xix. 5; Wisd. i. 11.

tribunals to which they make their appeal are the most solemn of any upon earth. And what other end do they propose by these investigations, except to move the Emperor to capital punishment?

4. Their own conduct therefore, and not that of Athanasius, is the fittest subject for lamentation and mourning, and one would more properly lament them, for such actions ought to be bewailed, since it is written, ' Weep ye not for the dead, neither bemoan him : but weep sore for him that goeth away, for he shall return no more [8].' For their whole letter contemplates nothing but death ; and their endeavour is to kill, whenever they may be permitted, or if not, to drive into exile. And this they were permitted to do by the most religious father of the Emperors, who gratified their fury by the banishment of Athanasius [9], instead of his death. Now that this is not the conduct even of ordinary Christians, scarcely even of heathens, much less of Bishops, who profess to teach others right-eousness, we suppose that your Christian consciences must at once perceive. How can they forbid others to accuse their brethren, who themselves become their accusers, and that to the Emperors? How can they teach compassion for the misfortunes of others, who cannot rest satisfied even with our banishment? For there was confessedly a general sentence of banishment against us Bishops, and we all looked upon ourselves as banished men : and now again we consider ourselves as restored with Athanasius to our native places, and instead of our former lamentations and mourning over him, as hav-ing the greatest encouragement and grace,— which may the Lord continue to us, nor suffer Eusebius and his fellows to destroy?

Even if their charges against him were true, here is a certain charge against them, that against the precept of Christianity, and after his banishment and trials, they have assaulted him again, and accuse him of murder, and butchery, and other crimes, which they sound in the royal ears against the Bishops. But how manifold is their wickedness, and what manner of men think you them, when every word they speak is false, every charge they bring a calumny, and there is no truth whatever either in their mouths or their writings ! Let us then at length enter upon these matters, and meet their last charges. This will prove, that in their former repre-sentations in the Council [1] and at the trial

their conduct was dishonourable, or rather their words untrue, besides exposing them for what they have now advanced.

5. We are indeed ashamed to make any defence against such charges. But since our reckless accusers lay hold of any charge, and allege that murders and butcheries were com-mitted after the return of Athanasius, we beseech you to bear with our answer though it be somewhat long ; for circumstances con-strain us. No murder has been committed either by Athanasius or on his account, since our accusers, as we said before, compel us to enter upon this humiliating defence. Slaughter and imprisonment are foreign to our Church. No one did Athanasius commit into the hands of the executioner ; and the prison, so far as he was concerned, was never disturbed. Our sanctuaries are now, as they have always been, pure, and honoured only with the Blood of Christ and His pious worship. Neither Pres-byter nor Deacon was destroyed by Athana-sius ; he perpetrated no murder, he caused the banishment of no one. Would that they had never caused the like to him, nor given him actual experience of it ! No one here has been banished on his account ; no one at all except Athanasius himself, the Bishop of Alexandria, whom they banished, and whom, now that he is restored, they again seek to entangle in the same or even a more cruel plot than before, setting their tongues to speak all manner of false and deadly words against him.

For, behold, they now attribute to him the acts of the magistrates ; and although they plainly confess in their letter that the Prefect of Egypt passed sentence upon certain persons, they now are not ashamed to impute this sentence to Athanasius ; and that, though he had not at the time entered Alexandria, but was yet on his return from his place of exile. Indeed he was then in Syria ; since we must needs adduce in defence his length of way from home, that a man may not be responsible for the actions of a Governor or Prefect of Egypt. But supposing Athanasius had been in Alexandria, what were the proceedings of the Prefect to Athanasius? However, he was not even in the country ; and what the Prefect of Egypt did was not done on ecclesiastical grounds, but for reasons which you will learn from the records, which, after we understood what they had written, we made diligent enquiry for, and have transmitted to you. Since then they now raise a cry against certain things which were never done either by him or for him, as though they had certainly taken place, and testify against such evils as though they were assured of their existence ; let them

---

[8] Jer. xxii. 10.   [9] Hist. Ar. 50.
[1] Of Tyre. See below, § 71.

inform us from what Council they obtained their knowledge of them, from what proofs, and from what judicial investigation? But if they have no such evidence to bring forward, and nothing but their own mere assertion, we leave it to you to consider as regards their former charges also, how the things took place, and why they so speak of them. In truth, it is nothing but calumny, and a plot of our enemies, and a temper of ungovernable mood, and an impiety in behalf of the Arian madmen, which is frantic against true godliness, and desires to root out the orthodox, so that henceforth the advocates of impiety may preach without fear whatever doctrines they please. The history of the matter is as follows :—

6. When Arius, from whom the heresy of the Arian madmen has its name, was cast out of the Church for his impiety by Bishop Alexander, of blessed memory, Eusebius and his fellows, who are the disciples and partners of his impiety, considering themselves also to have been ejected, wrote frequently to Bishop Alexander, beseeching him not to leave the heretic Arius out of the Church [2]. But when Alexander in his piety towards Christ refused to admit that impious man, they directed their resentment against Athanasius, who was then a Deacon, because in their busy enquiries they had heard that he was much in the familiarity of Bishop Alexander, and much honoured by him. And their hatred of him was greatly increased after they had experience of his piety towards Christ, in the Council assembled at Nicæa [3], wherein he spoke boldly against the impiety of the Arian madmen. But when God raised him to the Episcopate, their long-cherished malice burst forth into a flame, and fearing his orthodoxy and resistance of their impiety, they (and especially Eusebius [4], who was smitten with a consciousness of his own evil doings), engaged in all manner of treacherous designs against him. They prejudiced the Emperor against him; they frequently threatened him with Councils; and at last assembled at Tyre; and to this day they cease not to write against him, and are so implacable that they even find fault with his appointment to the Episcopate [5], taking every

means of shewing their enmity and hatred towards him, and spreading false reports for the sole purpose of thereby vilifying his character.

However, the very misrepresentations which they now are making do but convict their former statements of being falsehoods, and a mere conspiracy against him. For they say, that 'after the death of Bishop Alexander, a certain few having mentioned the name of Athanasius, six or seven Bishops elected him clandestinely in a secret place :' and this is what they wrote to the Emperors, having no scruple about asserting the greatest falsehoods. Now that the whole multitude and all the people of the Catholic Church assembled together as with one mind and body, and cried, shouted, that Athanasius should be Bishop of their Church, made this the subject of their public prayers to Christ, and conjured us to grant it for many days and nights, neither departing themselves from the Church, nor suffering us to do so; of all this we are witnesses, and so is the whole city, and the province too. Not a word did they speak against him, as these persons represented, but gave him the most excellent titles they could devise, calling him good, pious, Christian, an ascetic [5], a genuine Bishop. And that he was elected by a majority of our body in the sight and with the acclamations of all the people, we who elected him also testify, who are surely more credible witnesses than those who were not present, and now spread these false accounts.

But yet Eusebius finds fault with the appointment of Athanasius,—he who perhaps never received any appointment to his office at all; or if he did, has himself rendered it invalid [6]. For he had first the See of Berytus, but leaving that he came to Nicomedia. He left the one contrary to the law, and contrary to the law invaded the other; having deserted his own without affection, and holding possession of another's without reason; he

---

but that, fortifying himself in his position, he sent in his election to the Emperor, and by this means obtained its confirmation. *H. E.* ii. 16. It appears, in matter of fact, that S. Athan. was absent at the time of his election; as Socrates says, in order to avoid it, or as Epiphanius, on business at the Court; these reasons are compatible. [Cf. Prolegg. ch. ii. § 4, and Gwatkin's note, quoted there.]

5 It is contested whether S. Athan. was ever one of S. Antony's monks, the reading of a passage in the commencement of his *Vit. Ant.*, which would decide the question, varying in different MSS. The word "ascetic" is used of those who lived a life, as afterwards followed in Monasteries, in the Ante-Nicene times. [See D.C.B. i. 181ᵃ, and Prolegg. ch. ii. § 1 *ad fin*, and Introd. to *Vit. Ant.*]

6 The Canons of Nicæa and Sardica were absolute against translation, but, as Bingham observes, Antiqu. vi. 4. § 6. only as a general rule. The so-called Apostolical Canons except "a reasonable cause" and the sanction of a Council; one of the Councils of Carthage prohibits them when subserving ambitious views, and except for the advantage of the Church. Vid. list of translations in Socr. *Hist.* vii. 36. Cassiodor. *Hist.* xii. 8. Niceph. *Hist.* xiv. 39. Coteler. adds others *ad Can. Apost.* 14. [cf *Hist Ari. 7.*]

---

2 Cf. *de Syn.* 17.   3 Cf. Socr. i. 8.   4 Cf. Nicomedia.
5 The Eusebians alleged that, fifty-four Bishops of the two parties of S. Alexander and Meletius being assembled for the election, and having sworn to elect by the common voice, six or seven of these broke their oaths in favour of S. Athanasius, whom no one had thought of, and consecrated him in secret to the great surprise and scandal of both ecclesiastical and lay persons. vid. Socr. ii. 17. Philostorgius (A.D. 425) adds particulars, explanatory or corrective of this statement, of which the Bishops in the text do not seem to have heard; viz., that Athanasius with his party one night seized on the Church of St. Dionysius, and compelled two Bishops whom he found there to consecrate him against their will; that he was in consequence anathematized by all the other Bishops,

lost his love for the first in his lust for another, without even keeping to that which he obtained at the prompting of his lust. For, behold, withdrawing himself from the second, again he takes possession of another's [6a], casting an evil eye all around him upon the cities of other men, and thinking that godliness [7] consists in wealth and in the greatness of cities, and making light of the heritage of God to which he had been appointed; not knowing that 'where' even 'two or three are gathered in the name of the' Lord, 'there' is the Lord 'in the midst of them;' not considering the words of the Apostle, 'I will not boast in another man's labours;' not perceiving the charge which he has given, 'Art thou bound unto a wife? seek not to be loosed.' For if this expression applies to a wife, how much more does it apply to a Church, and to the same Episcopate; to which whosoever is bound ought not to seek another, lest he prove an adulterer according to holy Scripture.

7. But though conscious of these his own misdoings, he has boldly undertaken to arraign the appointment of Athanasius, to which honourable testimony has been borne by all, and he ventures to reproach him with his deposition, though he has been deposed himself, and has a standing proof of his deposition in the appointment of another in his room. How could either he or Theognius [8] depose another, after they had been deposed themselves, which is sufficiently proved by the appointment of others in their room? For you know very well that there were appointed instead of them Amphion to Nicomedia and Chrestus to Nicæa, in consequence of their own impiety and connection with the Arian madmen, who were rejected by the Ecumenic Council. But while they desire to set aside that true Council, they endeavour to give that name to their own unlawful combination [9]; while they are unwilling that the decrees of the Council should be enforced, they desire to enforce their own decisions; and they use the name of a Council, while they refuse to submit themselves to one so great as this. Thus they care not for Councils, but only pretend to do so in order that they may root out the orthodox, and annul the decrees of the true and great Council against the Arians, in support of whom, both now and heretofore, they have ventured to assert these falsehoods against

the Bishop Athanasius. For their former statements resembled those they now falsely make, viz., that disorderly meetings were held at his entrance [10], with lamentation and mourning, the people indignantly refusing to receive him. Now such was not the case, but, quite the contrary, joy and cheerfulness prevailed, and the people ran together, hastening to obtain the desired sight of him. The churches were full of rejoicings, and thanksgivings were offered up to the Lord everywhere; and all the Ministers and Clergy beheld him with such feelings, that their souls were possessed with delight, and they esteemed that the happiest day of their lives. Why need we mention the inexpressible joy that prevailed among us Bishops, for we have already said that we counted ourselves to have been partakers in his sufferings?

8. Now this being confessedly the truth of the matter, although it is very differently represented by them, what weight can be attached to that Council or trial of which they make their boast? Since they presume thus to interfere in a case which they did not witness, which they have not examined, and for which they did not meet, and to write as though they were assured of the truth of their statements, how can they claim credit respecting these matters for the consideration of which they say that they did meet together? Will it not rather be believed that they have acted both in the one case and in the other out of enmity to us? For what kind of a Council of Bishops was then held? Was it an assembly which aimed at the truth? Was not almost every one among them our enemy [1]? Did not the attack of Eusebius and his fellows upon us proceed from their zeal for the Arian madness? Did they not urge on the others of their party? Have we not always written against them as professing the doctrines of Arius? Was not Eusebius of Cæsarea in Palestine accused by our confessors of sacrificing to idols [2]? Was not George proved to have been deposed by the blessed Alexander[3]? Were not they charged with various offences, some with this, some with that?

How then could such men entertain the purpose of holding a meeting against us?

[6a] i.e. Constantinople, on the expulsion of Paul.
[7] 1 Tim. vi. 5; Matt. xviii. 20; 2 Cor. x. 15; 1 Cor. vii. 27.
[8] Or Theognis; he was, as well as Eusebius, a pupil of Lucian's, and was deposed together with him after the Nicene Council for communicating with Arians. [They were not ecclesiastically deposed, but exiled by the Emperor, see Prolegg. ch ii. §§ 3 (1) and (2) c, 6 (1).] Constantine banished them to Gaul; they were recalled in the course of two or three years. He was dead by the date of the Council of Sardica.
[9] Eusebian Council of Tyre, A.D. 335.

[10] On his return from Gaul, Nov. 23, A.D. 337. [Prolegg. ch. ii. § 6 (1).]   [1] Cf. § 77.
[2] At the Council of Tyre, Potamo, an Egyptian Bishop and Confessor asked Eusebius what had happened to *him* in prison during the persecution, Epiph. *Hær.* 68, 7, as if hinting at his cowardice. It appears that Eusebius was prisoner at Cæsarea with S. Pamphilus; yet he never mentions the fact himself, which is unlike him, if it was producible. [The insinuation of Potammon was groundless: see Dic. C. Biog. ii. 311.]
[3] George, Bishop of Laodicea, had been degraded when a priest by S. Alexander, for his profligate habits as well as his Arianism. Athan. speaks of him elsewhere as reprobated even by his party. *de Fug.* 26. [Cf. § 49, *de Syn.* 17. Prolegg. ch. ii. § 3 (2) c, 2.]

How can they have the boldness to call that a Council, at which a Count presided, which an executioner attended, and where an usher [4] instead of the Deacons of the Church introduced us into Court; and where the Count only spoke, and all present held their peace, or rather obeyed his directions [5]? The removal of those Bishops who seemed to deserve it, was prevented at his desire; and when he gave the order we were dragged about by soldiers ;—or rather Eusebius and his fellows gave the order, and he was subservient to their will. In short, dearly beloved, what kind of Council was that, the object of which was banishment and murder at the pleasure of the Emperor? And of what nature were their charges?—for here is matter of still greater astonishment. There was one Arsenius whom they declared to have been murdered ; and they also complained that a chalice belonging to the sacred mysteries had been broken.

Now Arsenius is alive, and prays to be admitted to our communion. He waits for no other testimony to prove that he is still living, but himself confesses it, writing in his own person to our brother Athanasius, whom they positively asserted to be his murderer. The impious wretches were not ashamed to accuse him of having murdered a man who was at a great distance from him, being separated by so great a distance, whether by sea or land, and whose abode at that time no one knew. Nay, they even had the boldness to remove him out of sight, and place him in concealment, though he had suffered no injury; and, if it had been possible, they would have transported him to another world, nay, or have taken him from life in earnest, so that either by a true or false statement of his murder they might in good earnest destroy Athanasius. But thanks to divine Providence for this also, which permitted them not to succeed in their injustice, but presented Arsenius [6] alive to the eyes of all men, who has clearly proved their conspiracy and calumnies. He does not withdraw from us as murderers, nor hate us as having injured him (for indeed he has suffered no evil at all) ; but he desires to hold communion with us ; he wishes to be numbered among us, and has written to this effect.

9. Nevertheless they laid their plot against Athanasius, accusing him of having murdered a person who was still alive ; and those same men are the authors of his banishment [7]. For it was not the father of the Emperors, but their calumnies, that sent him into exile. Consider whether this is not the truth. When nothing was discovered to the prejudice of

our fellow-minister Athanasius, but still the Count threatened him with violence, and was very zealous against him, the Bishop [8] fled from this violence and went up [9] to the most religious Emperor, where he protested against the Count and their conspiracy against him, and requested either that a lawful Council of Bishops might be assembled, or that the Emperor would himself receive his defence concerning the charges they brought against him. Upon this the Emperor wrote in anger, summoning them before him, and declaring that he would hear the cause himself, and for that purpose he also ordered a Council to be held. Whereupon Eusebius and his fellows went up and falsely charged Athanasius, not with the same offences which they had published against him at Tyre, but with an intention of detaining the vessels laden with corn, as though Athanasius had been the man to pretend that he could stop the exports of corn from Alexandria to Constantinople [10].

Certain of our friends were present at the palace with Athanasius, and heard the threats of the Emperor upon receiving this report. And when Athanasius cried out upon the calumny, and positively declared that it was not true, (for how, he argued, should he a poor man, and in a private station, be able to do such a thing?) Eusebius did not hesitate publicly to repeat the charge, and swore that Athanasius was a rich man, and powerful, and able to do anything; in order that it might thence be supposed that he had used this language. Such was the accusation these venerable Bishops proffered against him. But the grace of God proved superior to their wickedness, for it moved the pious Emperor to mercy, who instead of death passed upon him the sentence of banishment. Thus their calumnies, and nothing else, were the cause of this. For the Emperor, in the letter which he previously wrote, complained of their conspiracy, censured their machinations, and condemned the Meletians as unscrupulous and deserving of execration; in short, expressed himself in the severest terms concerning them. For he was greatly moved when he heard the story of the dead alive; he was moved at hearing of

---

[8] The circumstances of this appeal, which are related by Athan. below, § 86, are thus summed up by Gibbon; "Before the final sentence could be pronounced at Tyre, the intrepid primate threw himself into a bark which was ready to hoist sail for the imperial city. The request of a formal audience might have been opposed or eluded; but Athanasius concealed his arrival, watched the moment of Constantine's return from an adjacent villa, and boldly encountered his angry sovereign as he passed on horseback through the principal street of Constantinople. So strange an apparition excited his surprise and indignation ; and the guards were ordered to remove the importunate suitor ; but his resentment was subdued by involuntary respect; and the haughty spirit of the Emperor was awed by the courage and eloquence of a Bishop, who implored his justice and awakened his conscience." *Decl. and Fall*, xxi. Athan. was a small man in person. [9] i.e. to Constantinople. [10] § 87.

---

[4] Conventarius.   [5] *Hist. Ari.* 11, and below §§ 36, 71.
[6] § 65.   [7] By Constantine into Gaul, A.D. 336.

murder in the case of one alive, and not deprived of life. We have sent you the letter.

10. But these marvellous men, Eusebius and his fellows, to make a show of refuting the truth of the case, and the statements contained in this letter, put forward the name of a Council, and ground its proceedings upon the authority of the Emperor. Hence the attendance of a Count at their meeting, and the soldiers as guards of the Bishops, and royal letters compelling the attendance of any persons whom they required. But observe here the strange character of their machinations, and the inconsistency of their bold measures, so that by some means or other they may take Athanasius away from us. For if as Bishops they claimed for themselves alone the judgment of the case, what need was there for the attendance of a Count and soldiers? or how was it that they assembled under the sanction of royal letters? Or if they required the Emperor's countenance and wished to derive their authority from him, why were they then annulling his judgment? and when he declared in the letter which he wrote, that the Meletians were calumniators, unscrupulous, and that Athanasius was most innocent, and made much stir about the pretended murder of the living, how was it that they determined that the Meletians had spoken the truth, and that Athanasius was guilty of the offence; and were not ashamed to make the living dead, living both after the Emperor's judgment, and at the time when they met together, and who even until this day is amongst us? So much concerning the case of Arsenius.

11. And as for the cup belonging to the mysteries, what was it, or where was it broken by Macarius? for this is the report which they spread up and down. But as for Athanasius, even his accusers would not have ventured to blame him, had they not been suborned by them. However, they attribute the origin of the offence to him; although it ought not to be imputed even to Macarius who is clear of it. And they are not ashamed to parade the sacred mysteries before Catechumens, and worse than that, even before heathens[1]: whereas, they ought to attend to what is written, 'It is good to keep close the secret of a king[2];' and as the Lord has charged us, 'Give not that which is holy unto the dogs, neither cast ye your pearls before swine[3].' We ought not then to parade the holy mys-

teries before the uninitiated, lest the heathen in their ignorance deride them, and the Catechumens being over-curious be offended. However, what was the cup, and where and before whom was it broken? It is the Meletians who make the accusation, who are not worthy of the least credit, for they have been schismatics and enemies of the Church, not of a recent date, but from the times of the blessed Peter, Bishop and Martyr[4]. They formed a conspiracy against Peter himself; they calumniated his successor Achillas; they accused Alexander even before the Emperor; and being thus well versed in these arts, they have now transferred their enmity to Athanasius, acting altogether in accordance with their former wickedness. For as they slandered those that have been before him, so now they have slandered him. But their calumnies and false accusations have never prevailed against him until now, that they have got Eusebius and his fellows for their assistants and patrons, on account of the impiety which these have adopted from the Arian madmen, which has led them to conspire against many Bishops, and among the rest Athanasius.

Now the place where they say the **cup** was broken, was not a Church; there was no Presbyter in occupation of the place; and the day on which they say that Macarius did the deed, was not the Lord's day. Since then there was no church there; since there was no one to perform the sacred office; and since the day did not require the use of it[5]; what was this cup belonging to the mysteries, and when, or where was it broken? There are many cups, it is plain, both in private houses, and in the public market; and if a person breaks one of them, he is not guilty of impiety. But the cup which belongs to the mysteries, and which if it be broken intentionally, makes the perpetrator of the deed an impious person, is found only among those who lawfully preside. This is the only description that can be given of this kind of cup; there is none other; this you legally give to the people to drink; this you have received according to the canon of the Church[6]; this belongs only to those who preside over the Catholic Church, for to you only it appertains to administer the Blood of Christ, and to none besides. But as he who breaks the cup belonging to the mysteries is an impious person, much more impious is he who treats the

---

[1] This period, when Christianity was acknowledged by the state but not embraced by the population, is just the time when we hear most of this Reserve as a principle. While Christians were but a sect, persecution enforced a discipline, and when they were commensurate with the nation, faith made it unnecessary. **We are now** returned to the state of the fourth century.
[2] Tob. xii. 7.　　　[3] Matt. vii. 6.

[4] [Cf. § 59, and *Ep. Æg.* 22, Prolegg. ch. ii. § 2 *init.*]
[5] This seems to imply that the Holy Communion was only celebrated on Sundays in the Egyptian Churches. [Cf. §§ 63, 74, 76.]　　　[6] Vid. *Can. Ap.* 65.

Blood of Christ with contumely: and he does so who 'does this[7]' contrary to the rule of the Church. (We say this, not as if a cup even of the schismatics was broken by Macarius, for there was no cup there at all; how should there be? where there was neither Lord's house nor any one belonging to the Church, nay, it was not the time of the celebration of the mysteries). Now such a person is the notorious Ischyras, who was never appointed to his office by the Church, and when Alexander admitted the Presbyters that had been ordained by Meletius, he was not even numbered amongst them; and therefore did not receive ordination even from that quarter.

12. By what means then did Ischyras become a Presbyter? who was it that ordained him? was it Colluthus? for this is the only supposition that remains. But it is well known, and no one has any doubt about the matter, that Colluthus died a Presbyter, and that every ordination of his was invalid, and that all that were ordained by him during the schism were reduced to the condition of laymen, and in that rank appear in the congregation. How then can it be believed that a private person, occupying a private house, had in his possession a sacred chalice? But the truth is, they gave the name of Presbyter at the time to a private person, and gratified him with this title to support him in his iniquitous conduct towards us; and now as the reward of his accusations they procure for him the erection of a Church[8]. So that this man had then no Church; but as the reward of his malice and subserviency to them in accusing us, he receives now what he had not before; nay, perhaps they have even remunerated his services with the Episcopate, for so he goes about reporting, and accordingly behaves towards us with great insolence. Thus are such rewards as these now bestowed by Bishops upon accusers and calumniators; though indeed it is reasonable, in the case of an accomplice, that as they have made him a partner in their proceedings, so they should also make him their associate in their own Episcopate. But this is not all; give ear yet further to their proceedings at that time.

13. Being unable to prevail against the truth, though they had thus set themselves in array against it, and Ischyras having proved nothing at Tyre, but being shewn to be a calumniator, and the calumny ruining their plot, they defer proceedings for fresh evidence, and profess that they are going to send to the Mareotis certain of their party to enquire diligently into the matter. Accordingly they dispatched secretly, with the assistance of the civil power, persons to whom we openly objected on many accounts, as being of the party of Arius, and therefore our enemies; namely, Diognius[9], Maris, Theodorus, Macedonius, and two others, young both in years and mind[9], Ursacius and Valens from Pannonia; who, after they had undertaken this long journey for the purpose of sitting in judgment upon their enemy, set out again from Tyre for Alexandria. They did not shrink from becoming witnesses themselves, although they were the judges, but openly adopted every means of furthering their design, and undertook any labour or journey whatsoever in order to bring to a successful issue the conspiracy which was in progress. They left the Bishop Athanasius detained in a foreign country while they themselves entered their enemy's city, as if to have their revel both against his Church and against his people. And what was more outrageous still, they took with them the accuser Ischyras, but would not permit Macarius, the accused person, to accompany them, but left him in custody at Tyre. For 'Macarius the Presbyter of Alexandria' was made answerable for the charge far and near.

14. They therefore entered Alexandria alone with the accuser, their partner in lodging, board, and cup; and taking with them Philagrius the Prefect of Egypt they proceeded to the Mareotis, and there carried on the so-called investigation by themselves, all their own way, with the forementioned person. Although the Presbyters frequently begged that they might be present, they would not permit them. The Presbyters both of the city and of the whole country desired to attend, that they might detect who and whence persons were who were suborned by Ischyras. But they forbade the Ministers to be present, while they carried on the examination concerning church, cup, table, and the holy things, before the heathen; nay, worse than that, they summoned heathen witnesses during the enquiry concerning a cup belonging to the mysteries; and those persons who they affirmed were taken out of the way by Athanasius by summons of the Receiver-general, and they knew not where in the world they were, these same individuals they brought forward before themselves and the Prefect only, and avowedly used their testimony, whom they affirmed without shame to have been secreted by the Bishop Athanasius.

---

7 1 Cor. xi. 25.   8 Cf. § 85.

9 Vid. also *Ep. Æg.* 7. Euseb. *Vit. C.* iv. 43. Hilar. *ad Const* i. 5. *Fragm.* ii. 12 ['Diognius' is another form of 'Theognius' or Theognis. See Prolegg. ch. ii. § 5.]

But here too their only object is to effect his death, and so they again pretend that persons are dead who are still alive, following the same method they adopted in the case of Arsenius. For the men are living, and are to be seen in their own country; but to you who are at a great distance from the spot they make a great stir about the matter as though they had disappeared, in order that, as the evidence is so far removed from you, they may falsely accuse our brother-minister, as though he used violence and the civil power; whereas they themselves have in all respects acted by means of that power and the countenance of others. For their proceedings in the Mareotis were parallel to those at Tyre; and as there a Count attended with military assistance, and would permit nothing either to be said or done contrary to their pleasure, so here also the Prefect of Egypt was present with a band of men, frightening all the members of the Church, and permitting no one to give true testimony. And what was the strangest thing of all, the persons who came, whether as judges or witnesses, or, what was more likely, in order to serve their own purposes and those of Eusebius, lived in the same place with the accuser, even in his house, and there seemed to carry on the investigation as they pleased.

15. We suppose you are not ignorant what outrages they committed at Alexandria; for they are reported everywhere. Naked swords[10] were at work against the holy virgins and brethren; scourges were at work against their persons, esteemed honourable in the sight of God, so that their feet were lamed by the stripes, whose souls are whole and sound in purity and all good works[1]. The trades were excited against them; and the heathen multitude was set to strip them naked, to beat them, wantonly to insult them, and to threaten them with their altars and sacrifices. And one coarse fellow, as though license had now been given them by the Prefect in order to gratify the Bishops, took hold of a virgin by the hand, and dragged her towards an altar that happened to be near, imitating the practice of compelling to offer sacrifice in time of persecution. When this was done, the virgins took to flight, and a shout of laughter was raised by the heathen against the Church; the Bishops being in the place, and occupying the very house where this was going on; and from which, in order to obtain favour with them, the virgins were assaulted with naked swords, and were exposed to all kinds of danger, and insult, and wanton violence. And this treatment they received on a fast-day[2], and at the hands of persons who themselves were feasting with the Bishops indoors.

16. Foreseeing these things, and reflecting that the entrance of enemies into a place is no ordinary calamity, we protested against this commission. And Alexander[3], Bishop of Thessalonica, considering the same, wrote to the people residing there, discovering the conspiracy, and testifying of the plot. They indeed reckon him to be one of themselves, and account him a partner in their designs; but they only prove thereby the violence they have exercised towards him. For even the profligate Ischyras himself was only induced by fear and violence to proceed in the matter, and was obliged by force to undertake the accusation. As a proof of this, he wrote himself to our brother Athanasius[4], confessing that nothing of the kind that was alleged had taken place there, but that he was suborned to make a false statement. This declaration he made, though he was never admitted by Athanasius as a Presbyter, nor received such a title of grace from him, nor was entrusted by way of recompense with the erection of a Church, nor expected the bribe of a Bishopric; all of which he obtained from them in return for undertaking the accusation. Moreover, his whole family held communion with us[5], which they would not have done had they been injured in the slightest degree.

17. Now to prove that these things are facts and not mere assertions, we have the testimony[6] of all the Presbyters of the Mareotis[7], who always accompany the Bishop in his visitations, and who also wrote at the time against Ischyras. But neither those of them who came to Tyre were allowed to declare the truth[8], nor could those who remained in the Mareotis obtain permission to refute the calumnies of Ischyras[9]. The copies also of the letters of Alexander, and of the Presbyters, and of Ischyras will prove the same thing. We have sent also the letter of the father of the Emperors, in which he expresses his indignation that the murder of Arsenius was charged upon any one while the man was still alive; as also his astonishment at the variable and in-

---

2 [Not in Lent, for the commission were at Alexandria in September, see the date of the protest, *infra*, § 76.]
3 This Alexander had been one of the Nicene Fathers, in 325, and had the office of publishing their decrees in Macedonia, Greece, &c. He was at the Council of Jerusalem ten years after, at which the Church of the Holy Sepulchre was consecrated, and afterwards Arius admitted to communion. His influence with the Court party seems to have been great, judging from Count Dionysius's tone in speaking of him. Infr. §§ 66, 80, 81.   4 Infr. § 64.
5 Vid. infr. § 63 fin. § 85 fin.   6 Infr. § 74.
7 The district, called Mareotis from a neighbouring lake, lay in the territory and diocese of Alexandria, to the south-west. It consisted of various large villages, with handsome Churches, and resident Priests, and of hamlets which had none; of the latter was "Irene of Secontarurus," (infr. § 85.) where Ischyras lived.
8 Infr. § 79.   9 § 72 fin.

consistent character of their accusations with respect to the cup; since at one time they accused the Presbyter Macarius, at another the Bishop Athanasius, of having broken it with his hands. He declares also on the one hand that the Meletians are calumniators, and on the other that Athanasius is perfectly innocent.

And are not the Meletians calumniators, and above all John [10], who after coming into the Church, and communicating with us, after condemning himself, and no longer taking any part in the proceedings respecting the cup, when he saw Eusebius and his fellows zealously supporting the Arian madmen, though they had not the daring to co-operate with them openly, but were attempting to employ others as their masks, undertook a character, as an actor in the heathen theatres [1]? The subject of the drama was a contest of Arians; the real design of the piece being their success, but John and his partizans being put on the stage and playing the parts, in order that under colour of these, the supporters of the Arians in the garb of judges might drive away the enemies of their impiety, firmly establish their impious doctrines, and bring the Arians into the Church. And those who wish to drive out true religion strive all they can to prevail by irreligion; they who have chosen the part of that impiety which wars against Christ, endeavour to destroy the enemies thereof, as though they were impious persons; and they impute to us the breaking of the cup, for the purpose of making it appear that Athanasius, equally with themselves, is guilty of impiety towards Christ.

For what means this mention of a cup belonging to the mysteries by them? Whence comes this religious regard for the cup among those who support impiety towards Christ? Whence comes it that Christ's cup is known to them who know not Christ? How can they who profess to honour that cup, dishonour the God of the cup? or how can they who lament over the cup, seek to murder the Bishop who celebrates the mysteries therewith? for they would have murdered him, had it been in their power. And how can they who lament the loss of the throne that was Episcopally covered [2], seek to destroy the Bishop that sat upon it, to the end that both the throne may be without its Bishop, and that the people may be deprived of godly doctrine? It was not then the cup, nor the murder, nor any of those portentous deeds they talk about, that induced them to act thus; but the forementioned heresy of the Arians, for the sake of which they conspired against Athanasius and other Bishops, and still continue to wage war against the Church.

Who are they that have really been the cause of murders and banishments? Is it not these? Who are they that, availing themselves of external support, conspire against the Bishops? Are not Eusebius and his fellows the men, and not Athanasius, as they say in their letters? Both he and others have suffered at their hands. Even at the time of which we speak, four Presbyters [3] of Alexandria, though they had not even proceeded to Tyre, were banished by their means. Who then are they whose conduct calls for tears and lamentations? Is it not they, who after they have been guilty of one course of persecution, do not scruple to add to it a second, but have recourse to all manner of falsehood, in order that they may destroy a Bishop who will not give way to their impious heresy? Hence arises the enmity of Eusebius and his fellows; hence their proceedings at Tyre; hence their pretended trials; hence also now the letters which they have written even without any trial, expressing the utmost confidence in their statements; hence their calumnies before the father of the Emperors, and before the most religious Emperors themselves.

18. For it is necessary that you should know what is now reported to the prejudice of our fellow-minister Athanasius, in order that you may thereby be led to condemn their wickedness, and may perceive that they desire nothing else but to murder him. A quantity of corn was given by the father of the Emperors for the support of certain widows, partly of Libya, and partly certain out of Egypt. They have all received it up to this time, Athanasius getting nothing therefrom, but the trouble of assisting them. But now, although the recipients themselves make no complaint, but acknowledge that they have received it, Athanasius has been accused of selling all the corn, and appropriating the profits to his own use: and the Emperor wrote to this effect about it, charging him with the offence in consequence of the calumnies which had been raised against him. Now who are they which have raised these calumnies? Is it not those who after they have been guilty of one course of persecution, scruple not to set on foot another? Who are the authors of those letters which are said to have come from the Emperor? Are not the Arians, who are so zealous against Athanasius, and scruple not to speak and write anything against him? No one would pass over persons

---

[10] Arcaph. infr. 65 fin., head of the Meletians.
[1] Vid. infr. § 37, 46. and *de Syn.* 32, note.
[2] Cathedræ velatæ, see Bingh. viii. 6. § 10.

[3] Vid. their names infr. § 40.

who have acted as they have done, in order to entertain suspicion of others. Nay, the proof of their calumny appears to be most evident, for they are anxious under cover of it, to take away the corn from the Church, and to give it to the Arians. And this circumstance more than any other, brings the matter home to the authors of this design and their principals, who scrupled neither to set on foot a charge of murder against Athanasius, as a base means of prejudicing the Emperor against him, nor yet to take away from the Clergy of the Church the subsistence of the poor, in order that in fact they might make gain for the heretics.

19. We have sent also the testimony of our fellow-ministers in Libya, Pentapolis, and Egypt, from which likewise you may learn the false accusations which have been brought against Athanasius. And these things they do, in order that, the professors of true godliness being henceforth induced by fear to remain quiet, the heresy of the impious Arians may be brought in in its stead. But thanks be to your piety, dearly beloved, that you have frequently anathematized the Arians in your letters, and have never given them admittance into the Church. The exposure of Eusebius and his fellows is also easy and ready at hand. For behold, after their former letters concerning the Arians, of which also we have sent you copies, they now openly stir up the Arian madmen against the Church, though the whole Catholic Church has anathematized them; they have appointed a Bishop[1] over them; they distract the Churches with threats and alarms, that they may gain assistants in their impiety in every part. Moreover, they send Deacons to the Arian madmen, who openly join their assemblies; they write letters to them, and receive answers from them, thus making schisms in the Church, and holding communion with them; and they send to every part, commending their heresy, and repudiating the Church, as you will perceive from the letters they have addressed to the Bishop of Rome[2], and perhaps to yourselves also. You perceive therefore, dearly beloved, that these things are not undeserving of vengeance: they are indeed dreadful and alien from the doctrine of Christ.

Wherefore we have assembled together, and have written to you, to request of your Christian wisdom to receive this our declaration and sympathize with our brother Athanasius, and to shew your indignation against Eusebius and his fellows who have essayed such things, in order that such malice and wickedness may no longer prevail against the Church. We call upon you

to be the avengers of such injustice, reminding you of the injunction of the Apostle, 'Put away from among yourselves that wicked person[3].' Wicked indeed is their conduct, and unworthy of your communion. Wherefore give no further heed to them, though they should again write to you against the Bishop Athanasius (for all that proceeds from them is false); not even though they subscribe their letter with names[4] of Egyptian Bishops. For it is evident that it will not be we who write, but the Meletians[5], who have ever been schismatics, and who even unto this day make disturbances and raise factions in the Churches. For they ordain improper persons, and all but heathens; and they are guilty of such actions as we are ashamed to set down in writing, but which you may learn from those whom we have sent unto you, who will also deliver to you our letter.

20. Thus wrote the Bishops of Egypt to all Bishops, and to Julius, Bishop of Rome.

CHAPTER II.

Letter of Julius to the Eusebians at Antioch.

Eusebius and his fellows wrote also to Julius, and thinking to frighten me, requested him to call a council, and to be himself the judge, if he so pleased[6]. When therefore I went up to Rome, Julius wrote to Eusebius and his fellows as was suitable, and sent moreover two of his own Presbyters[7], Elpidius and Philoxenus[8]. But they, when they heard of me, were thrown into confusion, as not expecting my going up thither; and they declined the proposed Council, alleging unsatisfactory reasons for so doing, but in truth they were afraid lest the things should be proved against them which Valens and Ursacius afterwards confessed[9]. However, more than fifty Bishops assembled, in the place where the Presbyter Vito held his congregation; and they acknowledged my defence, and gave me the confirmation[1] both of their communion and their love. On

---

3 1 Cor. v. 13.
4 The Eusebians availed themselves of the subscriptions of the Meletians, as at Philippopolis, Hilar. *Fragm.* 3.   5 Infr. § 73.
6 A.D. 339. vid. *Hist. Arian.* § 11. [Socrates (iii. 5) and Sozomenus (ii. 8, &c.), confuse the Antiochene Synod, which sent the letter referred to, with the Synod of the 'Dedication' held in 341 A.D., after the receipt of the letter of Julius.]
7 Vito and Vincentius, Presbyters, had represented Silvester at Nicæa. Liberius sent Vincentius, Bishop, and Marcellus, Bishop, to Constantius; and again Lucifer, Bishop, and Eusebius, Bishop. [The practice was common to all bishops, not peculiar to that of Rome.] S. Basil suggests that Damasus should send legates into the East, Ep. 69. The Council of Sardica, Can. 5, recognised the Pope's power of sending legates into foreign Provinces to hear certain appeals; "ut de *Latere suo* Presbyterum mittat." [It *conferred* the power (1) upon Julius (2) without any right of initiative, in Can. 3; Can. 5 simply regulates the exercise of the power thus conferred. The genuineness of these Canons has been disputed: at Rome they were quoted in the fifth century as 'Nicene.'] vid. Thomassin. *de Eccl. Disc.* Part I. ii. 117. [D.C.B. iii. 530, D.C.A. 197, 1658.]
8 [Date uncertain; see Prolegg. ch. ii. § 6 (1) *sub fin.*, and note there.]   9 Infr. § 58.   1 Vid. infr. § 36.

---

1 Pistus.   2 Vid. infr. § 21.

the other hand, they expressed great indignation against Eusebius and his fellows, and requested that Julius would write to the following effect to those of their number who had written to him. Which accordingly he did, and sent it by the hand of Count Gabianus.

The Letter of Julius.

Julius to his dearly beloved brethren[2], Danius, Flacillus, Narcissus, Eusebius, Maris, Macedonius, Theodorus, and their friends, who have written to me from Antioch, sends health in the Lord.

21. I have read your letter[3] which was brought to me by my Presbyters Elpidius and Philoxenus, and I am surprised to find that, whereas I wrote to you in charity and with conscious sincerity, you have replied to me in an unbecoming and contentious temper; for the pride and arrogance of the writers is plainly exhibited in that letter. Yet such feelings are inconsistent with the Christian faith; for what was written in a charitable spirit ought likewise to be answered in a spirit of charity and not of contention. And was it not a token of charity to send Presbyters to sympathize with them that are in suffering, and to desire those who had written to me to come thither, that the questions at issue might obtain a speedy settlement, and all things be duly ordered, so that our brethren might no longer be exposed to suffering, and that you might escape further calumny? But something seems to shew that your temper is such, as to force us to conclude that even in the terms in which you appeared to pay honour to us, you have expressed yourselves under the disguise of irony. The Presbyters also whom we sent to you, and who ought to have returned rejoicing, did on the contrary return sorrowful on account of the proceedings they had witnessed among you. And I, when I had read your letter, after much consideration, kept it to myself, thinking that after all some of you would come, and there would be no need

to bring it forward, lest if it should be openly exhibited, it should grieve many of our brethren here. But when no one arrived, and it became necessary that the letter should be produced, I declare to you, they were all astonished, and were hardly able to believe that such a letter had been written by you at all; for it is expressed in terms of contention rather than of charity.

Now if the author of it wrote with an ambition of exhibiting his power of language, such a practice surely is more suitable for other subjects: in ecclesiastical matters, it is not a display of eloquence that is needed, but the observance of Apostolic Canons, and an earnest care not to offend one of the little ones of the Church. For it were better for a man, according to the word of the Church, that a millstone were hanged about his neck, and that he were drowned in the sea, than that he should offend even one of the little ones[4]. But if such a letter was written, because certain persons have been aggrieved on account of their meanness of spirit towards one another (for I will not impute it to all); it were better not to entertain any such feeling of offence at all, at least not to let the sun go down upon their vexation; and certainly not to give it room to exhibit itself in writing.

22. Yet what has been done that is a just cause of vexation? or in what respect was my letter to you such? Was it, that I invited you to be present at a council? You ought rather to have received the proposal with joy. Those who have confidence in their proceedings, or as they choose to term them, in their decisions, are not wont to be angry, if such decision is inquired into by others; they rather shew all boldness, seeing that if they have given a just decision, it can never prove to be the reverse. The Bishops who assembled in the great Council of Nicæa agreed, not without the will of God, that the decisions of one council should be examined in another[5], to the end that the judges, having before their eyes that other trial which was to follow, might be led to investigate matters with the utmost caution, and that the parties concerned in their sentence might have assurance that the judgment they received was just, and not dictated by the enmity of their

---

[2] By Danius, which had been considered the same name as Dianius, Bishop of Cæsarea in Cappadocia, Montfaucon *in loc.* understands the notorious Arian Bishop of Nicæa, called variously Diognius (supr. § 13.), Theognius (infr. § 28.), Theognis (Philost. *Hist.* ii. 7.) Theogonius, (Theod. *Hist.* i. 19.), and assigns some ingenious and probable reasons for his supposition. ['Danius' was the Bishop of Cæsarea in Cappad., he also signs at Philippopolis. See D.C.B. under DIANIUS and BASIL.] Flacillus, Arian Bishop of Antioch, as Athan. names him, is called Placillus (in S. Jerome's *Chronicon*, p. 785.), Placitus (Soz. iii. 5.), Flacitus (Theod. *Hist.* i. 21.). Theodorus was Arian Bishop of Heraclea, whose Comments on the Psalms are supposed to be those which bear his name in Corderius's Catena. [He was not a thorough Arian.]

[3] Some of the topics contained in the Eusebian Letter are specified in Julius's answer. It acknowledged, besides, the high dignity of the [church] of Rome, as being a "School (φροντιστήριον) of Apostles and a Metropolis of orthodoxy from the beginning," but added that "doctors came to it from the east; and they ought not themselves to hold the second place, for they were superior in virtue, though not in their Church." And they said that they would hold communion with Julius if he would agree to their depositions and substitutions in the Eastern Sees. Soz. iii. 8.

[4] Matt. xviii. 6.

[5] As this determination does not find a place among the now received Canons of the Council, the passage in the text becomes of great moment in the argument in favour of the twenty Canons extant in Greek being but a portion of those passed at Nicæa. vid. Alber. *Dissert. in Hist. Eccles.* vii. Abraham Ecchellensis has argued on the same side (apud Colet. *Concil.* t. ii. p. 399. Ed. Ven. 1728), also Baronius, though not so strongly, Ann. 325. nn. 157 &c. and Montfaucon *in loc.* Natalis Alexander, *Sæc.* 4. *Dissert.* 28 argues against the larger number, and Tillemont, *Mem.* vi. 674. [But it is far more likely that Julius is making a free use of Can. Nic. 5; the Arabic canons are apparently referred to in the above note: no one now defends them.]

former judges. Now if you are unwilling that such a practice should be adopted in your own case, though it is of ancient standing, and has been noticed and recommended by the great Council, your refusal is not becoming ; for it is unreasonable that a custom which had once obtained in the Church, and been established by councils, should be set aside by a few individuals.

For a further reason they cannot justly take offence in this point. When the persons whom you, Eusebius and his fellows, dispatched with your letters, I mean Macarius the Presbyter, and Martyrius and Hesychius the Deacons, arrived here, and found that they were unable to withstand the arguments of the Presbyters who came from Athanasius, but were confuted and exposed on all sides, they then requested me to call a Council together, and to write to Alexandria to the Bishop Athanasius, and also to Eusebius and his fellows, in order that a just judgment might be given in presence of all parties. And they undertook in that case to prove all the charges which had been brought against Athanasius. For Martyrius and Hesychius had been publicly refuted by us, and the Presbyters of the Bishop Athanasius had withstood them with great confidence : indeed, if one must tell the truth, Martyrius and his fellows had been utterly overthrown ; and this it was that led them to desire that a Council might be held. Now supposing that they had not desired a Council, but that I had been the person to propose it, in discouragement of those who had written to me, and for the sake of our brethren who complain that they have suffered injustice ; even in that case the proposal would have been reasonable and just, for it is agreeable to ecclesiastical practice, and well pleasing to God. But when those persons, whom you, Eusebius and his fellows, considered to be trustworthy, when even they wished me to call the brethren together, it was inconsistent in the parties invited to take offence, when they ought rather to have shewn all readiness to be present. These considerations shew that the display of anger in the offended persons is petulant, and the refusal of those who decline to meet the Council is unbecoming, and has a suspicious appearance. Does any one find fault, if he sees that done by another, which he would allow if done by himself ? If, as you write, each council has an irreversible force, and he who has given judgment on a matter is dishonoured, if his sentence is examined by others ; consider, dearly beloved, who are they that dishonour councils ? who are setting aside the decisions of former judges ? Not to inquire at present into every individual

case, lest I should appear to press too heavily on certain parties, the last instance that has occurred, and which every one who hears it must shudder at, will be sufficient in proof of the others which I omit.

23. The Arians who were excommunicated for their impiety by Alexander, the late Bishop of Alexandria, of blessed memory, were not only proscribed by the brethren in the several cities, but were also anathematised by the whole body assembled together in the great Council of Nicæa. For theirs was no ordinary offence, neither had they sinned against man, but against our Lord Jesus Christ Himself, the Son of the living God. And yet these persons who were proscribed by the whole world, and branded in every Church, are said now to have been admitted to communion again ; which I think even you ought to hear with indignation. Who then are the parties who dishonour a council ? Are not they who have set at nought the votes of the Three hundred [6], and have preferred impiety to godliness ? The heresy of the Arian madmen was condemned and proscribed by the whole body of Bishops everywhere ; but the Bishops Athanasius and Marcellus have many supporters who speak and write in their behalf. We have received testimony in favour of Marcellus [7], that he resisted the advocates of the Arian doctrines in the Council of Nicæa ; and in favour of Athanasius [8], that at Tyre nothing was brought home to him, and that in the Mareotis, where the Reports against him are said to have been drawn up, he was not present. Now you know, dearly beloved, that *ex parte* proceedings are of no weight, but bear a suspicious appearance. Nevertheless, these things being so, we, in order to be accurate, and neither shewing any prepossession in favour of yourselves, nor of those who wrote in behalf of the other party, invited those who had written to us to come hither ; that, since there were many who wrote in their behalf, all things might be enquired into in a council, and neither the guiltless might be condemned, nor the person on his trial be accounted innocent. We then are not the parties who dishonour a council, but they who at once and recklessly have received the Arians whom all had condemned, and contrary to the decision of the judges. The greater part of those judges have now departed, and are with Christ ; but some of them are still in this life of trial, and

---

6 The number of the Fathers at the Nicene Council is generally considered to have been 318, the number of Abraham's servants, Gen. xiv. 14. Anastasius (*Hodeg.* 3. fin.) referring to the first three Ecumenical Councils, speaks of the faith of the 318, the 150, and the 200. [Prolegg. ch. ii. § 3 (1).]
7 Cf. § 32.   8 Cf. § 73.

are indignant at learning that certain persons have set aside their judgment.

24. We have also been informed of the following circumstance by those who were at Alexandria. A certain Carpones, who had been excommunicated by Alexander for Arianism, was sent hither by one Gregory with certain others, also excommunicated for the same heresy. However, I had learnt the matter also from the Presbyter Macarius, and the Deacons Martyrius and Hesychius. For before the Presbyters of Athanasius arrived, they urged me to send letters to one Pistus at Alexandria, though at the same time the Bishop Athanasius was there. And when the Presbyters of the Bishop Athanasius came, they informed me that this Pistus was an Arian, and that he had been excommunicated[9] by the Bishop Alexander and the Council of Nicæa, and then ordained[1] by one Secundus, whom also the great Council excommunicated as an Arian. This statement Martyrius and his fellows did not gainsay, nor did they deny that Pistus had received his ordination from Secundus. Now consider, after this who are most justly liable to blame? I, who could not be prevailed upon to write to the Arian Pistus; or those, who advised me to do dishonour to the great Council, and to address the irreligious as if they were religious persons? Moreover, when the Presbyter Macarius, who had been sent hither by Eusebius with Martyrius and the rest, heard of the opposition which had been made by the Presbyters of Athanasius, while we were expecting his appearance with Martyrius and Hesychius, he departed in the night, in spite of a bodily ailment; which leads us to conjecture that his departure arose from shame on account of the exposure which had been made concerning Pistus. For it is impossible that the ordination of the Arian Secundus should be considered valid in the Catholic Church. This would indeed be dishonour to the Council, and to the Bishops who composed it, if the decrees they framed, as in the presence of God, with such extreme earnestness and care, should be set aside as worthless.

25. If, as you write[2], the decrees of all Councils ought to be of force, according to the precedent in the case of Novatus[3] and Paul of Samosata, all the more ought not the sentence of the Three hundred to be reversed, certainly a general Council ought not to be set at nought by a few individuals. For the Arians are heretics as they, and the like sentence has been passed both against one and the other. And, after such bold proceedings as these, who are they that have lighted up the flame of discord? for in your letter you blame us for having done this. Is it we, who have sympathised with the sufferings of the brethren, and have acted in all respects according to the Canon; or they who contentiously and contrary to the Canon have set aside the sentence of the Three hundred, and dishonoured the Council in every way? For not only have the Arians been received into communion, but Bishops also have made a practice of removing from one place to another[4]. Now if you really believe that all Bishops have the same and equal authority[5], and you do not, as you assert, account of them according to the magnitude of their cities; he that is entrusted with a small city ought to abide in the place committed to him, and not from disdain of his trust to remove to one that has never been put under him; despising that which God has given him, and making much of the vain applause of men. You ought then, dearly beloved, to have come and not declined, that the matter may be brought to a conclusion; for this is what reason demands.

But perhaps you were prevented by the time fixed upon for the Council, for you complain in your letter that the interval before the day we appointed[6] was too short. But this, beloved, is a mere excuse. Had the day forestalled any when on the journey, the interval allowed would then have been proved to be too short. But when persons do not wish to come, and detain even my Presbyters up to the month of January[7], it is the mere excuse of those who have no confidence in their cause; otherwise, as I said before, they would have come, not regarding the length of the journey, not considering the shortness of the time, but trusting to the justice and reasonableness of their cause. But perhaps they did not come on account of the aspect of the times[8], for again you declare in your letter, that we ought to have considered the present circumstances of the East, and not to have urged you to come. Now if as you say you did not come because the times were such, you ought to have considered such times beforehand, and not to have become the authors of schism, and of mourning and lamentation in the Churches. But as the matter stands, men, who have been

---

9 Cf. supr. *D fos. Ar.*   1 Cf. *Ep. Æg.* 7, 19, *Hist. Ar.* 63.
2 Vid. also Hilar. *Fragm.* iii. 20.
3 The instance of Novatian makes against the Eusebians, because for some time after Novatian was condemned in the West, his cause was abandoned in the East. Tillemont, *Mem.* t. 7. p. 277.

4 Vid. supr. §. 6.   5 Cyprian. *de Unit. Eccl.* 4.
6 προθεσμία.   7 A.D. 340.
8 The Persian war. *Hist. Arian.* § 11.

the cause of these things, shew that it is not the times that are to blame, but the determination of those who will not meet a Council.

26. But I wonder also how you could ever have written that part of your letter, in which you say, that I alone wrote, and not to all of you, but to Eusebius and his fellows only. In this complaint one may discover more of readiness to find fault than of regard for truth. I received the letters against Athanasius from none other than Martyrius, Hesychius and their fellows, and I necessarily wrote to them who had written against him. Either then Eusebius and his fellows ought not alone to have written, apart from you all, or else you, to whom I did not write, ought not to be offended that I wrote to them who had written to me. If it was right that I should address my letter to you all, you also ought to have written with them ; but now considering what was reasonable, I wrote to them, who had addressed themselves to me, and had given me information. But if you were displeased because I alone wrote to them, it is but consistent that you should also be angry, because they wrote to me alone. But for this also, beloved, there was a fair and not unreasonable cause. Nevertheless it is necessary that I should acquaint you that, although I wrote, yet the sentiments I expressed were not those of myself alone, but of all the Bishops throughout Italy and in these parts. I indeed was unwilling to cause them all to write, lest the others should be overpowered by their number. The Bishops however assembled on the appointed day, and agreed in these opinions, which I again write to signify to you ; so that, dearly beloved, although I alone address you, yet you may be assured that these are the sentiments of all. Thus much for the excuses, not reasonable, but unjust and suspicious, which some of you have alleged for your conduct.

27. Now although what has already been said were sufficient to shew that we have not admitted to our communion our brothers Athanasius and Marcellus either too readily, or unjustly, yet it is but fair briefly to set the matter before you. Eusebius and his fellows wrote formerly against Athanasius and his fellows, as you also have written now ; but a great number of Bishops out of Egypt and other provinces wrote in his favour. Now in the first place, your letters against him are inconsistent with one another, and the second have no sort of agreement with the first, but in many instances the former are answered by the latter, and the latter are impeached by the former. Now where there is this contradiction

in letters, no credit whatever is due to the statements they contain. In the next place if you require us to believe what you have written, it is but consistent that we should not refuse credit to those who have written in his favour ; especially, considering that you write from a distance, while they are on the spot, are acquainted with the man, and the events which are occurring there, and testify in writing to his manner of life, and positively affirm that he has been the victim of a conspiracy throughout.

Again, a certain Bishop Arsenius was said at one time to have been made away with by Athanasius, but we have learned that he is alive, nay, that he is on terms of friendship with him. He has positively asserted that the Reports drawn up in the Mareotis were *ex parte* ones ; for that neither the Presbyter Macarius, the accused party, was present, nor yet his Bishop, Athanasius himself. This we have learnt, not only from his own mouth, but also from the Reports which Martyrius, Hesychius and their fellows, brought to us [9] ; for we found on reading them, that the accuser Ischyras was present there, but neither Macarius, nor the Bishop Athanasius ; and that the Presbyters of Athanasius desired to attend, but were not permitted. Now, beloved, if the trial was to be conducted honestly, not only the accuser, but the accused also ought to have been present. As the accused party Macarius attended at Tyre, as well as the accuser Ischyras, when nothing was proved, so not only ought the accuser to have gone to the Mareotis, but also the accused, so that in person he might either be convicted, or by not being convicted might shew the falseness of the accusation. But now, as this was not the case, but the accuser only went out thither, with those to whom Athanasius objected, the proceedings wear a suspicious appearance.

28. And he complained also that the persons who went to the Mareotis went against his wish, for that Theognius, Maris, Theodorus, Ursacius, Valens, and Macedonius, who were the persons they sent out, were of suspected character. This he shewed not by his own assertions merely, but from the letter of Alexander who was Bishop of Thessalonica ; for he produced a letter written by him to Dionysius [1], the Count who presided in the Council, in which he shews most clearly that there was a conspiracy on foot against Athanasius. He has also brought forward a genuine document, all in the handwriting of the accuser Ischyras himself [2], in which he calls God Almighty to

---

9 Infr. § 83 fin.　　　1 Infr. § 80.　　　2 § 64.

witness that no cup was broken, nor table overthrown, but that he had been suborned by certain persons to invent these accusations. Moreover, when the Presbyters of the Mareotis arrived [3], they positively affirmed that Ischyras was not a Presbyter of the Catholic Church, and that Macarius had not committed any such offence as the other had laid to his charge. The Presbyters and Deacons also who came to us testified in the fullest manner in favour of the Bishop Athanasius, strenuously asserting that none of those things which were alleged against him were true, but that he was the victim of a conspiracy.

And all the Bishops of Egypt and Libya wrote and protested [4] that his ordination was lawful and strictly ecclesiastical, and that all that you had advanced against him was false, for that no murder had been committed, nor any persons despatched on his account, nor any cup broken, but that all was false. Nay, the Bishop Athanasius also shewed from the *ex parte* reports drawn up in the Mareotis, that a catechumen was examined and said [5], that he was within with Ischyras, at the time when they say Macarius the Presbyter of Athanasius burst into the place ; and that others who were examined said,— one, that Ischyras was in a small cell,—and another, that he was lying down behind the door, being sick at that very time, when they say Macarius came thither. Now from these representations of his, we are naturally led to ask the question, How was it possible that a man who was lying behind the door sick could get up, conduct the service, and offer ? and how could it be that Oblations were offered when catechumens were within [6]? for if there were catechumens present, it was not yet the time for presenting the Oblations. These representations, as I said, were made by the Bishop Athanasius, and he showed from the reports, what was also positively affirmed by those who were with him, that Ischyras has never been a presbyter at all in the Catholic Church, nor has ever appeared as a presbyter in the assemblies of the Church ; for not even when Alexander admitted those of the Meletian schism, by the indulgence of the great Council, was he named by Meletius among his presbyters, as they deposed [7] ; which is the strongest argument possible that he was not even a presbyter of Meletius ; for otherwise, he would certainly have been numbered with the rest. Besides, it was shewn also by Athanasius from the reports, that Ischyras had spoken falsely in other instances :

for he set up a charge respecting the burning of certain books, when, as they pretend, Macarius burst in upon them, but was convicted of falsehood by the witnesses he himself brought to prove it.

29. Now when these things were thus represented to us, and so many witnesses appeared in his favour, and so much was advanced by him in his own justification, what did it become us to do ? what did the rule of the Church require of us, but that we should not condemn him, but rather receive him and treat him like a Bishop, as we have done ? Moreover, besides all this he continued here a year and six months [8], expecting the arrival of yourselves and of whoever chose to come, and by his presence he put everyone to shame, for he would not have been here, had he not felt confident in his cause ; and he came not of his own accord, but on an invitation by letter from us, in the manner in which we wrote to you [9]. But still you complain after all of our transgressing the Canons. Now consider ; who are they that have so acted ? we who received this man with such ample proof of his innocence, or they who, being at Antioch at the distance of six and thirty posts [1], nominated a stranger to be Bishop, and sent him to Alexandria with a military force ; a thing which was not done even when Athanasius was banished into Gaul, though it would have been done then, had he been really proved guilty of the offence. But when he returned, of course he found his Church unoccupied and waiting for him.

30. But now I am ignorant under what colour these proceedings have been carried on. In the first place, if the truth must be spoken, it was not right, when we had written to summon a council, that any persons should anticipate its decisions : and in the next place, it was not fitting that such novel proceedings should be adopted against the Church. For what canon of the Church, or what Apostolical tradition warrants this, that when a Church was at peace, and so many Bishops were in unanimity with Athanasius the Bishop of Alexandria, Gregory should be sent thither, a stranger to the city, not having been baptized

---

8 Spring of 339 A.D. to autumn of 340.
9 *Hist. Ar.* 9.
1 Or rather, halts, μοναί. They are enumerated in the Itinerary of Antoninus, and are set down on Montfaucon's plate. The route passes over the Delta to Pelusium, and then coasts all the way to Antioch. These μοναί were day's journeys, Coustant in Hilar. Psalm 118, Lit. 5. 2. or half a day's journey, Herman. ibid ; and were at unequal intervals, Ambros. in Psalm 118, Serm. 5. § 5. Gibbon says that by the government conveyances, "it was easy to travel an 100 miles in a day along the Roman roads." ch. ii. Μονή or mansio properly means the building, where soldiers or other public officers rested at night (hence its application to monastic houses). Such buildings included granaries, stabling, &c. vid. Con. Theod. ed. Gothofr. 1665. t. 1. p. 47, t. 2. p. 507. Du Cange *Gloss.* t. 4. p. 426. Col. 2.

---

3 § 74.   4 Supr. § 6.   5 Infr. § 83.
6 Bingh. *Ant.* X. v. 8.   7 Infr. § 71.

I 2

there, nor known to the general body, and desired neither by Presbyters, nor Bishops, nor Laity—that he should be appointed at Antioch, and sent to Alexandria, accompanied not by presbyters, nor by deacons of the city, nor by bishops of Egypt, but by soldiers? for they who came hither complained that this was the case.

Even supposing that Athanasius was in the position of a criminal after the Council, this appointment ought not to have been made thus illegally and contrary to the rule of the Church, but the Bishops of the province ought to have ordained one in that very Church, of that very Priesthood, of that very Clergy[2]; and the Canons received from the Apostles ought not thus to be set aside. Had this offence been committed against any one of you, would you not have exclaimed against it, and demanded justice as for the transgression of the Canons? Dearly beloved, we speak honestly, as in the presence of God, and declare, that this proceeding was neither pious, nor lawful, nor ecclesiastical. Moreover, the account which is given of the conduct of Gregory on his entry into the city, plainly shews the character of his appointment. In such peaceful times, as those who came from Alexandria declared them to have been, and as the Bishops also represented in their letters, the Church was set on fire; Virgins were stripped; Monks were trodden under foot; Presbyters and many of the people were scourged and suffered violence; Bishops were cast into prison; multitudes were dragged about from place to place; the holy Mysteries[3], about which they accused the Presbyter Macarius, were seized upon by heathens and cast upon the ground; and all to constrain certain persons to admit the appointment of Gregory. Such conduct plainly shews who they are that transgress the Canons. Had the appointment been lawful, he would not have had recourse to illegal proceedings to compel the obedience of those who in a legal way resisted him. And notwithstanding all this, you write that perfect peace prevailed in Alexandria and Egypt. Surely not, unless the work of peace is entirely changed, and you call such doings as these peace.

31. I have also thought it necessary to point out to you this circumstance, viz. that Athanasius positively asserted that Macarius was kept at Tyre under a guard of soldiers, while only his accuser accompanied those who went to the Mareotis; and that the Presbyters who desired to attend the inquiry were not permitted to do so, while the said inquiry respecting the cup and the Table was carried on before the Prefect and his band, and in the presence of Heathens and Jews. This at first seemed incredible, but it was proved to have been so from the Reports; which caused great astonishment to us, as I suppose, dearly beloved, it does to you also. Presbyters, who are the ministers of the Mysteries, are not permitted to attend, but an enquiry concerning Christ's Blood and Christ's Body is carried on before an external judge, in the presence of Catechumens, nay, worse than that, before Heathens and Jews, who are in ill repute in regard to Christianity. Even supposing that an offence had been committed, it should have been investigated legally in the Church and by the Clergy, not by heathens who abhor the Word and know not the Truth. I am persuaded that both you and all men must perceive the nature and magnitude of this sin. Thus much concerning Athanasius.

32. With respect to Marcellus[5], forasmuch as you have charged him also of impiety towards Christ, I am anxious to inform you, that when he was here, he positively declared that what you had written concerning him was not true; but being nevertheless requested by us to give an account of his faith, he answered in his own person with the utmost boldness, so that we recognised that he maintains nothing outside the truth. He made a confession[6] of the same godly doctrines concerning our Lord and Saviour Jesus Christ as the Catholic Church confesses; and he affirmed that he had held these opinions for a very long time, and had not recently adopted them: as indeed our Presbyters[7], who were at a former date present at the Council of Nicæa, testified to his orthodoxy; for he maintained then, as he has done now, his opposition to Arianism (on which points it is right to admonish you, lest any of you admit such heresy, instead of abominating it as alien from sound doctrine[8]). Seeing then that he professed orthodox opinions, and had testimony to his orthodoxy, what, I ask again in his case, ought we to have done, except to receive him as a Bishop, as we did, and not reject him from our communion? These things I have written, not so much for the purpose of defending their cause,

---

[2] Vid. Bingh. *Ant.* II. xi.

[3] Athan. only suggests this, supr. *Encyc.* 3. S. Hilary says the same of the conduct of the Arians at Toulouse; "Clerks were beaten with clubs; Deacons bruised with lead; nay, even *on Christ Himself* (the Saints understand my meaning) hands were laid." Contr. Constant. 11.

[5] Julius here acquits Marcellus; but he is considered heretical by S. Epiphanius, *loc. cit.* S. Basil, *Epp.* 69, 125, 263, 265. S. Chyrsostom in *Hebr. Hom.* ii. 2. Theodoret, *Hær.* ii. 10. vid. Petav. *de Trin.* i. 13. who condemns him, and Bull far more strongly, *Def. F. N.* ii. 1. § 9. Montfaucon defends him (in a special Dissertation, *Collect. Nov.* tom. 2.) and Tillemont. *Mem.* tom. 7. p. 513, and Natalis Alex. Sæc. **iv.** Dissert. 30. [Prolegg. ch. ii. § 3 (2) c.]

[6] Vid. Epiph. *Hær.* 72. 2, 3. and § 47. *infr.*

[7] Vincentius and Vito.   [8] 1 Tim. i. 10.

as in order to convince you, that we acted justly and canonically in receiving these persons, and that you are contentious without a cause. But it is your duty to use your anxious endeavours and to labour by every means to correct the irregularities which have been committed contrary to the Canon, and to secure the peace of the Churches ; so that the peace of our Lord which has been given to us [9] may remain, and the Churches may not be divided, nor you incur the charge of being authors of schism. For I confess, your past conduct is an occasion of schism rather than of peace.

33. For not only the Bishops Athanasius and Marcellus and their fellows came hither and complained of the injustice that had been done them, but many other Bishops also [1], from Thrace, from Cœle-Syria, from Phœnicia and Palestine, and Presbyters, not a few, and others from Alexandria and from other parts, were present at the Council here, and in addition to their other statements, lamented before all the assembled Bishops the violence and injustice which the Churches had suffered, and affirmed that similar outrages to those which had been committed in Alexandria had occurred in their own Churches, and in others also. Again there lately came Presbyters with letters from Egypt and Alexandria, who complained that many Bishops and Presbyters who wished to come to the Council were prevented ; for they said that, since the departure of Athanasius [2] even up to this time, Bishops who are confessors [3] have been beaten with stripes, that others have been cast into prison, and that but lately aged men, who have been an exceedingly long period in the Episcopate, have been given up to be employed in the public works, and nearly all the Clergy of the Catholic Church with the people are the objects of plots and persecutions. Moreover they said that certain Bishops and other brethren had been banished for no other reason than to compel them against their will to communicate with Gregory and his Arian associates. We have heard also from others, what is confirmed by the testimony of the Bishop Marcellus, that a number of outrages, similar to those which were committed at Alexandria, have occurred also at Ancyra in Galatia [4]. And in addition to all this, those who came to the Council reported against some of you (for I will not mention names) certain charges of so dreadful a nature that I have declined setting them down in writing : perhaps you also have heard them from others. It was for this cause especially that I wrote to desire you to come, that you might be present to hear them, and that all irregularities might be corrected and differences healed. And those who were called for these purposes ought not to have refused, but to have come the more readily, lest by failing to do so they should be suspected of what was alleged against them, and be thought unable to prove what they had written.

34. Now according to these representations, since the Churches are thus afflicted and treacherously assaulted, as our informants positively affirmed, who are they that have lighted up a flame of discord [5]? We, who grieve for such a state of things and sympathize with the sufferings of the brethren, or they who have brought these things about? While then such extreme confusion existed in every Church, which was the cause why those who visited us came hither, I wonder how you could write that unanimity prevailed in the Churches. These things tend not to the edification of the Church, but to her destruction ; and those who rejoice in them are not sons of peace, but of confusion : but our God is not a God of confusion, but of peace [6]. Wherefore, as the God and Father of our Lord Jesus Christ knows, it was from a regard for your good name, and with prayers that the Churches might not fall into confusion, but might continue as they were regulated by the Apostles, that I thought it necessary to write thus unto you, to the end that you might at length put to shame those who through the effects of their mutual enmity have brought the Churches to this condition. For I have heard, that it is only a certain few [7] who are the authors of all these things.

Now, as having bowels of mercy, take ye care to correct, as I said before, the irregularities which have been committed contrary to the Canon, so that if any mischief has already befallen, it may be healed through your zeal. And write not that I have preferred the communion of Marcellus and Athanasius to yours, for such like complaints are no indications of peace, but of contentiousness and hatred of the brethren. For this cause I have written the foregoing, that you may understand that we acted not unjustly in admitting them to our communion, and so may cease this strife. If

---

[9] Joh. xiv. 27.
[1] The names of few are known ; perhaps Marcellus, Asclepas, Paul of Constantinople, Lucius of Adrianople. vid. Montf. *in loc.* Tillem. *Mem.* tom. 7. p. 272.
[2] These outrages took place immediately on the dismission of Elpidius and Philoxenus, the Pope's legates, from Antioch. Athan. *Hist. Ar.* 12.
[3] e.g. Sarapammon and Potamo, both Confessors, who were of the number of the Nicene Fathers, and had defended Athan. at Tyre, were, the former banished, the latter beaten to death. vid. infr. *Hist. Ar.* 12.
[4] The Pseudo-Sardican Council, i.e. that of Philippopolis, retort this accusation on the party of Marcellus ; Hilar. *Fragm.* iii. 9. but the character of the outrages fixes them on the Arians, vid. infr. § 45, note [There were doubtless outrages on both sides].
[5] Vid. supr. § 25.   [6] 1 Cor. xiv. 33.
[7] Ad *Ep. Æg.* 5. *de Syn.* 5.

you had come hither, and they had been condemned, and had appeared unable to produce reasonable evidence in support of their cause, you would have done well in writing thus. But seeing that, as I said before, we acted agreeably to the Canon, and not unjustly, in holding communion with them, I beseech you for the sake of Christ, suffer not the members of Christ to be torn asunder, neither trust to prejudices, but seek rather the peace of the Lord. It is neither holy nor just, in order to gratify the petty feeling of a few persons, to reject those who have never been condemned, and thereby to grieve the Spirit[8]. But if you think that you are able to prove anything against them, and to confute them face to face, let those of you who please come hither : for they also promised that they would be ready to establish completely the truth of those things which they have reported to us.

35. Give us notice therefore of this, dearly beloved, that we may write both to them, and to the Bishops who will have again to assemble, so that the accused may be condemned in the presence of all, and confusion no longer prevail in the Churches. What has already taken place is enough : it is enough surely that Bishops have been sentenced to banishment in the presence of Bishops ; of which it behoves me not to speak at length, lest I appear to press too heavily on those who were present on those occasions. But if one must speak the truth, matters ought not to have proceeded so far ; their petty feeling ought not to have been suffered to reach the present pitch. Let us grant the "removal," as you write, of Athanasius and Marcellus, from their own places, yet what must one say of the case of the other Bishops and Presbyters who, as I said before, came hither from various parts, and who complained that they also had been forced away, and had suffered the like injuries ? O beloved, the decisions of the Church are no longer according to the Gospel, but tend only to banishment and death[9]. Supposing, as you assert, that some offence rested upon those persons, the case ought to have been conducted against them, not after this manner, but according to the Canon of the Church. Word should have been written of it to us all[1], that so a just sentence might proceed from all. For the sufferers were Bishops, and Churches of no ordinary note, but those which the Apostles themselves had governed in their own persons[2].

And why was nothing said to us concerning the Church of the Alexandrians in particular ? Are you ignorant that the custom has been for word to be written first to us, and then for a just decision to be passed from this place[3] ? If then any such suspicion rested upon the Bishop there, notice thereof ought to have been sent to the Church of this place ; whereas, after neglecting to inform us, and proceeding on their own authority as they pleased, now they desire to obtain our concurrence in their decisions, though we never condemned him. Not so have the constitutions[4] of Paul, not so have the traditions of the Fathers directed ; this is another form of procedure, a novel practice. I beseech you, readily bear with me : what I write is for the common good. For what we have received from the blessed Apostle Peter[5], that I signify to you ; and I should not have written this, as deeming that these things were manifest unto all men, had not these proceedings so disturbed us. Bishops are forced away from their sees and driven into banishment, while others from different quarters are appointed in their place ; others are treacherously assailed, so that the people have to grieve for those who are forcibly taken from them, while, as to those who are sent in their room, they are obliged to give over seeking the man whom they desire, and to receive those they do not.

I ask of you, that such things may no longer be, but that you will denounce in writing those persons who attempt them ; so that the Churches may no longer be afflicted thus, nor any Bishop or Presbyter be treated with insult, nor any one be compelled to act contrary to his judgment, as they have represented to us, lest we become a laughing-stock among the heathen, and above all, lest we excite the wrath of God

---

Ep. 9.) at Alexandria. St. Paul at Ancyra in Galatia (Tertull. *contr. Marcion.* iv. 5.) vid. Coustant. *in loc.*

3 Socrates says somewhat differently, "Julius wrote back . . . . that they acted against the Canons, because they had not called him to a Council, the Ecclesiastical Canon commanding that the Churches ought not to make Canons beside the will of the Bishop of Rome." Hist. ii. 17. Sozomen in like manner, "for it was a sacerdotal law, to declare invalid whatever was transacted beside the will of the Bishop of the Romans." Hist. iii. 10. vid. Pope Damasus ap. Theod. Hist. v. 10. Leon. Epist. 14. &c. In the passage in the text the prerogative of the Roman see is limited, as Coustant observes, to the instance of Alexandria ; and we actually find in the third century a complaint lodged against its Bishop Dionysius with the Pope. [Prolegg. ch. iv. § 4.]

4 διατάξεις. St. Paul says οὕτως ἐν ταῖς ἐκκλησίαις διατάσσομαι. 1 Cor. vii. 17. τὰ δὲ λοιπὰ διατάξομαι. Ibid. xi. 34. vid. Pearson, Vind. Ignat. p. 298. Hence Coustant in col. Athan. would suppose Julius to refer to 1 Cor. v. 4. which Athan. actually quotes, *Ep. Encycl.* § 2. supr. p. 93. Pearson, *loc. cit.* considers the διατάξεις of the Apostles, as a collection of regulation and usages, which more or less represented, or claimed to represent, what may be called St. Paul's *rule*, or St. Peter's *rule*, &c. Cotelier considers the διατάξεις as the same as the διδαχαί, the "doctrine" or "teaching" of the Apostles. Praefat. in Const. Apost. So does Beveridge, Cod. Can. Illustr. ii. 9. § 5.

5 [Petri] in Sede sua vivit potestas et excellit auctoritas Leon. Serm. iii. 3. vid. contra Barrow on the Supremacy, p. 116. ed. 1836. "not one Bishop, but all Bishops together through the whole Church, do succeed St. Peter, or any other Apostle

---

8 Eph. iv 30.   9 *Hist. Arian.* § 67.
1 Coustant *in loc.* fairly insists on the word "all," as shewing that S. Julius does not here claim the prerogative of judging *by himself* all Bishops whatever, and that what follows relates merely to the Church of Alexandria.
2 St. Peter (Greg. M. Epist. vii. Ind. 15. 40.) or St. Mark (Leo

against us. For every one of us shall give account in the Day of judgment [6] of the things which he has done in this life. May we all be possessed with the mind of God! so that the Churches may recover their own Bishops, and rejoice evermore in Jesus Christ our Lord; through Whom to the Father be glory, for ever and ever. Amen.

I pray for your health in the Lord, brethren dearly beloved and greatly longed for.

36. Thus wrote the Council of Rome by Julius, Bishop of Rome.

CHAPTER III.

Letters of the Council of Sardica to the Churches of Egypt and of Alexandria, and to all Churches.

But when, notwithstanding, Eusebius and his fellows proceeded without shame, disturbing the Churches, and plotting the ruin of many, the most religious Emperors Constantius and Constans being informed of this, commanded the Bishops from both the West and East to meet together in the city of Sardica. In the meantime Eusebius [6a] died: but a great number assembled from all parts, and we challenged the associates of Eusebius and his fellows to submit to a trial. But they, having before their eyes the things that they had done, and perceiving that their accusers had come up to the Council, were afraid to do this; but, while all besides met with honest intentions, they again brought with them the Counts [7] Musonianus [8] and Hesychius the Castrensian [9], that, as their custom was, they might effect their own aims by their authority. But when the Council met without Counts, and no soldiers were permitted to be present, they were confounded, and conscience-stricken, because they could no longer obtain the judgment they wished, but such only as reason and truth required. We, however, frequently repeated our challenge, and the Council of Bishops called upon them to come forward, saying, " You have come for the purpose of undergoing a trial; why then do you now withdraw yourselves? Either you ought not to have come, or having come, not to conceal yourselves. Such conduct will prove your greatest condemnation. Behold, Athanasius and his fellows are here, whom you accused while

absent; if therefore you think that you have any thing against them, you may convict them face to face. But if you pretend to be unwilling to do so, while in truth you are unable, you plainly shew yourselves to be calumniators, and this is the decision the Council will give you." When they heard this they were self-condemned (for they were conscious of their machinations and fabrications against us), and were ashamed to appear, thereby proving themselves to have been guilty of many base calumnies.

The holy Council therefore denounced their indecent and suspicious flight [1], and admitted us to make our defence; and when we had related their conduct towards us, and proved the truth of our statements by witnesses and other evidence, they were filled with astonishment, and all acknowledged that our opponents had good reason to be afraid to meet the Council, lest their guilt should be proved before their faces. They said also, that probably they had come from the East, supposing that Athanasius and his fellows would not appear, but that, when they saw them confident in their cause, and challenging a trial, they fled. They accordingly received us as injured persons who had been falsely accused, and confirmed yet more towards us their fellowship and love. But they deposed Eusebius's associates in wickedness, who had become even more shameless than himself, viz., Theodorus [2] of Heraclea, Narcissus of Neronias, Acacius [3] of Cæsarea, Stephanus [4] of Antioch, Ursacius and Valens of Pannonia, Menophantus of Ephesus, and George [5] of Laodicæa; and they wrote to the Bishops in all parts of the world, and to the diocese of each of the injured persons, in the following terms.

Letter of the Council of Sardica to the Church of Alexandria.

The Holy Council, by the grace of God assembled at Sardica, from [6] Rome, Spain, Gaul, Italy, Campania, Calabria, Apulia, Africa, Sardinia, Pannonia, Moesia, Dacia, Noricum, Siscia, Dardania, the other Dacia, Macedonia, Thessaly, Achaia, Epirus, Thrace, Rhodope, Palestine, Arabia, Crete, and Egypt, to their beloved brothers, the Presbyters and Deacons, and to all the Holy Church of God abiding at Alexandria, sends health in the Lord.

37. We were not ignorant, but the fact was

---

6 Matt. xii. 36.   6a Of Nicodemia.   7 *Hist. Ar.* 15.
8 Musonian was originally of Antioch, and his name Strategius; he had been promoted and honoured with a new name by Constantine, for whom he had collected information about the Manichees. Amm. Marc. xv. 13, § 1. In 354, he was Prætorian Prefect of the East. (vid. *de Syn.* 1, note 1.) Libanius praises him.
9 The Castrensians were the officers of the palace; castra, as στρατόπεδον, infr. § 86. being at this time used for the Imperial Court. vid. Gothofred in Cod. Theod. vi. 30. p. 218. Du Cange *in voc.*

1 To Philippopolis.   2 p. 111, note 2.
3 [Prolegg. ch. ii. § 8 (2) b.]   4 *Hist. Arian.* § 20.
5 [Prolegg. ch. ii. § 3 (2) c. 1. and § 8 (2) c.]
6 Vid. supr. p. 100, where Isauria, Thessaly, Sicily, Britain, &c., added. Also Theod. *H. E.* ii. 6. vid. p. 120 note 9 a.

well known to us, even before we received the letters of your piety, that the supporters of the abominated heresy of the Arians were practising many dangerous machinations, rather to the destruction of their own souls, than to the injury of the Church. For this has ever been the object of their unprincipled craft; this is the deadly design in which they have been continually engaged; viz. how they may best expel from their places and persecute all who are to be found anywhere of orthodox sentiments, and maintaining the doctrine of the Catholic Church, which was delivered to them from the Fathers. Against some they have laid false accusations; others they have driven into banishment; others they have destroyed by the punishments inflicted on them. At any rate they endeavoured by violence and tyranny to surprise the innocence of our brother and fellow-Bishop Athanasius, and therefore conducted their enquiry into his case without any care, without any faith, without any sort of justice. Accordingly having no confidence in the part they had played on that occasion, nor yet in the reports they had circulated against him, but perceiving that they were unable to produce any certain evidence respecting the case, when they came to the city of Sardica, they were unwilling to meet the Council of all the holy Bishops. From this it became evident that the decision of our brother and fellow-Bishop Julius was a just one[7]; for after cautious deliberation and care he had determined, that we ought not to hesitate at all about communion with our brother Athanasius. For he had the credible testimony of eighty Bishops, and was also able to advance this fair argument in his support that by the mere means of our dearly beloved brethren his own Presbyters, and by correspondence, he had defeated the design of Eusebius and his fellows, who relied more upon violence than upon a judicial enquiry.

Wherefore all the Bishops from all parts determined upon holding communion with Athanasius on the ground that he was innocent. And let your charity also observe, that when he came to the holy Council assembled at Sardica, the Bishops of the East were informed of the circumstance, as we said before, both by letter, and by injunctions conveyed by word of mouth, and were invited by us to be present. But, being condemned by their own conscience, they had recourse to unbecoming excuses, and set themselves to avoid the enquiry. They demanded that an innocent man should be rejected from our communion, as a culprit, not considering how un-

becoming, or rather how impossible, such a proceeding was. And as for the Reports which were framed in the Mareotis by certain most wicked and most abandoned youths[8], to whose hands one would not commit the very lowest office of the ministry, it is certain that they were *ex parte* statements. For neither was our brother the Bishop Athanasius present on the occasion, nor the Presbyter Macarius who was accused by them. And besides, their enquiry, or rather their falsification of facts, was attended by the most disgraceful circumstances. Sometimes heathens, sometimes Catechumens, were examined, not that they might declare what they knew, but that they might assert those falsehoods which they had been taught by others. And when you Presbyters, who were in charge in the absence of your Bishop, desired to be present at the enquiry, in order that you might shew the truth, and disprove the falsehoods, no regard was paid to you; they would not permit you to be present, but drove you away with insult.

Now although their calumnies have been most plainly exposed before all men by these circumstances; yet we found also, on reading the Reports, that the most iniquitous Ischyras, who has obtained from them the empty title of Bishop as his reward for the false accusation, had convicted himself of calumny. He declares in the Reports that at the very time when, according to his positive assertions, Macarius entered his cell, he lay there sick; whereas Eusebius and his fellows had the boldness to write that Ischyras was standing up and offering when Macarius came in.

38. The base and slanderous charge which they next alleged against him, has become well-known to all men. They raised a great outcry, affirming that Athanasius had committed murder, and had made away with one Arsenius a Meletian Bishop, whose loss they pretended to deplore with feigned lamentations and fictitious tears, and demanded that the body of a living man, as if a dead one, should be given up to them. But their fraud was not undetected; one and all knew that the person was alive, and was numbered among the living. And when these men, who are ready upon any opportunity, perceived their falsehoods detected (for Arsenius shewed himself alive, and so proved that he had not been made away with, and was not dead), yet they would not rest, but proceeded to add other to their former calumnies[9], and to slander the man by a fresh expedient. Well; our brother Athanasius, dearly beloved, was not confounded, but again in the

---

present case also with great boldness challenged them to the proof, and we too prayed and exhorted them to come to the trial, and if they were able, to establish their charge against him. O great arrogance! O dreadful pride! or rather, if one must say the truth, O evil and accusing conscience! for this is the view which all men take of it.

Wherefore, beloved brethren, we admonish and exhort you, above all things to maintain the right faith of the Catholic Church. You have undergone many severe and grievous trials; many are the insults and injuries which the Catholic Church has suffered, but 'he that endureth to the end, the same shall be saved[1].' Wherefore even though they still recklessly assail you, let your tribulation be unto you for joy. For such afflictions are a sort of martyrdom, and such confessions and tortures as yours will not be without their reward, but ye shall receive the prize from God. Therefore strive above all things in support of the sound faith, and of the innocence of your Bishop and our fellow-minister Athanasius. We also have not held our peace, nor been negligent of what concerns your comfort, but have deliberated and done whatsoever the claims of charity demand. We sympathize with our suffering brethren, and their afflictions we consider as our own.

39. Accordingly we have written to beseech our most religious and godly Emperors, that their kindness would give orders for the release of those who are still suffering from affliction and oppression, and would command that none of the magistrates, whose duty it is to attend only to civil causes, give judgment upon Clergy[2], nor henceforward in any way, on pretence of providing for the Churches, attempt anything against the brethren; but that every one may live, as he prays and desires to do, free from persecution, from violence and fraud, and in quietness and peace may follow the Catholic and Apostolic Faith. As for Gregory, who has the reputation of being illegally appointed by the heretics, and has been sent by them to your city, we wish your unanimity to understand, that he has been deposed by a judgment of the whole sacred Council, although indeed he has never at any time been considered to be a Bishop at all. Wherefore receive gladly your Bishop Athanasius, for to this end we have dismissed him in peace. And we exhort all those who either through fear, or through the intrigues of certain persons, have held communion with

Gregory, that now being admonished, exhorted, and persuaded by us, they withdraw from that his detestable communion, and straightway unite themselves to the Catholic Church.

40. But forasmuch as we have learnt that Aphthonius, Athanasius the son of Capito, Paul, and Plutio, our fellow Presbyters[3], have also suffered from the machinations of Eusebius and his fellows, so that some of them have had trial of exile, and others have fled on peril of their lives, we have in consequence thought it necessary to make this known unto you, that you may understand that we have received and acquitted them also, being aware that whatever has been done by Eusebius and his fellows against the orthodox has tended to the glory and commendation of those who have been attacked by them. It were fitting that your Bishop and our brother Athanasius should make this known to you respecting them, to his own respecting his own; but as for more abundant testimony he wished the holy Council also to write to you, we deferred not to do so, but hastened to signify this unto you, that you may receive them as we have done, for they also are deserving of praise, because through their piety towards Christ they have been thought worthy to endure violence at the hands of the heretics.

What decrees have been passed by the holy Council against those who are at the head of the Arian heresy, and have offended against you, and the rest of the Churches, you will learn from the subjoined documents[4]. We have sent them to you, that you may understand from them that the Catholic Church will not overlook those who offend against her.

Letter of the Council of Sardica to the Bishops of Egypt and Libya.

The holy Council, by the grace of God assembled at Sardica, to the Bishops of Egypt and Libya, their fellow-ministers and dearly beloved brethren, sends health in the Lord.

41. We were not ignorant[5], but the fact was well known to us, even before we received the letters of your piety, that the supporters of the abominated heresy of the Arians were practising many dangerous machinations, rather to the destruction of their own souls, than to the injury of the Church. For this has ever been the object of their craft and villainy: this is the deadly design in which they have been continually engaged, viz. how they may best expel from their places and persecute all who are to be found anywhere of orthodox sentiments, and maintaining the doctrine of the

---

[1] Matt. x. 22.
[2] Vid. Bingham. Antiqu. V. ii. 5. &c. Gieseler *Eccl. Hist.* vol. I. p. 242. Bassi. *Biblioth. Jur.* t. l. p. 276. Bellarm. *de Cleric.* 28.

[3] Supr. p. 109.   [4] Vid. Encycl. Letter, *infr.* § 46.
[5] It will be observed that this Letter is nearly a transcript of the foregoing. It was first printed in the Benedictine Edition.

Catholic Church, which was delivered to them from the Fathers. Against some they have laid false accusations; others they have driven into banishment; others they have destroyed by the punishments inflicted on them. At any rate they endeavoured by violence and tyranny to surprise the innocence of our brother and fellow-Bishop Athanasius, and therefore conducted their enquiry into his case without any faith, without any sort of justice. Accordingly having no confidence in the part they had played on that occasion, nor yet in the reports they had circulated against him, but perceiving that they were unable to produce any certain evidence respecting the case, when they came to the city of Sardica, they were unwilling to meet the Council of all the holy Bishops. From this it became evident that the decision of our brother and fellow-Bishop Julius was a just one; for after cautious deliberation and care he had decided, that we ought not to hesitate at all about communion with our brother Athanasius. For he had the credible testimony of eighty Bishops, and was also able to advance this fair argument in his support, that by the mere means of our dearly beloved brethren his own Presbyters, and by correspondence, he had defeated the designs of Eusebius and his fellows, who relied more upon violence than upon a judicial inquiry.

Wherefore all the Bishops from all parts determined upon holding communion with Athanasius on the ground that he was innocent. And let your charity also observe, that when he came to the holy Council assembled at Sardica, the Bishops of the East were informed of the circumstance, as we said before, both by letter, and by injunctions conveyed by word of mouth, and were invited by us to be present. But, being condemned by their own conscience, they had recourse to unbecoming excuses, and began to avoid the enquiry. They demanded that an innocent man should be rejected from our communion, as a culprit, not considering how unbecoming, or rather how impossible, such a proceeding was. And as for the reports which were framed in the Mareotis by certain most wicked and abandoned youths, to whose hands one would not commit the very lowest office of the ministry, it is certain that they were *ex parte* statements. For neither was our brother the Bishop Athanasius present on the occasion, nor the Presbyter Macarius, who was accused by them. And besides, their enquiry, or rather their falsification of facts, was attended by the most disgraceful circumstances. Sometimes Heathens, sometimes Catechumens, were examined, not that they might declare what they knew, but that they

might assert those falsehoods which they had been taught by others. And when you Presbyters, who were in charge in the absence of your Bishop, desired to be present at the enquiry, in order that you might shew the truth, and disprove falsehood, no regard was paid to you; they would not permit you to be present, but drove you away with insult.

Now although their calumnies have been most plainly exposed before all men by these circumstances; yet we found also, on reading the Reports, that the most iniquitous Ischyras, who has obtained from them the empty title of Bishop as his reward for the false accusation, had convicted himself of calumny. He declares in the Reports, that at the very time when, according to his positive assertions, Macarius entered his cell, he lay there sick; whereas Eusebius and his fellows had the boldness to write that Ischyras was standing offering when Macarius came in.

42. The base and slanderous charge which they next alleged against him has become well known unto all men. They raised a great outcry, affirming that Athanasius had committed murder, and made away with one Arsenius a Meletian Bishop, whose loss they pretended to deplore with feigned lamentations, and fictitious tears, and demanded that the body of a living man, as if a dead one, should be given up to them. But their fraud was not undetected; one and all knew that the person was alive, and was numbered among the living. And when these men, who are ready upon any opportunity, perceived their falsehood detected (for Arsenius shewed himself alive, and so proved that he had not been made away with, and was not dead), yet they would not rest, but proceeded to add other to their former calumnies, and to slander the man by a fresh expedient. Well: our brother Athanasius, dearly beloved, was not confounded, but again in the present case also with great boldness challenged them to the proof, and we too prayed and exhorted them to come to the trial, and if they were able, to establish their charge against him. O great arrogance! O dreadful pride! or rather, if one must say the truth, O evil and accusing conscience! for this is the view which all men take of it.

Wherefore, beloved brethren, we admonish and exhort you, above all things, to maintain the right faith of the Catholic Church. You have undergone many severe and grievous trials; many are the insults and injuries which the Catholic Church has suffered, but 'he that endureth to the end, the same shall be saved[6].' Wherefore, even though they

---

6 Matt. x. 22.

shall still recklessly assail you, let your tribulation be unto you for joy. For such afflictions are a sort of martyrdom, and such confessions and tortures as yours will not be without their reward, but ye shall receive the prize from God. Therefore strive above all things in support of the sound Faith, and of the innocence of your Bishop and our brother Athanasius. We also have not held our peace, nor been negligent of what concerns your comfort, but have deliberated and done whatsoever the claims of charity demand. We sympathize with our suffering brethren, and their afflictions we consider as our own, and have mingled our tears with yours. And you, brethren, are not the only persons who have suffered: many others also of our brethren in ministry have come hither, bitterly lamenting these things.

43. Accordingly, we have written to beseech our most religious and godly Emperors, that their kindness would give orders for the release of those who are still suffering from affliction and oppression, and would command that none of the magistrates, whose duty it is to attend only to civil causes, give judgment upon Clergy, nor henceforward in any way, on pretence of providing for the Churches, attempt anything against the brethren, but that every one may live, as he prays and desires to do, free from persecution, from violence and fraud, and in quietness and peace may follow the Catholic and Apostolic Faith. As for Gregory, who has the reputation of being illegally appointed by the heretics, and who has been sent by them to your city, we wish your unanimity to understand, that he has been deposed by the judgment of the whole sacred Council, although indeed he has never at any time been considered to be a Bishop at all. Wherefore receive gladly your Bishop Athanasius; for to this end we have dismissed him in peace. And we exhort all those, who either through fear, or through intrigues of certain persons, have held communion with Gregory, that being now admonished, exhorted, and persuaded by us, they withdraw from his detestable communion, and straightway unite themselves to the Catholic Church.

What decrees have been passed by the holy Council against Theodorus, Narcissus, Stephanus, Acacius, Menophantus, Ursacius, Valens, and George[7], who are the heads of the Arian heresy, and have offended against you and the rest of the Churches, you will learn from the subjoined documents. We have sent them to you, that your piety may assent to our decisions, and that you may understand

from them, that the Catholic Church will not overlook those who offend against her.

Encyclical Letter of the Council of Sardica.

The holy Council[8], by the grace of God, assembled at Sardica, to their dearly beloved brethren, the Bishops and fellow-Ministers of the Catholic Church every where, sends health in the Lord.

44. The Arian madmen have dared repeatedly to attack the servants of God, who maintain the right faith; they attempted to substitute a spurious doctrine, and to drive out the orthodox; and at last they made so violent an assault against the Faith, that it became known even to the piety of our most religious Emperors. Accordingly, the grace of God assisting them, our most religious Emperors have themselves assembled us together out of different provinces and cities, and have permitted this holy Council to be held in the city of Sardica; to the end that all dissension may be done away, and all false doctrine being driven from us, Christian godliness may alone be maintained by all men. The Bishops of the East also attended, being exhorted to do so by the most religious Emperors, chiefly on account of the reports they have so often circulated concerning our dearly beloved brethren and fellow-ministers Athanasius, Bishop of Alexandria, and Marcellus, Bishop of Ancyro-Galatia. Their calumnies have probably already reached you, and perhaps they have attempted to disturb your ears, that you may be induced to believe their charges against the innocent, and that they may obliterate from your minds any suspicions respecting their own wicked heresy. But they have not been permitted to effect this to any great extent; for the Lord is the Defender of His Churches, Who endured death for their sakes and for us all, and provided access to heaven for us all through Himself. When therefore Eusebius and his fellows wrote long ago to Julius our brother and Bishop of the Church of the Romans, against our forementioned brethren, that is to say, Athanasius, Marcellus, and Asclepas[9], the Bishops from the other parts wrote also, testifying to the innocence of our fellow-minister Athana-

---

8 Vid. Theod. *Hist.* ii. 6. Hil. *Fragm.* ii.
9 Asclepas, or Asclepius of Gaza, Epiph. *Hær.* 69. 4. was one of the Nicene Fathers, and according to Theod. *Hist.* i. 27. was at the Council of Tyre, which Athan. also attended, but only by compulsion. According to the Eusebians at Philippopolis, they had deposed him [17 years previously, but the number must be corrupt, or the statement incorrect]. They state, however, at the same time, that he had been condemned by Athanasius and Marcellus, vid. Hilar. *Fragm.* iii. 13. Sozomen, *Hist.* iii. 8. says that they deposed him on the charge of having overturned an altar; and, after Athan. *infr.* § 47, that he was acquitted at Sardica on the ground that Eusebius of Cæsarea and others had reinstated him in his see (before 339). There is mention of a Church built by him in Gaza ap. Bolland. Febr. 26. Vit. L. Porphyr. n. 20. p. 648.

sius, and declaring that the representations of Eusebius and his fellows were nothing else but mere falsehood and calumny.

And indeed their calumnies were clearly proved by the fact that, when they were invited to a Council by our dearly beloved fellow-minister Julius, they would not come, and also by what was written to them by Julius himself. For had they had confidence in the measures and the acts in which they were engaged against our brethren, they would have come. And besides, they gave a still more evident proof of their conspiracy by their conduct in this great and holy Council. For when they arrived at the city of Sardica, and saw our brethren Athanasius, Marcellus, Asclepas, and the rest, they were afraid to come to a trial, and though they were repeatedly invited to attend, they would not obey the summons. Although all we Bishops met together, and above all that man of most happy old age, Hosius, one who on account of his age, his confession, and the many labours he has undergone, is worthy of all reverence; and although we waited and urged them to come to the trial, that in the presence of our fellow-ministers they might establish the truth of those charges which they had circulated and written against them in their absence; yet they would not come, when they were thus invited, as we said before, thus giving proof of their calumnies, and almost proclaiming to the world by this their refusal, the plot and conspiracy in which they have been engaged. They who are confident of the truth of their assertions are able to make them good against their opponents face to face. But as they would not meet us, we think that no one can now doubt, however they may again have recourse to their bad practices, that they possess no proof against our fellow-ministers, but calumniate them in their absence, while they avoid their presence.

45. They fled, beloved brethren, not only on account of the calumnies they had uttered, but because they saw that those had come who had various charges to advance against them. For chains and irons were brought forward which they had used; persons appeared who had returned from banishment; there came also our brethren, kinsmen of those who were still detained in exile, and friends of such as had perished through their means. And what was the most weighty ground of accusation, Bishops were present, one[1] of whom brought forward the irons and chains which they had caused him to wear, and others appealed to the death which had been brought

about by their calumnies. For they had proceeded to such a pitch of madness, as even to attempt to destroy Bishops; and would have destroyed them, had they not escaped their hands. Our fellow-ministers, Theodulus of blessed memory[2], died during his flight from their false accusations, orders having been given in consequence of these to put him to death. Others also exhibited sword-wounds; and others complained that they had been exposed to the pains of hunger through their means. Nor were they ordinary persons who testified to these things, but whole Churches, in whose behalf legates appeared[3], and told us of soldiers sword in hand, of multitudes armed with clubs, of the threats of judges, of the forgery of false letters. For there were read certain false letters of Theognius and his fellows against our fellow-ministers Athanasius, Marcellus, and Asclepas, written with the design of exasperating the Emperors against them; and those who had then been Deacons of Theognius proved the fact. From these men, we heard of virgins stripped naked, churches burnt, ministers in custody, and all for no other end, but only for the sake of the accursed heresy of the Arian madmen, whose communion whoso refused was forced to suffer these things.

When they perceived then how matters lay, they were in a strait what course to choose. They were ashamed to confess what they had done, but were unable to conceal it any longer. They therefore came to the city of Sardica, that by their arrival they might seem to remove suspicion from themselves of such offences. But when they saw those whom they had calumniated, and those who had suffered at their hands; when they had before their eyes their accusers and the proofs of their guilt, they were unwilling to come forward, though invited by our fellow-ministers Athanasius, Marcellus, and Asclepas, who with great freedom complained of their conduct, and urged and challenged them to the trial, promising not only to refute their calumnies, but also to bring proof of the offences which they had committed against

---

[1] Perhaps Lucius of Hadrianople, says Montfaucon, referring to Apol. de Fug. § 3. vid. also Hist. Arian. 19.

[2] Theodulus, Bishop of Trajanopolis in Thrace, who is here spoken of as deceased, seems to have suffered this persecution from the Eusebians upon their retreat from Sardica, vid. Athan. Hist. Arian. § 19. We must suppose then with Montfaucon, that the Council, from whom this letter proceeds, sat some considerable time after that retreat, and that the proceedings spoken of took place in the interval. Socrates, however, makes Theodulus survive Constans, who died 350. H. E. ii. 26.

[3] The usual proceeding of the Arians was to retort upon the Catholics the charges which they brought against them, supr. § 33, note 4. Accordingly, in their Encyclical from Philippopolis, they say that "a vast multitude had congregated at Sardica, of wicked and abandoned persons, from Constantinople and Alexandria; who lay under charges of murder, blood, slaughter, robbery, plunder, spoiling, and all nameless sacrileges and crimes; who had broken altars, burnt Churches, ransacked private houses," &c. &c. Hil. Fragm. iii. 19.

their Churches. But they were seized with such terrors of conscience, that they fled ; and in doing so they exposed their own calumnies, and confessed by running away the offences of which they had been guilty.

46. But although their malice and their calumnies have been plainly manifested on this as well as on former occasions, yet that they may not devise means of practising a further mischief in consequence of their flight, we have considered it advisable to examine the part they have played according to the principles of truth ; this has been our purpose, and we have found them calumniators by their acts, and authors of nothing else than a plot against our brethren in ministry. For Arsenius, who they said had been murdered by Athanasius, is still alive, and is numbered among the living ; from which we may infer that the reports they have spread abroad on other subjects are fabrications also. And whereas they spread abroad a rumour concerning a cup, which they said had been broken by Macarius the Presbyter of Athanasius, those who came from Alexandria, the Mareotis, and the other parts, testified that nothing of the kind had taken place. And the Egyptian Bishops[2] who wrote to Julius our fellow-minister, positively affirmed that there had not arisen among them even any suspicion whatever of such a thing.

Moreover, the Reports, which they say they have to produce against him, are, as is notorious, *ex parte* statements ; and even in the formation of these very Reports, Heathens and Catechumens were examined ; one of whom, a Catechumen, said[3] in his examination that he was present in the room when Macarius broke in upon them ; and another declared, that Ischyras of whom they speak so much, lay sick in his cell at the time ; from which it appears that the Mysteries were never celebrated at all, because Catechumens were present, and also that Ischyras was not present, but was lying sick on his bed. Besides, this most worthless Ischyras, who has falsely asserted, as he was convicted of doing, that Athanasius had burnt some of the sacred books, has himself confessed that he was sick, and was lying in his bed when Macarius came; from which it is plain that he is a slanderer. Nevertheless, as a reward for these his calumnies, they have given to this very Ischyras the title of Bishop, although he is not even a Presbyter. For two Presbyters, who were once associated with Meletius, but were afterwards received by the blessed Alexander, Bishop of Alexandria, and are now with

Athanasius, appeared before the Council, and testified that he was not even a Presbyter of Meletius, and that Meletius never had either Church or Minister in the Mareotis. And yet this man, who has never been even a Presbyter, they have now brought forward as a Bishop, that by this name they may have the means of overpowering those who are within hearing of his calumnies.

47. The book of our fellow-minister Marcellus was also read, by which the fraud of Eusebius and his fellows was plainly discovered. For what Marcellus had advanced by way of enquiry[4], they falsely represented as his professed opinion ; but when the subsequent parts of the book were read, and the parts preceding the queries themselves, his faith was found to be correct. He had never pretended, as they positively affirmed[5], that the Word of God had His beginning from holy Mary, nor that His kingdom had an end; on the contrary he had written that His kingdom was both without beginning and without end. Our fellow-minister Asclepas also produced Reports which had been drawn up at Antioch in the presence of his accusers and Eusebius of Cæsarea, and proved that he was innocent by the declarations of the Bishops who judged his cause[6]. They had good reason therefore, dearly beloved brethren, for not hearkening to our frequent summons, and for deserting the Council. They were driven to this by their own consciences ; but their flight only confirmed the proof of their own calumnies, and caused those things to be believed against them, which their accusers, who were present, were asserting and arguing. But besides all these things, they had not only received those who were formerly degraded and ejected on account of the heresy of Arius, but had even promoted them to a higher station, advancing Deacons to the Presbytery, and of Presbyters making Bishops, for no other end, but that they might disseminate and spread abroad impiety, and corrupt the orthodox faith.

48. Their leaders are now, after Eusebius and his fellows, Theodorus of Heraclea, Narcissus of Neronias in Cilicia, Stephanus of Antioch, George of Laodicea, Acacius of Cæsarea in Palestine, Menophantus of Ephesus in Asia, Ursacius of Singidunum in Mœsia, and Valens of Mursa in Pannonia[7]. These men would not permit those who came with them from the East to meet the holy Council, nor even to approach the Church of God ; but as they were coming to Sardica, they held Councils in

---

4 Cf. *de Decr.* § 25, note.   5 *De Syn.* § 25, note.
6 § 44, note 9.
7 Vid. supr. §§ 13, note, and 36. About Stephanus, vid. infr. *Hist. Arian.* § 20.

various places by themselves, and made an engagement under threats, that when they came to Sardica, they would not so much as appear at the trial, nor attend the assembling of the holy Council, but simply coming and making known their arrival as a matter of form, would speedily take to flight. This we have been able to ascertain from our fellow-ministers, Macarius of Palestine and Asterius of Arabia[8], who after coming in their company, separated themselves from their unbelief. These came to the holy Council, and complained of the violence they had suffered, and said that no right act was being done by them; adding that there were many among them who adhered to orthodoxy, but were prevented by those men from coming hither, by means of the threats and promises which they held out to those who wished to separate from them. On this account it was that they were so anxious that all should abide in one dwelling, and would not suffer them to be by themselves even for the shortest space of time.

49. Since then it became us not to hold our peace, nor to pass over unnoticed their calumnies, imprisonments, murders, wounds, conspiracies by means of false letters, outrages, stripping of the virgins, banishments, destruction of the Churches, burnings, translations from small cities to larger dioceses, and above all, the rising of the ill-named Arian heresy by their means against the orthodox faith; we have therefore pronounced our dearly beloved brethren and fellow-ministers Athanasius, Marcellus, and Asclepas, and those who minister to the Lord with them, to be innocent and clear of offence, and have written to the diocese of each, that the people of each Church may know the innocence of their own Bishop, and may esteem him as their Bishop and expect his coming.

And as for those who like wolves[9] have invaded their Churches, Gregory at Alexandria, Basil at Ancyra, and Quintianus at Gaza, let them neither give them the title of Bishop, nor hold any communion at all with them, nor receive letters[10] from them, nor write to them. And for Theodorus, Narcissus, Acacius, Stephanus, Ursacius, Valens, Menophantus, and George, although the last from fear did not come from the East, yet because he was deposed by the blessed Alexander, and because both he and the others were connected with the Arian madness, as well as on account of the charges which lie against them, the holy Council has unanimously deposed them from

the Episcopate, and we have decided that they not only are not Bishops, but that they are unworthy of holding communion with the faithful.

For they who separate the Son and alienate the Word from the Father, ought themselves to be separated from the Catholic Church and to be alien from the Christian name. Let them therefore be anathema to you, because they have 'corrupted the word of truth[1].' It is an Apostolic injunction[2], 'If any man preach any other Gospel unto you than that ye have received, let him be accursed.' Charge your people that no one hold communion with them, for there is no communion of light with darkness; put away from you all these, for there is no concord of Christ in Belial[3]. And take heed, dearly beloved, that ye neither write to them, nor receive letters from them; but desire rather, brethren and fellow-ministers, as being present in spirit[3a] with our Council, to assent to our judgments by your subscriptions[4], to the end that concord may be preserved by all our fellow-ministers everywhere. May Divine Providence protect and keep you, dearly beloved brethren, in sanctification and joy.

I, Hosius, Bishop, have subscribed this, and all the rest likewise.

This is the letter which the Council of Sardica sent to those who were unable to attend, and they on the other hand gave their judgment in accordance; and the following are the names both of those Bishops who subscribed in the Council, and of the others also.

50. Hosius of Spain[5], Julius of Rome by his Presbyters Archidamus and Philoxenus, Protogenes of Sardica, Gaudentius, Macedonius, Severus, Prætextatus, Ursicius, Lucillus, Eugenius, Vitalius, Calepodius, Florentius, Bassus, Vincentius, Stercorius, Palladius, Domitianus, Chalbis, Gerontius, Protasius, Eulogus, Porphyrius, Dioscorus, Zosimus, Januarius, Zosimus, Alexander, Eutychius, Socrates, Diodorus, Martyrius, Eutherius, Eucarpus, Athenodorus, Irenæus,

---

1 2 Cor. ii. 17.   2 Gal. i. 9.
3 2 Cor. vi. 14, 15.   3a 1 Cor. v. 3.
4 In like manner the Council of Chalcedon was confirmed by as many as 470 subscriptions, according to Ephrem (*Phot. Bibl.* p. 801) by 1600 according to Eulogius (ibid. p. 877), i.e. of Bishops, Archimandrites, &c.
5 Hosius is called by Athan. the father and the president of the Council. *Hist. Arian.* 15, 16. Roman controversialists here explain why Hosius does not sign himself as the Pope's legate, De Marc. *Concord.* v. 4. Alber. *Dissert.* ix. and Protestants why his legates rank before all the other Bishops, even before Protogenes, Bishop of the place. Basnage, *Ann.* 347. 5. Febronius considers that Hosius signed here and at Nicæa, as a sort of representative of the civil, and the Legates of ecclesiastical supremacy. *de Stat. Eccl.* vi. 4. And so Thomassin, "Imperator velut exterior Episcopus: præfuit autem summus Pontifex, ut Episcopus interior." Dissert. in Conc. x. 14. The popes never attended in person the Eastern Councils. St. Leo excuses himself on the plea of its being against usage. Epp. 37. and 93. [Silvester's absence from Nicæa was due solely to extreme old age. But Sardica was a *Western* council.]

---

8 [For Macarius, read Arius.] These two Bishops were soon after the Council banished by Eusebian influence into upper Libya, where they suffered extreme ill usage. vid. *Hist. Arian.* § 18.
9 Vid. Acts xx. 29.   10 p. 95, note 4.

Julianus, Alypius, Jonas, Aetius, Restitutus, Marcellinus, Aprianus, Vitalius, Valens, Hermogenes, Castus, Domitianus, Fortunatius, Marcus, Annianus, Heliodorus, Musæus, Asterius, Paregorius, Plutarchus, Hymenæus, Athanasius, Lucius, Amantius, Arius, Asclepius, Dionysius, Maximus, Tryphon, Alexander, Antigonus, Ælianus, Petrus, Symphorus, Musonius, Eutychus, Philologius, Spudasius, Zosimus, Patricius, Adolius, Sapricius[6].

From Gaul the following; Maximianus[6a], Verissimus[6b], Victurus, Valentinus[1], Desiderius, Eulogius, Sarbatius, Dyscolius[2], Superior, Mercurius, Declopetus, Eusebius, Severinus[3], Satyrus, Martinus, Paulus, Optatianus, Nicasius, Victor[4], Sempronius, Valerinus, Pacatus, Jesses, Ariston, Simplicius, Metianus, Amantus[5], Amillianus, Justinianus, Victorinus[6], Satornilus, Abundantius, Donatianus, Maximus.

From Africa; Nessus, Gratus[7], Megasius, Coldæus, Rogatianus, Consortius, Rufinus, Manninus, Cessilianus, Herennianus, Marianus, Valerius, Dynamius, Mizonius, Justus, Celestinus, Cyprianus, Victor, Honoratus, Marinus, Pantagathus, Felix, Baudius, Liber, Capito, Minervalis, Cosmus, Victor, Hesperio, Felix, Severianus, Optantius, Hesperus, Fidentius, Salustius, Paschasius.

From Egypt; Liburnius, Amantius, Felix, Ischyrammon, Romulus, Tiberinus, Consortius, Heraclides, Fortunatius, Dioscorus, Fortunatianus, Bastamon, Datyllus, Andreas, Serenus, Arius, Theodorus, Evagoras, Helias, Timotheus, Orion, Andronicus, Paphnutius, Hermias, Arabion, Psenosiris, Apollonius, Muis, Sarapampon[8], Philo, Philippus, Apollonius, Paphnutius, Paulus, Dioscorus, Nilammon, Serenus, Aquila, Aotas, Harpocration, Isac, Theodorus, Apollos, Ammonianus, Nilus, Heraclius, Arion, Athas, Arsenius, Agathammon, Theon, Apollonius, Helias, Paninuthius, Andragathius, Nemesion, Sarapion, Ammonius, Ammonius, Xenon, Gerontius, Quintus, Leonides, Sempronianus, Philo, Heraclides, Hieracys, Rufus, Pasophius, Macedonius, Apollodorus, Flavianus, Psaes, Syrus, Apphus, Sarapion, Esaias, Paphnutius, Timotheus, Elurion, Gaius, Musæus, Pistus, Heraclammon, Heron, Helias, Anagamphus, Apollonius, Gaius, Philotas, Paulus, Tithoes, Eudæmon, Julius.

Those on the road[9] of Italy are Proba-

tius, Viator, Facundinus, Joseph, Numedius, Sperantius, Severus, Heraclianus, Faustinus, Antoninus, Heraclius, Vitalius, Felix, Crispinus, Paulianus.

From Cyprus; Auxibius, Photius, Gerasius, Aphrodisius, Irenicus, Nunechius, Athanasius, Macedonius, Triphyllius, Spyridon, Norbanus, Sosicrates.

From Palestine; Maximus, Aetius, Arius, Theodosius, Germanus, Silvanus, Paulus, Claudius, Patricius, Elpidius, Germanus, Eusebius, Zenobius, Paulus, Petrus.

These are the names of those who subscribed to the acts of the Council; but there are very many beside, out of Asia, Phrygia, and Isauria[9a], who wrote in my behalf before this Council was held, and whose names, nearly sixty-three in number, may be found in their own letters. They amount altogether to three hundred and forty-four[10].

CHAPTER IV.

Imperial and Ecclesiastical Acts in consequence of the Decision of the Council of Sardica.

51. WHEN the most religious Emperor Constantius heard of these things, he sent for me, having written privately to his brother Constans of blessed memory, and to me three several times in the following terms.

Constantius Victor Augustus to Athanasius[1].

Our benignant clemency will not suffer you to be any longer tempest-tossed by the wild waves of the sea; for our unwearied piety has not lost sight of you, while you have been bereft of your native home, deprived of your goods, and have been wandering in savage wildernesses. And although I have for a long time deferred expressing by letter the purpose of my mind concerning you, principally because I expected that you would appear before us of your own accord, and would seek a relief of your sufferings; yet forasmuch as fear, it may be, has prevented you from fulfilling your intentions, we have therefore addressed to your fortitude letters full of our bounty, to the end that you may use all speed and without fear present yourself in our presence, thereby to obtain the enjoyment of your wishes, and that, having experience of our kindness, you may be

---

6 [The above names, with a few exceptions, comprise those present at the Council. See additional Note at the end of this Apology, where a list is given in alphabetical order of all bishops present, with their Sees.]
6a Of Treveri.
6b Of Lyons.   1 Of Arles.   2 Of Rheims.
3 Of Sens.   4 Of Worms.   5 Of Strassburg.
6 Of Paris.   7 Of Carthage.   8 §§ 33, note 3a, and 78.
9 οἱ ἐν τῷ καναλίῳ τῆς Ἰταλίας. "Canalis est, non via regia aut militaris, verum via tranversa, quæ in regiam seu basilicam influit, quasi aquæ canalis in alveum." Gothofred. in Cod. Theod. vi. *de Curiosis*, p. 196. who illustrates the word at length. Du Cange

on the contrary, *in voc.* explains it of "the high road." Tillemont professes himself unable to give a satisfactory sense to it. vol. viii. p. 685. [The word occurs in the XIth. Sardican canon, where the Greek version (Can. XX. in Bruns) glosses it καναλίῳ ἤτοι παρόδῳ.]
9a Cf. § 36.
10 Athan. says, supr. § 1. that the Letter of the Council was signed in all by more than 300. It will be observed, that Athan.'s numbers in the text do not accurately agree with each other. The subscriptions enumerated are 284, to which 63 being added, made a total of 347, not 344. [The enumeration of Ath. includes many who signed long afterwards. Those 'from Palestine' are simply the signatories of the synodal letter of 346, below § 57. The number, 170, mentioned by Ath. *Hist. Ar.* 15 gives an orthodox majority of 20. See additional Note at end of this Apology, and Gwatkin, *Studies*, p. 121, note.]
1 Written A.D. 345.

restored again to your own. For this purpose I have besought my lord and brother Constans Victor Augustus, in your behalf, that he would give you permission to come, in order that you may be restored to your country with the consent of us both, receiving this as a pledge of our favour.

The Second Letter.

Although we made it very plain to you in a former letter that you may without hesitation come to our Court, because we greatly wished to send you home, yet, we have further sent this present letter to your fortitude to exhort you without any distrust or apprehension, to place yourself in the public conveyances [2], and to hasten to us, that you may enjoy the fulfilment of your wishes.

The Third Letter.

Our pleasure was, while we abode at Edessa, and your Presbyters were there, that, on one of them being sent to you, you should make haste to come to our Court, in order that you might see our face, and straightway proceed to Alexandria. But as a very long period has elapsed since you received letters from us, and you have not yet come, we therefore hasten to remind you again, that you may endeavour even now to present yourself before us with speed, and so may be restored to your country, and obtain the accomplishment of your prayers. And for your fuller information we have sent Achitas the Deacon, from whom you will be able to learn the purpose of our soul, that you may now secure the objects of your prayers.

Such was the tenor of the Emperor's letters; on receiving which I went up to Rome to bid farewell to the Church and the Bishop : for I was at Aquileia [3] when the above was written. The Church was filled with all joy, and the Bishop Julius rejoiced with me in my return and wrote to the Church [4] ; and as we passed along, the Bishops of every place sent us on our way in peace. The letter of Julius was as follows.

---

[2] Gothof. in *Cod. Theod.* viii. 5. p. 507.   [3] *Apol. Const.* 3, 15.
[4] "They acquainted Julius the Bishop of Rome with their case ; and he, according to the prerogative (προνόμια) of the Church in Rome, fortified them with letters in which he spoke his mind, and sent them back to the East, restoring each to his own place, and remarking on those who had violently deposed them. They then set out from Rome, and on the strength (θαρροῦντες) of the letters of Bishop Julius, take possession of their Churches." Socr. ii. 15. It must be observed, that in the foregoing sentences Socrates has spoken of "(*imperial*) Rome." Sozomen says, "Whereas the care of all (κηδεμονίας) pertained to him on account of the dignity of his see, he restored each to his own Church." iii. 8. "I answer," says Barrow, "the Pope did not restore them *judicially*, but *declaratively*, that is, declaring his approbation of their right and innocence, did admit them to communion. . . . Besides, the Pope's proceeding was taxed, and protested against, as irregular : . . . and, lastly, the restitution of Athanasius and the other Bishops had no complete effect, till it was confirmed by the synod of Sardica, backed by the imperial authority." *Suprem.* p. 360. ed. 1836.

52. Julius to the Presbyters, Deacons, and people residing at Alexandria [5].

I congratulate you, beloved brethren, that you now behold the fruit of your faith before your eyes ; for any one may see that such indeed is the case with respect to my brother and fellow-Bishop Athanasius, whom for the innocency of his life, and by reason of your prayers, God is restoring to you again. Wherefore it is easy to perceive, that you have continually offered up to God pure prayers and full of love. Being mindful of the heavenly promises, and of the conversation that leads to them, which you have learnt from the teaching of my brother aforesaid, you knew certainly and understood by the right faith that is in you, that he, whom you always had as present in your most pious minds, would not be separated from you for ever. Wherefore there is no need that I should use many words in writing to you ; for your faith has already anticipated whatever I could say to you, and has by the grace of God procured the accomplishment of the common prayers of you all. Therefore, I repeat again, I congratulate you, because you have preserved your souls unconquered in the faith ; and I also congratulate no less my brother Athanasius, in that, though he is enduring many afflictions, he has at no time been forgetful of your love and earnest desires towards him. For although for a season he seemed to be withdrawn from you in body, yet he has continued to live as always present with you in spirit [6].

53. Wherefore he returns to you now more illustrious than when he went away from you. Fire tries and purifies the precious materials, gold and silver : but how can one describe the worth of such a man, who, having passed victorious through the perils of so many tribulations, is now restored to you, being pronounced innocent not by our voice only, but by the voice of the whole Council [7] ? Receive therefore, beloved brethren, with all godly honour and rejoicing, your Bishop Athanasius, together with those who have been partners with him in so many labours. And rejoice that you now obtain the fulfilment of your prayers, after that in your salutary letter you have given meat and drink to your Pastor, who, so to speak, longed and thirsted after your godliness. For while he sojourned in a foreign land, you were his consolation ; and you refreshed him during his persecutions by your most faithful minds and spirits. And it delights me now to conceive

---

[5] Written early in 346 A.D.
[6] Athan. here omits a paragraph in his own praise. vid. Socr. ii. 23.   [7] § 35, note 3.

and figure to my mind the joy of every one of you at his return, and the pious greetings of the concourse, and the glorious festivity of those that run to meet him. What a day will that be to you, when my brother comes back again, and your former sufferings terminate, and his much-prized and desired return inspires you all with an exhilaration of perfect joy! The like joy it is ours to feel in a very great degree, since it has been granted us by God, to be able to make the acquaintance of so eminent a man. It is fitting therefore that I should conclude my letter with a prayer. May Almighty God, and His Son our Lord and Saviour Jesus Christ, afford you continual grace, giving you a reward for the admirable faith which you displayed in your noble confession in behalf of your Bishop, that He may impart unto you and unto them that are with you, both here and hereafter, those better things, which 'the eye hath not seen, nor ear heard, neither hath entered into the heart of man, the things which God hath prepared for them that love Him[8],' through our Lord Jesus Christ, through Whom to Almighty God be glory for ever and ever. Amen. I pray, dearly beloved brethren, for your health and strength in the Lord.

54. The Emperor, when I came to him[9] with these letters, received me kindly, and sent me forth to my country and Church, addressing the following to the Bishops, Presbyters, and People.

Constantius, Victor, Maximus, Augustus, to the Bishops and Presbyters of the Catholic Church.

The most reverend Athanasius has not been deserted by the grace of God, but although for a brief season he was subjected to trial to which human nature is liable, he has obtained from the all-surveying Providence such an answer to his prayers as was meet, and is restored by the will of the Most High, and by our sentence, at once to his country and to the Church, over which by divine permission he presided. Wherefore, in accordance with this, it is fitting that it should be provided by our clemency, that all the decrees which have heretofore been passed against those who held communion with him, be now consigned to oblivion, and that all suspicions respecting them be henceforward set at rest, and that immunity, such as the Clergy who are associated with him formerly enjoyed, be duly confirmed to them. Moreover to our other acts of favour towards him we have thought good to add the following, that all persons of

the sacred catalogue[1] should understand, that an assurance of safety is given to all who adhere to him, whether Bishops, or other Clergy. And union with him will be a sufficient guarantee, in the case of any person, of an upright intention. For whoever, acting according to a better judgment and part, shall choose to hold communion with him, we order, in imitation of that Providence which has already gone before, that all such should have the advantage of the grace which by the will of the Most High is now offered to them from us. May God preserve you.

The Second Letter.

Constantius, Victor, Maximus, Augustus, to the people of the Catholic Church at Alexandria.

55. Having in view your welfare in all respects, and knowing that you have for a long time been deprived of episcopal superintendence, we have thought good to send back to you your Bishop Athanasius, a man known to all men for the uprightness that is in him, and for the good disposition of his personal character. Receive him, as you are wont to receive every one, in a suitable manner, and, using his advocacy as your succour in your prayers to God, endeavour to preserve continually that unanimity and peace according to the order of the Church which is at the same time becoming in you, and most advantageous for us. For it is not becoming that any dissension or faction should be raised among you, contrary to the prosperity of our times. We desire that this offence may be altogether removed from you, and we exhort you to continue stedfastly in your accustomed prayers, and to make him, as we said before, your advocate and helper towards God. So that, when this your determination, beloved, has influenced the prayers of all men, even those heathen who are still addicted to the false worship of idols may eagerly desire to come to the knowledge of our sacred religion. Again therefore we exhort you to continue in these things, and gladly to receive your Bishop, who is sent back to you by the decree of the Most High, and by our decision, and determine to greet him cordially with all your soul and with all your mind. For this is what is both becoming in you, and agreeable to our clemency. In order that all occasions of disturbance and sedition may be taken away from those who are maliciously disposed, we have by letter commanded the magistrates who are among you to subject to the vengeance of

---

[8] 1 Cor. ii. 9.
[9] [At Antioch September(?) 346. See Prolegg. ch. ii. § 6 (3).]

[1] Vid. Bingh. *Antiqu.* I v. 10.

the law all whom they find to be factious. Wherefore taking into consideration both these things, our decision in accordance with the will of the Most High, and our regard for you and for concord among you, and the punishment that awaits the disorderly, observe such things as are proper and suitable to the order of our sacred religion, and receiving the afore-mentioned Bishop with all reverence and honour, take care to offer up with him your prayers to God, the Father of all, in behalf of yourselves, and for the well-being of your whole lives.

56. Having written these letters, he also commanded that the decrees, which he had formerly sent out against me in consequence of the calumnies of Eusebius and his fellows, should be cancelled and struck out from the Orders of the Duke and the Prefect of Egypt; and Eusebius the Decurion[2] was sent to withdraw them from the Order-books. His letter on this occasion was as follows.

Constantius, Victor, Augustus, to Nestorius[3]. (*And in the same terms, to the Governors of Augustamnica, the Thebais, and Libya.*)

Whatever Orders are found to have been passed heretofore, tending to the injury and dishonour of those who hold communion with the Bishop Athanasius, we wish them to be now erased. For we desire that whatever immunities his Clergy possessed before, they should again possess the same. And we wish this our Order to be observed, that when the Bishop Athanasius is restored to his Church, those who hold communion with him may enjoy the immunities which they have always enjoyed, and which the rest of the Clergy enjoy; so that they may have the satisfaction of being on an equal footing with others.

57. Being thus set forward on my journey, as I passed through Syria, I met with the Bishops of Palestine, who when they had called a Council[4] at Jerusalem, received me cordially, and themselves also sent me on my way in peace, and addressed the following letter to the Church and the Bishops.

The Holy Council, assembled at Jerusalem, to the fellow-ministers in Egypt and Libya, and to the Presbyters, Deacons, and People at Alexandria, brethren beloved and greatly longed for, sends health in the Lord.

We cannot give worthy thanks to the God of all, dearly beloved, for the wonderful things which He has done at all times, and especially at this time for your Church, in restoring to you your pastor and lord, and our fellow-minister Athanasius. For who ever

hoped that his eyes would see what you are now actually obtaining? Of a truth, your prayers have been heard by the God of all, Who cares for His Church, and has looked upon your tears and groans, and has therefore heard your petitions. For ye were as sheep scattered and fainting, not having a shepherd[5]. Wherefore the true Shepherd, Who careth for His own sheep, has visited you from heaven, and has restored to you him whom you desire. Behold, we also, being ready to do all things for the peace of the Church, and being prompted by the same affection as yourselves, have saluted him before you; and communicating with you through him, we send you these greetings, and our offering of thanksgiving, that you may know that we also are united in the bond of love that joins you to him. You are bound to pray also for the piety of our most God-beloved Emperors, who, when they knew your earnest longings after him, and his innocency, determined to restore him to you with all honour. Wherefore receive him with uplifted hands, and take good heed that you offer up due thanksgiving on his behalf to God Who has bestowed these blessings upon you; so that you may continually rejoice with God and glorify our Lord, in Christ Jesus our Lord, through Whom to the Father be glory for ever. Amen.

I have set down here the names of those who subscribed this letter, although I have mentioned them before[6]. They are these; Maximus, Aetius, Arius, Theodorus[7], Germanus, Silvanus, Paulus, Patricius, Elpidius, Germanus, Eusebius, Zenobius, Paulus, Macrinus[8], Petrus, Claudius.

58. When Ursacius and Valens saw all this, they forthwith condemned themselves for what they had done, and going up to Rome, confessed their crime, declared themselves penitent, and sought forgiveness[9], addressing the following letters to Julius, Bishop of ancient Rome, and to ourselves. Copies of them were sent to me from Paulinus, Bishop of Treveri[10].

A Translation from the Latin of a Letter[1] to Julius, concerning the recantation of Ursacius and Valens[2].

Ursacius and Valens to the most blessed lord, pope Julius.

---

2 Member of the Curia or Council.   3 Prefect of Egypt, vid. *Vita Ant.* 86, *Fest. Ind.* xvii.—xxiv.   4 *Hist. Arian.* 25.

5 Matt. ix. 36.   6 § 50.   7 Theodosius, *supr.*   8 Not *supr.* 9 Cf. § 20, note 4.   10 Τριβέρων, Paul *infr. Hist. Ar.* 26. 1 *Hist. Arian.* 25. 26.

2 [Gibbon, ch. xxi. note 108, doubts the fact of this recantation on the ground of the dissimilar tone of the two letters that follow. Newman explains that they treat Julius as 'a superior,' Athanasius as 'an equal;' but surely he was something more than an equal. Fear of Constans, and the desire to secure themselves from attack, would make it important for them at any price to obtain the favour of the first bishop of the West. In order to do this they had to make their peace with Athanasius; but in doing so, they went no further than they could help.]

Whereas it is well known that we have heretofore in letters laid many grievous charges against the Bishop Athanasius, and whereas, when we were corrected by the letters of your Goodness, we were unable to render an account of the statement we had made; we do now confess before your Goodness, and in the presence of all the Presbyters our brethren, that all the reports which have heretofore come to your hearing respecting the case of the aforesaid Athanasius, are falsehoods and fabrications, and are utterly inconsistent with his character. Wherefore we earnestly desire communion with the aforesaid Athanasius, especially since your Piety, with your characteristic generosity, has vouchsafed to pardon our error. But we also declare, that if at any time the Eastern Bishops, or even Athanasius himself, ungenerously should wish to bring us to judgment for this matter, we will not depart contrary to your judgment. And as for the heretic Arius and his supporters, who say that once the Son was not, and that the Son was made of that which was not, and who deny that Christ is God and the Son of God before the worlds, we anathematize them both now and for evermore, as also we have set forth in our former declaration at Milan[3]. We have written this with our own hands, and we profess again, that we have renounced for ever, as we said before, the Arian heresy and its authors.

I Ursacius subscribed this my confession in person; and likewise I Valens.

Ursacius and Valens, Bishops, to their lord and brother, the Bishop Athanasius.

Having an opportunity of sending by our brother and fellow Presbyter Musæus, who is coming to your Charity, we salute you affectionately, beloved brother, through him, from Aquileia, and pray you, being as we trust in health, to read our letter. You will also give us confidence, if you will return to us an answer in writing. For know that we are at peace with you, and in communion with the Church, of which the salutation prefixed to this letter is a proof. May Divine Providence preserve you, my Lord, our beloved brother!

Such were their letters, and such the sentence and the judgment of the Bishops in my behalf. But in order to prove that they did not act thus to ingratiate themselves, or under compulsion in any quarter, I desire, with your permission, to recount the whole matter from the beginning, so that you may perceive that the bishops wrote as they did with upright and just intentions, and that Ursacius and

Valens, though they were slow to do so, at last confessed the truth.

PART II.

CHAPTER V.

Documents connected with the charges of the Meletians against S. Athanasius.

59. PETER was Bishop among us before the persecution, and during the course of it he suffered martyrdom. When Meletius, who held the title of bishop in Egypt, was convicted of many crimes, and among the rest of offering sacrifice to idols, Peter deposed him in a general council of the bishops. Whereupon Meletius did not appeal to another council, or attempt to justify himself before those who should come after, but made a schism, so that they who espoused his cause are even yet called Meletians instead of Christians[1]. He began immediately to revile the bishops, and made false accusations, first against Peter himself, and against his successor Achillas, and after Achillas, against Alexander[2]. And he thus practised craftily, following the example of Absalom, to the end that, as he was disgraced by his deposition, he might by his calumnies mislead the simple. While Meletius was thus employed, the Arian heresy also had arisen. But in the Council of Nicæa, while the heresy was anathematized, and the Arians were cast out, the Meletians on whatever grounds[3] (for it is not necessary now to mention the reason) were received. Five months however had not yet passed[4] when, the blessed Alexander having died, the Meletians, who ought to have remained quiet, and to have been grateful that they were received on any terms, like dogs unable to forget their vomit, were again troubling the Churches.

Upon learning this, Eusebius, who had the lead in the Arian heresy, sends and buys the Meletians with large promises, becomes their secret friend, and arranges with them for their assistance on any occasion when he might wish for it. At first he sent to me, urging me to admit Arius and his fellows to communion[5], and threatened me in his verbal communications, while in his letters he [merely] made a request. And when I refused, declaring that it was not right that those who had invented

---

[1] Cf. *Orat.* i. 2 and notes.   [2] Ad. *Ep. Æg.* § 22. supr. § 11.
[3] [Prolegg. ch. ii. § 3 (1) *ad fin.*] Athan. speaks more openly against this arrangement. infr. § 71.
[4] [According to the tenses in the original the five months mark the date not of Alexander's death (April 17, 328), but of the renewed Meletian troubles. The settlement did not keep them quiet for five months. The *terminus a quo* of the five months is somewhat doubtful; but it certainly is not the Council of Nicæa, see § 71, &c. Montf. *Monit. in Vit. S. Athanasii*, also Prolegg. ch. ii. § 3 (1) and ch. v. ᵟ 3 a.]   [5] Ad. *Ep. Æg.* 23.

heresy contrary to the truth, and had been anathematized by the Ecumenical [6] Council, should be admitted to communion, he caused the Emperor also, Constantine, of blessed memory, to write to me, threatening me, in case I should not receive Arius and his fellows, with those afflictions, which I have before undergone, and which I am still suffering. The following is a part of his letter. Syncletius and Gaudentius, officers of the palace [7], were the bearers of it.

Part of a Letter from the Emperor Constantine.

Having therefore knowledge of my will, grant free admission to all who wish to enter into the Church. For if I learn that you have hindered or excluded any who claim to be admitted into communion with the Church, I will immediately send some one who shall depose you by my command, and shall remove you from your place.

60. When upon this I wrote and endeavoured to convince the Emperor, that that anti-Christian heresy had no communion with the Catholic Church, Eusebius forthwith, availing himself of the occasion which he had agreed upon with the Meletians, writes and persuades them to invent some pretext, so that, as they had practised against Peter and Achillas and Alexander, they might devise and spread reports against us also. Accordingly, after seeking for a long time, and finding nothing, they at last agree together, with the advice of Eusebius and his fellows, and fabricate their first accusation by means of Ision, Eudæmon, and Callinicus [8], respecting the linen vestments [9], to the effect that I had imposed a law upon the Egyptians, and had required its observance of them first. But when certain Presbyters of mine were found to be present, and the Emperor took cognizance of the matter, they were condemned (the Presbyters were Apis and Macarius), and the Emperor wrote, condemning Ision, and ordering me to appear before him. His letters were as follows [1].

Eusebius, having intelligence of this, persuades them to wait; and when I arrive, they next accuse Macarius of breaking the cup, and bring against me the most heinous accusation possible, viz. that, being an enemy of the Emperor, I had sent a purse of gold to one Philumenus. The Emperor therefore heard us on this charge also in Psammathia [2], when they, as usual, were condemned, and

driven from the presence; and, as I returned, he wrote the following letter to the people.

Constantine, Maximus, Augustus, to the people of the Catholic Church at Alexandria.

61. Beloved brethren, I greet you well, calling upon God, Who is the chief witness of my intention, and on the Only-begotten, the Author of our Law, Who is Sovereign over the lives of all men, and Who hates dissensions. But what shall I say to you? That I am in good health? Nay, but I should be able to enjoy better health and strength, if you were possessed with mutual love one towards another, and had rid yourselves of your enmities, through which, in consequence of the storms excited by contentious men, we have left the haven of brotherly love. Alas! what perverseness is this! What evil consequences are produced every day by the tumult of envy which has been stirred up among you! Hence it is that evil reports have settled upon the people of God. Whither has the faith of righteousness departed? For we are so involved in the mists of darkness, not only through manifold errors, but through the faults of ungrateful men, that we bear with those who favour folly, and though we are aware of them, take no heed of those who set aside goodness and truth. What strange inconsistency is this! We do not convict our enemies, but we follow the example of robbery which they set us, whereby the most pernicious errors, finding no one to oppose them, easily, if I may so speak, make a way for themselves. Is there no understanding among us, for the credit of our common nature, since we are thus neglectful of the injunctions of the law?

But some one will say, that love is a thing brought out by nature. But, I ask, how is it that we who have got the law of God for our guide in addition to our natural advantages, thus tolerate the disturbances and disorders raised by our enemies, who seem inflamed, as it were, with firebrands? How is it, that having eyes, we see not, neither understand, though we are surrounded by the intelligence of the law? What a stupor has seized upon our life, that we are thus neglectful of ourselves, and that although God admonishes us! Is it not an intolerable evil? and ought we not to esteem such men as our enemies, and not the household and people of God? For they are infuriated against us, abandoned as they are: they lay grievous crimes to our charge, and make attacks upon us as enemies.

62. And I would have you yourselves to consider with what exceeding madness they do

---

[6] Supr. § 7, and *de Decr.* 27.
[7] παλατῖνοι, vid. *Apol. ad Const.* § 19.
[8] Infr. § 71 fin. Sozom. ii. 25.
[9] στιχάρια, ecclesiastical. [See D.C.A. p. 1933.]
[1] They are lost.
[2] Suburb of Nicomedia, infr. § 65.

this. The foolish men carry their maliciousness at their tongues' end. They carry about with them a sort of leaden anger, so that they reciprocally smite one another, and involve us by way of increasing their own punishment. The good teacher is accounted an enemy, while he who clothes himself with the vice of envy, contrary to all justice makes his gain of the gentle temper of the people; he ravages, and consumes, he decks himself out, and recommends himself with false praises; he subverts the truth, and corrupts the faith, until he finds out a hole and hiding-place for his conscience. Thus their very perverseness makes them wretched, while they impudently prefer themselves to places of honour, however unworthy they may be. Ah! what a mischief is this! they say "Such an one is too old; such an one is a mere boy; the office belongs to me; it is due to me, since it is taken away from him. I will gain over all men to my side, and then I will endeavour with my power to ruin him." Plain indeed is this proclamation of their madness to all the world; the sight of companies, and gatherings, and rowers under command[3] in their offensive cabals. Alas! what preposterous conduct is ours, if I may say it! Do they make an exhibition of their folly in the Church of God? And are they not yet ashamed of themselves? Do they not yet blame themselves? Are they not smitten in their consciences, so that they now at length shew that they entertain a proper sense of their deceit and contentiousness? Theirs is the mere force of envy, supported by those baneful influences which naturally belong to it. But those wretches have no power against your Bishop. Believe me, brethren, their endeavours will have no other effect than this, after they have worn down our days, to leave to themselves no place of repentance in this life. Wherefore I beseech you, lend help to yourselves; receive kindly our love, and with all your strength drive away those who desire to obliterate from among us the grace of unanimity; and looking unto God, love one another. I received gladly your Bishop Athanasius, and addressed him in such a manner, as being persuaded that he was a man of God. It is for you to understand these things, not for me to judge of them. I thought it becoming that the most reverend Athanasius himself should convey my salutation to you, knowing his kind care of you, which, in a manner worthy of that peaceable faith which I myself profess, is continually engaged in the good work of declaring saving knowledge, and

will be able to exhort you as is suitable, May God preserve you, beloved brethren.

Such was the letter of Constantine.

63. After these occurrences the Meletians remained quiet for a little time, but afterwards shewed their hostility again, and contrived the following plot, with the aim of pleasing those who had hired their services. The Mareotis is a country district of Alexandria, in which Meletius was not able to make a schism. Now while the Churches still existed within their appointed limits, and all the Presbyters had congregations in them, and while the people were living in peace, a certain person named Ischyras[4], who was not a clergyman, but of a worthless disposition, endeavoured to lead astray the people of his own village, declaring himself to be a clergyman. Upon learning this, the Presbyter of the place informed me of it when I was going through my visitation of the Churches, and I sent Macarius the Presbyter with him to summon Ischyras. They found him sick and lying in a cell, and charged his father to admonish his son not to continue any such practices as had been reported against him. But when he recovered from his sickness, being prevented by his friends and his father from pursuing the same course, he fled over to the Meletians; and they communicate with Eusebius and his fellows, and at last that calumny is invented by them, that Macarius had broken a cup, and that a certain Bishop named Arsenius had been murdered by me. Arsenius they placed in concealment, in order that he might seem made away with, when he did not make his appearance; and they carried about a hand, pretending that he had been cut to pieces. As for Ischyras, whom they did not even know, they began to spread a report that he was a Presbyter, in order that what he said about the cup might mislead the people. Ischyras, however, being censured by his friends, came to me weeping, and said that no such thing as they had reported had been done by Macarius, and that himself had been suborned by the Meletians to invent this calumny. And he wrote the following letter.

To the Blessed pope[5] Athanasius, Ischyras sends health in the Lord.

64. As when I came to you, my Lord Bishop, desiring to be received into the Church, you reproved me for what I formerly said, as though I had proceeded to such lengths of my own free choice, I therefore

---

4 Cf. §§ 46, 72, 77.

5 Cf. de Syn. 16, [and Fest. Ind. passim].

submit to you this my apology in writing, in order that you may understand, that violence was used towards me, and blows inflicted on me by Isaac and Heraclides, and Isaac of Letopolis, and those of their party. And I declare, and take God as my witness in this matter, that of none of the things which they have stated, do I know you to be guilty. For no breaking of a cup or overturning of the Holy Table ever took place, but they compelled me by violent usage to assert all this. And this defence I make and submit to you in writing, desiring and claiming for myself to be admitted among the members of your congregation. I pray that you may have health in the Lord.

I submit this my handwriting to you the Bishop Athanasius in the presence of the Presbyters, Ammonas of Dicella, Heraclius of Phascos, Boccon of Chenebri, Achillas of Myrsine, Didymus of Taphosiris, and Justus from Bomotheus [6]; and of the Deacons, Paul, Peter, and Olympius, of Alexandria, and Ammonius, Pistus, Demetrius, and Gaius, of the Mareotis.

65. Notwithstanding this statement of Ischyras, they again spread abroad the same charges against me everywhere, and also reported them to the Emperor Constantine. He too had heard before of the affair of the cup in Psammathia [7], when I was there, and had detected the falsehood of my enemies. But now he wrote to Antioch to Dalmatius [8] the Censor requiring him to institute a judicial enquiry respecting the murder. Accordingly the Censor sent me notice to prepare for my defence against the charge. Upon receiving his letters, although at first I paid no regard to the thing because I knew that nothing of what they said was true, yet seeing that the Emperor was moved, I wrote to my fellow-ministers into Egypt, and sent a deacon, desiring to learn something of Arsenius, for I had not seen the man for five or six years. Well, not to relate the matter at length, Arsenius was found in concealment, in the first instance in Egypt, and afterwards my friends discovered him again in concealment in Tyre also. And what was most remarkable, even when he was discovered he would not confess that he was Arsenius, until he was convicted in court before

Paul, who was then Bishop of Tyre, and at last out of very shame could not deny it.

This he did in order to fulfil his contract with Eusebius and his fellows, lest, if he were discovered, the game they were playing should at length be broken up ; which in fact came to pass. For when I wrote the Emperor word, that Arsenius was discovered, and reminded him of what he had heard in Psammathia concerning Macarius the Presbyter, he stopped the proceedings of the Censor's court, and wrote condemning the proceedings against me as calumnious, and commanded Eusebius and his fellows, who were coming into the East to appear against me, to return. Now in order to shew that they accused me of having murdered Arsenius (not to bring forward the letters of many persons on the subject), it shall be sufficient only to produce one from Alexander the Bishop of Thessalonica, from which the tenor of the rest may be inferred. He then being acquainted with the reports which Archaph, who is also called John, circulated against me on the subject of the murder, and having heard that Arsenius was alive, wrote as follows.

Letter of Alexander.

To his dearly beloved son and fellow-minister like-minded, the lord Athanasius, Alexander the Bishop sends health in the Lord.

66. I congratulate the most excellent Sarapion, that he is striving so earnestly to adorn himself with holy habits, and is thus advancing to higher praise the memory of his father. For, as the Holy Scripture somewhere says, ' though his father die, yet he is as though he were not dead [9]:' for he has left behind him a memorial of his life. What my feelings were towards the ever memorable Sozon, you yourself, my lord [10], are not ignorant, for you know the sacredness of his memory, as well as the goodness of the young man. I have received only one letter from your reverence, which I had by the hands of this youth. I mention this to you, my lord, in order that you may know. Our dearly beloved brother and deacon Macarius, afforded me great pleasure by writing to me from Constantinople, that the false accuser Archaph had met with disgrace, for having given out before all men that a live man had been murdered. That he will receive from the righteous Judge, together with all the tribe of his associates, that punishment, which his crimes deserve, the unerring Scriptures assure us. May the Lord of all preserve you for

---

6 [Cf. the list of Mareotic clergy *supr.*, p. 72. The three deacons of Alexandria are in the list, p. 71].

7 Vid. § 60.

8 Dalmatius was the name of father and son, the brother and nephew of Constantine. Socrates, *Hist.* i. 27. gives the title of Censor to the son ; but the *Chron. Pasch.* p. 531 (Dind.) gives it to the father. Valesius, and apparently Tillemont (*Empereurs*, vol. 4. p. 657) think Socrates mistaken. The younger Dalmatius was created Cæsar by Constantine a few year before his death ; and as well as his brother Hannibalian, and a number of other relatives, was put to death by the soldiery, on the death of Constantine. vid. *Hist. Ar.* 69. [Gwatkin, p. 108 note].

9 Ecclus. 30. 4   10 δέσποτα. Theod. *H E.* i. 5. init.

very many years, my lord, in every way most kind.

67. And they who lived with Arsenius bear witness, that he was kept in concealment for this purpose, that they might pretend his death; for in searching after him we found the person [who had done so], and he in consequence wrote the following letter to John, who played the chief part in this false accusation.

To his dearly beloved brother John, Pinnes, Presbyter of the Monastery [11] of Ptemencyrcis, in the nome of Anteopolis, sends greeting.

I wish you to know, that Athanasius sent his deacon into the Thebais, to search everywhere for Arsenius; and Pecysius the Presbyter, and Silvanus the brother of Helias, and Tapenacerameus, and Paul monk of Hypsele, whom he first fell in with, confessed that Arsenius was with us. Upon learning this we caused him to be put on board a vessel, and to sail to the lower countries with Helias the monk. Afterwards the deacon returned again suddenly with certain others, and entered our monastery, in search of the same Arsenius, and him they found not, because, as I said before, we had sent him away to the lower countries; but they conveyed me together with Helias the monk, who took him out of the way, to Alexandria, and brought us before the Duke [1]; when I was unable to deny, but confessed that he was alive, and had not been murdered: the monk also who took him out of the way confessed the same. Wherefore I acquaint you with these things, Father, lest you should determine to accuse Athanasius; for I said that he was alive, and had been concealed with us, and all this is become known in Egypt, and it cannot any longer be kept secret.

I, Paphnutius, monk of the same monastery, who wrote this letter, heartily salute you. I pray for your health.

The following also is the letter which the Emperor wrote when he learnt that Arsenius was found to be alive.

Constantine, Victor, Maximus, Augustus, to the pope Athanasius.

68. Having read the letters of your wisdom, I felt the inclination to write in return to your fortitude, and to exhort you that you would endeavour to restore the people of God to tranquillity, and to merciful feelings. For in my own mind I hold these things to be of the greatest importance, that we should cultivate truth, and ever keep righteousness in our thoughts, and have pleasure especially in those who walk in the right way of life. But as concerning those who are deserving of all execration, I mean the most perverse and ungodly Meletians, who have at last stultified themselves by their folly, and are now raising unreasonable commotions by envy, uproar, and tumult, thus making manifest their own ungodly dispositions, I will say thus much. You see that those who they pretended had been slain with the sword, are still amongst us, and in the enjoyment of life. Now what could be a stronger presumption against them, and one so manifestly and clearly tending to their condemnation, as that those whom they declared to have been murdered, are yet in the enjoyment of life, and accordingly will be able to speak for themselves?

But this further accusation was advanced by these same Meletians. They positively affirmed that you, rushing in with lawless violence, had seized upon and broken a cup, which was deposited in the most Holy Place; than which there certainly could not be a more serious charge, nor a more grievous offence, had such a crime actually been perpetrated. But what manner of accusation is this? What is the meaning of this change and variation and difference in the circumstances of it, insomuch that they now transfer this same accusation to another person [2], a fact which makes it clearer, so to speak, than the light itself, that they designed to lay a plot for your wisdom? After this, who can be willing to follow them, men that have fabricated such charges to the injury of another, seeing too that they are hurrying themselves on to ruin, and are conscious that they are accusing you of false and feigned crimes? Who then, as I said, will follow after them, and thus go headlong in the way of destruction; in that way in which it seems they alone suppose that they have hope of safety and of help? But if they were willing to walk according to a pure conscience, and to be directed by the best wisdom, and to go in the way of a sound mind, they would easily perceive that no help can come to them from Divine Providence, while they are given up to such doings, and tempt their own destruction. I should not call this a harsh judgment of them, but the simple truth.

---

[11] [The μονή here is not a monastery in the later sense, but a village or cluster of cells. This intercepted letter demonstrates the existence of *Meletian* monks, of which there is other evidence also: (see below, Introd. to *Vit. Ant.* The objection of Weingarten to the genuineness of this letter is purely arbitrary)].

[1] According to the system of government introduced by Diocletian and Constantine, there were thirty-five military commanders of the troops, under the Magistri militum, and all of these bore the name of duces or dukes; the comites, or counts, were ten out of the number, who were distinguished as companions of the Emperor. vid. Gibbon, ch. 17. Three of these dukes were stationed in Egypt [i.e. in the whole prefecture; one only in the province of Egypt in the narrower sense].

[2] Cf. § 28.

And finally, I will add, that I wish this letter to be read frequently by your wisdom in public, that it may thereby come to the knowledge of all men, and especially reach the ears of those who thus act, and thus raise disturbances; for the judgment which is expressed by me according to the dictates of equity is confirmed also by real facts. Wherefore, seeing that in such conduct there is so great an offence, let them understand that I have thus judged; and that I have come to this determination, that if they excite any further commotion of this kind, I will myself in person take cognizance of the matter, and that not according to the ecclesiastical, but according to the civil laws, and so I will in future find them out, because they clearly are robbers, so to speak, not only against human kind, but against the divine doctrine itself. May God ever preserve you, beloved brother!

69. But that the wickedness of the calumniators might be more fully displayed, behold Arsenius also wrote to me after he was discovered in his place of concealment; and as the letter which Ischyras had written confessed the falsehood of their accusation, so that of Arsenius proved their maliciousness still more completely.

To the blessed Pope Athanasius, Arsenius, Bishop of those who were heretofore under Meletius in the city of the Hypselites, together with the Presbyters and Deacons, wishes much health in the Lord.

Being earnestly desirous of peace and union with the Catholic Church, over which by the grace of God you preside, and wishing to submit ourselves to the Canon of the Church, according to the ancient rule[3], we write unto you, dearly beloved Pope, and declare in the name of the Lord, that we will not for the future hold communion with those who continue in schism, and are not yet at peace with the Catholic Church, whether Bishops, Presbyters, or Deacons. Neither will we take part with them if they wish to establish anything in a Council; neither will we send letters of peace[3a] unto them nor receive such from them; neither yet without the consent of you, the bishop of the metropolis, will we publish any determination concerning Bishops, or on any other general ecclesiastical question; but we will yield obedience to all the canons that have heretofore been ordained, after the example of the Bishops[4] Ammonian, Ty-

rannus, Plusian, and the rest. Wherefore we beseech your goodness to write to us speedily in answer, and likewise to our fellow-ministers concerning us, informing them that we will henceforth abide by the fore-mentioned resolution and will be at peace with the Catholic Church, and at unity with our fellow-ministers in the [various] districts. And we are persuaded that your prayers, being acceptable unto God, will so prevail with Him, that this peace shall be firm and indissoluble unto the end, according to the will of God the Lord of all, through Jesus Christ our Lord.

The sacred Ministry that is under you, we and those that are with us salute. Very shortly, if God permit, we will come to visit your goodness. I, Arsenius, pray for your health in the Lord for many years, most blessed Pope.

70. But a stronger and clearer proof of the calumny against us is the recantation of John, of which the most God-beloved Emperor Constantine of blessed memory is a witness, for knowing how John had accused himself, and having received letters from him expressing his repentance, he wrote to him as follows.

Constantine, Maximus, Augustus to John.

The letters which I have received from your prudence were extremely pleasing to me, because I learned from them what I very much longed to hear, that you had laid aside every petty feeling, had joined the Communion of the Church as became you, and were now in perfect concord with the most reverend Bishop Athanasius. Be assured therefore that so far I entirely approve of your conduct; because, giving up all skirmishing, you have done that which is pleasing to God, and have embraced the unity of His Church. In order therefore that you may obtain the accomplishment of your wishes, I have thought it right to grant you permission to enter the public conveyance[5], and to come

---

[3] Vid. *supr.* p. 92, note 3: the (so-called) Apostolical Canon apparently referred to here, is Can. 27. according to Beveridge.

[3a] Cf. p. 95, note 4.

[4] i.e. Meletian Bishops who had conformed; or, since they are not in the list, § 71. Catholic Bishops with whom the conforming party were familiar; or Meletians after the return of Meletius. vid. Tillemont, *Mem.* vol. 8. p. 658

[5] On the "cursus publicus," vid. Gothofred. *in Cod. Theod.* viii. tit. 5. It was provided for the journeys of the Emperor, for persons whom he summoned, for magistrates, ambassadors, and for such private persons as the Emperor indulged in the use of it, which was gratis. The use was granted by Constantine to the Bishops who were summoned to Nicæa, as far as it went, in addition (though aliter Valesius in loc.) to other means of travelling. Euseb. *v. Const.* iii. 6. The cursus publicus brought the Bishops to the Council of Tyre. *ibid.* iv. 43. In the conference between Liberius and Constantius, Theod. *Hist.* ii. 13. it is objected that the cursus publicus is not sufficient to convey Bishops to the Council which Liberius proposes; he answers that the Churches are rich enough to convey their Bishops as far as the sea. Thus S. Hilary was compelled (data evectionis copia, Sulp. Sev. *Hist.* ii. 57.) to attend at Seleucia, as Athan. at Tyre. Julian complains of the abuse of the cursus publicus, perhaps with an allusion to these Councils of Constantius. vid. *Cod. Theod.* viii. tit. 5. l. 12. where Gothofred quotes Liban. *Epitaph. in Julian.* (vol. i. p. 569. ed. Reiske.) Vid. the well-known passage of Ammianus, who speaks of the Councils being the ruin of the res vehicularia *Hist.* xxi. 16. The Eusebians at Philippopolis say the same thing. Hilar. *Frag.* iii. 25. The Emperor provided board and perhaps

to the court[6] of my clemency. Let it then be your care to make no delay; but as this letter gives you authority to use the public conveyance, come to me immediately, that you may have your desires fulfilled, and by appearing in my presence may enjoy that pleasure which it is fit for you to receive. May God preserve you continually, dearly beloved brother.

CHAPTER VI.

Documents connected with the Council of Tyre.

71. Thus ended the conspiracy. The Meletians were repulsed and covered with shame; but notwithstanding this Eusebius and his fellows still did not remain quiet, for it was not for the Meletians but for Arius and his fellows, that they cared, and they were afraid lest, if the proceedings of the former should be stopped, they should no longer find persons to play the parts[1], by whose assistance they might bring in that heresy. They therefore again stirred up the Meletians, and persuaded the Emperor to give orders that a Council should be held afresh at Tyre, and Count Dionysius was despatched thither, and a military guard was given to Eusebius and his fellows. Macarius also was sent as a prisoner to Tyre under a guard of soldiers; and the Emperor wrote to me, and laid a peremptory command upon me, so that, however unwilling, I set out. The whole conspiracy may be understood from the letters which the Bishops of Egypt wrote; but it will be necessary to relate how it was contrived by them in the outset, that so may be perceived the malice and wickedness that was exercised against me. There are in Egypt, Libya, and Pentapolis, nearly one hundred Bishops; none of whom laid anything to my charge; none of the Presbyters found any fault with me; none of the people spoke aught against me; but it was the Meletians who were ejected by Peter, and the Arians, that divided the plot between them, while the one party claimed to themselves the right of accusing me, the other of

sitting in judgment on the case. I objected to Eusebius and his fellows as being my enemies on account of the heresy; next, I shewed in the following manner that the person who was called my accuser was not a Presbyter at all. When Meletius was admitted into communion (would that he had never been so admitted[2]!) the blessed Alexander who knew his craftiness required of him a schedule of the Bishops whom he said he had in Egypt, and of the presbyters and deacons that were in Alexandria itself, and if he had any in the country district. This the Pope Alexander has done, lest Meletius, having received the freedom of the Church, should tender[3] many, and thus continually, by a fraudulent procedure, foist upon us whomsoever he pleased. Accordingly he has made out the following schedule of those in Egypt.

A schedule presented by Meletius to the Bishop Alexander.

I, Meletius of Lycopolis, Lucius of Antinopolis, Phasileus of Hermopolis, Achilles of Cusæ, Ammonius of Diospolis.

In Ptolemais, Pachymes of Tentyræ.

In Maximianopolis, Theodorus of Coptus.

In Thebais, Cales of Hermethes, Colluthus of Upper Cynopolis, Pelagius of Oxyrynchus, Peter of Heracleopolis, Theon of Nilopolis, Isaac[4] of Letopolis, Heraclides of Niciopolis[4], Isaac of Cleopatris, Melas of Arsenoitis.

In Heliopolis, Amos of Leontopolis, Ision of Athribis.

In Pharbethus, Harpocration of Bubastus, Moses of Phacusæ, Callinicus[5] of Pelusium, Eudæmon of Tanis[5], Ephraim of Thmuis.

In Sais, Hermæon of Cynopolis and Busiris, Soterichus of Sebennytus, Pininuthes of Phthenegys, Cronius of Metelis, Agathammon of the district of Alexandria.

In Memphis, John who was ordered by the Emperor to be with the Archbishop[6]. These are those of Egypt.

And the Clergy that he had in Alexandria were Apollonius Presbyter, Irenæus Presbyter, Dioscorus Presbyter, Tyrannus Presbyter. And Deacons; Timotheus Deacon, Antinous Deacon, Hephæstion Deacon. And Macarius Presbyter of Parembole[7].

72. These Meletius presented actually in person[8] to the Bishop Alexander, but he made no mention of the person called Ischyras, nor ever

---

lodging for the Bishops at Ariminum; which the Bishops of Aquitaine, Gaul, and Britain, declined, except three British from poverty. Sulp. *Hist.* ii. 56. Hunneric in Africa, after assembling 466 Bishops at Carthage, dismissed them without modes of conveyance, provision, or baggage. Victor Utic. *Hist.* iii. init. In the Emperor's letter previous to the assembling of the sixth Ecumenical Council, A.D. 678, (Harduin, *Conc.* t. 3. p. 1048 fin.) he says he has given orders for the conveyance and maintenance of its members. Pope John VIII. reminds Ursus, Duke of Venice (A.D. 876.), of the same duty of providing for the members of a Council, "secundum pios principes, qui in talibus munifice semper erant intenti." Colet. *Concil.* (Ven. 1730,) t. xi. p. 14.
6 στρατόπεδον· vid. Chrys. *on the Statues*, p. 382, note 6. Gothofr. in Cod. Theod. vi. 32, 1. 1. Castra sunt ubi Princeps est. ibid. 35, l. 15. also Kiesling. *de Discipl. Cler.* i. 5. p. 16. Beveridge *in Can. Apost.* 83. interprets στρατεία of any civil engagement as opposed to clerical.　　　　　 1 Cf. § 17, note 1.

---

2 Cf. § 59.
3 [πωλήσῃ: i.e. palm them off on the church. Cf. Lat. *venditare.*]　　4 Cf. § 64.　　　　5 Cf. § 60.
6 [The 'archbishop' is Meletius; this is the first occurrence of the word; it evidently has not its later fixed sense. The historical allusion is obscure.]
7 A village on the Mareotic lake. vid. Socr. iv. 23. Athan Opp. ed. Pat. t. 3. p. 86—89.
8 [Prolegg. ch. ii. § 3 (1) *sub. fin.* and ch. v. § 3 a.]

professed at all that he had any Clergy in the Mareotis. Notwithstanding our enemies did not desist from their attempts, but still he that was no Presbyter was feigned to be one, for there was the Count ready to use compulsion towards us, and soldiers were hurrying us about. But even then the grace of God prevailed: for they could not convict Macarius in the matter of the cup; and Arsenius, whom they reported to have been murdered by me, stood before them alive and shewed the falseness of their accusation. When therefore they were unable to convict Macarius, Eusebius and his fellows, who became enraged that they had lost the prey of which they had been in pursuit, persuaded the Count Dionysius, who is one of them, to send to the Mareotis, in order to see whether they could not find out something there against the Presbyter, or rather that they might at a distance patch up their plot as they pleased in our absence: for this was their aim. However,—when we represented that the journey to the Mareotis was a superfluous undertaking (for that they ought not to pretend that statements were defective which they had been employed upon so long, and ought not now to defer the matter; for they had said whatever they thought they could say, and now being at a loss what to do, they were making pretences); or if they must needs go to the Mareotis, that at least the suspected parties should not be sent,—the Count was convinced by my reasoning, with respect to the suspected persons; but they did anything rather than what I proposed, for the very persons whom I objected against on account of the Arian heresy, these were they who promptly went off, viz. Diognius, Maris, Theodorus, Macedonius, Ursacius, and Valens. Again, letters were written to the Prefect of Egypt, and a military guard was provided; and, what was remarkable and altogether most suspicious, they caused Macarius the accused party to remain behind under a guard of soldiers, while they took with them the accuser[9]. Now who after this does not see through this conspiracy? Who does not clearly perceive the wickedness of Eusebius and his fellows? For if a judicial enquiry must needs take place in the Mareotis, the accused also ought to have been sent thither. But if they did not go for the purpose of such an enquiry, why did they take the accuser? It was enough that he had not been able to prove the fact. But this they did in order that they might carry on their designs against the absent Presbyter, whom they could not convict when present, and might concoct a plan as they pleased. For when the Presbyters of Alexandria and

of the whole district found fault with them because they were there by themselves, and required that they too might be present at their proceedings (for they said that they knew both the circumstances of the case, and the history of the person named Ischyras), they would not allow them; and although they had with them Philagrius the Prefect of Egypt[1], who was an apostate, and heathen soldiers, during an enquiry which it was not becoming even for Catechumens to witness, they would not admit the Clergy, lest there as well as at Tyre there might be those who would expose them.

73. But in spite of these precautions they were not able to escape detection: for the Presbyters of the City and of the Mareotis, perceiving their evil designs, addressed to them the following protest.

To Theognius, Maris, Macedonius, Theodorus, Ursacius, and Valens, the Bishops who have come from Tyre, these from the Presbyters and Deacons of the Catholic Church of Alexandria under the most reverend Bishop Athanasius.

It was incumbent upon you when you came hither and brought with you the accuser, to bring also the Presbyter Macarius; for trials are appointed by Holy Scripture to be so constituted, that the accuser and accused may stand up together. But since neither you brought Macarius, nor our most reverend Bishop Athanasius came hither with you, we claimed for ourselves the right of being present at the investigation, that we might see that the enquiry was conducted impartially, and might ourselves be convinced of the truth. But when you refused to allow this, and wished, in company only with the Prefect of Egypt and the accuser, to do whatever you pleased, we confess that we saw a suspicion of evil in the affair, and perceived that your coming was only the act of a cabal and a conspiracy. Wherefore we address to you this letter, to be a testimony before a genuine Council, that it may be known to all men, that you have carried on an *ex parte* proceeding and for your own ends, and have desired nothing else but to form a conspiracy against us. A copy of this, lest it should be kept secret by you, we have handed in to Palladius also the Controller[2] of Augustus. For what you have already done causes us to suspect you, and to

---

[1] Cf. *Encycl.* § 3.
[2] Curiosus; the Curiosi (in curis agendis) were properly the overseers of the public roads, Du Cange in voc., but they became in consequence a sort of imperial spy, and were called the Emperor's eyes. Gothofr. *in Cod. Theod.* t. 2. p. 194. ed. 1665. Constantius confined them to the school of the Agentes in rebus (infr. *Apol. ad Const.* § 10.), under the Master of the Offices. Gothofr. *ibid.* p. 192.

reckon on the like conduct from you hereafter.

I Dionysius Presbyter have handed in this letter. Alexander Presbyter, Nilaras Presbyter, Longus Presbyter, Aphthonius Presbyter, Athanasius Presbyter, Amyntius Presbyter, Pistus Presbyter, Plution Presbyter, Dioscorus Presbyter, Apollonius Presbyter, Sarapion Presbyter, Ammonius Presbyter, Gaius Presbyter, Rhinus Presbyter, Æthales Presbyter.

Deacons; Marcellinus Deacon, Appianus Deacon, Theon Deacon, Timotheus Deacon, a second Timotheus Deacon.

74. This is the letter, and these the names of the Clergy of the city; and the following was written by the Clergy of the Mareotis, who know the character of the accuser, and who were with me in my visitation.

To the holy Council of blessed Bishops of the Catholic Church, all the Presbyters and Deacons of the Mareotis send health in the Lord.

Knowing that which is written, 'Speak that thine eyes have seen,' and, 'A false witness shall not be unpunished[3],' we testify what we have seen, especially since the conspiracy which has been formed against our Bishop Athanasius has made our testimony necessary. We wonder how Ischyras ever came to be reckoned among the number of the Ministers of the Church, which is the first point we think it necessary to mention. Ischyras never was a Minister of the Church; but when formerly he represented himself to be a Presbyter of Colluthus, he found no one to believe him, except only his own relations[4]. For he never had a Church, nor was ever considered a Clergyman by those who lived but a short distance from his village, except only, as we said before, by his own relations. But, notwithstanding he assumed this designation, he was deposed in the presence of our Father Hosius at the Council which assembled at Alexandria[5], and was admitted to communion as a layman, and so he continued subsequently, having fallen from his falsely reputed rank of presbyter. Of his character we think it unnecessary to speak, as all men have it in their power to become acquainted therewith. But since he has falsely accused our Bishop Athanasius of breaking a cup and overturning a table, we are necessarily obliged to address you on this point. We have said already that he never had a Church in the Mareotis; and we declare before God as our witness, that no cup was broken, nor table overturned by our Bishop, nor by any one of those who accompanied

him; but all that is alleged respecting this affair is mere calumny. And this we say, not as having been absent from the Bishop, for we are all with him when he makes his visitation of the Mareotis, and he never goes about alone, but is accompanied by all of us Presbyters and Deacons, and by a considerable number of the people. Wherefore we make these assertions as having been present with him in every visitation which he has made amongst us, and testify that neither was a cup ever broken, nor table overturned, but the whole story is false, as the accuser himself also witnesses under his own hand[6]. For when, after he had gone off with Meletians, and had reported these things against our Bishop Athanasius, he wished to be admitted to communion, he was not received, although he wrote and confessed under his own hand that none of these things were true, but that he had been suborned by certain persons to say so.

75. Wherefore also Theognius, Theodorus, Maris, Macedonius, Ursacius, Valens, and their fellows came into the Mareotis, and when they found that none of these things were true, but it was likely to be discovered that they had framed a false accusation against our Bishop Athanasius, Theognius and his fellows being themselves his enemies, caused the relations of Ischyras and certain Arian madmen to say whatever they wished. For none of the people spoke against the Bishop; but these persons, through fear of Philagrius the Prefect of Egypt, and by threats and with the support of the Arian madmen, accomplished whatever they desired. For when we came to disprove the calumny, they would not permit us, but cast us out, while they admitted whom they pleased to a participation in their schemes, and concerted matters with them, influencing them by fear of the Prefect Philagrius. Through his means they prevented us from being present, that we might discover whether those who were suborned by them were members of the Church or Arian madmen. And you also, dearly beloved Fathers, know, as you teach us, that the testimony of enemies avails nothing. That what we say is the truth the handwriting[7] of Ischyras testifies, as do also the facts themselves, because when we were conscious that no such thing as was pretended had taken place, they took with them Philagrius, that through fear of the sword and by threats they might frame whatever plots they wished. These things we testify as in the presence of God; we make these assertions as knowing

---

that there will be a judgment held by God; desiring indeed all of us to come to you, but being content with certain of our number, so that the letters may be instead of the presence of those who have not come.

I, Ingenius Presbyter, pray you health in the Lord, beloved fathers. Theon Presbyter, Ammonas P., Heraclius P., Boccon P., Tryphon P., Peter P., Hierax P., Sarapion P., Marcus P., Ptollarion P., Gaius P., Dioscorus P., Demetrius P., Thyrsus P.

Deacons; Pistus Deacon, Apollos D., Serras D., Pistus D., Polynicus D., Ammonius D., Maurus D., Hephæstus D., Apollos D., Metopas D., Apollos D., Serapas D., Meliphthongus D., Lucius D., Gregoras D.

76. *The same to the Controller, and to Philagrius, at that time Prefect of Egypt.*

To Flavius Philagrius, and to Flavius Palladius, Ducenary[8], Officer of the Palace, and Controller, and to Flavius Antoninus, Commissary of Provisions, and Centenary of my lords the most illustrious Prefects of the sacred Prætorium, these from the Presbyters and Deacons of the Mareotis, a nome of the Catholic Church which is under the most Reverend Bishop Athanasius, we address this testimony by those whose names are underwritten :—

Whereas Theognius, Maris, Macedonius, Theodorus, Ursacius, and Valens, as if sent by all the Bishops who assembled at Tyre, came into our Diocese alleging that they had received orders to investigate certain ecclesiastical affairs, among which they spoke of the breaking of a cup of the Lord, of which information was given them by Ischyras, whom they brought with them, and who says that he is a Presbyter, although he is not,— for he was ordained by the Presbyter Colluthus who pretended to the Episcopate, and was afterwards ordered by a whole Council, by Hosius and the Bishops that were with him, to take the place of a Presbyter, as he was before; and accordingly all that were ordained by Colluthus resumed the same rank which they held before, and so Ischyras himself proved to be a layman,—and the church which he says he has, never was a church at all, but a quite small private house belonging to an orphan boy of the name of Ision;—for this reason we have offered this testimony, adjuring you by Almighty God, and by our Lords Constantine Augustus, and the most illustrious Cæsars his sons, to bring these things to the knowledge of

their piety. For neither is he a Presbyter of the Catholic Church nor does he possess a church, nor has a cup ever been broken, but the whole story is false and an invention.

Dated in the Consulship of Julius Constantius the most illustrious Patrician[9], brother of the most religious Emperor Constantine Augustus, and of Rufinus Albinus, most illustrious men, on the tenth day of the month Thoth[10].

These were the letters of the Presbyters.

77. The following also are the letters and protests of the Bishops who came with us to Tyre, when they became aware of the conspiracy and plot.

To the Bishops assembled at Tyre, most honoured Lords, those of the Catholic Church who have come from Egypt with Athanasius send greeting in the Lord.

We suppose that the conspiracy which has been formed against us by Eusebius, Theognius, Maris, Narcissus, Theodorus, Patrophilus, and their fellows is no longer uncertain. From the very beginning we all demurred, through our fellow-minister Athanasius, to the holding of the enquiry in their presence, knowing that the presence of even one enemy only, much more of many, is able to disturb and injure the hearing of a cause. And you also yourselves know the enmity which they entertain, not only towards us, but towards all the orthodox, how that for the sake of the madness of Arius, and his impious doctrine, they direct their assaults, they form conspiracies against all. And when, being confident in the truth, we desired to shew the falsehood, which the Meletians had employed against the Church, Eusebius and his fellows endeavoured by some means or other to interrupt our representations, and strove eagerly to set aside our testimony, threatening those who gave an honest judgment, and insulting others, for the sole purpose of carrying out the design they had against us. Your godly piety, most honoured Lords, was probably ignorant of their conspiracy, but we suppose that it has now been made manifest. For indeed they have themselves plainly disclosed it; for they desired to send to the Mareotis those of their party who are suspected by us, so that, while we were absent and remained here, they might disturb the people and accomplish what they wished. They knew

---

[8] On the different kinds of Ducenaries, vid. Gothofr. in *Cod. Theod.* XI. vii. 1. Here, as in Euseb. *Hist.* vii. 30. the word stands for a Procurator, whose annual pay amounted to 200 sestertia, vid. Salmas. *Hist. Aug.* t. l. p. 533. In like manner a Centenary is one who receives 100.

[9] The title Patrician was revived by Constantine as a personal distinction. It was for life, and gave precedence over all the great officers of state except the Consul. It was usually bestowed on favourites, or on ministers as a reward of services. Gibbon, *Hist.* ch. 17. This Julius Constantius, who was the father of Julian, was the first who bore the title, with L. Optatus, who had been consul the foregoing year. Illustrissimus was the highest of the three ranks of honour. *ibid.*

[10] [Sep. 8. 335 A.D. See note on leap-year at the end of the table of Egyptian months, below, Introd. to *Letters.*]

that the Arian madmen, and Colluthians[1] and Meletians, were enemies of the Catholic Church, and therefore they were anxious to send them, that in the presence of our enemies they might devise against us whatever schemes they pleased. And those of the Meletians who are here, even four days previously (as they knew that this enquiry was about to take place), despatched at evening certain of their party, as couriers, for the purpose of collecting Meletians out of Egypt into the Mareotis, because there were none at all there, and Colluthians and Arian madmen, from other parts, and to prepare them to speak against us. For you also know that Ischyras himself confessed before you, that he had not more than seven persons in his congregation. When therefore we heard that, after they had made what preparations they pleased against us, and had sent these suspected persons, they were going about to each of you, and requiring your subscriptions, in order that it might appear as if this had been done with the consent of you all; for this reason we hastened to write to you, and to present this our testimony; declaring that we are the objects of a conspiracy under which we are suffering by and through them, and demanding that having the fear of God in your minds, and condemning their conduct in sending whom they pleased without our consent, you would refuse your subscriptions, lest they pretend that those things are done by you, which they are contriving only among themselves. Surely it becomes those who are in Christ, not to regard human motives, but to prefer the truth before all things. And be not afraid of their threatenings, which they employ against all, nor of their plots, but rather fear God. If it was at all necessary that persons should be sent to the Mareotis, we also ought to have been there with them, in order that we might convict the enemies of the Church, and point out those who were aliens, and that the investigation of the matter might be impartial. For you know that Eusebius and his fellows contrived that a letter should be presented, as coming from the Colluthians, the Meletians, and Arians, and directed against us: but it is evident that these enemies of the Catholic Church speak nothing that is true concerning us, but say everything against us. And the law of God forbids an enemy to be either a witness or a judge. Wherefore as you will have to give an account in the day of judgment, receive this testimony, and recognising the conspiracy which has been framed against us, beware, if you are requested by them, of doing anything against us, and of taking part in the designs of Eusebius and his fellows. For you know, as we said before, that they are our enemies, and you are aware why Eusebius of Cæsarea became such last year[2]. We pray that you may be in health, greatly beloved Lords.

78. To the most illustrious Count Flavius Dionysius, from the Bishops of the Catholic Church in Egypt who have come to Tyre.

We suppose that the conspiracy which has been formed against us by Eusebius, Theognius, Maris, Narcissus, Theodorus, Patrophilus and their fellows, is no longer uncertain. From the very beginning we all demurred, through our fellow-minister Athanasius, to the holding of the enquiry in their presence, knowing that the presence of even one enemy only, much more of many, is able to disturb and injure the hearing of a cause. For their enmity is manifest which they entertain, not only towards us, but also towards all the orthodox, because they direct their assaults, they form conspiracies against all. And when, being confident in the truth, we desired to shew the falsehood which the Meletians had employed against the Church, Eusebius and his fellows endeavoured by some means or other to interrupt our representations, and strove eagerly to set aside our testimony, threatening those who gave an honest judgment and insulting others, for the sole purpose of carrying out the design they had against us. Your goodness was probably ignorant of the conspiracy which they have formed against us, but we suppose that it has now been made manifest. For indeed they have themselves plainly disclosed it; for they desired to send to the Mareotis those of their party who are suspected by us, so that, while we were absent and remained here, they might disturb the people and accomplish what they wished. They knew that Arian madmen, Colluthians, and Meletians were enemies of the Church, and therefore they were anxious to send them, that in the presence of our enemies, they might devise against us whatever schemes they pleased. And those of the Meletians who are here, even four days previously (as they knew that this enquiry was about to take place), despatched at evening two individuals of their own party, as couriers, for the purpose of collecting Meletians out of Egypt into the Mareotis, because there were none at all there, and Colluthians, and Arian madmen, from other

---

[1] Colluthus formed a schism on the doctrine that God was not the cause of any sort of evil, e.g. did not inflict pain and suffering. Though a Priest, he took on himself to ordain, even to the Priesthood [§ 12]. St. Alexander even seems to imply that he did so for money. Theod. *H.E.* i. 3. [Prolegg. ch. ii. § 2.]

[2] [Ath. had refused to attend a synod at Cæsarea, A.D. 334. See Thdt. *H.E.* i. 28, Prolegg. ch. ii. § 4. and D.C.B. ii. 315 b.]

parts, and to prepare them to speak against us. And your goodness knows that he himself confessed before you, that he had not more than seven persons in his congregation. When therefore we heard that, after they had made what preparations they pleased against us, and had sent these suspected persons, they were going about to each of the Bishops and requiring their subscriptions, in order that it might appear that this was done with the consent of them all; for this reason we hastened to refer the matter to your honour, and to present this our testimony, declaring that we are the objects of a conspiracy, under which we are suffering by and through them, and demanding of you that having in your mind the fear of God, and the pious commands of our most religious Emperor, you would no longer tolerate these persons, but condemn their conduct in sending whom they pleased without our consent.

I Adamantius Bishop have subscribed this letter, Ischyras, Ammon, Peter, Ammonianus, Tyrannus, Taurinus, Sarapammon, Ælurion, Harpocration, Moses, Optatus, Anubion, Saprion, Apollonius. Ischyrion, Arbæthion, Potamon, Paphnutius, Heraclides, Theodorus, Agathammon, Gaius, Pistus, Athas, Nicon, Pelagius, Theon, Paninuthius, Nonnus, Ariston, Theodorus, Irenæus, Blastammon, Philippus, Apollos, Dioscorus, Timotheus of Diospolis, Macarius, Heraclammon, Cronius, Myis, Jacobus, Ariston, Artemidorus, Phinees, Psais, Heraclides.

Another from the same.

79. The Bishops of the Catholic Church who have come from Egypt to Tyre, to the most illustrious Count Flavius Dionysius.

Perceiving that many conspiracies and plots are being formed against us through the machinations of Eusebius, Narcissus, Flacillus, Theognius, Maris, Theodorus, Patrophilus, and their fellows (against whom we wished at first to enter añ objection, but were not permitted), we are constrained to have recourse to the present appeal. We observe also that great zeal is exerted in behalf of the Meletians, and that a plot is laid against the Catholic Church in Egypt in our persons. Wherefore we present this letter to you, beseeching you to bear in mind the Almighty Power of God, who defends the kingdom of our most religious and godly Emperor Constantine, and to reserve the hearing of the affairs which concern us for the most religious Emperor himself. For it is but reasonable, since you were commissioned by his Majesty, that you should reserve the matter for him upon our appealing to his piety. We can no longer endure to be the objects of the

treacherous designs of the fore-mentioned Eusebius and his fellows, and therefore we demand that the case be reserved for the most religious and God-beloved Emperor, before whom we shall be able to set forth our own and the Church's just claims. And we are convinced that when his piety shall have heard our cause, he will not condemn us. Wherefore we again adjure you by Almighty God, and by our most religious Emperor, who, together with the children of his piety, has thus ever been victorious [3] and prosperous these many years, that you proceed no further, nor suffer yourselves to move at all in the Council in relation to our affairs, but reserve the hearing of them for his piety. We have likewise made the same representations to my Lords the orthodox Bishops.

80. Alexander [4], Bishop of Thessalonica, on receiving these letters, wrote to the Count Dionysius as follows.

The Bishop Alexander to my master Dionysius.

I see that a conspiracy has evidently been formed against Athanasius; for they have determined, I know not on what grounds, to send all those to whom he has objected, without giving any information to us, although it was agreed that we should consider together who ought to be sent. Take care therefore that nothing be done rashly (for they have come to me in great alarm, saying that the wild beasts have already roused themselves, and are going to rush upon them; for they had heard it reported, that John had sent certain [5]), lest they be beforehand with us, and concoct what schemes they please. For you know that the Colluthians who are enemies of the Church, and the Arians, and Meletians, are all of them leagued together, and are able to work much evil. Consider therefore what is best to be done, lest some mischief arise, and we be subject to censure, as not having judged the matter fairly. Great suspicions are also entertained of these persons, lest, as being devoted to the Meletians, they should go through those Churches whose Bishops are here [6], and raise an alarm amongst them, and so disorder the whole of Egypt. For they see that this is already taking place to a great extent.

Accordingly the Count Dionysius wrote to Eusebius and his fellows as follows.

81. This is what I have already mentioned to my lords, Flacillus [7] and his fellows, that Athanasius has come forward and complained

3 Cf. Euseb. *v. Const.* ii. 48.   4 Cf. § 16.
5 Cf. §§ 17, 65, 70.   6 At Tyre.
7 Perhaps president of the Council, cf. § 20. [But see Prolegg. ch. ii. § 5.]

that those very persons have been sent whom he objected to; and crying out that he has been wronged and deceived. Alexander the lord of my soul [7a] has also written to me on the subject; and that you may perceive that what his Goodness has said is reasonable, I have subjoined his letter to be read by you. Remember also what I wrote to you before: I impressed upon your Goodness, my lords, that the persons who were sent ought to be commissioned by the general vote and decision of all. Take care therefore lest our proceedings fall under censure, and we give just grounds of blame to those who are disposed to find fault with us. For as the accuser's side ought not to suffer any oppression, so neither ought the defendant's. And I think that there is no slight ground of blame against us, when my lord Alexander evidently disapproves of what we have done.

82. While matters were proceeding thus we withdrew from them, as from an assembly of treacherous men [8], for whatsoever they pleased they did, whereas there is no man in the world but knows that *ex parte* proceedings cannot stand good. This the divine law determines; for when the blessed Apostle was suffering under a similar conspiracy and was brought to trial, he demanded, saying, 'The Jews from Asia ought to have been here before thee, and object, if they had aught against me [9].' On which occasion Festus also, when the Jews wished to lay such a plot against him, as these men have now laid against me, said, ' It is not the manner of Romans to deliver any man to die, before that he which is accused have the accuser face to face, and have licence to answer for himself concerning the crime laid against him [10].' But Eusebius and his fellows both had the boldness to pervert the law, and have proved more unjust even than those wrong-doers. For they did not proceed privately at the first, but when in consequence of our being present they found themselves weak, then they straightway went out, like the Jews, and took counsel together alone, how they might destroy us and bring in their heresy, as those others demanded Barabbas. For this purpose it was, as they have themselves confessed, that they did all these things.

83. Although these circumstances were amply sufficient for our vindication, yet in order that the wickedness of these men and the freedom of the truth might be more fully exhibited, I have not felt averse to repeat them again, in order to shew that they have acted in a manner inconsistently with themselves, and as men

scheming in the dark have fallen foul of their own friends, and while they desired to destroy us have like insane persons wounded themselves. For in their investigation of the subject of the Mysteries, they questioned Jews, they examined Catechumens [1]; 'Where were you,' they said, ' when Macarius came and overturned the Table?' They answered, ' We were within;' whereas there could be no oblation if Catechumens were present. Again, although they had written word everywhere, that Macarius came and overthrew everything, while the Presbyter was standing and celebrating the Mysteries, yet when they questioned whomsoever they pleased, and asked them, 'Where was Ischyras when Macarius rushed in?' those persons answered that he was lying sick in a cell. Well, then, he that was lying was not standing, nor was he that lay sick in his cell offering the oblation. Besides whereas Ischyras said that certain books had been burnt by Macarius, they who were suborned to give evidence, declared that nothing of the kind had been done, but that Ischyras spoke falsely. And what is most remarkable, although they had again written word everywhere, that those who were able to give evidence had been concealed by us, yet these persons made their appearance, and they questioned them, and were not ashamed when they saw it proved on all sides that they were slanderers, and were acting in this matter clandestinely, and according to their pleasure. For they prompted the witnesses by signs, while the Prefect threatened them, and the soldiers pricked them with their swords; but the Lord revealed the truth, and shewed them to be slanderers. Therefore also they concealed the minutes of their proceedings, which they retained themselves, and charged those who wrote them to put out of sight, and to commit to no one whomsoever. But in this also they were disappointed; for the person who wrote them was Rufus, who is now public executioner in the Augustalian [2] prefecture, and is able to testify to the truth of this; and Eusebius and his fellows sent them to Rome by the hands of their own friends, and Julius the Bishop transmitted them to me. And now they are mad, because we obtained and read what they wished to conceal.

84. As such was the character of their machinations, so they very soon shewed plainly the reasons of their conduct. For when they went away, they took the Arians with them to Jerusalem, and there admitted them to communion, having sent out a letter concerning

---

[7a] i.e. my beloved lord.
[9] Acts xxiv. 18, 19.
[8] Jer. ix. 2.
[10] Acts xxv. 16.
[1] Vid. § 46.
[2] Vid. *Encyc.* § 5, p. 93, note 2.

them, part[3] of which, and the beginning, is as follows.

The holy Council by the grace of God assembled at Jerusalem, to the Church of God which is in Alexandria, and to the Bishops, Presbyters, and Deacons, in all Egypt, the Thebais, Libya, Pentapolis, and throughout the world, sends health in the Lord.

Having come together out of different Provinces to a great meeting which we have held for the consecration of the Martyry [3a] of the Saviour, which has been appointed to the service of God the King of all and of His Christ, by the zeal of our most God-beloved Emperor Constantine, the grace of God hath afforded us more abundant rejoicing of heart; which our most God-beloved Emperor himself hath occasioned us by his letters, wherein he hath stirred us up to do that which is right, putting away all envy from the Church of God, and driving far from us all malice, by which the members of God have been heretofore torn asunder, and that we should with simple and peaceable minds receive Arius and his fellows, whom envy, that enemy of all goodness, has caused for a season to be excluded from the Church. Our most religious Emperor has also in his letter testified to the correctness of their faith, which he has ascertained from themselves, himself receiving the profession of it from them by word of mouth, and has now made manifest to us by subjoining to his own letters the men's orthodox opinion in writing.

85. Every one that hears of these things must see through their treachery. For they made no concealment of what they were doing; unless perhaps they confessed the truth without wishing it. For if I was the hindrance to the admittance of Arius and his fellows into the Church, and if they were received while I was suffering from their plots, what other conclusion can be arrived at, than that these things were done on their account, and that all their proceedings against me, and the story which they fabricated about the breaking of the cup and the murder of Arsenius, were for the sole purpose of introducing impiety into the Church, and of preventing their being condemned as heretics? For this was what the Emperor threatened formerly in his letters to me. And they were not ashamed to write in the manner they did, and to affirm that those persons whom the whole Ecumenical Council anathematized held orthodox sentiments. And as they undertook to say and do anything without scruple, so they were not afraid to meet together 'in a

corner,' in order to overthrow, as far as was in their power, the authority of so great a Council.

Moreover, the price which they paid for false testimony yet more fully manifests their wickedness and impious intentions. The Mareotis, as I have already said, is a country district of Alexandria, in which there has never been either a Bishop or a Chorepiscopus[4]; but the Churches of the whole district are subject to the Bishop of Alexandria, and each Presbyter has under his charge one of the largest villages, which are about ten or more in number[5]. Now the village in which Ischyras lives is a very small one, and possesses so few inhabitants, that there has never been a church built there, but only in the adjoining village. Nevertheless, they determined, contrary to ancient usage[6], to nominate a Bishop for this place, and not only so, but even to appoint one, who was not so much as a Presbyter. Knowing as they did the unusual nature of such a proceeding, yet being constrained by the promises they had given in return for his false impeachment of me, they submitted even to this, lest that abandoned person, if he were ungratefully treated by them, should disclose the truth, and thereby shew the wickedness of Eusebius and his fellows. Notwithstanding this he has no church, nor a people to obey him, but is scouted by them all, like a dog[7], although they have even caused the Emperor to write to the Receiver-General (for everything is in their power), commanding that a church should be built for him, that being possessed of that, his statement may appear credible about the cup and the table. They caused him immediately to be nominated a Bishop also, because if he were without a church, and not even a Presbyter, he would appear to be a false accuser, and a fabricator of the whole matter. At any rate he has no people, and even his own relations are not obedient to him, and as the name which he retains is an empty one, so also the following letter is ineffectual, which he keeps, making a display of it as an exposure of the utter

---

[4] That Chorepiscopi were real Bishops, vid. Bevereg. in Conc. Ancyr. Can. 13. Routh in Conc. Neocæs. Can. 13. referring to Rhabanus Maurus. Thomassin on the other hand denies that they were Bishops, *Discipl. Eccl.* i. 2. c. 1. [see D.C.A. s.v.]

[5] Ten under each Presbyter. Vales ad Socr. *Hist.* i. 27. Ten altogether, Montfaucon in loc. with more probability; and so Tillemont, vol. 8. p. 20. [Six villages are mentioned *supr.* § 64, *fin.*]

[6] It was against the Canon of Sardica, and doubtless against ancient usage, to ordain a Bishop for so small a village, vid. Bingham, Antiqu. II. xii., who, however, maintains by instances, that at least small towns might be sees. Also it was against usage that a layman, as Ischyras, should be made a Bishop. ibid. x. 4, &c. St. Hilary, however, makes him a Deacon. *Fragm.* ii. 16.

[7] Dogs without owners, and almost in a wild state, abound, as is well known, in Eastern cities; vid. Psalm lix. 6, 14, 15. 2 Kings ix. 35, 36. and for the view taken in Scripture of dogs, vid. Bochart, *Hieroz.* ii. 56 [and Dict. Bib. s.v.].

---

[3] Vid. *de Syn.* § 21. [3a] [i.e. Church, see D.C.A. s.v. Martyrium.]

wickedness of himself and of Eusebius and his fellows.

The Letter of the Receiver-General[8].

Flavius Hemerius sends health to the Tax-collector of the Mareotis.

Ischyras the Presbyter having petitioned the piety of our Lords, Augusti and Cæsars, that a Church might be built in the district of Irene, belonging to Secontarurus[9], their divinity has commanded that this should be done as soon as possible. Take care therefore, as soon as you receive the copy of the sacred Edict, which with all due veneration is placed above, and the Reports which have been formed before my devotion, that you quickly make an abstract of them, and transfer them to the Order book, so that the sacred command may be put in execution.

86. While they were thus plotting and scheming, I went up[10] and represented to the Emperor the unjust conduct of Eusebius and his fellows, for he it was who had commanded the Council to be held, and his Count presided at it. When he heard my report, he was greatly moved, and wrote to them as follows.

Constantine, Victor[1], Maximus, Augustus, to the Bishops assembled at Tyre.

I know not what the decisions are which you have arrived at in your Council amidst noise and tumult: but somehow the truth seems to have been perverted in consequence of certain confusions and disorders, in that you, through your mutual contentiousness, which you are resolved should prevail, have failed to perceive what is pleasing to God. However, it will rest with Divine Providence to disperse the mischiefs which manifestly are found to arise from this contentious spirit, and to shew plainly to us, whether you, while assembled in that place, have had any regard for the truth, and whether you have made your decisions uninfluenced by either favour or enmity. Wherefore I wish you all to assemble with all speed before my piety, in order that you may render in person a true account of your proceedings.

The reason why I have thought good to write thus to you, and why I summon you before me by letter, you will learn from what I am going to say. As I was entering on a late occasion our all-happy home of Constantinople, which bears our name (I chanced at the time to be on horseback), on a sudden the Bishop Athanasius, with certain others whom he had

with him, approached me in the middle of the road, so unexpectedly, as to occasion me much amazement. God, who knoweth all things, is my witness, that I should have been unable at first sight even to recognise him, had not some of my attendants, on my naturally inquiring of them, informed me both who it was, and under what injustice he was suffering. I did not however enter into any conversation with him at that time, nor grant him an interview; but when he requested to be heard I was refusing, and all but gave orders for his removal; when with increasing boldness he claimed only this favour, that you should be summoned to appear, that he might have an opportunity of complaining before me of the ill-treatment he has met with. As this appeared to me to be a reasonable request, and suitable to the times, I willingly ordered this letter to be written to you, in order that all of you, who constituted the Council which was held at Tyre, might hasten without delay to the Court[2] of my clemency, so as to prove by facts that you had passed an impartial and uncorrupt judgment. This, I say, you must do before me, whom not even you will deny to be a true servant of God.

For indeed through my devotion to God, peace is preserved everywhere, and the Name of God is truly worshipped even by the barbarians, who have hitherto been ignorant of the truth. And it is manifest, that he who is ignorant of the truth, does not know God either. Nevertheless, as I said before, even the barbarians have now come to the knowledge of God, by means of me, His true servant[3], and have learned to fear Him Whom they perceive from actual facts to be my shield and protector everywhere. And from this chiefly they have come to know God, Whom they fear through the dread which they have of me. But we, who are supposed to set forth (for I will not say to guard) the holy mysteries of His Goodness, we, I say, engage in nothing but what tends to dissension and hatred, and, in short, whatever contributes to the destruction of mankind. But hasten, as I said before, and all of you with all speed come to us, being persuaded that I shall endeavour with all my might to amend what is amiss, so that those things specially may be preserved and firmly established in the law of God, to which no blame nor dishonour may attach; while the enemies of the law, who under pretence of His holy Name bring in manifold and divers blasphemies, shall be

---

8 Catholicus, § 14, *Apol. Const.* § 10. [The mention, below, of 'Augusti and Cæsars' makes 337 the earliest likely date for this letter.]   9 Cf. § 17. note 7.   [Prolegg. ch. ii. § 4.]
10 Cf. § 9.   1 Euseb. *v. Const.* ii. 48.

2 στρατόπεδον, § 70. note 6.
3 "Once in an entertainment, at which he (Constantine) received Bishops, he made the remark that he too was a Bishop; using pretty much these words in my hearing, 'You are Bishops of matters within the Church, I am appointed by God to be Bishop of matters external to it." Euseb. *Vit. Const.* iv. 24.

scattered abroad, and entirely crushed, and utterly destroyed.

87. When Eusebius and his fellows read this letter, being conscious of what they had done, they prevented the rest of the Bishops from going up, and only themselves went, viz. Eusebius, Theognius, Patrophilus, the other Eusebius, Ursacius, and Valens. And they no longer said anything about the cup and Arsenius (for they had not the boldness to do so), but inventing another accusation which concerned the Emperor himself, they declared before him, that Athanasius had threatened that he would cause the corn to be withheld which was sent from Alexandria to his own home [4]. The Bishops Adamantius, Anubion, Agathammon, Arbethion, and Peter, were present and heard this. It was proved also by the anger of the Emperor; for although he had written the preceding letter, and had condemned their injustice, as soon as he heard such a charge as this, he was immediately incensed, and instead of granting me a hearing, he sent me away into Gaul. And this again shews their wickedness further; for when the younger Constantine, of blessed memory, sent me back home, remembering what his father had written [5], he also wrote as follows.

Constantine Cæsar, to the people of the Catholic Church of the city of Alexandria.

I suppose that it has not escaped the knowledge of your pious minds, that Athanasius, the interpreter of the adorable Law, was sent away into Gaul for a time, with the intent that, as the savageness of his bloodthirsty and inveterate enemies persecuted him to the hazard of his sacred life, he might thus escape suffering some irremediable calamity, through the perverse dealing of those evil men. In order therefore to escape this, he was snatched out of the jaws of his assailants, and was ordered to pass some time under my government, and so was supplied abundantly with all necessaries in this city, where he lived, although indeed his celebrated virtue, relying entirely on divine assistance, sets at nought the sufferings of adverse fortune. Now seeing that it was the fixed intention of our master Constantine Augustus, my Father, to restore the said Bishop to his own place, and to your most beloved piety, but he was taken away by that fate which is common to all men, and went to his rest before he could accomplish his wish; I have thought proper to fulfil that intention of the Emperor of sacred

memory which I have inherited from him. When he comes to present himself before you, you will learn with what reverence he has been treated. Indeed it is not wonderful, whatever I have done on his behalf; for the thoughts of your longing desire for him, and the appearance of so great a man, moved my soul, and urged me thereto. May Divine Providence continually preserve you, beloved brethren.

Dated from Treveri the 15th before the Calends of July [6].

88. This being the reason why I was sent away into Gaul, who, I ask again, does not plainly perceive the intention of the Emperor, and the murderous spirit of Eusebius and his fellows, and that the Emperor had done this in order to prevent their forming some more desperate scheme? for he listened to them in simplicity [7]. Such were the practices of Eusebius and his fellows, and such their machinations against me. Who that has witnessed them will deny that nothing has been done in my favour out of partiality, but that that great number of Bishops both individually and collectively wrote as they did in my behalf and condemned the falsehood of my enemies justly, and in accordance with the truth? Who that has observed such proceedings as these will deny that Valens and Ursacius had good reason to condemn themselves, and to write [8] as they did, to accuse themselves when they repented, choosing rather to suffer shame for a short time, than to undergo the punishment of false accusers for ever and ever [9]?

89. Wherefore also my blessed fellow-ministers, acting justly and according to the laws of the Church, while certain affirmed that my case was doubtful, and endeavoured to compel them to annul the sentence which was passed in my favour, have now endured all manner of sufferings, and have chosen rather to be banished than to see the judgment of so many Bishops reversed. Now if those genuine Bishops had withstood by words only those who plotted against me, and wished to undo all that had been done in my behalf; or if they had been ordinary men, and not the

---

[4] Constantinople. [5] [See Bright, *Hist. Writ.* p. xii. note 3, and on the date of this letter, Prolegg. ch. v. § 3 b, and note 6 below.]

[6] June 17. A.D. 337 [see Gwatk. *Stud.*, 136]. [7] ἐπήκουσε γὰρ ἁπλῶς. Montfaucon in Onomast. (Athan. t. 2. ad calc.) points out some passages in his author, where ἐπακούειν, like ὑπακούειν, means "to answer." vid. *Apol. Const.* § 16 init. *Orat.* iii. 27 fin. [8] Cf. § 58. [9] Here ends the second part of the Apology, as is evident by turning back to § 58. (supr. p. 130) to which this paragraph is an allusion. The express object of the second part was to prove, what has now been proved by documents, that Valens and Ursacius did but succumb to plain facts which they could not resist. It is observable too from this passage that the Apology was written before their relapse, i.e. before A.D. 351 or 352. The remaining two sections are written after 357, as they mention the fall of Liberius and Hosius, and speak of Constantius in different language from any which has been found above. [Introdd. to *Apol. Const.* and *Hist. Ar.*]

Bishops of illustrious cities, and the heads of great Churches, there would have been room to suspect that in this instance they too had acted contentiously and in order to gratify me. But when they not only endeavoured to convince by argument, but also endured banishment, and one of them is Liberius, Bishop of Rome, (for although he did not endure [10] to the end the sufferings of banishment, yet he remained in his exile for two years, being aware of conspiracy formed against us), and since there is also the great Hosius, together with the Bishops of Italy, and of Gaul, and others from Spain, and from Egypt, and Libya, and all those from Pentapolis (for although for a little while, through fear of the threats of Constantius, he seemed not to resist them [1], yet the great violence and tyrannical power exercised by Constantius, and the many insults and stripes inflicted upon him, proved that it was not because he gave up my cause, but through the weakness of old age, being unable to bear the stripes, that he yielded to them for a season), therefore I say, it is altogether right that all, as being fully convinced, should hate and abominate the injustice and the violence which they have used towards me; especially as it is well known that I have suffered these things on account of nothing else but the Arian impiety.

90. Now if anyone wishes to become acquainted with my case, and the falsehood of Eusebius and his fellows, let him read what has been written in my behalf, and let him hear the witnesses, not one, or two, or three, but that great number of Bishops; and again let him attend to the witnesses of these proceedings, Liberius and Hosius, and their fellows, who when they saw the attempts made against us, chose rather to endure all manner of sufferings than to give up the truth, and the judgment which had been pronounced in our favour. And this they did with an honourable and righteous intention, for what they suffered proves to what straits the other Bishops were reduced. And they are memorials and records against the Arian heresy, and the wickedness of false accusers, and afford a pattern and model for those who come after, to contend for the truth unto death [2], and to abominate the Arian heresy which fights against Christ, and is a forerunner of Antichrist, and not to believe those who attempt to speak against me. For the defence put forth, and the sentence given, by so many Bishops of high character, are a trustworthy and sufficient testimony in our behalf.

---

[10] See *Hist. Ar.* § 41.
[1] Cf. *Apol. Fug.*, § 5, and *Hist. Ar.* § 45.

[2] Ecclus. iv. 28.

ADDITIONAL NOTE ON *APOL. C. ARIANOS*, § 50.

LIST OF BISHOPS PRESENT AT SARDICA.

[THE materials for an authentic list are (1) the names given by Athanasius, *Apol. c. Ar.* 50, *previous* to the lists of bishops from various provinces who signed the letter of the council when in circulation. These names, given with no specification of their sees, are 77 in number. (2) The list of signatures to the letter of the council to Julius, given by Hilary, *Fragm.* ii., 59 in number. The signatures to the letters discovered by Maffei and printed in Migne, *Patr. Gr.* xxvi. 1331, sqq. Of these, 26 sign (3) the council's letter to the Mareotic Churches, and 61, in part the same, sign (4) the letter of Athanasius to the same (*Letter* 46 in this volume). These signatures comprise 30 *names not given by Hilary*, while those in (1) add six which are absent from (2) and (3) alike. This raises the total to 95. We add (5) Gratus of Carthage, present according to the Greek text of the Canons, although he afterward signed the letter in a local council of his own, like Maximin of Treveri, Verissimus of Lyons, and Arius of Palestine, who are therefore given by Athanasius in his second list (the former two being omitted from the first) : also Euphrates of Cologne, who was sent by Constans to Antioch with the council's decisions (Prolegg. ch. ii. § 6), and was therefore most likely present at the council itself. We thus get 97 in all.

This total is confirmed if we subtract from the '170 more or less' of *Hist. Arian.* 15 the 76 seceders to Philippopolis (Sabinus in Socr. ii. 16), 73 of whom sign their letter, given by Hilary. This leaves 94 'more or less,' so that the list now to be given, in elucidation of that of Athanasius, has strong claims to rank as approximately correct. The numbers *after* the names refer to the sources (1, 2, 3, 4, 5) specified above.

1. ADOLIUS (1), *See unknown*; 2. AETIUS (1, 3), *Thessalonica in Macedonia*; 3. ALEXANDER (1, 4), *Cypara (i.e. Cyparissus?) in Achaia*; 4. ALEXANDER (2), *Montemnae (?) in Achaia*; 5. ALEXANDER (1, 2, 3), *Larissa in Thessaly*; 6. ALYPIUS (1, 2, 3), *Megara in Achaia*; 7. AMANTIUS (1, 4), *Viminacium*, by deputy; 8. AMMONIUS (4), *See unknown*; 9. ANIANUS (1, 2, 4), *Casiulo in Spain*; 10. ANTIGONUS (1, 4), *Pella, or Pallene in Macedonia*; 11. APPIANUS (4), *See unknown*; 12. APRIANUS (1, 4), *Feiabio (Petovio) in*

Pannonia; 13. APRIANUS (4), *See unknown*; 14. ARIUS (1, 2, 3), *of Palestine, See unknown* (see note on *Hist. Ar.* 18); 15. ASCLEPAS (1, 2, 4), *Gaza*; 16. ASTERIUS (1, 2, 3), [*Petra in*] *Arabia*; 17. ATHANASIUS (1, 2, 3, 4), *Alexandria*; 18. ATHENODORUS (1, 2, 3, 4), *Platæa in Achaia*; 19. BASSUS (1, 2, 3), *Diocletianapolis* "in Macedonia" (really in *Thrace*); 20. CALEPODIUS (1, 2, 3), *of Campania* (? *Naples*); 21. CALVUS (2, 4), *Castrum Martis in Dacia* Ripensis; 22. CALOES or 'Chalbis' (1, 4), *See unknown*; 23. CASTUS (1, 2, 4), *Saragossa in Spain*; 24. COCRAS (2), *Asapofebiae in Achaia* (= Asopus), perhaps the 'Socrates' of (1); 25. CYDONIUS (4), *Cydon in Crete*; 26. DIODORUS (1, 2, 4), *Tenedos*; 27. DIONYSIUS (1, 2, 3), *Elida* (Elis?) *in Achaia*; 28. DIOSCORUS (1, 2, 3), *Thrace, See unknown*; 29. DOMETIUS (or Domitianus) (1, 4), *Acaria Constantias* (possibly *Castra Constantia* = Coutances); 30. DOMITIANUS (1, 2, 3), *Asturica in Spain*; 31. ELIODORUS (1, 2, 3), *Nicopolis*; 32. EUCARPUS (1, 4), *Opus in Achaia*; 33. EUCARPUS (4), *See unknown*; 34. EUCISSUS (4), *Cissamus in Crete*; 35. EUGENIUS (4 = EUAGRIUS in 2?), *Heraclea* (in Lucania? texts very corrupt); 36. EUGENIUS (1?, 4), *See unknown*; 37. EULOGIUS (1, 4), *See unknown*; EUPHRATES, see below (97); 38. EUTASIUS (2), *Pannonia, See unknown*; 39. EUTERIUS (1, 2), '*Procia de Cayndo*' (corrupt); 40. EUTYCHIUS (1, 4), *Methone in Achaia*; 41. EUTYCHIUS (1, 2), *Achaia, See unknown*; 42. FLORENTIUS (1, 2, 4), *Emerita in Spain*; 43. FORTUNATIANUS (1, 2), *Aquileia*; GALBA (see above (22); 44. GAUDENTIUS (1, 2, 4), *Naissus*; 45. GERONTIUS (1, 2, 3, 4), *a Macedonia in Brevi*(?) in Hil.; GRATUS, see below (96); 46. HELIANUS (1, 4), *Tyrtana* (?); HELIODORUS, see above (31); 47. HERMOGENES (1, 4), *Sicyai* (?); 48. HYMENAEUS (1, 2, 4), *Hypata in Thessaly*; 49. JANUARIUS (1, 2, 4), *Beneventum in Campania*; 50. JOHN (3), *See unknown*; 51. JONAS (1, 2, 3), *Particopolis in Macedonia*; 52. IRENAEUS (1, 2, 4), *Scyros in Achaia*; 53. JULIANUS (1, 2, 4), *of Thebes in Achaia* (or Thera? see note to *Letter* 46); 54. JULIANUS (1, 4), *See unknown*; JULIUS, see below (95); LERENIUS (2), see above (52); 55. LUCIUS (1, 2, 3, 4), *Hadrianople in Thrace*; 56. LUCIUS ('LUCILLUS' Ath. twice) (1, 2, 4), *Verona*; 57. MACEDONIUS (1, 2, 4), *Ulpiana in Dardania*; 58. MARCELLUS (2, 4, Marcellinus in 1), *Ancyra*; 59. MARCUS (1, 2, 4), *Siscia on the Save*; 60. MARTYRIUS (2, 4), *Naupactus in Achaia*; 61. MARTYRIUS (1, 4), *See unknown*; 62. MAXIMUS (1, 2), *Luca in Tuscany*; 63. MAXIMUS (i.e. MAXIMINUS) (4), *Treviri*; 64. MUSONIUS (1, 4), *Heraclea in Crete*; 65. MOYSES (or Musaeus, 1, 2), *Thebes in Thessaly*; 66. OLYMPIUS (4), *Aeni in Thrace*; 67. Osius (HOSIUS), (1, 2, 3), *Cordova*; 68. PALLADIUS (1, 2, 4), *Dium in Macedonia*; 69. PAREGORIUS (1, 2, 3, 4), *Scupi in Dardania*; 70. PATRICIUS (1), *See unknown*; 71. PETER (1), *See unknown*; 72. PHILOLOGIUS (1), *See unknown*; 73. PLUTARCHUS (1, 2, 3), *Patrae in Achaia*; 74. PORPHYRIUS (1, 2, 3, 4), *Philippi in Macedonia*; 75. PRAETEXTATUS (1, 2, 4), *Barcelona*; 76. PROTASIUS (1, 2, 4), *Milan*; 77. PROTOGENES (1, 2, 4), *Sardica*; 78. RESTITUTUS (1, 3), *See unknown*; 79. SAPRICIUS (1), *See unknown*; 80. SEVERUS (4), *Chalcis in Thessaly* (Euboea); 81. SEVERUS (1, 2, 3), *Ravenna*; SOCRATES (1), see above, no. 24; 82. SPUDASIUS (1), *See unknown*; 83. STERCORIUS (1, 2, 4), *Canusium in Apulia*; 84. SYMPHORUS (1, 4), *Hierapythna in Crete*; TITIUS (2), see above (40); 85. TRYPHO (1, 2, 4), *Achaia* (*See uncertain* from corruption of text); 86. VALENS (1, 2, 3), '*Scio*' *in Dacia Ripensis*; 87. VERISSIMUS (2, 4, text of latter gives 'Broseus' corruptly), *Lyons*; 88. VINCENTIUS (1, 2, 3), *Capua*; 89. VITALIS (1, 2, 4), *Aquae in Dacia Ripensis*; 90. VITALIS 1, 3, 4), *Vertara in Africa*; 91. URSACIUS (1, 2, 4), *Brixia in Italy*; 92. ZOSIMUS (1, 2, 4), *Lychnidus or Lignidus in Dacia*; 93. ZOSIMUS (1, 4), *Horrea Margi in Moesia*; 94. ZOSIMUS (1, 4), *See unknown*; 95. JULIUS (1, 4), *Rome* (by deputies); 96. GRATUS (5), *Carthage*; 97. EUPHRATES (5), *Cologne*.

The names, both of bishops and of sees, have suffered much in transcription, and the above list is the result of comparing the divergent errors of the various lists. The details of the latter will be found in the originals, and in the discussion of the Ballerini, on whose work (in Leonis M. Opp. vol. iii. pp. xlii. sqq.) our list is founded. In some cases the names of the see are clearly corrupt beyond all recognition. The signatures appended to the canons in the collections of councils, are taken (with certain uncritical adaptations) from the Hilarian list, with the addition, in some copies, of Alexander (3 supra), whose name, therefore, has probably dropped out of the Hilarian text in course of transmission.]

DE DECRETIS

OR

DEFENCE OF THE NICENE DEFINITION

THIS letter must have been written in the interval between the return of Athanasius in 346 and his flight in 356. Acacius was already (§ 3) Bishop of Cæsarea (339); Eusebius of Nicomedia is not referred to as though still living (he died 342). Moreover the language of § 2 ("for in no long time they will turn to outrage," &c.) implies a period of actual peace, but with a prospect of the repetition of the scenes of the year 339. This actually occurred in 356. Accordingly we must probably place the tract under the sole reign of Constantius, between 351 and the end of 355.

It is written in answer to a friend who in disputing with Arians had been posed by their objection to the use of non-scriptural terms in the Nicene Definition. He accordingly asks for some account of what the council had done.

Athanasius begins his answer by stigmatising the evasions and inconsistency of the Arianisers, and describing their conduct at the council, and how they eventually subscribed to the terms now complained of (1—5). He then investigates the meaning of the divine Sonship (6—14), and how its true meaning is brought out by the other titles of the Son (15—17). Coming to the non-scriptural expressions he shews how they were forced upon the council by the evasions of the Arians (18—20), and that they express no sense not to be found in Scripture (21—24). Moreover, they had already been in use in the Church, as is shewn by extracts from Theognostus, the two Dionysii, and Origen (25—27). Lastly (28—32) he discusses the term ἀγένητος, applied by the Arians (especially Asterius) to the Father, in contrast, not to the creation, but to the Son, who is thereby implied to be γένητος. He insists on 'Father' not 'ἀγένητος' as the divine title authorised by Scripture. Lastly he appends, in proof of what he states in § 3, the letter of Eusebius to the people of Cæsarea, containing the creed of the council, which, for reasons there stated, we have inserted above, pp. 73—76.

The interest of the letter is principally threefold; first on account of its notice of the proceedings at Nicæa (cf. *ad Afr.* 5), one of the few primary sources of our knowledge of what took place there: secondly, on account of its fragments of early writers, especially the Dionysii, of whom more will be said in the introduction to the next tract. With regard to Theognostus, the quotations in this tract and in *Serap.* iv. 9 are important in view of the somewhat damaging accounts of his teaching in the few other writers (Gregory of Nyssa, Photius) who mention him.

Thirdly, the term ἀγένητος demands attention. It is impossible to give its exact force in idiomatic English: the rendering 'Ingenerate' adopted by Newman is perhaps the most unfortunate one imaginable. 'Uncreated,' a possible substitute, is also open to objection, firstly, as not distinguishing the word from the derivatives of κτίζειν, ποιεῖν, δημιουργεῖν, secondly, as giving it a passive sense, which does not inherently attach to it. For lack of a better word, 'Unoriginate' may perhaps be adopted. 'That which has not (or cannot) come to be,' 'that which is *not* the result of a process,'—is what the word strictly signifies'—'*das Ungewordene.*' It was therefore strictly applicable to the Son as well as to the Father. But throughout the earlier stages of the Arian controversy the question was embarrassed by the homophones γέννητος and ἀγέννητος, generate or begotten, and unbegotten. The confusion of thought due to the resemblance of sound is reflected, in the confusion of readings in the MSS. Athanasius himself (*Orat.* i. 56) perceives the distinctive sense of ἀγέννητος. In the present tract and in *Orat.* i. 30, he has ἀγένητος only in view, the idea of begetting being absent. Here (and cf. *de Syn.* 46, note 5) he is denying that the Father is alone ἀγένητος, uncreated or without a 'becoming.' Accordingly although the word γεννηθέντα was consecrated and safeguarded in the Creed of Nicæa (Begotten not made), and although the distinctness of the derivatives of the two verbs was felt by Athanasius, and pointed out by others (Epiph. *Hær.* 64, 8), the use of either group of words was avoided by Catholics as dangerous. A clear distinction of the words and of their respective applicability is made by John Damascene *Fid. Orth.* I. viii. (see Lightfoot, *Ignat.* vol. 2, excursus on Eph. § 7, Thilo, *ubi supra*, Introd. p. 14, and Harnack, *Dg.* 2, p. 193 note).

DE DECRETIS

OR

DEFENCE OF THE NICENE DEFINITION

CHAPTER I.

INTRODUCTION.

The complaint of the Arians against the Nicene Council; their fickleness; they are like Jews; their employment of force instead of reason.

1. THOU hast done well, in signifying to me the discussion thou hast had with the advocates of Arianism, among whom were certain of the friends of Eusebius, as well as very many of the brethren who hold the doctrine of the Church. I hailed thy vigilance for the love of Christ, which excellently exposed the irreligion [1] of their heresy; while I marvelled at the effrontery which led the Arians, after all the past detection of unsoundness and futility in their arguments, nay, after the general conviction of their extreme perverseness, still to complain like the Jews, "Why did the Fathers at Nicæa use terms not in Scripture [2], 'Of the essence' and 'One in essence?'" Thou then, as a man of learning, in spite of their subterfuges, didst convict them of talking to no purpose; and they in devising them were but acting suitably to their own evil

disposition. For they are as variable and fickle in their sentiments, as chameleons in their colours [3]; and when exposed they look confused, and when questioned they hesitate, and then they lose shame, and betake themselves to evasions. And then, when detected in these, they do not rest till they invent fresh matters which are not, and, according to the Scripture, 'imagine a vain thing [4]'; and all that they may be constant to their irreligion.

Now such endeavours [5] are nothing else than an obvious token of their defect of reason [6], and a copying, as I have said, of Jewish malignity. For the Jews too, when convicted by the Truth, and unable to confront it, used evasions, such as, 'What sign doest Thou, that we may see and believe Thee? What dost Thou work [7]? though so many signs were given, that they said themselves, 'What do we? for this man doeth many miracles [8].' In truth, dead men were raised, lame walked, blind saw afresh, lepers were cleansed, and the water became wine, and five loaves satisfied five thousand, and all wondered and worshipped the Lord, confessing that in Him were fulfilled the prophecies, and that He was God the Son of God; all but the Pharisees, who, though the signs shone brighter than the sun, yet complained still, as ignorant men, 'Why dost Thou, being a man, make

---

[1] εὐσέβεια, ἀσέβεια, &c., here translated "religion, irreligion, religious, &c. &c." are technical words throughout, being taken from S. Paul's text, "Great is the mystery of *godliness*," εὐσεβείας, i.e. orthodoxy. Such too seems to be the meaning of "godly admonitions," and "godly judgments," and "this godly and well-learned man," in our Ordination Services. The Latin translation is "pius," "pietas." It might be in some respects suitably rendered by "devout" and its derivatives. On its familiar use in controversy depends the blasphemous jest of Eudoxius, Arian Bishop of Constantinople, which was received with loud laughter in the Cathedral, and remained in esteem down to Socrates' day, "The Father is ἀσεβής, as being without devotion, the Son εὐσεβής, devout, as paying devotion to the Father." Socr. *Hist.* ii. 43. Hence Arius ends his Letter to Eusebius with ἀληθῶς εὐσέβιε. Theod. *Hist.* i. 4.

[2] It appears that the Arians did not venture to speak disrespectfully of the definition of the Council till the date (A.D. 352) of this work, when Acacius headed them. Yet the plea here used, the unscriptural character of its symbol, had been suggested to Constantius on his accession, A.D. 337, by the Arian priest, the favourite of Constantia, to whom Constantine had entrusted his will, Theod. *Hist.* ii. 3; and Eusebius of Cæsarea glances at it, at the time of the Council, in the letter to his Church, which is subjoined to this Treatise.

[3] Alexander also calls them chameleons, Socr. i. 6. p. 12. Athanasius so calls the Meletians, *Hist. Arian.* § 79. Cyril compares them to "the leopard which cannot change his spots." Dial. ii. init. t. v. i. Aub., *Naz. Or.* 28. 2. On the fickleness of the Arians, vid. infra, § 4. &c. *Orat.* ii. 40. He says, ad *Ep. Æg.* 6. that they considered Creeds as yearly covenants; and *de Synod.* § 3. 4. as State Edicts. vid. also § 14. and *passim.* "What wonder that they fight against their fathers, when they fight against themselves?" § 37.   [4] Ps. ii. 1.

[5] ἐπιχείρημα. and so *Orat.* i. § 44. init. but infra. § 25. ἐπιχειρήματα means more definitely reasonings or argumentations.

[6] ἀλογίας; an allusion frequent in Athanasius to the judicial consequence of their denying the Word of God. Thus, just below, n. 3. "Denying the Word" or Reason " of God, reason have they none." Also *Orat.* i. § 35. fin. § 40. init. § 62. *Orat.* ii. § 7. init. Hence he so often calls the Arians "mad" and "deranged;" e.g. "not aware how 'mad' their 'reason' is." *Orat.* i. § 37.

[7] John vi. 30.   [8] Ib. xi. 47.

Thyself God[9]? Insensate, and verily blind in understanding! they ought contrariwise to have said, "Why hast Thou, being God, become man?" for His works proved Him God, that they might both worship the goodness of the Father, and admire the Son's Economy for our sakes. However, this they did not say; no, nor liked to witness what He was doing; or they witnessed indeed, for this they could not help, but they changed their ground of complaint again, "Why healest Thou the paralytic, why makest Thou the born-blind to see, on the sabbath day?" But this too was an excuse, and mere murmuring; for on other days as well did the Lord heal 'all manner of sickness, and all manner of disease [1],' but they complained still according to their wont, and by calling Him Beelzebub, preferred the suspicion of Atheism [2], to a recantation of their own wickedness. And though in such sundry times and divers manners the Saviour shewed His Godhead and preached the Father to all men, nevertheless, as kicking against the pricks, they contradicted in the language of folly, and this they did, according to the divine proverb, that by finding occasions, they might separate themselves from the truth [3].

2. As then the Jews of that day, for acting thus wickedly and denying the Lord, were with justice deprived of their laws and of the promise made to their fathers, so the Arians, Judaizing now, are, in my judgment, in circumstances like those of Caiaphas and the contemporary Pharisees. For, perceiving that their heresy is utterly unreasonable, they invent excuses, "Why was this defined, and not that?" Yet wonder not if now they practise thus; for in no long time they will turn to outrage, and next will threaten 'the band and the captain [4].' Forsooth in these their heterodoxy has its support, as we see; for denying the Word of God, reason have they none at all, as is equitable. Aware then of this, I would have made no reply to their interrogations: but, since thy friendliness [5] has asked to know the transactions of the Council, I have without any delay related at once what then took place, shewing in few words, how destitute Arianism is of a religious spirit, and how their one business is to frame evasions.

CHAPTER II.

CONDUCT OF THE ARIANS TOWARDS THE NICENE COUNCIL.

Ignorant as well as irreligious to attempt to reverse an Ecumenical Council: proceedings at Nicæa: Eusebians then signed what they now complain of: on the unanimity of true teachers and the process of tradition: changes of the Arians.

AND do thou, beloved, consider whether it be not so. If, the devil having sowed their hearts with this perverseness[6], they feel confidence in their bad inventions, let them defend themselves against the proofs of heresy which have been advanced, and then will be the time to find fault, if they can, with the definition framed against them[7]. For no one, on

---

9 Ib. x. 33.   **1** Matt. iv. 23.

2 Or ungodliness, ἀθεότητος. Thus Aetius was called ὁ ἄθεος, the ungodly. *de Synod.* § 6; and Arius complains that Alexander had expelled him and his from Alexandria, ὡς ἀνθρώπους ἀθέους. Theodor. *Hist.* i. 4. "Atheism" and "Atheist" imply intention, system, and profession, and are so far too strong a rendering of the Greek. Since Christ was God, to deny Him was to deny God. The force of the term, however, seems to be, that, whereas the Son had revealed the "unknown God," and destroyed the reign of idols, the denial of the Son was bringing back idolatry and its attendant spiritual ignorance. Thus *contr. Gent.* § 29. fin. he speaks of "the Greek idolatry as full of all Atheism" or ungodliness, and contrasts with it the knowledge of "the Guide and Framer of the Universe, the Father's Word," "that through Him 'we may discern His Father,' and the Greeks may know 'how far they have separated themselves from the truth.'" And *Orat.* ii. 43. he classes Arians with the Greeks, who "though they have the name of God in their mouths, incur the charge of 'Atheism,' because they know not the real and true God, 'the Father of our Lord Jesus Christ.'" (vid. also Basil in *Eunom.* ii. 22.) Shortly afterwards he gives a further reason for the title, observing that Arianism was worse than previous heresies, such as Manicheism. inasmuch as the latter denied the Incarnation, but Arianism tore from God's substance His connatural Word, and, as far as its words went, infringed upon the perfections and being of the first Cause. And so ad *Ep. Æg.* § 17. fin. he says, that it alone, beyond other heresies, "has been bold against the Godhead Itself in a mad way (μανικώτερον, vid. foregoing note), denying that there is a Word, and that the Father was always Father." Elsewhere he speaks more generally, as if Arianism introduced "an Atheism or rather Judaism 'against the Scriptures,' being next door to Heathenism, so that its disciple cannot be even named Christian; for all such tenets are 'contrary to the Scriptures;'" and he makes this the reason why the Nicene Fathers stopped their ears and condemned it. ad *Ep. Æg.* § 13. For the same reason he calls the heathen ἄθεοι, atheistical or ungodly, "who are arraigned of irreligion by Divine Scripture." *contr. Gent.* § 14. vid. εἰδώλων ἀθεότητα. § 46. init. Moreover, he calls the Arian persecution worse than the pagan 'cruelties,' and therefore "a Babylonian Atheism," *Ep. Encycl.* § 5. as not allowing the Catholics the use of prayer and baptism, with a reference to Dan. vi. 11, &c. Thus too he calls Constantius atheist, for his treatment of Hosius; οὔτε τὸν θεὸν φοβηθεὶς ὁ ἄθεος. *Hist. Arian.* 45. Another reason for the title seems to have lain in the idolatrous character of Arian worship 'on its own shewing,' viz. as worshipping One whom they yet maintained to be a creature. [Prolegg. ch. ii. § 3 (2) a, *sub. fin.*]

3 A reference to Prov. xviii. 1. which runs in the LXX. "a man seeketh occasions, when desirous of separating himself from friends."

4 Apparently an allusion to Joh. xviii. 12. Elsewhere, he speaks of "the chief captain" and "the governor," with an allusion to Acts xxiii. 22—24. &c. *Hist. Arian.* § 66. fin. vid. also § 2. *Apol. contr. Arian.* §8. also § 10. and 45. *Orat.* ii. § 43. *Ep. Encycl.* § 5. Against the use of violence in religion, vid. *Hist. Arian.* § 33. 67. (Hil. *ad Const.* i. 2.) On the other hand, he observes, that at Nicæa, "it was not necessity which drove the judges to" their decision, "but all vindicated the Truth from deliberate purpose." ad *Ep. Æg.* 13.

5 διάθεσις. vid. also *Hist. Arian.* § 45. *Orat.* ii. § 4. where Parker maintains without reason that it should be translated, "external condition." vid. also Theod. *Hist.* i. 4. init.

6 ἐπισπείραντος τοῦ διαβόλου, the allusion is to Matt. xiii. 25, and is very frequent in Athan., chiefly with a reference to Arianism. He draws it out at length, *Orat.* ii. § 34. Elsewhere, he uses the image for the evil influences introduced into the soul upon Adam's fall, *contr. Apoll.* i. § 15. as does S. Irenæus, *Hær.* iv. 40. n. 3. using it of such as lead to back-sliding in Christians. ibid. v. 10. n. 1. Gregory Nyssen, of the natural passions and of false reason misleading them, *de An. et Resurr.* p. 640. vid. also Leon. *Ep.* 156. c. 2.

7 The Council did two things, anathematise the Arian positions (at the end of the Creed), and establish the true doctrine by the insertion of the phrases, "of the substance" and "one in substance." Athan. says that the Arians must not criticise the latter

being convicted of murder or adultery, is at liberty after the trial to arraign the sentence of the judge, why he spoke in this way and not in that[8]. For this does not exculpate the convict, but rather increases his crime on the score of petulance and audacity. In like manner, let these either prove that their sentiments are religious (for they were then accused and convicted, and their complaints are subsequent, and it is just that those who are under a charge should confine themselves to their own defence), or if they have an unclean conscience, and are aware of their own irreligion, let them not complain of what they do not understand, or they will bring on themselves a double imputation, of irreligion and of ignorance. Rather let them investigate the matter in a docile spirit, and learning what hitherto they have not known, cleanse their irreligious ears with the spring of truth and the doctrines of religion [9].

3. Now it happened to Eusebius and his fellows in the Nicene Council as follows:— while they stood out in their irreligion, and attempted their fight against God[1], the terms they used were replete with irreligion; but the assembled Bishops who were three hundred more or less, mildly and charitably required of them to explain and defend themselves on religious grounds. Scarcely, however, did they begin to speak, when they were condemned[2], and one differed from another; then perceiving the straits in which their heresy lay, they remained dumb, and by their silence confessed the disgrace which came upon their heterodoxy. On this the Bishops, having negatived the terms they had invented, published against them the sound and ecclesiastical faith; and, as all subscribed it, Eusebius and his fellows subscribed it also in those very words, of which they are

now complaining, I mean, "of the essence" and "one in essence," and that "the Son of God is neither creature or work, nor in the number of things originated[3], but that the Word is an offspring from the substance of the Father." And what is strange indeed, Eusebius of Cæsarea in Palestine, who had denied the day before, but afterwards subscribed, sent to his Church a letter, saying that this was the Church's faith, and the tradition of the Fathers; and made a public profession that they were before in error, and were rashly contending against the truth. For though he was ashamed at that time to adopt these phrases, and excused himself to the Church in his own way, yet he certainly means to imply all this in his Epistle, by his not denying the "one in essence," and "of the essence." And in this way he got into a difficulty; for while he was excusing himself, he went on to attack the Arians, as stating that "the Son was not before His generation," and as thereby rejecting His existence before His birth in the flesh. And this Acacius is aware of also, though he too through fear may pretend otherwise because of the times and deny the fact. Accordingly I have subjoined at the end the letter of Eusebius, that thou mayest know from it the disrespect towards their own doctors shewn by Christ's enemies, and singularly by Acacius himself[4].

4. Are they not then committing a crime, in their very thought to gainsay so great and ecumenical a Council? are they not in transgression, when they dare to confront that good definition against Arianism, acknowledged, as it is, by those who had in the first instance taught them irreligion? And supposing, even after subscription, Eusebius and his fellows did change again, and return like dogs to their own vomit of irreligion, do not the present gainsayers deserve still greater detestation, because they thus sacrifice[5] their souls' liberty to others; and are willing to take these persons as masters of their heresy, who are, as James[6] has said, double-minded men, and unstable in all their ways, not having one opinion, but changing to and fro, and now recommending certain statements, but soon dishonouring them, and in turn recommending what just now they were blaming? But this, as the

---

before they had cleared themselves of the former. Thus he says presently, that they were at once irreligious in their faith and ignorant in their criticism; and speaks of the Council negativing their formulæ, and substituting those which were "sound and ecclesiastical." vid. also n. 4.

[8] And so S. Leo *passim* concerning the Council of Chalcedon, "Concord will be easily established, if the hearts of all concur in that faith which, &c., no discussion being allowed whatever concerning any retractation," *Ep.* 94. He calls such an act a "magnum sacrilegium," *Ep.* 157. c. 3. "To be seeking for what has been disclosed, to retract what has been perfected, to tear up what has been laid down (definita), what is this but to be unthankful for what we gained?" *Ep.* 162. vid. the whole of it. He says that the attempt is "no mark of a peace-maker but a rebel." *Ep.* 164. c. l. fin. vid. also Epp. 145, and 156, where he says, none can assail what is once determined, but "aut antichristus aut diabolus." c. 2.

[9] Vid. *Orat.* iii. § 28.

[1] θεομαχεῖν, θεομάχοι. vid. Acts v. 39, xxiii. 9. are of very frequent use in Athan. as is χριστομάχοι, in speaking of the Arians, vid. *infra passim.* also ἀντιμαχόμενοι τῷ σωτῆρι, *Ep. Encycl.* § 5. And in the beginning of the controversy, Alexander *ap. Socr.* i. 6. p. 10. b. c. p. 12. p. 13. Theod. *Hist.* i. 3. p. 729. And so θεομάχος γλῶσσα, Basil. *contr. Eunom.* ii. 27. fin. χριστομάχων. *Ep.* 236. init. vid. also Cyril (Thesaurus, p. 19 e. p. 24 e.). θεομάχοι is used of other heretics, e.g. the Manichees, by Greg. Naz. *Orat.* 45. § 8.

[2] i.e. "convicted *themselves,*" infr. § 18. init. ἑαυτῶν ἀεὶ κατήγοροι, ad. *Ep. Æg.* § 6. i.e. by their variations, vid. Tit. iii. 11. αὐτοκατάκριτος.

[3] γενητῶν.

[4] The party he is writing against is the Acacian, of whom he does not seem to have had much distinct knowledge. He contrasts them again and again in the passages which follow with the Eusebians of the Nicene Council, and says that he is sure that the ground they take when examined will be found substantially the same as the Eusebian. vid. § 6 *init. et alib.* § 7. *init.* § 9. *circ. fin.* § 10. *circ. fin.* § 13. *init.* τότε καὶ νῦν. § 18. *circ. fin.* § 28. *fin* [On Acacius see Prolegg. ch. ii. § 8 (2) b.]

[5] προπίνοντες vid. *de Syn.* § 14.

[6] James i. 8.

Shepherd has said, is "the child of the devil[7]," and the note of hucksters rather than of doctors. For, what our Fathers have delivered, this is truly doctrine; and this is truly the token of doctors, to confess the same thing with each other, and to vary neither from themselves nor from their fathers; whereas they who have not this character are to be called not true doctors but evil. Thus the Greeks, as not witnessing to the same doctrines, but quarrelling one with another, have no truth of teaching; but the holy and veritable heralds of the truth agree together, and do not differ. For though they lived in different times, yet they one and all tend the same way, being prophets of the one God, and preaching the same Word harmoniously[8].

5. And thus what Moses taught, that Abraham observed; and what Abraham observed, that Noah and Enoch acknowledged, discriminating pure from impure, and becoming acceptable to God. For Abel too in this way witnessed, knowing what he had learned from Adam, who himself had learned from that Lord, who said, when He came at the end of the ages for the abolishment of sin, "I give no new commandment unto you, but an old commandment, which ye have heard from the beginning[9]." Wherefore also the blessed Apostle Paul, who had learned it from Him, when describing ecclesiastical functions, forbade that deacons, not to say bishops, should be double-tongued[10]; and in his rebuke of the Galatians, he made a broad declaration, "If anyone preach any other Gospel unto you than that ye have received, let him be anathema, as I have said, so say I again. If even we, or an Angel from heaven should preach unto you any other Gospel than that ye have received, let him be anathema[1]." Since then the Apostle thus speaks, let these men either anathematise Eusebius and his fellows, at least as changing round and professing what is contrary to their subscriptions; or, if they acknowledge that their subscriptions were good, let them not utter complaints against so great a Council. But if they do neither the one nor the other, they are themselves too plainly the sport of every wind and surge, and are influenced by opinions, not their own, but of others, and being such, are as little worthy of deference now as before, in what they allege. Rather let them cease to carp at what they understand

not; lest so be that not knowing to discriminate, they simply call evil good and good evil, and think that bitter is sweet and sweet is bitter. Doubtless, they desire that doctrines which have been judged wrong and have been reprobated should gain the ascendancy, and they make violent efforts to prejudice what was rightly defined. Nor should there be any reason on our part for any further explanation, or answer to their excuses, neither on theirs for further resistance, but for an acquiescence in what the leaders of their heresy subscribed; for though the subsequent change of Eusebius and his fellows was suspicious and immoral, their subscription, when they had the opportunity of at least some little defence of themselves, is a certain proof of the irreligion of their doctrine. For they would not have subscribed previously had they not condemned the heresy, nor would they have condemned it, had they not been encompassed with difficulty and shame; so that to change back again is a proof of their contentious zeal for irreligion. These men also ought therefore, as I have said, to keep quiet; but since from an extraordinary want of modesty, they hope perhaps to be able to advocate this diabolical[2] irreligion better than the others, therefore, though in my former letter written to thee, I have already argued at length against them, notwithstanding, come let us now also examine them, in each of their separate statements, as their predecessors; for now not less than then their heresy shall be shewn to have no soundness in it, but to be from evil spirits.

CHAPTER III.

Two senses of the word Son, 1. adoptive; 2. essential; attempts of Arians to find a third meaning between these; e.g. that our Lord only was created immediately by God (Asterius's view), or that our Lord alone partakes the Father. The second and true sense; God begets as He makes, really; though His creation and generation are not like man's; His generation independent of time; generation implies an internal, and therefore an eternal, act in God; explanation of Prov. viii. 22.

6. THEY say then what the others held and dared to maintain before them; "Not always

---

[7] Hermas, *Mand.* ix., who is speaking immediately, as S. James, of wavering in prayer.
[8] Thus S. Basil says the same of the Grecian Sects, "We have not the task of refuting their tenets, for they suffice for the overthrow of each other." *Hexaem.* i. 2. vid. also Theod. *Græc. Affect.* i. p. 707. &c. August. *Civ. Dei*, xviii. 41. and Vincentius's celebrated Commonitorium *passim.*
[9] 1 John ii. 7. [10] 1 Tim. iii. 8. [1] Gal. i. 8, 9.

[2] This is Athan.'s deliberate judgment. vid. *de Sent. Dion.* fin., *ib.* § 24. he speaks of Arius's "hatred of the truth." Again, "though the diabolical men rave" *Orat.* iii. § 8. "friends of the devil, and his spirits," Ad *Ep. Æg.* 5. Another reason of his so accounting them, was their atrocious cruelty towards Catholics; this leads him elsewhere to break out: "O new heresy, that has put on the whole devil in irreligious doctrine *and conduct!" Hist. Arian.* § 66, also Alexander, 'diabolical,' ap Theod. *Hist.* i. 3, p. 731. 'satanical,' ibid. p. 741. vid. also Socr. i. 9. p. 30 fin. Hilar. *contr. Const.* 17.

Father, not always Son; for the Son was not before His generation, but, as others, came to be from nothing; and in consequence God was not always Father of the Son; but, when the Son came to be and was created, then was God called His Father. For the Word is a creature and a work, and foreign and unlike the Father in essence; and the Son is neither by nature the Father's true Word, nor His only and true Wisdom; but being a creature and one of the works, He is improperly[3] called Word and Wisdom; for by the Word which is in God was He made, as were all things. Wherefore the Son is not true God[4].''

Now it may serve to make them understand what they are saying, to ask them first this, what in fact a son is, and of what is that name significant[5]. In truth, Divine Scripture acquaints us with a double sense of this word:—one which Moses sets before us in the Law, 'When ye shall hearken to the voice of the Lord thy God, to keep all His commandments which I command thee this day, to do that which is right in the eyes of the Lord thy God, ye are children of the Lord your God[6];' as also in the Gospel, John says, 'But as many as received Him, to them gave He power to become the sons of God[7]:'—and the other sense, that in which Isaac is son of Abraham, and Jacob of Isaac, and the Patriarchs of Jacob. Now in which of these two senses do they understand the Son of God that they relate such fables as the foregoing? for I feel sure they will issue in the same irreligion with Eusebius and his fellows.

If in the first, which belongs to those who gain the name by grace from moral improvement, and receive power to become sons of God (for this is what their predecessors said), then He would seem to differ from us in nothing; no, nor would He be Only-begotten, as having obtained the title of Son as others from His virtue. For granting what they say, that, whereas His qualifications were foreknown[8], He therefore received grace from the first, the name, and the glory of the name, from His very first beginning, still there will be no difference between Him and those who receive the name after their actions, so long as this is the ground on which He as others has the character of son. For Adam too, though he received grace from the first, and upon his creation was at once placed in paradise, differed in no respect either from Enoch, who was translated thither after some time from his birth on his pleasing God, or from the Apostle, who likewise was caught up to Paradise after his actions; nay, not from him who once was a thief, who on the ground of his confession, received a promise that he should be forthwith in paradise.

7. When thus pressed, they will perhaps make an answer which has brought them into trouble many times already; "We consider that the Son has this prerogative over others, and therefore is called Only-begotten, because He alone was brought to be by God alone, and all other things were created by God through the Son[1]." Now I wonder who it was[2] that suggested to you so futile and novel an idea as that the Father alone wrought with His own hand the Son alone, and that all other things were brought to be by the Son as by an under-worker. If for the toil's sake God was content with making the Son only, instead of making all things at once, this is an irreligious thought, especially in those who know the words of Esaias, 'The everlasting God, the Lord, the Creator of the ends of the earth, hungereth not, neither is weary; there is no searching of His understanding[3].' Rather it is He who gives strength to the hungry, and through His Word refreshes the labouring[4]. Again, it is irreligious to suppose that He disdained, as if a humble task, to form the creatures Himself which came after the Son; for there is no pride in that God, who goes down with Jacob into Egypt, and for Abraham's sake corrects Abim-

---

3 καταχρηστικῶς. This word is noticed and protested against by Alexander, Socr. *Hist.* i. 6. p. 11 a. by the Semiarians at Ancyra, Epiph. *Hær.* 73. n. 5. by Basil. *contr. Eunom.* ii. 23. and by Cyril, *Dial.* ii. t. v. i. pp. 432, 3.

4 Vid. *Ep. Æg.* 12. *Orat.* i. § 5. 6. *de Synod.* 15, 16. Athanas. seems to have had in mind Socr. i. 6. p. 10, 11, or the like.

5 Vid. *Orat.* i. § 38. The controversy turned on the question what was meant by the word 'Son.' Though the Arians would not allow with the Catholics that our Lord was Son *by nature*, and maintained that the word implied *a beginning of existence*, they did not dare to say that He was Son merely in the sense in which we are sons, though, as Athan. contends, they necessarily tended to this conclusion, directly they receded from the Catholic view. Thus Arius said that He was a creature, 'but not as one of the creatures.' *Orat.* ii. § 19. Valens at Ariminum said the same, Jerom. adv. *Lucifer.* 18. Hilary says, that not daring directly to deny that He was God, the Arians merely asked 'whether He was a Son.' *de Trin.* viii. 3. Athanasius remarks upon this reluctance to speak out, challenging them to present 'the heresy naked,' *de Sent. Dionys.* 2. *init.* 'No one,' he says elsewhere, 'puts a light under a bushel; let them shew the world their heresy naked.' *Ep. Æg.* 18. vid. ibid. 10. In like manner, Basil says that (though Arius was really like Eunomius, in faith, *contr. Eunom.* i. 4) Aetius his master was the first to teach openly (φανερῶς), that the Father's substance was unlike, ἀνόμοιος, the Son's. ibid. i. 1. Epiphanius *Hær.* 76. p. 949. seems to say that the elder Arians held the divine generation in a sense in which Aetius did not, that is, they were not so consistent and definite as he. Athan. goes on to mention some of the attempts of the Arians to find some theory short of orthodoxy, yet short of that extreme heresy, on the other hand, which they felt ashamed to avow.

6 Deut. xiii. 18; xiv. 1.   7 John. i. 12.

8 Theod. *Hist.* i. 3.

1 This is celebrated as an explanation of the Anomœans. vid. Basil. *contr. Eunom.* ii. 20, 21. though Athan. speaks of it as belonging to the elder Arians. vid. Socr. *Hist.* i. 6.

2 i.e. what is your *authority?* is it not a *novel,* and therefore a wrong doctrine? vid. infr. § 13. *ad Serap.* i. 3. Also *Orat.* i. § 8. 'Who ever *heard* such doctrine? or *whence* or *from whom* did they hear it? who, *when they were under catechising, spoke* thus to them? If they themselves confess that they now hear it for the first time, they must grant that their heresy is alien, and *not from the Fathers.*' vid. ii. § 34. and Socr. i. 6. p. 11 c.

3 Is. xl. 28.   4 Ib. 29.

elek because of Sara, and speaks face to face with Moses, himself a man, and descends upon Mount Sinai, and by His secret grace fights for the people against Amalek. However, you are false even in this assertion, for 'He made us, and not we ourselves[5].' He it is who through His Word made all things small and great, and we may not divide the creation, and says this is the Father's, and this the Son's, but they are of one God, who uses His proper Word as a Hand[6], and in Him does all things. This God Himself shews us, when He says, 'All these things hath My Hand made[7];' while Paul taught us as he had learned[8], that 'There is one God, from whom all things; and one Lord Jesus Christ, through whom all things[9].' Thus He, always as now, speaks to the sun and it rises, and commands the clouds and it rains upon one place; and where it does not rain, it is dried up. And He bids the earth yield her fruits, and fashions Jeremias[10] in the womb. But if He now does all this, assuredly at the beginning also He did not disdain to make all things Himself through the Word; for these are but parts of the whole.

8. But let us suppose that the other creatures could not endure to be wrought by the absolute Hand of the Unoriginate[1], and therefore the Son alone was brought into being by the Father alone, and other things by the Son as an underworker and assistant, for this is what Asterius the sacrificer[2] has written, and Arius has transcribed[3] and bequeathed to his own friends, and from that time they use this form of words, broken reed as it is, being ignorant, the bewildered men, how brittle it is. For if it was impossible for things originate to bear the hand of God, and you hold the Son to be one of their number, how was He too equal to this formation by God alone? and if a Mediator became necessary that things originate might come to be, and you hold the Son to be originated, then must there have been some medium before Him, for His creation; and that Mediator himself again being a creature, it follows that he too needed another Mediator for his own constitution. And though we were to devise another, we must first devise his Mediator, so that we shall never come to an end. And thus a Mediator being ever in request, never will the creation be constituted, because nothing originate, as you say, can bear the absolute hand of the Unoriginate[4]. And if, on your perceiving the extravagance of this, you begin to say that the Son, though a creature, was made capable of being made by the Unoriginate, then it follows that other things also, though originated, are capable of being wrought immediately by the Unoriginate; for the Son too is but a creature in your judgment, as all of them. And accordingly the origination of the Word is superfluous, according to your irreligious and futile imagination, God being sufficient for the immediate formation of all things, and all things originate being capable of sustaining His absolute hand.

These irreligious men then having so little mind amid their madness, let us see whether this particular sophism be not even more irrational than the others. Adam was created alone by God alone through the Word; yet no one would say that Adam had any prerogative over other men, or was different from those who came after him, granting that he alone was made and fashioned by God alone, and we all spring from Adam, and consist according to succession of the race, so long as he was fashioned from the earth as others, and at first not being, afterwards came to be.

9. But though we were to allow some prerogative to the Protoplast as having been deemed worthy of the hand of God, still it must be one of honour not of nature. For he came of the earth, as other men; and the hand which then fashioned Adam, is also both now and ever fashioning and giving entire consistence to those who come after him. And God Himself declares this to Jeremiah, as I said before; 'Before I formed thee in the womb, I knew thee[5];' and so He says of all, 'All those things hath My hand made[6];' and again by Isaiah, 'Thus saith the Lord, thy redeemer, and He that formed thee from the womb, I am the Lord that maketh all things; that stretcheth forth the heavens alone; that spreadeth abroad the earth by Myself[7].' And David, knowing this, says in the Psalm, 'Thy hands have made me and fashioned me[8];' and he who says in Isaiah, 'Thus saith the Lord who formed me from the womb to be His servant[9],' signifies the same. Therefore, in respect of nature, he differs nothing from us though he precede us in time, so long as we all consist and are created by the same hand. If then these be your thoughts, O Arians, about

5 Ps. c. 3.
6 Vid. infr. § 17. *Orat.* ii. § 31. 71. Irenæus calls the Son and Holy Spirit the Hands of God. *Hær.* iv. *præf.* vid. also Hilar. *de Trin.* vii. 22. This image is in contrast to that of *instrument*, ὄργανον, which the Arians would use of the Son, vid Socr. i. 6. p. 11, as implying He was external to God, whereas the word *Hand* implies His consubstantiality with the Father.
7 Is. lxvi. 2.
8 μαθὼν ἐδίδασκεν, implying the traditional nature of the teaching. And so S. Paul himself, 1 Cor. xv. 3, vid. for an illustration, supr. § 5. init. also note 2.
9 1 Cor. viii. 6.   10 Jer. i. 5.   1 *Orat.* ii. § 24. fin.
2 Vid. infr. 20. *Orat.* i. § 31. ii. §§ 24, 28. 37. 40. iii. §§ 2. 60. *de Synod* §§ 18. 19. [Prolegg. ch. ii. § 3 (2) a.]
3 Vid. also infr. § 20. *de Synod.* § 17.

4 Vid. infr. § 24. *Orat.* i. § 15. fin. ii. § 29. Epiph. *Hær.* 76. p. 951.   5 Jer. i. 5.   6 Is. lxvi. 2.
7 Ib. xliv. 2.   8 Ps. cxix. 73.   9 Is. xlix. 5.

the Son of God too, that thus He subsists and came to be, then in your judgment He will differ nothing on the score of nature from others, so long as He too was not, and came to be, and the name was by grace united to Him in His creation for His virtue's sake. For He Himself is one of those, from what you say, of whom the Spirit says in the Psalms, 'He spake the word, and they were made; He commanded, and they were created [1].' If so, who was it by whom God gave command [2] for the Son's creation? for a Word there must be by whom God gave command, and in whom the works are created; but you have no other to shew than the Word you deny, unless indeed you should devise again some new notion.

"Yes," they will say, "we have another;" (which indeed I formerly heard Eusebius and his fellows use), "on this score do we consider that the Son of God has a prerogative over others, and is called Only-begotten, because He alone partakes the Father, and all other things partake the Son." Thus they weary themselves in changing and in varying their phrases like colours [3]; however, this shall not save them from an exposure, as men that are of the earth, speaking vainly, and wallowing in their own conceits as in mire.

10. For if He were called God's Son, and we the Son's sons, their fiction were plausible; but if we too are said to be sons of that God, of whom He is Son, then we too partake the Father [4], who says, 'I have begotten and exalted children [5].' For if we did not partake Him, He had not said, 'I have begotten;' but if He Himself begat us, no other than He is our Father [6]. And, as before, it matters not, whether the Son has something more and was made first, but we something less, and were made afterwards, as long as we all partake, and are called sons, of the same Father [7]. For

the more or less does not indicate a different nature; but attaches to each according to the practice of virtue; and one is placed over ten cities, another over five; and some sit on twelve thrones judging the twelve tribes of Israel; and others hear the words, 'Come, ye blessed of My Father,' and, 'Well done, good and faithful servant [8].' With such ideas, however, no wonder they imagine that of such a Son God was not always Father, and such a Son was not always in being, but was generated from nothing as a creature, and was not before His generation; for such an one is other than the True Son of God.

But to persist in such teaching does not consist with piety [9], for it is rather the tone of thought of Sadducees and the Samosatene [10]; it remains then to say that the Son of God is so called according to the other sense, in which Isaac was son of Abraham; for what is naturally begotten from any one and does not accrue to him from without, that in the nature of things is a son, and that is what the name implies [1]. Is then the Son's generation one of human affection? (for this perhaps, as their predecessors [2], they too will be ready to object in their ignorance;)—in no wise; for God is not as man, nor men as God. Men were created of matter, and that passible; but God is immaterial and incorporeal. And if so be the same terms are used of God and man in divine Scripture, yet the clear-sighted, as Paul enjoins, will study it, and thereby discriminate, and dispose of what is written according to the nature of each subject, and avoid any confusion of sense, so as neither to conceive of the things of God in a human way, nor to ascribe the things of man to God [3].

---

them; for even in those things which are of a created nature, we may find some things surpassing others. Star, for instance, differs from star in glory, yet it does not follow that some are sovereign, and others serve, &c.' ii. § 20. And so Gregory Nyssen *contr. Eunom.* iii. p. 132 D. Epiph. *Hær.* 76. p. 970.

[8] Matt. xxv. 21, 23, 34.

[9] i.e. since it is impossible they can persist in evasions so manifest as these, nothing is left but to take the other sense of the word.

[10] Paul of Samosata [see Prolegg. ch. ii. § 3 (2) a.]

[1] The force lies in the word φύσει, 'naturally,' which the Council expressed still more definitely by 'essence.' Thus Cyril says, 'the term "Son" denotes the essential origin from the Father.' *Dial.* 5. p. 573. And Gregory Nyssen, 'the title "Son" does not simply express the being *from* another' vid. infra.§ 19.), but *relationship according to nature. contr. Eunom.* ii. p. 91. Again S. Basil says, that Father is 'a term of relationship,' οἰκειώσεως. *contr. Eunom.* ii. 24. init. And hence he remarks, that we too are properly, κυρίως, sons of God, as becoming related to Him through works of the Spirit. ii. 23. So also Cyril, *loc. cit.* Elsewhere S. Basil defines father 'one who gives to another the origin of being according to a nature like his own;' and a son 'one who possesses the origin of being from another by generation,' *contr Eun.* ii. 22. On the other hand, the Arians at the first denied that 'by nature there was any Son of God.' Theod. *H. E.* i. 3. p. 732.

[2] vid. Eusebius, in his *Letter, supr.* p. 73 *sq.:* also Socr. *Hist.* i 8. Epiphan. *Hær.* 69. n 8 and 15.

[3] One of the characteristic points in Athanasius is his constant attention to the *sense* of doctrine, or the *meaning* of writers, in preference to the words used. Thus he scarcely uses the symbol ὁμοούσιον, one in substance, throughout his *Orations*, and in the *de Synod.* acknowledges the Semiarians as brethren. Hence

---

[1] Ps. cxlviii. 5 (LXX).

[2] In like manner, 'Men were made through the Word, when the Father Himself *willed.' Orat.* i. 63. 'The Word forms matter as injoined by, and ministering to, God.' προστατόμενος καὶ ὑπουργῶν. ibid. ii. § 22. *contr. Gent.* 46. vid. note on *Orat.* ii. 22.

[3] *ad Serap.* i. 3.

[4] His argument is, that if the Son but partook the Father in the sense in which we partake the Son, then the Son would not impart to us the Father, but Himself, and would be a separating as well as uniting medium between the Father and us; whereas He brings us so near to the Father, that we are the Father's children, not His, and therefore He must be Himself one with the Father, or the Father must be in Him with an incomprehensible completeness. vid. *de Synod.* § 51. *contr. Gent.* 46. fin. Hence S. Augustin says, 'As the Father has life in Himself, so hath He given also to the Son to have life in Himself, *not by participating,* but in Himself. For we have not life in ourselves, but in our God. But that Father, who has life in Himself, begat a Son such, as to have life in Himself, not to become partaker of life, but *to be Himself life; and of that life to make us partakers.' Serm.* 127. *de Verb. Evang.* 9.

[5] Is. i. 2.

[6] 'To say God is *wholly partaken,* is the same as saying that *God begets.' Orat.* i. § 16. And in like manner, our inferior participation involves such sonship as is vouchsafed to us.

[7] And so in *Orat.* ii. § 19—22. 'Though the Son surpassed other things on a comparison, yet He were equally a creature with

For this were to mix wine with water[4], and to place upon the altar strange fire with that which is divine.

11. For God creates, and to create is also ascribed to men; and God has being, and men are said to be, having received from God this gift also. Yet does God create as men do? or is His being as man's being? Perish the thought; we understand the terms in one sense of God, and in another of men. For God creates, in that He calls what is not into being, needing nothing thereunto; but men work some existing material, first praying, and so gaining the wit to make, from that God who has framed all things by His proper Word. And again men, being incapable of self-existence, are enclosed in place, and consist in the Word of God; but God is self-existent, enclosing all things, and enclosed by none; within all according to His own goodness and power, yet without all in His proper nature[5]. As then men create not as God creates, as their being is not such as God's being, so men's generation is in one way, and the Son is from the Father in another[6]. For the offspring of men are portions of their fathers, since the very nature of bodies is not uncompounded, but in a state of flux[7], and composed of parts; and men lose their substance in begetting, and again they gain substance from the accession of food. And on this account men in their time become fathers of many children; but God, being without parts, is Father of the Son without partition or passion; for there is neither effluence[8] of the Immaterial, nor influx from without, as among men; and being uncompounded in nature, He is Father of One Only Son. This is why He is Only-begotten, and alone in the Father's bosom, and alone is acknowledged by the Father to be from Him, saying, 'This is My beloved Son, in whom I am well pleased[9].' And He too is the Father's Word, from which may be understood the impassible and impartitive nature of the Father, in that not even a human word is begotten with passion or partition, much less the Word of God[1]. Wherefore also He sits, as Word, at the Father's right hand; for where the Father is, there also is His Word; but we, as His works, stand in judgment before Him; and, while He is adored, because He is Son of the adorable Father, we adore, confessing Him Lord and God, because we are creatures and other than He.

12. The case being thus, let who will among them consider the matter, so that one may abash them by the following question; Is it right to say that what is God's offspring and proper to Him is out of nothing? or is it reasonable in the very idea, that what is from God has accrued to Him, that a man should dare to say that the Son is not always? For in this again the generation of the Son exceeds and transcends the thoughts of man, that we become fathers of our own children in time, since we ourselves first were not and then came into being; but God, in that He ever is, is ever Father of the Son[2]. And the origination

---

infr. § 18. he says, that orthodox doctrine 'is revered by all though expressed in strange language, provided the speaker means religiously, and wishes to convey by it a religious sense.' vid. also § 21. He says, that Catholics are able to 'speak freely,' or to expatiate, παρρησιαζόμεθα, 'out of Divine Scripture.' *Orat.* i. § 9. vid. *de Sent. Dionys.* § 20. init. Again: 'The devil spoke from Scripture, but was silenced by the Saviour; Paul spoke from profane writers, yet, being a saint, he has a religious meaning.' *de Syn.* § 39. also ad *Ep. Æg.* 8. Again, speaking of the apparent contrariety between two Councils, 'It were unseemly to make the one conflict with the other, for all their members are fathers; and it were profane to decide that these spoke well and those ill, for all of them have slept in Christ.' § 43. also § 47. Again: 'Not the phrase, but the meaning and the religious life, is the recommendation of the faithful.' ad *Ep. Æg.* § 9.

4 vid. *Orat.* iii. § 35, and Isa. i. 22.

5 Vid. also *Incarn.* § 17. This contrast is not commonly found in ecclesiastical writers, who are used to say that God is present everywhere, in substance as well as by energy or power. S. Clement, however, expresses himself still more strongly in the same way, 'In substance far off (for how can the originate come close to the Unoriginate?), but most close in power, in which the universe is embosomed.' *Strom.* 2. *circ. init.* but the parenthesis explains his meaning. Vid. Cyril. *Thesaur.* 6. p. 44. The common doctrine of the Fathers is, that God is present everywhere in *substance*. Vid. Petav. *de Deo*, iii. 8. and 9. It may be remarked, that S. Clement continues '*neither enclosing* nor enclosed.'

6 In Almighty God is the perfection and first pattern of what is seen in shadow in human nature, according to the imperfection of the subject matter; and this remark applies, as to creation, so to generation. Athanasius is led to state this more distinctly in another connection in *Orat.* i. § 21. fin. 'It belongs to the Godhead alone, *that the Father is properly* (κυρίως) *Father, and the Son properly* (κυρίως) *Son;* and in Them and Them only does it hold that the Father is ever Father, and the Son ever Son.' Accordingly he proceeds, shortly afterwards, as in the text, to argue, '*For God does not make men His pattern,* but rather we men, for that God *is properly* and alone truly Father of His own Son, are also called fathers of our own children, for "of Him is every father-hood in heaven and on earth named,"' § 23. The Semiarians at Ancyra quote the same text for the same doctrine. Epiphan. *Hær.* 73. 5. As do Cyril in *Joan.* i. p. 24. *Thesaur.* 32. p. 281. and Damascene *de Fid. Orth.* i. 8. The same parallel, as existing between creation and generation, is insisted on by Isidor. Pel. *Ep.* iii. 355. Basil *contr. Eun.* iv. p. 280 A., Cyril *Thesaur.* 6. p. 43. Epiph. *Hær.* 69. 36. and Gregor. Naz. *Orat.* 20. 9. who observes that God creates with a *word*, Ps. cxlviii. 5, which evidently transcends human creations. Theodorus Abucara, with the same object, draws out the parallel of life, ζωὴ, as Athan. that of being, εἶναι. *Opusc.* iii. p. 420—422.

7 Vid. *de Synod.* § 51. *Orat.* i. § 15, 16. ῥευστὴ. vid. *Orat.* i. § 28. Bas. in *Eun.* ii. 23. ῥύσιν. Bas. in *Eun.* ii. 6. Greg. Naz. *Orat.* 28, 22. Vid. *contr. Gentes*, §§ 41, 42; where Athan. without reference to the Arian controversy, draws out the contrast between the Godhead and human nature.

8 S. Cyril, *Dial.* iv. init. p. 505 E. speaks of the θρυλλουμένη ἀπορροὴ, and disclaims it, *Thesaur.* 6. p. 43. Athan. disclaims it, *Expos.* § 1. *Orat.* i. § 21. So does Alexander, ap. Theod. *Hist.* i 3. p. 743. On the other hand, Athanasius quotes it in a passage which he adduces from Theognostus, *infr.* § 25. and from Dionysius, *de Sent. D.* § 23. and Origen uses it, *Periarchon*, i. 2. It is derived from Wisd. vii. 25. 9 Matt. iii. 17.

1 The title 'Word' implies the ineffable mode of the Son's generation, as distinct from *material* parallels, vid. Gregory Nyssen, *contr. Eunom.* iii. p. 107. Chrysostom in *Joan.* Hom. 2. § 4. Cyril Alex. *Thesaur.* 5. p. 37. Also it implies that there is but *One* Son. vid. infr. § 16. 'As the Origin is one essence, so its Word and Wisdom is one, essential and subsisting.' *Orat.* iv. 1. fin.

2 'Man,' says S. Cyril, 'inasmuch as he had a beginning of being, also has of necessity a beginning of begetting, as what is from him is a thing generate, but . . . . if God's essence transcend time, or origin, or interval, His generation too will transcend these; nor does it deprive the Divine Nature of the power of generating, that it doth not this in time. For other than human is the manner of divine generation; and together with God's existing is His generating implied, and the Son was in Him by generation, nor did His generation precede His existence, but He was always, and that by generation.' *Thesaur.* v. p. 35.

of mankind is brought home to us from things that are parallel; but, since 'no one knoweth the Son but the Father, and no one knoweth the Father but the Son, and he to whomsoever the Son will reveal Him[3],' therefore the sacred writers to whom the Son has revealed Him, have given us a certain image from things visible, saying, 'Who is the brightness of His glory, and the Expression of His Person[4];' and again, 'For with Thee is the well of life, and in Thy light shall we see light[5];' and when the Word chides Israel, He says, 'Thou hast forsaken the Fountain of wisdom[6];' and this Fountain it is which says, 'They have forsaken Me the Fountain of living waters[7].' And mean indeed and very dim is the illustration[8] compared with what we desiderate; but yet it is possible from it to understand something above man's nature, instead of thinking the Son's generation to be on a level with ours. For who can even imagine that the radiance of light ever was not, so that he should dare to say that the Son was not always, or that the Son was not before His generation? or who is capable of separating the radiance from the sun, or to conceive of the fountain as ever void of life, that he should madly say, 'The Son is from nothing,' who says, 'I am the life[9],' or 'alien to the Father's essence,' who says, 'He that hath seen Me, hath seen the Father[10]?' for the sacred writers wishing us thus to understand, have given these illustrations; and it is unseemly and most irreligious, when Scripture contains such images, to form ideas concerning our Lord from others which are neither in Scripture, nor have any religious bearing.

13. Therefore let them tell us, from what teacher or by what tradition they derived these notions concerning the Saviour? "We have read," they will say, "in the Proverbs, 'The Lord created me a beginning of His ways unto His works[1];'" this Eusebius and his fellows used to insist on[2], and you write me word, that the present men also, though overthrown and confuted by an abundance of arguments, still were putting about in every quarter this passage, and saying that the Son was one of the creatures, and reckoning Him

with things originated. But they seem to me to have a wrong understanding of this passage also; for it has a religious and very orthodox sense, which had they understood, they would not have blasphemed the Lord of glory. For on comparing what has been above stated with this passage, they will find a great difference between them[3]. For what man of right understanding does not perceive, that what are created and made are external to the maker; but the Son, as the foregoing argument has shewn, exists not externally, but from the Father who begat Him? for man too both builds a house and begets a son, and no one would reverse things, and say that the house or the ship were begotten by the builder[4], but the son was created and made by him; nor again that the house was an image of the maker, but the son unlike him who begat him; but rather he will confess that the son is an image of the father, but the house a work of art, unless his mind be disordered, and he beside himself. Plainly, divine Scripture, which knows better than any the nature of everything, says through Moses, of the creatures, 'In the beginning God created the heaven and the earth[5];' but of the Son it introduces not another, but the Father Himself saying, 'I have begotten Thee from the womb before the morning star[6];' and again, 'Thou art My Son, this day have I begotten Thee[7].' And the Lord says of Himself in the Proverbs, 'Before all the hills He begets me[8];' and concerning things originated and created John speaks, 'All things were made by Him[9];' but preaching of the Lord, he says, 'The Only-begotten Son, who is in the bosom of the Father, He declared Him[10].' If then son, therefore not creature; if creature, not son; for great is the difference between them, and son and creature cannot be the same, unless His essence be considered to be at once from God, and external to God.

14. 'Has then the passage no meaning?' for this, like a swarm of gnats, they are droning about us[1]. No surely, it is not without meaning, but has a very apposite one; for it is true to say that the Son was created too, but this took place when He became man; for creation

---

3 Matt. xi. 27.　　　　4 Heb. i. 3.
5 Ps. xxxvi. 9.　　　　6 Bar. iii. 12.
7 Jer. ii. 13. Vid. *infr. passim.* All these titles, 'Word, Wisdom, Light,' &c., serve to guard the title 'Son' from any notions of parts or dimensions, e.g. 'He is not composed of parts, but being impassible and single, He is impassibly and indivisibly Father of the Son ... for ... the Word and Wisdom is neither creature, nor part of Him Whose Word He is, nor an offspring passibly begotten.' *Orat.* i. § 28.
8 *Ad Serap.* 20.　　　9 John xiv. 6.　　　10 Ib. 9.
1 Prov. viii. 22, and cf. *Orat.* ii. throughout
2 Eusebius of Nicomedia quotes it in his Letter to Paulinus, ap. Theodor. *Hist.* i. 5. And Eusebius of Cæsarea, *Demonstr. Evang.* v. 1.

3 i.e. 'Granting that the *primâ facie* impression of this text is in favour of our Lord's being a creature, yet so many arguments have been already brought, and may be added, against His creation, that we must interpret this text by them. It cannot mean that our Lord was simply created, *because* we have already shewn that He is not external to His Father.'
4 *Serap.* 2, 6. *Sent. Dion.* 4.　　　5 Gen. i. 1.
6 Ps. cx. 3.　　　7 Ps. ii. 7.　　　8 Prov. viii. 25.
9 John i. 3.　　　10 Ib. 18.
1 περιβομβοῦσιν. So in ad Afros. 5. init. And Sent. D. § 19. περιέρχονται περιβομβοῦντες. And Gregory Nyssen. *contr. Eun.* viii. p. 234 C. ὡς ἂν τοὺς ἀπείρους ταῖς πλατωνικαῖς καλλιφωνίαι περιβομβήσειεν. vid. also περιέρχονται ὡς οἱ κάνθαροι. Orat iii. fin.

belongs to man. And any one may find this sense duly given in the divine oracles, who, instead of accounting their study a secondary matter, investigates the time and characters[2], and the object, and thus studies and ponders what he reads. Now as to the season spoken of, he will find for certain that, whereas the Lord always is, at length in fulness of the ages He became man; and whereas He is Son of God, He became Son of man also. And as to the object he will understand, that, wishing to annul our death, He took on Himself a body from the Virgin Mary; that by offering this unto the Father a sacrifice for all, He might deliver us all, who by fear of death were all our life through subject to bondage[3]. And as to the character, it is indeed the Saviour's, but is said of Him when He took a body and said, 'The Lord created me a beginning of His ways unto His works[4].' For as it properly belongs to God's Son to be everlasting, and in the Father's bosom, so on His becoming man, the words befitted Him, 'The Lord created me.' For then it is said of Him, as also that He hungered, and thirsted, and asked where Lazarus lay, and suffered, and rose again[5]. And as, when we hear of Him as Lord and God and true Light, we understand Him as being from the Father, so on hearing, 'The Lord created,' and 'Servant,' and 'He suffered,' we shall justly ascribe this, not to the Godhead, for it is irrelevant, but we must interpret it by that flesh which He bore for our sakes: for to it these things are proper, and this flesh was none other's than the Word's. And if we wish to know the object attained by this, we shall find it to be as follows: that the Word was made flesh in order to offer up this body for all, and that we, partaking of His Spirit, might be deified[6], a gift which we could not otherwise have gained than by His clothing Himself in our created body[7], for hence we derive our name of "men of God" and "men in Christ." But as we, by receiving the Spirit, do not lose our own proper substance, so the Lord, when made man for us, and bearing a body, was no less God; for He was not lessened by the envelopment of the body, but rather deified it and rendered it immortal[8].

CHAPTER IV.

PROOF OF THE CATHOLIC SENSE OF THE WORD SON.

Power, Word or Reason, and Wisdom, the names of the Son, imply eternity; as well as the Father's title of Fountain. The Arians reply that these do not formally belong to the essence of the Son, but are names given Him; that God has many words, powers, &c. Why there is but one Son and Word, &c. All the titles of the Son coincide in Him.

15. THIS then is quite enough to expose the infamy of the Arian heresy; for, as the Lord has granted, out of their own words is irreligion brought home to them[1]. But come now and let us on our part act on the offensive, and call on them for an answer; for now is fair time, when their own ground has failed them, to question them on ours; perhaps it may abash the perverse, and disclose to them whence they have fallen. We have learned from divine Scripture, that the Son of God, as was said above, is the very Word and Wisdom of the Father. For the Apostle says, 'Christ the power of God and the Wisdom of God[2];' and John after saying, 'And the Word was made flesh,' at once adds, 'And we saw His glory, the glory as of the Only-begotten of the Father, full of grace and truth[3],' so that, the Word being the Only-begotten Son, in this Word and in Wisdom heaven and earth and all that is therein were made. And of this Wisdom that God is Fountain we have learned from[4] Baruch, by Israel's being charged with having forsaken the Fountain of Wisdom. If then they deny Scripture, they are at once aliens to their name, and may fitly be called of all men atheists[5], and Christ's enemies, for they have brought upon themselves these names. But if they agree with us that the sayings of Scripture are divinely inspired, let them dare to say openly what they think in secret that God was once wordless and wisdomless[6]; and

---

2 πρόσωπα. vid. *Orat.* i. § 54. ii. § 8. *Sent. D.* 4. not *persons*, but *characters*; which must also be considered the meaning of the word, *contr. Apoll.* ii. 2. and 10; though it there approximates (even in phrase, οὐκ ἐν διαιρέσει προσώπων) to its ecclesiastical use, which seems to have been later. Yet persona occurs in Tertull. *in Prax.* 27; it may be questioned, however, whether in any genuine Greek treatise till the Apollinarians.
3 Heb. ii. 15.   4 Prov. viii. 22.
5 *Sent. D.* 9. *Orat.* 3, §§ 26—41.
6 [See *de Incar.* § 54. 3, and note.]
7 *Orat.* 2, § 70.
8 Cf. *Orat.* ii. 6. [See also *de Incar.* § 17.]

---

1 The main argument of the Arians was that our Lord was a Son, and *therefore* was not eternal, but of a substance which had a beginning. [Prolegg. ch. ii. § 3 (2) a.] Accordingly Athanasius says, 'Having argued with them as to the meaning of their own selected term "Son," let us go on to others, which on the very face make for us, such as Word, Wisdom, &c.'
2 1 Cor. i. 24.
3 John i. 14.
4 Vid. supr. § 12.   5 Vid. supr. § 1. note 2, bis.
6 ἄλογος, ἄσοφος. Vid. infr., § 26. This is a frequent argument in the controversy, viz. that to deprive the Father of His Son or substantial Word (Λόγος), is as great a sacrilege as to deny His Reason, λόγος, from which the Son receives His name. Thus *Orat.* i. § 14. fin. Athan. says, 'imputing to God's nature an absence of His Word (ἀλογίαν or irrationality), they are most irreligious.' Vid. § 19. fin. 24. Elsewhere, he says, 'Is a man not mad himself, who even entertains the thought that God is word-less and wisdom-less? for such illustrations and such images Scripture hath proposed, that, considering the inability of human nature to comprehend concerning God, we might even from these, however poorly and dimly, discern as far as is attainable.' *Orat.* ii 32. vid also iii. 63. iv. 1. *Serap.* ii. 2.

let them in their madness[7] say, 'There was once when He was not,' and, 'before His generation, Christ was not[8];' and again let them declare that the Fountain begat not Wisdom from itself, but acquired it from without, till they have the daring to say, 'The Son came of nothing;' whence it will follow that there is no longer a Fountain, but a sort of pool, as if receiving water from without, and usurping the name of Fountain[9].

16. How full of irreligion this is, I consider none can doubt who has ever so little understanding. But since they mutter something about Word and Wisdom being only names of the Son[10], we must ask then, If these are only names of the Son, He must be something else beside them. And if He is higher than the names, it is not lawful from the lesser to denote the higher; but if He be less than the names, yet He surely must have in Him the principle of this more honourable appellation; and this implies his advance, which is an irreligion equal to anything that has gone before. For He who is in the Father, and in whom also the Father is, who says, 'I and the Father are one[1],' whom he that hath seen, hath seen the Father, to say that He has been exalted[2] by anything external, is the extreme of madness. However, when they are beaten hence, and like Eusebius and his fellows, are in these great straits, then they have this remaining plea, which Arius too in ballads, and in his own Thalia[3], fabled, as a new difficulty: 'Many words speaketh God; which then of these are we to call Son and Word, Only-begotten of the Father[4]?'

Insensate, and anything but Christians[5]! for first, on using such language about God, they conceive of Him almost as a man, speaking and reversing His first words by His second, just as if one Word from God were not sufficient for the framing of all things at the Father's will, and for His providential care of all. For His speaking many words would argue a feebleness in them all, each needing the service of the other. But that God should have one Word, which is the true doctrine, both shews the power of God, and the perfection of the Word that is from Him, and the religious understanding of them who thus believe.

17. O that they would consent to confess the truth from this their own statement! for if they once grant that God produces words, they plainly know Him to be a Father; and acknowledging this, let them consider that, while they are loth to ascribe one Word to God, they are imagining that He is Father of many; and while they are loth to say that there is no Word of God at all, yet they do not confess that He is the Son of God,— which is ignorance of the truth, and inexperience in divine Scripture. For if God is Father of a word at all, wherefore is not He that is begotten a Son? And again, who should be Son of God, but His Word? For there are not many words, or each would be imperfect, but one is the Word, that He only may be perfect, and because, God being one, His Image too must be one, which is the Son. For the Son of God, as may be learnt from the divine oracles themselves, is Himself the Word of God, and the Wisdom, and the Image, and the Hand, and the Power; for God's offspring is one, and of the generation from the Father these titles are tokens[6]. For if you say the Son, you have declared what is from the Father by nature; and if you think of the Word, you are thinking again of what is

---

[7] Vid. above, § 1, note 6.

[8] These were among the original positions of the Arians; for the former, see above, note 1; the latter is one of those specified in the Nicene Anathema.

[9] And so πηγὴ ξηρά. Serap. ii. 2. Orat. i. § 14 fin. also ii. § 2, where Athanasius speaks as if those who deny that Almighty God is Father, cannot really believe in Him as a Creator. If the divine substance be not fruitful (καρπογόνος), but barren, as they say, as a light which enlightens not, and a dry fountain, are they not ashamed to maintain that He possesses the creative energy?' Vid. also πηγὴ θεότητος, Pseudo-Dion. Div. Nom. c. 2. πηγὴ ἐκ πηγῆς, of the Son, Epiphan. Ancor. 19. And Cyril, 'If thou take from God His being Father, thou wilt deny the generative power (καρπογόνον) of the divine nature, so that It no longer is perfect. This then is a token of its perfection, and the Son who went forth from Him apart from time, is a pledge (σφραγίς) to the Father that He is perfect.' Thesaur. p. 37.

[10] Arius said, as the Eunomians after him, that the Son was not really, but only called, Word and Wisdom, which were simply attributes of God, and the prototypes of the Son. Vid. Socr. i. 6. Theod. H.E. i. 3, and infr. Orat. ii. 37, 38.

[1] John x. 30.   [2] βελτιοῦσθαι.   [3] Vid. de Syn. § 15.

[4] As the Arians took the title Son in that part of its earthly sense in which it did not apply to our Lord, so they misinterpreted the title Word also; which denoted the Son's immateriality and indivisible presence in the Father, but did not express His perfection. Vid. Orat. ii. § 34—36. contr. Gent. 41. ad Ep. Æg. 16. Epiph. Hær. 65. 3. Nyss. in Eun. xii. p. 349. Origen (in a passage, however, of questionable doctrine), says, 'As there are gods many, but to us one God the Father, and many lords, but to us one Lord Jesus Christ, so there are many words, but we pray that in us may exist the Word that was in the beginning, with God, and was God.' In Joan. tom. ii. 3. 'Many things, it is acknowledged, does the Father speak to the Son,' say the Semiarians at Ancyra, 'but the words which God speaks to the Son, are not sons. They are not substances of God, but vocal

energies; but the Son, though a Word, is not such, but, being a Son, is a substance.' Epiph. Hær. 73. 12. The Semiarians are speaking against Sabellianism, which took the same ground here as Arianism; so did the heresy of the Samosatene, who according to Epiphanius, considered our Lord as the internal Word, or thought. Hær. 65. The term word in this inferior sense is often in Greek ῥῆμα. Epiph. supr. and Cyril, de Incarn. Unig. init. t. v. i. p. 679.

[5] 'If they understood and acknowledged the characteristic idea (χαρακτῆρα) of Christianity, they would not have said that the Lord of glory was a creature.' Ad Serap. ii. 7. In Orat. i. § 2, he says, Arians are not Christians because they are Arians, for Christians are called, not from Arius, but from Christ, who is their only Master. Vid. also de Syn. § 38. init. Sent. D. fin. Ad Afros. 4. Their cruelty and co-operation with the heathen populace was another reason. Greg. Naz. Orat. 25. 12.

[6] All the titles of the Son of God are consistent with each other, and variously represent one and the same Person. 'Son' and 'Word,' denote His derivation; 'Word' and 'Image,' His Similitude; 'Word' and 'Wisdom,' His immateriality; 'Wisdom' and 'Hand,' His co-existence. 'If He is not Son, neither is He Image.' Orat. ii. § 2. 'How is there Word and Wisdom, unless He be a proper offspring of His substance? ii. § 22. Vid. also Orat. i. § 20. 21. and at great length Orat. iv. § 20, &c. vid. also Naz. Orat. 30. n. 20. Basil. contr. Eunom. i. 18. Hilar. de Trin. vii. 11. August. in Joan. xlviii. 6. and in Psalm. xliv. (xlv.) 5.

from Him, and what is inseparable; and, speaking of Wisdom, again you mean just as much, what is not from without, but from Him and in Him; and if you name the Power and the Hand, again you speak of what is proper to essence; and, speaking of the Image, you signify the Son: for what else is like God but the offspring from Him? Doubtless the things, which came to be through the Word, these are 'founded in Wisdom' and what are 'founded in Wisdom,' these are all made by the Hand, and came to be through the Son. And we have proof of this, not from external sources, but from the Scriptures; for God Himself says by Isaiah the Prophet; 'My hand also hath laid the foundation of the earth, and My right hand hath spanned the heavens[7].' And again, 'And I will cover thee in the shadow of My Hand, by which I planted the heavens, and laid the foundations of the earth[8].' And David being taught this, and knowing that the Lord's Hand was nothing else than Wisdom, says in the Psalm, 'In wisdom hast Thou made them all; the earth is full of Thy creation[9].' Solomon also received the same from God, and said, 'The Lord by wisdom founded the earth[10],' and John, knowing that the Word was the Hand and the Wisdom, thus preached, 'In the beginning was the Word, and the Word was with God, and the Word was God; the same was in the beginning with God: all things were made by Him, and without Him was not anything made[1].' And the Apostle, seeing that the Hand and the Wisdom and the Word was nothing else than the Son, says, 'God, who at sundry times and in divers manners spake in time past unto the Fathers by the Prophets, hath in these last days spoken unto us by His Son, whom He hath appointed Heir of all things, by whom also He made the ages[2].' And again, 'There is one Lord Jesus Christ, through whom are all things, and we through Him[3].' And knowing also that the Word, the Wisdom, the Son Himself was the Image of the Father, he says in the Epistle to the Colossians, 'Giving thanks to God and the Father, which hath made us meet to be partakers of the inheritance of the Saints in light, who hath delivered us from the power of darkness, and hath translated us into the kingdom of His dear Son; in whom we have redemption, even the remission of sins; who is the Image of the Invisible God, the First-born of every creature; for by Him were all things created, that are in heaven, and that are in earth, visible and invisible, whether they be thrones,

or dominions, or principalities, or powers; all things were created by Him and for Him; and He is before all things, and in Him all things consist[4].' For as all things are created by the Word, so, because He is the Image, are they also created in Him[5]. And thus anyone who directs his thoughts to the Lord, will avoid stumbling upon the stone of offence, but rather will go forward to the brightness in the light of truth; for this is really the doctrine of truth, though these contentious men burst with spite[6], neither religious toward God, nor abashed at their confutation.

CHAPTER V.

DEFENCE OF THE COUNCIL'S PHRASES, "FROM THE ESSENCE," AND "ONE IN ESSENCE."

Objection that the phrases are not scriptural; we ought to look at the sense more than the wording; evasion of the Arians as to the phrase "of God" which is in Scripture; their evasion of all explanations but those which the Council selected, which were intended to negative the Arian formulæ; protest against their conveying any material sense.

18. Now Eusebius and his fellows were at the former period examined at great length, and convicted themselves, as I said before; on this they subscribed; and after this change of mind they kept in quiet and retirement[1]; but since the present party, in the fresh arrogance of irreligion, and in dizziness about the truth, are full set upon accusing the Council, let them tell us what are the sort of Scriptures from which they have learned, or who is the Saint[2] by whom they have been taught, that they have heaped together the phrases, 'out of nothing[3],' and 'He was not before His generation,' and 'once He was not,' and 'alterable,' and 'pre-existence,' and 'at the will;' which are their fables in mockery of the Lord. For the blessed Paul in his Epistle to the Hebrews says, 'By faith we understand that the ages were framed by the Word of God, so that that which is seen was not made of things which do appear[4].' But nothing is common to the Word with the ages[5]; for He it is who is in existence before

---

[4] Col. i. 12—17.
[5] Vid. a beautiful passage, *contr. Gent.* 42, &c. Again, of men, *de Incarn.* 3. 3; also *Orat.* ii. 78. where he speaks of Wisdom as being infused into the world on its creation, that it might possess 'a type and semblance of its Image.'
[6] διαρρ̀ωσιν, and so *Serap.* ii. fin. διαρρηγνύωνται. *de Syn.* 34. διαρρηγνύωσιν ἑαυτούς. *Orat.* ii. § 23. σπαραττέτωσαν ἑαυτούς. *Orat.* ii. § 64. τριζέτω τοὺς ὀδόντας. *Sent. D.* 16.
[1] [Prolegg. ch. ii. § 6 (2).] [2] *supr.* § 7, note 2.
[3] ἐξ οὐκ ὄντων. [4] Heb. xi. 3.
[5] By αἰών, age, seems to be meant duration, or the measure of duration, before or independent of the existence of motion, which is in measure of time. As motion, and therefore time, are creatures, so are the ages. Considered as the measure of duration, an age has a sort of positive existence, though not an οὐσία or

---

[7] Is. xlviii. 13. [8] Is li. 16. [9] Ps. civ. 24.
[10] Prov. iii. 19. [1] John i. 1—3. [2] Heb. i. 1, 2.
[3] 1 Cor. viii. 6.

the ages, by whom also the ages came to be. And in the Shepherd [6] it is written (since they allege this book also, though it is not of the Canon [7]), 'First of all believe, that God is one, who created all things, and arranged them, and brought all things from nothing into being;' but this again does not relate to the Son, for it speaks concerning all things which came to be through Him, from whom He is distinct; for it is not possible to reckon the Framer of all with the things made by Him, unless a man is so beside himself as to say that the architect also is the same as the buildings which he rears.

Why then, when they have invented on their part unscriptural phrases, for the purposes of irreligion, do they accuse those who are religious in their use of them [8]? For irreligiousness is utterly forbidden, though it be attempted to disguise it with artful expressions and plausible sophisms; but religiousness is confessed by all to be lawful, even though presented in strange phrases [9], provided only they are used with a religious view, and a wish to make them the expression of religious thoughts. Now the aforesaid grovelling phrases of Christ's enemies have been shewn in these remarks to be both formerly and now replete with irreligion; whereas the definition of the Council against them, if accurately examined, will be found to be altogether a representation of the truth, and especially if diligent attention be paid to the occasion which gave rise to these expressions, which was reasonable, and was as follows:—

19. The Council [10] wishing to do away with the irreligious phrases of the Arians, and to use instead the acknowledged words of the Scriptures, that the Son is not from nothing but 'from God,' and is 'Word' and ' Wisdom,' and not creature or work, but a proper offspring from the Father, Eusebius and his fellows, led by their inveterate heterodoxy, understood the phrase 'from God' as belonging to us, as if in respect to it the Word of God differed nothing from us, and that because it is written, 'There is one God, from whom all things [1];' and again, ' Old things are passed away, behold, all things are become new, and all things are from God [2].' But the Fathers, perceiving their craft and the cunning of their irreligion, were forced to express more distinctly the sense of the words 'from God.' Accordingly, they wrote 'from the essence of God [3],' in order that 'from God' might not be considered common and equal in the Son and in things originate, but that all others might be acknowledged as creatures, and the Word alone as from the Father. For though all things be said to be from God, yet this is not in the sense in which the Son is from Him; for as to the creatures, ' of God ' is said of them on this account, in that they exist not at random or spontaneously, nor come to be by chance [4], according to those philosophers who refer them to the combination of atoms, and to elements of similar structure,—nor as certain heretics speak of a distinct Framer,—nor as others again say that the

---

substance, and means the same as 'world,' or an existing system of things viewed apart from time and motion. Vid. Theodt. in Hebr. i. 2. Our Lord then is the Maker of the ages thus considered, as the Apostle also tells us, Hebr. xi. 3. and God is the King of the ages, 1 Tim. i. 17. or is before all ages, as being eternal, or προαιώνιος. However, sometimes the word is synonymous with eternity; ' as time is to things which are under time, so ages to things which are everlasting.' Damasc. Fid. Orth. ii. 1, and 'ages of ages' stands for eternity; and then the 'ages' or measures of duration may be supposed to stand for the ἰδέαι or ideas in the Divine Mind, which seems to have been a Platonic or Gnostic notion. Hence Synesius, Hymn iii. addresses the Almighty as αἰωνότοκε, parent of the ages. Hence sometimes God Himself is called the Age, Clem. Alex. Hymn. Pæd. iii. fin. or, the Age of ages, Pseudo-Dion. de Div. Nom. 5. p. 580. or again, αἰώνιος. Theodoret sums up what has been said thus: 'Age is not any subsisting substance, but is an interval indicative of time, now infinite, when God is spoken of, now commensurate with creation, now with human life.' Hær. v. 6. If then, as Athan. says in the text, the Word is Maker of the ages, He is independent of duration altogether; He does not come to be in time, but is above and beyond it, or eternal. Elsewhere he says, 'The words addressed to the Son in the 144th Psalm, 'Thy kingdom is a kingdom of all ages,' forbid any one to imagine any interval at all in which the Word did not exist. For if every interval is measured by ages, and of all the ages the Word is King and Maker, therefore, whereas no interval at all exists prior to Him, it were madness to say, "There was once when the Everlasting (αἰώνιος) was not." Orat. i. 12. And so Alexander; 'Is it not unreasonable that He who made times, and ages, and seasons, to all of which belongs 'was not,' should be said not to be? for, if so, that interval in which they say the Son was not yet begotten by the Father, precedes that Wisdom of God which framed all things.' Theod. Hist. i. 4. vid also Basil de Sp. S. n. 14. Hilar. de Trin. xii. 34.

6 Herm. Mand. 1. vid. ad Afr. 5.

7 [Letter 39, and Prolegg. ch. iv. § 4.] He calls it elsewhere a most profitable book. Incarn. 3.

8 Athan. here retorts, as it was obvious to do, the charge brought against the Council which gave occasion for this Treatise. If the Council went beyond Scripture in the use of the word ' essence' (which however can hardly be granted), who made this necessary, but they who had already introduced the phrases, ' the Son was out of nothing,' &c., &c. ? ' Of the essence,' and ' one in essence,' were directly intended to contradict and supplant the Arian unscriptural innovations, as he says below, § 20. fin. 21. init. vid. also ad Afros. 6. de Synod. § 36, 37. He observes in like manner that the Arian ἀγένητος, though allowable as used by religious men, de Syn. § 40. was unscriptural, Orat. i. § 30, 34. Also Epiph. Hær. 76. p. 941. Basil. contr. Eunom. i. 5. Hilar. contr. Const. 16. Ambros. Incarn. 80.　　9 Vid. § 10, note 3.

10 vid. ad. Afr. 5.　　1 1 Cor. viii. 6.　　2 2 Cor. v. 17.

3 Hence it stands in the Creed, 'from the Father, that is, from the essence of the Father.' vid. Eusebius's Letter, infr. According to the received doctrine of the Church all rational beings, and in one sense all beings whatever, are 'from God,' over and above the fact of their creation; and of this truth the Arians made use to deny our Lord's proper divinity. Athan. lays down elsewhere that nothing remains in consistence and life, except from a participation of the Word, which is to be considered a gift from Him, additional to that of creation, and separable in idea from it; vid. above, § 17, note 5. contr. Gent. 42, de Incarn. 5. Man thus considered is, in his first estate, a son of God and born of God, or, to use the term which occurs so frequently in the Arian controversy, in the number, not only of the creatures, but of things generate, γεννητά. This was the sense in which the Arians said that our Lord was Son of God; whereas, as Athan. says, 'things originate, being works, cannot be called generate, except so far as, after their making, they partake of the begotten Son,' and are therefore said to have been generated also; not at all in their own nature, but because of their participation of the Son in the Spirit.' Orat. i. 56. The question then was, as to the distinction of the Son's divine generation over that of holy men; and the Catholics answered that He was ἐξ οὐσίας, from the essence of God; not by participation of grace, not by resemblance, not in a limited sense, but really and simply, and therefore by an internal divine act. vid. below, § 22. and infr. § 31. [The above note has been modified so as to eliminate the erroneous identification of γεννητὸς and γενητός.]　　4 Cf. de Syn. § 35.

constitution of all things is from certain Angels;—but in that (whereas God is), it was by Him that all things were brought into being, not being before, through His Word; but as to the Word, since He is not a creature, He alone is both called and is 'from the Father;' and it is significant of this sense to say that the Son is 'from the essence of the Father,' for to nothing originate does this attach. In truth, when Paul says that 'all things are from God,' he immediately adds, 'and one Lord Jesus Christ, through whom all things [5],' in order to shew all men, that the Son is other than all these things which came to be from God (for the things which came to be from God, came to be through His Son); and that he had used his foregoing words with reference to the world as framed by God [6], and not as if all things were from the Father as the Son is. For neither are other things as the Son, nor is the Word one among others, for He is Lord and Framer of all; and on this account did the Holy Council declare expressly that He was of the essence [7] of the Father, that we might believe the Word to be other than the nature of things originate, being alone truly from God; and that no subterfuge should be left open to the irreligious. This then was the reason why the Council wrote 'of the essence.'

20. Again, when the Bishops said that the Word must be described as the True Power and Image of the Father, in all things exact [8] and like the Father, and as unalterable, and as always, and as in Him without division (for never was the Word not, but He was always, existing everlastingly with the Father, as the radiance of light), Eusebius and his fellows endured indeed, as not daring to contradict, being put to shame by the arguments which were urged against them; but withal they were caught whispering to each other and winking with their eyes, that 'like,' and 'always,' and 'power,' and 'in Him,' were, as before, common to us and the Son, and that it was no difficulty to agree to these. As to 'like,' they said that it is written of us, 'Man is the image and glory of God [9]:' 'always,' that it was written, 'For we which live are alway [10]:' 'in Him,' 'In Him we live and move and have our being [1]:' 'unalterable,' that it is written, 'Nothing shall separate us from the love of Christ [2]:' as to 'power,' that the caterpillar and the locust are called 'power' and 'great power [3],' and that it is often said of the people, for instance, 'All the power of the Lord came out of the land of Egypt [4]:' and there are others also, heavenly ones, for Scripture says, 'The Lord of powers is with us, the God of Jacob is our refuge [5].' Indeed Asterius, by title the sophist, had said the like in writing, having learned it from them, and before him Arius [6] having learned it also, as has been said. But the Bishops discerning in this too their dissimulation, and whereas it is written, 'Deceit is in the heart of the irreligious that imagine evil [7],' were again compelled on their part to collect the sense of the Scriptures, and to re-say and re-write what they had said before, more distinctly still, namely, that the Son is 'one in essence [8]' with the Father; by way of signifying, that the Son was from the Father, and not merely like, but the same in likeness [9], and

---

5 1 Cor. viii. 6.
6 When characteristic attributes and prerogatives are ascribed to God, or to the Father, this is done only to the exclusion of creatures, or of false gods, not to the exclusion of His Son who is implied in the mention of Himself. Thus when God is called only wise, or the Father the only God, or God is said to be unoriginate, ἀγένητος, this is not in contrast to the Son, but to all things which are distinct from God. vid. *Orat.* iii. 8. Naz. *Orat.* 30, 13. Cyril. *Thesaur.* p. 142. 'The words "one" and "only" ascribed to God in Scripture,' says S. Basil, 'are not used in contrast to the Son or the Holy Spirit, but with reference to those who are not God, and falsely called so.' *Ep.* 8. n. 3. On the other hand, when the Father is mentioned, the other Divine Persons are implied in Him, 'The Blessed and Holy Trinity,' says S. Athan. 'is indivisible and one in itself; and when the Father is mentioned, His Word is added, and the Spirit in the Son; and if the Son is named, in the Son is the Father, and the Spirit is not external to the Word.' *ad Serap.* i. 14.
7 Vid. also *ad Afros.* 4. Again, '"I am," τὸ ὄν, is really proper to God and is a whole, bounded or mutilated neither by aught before Him, nor after Him, for He neither was, nor shall be.' Naz. *Orat.* 30. 18 fin. Also Cyril *Dial.* i. p. 392. Damasc. *Fid. Orth.* i. 9. and the Semiarians at Ancyra, Epiph. *Hær.* 73. 12 init. By the 'essence,' however, or, 'substance' of God, the Council did not mean any thing distinct from God, vid. note 3 *infr.* but God Himself viewed in His self-existing nature (vid. Tert. in *Hermog,* 3.) nay, it expressly meant to negative the contrary notion of the Arians, that our Lord was from something distinct from God, and in consequence of created substance. Moreover the term expresses the idea of God *positively,* in contradistinction to negative epithets, such as infinite, immense, eternal, &c. Damasc. *Fid. Orthod.* i. 4. and as little implies any thing distinct from God as those epithets do.   8 ἀπαράλλακτον.

9 1 Cor. xi. 7.   10 2 Cor. iv. 11.
1 Acts xvii. 28.   2 Rom. viii. 35, *who shall separate.*
3 Joel ii. 25.   4 Ex. xii. 41.   5 Ps. xlvi. 7.
6 vid. supr. § 8, note 3.   7 Prov. xii. 20.
8 vid. *ad Afros.* 5. 6. *ad Serap.* ii. 5. S. Ambrose tells us, that a Letter written by Eusebius of Nicomedia, in which he said, 'If we call Him true Son of the Father and uncreate, then are we granting that He is one in essence, ὁμοούσιον,' determined the Council on the adoption of the term. *de Fid.* iii. n. 125. He had disclaimed 'of the essence,' in his Letter to Paulinus. Theod. *Hist.* i. 4. Arius, however, had disclaimed ὁμοούσιον already Epiph. *Hær.* 69. 7. It was a word of old usage in the Church, as Eusebius of Cæsarea confesses in his Letter, infr. Tertullian in *Prax.* 13 fin. has the translation 'unius substantiæ' (vid. Lucifer *de non Parc.* p. 218.) as he has 'de substantia Patris,' in *Prax.* 4. and Origen perhaps used the word, vid. Pamph. *Apol.* 5. and Theognostus and the two Dionysii, *infr.* § 25, 26. And before them Clement had spoken of the ἕνωσις τῆς μοναδικῆς οὐσίας, 'the union of the single essence,' vid. Le Quien in Damasc. *Fid. Orth.* i. 8. Novatian too has 'per substantiæ communionem,' *de Trinit.* 31.
9 The Arians allowed that our Lord was like and the image of the Father, but in the sense in which a picture is like the original, differing from it in substance and in fact. In this sense they even allowed the strong word ἀπαράλλακτος *unvarying* [or rather *exact*] image, vid. beginning of § 20. which had been used by the Catholics (vid. Alexander, ap. Theod. *Hist.* i. 3. p. 740.) as by the Semiarians afterwards (who even added the words κατ' οὐσίαν, or 'according to substance.' Even this strong phrase, however, κατ' οὐσίαν ἀπαράλλακτος εἰκών, or ἀπαράλλακτως ὅμοιος, did not appear to the Council an adequate safeguard of the doctrine. Athan. notices *de Syn.* that 'like' applies to qualities rather than to essence, § 53. Also Basil. *Ep.* 8. n. 3. 'while in itself,' says the same Father, 'it is frequently used of faint similitudes, and falling very far short of the original.' *Ep.* 9. n. 3. Accordingly, the Council determined on the word ὁμοούσιον as implying, as the

of shewing that the Son's likeness and unalterableness was different from such copy of the same as is ascribed to us, which we acquire from virtue on the ground of observance of the commandments. For bodies which are like each other may be separated and become at distances from each other, as are human sons relatively to their parents (as it is written concerning Adam and Seth, who was begotten of him, that he was like him after his own pattern[10]); but since the generation of the Son from the Father is not according to the nature of men, and not only like, but also inseparable from the essence of the Father, and He and the Father are one, as He has said Himself, and the Word is ever in the Father and the Father in the Word, as the radiance stands towards the light (for this the phrase itself indicates), therefore the Council, as understanding this, suitably wrote 'one in essence,' that they might both defeat the perverseness of the heretics, and shew that the Word was other than originated things. For, after thus writing, they at once added, 'But they who say that the Son of God is from nothing, or created, or alterable, or a work, or from other essence, these the Holy Catholic Church anathematizes[1].' And by saying this, they shewed clearly that 'of the essence,' and 'one in essence,' are destructive of those catchwords of irreligion, such as 'created,' and 'work,' and 'originated,' and 'alterable,' and 'He was not before His generation.' And he who holds these, contradicts the Council; but he who does not hold with Arius, must needs hold and intend the decisions of the Council, suitably regarding them to signify the relation of the radiance to the light, and from thence gaining the illustration of the truth.

21. Therefore if they, as the others, make an excuse that the terms are strange, let them consider the sense in which the Council so wrote, and anathematize what the Council anathematized; and then if they can, let them find fault with the expressions. But I well know that, if they hold the sense of the Council, they will fully accept the terms in which it is conveyed; whereas if it be the sense which they wish to complain of, all must see that it is idle in them to discuss the wording, when they are but seeking handles for irreligion. This then was the reason of these expressions; but if they still complain that such are not scriptural, that very complaint is a reason why they should be cast out, as talking idly and disordered in mind. And let them blame themselves in this matter, for they set the example, beginning their war against God with words not in Scripture. However, if a person is interested in the question, let him know, that, even if the expressions are not in so many words in the Scriptures, yet, as was said before, they contain the sense of the Scriptures, and expressing it, they convey it to those who have their hearing unimpaired for religious doctrine. Now this circumstance is it for thee to consider, and for those ill-instructed men to give ear to. It has been shewn above, and must be believed as true, that the Word is from the Father, and the only Offspring[2] proper to Him and natural. For whence may one conceive the Son to be, who is the Wisdom and the Word, in whom all things came to be, but from God Himself? However, the Scriptures also teach us this, since the Father says by David, 'My heart uttered a good Word[3],' and, 'From the womb before the morning star I begat Thee[4];' and the Son signifies to the Jews about Himself, 'If God were your Father, ye would love Me; for I proceeded forth from the Father[5].' And again; 'Not that anyone has seen the Father, save He which is from God, He hath seen the Father[6].' And moreover, 'I and My Father are one,' and, 'I in the Father and the Father in Me[7],' is equivalent to saying, 'I am from the Father, and inseparable from Him.' And John in saying, 'The Only-begotten Son which is in the bosom of the Father, He hath declared Him[8],' spoke of what He had learned from the Saviour. Besides, what else does 'in the bosom' intimate, but the Son's genuine generation from the Father?

22. If then any man conceives God to be compound, as accident[9] is in essence, or

---

text expresses it, 'the same in likeness,' ταὐτὸν τῇ ὁμοιώσει, that the likeness might not be analogical. vid. the passage about gold and brass, § 23 below, Cyril in Joan. I. iii. c. v. p. 302. [See below de Syn. 15, note 2.]　　　[10] Gen. v. 3.
[1] vid. Euseb.'s Letter, supr.

[2] γέννημα, offspring; this word is of very frequent occurrence in Athan. He speaks of it, Orat. iv. 3. as virtually Scriptural. Yet Basil, contr. Eunom. ii. 6—8. expl·citly disavows the word, as an unscriptural invention of Eunomius. 'That the Father begat we are taught in many places: that the Son is an offspring we never heard up to this day, for Scripture says, "unto us a child is born, unto us a son is given."' c. 7. He goes on to say that 'it is fearful to give Him names of our own to whom God has given a name which is above every name;' and observes that offspring is not the word which even a human father would apply to his son, as for instance we read, 'Child, (τέκνον,) go into the vineyard,' and 'Who art thou, my son?' moreover that fruits of the earth are called offspring ('I will not drink of the offspring of this vine'), rarely animated things, except indeed in such instances as, 'Ὁ generation (offspring) of vipers.' Nyssen defends his brother, contr. Eunom. Orat. iii. p. 105. In the Arian formula 'an offspring, but not as one of the offsprings,' it is synonymous with 'work' or 'creature.' On the other hand Epiphanius uses it, e.g. Hær. 76. n. 8. and Naz. Orat. 29. n. 2. Eusebius, Demonstr. Ev. iv. 2. Pseudo-Basil. adv. Eunom. iv. p. 280. fin.
[3] Ps. xiv. 1.　　　[4] Ib. cx. 3.　　　[5] John viii. 42.
[6] Ib. vi. 46.　　[7] Ib. x. 30, and xiv. 10.　　[8] Ib. i. 18.
[9] συμβεβηκός. Cf. Orat. iv. 2. also Orat. i. 36. The text embodies the common doctrine of the Fathers. Athenagoras, however, speaks of God's goodness as an accident, 'as colour to the body,' 'as flame is ruddy and the sky blue,' Legat. 24. This, however, is but a verbal difference, for shortly before he speaks of His

to have any external envelopement[1] and to be encompassed, or as if there is aught about Him which completes the essence, so that when we say 'God,' or name 'Father,' we do not signify the invisible and incomprehensible essence, but something about it, then let them complain of the Council's stating that the Son was from the essence of God; but let them reflect, that in thus considering they utter two blasphemies; for they make God corporeal, and they falsely say that the Lord is not Son of the very Father, but of what is about Him. But if God be simple, as He is, it follows that in saying 'God' and naming 'Father,' we name nothing as if about Him, but signify his essence itself. For though to comprehend what the essence of God is be impossible, yet if we only understand that God is, and if Scripture indicates Him by means of these titles, we, with the intention of indicating Him and none else, call Him God and Father and Lord. When then He says, 'I am that I am,' and 'I am the Lord God[2],' or when Scripture says, 'God,' we understand nothing else by it but the intimation of His incomprehensible essence Itself, and that He Is, who is spoken of[3]. Therefore let no one be startled on hearing that the Son of God is from the Essence of the Father; but rather let him accept the explanation of the Fathers, who in more explicit but equivalent language have for 'from God' written 'of the essence.' For they considered it the same thing to say that the Word was 'of God' and 'of the essence of God,' since

the word 'God,' as I have already said, signifies nothing but the essence of Him Who Is. If then the Word is not in such sense from God, as a son, genuine and natural, from a father, but only as creatures because they are framed, and as 'all things are from God,' then neither is He from the essence of the Father, nor is the Son again Son according to essence, but in consequence of virtue, as we who are called sons by grace. But if He only is from God, as a genuine Son, as He is, then the Son may reasonably be called from the essence of God.

23. Again, the illustration of the Light and the Radiance has this meaning. For the Saints have not said that the Word was related to God as fire kindled from the heat of the sun, which is commonly put out again, for this is an external work and a creature of its author, but they all preach of Him as Radiance[4], thereby to signify His being from the essence, proper and indivisible, and His oneness with the Father. This also will secure His true unchangableness and immutability; for how can these be His, unless He be proper Offspring of the Father's essence? for this too must be taken to confirm His identity with His own Father. Our explanation then having so religious an aspect, Christ's enemies should not be startled at the 'One in essence,' either, since this term also has a sound sense and good reasons. Indeed, if we say that the Word is from the essence of God (for after what has been said this must be a phrase admitted by them), what does this mean but the truth and eternity of the essence from which He is begotten? for it is not different in kind, lest it be combined with the essence of God, as something foreign and unlike it. Nor is He like only outwardly, lest He seem in some respect or wholly to be other in essence, as brass shines like gold and silver like tin. For these are foreign and of other nature, are separated off from each other in nature and virtues, nor is brass proper to gold, nor is the pigeon born from the dove[5]; but

being, τὸ ὄντως ὄν, and His unity of nature, τὸ μονοφυὲς, as in the number of ἐπισυμβεβηκότα αὐτῷ. Eusebius uses the word συμβεβηκὸς in the same way [but see *Orat.* iv. 2, note 8], Demonstr. *Evang.* iv. 3. And hence S. Cyril, in controversy with the Arians, is led by the course of their objections to observe, 'There are cogent reasons for considering these things *as accidents* συμβεβηκότα in God, though they be not.' *Thesaur.* p. 263. vid. the following note.

[1] περιβολὴ, and so *de Syn.* § 34. which is very much the same passage. Some Fathers, however, seem to say the reverse. E.g. Nazianzen says that 'neither the immateriality of God nor ingenerateness, present to us His essence.' *Orat.* 28. 9. And S. Augustine, arguing on the word ingenitus, says, that 'not every thing which is said to be in God is said according to essence.' *de Trin.* v. 6. And hence, while Athan. in the text denies that there are qualities or the like belonging to Him, περὶ αὐτὸν, it is still common in the Fathers to speak of qualities, as in the passage of S. Gregory just cited, in which the words περὶ θεὸν occur. There is no difficulty in reconciling these statements, though it would require more words than could be given to it here. Petavius has treated the subject fully in his work *de Deo* i. 7—11. and especially ii. 3. When the Fathers say that there is no difference between the divine 'proprietates' and essence, they speak of the fact, considering the Almighty as He is; when they affirm a difference, they speak of Him as contemplated by us, who are unable to grasp the idea of Him as one and simple, but view His Divine Nature as if *in projection* (if such a word may be used), and thus divided into substance and quality as man may be divided into genus and difference. [2] Ex. iii. 14, 15.

[3] In like manner *de Synod.* § 34. Also Basil, 'The essence is not any one of things which do not attach, but is the very being of God.' *contr. Eun.* i. 10 fin. 'The nature of God is no other than Himself, for He is simple and uncompounded.' Cyril *Thesaur.* p. 59. 'When we say the power of the Father, we say nothing else than the essence of the Father.' August. *de Trin.* vii. 6. And so Numenius in Eusebius, 'Let no one deride, if I say that the name of the Immaterial is essence and being.' *Præp. Evang.* xi. 10.

[4] Athan.'s ordinary illustration is, as here, not from 'fire,' but from 'radiance,' ἀπαύγασμα, after S. Paul [i.e. Hebrews] and the Author of the Book of Wisdom, meaning by radiance the light which a light diffuses by means of the atmosphere. On the other hand Arius in his letter to Alexander, Epiph. *Hær.* 69. 7. speaks against the doctrine of Hieracas that the Son was from the Father as a light from a light or as a lamp divided into two, which after all was Arian doctrine. Athanasius refers to fire, *Orat.* iv. § 2 and 10, but still to fire and its radiance. However we find the illustration of fire from fire, Justin. *Tryph.* 61. Tatian *contr. Græc.* 5. At this early day the illustration of radiance might have a Sabellian bearing, as that of fire in Athan.'s had an Arian. Hence Justin protests against those who considered the Son as 'like the sun's light in the heaven,' which 'when it sets, goes away with it,' whereas it is as 'fire kindled from fire.' *Tryph.* 128. Athenagoras, however, like Athanasius, says 'as light from fire,' using also the word ἀπόρροια, effluence: vid. also Orig. *Periarch.* i. 2. n. 4. Tertull. *Ap.* 21. Theognostus, quoted *infr.* § 25.

[5] vid. *de Syn.* § 41.

though they are considered like, yet they differ in essence. If then it be thus with the Son, let Him be a creature as we are, and not One in essence; but if the Son is Word, Wisdom, Image of the Father, Radiance, He must in all reason be One in essence. For unless it be proved that He is not from God, but an instrument different in nature and different in essence, surely the Council was sound in its doctrine and correct in its decree[6].

24. Further, let every corporeal inference be banished on this subject; and transcending every imagination of sense, let us, with pure understanding and with mind alone, apprehend the genuine relation of son to father, and the Word's proper relation towards God, and the unvarying likeness of the radiance towards the light: for as the words 'Offspring' and 'Son' bear, and are meant to bear, no human sense, but one suitable to God, in like manner when we hear the phrase 'one in essence,' let us not fall upon human senses, and imagine partitions and divisions of the Godhead, but as having our thoughts directed to things immaterial, let us preserve undivided the oneness of nature and the identity of light; for this is proper to a son as regards a father, and in this is shewn that God is truly Father of the Word. Here again, the illustration of light and its radiance is in point[7]. Who will presume to say that the radiance is unlike and foreign to the sun? rather who, thus considering the radiance relatively to the sun, and the identity of the light, would not say with confidence, 'Truly the light and the radiance are one, and the one is manifested in the other, and the radiance is in the sun, so that whoso sees this, sees that also?' but such a oneness and natural property, what should it be named by those who believe and see aright, but Offspring one in essence? and God s Offspring what should we fittingly and suitably consider, but Word, and Wisdom, and Power? which it were a sin to say was foreign to the Father, or a crime even to imagine as other than with Him everlastingly. For by this Offspring the Father made all things, and extended His Providence unto all things; by Him He exercises His love to man, and thus He and the Father are one, as has been said; unless indeed these perverse

men make a fresh attempt, and say that the essence of the Word is not the same as the Light which is in Him from the Father, as if the Light in the Son were one with the Father, but He Himself foreign in essence as being a creature. Yet this is simply the belief of Caiaphas and the Samosatene, which the Church cast out, but these now are disguising; and by this they fell from the truth, and were declared to be heretics. For if He partakes in fulness the light from the Father, why is He not rather that which others partake[8], that there be no medium introduced between Him and the Father? Otherwise, it is no longer clear that all things were generated by the Son, but by Him, of whom He too partakes[9]. And if this is the Word, the Wisdom of the Father, in whom the Father is revealed and known, and frames the world, and without whom the Father doth nothing, evidently He it is who is from the Father: for all things originated partake of Him, as partaking of the Holy Ghost. And being such, He cannot be from nothing, nor a creature at all, but rather a proper Offspring from the Father, as the radiance from light.

CHAPTER VI.

AUTHORITIES IN SUPPORT OF THE COUNCIL.

Theognostus; Dionysius of Alexandria; Dionysius of Rome; Origen.

25. THIS then is the sense in which they who met at Nicæa made use of these expressions. But next that they did not invent them for themselves (since this is one of their excuses), but spoke what they had received from their predecessors, proceed we to prove this also, to cut off even this excuse from them. Know then, O Arians, foes of Christ, that Theognostus[1], a learned man, did not decline the phrase 'of the essence,' for in the second book of his Hypotyposes, he writes thus of the Son:—

"The essence of the Son is not one procured

---

6 As 'of the essence' declared that our Lord was *uncreate*, so 'one in essence' declared that He was *equal* with the Father; no term derived from 'likeness,' even 'like in essence' answering for this purpose, for such phrases might all be understood of *resemblance* or *representation*. vid. § 20, notes 8, 9.
7 Athan. has just used the illustration of radiance in reference to 'of the essence:' and now he says that it equally illustrates 'one in essence;' the light diffused from the sun being at once contemporaneous and homogeneous with its original.

8 Vid. § 10 *init.* note 4.
9 The point in which perhaps all the ancient heresies concerning our Lord's divine nature agreed, was in considering His different titles to be those of different beings or subjects, or not really and properly to belong to one and the same person; so that the Word was not the Son, or the Radiance not the Word, or our Lord was the Son, but only improperly the Word, not the true Word, Wisdom, or Radiance. Paul of Samosata, Sabellius [?], and Arius, agreed in considering that the Son was a creature, and that He was called, made after, or inhabited by the impersonal attribute called the Word or Wisdom. When the Word or Wisdom was held to be personal, it became the doctrine of Nestorius.
1 Athanasius elsewhere calls him 'the admirable and excellent.' *ad Serap.* iv. 9. He was Master of the Catechetical school of Alexandria towards the end of the third century, being a scholar, or at least a follower of Origen. His seven books of Hypotyposes treated of the Holy Trinity, of angels, and evil spirits, of the Incarnation, and the Creation. Photius, who gives this account, Cod. 106, accuses him of heterodoxy on these points; which Athanasius in a measure admits, as far as the wording of his treatise went, when he speaks of his 'investigating by way of exercise.' Eusebius does not mention him at all. [His remains in Routh, *Rell.* iii. 409—414.]

from without, nor accruing out of nothing [2], but it sprang from the Father's essence, as the radiance of light, as the vapour [3] of water; for neither the radiance, nor the vapour, is the water itself or the sun itself, nor is it alien; but it is an effluence of the Father's essence, which, however, suffers no partition. For as the sun remains the same, and is not impaired by the rays poured forth by it, so neither does the Father's essence suffer change, though it has the Son as an Image of Itself [4]."

Theognostus then, after previously investigating in the way of an exercise [5], proceeds to lay down his sentiments in the foregoing words. Next, Dionysius, who was Bishop of Alexandria, upon his writing against Sabellius and expounding at large the Saviour's Economy according to the flesh, and thence proving against the Sabellians that not the Father but His Word became flesh, as John has said, was suspected of saying that the Son was a thing made and originated, and not one in essence with the Father; on this he writes to his namesake Dionysius, Bishop of Rome, to allege in his defence that this was a slander upon him. And he assured him that he had not called the Son made, nay, did confess Him to be even one in essence. And his words ran thus :—

" And I have written in another letter a refutation of the false charge they bring against me, that I deny that Christ was one in essence with God. For though I say that I have not found this term anywhere in Holy Scripture, yet my remarks which follow, and which they have not noticed, are not inconsistent with that belief. For I instanced human birth as being evidently homogeneous, and I observed that undeniably parents differed from their children only in not being the same individuals, otherwise there could be neither parents nor children. And my letter, as I said before, owing to present circumstances I am unable to produce ; or I would have sent you the very words I used, or rather a copy of it all, which, if I have an opportunity, I will do still. But I am sure from recollection that I adduced parallels

of things kindred with each other ; for instance, that a plant grown from seed or from root, was other than that from which it sprang, yet was altogether one in nature with it [6]: and that a stream flowing from a fountain, gained a new name, for that neither the fountain was called stream, nor the stream fountain, and both existed, and the stream was the water from the fountain."

26. And that the Word of God is not a work or creature, but an offspring proper to the Father's essence and indivisible, as the great Council wrote, here you may see in the words of Dionysius, Bishop of Rome, who, while writing against the Sabellians, thus inveighs against those who dared to say so :—

" Next, I may reasonably turn to those who divide and cut to pieces and destroy that most sacred doctrine of the Church of God, the Divine Monarchy [7], making it as it were three powers and partitive subsistences [7a] and godheads three. I am told that some among you who are catechists and teachers of the Divine Word, take the lead in this tenet, who are diametrically opposed, so to speak, to Sabellius's opinions ; for he blasphemously says that the Son is the Father, and the Father the Son, but they in some sort preach three Gods, as dividing the sacred Monad into three subsistences foreign to each other and utterly separate. For it must needs be that with the God of the Universe, the Divine Word is united, and the Holy Ghost must repose [8] and habitate in God ; thus in one as in a summit, I mean the God of the Universe, must the Divine Triad [9] be gathered up and brought together.

---

[2] Vid. above § 15. fin. 'God was alone,' says Tertullian, 'because there was nothing external to Him, *extrinsecus; yet* not even then alone, for He had with Him, what He had in Himself, His Reason.' in *Prax.* 5. Non per adoptionem spiritus filius fit *extrinsecus*, sed naturâ filius est. Origen. *Periarch.* i. 2. n. 4.
[3] From Wisdom vii. 25. and so Origen, *Periarch.* i. 2. n. 5. and 9. and Athan. *de Sent. Dionys.* 15.
[4] It is sometimes erroneously supposed that such illustrations as this are intended to *explain* how the Sacred Mystery in question is possible, whereas they are merely intended to shew that the words we use concerning it are not *self-contradictory*, which is the objection most commonly brought against them. To say that the doctrine of the Son's generation does not intrench upon the Father's perfection and immutability, or negative the Son's eternity, seems at first sight inconsistent with what the words Father and Son mean, till another image is adduced, such as the sun and radiance, in which that alleged inconsistency is seen to exist in fact. Here one image corrects another ; and the accumulation of images is not, as is often thought, the restless and fruitless effort of the mind to *enter into the Mystery*, but is a *safeguard* against any one image, nay, any collection of images being supposed *sufficient*. If it be said that the language used concerning the sun and its radiance is but popular not philosophical, so again the Catholic language concerning the Holy Trinity may, nay must be, economical, not adequate, conveying the truth, not in the tongues of angels, but under human modes of thought and speech.
[5] ἐν γυμνασίᾳ ἐξέτασας. And so § 27. of Origen, ζητῶν καὶ γυμνάζων. Constantine too, writing to Alexander and Arius, speaks of altercation, φυσικῆς τινος γυμνασίας ἕνεκα. Socr. i. 7. In somewhat a similar way, Athanasius speaks of Dionysius writing κατ' οἰκονομίαν, economically, or with reference to certain persons addressed or objects contemplated, *de Sent.* D. 6. and 26.

[6] The Arians at Nicæa objected to this image, Socr. i. 8. as implying that the Son was a προβολὴ, issue or development, as Valentinus taught. Epiph. *Hær.* 69. 7. Athanasius elsewhere uses it himself.
[7] By the Monarchy is meant the doctrine that the Second and Third Persons in the Ever-blessed Trinity are ever to be referred in our thoughts to the First as the Fountain of Godhead, vid. § 15. note 9. and § 19, note 6. It is one of the especial senses in which God is said to be one. Cf. *Orat.* iii. § 15. vid. also iv. § 1. 'The Father is *union*, ἕνωσις,' says S. Greg. Naz. 'from whom and unto whom are the others.' *Orat.* 42. 15. also *Orat.* 20. 7. and Epiph. *Hær.* 57. 5. Tertullian, before Dionysius, uses the word Monarchia, which Praxeas had perverted into a kind of Unitarianism or Sabellianism, in *Prax.* 3. Irenæus too wrote on the Monarchy, i.e. against the doctrine that God is the author of evil. Eus. *Hist.* v. 20. [see S. Iren. *fragment* 33, Ante-Nic. Lib.] And before him was Justin's work *de Monarchia,* where the word is used in opposition to Polytheism. The Marcionites, whom Dionysius presently mentions, are also specified in the above extract by Athan. vid. also Cyril. *Hier. Cat.* xvi. 3. Epiphanius says that their three origins were God, the Creator, and the evil spirit. *Hær.* 42, 3. or as Augustine says, the good, the just, and the wicked, which may be taken to mean nearly the same thing. *Hær.* 22. The Apostolical Canons denounce those who baptize into Three Unoriginate ; vid. also Athan. Tom. *ad Antioch.* 5. Naz. *Orat.* 20. 6. Basil denies τρεῖς ἀρχικαὶ ὑποστάσεις, *de Sp. S.* 38. which is a Platonic phrase.
[7a] And so Dionysius Alex. in a fragment preserved by S. Basil, 'If because the subsistences are three, they say that they are partitive, μεμερισμένας, still three there are, though these persons dissent, or they utterly destroy the Divine Trinity.' *de Sp. S.* n. 72. Athan. expresses the same more distinctly, οὐ τρεῖς ὑποστάσεις μεμερισμένας, Expos. *Fid.* § 2. In S. Greg. Naz. we find ἀμέριστος ἐν μεμερισμένοις ἡ θεότης. *Orat.* 31. 14. Elsewhere for μεμ. he substitutes ἀπερρηγμένας. *Orat.* 20. 6. ἀπεξενωμένας ἀλλήλων καὶ διεσπασμένας. *Orat.* 23. 6. as infr. ξένας ἀλλήλων παντάπασι κεχωρισμένας. The passage in the text comes into question in the controversy about the ἐξ ὑποστάσεως ἢ οὐσίας of the Nicene Creed, of which infr. on the Creed itself in Eusebius's Letter. [8] ἐμφιλοχωρεῖν.
[9] The word τριὰς, usually translated Trinity, is first used by Theophilus, *ad Autol.* ii. 15. Gibbon remarks that the doctrine of 'a numerical rather than a generical unity,' which has been explicitly put forth by the Latin Church, is favoured by the Latin language ; τριὰς seems to excite the idea of substance, *trinitas* of qualities.' ch. 21. note 74. It is certain that the Latin view of the sacred truth, when perverted, becomes Sabellianism ; and that the Greek, when perverted, becomes Arianism ; and we find Arius arising in the East. Sabellius in the West. It is also certain that the word Trinitas is properly abstract ; and expresses τριὰς or 'a three,' only in an ecclesiastical

For it is the doctrine of the presumptuous Marcion, to sever and divide the Divine Monarchy into three origins,—a devil's teaching, not that of Christ's true disciples and lovers of the Saviour's lessons. For they know well that a Triad is preached by divine Scripture, but that neither Old Testament nor New preaches three Gods. Equally must one censure those who hold the Son to be a work, and consider that the Lord has come into being, as one of things which really came to be; whereas the divine oracles witness to a generation suitable to Him and becoming, but not to any fashioning or making. A blasphemy then is it, not ordinary, but even the highest, to say that the Lord is in any sort a handiwork. For if He came to be Son, once He was not; but He was always, if (that is) He be in the Father, as He says Himself, and if the Christ be Word and Wisdom and Power (which, as ye know, divine Scripture says), and these attributes be powers of God. If then the Son came into being, once these attributes were not; consequently there was a time, when God was without them; which is most absurd. And why say more on these points to you, men full of the Spirit and well aware of the absurdities which come to view from saying that the Son is a work? Not attending, as I consider, to this circumstance, the authors of this opinion have entirely missed the truth, in explaining, contrary to the sense of divine and prophetic Scripture in the passage, the words, 'The Lord created me a beginning of His ways unto His works[1].' For the sense of 'He created,' as ye know, is not one, for we must understand 'He created' in this place, as 'He set over the works made by Him,' that is, 'made by the Son Himself.' And 'He created' here must not be taken for 'made,' for creating differs from making. 'Is not He thy Father that hath bought thee? hath He not made thee and created thee[2]?' says Moses in his great song in Deuteronomy. And one may say to them, O reckless men, is He a work, who is 'the First-born of every creature, who is born from the womb before the morning star[3],' who said, as Wisdom, 'Before all the hills He begets me[4]?' And in many passages of the divine oracles is the Son said to have been[5] generated, but nowhere to have[6] come into being; which manifestly convicts those of misconception about the Lord's generation, who presume to call His divine and ineffable generation a making[6]. Neither then may we divide into three Godheads the wonderful and divine Monad; nor disparage with the name of 'work' the dignity and exceeding majesty of the Lord; but we must believe in God the Father Almighty, and in Christ Jesus His Son, and in the Holy Ghost, and hold that to the God of the universe the Word is united[7]. For 'I,' says He, 'and the Father are one;'

and, 'I in the Father and the Father in Me.' For thus both the Divine Triad, and the holy preaching of the Monarchy, will be preserved."

27. And concerning the everlasting co-existence of the Word with the Father, and that He is not of another essence or subsistence, but proper to the Father's, as the Bishops in the Council said, you may hear again from the labour-loving[8] Origen also. For what he has written as if inquiring and by way of exercise, that let no one take as expressive of his own sentiments, but of parties who are contending in investigation, but what he[9] definitely declares, that is the sentiment of the labour-loving man. After his prolusions then (so to speak) against the heretics, straightway he introduces his personal belief, thus :—

"If there be an Image of the Invisible God, it is an invisible Image; nay, I will be bold to add, that, as being the likeness of the Father, never was it not. For when was that God, who, according to John, is called Light (for 'God is Light'), without a radiance of His proper glory, that a man should presume to assert the Son's origin of existence, as if before He was not? But when was not that Image of the Father's Ineffable and Nameless and Unutterable subsistence, that Expression and Word, and He that knows the Father? for let him understand well who dares to say, 'Once the Son was not,' that he is saying, 'Once Wisdom was not,' and 'Word was not,' and 'Life was not.'"

And again elsewhere he says :—

"But it is not innocent nor without peril, if because of our weakness of understanding we deprive God, as far as in us lies, of the Only-begotten Word ever co-existing with Him; and the Wisdom in which He rejoiced; else He must be conceived as not always possessed of joy."

See, we are proving that this view has been transmitted from father to father; but ye, O modern Jews and disciples of Caiaphas, how many fathers can ye assign to your phrases? Not one of the understanding and wise; for all abhor you, but the devil alone[9a]; none but he is your father in this apostasy, who both in the beginning sowed you with the seed of this

---

sense. But Gibbon does not seem to observe that Unitas is abstract as well as Trinitas; and that we might just as well say in consequence, that the Latins held an abstract unity or a unity of qualities, while the Greeks by μονάς taught the doctrine of 'a one' or a numerical unity. 'Singularitatem hanc dico (says S. Ambrose), quod Græce μονότης dicitur; singularitas ad personam pertinet, unitas ad naturam.' *de Fid.* v. 1. It is important, however, to understand, that 'Trinity' does not mean the *state* or *condition* of being three, as humanity is the condition of being man, but is synonymous with 'three persons.' Humanity does not exist and cannot be addressed, but the Holy Trinity is a three, or a unity which exists in three. Apparently from not considering this, Luther and Calvin objected to the word Trinity, 'It is a common prayer,' says Calvin: 'Holy Trinity, one God, have mercy on us.' It displeases me, and savours throughout of barbarism.' *Ep. ad Polon.* p. 796.
    1 Prov. viii. 22.   2 Deut. xxxii. 6.   3 Col. i. 15, and Ps. cx. 3.   4 Prov. viii. 25.   5 γεγεννῆσθαι.   6 γεγονέναι.
    7 This extract discloses to us (in connexion with the passages from Dionysius Alex. here and in the *de Sent. D.*) a remarkable anticipation of the Arian controversy in the third century.   1. It appears that the very symbol of ἦν ὅτε οὐκ ἦν, 'onte He was not,' was asserted or implied; vid. also the following extract from Origen, § 27. and Origen *Periarchon,* iv. 28. where mention is also made of the ἐξ οὐκ ὄντων, 'out of nothing,' which was the Arian symbol in opposition to 'of the substance.' Allusions are made

besides, to 'the Father not being always Father,' *de Sent. D.* 15. and 'the Word being brought to be by the true Wisdom,' ibid. 25.   2. The same special text is used in defence of the heresy, and that not at first sight an obvious one, which is found among the Arians, Prov. viii. 22.   3. The same texts were used by the Catholics, which occur in the Arian controversy. e.g. Deut. xxxii. 6. against Prov. viii. 22. and such as Ps. cx. 3. Prov. viii. 25. and the two John x. 30. and xiv. 10.   4. The same Catholic symbols and statements are found, e.g. 'begotten not made,' 'one in essence,' 'Trinity,' ἀδιαίρετον, ἄναρχον, ἀειγενές, 'light from light,' &c. Much might be said on this circumstance, as forming part of the proof of the very early date of the development and formation of the Catholic theology, which we are at first sight apt to ascribe to the 4th and 5th centuries. [But see Introd. to *de Sent. Dion.*]
    8 φιλοπόνου, and so *Serap.* iv. 9. [This place is referred to by *Socr.* vi. 13.]
    9 ἃ μὲν ὡς ζητῶν καὶ γυμνάζων ἔργαψε, ταῦτα μὴ ὡς αὐτοῦ φρονοῦντος δεχέσθω τις, ἀλλὰ τῶν πρὸς ἔριν φιλονεικούντων ἐν τῷ ζητεῖν, ἀδεῶς ὁρίζων ἀποφαίνεται, τοῦτο τοῦ φιλοπόνου τὸ φρόνημά ἐστι. 'ἀλλὰ. Certe legendum ἀλλ' ἃ, idque omnino exigit sensus. Montfaucon. Rather for ἀδεῶς read ἃ δὲ ὡς, and put the stop at ζητεῖν instead of δεχέσθω τις.
    9a Supr. § 5.

irreligion, and now persuades you to slander the Ecumenical Council[1], for committing to writing, not your doctrines, but that which from the beginning those who were eye-witnesses and ministers of the Word have handed down to us[2]. For the faith which the Council has confessed in writing, that is the faith of the Catholic Church; to assert this, the blessed Fathers so expressed themselves while condemning the Arian heresy; and this is a chief reason why these apply themselves to calumniate the Council. For it is not the terms which trouble them[2a], but that those terms prove them to be heretics, and presumptuous beyond other heresies.

CHAPTER VII.

On the Arian Symbol. "Unoriginate."

This term afterwards adopted by them; and why; three senses of it. A fourth sense. Unoriginate denotes God in contrast to His creatures, not to His Son; Father the scriptural title instead; Conclusion.

28. This in fact was the reason, when the

---

[1] vid. supr. § 4. *Orat.* i. § 7. *Ad Afros.* 2, twice. Apol. *contr. Arian.* 7. *ad Ep. Æg.* 5. Epiph. *Hær.* 70. 9. Euseb. *Vit. Const.* iii. 6. The Council was more commonly called μεγάλη, vid. supr. § 26. The second General Council, A. D. 381, took the name of ecumenical. vid. Can. 6. fin. but incidentally. The Council of Ephesus so styles itself in the opening of its Synodical Letter.
[2] The profession under which the decrees of Councils come to us is that of setting forth in writing what has ever been held orally or implicitly in the Church. Hence the frequent use of such phrases as ἐγγραφῶς ἐξετέθη with reference to them. Thus Damasus, Theod. *H. E.* v. 10. speaks of that 'apostolical faith, which was *set forth in writing* by the Fathers in Nicæa.' On the other hand, Ephrem of Antioch speaks of the doctrine of our Lord's perfect humanity being 'inculcated by our Holy Fathers, but not as yet [i.e. till the Council of Chalcedon] being *confirmed* by the decree of an ecumenical Council.' *Phot.* 229. p. 801. (ἐγγραφῶς, however, sometimes relates to the act of subscribing. Phot. *ibid.* or to Scripture, Clement. *Strom.* i. init. p. 321.) Hence Athan. says *ad Afros.* 1. and 2. that 'the Word of the Lord which was given through the ecumenical Council in Nicæa *remaineth for ever*;' and uses against its opposers the texts, 'Remove not the ancient landmark which thy fathers have set' (vid. also Dionysius in Eus. *H. E.* vii. 7.), and 'He that curseth his father or his mother, shall surely be put to death.' Prov. xxii. 28. Ex. xxi. 17. vid. also Athan. *ad Epict.* 1. And the Council of Chalcedon professes to 'drive away the doctrines of error by a common decree, and *renew* the unswerving faith of the Fathers,' Act. v. p. 452. [t. iv. 1453 ed. Col.] 'as,' they proceed, 'from of old the prophets spoke of Christ, and He Himself instructed us, and the creed of the Fathers has delivered to us,' whereas 'other faith it is not lawful for any to bring forth, or to write, or to draw up, or to hold, or to teach.' p. 456. [1460 ed. Col.] vid. S. Leo. supr. p. 5. note m. This, however, did not interfere with their *adding* without *undoing*. 'For,' says Vigilius, 'if it were unlawful to receive aught further after the Nicene statutes, on what authority venture we to assert that the Holy Ghost is of one substance with the Father, which it is notorious was there omitted?' *contr. Eutych.* v. init.; he gives other instances, some in point, others not. vid. also Eulogius, *apud Phot. Cod.* 23. pp. 829. 853. Yet to add to the *confession* of the Church is not to add to the *faith*, since nothing can be added to the faith. Leo, *Ep.* 124. p. 1237. Nay, Athan. says that the Nicene faith is sufficient to refute every heresy, *ad Max.* 5. fin. (also Leo. *Ep.* 54. p. 956. and Naz. *Ep.* 102. init.) *excepting, however*, the doctrine of the Holy Spirit; which explains his meaning. The Henoticon of Zeno says the same, but with the intention of dealing a blow at the Council of Chalcedon. Evagr. iii. 14. p. 345. Aetius at Chalcedon says that at Ephesus and Chalcedon the Fathers did not profess to draw up an exposition of faith, and that Cyril and Leo did but *interpret* the Creed. Conc. t. 2. p. 428. [t. iv. 1430, 1431 ed. Col. See this whole subject very amply treated in Dr. Pusey's *On the Clause, And the Son*, pp. 76 sqq.] Leo even says that the Apostles' Creed is sufficient against all heresies, and that Eutyches erred on a point ' of which our Lord wished no one of either sex in the Church to be ignorant,' and he wishes Eutyches to take the plentitude of the Creed 'puro et simplici corde.' *Ep.* 31. p. 857, 8.   [2a] Supr. § 21. init.

unsound nature of their phrases had been exposed at that time, and they were henceforth open to the charge of irreligion, that they proceeded to borrow of the Greeks the term Unoriginate[1], that, under shelter of it, they might reckon among the things originated and the creatures, that Word of God, by whom these very things came to be; so unblushing are they in their irreligion, so obstinate in their blasphemies against the Lord. If then this want of shame arises from ignorance of the term, they ought to have learned of those who gave it them, and who have not scrupled to say that even intellect, which they derive from Good, and the soul which proceeds from intellect, though their respective origins be known, are notwithstanding unoriginated, for they understand that by so saying they do not disparage that first Origin of which the others come[2]. This being the case, let them say the like themselves, or else not speak at all of what they do not know. But if they consider they are acquainted with the subject, then they must be interrogated; for[3] the expression is not from divine Scripture[4], but they are contentious, as elsewhere, for unscriptural positions. Just as I have related the reason and sense, with which the Council and the Fathers before it defined and published 'of the essence,' and 'one in essence,' agreeably to what Scripture says of the Saviour; so now let them, if they can, answer on their part what has led them to this unscriptural phrase, and in what sense they call God Unoriginated? In truth, I am told[4a], that the name has

---

[1] ἀγένητον. Opportunity will occur for noticing this celebrated word on *Orat.* i. 30—34. where the present passage is partly re-written, partly transcribed. Mention is also made of it in the *De Syn.* 46, 47. Athanasius would seem to have been but partially acquainted with the writings of the Anomœans, whose symbol it was, and to have argued with them from the writings of the elder Arians, who had also made use of it. [On Newman's unfortunate confusion of ἀγένητον and ἀγέννητον, see Lightfoot, as quoted in the note on *Exp. Fid.* § 1. Newman's reasons are stated in note 7 to *Orat.* i. 56.]
[2] Montfaucon quotes a passage from Plato's Phædrus, in which the human soul is called 'unoriginate and immortal [246 a.];' but Athan. is referring to another subject, the Platonic, or rather the Eclectic [i.e. Neo-Platonic] Trinity. Thus Theodoret, 'Plotinus, and Numenius, explaining the sense of Plato, say, that he taught Three principles beyond time and eternal, Good, Intellect, and the Soul of all,' *de Affect. Cur.* ii. p. 750. And so Plotinus himself, 'It is as if one were to place Good as the centre, Intellect like an immoveable circle round, and Soul a moveable circle, and moveable by appetite.' 4 *Ennead.* iv. c. 16. vid. Porphyry in Cyril. *contr. Julian.* viii. t. ult. p. 271. vid. ibid. i. p. 32. *Plot.* 3 *Ennead.* v. 2 and 3. Athan.'s testimony that the Platonists considered three ὑποστάσεις all unoriginate is perhaps a singular one. In 5 *Ennead.* iv. 1. Plotinus says what seems contrary to it, ἡ δὲ ἀρχὴ ἀγέννητος, speaking of his τἀγαθόν. Yet Plato, quoted by Theodoret, ibid. p. 749, speaks of εἴτε ἀρχὴν εἴτε ἀρχάς.
[3] ἐπεὶ μάλισται, ὅτι μάλιστα, *Orat.* i. § 36. *de Syn.* § 21. fin. ὅταν μάλιστα, *Apol. ad Const.* 23. καὶ μάλιστα, *de Syn.* § 42, 54.
[4] Cf. § 18, n. 8.
[4a] And so *de Syn.* § 46. 'we have on *careful inquiry* ascertained, &c.' Again, 'I have acquainted myself on their account [the Arians] with the meaning of ἀγένητον.' *Orat.* i. § 30. This is remarkable. for Athan. was a man of liberal education, as his *Orat. contr. Gent.* and '*de Incarn.* shew, especially, his acquaintance with the Platonic philosophy. Sulpicius too speaks of him as a jurisconsultus, Sacr. *Hist.* ii. 50. S. Gregory Naz. says, that he gave some attention, but not much, to the subjects of general education, τῶν ἐγκυκλίων, that he might not be altogether ig-

different senses; philosophers say that it means, first, 'what has not yet, but may, come to be;' next, 'what neither exists, nor can come into being;' and thirdly, 'what exists indeed, but was neither originated nor had origin of being, but is everlasting and indestructible⁵.' Now perhaps they will wish to pass over the first two senses, from the absurdity which follows; for according to the first, things that already have come to be, and things that are expected to come to be, are unoriginated; and the second is more absurd still; accordingly they will proceed to the third sense, and use the word in it; though here, in this sense too, their irreligion will be quite as great. For if by unoriginated they mean what has no origin of being, nor is originated or created, but eternal, and say that the Word of God is contrary to this, who comprehends not the craft of these foes of God? who but would stone⁶ such madmen? for, when they are ashamed to bring forward again those first phrases which they fabled, and which were condemned, the wretches have taken another way to signify them, by means of what they call unoriginate. For if the Son be of things originate, it follows, that He too came to be from nothing; and if He has an origin of being, then He was not before His generation; and if He is not eternal, there was once when He was not⁷.

29. If these are their sentiments they ought to signify their heterodoxy in their own phrases, and not to hide their perverseness under the cloke of the Unoriginate. But instead of this, the evil-minded men do all things with craftiness like their father, the devil; for as he attempts to deceive in the guise of others, so these have broached the term Unoriginate, that they might pretend to speak piously of God, yet might cherish a concealed blasphemy against the Lord, and under a veil might teach it to others. However, on the detecting of this sophism, what remains to them? 'We have found another,' say the evildoers; and then proceed to add to what they have said already, that Unoriginate means what has no author of being, but stands itself in this relation to things originated. Unthankful, and in truth deaf to the Scriptures! who do everything, and say everything, not to honour God, but to dishonour the Son, ignorant that he who dishonours the Son, dishonours the Father. For first, even though they denote God in this way, still the Word is not proved to be of things originated. For again, as being an offspring of the essence of the Father, He is of consequence with Him eternally. For this name of offspring does not detract from the nature of the Word, nor does Unoriginated take its sense from contrast with the Son, but with the things which come to be through the Son; and as he who addresses an architect, and calls him framer of house or city, does not under this designation allude to the son who is begotten from him, but on account of the art and science which he displays in his work, calls him artificer, signifying thereby that he is not such as the things made by him, and while he knows the nature of the builder, knows also that he whom he begets is other than his works; and in regard to his son calls him father, but in regard to his works, creator and maker; in like manner he who says in this sense that God is unoriginate, names Him from His works, signifying, not only that He is not originated, but that He is maker of things which are so; yet is aware withal that the Word is other than the things originate, and alone a proper offspring of the Father, through whom all things came to be and consist⁸.

30. In like manner, when the Prophets spoke of God as All-ruling, they did not so name Him, as if the Word were included in that All; (for they knew that the Son was

norant, of what he nevertheless despised, *Orat.* 21. 6. In the same way S. Basil, whose cultivation of mind none can doubt, speaks slightingly of his own philosophical knowledge. He writes of his 'neglecting his own weakness, and being utterly unexercised in such disquisitions;' *contr. Eunom.* init. And so in *de Sp.* § 5. he says, that 'they who have given vent' to vain philosophy, 'divide causes into principal, cooperative,' &c. Elsewhere he speaks of having 'expended much time on vanity, and wasted nearly all his youth in the vain labour of pursuing the studies of that wisdom which God has made foolishness,' *Ep.* 223. 2. In truth, Christianity has a philosophy of its own. Thus in the commencement of his *Viæ Dux* Anastasius says, 'It is a first point to be understood, that the tradition of the Catholic Church does not proceed upon, or follow, the philosophical definitions in all respects, and especially as regards the mystery of Christ, and the doctrine of the Trinity, but a certain rule of its own, evangelical and apostolical.' p. 20.

5 Four senses of ἀγένητον are enumerated, *Orat.* i. § 30. 1. What is not as yet, but is possible; 2. what neither has been nor can be; 3. what exists, but has not come to be from any cause; 4. what is not made, but is ever. Only two senses are specified in the *de Syn.* § 46. and in these the question really lies; 1. what is, but without a cause; 2. uncreate.

6 Βαλλέσθωσαν παρὰ πάντων, *Orat.* ii. § 28. An apparent allusion to the punishment of blasphemy and idolatry under the Jewish Law. vid. [Ex. xix. 13. and] reference to Ex. xxi. 17, in § 27, note 2. Thus, e.g. Nazianzen : 'While I go up the mount with good heart, that I may become within the cloud, and may hold converse with God, for so God bids; if there be any Aaron, let him go up with me and stand near. And if there be any Nadab or Abihu, or of the elders, let him go up, but stand far off, according to the measure of his purification. . . . But if any one is an evil and savage beast, and quite incapable of science and theology; let him stand off still further, and depart from the mount . *or he will be stoned* and crushed ; for the wicked shall be miserably destroyed. For as stones for the bestial are true words and strong. Whether he be leopard, let him die spots and all,' &c. &c. *Orat.* 28. 2.

7 The Arians argued that the word *unoriginate* implied *originate* or *creature* as its correlative, and therefore indirectly signified *Creator;* so that the Son being not unoriginate, was not the Creator. Athan. answers, that in the use of the word, whether there be a Son does not come into the question. As the idea of Father and Son does not include creation, so that of creator and creature does not include generation; and it would be as illogical to infer that there are no creatures because there is a Son as that there is no Son because there are creatures.

8 The whole of this passage is repeated in *Orat.* i. 32. &c. vid. for this particular argument, Basil also, *contr. Eunom.* i. 16.

other than things originated, and Sovereign over them Himself, according to His likeness to the Father); but because He is Ruler over all things which through the Son He has made, and has given the authority of all things to the Son, and having given it, is Himself once more the Lord of all things through the Word. Again, when they called God, Lord of the powers[9], they said not this as if the Word was one of those powers, but because, while He is Father of the Son, He is Lord of the powers which through the Son have come to be. For again, the Word too, as being in the Father, is Lord of them all, and Sovereign over all ; for all things, whatsoever the Father hath, are the Son's. This then being the force of such titles, in like manner let a man call God unoriginated, if it so please him ; not however as if the Word were of originated things, but because, as I said before, God not only is not originated, but through His proper Word is He the maker of things which are so. For though the Father be called such, still the Word is the Father's Image, and one in essence with Him ; and being His Image, He must be distinct from things originated, and from everything ; for whose Image He is, His property and likeness He hath: so that he who calls the Father unoriginated and almighty, perceives in the Unoriginated and the Almighty, His Word and His Wisdom, which is the Son. But these wondrous men, and prompt for irreligion, hit upon the term Unoriginated, not as caring for God's honour, but from malevolence towards the Saviour ; for if they had regard to honour and reverent language, it rather had been right and good to acknowledge and to call God Father, than to give Him this name ; for in calling God unoriginated, they are, as I said before, calling Him from things which came to be, and as a Maker only, that so they may imply the Word to be a work after their own pleasure ; but he who calls God Father, in Him withal signifies His Son also, and cannot fail to know that, whereas there is a Son, through this Son all things that came to be were created.

31. Therefore it will be much more accurate to denote God from the Son and to call Him Father, than to name Him and call Him Unoriginated from His works only ; for the latter term refers to the works that have come to be at the will of God through the Word, but the name of Father points out the proper offspring from His essence. And whereas the Word surpasses things originated, by so much and more also doth calling God Father surpass

the calling Him Unoriginated; for the latter is non-scriptural and suspicious, as it has various senses; but the former is simple and scriptural, and more accurate, and alone implies the Son. And 'Unoriginated' is a word of the Greeks who know not the Son : but 'Father' has been acknowledged and vouchsafed by our Lord; for He knowing Himself whose Son He was, said, 'I in the Father and the Father in Me[1];' and, 'He that hath seen Me hath seen the Father;' and, 'I and the Father are one[2];' but nowhere is He found to call the Father Unoriginated. Moreover, when He teaches us to pray, He says not, 'When ye pray, say, O God Unoriginated,' but rather, 'When ye pray, say, Our Father, which art in heaven[3].' And it was His Will, that the Summary of our faith should have the same bearing. For He has bid us be baptized, not in the name of Unoriginate and Originate, not into the name of Uncreate and Creature, but into the name of Father, Son, and Holy Spirit[4], for with such an initiation we too are made sons verily[5], and using the name of the Father, we acknowledge from that name

---

[1] John xiv. 9, 10.   [2] Ib. x. 30.   [3] Matt. vi. 9.
[4] And so S. Basil, 'Our faith was not in Framer and Work, but in Father and Son were we sealed through the grace in baptism.' contr. Eunom. ii. 22. And a somewhat similar passage occurs Orat. ii. § 41.
[5] υἱοποιούμεθα ἀληθῶς. This strong term 'truly' or 'verily' seems taken from such passages as speak of the 'grace and truth' of the Gospel, John i. 12—17. Again S. Basil says, that we are sons, κυρίως, 'properly,' and πρώτως 'primarily,' in opposition to τροπικῶς, 'figuratively,' contr. Eunom. ii. 23. S. Cyril too says, that we are sons 'naturally' φυσικῶς as well as κατὰ χάριν, vid. Suicer Thesaur. v. υἱός. i. 3. Of these words, ἀληθῶς, φυσικῶς, κυρίως, and πρώτως, the first two are commonly reserved for our Lord: e.g. τὸν ἀληθῶς υἱὸν, Orat. ii. § 37. ἡμεῖς υἱοί, οὐκ ὡς ἐκεῖνος φύσει καὶ ἀληθείᾳ, iii. § 19. Hilary seems to deny us the title of 'proper' sons; de Trin. xii. 15 ; but his 'proprium' is a translation of ἴδιον, not κυρίως. And when Justin says of Christ ὁ μόνος λεγόμενος κυρίως υἱός, Apol. ii. 6. κυρίως seems to be used in reference to the word κύριος, Lord, which he has just been using, κυριολογεῖν being sometimes used by him as others in the sense of 'naming as Lord,' like θεολογεῖν. vid. Tryph. 56. There is a passage in Justin's ad Græc. 21. where he (or the writer) when speaking of ἐγώ εἰμι ὁ ὤν, uses the word in the same ambiguous sense; οὐδὲν γὰρ ὄνομα ἐπὶ θεοῦ κυριολογεῖσθαι δυνατὸν, 21 ; as if κύριος, the Lord, by which 'I am' is translated, were a sort of symbol of that proper name of God which cannot be given. But to return: the true doctrine then is, that, whereas there is a primary and secondary sense in which the word Son is used, primary when it has its formal meaning of continuation of nature, and secondary when it is used nominally, or for an external resemblance to the first meaning, it is applied to the regenerate, not in the secondary sense, but in the primary. S. Basil and S. Gregory Nyssen consider Son to be 'a term of relationship according to nature' (vid. supr. § 10, note 1.), also Basil in Psalm xxviii. 1. The actual presence of the Holy Spirit in the regenerate in substance (vid. Cyril, Dial. 7. p. 638.) constitutes this relationship of nature ; and hence after the words quoted from S. Cyril in the beginning of the note, in which he says, that we are sons, φυσικῶς, he proceeds, 'naturally, because we are in Him, and in Him alone.' vid. Athan.'s words which follow in the text at the end of § 31. And hence Nyssen lays down, as a received truth, that 'to none does the term "proper," κυριώτατον, apply, but to one in whom the name responds with truth to the nature,' contr. Eunom. iii. p. 123. And he also implies, p. 117, the intimate association of our sonship with Christ's, when he connects together regeneration with our Lord's eternal generation, neither being διὰ πάθους, or, of the will of the flesh. If it be asked, what the distinctive words are which are incommunicably the Son's, since so much is man's, it is obvious to answer, ἴδιος υἱὸς and μονογενὴς, which are in Scripture, and the symbols 'of the essence,' and 'one in essence,' of the Council ; and this is the value of the Council's phrases, that, while they guard the Son's divinity, they allow full scope, without risk of entrenching on it, to the Catholic doctrine of the fulness of the Christian privileges. vid. supr. § 19, note.

---

the Word in the Father. But if He wills that we should call His own Father our Father, we must not on that account measure ourselves with the Son according to nature, for it is because of the Son that the Father is so called by us; for since the Word bore our body and came to be in us, therefore by reason of the Word in us, is God called our Father. For the Spirit of the Word in us names through us His own Father as ours, which is the Apostle's meaning when he says, 'God hath sent forth the Spirit of His Son into your hearts, crying, Abba, Father[6].'

32. But perhaps being refuted as touching the term Unoriginate also, they will say according to their evil nature, 'It behoved, as regards our Lord and Saviour Jesus Christ also, to state from the Scriptures what is there written of Him, and not to introduce nonscriptural expressions.' Yes, it behoved, say I too; for the tokens of truth are more exact as drawn from Scripture, than from other sources[7]; but the ill disposition and the versatile and crafty irreligion of Eusebius and his fellows, compelled the Bishops, as I said before, to publish more distinctly the terms which overthrew their irreligion; and what the Council did write has already been shewn to have an orthodox sense, while the Arians have been shewn to be corrupt in their phrases, and evil in their dispositions. The term Unoriginate, having its own sense, and admitting of a religious use, they nevertheless, according to their own idea, and as they will, use for the dishonour of the Saviour, all for the sake of contentiously maintaining, like giants[8], their fight with God. But as they did not escape condemnation when they adduced these former phrases, so when they misconceive of the Unoriginated which in itself admits of being used well and religiously, they were detected, being disgraced before all, and their heresy everywhere proscribed. This then, as I could, have I related, by way of explaining what was formerly done in the Council; but I know that the contentious among Christ's foes will not be disposed to change even after hearing this, but will ever search about for other pretences, and for others again after those. For as the Prophet speaks, 'If the Ethiopian change his skin, or the leopard his spots[9], then will they be willing to think religiously, who have been instructed in irreligion. Thou however, beloved, on receiving this, read it by thyself; and if thou approvest of it, read it also to the brethren who happen to be present, that they too on hearing it, may welcome the Council's zeal for the truth, and the exactness of its sense; and may condemn that of Christ's foes, the Arians, and the futile pretences, which for the sake of their irreligious heresy they have been at the pains to frame among themselves; because to God and the Father is due the glory, honour, and worship with His co-existent Son and Word, together with the All-holy and Life-giving Spirit, now and unto endless ages of ages. Amen.

---

6 Gal. iv. 6.
7 Cf. *contr. Gent.* init. *Incarn.* 57. *ad Ep. Æg.* 4. *Vit. Ant.* 16. And *passim* in Athan.

8 And so, *Orat.* ii. § 32, κατὰ τοὺς μυθευομένους γίγαντας. And so Nazianzen, *Orat.* 43. 26. speaking of the disorderly Bishops during the Arian ascendancy. Also Socr. v. 10. Sometimes the Scripture giants are spoken of, sometimes the mythological.
9 Jer. xiii. 23.

DE SENTENTIA DIONYSII

THE following tract, like the last, is a letter to a person engaged in discussion with Arians, who were openly finding fault with the Definition of Nicæa, and especially with the word Co-essential (§ 19). Montfaucon suggests that both epistles were addressed to the same person, the *de Decretis* (§ 25) having as it were challenged the Arians to cite passages from Dionysius on behalf of their own doctrine, whereupon their opponent came back to Athanasius with a request for further help. But the language of the first sentence of our present tract seems to imply that Athanasius had not previously heard of the discussions in question. However, slender as such grounds are, the tract furnishes no more decisive indication of date. (On certain expressions which might seem to carry the date back to the lifetime of Arius, see Prolegg. ch. ii. § 7.)

Dionysius 'the Great,' Bishop of Alexandria 233—265, was a pupil of Origen (Eus. *H. E.* vi. 29), and equally distinguished as a ruler of the Church and as a theologian. In all the controversies of his age (the lapsed, rebaptism, Easter, Paul of Samosata, Sabellianism, the authorship of the Apocalypse) his influence made itself felt, and his writings were very numerous (Westcott in D. C. B. i. p. 851 sq.; a good account of Dionysius in vol. I. of this series, p. 281, note). The most celebrated controversy in which he was involved was that which, a century later, gave rise to the tract before us.

About the period when personal attacks on the Nicene leaders began to be exchanged for overt objections to the Nicene Definitions, the claim was freely made that 'the fathers' had been condemned by the latter: in other words, that they had held with the Arians (see below § 1, ἀεὶ μὲν προφάσεις . . . . νῦν δὲ καὶ διαβάλλειν τοὺς πατέρας τετολμήκασι). Accordingly we find Athanasius at about the same date, viz. early in the sole reign of Constantius, vindicating on the one hand the work of the Council, on the other the orthodox reputation of Dionysius. The Arians found material for their appeal to the latter in a letter addressed by him to certain bishops in Pentapolis, called Ammon and Euphranor. Whether or no Sabellius had been a native of that province, at any rate his doctrine was at that time so popular there 'that the Son of God was scarcely any longer preached in the Churches.' Exercising the right of supervision over those districts which had already become vested by prescription in the Alexandrian See, Dionysius wrote to Ammon, Bishop of Berenice, (Euseb. *H. E.* vii. 26, who enumerates three several letters to Ammon, Telesphorus, and Euphranor, and a fourth to Ammon and Euporus: he also refers to his letters to Dionysius of Rome: Montfaucon is therefore scarcely fair in charging Eusebius with suppressing the episode 'ne verbum quidem de hac historia fecerit!') insisting on the distinctness of the Son from the Father. In doing so he used strong expressions akin to the language of Origen on the subordination of the Son. These expressions were at once objected to by certain orthodox churchmen (§ 13, it is not clear whether they belonged to Pentapolis or Alexandria), who without consulting Dionysius went to Rome (about 260), and spoke against him in the presence of his namesake, the Roman Bishop. The latter, true to the traditions of his See since the time of Callistus (see Hipp. *Philos* IX. vii. δίθεοι ἐστε), while steering clear of Sabellianism, was especially jealous of error in the opposite direction. Accordingly he assembled a synod (*de Synod*. 44), and drew up a letter to Alexandria, in which he rebuked firstly the Sabellians, but secondly and more fully those who separate the Godhead or speak of the Son as a work, including under this category certain *unnamed* catechists and teachers of Alexandria (*De Decr.* 26). At the same time he wrote personally to Dionysius, informing him that he was accused of maintaining the opinions in question. In answer to this letter, Dionysius of Alexandria drew up a treatise in four books, entitled 'Refutation and Defence,' and addressed to his namesake of Rome, in which he explained his language, and stated his belief in a manner which put an end to the controversy. He had been charged with maintaining that the Son was made, that He was not eternal (οὐκ ἀεὶ ἦν ὁ θεὸς πατήρ, οὐκ ἀεὶ ἦν ὁ υἱός, ... οὐκ ἦν πρὶν γεννήθη, ἀλλ' ἦν ποτὲ ὅτε οὐκ ἦν κ.τ.λ. § 14), that he denied the co-essentiality (ὁμοούσιον) of the Son, and separated Him from the Father (§§ 16, 18, cf. § 4, ξένον κατ' οὐσίαν κ.τ.λ.). In his Refutation and Defence, Dionysius admits the use of these expressions, withdraws the first (§ 15, line 1), and admits the propriety of the ὁμοούσιον, although he himself prefers Scriptural language (§. 18. The section shews the unfixed use of the word. Dionysius had formerly used οὐσία in the sense of πρώτη οὐσία, nearly as equivalent to ὑπόστασις: but now he clearly takes it as δευτέρα οὐσία, indicative not of Person but of Nature). That the Son was made, he explains as an inadequate formula, the word being applicable (in one of its many senses) to the relation of son to father (§ 20. The defence of Athanasius, that Dionysius referred to the Human Nature of Christ, is scarcely tenable. It is not supported by what Dionysius himself says, rather the contrary: and if his language did not refer to the Trinity, where would be its relevancy against Sabellianism?). The words ἦν ὅτε οὐκ ἦν, and οὐκ ἦν πρὶν γεννήθη, he does not explain, but professes his belief in the eternal union of the Word with the Father (§§ 24, 25). Lastly, he repudiates the charge of dividing the Holy Trinity, or of mentioning Father and Son as though separate Beings: When I mention the Father, I have already mentioned the Son, before I pronounce His Name (§ 17, the closing words of the section are a complete formula of agreement with all that his Roman namesake could possibly require of him).

That Dionysius in his 'Refutation and Defence' merely restated, and did not (κατ' οἰκονομίαν) alter, his theological position is open to no doubt. Athanasius, not the Arians, had the right to claim him as his own. He is clearly speaking *optima fide* when he deprecates the pressing of statements in which he had given expression to one side only, and that the less essential side, of his convictions. At the same time we cannot but see that the Arians had good *prima facie* ground for their appeal. Here were their special formulæ, those anathematised at Nicæa, ἦν ποτὲ ὅτε οὐκ ἦν and the rest, adopted, and the ὁμοούσιον implicitly rejected, by the most renowned bishop Alexandria had yet had. (Newman, in *de Decr.* 26, note 7, fails to appreciate the reference to the language of Dion. Alex.) Moreover it is only fair to admit that not only in language, but in thought also, Athanasius had advanced upon his predecessors of the Alexandrian School. The rude shock of Arianism had shewn him and the other Nicene leaders the necessity of greater consistency than had characterised the theology of Origen and his school, a consistency to be gained only by breaking with one side of it altogether. While on the one hand Origen held fast to the Godhead of the Logos (κατ' οὐσίαν ἐστὶ θεός), and to His coeternity with the Father (ἀεὶ γεννᾶται ὁ σωτὴρ ὑπὸ τοῦ πατρός, and see *de Decr.* § 27); he had yet, using οὐσία in its 'first' sense, spoken of Him as ἕτερος κατ' οὐσίαν τοῦ πατρός (*de Orat.* 15), and placed him, after the manner of Philo, as an intermediary between God and the Universe. He had spoken of the unity of the Father and the Son as moral (*Cels.* viii. 12, τῇ ὁμονοίᾳ καὶ τῇ συμφωνίᾳ), insisted upon the ὑπεροχὴ of the Father (i.e. 'subordination' of the Son), and spoken (*De Orat.*) as though the highest worship of all were to be reserved for the Father (Jerome ascribes still stronger language to him). Yet there is no real doubt that, as regards the core of the question, Athanasius and not his opponents is the true successor of Origen. The essential difference between Athanasius and the 'Conservatives' of the period following the great council consisted in the fact that the former saw clearly what the latter failed to realise, namely the insufficiency of the formulæ of the third century to meet the problem of the fourth. We may then, without disparagement to Dionysius, admit that he was not absolutely consistent in his language; that he failed to distinguish the ambiguities which beset the words οὐσία, ὑπόστασις, and even ποιεῖν and γένεσθαι, and that he used language (οὐκ ἦν πρὶν γεννήθη and the like) which we, with our minds cleared by the Arian controversy, cannot reconcile with the more deliberate and guarded statements of the 'Refutation and Defence[1].'

The controversy of the two Dionysii has another interesting side, as bearing upon the means then employed for dealing with questions affecting the Church as a whole,—and in particular upon the position of the Roman Church as the natural referee in such questions. (Cf. Prolegg. ch. iv. § 4.) This is not the place for a general discussion of the question, or for an attempt to trace its history previous to the case before us. But it should be noted, firstly, that when the Pentapolite (?) opponents of Dionysius desire a lever against him, their first resource is not a council of local bishops, but the Roman Church : secondly, that the Roman bishop takes up the case, and writes to his Alexandrian namesake for an explanation : thirdly, that the explanation asked for is promptly given. Unfortunately the fragment of the Roman letter preserved to us by Athanasius tells us nothing of the form of the intervention, whether it was the request of one co-trustee to another for an explanation of the latter's action in a matter concerning their common trust, or whether it was coupled with any assumption of jurisdiction at all like that involved in the letter of the Bishop of Alexandria to those of Libya. At any rate, the latter alternative has no positive evidence in our documents ; and the fragments of the Refutation and Defence 'shew the most complete and resolute independence. There is nothing in the narrative of Athanasius which implies that the Alexandrine Bishop recognised or that the Roman Bishop claimed any dogmatic authority as belonging to the Imperial See.' The letter of Dionysius of Rome is certainly highly characteristic of the indifference to theological reasoning and the close adherence to the rule of faith as the authoritative solution of all questions of doctrine which marks the genius of Rome as contrasted with that of Alexandria (see Gore, *The Church and the Ministry*, ch. i. *sub fin.*, and Harnack, *Dg.* i. 686, who observes upon the striking family likeness between this letter and that of Leo to Flavian, and of Agatho to the Sixth Ecumenical Council). Lastly, the Roman Church, which never troubled about a precedent adverse to her imperial instinct, never forgot one which favoured it. The intervention of Dionysius was treasured up in her memory, and, when the time came, fully exploited (*supr.* p. 11?, note 3, where the note distinguishes somewhat too carefully between the 'Pope' of Rome and the 'Bishop,' πάπας, of Alexandria).

The tract of Athanasius, with his extracts in *de Decr.* and *de Syn.*, tell us all that we know of the history of this important controversy. Dionysius had previously (Eus. *H. E.* vii. 6) had some correspondence with Xystus, the previous Bishop of Rome, on the subject of the Sabellian teaching current in the Pentapolis. He was in fact during his episcopate in constant communication with Rome and with the other important churches of the Christian World. His letters are much used in the sixth and seventh books of the History of Eusebius, to whom we are indebted for most of our knowledge of his writings.

The general arrangement of the tract is as follows :—

§§ 1—4 are prefatory, the fourth section broadly indicates the line of the defence. §§ 5—12 deal with the incriminated passages : Athan. gives the history of them, and lays stress on their incomplete presentation of the belief of Dionysius, as having been written for a special purpose,—as may also be said of much of the language of the Apostles. But even in themselves the expressions of Dionysius are orthodox, referring (as Athanasius claims) to Christ as man. In §§ 13—23 he turns to the Refutation and Defence, from which he makes copious extracts, bringing out the diametrical opposition between Dionysius and the Arians. In §§ 24, 25 the anti-Arian doctrine of Dionysius is summed up, and § 26 recapitulates the main points of §§ 5—12. He concludes (§ 27) by claiming a verdict upon the evidence, and urging upon the Arians the alternative of abandoning their error, or of being left with the devil as their only partisan.

---

[1] It may be added that the letter to Paul of Samosata quoted by Bull, *Def.* III. iv. 3, Petavius, *Trin.* I. iv. is not genuine. Posterity, which enveloped the name of Origen with storms of controversy, did not entirely spare his pupil : Basil (*Ep.* 41) taxes him with sowing the first seeds of the Anomœan heresy, Gennadius (*Eccl. Dogm.* iv.) calls him ' Fons Arii.'

ON THE OPINION OF DIONYSIUS

LETTER of Athanasius concerning Dionysius, Bishop of Alexandria, shewing that he too was against the Arian heresy, like the Synod of Nicæa, and that the Arians in vain libel him in claiming him as on their side.

1. *The Arian appeal to Dionysius a slander against him.*

You have been tardy in informing me of the present argument between yourself and the enemies of Christ; for even before your courtesy wrote to me, I had made diligent enquiry, and learnt about the matter, of which I heard with pleasure. I approved of the right opinion entertained by your piety concerning our blessed fathers, while on the present occasion I once more recognise the unreasonableness of the Arian madmen. For whereas their heresy has no ground in reason, nor express proof from holy writ, they were always resorting to shameless subterfuges and plausible fallacies. But they have now also ventured to slander the fathers: and this is not inconsistent, but fully of a piece with their perversity. For what marvel is it if men who have presumed to 'take counsel against the Lord and against His Christ,' are also vilifying the blessed Dionysius, Bishop of Alexandria, as a partisan and accomplice of their own? For if they are pleased to extol a man, for the support of their own heresy, even if they call him blessed, they cast upon him no slight affront, but a great one indeed; just like robbers or men of evil life who, when branded for their own practices, claim sober persons as being of their number, and thus defame their sober character.

2. *The Arian position inconsistent with Holy Scripture.*

If then they have confidence in their opinions and statements, let them broach their heresy nakedly, and shew from it if they think they have any religious argument whether from Scripture, or from human reason, in their defence. But if they have nothing of the kind, let them hold their peace. For they will find nothing from any quarter except the greater condemnation of themselves. Firstly from the Scriptures, in that John says, 'In the beginning was the Word;' whereas they say, 'he was not before he was begotten:' while David sings, in the character of the Father, 'my heart uttered a good Word' (Ps. xlv. 1, LXX.), whom they allege to be in thought only, and originated from nothing. Further, whereas John once more says in the Gospel (i. 3), 'all things were made by Him, and without Him was not anything made,' while Paul writes, 'there is one Lord Jesus Christ by whom are all things' (1 Cor. viii. 6), and elsewhere, 'all things were created in Him' (Col. i. 16), how will they have the boldness (or rather how will they escape disgrace) to oppose the sayings of the saints, by saying that the artificer of all things is a creature, and that He is a created thing in whom all things created have come into being and subsist? Nor, secondly, is any religious argument from human reason left them in their defence. For what man, Greek or barbarian, presumes to call one, whom he confesses to be God, a created thing, or to say that he was not before he was made? or what man, when he has heard Him whom he believes to be God alone say, 'This is My beloved Son' (Mat. iii. 17), and 'my heart uttered a good Word,' will venture even to say that the Word out of the heart of God has come into being out of nothing? or that the Son is a created thing and not the very offspring of Him that speaks? or again, who that hears Him whom he believes to be Lord and Saviour say, 'I am in the Father and the Father in Me,' and 'I and the Father are one' (John xiv. 10, x. 30), will presume to put asunder what He has made one and maintained indivisible?

3. *The Arians appeal to Dionysius as the Jews did to Abraham: but with equally little reason.*

Seeing this themselves, accordingly, and having no confidence in their own position, they utter falsehoods against religious men. But it would be better for them, when isolated, and perceiving that under examination they were at a loss and put to silence on all sides, rather to have turned back from the way of error and not to claim men whom they do not know, lest being confuted by them also they should carry off all the more disgrace. But perhaps they do not wish ever to depart from this wickedness of theirs ; for they emulate this characteristic of Caiaphas and his party, just as they have learned from them to deny Christ. For they too, when the Lord had done so many works, by which He shewed Himself to be the Christ the Son of the Living God, and being convicted by him, from thenceforth in all things thinking and speaking against the Scriptures, and unable for a moment to face the proofs against themselves, betook themselves to the patriarch with the words, 'We have Abraham to our father' (Matt. iii. 9), thus thinking to cloke their own unreasonableness. But neither did they gain anything by these words, nor will these men, by speaking of Dionysius, be able to escape the guilt of the others. For the Lord convicted the latter of their wicked deeds by the words, 'This did not Abraham' (John viii. 40), while the same truth again shall convict these men of their impiety and falsehood. For the Bishop Dionysius did not hold with Arius, nor was he ignorant of the truth. On the contrary, both the Jews of that day, and the new Jews of the present day inherited their mad enmity against Christ from their father the devil. Well then, a strong proof that here once more these men are saying what is not true, but are maligning the man, is the fact that neither was he condemned and expelled from the church for impiety by other bishops, as these men have been from the clergy, nor did he of his own accord leave the church as the partisan of a heresy, but died honourably within it, and his memory is retained and registered along with the fathers to the present day. For if he had held with these men, or not vindicated what he had written, without doubt he too would have been treated as these men have been.

4. The Arian appeal to Dionysius based upon an isolated fragment of his teaching to the neglect of the rest.

And indeed this would suffice for the entire refutation of the new Jews, who both deny the Lord and slander the fathers and attempt to deceive all Christians. But since they think they have, in certain parts of the bishop's letter, pretexts for their slander of him, come let us look at these also, so that even from them the futility of the reasoning may be exposed, and they may at length cease from their blasphemy against the Lord, and at any rate with the soldiers (Mat. xxvii. 54), when they see creation witnessing, confess that truly He is the Son of God, and not one of created things. They say then that in a letter the blessed Dionysius has said, ' that the Son of God is a creature and made, and not His own by nature, but in essence alien from the Father, just as the husbandman is from the vine, or the ship-builder from the boat, for that, being a creature, He was not before He came to be.' Yes, he wrote it, and we too admit that his letter runs thus. But just as he wrote this, he also wrote very many other letters, and they ought to consult those also ; in order that the faith of the man may be made clear from them all, and not from this alone. For the art of a ship-builder who has constructed many triremes is judged of not from one, but from all. If therefore he simply wrote this letter of which they speak as an exposition of his faith, or if this was his only letter, let them accuse him to their hearts' content,—for this suggestion really amounts to an accusation,—but if he was led to write as he did by the occasion and the person [1] concerned, while he also wrote other letters, defending himself where he had been suspected, in that case they ought not to have neglected the reasons, and hastily cast a slur upon the man, lest they should appear to be hunting merely stray expressions, while passing over the truth to be found in his other letters. For a husbandman also treats trees of the same sort now in one way now in another, according to the character of the soil he has to do with : nor would any one blame him because he cuts one, grafts another, plants another, and another again takes up. On the contrary, upon learning the reason, he all the more admires the versatility of his skill. Well then, unless they have consulted the writing superficially let them state the main subject of the letter ; for so the malignity and unscrupulous character of their design will come out. But since they do not know, or are ashamed to state it, we must state it ourselves.

5. The occasion of Dionysius' writing against the Sabellians.

At that date certain of the Bishops in Pentapolis, Upper Libya, held with Sabellius. And they were so successful with their opinions that the Son of God was scarcely any longer preached in the churches. Dionysius

---

1 προσώπου : but see also Newman's note 2 on de Decr. § 14.

having heard of this, as he had the charge [2] of those churches, sends men to counsel the guilty ones to cease from their error, but as they did not cease, but waxed more shameless in their impiety, he was compelled to meet their shameless conduct by writing the said letter, and to expound from the Gospels the human nature of the Saviour, in order that since those men waxed bolder in denying the Son, and in ascribing His human actions to the Father, he accordingly by demonstrating that it was the Son and not the Father that was made man for us, might persuade the ignorant persons that the Father is not a Son, and so by degrees lead them up to the true Godhead of the Son, and the knowledge of the Father. This is the main subject of the letter, and this is the reason why he wrote it, by reason of those who so shamelessly had chosen to alter the true faith.

6. Dionysius did not express his full opinion in the passages alleged.

Well then, what is there in common between the heresy of Arius and the opinion of Dionysius: or why is Dionysius to be called like Arius, when they differ widely? For the one is a teacher of the Catholic Church, while the other has been the inventor of a new heresy. And while Arius to expound his own error wrote a Thaleia in an effeminate and ridiculous style like Sotades the Egyptian, Dionysius not only wrote other letters also, but composed a defence of himself upon the suspicious points, and came out clearly as of right opinions. If then his writings are inconsistent, let them not draw him to their side, for on this assumption he is not worthy of credit. But if, when he had written his letter to Ammonius, and fallen under suspicion, he made his defence so as to better [3] what he had previously said, but did so without changing, it must be evident that he wrote the suspected passages in a qualified sense [4]. But what is

---

[2] See Epiphanius, *Hær.* lxviii. 1. The arrangement is recognised as one of old standing in the sixth canon of Nicæa, 'Let the old customs which exist in Egypt, Libya, and Pentapolis remain in force, namely that the Bishop of Alexandria should have authority over all these regions; since this is also customary for the Bishop of Rome. Likewise also at Antioch and in the other prefectures (it is decreed) that their prerogatives should be maintained to those churches.' The canon points to the natural explanation of the arrangement: the bishops of the capitals began from a very early date to exercise a loosely defined but gradually strengthening supervision over those of the rest of the province. In particular, they came to exercise a veto (and latterly more than a veto) upon the appointments to the provincial sees (εἰ τις χωρὶς γνώμης, ib.). The bishops of Alexandria as well as Rome had even at this date acquired something of the rank of secular potentates (δυναστεία, *Socr.* vii. 11, ἤδη πάλαι), but not to the extent to which it went later on (ib. 7. and supr. *Apol. Ar.* § 9).

[3] θεραπεύειν. For the word, cf. Hatch, *Hibb. Lect.* p. 80 note.

[4] κατ᾽ οἰκονομίαν, as below § 24. Cf. *de Decr.* § 25, note 5. The word οἰκονομία has two main senses in Athanasius, both derived from the classical sense of *management* or *dispensation*, the adapting of means toward an end. (1) As in the present passage (cf. Origen in *Migne* XI. p. 77 b, οἰκονομικῶς): a use which

written or done in such a sense men have no business to construe maliciously, or wrest each one to a meaning of his own. For even a physician frequently in accordance with his knowledge applies to the wounds he has to deal with, remedies which to some seem unsuitable, with a view to nothing but health. In like manner it is the practice of a wise teacher to arrange and deliver his lessons with reference to the characters of his pupils, until he has brought them over to the way of perfection.

7. The language of the Apostles needs similar caution in particular passages.

But if they accuse the blessed man (for the arguments of the Arians about him are in fact accusations against him) simply for writing thus, what will they do when they hear even the great and blessed Apostles in the Acts, firstly Peter saying (Acts ii. 22), 'Ye men of Israel hear these words: Jesus of Nazareth, a man approved of God unto us by mighty works and wonders and signs which God did by Him in the midst of you, as ye yourselves know: Him, being delivered up by the determinate counsel and foreknowledge of God, ye by the hand of lawless men did crucify and slay;' and again (ib. iv. 10), 'In the name of Jesus Christ of Nazareth, Whom ye crucified, Whom God raised from the dead, even in Him doth this man stand here before you whole;' and Paul, relating (ib. xiii. 22) in Antioch of Pisidia how God, 'when He had removed Saul, raised up David to be king; to whom also He bare witness and said, I have found David the Son of Jesse, a man after my heart, who shall do My will. Of this man's seed hath God according to promise brought unto Israel a Saviour, Jesus;' and again at Athens (ib. xvii. 30), 'The times of ignorance therefore God overlooked; but now He commandeth men that they should all everywhere repent: inasmuch as He hath appointed a day in the which He will judge the world in righteousness by means of the man whom He hath ordained, whereof He hath given assurance unto all men, in that He hath raised Him from the dead;' or Stephen, the great martyr, when he says, 'Behold I see the heavens opened and the Son of man standing on the right hand of God.' Why, it is high time for them to brazen it out (for there is nothing too

---

is the lineal ancestor of the ill-sounding word 'economy' as a term in casuistry; (2) as applied to the Incarnation of our Lord, regarded as *the* Dispensation, the Divine Method for the salvation of mankind. This use is very frequent in St. Athanasius (compare *Ep. Æg.* 2. and *Orat.* ii. 11), and in earlier Fathers from Ignatius (*Eph.* 18 ἐκυοφορήθη ὑπὸ Μαρίας κατ᾽ οἰκονομίαν, where Lightfoot refers to a more detailed history of the word in his unpublished note on Eph. i. 10) downwards (references in Soph. *Lex. s.v.*).

daring for them) and claim that the very apostles held with Arius: for they declare Christ to have been a man from Nazareth, and passible.

8. *The Apostles spoke of Christ as man, but also as God.*

Well then, such being the imaginations of these men, did the Apostles, since they used the above language, regard Christ as only a man and nothing more? God forbid. The very idea is out of the question. But here too they have acted as wise master-builders and stewards of the mysteries of God. And they have good reason for it. For inasmuch as the Jews of that day, in error themselves and misleading the Gentiles, thought that the Christ was coming as a mere man of the seed of David, after the likeness of the rest of the children of David's descent, and would neither believe that He was God nor that the Word was made flesh; for this reason it was with much wisdom that the blessed Apostles began by proclaiming to the Jews the human characteristics of the Saviour, in order that by fully persuading them from visible facts, and from miracles which were done, that the Christ was come, they might go on to lead them up to faith in His Godhead, by shewing that the works He had done were not those of a man, but of God. Why, Peter, who calls Christ a man capable of suffering, at once went on (Act. iii. 15) to add, 'He is Prince of Life,' while in the Gospel he confesses, 'Thou art the Christ, the Son of the living God.' But in his Epistle he calls Him Bishop of souls, and Lord both of himself and of angels and Powers. Paul, again, who calls Christ a man of the seed of David, wrote thus to the Hebrews (i. 3), 'Who being the brightness of His glory and the very image of His subsistence,' and to the Philippians (ii. 6), 'Who being in the form of God counted it not a prize to be on an equality with God.' But what can it mean to call him Prince of Life, Son of God, brightness, express image, on an equality with God, Lord, and Bishop of souls, if not that in the body He was Word of God, by whom all things were made, and is as indivisible from the Father as is the brightness from the light?

9. *Dionysius must be interpreted like the Apostles.*

And Dionysius accordingly acted as he learned from the Apostles. For as the heresy of Sabellius was creeping on, he was compelled, as I said before, to write the aforesaid letter, and to hurl at them what is said of the Saviour in reference to His manhood and His humiliation, so as to bar them by reason of His human attributes from saying that the Father was a son, and so render easier for them the teaching concerning the Godhead of the Son, when in his other letters he calls Him from the Scriptures the word, wisdom, power, breath (Wisd. vii. 25), and brightness of the Father. For example, in the letters written in his defence, speaking as I have described, he waxes bold in the faith, and in piety towards Christ. As then the Apostles are not to be accused by reason of their human language about the Lord,—because the Lord has been made man,—but are all the more worthy of admiration for their wise reserve and seasonable teaching, so Dionysius is no Arian on account of his letter to Euphranor and Ammonius against Sabellius. For even if he did use humble phrases and examples, yet they too are from the Gospels, and his justification for them is the Saviour's coming in the flesh, on account of which not only these things, but others like them are written. For just as He is Word of God, so afterwards 'the Word was made flesh;' and while 'in the beginning was the Word,' the Virgin at the consummation of the ages conceived, and the Lord has become man. And He who is indicated by both statements is one Person, for 'the Word was made flesh.' But the expressions used about His Godhead, and His becoming man, are to be interpreted with discrimination and suitably to the particular context. And he that writes of the human attributes of the Word knows also what concerns His Godhead: and he who expounds concerning His Godhead is not ignorant of what belongs to His coming in the flesh: but discerning each as a skilled and 'approved money-changer[4],' he will walk in the straight way of piety; when therefore he speaks of His weeping, he knows that the Lord, having become man, while he exhibits his human character in weeping, as God raises up Lazarus; and He knows that He used to hunger and thirst physically, while divinely He fed five thousand persons from five loaves; and knows that while a human body lay in the tomb, it was raised as God's body by the Word Himself.

10. *The expressions of Dionysius claimed by the Arians refer to Christ as Man.*

Dionysius, teaching exactly thus, in his letter to Euphranor and Ammonius wrote in view of Sabellius concerning the human pre-

---

4 See Westcott, *Introduction to the Gospels*, Appendix C, 5.

N 2

dicates of the Saviour. For to the latter class belong the sayings, 'I am the Vine and My Father the Husbandman' (Joh. xv. 1), and 'faithful to Him that made Him' (Heb. iii. 2), and 'He created me' (Prov. viii. 22), and 'made so much better than the angels' (Heb. i. 4). But He was not ignorant of the passages, 'I am in the Father and the Father in Me' (Joh. xiv. 10), and 'He that hath seen Me hath seen the Father.' For we know that he mentioned them in his other Epistles. For while mentioning them there, he made mention also of the human attributes of the Lord. For just as 'being in the form of God He counted it not a prize to be on an equality with God, but emptied Himself, taking the form of a slave' (Phil. ii. 6), and 'though He was rich, yet for our sakes He became poor,' so while there are high and rich descriptions of His Deity, there are also those which relate to His coming in the flesh, humble expressions and poor. But that these are used of the Saviour as man is apparent on the following grounds. The husbandman is different in essence from the vine, while the branches are of one essence and akin to it, and are in fact undivided from the vine, it and they having one and the same origin. But, as the Lord said, He is the vine, we are the branches. If then the Son is of one essence with ourselves, and has the same origin as we, let us grant that in this respect the Son is diverse in essence from the Father, like as the vine is from the husbandman. But if the Son is different from what we are, and He is the Word of the Father while we are made of earth, and are descendants of Adam, then the above expression ought not to be referred to the deity of the Word, but to His human coming. Since thus also has the Saviour said : 'I am the vine, ye are the branches, My Father is the husbandman.' For we are akin to the Lord according to the body, and for that reason he said (Heb. ii. 12, Ps. xxii. 22), 'I will declare thy name unto my brethren.' And just as the branches are of one essence with the vine, and are from it, so we also having our bodies homogeneous with the Lord's body, receive of His fulness (Joh. i. 16), and have that body as our root [4a] for our resurrection and our salvation. But the Father is called the husbandman, for He it was who by His Word cultivated the Vine, namely the manhood of the Saviour, and who by His own Word prepared for us a way to a kingdom ; and none cometh to the Lord except the Father draw him to Him (Joh. vi. 44).

[4a] Cf. *Orat.* i. 48, note 7, and ii. 56, note 5.

11. *The same is true of the analogous language of the Apostles.*

This then being the sense of the expression, it follows that it is of the vine, so understood, that it is written : 'Who was faithful to Him that had created Him' (Heb. iii. 2), and 'made so much better than the angels' (ib. i. 4), and 'He created me' (Prov. viii. 22). For when He had taken that which He had to offer on our behalf, namely His body of the Virgin Mary, then it is written of Him that He had been created, and formed, and made : for such phrases are applicable to men. Moreover not after (His taking) the body has He been made better than the angels, lest He should appear to have been previously less than or equal to them. But writing to Jews, and comparing the human ministry of the Lord to Moses, he said, 'having been made so much better than the angels,' for by means of angels the law was spoken, because 'the law was given by Moses, but grace came by Jesus Christ' (Joh. i. 17), and the gift of the Spirit. And whereas in those days the law was preached from Dan to Beersheba, now 'their sound is gone out into all lands' (Rom. x. 18; Ps. xix. 3), and the Gentiles worship Christ, and through Him know the Father. The above things then are written of the Saviour as man, and not otherwise.

12. *The passages alleged from Dionysius are, when rightly understood, strictly orthodox.*

Well then, did Dionysius, as the adversaries of Christ reiterate, when writing of the human characteristics of the Son, and so calling Him a creature, mean that he was one man among others? Or when he said that the Word was not proper to the essence of the Father, did he hold that He was of one essence with us men? Certainly he did not write thus in his other epistles, but in them not only manifests a correct opinion, but as good as cries out by them against these people, saying as it were : I am not of the same opinion as you, you adversaries of God, nor did my writings furnish Arius with a pretext for impiety. But writing to Ammon and Euphranor on account of the Sabellianisers, I made mention of the vine and the husbandman and used other like expressions, in order that, by pointing out the human characteristics of the Lord, I might persuade those men not to say that it is the Father who was made man. For like as the husbandman is not the vine, so He that came in the body was not the Father but the Word ; and the Word having come to be in the Vine was called the Vine, because of His bodily kinship with the branches, namely ourselves. In this sense, then, I wrote as I did to Euphranor and Ammonius, but your shamelessness I confront with the other letters written by me, so that men of sound mind may know the defence they contain, and my right mind in the faith of Christ. The Arians then ought, if their intelligence were sound, thus to have thought and held concerning the Bishop: 'for all things are manifest to them that understand, and right to them that find knowledge' (Prov. viii. 9). But since, not having understood the faith of the Catholic Church, they have fallen into impiety, and consequently, maimed in their intelligence, think that even straight things are crooked and call light darkness, while they think that darkness is light, it is necessary to quote also from the other letters of Dionysius, and state why they were written, to the greater condemnation of the heretics. For it was from them that we ourselves have learned to think and write as we are doing about the man.

13. But other writings of Dionysius have to be considered also. Their history.

The following is the occasion of his writing the other letters. The Bishop Dionysius having heard of the affairs in Pentapolis, and having written, in zeal for religion, as I said above, his letter to Euphranor and Ammonius against the heresy of Sabellius, some of the brethren belonging to the Church, of right opinions, but without asking him, so as to learn from himself how he had written, went up to Rome; and they spoke against him in the presence of his namesake Dionysius the Bishop of Rome. And he, upon hearing it, wrote simultaneously against the partisans of Sabellius and against those who held the very opinions for uttering which Arius was cast out of the Church; calling it an equal and opposite impiety to hold with Sabellius, or with those who say that the Word of God is a thing made and formed and originated. And he wrote also to Dionysius to inform him of what they had said about him. And the latter straightway wrote back, and inscribed his books 'a Refutation and a Defence.' Here mark the detestable gang of the adversaries of Christ, and how they themselves have stirred up their disgrace against themselves. For Dionysius, Bishop of Rome, having written also against those who said that the Son of God was a creature and a created thing, it is manifest that not now for the first time but from of old the heresy of the Arian adversaries of Christ has been anathematised by all. And Dionysius, Bishop of Alexandria, making his defence concerning the letter he had written, appears in his turn as neither thinking as they

allege, nor having held the Arian error at all.

14. Object and general method of Dionysius in his ' Refutation and Defence.'

And the mere fact of Dionysius having made his defence about the matters on which these people harp suffices completely to condemn the Arians, and to demonstrate their malignity. For he wrote, not in angry controversy, but to defend himself on the points where he was under suspicion. But in defending himself against charges, what does he do if not, while disposing of every charge of which he was suspected, by this very fact convict the Arian madmen of malignity? But, to complete their confusion by means of what he wrote in his defence, come, let me set before you his actual words. For from them you will learn firstly that the Arians are malicious, secondly that Dionysius has nothing to do with their error. To begin with, then, he wrote his letter as in Refutation and in Defence. But this means, surely, that he aims at refuting false statements, and defends himself for what he has written; shewing that he wrote not as Arius supposed, but that in mentioning what is said concerning the Lord in His human aspect, he was not ignorant that He was the Word and Wisdom undivided from the Father. Then he blames those who spoke against him for not quoting his language as a whole, but garbling it, and speaking not in good faith but disingenuously and arbitrarily. And he compares them to those who used to impeach the letters of the blessed Apostle. But this complaint of his entirely clears him from sinister suspicion. For if he considers the detractors of Paul to be like his own, he shews precisely this, that he wrote as he did in Paul's sense. At any rate, in meeting severally the charges of his opponents, he explains all the passages cited by them: and, whereas in these latter he upsets Sabellius, in his subsequent letters he shews how sound and pious is his own faith. Accordingly whereas they would have it that Dionysius held that 'God was not always a Father, the Son did not always exist, but God existed apart from the Word, while the Son Himself was not before He was begotten: on the contrary, there was a time when He was not, for He is not eternal but has come later into being,'—see how he replies! Most of what he said, whether in the form of investigations, or collective inferences, or interrogatory refutations, or charges against his accusers, I omit because of the length of his discourses, inserting only what is strictly relevant to the charges against him. In answer to these, he writes after certain prefatory matter, in the first book inscribed 'Refutation and Defence' in the following terms.

15. Extracts from the ' Refutation and Defence.'

'For never was there a time when God was not a father.' And this he acknowledges in what follows, 'that Christ is for ever, being Word and Wisdom and Power. For it is not to be supposed that God, having at first no such issue, afterwards begat a Son, but that the Son has His being not of Himself but of the Father.' And a little way on he adds on the same subject, ' But being the brightness of light eternal, certainly He is Himself eternal; for as the light exists always, it is evident that the brightness must exist always as well. For it is by the fact of its shining that the existence of light is perceived, and there cannot be light that does not give light. For let us come back to our examples. If there is sun, there is sunlight, there is day. If there is none of these things, it is quite impossible for there to be sun. If then the sun were eternal, the day also would be unceasing. But in fact, as that is not so, the day begins and ceases with the sun. But God is light eternal, never beginning nor ceasing. The brightness then lies before Him eternally, and is with Him without beginning and ever-begotten, shining in His Presence, being that Wisdom which said, " I was that wherein he rejoiced, and daily I was glad in his presence at all times" (Prov. viii. 30).' And again after a little he resumes the same subject with the words, ' The Father then being eternal, the Son is eternal, being Light of Light: for if there is a parent there is also a child. But if there were not a child, how and of whom can there be a parent? But there are both, and that eternally.' Then again he adds, 'God then being light, Christ is brightness; and being Spirit, for " God is a Spirit " (John iv. 24),—in like manner Christ is called the breath, for He is the " breath of the power of God " (Wisd. vii. 25).' And again, to quote the second book, he says, ' But only the Son, who always is with the Father and is filled of Him that IS, Himself also IS from the Father.'

16. Contrast of the language of Dionysius with that of Arius.

Now if the sense of the above statements were doubtful, there would be need of an interpreter. But since he wrote plainly and repeatedly on the same subject, let Arius gnash his teeth when he sees his own heresy subverted by Dionysius, and hears him say what he does not wish to hear : 'God was always Father, and the Son is not absolutely eternal,

but His eternity flows from the eternity of the Father, and He coexists with Him as brightness with the light.' But let these, who have so much as imagined that Dionysius held with Arius, lay aside such a slander against him. For what have they in common, when Arius says, ' The Son was not before He was begotten, but there was once a time when He was not,' whereas Dionysius teaches, ' Now God is Light eternal, neither beginning, nor ever to end : accordingly the brightness lies before Him eternally, and coexists with Him, shining before Him without beginning and ever-begotten.' For in fact to meet the suspicion of others who allege that Dionysius in speaking of the Father does not name the Son, and again in speaking of the Son does not name the Father, but divides, removes, and separates the Son from the Father, he replies and puts them to shame in the second book, as follows.

17. Dionysius did not separate the Persons of the Holy Trinity.

'Each of the names I have mentioned is inseparable and indivisible [4b] from that next to it. I spoke of the Father, and before referring to the Son I designated Him too in the Father. I referred to the Son,—and even if I did not also expressly mention the Father, certainly He was to be understood beforehand in the Son. I added the Holy Spirit, but at the same time I further added both whence and through whom He proceeded. But they are ignorant that neither is the Father, quâ Father, separated from the Son,— for the name carries that relationship with it,—nor is the Son expatriated from the Father. For the title Father denotes the common bond. But in their hands is the Spirit, who cannot be parted either from Him that sent or from Him that conveyed Him : How then can I, who use these names, imagine that they are sundered and utterly [5] separated from one another?' And after a little he goes on, 'Thus then we extend the Monad [6] indivisibly into the Triad, and conversely gather together the Triad without diminution into the Monad.'

[4b] This passage is somewhat differently rendered by Dr. Pusey in his letter on the Filioque (1876), p. 112.

[5] The παντελῶς somewhat qualifies the repudiation. Dionysius expressly maintained three Hypostases in the Holy Trinity, in contrast to the language of Rome (de Decr. 26 note 7a) and the later use of Athanasius himself. But see the Tom. ad Antioch. of 362, below, and supra p. 90, note 2. Dionysius of Rome repudiates τρεῖς μεμερισμένας ὑποστάσεις, while Dionysius of Alexandria (in Bas. de Sp. S.) maintains that unless three Hypostases be recognised, the divine Triad is denied.

[6] As pointed out by Newman on De Decr. 26, note 9, Τριάς and Μονάς are concrete, Trinitas and Unitas abstract terms ; so that while Trinitas (and Μονάς) lend themselves to a Sabellian, Τριάς and Unitas may be pressed into an Arian sense : but each pair of terms (Greek and Latin) holds the balance evenly between the opposite misinterpretations.

18. *Dionysius did not hold that the Son was not of one essence with the Father.*

Next he confutes them upon their charge that he called the Son one of the things originated, and not of one essence with the Father (once more in the first book) as follows: ' Only in saying that certain things were perceived to be originated and created, I gave them as examples cursorily, as being less adequate, saying that neither was the plant [of one essence] with the husbandman, nor the boat with its builder. Then I dwelt more upon more apposite and suitable comparisons, and went at greater length into those nearer the truth, making out various proofs, which I wrote to you[6a] in another letter, by means of which proofs I shewed also that the charge they allege against me is untrue, namely, that I denied Christ to be of one essence with God. For even if I argue that I have not found this word (ὁμοούσιον) nor read it anywhere in the Holy Scriptures, yet my subsequent reasonings, which they have suppressed, do not discord with its meaning. For I gave the example of human birth, evidently as being homogeneous, and saying that certainly the parents only differed from their children in not being themselves the children, else it would follow that there was no such thing as parents or children. And the letter, as I said before, I am prevented by circumstances from producing, else I would have sent you the exact words I then used, or rather a copy of all the letter: which I will do if I have an opportunity. But I know, and recollect, that I added several similitudes from kindred relations. For I said that a plant, sprung from a seed or root, was different from that whence it sprung, and at the same time entirely of one nature with it: and that a stream flowing from a well receives another form and name,—for the well is not called a river, nor the river a well,—and that both existed, and that the well was as it were a father, while the river was water from the well. But they pretend not to see these and the like written statements, but to be as it were blind, while they try to pelt me with two unconnected expressions like stones, from a distance, not knowing that in matters beyond our knowledge, and which require training to apprehend, frequently not only foreign, but even contrary examples serve to illustrate the problem in hand.' And in the third book he says, 'Life was begotten of Life, and flowed as a river from a well, and from Light unquenchable bright Light was kindled.'

19. *Inconsistency of the Arian appeal to Dionysius.*

Who that hears this will not set down as mad those who suspect Dionysius of holding with Arius? For lo! in these words, by arguments based on truth, he tramples upon his entire heresy. For by the simile of the Brightness he destroys the statements that ' He was not before He was begotten,' and ' There was a time when He was not,' as also by saying that His Father was never without issue. But their allegation that He was made ' of nothing' he destroys by saying that the Word was like a river from a well, and a shoot from a stock, and a child from a parent, and Light from Light, and Life from Life. And their barring off and separating the Word from God, he overthrows by saying that the Triad is without division and without diminution gathered together into the Monad. While their statement that the Son has no part in the Father's essence, he unequivocally tramples down by saying that the Son is of one essence with the Father. Wherein one must wonder at the impudence of the irreligious persons. How can they, when Dionysius whom they claim as their partisan says that the Son is of one essence[6b], themselves go about buzzing like gnats with the complaint that the Synod was wrong in writing ' of one essence?' For if Dionysius is a friend of theirs, let them not deny what their partisan holds. But if they think that the expression was wrongly used, how can they reiterate that Dionysius, who used it, held with them? the more so as he does not appear to have written these things merely by the way, but having previously written other letters[7], he convicts of falsehood those who had charged him with not saying that the Son was of one Essence with the Father, while he refutes those who thought that he said that the Word was originated, shewing that he did not hold what they supposed, but even if he had used the expressions, he had done so merely in order to shew that it was the Son, not the Father, who had put on the originated, formed, created body; for which reason the Son also is said to have been originated, created, and formed.

20. *Dionysius must be fairly interpreted, and allowed the benefit of his own explanatory statements.*

Clearly since he had previously used such

6a ' To you' is omitted in the extract *de Decr.* 25.

6b It should be noted that Dionysius, while assenting to this word, does not use it as his own.
7 Possibly to other bishops who had questioned his teaching (Routh, *Reil.* iii. p. 380).

expressions, while bidding a long farewell to the Arians, he demands a good conscience from his hearers,—being entitled to plead the difficulty, or perhaps one may say the incomprehensibleness of the problems concerned,—namely that they may judge not of the words but of the meaning of the writer, and the more so as there is very much to shew his intention. For instance he says himself: ' I used the examples of such relations cursorily, as being less adequate, the plant and the husbandman for instance ; while I dwelt upon the more pertinent examples, and went at greater length into those nearer the truth.' But a man who says this shews that it is nearer the truth to say that the Son is eternal and of the Father, than to say that He is originated. For by the latter the bodily nature of the Lord is denoted, but by the former, the eternity of His Godhead. In the following words, for instance, he maintains, and not only so, but deliberately and with genuine demonstrative force, that they are refuted who charged him with not saying that the Son is of one essence with the Father: ' even if I did not find this expression in the Scriptures, yet collecting from the actual Scriptures their general sense, I knew that, being Son and Word, He could not be outside the Essence of the Father.' For that he does not hold the Son to be a thing created or formed,—for on this point also they have quoted him repeatedly—he says in the second book as follows : ' But if any one of my traducers, because I called God the Creator the maker of all things, thinks that I mean that He is Maker of Christ also, let him mark that I previously called Him Father, in which term the Son also is implied. For after I said that the Father is Maker, I added neither is He Father of the things He created, if He that begat is to be called Father in the strict sense. For the wider sense of the term Father we will work out in what follows. Neither is the Father a maker, if by maker is meant simply the artificer. For among the Greeks, philosophers are called "makers" of their own discourses. And the Apostle speaks of a "doer" ($\pi o \iota \eta \tau \eta s$) "of the law" (Rom. ii. 13), for men are called " doers " of inward qualities, such as virtue and vice ; as God said, " I looked for one to do justice, but he did wickedness " ' (Isa. v. 7, LXX.).

21. In what sense Dionysius said that the Son was ' made.'

Of a truth one that hears this is reminded of the divine oracle which says, ' whithersoever the impious turns, he is destroyed ' (Prov. xii. 7, LXX.). For lo ! turning subtly in each direc-

tion these impious men are destroyed, having even here no excuse as touching Dionysius. For he teaches openly that the Son is not a thing made or created, while he taxes and corrects those who accuse him of having said that God was the creator (of Christ), in that they failed to notice that he had previously spoken of God as Father, in which expression the Son also is implied. But in saying thus, he shews that the Son is not one of the creatures, and that God is not the maker but the Father of His own Word. And since certain had ignorantly objected to him that he called God the maker of Christ, he defends himself in various ways, shewing that not even here is what he said open to blame. For he had said that God was the maker of Christ in regard to His flesh, which the Word took, and which was in itself created. But if any one were to suspect that this referred to the Word, here too they were bound to give him a fair hearing. ' For as I do not hold that the Word is a creature, and call God not His maker but His Father, even if I in passing, while referring to the Son, call God a creator, yet even here I am able to defend myself. For the Greek philosophers call themselves makers ($\pi o \iota \eta \tau a \iota$) of their own discourses ($\lambda \acute{o} \gamma o \iota$), although they are their fathers ; while the Divine Scripture describes us as makers (doers) even of the motions of our hearts, speaking of " doers " of the law and of judgment and justice.' So that on all sides he demonstrates not only that the Son is not a thing made or created, but also that he himself has nothing to do with Arian error.

22. The relation of the Son to the Father is essential, according to Dionysius.

For let not any Arian suppose that he says even anything of the following kind : The Son coexists with the Father, so that while the names are correlated, the things are widely removed ; and whereas the Son did not always coexist with the Father, since the Son came into being, God received from that fact the additional name of Father, and His coexistence with Him dates from that time as happens in the case of men. On the contrary, let him observe and bear in mind what we have said before, and he will see that the faith of Dionysius is correct. For in saying, ' For there was no time when God was not Father,' and again, ' God at any rate is light eternal without beginning nor ever to end, accordingly the brightness is eternally before Him and coexists with Him, without beginning and ever-begotten, shining in His presence,' he should make it impossible for any one to entertain any such suspicion against him. Moreover the examples of the well and the river, and the root and the branch, and the breath and the vapour, put to shame the adversaries of Christ when they reiterate the contrary against him.

23. *Dionysius did not hold that there are two Words.*

But since in addition to all his own iniquities Arius has raked up this expression also as if from a dunghill, adding that, 'The Word is not the Father's own, but the Word that is in God is different, while this one, the Lord, is outside of and has nothing to do with the Essence of the Father, and is only called "Word" conceptually[8], and is not by nature and of a truth Son of God, but is called Son, He too, by adoption, as a creature;'—and since saying thus he boasts among the ignorant as though here too he has Dionysius as His partisan;—look at the faith of Dionysius on these points also, how he contradicts these perversities of Arius. For in the first book he writes as follows: 'Now I have said that God is the well of all that is good: while the Son has been described as the river which proceeds from Him. For word is an efflux of intelligence, and, to borrow language applicable to men, the intelligence that issues by the tongue is derived from the heart through the mouth, coming out different from the word in the heart. For the latter remains, after sending forth the other, as it was. But the other is sent forth and flies forth, and is borne in every direction. And so each is in the other, and each distinct from the other: and they are one, and at the same time two. Likewise the Father and the Son were said to be one, and the One in the other.' And in the fourth book he says: 'For as our intelligence utters the word from itself, as the prophet says, My heart uttered a good word (Ps. xlv. 1), and, while either is distinct from the other, occupying a place of its own distinct from the other, the one dwelling and stirring in the heart, the other upon the tongue,—yet they are not separated, not for a moment lost to one another, nor is the intelligence without utterance (ἄλογος), nor the word without intelligence, but the intelligence creates the Word being manifested in it, and the Word shews forth the intelligence having originated in it, and the intelligence is as it were an internal word, and the word an issuing intelligence; the intelligence passing over into the word, while the word circulates the intelligence among the hearers: and so the intelligence through the word gains a lodgment in the

souls of the hearers, entering in along with the word; and the intelligence is as it were the father of the word, existing in itself, while the word is as it were the son of the intelligence, having its origin, not of course before the latter, nor yet concurrently with it from some external source, but by springing out of it;—so the mighty Father and universal Intelligence has the Son before all things as His Word, Interpreter and Messenger.'

24. *If the Arians agree with Dionysius let them use his language.*

These things Arius either never heard, or heard and in his ignorance did not understand. For otherwise, had he understood, he would not have so grossly libelled the Bishop, but certainly would revile him also, as he did ourselves, because of his hatred of the truth. For being an adversary of Christ, he will not hesitate to persecute also those who hold the doctrine of Christ, as the Lord Himself has said beforehand: 'If they persecuted Me, they will also persecute you' (Joh. xv. 20). Or, if the leaders of impiety think Dionysius was a partisan of theirs, let them write and confess what he did. Let them write about the vine and the husbandman, the boat and the shipbuilder; and let them at the same time confess, as he did in his defence, the Unity of Essence, and that the Son is of the Father's Substance, and eternal; and the relation of intelligence and word, and the well and the river, and the rest; in order that they may see from the very contrast that he used the former class of language for a special purpose, but the latter as expressing the full meaning of the Christian Faith. And consequently let them, by adopting this language, revoke what they have held inconsistently with it. For in what way does the faith of Dionysius even approximate to the mischief of Arius? Does not Arius restrict the term Word to a conceptual sense, while Dionysius calls Him the true Word of God by nature? and while the one banishes the Word from the Father, the other teaches that He is the Father's own, and inseparable from His Essence, as the word is to the intelligence and the river to the well. If then any one is able to separate and banish the word from the intelligence, or to put asunder the river and the well, and wall them off, or to say that the river is of another essence than the well, and to shew that the water is from elsewhere, or ventures to divide the brightness from the light and to say that the brightness is from another essence, then let him join Arius in his madness. For such an one will cease to have the semblance even of human intelligence. But if Nature knows

8 See *Orat.* ii. 37. note 7.

that these are indivisible, and that the off-spring of those objects is their very own, then let no one any longer hold with Arius or slander Dionysius, but rather on these grounds admire the plainness of his language and the correctness of his faith.

25. The teaching of Dionysius on the Word (continued).

For with reference to the madness of Arius when he says that the Word which is in God is distinct from that one of which John said, 'In the beginning was the Word' (Joh. i. 1), and that God's own wisdom within Himself is not the same as that to which the Apostle refers as 'Christ the power of God and the wisdom of God' (1 Cor. i. 24), Dionysius resists and denounces any such error, as you may see in the second book where he writes on the subject as follows : '"In the beginning was the Word;" but it was not Word that sent forth the Word, for "the Word was with God." The Lord has been made wisdom (cf. 1 Cor. i. 30): He then that sent out Wisdom was not Wisdom, for "I was she," saith Wisdom, "in whom He delighted." Christ is truth: but "Blessed," saith He, "be the God of truth"' (1 Esdr. iv. 40). There He over-throws both Sabellius and Arius, and shews both heresies to be equal in impiety. For neither is the Father of the Word Himself Word, nor is the offspring of the Father a creature, but the Own-begotten of His essence. And again the Word that proceeded forth is not Father, nor again is He one word out of many ; but He alone is the Father's Son, the true and genuine Son by nature, Who both now is in Him, and is eternally and indivisibly from within Him. Thus the Lord is both Wisdom and Truth, and is not in the second place after another wisdom ; but He alone it is through whom the Father made all things, and in Him He made the manifold essences of created things, and through Him He is made known to whom He will, and in Him He carries on and effects His universal pro-vidence. For Him alone does Dionysius re-cognise as Word of God. This is the faith of Dionysius : for I have collected and copied a few statements from his letters, enough to induce you to add to their number, but to put the Arians to utter shame on account of their libel upon the Bishop. For in all, even the details, of what he wrote, he exposed their error and branded their heresy.

26. How Dionysius dealt with the Sabellians.

Hence too it is manifest that even the letter to Euphranor and Ammonius was written by him in a different sense and for a special pur-pose. For this his defence makes plain. And in truth this is an effective form of argument for the subversion of the madness of Sabellius, for him that wishes for a short way with those heretics, not to start from expressions applicable to the deity of the Word, such as that the Son is God's Word and Wisdom and Power, and that 'I and the Father are one' (John x. 30), lest they, perverting what is well said should use such expressions as a pretext for their un-blushing contentiousness, when they hear the texts, 'I and the Father are one,' and 'he that hath seen Me hath seen the Father.' (John x. 30, xiv. 9) ; but to emphasize what is said of the Saviour as Man, as He Himself has done, such as His hungering and thirsting, and being weary, and how He is the Vine, and how He prayed and has suffered. For in so far as these are lowly expressions, it becomes all the clearer that it was not the Father that was made man. For it follows, when the Lord is called the Vine, that there must also be a hus-bandman : and when He prayed, that there was one to hear, and when He asked, that there was one to give. Now such things shew far more readily the madness of the Sabellians, because He that prayed was one, He that heard another, one the Vine and another the Husbandman. For whatever expressions are cited to dis-tinguish between the Son and the Father are used of Him by reason of the flesh which He bore for our sake. For created things are dis-tinct in nature from God. Accordingly since, the flesh being a created thing, 'the Word,' as John says, 'was made flesh' (John i. 14), although He is by nature the Father's own and inseparable from Him, yet by reason of the flesh the Father is widely distinguished from Him. For He Himself permits that what is ap-propriate to the flesh should be said of him, that it may be made plain that the body was His own and not that of any other. But this being the sense of these sayings, Sabellius will be the more quickly confuted, it being proved that it was not the Father that was made flesh, but His Word, who also redeemed the flesh and offered it to the Father. But thus having con-futed and persuaded him, he will next be able more readily to teach him concerning the deity of the Word, how that He is the Word and Wisdom, Son and Power, Brightness and Express Image. For it is here again a neces-sary inference that as the Word exists, there must also exist the Father of the Word, and as Wisdom exists, there exists also its Parent, and as Brightness exists so also does the Light ; and that in this manner the Son and the Father are one.

27. *Conclusion.*

Dionysius knew this when he wrote.   And by his first letters he silenced Sabellius, and in his others he overcame the heresy of Arius. For just as the human attributes of the Saviour overthrew Sabellius, so against the Arian madmen one must use proofs drawn not from the human attributes but from what betokens the deity of the Word, lest they pervert what is said of the Lord by reason of His Body, and think that the Word is of like nature with us men, and so abide still in their madness. But if they also are taught about His deity they will condemn their own error ; and when they understand that the Word was made flesh, they too will the more easily distinguish in future the human characteristics from those which fit His deity.   But this being so, and the Bishop Dionysius having been shewn by his writings to be pious, what will the Arian madmen do next ? Convicted on this evidence, whom will they again venture to malign ? For they needs must, since they have fallen from the foundation of the Apostles and have no settled mind of their own, seek some support, and if they can find none, then malign the fathers.   But no one will believe them any more even if they make efforts to libel them, for the heresy is condemned on all hands.   Unless perchance they will henceforth speak of the devil, for he is their only partisan, or rather he it is who suggested their heresy to them.   Who then can any longer call men 'Christians' whose leader is the devil, and not rather 'Diabolici,' so that they may bear the name not merely of adversaries of Christ, but of partisans of the devil ? Unless indeed they change round, and, rejecting the impiety they have contrived, come to know the truth.   For this will at once be for their own good, and it is thus that it beseems us to pray for all those that are in error.

VITA S. ANTONI

(WRITTEN BETWEEN 356 AND 362)

THE Life of St. Antony is included in the present collection partly on account of the important influence it has exercised upon the development of the ascetic life in the Church, partly and more especially on the ground of its strong claim to rank as a work of Athanasius. If that claim were undisputed, no apology would be needed for its presence in this volume. If on the other hand its spurious and unhistorical character had been finally demonstrated, its insertion would be open to just objections. As it is, the question being still in dispute, although the balance of qualified opinion is on the side of the Athanasian authorship, it is well that the reader should have the work before him and judge for himself. To assist his judgment, it will be attempted in the following paragraphs to state the main reasons on either side. In doing so, I can honestly disclaim any bias for or against the *Vita*, or monasticism. Monasticism, with all its good and evil, is a great outgrowth of human life and instinct, a great fact in the history of the Christian religion; and whether its origin is to be put fifty years earlier or later (for that is the net value of the question at issue) is a somewhat small point relatively to the great problems which it offers to the theologian, the historian, and the moralist. But the point is at any rate worthy of careful and dispassionate examination. In attempting this, while holding no brief for either side, I may as well at once state my opinion on the evidence, namely that, genuine as are many of the difficulties which surround the question, the external evidence for the *Vita* is too strong to allow us to set it aside as spurious, and that in view of that evidence the attempts to give a positive account of the book as a spurious composition have failed.

1. BIBLIOGRAPHY. *a. Sources.* The only reference to Antony in other writings of Athanasius is in *Hist. Ar.* 14. See also *Fest. Index* x. *Vita Pachomii* in *Act. SS. Mai.*, Tom. iii. Appx. (written late in the fourth century, but by a person who had known Pachomius). *Coptic fragments and documents* (for early history of Egyptian monasticism with occasional details about Antony) in Zoega, *Catalogus codd. Copticorum*, (Rome, 1810), Mingarelli, *Codd. copticorum reliquiæ*, (Bologna, 1785), Revillout, *Rapport sur une mission*, etc. (in *Archives des Missions scientifiques et littéraires*, 3ᵐᵉ série, 1879, vol. 4), Amélineau, *Hist. de S. Pakhôme*, &c. (Annales du Musée Guimet, vol. xvii. Paris, 1889).

b. Modern discussions. Since the Reformation the general tendency of protestant writers has been to discredit, of Roman Catholics to maintain the authority of the Vita. To the former class belong the Magdeburg Centuriators, Rivet, Basnage, Casimir Oudin; to the latter, Bellarmin, Noel Alexandre, and above all Montfaucon in the Benedictine edition of Athanasius (especially in the *Vita Athanasii, Animadversio II. in Vitam et Scripta S.A.*, and the *Monitum in Antonii Vitam*, which latter may still claim the first rank in critical discussions of the problem). We may add, as more or less unbiassed defenders of the *Vita*, Cave (*Hist. Lit.* i. 193), and Tillemont (*Mem.* vol. vii.). All the above belong to the period before 1750. In more recent times the attack has been led by Weingarten (*Ursprung des Mönchtums in nachkonst. zeitalter*, reprinted in 1877 from *Zeitschrift für K.G.* 1876, and in Herzog, vol. x. pp. 758 sqq.), followed by Gass (in *Ztsch. K.G.* II. 274), and Gwatkin (*Studies*, &c. pp. 98—103). Israel, in *Zeitsch. Wiss. Theol.* 1880, p. 130, &c., characterises Weingarten's attack on the *Vita* as 'too bold.' Keim (*Aus dem Urchr.* 207 sqq.) and Hilgenfeld (*in Zeitsch. f. Wiss. Theol.* 1878) put the book in the lifetime of Ath. without absolutely pronouncing for him as the author, while Hase (*J. Prot. Th.* 1880), Harnack (especially in *Th. Ltz.* xi. 391, see also ' *Das Mönchtum*' *u.s.w.*, Giessen, 1886), Möller, *Lehrb. der K.G.* i. 372, and Eichhorn ('*Athanasii de vita ascetica testimonia*,' Halle, 1886, the most convincing discussion of recent date, and indispensable) decide without hesitation in its favour. The discussion of Bornemann (*In investigando monachatus origine, quibus de causis ratio habenda sit Origenis*, Leipzig, 1885) may also be mentioned as bearing on the general subject; also the articles 'Monastery,' 'Cœnobium,' and 'Hermits' in D.C.A. The article 'Antony' in D.C.B. passes over the question without discussion, excepting the trite, but untenable, statement that the *Vita* 'is probably interpolated.' Farrar (*Lives of the Fathers*, and *Contemp. Review*, Nov. 1887) follows Gwatkin. Picturesque representations of Antony (from the *Vita*) in Kingsley's *Hermits* and Newman's *Historical Sketches*, vol. 2.

2. EXTERNAL EVIDENCE AS TO AUTHORSHIP AND DATE. This is given by Montfaucon in the *Monitum* and reproduced by Eichhorn, pp. 36 sqq.

i. *The Version of Evagrius.* Evagrius, presbyter (Eustathian) and subsequently (388) Bishop at Antioch (in Italy 364—373), translated the *Vita Antonii* into Latin. He prefaced it with a short apology (see below, *Vit. Ant.* § 1, note 1) for the freedom of his rendering, addressed 'Innocentio carissimo filio.' Now this Innocent, the friend of Jerome and Evagrius, died in the summer of 374, almost exactly a year after the death of Athanasius (D.C.B. iii. 31, 251). Of this identification there is no reason to doubt; still less ground is there for the hesitation (*Hist. Lit.* I. 283, 'non una est dubitandi ratio') of Cave and others as to the identity of the version, printed by Montfaucon and transmitted by very numerous MSS. ('quæ ingenti numero vidi,' Migne xxv. p. clviii.) with that actually made by Evagrius. Therefore, even if we make the two very improbable assumptions that the Dedication to Innocentius falls within a few weeks or days of his death (i.e. during the journey from Italy to Syria!), and that the *Vita* was translated by Evagrius almost immediately upon its composition, the composition of the *Vita* falls within a few months of the death of Athanasius. Its antiquity then 'is fully conceded' even by Mr. Gwatkin (*Studies*, p. 103, who yet, p. 98, puts it down to 'the generation after Athanasius!'). The translation of Evagrius also preserves what looks like the original heading. It should be added that the Evagrian version (read in the light of its preface), entirely excludes the hypothesis that the Greek text of the *Vita* is interpolated. Evagrius avowedly abridges at times, while in some cases he embellishes (see § 82, note 16).

ii. Jerome wrote his *Vita Pauli* in the Syrian desert, between 374 and 379. He mentions both the *Vita* and its Latin Version in the prologue: if he had seen the latter he can scarcely have been ignorant of its heading. The non-mention of Athanasius as the author is an *argumentum ex silentio* of the most precarious kind. Some fifteen years later (*de Script. Eccles.* 87, 88, 125) he repeatedly mentions Athanasius as the author, and specifies Evagrius as the translator.

iii. Ephrem the Syrian (Opp. ed. 1732-43, I. p. 249) quotes 'Saint' Athanasius by name as the biographer of Antony. Ephrem died in 373. But little stress can be laid upon this testimony, in view of the lack of a critical sifting of the works which bear the name of this saint (so Tillemont viii. 229, and vii. 138). More important is

iv. Gregory Naz. *Or.* 21, 'Athanasius compiled the biography of the divine Antony τοῦ μοναδικοῦ βίου νομοθεσίαν ἐν πλάσματι διηγήσεως' (cf. *Vita*, Prologue). This oration was delivered in 380, seven years after the death of Athanasius. Gregory, it is true, is not a good judge on a point of criticism. But he expresses the opinion of his time, and confirms and is confirmed by the evidence of Evagrius and Jerome.

v. Rufinus, *Hist. Eccl.* I. viii. He would give an account of Antony, but 'ille libellus exclusit qui ab Athanasio scriptus etiam Latino Sermone editus est.' This was written 400 A.D.: if in a later work (*Hist. Mon.* 30, and see also 29) he happens to allude to the Vita without mentioning its author, we are not entitled to say that to Rufinus 'the work is anonymous' (Gwatkin, p. 103).

vi. The *Life of Pachomius*, which (as above mentioned) has details of Antony's life independent of the Vita, also mentions the latter (c. 1) as the work of Athanasius. Though written perhaps as late as 390, this document is of great weight as evidence in the case (see Krüger in *Theol. Ltzg.* 1890, p. 620).

vii. Paulinus in his prologue to the Life of Ambrose (after 400) refers to the *Vita* as written by Athanasius.

viii. Fifth-century historians, Palladius, *Hist. Laus.* 8, Socrates (*H. E.*, i. 21) Sozomenus (i. 13) attest the established tradition of their day that Athanasius was the author of the Life.

ix. Augustine (*Conf.* viii. 14, 15, 19, 29) and Chrysostom (*Hom.* 8 on S. Matthew) mention the *Vita* without giving the name of the author. But we are not entitled to cite them as witnesses to its (alleged) anonymity, which they neither affirm nor imply.

The above witnesses, all of whom excepting No. viii. come within 50 years of the death of Athanasius, are a formidable array. No other work of Athanasius can boast of such external evidence in its favour. And in the face of such evidence it is impossible to place the composition later than the lifetime of the great Bishop. We have therefore to ask whether the contents of the *Vita* are in irreconcileable conflict with the result of the external evidence: whether they point, not indeed to a later age, for the external evidence excludes this, but to an author who during the lifetime of Athanasius (i.e. not later than the year of his death) ventured to publish a hagiographic romance in his name (' Evagrian' heading, and §§ 71, 82).

3. INTERNAL EVIDENCE. It may be remarked *in limine* that for the existence of Antony there is not only the evidence of the *Vita* itself, but also that of many other fourth-century documents (see above 1. a. under ' sources '). Weingarten quite admits this (*R.E.,* X. 774, but he implies the contrary in his *Zeit-tafeln,* ed. 3, p. 228); and Mr. Gwatkin is certainly far ahead of his evidence when he pronounces (Arian Controversy, p. 48) that Antony ' never existed.'

a. *Origin and early history of Monasticism.* According to the *Vita,* the desert was unknown to μοναχοί (solitary ascetics) at the time (about 275? *Vit.* § 3) when Antony first adopted the ascetic life. About the year 285 he began his twenty years' sojourn in the ruined fort. To the end of this sojourn belongs the first great wave of Monastic settlement in the desert. During the later part of the great persecution ' monasteries ' and monks begin to abound (§ 44, 46). The remainder of his long life (311—356) is passed mainly in his ' inner mountain,' where he forms the head and centre of Egyptian monasticism. Now it is contended by Weingarten and his followers that the *Vita* is contradicted in this important particular by all the real evidence as to the origin of monasticism, which cannot be proved to have originated before the death of Constantine. But Eichhorn has I think conclusively shewn the hastiness of this assumption. Passing over the disputable evidence of the *De Vita Contemplativa* ascribed to Philo, (which Weingarten endeavours, against Lucius and others, to put back to a date much earlier than the third century and out of relation to Christian asceticism[1]), the writings of Athanasius himself are the sufficient refutation of the late date assigned to the rise of monachism.

In the writings of the supposed date (356—362) of the *Vita,* references to monks are very frequent (e.g. *Apol. Fug.* 4, *Apol. Const.* 29): but previous to this (339) we find them mentioned in *Encyl.* § 3, and yet earlier, *Apol. Ar.* 67 (see below). In the letter to Dracontius (*Letter* 49 in this vol.), corporate monasticism is implied to be no novel institution. Dracontius himself (about 354) is president of a monastery, and many other similar communities are referred to. (Gwatkin deals with this letter in an unsatisfactory fashion, p. 102, see the letter itself, §§ 7, 9, and notes.) The letter to Amun, probably earlier than that just mentioned, is clearly (sub. fin.) addressed to the head of a monastic society. Again, the bishops Muis and Paulus of *Letter* 49, § 7, who were monks before their consecration, had been in the monastery of Tabennæ before the death of Pachomius, which occurred almost certainly in 346 (Eichhorn 12, 13. The whole history of Pachomius, who was only a year or two older than Athanasius, although personally but little known to him, his monastery being at Tabennæ, an island near Philæ, is in conflict with Weingarten's theory). Lastly[2] one of the most characteristic and life-like of the documents relating to the case of Arsenius and the Council of Tyre, namely the letter of Pinnes to John Arcaph (*Apol. Ar.* 67) carries back the evidence earlier still. Pinnes is ' presbyter of a monastery ' (μονή): that μονή here means a society of monks, and not a posting station (Weing. in *R.E.,* X. p. 775) is clear from the mention of ' Helias the monk,' and ' I, Paphnutius, monk *of the same monastery.*' This letter proves that there were not only Catholic but Meletian monks, and these not hermits but in societies: and thus the origin of the solitary type of monasticism goes back as far as the Meletian schism. (The existence of Meletian monks is attested independently of this letter, see Eich. p. 347.) Weingarten is quite unable to deal with this obstacle to his theory. His argument is simply this: either the letter has nothing to do with monks and monasteries (he overlooks Paphnutius),

---

[1] See the note in Vol. I. of this Series, p. 117, D.C.B. iv. 368, *Theod. Ltzg.* xiii. 493—499.
[2] The silence of *Ep. Fest.* X. (338) is made much of by Weingarten, but there is nothing there to lead up to a reference to desert monasticism.

or it must be rejected as spurious! What *reductio ad absurdum* could be more complete? In an equally desperate way he deals with the clear evidence of Aphraates, *Hom.* vi., as to the existence of (at any rate) solitary monasticism in Eastern Syria as early as 336. See *Texte und Unter-suchungen* iii. 3, pp. xvi. 89, &c. (Leipzig, 1888.)

b. Historical misstatements. i. It is better to include under this head rather than under the last the title *ad peregrinos fratres*. Who were the 'foreign monks' (τοὺς ἐν τῇ ξένῃ μοναχούς)? The introduction of monasticism into the West seems to belong to the time of S. Ambrose (Aug. *Conf.* viii. 6, cf. Sozom. III. 14, 'the European nations [before 361] had no experience of monastic societies') or rather Martin of Tours (D.C.B. iii. p. 840). The statement (*Encycl. Brit.* 'Monachism') that Athanasius carried the *Vita Antonii* to Rome in 340 is based on a misunderstanding of Jerome (*Ep.* 127), who really says no more than that the existence of monachism in Egypt first became known at Rome from the visits of Athanasius and of his successor Peter. If then the 'peregrini fratres' are to be looked for in the West, we have a serious difficulty, and must choose between the *Vita* and Sozomen. But the foreign monks may have belonged to the East. (I cannot see that § 93 'assumes,' as Mr. Gwatkin maintains, 'the existence of numerous monks in the West.' What is said is simply that Antony had *been heard of* —ἠκούσθη—in Spain, Gaul, and Africa.) However, the point must be left uncertain, and so far allowed to weigh against the *Vita*.

ii. Early intercourse of Athanasius with Antony (Prologue, and note 2). If the Benedictine text is correct, the reference must be to the period before Athanasius became deacon to Bishop Alexander, in fact to a period previous to 318 A.D. Tillemont (viii. 652), who maintains the other reading, mainly relies upon the impossibility of finding room for the intercourse in question in the early life of Athanasius. But his only source of knowledge of that period is Rufinus, a very poor authority, and Montfaucon replies with some force (*Animadv.* 11) that we have no sufficient information as to how Athanasius passed the years previous to his ordination by Alexander. He also suggests that Athanasius may have been one of those who followed Antony's example (§ 46, cf. *Apol. c. Ar.* 6) after his first visit to Alexandria. I may add that the notes to the *Vita* will call attention to several points of contact between the teaching of Antony and the earliest treatises of Athanasius. Yet the impression left on the mind is here again one of uncertainty (cf. Prolegg. ch. ii. § 1 *fin.*).

iii. The narrative about Duke Balacius (§ 86 : see note there) is another genuine difficulty, only to be got over if we suppose *either* that Athanasius in one place tells the story inaccurately, and corrects himself in the other, *or* that the *Hist. Arian.* was partly written for Athanasius by a secretary.

iv. Supposed learning of Antony. His ignorance of letters and of the Greek language does not prevent his forcibly employing the most effective arguments against Arianism (69), vindicating the Incarnation (74) much in the manner of Athanasius, and above all showing a fair acquaintance (72—74) with Platonic philosophy (see notes there). But everything in the biography points to a man of robust mind, retentive memory (3) and frequent intercourse with visitors. If he were so, he can scarcely have been ignorant of the theological controversies of his day, or of the current philosophical ideas. Nor can I see that the philosophy of his argument against the Greeks goes beyond what that would imply. His allusion to Plato does not look like a first-hand citation. And even an Athanasius would not so entirely rise out of the biographical habits of his day as to mingle nothing of his own with the speeches of his hero ('Equidem quid Antonio quid Athanasio tribuendum sit uix diiudicari posse concedo,' Eich. p. 52).

c. Inconsistencies with Athanasius. It is the most serious objection to the Athanasian authorship of the *Vita* that Athanasius (with the exception of the 'antilegomenon' *Hist. Ar.* 14) nowhere else mentions Antony by name. Especially in the letter to Dracontius, who at first refused the Episcopate in the supposed interests of his soul, we might, it is argued, have expected a reference to the deep reverence of Antony (§ 67) for even the lowest clergy (the persons enumerated, *Letter* 49, § 7, are *bishops* who had previously been monks, and have nothing to do with this question). That is true. We *might* have expected it. But as a matter of fact Athanasius uses another argument instead (see *Letter* 49, § 3, note 8ª). It does not follow that he *did not know* of the Antony of the Vita. But although the letter in question has been pressed unduly, the general objection, as an *argumentum ex silentio* on a rather large scale, remains[3]. Some more detailed points must now be considered.

---

[3] It is fortified by the 'silence of Eusebius' (1) as to monks in general (but yet see *H. E.* II. 17, vol. 1, p. 116, note in this series)**;** (2) as to the part played by Antony at Alexandria during the persecution (*H. E.* VII. 32, VIII. 13, IX. 6) ; (3) as to Constantine's letter to Antony (§ 81).

a. Demons and Miracles. The writings of Athanasius are singularly free from the tendency to indulge in the marvellous. The death of Arius he regards as a judgment, and relates it with a certain awe-struck sobriety. The φήμη of Julian's death in the *Narrat. ad Ammon.* comes less under the head of ecclesiastical miracle than under that of τὰ θεῖα τῶν πρηγμάτων (Herod. ix. 100, cf. Grote v. 260 sq.); whereas the *Vita* swarms with miraculous and demoniacal stories, some (passed over in silence by Newman and other apologists for the Life) indescribably silly (e.g. §§ 53, 63). Hence even Cave allows that the *Vita* contains things 'tanto viro indigna.' But it must be observed (1) that Antony disclaims, and his biographer disclaims for him, inherent miraculous power. His miracles are wrought by Christ in answer to prayer, and he prefers that those who desire his help should obtain what they want by praying for themselves (cf. also § 49). (2) That again and again (esp. §§ 16—43) he insists on the absolute subjection of all evil powers to God, and their powerlessness to injure believers in Christ. (3) That Athanasius recognises σημεῖα (in the sense of miracles, see *Letter* 49, § 9, note 9) as a known phenomenon in the case both of bishops and of monks. (4) That his language about demons and the power of the sign of the Cross in dispersing them is quite of a piece with what is related in the *Vita* (see notes *passim*). (5) On the *clairvoyance* of Antony, and one or two kindred matters which offer points of contact with phenomena that have been recently the subject of careful research, notes will be found below giving modern references. On the whole, one could wish that Athanasius, who is in so many ways suprisingly in touch with the modern mind (*supra*, introd. to *de Incar.* and Prolegg. ch. iv. § 2 d and § 3), had not written a biography revealing such large credulity. But we must measure this credulity of his not by the evidential methods of our own day, but by those of his own. If we compare the *Vita*, not with our modern biographies but with those, say, of Paul and Hilarion by Jerome, its superiority is striking (this is pointed out by W. Israël in *Zeitschr. für Wiss. Theol.* 1878, pp. 130, 137, 145, 153). For myself, I should certainly prefer to believe that Athanasius had not written many things in the *Vita*: but I would far rather he had written them all than the one passage *Hist. Ar.* § 38 fin.

β. Theology. That there should be certain characteristic differences from the theology of Athanasius is what one would expect in an account of Antony that bore any relation to the historical person. Such is the anthropomorphic tendency, shewn especially in the corporeal nature ascribed to demons. Such perhaps is a tinge of naive semi-pelagianism about the Hermit's language (§ 20 and elsewhere); we cannot forget the connection of Cassian's Collations with Egyptian monasticism. Once again, 'Antony's shame of the body is not in the spirit of the writer *ad Amunem*' (Gwatkin, *Studies*, p. 102). Lastly, in Antony's account of the heathen gods (§ 76) we miss the characteristic Euhemerism of Athanasius (see *supra*, pp. 10, 62, &c.). Throughout, in fact, the ruder monastic instinct crops up from under the Athanasian style and thought of the biographer. But the latter is also unmistakeable (see the notes *passim*), and the differences have been certainly made too much of. I will give one example from Mr. Gwatkin, who says (*ubi supra*), 'Athanasius does not speak of πρόνοια like the *Vita* (*c.* 49, 66, 74), for *de Fuga* 25 specially refers to his providential escape from Syrianus, and *c. Gent.* 47, πρόνοια τῶν πάντων is very incidental.' Now certainly the constant introduction of πρόνοια, which Mr. Gwatkin has understated, is a marked feature of the *Vita*. But I am not prepared to say that Athanasius could not speak in this way. The word is common, and even characteristic, in his writings. A few examples will support this statement; more will be referred to in the index to this volume.

De Incarn. 2. 1.   τὴν τῶν ὅλων πρόνοιαν καθ᾽ ἑαυτῶν οὐκ εἶναι μυθολογοῦσιν.

14. 6.   τοῦ διὰ τῆς ἰδίας προνοίας . . . διδάσκοντος περὶ τοῦ πατρός.

Epist. Æg. 15.   βλέποντες . . . πάντα τάξει καὶ προνοίᾳ κινούμενα.

Apol. Fug. 17.   ἔμελε γὰρ αὐτοῖς . . . μήτε τὴν ὡρισμένην παρὰ τῆς Προνοίας κρίσιν προλαμβάνειν (and so in §§ 9, 16, 22, 25 of this short tract).

Orat. iii. 37.   ʽΟ Πατὴρ ἐν τῷ Ὑιῷ τῶν πάντων τὴν πρόνοιαν ποιεῖται.

If each one of these and numberless other references to Providence is 'very incidental,' those in the *Vita* may surely claim the benefit (whatever that may be) of the same formula.

The above are the principal materials for a decision as to the genuineness of the *Vita*: and I do not see how they can justify any opinion but that stated at the outset. Against the *Vita* we have certain historical difficulties (intercourse with Athanasius, peregrini fratres, Balacius), and arguments *ex silentio*, a kind of evidence seldom conclusive. For it, we have a quite unusual array of external evidence, including an almost contemporary version, the absence of any room for its date at a safe distance from its traditional author, and the many points of contact, as well as the characteristic differences between the *Vita* and the writings of Athanasius. Moreover on the kindred question of the origin of monasticism, Weingarten's theory breaks down, and leads him to suicidal steps in more than one direction. Although, therefore, it is permissible to keep an open mind on the subject, we must recognise that the enterprise of the recent assailants of the *Vita* is at present at a dead halt, that overwhelming probability is against them.

But if Athanasius wrote the *Vita*, it does not follow that all its less edifying details are true, nor that its portraiture is free from subjectivity[4]. At the same time, to the present writer at least, the lineaments of a genuine man, ὁμοιοπαθοῦς ἡμῖν, stand out from the story. Doubtless there is idealisation, panegyric, an absence of sinfulness (Gwatkin, *Studies*, p. 100). But the moderate value set on miracles (38, 56), the absence of the element of fear from his religion (42, &c.), his serene courtesy (73) and uniform cheerfulness (67, 70), the caution against being tempted to excess in ascetic exercises (25), the ready half-humorous good sense (73, 85) of the man, are human touches which belong to flesh and blood, not to hagiographic imagination. But here the question is one of individual taste. At any rate the *Vita* embodies the best spirit of early monasticism. It was the pure desire to serve God and fulfil the spirit of the Gospel that led Antony to part with all that might make the world precious to him, and to betake himself to his long voluntary martyrdom of solitude, privation, and prayer. We see nothing but tenderness and love of men in his character, nothing of the fierce bloodthirsty fanaticism which in persons like Senuti made fifth-century monasticism a reproach to the Christian name. Had Antony lived in our time, he might have felt that the solitary life was a renunciation of the highest vocation of which man is capable, the ministry to the material and spiritual needs of others. But it is not given to man to see all aspects of truth at once ; and to our bustling, comfort-loving age, even the life of Antony has its lesson.

The *Vita* has undoubtedly exercised a powerful and wide-spread influence. Upon it Jerome modelled his highly idealised tales of Paul and Hilarion ; at Rome and all over the West it kindled the flame of monastic aspirations ; it awoke in Augustine (*Conf.* viii. *ubi supra*) the resolution to renounce the world and give himself wholly to God. The *ingens numerus* of Latin manuscripts, and the imitation of its details in countless monastic biographies, testify to its popularity in the middle ages. Like monasticism itself, its good influence was not without alloy ; but on the whole we may claim for it that it tended to stimulate the nobler of the impulses which underlie the monastic life.

A few words may be added on the evidence of the *Vita* as to the form and motive of early monachism. In the Life of Antony, the stages are (1) ascetics living in the towns and villages, not withdrawn from society (§§ 3, 4) ; (2) solitary monasticism in the desert, away from human society ; and, as the fame of Antony increases, (3) the formation (§ 44) of clusters of cells centering round some natural leader, the *germ* of the λαύρα (such as the community of Tabennæ under Pachomius). Of organised monastic communities the *Vita* tells us nothing. With regard to the *motive* of the earliest monasticism, this has been variously sought in (1) the development of the ascetic element present in Christianity from the very first ; (2) in the influence of the Alexandrian School, especially Origen, who again is influenced by the spirit of revolt against the body and detachment from the world which characterised neo-Platonism (see Bornemann's work mentioned above) ; (3) in the persecutions, which drove Christians to the desert (Eus. *H. E.* vi. 42), which some adopted as their home ; (4) to the (not necessarily conscious) imitation of analogous heathen institutions, especially the societies of ἀγνεύοντες which were gathered round or in the temples of Serapis (Weingarten, *R.E.*, X. 779—785. Revillout, p. 480 n, refers to Zoega, p. 542, for the fact that Pachomius himself was a monk of Serapis before his forced baptism by his Christian neighbours ; and that after it he continued his ascetic life with no external difference. (5) To the desire to avoid civil obligations, already marked in the Rescript of Valens (*Cod. Th.* xii. 1. 63, quidam ignauiæ sectatores desertis civitatum muneribus, &c.). Of the above motives the *Vita* gives no support to any but the first, which it directly confirms, and perhaps indirectly to the second. The date of the *Vita* depends mainly on the view to be taken of § 82, where see note 16.

---

4 The life of Senuti (or 'Schnoudi'), by his disciple Visa, may be consulted in illustration of this point. See edition by Amélineau in vol. 4 of the *Memoires de la Mission archéologique Française au Caire*, 1888.

LIFE OF ANTONY

TABLE OF CONTENTS

[Antony's answers to a philosopher, and to Didymus, are given by Socrates IV. 23, 25: the following is from Hanmer's translation of Socr. I. 21: 'The same time lived Antony the monk in the deserts of Ægypt. But inasmuch as Athanasius, Bishop of Alexandria, hath lately set forth in a severall volume, intituled of his life, his manners and conversation, how openly he buckled with divils, how he over-reached their sleights and subtle combats, and wrought many marvellous and strange miracles, I think it superfluous on my part to intreat thereof.']

For the translation of the text I am indebted to my friend and colleague the Rev. H. Ellershaw, jun.

LIFE OF ANTONY

THE life and conversation of our holy Father, Antony: written and sent to the monks in foreign parts by our Father among the Saints, Athanasius, Bishop of Alexandria.

Athanasius [1] the bishop to the brethren in foreign parts.

You have entered upon a noble rivalry with the monks of Egypt by your determination either to equal or surpass them in your training in the way of virtue. For by this time there are monasteries among you, and the name of monk receives public recognition. With reason, therefore, all men will approve this determination, and in answer to your prayers God will give its fulfilment. Now since you asked me to give you an account of the blessed Antony's way of life, and are wishful to learn how he began the discipline, who and what manner of man he was previous to this, how he closed his life, and whether the things told of him are true, that you also may bring yourselves to imitate him, I very readily accepted your behest, for to me also the bare recollection of Antony is a great accession of help. And I know that you, when you have heard, apart from your admiration of the man, will be wishful to emulate his determination; seeing that for monks the life of Antony is a sufficient pattern of discipline. Wherefore do not refuse credence to what you have heard from those who brought tidings of him ; but think rather that they have told you only a few things, for at all events they scarcely can have given circumstances of so great import in any detail. And because I at your request have called to mind a few circumstances about him, and shall send as much as I can tell in a letter, do not neglect to question those who sail from here: for possibly when all have told their tale, the account will hardly be in proportion to his merits. On account of this I was desirous, when I received your letter, to send for certain of the monks, those especially who were wont to be more frequently with him, that if I could learn any fresh details I might send them to you. But since the season for sailing was coming to an end and the letter-carrier urgent, I hastened to write to your piety what I myself know, having seen him many times, and what I was able to learn from him, for I was his attendant for a long time, and poured water on his hands [2] ; in all points being mindful of the truth, that no one should disbelieve through hearing too much, nor on the other hand by hearing too little should despise the man.

1. Antony you must know was by descent an Egyptian : his parents were of good family and possessed considerable wealth [2a], and as they were Christians he also was reared in the same Faith. In infancy he was brought up with his parents, knowing nought else but them and his home. But when he was grown and arrived at boyhood, and was advancing in years, he could not endure to learn [2b] letters, not caring to associate with other boys; but all his desire was, as it is written of Jacob, to live a plain man at home [3]. With his parents he used to attend the Lord's House, and neither as a child was he idle nor when older did he despise them ; but was both obedient to his father and mother and attentive to what was read, keeping in his heart what was profitable in what he heard. And though as a child brought up in moderate affluence, he did not trouble his parents for varied or

---

[1] This heading, preserved in the Evagrian version, is probably the original one. Compare the statement to the same effect in *Vit. Pachom.* 63. The preface to the Evagrian version is important as bearing on the question of interpolation. It runs as follows: 'Evagrius, presbyter, to his dearest son Innocent, greeting in the Lord. A word-for-word translation from one language to another obscures the sense and as it were chokes the corn with luxuriant grass. For in slavishly following cases and constructions, the language scarcely explains by lengthy periphrasis what it might state by concise expression. To avoid this, I have at your request rendered the Life of the blessed Antony in such a way as to give the full sense, but cut short somewhat of the words. Let others try to catch syllables and letters ; do you seek the meaning.'

[2] Cf. 2 Kings iii. 11 : the expression merely refers to personal attendance (contrast §§ 47, 93). The text is uncertain, as some MSS. both Greek and Latin read, 'was able to learn *from him who* was his attendant,' &c. The question of textual evidence requires further sifting. In support of the statement in the text we may cite *Ap. c. Ar.* 6, where Ath. is called 'one of the ascetics,' which may, but need not, refer to something of the kind.
[2a] At Coma in Upper Egypt, see *Sozom.* i. 13.
[2b] Cf. St. Aug. *de Doctr. Christ.* Prologue.
[3] Gen. xxv. 27.

luxurious fare, nor was this a source of pleasure to him ; but was content simply with what he found nor sought anything further.

2. After the death of his father and mother he was left alone with one little sister : his age was about eighteen or twenty, and on him the care both of home and sister rested. Now it was not six months after the death of his parents, and going according to custom into the Lord's House, he communed with himself and reflected as he walked how the Apostles[4] left all and followed the Saviour ; and how they in the Acts[5] sold their possessions and brought and laid them at the Apostles' feet for distribution to then eedy, and what and how great a hope was laid up for them in heaven. Pondering over these things he entered the church, and it happened the Gospel was being read, and he heard the Lord saying to the rich man[6], 'If thou wouldest be perfect, go and sell that thou hast and give to the poor ; and come follow Me and thou shalt have treasure in heaven.' Antony, as though God had put him in mind of the Saints, and the passage had been read on his account, went out immediately from the church, and gave the possessions of his forefathers to the villagers—they were three hundred acres[7], productive and very fair —that they should be no more a clog upon himself and his sister[8]. And all the rest that was movable he sold, and having got together much money he gave it to the poor, reserving a little however for his sister's sake.

3. And again as he went into the church, hearing the Lord say in the Gospel[9], 'be not anxious for the morrow,' he could stay no longer, but went out and gave those things also to the poor. Having committed his sister to known and faithful virgins, and put her into a convent[10] to be brought up, he henceforth devoted himself outside his house to discipline[11], taking heed to himself and training himself with patience. For there were not yet so many monasteries[12] in Egypt, and no monk at all knew of the distant desert ; but all who wished to give heed to themselves practised the discipline in solitude near their own village. Now there was then in the next village an old man who had lived the life of a

hermit from his youth up. Antony, after he had seen this man, imitated him in piety. And at first he began to abide in places outside the village : then if he heard of a good man anywhere, like the prudent bee, he went forth and sought him, nor turned back to his own place until he had seen him ; and he returned, having got from the good man as it were supplies for his journey in the way of virtue. So dwelling there at first, he confirmed his purpose not to return to the abode of his fathers nor to the remembrance of his kinsfolk ; but to keep all his desire and energy for perfecting his discipline. He worked, however, with his hands, having heard, 'he who is idle let him not eat[13],' and part he spent on bread and part he gave to the needy. And he was constant in prayer, knowing that a man ought to pray in secret unceasingly[14]. For he had given such heed to what was read that none of the things that were written fell from him to the ground, but he remembered all, and afterwards his memory served him for books.

4. Thus conducting himself, Antony was beloved by all. He subjected himself in sincerity to the good men whom he visited, and learned thoroughly where each surpassed him in zeal and discipline. He observed the graciousness of one ; the unceasing prayer of another ; he took knowledge of another's freedom from anger and another's loving-kindness ; he gave heed to one as he watched, to another as he studied ; one he admired for his endurance, another for his fasting and sleeping on the ground ; the meekness of one and the long-suffering of another he watched with care, while he took note of the piety towards Christ and the mutual love which animated all. Thus filled, he returned to his own place of discipline, and henceforth would strive to unite the qualities of each, and was eager to show in himself the virtues of all. With others of the same age he had no rivalry ; save this only, that he should not be second to them in higher things. And this he did so as to hurt the feelings of nobody, but made them rejoice over him. So all they of that village and the good men in whose intimacy he was, when they saw that he was a man of this sort, used to call him God-beloved. And some welcomed him as a son, others as a brother.

5. But the devil, who hates and envies what is good, could not endure to see such a resolution in a youth, but endeavoured to carry out against him what he had been wont to effect against others. First of all he tried to lead him away from the discipline, whispering to him the remembrance of

---

4 Matt. iv. 20.　　5 Acts iv. 35.　　6 Matt. xix. 21.
7 ἄρουραι. The arura was 100 Egyptian cubits square, see *Herod.* ii. 168.
8 Or, perhaps, 'in order that they (the villagers) might have no occasion to trouble himself and his sister,' i.e. on condition of future immunity from taxes, &c. (so Neander).
9 Matt. vi. 34.
10 Παρθενών : the earliest use of the word in this sense. Perhaps a house occupied by Virgins is implied in *Apol. c. Ar.* 15. But at this time virgins generally lived with their families. See D.C.A. 2021ᵇ (the reference to Tertullian there is not relevant), Eichhorn, pp. 4, sqq., 28—30.
11 ἄσκησις (so throughout the *Vita*).
12 Probably the word has in this place the sense of a monk's cell (D.C.A. 1220), as below, § 39.

13 2 Thess. iii. 10.　　14 Matt. vi. 7 ; 1 Thess. v. 17.

his wealth, care for his sister, claims of kindred, love of money, love of glory, the various pleasures of the table and the other relaxations of life, and at last the difficulty of virtue and the labour of it; he suggested also the infirmity of the body and the length of the time. In a word he raised in his mind a great dust of debate, wishing to debar him from his settled purpose. But when the enemy saw himself to be too weak for Antony's determination, and that he rather was conquered by the other's firmness, overthrown by his great faith and falling through his constant prayers, then at length putting his trust in the weapons which are [15] 'in the navel of his belly' and boasting in them—for they are his first snare for the young—he attacked the young man, disturbing him by night and harassing him by day, so that even the onlookers saw the struggle which was going on between them. The one would suggest foul thoughts and the other counter them with prayers: the one fire him with lust, the other, as one who seemed to blush, fortify his body with faith, prayers, and fasting. And the devil, unhappy wight, one night even took upon him the shape of a woman and imitated all her acts simply to beguile Antony. But he, his mind filled with Christ and the nobility inspired by Him, and considering the spirituality of the soul, quenched the coal of the other's deceit. Again the enemy suggested the ease of pleasure. But he like a man filled with rage and grief turned his thoughts to the threatened fire and the gnawing worm, and setting these in array against his adversary, passed through the temptation unscathed. All this was a source of shame to his foe. For he, deeming himself like God, was now mocked by a young man; and he who boasted himself against flesh and blood was being put to flight by a man in the flesh. For the Lord was working with Antony—the Lord who for our sake took flesh [16] and gave the body victory over the devil, so that all who truly fight can say [17], 'not I but the grace of God which was with me.'

6. At last when the dragon could not even thus overthrow Antony, but saw himself thrust out of his heart, gnashing his teeth as it is written, and as it were beside himself, he appeared to Antony like a black boy, taking a visible shape [17a] in accordance with the colour of his mind. And cringing to him, as it were, he plied him with thoughts no longer, for guileful as he was, he had been worsted, but at last spoke in human voice and said, 'Many I deceived, many I cast down; but now attacking thee and thy labours as I had many others, I proved weak.' When Antony asked, Who art thou who speakest thus with me? he answered with a lamentable voice, 'I am the friend of whoredom, and have taken upon me incitements which lead to it against the young. I am called the spirit of lust. How many have I deceived who wished to live soberly, how many are the chaste whom by my incitements I have over-persuaded! I am he on account of whom also the prophet reproves those who have fallen, saying [17b], "Ye have been caused to err by the spirit of whoredom." For by me they have been tripped up. I am he who have so often troubled thee and have so often been overthrown by thee.' But Antony having given thanks to the Lord, with good courage said to him, 'Thou art very despicable then, for thou art black-hearted and weak as a child. Henceforth I shall have no trouble from thee [18], "for the Lord is my helper, and I shall look down on mine enemies."' Having heard this, the black one straightway fled, shuddering at the words and dreading any longer even to come near the man.

7. This was Antony's first struggle against the devil, or rather this victory was the Saviour's work in Antony [19], 'Who condemned sin in the flesh that the ordinance of the law might be fulfilled in us who walk not after the flesh but after the spirit.' But neither did Antony, although the evil one had fallen, henceforth relax his care and despise him; nor did the enemy as though conquered cease to lay snares for him. For again he went round as a lion seeking some occasion against him. But Antony having learned from the Scriptures that the devices [20] of the devil are many, zealously continued the discipline, reckoning that though the devil had not been able to deceive his heart by bodily pleasure, he would endeavour to ensnare him by other means. For the demon loves sin. Wherefore more and more he repressed the body and kept it in subjection [1], lest haply having conquered on one side, he should be dragged down on the other. He therefore planned to accustom himself to a severer mode of life. And many marvelled, but he himself used to bear the labour easily; for the eagerness of soul, through the length of time it had abode in him, had wrought a good habit in him, so that taking but little initiation from others he shewed great zeal in this matter. He kept vigil to such an extent that he often continued the

---

[15] Job xl. 16 (*v.* 11, LXX): the descriptions of behemoth and leviathan are allegorically referred to Satan, cf. *Orat.* i. 1, note 5. and below, § 24, *Ep. Æg.* 3.

[16] Cf. *de Incar.* 8. 2; 10. 5.   [17] 1 Cor. xv. 10.

[17a] For visible appearances of devils, see 'Phantasms of the Living,' vol. 2, p. 266, &c. (Trübner, 1886).

[17b] Hosea iv. 12.   [18] Ps. cxviii. 7.
[19] Rom. viii. 3 and 4.   [20] Eph. vi. 11.
[1] 1 Cor. ix. 27; Ath. (with many fathers and uncials) appears to have read ὑπωπιάζω, the reading which is followed by the Authorised Version.

whole night without sleep; and this not once but often, to the marvel of others. He ate once a day, after sunset, sometimes once in two days, and often even in four. His food was bread and salt, his drink, water only. Of flesh and wine it is superfluous even to speak, since no such thing was found with the other earnest men. A rush mat served him to sleep upon, but for the most part he lay upon the bare ground. He would not anoint himself with oil, saying it behoved young men to be earnest in training and not to seek what would enervate the body; but they must accustom it to labour, mindful of the Apostle's words[2], 'when I am weak, then am I strong.' 'For,' said he, 'the fibre of the soul is then sound when the pleasures of the body are diminished.' And he had come to this truly wonderful conclusion, 'that progress in virtue, and retirement from the world for the sake of it, ought not to be measured by time, but by desire and fixity of purpos . He at least gave no thought to the past, but day by day, as if he were at the beginning of his discipline, applied greater pains for advancement, often repeating to himself the saying of Paul[3]: 'Forgetting the things which are behind and stretching forward to the things which are before.' He was also mindful of the words spoken by the prophet Elias[4], 'the Lord liveth before whose presence I stand to-day.' For he observed that in saying 'to-day' the prophet did not compute the time that had gone by: but daily as though ever commencing he eagerly endeavoured to make himself fit to appear before God, being pure in heart and ever ready to submit to His counsel, and to Him alone. And he used to say to himself that from the life of the great Elias the hermit ought to see his own as in a mirror.

8. Thus tightening his hold upon himself, Antony departed to the tombs, which happened to be at a distance from the village; and having bid one of his acquaintances to bring him bread at intervals of many days, he entered one of the tombs, and the other having shut the door on him, he remained within alone. And when the enemy could not endure it, but was even fearful that in a short time Antony would fill the desert with the discipline, coming one night with a multitude of demons, he so cut him with stripes that he lay on the ground speechless from the excessive pain. For he affirmed that the torture had been so excessive that no blows inflicted by man could ever have caused him such torment. But by the Providence of God—for the Lord never overlooks them that hope

in Him—the next day his acquaintance came bringing him the loaves. And having opened the door and seeing him lying on the ground as though dead, he lifted him up and carried him to the church in the village, and laid him upon the ground. And many of his kinsfolk and the villagers sat around Antony as round a corpse. But about midnight he came to himself and arose, and when he saw them all asleep and his comrade alone watching, he motioned with his head for him to approach, and asked him to carry him again to the tombs without waking anybody.

9. He was carried therefore by the man, and as he was wont, when the door was shut he was within alone. And he could not stand up on account of the blows, but he prayed as he lay. And after he had prayed, he said with a shout, Here am I, Antony; I flee not from your stripes, for even if you inflict more nothing shall separate me[5] from the love of Christ. And then he sang, 'though a camp be set against me, my heart shall not be afraid[6].' These were the thoughts and words of this ascetic. But the enemy, who hates good, marvelling that after the blows he dared to return, called together his hounds and burst forth, 'Ye see,' said he, 'that neither by the spirit of lust nor by blows did we stay the man, but that he braves us, let us attack him in another fashion.' But changes of form for evil are easy for the devil, so in the night they made such a din that the whole of that place seemed to be shaken by an earthquake, and the demons as if breaking the four walls of the dwelling seemed to enter through them, coming in the likeness of beasts and creeping things. And the place was on a sudden filled with the forms of lions, bears, leopards, bulls, serpents, asps, scorpions, and wolves, and each of them was moving according to his nature. The lion was roaring, wishing to attack, the bull seeming to toss with its horns, the serpent writhing but unable to approach, and the wolf as it rushed on was restrained; altogether the noises of the apparitions, with their angry ragings, were dreadful. But Antony, stricken and goaded by them, felt bodily pains severer still. He lay watching, however, with unshaken soul, groaning from bodily anguish; but his mind was clear, and as in mockery he said, 'If there had been any power in you, it would have sufficed had one of you come, but since the Lord hath made you weak you attempt to terrify me by numbers: and a proof of your weakness is that you take the shapes of brute beasts.' And again with boldness he said, ' If you are able, and have received power

[2] 2 Cor xii. 10.   [3] Phil. iii. 14.   [4] 1 Kings xviii. 15.   [5] Rom. viii. 35.   [6] Ps. xxvii. 3.

against me, delay not to attack ; but if you are unable, why trouble me in vain ? For faith in our Lord is a seal and a wall of safety to us.' So after many attempts they gnashed their teeth upon him, because they were mocking themselves rather than him.

10. Nor was the Lord then forgetful of Antony's wrestling, but was at hand to help him. So looking up he saw the roof as it were opened, and a ray of light descending to him. The demons suddenly vanished, the pain of his body straightway ceased, and the building was again whole. But Antony feeling the help, and getting his breath again, and being freed from pain, besought the vision which had appeared to him, saying, 'Where wert thou ? Why didst thou not appear at the beginning to make my pains to cease?' And a voice came to him, 'Antony, I was here, but I waited to see thy fight ; wherefore since thou hast endured, and hast not been worsted, I will ever be a succour to thee, and will make thy name known everywhere.' Having heard this, Antony arose and prayed, and received such strength that he perceived that he had more power in his body than formerly. And he was then about thirty-five years old.

11. And on the day following he went forth still more eagerly bent on the service of God, and having fallen in with the old man he had met previously, he asked him to dwell with him in the desert. But when the other declined on account of his great age, and because as yet there was no such custom, Antony himself set off forthwith to the mountain. And yet again the enemy seeing his zeal and wishing to hinder it, cast in his way what seemed to be a great silver dish. But Antony, seeing the guile of the Evil One, stood, and having looked on the dish, he put the devil in it to shame, saying, 'Whence comes a dish in the desert? This road is not well-worn, nor is there here a trace of any wayfarer ; it could not have fallen without being missed on account of its size ; and he who had lost it having turned back to seek it, would have found it, for it is a desert place. This is some wile of the devil. O thou Evil One, not with this shalt thou hinder my purpose ; let it go with thee to destruction.[3]' And when Antony had said this it vanished like smoke from the face of fire.

12. Then again as he went on he saw what was this time not visionary, but real gold scattered in the way. But whether the devil showed it, or some better power to try the athlete and show the Evil One that Antony truly cared nought for money, neither he told nor do we know. But it is certain that that which

appeared was gold. And Antony marvelled at the quantity, but passed it by as though he were going over fire ; so he did not even turn, but hurried on at a run to lose sight of the place. More and more confirmed in his purpose, he hurried to the mountain, and having found a fort, so long deserted that it was full of creeping things, on the other side of the river ; he crossed over to it and dwelt there. The reptiles, as though some one were chasing them, immediately left the place. But he built up the entrance completely, having stored up loaves for six months—this is a custom of the Thebans, and the loaves often remain fresh a whole year—and as he found water within, he descended as into a shrine, and abode within by himself, never going forth nor looking at any one who came. Thus he employed a long time training himself, and received loaves, let down from above, twice in the year.

13. But those of his acquaintances who came, since he did not permit them to enter, often used to spend days and nights outside, and heard as it were crowds within clamouring, dinning, sending forth piteous voices and crying, ' Go from what is ours. What dost thou even in the desert? Thou canst not abide our attack.' So at first those outside thought there were some men fighting with him, and that they had entered by ladders ; but when stooping down they saw through a hole there was nobody, they were afraid, accounting them to be demons, and they called on Antony. Them he quickly heard, though he had not given a thought to the demons, and coming to the door he besought them to depart and not to be afraid, 'for thus,' said he, 'the demons make their seeming onslaughts against those who are cowardly. Sign yourselves therefore with the cross [4], and depart boldly, and let these make sport for themselves.' So they departed fortified with the sign of the Cross. But he remained in no wise harmed by the evil spirits, nor was he wearied with the contest, for there came to his aid visions from above, and the weakness of the foe relieved him of much trouble and armed him with greater zeal. For his acquaintances used often to come expecting to find him dead, and would hear him singing [5], ' Let God arise and let His enemies be scattered, let them also that hate Him flee before His face. As smoke vanisheth, let them vanish ; as wax melteth before the face of fire, so let the sinners perish from the face of God ;' and again, ' All nations compassed me about, and in the name of the Lord I requited them [6].'

---

3 Cf. Acts viii. 20.

4 Cf. de Incarn. xlvii. 2.   5 Ps. lxviii. 1.
6 Ps. cxviii. 10. Evagr. renders by ' vindicavi in eis.

14. And so for nearly twenty years he continued training himself in solitude, never going forth, and but seldom seen by any. After this, when many were eager and wishful to imitate his discipline, and his acquaintances came and began to cast down and wrench off the door by force, Antony, as from a shrine, came forth initiated in the mysteries and filled with the Spirit of God. Then for the first time he was seen outside the fort by those who came to see him. And they, when they saw him, wondered at the sight, for he had the same habit of body as before, and was neither fat, like a man without exercise, nor lean from fasting and striving with the demons, but he was just the same as they had known him before his retirement. And again his soul was free from blemish, for it was neither contracted as if by grief, nor relaxed by pleasure, nor possessed by laughter or dejection, for he was not troubled when he beheld the crowd, nor overjoyed at being saluted by so many. But he was altogether even as being guided by reason, and abiding in a natural state. Through him the Lord healed the bodily ailments of many present, and cleansed others from evil spirits. And He gave grace to Antony in speaking, so that he consoled many that were sorrowful, and set those at variance at one, exhorting all to prefer the love of Christ before all that is in the world. And while he exhorted and advised them to remember the good things to come, and the loving-kindness of God towards us, 'Who spared not His own Son, but delivered Him up for us all 7,' he persuaded many to embrace the solitary life. And thus it happened in the end that cells arose even in the mountains, and the desert was colonised by monks, who came forth from their own people, and enrolled themselves for the citizenship in the heavens.

15. But when he was obliged to cross the Arsenoitic Canal 8—and the occasion of it was the visitation of the brethren—the canal was full of crocodiles. And by simply praying, he entered it, and all they with him, and passed over in safety. And having returned to his cell, he applied himself to the same noble and valiant exercises ; and by frequent conversation he increased the eagerness of those already monks, stirred up in most of the rest the love of the discipline, and speedily by the attraction of his words. cells multiplied, and he directed them all as a father.

16. One day when he had gone forth because all the monks had assembled to him and asked to hear words from him, he spoke to them in the Egyptian tongue as follows: 'The Scriptures are enough for instruction 9, but it is a good

thing to encourage one another in the faith, and to stir up with words. Wherefore you, as children, carry that which you know to your father ; and I as the elder share my knowledge and what experience has taught me with you. Let this especially be the common aim of all, neither to give way having once begun, nor to faint in trouble, nor to say : We have lived in the discipline a long time : but rather as though making a beginning daily let us increase our earnestness. For the whole life of man is very short, measured by the ages to come, wherefore all our time is nothing compared with eternal life. And in the world everything is sold at its price, and a man exchanges one equivalent for another; but the promise of eternal life is bought for a trifle. For it is written, " The days of our life in them are threescore years and ten, but if they are in strength, fourscore years, and what is more than these is labour and sorrow 10." Whenever, therefore, we live full fourscore years, or even a hundred in the discipline, not for a hundred years only shall we reign, but instead of a hundred we shall reign for ever and ever. And though we fought on earth, we shall not receive our inheritance on earth, but we have the promises in heaven ; and having put off the body which is corrupt, we shall receive it incorrupt.

17. 'Wherefore, children, let us not faint nor deem that the time is long, or that we are doing something great, "for the sufferings of this present time are not worthy to be compared with the glory which shall be revealed to us-ward 11." Nor let us think, as we look at the world, that we have renounced anything of much consequence, for the whole earth is very small compared with all the heaven. Wherefore if it even chanced that we were lords of all the earth and gave it all up, it would be nought worthy of comparison with the kingdom of heaven. For as if a man should despise a copper drachma to gain a hundred drachmas of gold ; so if a man were lord of all the earth and were to renounce it, that which he gives up is little, and he receives a hundredfold. But if not even the whole earth is equal in value to the heavens, then he who has given up a few acres leaves as it were nothing ; and even if he have given up a house or much gold he ought not to boast nor be low-spirited. Further, we should consider that even if we do not relinquish them for virtue's sake, still afterwards when we die we shall leave them behind—very often, as the Preacher saith 12, to those to whom we do not wish. Why then should we not give them up for virtue's sake, that we may inherit even a kingdom? Therefore let the

Rom. viii. 32.   8 Between the Nile and the Fayûm.
9 Compare c. Gent. 1, de Synod. 6.

10 Ps. xc. 10. LXX.   11 Rom. viii. 18.   12 Eccl. iv. 8, vi. 2.

desire of possession take hold of no one, for what gain is it to acquire these things which we cannot take with us? Why not rather get those things which we can take away with us—to wit, prudence, justice, temperance, courage, understanding, love, kindness to the poor, faith in Christ, freedom from wrath, hospitality? If we possess these, we shall find them of themselves preparing for us a welcome there in the land of the meek-hearted.

18. 'And so from such things let a man persuade himself not to make light of it, especially if he considers that he himself is the servant of the Lord, and ought to serve his Master. Wherefore as a servant would not dare to say, because I worked yesterday, I will not work to-day; and considering the past will do no work in the future; but, as it is written in the Gospel, daily shows the same readiness to please his master, and to avoid risk: so let us daily abide firm in our discipline, knowing that if we are careless for a single day the Lord will not pardon us, for the sake of the past, but will be wrath against us for our neglect. As also we have heard in Ezekiel[13]; and as Judas because of one night destroyed his previous labour.

19. 'Wherefore, children, let us hold fast our discipline, and let us not be careless. For in it the Lord is our fellow-worker, as it is written, "to all that choose the good, God worketh with them for good[14]." But to avoid being heedless, it is good to consider the word of the Apostle, "I die daily[15]." For if we too live as though dying daily, we shall not sin. And the meaning of that saying is, that as we rise day by day we should think that we shall not abide till evening; and again, when about to lie down to sleep, we should think that we shall not rise up. For our life is naturally uncertain, and Providence allots it to us daily. But thus ordering our daily life, we shall neither fall into sin, nor have a lust for anything, nor cherish wrath against any, nor shall we heap up treasure upon earth. But, as though under the daily expectation of death, we shall be without wealth, and shall forgive all things to all men, nor shall we retain at all the desire of women or of any other foul pleasure. But we shall turn from it as past and gone, ever striving and looking forward to the day of Judgment. For the greater dread and danger of torment ever destroys the ease of pleasure, and sets up the soul if it is like to fall.

20. 'Wherefore having already begun and set out in the way of virtue, let us strive the more that we may attain those things that are before. And let no one turn to the things behind, like Lot's wife, all the more so that the Lord hath said, "No man, having put his hand to the plough, and turning back, is fit for the kingdom of heaven[16]." And this turning back is nought else but to feel regret, and to be once more worldly-minded. But fear not to hear of virtue, nor be astonished at the name. For it is not far from us, nor is it without ourselves, but it is within us, and is easy if only we are willing. That they may get knowledge, the Greeks live abroad and cross the sea, but we have no need to depart from home for the sake of the kingdom of heaven, nor to cross the sea for the sake of virtue. For the Lord aforetime hath said, "The kingdom of heaven is within you[17]." Wherefore virtue hath need at our hands of willingness alone, since it is in us and is formed from us. For when the soul hath its spiritual faculty in a natural state virtue is formed. And it is in a natural state when it remains as it came into existence. And when it came into existence it was fair and exceeding honest. For this cause Joshua, the son of Nun, in his exhortation said to the people, "Make straight your heart unto the Lord God of Israel[18]," and John, "Make your paths straight[19]." For rectitude of soul consists in its having its spiritual part in its natural state as created. But on the other hand, when it swerves and turns away from its natural state, that is called vice of the soul. Thus the matter is not difficult. If we abide as we have been made, we are in a state of virtue, but if we think of ignoble things we shall be accounted evil. If, therefore, this thing had to be acquired from without, it would be difficult in reality; but if it is in us, let us keep ourselves from foul thoughts. And as we have received the soul as a deposit, let us preserve it for the Lord, that He may recognise His work as being the same as He made it.

21. 'And let us strive that wrath rule us not nor lust overcome us, for it is written, "The wrath of man worketh not the righteousness of God. And lust, when it hath conceived, beareth sin, and the sin when it is full grown bringeth forth death[20]." Thus living, let us keep guard carefully, and as it is written, "keep our hearts with all watchfulness[1]." For we have terrible and crafty foes—the evil spirits—and against them we wrestle, as the Apostle said, "Not against flesh and blood, but against the principalities and against the powers, against the world-rulers of this darkness, against the spiritual hosts of wickedness in the heavenly places[1a]." Great is their

---

13 Ezek. xviii. 26. 14 Rom. viii. 28, R.V. Marg.
15 1 Cor. xv. 31.

16 Phil. iii. 13; Gen. xix. 26; Luke ix. 62.
17 Luke xvii. 21 (from memory). 18 Josh. xxiv. 23.
19 Matt. iii. 3. 20 James i. 20 and 15.
1 Prov. iv. 23. 1a Eph. vi. 12.

number in the air around us[a], and they are not far from us. Now there are great distinctions among them; and concerning their nature and distinctions much could be said, but such a description is for others of greater powers than we possess. But at this time it is pressing and necessary for us only to know their wiles against ourselves.

22. 'First, therefore, we must know this: that the demons have not been created like what we mean when we call them by that name; for God made nothing evil, but even they have been made good. Having fallen, however, from the heavenly wisdom, since then they have been grovelling on earth. On the one hand they deceived the Greeks with their displays, while out of envy of us Christians they move all things in their desire to hinder us from entry into the heavens; in order that we should not ascend up thither from whence they fell. Thus there is need of much prayer and of discipline, that when a man has received through the Spirit the gift of discerning spirits, he may have power to recognise their characteristics: which of them are less and which more evil; of what nature is the special pursuit of each, and how each of them is overthrown and cast out. For their villainies and the changes in their plots are many. The blessed Apostle and his followers knew such things when they said, "for we are not ignorant of his devices[3];" and we, from the temptations we have suffered at their hands, ought to correct one another under them. Wherefore I, having had proof of them, speak as to children.

23. 'The demons, therefore, if they see all Christians, and monks especially, labouring cheerfully and advancing, first make an attack by temptation and place hindrances to hamper our way, to wit, evil thoughts. But we need not fear their suggestions, for by prayer, fasting, and faith in the Lord their attack immediately fails. But even when it does they cease not, but knavishly by subtlety come on again. For when they cannot deceive the heart openly with foul pleasures they approach in different guise, and thenceforth shaping displays they attempt to strike fear, changing their shapes, taking the forms of women, wild beasts, creeping things, gigantic bodies, and troops of soldiers. But not even then need ye fear their deceitful displays. For they are nothing and quickly disappear, especially if a man fortify himself beforehand with faith and the sign of the cross[4]. Yet are

they bold and very shameless, for if thus they are worsted they make an onslaught in another manner, and pretend to prophesy and foretell the future, and to shew themselves of a height reaching to the roof and of great breadth; that they may stealthily catch by such displays those who could not be deceived by their arguments. If here also they find the soul strengthened by faith and a hopeful mind, then they bring their leader to their aid.

24. 'And he said they often appeared as the Lord revealed the devil to Job, saying, "His eyes are as the morning star. From his mouth proceed burning lamps and hearths of fire are cast forth. The smoke of a furnace blazing with the fire of coals proceeds from his nostrils. His breath is coals and from his mouth issues flame[5]." When the prince of the demons appears in this wise, the crafty one, as I said before, strikes terror by speaking great things, as again the Lord convicted him saying to Job, for "he counteth iron as straw, and brass as rotten wood, yea he counteth the sea as a pot of ointment, and the depth of the abyss as a captive, and the abyss as a covered walk[6]." And by the prophet, "the enemy said, I will pursue and overtake[7]," and again by another, "I will grasp the whole world in my hand as a nest, and take it up as eggs that have been left[8]." Such, in a word, are their boasts and professions that they may deceive the godly. But not even then ought we, the faithful, to fear his appearance or give heed to his words. For he is a liar and speaketh of truth never a word. And though speaking words so many and so great in his boldness, without doubt, like a dragon he was drawn with a hook by the Saviour[9], and as a beast of burden he received the halter round his nostrils, and as a runaway his nostrils were bound with a ring, and his lips bored with an armlet[10]. And he was bound by the Lord as a sparrow, that we should mock him. And with him are placed the demons his fellows, like serpents and scorpions to be trodden underfoot by us Christians. And the proof of this is that we now live opposed to him. For he who threatened to dry the sea and seize upon the world, behold now cannot stay our discipline, nor even me speaking against him. Let us then heed not his words, for he is a liar: and let us not fear his visions, seeing that they themselves are deceptive. For that which appears in them is no true light, but they are rather the preludes and likenesses of the fire prepared for the demons who attempt to terrify men with those flames in which they themselves will be burned. Doubt-

---

[a] This is not quite the view of Athanasius himself, who regards the air as cleared of evil spirits by the Death of Christ, *de Incar.* xxv. 5: but Athan. does not mean that their power *over the wicked* is done away; nor does Antony ascribe to them any power over the Christian, see §§ 24, 28, 41.

[3] 2 Cor. ii. 11.   [4] See above, § 13.

[5] Job xli. 18, 19, 20 (vv. 9—11, LXX.), see above § 5, note 15.
[6] Job xli. 27 sq.   [7] Exod. xv. 9.   [8] Isai. x. 14, cf. *Ep. Æg.* 2.
[9] Job xli. 1.   [10] Ibid. 2. Cf. Job xl. 19—24.

less they appear; but in a moment disappear again, hurting none of the faithful, but bringing with them the likeness of that fire which is about to receive themselves. Wherefore it is unfitting that we should fear them on account of these things; for through the grace of Christ all their practices are in vain.

25. 'Again they are treacherous, and are ready to change themselves into all forms and assume all appearances. Very often also without appearing they imitate the music of harp and voice, and recall the words of Scripture. Sometimes, too, while we are reading they immediately repeat many times, like an echo, what is read. They arouse us from our sleep to prayers; and this constantly, hardly allowing us to sleep at all. At another time they assume the appearance of monks and feign the speech of holy men, that by their similarity they may deceive and thus drag their victims where they will. But no heed must be paid them even if they arouse to prayer, even if they counsel us not to eat at all, even though they seem to accuse and cast shame upon us for those things which once they allowed. For they do this not for the sake of piety or truth, but that they may carry off the simple to despair; and that they may say the discipline is useless, and make men loathe the solitary life as a trouble and burden, and hinder those who in spite of them walk in it.

26. 'Wherefore the prophet sent by the Lord declared them to be wretched, saying : "Wo is he who giveth his neighbours to drink muddy destruction¹¹." For such practices and devices are subversive of the way which leads to virtue. And the Lord Himself, even if the demons spoke the truth,—for they said truly : "Thou art the Son of God¹²"—still bridled their mouths and suffered them not to speak ; lest haply they should sow their evil along with the truth, and that He might accustom us never to give heed to them even though they appear to speak what is true. For it is unseemly that we, having the holy Scriptures and freedom from the Saviour, should be taught by the devil who hath not kept his own order but hath gone from one mind to another¹³. Wherefore even when he uses the language of Scripture He forbids him, saying: "But to the sinner said God, Wherefore dost thou declare My ordinances and takest My covenant in thy mouth¹⁴ ?" For the demons do all things —they prate, they confuse, they dissemble, they confound— to deceive the simple. They din, laugh madly, and whistle ; but if no heed

is paid to them forthwith they weep and lament as though vanquished.

27. 'The Lord therefore, as God, stayed the mouths of the demons : and it is fitting that we, taught by the saints, should do like them and imitate their courage. For they when they saw these things used to say : "When the sinner rose against me, I was dumb and humble, and kept silence from good words¹⁵." And again : "But I was as a deaf man and heard not, and as a dumb man who openeth not his mouth, and I became as a man who heareth not¹⁶." So let us neither hear them as being strangers to us, nor give heed to them even though they arouse us to prayer and speak concerning fasting. But let us rather apply ourselves to our resolve of discipline, and let us not be deceived by them who do all things in deceit, even though they threaten death. For they are weak and can do nought but threaten.

28. 'Already in passing I have spoken on these things, and now I must not shrink from speaking on them at greater length, for to put you in remembrance will be a source of safety. Since the Lord visited earth¹⁷, the enemy is fallen and his powers weakened. Wherefore although he could do nothing, still like a tyrant, he did not bear his fall quietly, but threatened, though his threats were words only. And let each one of you consider this, and he will be able to despise the demons. Now if they were hampered with such bodies as we are, it would be possible for them to say, "Men when they are hidden we cannot find, but whenever we do find them we do them hurt." And we also by lying in concealment could escape them, shutting the doors against them. But if they are not of such a nature as this, but are able to enter in, though the doors be shut, and haunt all the air, both they and their leader the devil, and are wishful for evil and ready to injure ; and, as the Saviour said, "From the beginning the devil is a manslayer and a father of vice¹⁸ ;" while we, though this is so, are alive, and spend our lives all the more in opposing him ; it is plain they are powerless. For place is no hindrance to their plots, nor do they look on us as friends that they should spare us ; nor are they lovers of good that they should amend. But on the contrary they are evil, and nothing is so much sought after by them as wounding them that love virtue and fear God. But since they have no power to effect anything, they do nought but threaten. But if they could, they would not

¹¹ Habak. ii. 15. LXX. ¹² Luke iv. 41. ¹³ ἕτερα ἀνθ' ἑτέρων, as in de Incar. 11. 4. ¹⁴ Ps. l. 16, Ep. Æg. 3. ¹⁵ Ps. xxxix. 2. ¹⁶ Ps. xxxviii. 14. ¹⁷ Cf. de Incar. 47, 48. ¹⁸ John viii. 44.

hesitate, but forthwith work evil (for all their desire is set on this), and especially against us. Behold now we are gathered together and speak against them, and they know when we advance they grow weak. If therefore they had power they would permit none of us Christians to live, for godliness is an abomination to a sinner[9]. But since they can do nothing they inflict the greater wounds on themselves; for they can fulfil none of their threats. Next this ought to be considered, that we may be in no fear of them: that if they had the power they would not come in crowds, nor fashion displays, nor with change of form would they frame deceits. But it would suffice that one only should come and accomplish that which he was both able and willing to do: especially as every one who has the power neither slays with display nor strikes fear with tumult, but forthwith makes full use of his authority as he wishes. But the demons as they have no power are like actors on the stage changing their shape and frightening children with tumultuous apparition and various forms: from which they ought rather to be despised as shewing their weakness. At least the true angel of the Lord sent against the Assyrian had no need for tumults, nor displays from without, nor noises nor rattlings, but in quiet he used his power and forthwith destroyed a hundred and eighty-five thousand. But demons like these, who have no power, try to terrify at least by their displays[20].

29. 'But if any one having in mind the history of Job[1] should say, Why then hath the devil gone forth and accomplished all things against him; and stripped him of all his possessions, and slew his children, and smote him with evil ulcers? let such a one, on the other hand, recognise that the devil was not the strong man, but God who delivered Job to him to be tried. Certainly he had no power to do anything, but he asked, and having received it, he hath wrought what he did. So also from this the enemy is the more to be condemned, for although willing he could not prevail against one just man. For if he could have, he would not have asked permission. But having asked not once but also a second time, he shows his weakness and want of power. And it is no wonder if he could do nothing against Job, when destruction would not have come even on his cattle had not God allowed it. And he has not the power over swine, for as it is written in the Gospel, they besought the Lord, saying, "Let us enter the swine[2]." But if they had power not even against swine, much less have they any over men formed[3] in the image of God.

30. 'So then we ought to fear God only, and despise the demons, and be in no fear of them. But the more they do these things the more let us intensify our discipline against them, for a good life and faith in God is a great weapon. At any rate they fear the fasting, the sleeplessness, the prayers, the meekness, the quietness, the contempt of money and vainglory, the humility, the love of the poor, the alms, the freedom from anger of the ascetics, and, chief of all, their piety towards Christ. Wherefore they do all things that they may not have any that trample on them, knowing the grace given to the faithful against them by the Saviour, when He says, "Behold I have given to you power to tread upon serpents and scorpions, and upon all the power of the enemy[4]."

31. 'Wherefore if they pretend to foretell the future, let no one give heed, for often they announce beforehand that the brethren are coming days after. And they *do* come. The demons, however, do this not from any care for the hearers, but to gain their trust, and that then at length, having got them in their power, they may destroy them. Whence we must give no heed to them, but ought rather to confute them when speaking, since we do not need them. For what wonder is it, if with more subtle bodies than men have[5], when they have seen them start on their journey, they surpass them in speed, and announce their coming? Just as a horseman getting a start of a man on foot announces the arrival of the latter beforehand, so in this there is no need for us to wonder at them. For they know none of those things which are not yet in existence; but God only is He who knoweth all things before their birth[6]. But these, like thieves, running off first with what they see, proclaim it: to how many already have they announced our business—that we are assembled together, and discuss measures against them, before any one of us could go and tell these things. This in good truth a fleet-footed boy could do, getting far ahead of one less swift. But what I mean is this. If any one begins to walk from the Thebaid, or from any other district, before he begins to walk, they do not know whether he will walk. - But when they have seen him walking they run on, and before he comes up report his approach. And so it

---

[9] Ecclesiasticus i. 25.   [20] 2 Kings xix. 35.
     [1] Job i. and ii.

[2] Matt. viii. 31.   [3] Cf. *de Incar.* 3. 3, and *passim.*
[4] Luke x. 19.
[5] This materialistic view of demons may be paralleled from Origen and other fathers (D.C.B. i. 809), but is not Athanasian. But it would be congenial to the Coptic mind; compare the story told by Cassian of the Monk Serapion, who, on being convinced that 'God is a Spirit,' cried out, 'You have taken my God from me' (and see D.C.B. i. p. 120).   [6] Susann. 42.

falls out that after a few days the travellers arrive. But often the walkers turn back, and the demons prove false.

32. 'So, too, with respect to the water of the river, they sometimes make foolish statements. For having seen that there has been much rain in the regions of Ethiopia, and knowing that they are the cause of the flood of the river, before the water has come to Egypt they run on and announce it. And this men could have told, if they had as great power of running as the demons. And as David's spy[7] going up to a lofty place saw the man approaching better than one who stayed down below, and the forerunner himself announced, before the others came up, not those things which had not taken place, but those things which were already on the way and were being accomplished, so these also prefer to labour, and declare what is happening to others simply for the sake of deceiving them. If, however, Providence meantime plans anything different for the waters or wayfarers—for Providence can do this—the demons are deceived, and those who gave heed to them cheated.

33. 'Thus in days gone by arose the oracles of the Greeks, and thus they were led astray by the demons. But thus also thenceforth their deception was brought to an end by the coming of the Lord[8], who brought to nought the demons and their devices. For they know nothing of themselves, but, like thieves, what they get to know from others they pass on, and guess at rather than foretell things. Therefore if sometimes they speak the truth, let no one marvel at them for this. For experienced physicians also, since they see the same malady in different people, often foretell what it is, making it out by their acquaintance with it. Pilots, too, and farmers, from their familiarity with the weather, tell at a glance the state of the atmosphere, and forecast whether it will be stormy or fine. And no one would say that they do this by inspiration, but from experience and practice. So if the demons sometimes do the same by guesswork, let no one wonder at it or heed them. For what use to the hearers is it to know from them what is going to happen before the time? Or what concern have we to know such things, even if the knowledge be true? For it is not productive of virtue, nor is it any token of goodness. For none of us is judged for what he knows not, and no one is called blessed because he hath learning and knowledge. But each one will be called to judgment in these points—whether he have kept the faith and truly observed the commandments.

34. 'Wherefore there is no need to set much value on these things, nor for the sake of them to practise a life of discipline and labour; but that living well we may please God. And we neither ought to pray to know the future, nor to ask for it as the reward of our discipline; but our prayer should be that the Lord may be our fellow-helper for victory over the devil. And if even once we have a desire to know the future, let us be pure in mind, for I believe that if a soul is perfectly pure and in its natural state, it is able[9], being clear-sighted, to see more and further than the demons—for it has the Lord who reveals to it—like the soul of Elisha, which saw what was done[10] by Gehazi, and beheld the hosts[11] standing on its side.

35. 'When, therefore, they come by night to you and wish to tell the future, or say, " we are the angels," give no heed, for they lie. Yea even if they praise your discipline and call you blessed, hear them not, and have no dealings with them; but rather sign yourselves and your houses, and pray, and you shall see them vanish. For they are cowards, and greatly fear the sign of the Lord's Cross, since of a truth in it the Saviour stripped them, and made an example of them[11a]. But if they shamelessly stand their ground, capering and changing their forms of appearance, fear them not, nor shrink, nor heed them as though they were good spirits. For the presence either of the good or evil by the help of God can easily be distinguished. The vision of the holy ones is not fraught with distraction: "For they will not strive, nor cry, nor shall any one hear their voice[12]." But it comes so quietly and gently that immediately joy, gladness and courage arise in the soul. For the Lord who is our joy is with them, and the power of God the Father. And the thoughts of the soul remain unruffled and undisturbed, so that it, enlightened as it were with rays, beholds by itself those who appear. For the love of what is divine and of the things to come possesses it, and willingly it would be wholly joined with them if it could depart along with them. But if, being men, some fear the vision of the good, those who appear immediately take fear away; as Gabriel[13] did in the case of Zacharias, and as the angel[14] did who appeared to the women at the holy

---

9 Compare below, §§ 59, 62, for examples. This quite goes beyond any teaching of Athanasius himself; at the same time it finds a point of contact in what he says about dreams in *c. Gent.* 30 (μαντευόμενος καὶ προγιγνώσκων), and about the soul's capacity for objective thought, ib. 33, *de Incar.* 17. 3.
10 2 Kings v. 26.   11 2 Kings vi. 17.   11a Col. ii. 15.
12 Matt. xii. 19, cf. Isai. xlii. 2.   13 Luke i. 13.
14 Matt. xxviii. 5.

7 2 Sam. xviii. 24.   8 *De Incar.* 47.

sepulchre, and as He did who said to the shepherds in the Gospel, "Fear not." For their fear arose not from timidity, but from the recognition of the presence of superior beings. Such then is the nature of the visions of the holy ones.

36. 'But the inroad and the display of the evil spirits is fraught with confusion, with din, with sounds and cryings such as the disturbance of boorish youths or robbers would occasion. From which arise fear in the heart, tumult and confusion of thought, dejection, hatred towards them who live a life of discipline, indifference, grief, remembrance of kinsfolk and fear of death, and finally desire of evil things, disregard of virtue and unsettled habits. Whenever, therefore, ye have seen ought and are afraid, if your fear is immediately taken away and in place of it comes joy unspeakable, cheerfulness, courage, renewed strength, calmness of thought and all those I named before, boldness and love toward God,—take courage and pray. For joy and a settled state of soul show the holiness of him who is present. Thus Abraham beholding the Lord rejoiced [14]; so also John [15] at the voice of Mary, the God-bearer [16], leaped for gladness. But if at the appearance of any there is confusion, knocking without, worldly display, threats of death and the other things which I have already mentioned, know ye that it is an onslaught of evil spirits.

37. 'And let this also be a token for you: whenever the soul remains fearful there is a presence of the enemies. For the demons do not take away the fear of their presence as the great archangel Gabriel did for Mary and Zacharias, and as he did who appeared to the women at the tomb; but rather whenever they see men afraid they increase their delusions that men may be terrified the more; and at last attacking they mock them, saying, "fall down and worship." Thus they deceived the Greeks, and thus by them they were considered gods, falsely so called. But the Lord did not suffer us to be deceived by the devil, for He rebuked him whenever he framed such delusions against Him, saying: "Get behind me, Satan: for it is written, Thou shalt worship the Lord thy God, and Him only shalt thou serve [17]." More and more, therefore, let the deceiver be despised by us; for what the Lord hath said, this for our sakes He hath done: that the demons hearing like words from us may be put to flight through the Lord who rebuked them in those words.

38. 'And it is not fitting to boast at the casting forth of the demons, nor to be uplifted by the healing of diseases: nor is it fitting that he who casts out devils should alone be highly esteemed, while he who casts them not out should be considered nought. But let a man learn the discipline of each one and either imitate, rival, or correct it. For the working of signs is not ours but the Saviour's work: and so He said to His disciples: "Rejoice not that the demons are subject to you, but that your names are written in the heavens [18]." For the fact that our names are written in heaven is a proof of our virtuous life, but to cast out demons is a favour of the Saviour who granted it. Wherefore to those who boasted in signs but not in virtue, and said: "Lord, in Thy name did we not cast out demons, and in Thy name did many mighty works [19]?" He answered, "Verily I say unto you, I know you not;" for the Lord knoweth not the ways of the wicked. But we ought always to pray, as I said above, that we may receive the gift of discerning spirits; that, as it is written [20], we may not believe every spirit.

39. 'I should have liked to speak no further and to say nothing from my own promptings, satisfied with what I have said: but lest you should think that I speak at random and believe that I detail these things without experience or truth; for this cause even though I should become as a fool, yet the Lord who heareth knoweth the clearness of my conscience, and that it is not for my own sake, but on account of your affection towards me and at your petition that I again tell what I saw of the practices of evil spirits. How often have they called me blessed and I have cursed them in the name of the Lord! How often have they predicted the rising of the river, and I answered them, "What have you to do with it?" Once they came threatening and surrounded me like soldiers in full armour. At another time they filled the house with horses, wild beasts and creeping things, and I sang: "Some in chariots and some in horses, but we will boast in the name of the Lord our God [1];" and at the prayers they were turned to flight by the Lord. Once they came in darkness, bearing the appearance of a light, and said, "We are come to give thee a light, Antony." But I closed my eyes and prayed, and immediately the light of the wicked ones was quenched. And a few months after they came as though singing psalms and babbling the words of Scripture, "But I like a deaf man, heard not [2]." Once they shook the cell [3] with an earthquake, but I continued praying with unshaken heart. And

---

[14] John viii. 56.   [15] Luke i. 41.
[16] θεοτόκος, as in *Orat.* iii. 14 (where see note 3).
[17] Matt. iv. 10.

[18] Luke x. 20.   [19] Matt. vii. 22.
[20] 1 John iv. 1.   [1] Ps. xx. 7.
[2] Ps. xxxviii. 14.   [3] μοναστήριον.

after this they came again making noises, whistling and dancing. But as I prayed and lay singing psalms to myself they forthwith began to lament and weep, as if their strength had failed them. But I gave glory to the Lord, who had brought down and made an example of their daring and madness.

40. 'Once a demon exceeding high appeared with pomp, and dared to say, "I am the power of God and I am Providence, what dost thou wish that I shall give thee?" But I then so much the more breathed upon him [3a], and spoke the name of Christ, and set about to smite him. And I seemed to have smitten him, and forthwith he, big as he was, together with all his demons, disappeared at the name of Christ. At another time, while I was fasting, he came full of craft, under the semblance of a monk, with what seemed to be loaves, and gave me counsel, saying, "Eat and cease from thy many labours. Thou also art a man and art like to fall sick." But I, perceiving his device, rose up to pray; and he endured it not, for he departed, and through the door there seemed to go out as it were smoke. How often in the desert has he displayed what resembled gold, that I should only touch it and look on it. But I sang psalms against him, and he vanished away. Often they would beat me with stripes, and I repeated again and again, "Nothing shall separate me from the love of Christ [4]," and at this they rather fell to beating one another. Nor was it I that stayed them and destroyed their power, but it was the Lord, who said, "I beheld Satan as lightning fall from Heaven [5];" but I, children, mindful of the Apostle's words, transferred [6] this to myself, that you might learn not to faint in discipline, nor to fear the devil nor the delusions of the demons.

41. 'And since I have become a fool in detailing these things, receive this also as an aid to your safety and fearlessness; and believe me for I do not lie. Once some one knocked at the door of my cell, and going forth I saw one who seemed of great size and tall. Then when I enquired, "Who art thou?" he said, "I am Satan." Then when I said, "Why art thou here?" he answered, "Why do the monks and all other Christians blame me undeservedly? Why do they curse me hourly?" Then I answered, "Wherefore dost thou trouble them?" He said, "I am not he who troubles them, but they trouble themselves, for I am become weak. Have they not read [7], "The swords of the enemy have come to an end, and thou hast destroyed the cities?" I have no longer a place, a weapon, a city.

The Christians are spread everywhere, and at length even the desert is filled with monks. Let them take heed to themselves, and let them not curse me undeservedly." Then I marvelled at the grace of the Lord, and said to him: "Thou who art ever a liar and never speakest the truth, this at length, even against thy will, thou hast truly spoken. For the coming of Christ hath made thee weak, and He hath cast thee down and stripped thee." But he having heard the Saviour's name, and not being able to bear the burning from it, vanished.

42. 'If, therefore, the devil himself confesses that his power is gone, we ought utterly to despise both him and his demons; and since the enemy with his hounds has but devices of this sort, we, having got to know their weakness, are able to despise them. Wherefore let us not despond after this fashion, nor let us have a thought of cowardice in our heart, nor frame fears for ourselves, saying, I am afraid lest a demon should come and overthrow me; lest he should lift me up and cast me down; or lest rising against me on a sudden he confound me. Such thoughts let us not have in mind at all, nor let us be sorrowful as though we were perishing; but rather let us be courageous and rejoice always, believing that we are safe. Let us consider in our soul that the Lord is with us, who put the evil spirits to flight and broke their power. Let us consider and lay to heart that while the Lord is with us, our foes can do us no hurt. For when they come they approach us in a form corresponding to the state in which they discover us [8], and adapt their delusions to the condition of mind in which they find us. If, therefore, they find us timid and confused, they forthwith beset the place, like robbers, having found it unguarded; and what we of ourselves are thinking, they do, and more also. For if they find us faint-hearted and cowardly, they mightily increase our terror, by their delusions and threats; and with these the unhappy soul is thenceforth tormented. But if they see us rejoicing in the Lord, contemplating the bliss of the future, mindful of the Lord, deeming all things in His hand, and that no evil spirit has any strength against the Christian, nor any power at all over any one— when they behold the soul fortified with these thoughts—they are discomfited and turned backwards. Thus the enemy, seeing Job fenced round with them, withdrew from him; but finding Judas unguarded, him he took captive. Thus if we are wishful to despise the enemy, let us ever ponder over the things of the Lord, and let the soul ever rejoice in hope. And we

---

3a See D.C.A. p. 652.   4 Rom. viii. 35.
5 Luke x. 18.   6 1 Cor. iv. 6.   7 Ps. ix. 6.

8 'An important psychological observation.' (Schaff, *Ch. Hist.*)

shall see the snares of the demon are like smoke, and the evil ones themselves flee rather than pursue. For they are, as I said before, exceeding fearful, ever looking forward to the fire prepared for them.

43. 'And for your fearlessness against them hold this sure sign—whenever there is any apparition, be not prostrate with fear, but whatsoever it be, first boldly ask, Who art thou? And from whence comest thou? And if it should be a vision of holy ones they will assure you, and change your fear into joy. But if the vision should be from the devil, immediately it becomes feeble, beholding your firm purpose of mind. For merely to ask, Who art thou? and whence comest thou? is a proof of coolness. By thus asking, the son of Nun learned who his helper was; nor did the enemy escape the questioning of Daniel [10].'

44. While Antony was thus speaking all rejoiced; in some the love of virtue increased, in others carelessness was thrown aside, the self-conceit of others was stopped; and all were persuaded to despise the assaults of the Evil One, and marvelled at the grace given to Antony from the Lord for the discerning of spirits. So their cells were in the mountains, like tabernacles, filled with holy bands of men who sang psalms, loved reading, fasted, prayed, rejoiced in the hope of things to come, laboured in alms-giving, and preserved love and harmony one with another. And truly it was possible, as it were, to behold a land set by itself, filled with piety and justice. For then there was neither the evil-doer, nor the injured, nor the reproaches of the tax-gatherer: but instead a multitude of ascetics; and the one purpose of them all was to aim at virtue. So that any one beholding the cells again, and seeing such good order among the monks, would lift up his voice and say, 'How goodly are thy dwellings, O Jacob, and thy tents, O Israel; as shady glens and as a garden[11] by a river; as tents which the Lord hath pitched, and like cedars near waters[12].'

45. Antony, however, according to his custom, returned alone to his own cell, increased his discipline, and sighed daily as he thought of the mansions in Heaven, having his desire fixed on them, and pondering over the shortness of man's life. And he used to eat and sleep, and go about all other bodily necessities with shame when he thought of the spiritual faculties of the soul. So often, when about to eat with any other hermits, recollecting the spiritual food, he begged to be excused, and departed far off from them, deeming it a matter for shame if he should be seen eating by others. He used, however, when by himself, to eat through bodily necessity, but often also with the brethren; covered with shame on these occasions, yet speaking boldly words of help. And he used to say that it behoved a man to give all his time to his soul rather than his body, yet to grant a short space to the body through its necessities; but all the more earnestly to give up the whole remainder to the soul and seek its profit, that it might not be dragged down by the pleasures of the body, but, on the contrary, the body might be in subjection to the soul. For this is that which was spoken by the Saviour: 'Be not anxious for your life what ye shall eat, nor for your body what ye shall put on. And do ye seek not what ye shall eat, or what ye shall drink, and be not of a doubtful mind. For all these things the nations of the world seek after. But your Father knoweth that ye have need of all these things. Howbeit seek ye first His Kingdom, and all these things shall be added unto you[13].'

46. After this the Church was seized by the persecution which then[14] took place under Maximinus, and when the holy martyrs were led to Alexandria, Antony also followed, leaving his cell, and saying, Let us go too, that if called, we may contend or behold them that are contending. And he longed to suffer martyrdom, but not being willing to give himself up, he ministered to the confessors in the mines and in the prisons. And he was very zealous in the judgment hall to stir up to readiness those who were summoned when in their contest, while those who were being martyred he received and brought on their way until they were perfected. The judge, therefore, beholding the fearlessness of Antony and his companions, and their zeal in this matter, commanded that no monk should appear in the judgment hall, nor remain at all in the city. So all the rest thought it good to hide themselves that day, but Antony gave so little heed to the command that he washed his garment, and stood all next day on a raised place before them, and appeared in his best before the governor. Therefore when all the rest wondered at this, and the governor saw and passed by with his array, he stood fearlessly, shewing the readiness of us Christians. For, as I said before, he prayed himself to be a martyr, wherefore he seemed as one grieved that he had not borne his witness. But the Lord was keeping him for our profit and that of others, that he should become a teacher to many of the discipline which he had learned from the Scriptures. For many only beholding his manner of life were eager to be imitators

of his ways. So he again ministered as usual to the confessors, and as though he were their fellow captive he laboured in his ministry.

47. And when at last the persecution ceased, and the blessed Bishop Peter[15] had borne his testimony, Antony departed, and again withdrew to his cell, and was there daily a martyr to his conscience, and contending in the conflicts of faith. And his discipline was much severer, for he was ever fasting, and he had a garment of hair on the inside, while the outside was skin, which he kept until his end. And he neither bathed his body with water to free himself from filth, nor did he ever wash his feet, nor even endure so much as to put them into water, unless compelled by necessity. Nor did any one even see him unclothed, nor his body naked at all, except after his death, when he was buried.

48. When therefore he had retired and determined to fix a time, after which neither to go forth himself nor admit anybody, Martinian, a military officer, came and disturbed Antony. For he had a daughter afflicted with an evil spirit. But when he continued for a long while knocking at the door, and asking him to come out and pray to God for his child, Antony, not bearing to open, looked out from above and said, 'Man, why dost thou call on me? I also am a man even as you. But if you believe on Christ whom I serve, go, and according as you believe, pray to God, and it shall come to pass.' Straightway, therefore, he departed, believing and calling upon Christ, and he received his daughter cleansed from the devil. Many other things also through Antony the Lord did, who saith, 'Seek and it shall be given unto you[16].' For many of the sufferers, when he would not open his door, slept outside his cell, and by their faith and sincere prayers were healed.

49. But when he saw himself beset by many, and not suffered to withdraw himself according to his intent as he wished, fearing because of the signs which the Lord wrought by him, that either he should be puffed up, or that some other should think of him above what he ought to think, he considered and set off to go into the upper Thebaid, among those to whom he was unknown. And having received loaves from the brethren, he sat down by the bank of the river, looking whether a boat would go by, that, having embarked thereon, he might go up the river with them. While he was considering these things, a voice came to him from above, 'Antony, whither goest thou and wherefore?' But he no way disturbed, but as he had been accustomed to be called[16a] often thus,

giving ear to it, answered, saying, 'Since the multitude permit me not to be still, I wish to go into the upper Thebaid on account of the many hindrances that come upon me here, and especially because they demand of me things beyond my power.' But the voice said unto him, 'Even though you should go into the Thebaid, or even though, as you have in mind, you should go down to the Bucolia[17], you will have to endure more, aye, double the amount of toil. But if you wish really to be in quiet, depart now into the inner desert.' And when Antony said, 'Who will show me the way for I know it not?' immediately the voice pointed out to him Saracens about to go that way. So Antony approached, and drew near them, and asked that he might go with them into the desert. And they, as though they had been commanded by Providence, received him willingly. And having journeyed with them three days and three nights, he came to a very lofty mountain, and at the foot of the mountain ran a clear spring, whose waters were sweet and very cold; outside there was a plain and a few uncared-for palm trees.

50. Antony then, as it were, moved by God, loved the place[18], for this was the spot which he who had spoken with him by the banks of the river had pointed out. So having first received loaves from his fellow travellers, he abode in the mountain alone, no one else being with him. And recognising it as his own home, he remained in that place for the future. But the Saracens, having seen the earnestness of Antony, purposely used to journey that way, and joyfully brought him loaves, while now and then the palm trees also afforded him a poor and frugal relish. But after this, the brethren learning of the place, like children mindful of their father, took care to send to him. But when Antony saw that the bread was the cause of trouble and hardships to some of them, to spare the monks this, he resolved to ask some of those who came to bring him a spade, an axe, and a little corn. And when these were brought, he went over the land round the mountain, and having found a small plot of suitable ground, tilled it; and having a plentiful supply of water for watering, he sowed. This doing year by year, he got his bread from thence, rejoicing that thus he would be troublesome to no one, and because he kept himself from being a burden to anybody. But after this, seeing again that people came, he cultivated a few pot-herbs, that he who came to him might have some slight solace after the labour

15 Martyred on Nov. 25, 311, cf. Eus. H.E. vii. 32.
16 Luke xi. 9   16a See on this subject 'Phantasms of the Living,' vol. 1, p. 480 sq (Trübner, 1886).

17 In Lower Egypt.
18 Mount Colzim, seven hours distant from the Red Sea, where an old cloister still preserves his name and memory (Schaff, Ch. Hist. Nic. p. 183).

of that hard journey. At first, however, the wild beasts in the desert, coming because of the water, often injured his seeds and husbandry. But he, gently laving hold of one of them, said to them all, 'Why do you hurt me, when I hurt none of you? Depart, and in the name of the Lord come not nigh this spot.' And from that time forward, as though fearful of his command, they no more came near the place.

51. So he was alone in the inner mountain, spending his time in prayer and discipline. And the brethren who served him asked that they might come every month and bring him olives, pulse and oil, for by now he was an old man. There then he passed his life, and endured such great wrestlings, 'Not against flesh and blood [19],' as it is written, but against opposing demons, as we learned from those who visited him. For there they heard tumults, many voices, and, as it were, the clash of arms. At night they saw the mountain become full of wild beasts, and him also fighting as though against visible beings, and praying against them. And those who came to him he encouraged, while kneeling he contended and prayed to the Lord. Surely it was a marvellous thing that a man, alone in such a desert, feared neither the demons who rose up against him, nor the fierceness of the four-footed beasts and creeping things, for all they were so many. But in truth, as it is written, 'He trusted in the Lord as Mount Sion [20],' with a mind unshaken and undisturbed; so that the demons rather fled from him, and the wild beasts, as it is written [21], 'kept peace with him.'

52. The devil, therefore, as David says in the Psalms [1], observed Antony and gnashed his teeth against him. But Antony was consoled by the Saviour and continued unhurt by his wiles and varied devices. As he was watching in the night the devil sent wild beasts against him. And almost all the hyenas in that desert came forth from their dens and surrounded him; and he was in the midst, while each one threatened to bite. Seeing that it was a trick of the enemy he said to them all: 'If ye have received power against me I am ready to be devoured by you; but if ye were sent against me by demons, stay not, but depart, for I am a servant of Christ.' When Antony said this they fled, driven by that word as with a whip.

53. A few days after, as he was working (for he was careful to work hard), some one stood at the door and pulled the plait which he was working, for he used to weave baskets, which he gave to those who came in return for what

they brought him. And rising up he saw a beast like a man to the thighs but having legs and feet like those of an ass. And Antony only signed himself and said, 'I am a servant of Christ. If thou art sent against me, behold I am here.' But the beast together with his evil spirits fled, so that, through his speed, he fell and died. And the death of the beast was the fall of the demons. For they strove in all manner of ways to lead Antony from the desert and were not able.

54. And once being asked by the monks to come down and visit them and their abodes after a time, he journeyed with those who came to him. And a camel carried the loaves and the water for them. For all that desert is dry, and there is no water at all that is fit to drink, save in that mountain from whence they drew the water, and in which Antony's cell was. So when the water failed them on their way, and the heat was very great, they all were in danger. For having gone round the neighbourhood and finding no water, they could walk no further, but lay on the ground and despairing of themselves, let the camel go. But the old man seeing that they were all in jeopardy, groaning in deep grief, departed a little way from them, and kneeling down he stretched forth his hands and prayed. And immediately the Lord made water to well forth where he had stood praying, and so all drank and were revived. And having filled their bottles they sought the camel and found her, for the rope happened to have caught in a stone and so was held fast. Having led it and watered it they placed the bottles on its back and finished their journey in safety. And when he came to the outer cells all saluted him, looking on him as a father. And he too, as though bringing supplies from the mountain, entertained them with his words and gave them a share of help. And again there was joy in the mountains, zeal for improvement and consolation through their mutual faith. Antony also rejoiced when he beheld the earnestness of the monks, and his sister grown old in virginity, and that she herself also was the leader of other virgins.

55. So after certain days he went in again to the mountain. And henceforth many resorted to him, and others who were suffering ventured to go in. To all the monks therefore who came to him, he continually gave this precept: 'Believe on the Lord and love Him; keep yourselves from filthy thoughts and fleshly pleasures, and as it is written in the Proverbs, be not deceived "by the fulness of the belly [2]." Pray continually; avoid vain-

---

[19] Eph. vi. 12.   [20] Ps. cxxv. 1.   [21] Job v. 23.
[1] Ps. xxxv. 16.

[2] Prov. xxiv. 15, LXX.

glory; sing psalms before sleep and on awaking; hold in your heart the commandments of Scripture ; be mindful of the works of the saints that your souls being put in remembrance of the commandments may be brought into harmony with the zeal of the saints.' And especially he counselled them to meditate continually on the apostle's word, 'Let not the sun go down upon your wrath[3].' And he considered this was spoken of all commandments in common, and that not on wrath alone, but not on any other sin of ours, ought the sun to go down. For it was good and needful that neither the sun should condemn us for an evil by day nor the moon for a sin by night, or even for an evil thought. That this state may be preserved in us it is good to hear the apostle and keep his words, for he says, 'Try your own selves and prove your own selves[4].' Daily, therefore, let each one take from himself the tale of his actions both by day and night ; and if he have sinned, let him cease from it ; while if he have not, let him not be boastful. But let him abide in that which is good, without being negligent, nor condemning his neighbours, nor justifying himself, 'until the Lord come who searcheth out hidden things[5],' as saith the blessed apostle Paul. For often unawares we do things that we know not of ; but the Lord seeth all things. Wherefore committing the judgment to Him, let us have sympathy one with another. Let us bear each other's burdens[6] : but let us examine our own selves and hasten to fill up that in which we are lacking. And as a safeguard against sin let the following be observed. Let us each one note and write down our actions and the impulses of our soul as though we were going to relate them to each other. And be assured that if we should be utterly ashamed to have them known, we shall abstain from sin and harbour no base thoughts in our mind. For who wishes to be seen while sinning? or who will not rather lie after the commission of a sin, through the wish to escape notice? As then while we are looking at one another, we would not commit carnal sin, so if we record our thoughts as though about to tell them to one another, we shall the more easily keep ourselves free from vile thoughts through shame lest they should be known. Wherefore let that which is written be to us in place of the eyes of our fellow hermits, that blushing as much to write as if we had been caught, we may never think of what is unseemly. Thus fashioning ourselves we shall be able to keep the body in subjection, to please the Lord, and to trample on the devices of the enemy.

56. This was the advice he gave to those who came to him. And with those who suffered he sympathised and prayed. And ofttimes the Lord heard him on behalf of many : yet he boasted not because he was heard, nor did he murmur if he were not. But always he gave the Lord thanks and besought the sufferer to be patient, and to know that healing belonged neither to him nor to man at all, but only to the Lord, who doeth good when and to whom He will. The sufferers therefore used to receive the words of the old man as though they were a cure, learning not to be downhearted but rather to be long-suffering. And those who were healed were taught not to give thanks to Antony but to God alone.

57. Wherefore a man, Fronto by name, who was an officer of the Court and had a terrible disease, for he used to bite his own tongue and was in danger of injury to his eyes, having come to the mountain, asked Antony to pray for him. But Antony said to him, 'Depart and thou shalt be healed.' But when he was violent and remained within some days, Antony waited and said, 'If thou stayest here, thou canst not be healed. Go, and having come into Egypt thou shall see the sign wrought in thee.' And he believed and went. And as soon as he set eyes on Egypt his sufferings ceased, and the man became whole according to the word of Antony, which the Saviour had revealed to him in prayer.

58. There was also a maiden from Busiris Tripolitana, who had a terrible and very hideous disorder. For the runnings of her eyes, nose, and ears fell to the ground and immediately became worms. She was paralysed also and squinted. Her parents having heard of monks going to Antony, and believing on the Lord who healed [7] the woman with the issue of blood, asked to be allowed, together with their daughter, to journey with them. And when they suffered them, the parents together with the girl, remained outside the mountain with Paphnutius, the confessor and monk ; but the monks went in to Antony. And when they only wished to tell about the damsel, he anticipated them, and detailed both the sufferings of the child and how she journeyed with them. Then when they asked that she should be admitted, Antony did not allow it, but said, 'Go, and if she be not dead, you will find her healed: for the accomplishment of this is not mine, that she should come to me, wretched man that I am,

---

3 Eph. iv. 26. 4 2 Cor. xiii. 5.
5 1 Cor. iv. 5 ; Rom. ii. 16. 6 Gal. vi. 6.

7 Matt. ix. 20.

but her healing is the work of the Saviour, who in every place sheweth His pity to them that call upon Him. Wherefore the Lord hath inclined to her as she prayed, and His loving-kindness hath declared to me that He will heal the child where she now is.' So the wonder took place; and going out they found the parents rejoicing and the girl whole.

59. But when two brethren were coming to him, the water failed on the way, and one died and the other was at the point of death, for he had no strength to go on, but lay upon the ground expecting to die. But Antony sitting in the mountain called two monks, who chanced to be there, and urged them saying, 'Take a pitcher of water and run on the road towards Egypt. For of two men who were coming, one is already dead and the other will die unless you hasten. For this has been revealed to me as I was praying.' The monks therefore went, and found one lying dead, whom they buried, and the other they restored with water and led him to the old man. For it was a day's journey[7a]. But if any one asks, why he did not speak before the other died, the question ought not to be asked. For the punishment of death was not Antony's but God's, who also judged the one and revealed the condition of the other. But the marvel here was only in the case of Antony: that he, sitting in the mountain had his heart watchful, and had the Lord to show him things afar off.

60. And this is so, for once again he was sitting on the mountain, and looking up saw in the air some one being borne upwards, and there was much joy among those who met him. Then wondering and deeming a company of that kind to be blessed, he prayed to learn what this might be. And immediately a voice came to him : 'This is the soul of Amun, the monk at Nitria.' Now Amun had persevered in the discipline up to old age; and the distance from Nitria to the mountain where Antony was, was thirteen days' journey. The companions of Antony therefore, seeing the old man amazed, asked to learn, and heard that Amun was just dead[8]. And he was well known, for he had stayed there very often, and many signs had been wrought by his means. And this is one of them. Once when he had need to cross the river called Lycus (now it was the season of the flood), he asked his comrade Theodorus to remain at a distance, that they should not see one another naked as they swam the water. Then when Theodorus was departed he again felt ashamed even to see

himself naked. While, therefore, he was pondering filled with shame, on a sudden he was borne over to the other side. Theodorus, therefore, himself being a good man, approached, and seeing Amun across first without a drop of water falling from him, enquired how he had got over. And when he saw that Amun was unwilling to tell him, he held him by the feet and declared that he would not let him go before he had learned it from him. So Amun seeing the determination of Theodorus especially from what he had said, and having asked him to tell no man before his death, told him that he had been carried and placed on the further side. And that he had not even set foot on the water, nor was that possible for man, but for the Lord alone and those whom He permits, as He did for the great apostle Peter[9]. Theodorus therefore told this after the death of Amun. And the monks to whom Antony spoke concerning Amun's death marked the day; and when the brethren came up from Nitria thirty days after, they enquired of them and learned that Amun had fallen asleep at that day and hour in which the old man had seen his soul borne upwards. And both these and the others marvelled at the purity of Antony's soul, how he had immediately learned that which was taking place at a distance of thirteen days' journey, and had seen the soul as it was taken up.

61. And Archelaus too, the Count, on a time having found him in the outer mountain, asked him merely to pray for Polycratia of Laodicea, an excellent and Christian[9a] maiden, for she suffered terribly in the stomach and side through over much discipline, and was altogether weakly of body. Antony prayed therefore, and the Count noted the day in which the prayer was made, and having departed to Laodicea he found the maiden whole. And having enquired when and on what day she was relieved of her infirmity, he produced the paper on which he had written the time of the prayer, and having read it he immediately shewed the writing on the paper. And all wondered when they knew that the Lord had relieved her of pain at the time when Antony was praying and invoking the goodness of the Saviour on her behalf.

62. And concerning those who came to him, he often foretold some days or sometimes a month beforehand what was the cause of their coming. For some came only for the sake of seeing him, others through sickness, and others suffering from evil spirits. And all thought the labour of the journey neither trouble nor loss. For each one returned

---

[7a] For similar cases, cf. 'Phantasms of the Living,' vol. 2, p. 368, &c.
[8] The same story is told (by Bede in his Life) of St. Cuthbert, who saw the soul of St. Aidan being carried to heaven. Amun was probably the recipient of the letter, No. 48 in this volume.

[9] Matt. xiv. 28.　　[9a] Χριστοφόρος, lit. Christ-bearing.

aware that he had received benefit. But though saying such things and beholding such sights, he used to ask that no one should wonder at him for this; but should rather marvel at the Lord for having granted to us men to know Him as far as our powers extended.

63. Afterwards, on another occasion, having descended to the outer cells, he was asked to enter a vessel and pray with the monks, and he alone perceived an exceedingly unpleasant smell. But those on board said that the stench arose from the fish and salt meat in the ship. He replied however, the smell was different from that; and while he was speaking, a youth with an evil spirit, who had come and hidden himself in the ship, cried out. But the demon being rebuked in the name of the Lord Jesus Christ departed from him, and the man became whole. And all knew that the evil smell arose from the demon.

64. And another, a person of rank, came to him, possessed by a demon; and the demon was so terrible that the man possessed did not know that he was coming to Antony. But he even ate the excreta from his body. So those who brought him besought Antony to pray for him. And Antony pitying the young man prayed and kept watch with him all the night. And about dawn the young man suddenly attacked Antony and gave him a push. But when those who came with him were angry, Antony said, 'Be not angry with the young man, for it is not he, but the demon which is in him. And being rebuked and commanded to go into dry places, the demon became raging mad, and he has done this. Wherefore give thanks to the Lord, for his attack on me thus is a sign of the departure of the evil spirit.' When Antony had said this, straightway the young man had become whole, and having come at last to his right mind, knew where he was, and saluted the old man and gave thanks to God.

65. And many monks have related with the greatest agreement and unanimity that many other such like things were done by him. But still these do not seem as marvellous as certain other things appear to be. For once, when about to eat, having risen up to pray about the ninth hour, he perceived that he was caught up in the spirit, and, wonderful to tell, he stood and saw himself, as it were, from outside himself, and that he was led in the air by certain ones. Next certain bitter and terrible beings stood in the air and wished to hinder him from passing through. But when his conductors opposed them, they demanded whether he was not accountable to them. And when they wished to sum up the account from his

birth, Antony's conductors stopped them, saying, 'The Lord hath wiped out the sins from his birth, but from the time he became a monk, and devoted himself to God, it is permitted you to make a reckoning.' Then when they accused him and could not convict him, his way was free and unhindered. And immediately he saw himself, as it were, coming and standing by himself, and again he was Antony as before. Then forgetful of eating, he remained the rest of the day and through the whole of the night groaning and praying. For he was astonished when he saw against what mighty opponents our wrestling is, and by what labours we have to pass through the air. And he remembered that this is what the Apostle said, 'according to the prince of the power of the air [10].' For in it the enemy hath power to fight and to attempt to hinder those who pass through. Wherefore most earnestly he exhorted, 'Take up the whole armour of God, that ye may be able to withstand in the evil day [11],' that the enemy, 'having no evil thing to say against us, may be ashamed [12].' And we who have learned this, let us be mindful of the Apostle when he says, 'whether in the body I know not, or whether out of the body I know not; God knoweth [13].' But Paul was caught up unto the third heaven, and having heard things unspeakable he came down; while Antony saw that he had come to the air, and contended until he was free.

66. And he had also this favour granted him. For as he was sitting alone on the mountain, if ever he was in perplexity in his meditations, this was revealed to him by Providence in prayer. And the happy man, as it is written, was taught of God [14]. After this, when he once had a discussion with certain men who had come to him concerning the state of the soul and of what nature its place will be after this life, the following night one from above called him, saying, 'Antony, rise, go out and look.' Having gone out therefore (for he knew whom he ought to obey) looking up, he beheld one standing and reaching to the clouds, tall, hideous, and fearful, and others ascending as though they were winged. And the figure stretched forth his hands, and some of those who were ascending were stayed by him, while others flew above, and having escaped heavenward, were borne aloft free from care. At such, therefore, the giant gnashed his teeth, but rejoiced over those who fell back. And forthwith a voice came to Antony, 'Understandest thou what thou seest?' And his understanding was

---

10 Eph. ii. 2.   11 Eph. vi. 13.   12 Tit. ii. 8.
13 2 Cor. xii. 2.   14 Isai. liv. 13; John vi. 45.

opened, and he understood that it was the passing of souls, and that the tall being who stood was the enemy who envies the faithful. And those whom he caught and stopped from passing through are accountable to him, while those whom he was unable to hold as they passed upwards had not been subservient to him. So having seen this, and as it were being reminded, he struggled the more daily to advance towards those things which were before. And these visions he was unwilling to tell, but as he spent much time in prayer, and was amazed, when those who were with him pressed him with questions and forced him, he was compelled to speak, as a father who cannot withhold ought from his children. And he thought that as his conscience was clear, the account would be beneficial for them, that they might learn that discipline bore good fruit, and that visions were oftentimes the solace of their labours.

67. Added to this he was tolerant in disposition and humble in spirit. For though he was such a man, he observed the rule of the Church most rigidly, and was willing that all the clergy should be honoured above himself [17]. For he was not ashamed to bow his head to bishops and presbyters, and if ever a deacon came to him for help he discoursed with him on what was profitable, but gave place to him in prayer, not being ashamed to learn himself. For often he would ask questions, and desired to listen to those who were present, and if any one said anything that was useful he confessed that he was profited. And besides, his countenance had a great and wonderful grace. This gift also he had from the Saviour. For if he were present in a great company of monks, and any one who did not know him previously, wished to see him, immediately coming forward he passed by the rest, and hurried to Antony, as though attracted by his appearance. Yet neither in height nor breadth was he conspicuous above others, but in the serenity of his manner and the purity of his soul. For as his soul was free from disturbances, his outward appearance was calm; so from the joy of his soul he possessed a cheerful countenance, and from his bodily movements could be perceived the condition of his soul, as it is written, 'When the heart is merry the countenance is cheerful, but when it is sorrowful it is cast down [18].' Thus Jacob recognised the counsel Laban had in his heart, and said to his wives, 'The countenance of your father is not as it was yesterday and the day before [19].' Thus Samuel recognised David,

for he had mirthful eyes, and teeth white as milk. Thus Antony was recognised, for he was never disturbed, for his soul was at peace; he was never downcast, for his mind was joyous.

68. And he was altogether wonderful in faith and religious, for he never held communion with the Meletian schismatics, knowing their wickedness and apostacy from the beginning; nor had he friendly dealings with the Manichæans or any other heretics; or, if he had, only as far as advice that they should change to piety. For he thought and asserted that intercourse with these was harmful and destructive to the soul. In the same manner also he loathed the heresy of the Arians, and exhorted all neither to approach them nor to hold their erroneous belief. And once when certain Arian madmen came to him, when he had questioned them and learned their impiety, he drove them from the mountain, saying that their words were worse than the poison of serpents.

69. And once also the Arians having lyingly asserted that Antony's opinions were the same as theirs, he was displeased and wroth against them. Then being summoned by the bishops and all the brethren, he descended from the mountain, and having entered Alexandria [19a], he denounced the Arians, saying that their heresy was the last of all and a forerunner of Antichrist. And he taught the people that the Son of God was not a created being, neither had He come into being from non-existence, but that He was the Eternal Word and Wisdom of the Essence of the Father. And therefore it was impious to say, 'there was a time when He was not,' for the Word was always co-existent with the Father. Wherefore have no fellowship with the most impious Arians. For there is no communion between light and darkness [20]. For you are good Christians, but they, when they say that the Son of the Father, the Word of God, is a created being, differ in nought from the heathen, since they worship that which is created, rather than God the creator [1]. But believe ye that the Creation itself is angry with them because they number the Creator, the Lord of all, by whom all things came into being, with those things which were originated.

70. All the people, therefore, rejoiced when they heard the anti-Christian heresy anathematised by such a man. And all the people in the city ran together to see Antony; and the Greeks and those who are called their Priests,

[17] This was by no means universal among monks: Athan. argues to Dracontius (cc. 8, 9) against the monastic tendency to think little of the clergy. Here, he propounds the example of Antony for the imitation of the 'peregrini fratres.'
[18] Prov. xv. 13.   [19] Gen. xxxi. 5; 1 Sam. xvi. 12, xvii. 32.

[19a] July 25—27, 338, Fest. Ind. x.   [20] 2 Cor. vi. 14.
[1] Orat. ii. 23, &c. This was an argument much used against Arianism. Antony's arguments may be compared with those of Ath. in Ep. Æg 13

came into the church, saying, 'We ask to see the man of God,' for so they all called him. For in that place also the Lord cleansed many of demons, and healed those who were mad. And many Greeks asked that they might even but touch the old man, believing that they should be profited. Assuredly as many became Christians in those few days as one would have seen made in a year. Then when some thought that he was troubled by the crowds, and on this account turned them all away from him, he said, undisturbedly, that there were not more of them than of the demons with whom he wrestled in the mountain.

71. But when he was departing, and we were setting him forth on his way, as we[2] arrived at the gate a woman from behind cried out, 'Stay, thou man of God, my daughter is grievously vexed by a devil. Stay, I beseech thee, lest I too harm myself with running.' And the old man when he heard her, and was asked by us, willingly stayed. And when the woman drew near, the child was cast on the ground. But when Antony had prayed and called upon the name of Christ, the child was raised whole, for the unclean spirit was gone forth. And the mother blessed God, and all gave thanks. And Antony himself also rejoiced, departing to the mountain as though it were to his own home.

72. And Antony also was exceeding prudent, and the wonder was that although he had not learned letters, he was a ready-witted and sagacious man. At all events two Greek philosophers once came, thinking they could try their skill on Antony; and he was in the outer mountain, and having recognised who they were from their appearance, he came to them and said to them by means of an interpreter, 'Why, philosophers, did ye trouble yourselves so much to come to a foolish man?' And when they said that he was not a foolish man, but exceedingly prudent, he said to them, 'If you came to a foolish man, your labour is superfluous; but if you think me prudent become as I am, for we ought to imitate what is good. And if I had come to you I should have imitated you; but if you to me, become as I am, for I am a Christian.' But they departed with wonder, for they saw that even demons feared Antony.

73. And again others such as these met him in the outer mountain and thought to mock[3] him because he had not learned letters. And Antony said to them, 'What say ye? which is first, mind or letters? And which is the cause of which—mind of letters or letters of mind?'

And when they answered mind is first and the inventor of letters, Antony said, 'Whoever, therefore, hath a sound mind hath not need of letters.' This answer amazed both the bystanders and the philosophers, and they departed marvelling that they had seen so much understanding in an ignorant man. For his manners were not rough as though he had been reared in the mountain and there grown old, but graceful and polite, and his speech was seasoned with the divine salt, so that no one was envious, but rather all rejoiced over him who visited him.

74. After this again certain others came; and these were men who were deemed wise among the Greeks, and they asked him a reason for our faith in Christ. But when they attempted to dispute concerning the preaching of the divine Cross and meant to mock, Antony stopped for a little, and first pitying their ignorance, said, through an interpreter, who could skilfully interpret his words, 'Which is more beautiful, to confess the Cross or to attribute to those whom you call gods adultery and the seduction of boys? For that which is chosen by us is a sign of courage and a sure token of the contempt of death, while yours are the passions of licentiousness. Next, which is better, to say that the Word of God was not changed, but, being the same, He took a human body for the salvation and well-being of man, that having shared in human birth He might make man partake in the divine and spiritual nature[4]; or to liken the divine to senseless animals and consequently to worship four-footed beasts, creeping things and the likenesses of men? For these things, are the objects of reverence of you wise men. But how do you dare to mock us, who say that Christ has appeared as man, seeing that you, bringing the soul from heaven, assert that it has strayed and fallen from the vault of the sky into body[5]? And would that you had said that it had fallen into human body alone, and not asserted that it passes and changes into four-footed beasts and creeping things. For our faith declares that the coming of Christ was for the salvation of men. But you err because you speak of soul as not generated. And we, considering the power and loving-kindness of Providence, think that the coming of Christ in the flesh was not impossible with God. But you, although calling the soul the likeness of Mind[6], connect it with falls and

---

[2] This seems to imply Athanasius as the (real or ostensible) narrator.

[3] Cf. *c. Gent. 1, de Incar.* 1, 41, 48. 7.

[4] Cf. *de Incar.* 54. 3; 2 Pet. i. 4.

[5] Cf. Plat. *Phædr.* 274 B: but the resemblances is not close and the relation of this passage to the Phædrus is probably mediate. I cannot see that the doctrine referred to here is necessarily different from that of Plotinus (*Enn.* IV. iii. 15).

[6] Plotinus (*Enn.* V. i. 3) taught that the soul was, as it were, an image of Mind, as the uttered word is of the word in the soul (cf Philo. *Vit. Mos.* iii. 13).

feign in your myths that it is changeable, and consequently introduce the idea that Mind itself is changeable by reason of the soul. For whatever is the nature of a likeness, such necessarily is the nature of that of which it is a likeness. But whenever you think such a thought concerning Mind, remember that you blaspheme even the Father of Mind Himself[7].

75. But concerning the Cross, which would you say to be the better, to bear it, when a plot is brought about by wicked men, nor to be in fear of death brought about under any form whatever[8]; or to prate about the wanderings of Osiris and Isis, the plots of Typhon, the flight of Cronos, his eating his children and the slaughter of his father. For this is your wisdom. But how, if you mock the Cross, do you not marvel at the resurrection? For the same men who told us of the latter wrote the former. Or why when you make mention of the Cross are you silent about the dead who were raised, the blind who received their sight, the paralytics who were healed, the lepers who were cleansed, the walking upon the sea, and the rest of the signs and wonders, which shew that Christ is no longer a man but God? To me you seem to do yourselves much injustice and not to have carefully read our Scriptures. But read and see that the deeds of Christ prove Him to be God come upon earth for the salvation of men.

76. But do you tell us *your* religious beliefs. What can you say of senseless creatures except senselessness and ferocity? But if, as I hear, you wish to say that these things are spoken of by you as legends, and you allegorize the rape of the maiden Persephone of the earth; the lameness of Hephaestus of fire; and allegorize the air as Hera, the sun as Apollo, the moon as Artemis, and the sea as Poseidon; none the less, you do not worship God Himself, but serve the creature rather than God who created all things. For if because creation is beautiful you composed such legends, still it was fitting that you should stop short at admiration and not make gods of the things created; so that you should not give the honour of the Creator to that which is created. Since, if you do, it is time for you to divert the honour of the master builder to the house built by him; and of the general to the soldier. What then can you reply to these things, that we may know whether the Cross hath anything worthy of mockery?'

77. But when they were at a loss, turning hither and thither, Antony smiled and said— again through an interpreter—'Sight itself carries the conviction of these things. But as you prefer to lean upon demonstrative arguments, and as you, having this art, wish us also not to worship God, until after such proof, do you tell first how things in general and specially the recognition of God are accurately known. Is it through demonstrative argument or the working of faith? And which is better, faith which comes through the inworking (of God) or demonstration by arguments?' And when they answered that faith which comes through the inworking was better and was accurate knowledge, Antony said, 'You have answered well, for faith arises from disposition of soul, but dialectic from the skill of its inventors. Wherefore to those who have the inworking through faith, demonstrative argument is needless, or even superfluous. For what we know through faith this you attempt to prove through words, and often you are not even able to express what we understand. So the inworking through faith is better and stronger than your professional arguments.

78. 'We Christians therefore hold the mystery not in the wisdom of Greek arguments, but in the power of faith richly supplied to us by God through Jesus Christ. And to show that this statement is true, behold now, without having learned letters, we believe in God, knowing through His works His providence over all things. And to show that our faith is effective, so now we are supported by faith in Christ, but you by professional logomachies. The portents of the idols among you are being done away, but our faith is extending everywhere. You by your arguments and quibbles have converted none from Christianity to Paganism. We, teaching the faith on Christ, expose your superstition, since all recognise that Christ is God and the Son of God. You by your eloquence do not hinder the teaching of Christ. But we by the mention of Christ crucified put all demons to flight, whom you fear as if they were gods. Where the sign of the Cross is[9], magic is weak and witchcraft has no strength.

79. 'Tell us therefore where your oracles are now? Where are the charms of the Egyptians? Where the delusions of the magicians? When did all these things cease and grow weak except when the Cross of Christ arose? Is It then a fit subject for mockery, and not rather the things brought to nought by it, and convicted of weakness? For this is a marvellous thing, that your religion was never persecuted, but even was honoured by men in every city, while

---

[7] It is certainly startling to find Antony, ignorant of Greek and of letters, reasoning with philosophers upon the doctrines of Neoplatonism. His whole life, excepting two short visits to Alexandria, had been spent out of ear-shot of such discussions. Yet it is not easy to say exactly how much a man of strong mind and retentive memory may have picked up from the conversation of those who visited him upon subjects so widely discussed as these speculations were.   [8] *De Incar.* 24. 3.

[9] *De Incar.* 47. 4.

the followers of Christ are persecuted, and still our side flourishes and multiplies over yours. What is yours, though praised and honoured, perishes, while the faith and teaching of Christ, though mocked by you and often persecuted by kings, has filled the world. For when has the knowledge of God so shone forth? or when has self-control and the excellence of virginity appeared as now? or when has death been so despised except when the Cross of Christ has appeared? And this no one doubts when he sees [10] the martyr despising death for the sake of Christ, when he sees for Christ's sake the virgins of the Church keeping themselves pure and undefiled.

80. 'And these signs are sufficient to prove that the faith of Christ alone is the true religion. But see! you still do not believe and are seeking for arguments. We however make our proof "not in the persuasive words of Greek wisdom [11]," as our teacher has it, but we persuade by the faith which manifestly precedes argumentative proof. Behold there are here some vexed with demons;'—now there were certain who had come to him very disquieted by demons, and bringing them into the midst he said,—'Do you cleanse them either by arguments and by whatever art or magic you choose, calling upon your idols, or if you are unable, put away your strife with us and you shall see the power of the Cross of Christ.' And having said this he called upon Christ, and signed the sufferers two or three times with the sign of the Cross. And immediately the men stood up whole, and in their right mind, and forthwith gave thanks unto the Lord. And the philosophers, as they are called, wondered, and were astonished exceedingly at the understanding of the man and at the sign which had been wrought. But Antony said, 'Why marvel ye at this? We are not the doers of these things, but it is Christ who worketh them by means of those who believe on Him. Believe, therefore, also yourselves, and you shall see that with us there is no trick of words, but faith through love which is wrought in us towards Christ; which if you yourselves should obtain you will no longer seek demonstrative arguments, but will consider faith in Christ sufficient.' These are the words of Antony. And they marvelling at this also, saluted him and departed, confessing the benefit they had received from him [12].

81. And the fame of Antony came even unto kings. For Constantine Augustus, and his sons Constantius and Constans the Augusti wrote letters to him, as to a father, and begged an answer from him. But he made nothing very much of the letters, nor did he rejoice at the messages, but was the same as he had been before the Emperors wrote to him. But when they brought him the letters he called the monks and said, 'Do not be astonished if an emperor writes to us, for he is a man; but rather wonder that God wrote the Law for men and has spoken to us [13] through His own Son.' And so he was unwilling to receive the letters, saying that he did not know how to write an answer to such things. But being urged by the monks because the emperors were Christians, and lest they should take offence on the ground that they had been spurned, he consented that they should be read, and wrote an answer approving them because they worshipped Christ, and giving them counsel on things pertaining to salvation: 'not to think much of the present, but rather to remember the judgment that is coming, and to know that Christ alone was the true and Eternal King.' He begged them to be merciful and to give heed to justice and the poor. And they having received the answer rejoiced. Thus he was dear to all, and all desired to consider him as a father.

82. Being known to be so great a man, therefore, and having thus given answers to those who visited him, he returned again to the inner mountain, and maintained his wonted discipline. And often when people came to him, as he was sitting or walking, as it is written in Daniel [14], he became dumb, and after a season he resumed the thread of what he had been saying before to the brethren who were with him. And his companions perceived that he was seeing a vision. For often when he was on the mountains he saw what was happening in Egypt, and told it to Serapion the bishop [15], who was indoors with him, and who saw that Antony was wrapped in a vision. Once as he was sitting and working, he fell, as it were, into a trance, and groaned much at what he saw. Then after a time, having turned to the bystanders with groans and trembling, he prayed, and falling on his knees remained so a long time. And having arisen the old man wept. His companions, therefore, trembling and terrified, desired to learn from him what it was. And they troubled him much, until he was forced to speak. And with many groans he spake as follows: 'O, my children, it were better to die before what has appeared in the vision come to

[10] Compare *de Incar.* 48. 2.   [11] 1 Cor. ii. 4.
[12] The above argument with the philosophers runs upon the general lines of that of Athanasius *c. Gent.* The point which we miss here is the Euhemerism upon which Athanasius so strongly insists. This latter view would be naturally less congenial to Antony's mind than the view that the gods were merely demons.

[13] Heb. i. 2.   [14] Dan. iv. 19 (*v.* 16 LXX).
[15] Of Thmuis, the friend and correspondent of Athanasius; see below, § 91.

pass.' And when again they asked him, having burst into tears, he said, ' Wrath is about to seize the Church, and it is on the point of being given up to men who are like senseless beasts. For I saw the table of the Lord's House, and mules standing around it on all sides in a ring, and kicking the things therein, just like a herd kicks when it leaps in confusion. And you saw,' said he, ' how I groaned, for I heard a voice saying, " My altar shall be defiled." ' These things the old man saw, and after two years the present [16] inroad of the Arians and the plunder of the churches took place, when they violently carried off the vessels, and made the heathen carry them ; and when they forced the heathen from the prisons to join in their services, and in their presence did upon the Table as they would. Then we all understood that these kicks of the mules signified to Antony what the Arians, senselessly like beasts, are now doing. But when he saw this vision, he comforted those with him, saying, ' Be not downcast, my children ; for as the Lord has been angry, so again will He heal us, and the Church shall soon again receive her own order, and shall shine forth as she is wont. And you shall behold the persecuted restored, and wickedness again withdrawn to its own hiding-place, and pious faith speaking boldly in every place with all freedom. Only defile [17] not yourselves with the Arians, for

---

[16] Cf. below, ' what the Arians are *now* doing.' This incidental notice of time fixes the date of the present passage. Weingarten in vain attempts to extract some other sense from the Greek, which is plainness itself. It also fixes the date of Antony's death to within two years of the troubles in question. The Benedictines refer the troubles to the intrusion of Gregory ' in 341' (really 339), and the apparently unprecedented character ascribed to the outrages by Antony is in favour of this, as well as the fact (*Encyc.* 3) that in 339 the heathen are said to have offered sacrifice in the churches. But the latter is only in superficial agreement with the Greek text of the present passage, which speaks of *Arian συνάξεις* at which heathen were impressed to be present, apparently to make some show of a congregation. The Evagrian version, indeed, adds that the Gentiles on this occasion also carried on idolatrous rites in the Church and polluted the baptisteries ; but Evagrius is in the habit of interpolating little details from his own knowledge or opinion (e.g. 16, ' Ita exorsus,' &c., 26, 'qui vinctas hominum linguas solvebat,' 58, 'qui effosso pro Christo oculo sub Maximiano,' &c.), and in this case appears to borrow from *Encycl.* 3. Again, the writer of the *Vita* was not present (' the bystanders' *supra;* ' *they* troubled him ;' ' *they* asked him ;' . . . and *infr.* ' those with him') when the Vision took place : but when, two years later, it was interpreted by events, he was in the company of those who had been with Antony at the time (*infr.* ' then *we all* understood'). This (on the assumption of Athanasian authorship) excludes the year 339, when Athanasius fled to Italy, and compels us to refer the Vision to the troubles of 356 (*Apol. Fug.* 6, 7. *Hist. Ar.* 55, 56, *Ep. ad Lucif.*), after which Athanasius fled to the desert and was in the company of the monks. This conclusion is in independent agreement with (1) the fact, decisive by itself, that Antony is still alive in 345, when Nestorius became Prefect of Egypt (§ 86, note 3), i.e. six years after the troubles of 339 ; (2) the evidence that Antony was still living about 353 A.D. (*Epist. Ammon. de Pachom. et Theod.* 20, 21, in *Act. SS. Mai.* tom. iii. Appendix 70 C E, Tillemont vii. 123), and (3) the statement of Jerome (Chron.) that Antony died in 356. Against it Weingarten urges the prophecy of restored peace to the Church (*infr.*), as pointing to a time after the overthrow of Arianism. This is of little weight, for the prophecy expresses only what must have been the hope and belief of all. The prologue, which Tillemont (viii. 227) thinks must have been written in a time of peace at Alexandria, is not sufficiently explicit on the point to weigh against the plain sense of the present passage.

[17] Cf. the Second Letter to monks (Letter 53).

---

their teaching is not that of the Apostles, but that of demons and their father the devil ; yea, rather, it is barren and senseless, and without light understanding, like the senselessness of these mules.'

83. Such are the words of Antony, and we ought not to doubt whether such marvels were wrought by the hand of a man. For it is the promise of the Saviour, when He saith, ' If ye have faith as a grain of mustard seed, ye shall say to this mountain, remove hence and it shall remove ; and nothing shall be impossible unto you [18].' And again, ' Verily, verily, I say unto you, if ye shall ask the father in My name He will give it you. Ask and ye shall receive [19].' And He himself it is who saith to His disciples and to all who believe on Him, ' Heal the sick, cast out demons ; freely ye have received, freely give [20].'

84. Antony, at any rate, healed not by commanding, but by prayer and speaking the name of Christ. So that it was clear to all that it was not he himself who worked, but the Lord who showed mercy by his means and healed the sufferers. But Antony's part was only prayer and discipline, for the sake of which he stayed in the mountain, rejoicing in the contemplation of divine things, but grieving when troubled by much people, and dragged to the outer mountain. For all judges used to ask him to come down, because it was impossible for them to enter on account of their following of litigants. But nevertheless they asked him to come that they might but see him. When therefore he avoided it and refused to go to them, they remained firm, and sent to him all the more the prisoners under charge of soldiers, that on account of these he might come down. Being forced by necessity, and seeing them lamenting, he came into the outer mountain, and again his labour was not unprofitable. For his coming was advantageous and serviceable to many ; and he was of profit to the judges, counselling them to prefer justice to all things ; to fear God, and to know, ' that with what judgment they judged, they should be judged [1].' But he loved more than all things his sojourn in the mountain.

85. At another time, suffering the same compulsion at the hands of them who had need, and after many entreaties from the commander of the soldiers, he came down, and when he was come he spoke to them shortly of the things which make for salvation, and concerning those who wanted him, and was hastening away. But when the duke, as he is called, entreated him to stay, he replied that he could not linger among them, and persuaded him by a pretty simile, say-

---

[18] Matt. xvii. 20.　　[19] John xvi. 23.　　[20] Matt. x. 8.
[1] Matt. vii. 2.

ing, 'Fishes, if they remain long on dry land, die. And so monks lose their strength if they loiter among you and spend their time with you. Wherefore as fish must hurry to the sea, so must we hasten to the mountain. Lest haply if we delay we forget the things within us.' And the general having heard this and many other things from him, was amazed and said, 'Of a truth this man is the servant of God. For, unless he were beloved of God, whence could an ignorant man have such great understanding?'

86. And a certain general, Balacius by name, persecuted us Christians bitterly on account of his regard for the Arians—that name of ill-omen. And as his ruthlessness was so great that he beat virgins, and stripped and scourged monks, Antony at this time wrote a letter as follows, and sent it to him. 'I see wrath coming upon thee, wherefore cease to persecute the Christians, lest haply wrath catch hold of thee, for even now it is on the point of coming upon thee[2].' But Balacius laughed and threw the letter on the ground, and spit on it, and insulted the bearers, bidding them tell this to Antony: 'Since thou takest thought for the monks, soon I will come after thee also.' And five days had not passed before wrath came upon him. For Balacius and Nestorius, the Prefect of Egypt[3], went forth to the first halting-place from Alexandria, which is called Chæreu, and both were on horseback, and the horses belonged to Balacius, and were the quietest of all his stable. But they had not gone far towards the place when the horses began to frisk with one another as they are wont to do ; and suddenly the quieter, on which Nestorius sat[4], with a bite dismounted Balacius, and attacked him, and tore his thigh so badly with its teeth that he was borne straight back to the city, and in three days died. And all wondered because what Antony had foretold had been so speedily fulfilled.

87. Thus, therefore, he warned the cruel. But the rest who came to him he so instructed that they straightway forgot their lawsuits, and felicitated those who were in retirement from the world. And he championed those who were wronged in such a way that you would imagine that he, and not the others, was the sufferer. Further, he was able to be of such use to all, that many soldiers and men who had great possessions laid aside the burdens of life, and became monks for the rest of their days. And it was as if a physician had been given by God

to Egypt. For who in grief met Antony and did not return rejoicing ? Who came mourning for his dead and did not forthwith put off his sorrow ? Who came in anger and was not converted to friendship ? What poor and low-spirited man met him who, hearing him and looking upon him, did not despise wealth and console himself in his poverty ? What monk, having being neglectful, came to him and became not all the stronger ? What young man having come to the mountain and seen Antony, did not forthwith deny himself pleasure and love temperance ? Who when tempted by a demon, came to him and did not find rest ? And who came troubled with doubts and did not get quietness of mind ?

88. For this was the wonderful thing in Antony's discipline, that, as I said before, having the gift of discerning spirits, he recognised their movements, and was not ignorant whither any one of them turned his energy and made his attack. And not only was he not deceived by them himself, but cheering those who were troubled with doubts, he taught them how to defeat their plans, telling them of the weakness and craft of those who possessed them. Thus each one, as though prepared by him for battle, came down from the mountain, braving the designs of the devil and his demons. How many maidens who had suitors, having but seen Antony from afar, remained maidens for Christ's sake. And people came also from foreign parts to him, and like all others, having got some benefit, returned, as though set forward by a father. And certainly when he died, all as having been bereft of a father, consoled themselves solely by their remembrances of him, preserving at the same time his counsel and advice.

89. It is worth while that I should relate, and that you, as you wish it, should hear what his death was like. For this end of his is worthy of imitation. According to his custom he visited the monks in the outer mountain, and having learned from Providence that his own end was at hand, he said to the brethren, 'This is my last visit to you which I shall make. And I shall be surprised if we see each other again in this life. At length the time of my departure is at hand, for I am near a hundred and five years old.' And when they heard it they wept, and embraced, and kissed the old man. But he, as though sailing from a foreign city to his own, spoke joyously, and exhorted them 'Not to grow idle in their labours, nor to become faint in their training, but to live as though dying daily. And as he had said before, zealously to guard the soul from foul thoughts, eagerly to imitate the Saints, and to have nought to do with the Meletian

[2] In *Hist. Ar.* 14 the letter is sent not to Balacius but to Gregory, who died on June 26, 345 (Gwatkin, p. 105).
[3] Nestorius was prefect '345—352' (Index to **Fest. Letters,** where the year '345' is from August 344 to August 345).
[4] In the *Hist. Ar.* it is simply stated that Balacius was bitten by *his own* horse. The present passage looks like a more careful restatement.

schismatics, for you know their wicked and profane character. Nor have any fellowship with the Arians, for their impiety is clear to all. Nor be disturbed if you see the judges protect them, for it shall cease, and their pomp is mortal and of short duration. Wherefore keep yourselves all the more untainted by them, and observe the traditions of the fathers, and chiefly the holy faith in our Lord Jesus Christ, which you have learned from the Scripture, and of which you have often been put in mind by me.'

90. But when the brethren were urging him to abide with them and there to die, he suffered it not for many other reasons, as he showed by keeping silence, and especially for this :—The Egyptians are wont to honour with funeral rites, and to wrap in linen cloths at death the bodies of good men, and especially of the holy martyrs; and not to bury them underground, but to place them on couches, and to keep them in their houses, thinking in this to honour the departed. And Antony often urged the bishops to give commandment to the people on this matter. In like manner he taught the laity and reproved the women, saying, 'that this thing was neither lawful nor holy at all. For the bodies of the patriarchs and prophets are until now preserved in tombs, and the very body of the Lord was laid in a tomb, and a stone was laid upon it, and hid it until He rose on the third day[4a].' And thus saying, he showed that he who did not bury the bodies of the dead after death transgressed the law, even though they were sacred. For what is greater or more sacred than the body of the Lord? Many therefore having heard, henceforth buried the dead underground, and gave thanks to the Lord that they had been taught rightly.

91. But he, knowing the custom, and fearing that his body would be treated this way, hastened, and having bidden farewell to the monks in the outer mountain entered the inner mountain, where he was accustomed to abide. And after a few months he fell sick. Having summoned those who were there— they were two in number who had remained in the mountain fifteen years, practising the discipline and attending on Antony on account of his age—he said to them, 'I, as it is written[5], go the way of the fathers, for I perceive that I am called by the Lord. And do you be watchful and destroy not your long discipline, but as though now making a beginning, zealously preserve your determination. For ye know the treachery of the demons, how fierce they are, but how little power they have. Wherefore fear them not, but rather ever breathe Christ, and trust Him. Live as though dying

daily. Give heed to yourselves, and remember the admonition you have heard from me. Have no fellowship with the schismatics, nor any dealings at all with the heretical Arians. For you know how I shunned them on account of their hostility to Christ, and the strange doctrines of their heresy. Therefore be the more earnest always to be followers first of God and then of the Saints; that after death they also may receive you as well-known friends into the eternal habitations. Ponder over these things and think of them, and if you have any care for me and are mindful of me as of a father, suffer no one to take my body into Egypt, lest haply they place me in the houses[6], for to avoid this I entered into the mountain and came here. Moreover you know how I always put to rebuke those who had this custom, and exhorted them to cease from it. Bury my body, therefore, and hide it underground yourselves, and let my words be observed by you that no one may know the place[6a] but you alone. For at the resurrection of the dead I shall receive it incorruptible from the Saviour. And divide my garments. To Athanasius the bishop give one sheepskin and the garment whereon I am laid, which he himself gave me new, but which with me has grown old. To Serapion the bishop give the other sheepskin, and keep the hair garment yourselves[7]. For the rest fare ye well, my children, for Antony is departing, and is with you no more.'

92. Having said this, when they had kissed him, he lifted up his feet, and as though he saw friends coming to him and was glad because o them—for as he lay his countenance appeared joyful—he died and was gathered to the fathers. And they afterward, according to his commandment, wrapped him up and buried him, hiding his body underground. And no one knows to this day where it was buried, save those two only. But each of those who received the sheepskin of the blessed Antony and the garment worn by him guards it as a precious treasure. For even to look on them is as it were to behold Antony; and he who is clothed in them seems with joy to bear his admonitions.

93. This is the end of Antony's life in the body

4a Cf. John xix. 41; Matt. xxvii. 60.   5 Josh. xxiii. 14.

6 Cf. St. Aug. *Serm.* 361. 12, D.C.A. p. 251.

6a The body of Antony was discovered 'by a revelation' in 561, and translated to Alexandria. When the Saracens conquered Egypt it was transferred to Constantinople, and lastly in the tenth century was carried to Vienne by a French Seigneur. The first and last links of this history are naturally precarious. The translation to Alexandria is vouched for by Victor of Tunis (*Chron.*) who was in the neighbourhood at the time.

7 Jerome, in his life of Paul of Thebes, relates that Antony received from Paul, and ever afterwards wore on festivals, his tunic of palm-leaves. If this 'legacy more glorious than the purple of a king' (*Vit. Paul.* c. 13) had any existence, it would certainly not have been forgotten by Antony in disposing of his worldly goods. The silence of the Life of Antony throws discredit on Jerome's whole account of Paul.

and the above was the beginning of the discipline. Even if this account is small compared with his merit, still from this reflect how great Antony, the man of God, was. Who from his youth to so great an age preserved a uniform zeal for the discipline, and neither through old age was subdued by the desire of costly food, nor through the infirmity of his body changed the fashion of his clothing, nor washed even his feet with water, and yet remained entirely free from harm. For his eyes were undimmed and quite sound and he saw clearly; of his teeth he had not lost one, but they had become worn to the gums through the great age of the old man. He remained strong both in hands and feet; and while all men were using various foods, and washings and divers garments, he appeared more cheerful and of greater strength. And the fact that his fame has been blazoned everywhere; that all regard him with wonder, and that those who have never seen him long for him, is clear proof of his virtue and God's love of his soul. For not from writings, nor from worldly wisdom, nor through any art, was Antony renowned, but solely from his piety towards God. That this was the gift of God no one will deny. For from whence into Spain and into Gaul, how into Rome and Africa, was the man heard of who abode hidden in a mountain, unless it was God who maketh His own known everywhere, who also promised this to Antony at the beginning? For even if they work secretly, even if they wish to remain in obscurity, yet the Lord shows them as lamps to lighten all, that those who hear may thus know that the precepts of God are able to make men prosper and thus be zealous in the path of virtue.

94. Read these words, therefore, to the rest of the brethren that they may learn what the life of monks ought to be; and may believe that our Lord and Saviour Jesus Christ glorifies those who glorify Him: and leads those who serve Him unto the end, not only to the kingdom of heaven, but here also—even though they hide themselves and are desirous of withdrawing from the world—makes them illustrious and well known everywhere on account of their virtue and the help they render others. And if need be, read this among the heathen, that even in this way they may learn that our Lord Jesus Christ is not only God and the Son of God, but also that the Christians who truly serve Him and religiously believe on Him, prove, not only that the demons, whom the Greeks themselves think to be gods, are no gods, but also tread them under foot and put them to flight, as deceivers and corrupters of mankind, through Jesus Christ our Lord, to whom be glory for ever and ever. Amen.

AD EPISCOPOS ÆGYPTI

ET LIBYÆ

EPISTOLA ENCYCLICA

WRITTEN A.D. 356.

THIS letter was addressed by St. Athanasius to the bishops of his Province after his expulsion by Syrianus (Feb. 8, 356), and when the nomination of George the contractor to the Alexandrian See was already known (§ 7). But no details of the persecution of the orthodox in Egypt had reached Athanasius when he wrote, in fact he mentions it as only beginning (§ 5). This points to about the Easter of 356; see Prolegg. ch. ii. § 8 (1). The tract thus opens the series of anti-Arian works composed during the 'third exile.' It has indeed been inferred (by Baronius and others) from § 22 that the letter was written thirty-six years after the Nicene Synod, i.e. in 361. But it was certainly written before the arrival of George, and in the passage referred to it is the first condemnation of Arius by Alexander, and not the Council of Nicæa, that is placed thirty-six years ago. The primary purpose of the letter is to warn the bishops against a formulary which was on the point of being circulated for their acceptance on pain of banishment (§ 5). The creed in question cannot now be identified,—but it was very possibly the Sirmian Creed of 351 (de Synod. 27), not formally Arian, but evading the Nicene test (§ 10). He begins, accordingly, after a general warning (1—4) against being imposed upon by mere words, and a statement (5) of the tactics of his opponents, by urging the bishops to hold to the faith of Nicæa, in contrast to the shifting professions of its opponents (6—8), and to be satisfied with nothing short of an explicit repudiation of Arianism (9—11). In the Second Part of the Letter he turns to doctrine. He states (12) the original Arian position, and confronts it (13) with passages from Scripture. He challenges the Arians (14) to state any clear belief as to the nature of the Word, which shall reconcile their premises with the language of Holy Writ (15, 16). He explains Prov. viii. 22 of the Incarnation, and taxes the Arians with denying this truth, like the heathen (17). He next taxes them with dissimulation, especially Arius in his profession to Constantine (18); he describes the death of Arius, and presses the charge of complicity with a man already judged by God (19). He urges the bishops (20, 21) to steadfastness and confessorship, reprobates the coalition of Meletians (22) and Arians, and finally expresses the conviction (23) that the Emperor Constantius will put an end to these outrages when informed of the true facts of the case.

The last section is an anticipation of the *Apol. ad Constantium*, which Athanasius was probably preparing at the same time. Not till two years later does he cast aside all hope of the Emperor and launch out in the bitter invective of the 'Arian History' (see *Apol. pro Fuga* 26, note 7).

The place where this Encyclical was written is quite uncertain, but it was most probably in the Libyan desert, or in Cyrenaica (Prolegg. *ubi supr.* note 10). His language (*infr.* § 5, note 7) would naturally be such as not to give, through so public a document, a clue to his pursuers.

It may be added that in many MSS., and in the editions previous to 1698, this tract was counted as the first of the 'five' (or in some cases 'six') *Orationes contra Arianos*. For a discussion of this error, see Montfaucon's *Monita* to this tract and to the four *Orationes*.

TO THE BISHOPS OF EGYPT

CHAPTER I.

1. *Christ warned His followers against false prophets.*

ALL things whatsoever our Lord and Saviour Jesus Christ, as Luke wrote, 'both hath done and taught[1],' He effected after having appeared for our salvation; for He came, as John saith, 'not to condemn the world, but that the world through Him might be saved[2].' And among the rest we have especially to admire this instance of His goodness, that He was not silent concerning those who should fight against us, but plainly told us beforehand, that, when those things should come to pass, we might straightway be found with minds established by His teaching. For He said, 'There shall arise false prophets and false Christs, and shall shew great signs and wonders; insomuch that, if it were possible, the very elect shall be deceived. Behold, I have told you before[3].' Manifold indeed and beyond human conception are the instructions and gifts of grace which He has laid up in us; as the pattern of heavenly conversation, power against demons, the adoption of sons, and that exceeding great and singular grace, the knowledge of the Father and of the Word Himself, and the gift of the Holy Ghost. But the mind of man is prone to evil exceedingly; moreover, our adversary the devil, envying us the possession of such great blessings, goeth about seeking to snatch away the seed of the word which is sown within us. Wherefore as if by His prophetic warnings He would seal up His instructions in our hearts as His own peculiar treasure, the Lord said, 'Take heed that no man deceive you: for many shall come in My name, saying, I am he; and the time draweth near; and they shall deceive many: go ye not therefore after them[4].' This is a great gift which the Word has bestowed upon us, that we should not be deceived by appearances, but that, howsoever these things are concealed, we should all the more distinguish them by the grace of the Spirit. For whereas the inventor of wickedness and great spirit of evil, the devil, is utterly hateful, and as soon as he shews himself is rejected[5] of all men,—as a serpent, as a dragon, as a lion seeking whom he may seize upon and devour,—therefore he conceals and covers what he really is, and craftily personates that Name which all men desire, so that deceiving by a false appearance, he may thenceforth fix fast in his own chains those whom he has led astray. And as if one that desired to kidnap the children of others during the absence of their parents, should personate their appearance, and so putting a cheat on the affections of the offspring, should carry them far away and destroy them; in like manner this evil and wily spirit the devil, having no confidence in himself, and knowing the love which men bear to the truth, personates its appearance, and so spreads his own poison among those that follow after him.

2. *Satan pretending to be holy, is detected by the Christian.*

Thus he deceived Eve, not speaking his own, but artfully adopting the words of God, and perverting their meaning. Thus he suggested evil to the wife of Job, persuading her to feign affection for her husband, while he taught her to blaspheme God. Thus does the crafty spirit mock men by false displays, deluding and drawing each into his own pit of wickedness. When of old he deceived the first man Adam, thinking that through him he should have all men subject unto him, he exulted with great boldness and said, 'My hand hath found as a nest the riches of the people; and as one gathereth eggs that are left, have I gathered all the earth; and there is none that shall escape me or speak against

---

Acts i. 1.   [2] John iii. 17.   [3] Matt. xxiv. 24, 25.   [4] Luke xxi. 8.   [5] βάλλεται, vid. p. 170, note 6.

me[6].' But when the Lord came upon earth, and the enemy made trial of His human Economy, being unable to deceive the flesh which He had taken upon Him, from that time forth he, who promised himself the occupation of the whole world, is for His sake mocked even by children: that proud one is mocked as a sparrow[7]. For now the infant child lays his hand upon the hole of the asp, and laughs at him that deceived Eve[8]; and all that rightly believe in the Lord tread under foot him that said, 'I will ascend above the heights of the clouds: I will be like the Most High[9].' Thus he suffers and is dishonoured; and although he still ventures with shameless confidence to disguise himself, yet now, wretched spirit, he is detected the rather by them that bear the Sign on their foreheads[1]; yea, more, he is rejected of them, and is humbled, and put to shame. For even if, now that he is a creeping serpent, he shall transform himself into an angel of light, yet his deception will not profit him; for we have been taught that 'though an angel from heaven preach unto us any other gospel than that we have received, he is anathema[2].'

3. And although, again, he conceal his natural falsehood, and pretend to speak truth with his lips; yet are we 'not ignorant of his devices[3],' but are able to answer him in the words spoken by the Spirit against him; 'But unto the ungodly, said God, why dost thou preach My laws?' and, 'Praise is not seemly in the mouth of a sinner[4].' For even though he speak the truth, the deceiver is not worthy of credit. And whereas Scripture shewed this, when relating his wicked artifices against Eve in Paradise, so the Lord also reproved him,—first in the mount, when He laid open 'the folds of his breast-plate[5],' and shewed who the crafty spirit was, and proved that it was not one of the saints[6], but Satan that was tempting Him. For He said, 'Get thee behind Me Satan; for it is written, Thou shalt worship the Lord thy God, and Him only shalt thou serve[7].' And again, when He put a curb in the mouths of the demons that cried after Him from the tombs. For although what they said was true, and they lied not then, saying, 'Thou art the Son of God,' and 'the Holy One of God[8];' yet He would not that the truth should proceed from an unclean mouth, and especially from such as them, lest under pretence thereof they should mingle with it their own malicious devices, and sow these also while

men slept. Therefore He suffered them not to speak such words, neither would He have us to suffer such, but hath charged us by His own mouth, saying, 'Beware of false prophets, which come to you in sheeps' clothing, but inwardly they are ravening wolves[9];' and by the mouth of His Holy Apostles, 'Believe not every spirit[10].' Such is the method of our adversary's operations; and of the like nature are all these inventions of heresies, each of which has for the father of its own device the devil, who changed and became a murderer and a liar from the beginning. But being ashamed to profess his hateful name, they usurp the glorious Name of our Saviour 'which is above every name[1],' and deck themselves out in the language of Scripture, speaking indeed the words, but stealing away the true meaning thereof; and so disguising by some artifice their false inventions, they also become the murderers of those whom they have led astray.

4. It profits not to receive part of Scripture, and reject part.

For whence do Marcion and Manichæus receive the Gospel while they reject the Law? For the New Testament arose out of the Old, and bears witness to the Old; if then they reject this, how can they receive what proceeds from it? Thus Paul was an Apostle of the Gospel, 'which God promised afore by His prophets in the holy Scriptures[3]:' and our Lord Himself said, 'ye search the Scriptures, for they are they which testify of Me[4].' How then shall they confess the Lord unless they first search the Scriptures which are written concerning Him? And the disciples say that they have found Him, 'of whom Moses and the Prophets did write[5].' And what is the Law to the Sadducees if they receive not the Prophets[6]? For God who gave the Law, Himself promised in the Law that He would raise up Prophets also, so that the same is Lord both of the Law and of the Prophets, and he that denies the one must of necessity deny the other also. And again, what is the Old Testament to the Jews, unless they acknowledge the Lord whose coming was expected according to it? For had they believed the writings of Moses, they would have believed the words of the Lord; for He said, 'He wrote of Me[7].' Moreover, what are the Scriptures to him[8] of Samosata, who denies the Word of God and His incarnate

---

[6] Is. x. 14. LXX., cf. p. 202, note 8.   [7] Vid. Job xli. 5;
xl. 24. LXX.   [8] Isa. xi. 8; 2 Cor. xi. 3.   [9] Is. xiv. 14.
[1] Ezek. ix. 4. LXX.   [2] Gal. i. 8, 9.   [3] 2 Cor. ii. 11.   [4] Ps. l.
16: Ecclus. xv. 9.   [5] Job xli. 13, v. 4. LXX. and cf. Orat. i. 1,
and Vit. Ant. supr. p. 197, note 15.   [6] Or sacred writers, ἁγίων.
[7] Matt. iv. 10.   [8] Matt. viii. 29; Mark i. 24.

[9] Matt. vii. 15.   [10] 1 John iv. 1.   [1] Phil. ii. 9.
[3] Rom. i. 2.   [4] John v. 39.   [5] John i. 45.
[6] Vid. Prideaux, Conn. ii. 5. (vol. 3, p. 474. ed. 1725).
[7] John v. 46.   [8] See Prolegg. ch. ii. § 3 (2) a.

Presence[9], which is signified and declared both in the Old and New Testament? And of what use are the Scriptures to the Arians also, and why do they bring them forward, men who say that the Word of God is a creature, and like the Gentiles 'serve the creature more than' God 'the Creator[1]?' Thus each of these heresies, in respect of the peculiar impiety of its invention, has nothing in common with the Scriptures. And their advocates are aware of this, that the Scriptures are very much, or rather altogether, opposed to the doctrines of every one of them; but for the sake of deceiving the more simple sort (such as are those of whom it is written in the Proverbs, 'The simple believeth every word[2]),' they pretend like their 'father the devil[3]' to study and to quote the language of Scripture, in order that they may appear by their words to have a right belief, and so may persuade their wretched followers to believe what is contrary to the Scriptures. Assuredly in every one of these heresies the devil has thus disguised himself, and has suggested to them words full of craftiness. The Lord spake concerning them, that 'there shall arise false Christs and false prophets, so that they shall deceive many[4].' Accordingly the devil has come, speaking by each and saying, 'I am Christ, and the truth is with me;' and he has made them, one and all, to be liars like himself. And strange it is, that while all heresies are at variance with one another concerning the mischievous inventions which each has framed, they are united together only by the common purpose of lying[5]. For they have one and the same father that has sown in them all the seeds of falsehood. Wherefore the faithful Christian and true disciple of the Gospel, having grace to discern spiritual things, and having built the house of his faith upon a rock, stands continually firm and secure from their deceits. But the simple person, as I said before, that is not thoroughly grounded in knowledge, such an one, considering only the words that are spoken and not perceiving their meaning, is immediately drawn away by their wiles. Wherefore it is good and needful for us to pray that we may receive the gift of discerning spirits, so that every one may know, according to the precept of John, whom he ought to reject, and whom to receive as friends and of the same faith. Now one might write at great length concerning these things, if one desired to go into details respecting them; for the impiety and perverseness of heresies will appear to be manifold and various, and the craft of the deceivers to be very terrible. But since holy

Scripture is of all things most sufficient[6] for us, therefore recommending to those who desire to know more of these matters, to read the Divine word, I now hasten to set before you that which most claims attention, and for the sake of which principally I have written these things.

5. *Attempt of Arians to substitute a Creed for the Nicene.*

I heard during my sojourn in these parts[7] (and they were true and orthodox brethren that informed me), that certain professors of Arian opinions had met together, and drawn a confession of faith to their own liking, and that they intend to send word to you, that you must either subscribe to what pleases them, or rather to what the devil has inspired them with, or in case of refusal must suffer banishment. They are indeed already beginning to molest the Bishops of these parts; and thereby are plainly manifesting their disposition. For inasmuch as they frame this document only for the purpose of inflicting banishment or other punishments, what does such conduct prove them to be, but enemies of the Christians, and friends of the devil and his angels? and especially since they spread abroad what they like contrary to the mind of that gracious Prince, our most religious Emperor Constantius[8]. And this they do with great craftiness, and, as appears to me, chiefly with two ends in view; first, that by obtaining your subscriptions, they may seem to remove the evil repute that rests upon the name of Arius, and may escape notice themselves as if not professing his opinions; and again, that by putting forth these statements they may cast a shade over the Council of Nicæa[9], and the confession of faith which was then put forth against the Arian heresy. But this proceeding does but prove the more plainly their own maliciousness and heterodoxy. For had they believed aright, they would have been satisfied with the confession put forth at Nicæa by the whole Ecumenic Council; and had they considered themselves calumniated and falsely called Arians, they ought not to have been so eager to innovate upon what was written against Arius, lest what was directed against him might seem to be aimed at them also. This, however, is not the course they pursue, but they conduct the struggle in their own behalf, just as if they were Arius. Observe how entirely they disregard the truth, and how everything they say and do is for the sake of the Arian heresy. For in that they dare to question those sound

---

9 See *Orat* i. 49.   1 Rom. i. 25.   2 Prov. xiv. 15.   6 Cf. p. 4, note 2.   7 [Probably Cyrenaica, see above, Introd. *sub. fin.*]   8 Cf. § 23, and *Apol. Const.* 32.   9 Cf. *de Syn.* 7.
3 John viii. 44.   4 Matt. xxiv. 24.   5 vid. *Orat.* ii. § 18.

VOL. IV.   Q

definitions of the faith, and take upon them-selves to produce others contrary to them, what else do they but accuse the Fathers, and stand up in defence of that heresy which they opposed and protested against? And what they now write proceeds not from any regard for the truth, as I said before, but rather they do it as in mockery and by an artifice, for the purpose of deceiving men; that by sending about their letters they may engage the ears of the people to listen to these notions, and so put off the time when they will be brought to trial; and that by concealing their impiety from observa-tion, they may have room to extend their heresy, which, 'like a gangrene[10],' eats its way everywhere.

6. Accordingly they disturb and disorder everything, and yet not even thus are they satis-fied with their own proceedings. For every year, as if they were going to draw up a contract, they meet together and pretend to write about the faith, whereby they expose themselves the more to ridicule and disgrace, because their exposi-tions are rejected, not by others, but by them-selves. For had they had any confidence in their previous statements, they would not have desired to draw up others; nor again, leaving these last, would they now have set down the one in question, which no doubt true to their custom they will again alter, after a very short interval, and as soon as they shall find a pretence for their customary plotting against certain persons. For when they have a design against any, then it is that they make a great show of writing about the faith; that, as Pilate washed his hands, so they by writing may destroy those who rightly believe in Christ, hoping that, as making definitions about the faith, they may appear, as I have repeatedly said, to be free from the charge of false doctrine. But they will not be able to hide themselves, nor to escape; for they continually become their own accusers even while they defend themselves. Justly so, since instead of answering those who bring proof against them, they do but persuade themselves to believe whatever they wish. And when is an acquittal obtained, upon the criminal becoming his own judge? Hence it is that they are always writing, and always altering their own previous statements, and thus they shew an uncertain faith[1],' or rather a manifest unbelief and per-verseness. And this, it appears to me, must needs be the case with them; for since, having fallen away from the truth, and desiring to overthrow that sound confession of faith which was drawn up at Nicæa, they have, in the language of Scripture, 'loved to wander, and

have not refrained their feet[2];' therefore, like Jerusalem of old, they labour and toil in their changes, sometimes writing one thing, and sometimes another, but only for the sake of gaining time, and that they may continue enemies of Christ, and deceivers of mankind.

7. The party of Acacius really Arians.

Who, then, that has any real regard for truth, will be willing to suffer these men any longer? who will not justly reject their writing? who will not denounce their audacity, that being but few[3] in number, they would have their decisions to prevail over everything, and as desiring the supremacy of their own meetings, held in corners and suspicious in their circum-stances, would forcibly cancel the decrees of an uncorrupt, pure, and Ecumenic Council? Men who have been promoted by Eusebius and his fellows for advocating this Antichristian heresy, venture to define articles of faith, and while they ought to be brought to judgment as crimi-nals, like Caiaphas, they take upon themselves to judge. They compose a Thalia, and would have it received as a standard of faith, while they are not yet themselves determined what they believe. Who does not know that Secun-dus[4] of Pentapolis, who was several times de-graded long ago, was received by them for the sake of the Arian madness; and that George[5], now of Laodicea, and Leontius the Eunuch, and before him Stephanus, and Theodorus of Hera-clea[6], were promoted by them? Ursacius and Valens also, who from the first were instructed by Arius as young men[7], though they had been formerly degraded from the Priesthood, after-wards got the title of Bishops on account of their impiety; as did also Acacius, Patro-philus[8], and Narcissus, who have been most forward in all manner of impiety. These were degraded in the great Synod of Sardica; Eusta-thius also now of Sebastea, Demophilus and Germinius[9], Eudoxius, and Basil, who are sup-porters of that impiety, were advanced in the same manner. Of Cecropius[10], and him they called Auxentius, and of Epictetus[11] the im-postor, it were superfluous for me to speak, since it is manifest to all men, in what manner, on what pretexts, and by what enemies of ours these were promoted, that they might bring their false charges against the orthodox Bishops who were the objects of their designs. For although they resided at the distance of eighty posts, and were unknown to the people, yet on the ground of their impiety they pur-chased for themselves the title of Bishop. For

---

[10] 2 Tim. ii. 17. [1] Cf. de Syn. §§ 3, 6.

[2] Jer. xiv. 10. [3] Cf. de Syn. 5, note. [4] Cf. de Syn. 12; Prolegg. ch. ii. § 3 (1), &c. [5] p. 104, note 3. [6] Supr. p. 119. [7] Supr. p. 107, note 9. [8] Omitted supr. p. 123. [9] De Syn. § 9. [10] Of Nicomedia, see D. C. B. s.v. [11] Vid. Hist. Ar. § 74 fin.

the same reason also they have now[1] hired one George of Cappadocia, whom they wish to impose upon you. But no respect is due to him any more than to the rest; for there is a report in these parts that he is not even a Christian, but is devoted to the worship of idols; and he has a hangman's temper[2]. And this person, such as he is described to be, they have taken into their ranks, that they may be able to injure, to plunder, and to slay; for in these things he is a great proficient, but is ignorant of the very principles of the Christian faith.

8. Words are bad, though Scriptural, which proceed from bad men.

Such are the machinations of these men against the truth: but their designs are manifest to all the world, though they attempt in ten thousand ways, like eels, to elude the grasp, and to escape detection as enemies of Christ. Wherefore I beseech you, let no one among you be deceived, no one seduced by them; rather, considering that a sort of judaical impiety is invading the Christian faith, be ye all zealous for the Lord; hold fast, every one, the faith we have received from the Fathers, which they who assembled at Nicæa recorded in writing, and endure not those who endeavour to innovate thereon. And however they may write phrases out of the Scripture, endure not their writings; however they may speak the language of the orthodox, yet attend not to what they say; for they speak not with an upright mind, but putting on such language like sheeps' clothing, in their hearts they think with Arius, after the manner of the devil, who is the author of all heresies. For he too made use of the words of Scripture, but was put to silence by our Saviour. For if he had indeed meant them as he used them, he would not have fallen from heaven; but now having fallen through his pride, he artfully dissembles in his speech, and oftentimes maliciously endeavours to lead men astray by the subtleties and sophistries of the Gentiles. Had these expositions of theirs proceeded from the orthodox, from such as the great Confessor Hosius, and Maximinus[3] of Gaul, or his successor[3a], or from such as Philogonius and Eustathius[4], Bishops of the East[5], or Julius and Liberius of Rome, or Cyriacus of Mœsia[6], or Pistus and Aristæus of Greece, or Silvester and Protogenes of Dacia, or Leontius and Eupsychius of Cappadocia, or Cæcilianus of Africa, or Eustorgius of Italy, or Capito of Sicily, or

Macarius of Jerusalem, or Alexander of Constantinople, or Pæderos of Heraclea, or those great Bishops Meletius, Basil, and Longianus, and the rest from Armenia and Pontus, or Lupus and Amphion from Cilicia, or James[6a] and the rest from Mesopotamia, or our own blessed Alexander, with others of the same opinions as these;—there would then have been nothing to suspect in their statements, for the character of apostolical men is sincere and incapable of fraud.

9. For such words do but serve as their cloak.

But when they proceed from those who are hired to advocate the cause of heresy, and since, according to the divine proverb, 'The words of the wicked are to lie in wait,' and 'The mouth of the wicked poureth out evil things,' and 'The counsels of the wicked are deceit[7]:' it becomes us to watch and be sober, brethren, as the Lord has said, lest any deception arise from subtlety of speech and craftiness; lest any one come and pretend to say, 'I preach Christ,' and after a little while he be found to be Antichrist. These indeed are Antichrists, whosoever come to you in the cause of the Arian madness. For what defect is there among you, that any one need to come to you from without? Or, of what do the Churches of Egypt and Libya and Alexandria stand so much in need, that these men should make a purchase[8] of the Episcopate instead of wood and goods, and intrude into Churches which do not belong to them? Who is not aware, who does not perceive clearly, that they do all this in order to support their impiety? Wherefore although they should make themselves dumb, or although they should bind on their garments larger borders than the Pharisees, and pour themselves forth in long speeches, and practise the tones of their voice[9], they ought not to be believed; for it is not the mode of speaking, but the intentions of the heart and a godly conversation that recommend the faithful Christian. And thus the Sadducees and Herodians, although they have the law in their mouths, were put to rebuke by our Saviour, who said unto them, 'Ye do err, not knowing the Scriptures, nor the power of God[10]:' and all men witnessed the exposure of those who pretended to quote the words of the Law, as being in their minds heretics and enemies of God[11]. Others indeed they deceived by these professions, but when our Lord became man they were not able to deceive Him; 'for

---

[1] Hist. Ar. 75.   [2] Cf. de Syn. 37.   [3] Supr. Apol. Ar. 50.
[3a] Paulinus of Treveri, cf. supr. p. 130, note 10.
[4] At Nicæa, as most of the others.   [5] i.e. of Antioch.
[6] [Unknown.]

[6a] [Of Nisibis. See D.C.B. iii. p. 325 and foll.]
[7] Prov. xii. 6; xv. 28; xii. 5.   [8] Ap. ad Const. § 28.
Hist. Arian. § 73, supr.   [9] Vid. Basil. Ep. 22⟨.⟩ 3.
[10] Matt. xxii. 29.   [11] θεομάχοι.

the Word was made Flesh,' who 'knoweth the thoughts of men that they are vain.' Thus He exposed the carping of the Jews, saying, ' If God were your Father, ye would love Me, for I proceeded forth from the Father, and am come to you[1].' In like manner these men seem now to act ; for they disguise their real sentiments, and then make use of the language of Scripture for their writings, which they hold forth as a bait for the ignorant, that they may inveigle them into their own wickedness.

10. They ought first to condemn Arius, if they are to be heard.

Consider, whether this be not so. If, when there is no reason for their doing so, they write confessions of faith, it is a superfluous, and perhaps also a mischievous proceeding, because, when there is no enquiry, they offer occasion for controversy of words, and unsettle the simple hearts of the brethren, disseminating among them such notions as have never entered into their minds. And if they are attempting to write a defence of themselves in regard to the Arian heresy, they ought first to have removed the seeds of those evils which have sprung up, and to have proscribed those who produced them, and then in the room of former statements to set forth others which are sound ; or else let them openly vindicate the opinions of Arius, that they may no longer covertly but openly shew themselves enemies of Christ, and that all men may fly from them as from the face of a serpent. But now they keep back those opinions, and for a pretence write on other matters ; just as if a surgeon, when summoned to attend a person wounded and suffering, should upon coming in to him say not a word concerning his wounds, but proceed to discourse about his sound limbs. Such an one would be chargeable with utter stupidity, for saying nothing on the matter for which he came, but discoursing on those other points in which he was not needed. Yet just in the same manner these men omit those matters which concern their heresy, and take upon themselves to write on other subjects ; whereas if they had any regard for the Faith, or any love for Christ, they ought first to have removed out of the way those blasphemous expressions uttered against Him, and then in the room of them to speak and to write the sound words. But this they neither do themselves, nor permit those that desire to do so, whether it be from ignorance, or through craft and artifice.

11. No profit to do right in one way, if we do wrong in another.

If they do this from ignorance they must be charged with rashness, because they affirm positively concerning things that they know not ; but if they dissemble knowingly, their condemnation is the greater, because while they overlook nothing in consulting for their own interests, in writing about faith in our Lord they make a mockery, and do anything rather than speak the truth ; they keep back those particulars respecting which their heresy is accused, and merely bring forward the language of the Scriptures. Now this is a manifest theft of the truth, and a practice full of all iniquity ; and so I am sure your piety will readily perceive it to be from the following illustrations. No person being accused of adultery defends himself as innocent of theft ; nor would any one in prosecuting a charge of murder suffer the accused parties to defend themselves by saying, 'We have not committed perjury, but have preserved the deposit which was entrusted to us.' This would be mere child's play, instead of a refutation of the charge and a demonstration of the truth. For what has murder to do with a deposit, or adultery with theft ? The vices are indeed related to each other as proceeding from the same heart ; yet in respect to the refutation of an alleged offence, they have no connection with each other. Accordingly as it is written in the Book of Joshua[2] the son of Nun, when Achan was charged with theft, he did not excuse himself with the plea of his zeal in the wars ; but being convicted of the offence was stoned by all the people. And when Saul was charged with negligence and a breach of the law, he did not benefit his cause by alleging his conduct on other matters[3]. For a defence on one count will not operate to obtain an acquittal on another count ; but if all things should be done according to law and justice, a man must defend himself in those particulars wherein he is accused, and must either disprove the past, or else confess it with the promise that he will desist, and do so no more. But if he is guilty of the crime, and will not confess, but in order to conceal the truth speaks on other points instead of the one in question, he shews plainly that he has acted amiss, nay, and is conscious of his delinquency. But what need of many words, seeing that these persons are themselves accusers of the Arian heresy ? For since they have not the boldness to speak out, but conceal their blasphemous expressions, it is plain that they know

---

[1] John i. 14 ; Ps. xciv. 11 ; John viii. 42, ἥκω, vid. Hipp. contr. Noet. 16. and de Syn. 16.

[2] Josh. vii. 20, &c.　　[3] 1 Sam. xv.

that this heresy is separate and alien from the truth. But since they themselves conceal it and are afraid to speak, it is necessary for me to strip off the veil from their impiety, and to expose the heresy to public view, knowing as I do the statements which Arius and his fellows formerly made, and how they were cast out of the Church, and degraded from the Clergy. But here first I ask for pardon[4] of the foul words which I am about to produce, since I use them, not because I thus think, but in order to convict the heretics.

CHAPTER II.

12. *Arian statements.*

Now the Bishop Alexander of blessed memory cast Arius out of the Church for holding and maintaining the following opinions: 'God was not always a Father: The Son was not always: But whereas all things were made out of nothing, the Son of God also was made out of nothing: And since all things are creatures, He also is a creature and a thing made: And since all things once were not, but were afterwards made, there was a time when the Word of God Himself was not; and He was not before He was begotten, but He had a beginning of existence: For He has then originated when God has chosen to produce Him: For He also is one among the rest of His works. And since He is by nature changeable, and only continues good because He chooses by His own free will, He is capable of being changed, as are all other things, whenever He wishes. And therefore God, as foreknowing that He would be good, gave Him by anticipation that glory which He would have obtained afterwards by His virtue; and He is now become good by His works which God foreknew.' Accordingly they say, that Christ is not truly God, but that He is called God on account of His participation in God's nature, as are all other creatures. And they add, that He is not that Word which is by nature in the Father, and is proper to His Essence, nor is He His proper wisdom by which He made this world; but that there is another Word[5] which is properly in the Father, and another Wisdom which is properly in the Father, by which Wisdom also He made this Word; and that the Lord Himself is called the Word (Reason) conceptually in regard of things endued with reason, and is called Wisdom conceptually in regard of things endued with wisdom. Nay, they say that as all things are in essence separate and alien from the Father, so He also is in all respects separate and alien from the essence

of the Father, and properly belongs to things made and created, and is one of them; for He is a creature, and a thing made, and a work. Again, they say[6] that God did not create us for His sake, but Him for our sakes. For they say, 'God was alone, and the Word was not with Him, but afterwards when He would produce us, then He made Him; and from the time He was made, He called Him the Word, and the Son, and the Wisdom, in order that He might create us by Him. And as all things subsisted by the will of God, and did not exist before; so He also was made by the will of God, and did not exist before. For the Word is not the proper and natural Offspring of the Father, but has Himself originated by grace: for God who existed made by His will the Son who did not exist, by which will also He made all things, and produced, and created, and willed them to come into being.' Moreover they say also, that Christ is not the natural and true power of God; but as the locust and the cankerworm are called a power[7], so also He is called the power of the Father. Furthermore he said, that the Father is secret from the Son, and that the Son can neither see nor know the Father perfectly and exactly. For having a beginning of existence, He cannot know Him that is without beginning; but what He knows and sees, He knows and sees in a measure proportionate to His own measure, as we also know and see in proportion to our powers. And he added also, that the Son not only does not know His own Father exactly, but that He does not even know His own essence.

13. *Arguments from Scripture against Arian statements.*

For maintaining these and the like opinions Arius was declared a heretic; for myself, while I have merely been writing them down, I have been cleansing myself by thinking of the contrary doctrines, and by holding fast the sense of the true faith. For the Bishops who all assembled from all parts at the Council of Nicæa, began to hold their ears at these statements, and all with one voice condemned this heresy on account of them, and anathematized it, declaring it to be alien and estranged from the faith of the Church. It was no compulsion which led the judges to this decision, but they all deliberately vindicated the truth[8]: and they did so justly and

---

4 Cf. *Orat.* i. § 25 note.   5 Cf. *De Syn.* §§ 15, 18.

6 *De Syn.* 15—19.
7 Joel ii. 25. [With this entire section, compare *Socr.* i. 5, *de Decr.* 6, *de Syn.* 15, *Orat.* i. 5. 6, *ad Afros* 5, *Vit. Ant.* 69, and the *Depositio Arii.*']
8 Cf. *Ep. ad Jov.* (Letter 56, below), § 2. Theod. *H. E.* v. 9. p. 205, l. 17. vid. Keble on Primitive Trad. p. 122. 10. 'Let each boldly set down his faith in writing, having the fear of God before

rightly. For infidelity is coming in through these men, or rather a Judaism counter to the Scriptures, which has close upon it Gentile superstition, so that he who holds these opinions can no longer be even called a Christian, for they are all contrary to the Scriptures. John, for instance, saith, 'In the beginning was the Word[9];' but these men say, 'He was not, before He was begotten.' And again he wrote, 'And we are in Him that is true, even in His Son Jesus Christ; this is the true God, and eternal life[10];' but these men, as if in contradiction to this, allege that Christ is not the true God, but that He is only called God, as are other creatures, in regard of His participation in the divine nature. And the Apostle blames the Gentiles, because they worship the creatures, saying, 'They served the creature more than' God 'the Creator[1].' But if these men say that the Lord is a creature, and worship Him as a creature, how do they differ from the Gentiles? If they hold this opinion, is not this passage also against them; and does not the blessed Paul write as blaming them? The Lord also says, 'I and My Father are One:' and 'He that hath seen Me, hath seen the Father[2];' and the Apostle who was sent by Him to preach, writes, 'Who being the Brightness of His glory, and the express Image of His Person[3].' But these men dare to separate them, and to say that He is alien from the essence and eternity of the Father; and impiously to represent Him as changeable, not perceiving, that by speaking thus, they make Him to be, not one with the Father, but one with created things. Who does not see, that the brightness cannot be separated from the light, but that it is by nature proper to it, and co-existent with it, and is not produced after it? Again, when the Father says, 'This is My beloved Son[4],' and when the Scriptures say that 'He is the Word' of the Father, by whom 'the heavens were established[5],' and in short, 'All things were made by Him[6];' these inventors of new doctrines and fictions represent that there is another Word, and another Wisdom of the Father, and that He is only called the Word and the Wisdom conceptually on account of things endued with reason, while they perceive not the absurdity of this.

14. Arguments from Scripture against Arian statements.

But if He be styled the Word and the Wisdom by a fiction on our account, what He really is they cannot tell[7]. For if the Scriptures affirm that the Lord is both these, and yet these men will not allow Him to be so, it is plain that in their godless opposition to the Scriptures they would deny His existence altogether. The faithful are able to conclude this truth both from the voice of the Father Himself, and from the Angels that worshipped Him, and from the Saints that have written concerning Him; but these men, as they have not a pure mind, and cannot bear to hear the words of divine men who teach of God, may be able to learn something even from the devils who resemble them, for they spoke of Him, not as if there were many besides, but, as knowing Him alone, they said, 'Thou art the Holy One of God,' and 'the Son of God[8].' He also who suggested to them this heresy, while tempting Him, in the mount, said not, 'If Thou also be a Son of God,' as though there were others besides Him, but, 'If Thou be the[8a] Son of God,' as being the only one. But as the Gentiles, having fallen from the notion of one God, have sunk into polytheism, so these wonderful men, not believing that the Word of the Father is one, have come to adopt the idea of many words, and they deny Him that is really God and the true Word, and have dared to conceive of Him as a creature, not perceiving how full of impiety is the thought. For if He be a creature, how is He at the same time the Creator of creatures? or how the Son and the Wisdom and the Word? For the Word is not created, but begotten; and a creature is not a Son, but a production. And if all creatures were made by Him, and He is also a creature, then by whom was He made? Things made must of necessity originate through some one; as in fact they have originated through the Word; because He was not Himself a thing made, but the Word of the Father. And again, if there be another wisdom in the Father beside the Lord, then Wisdom has originated in wisdom: and if the Word of God be the Wisdom of God, then the Word has originated in a word: and if the Son be the Word of God, then the Son must have been made in the Son.

15. Arguments from Scripture against Arian statements.

How is it that the Lord has said, 'I am in the Father, and the Father in Me[9],' if there be another in the Father, by whom the Lord Himself also was made? And how is it that John, passing over that other, relates of this

his eyes.' Conc. Chalced. Sess. 1. *Hard.* t. 2. 273. 'Give diligence without fear, favour, or dislike, to set out the faith in its purity.' ibid. p. 285.   9 John i. 1.   10 1 John v. 20.
1 Rom. i. 25. supr. § 4, and note on *Or.* i. 8, also *Vit. Ant.* 69.
2 John x. 30; xiv. 9, and *Or.* i. 34. note.   3 Heb. i. 3.
4 Matt. xvii. 5.   5 Ps. xxxiii. 6.   6 John . 3.

7 Cf. *de. Decr.* 6, note 5.   8 Mark i. 24; Matt. viii. 29.
8a [Matt. iv. 3; Luke iv. 3. No existing text appears to bear out Athanasius in his insertion of the definite article.]
9 John xiv. 10.

One, saying, 'All things were made by Him; and without Him was not any thing made [10]?' If all things that were made by the will of God were made by Him, how can He be Himself one of the things that were made? And when the Apostle says, 'For whom are all things, and by whom are all things [1],' how can these men say, that we were not made for Him, but He for us? If it be so, He ought to have said, 'For whom the Word was made;' but He saith not so, but, 'For whom are all things, and by whom are all things,' thus proving these men to be heretical and false. But further, as they have had the boldness to say that there is another Word in God, and since they cannot bring any clear proof of this from the Scriptures, let them but shew one work of His, or one work of the Father that was done without this Word; so that they may seem to have some ground at least for their own idea. The works of the true Word are manifest to all, so as for Him to be contemplated by analogy from them. For as, when we see the creation, we conceive of God as the Creator of it; so when we see that nothing is without order therein, but that all things move and continue with order and providence, we infer a Word of God who is over all and governs all. This too the holy Scriptures testify, declaring that He is the Word of God, and that 'all things were made by Him, and without Him was not any thing made [2].' But of that other Word, of whom they speak, there is neither word nor work that they have to shew. Nay, even the Father Himself, when He says, 'This is My beloved Son [3],' signifies that besides Him there is none other

16. *Arians parallel to the Manichees.*

It appears then that so far as these doctrines are concerned, these wonderful men have now joined themselves to the Manichees. For these also confess the existence of a good God, so far as the mere name goes, but they are unable to point out any of His works either visible or invisible. But inasmuch as they·deny Him who is truly and indeed God, the Maker of heaven and earth, and of all things invisible, they are mere inventors of fables. And this appears to me to be the case with these evil-minded men. They see the works of the true Word who alone is in the Father, and yet they deny Him, and make to themselves another Word [4], whose · existence they are unable to prove either by His Works or by the testimony of others. Unless it be that they have adopted

a fabulous notion of God, that He is a composite being like man, speaking and then changing His words, and as a man exercising understanding and wisdom; not perceiving to what absurdities they are reduced by such an opinion. For if God has a succession of words [5], they certainly must consider Him as a man. And if those words proceed from Him and then vanish away, they are guilty of a greater impiety, because they resolve into nothing what proceeds from the self-existent God. If they conceive that God doth at all beget, it were surely better and more religious to say that He is the begetter of One Word, who is the fulness of His Godhead, in whom are hidden the treasures of all knowledge [6], and that He is co-existent with His Father, and that all things were made by Him; rather than to suppose God to be the Father of many words which are nowhere to be found, or to represent Him who is simple in His nature as compounded of many [7], and as being subject to human passions and variable. Next whereas the Apostle says, 'Christ the power of God and the wisdom of God [8],' these men reckon Him but as one among many powers; nay, worse than this, they compare Him, transgressors as they are, with the cankerworm and other irrational creatures which are sent by Him for the punishment of men. Next, whereas the Lord says, 'No one knoweth the Father, save the Son [9];' and again, 'Not that any man hath seen the Father save He which is of the Father [10];' are not these indeed enemies of God which say that the Father is neither seen nor known of the Son perfectly? If the Lord says, 'As the Father knoweth Me, even so know I the Father [11],' and if the Father knows not the Son partially, are they not mad to say idly that the Son knows the Father only partially, and not fully? Next, if the Son has a beginning of existence, and all things likewise have a beginning, let them say, which is prior to the other. But indeed they have nothing to say, neither can they with all their craft prove such a beginning of the Word. For He is the true and proper Offspring of the Father, and 'in the beginning was the Word, and the Word was with God, and the Word was God [1].' For with regard to their assertion, that the Son knows not His own essence, it is superfluous to reply to it, except only so far as to condemn their madness; for how does not the Word know Himself, when He imparts to all men the knowledge of His Father and of Himself, and blames those who know not themselves?

---

[10] John i. 3.   [1] Heb. ii. 10.   [2] Joh. i. 3.
[3] Matt. xvii. 5.   [4] Vid. passage in *Orat.* ii. 39 fin.

[5] *de Decr.* 16, note 4.   [6] Cf. Col. ii. 3, 9,   [7] *de Decr.* 22
note 9.   [8] 1 Cor. i. 24.   [9] Matt. xi. 27.   [10] John vi. 46.
[11] John x. 15.   [1] John i. 1.

17. *Arguments from Scripture against Arian statements.*

But it is written [2], say they, 'The Lord created me in the beginning of His ways for His works.' O untaught and insensate that ye are! He is called also in the Scriptures, 'servant [3],' and 'son of a handmaid,' and 'lamb,' and 'sheep,' and it is said that He suffered toil, and thirst, and was beaten, and has suffered pain. But there is plainly a reasonable ground and cause [4], why such representations as these are given of Him in the Scriptures; and it is because He became man and the Son of man, and took upon Him the form of a servant, which is the human flesh: for 'the Word,' says John, 'was made flesh [5].' And since He became man, no one ought to be offended at such expressions; for it is proper to man to be created, and born, and formed, to suffer toil and pain, to die and to rise again from the dead. And as, being Word and Wisdom of the Father, He has all the attributes of the Father, His eternity, and His unchangeableness, and the being like Him in all respects and in all things [6], and is neither before nor after, but co-existent with the Father, and is the very form [7] of the Godhead, and is the Creator, and is not created: (for since He is in essence like [8] the Father, He cannot be a creature, but must be the Creator, as Himself hath said, 'My Father worketh hitherto, and I work [9]:') so being made man, and bearing our flesh, He is necessarily said to be created and made, and that is proper to all flesh; however, these men, like Jewish vintners, who mix their wine with water [1], debase the Word, and subject His Godhead to their notions of created things. Wherefore the Fathers were with reason and justice indignant, and anathematized this most impious heresy; which these persons are now cautious of and keep back, as being easy to be disproved and unsound in every part of it. These that I have set down are but a few of the arguments which go to condemn their doctrines; but if any one desires to enter more at large into the proof against them, he will find that this heresy is not far removed from heathenism, and that it is the lowest and the very dregs of all the other heresies. These last are in error either concerning the body or the incarnation of the Lord, falsifying the truth, some in one way and some in another, or else they deny that the Lord has sojourned here at all, as the Jews erroneously suppose. But this one alone more madly than the rest has dared to assail the very Godhead, and to assert that the Word is not at all, and that the Father was not always a father; so that one might reasonably say that that Psalm was written against them; 'The fool hath said in his heart, there is no God [2]. Corrupt are they, and become abominable in their doings.'

18. *If the Arians felt they were right, they would speak openly.*

'But,' say they, 'we are strong, and are able to defend our heresy by our many devices.' They would have a better answer to give, if they were able to defend it, not by artifice nor by Gentile sophisms, but by the simplicity of their faith. If however they have confidence in it, and know it to be in accordance with the doctrines of the Church, let them openly express their sentiments; for no man when he hath lighted a candle putteth it under the bushel [3], but on the candlestick, and so it gives light to all that come in. If therefore they are able to defend it, let them record in writing the opinions above imputed to them, and expose their heresy bare to the view of all men, as they would a candle, and let them openly accuse the Bishop Alexander, of blessed memory, as having unjustly ejected [4] Arius for professing these opinions; and let them blame the Council of Nicæa for putting forth a written confession of the true faith in place of their impiety. But they will not do this, I am sure, for they are not so ignorant of the evil nature of those notions which they have invented and are ambitious of sowing abroad; but they know well enough, that although they may at first lead astray the simple by vain deceit, yet their imaginations will soon be extinguished, 'as the light of the ungodly [4a],' and themselves branded everywhere as enemies of the Truth. Therefore although they do all things foolishly, and speak as fools, yet in this at least they have acted wisely, as 'children of this world [5],' hiding their candle under the bushel, that it may be supposed to give light, and lest, if it appear, it be condemned and extinguished. Thus when Arius himself, the author of this heresy, and the associate of Eusebius, was summoned through the interest of Eusebius and his fellows to appear before Constantine Augustus of blessed memory [6], and was required to present a written declaration of his faith, the wily man wrote one, but kept out of sight the peculiar expressions of his impiety, and pretended, as the Devil did, to quote the simple words of Scripture, just as they are written. And when the blessed Constantine said to him, 'If thou

---

[2] *Orat.* ii. 18—72; Prov. viii. 22.   [3] Ps. cxvi. 16, &c.
[4] *de Decr.* 14.   [5] John i. 14.   [6] *De Syn.* 26, and note.
[7] εἶδος, ibid. § 52, note.   [8] *Orat.* i. 20, note.   [9] John v. 17.
[1] Isa. i. 22, cf. *Orat.* iii. § 35, also *de Decr.* 10 end.

[2] Ps. liii. 1.   [3] Matt. v. 15.   [4] Infr. § 21, note.
[4a] Job xviii. 5.   [5] Luke xvi. 8.   [6] Vid. *Letter* 54.

holdest no other opinions in thy mind besides these, take the Truth to witness for thee; the Lord is thy avenger if thou swear falsely:' the unfortunate man swore that he held no other, and that he had never either spoken or thought otherwise than as he had now written. But as soon as he went out he dropped down, as if paying the penalty of his crime, and 'falling headlong burst asunder in the midst [7].'

19. Significance of the death of Arius.

Death, it is true, is the common end of all men, and we ought not to insult the dead, though he be an enemy, for it is uncertain whether the same event may not happen to ourselves before evening. But the end of Arius was not after an ordinary manner, and therefore it deserves to be related. Eusebius and his fellows threatening to bring him into the Church, Alexander, the Bishop of Constantinople, resisted them; but Arius trusted to the violence and menace of Eusebius. It was the Sabbath, and he expected to join communion on the following day. There was therefore a great struggle between them; the others threatening, Alexander praying. But the Lord being judge of the case, decided against the unjust party: for the sun had not set, when the necessities of nature compelled him to that place, where he fell down, and was forthwith deprived of communion with the Church and of his life together. The blessed Constantine hearing of this at once, was struck with wonder to find him thus convicted of perjury. And indeed it was then evident to all that the threats of Eusebius and his fellows had proved of no avail, and the hope of Arius had become vain. It was shewn too that the Arian madness was rejected from communion by our Saviour both here and in the Church of the first-born in heaven. Now who will not wonder to see the unrighteous ambition of these men, whom the Lord has condemned;—to see them vindicating the heresy which the Lord has pronounced· excommunicate (since He did not suffer its author to enter into the Church), and not fearing that which is written, but attempting impossible things? 'For the Lord of hosts hath purposed, and who shall disannul it [8]?' and whom God hath condemned, who shall justify? Let them however in defence of their own imaginations write what they please; but do you, brethren, as 'bearing the vessels of the Lord [9],' and vindicating the doctrines of the Church, examine this matter, I beseech you; and if they write in other terms than those above recorded as the language of Arius, then condemn them as hypocrites, who hide the poison of their opinions, and like the serpent flatter with the words of their lips. For, though they thus write, they have associated with them those who were formerly rejected with Arius, such as Secundus of Pentapolis, and the clergy who were convicted at Alexandria; and thay write to them in Alexandria. But what is most astonishing, they have caused us and our friends to be persecuted, although the most religious Emperor Constantine sent us back in peace to our country and Church, and shewed his concern for the harmony of the people. But now they have caused the Churches to be given up to these men, thus proving to all that for their sake the whole conspiracy against us and the rest has been carried on from the beginning.

20. While they are friends of Arius, in vain their moderate words.

Now while such is their conduct, how can they claim credit for what they write? Had the opinions they have put in writing been orthodox, they would have expunged from their list of books the Thalia of Arius, and have rejected the scions of the heresy, viz. those disciples of Arius, and the partners of his impiety and his punishment. But since they do not renounce these, it is manifest to all that their sentiments are not orthodox, though they write them over ten thousand times [1]. Wherefore it becomes us to watch, lest some deception be conveyed under the clothing of their phrases, and they lead away certain from the true faith. And if they venture to advance the opinions of Arius, when they see themselves proceeding in a prosperous course, nothing remains for us but to use great boldness of speech, remembering the predictions of the Apostle, which he wrote to forewarn us of such like heresies, and which it becomes us to repeat. For we know that, as it is written, 'in the latter times some shall depart from the sound faith, giving heed to seducing spirits, and doctrines of devils, that turn from the truth [2];' and, 'as many as will live godly in Christ shall suffer persecution. But evil men and seducers shall wax worse and worse, deceiving and being deceived.' But none of these things shall prevail over us, nor 'separate us from the love of Christ [3],' though the heretics threaten us with death. For we are Christians, not Arians [4]; would that they too, who have written these things, had not embraced the doctrines of Arius! Yea, brethren, there is need now of such boldness of speech; for we have not received 'the

---

[7] Acts i. 18.   [8] Is. xiv. 27.   [9] Is. lii. 11.

[1] Cf. De Syn. 6, 9.   [2] 1 Tim. iv. 1; Tit. i. 14; 2 Tim. iii. 12.
[3] Rom. viii. 35.   [4] Orat. i. 2, 10.

spirit of bondage again to fear [5],' but God hath called us 'to liberty [6].' And it were indeed disgraceful to us, most disgraceful, were we, on account of Arius or of those who embrace and advocate his sentiments, to destroy the faith which we have received from our Saviour through His Apostles. Already very many in these parts, perceiving the craftiness of these writers, are ready even unto blood to oppose their wiles, especially since they have heard of your firmness. And seeing that the refutation of the heresy has gone forth from you [7], and it has been drawn forth from its concealment, like a serpent from his hole, the Child that Herod sought to destroy is preserved among you, and the Truth lives in you, and the Faith thrives among you.

21. To make a stand for the Faith equivalent to martyrdom.

Wherefore I exhort you, keeping in your hands the confession which was framed by the Fathers at Nicæa, and defending it with great zeal and confidence in the Lord, be ensamples to the brethren everywhere, and shew them that a struggle is now before us in support of the Truth against heresy, and that the wiles of the enemy are various. For the proof of a martyr lies [8] not only in refusing to burn incense to idols; but to refuse to deny the Faith is also an illustrious testimony of a good conscience. And not only those who turned aside unto idols were condemned as aliens, but those also who betrayed the Truth. Thus Judas was degraded from the Apostolical office, not because he sacrificed to idols, but because he proved a traitor; and Hymenæus and Alexander fell away not by betaking themselves to the service of idols, but because they 'made shipwreck concerning the faith [9].' On the other hand, the Patriarch Abraham received the crown, not because he suffered death, but because he was faithful unto God; and the other Saints, of whom Paul speaks [10], Gideon, Barak, Samson, Jephtha, David and Samuel, and the rest, were not made perfect by the shedding of their blood, but by faith they were justified; and to this day they are the objects of our admiration, as being ready even to suffer death for piety towards the Lord. And if one may add an instance from our own country, ye know how the blessed Alexander contended even unto death against this heresy, and what great afflictions and labours, old man as he was, he sustained, until in extreme age he also was gathered to his fathers. And how many beside have undergone great toil, in their

teachings against this impiety, and now enjoy in Christ the glorious reward of their confession! Wherefore, let us also, considering that this struggle is for our all, and that the choice is now before us, either to deny or to preserve the faith, let us also make it our earnest care and aim to guard what we have received, taking as our instruction the Confession drawn up at Nicæa, and let us turn away from novelties, and teach our people not to give heed to 'seducing spirits [1],' but altogether to withdraw from the impiety of the Arian madmen, and from the coalition which the Meletians have made with them.

22. Coalition of sordid Meletians with insane Arians.

For you perceive how, though they were formerly at variance with one another, they have now, like Herod and Pontius, agreed together in order to blaspheme our Lord Jesus Christ. And for this they truly deserve the hatred of every man, because they were at enmity with one another on private grounds, but have now become friends and join hands, in their hostility to the Truth and their impiety towards God. Nay, they are content to do or suffer anything, however contrary to their principles, for the satisfaction of securing their several aims; the Meletians for the sake of pre-eminence and the mad love of money, and the Arian madmen for their own impiety. And thus by this coalition they are able to assist one another in their malicious designs, while the Meletians put on the impiety of the Arians, and the Arians from their own wickedness concur in their baseness, so that by thus mingling together their respective crimes, like the cup of Babylon [1a], they may carry on their plots against the orthodox worshippers of our Lord Jesus Christ. The wickedness and falsehood of the Meletians were indeed even before this evident unto all men; so too the impiety and godless heresy of the Arians have long been known everywhere and to all; for the period of their existence has not been a short one. The former became schismatics five and fifty years ago, and it is thirty-six years since the latter were pronounced heretics [2], and they were rejected from the Church by the judgment of the whole Ecumenic Council. But by their present proceedings they have proved at length, even to those who seem openly to favour them, that they have carried on their

---

[1] 1 Tim. iv. 1.   [1a] Rev. xviii. 6.

[2] This ἀποδείξις or declaration is ascribed to S. Alexander (as Montfaucon would explain it, supr. introd. p. 222). Cf. *Ap. Ar.* 23, above, §§ 18, 19. It should be observed that an additional reason for assigning this Letter to the year 356, is its resemblance in parts to the Orations which were written not long after. [This is not a strong reason, there being no proof that the Orations were written early in the exile.]

[5] Rom. viii. 15.   [6] Gal. v. 13.   [7] i.e. from Egypt.
[8] Vid. Suicer *Thes. in voc.* μαρτ. iii. [D.C.A. 1118 sqq.]
[9] 1 Tim. i. 19.   [10] Heb. xi. 32, &c.

designs against me and the rest of the orthodox Bishops from the very first solely for the sake of advancing their own impious heresy. For observe, that which was long ago the great object of Eusebius and his fellows is now brought about. They have caused the Churches to be snatched out of our hands, they have banished, as they pleased, the Bishops and Presbyters who refused to communicate with them ; and the people who withdrew from them they have excluded from the Churches, which they have given up into the hands of the Arians who were condemned so long ago, so that with the assistance of the hypocrisy of the Meletians they can without fear pour forth in them their impious language, and make ready, as they think, the way of deceit for Antichrist[3], who sowed among them the seeds of this heresy.

23. *Conclusion.*

Let them however thus dream and imagine vain things. We know that when our gracious Emperor shall hear of it, he will put a stop to their wickedness, and they will not continue long, but according to the words of Scripture, 'the hearts of the impious shall quickly fail them[4].' But let us, as it is written, 'put on the words of holy Scripture[5],' and resist them as apostates who would set up fanaticism in the house of the Lord. And let us not fear the death of the body, nor let us emulate their ways ; but let the word of Truth be preferred before all things. We also, as you all know, were formerly required[6] by Eusebius and his fellows either to put on their impiety, or to expect their hostility ; but we would not engage

ourselves with them, but chose rather to be persecuted by them, than to imitate the conduct of Judas. And assuredly they have done what they threatened ; for after the manner of Jezebel, they engaged the treacherous Meletians to assist them, knowing how the latter resisted the blessed martyr Peter, and after him the great Achillas, and then Alexander, of blessed memory, in order that, as being practised in such matters, the Meletians might pretend against us also whatever might be suggested to them, while Eusebius and his fellows gave them an opening for persecuting and for seeking to kill me. For this is what they thirst after ; and they continue to this day to desire to shed my blood. But of these things I have no care ; for I know and am persuaded that they who endure shall receive a reward from our Saviour ; and that ye also, if ye endure as the Fathers did, and shew yourselves examples to the people, and overthrow these strange and alien devices of impious men, shall be able to glory, and say, We have 'kept the Faith[7];' and ye shall receive the 'crown of life,' which God 'hath promised to them that love Him[8].' And God grant that I also together with you may inherit the promises, which, were given, not to Paul only, but also to all them that 'have loved the appearing[9]' of our Lord, and Saviour, and God, and universal King, Jesus Christ ; through whom to the Father be glory and dominion in the Holy Spirit, both now and for ever, world without end[10]. Amen.

---

3 *De Syn.* 5, note 10.
5 2 Kings xvii. 9, LXX.
4 Prov. x. 20, LXX.
6 *Apol. Ar.* § 59.

7 2 Tim. iv. 7.   8 James i. 12.   9 2 Tim. iv. 8.
10 [Cf. the doxology at the end of *Apol. pro Fuga*, and (with a difference) that of *Hist. Ar.* 80, contrasting that in *de Decr.* 32. Dr. Bright observes that Athan. 'felt himself free to use both forms, although at Antioch they became symbols respectively of the Arianisers and the Orthodox.']

APOLOGIA AD CONSTANTIUM

This address to the Emperor in defence against certain serious charges (see below) was completed about the time of the intrusion of George, who arrived at Alexandria on Feb. 24, 357. The main, or apologetic, part of the letter was probably composed before George's actual arrival, in fact at about the same date as the encyclical letter which immediately precedes; §§ 27 and following (see 27, note 2) forming an added expostulation upon hearing of the general expulsion of Catholic Bishops, and of the outrages[1] at Alexandria. It is quite uncertain whether it ever reached the emperor; whether it did so or not, his attitude toward Athanasius was in no way affected by it. It had probably been begun with the idea of its being actually delivered in the presence of Constantius (see §§ 3, 6, 8, 16 'I see you smile,' 22), but, although by a rhetorical fiction the form of an oral defence is kept up to the end, the concluding sections (27, 32 *init.*) shew that any such idea had been renounced before the Apology was completed. The first 26 sections are directed to the refutation of four personal charges, quite different from those of the earlier period, rebutted in the Apology against the Arians. They were (1) that Athanasius had poisoned the mind of Constans against his brother (2—5). To this Ath. replies that he had never spoken to the deceased Augustus except in the presence of witnesses, and that the history of his own movements when in the West entirely precluded any such possibility. The third and fourth sections thus incidentally supply important details for the life of Athanasius. (2) That he had written letters to the 'tyrant' Magnentius (6—13), a charge absurd in itself, and only to be borne out by forgery, but also amply disproved by his known affection toward Constans, the victim of the 'tyrant.' (3) That he had (14—18) used the new church in the 'Cæsareum,' before it was completed or dedicated, for the Easter festival of 355 (Tillem. viii. 149). This Athanasius admits, but pleads necessity and precedent, adding that no disrespect was intended toward the donor, nor any anticipation of its formal consecration. (4) That he had disobeyed an imperial order to leave Alexandria and go to Italy (19—26, see esp. 19, n. 4, and *Fest. Ind.* xxvi. Constantius is at Milan July 21, 353—Gwatkin p. 292). This charge involves the whole history of the attempts to dislodge Athanasius from Alexandria, which culminated in the events of 356. He replies to the charge, that the summons in question had come in the form of an invitation in reply to an alleged letter of his own asking leave to go to Italy, a letter which, as his amanuenses would testify, he had never written. Of the later visit (355, *Fest. Ind.* xxvii.) of Diogenes, he merely says that Diogenes brought neither letter nor orders. Syrianus, he seems to allow, had verbally ordered him to Italy (Constantius was again at Milan,—Gwatkin *ubi supra*) but without written authority. As against these supposed orders, Ath. had a letter from the emperor (§ 23) exhorting him to remain at Alexandria, whatever reports he might hear. Syrianus had, at the urgent remonstrance of the clergy and people, consented to refer the matter back to Constantius (24), but without waiting to do this, he had suddenly made his famous night attack upon the bishop when holding a vigil service in the Church of Theonas. Thereupon Athanasius had set out for Italy to lay the matter before the emperor in person (27 *init.*). But on reaching, as it would seem, the Libyan portion of his Province, he was turned back by the news of the Council of Milan, and the wholesale banishment which followed. Here we pass to the second part of the Apology. He explains his return to the desert by the three reports which had reached him: first, that just mentioned; secondly, that of further military outrages, about Easter 356 (or possibly those of George in 357, see *Apol. Fug.* 6; the clear statements of *Fest. Ind.* and *Hist. Aceph.* compel us[2] to place these in the latter year,

---

1 See *Apol. Fug.* 6, note 5.   2 See also note 1, *supr.*, and the discussion Prolegg. ch. ii. § 8 (1).

although on *à priori* grounds we might have followed Tillem., Bright, &c., in placing them in 356), and of the nomination of George; thirdly, of the letters of Constantius to the Alexandrians and to the Princes of Abyssinia. He had accordingly gone into hiding, in fear, not of the Emperor, but of the violence of his officers, and as of bounden duty to all (32). He concludes with an outspoken denunciation of the treatment of the virgins, and by an urgent entreaty to Constantius 'which supposes the imperial listener to be already more than half appeased' (Bright). The Apology is the most carefully written work of Athanasius, and 'has been justly praised for its artistic finish and its rhetorical skill' as well as for the force and the sustained calmness and dignity of its diction. (So Montfaucon, Newman, Gwatkin, &c. Fialon, pp. 286, 292, gives some interesting examples of apparent imitation of Demosthenes in this and in the two following tracts.) But the violent contrast between its almost affectionate respectfulness and the chilly reserve of the *Apol. pro Fuga*, or still more the furious invective of the Arian History, is startling, and gives a *prima facie* justification to Gibbon, who (vol. 3, p. 87, Smith's Ed.) charges the great bishop with simulating respect to the emperor's face while denouncing him behind his back. But although the *de Fuga* (see introd. there) was written very soon after our present Apology, there is no ground for making them simultaneous, while its tone (see *Ap. Fug.* 26, note 7) is very different from that of the later *Hist. Arian.* Doubtless much of the material for the invectives of the latter was already ancient history when the tract before us was composed. But Constantius was the Emperor, the first personage in the Christian world, and Athanasius with the feeling of his age, with the memory of the solemn assurances he had received from the Emperor (§§ 23, 25, 27, *Apol. Ar.* 51—56, *Hist. Ar.* 21—24), would 'hope all things,' even 'against hope,' so long as there was any apparent chance of influencing Constantius for good; would hope in spite of all appearances that the outrages, banishments, and intrigues against the faith of Nicæa were the work of the officers, the Arian bishops, the eunuchs of the Court, and not of 'Augustus' himself (see Bright, Introd. to this Apology, pp. lxiii.—lxv.).

DEFENCE BEFORE CONSTANTIUS

1. Knowing that you have been a Christian for many years [1], most religious Augustus, and that you are godly by descent, I cheerfully undertake to answer for myself at this time ;— for I will use the language of the blessed Paul, and make him my advocate before you, considering that he was a preacher of the truth, and that you are an attentive hearer of his words.

With respect to those ecclesiastical matters, which have been made the ground of a conspiracy against me, it is sufficient to refer your Piety to the testimony of the many Bishops who have written in my behalf [2]; enough too is the recantation of Ursacius and Valens [3], to prove to all men, that none of the charges which they set up against me had any truth in them. For what evidence can others produce so strong, as what they declared in writing? 'We lied, we invented these things; all the accusations against Athanasius are full of falsehood.' To this clear proof may be added, if you will vouchsafe to hear it, this circumstance, that the accusers brought no evidence against Macarius the presbyter while we were present; but in our absence [4], when they were by themselves, they managed the matter as they pleased. Now, the Divine Law first of all, and next our own Laws [5], have expressly declared, that such proceedings are of no force whatsoever. From these things your piety, as a lover of God and of the truth, will, I am sure, perceive that we are free from all suspicion, and will pronounce our opponents to be false accusers.

2. The first charge, of setting Constans against Constantius.

But as to the slanderous charge which has been preferred against me before your Grace, respecting correspondence with the most pious Augustus, your brother Constans [6], of blessed and everlasting memory (for my enemies report this of me, and have ventured to assert it in writing), the former events [7] are sufficient to prove this also to be untrue. Had it been alleged by another set of persons, the matter would indeed have been a fit subject of enquiry, but it would have required strong evidence, and open proof in presence of both parties : but when the same persons who invented the former charge, are the authors also of this, is it not reasonable to conclude from the issue of the one, the falsehood of the other? For this cause they again conferred together in private, thinking to be able to deceive your Piety before I was aware. But in this they failed : you would not listen to them as they desired, but patiently gave me an opportunity to make my defence. And, in that you were not immediately moved to demand vengeance, you acted only as was righteous in a Prince, whose duty it is to wait for the defence of the injured party. Which if you will vouchsafe to hear, I am confident that in this matter also you will condemn those reckless men, who have no fear of that God, who has commanded us not to speak falsely before the king [8].

3. He never saw Constans alone.

But in truth I am ashamed even to have to defend myself against charges such as these, which I do not suppose that even the accuser himself would venture to make mention of in my presence. For he knows full well that he speaks untruly, and that I was never so mad, so reft of my senses, as even to be open to the suspicion of having conceived any such thing. So that had I been questioned by any other on this subject, I would not even have answered, lest, while I was making my defence, my hearers should for a time have suspended their judgment concerning me. But to your Piety I answer with a loud and clear voice, and

---

[1] [cf. Acts xxvi. 2.] Constantius, though here called a Christian, was not baptized till his last illness, A.D. 361, and then by the Arian Bishop of Antioch, Euzoius. At this time he was 39 years of age. Theodoret represents him making a speech to his whole army on one occasion, exhorting them to Baptism previous to going to war ; and recommending all to go thence who could not make up their mind to the Sacrament. *H. E.* iii. 1. Constantius, his grandfather, had rejected idolatry and acknowledged the One God, according to Eusebius, *V. Const.* i. 14, though it does not appear that he had embraced Christianity.

[2] *Supr. Apol. Ar.* 1.   [3] *Apol. Ar.* 1, 58.
[4] ib. 13, 27, &c.   [5] Cf. *Apol. Ar.* ii. 51.

[6] Prolegg. ch. ii. § 6 (3) ; cf. Lucifer. *Op.* p. 91. (ed. Ven. 1778.) Theod. *H. E.* ii. 13 ; infr. *Hist. Arian.* § 50.
[7] Vid. *Apol. contr. Arian.* passim.   [8] Vid. Ecclus. vii. 5.

stretching forth my hand, as I have learned from the Apostle, 'I call God for a record upon my soul[9],' and as it is written in the histories of the Kings (let me be allowed to say the same), 'The Lord is witness, and His Anointed is witness[10],' I have never spoken evil of your Piety before your brother Constans, the most religious Augustus of blessed memory. I did not exasperate him against you, as these have falsely accused me. But whenever in my interviews with him he has mentioned your Grace (and he did mention you at the time that Thalassus[1] came to Pitybion, and I was staying at Aquileia), the Lord is witness, how I spoke of your Piety in terms which I would that God would reveal unto your soul, that you might condemn the falsehood of these my calumniators. Bear with me, most gracious Augustus, and freely grant me your indulgence while I speak of this matter. Your most Christian brother was not a man of so light a temper, nor was I a person of such a character, that we should communicate together on a subject like this, or that I should slander a brother to a brother, or speak evil of an emperor before an emperor. I am not so mad, Sire, nor have I forgotten that divine utterance which says, 'Curse not the king, no, not in thy thought; and curse not the rich in thy bedchamber: for a bird of the air shall carry the voice, and that which hath wings shall tell the matter[2].' If then those things, which are spoken in secret against you that are kings, are not hidden, it is not incredible that I should have spoken against you in the presence of a king, and of so many bystanders? For I never saw your brother by myself, nor did he ever converse with me in private, but I was always introduced in company with the Bishop of the city where I happened to be, and with others that chanced to be there. We entered the presence together, and together we retired. Fortunatian[3], Bishop of Aquileia, can testify this, the father Hosius is able to say the same, as also are Crispinus, Bishop of Padua, Lucillus of Verona, Dionysius of Lëis, and Vincentius of Campania. And although Maximinus of Treveri, and Protasius of Milan, are dead, yet Eugenius, who was Master of the Palace[4], can bear witness for me; for he stood before

the veil[5], and heard what we requested of the Emperor, and what he vouchsafed to reply to us.

4. *The movements of Athanasius refute this charge.*

This certainly is sufficient for proof, yet suffer me nevertheless to lay before you an account of my travels, which will further lead you to condemn the unfounded calumnies of my opponents. When I left Alexandria[6], I did not go to your brother's head-quarters, or to any other persons, but only to Rome; and having laid my case before the Church (for this was my only concern), I spent my time in the public worship. I did not write to your brother, except when Eusebius and his fellows had written to him to accuse me, and I was compelled while yet at Alexandria to defend myself; and again when I sent to him volumes[7] containing the holy Scriptures, which he had ordered me to prepare for him. It behoves me, while I defend my conduct, to tell the truth to your Piety. When however three years had passed away, he wrote to me in the fourth year[7a], commanding me to meet him (he was then at Milan); and upon enquiring the cause (for I was ignorant of it, the Lord is my witness), I learnt that certain Bishops[8] had gone up and requested him to write to your Piety, desiring that a Council might be called. Believe me, Sire, this is the truth of the matter; I lie not. Accordingly I went down to Milan, and met with great kindness from him; for he condescended to see me, and to say that he had despatched letters to you, requesting that a Council might be called. And while I remained in that city, he sent for me again into Gaul (for the father Hosius was going thither), that we might travel from thence to Sardica. And after the Council, he wrote to me while I continued at Naissus[9], and I went up, and abode afterwards at Aquileia; where the

---

5 πρὸ τοῦ βήλου. The Veil, which in the first instance was an appendage to the images of pagan deities, formed at this time part of the ceremonial of the imperial Court. It hung over the entrance of the Emperor's bedchamber, where he gave his audiences. It also hung before the secretarium of the Judges. vid. Hofman *in voc.* Gothofred *in Cod. Theod.* i. tit. vii. 1.

6 [A.D. 339.]

7 πύκτια, a bound book, vid. Montf. *Coll. Nov. infr.* Tillemont (t. viii. p. 86.) considers that Athan. alludes in this passage to the *Synopsis Scr. Sacr.* which is among his works; but Montfaucon, *Collect. Nov.* t. 2. p. xxviii. contends that a copy of the Gospels is spoken of. [cf. D.C.B. i. 651.]

7a [A.D. 342.]

8 Tillemont supposes that Constans was present at the Council of Milan [345], at which Eudoxius, Martyrius, and Macedonius, sent to the west with the Eusebian Creed, made their appearance to no purpose. [But this was long after the events related in the text, cf. Prolegg. ii. § 6, *sub. fin.*]

9 [Easter 344, see *Fest. Ind.* xvi.] Naissus was situated in Upper Dacia, and according to some was the birthplace of Constantine. The Bishop of the place, Gaudentius, whose name occurs among the subscriptions at Sardica, had protected S. Paul of Constantinople and incurred the anathemas of the Easterns at Philippopolis. Hil. *Fragm.* iii. 27.

---

9 2 Cor. i. 23.   10 1 Sam. xii. 5.

1 *Hist. Arian.* 22. vid. *Apol. Ar.* 51. ['Pitybion' is Patavia, now Padua.]   2 Eccles. x. 20.

3 All these names of Bishops occur among the subscriptions at Sardica. supr. *Ap. Ar.* 50. [See also D.C.B. *s. vv.*] Leis is Lauda, or Laus Pompeia, *hodie* Lodi Vecchio; Ughelli, *Ital. Sacr.* t. 4. p. 656.

4 Or, master of the offices; one of the seven Ministers of the Court under the Empire; 'He inspected the discipline of the civil and military schools, and received appeals from all parts of the Empire.' Gibbon, ch. 17. [cf. Gwatkin, p. 285.]

letters of your Piety found me. And again, being invited thence by your departed brother, I returned into Gaul, and so came at length to your Piety.

5. No possible time or place for the alleged offence.

Now what place and time does my accuser specify, at which I made use of these expressions according to his slanderous imputation? In whose presence was I so mad as to give utterance to the words which he has falsely charged me with speaking? Who is there ready to support the charge, and to testify to the fact? What his own eyes have seen that ought to he speak[1], as holy Scripture enjoins. But no; he will find no witnesses of that which never took place. But I take your Piety to witness, together with the Truth, that I lie not. I request you, for I know you to be a person of excellent memory, to call to mind the conversation I had with you, when you condescended to see me, first at Viminacium[2], a second time at Cæsarea in Cappadocia, and a third[3] time at Antioch. Did I speak evil before you even of Eusebius and his fellows who had persecuted me? Did I cast imputations upon any of those that have done me wrong? If then I imputed nothing to any of those against whom I had a right to speak, how could I be so possessed with madness as to slander an Emperor before an Emperor, and to set a brother at variance with a brother? I beseech you, either cause me to appear before you that the thing may be proved, or else condemn these calumnies, and follow the example of David, who says, 'Whoso privily slandereth his neighbour, him will I destroy[4].' As much as in them lies, they have slain me; for 'the mouth that belieth, slayeth the soul[5].' But your long-suffering has prevailed against them, and given me confidence to defend myself, that they may suffer condemnation, as contentious and slanderous persons. Concerning your most religious brother, of blessed memory, this may suffice: for you will be able, according to the wisdom which God has given you, to gather much from the little I have said, and to recognise the fictitious charge.

6. The second charge, of corresponding with Magnentius.

With regard to the second calumny, that I have written letters to the tyrant[6] (his name I am unwilling to pronounce), I beseech you

investigate and try the matter, in whatever way you please, and by whomsoever you may approve of. The extravagance of the charge so confounds me, that I am in utter uncertainty how to act. Believe me, most religious Prince, many times did I weigh the matter in my mind, but was unable• to believe that any one could be so mad as to utter such a falsehood. But when this charge was published abroad by the Arians, as well as the former, and they boasted that they had delivered to you a copy of the letter, I was the more amazed, and I used to pass sleepless nights contending against the charge, as if in the presence of my accusers; and suddenly breaking forth into a loud cry, I would immediately fall to my prayers, desiring with groans and tears that I might obtain a favourable hearing from you. And now that by the grace of the Lord, I have obtained such a hearing, I am again at a loss how I shall begin my defence; for as often as I make an attempt to speak, I am prevented by my horror at the deed. In the case of your departed brother, thè slanderers had indeed a plausible pretence for what they alleged; because I had been admitted to see him, and he had condescended to write to your brotherly affection concerning me; and he had often sent for me to come to him, and had honoured me when I came. But for the traitor Magnentius, 'the Lord is witness, and His Anointed is witness[6a],' I know him not, nor was ever acquainted with him. What correspondence then could there be between persons so entirely unacquainted with each other? What reason was there to induce me to write to such a man? How could I have commenced my letter, had I written to him? Could I have said, 'You have done well to murder the man who honoured me, whose kindness I shall never forget?' Or, 'I approve of your conduct in destroying our Christian friends, and most faithful brethren?' or, 'I approve of your proceedings in butchering those who so kindly entertained me at Rome; for instance, your departed Aunt Eutropia[6b], whose disposition answered to her name, that worthy man, Abuterius, the most faithful Spirantius, and many other excellent persons?'

7. This charge utterly incredible and absurd.

Is it not mere madness in my accuser even to suspect me of such a thing? What, I ask again, could induce me to place confidence in this man? What trait did I perceive in his character on which I could rely? He had

---

[1] Prov. xxv. 7, LXX.   [2] In Mœsia.   [3] [Prolegg. ch. ii. § 5 fin., § 6 (3).]   [4] Ps. ci. 5.   [5] Wisd. i. 11.
[6] [On Magnentius, see Prolegg. ch. ii. § 7 sub. fin.; Gwatkin, Studies, p. 143 sq.]

[6a] 1 Sam. xii. 5.
[6b] Nepotian, the son of Eutropia, Constantine's sister, had taken up arms against Magnentius, got possession of Rome, and enjoyed the title of Augustus for about a month. Magnentius put him to death, and his mother, and a number of his adherents, some of whom are here mentioned.

murdered his own master; he had proved faithless to his friends; he had violated his oath; he had blasphemed God, by consulting poisoners and sorcerers[7] contrary to his Law. And with what conscience could I send greeting to such a man, whose madness and cruelty had afflicted not me only, but all the world around me? To be sure, I was very greatly indebted to him for his conduct, that when your departed brother had filled our churches with sacred offerings, he murdered him. For the wretch was not moved by the sight of these his gifts, nor did he stand in awe of the divine grace which had been given to him in baptism: but like an accursed and devilish spirit, he raged against him, till your blessed brother suffered martyrdom at his hands; while he, henceforth a criminal like Cain, was driven from place to place, 'groaning and trembling[8],' to the end that he might follow the example of Judas in his death, by becoming his own executioner, and so bring upon himself a double weight of punishment in the judgment to come.

8. *Disproof of it.*

With such a man the slanderer thought that I had been on terms of friendship, or rather he did not think so, but like an enemy invented an incredible fiction: for he knows full well that he has lied. I would that, whoever he is, he were present here, that I might put the question to him on the word of Truth itself (for whatever we speak as in the presence of God, we Christians consider as an oath[9]); I say, that I might ask him this question, which of us rejoiced most in the well-being of the departed Constans? who prayed for him most earnestly? The facts of the foregoing charge prove this; indeed it is plain to every one how the case stands. But although he himself knows full well, that no one who was so disposed towards the departed Constans, and who truly loved him, could be a friend to his enemy, I fear that being possessed with other feelings towards him than I was, he has falsely attributed to me those sentiments of hatred which were entertained by himself.

9. *Athanasius could not write to one who did not even know him.*

For myself, I am so surprised at the enormity of the thing, that I am quite uncertain what I ought to say in my defence. I can only declare, that I condemn myself to die ten thousand deaths, if even the least sus-

picion attaches to me in this matter. And to you, Sire, as a lover of the truth, I confidently make my appeal. I beseech you, as I said before, investigate this affair, and especially with the testimony of those who were once sent by him as ambassadors to you. These are the Bishops Sarvatius[1] and Maximus and the rest, with Clementius and Valens. Enquire of them, I beseech you, whether they brought letters to me. If they did, this would give me occasion to write to him. But if he did not write to me, if he did not even know me, how could I write to one with whom I had no acquaintance? Ask them whether, when I saw Clementius and his fellows, and spoke of your brother of blessed memory, I did not, in the language of Scripture, wet my garments with tears[2], when I remembered his kindness of disposition and his Christian spirit. Learn of them how anxious I was, on hearing of the cruelty of the beast, and finding that Valens and his company had come by way of Libya, lest he should attempt a passage also, and like a robber murder those who held in love and memory the departed Prince, among whom I account myself second to none.

10. *His loyalty towards Constantius and his brother.*

How with this apprehension of such a design on their part, was there not an additional probability of my praying for your Grace? Should I feel affection for his murderer, and entertain dislike towards you his brother who avenged his death? Should I remember his crime, and forget that kindness of yours which you vouchsafed to assure me by letter[3] should remain the same towards me after your brother's death of happy memory, as it had been during his lifetime? How could I have borne to look upon the murderer? Must I not have thought that the blessed Prince beheld me, when I prayed for your safety? For brothers are by nature mirrors of each other. Wherefore as seeing you in him, I never should have slandered you before him; and as seeing him in you, never should I have written to his enemy, instead of praying for your safety. Of this my witnesses are, first of all, the Lord who has heard and has given to you entire the kingdom of your forefathers: and next those persons who were present at the time, Felicissimus, who was Duke of

---

7 Bingh. *Antiqu.* xvi. 5. § 5, &c.
8 Gen. iv. 12. LXX. vid. *Hist. Ar.* § 7.
9 Vid. Chrys. *in Eph.* Nicene Lib., Series I. vol. xiii. p. 58.

1 Sarbatius, or Servatius, and Maximus occur in the lists of Gallic subscriptions [*supr.* p. 127]. The former is supposed to be S. Servatius or Servatio of Tungri, concerning whom at Ariminum, vid. Sulp. Sev. *Hist.* ii. 59. vid. also Greg.Turon. *Hist. Franc* ii. 5. where however the Bened. Ed. prefers to read Aravatius, a Bishop, as he considers, of the fifth century.
2 Ps. vi. 6.   3 Cf. § 23.

Egypt, Rufinus, and Stephanus, the former of whom was Receiver-general, the latter, Master there; Count Asterius, and Palladius Master of the palace, Antiochus and Evagrius Official Agents[4]. I had only to say, 'Let us pray for the safety of the most religious Emperor, Constantius Augustus,' and all the people immediately cried out with one voice, 'O Christ send help to Constantius;' and they continued praying thus for some time[5].

11. Challenge to the accusers as to the alleged letter.

Now I have already called upon God, and His Word, the Only-begotten Son our Lord Jesus Christ, to witness for me, that I have never written to that man, nor received letters from him. And as to my accuser, give me leave to ask him a few short questions concerning this charge also. How did he come to the knowledge of this matter? Will he say that he has got copies of the letter? for this is what the Arians laboured to prove. Now in the first place, even if he can shew writing resembling mine, the thing is not yet certain; for there are forgers, who have often imitated the hand[6] even of you who are Emperors. And the resemblance will not prove the genuineness of the letter, unless my customary amanuensis shall testify in its favour. I would then again ask my accusers, Who provided you with these copies? and whence were they obtained? I had my writers[6a], and he his servants, who received his letters from the bearers, and gave them into his hand. My assistants are forthcoming; vouchsafe to summon the others (for they are most probably still living), and enquire concerning these letters. Search into the matter, as though Truth were the partner of your throne. She is the defence of Kings, and especially of Christian Kings; with her

you will reign most securely, for holy Scripture says, 'Mercy and truth preserve the king, and they will encircle his throne in righteousness[7].' And the wise Zorobabel gained a victory over the others by setting forth the power of Truth, and all the people cried out, 'Great is the truth, and mighty above all things[8].'

12. Truth the defence of Thrones.

Had I been accused before any other, I should have appealed to your Piety; as once the Apostle appealed unto Cæsar, and put an end to the designs of his enemies against him. But since they have had the boldness to lay their charge before you, to whom shall I appeal from you? to the Father of Him who says, 'I am the Truth[9],' that He may incline your heart into clemency:—

O Lord Almighty, and King of eternity, the Father of our Lord Jesus Christ, who by Thy Word hast given this Kingdom to Thy servant Constantius; do Thou shine into his heart, that he, knowing the falsehood that is set against me, may both favourably receive this my defence; and may make known unto all men, that his ears are firmly set to hearken unto the Truth, according as it is written, 'Righteous lips alone are acceptable unto the King[10].' For Thou hast caused it to be said by Solomon, that thus the throne of the kingdom shall be established.

Wherefore at least enquire into this matter, and let the accusers understand that your desire is to learn the truth; and see, whether they will not shew their falsehood by their very looks; for the countenance is a test of the conscience as it is written, 'A merry heart maketh a cheerful countenance, but by sorrow of the heart the spirit is broken[1].' Thus they who had conspired against Joseph[2] were convicted by their own consciences; and the craft of Laban towards Jacob was shewn in his countenance[3]. And thus you see the suspicious alarm of these persons, for they fly and hide themselves; but on our part frankness in making our defence. And the question between us is not one regarding worldly wealth, but concerning the honour of the Church. He that has been struck by a stone, applies to a physician; but sharper than a stone are the strokes of calumny; for as Solomon has said, 'A false witness is a maul, and a sword, and a sharp arrow[4],' and its wounds Truth alone is able to cure; and if Truth be set at nought, they grow worse and worse.

---

4 1. The Rationales or Receivers, in Greek writers Catholici (λογοθεταὶ being understood, Vales. ad Euseb. vii. 10.), were the same as the Procurators (Gibbon, Hist. ch. xvii. note 148.), who succeeded the Provincial Quæstors in the early times of the Empire. They were in the department of the Comes Sacrarum Largitionum, or High Treasurer of the Revenue (Gothofr. Cod. Theod. t. 6. p. 327). Both Gothofr. however and Pancirolus, p. 134. Ed. 1623, place Rationales also under the Comes Rerum Privatarum. Pancirolus, p. 120. mentions the Comes Rationalis Summarum Ægypti as distinct from other functionaries. Gibbon, ch. xvii. seems to say that there were in all 29, of whom 18 were counts. 2. Stephanus, μάγιστρος ἐκεῖ. Tillemont translates, 'Master of the camp of Egypt,' vol. viii. p. 137. 3. The Master of the offices or of the palace has been noticed above, p. 239, note 4. 4. ἀγεντισπρίβους, agentes in rebus. These were functionaries under the Master of the offices, whose business it was to announce the names of the consuls and the edicts and victories of the Empire. They at length became spies of the Court, vid. Gibbon, ch. xvii Gothofr. Cod. Th. vi. 27.

5 'Presbyterum Eraclium mihi successorem volo. A populo acclamatum est, Deo gratias, Christo laudes; dictum est vicies terties. Exaudi Christe, Augustino vita; dictum est sexies decies. Te patrem, te episcopum; dictum est octies.' August. Ep. 213.

6 Apol. Ar. 45.

6a Vid. Rom. xvi. 22. Lucian is spoken of as the amanuensis of the Confessors, who wrote to S. Cyprian, Ep. 16. Ed. Ben. Jader perhaps of Ep. 80. [Epp. 23, 79, Hartel.] S. Jerome was either secretary or amanuensis to Pope Damasus, vid. Ep. ad Ageruch. (123. n. 10. Ed. Vallars.) vid. Lami de Erud. Ap. p. 258.

---

7 Prov. xx. 28.　　8 1 Esdr. iv. 41.　　9 John xiv. 6.
10 Prov. xvi. 13, xxv. 5.　　1 Prov. xv. 13.
2 Gen. xlii. 21; xxxi. 2.　　3 Vid. Vit. Ant. § 67.
4 Prov. xxv. 18.

13. *This charge rests on forgery.*

It is this that has thrown the Churches every-where into such confusion; for pretences have been devised, and Bishops of great authority, and of advanced age [5], have been banished for holding communion with me. And if matters had stopped here, our prospect would be favour-able through your gracious interposition. But that the evil may not extend itself, let Truth prevail before you; and leave not every Church under suspicion, as though Christian men, nay even Bishops, could be guilty of plotting and writing in this manner. Or if you are unwilling to investigate the matter, it is but right that we who offer our defence, should be believed, rather than our calumniators. They, like ene-mies, are occupied in wickedness; we, as earn-estly contending for our cause, present to you our proofs. And truly I wonder how it comes to pass, that while we address you with fear and reverence, they are possessed of such an impudent spirit, that they dare even to lie be-fore the Emperor. But I pray you, for the Truth's sake, and as it is written [5a], 'search dili-gently' in my presence, on what grounds they affirm these things, and whence these letters were obtained. But neither will any of my servants be proved guilty, nor will any of his people be able to tell whence they came; for they are forgeries. And perhaps one had better not enquire further. They do not wish it, lest the writer of the letters should be cer-tain of detection. For the calumniators alone, and none besides, know who he is.

14. *The third charge, of using an undedicated Church.*

But forasmuch as they have informed against me in the matter of the great Church [5b], that a communion was holden there before it was completed, I will answer to your Piety on this charge also; for the parties who are hostile towards me constrain me to do so. I con-fess this did so happen; for, as in what I have hitherto said, I have spoken no lie, I will not now deny this. But the facts are far otherwise than they have represented them. Suffer me to declare to you, most religious Augustus, that we kept no day of dedication (it would certainly have been unlawful to do so, before receiving orders from you), nor were we led to act as we did through premeditation. No Bishop or other Clergyman was invited to join in our proceedings; for much was yet wanting to complete the building. Nay the congregation was not held on a previous notice,

which might give them a reason for informing against us. Every one knows how it happened; hear me, however, with your accustomed equity and patience. It was the feast of Easter [5c], and the multitude assembled together was ex-ceeding great, such as Christian kings would desire to see in all their cities. Now when the Churches were found to be too few to contain them, there was no little stir among the people, who desired that they might be allowed to meet together in the great Church, where they could all offer up their prayers for your safety. And this they did; for although I exhorted them to wait awhile, and to hold service in the other Churches, with whatever inconvenience to themselves, they would not listen to me; but were ready to go out of the city, and meet in desert places in the open air, thinking it better to endure the fatigue of the journey, than to keep the feast in such a state of discomfort.

15. *Want of room the cause, precedent the justification.*

Believe me, Sire, and let Truth be my wit-ness in this also, when I declare that in the congregations held during the season of Lent, in consequence of the narrow limits of the places, and the vast multitude of people as-sembled, a great number of children, not a few of the younger and very many of the older women, besides several young men, suf-fered so much from the pressure of the crowd, that they were obliged to be carried home; though by the Providence of God, no one is dead. All however murmured, and de-manded the use of the great Church. And if the pressure was so great during the days which preceded the feast, what would have been the case during the feast itself? Of course matters would have been far worse. It did not there-fore become me to change the people's joy into grief, their cheerfulness into sorrow, and to make the festival a season of lamentation.

And that the more, because I had a pre-cedent in the conduct of our Fathers. For the blessed Alexander, when the other places were too small, and he was engaged in the erection of what was then considered a very large one, the Church of Theonas [6], held

---

5 *Hist. Arian.* 72, &c.   5a Joel i. 7, LXX.

5b [In the Cæsareum, see *Hist. Ar.* 55, and *Fest. Ind.* xxxviii. xl. It had been begun by Gregory, and was built at the expense of Constantius (*infr.* end of § 18).]

5c A.D. 355.

6 S. Epiphanius mentions nine Churches in Alexandria. *Hær.* 69. 2. Athan. mentions in addition that of Quirinus. *Hist. Arian.* § 10. [See the plan of Larsow, appended to his *Fest-briefe.*] The Church mentioned in the text was built at the Emperor's expense; and apparently upon the Emperor's ground, as on the site was or had been a Basilica, which bore first the name of Hadrian, then of Licinius, Epiph. *ibid.* Hadrian had built in many cities temples without idols, which were popularly considered as intended by him for Christian worship, and went after his name. Lamprid. *Vit. Alex. Sev.* 43. The Church in question was built in the Cæsa-reum. *Hist. Arian.* 74. There was a magnificent Temple, dedi-cated to Augustus, as ἐπιβατήριος, on the harbour of Alexandria, Philon. *Legat. ad Caium,* pp. 1013, 4. ed. 1691, and called the

his congregations there on account of the number of the people, while at the same time he proceeded with the building. I have seen the same thing done at Treveri and at Aquileia, in both which places, while the building was proceeding, they assembled there during the feasts, on account of the number of the people; and they never found any one to accuse them in this manner. Nay, your brother of blessed memory was present, when a communion was held under these circumstances at Aquileia. I also followed this course. There was no dedication, but only a service of prayer. You, at least I am sure, as a lover of God will approve of the people's zeal, and will pardon me for being unwilling to hinder the prayers of so great a multitude.

16. Better to pray together than separately.

But here again I would ask my accuser, where was it right that the people should pray? in the deserts, or in a place which was in course of building for the purpose of prayer? Where was it becoming and pious that the people should answer, Amen[7]? in the deserts, or in what was already called the Lord's house? Where would you, most religious Prince, have wished your people to stretch forth their hands, and to pray for you? Where Greeks, as they passed by, might stop and listen, or in a place named after yourself, which all men have long called the Lord's house, even since the foundations of it were laid? I am sure that you prefer your own place; for you smile, and that tells me so. 'But,' says the accuser, 'it ought to have been in the Churches. They were all, as I said before, too small and confined to admit the multitude. Then again, in which way was it most becoming that their prayers should be made? Should they meet together in parts and separate companies, with danger from the crowded state of the congregation? or, when there was now a place that would contain them all, should they assemble in it, and speak as with one and the same voice in perfect harmony? This was the better course, for this shewed the unanimity of the multitude: in this way God will readily hear prayer. For if, according to the promise of our Saviour Himself[8], where two shall agree together as touching anything that they shall ask, it shall be done for them, how shall it be when so great an assembly of people with one voice utter their Amen to God? Who indeed was there

that did not marvel at the sight? Who but pronounced you happy when they saw so great a multitude met together in one place? How did the people themselves rejoice to see each other, having been accustomed heretofore to assemble in separate places! The circumstance was a source of pleasure to all; of vexation to the calumniator alone.

17. Better to pray in a building than in the desert.

Now then, I would also meet the other and only remaining objection of my accuser. He says, the building was not completed, and prayer ought not to have been made there. But the Lord said, 'But thou, when thou prayest, enter into thy closet, and shut the door[9].' What then will the accuser answer? or rather what will all prudent and true Christians say? Let your Majesty ask the opinion of such: for it is written of the other, 'The foolish person will speak foolishness[10];' but of these, 'Ask counsel of all that are wise[1].' When the Churches were too small, and the people so numerous as they were, and desirous to go forth into the deserts, what ought I to have done? The desert has no doors, and all who choose may pass through it, but the Lord's house is enclosed with walls and doors, and marks the difference between the pious and the profane. Will not every wise person then, as well as your Piety, Sire, give the preference to the latter place? For they know that here prayer is lawfully offered, while a suspicion of irregularity attaches to it there. Unless indeed no place proper for it existed, and the worshippers dwelt only in the desert, as was the case with Israel; although after the tabernacle was built, they also had thenceforth a place set apart for prayer. O Christ, Lord and true King of kings, Only-begotten Son of God, Word and Wisdom of the Father, I am accused because the people prayed Thy gracious favour, and through Thee besought Thy Father, who is God over all, to save Thy servant, the most religious Constantius. But thanks be to Thy goodness, that it is for this that I am blamed, and for the keeping of Thy laws. Heavier had been the blame, and more true had been the charge, had we passed by the place which the Emperor was building, and gone forth into the desert to pray. How would the accuser then have vented his folly! With what apparent reason would he have said, 'He despised the place which you are building; he does not approve of your undertaking; he passed it by in derision; he pointed to the desert to supply the want of

---

Cæsareum. It was near the Emperor's palace, vid. *Acad. des. Inscript.* vol. 9. p. 416. [Vid. *supr.* note 5[b], and cf. *Apol. de Fuga* 24.]
7 Bingham, *Antiqu.* xv. 3. § 25. [D.C.A. 75.] Suicer, *Thesaur. in voc.* ἀμήν, Gavanti, *Thesaur.* vol. i. p. 89. ed. 1763.
8 Matt. xviii. 19.

---

9 Matt. vi. 6.   10 Is. xxxii. 6. Sept.   1 Tob. iv. 18.

room; he prevented the people when they wished to offer up their prayers.' This is what he wished to say, and sought an occasion of saying it; and finding none he is vexed, and so forthwith invents a charge against me. Had he been able to say this, he would have confounded me with shame; as now he injures me, copying the accuser's ways, and watching for an occasion against those that pray. Thus has he perverted to a wicked purpose his knowledge of Daniel's [2] history. But he has been deceived; for he ignorantly imagined, that Babylonian practices were in fashion with you, and knew not that you are a friend of the blessed Daniel, and worship the same God, and do not forbid, but wish all men to pray, knowing that the prayer of all is, that you may continue to reign in perpetual peace and safety.

18. Prayers first do not interfere with dedication afterwards.

This is what I have to complain of on the part of my accuser. But may you, most religious Augustus, live through the course of many years to come, and celebrate the dedication of the Church. Surely the prayers which have been offered for your safety by all men, are no hindrance to this celebration. Let these unlearned persons cease such misrepresentations, but let them learn from the example of the Fathers; and let them read the Scriptures. Or rather let them learn of you, who are so well instructed in such histories, how that Joshua the son of Josedek the priest, and his brethren, and Zorobabel the wise, the son of Salathiel, and Ezra the priest and scribe of the law, when the temple was in course of building after the captivity, the feast of tabernacles being at hand (which was a great feast and time of assembly and prayer in Israel), gathered [3] the people together with one accord in the great court within the first gate, which is toward the East, and prepared the altar to God, and there offered their gifts, and kept the feast. And so afterwards they brought hither their sacrifices, on the sabbaths and the new moons, and the people offered up their prayers. And yet the Scripture says expressly, that when these things were done, the temple of God was not yet built; but rather while they thus prayed, the building of the house was advancing. So that neither were their prayers deferred in expectation of the dedication, nor was the dedication prevented by the assemblies held for the sake of prayer. But the people thus continued to pray; and when the house was entirely finished, they celebrated the dedication, and brought their gifts for that purpose, and all kept the

feast for the completion of the work. And thus also have the blessed Alexander, and the other Fathers done. They continued to assemble their people, and when they had completed the work they gave thanks unto the Lord, and celebrated the dedication. This also it befits you to do, O Prince, most careful in your inquiries. The place is ready, having been already sanctified by the prayers which have been offered in it, and requires only the presence of your Piety. This only is wanting to its perfect beauty. Do you then supply this deficiency, and there make your prayers unto the Lord, for whom you have built this house. That you may do so is the prayer of all men.

19. Fourth charge, of having disobeyed an Imperial order.

And now, if it please you, let us consider the remaining accusation, and permit me to answer it likewise. They have dared to charge me with resisting your commands, and refusing to leave my Church. Truly I wonder they are not weary of uttering their calumnies; I however am not yet weary of answering them, I rather rejoice to do so; for the more abundant my defence is, the more entirely must they be condemned. I did not resist the commands of your Piety, God forbid; I am not a man that would resist even the Quæstor [3a] of the city, much less so great a Prince. On this matter I need not many words, for the whole city will bear witness for me. Nevertheless, permit me again to relate the circumstances from the beginning; for when you hear them, I am sure you will be astonished at the presumption of my enemies. Montanus, the officer of the Palace [4], came and brought me a letter, which purported to be an answer to one from me, requesting that I might go into Italy, for the purpose of obtaining a supply of the deficiencies which I thought existed in the condition of our Churches. Now I desire to thank your Piety, which condescended to assent to my request, on the supposition that I had written to you, and has made provision [5] for me to undertake the journey, and to accomplish it without trouble. But here again I am astonished at those who have spoken falsehood in your ears, that they were not afraid, seeing that lying belongs to the Devil, and that liars are alien from Him who says, 'I am the Truth [6].' For I never wrote to you, nor will my accuser be able to find any such letter; and though I ought to have written every day, if I might thereby

---

[2] Dan. vi. 11.   [3] Ezr. iii. 6; Neh. viii.

[3a] λογιστῇ, auditor of accounts? vid. Demosth. de Corona, p. 290. ed. 1823. Arist. Polit. vi. 8.
[4] Vid. Cod. Theod. vi. 30 [summer of 353 A.D. Prolegg. ch. ii. § 7 fin.]
[5] Apol. Ar. 70, note 5.   [6] John xiv. 6.

behold your gracious countenance, yet it would neither have been pious to desert the Churches, nor right to be troublesome to your Piety, especially since you are willing to grant our requests in behalf of the Church, although we are not present to make them. Now may it please you to order me to read what Montanus commanded me to do. This is as follows[7]. * * *

20. *History of his disobeying it.*

Now I ask again, whence have my accusers obtained this letter also? I would learn of them who it was that put it into their hands? Do you cause them to answer. By this you may perceive that they have forged this, as they spread abroad also the former letter, which they published against me, with reference to the ill-named Magnentius. And being convicted in this instance also, on what pretence next will they bring me to make my defence? Their only concern is, to throw everything into disorder and confusion; and for this end I perceive they exercise their zeal. Perhaps they think that by frequent repetition of their charges, they will at last exasperate you against me. But you ought to turn away from such persons, and to hate them; for such as themselves are, such also they imagine those to be who listen to them; and they think that their calumnies will prevail even before you. The accusation of Doeg[8] prevailed of old against the priests of God: but it was the unrighteous Saul, who hearkened unto him. And Jezebel was able to injure the most religious Naboth[9] by her false accusations; but then it was the wicked and apostate Ahab who hearkened unto her. But the most holy David, whose example it becomes you to follow, as all pray that you may, favours not such men, but was wont to turn away from them and avoid them, as raging dogs. He says, 'Whoso privily slandereth his neighbour, him will I destroy[10].' For he kept the commandment which says, 'Thou shalt not receive a false report[11].' And false are the reports of these men in your sight. You, like Solomon, have required of the Lord (and you ought to believe yourself to have obtained your desire), that it would seem good unto Him to remove far from you vain and lying words[12].

21. Forasmuch then as the letter owed its origin to a false story, and contained no order that I should come to you, I concluded that it was not the wish of your Piety that I should come. For in that you gave me no absolute command, but merely wrote as in answer to

a letter from me, requesting that I might be permitted to set in order the things which seemed to be wanting, it was manifest to me (although no one told me this) that the letter which I had received did not express the sentiments of your Clemency. All knew, and I also stated in writing, as Montanus is aware, that I did not refuse to come, but only that I thought it unbecoming to take advantage of the supposition that I had written to you to request this favour, fearing also lest the false accusers should find in this a pretence for saying that I made myself troublesome to your Piety. Nevertheless, I made preparations, as Montanus also knows, in order that, should you condescend to write to me, I might immediately leave home, and readily answer your commands; for I was not so mad as to resist such an order from you. When then in fact your Piety did not write to me, how could I resist a command which I never received? or how can they say that I refused to obey, when no orders were given me? Is not this again the mere fabrication of enemies, pretending that which never took place? I fear that even now, while I am engaged in this defence of myself, they may allege against me that I am doing that which I have never obtained your permission to do. So easily is my conduct made matter of accusation by them, and so ready are they to vent their calumnies in despite of that Scripture, which says, 'Love not to slander another, lest thou be cut off[1].'

22. *Arrivals of Diogenes and of Syrianus.*

After a period of six and twenty months, when Montanus had gone away, there came Diogenes the Notary[2]; but he brought me no letter, nor did we see each other, nor did he charge me with any commands as from you. Moreover when the General Syrianus entered Alexandria[3], seeing that certain reports were spread abroad by the Arians, who declared that matters would now be as they wished, I enquired whether he had brought any letters on the subject of these statements of theirs. I confess that I asked for letters containing your commands. And when he said that he had brought none, I requested that Syrianus himself, or Maximus the Prefect of Egypt, would write to me concerning this matter. Which request I made, because your Grace has written

---

[7] Lost, or never introduced.
[8] 1 Sam. xxii. 9.　[9] 1 Kings xxi. 10.　[10] Ps. ci. 5.
[11] Ex. xxiii. 1.　[12] Prov. xxx. 8

[1] Prov. xx. 13, LXX.
[2] [August, 355 A.D. See *Hist. Aceph.* iii. *Fest. Ind.* xxv., xxvii.] Notaries were the immediate attendants on magistrates, whose judgments, &c., they recorded and promulgated. Their office was analogous in the Imperial Court. vid. Gothofred in *Cod. Theod.* VI. x. Ammian. Marcell. tom. 3. p. 464. ed. Erfurt, 1808. Pancirol. *Notit.* p. 143. Hofman *in voc.* Scharl enumerates with references the civil officers, &c., to whom they were attached in Dissert. 1, *de Notariis Ecclesiæ*, p. 49.
[3] [Jan. 5, 356.]

to me, desiring that I would not suffer myself to be alarmed by any one, nor attend to those who wished to frighten me, but that I would continue to reside in the Churches without fear. It was Palladius, the Master of the Palace, and Asterius, formerly Duke of Armenia, who brought me this letter. Permit me to read a copy of it. It is as follows :

23. A copy [4] of the letter as follows :
Constantius Victor Augustus to Athanasius [5].

It is not unknown to your Prudence, how constantly I prayed that success might attend my late brother Constans in all his undertakings, and your wisdom will easily judge how greatly I was afflicted, when I learnt that he had been cut off by the treachery of villains. Now forasmuch as certain persons are endeavouring at this time to alarm you, by setting before your eyes that lamentable tragedy, I have thought good to address to your Reverence this present letter, to exhort you, that, as becomes a Bishop, you would teach the people to conform to the established [6] religion, and, according to your custom, give yourself up to prayer together with them. For this is agreeable to our wishes ; and our desire is, that you should at every season be a Bishop in your own place.

And in another hand :—May divine Providence preserve you, beloved Father, many years.

24. *Why Athanasius did not obey the Imperial Order.*

On the subject of this letter, my opponents conferred with the magistrates. And was it not reasonable that I, having received it, should demand their letters, and refuse to give heed to mere pretences? And were they not acting in direct contradiction to the tenor of your instructions to me, while they failed to shew me the commands of your Piety? I therefore, seeing they produced no letters from you, considered it improbable that a mere verbal communication should be made to them, especially as the letter of your Grace had charged me not to give ear to such persons. I acted rightly then, most religious Augustus, that as I had returned to my country under the authority of your letters, so I should only leave it by your command ; and might not render myself liable hereafter to a charge of having deserted the Church, but as receiving your order might have a reason for my retiring. This was demanded for me by all my people, who went to Syrianus together

with the Presbyters, and the greatest part, to say the least, of the city with them. Maximus, the Prefect of Egypt, was also there : and their request was that either he would send me a declaration of your wishes in writing, or would forbear to disturb the Churches, while the people themselves were sending a deputation to you respecting the matter. When they persisted in their demand, Syrianus at last perceived the reasonableness of it, and consented, protesting by your safety (Hilary was present and witnessed this) that he would put an end to the disturbance, and refer the case to your Piety. The guards of the Duke, as well as those of the Prefect of Egypt, know that this is true ; the Prytanis [7] of the city also remembers the words ; so that you will perceive that neither I, nor any one else, resisted your commands.

25. *The irruption of Syrianus.*

All demanded that the letters of your Piety should be exhibited. For although the bare word of a King is of equal weight and authority with his written command, especially if he who reports it, boldly affirms in writing that it has been given him ; yet when they neither openly declared that they had received any command, nor, as they were requested to do, gave me assurance of it in writing, but acted altogether as by their own authority ; I confess, I say it boldly, I was suspicious of them. For there were many Arians about them, who were their companions at table, and their counsellors ; and while they attempted nothing openly, they were preparing to assail me by stratagem and treachery. Nor did they act at all as under the authority of a royal command, but, as their conduct betrayed, at the solicitation of enemies. This made me demand more urgently that they should produce letters from you, seeing that all their undertakings and designs were of a suspicious nature ; and because it was unseemly that after I had entered the Church, under the authority of so many letters from you, I should retire from it without such a sanction. When however Syrianus gave his promise, all the people assembled together in the Churches with feelings of joyfulness and security. But three and twenty days after [8], he burst into the Church with his soldiers, while we were engaged in our usual services, as those who entered in there witnessed ; for it was a vigil, preparatory to a communion on the morrow. And such things were done that night as the Arians desired and had beforehand denounced against us. For the

---

4 Vid. another translation of the Latin, *Hist. Arian.* § 24.
5 Spring of 350.
6 κεχρεωστημένην vid. κρατούσῃ πίστει, infr. § 31.

7 The Mayor, Tillem. vol. viii. p. 152.
8 [Feb. 8, 356 : cf. *Apol. Fug.* 24.]

General brought them with him; and they were the instigators and advisers of the attack. This is no incredible story of mine, most religious Augustus; for it was not done in secret, but was noised abroad everywhere. When therefore I saw the assault begun, I first exhorted the people to retire, and then withdrew myself after them, God hiding and guiding me, as those who were with me at the time witness. Since then, I have remained by myself, though I have all confidence to answer for my conduct, in the first place before God, and also before your Piety, for that I did not flee and desert my people, but can point to the attack of the General upon us, as a proof of persecution. His proceedings have caused the greatest astonishment among all men; for either he ought not to have made a promise, or not to have broken it after he had made it.

26. How Athanasius acted when this took place.

Now why did they form this plot against me, and treacherously lay an ambush to take me, when it was in their power to enforce the order by a written declaration? The command of an Emperor is wont to give great boldness to those entrusted with it; but their desire to act secretly made the suspicion stronger that they had received no command. And did I require anything so very absurd? Let your Majesty's candour decide. Will not every one say, that such a demand was reasonable for a Bishop to make? You know, for you have read the Scriptures, how great an offence it is for a Bishop to desert his Church, and to neglect the flocks of God. For the absence of the Shepherd gives the wolves an opportunity to attack the sheep. And this was what the Arians and all the other heretics desired, that during my absence they might find an opportunity to entrap the people into impiety. If then I had fled, what defence could I have made before the true Bishops? or rather before Him Who has committed to me His flock? He it is Who judges the whole earth, the true King of all, our Lord Jesus Christ, the Son of God. Would not every one have rightly charged me with neglect of my people? Would not your Piety have blamed me, and have justly asked, 'After you had returned under the authority of our letters, why did you withdraw without such authority, and desert your people?' Would not the people themselves at the day of judgment have reasonably imputed to me this neglect of them, and have said, 'He that had the oversight of us fled, and we were neglected, there being no one to

put us in mind of our duty?' When they said this, what could I have answered? Such a complaint was made by Ezekiel against the Pastors of old[9]; and the blessed Apostle Paul, knowing this, has charged every one of us through his disciple, saying, 'Neglect not the gift that is in thee, which was given thee, with the laying on of the hands of the presbytery[10].' Fearing this, I wished not to flee, but to receive your commands, if indeed such was the will of your Piety. But I never obtained what I so reasonably requested, and now I am falsely accused before you; for I resisted no commands of your Piety; nor will I now attempt to return to Alexandria, until your Grace shall desire it. This I say beforehand, lest the slanderers should again make this a pretence for accusing me.

27. Athanasius leaves Alexandria to go to Constantius, but is stopped by the news of the banishment of the Bishops.

Observing these things, I did not give sentence against myself, but hastened to come to your Piety, with this my defence, knowing your goodness, and remembering your faithful promises, and being confident that, as it is written in the divine Proverbs, 'Just speeches are acceptable to a gracious king[1].' But when I had already entered upon my journey, and had passed through the desert[1a], a report suddenly reached me[2], which at first I thought to be incredible, but which afterwards proved to be true. It was rumoured everywhere that Liberius, Bishop of Rome, the great Hosius of Spain, Paulinus of Gaul, Dionysius and Eusebius of Italy, Lucifer of Sardinia, and certain other Bishops and Presbyters and Deacons, had been banished[3] because they refused to subscribe to my condemnation. These had been banished: and Vincentius of Capua, Fortunatian of Aquileia, Heremius of Thessalonica, and all the Bishops of the West, were treated with no ordinary force, nay were suffering extreme violence and grievous injuries, until they could be induced to promise that they would not communicate with me. While I was astonished and perplexed at these tidings, behold another report[8] overtook me, respecting them of Egypt and Libya, that nearly ninety Bishops had been under persecution, and that their Churches were given up to the professors of Arianism; that sixteen had been banished, and of the rest, some had

---

9 Ez. xxxiv. 2, &c.　　10 1 Tim. iv. 14.
1 Prov. xvi. 13. quoted otherwise, supr. § 12.
1a [Probably the Libyan desert, as Const. was now in Italy.]
2 In this chapter he breaks off his Oratorical form, and ends his Apology much more in the form of a letter. vid. however τῶν λόγων καιρόν, infr. §§ 34. 35 init. προσφωνήσω, § 35.
3 Council of Milan 355, see *Apol. Fug.* 5.
8 Vid. *Hist. Ar.* §§ 31, 32, 54, 70, &c. [Prolegg. ch. ii. § 8 (1).]

fled, and others were constrained to dissemble. For the persecution was said to be so violent in those parts, that at Alexandria, while the brethren were praying during Easter and on the Lord's days in a desert place near the cemetery, the General came upon them with a force of soldiery, more than three thousand in number, with arms, drawn swords, and spears; whereupon outrages, such as might be expected to follow so unprovoked an attack, were committed against women and children, who were doing nothing more than praying to God. It would perhaps be unseasonable to give an account of them now, lest the mere mention of such enormities should move us all to tears. But such was their cruelty, that virgins were stripped, and even the bodies of those who died from the blows they received were not immediately given up for burial, but were cast out to the dogs, until their relatives, with great risk to themselves, came secretly and stole them away, and much effort was necessary, that no one might know it.

28. *The news of the intrusion of George.*

The rest of their proceedings will perhaps be thought incredible, and will fill all men with astonishment, by reason of their extreme atrocity. It is necessary however to speak of them, in order that your Christian zeal and piety may perceive that their slanders and calumnies against us are framed for no other end, than that they may drive us out of the Churches, and introduce their own impiety in our place. For when the lawful Bishops, men of advanced age, had some of them been banished, and others forced to fly, heathens and catechumens, those who hold the first places in the senate, and men who are notorious for their wealth, were straightway commissioned by the Arians to preach the holy faith instead of Christians[9]. And enquiry was no longer made, as the Apostle enjoined, ' if any be blameless[10]:' but according to the practice of the impious Jeroboam, he who could give most money was named Bishop; and it made no difference to them, even if the man happened to be a heathen, so long as he furnished them with money. Those who had been Bishops from the time of Alexander, monks and ascetics, were banished: and men practised only in calumny corrupted, as far as in them lay, the Apostolic rule, and polluted the Churches. Truly their false accusations against us have gained them much, that they should be able to commit iniquity, and to do such things as these in your time; so that

the words of Scripture may be applied to them, 'Woe unto those through whom My name is blasphemed among the Gentiles[1].'

29. *Athanasius has heard of his own proscription.*

Such were the rumours that were noised abroad; and although everything was thus turned upside down, I still did not relinquish my earnest desire of coming to your Piety, but was again setting forward on my journey. And I did so the more eagerly, being confident that these proceedings were contrary to your wishes, and that if your Grace should be informed of what was done, you would prevent it for the time to come. For I could not think that a righteous king could wish Bishops to be banished, and virgins to be stripped, or the Churches to be in any way disturbed. While I thus reasoned and hastened on my journey, behold a third report reached me, to the effect that letters had been written to the Princes of Auxumis, desiring that Frumentius[2], Bishop of Auxumis, should be brought from thence, and that search should be made for me even as far as the country of the Barbarians, that I might be handed over to the Commentaries[3] (as they are called) of the Prefects, and that all the laity and clergy should be compelled to communicate with the Arian heresy, and that such as would not comply with this order should be put to death. To shew that these were not merely idle rumours, but that they were confirmed by facts, since your Grace has given me leave, I produce the letter. My enemies were constantly reading it, and threatening each one with death.

30. *A copy of the letter of Constantius against Athanasius.*

Victor Constantius Maximus Augustus to the Alexandrians.

Your city, preserving its national character, and remembering the virtue of its founders, has habitually shewn itself obedient unto us, as it does at this day; and we on our part should consider ourselves greatly wanting in our duty, did not our good will eclipse even that of Alexander himself. For as it belongs to a temperate mind, to behave itself orderly in all respects, so it is the part of royalty, on account of virtue, permit me to say, such as yours, to embrace you above all others; you,

---

9 *Hist Ar.* § 73.   10 Tit. i. 8.

1 Rom. ii. 24.   2 [Prolegg. ch. ii. §§ 4, 7, 8 (1).]
3 That is, the prison. 'The official books,' Montfaucon (apparently) in *Onomast.* vid. Gothofr. *Cod. Theod.* ix. 3. 1. 5. However, in ix. 30. p. 243. he says, Malim pro ipsa custodia accipere. And so Du Cange *in voc.*, and this meaning is here followed. vid. supr. *Apol. contr. Arian.* § 8, where commentarius is translated ' jailor.'

who rose up as the first teachers of wisdom; who were the first to acknowledge [3a] God; who moreover have chosen for yourselves the most consummate masters; and have cordially acquiesced in our opinion, justly abominating that impostor and cheat, and dutifully uniting yourselves to those venerable men who are beyond all admiration. And yet, who is ignorant, even among those who live in the ends of the earth, what violent party spirit was displayed in the late proceedings? with which we know not anything that has ever happened, worthy to be compared. The majority of the citizens had their eyes blinded, and a man who had come forth from the lowest dens of infamy obtained authority among them, entrapping into falsehood, as under cover of darkness, those who were desirous to know the truth;—one who never provided for them any fruitful and edifying discourse, but corrupted their minds with unprofitable subtleties. His flatterers shouted and applauded him; they were astonished at his powers, and they still probably murmur secretly; while the majority of the more simple sort took their cue from them. And thus all went with the stream, as if a flood had broken in, while everything was entirely neglected. One of the multitude was in power;—how can I describe him more truly than by saying, that he was superior in nothing to the meanest of the people, and that the only kindness which he shewed to the city was, that he did not thrust her citizens down into the pit. This noble-minded and illustrious person did not wait for judgment to proceed against him, but sentenced himself to banishment, as he deserved. So that now it is for the interest of the Barbarians to remove him out of the way, lest he lead some of them into impiety, for he will make his complaint, like distressed characters in a play, to those who first fall in with him. To him however we will now bid a long farewell. For yourselves there are few with whom I can compare you: I am bound rather to honour you separately above all others, for the great virtue and wisdom which your actions, that are celebrated almost through the whole world, proclaim you to possess. Go on in this sober course. I would gladly have repeated to me a description of your conduct in such terms of praise as it deserves; O you who have eclipsed your predecessors in the race of glory, and will be a noble example both to those who are now alive, and to all who shall come after, and alone have chosen for yourselves the most perfect of beings as guide for your conduct, both in word and deed, and hesitated not a moment, but man-

fully transferred your affections, and gave yourselves up to the other side, leaving those grovelling [4] and earthly teachers, and stretching forth towards heavenly things, under the guidance of the most venerable George [5], than whom no man is more perfectly instructed therein. Under him you will continue to have a good hope respecting the future life, and will pass your time in this present world, in rest and quietness. Would that all the citizens together would lay hold on his words, as a sacred anchor, so that we might need neither knife nor cautery for those whose souls are diseased! Such persons we most earnestly advise to renounce their zeal in favour of Athanasius, and not even to remember the foolish things which he spoke so plentifully among them. Otherwise they will bring themselves before they are aware into extreme peril, from which we know not any one who will be skilful enough to deliver such factious persons. For while that pestilent fellow Athanasius is driven from place to place, being convicted of the basest crimes, for which he would only suffer the punishment he deserves, if one were to kill him ten times over, it would be inconsistent in us to suffer those flatterers and juggling ministers of his to exult against us: men of such a character as it is a shame even to speak of, respecting whom orders have long ago been given to the magistrates, that they should be put to death. But even now perhaps they shall not die, if they desist from their former offences, and repent at last. For that most pestilent fellow Athanasius led them on, and corrupted the whole state, and laid his impious and polluted hands upon the most holy things.

31. *Letter of Constantius to the Ethiopians against Frumentius.*

The following is the letter which was written to the Princes of Auxumis respecting Frumentius, Bishop of that place.

Constantius Victor Maximus Augustus, to Æzanes and Sazanes.

It is altogether a matter of the greatest care and concern to us, to extend the knowledge of the supreme God [6]; and I think that the whole race of mankind claims from us equal regard in this respect, in order that they may pass their lives in hope, being brought to a proper knowledge of God, and having no

---

3a On the reading, cf. infr. note 6.

4 τῶν χαμαί, vid. *contr.* Euseb. *H.E.* vii. **27.**
5 Of Cappadocia, *de Syn.* 37, note 3.
6 ἡ τοῦ κρείττονος γνῶσις, vid. τὸν κρείττονα, infr. And so in Arius's Thalia, the Eternal Father, in contrast to the Son, is called ὁ κρείττων, τὸν κρείττονα, *de Synod.* § 15. So again, θεὸν τὸν [ὄντα] συνιέντας, supr. § 30, and συνετῶν θεοῦ in the Thalia, *Orat.* i. 5. Again, σοφίας ἐξηγητὰς, supr. § 30. and τῶν σοφίας μεταχόντων, κατὰ πάντα σοφῶν in the Thalia, ibid. And τῶν ἐξηγητῶν τοὺς ἄκρους εἴλεσθε, supr. § 30, and τούτων κατ᾽ ἴχνος ἦλθον in the Thalia.

differences with each other in their enquiries concerning justice and truth. Wherefore considering that you are deserving of the same provident care as the Romans, and desiring to shew equal regard for your welfare, we command that the same doctrine be professed in your Churches as in theirs. Send therefore speedily into Egypt the Bishop Frumentius to the most venerable Bishop George, and the rest who are there, who have especial authority to appoint to these offices, and to decide questions concerning them. For of course you know and remember (unless you alone pretend to be ignorant of that which all men are well aware of) that this Frumentius was advanced to his present rank by Athanasius, a man who is guilty of ten thousand crimes; for he has not been able fairly to clear himself of any of the charges brought against him, but was at once deprived of his see, and now wanders about destitute of any fixed abode, and passes from one country to another, as if by this means he could escape his own wickedness. Now if Frumentius shall readily obey our commands, and shall submit to an enquiry into all the circumstances of his appointment, he will shew plainly to all men, that he is in no respect opposed to the laws of the Church and the established [7] faith. And being brought to trial, when he shall have given proof of his general good conduct, and submitted an account of his life to those who are to judge of these things, he shall receive his appointment from them, if it shall indeed appear that he has any right to be a Bishop. But if he shall delay and avoid the trial, it will surely be very evident, that he has been induced by the persuasions of the wicked Athanasius, thus to indulge impiety against God, choosing to follow the course of him whose wickedness has been made manifest. And our fear is lest he should pass over into Auxumis and corrupt your people, by setting before them accursed and impious statements, and not only unsettle and disturb the Churches, and blaspheme the supreme God, but also thereby cause utter overthrow and destruction to the several nations whom he visits. But I am sure that Frumentius will return home, perfectly acquainted with all matters that concern the Church, having derived much instruction, which will be of great and general utility, from the conversation of the most venerable George, and such other of the Bishops, as are excellently qualified to communicate such knowledge. May God continually preserve you, most honoured brethren.

32. *He defends his Flight.*

Hearing, nay almost seeing, these things, through the mournful representations of the messengers, I confess I turned back again into the desert, justly concluding, as your Piety will perceive, that if I was sought after, that I might be sent as soon as I was discovered to the Prefects[8], I should be prevented from ever coming to your Grace; and that if those who would not subscribe against me, suffered so severely as they did, and the laity who refused to communicate with the Arians were ordered for death, there was no doubt at all but that ten thousand new modes of destruction would be devised by the calumniators against me; and that after my death, they would employ against whomsoever they wished to injure, whatever means they chose, venting their lies against us the more boldly, for that then there would no longer be any one left who could expose them. I fled, not because I feared your Piety (for I know your long-suffering and goodness), but because from what had taken place, I perceived the spirit of my enemies, and considered that they would make use of all possible means to accomplish my destruction, from fear that they would be brought to answer for what they had done contrary to the intentions of your Excellency. For observe, your Grace commanded that the Bishops should be expelled only out of the cities and the province. But these worthy persons presumed to exceed your commands, and banished aged men and Bishops venerable for their years into desert and unfrequented and frightful places, beyond the boundaries of three provinces [9]. Some of them were sent off from Libya to the great Oasis; others from the Thebais to Ammoniaca in Libya [10]. Neither was it from fear of death that I fled; let none of them condemn me as guilty of cowardice; but because it is the injunction of our Saviour [1] that we should flee when we are persecuted, and hide ourselves when we are sought after, and not expose ourselves to certain dangers, nor by appearing before our persecutors inflame still more their rage against us. For to give one's self up to one's enemies to be murdered, is the same thing as to murder one's self; but to flee, as our Saviour has enjoined, is to know our time, and to manifest a real concern for our persecutors, lest if they proceed to the shedding of blood, they become guilty of the transgression of the law, ' Thou

---

7 κρατούσῃ, supr. § 23, note 6.

8 Supr. § 29.
9 Egypt was divided into three Provinces till Hadrian's time, Egypt, Libya, and Pentapolis; Hadrian made them four; Epiphanius speaks of them as seven. *Hær.* 68. i. By the time of Arcadius they had become eight. vid. Orlendini *Orbis Sacer et Prof.* vol. i. p. 118. vid. supr. *Encyc.* § 3, n. 2, *Apol. Ar.* § 83.
10 *Hist. Ar.* 72. 1 Vid. *Apol. de Fug.* init.; Matt. x. 23.

shalt not kill [2].' And yet these men by their calumnies against me, earnestly wish that I should suffer death. What they have again lately done proves that this is their desire and murderous intention. You will be astonished, I am sure, Augustus, most beloved of God, when you hear it; it is indeed an outrage worthy of amazement. What it is, I pray you briefly to hear.

33. Conduct of the Arians towards the consecrated Virgins.

The Son of God, our Lord and Saviour Jesus Christ, having become man for our sakes, and having destroyed death, and delivered our race from the bondage of corruption [3], in addition to all His other benefits bestowed this also upon us, that we should possess upon earth, in the state of virginity [3a], a picture of the holiness of Angels. Accordingly such as have attained this virtue, the Catholic Church has been accustomed to call the brides of Christ. And the heathen who see them express their admiration of them as the temples of the Word. For indeed this holy and heavenly profession is nowhere [3b] established, but only among us Christians, and it is a very strong argument that with us is to be found the genuine and true religion. Your most religious father Constantine Augustus, of blessed memory, honoured the Virgins above all the rest, and your Piety in several letters has given them the titles of the honourable and holy women. But now these worthy Arians who have slandered me, and by whom conspiracies have been formed against most of the Bishops, having obtained the consent and co-operation of the magistrates, first stripped them, and then caused them to be suspended upon what are called the Hermetaries [4], and scourged them on the ribs so severely three several times, that not even real malefactors have ever suffered the like. Pilate, to gratify the Jews of old, pierced one of our Saviour's sides with a spear. These men have exceeded the madness of Pilate, for they have scourged not one but both His sides; for the limbs of the Virgins are in an especial manner the Saviour's own. All men shudder at hearing the bare recital of deeds like these. These men alone not only did not fear to strip and to scourge those undefiled limbs, which the Virgins had dedicated solely to our Saviour Christ; but, what is worse than all, when they were reproached by every one for such extreme cruelty, instead of

manifesting any shame, they pretended that it was commanded by your Piety. So utterly presumptuous are they and full of wicked thoughts and purposes. Such a deed as this was never heard of in past persecutions [5]: or supposing that it ever occurred before, yet surely it was not befitting either that Virginity should suffer such outrage and dishonour, in the time of your Majesty, a Christian, or that these men should impute to your Piety their own cruelty. Such wickedness belongs only to heretics, to blaspheme the Son of God, and to do violence to His holy Virgins.

34. He expostulates with Constantius.

Now when such enormities as these were again perpetrated by the Arians, I surely was not wrong in complying with the direction of Holy Scripture, which says, 'Hide thyself for a little moment, until the wrath of the Lord be overpast [6].' This was another reason for my withdrawing myself, Augustus, most beloved of God; and I refused not, either to depart into the desert, or, if need were, to be let down from a wall in a basket [7]. I endured everything, I even dwelt among wild beasts, that your favour might return to me, waiting for an opportunity to offer to you this my defence, confident as I am that they will be condemned, and your goodness manifested unto me. O, Augustus, blessed and most beloved of God, what would you have had me to do? to come to you while my calumniators were inflamed with rage against me, and were seeking to kill me; or, as it is written, to hide myself a little, that in the mean time they might be condemned as heretics, and your goodness might be manifested unto me? or would you have had me, Sire, to appear before your magistrates, in order that though you had written merely in the way of threatening, they not understanding your intention, but being exasperated against me by the Arians, might kill me on the authority of your letters, and on that ground ascribe the murder to you? It would neither have been becoming in me to surrender, and give myself up that my blood might be shed, nor in you, as a Christian King, to have the murder of Christians, and those too Bishops, imputed unto you.

35. It was therefore better for me to hide myself, and to wait for this opportunity. Yes, I am sure that from your knowledge of the sacred Scriptures you will assent and approve of my conduct in this respect. For you will perceive that, now those who exasperated you against us have been silenced, your righteous clemency is apparent, and it is proved to all

---

[2] Exod. xx. 13.   [3] 2 Tim. i. 10; Rom. viii. 21.
[3a] Cf. Ep. Fest. i. 3, Ep. ad Amun, also de Incar. 27, 48, 51.
[3b] [Revillout (in the work quoted supr. p. 188), p. 479 sq. states the contrary with regard to Egypt. He refers to the opening of Plutarch's de Is. et Osir., also to Brunet de Presle Serapeum.]
[4] A rack, or horse, Tillemont. vol. viii. p. 169.

[5] Vid. Hist. Ar. §§ 40, 64.   [6] Is. xxvi. 20, LXX.
[7] 2 Cor. xi. 33.

men that you never persecuted the Christians at all, but that it was they who made the Churches desolate, that they might sow the seeds of their own impiety everywhere; on account of which I also, had I not fled, should long ago have suffered from their treachery. For it is very evident that they who scrupled not to utter such calumnies against me, before the great Augustus, and who so violently assailed Bishops and Virgins, sought also to compass my death. But thanks be to the Lord who has given you the kingdom. All men are confirmed in their opinion of your goodness, and of their wickedness, from which I fled at the first, that I might now make this appeal unto you, and that you might find some one towards whom you may shew kindness. I beseech you, therefore, forasmuch as it is written, 'A soft answer turneth away wrath,' and 'righteous thoughts are acceptable unto the King[8];' receive this my defence, and restore all the Bishops and the rest of the Clergy to their countries and their Churches; so that the wickedness of my accusers may be made manifest, and that you, both now and in the day of judgment, may have boldness to say to our Lord and Saviour Jesus Christ, the King of all, ' " None of Thine have I lost[9]," but these are they who designed the ruin of all, while I was grieved for those who perished, and for the Virgins who were scourged, and for all other things that were committed against the Christians; and I brought back them that were banished, and restored them to their own Churches.'

---

[8] Prov. xv. 1; xvi. 13. vid. § 27. note 1. [9] John xviii. 9.

APOLOGIA DE FUGA

THE date of this Defence of his Flight must be placed early enough to fall within the lifetime, or very close to the death (§ 1. n. 1), of Leontius of Antioch, and late enough to satisfy the references (§ 6) to the events at the end of May 357 (see notes there), and to the lapse of Hosius, the exact date of which again depends upon that of the Sirmian Council of 357, which, *if held in the presence of Constantius*, must have fallen as late as August (Gwatk. *Stud.* 157, n. 3). Athanasius not only refers to the lapse of Hosius, but by the quotation he makes from Gal. ii. 5, appears to know of its merely temporary nature (see D.C.B. iii. 173). How early, then, does the first-named condition compel us to place the 'Defence?' Upon the news of the death of Leontius reaching Italy (Soz. iv. 12), Eudoxius obtained the leave of Constantius (who was in Italy, April 28 to July 3, 357, and again, Nov. 10 to Dec. 10, Gwatk. p. 292), to repair to Antioch. There he got himself elected bishop, assembled a council (Acacius and other Homœans), and wrote a synodal letter, expelling from the Antiochene Church those who dissented. Some of the latter repaired to Ancyra with a letter from the semi-Arian George of Laodicea; at Ancyra, Basil assembled a small council (before Easter, April 12, 358, see D.C.B. i. 281, Epiph. *Hær.* 73), which wrote to the Emperor protesting against the proceedings of Eudoxius. To gain room for these events, at the very least five months, and probably more, must be allowed to elapse between the death of Leontius and April 12, 358. Leontius must therefore have died in the summer (Gwatk. p. 153, note), or at the very latest in October, 357. We cannot, therefore, place the Apology much after this date, for the reference to Hosius shews—in addition to many other indications—how quickly Athanasius in his hiding-place was informed of current events.

The Apology was drawn forth by the charge of cowardice circulated against him by the Arianising party, especially by the three bishops named in § 1. After a preamble upon the motives of his accusers (1, 2), he shews that his own case is but part of a general system (3—5) of expatriation directed against orthodox bishops. He then refers to the circumstance of the attack upon himself, and dwells at length upon the tyranny of George (6, 7) and the banishment of Egyptian and Libyan bishops. This brings him to the argument (8—22) which gives its name to the tract. After pressing the point that if flight be evil, those who persecute are the responsible cause (8, 9), and hinting at the real motive of their mortification at his escape (10), he defends his flight by the example first (10, 11) of the Scripture Saints, secondly of the Lord Himself (12—15). From the latter, he returns to the conduct of the Saints, who, unlike the Lord (16), were unaware of their appointed time, yet fled or not (17) as circumstances and the direction of the Spirit required them to do. The Saints if they fled were not moved to do so by cowardice, else how could their flight so frequently have been the occasion of divine communications (18—20), and how could such good (21, 22) have resulted from it? As a pendant to this vindication of flight on principle comes a short (23) but weighty rebuke of persecution as inherently devilish τὸ δὲ διώκειν διαβολικόν ἐστιν ἐπιχείρημα. From principle, Athanasius now passes to fact. He gives a graphic description (24) of the night attack on the Church of Theonas, and shews (25, 26) how fully his action on that occasion is covered by the examples of the ancient Saints of God. He concludes (26, 27) with a somewhat exasperated denunciation of his opponents, and a prayer for the frustration of their intrigues.

The Apology is a *locus classicus* on the duty of Christians under persecution. Athanasius was not the first great bishop who felt called upon to defend his conduct in retreating 'until the tyranny be overpast' (see Cyprian, *Ep.* 20. August. *Ep.* 228). His principles are laid down with regard to the common welfare. Rashness must be avoided, with its tendency to a reaction (17, end), and its presumption in forestalling the time appointed by Providence for our death. But neither must that time be evaded. When our end must come, we must face it quietly. Accordingly (22) it is a duty to escape when we can, and to hide when sought for rather than to follow the exceptional (ib.) action of certain martyrs in courting death.

It is uncertain to whom the 'Defence' was addressed: it was perhaps a 'memorandum' to be circulated wherever opportunity offered. The tract has always been justly admired for its lucidity, force, and dignity. It is quoted largely by Socrates (ii. 28, iii. 8) and by Theodoret (*H.E.* ii. 15).

DEFENCE OF HIS FLIGHT

1. *Athanasius charged with cowardice for escaping.*

I HEAR that Leontius[1], now at Antioch, and Narcissus[2] of the city of Nero, and George[3], now at Laodicea, and the Arians who are with them, are spreading abroad many slanderous reports concerning me, charging me with cowardice, because forsooth, when I myself was sought by them, I did not surrender myself into their hands. Now as to their imputations and calumnies, although there are many things that I could write, which even they are unable to deny, and which all who have heard of their proceedings know to be true, yet I shall not be prevailed upon to make any reply to them, except only to remind them of the words of our Lord, and of the declaration of the Apostle, that 'a lie is of the Devil,' and that, 'revilers shall not inherit the kingdom of God[4].' For it is sufficient thereby to prove, that neither their thoughts nor their words are according to the Gospel, but that after their own pleasure, whatsoever themselves desire, that they think to be good.

2. *Insincerity of this charge.*

But forasmuch as they pretend to charge me with cowardice, it is necessary that I should write somewhat concerning this, whereby it shall be proved that they are men of wicked minds, who have not read the sacred Scriptures: or if they have read them, that they do not believe the divine inspiration of the oracles they contain. For had they believed this, they would not dare to act contrary to them, nor imitate the malice of the Jews who slew the Lord. For God having given them a commandment, 'Honour thy father and thy mother,' and, 'He that curseth father or mother, let him die the death[5];' that people established a contrary law, changing the honour into dishonour, and alienating to other uses the money which was due from the children to their parents. And though they had read what David did, they acted in contradiction to his example, and accused the guiltless for plucking the ears of corn, and rubbing them in their hands on the Sabbath day[6]. Not that they cared either for the laws, or for the Sabbath, for they were guilty of greater transgressions of the law on that day: but being wicked-minded, they grudged the disciples the way of salvation, and desired that their own private notions should have the sole pre-eminence. They however have received the reward of their iniquity, having ceased to be an holy nation, and being counted henceforth as the rulers of Sodom, and as the people of Gomorrah[7]. And these men likewise, not less than they, seem to me to have received their punishment already in their ignorance of their own folly. For they understand not what they say, but think that they know things of which they are ignorant; while the only knowledge that is in them is to do evil, and to frame devices more and more wicked day by day. Thus they reproach us with our present flight, not for the sake of virtue, as wishing us to shew manliness by coming forward (how is it possible that such a wish can be entertained by enemies in behalf of those who run not with them in the same career of madness?); but being full of malice, they pretend this, and buzz[8] all around that such is the case, thinking, foolish as indeed they are, that through fear of their revilings, we shall yet be induced to give ourselves up to them. For this is what they desire: to accomplish this they have recourse to all kinds of schemes: they pretend themselves to be friends, while they search as enemies, to the end that they may glut themselves with our blood, and put us also out of the way, because we have always opposed and do still oppose their impiety, and confute and brand their heresy.

[1] Leontius died in the summer of 357, probably before Ath. wrote.   [2] *De Syn.* 17.   [3] *Apol. Ar.* 48.
[4] John viii. 44; 1 Cor. vi. 10.   [5] Matt. xv. 4.

[6] Luke vi. 1. *sqq.*   [7] Isa. i. 10, 11.   [8] περιβομβεῖν, *Nic. Def.* 14, note 1; Greg. Naz. *Orat.* 27. n. 2.

3. *Outrages of the Arians against the Bishops.*

For whom have they ever persecuted and taken, that they have not insulted and injured as they pleased? Whom have they ever sought after and found, that they have not handled in such a manner, that either he has died a miserable death, or has been ill-treated in every way? Whatever the magistrates appear to do, it is their work; and the others are merely the tools of their will and wickedness. In consequence, where is there a place that has not some memorial of their malice? Who has ever opposed them, without their conspiring against him, inventing pretexts for his ruin after the manner of Jezebel? Where is there a Church that is not at this moment lamenting the success of their plots against her Bishops? Antioch is mourning for the orthodox Confessor Eustathius[9]; Balaneæ for the most admirable Euphration[10]; Paltus and Antaradus for Kymatius[11] and Carterius; Adrianople for that lover of Christ, Eutropius, and his successor Lucius, who was often loaded with chains by their means, and so perished; Ancyra mourns for Marcellus, Berrhœa[1] for Cyrus[11], Gaza for Asclepas. Of all these, after inflicting many outrages, they by their intrigues procured the banishment; but for Theodulus and Olympius, Bishops of Thrace, and for us and our Presbyters, they caused diligent search to be made, to the intent that if we were discovered we should suffer capital punishment: and probably we should have so perished, had we not fled at that very time contrary to their intentions. For letters to that effect were delivered to the Proconsul Donatus against Olympius and his fellows, and to Philagrius against me. And having raised a persecution against Paul, Bishop of Constantinople, as soon as they found him, they caused him to be openly strangled[2] at a place called Cucusus in Cappadocia, employing as their executioner for the purpose Philip, who was Prefect. He was a patron of their heresy, and the tool of their wicked designs.

4. *Proceedings after the Council of Milan.*

Are they then satisfied with all this, and content to be quiet for the future? By no means; they have not given over yet, but like the horseleach[3] in the Proverbs, they revel more and more in their wickedness, and fix themselves upon the larger dioceses. Who can adequately describe the enormities they have already perpetrated? who is able to recount all the deeds that they have done? Even very lately, while the Churches were at peace, and the people worshipping in their congregations, Liberius, Bishop of Rome, Paulinus[4], Metropolitan of Gaul, Dionysius[5], Metropolitan of Italy, Lucifer[6], Metropolitan of the Sardinian islands, and Eusebius[7] of Italy, all of them good Bishops and preachers of the truth, were seized and banished[8], on no pretence whatever, except that they would not unite themselves to the Arian heresy, nor subscribe to the false accusations and calumnies which they had invented against me.

5. *In praise of Hosius.*

Of the great Hosius[9], who answers to his name, that confessor of a happy old age, it is superfluous for me to speak, for I suppose it is known unto all men that they caused him also to be banished; for he is not an obscure person, but of all men the most illustrious, and more than this. When was there a Council held, in which he did not take the lead[10], and by right counsel convince every one? Where is there a Church that does not possess some glorious monuments of his patronage? Who has ever come to him in sorrow, and has not gone away rejoicing? What needy person ever asked his aid, and did not obtain what he desired? And yet even on this man they made their assault, because knowing the calumnies which they invent in behalf of their iniquity, he would not subscribe to their designs against us. And if afterwards, upon the repeated stripes above measure that were inflicted upon him, and the conspiracies that were formed against his kinsfolk, he yielded[1] to them for a time[2], as being old and infirm in body, yet at least their wickedness is shewn even in this circumstance; so zealously did they endeavour by all means to prove that they were not truly Christians.

6. *Outrages of George upon the Alexandrians.*

After this they again fastened themselves upon Alexandria, seeking anew to put us to death: and their proceedings were now worse than before. For on a sudden the Church

---

9 Vid. *Hist. Arian.* § 4. also Theodoret *Hist.* i. 20. [Prolegg. ch. ii. § 4.] The name of Euphration occurs *de Syn.* 17. as the Bishop to whom Eusebius of Cæsarea wrote an heretical letter. Balaneæ is on the Syrian coast. Paltus also and Antaradus are in Syria, and these persecutions took place about A.D. 338; that of Eutropius, and of Lucius his successor, about 331, shortly after the proceedings against Eustathius. Cyrus too was banished under pretence of Sabellianism about 338. For Asclepas, Theodulus, and Olympius vid. *Hist. Arian.* § 19. and supr. *Apol. Ar.* 44, 45. 10 *Hist. Arian.* 5. 11 *Tom. ad Ant.* 1 Berœa, *Hist. Ar.* 5. 2 A.D. 350, infr. *Hist. Arian.* § 4; for Cucusus, see D.C.B. i. 529, 530.

3 *Hist. Arian.* § 65; Prov. xxx. 15. 4 Of Treveri. 5 Of Milan. 6 Of Cagliäri. 7 Of Vercellæ. 8 [Council of Milan, 355.] 9 *Hist. Ar.* 42. 10 [Nicæa and Sardica are specially referred to, but see Prolegg. ch. ii. § 3 (1) note 5, *sub. fin.*] 1 [*Apol. Ar.* 89, *Hist. Ar.* 45, 357 A.D.] 2 Gal. ii. 5.

was surrounded by soldiers, and sounds of war took the place of prayers. Then George[3] of Cappadocia who was sent by them, having arrived during the season of Lent[4], brought an increase of evils which they had taught him. For after Easter week, Virgins were thrown into prison; Bishops were led away in chains by soldiers; houses of orphans and widows were plundered, and their loaves taken away; attacks were made upon houses, and Christians thrust forth in the night, and their dwellings sealed up: brothers of clergymen were in danger of their lives on account of their brethren. These outrages were sufficiently dreadful, but more dreadful than these followed. For on the week that succeeded the Holy Pentècost [May 11], when the people after their fast had gone out to the cemetery to pray, because that all refused communion with George, that abandoned person, on learning this, stirred up against them the commander Sebastian, a Manichee; who straightway with a multitude of soldiers with arms, drawn swords, bows, and spears, proceeded to attack the people, though it was the Lord's day[5]: and finding a few praying (for the greater part had already retired on account of the lateness of the hour), he committed such outrages as became a disciple of these men. Having lighted a pile, he placed certain virgins near the fire, and endeavoured to force them to say that they were of the Arian faith: and when he saw that they were getting the mastery, and cared not for the fire, he immediately stripped them naked, and beat them in the face in such a manner, that for some time they could hardly be recognised.

7. Outrages of George.

And having seized upon forty men, he beat them after a new fashion. Cutting some sticks fresh from the palm tree, with the thorns still upon them[6], he scourged them on the back so severely, that some of them were for a long time under surgical treatment on account of the thorns which had broken off in their flesh, and others unable to bear up under their sufferings died. All those whom they had taken, and the virgin, they sent away together into banishment to the great Oasis. And the bodies of those who had perished they would not at first suffer to be given

up to their friends, but concealed them in any way they pleased, and cast them out without burial[7], in order that they might not appear to have any knowledge of these cruel proceedings. But herein their deluded minds greatly misled them. For the relatives of the dead, both rejoicing at the confession, and grieving for the bodies of their friends, published abroad so much the more this proof of their impiety and cruelty. Moreover they immediately banished out of Egypt and Libya the following Bishops[8], Ammonius, Muïus[9], Gaïus, Philo[9], Hermes, Plenius, Psenosiris, Nilammon, Agathus, Anagamphus, Marcus, Ammonius, another Marcus, Dracontius[1], Adelphius[2], Athenodorus, and the Presbyters, Hierax[3], and Dioscorus; whom they drove forth under such cruel treatment, that some of them died on the way, and others in the place of their banishment. They caused also more than thirty Bishops to take to flight; for their desire was, after the example of Ahab, if it were possible, utterly to root out the truth. Such are the enormities of which these impious men have been guilty.

8. If it is wrong to flee, it is worse to persecute.

But although[4] they have done all this, yet they are not ashamed of the evils they have already contrived against me, but proceed now to accuse me, because I have been able to escape their murderous hands. Nay, they bitterly bewail themselves, that they have not effectually put me out of the way; and so they pretend to reproach me with cowardice, not perceiving that by thus murmuring against me, they rather turn the blame upon themselves. For if it be a bad thing to flee, it is much worse to persecute; for the one party hides himself to escape death, the other persecutes with a desire to kill; and it is written in the Scriptures that we ought to flee; but he that seeks to destroy transgresses the law, nay, and is himself the occasion of the other's flight. If then they reproach me with my flight, let them be more ashamed of their own persecution[5]. Let them cease to conspire, and they who flee will forthwith cease to do so. But they, instead of giving over their wickedness, are employing every means to obtain possession of my person, not perceiving that the flight of those who are persecuted is a strong argument against those who persecute. For no man flees from the gentle and the humane, but from the cruel and the evil-

3 *Apol. Const.* 30, note 5, and reff.
4 [Comp. *Encyc.* § 4. The present passage certainly appears to put the arrival of George in the Lent immediately following the irruption of Syrianus: but see Prolegg. ch. ii. § 8 (1), note 5, below, *Fest. Index*, xxix., and the explanation in *Chron. Aceph.* that the *party* of George took possession of the Churches (in June 356), eight months before George arrived in person. Cf. Introd. to *Apol. Const.*]
5 [Sunday, May 18, 357. The Roman martyrology celebrates these victims on May 21, which suits the reference of the present passage to 357.] 6 *Hist. Arian.* § 72.

7 Ibid. § 72 fin. *Apol. Const.* 27. 8 Ibid. and see *Hist. Ar.* § 72. 9 Hieron. *V. Hilar.* § 30. [Rather see *Letter* 49. 7, notes 3 (a and b), and *Vit. Pachom.* 72, where the same names occur together.] 1 *Letter* 49. 2 *Letter* 60. 3 *Letter* 49. 10. 4 Cited by Socrates iii. 8. 5 *Apol. Ar.* § 4.

minded. 'Every one that was in distress, and every one that was in debt[6],' fled from Saul, and took refuge with David. But this is the reason why these men desire to cut off those who are in concealment, that there may be no evidence forthcoming of their wickedness. But herein their minds seem to be blinded with their usual error. For the more the flight of their enemies becomes known, so much the more notorious will be the destruction or the banishment which their treachery has brought upon them[7]; so that whether they kill them outright, their death will be the more loudly noised abroad against them, or whether they drive them into banishment, they will but be sending forth everywhere monuments of their own iniquity.

9. The accusation shews the mind of the accusers.

Now if they had been of sound mind, they would have seen that they were in this strait, and that they were falling foul of their own arguments. But since they have lost all judgment, they are still led on to persecute, and seek to destroy, and yet perceive not their own impiety. It may be they even venture to accuse Providence itself (for nothing is beyond the reach of their presumption), that it does not deliver up to them those whom they desire; certain as it is, according to the saying of our Saviour, that not even a sparrow can fall into the snare without our Father which is in heaven[8]. But when these accursed ones obtain possession of any one, they immediately forget not only all other, but even themselves; and raising their brow in very haughtiness, they neither acknowledge times and seasons, nor respect human nature in those whom they injure. Like the tyrant of Babylon[9], they attack more furiously; they shew pity to none, but mercilessly 'upon the ancient,' as it is written, 'they very heavily lay the yoke,' and 'they add to the grief of them that are wounded[1].' Had they not acted in this manner; had they not driven into banishment those who spoke in my defence against their calumnies, their representations might have appeared to some persons sufficiently plausible. But since they have conspired against so many other Bishops of high character, and have spared neither the great confessor Hosius, nor the Bishop of Rome, nor so many others from the Spains and the Gauls, and Egypt, and Libya, and the other countries, but have committed such cruel outrages against all who have in any way opposed them in my behalf; is it not plain

that their designs have been directed rather against me than against any other, and that their desire is miserably to destroy me as they have done others? To accomplish this they vigilantly watch for an opportunity, and think themselves injured, when they see those safe, whom they wished not to live.

10. Their real grievance is not that Athanasius is a coward, but that he is free.

Who then does not perceive their craftiness? Is it not very evident to every one that they do not reproach me with cowardice from regard to virtue, but that being athirst for blood, they employ these their base devices as nets, thinking thereby to catch those whom they seek to destroy? That such is their character is shewn by their actions, which have convicted them of possessing dispositions more savage than wild beasts, and more cruel than Babylonians. But although the proof against them is sufficiently clear from all this, yet since they still dissemble with soft words after the manner of their 'father the devil[2],' and pretend to charge me with cowardice, while they are themselves more cowardly than hares; let us consider what is written in the Sacred Scriptures respecting such cases as this. For thus they will be shewn to fight against the Scriptures no less than against me, while they detract from the virtues of the Saints.

For if they reproach men for hiding themselves from those who seek to destroy them, and accuse those who flee from their persecutors, what will they do when they see Jacob fleeing from his brother Esau, and Moses withdrawing into Midian for fear of Pharaoh? What excuse will they make for David, after all this idle talk, for fleeing from his house on account of Saul, when he sent to kill him, and for hiding himself in the cave, and for changing his appearance, until he withdrew from Abimelech[4], and escaped his designs against him? What will they say, they who are ready to say anything, when they see the great Elijah, after calling upon God and raising the dead, hiding himself for fear of Ahab, and fleeing from the threats of Jezebel? At which time also the sons of the prophets, when they were sought after, hid themselves with the assistance of Obadiah, and lay concealed in caves[5].

11. Examples of Scripture Saints in defence of flight.

Perhaps they have not read these histories; as being out of date; yet have they no recol-

---

6 1 Sam. xxii. 2.   7 Hist. Arian. §§ 34, 35.
8 Matt. x. 29.   9 Encyc. 5.   1 Is. xlvii. 6; Ps. lxix. 26.

2 John viii. 44.   4 Achish, 1 Sam. xxi. 13 [but cf. title of
Ps. xxxiv.]   5 1 Kings xviii. 15; Hist. Ar. § 52.

lection of what is written in the Gospel? For the disciples also withdrew and hid themselves for fear of the Jews; and Paul, when he was sought after by the governor at Damascus, was let down from the wall in a basket, and so escaped his hands. As the Scripture then relates these things of the Saints, what excuse will they be able to invent for their wickedness? To reproach them with cowardice would be an act of madness, and to accuse them of acting contrary to the will of God, would be to shew themselves entirely ignorant of the Scriptures. For there was a command under the law [6] that cities of refuge should be appointed, in order that they who were sought after to be put to death, might at least have some means of saving themselves. And when He Who spake unto Moses, the Word of the Father, appeared in the end of the world, He also gave this commandment, saying, 'But when they persecute you in this city, flee ye into another:' and shortly after He says, 'When ye therefore shall see the abomination of desolation, spoken of by Daniel the prophet, stand in the holy place (whoso readeth, let him understand); then let them which be in Judæa flee into the mountains: let him which is on the housetop not come down to take any thing out of his house: neither let him which is in the field return back to take his clothes [7].' Knowing these things, the Saints regulated their conduct accordingly. For what our Lord has now commanded, the same also He spoke by His Saints before His coming in the flesh: and this is the rule which is given unto men to lead them to perfection— what God commands, that to do.

12. *The Lord an example of timely flight.*

Wherefore also the Word Himself, being made man for our sakes, condescended to hide Himself when He was sought after, as we do: and also when He was persecuted, to flee and avoid the designs of His enemies. For it became Him, as by hunger and thirst and suffering, so also by hiding Himself and fleeing, to shew that He had taken our flesh, and was made man. Thus at the very first, as soon as He became man, when He was a little child, He Himself by His Angel commanded Joseph, 'Arise, and take the young Child and His Mother, and flee into Egypt; for Herod will seek the young Child's life [8].' And when Herod was dead, we find Him withdrawing to Nazareth by reason of Archelaus his son. And when afterwards He was shewing Himself to be God, and made whole the withered hand, the Pharisees went out, and held a council against Him, how they might destroy Him; but when Jesus knew it, He withdrew Himself from thence [9]. So also when He raised Lazarus from the dead, 'from that day forth,' says the Scripture, 'they took counsel for to put Him to death. Jesus therefore walked no more openly among the Jews; but went thence into the country near to the wilderness [10].' Again, when our Saviour said, 'Before Abraham was, I am,' 'the Jews took up stones to cast at Him; but Jesus hid Himself, and went out of the temple [1].' And 'going through the midst of them, He went His way,' and 'so passed by [2].'

13. *Example of our Lord.*

When they see these things, or rather even hear of them, for see they do not, will they not desire, as it is written, to become 'fuel of fire [2a],' because their counsels and their words are contrary to what the Lord both did and taught? Also when John was martyred, and his disciples buried his body, 'when Jesus heard of it, He departed thence by ship into a desert place apart [3].' Thus the Lord acted, and thus He taught. Would that these men were even now ashamed of their conduct, and confined their rashness to man, nor proceeded to such extreme madness as even to charge our Saviour with cowardice! for it is against Him that they now utter their blasphemies. But no one will endure such madness; nay it will be seen that they do not understand the Gospels. The cause must be a reasonable and just one, which the Evangelists represent as weighing with our Saviour to withdraw and to flee; and we ought therefore to assign the same for the conduct of all the Saints. (For whatever is written concerning our Saviour in His human nature, ought to be considered as applying to the whole race of mankind [4]; because He took our body, and exhibited in Himself human infirmity.) Now of this cause John has written thus, 'They sought to take Him: but no man laid hands on Him, because His hour was not yet come [5].' And before it came, He Himself said to His Mother, 'Mine hour is not yet come [6]:' and to them who were called His brethren, 'My time is not yet come [7].' And again, when His time was come, He said to the disciples, 'Sleep on now, and take your rest: for behold, the hour is at hand, and the Son of man is betrayed into the hands of sinners [8].'

14. *An hour and a time for all men.*

Now in so far as He was God and the Word

---

[6] Ex. xxi. 13.   [7] Matt. x. 23; xxiv. 15.   [8] Matt. ii. 13.

[9] Matt. xii. 15.   [10] John xi. 53, 54.   [1] John viii. 58, 59.
[2] Luke iv. 30.   [2a] Is. ix. 5.   [3] Matt. xiv. 13.   [4] Cf. *Orat.* i. 43.
[5] John vii. 30.   [6] John ii. 4.   [7] John vii. 6.
[8] Matt. xxvi. 45.

of the Father, He had no time ; for He is Himself the Creator of times [9]. But being made man, He shews by speaking in this manner that there is a time allotted to every man ; and that not by chance, as some of the Gentiles imagine in their fables, but a time which He, the Creator, has appointed to every one according to the will of the Father. This is written in the Scriptures, and is manifest to all men. For although it be hidden and unknown to all, what period of time is allotted to each, and how it is allotted ; yet every one knows this, that as there is a time for spring and for summer, and for autumn and for winter, so, as it is written [10], there is a time to die, and a time to live. And so the time of the generation which lived in the days of Noah was cut short, and their years were contracted, because the time of all things was at hand. But to Hezekiah were added fifteen years. And as God promises to them that serve Him truly, 'I will fulfil the number of thy days [1],' Abraham dies 'full of days,' and David besought God, saying, 'Take me not away in the midst of my days [2].' And Eliphaz, one of the friends of Job, being assured of this truth, said, 'Thou shalt come to thy grave like ripe corn, gathered in due time, and like as a shock of corn cometh in in his season [3].' And Solomon confirming his words, says, 'The souls of the unrighteous are taken away untimely [4].' And therefore he exhorts in the book of Ecclesiastes, saying, 'Be not overmuch wicked, neither be thou hard : why shouldest thou die before thy time [5]?'

15. The Lord's hour and time.

Now as these things are written in the Scriptures, the case is clear, that the saints know that a certain time is measured to every man, but that no one knows the end of that time is plainly intimated by the words of David, 'Declare unto me the shortness of my days [6].' What he did not know, that he desired to be informed of. Accordingly the rich man also, while he thought that he had yet a long time to live, heard the words, 'Thou fool, this night they are requiring thy soul : then whose shall those things be which thou hast provided [7]?' And the Preacher speaks confidently in the Holy Spirit, and says, 'Man also knoweth not his time [8].' Wherefore the Patriarch Isaac said to his son Esau, 'Behold, I am old, and I know not the day of my death [9].' Our Lord therefore, although as God, and the Word of the Father, He both knew

the time measured out by Him to all, and was conscious of the time for suffering, which He Himself had appointed also to His own body ; yet since He was made man for our sakes, He hid Himself when He was sought after before that time came, as we do ; when He was persecuted, He fled ; and avoiding the designs of His enemies He passed by, and 'so went through the midst of them [1].' But when He had brought on that time which He Himself had appointed, at which He desired to suffer in the body for all men, He announces it to the Father, saying, 'Father, the hour is come ; glorify Thy Son [2].' And then He no longer hid Himself from those who sought Him, but stood willing to be taken by them ; for the Scripture says, He said to them that came unto Him, 'Whom seek ye [3]?' and when they answered, 'Jesus of Nazareth,' He saith unto them, 'I am He whom ye seek.' And this He did even more than once ; and so they straightway led Him away to Pilate. He neither suffered Himself to be taken before the time came, nor did He hide Himself when it was come ; but gave Himself up to them that conspired against Him, that He might shew to all men that the life and death of man depend upon the divine sentence ; and that without our Father which is in heaven, neither a hair of man's head can become white or black, nor a sparrow ever fall into the snare [4].

16. The Lord's example followed by the Saints.

Our Lord therefore, as I said before, thus offered Himself for all ; and the Saints having received this example from their Saviour (for all of them before His coming, nay always, were under His teaching), in their conflicts with their persecutors acted lawfully in flying, and hiding themselves when they were sought after. And being ignorant, as men, of the end of the time which Providence had appointed unto them, they were unwilling at once to deliver themselves up into the power of those who conspired against them. But knowing on the other hand what is written, that 'the portions' of man 'are in God's hand [5],' and that 'the Lord killeth [6],' and the Lord 'maketh alive,' they the rather endured unto the end, 'wandering about [7],' as the Apostle has said, 'in sheepskins, and goatskins, being destitute, tormented, wandering in deserts,' and hiding themselves 'in dens and caves of the earth ;' until either the appointed time of death arrived, or God who had appointed their time spake unto them, and stayed the designs of their enemies, or else delivered up the perse-

---

[9] *De Decr.* 18, note 5.　　[10] Eccles. iii. 2.　　[1] Ex. xxiii. 26 ;
Gen. xxv. 8.　　[2] Ps. cii. 24.　　[3] Job v. 26, LXX.
[4] Vid. Prov. x. 27.　　[5] Eccles. vii. 17.　　[6] Ps. cii. 23, LXX.
[7] Luke xii. 20.　　[8] Eccles. ix. 12.　　[9] Gen. xxvii. 2.

[1] Luke iv. 30.　　[2] John xvii. 1.　　[3] John xviii. 4, 5.
[4] Matt. v. 36 ; x. 29.　　[5] Ps. xxxi. 15.　　[6] 1 Sam. ii. 6.
[7] Heb. xi. 37, 38.

cuted to their persecutors, according as it seemed to Him to be good. This we may well learn respecting all men from David : for when Joab instigated him to slay Saul, he said, ' As the Lord liveth, the Lord shall smite him ; or his day shall come to die ; or he shall descend into battle, and be delivered to the enemies ; the Lord forbid that I should stretch forth my hand against the Lord's anointed[8].'

17. *A time to flee and a time to stay.*

And if ever in their flight they came unto those that sought after them, they did not do so without reason : but when the Spirit spoke unto them, then as righteous men they went and met their enemies ; by which they also shewed their obedience and zeal towards God. Such was the conduct of Elijah, when, being commanded by the Spirit, he shewed himself unto Ahab[9] ; and of Micaiah the prophet when he came to the same Ahab ; and of the prophet who cried against the altar in Samaria, and rebuked Rehoboam[10] ; and of Paul when he appealed unto Cæsar. It was not certainly through cowardice that they fled : God forbid. The flight to which they submitted was rather a conflict and war against death. For with wise caution they guarded against these two things ; either that they should offer themselves up without reason (for this would have been to kill themselves, and to become guilty of death, and to transgress the saying of the Lord, 'What God hath joined let not man put asunder[1]'), or that they should willingly subject themselves to the reproach of negligence, as if they were unmoved by the tribulations which they met with in their flight, and which brought with them sufferings greater and more terrible than death. For he that dies, ceases to suffer ; but he that flies, while he expects daily the assaults of his enemies, esteems death lighter. They therefore whose course was consummated in their flight did not perish dishonourably, but attained as well as others the glory of martyrdom. Therefore it is that Job was accounted a man of mighty fortitude, because he endured to live under so many and such severe sufferings, of which he would have had no sense, had he come to his end. Wherefore the blessed Fathers thus regulated their conduct also ; they shewed no cowardice in fleeing from the persecutor, but rather manifested their fortitude of soul in shutting themselves up in close and dark places, and living a hard life. Yet did they not desire to avoid the time of death when it arrived ; for their concern was neither to

shrink from it when it came, nor to forestall the sentence determined by Providence, nor to resist His dispensation, for which they knew themselves to be preserved ; lest by acting hastily, they should become to themselves the cause of terror : for thus it is written, ' He that is hasty with his lips, shall bring terror upon himself[2].'

18. *The Saints who fled were no cowards.*

Of a truth no one can possibly doubt that they were well furnished with the virtue of fortitude. For the Patriarch Jacob who had before fled from Esau, feared not death when it came, but at that very time blessed the Patriarchs, each according to his deserts. And the great Moses, who previously had hid himself from Pharaoh, and had withdrawn into Midian for fear of him, when he received the commandment, 'Return into Egypt[3],' feared not to do so. And again, when he was bidden to go up into the mountain Abarim[4] and die, he delayed not through cowardice, but even joyfully proceeded thither. And David, who had before fled from Saul, feared not to risk his life in war in defence of his people ; but having the choice of death or of flight set before him, when he might have fled and lived, he wisely preferred death. And the great Elijah, who had at a former time hid himself from Jezebel, shewed no cowardice when he was commanded by the Spirit to meet Ahab, and to reprove Ahaziah. And Peter, who had hid himself for fear of the Jews, and the Apostle Paul who was let down in a basket, and fled, when they were told, ' Ye must bear witness at Rome[5],' deferred not the journey ; yea, rather, they departed rejoicing[6] ; the one as hastening to meet his friends, received his death with exultation ; and the other shrunk not from the time when it came, but gloried in it, saying, ' For I am now ready to be offered, and the time of my departure is at hand[7].'

19. *The Saints courageous in their flight, and divinely favoured.*

These things both prove that their previous flight was not the effect of cowardice ; and testify that their after conduct also was of no ordinary character : and they loudly proclaim that they possessed in a high degree the virtue of fortitude. For neither did they withdraw themselves on account of a slothful timidity, on the contrary, they were at such times under the practice of a severer discipline than at others ; nor were they con-

---

[8] 1 Sam. xxvi. 10, 11.   [9] 1 Kings xxi. 18
[10] i.e. Jeroboam 1 Kings xiii. 2.   [1] Matt. xix. 6.

[2] Prov. xiii. 3, LXX.   [3] Vid. Ex. iii. 10.   [4] Deut. xxxii. 49.
[5] Vid. Acts xxiii. 11. [The reference to the Roman martyrdom of the *two* great Apostles should be noted. The tradition is as old as Clem. Rom. ; much older than that or the Roman *Episcopate* of one of them.]   [6] Vid. Euseb. *Hist.* ii. 25.   [7] 2 Tim. iv. 6.

demned for their flight, or charged with cowardice, by such as are now so fond of criminating others. Nay they were blessed through that declaration of our Lord, 'Blessed are they which are persecuted for righteousness sake [8].' Nor yet were these their sufferings without profit to themselves; for having tried them as 'gold in the furnace,' as Wisdom has said, God found them worthy of Himself [9]. And then they shone the more 'like sparks,' being saved from them that persecuted them, and delivered from the designs of their enemies, and preserved to the end that they might teach the people; so that their flight and escape from the rage of them that sought after them, was according to the dispensation of the Lord. And so they became dear in the sight of God, and had the most glorious testimony to their fortitude.

20. *Same subject continued.*

Thus, for example, the Patriarch Jacob was favoured in his flight with many, even divine visions, and remaining quiet himself, he had the Lord on his side, rebuking Laban, and hindering the designs of Esau; and afterwards he became the Father of Judah, of whom sprang the Lord according to the flesh; and he dispensed the blessings to the Patriarchs. And when Moses the beloved of God was in exile, then it was that he saw that great sight, and being preserved from his persecutors, was sent as a prophet into Egypt, and being made the minister of those mighty wonders and of the Law, he led that great people in the wilderness. And David when he was persecuted wrote the Psalm, 'My heart uttered a good word [1];' and, 'Our God shall come even visibly, and shall not keep silence [2].' And again he speaks more confidently, saying, ' Mine eye hath seen his desire upon mine enemies [3];' and again, 'In God have I put my trust; I will not be afraid what man can do unto me [4].' And when he fled and escaped from the face of Saul 'to the cave,' he said, 'He hath sent from heaven, and hath saved me. He hath given them to reproach that would tread me under their feet. God hath sent His mercy and truth, and hath delivered my soul from the midst of lions [5].' Thus he too was saved according to the dispensation of God, and afterwards became king, and received the promise, that from his seed our Lord should issue. And the great Elijah, when he withdrew to mount Carmel, called upon God, and destroyed at once more than four hundred prophets of Baal; and when there were sent to

take him two captains of fifty with their hundred men, he said, ' Let fire come down from heaven [6],' and thus rebuked them. And he too was preserved, so that he anointed Elisha in his own stead, and became a pattern of discipline for the sons of the prophets. And the blessed Paul, after writing these words, ' what persecutions I endured; but out of them all the Lord delivered me, and will deliver [7];' could speak more confidently and say, ' But in all these things we are more than conquerors, for nothing shall separate us from the love of Christ [8].' For then it was that he was caught up to the third heaven, and admitted into paradise, where he heard 'unspeakable words, which it is not lawful for a man to·utter [9].' And for this end was he then preserved, that ' from Jerusalem even unto Illyricum ' he might ' fully preach the Gospel [10].'

21. *The Saints fled for our sakes.*

The flight of the saints therefore was neither blameable nor unprofitable. If they had not avoided their persecutors, how would it have come to pass that the Lord should spring from the seed of David? Or who would have preached the glad tidings of the word of truth? It was for this that the persecutors sought after the saints, that there might be no one to teach, as the Jews charged the Apostles; but for this cause they endured all things, that the Gospel might be preached. Behold, therefore, in that they were thus engaged in conflict with their enemies, they passed not the time of their flight unprofitably, nor while they were persecuted, did they forget the welfare of others: but as being ministers of the good word, they grudged not to communicate it to all men; so that even while they fled, they preached the Gospel, and gave warning of the wickedness of those who conspired against them, and confirmed the faithful by their exhortations. Thus the blessed Paul, having found it so by experience, declared beforehand, ' As many as will live godly in Christ, shall suffer persecution [1].' And so he straightway prepared them that fled for the trial, saying, 'Let us run with patience the race that is set before us [2];' for although there be continual tribulations, 'yet tribulation worketh patience, and patience experience, and experience hope, and hope maketh not ashamed [3].' And the Prophet Isaiah when such-like affliction was expected, exhorted and cried aloud, ' Come, my people, enter thou into thy chambers, and shut thy doors; hide thyself as it were for a little moment, until the indignation be overpast [4].' And so also the Preacher,

---

[8] Matt. v. 10.　　　[9] Wisd. iii. 57.　　　[1] Ps. xlv. 1.
[9] Ps. l. 3, LXX.　[3] Ps. liv. 7.　[4] Ps. lvi. 11.　[5] Ps. lvii. 3.

[6] 2 Kings i. 10.　[7] 2 Tim. iii. 11.　[8] Rom. viii. 35, 37
[9] 2 Cor. xii. 4.　[10] Rom. xv. 19.　[1] 2 Tim. iii. 12
[2] Heb. xii. 1.　[3] Rom. v. 4.　[4] Is. xxvi. 20.

who knew the conspiracies against the righteous, and said, 'If thou seest the oppression of the poor, and violent perverting of judgment and justice in a province, marvel not at the matter : for He that is higher than the highest regardeth, and there be higher than they: moreover there is the profit of the earth[5].' He had his own father David for an example, who had himself experienced the sufferings of persecution, and who supports them that suffer by the words, 'Be of good courage, and He shall strengthen your heart, all ye that put your trust in the Lord[6];' for them that so endure, not man, but the Lord Himself (he says), 'shall help them, and deliver them, because they put their trust in Him :' for I also 'waited patiently for the Lord, and He inclined unto me, and heard my calling ; He brought me up also out of the lowest pit, and out of the mire and clay[7].' Thus is shewn how profitable to the people and productive of good is the flight of the Saints, howsoever the Arians may think otherwise.

22. *Same subject concluded.*

Thus the Saints, as I said before, were abundantly preserved in their flight by the Providence of God, as physicians for the sake of them that had need. And to all men generally, even to us, is this law given, to flee when persecuted, and to hide when sought after, and not rashly tempt the Lord, but wait, as I said above, until the appointed time of death arrive, or the Judge determine something concerning them, according as it shall seem to Him to be good : that men should be ready, that, when the time calls, or when they are taken, they may contend for the truth even unto death. This rule the blessed Martyrs observed in their several persecutions. When persecuted they fled, while concealing themselves they shewed fortitude, and when discovered they submitted to martyrdom. And if some of them came and presented themselves to their persecutors[8], they did not do so without reason ; for immediately in that case they were martyred, and thus made it evident to all that their zeal, and this offering up of themselves to their enemies, were from the Spirit.

23. *Persecution is from the Devil.*

Seeing therefore that such are the commands of our Saviour, and that such is the conduct of the Saints, let these persons, to whom one cannot give a name suitable to their character,—let them, I say, tell us, from whom they learnt to persecute? They cannot say,

from the Saints[9]. No, but from the Devil (that is the only answer which is left them) ;—from him who says, 'I will pursue, I will overtake[10].' Our Lord commanded to flee, and the saints fled : but persecution is a device of the Devil, and one which he desires to exercise against all. Let them say then, to which we ought to submit ourselves ; to the words of the Lord, or to their fabrications? Whose conduct ought we to imitate, that of the Saints, or that of those whose example these men have adopted? But since it is likely they cannot determine this question (for, as Esaias said, their minds and their consciences are blinded, and they think 'bitter to be sweet,' and 'light darkness[1]'), let some one come forth from among us Christians, and put them to rebuke, and cry with a loud voice, 'It is better to trust in the Lord, than to attend to the foolish sayings of these men ; for the "words" of the Lord have "eternal life[2]," but the things which these utter are full of iniquity and blood.'

24. *Irruption of Syrianus.*

This were sufficient to put a stop to the madness of these impious men, and to prove that their desire is for nothing else, but only through a love of contention to utter revilings and insults. But forasmuch as having once dared to fight against Christ, they have now become officious, let them enquire and learn into the manner of my withdrawal from their own friends. For the Arians were mixed with the soldiers in order to exasperate them against me, and, as they were unacquainted with my person, to point me out to them. And although they are destitute of all feelings of compassion, yet when they hear the circumstances they will surely be quiet for very shame. It was now night[3], and some of the people were keeping a vigil preparatory to a communion on the morrow, when the General Syrianus suddenly came upon us with more than five thousand soldiers, having arms and drawn swords, bows, spears, and clubs, as I have related above. With these he surrounded the Church, stationing his soldiers near at hand, in order that no one might be able to leave the Church and pass by them. Now I considered that it would be unreasonable in me to desert the people during such a disturbance, and not to endanger myself in their behalf ; therefore I sat down upon my throne, and desired the Deacon to read a Psalm, and the people to answer, 'For His mercy endureth for ever[4],' and then all to withdraw and depart home. But the General having now

---

[5] Eccles. v. 8, 9. LXX.   [6] Ps. xxxi. 24.
[7] Ps. xxxvii. 40; xl. 1.
[8] Vid. instances and passages collected in Pearson's *Vind. Ignat.* part ii. o. 9; also Gibbon, ch. xvi. p. 428. Mosheim *de Reb. Ante Const.* p. 941. [See D.C.A. p. 1119 (3).]

[9] *Hist. Arian.* §§ 33, 67.   [10] Ex. xv. 9.   [1] Is. v. 20.
[2] John vi. 68.   [3] *Apol. Const.* 25.   [4] Ps. cxxxvi. 1
[on psalmody at Alexandria, cf. Aug. *Conf.* x. 33.]

made a forcible entry, and the soldiers having surrounded the sanctuary for the purpose of apprehending us, the Clergy and those of the laity, who were still there, cried out, and demanded that we too should withdraw. But I refused, declaring that I would not do so, until they had retired one and all. Accordingly I stood up, and having bidden prayer, I then made my request of them, that all should depart before me, saying that it was better that my safety should be endangered, than that any of them should receive hurt. So when the greater part had gone forth, and the rest were following, the monks who were there with us and certain of the Clergy came up and dragged us away. And thus (Truth is my witness), while some of the soldiers stood about the sanctuary, and others were going round the Church, we passed through, under the Lord's guidance, and with His protection withdrew without observation, greatly glorifying God that we had not betrayed the people, but had first sent them away, and then had been able to save ourselves, and to escape the hands of them which sought after us.

25. *Athanasius's wonderful escape.*

Now when Providence had delivered us in such an extraordinary manner, who can justly lay any blame upon me, because we did not give ourselves up into the hands of them, that sought after us, nor return and present ourselves before them? This would have been plainly to shew ingratitude to the Lord, and to act against His commandment, and in contradiction to the practice of the Saints. He who censures me in this matter must presume also to blame the great Apostle Peter, because though he was shut up and guarded by soldiers, he followed the angel that summoned him, and when he had gone forth from the prison and escaped in safety, he did not return and surrender himself, although he heard what Herod had done. Let the Arian in his madness censure the Apostle Paul, because when he was let down from the wall and had escaped in safety, he did not change his mind, and return and give himself up; or Moses, because he returned not out of Midian into Egypt, that he might be taken of them that sought after him; or David, because when he was concealed in the cave, he did not discover himself to Saul. As also the sons of the prophets remained in their caves, and did not surrender themselves to Ahab. This would have been to act contrary to the commandment, since the Scripture says, 'Thou shalt not tempt the Lord thy God[5].'

---

5 Deut. vi. 16 ; Matt. iv. 7.

26. *He acted according to the example of the Saints. Character of his accusers.*

Being careful to avoid such an offence, and instructed by these examples, I so ordered my conduct; and I do not undervalue the favour and the help which have been shewn me of the Lord, howsoever these in their madness may gnash their teeth[5a] against us. For since the manner of our retreat was such as we have described, I do not think that any blame whatever can attach to it in the minds of those who are possessed of a sound judgment: seeing that according to holy Scripture, this pattern has been left us by the Saints for our instruction. But there is no atrocity, it would seem, which these men neglect to practise, nor will they leave anything undone which may shew their own wickedness and cruelty. And indeed their lives are only in accordance with their spirit and the follies of their doctrines ; for there are no sins that one could charge them with, how heinous soever, that they do not commit without shame. Leontius[6] for instance, being censured for his intimacy with a certain young woman, named Eustolium, and prohibited from living with her, mutilated himself for her sake, in order that he might be able to associate with her freely. He did not however clear himself from suspicion, but rather on this account he was degraded from his rank as Presbyter. [Although the heretic Constantius by violence caused him to be named a Bishop[7].] Narcissus[8], besides being charged with many other transgressions, was degraded three times by different Councils ; and now he is among them, most wicked man. And George[9], who was a Presbyter, was deposed for his wickedness, and although he had nominated himself a Bishop, he was nevertheless a second time deposed in the great Council of Sardica. And besides all this, his dissolute life was notorious, for he is condemned even by his own friends, as making the end of existence, and its happiness, to consist in the commission of the most disgraceful crimes.

27. *Conclusion.*

Thus each surpasses the other in his own peculiar vices But there is a common blot that attaches to them all, in that through their heresy they are enemies of Christ, and are no

---

5a *Sent. Dion.* 16. *Hist. Ar.* §§ 68. 72.
6 *Hist. Arian.* § 28 [but see D.C.B. iii. 688].
7 [The bracketed passage is omitted by some good witnesses to the text. The respectful tone of the 'Apology to Const.' is exchanged for cold reserve in this 'Apology,' and for unmeasured invective in *Hist. Ar.*]   8 *De Syn.* 17, &c.
9 *Apol. Ar.* 8, note 3.

longer called Christians[10], but Arians. They ought indeed to accuse each other of the sins they are guilty of, for they are contrary to the faith of Christ; but they rather conceal them for their own sakes. And it is no wonder, that being possessed of such a spirit, and implicated in such vices, they persecute and seek after those who follow not the same impious heresy as themselves; that they delight to destroy them, and are grieved if they fail of obtaining their desires, and think themselves injured, as I said before, when they see those alive whom they wish to perish. May they continue to be injured in such sort, that they may lose the power of inflicting injuries, and that those whom they persecute may give thanks unto the Lord, and say in the words of the twenty-sixth Psalm, 'The Lord is my light and my salvation; whom then shall I fear? The Lord is the strength of my life; of whom then shall I be afraid? When the wicked, even mine enemies and my foes, came upon me to eat up my flesh, they stumbled and fell[11];' and again the thirtieth Psalm, 'Thou hast saved my soul from adversities; thou hast not shut me up into the hands of mine enemies; thou hast set my foot in a large room[12],' in Christ Jesus our Lord, through whom to the Father in the Holy Spirit be glory and power for ever and ever. Amen.

---

[10] Vid. supr. *Ep. Æg.* 20 infr. *Hist. Arian.* §§ 17. 34 fin. 41 init. 59 fin. 64 init. *De. Decr.* 16, note 5.

[11] Ps xxvii. 2.

[12] Ps. xxxi. 7, 8.

HISTORIA ARIANORUM

(WRITTEN 358.)

THIS History takes up the narrative from the admission of Arius to communion at the 'dedication' synod of Jerusalem (adjourned Council of Tyre) in 335, as described in *Apol. c. Ar.* 84. It has been commonly assumed from its abrupt beginning (the ταῦτα, referring to an antecedent narrative) that the History has lost its earlier chapters, which contained the story of Arianism *ab ovo*. Montfaucon suggests in fact that the copyists omitted the first chapters on account of their identity in substance with the great Apology. But this seems to require reconsideration. If the alleged missing chapters were different[1] in form from the second part of the Apology, they would not have been omitted: for such repetitions of the same matter in other words are very frequent in the works of Athanasius: but if they were identical in form, they are not lost, and the conclusion is that the History was written with the express intention of continuing the Apology. The customary inference from the abrupt commencement of the History may be dismissed with a *non sequitur*. Such a commencement was natural under the circumstances: we may compare the case of Xenophon, whose 'Hellenica' begin with the words Μετὰ δὲ ταῦτα, οὐ πολλαῖς ἡμέραις ὕστερον . . ., the reference being to the end of the history of Thucydides. The view here maintained is clinched by the fact that Athanasius at this very time *reissued* his Apology against the Arians with an appendix (§§ 89, 90) on the lapse of Hosius and Liberius[2].

The History of the Arians, then, is a complete work, and written to continue the narrative of the second part of the Apology. Being in fact a manifesto against Constantius, it naturally takes up the tale just before his entry upon the scene as the patron of Arianism. The substantially Athanasian authorship of the History cannot be questioned. The writer occasionally, like many others ancient and modern, speaks of himself in the third person (references § 21, note 5, see also *Orat.* i. 3); but in other places he clearly identifies himself with Athanasius. The only passage which appears to distinguish the writer from Athanasius (§ 52, see note), may be due to the bishop's habitual (*Apol. Const.* 11) employment of an amanuensis, but more probably the text is corrupt; in any case the passage cannot weigh against the clear sense of § 21. The *immediate* Athanasian authorship of the piece has been questioned partly on the ground of its alleged incompleteness, partly on that of several slight discrepancies with other writings. On this twofold ground it is inferred that the Arian History has passed through some obscure process of re-editing (Gwatkin, *Studies*, p. 99, § 14 'dependent on the *Vita [Antonii]* 86,' p. 127, 'not an uncorrupted work') by a later hand. I am quite unconvinced of this. The incompleteness of the work is, as I think I have shewn above, an unnecessary hypothesis, while the mistakes or inconsistencies may well be due to circumstances of composition. It was written in hiding, perhaps while moving from place to place, certainly under more pressure of highly wrought agitation and bitterness of spirit than any other work of Athanasius. The most accurate of men when working at leisure make strange slips at times (e.g. § 13, note 4); the mistakes in the History are not more than one might expect in such a work. The principal are, § 21 (see note 3), § 14 (reference in note 8), § 11, πρὶν γενέσθαι ταῦτα (cf. *Encycl.* 5), § 47 (inverting order of events in § 39).

The date of the History is at first sight a difficulty. The fall of Liberius is dealt with in Part V., which must therefore have been written not earlier than 358 (the exact chronology of the lapse of Liberius is not certain), while yet in § 4 Leontius, who died in the summer or autumn of 357, is still bishop of Antioch. We must therefore suppose that the History was begun at about the time when the *Apologia de Fuga* was finished (cf. the bitter conclusion

---

i.e. slight modifications excepted, see Montf. in *Migne*, P.G. xxv. 318, note 46, and 389, note 60.
² For another example of hastily inferred mutilation, see § 48, note 3.

of that tract) and completed when the lapse of Liberius was known in Egypt. A more accurate determination of date is not permitted by our materials.

The tract before us is in effect a fierce anonymous pamphlet against Constantius. Even apart from the references in the letters to the Monks and to Serapion (see below), the work bears clear marks of having been intended for secret circulation (for the practice, see Fialon, pp. 193—199). 'Instead of the "pious" Emperor who was so well versed in Scripture, whose presence would gladden a dedication festival, whose well-known humanity forbade the supposition that he could have perpetrated a deliberate injustice, we find a Costyllius (or "Connikin") whose misdeeds could only be palliated by the imbecility which rendered him the slave of his own servants—inhuman towards his nearest of kin,—false and crafty, a Pharaoh, a Saul, an Ahab, a Belshazzar, more cruel than Pilate or Maximian, ignorant of the Gospels, a patron of heresy, a precursor of Antichrist, an enemy of Christ, as if himself Antichrist, and—the words must be written—self-abandoned to the future doom of fire' (Bright, *Introd.* p. lxxviii., and see §§ 9, 30, 32, 34, 40, 45, 46, 51, 53, 67—70, 74, 80). There are certainly many passages which one could wish that Athanasius had not written,—one, not necessary to specify, in which he fully condescends to the coarse brutality of the age, mingling it unpardonably with holy things. But Athanasius was human, and exasperated by inhuman vindictiveness and perfidy. If in the passages referred to he falls below himself, and speaks in the spirit of his generation, there are not wanting passages equal in nobility to anything he ever wrote. Once more to quote Dr. Bright: 'The beautiful description of the Archbishop's return from his second exile, and of its moral and religious effect upon Alexandrian Church society (25), the repeated protests against the principle of persecution as alien to the mind of the Church of Christ (29, 33, 67), the tender allusion to sympathy for the poor as instinctive in human nature (63), the vivid picture—doubtless somewhat coloured by imagination—of the stand made by Western bishops, and notably for a time by Liberius, against the tyrannous dictation of Constantius in matters ecclesiastical (34 *sqq.* 76), the generous estimate of Hosius and Liberius in the hour of their infirmity (41, 45), the three golden passages which describe the union maintained by a common faith and a sincere affection between friends who are separated from each other (40), the all-sufficient presence of God with His servants in their extremest solitude (47), and the future joy when heaven would be to sufferers for the truth as a calm haven to sailors after a storm (79). It is in such contexts that we see the true Athanasius, and touch the source of his magnificent insuperable constancy' (p. lxxix.). Nothing could be more just, or more happily put. It ought to be noted before leaving this part of the subject, that the language put into the mouth of Constantius and the Arians (33 fin., 1, 3, 9, 12, 15, 30, 42, 45, 60), is not so much a report of their words as 'a representation *ad invidiam* of what is assumed to have been in their minds.' Other instances of this are to be found in Athanasius (*Ep. Æg.* 18, *Orat.* iii. 17), and he uses the device advisedly (*de Syn.* 7, *middle*).

The letter to Serapion on the death of Arius, and the letter to Monks, which in MSS. and printed editions are prefixed to this treatise, will be found in the collection of letters below (No. 54 and 52). They have been removed from their time-honoured place in accordance with the general arrangement of this volume, though not without hesitation, and apart from any intention to dogmatise on the relation they bear to the present tract.

The 'Arian History' has commonly been called the 'Hist. Arianorum ad Monachos,' or even the 'Epistola ad Monachos;' even at the present day it is sometimes cited simply as 'ad Monachos.' The History has derived this title from the fact, that in the Codices and editions, the Letter and History are frequently joined together without any sign of division. At the same time the correctness of this collocation is not entirely free from doubt.

Serapion (*Letter* 54 § 1) had written to Athanasius asking for three things,—a history of recent events relating to himself, an *exposé* of the Arian heresy, and an exact account of the death of Arius. The latter Athanasius furnishes in the letter just referred to. For the two former, he refers Serapion to a document he had written for the monks (ἅπερ ἔγραψα τοῖς μοναχοῖς), and which he now sends to Serapion. He begs Serapion at the end of his letter not on any account to part with the letters he has received, nor to copy them (he gave, he adds, the same directions to the monks, cf. *Letter* 52. 3), but to send them back with such corrections and additions as he might think desirable. He refers him to his letter to the monks for an explanation of the circumstances which render this precaution necessary. The monks (*ib.* 1) had apparently made the same request as Serapion afterwards made. It has been conjectured that the four 'Orations' against Arianism, or the first three, are the treatise on the heresy addressed to the monks and subsequently sent to Serapion. But the description of that treatise ἔγραψα δι ὀλίγων (*Letter* 52. 1) is quite inapplicable to the longest treatise extant among the works of Athanasius. Still less, even if the Arian History were a fragment (see above), could we suppose that the accompanying treatise formed the missing first part. We must therefore acquiesce in the conclusion that the treatise in question has perished. Accordingly we cannot be sure (although it is generally regarded as highly probable[3]) that the historical portion is preserved to us in the 'Arian History.' In any case the Letter to Monks is quite unconnected with it in its subject matter, and ends with the blessing, as the History does with the doxology, in the form of an independent document.

While admitting, therefore, the naturalness of the traditional arrangement, we may fairly treat the two as distinct, and permit the Arian History to launch the reader without preamble *in medias res*.

As the tract is long, and various in its subject-matter, the following scheme of contents may be found useful. It will be noted that chronological order is observed in Parts I.—IV., i.e. till 355, when the existing persecution of Constantius, the main theme of the History (*Letter* 52, § 1), is reached. The history of this persecution is dealt with (Parts V.—VII.) with much more fulness, and is grouped round subjects each of which covers more or less the same period. Part VIII. deals with the more recent events in Egypt.

PART I. PROCEEDINGS OF THE ARIANS FROM THE COUNCIL OF TYRE TILL THE RETURN OF THE EXILES (335—337).

§§ 1—3. General character of their proceedings.
§§ 4—7. Persecution of the orthodox bishops.
§ 8. Restoration of the exiles after Constantine's death.

PART II. SECOND EXILE OF ATHANASIUS, TILL THE COUNCIL OF SARDICA (337—343).

§ 9. Renewed intrigues against Athanasius.
§ 10. Gregory intruded by Constantius as bishop.
§ 11. Athanasius at Rome. Negotiations for a Council there.
§§ 12—14. Violent proceedings of Gregory. Case of Duke Balacius.

PART III. FROM SARDICA TILL THE DEATH OF CONSTANS (343—350).

§ 15. The meeting of the Synod. Dismay of the Arianising bishops.
§ 16. Their flight from the Synod.
§ 17. Proceedings of the Synod.
§§ 18, 19. Continued persecution after it.
§ 20. The infamous plot of Stephen against the Sardican legates at Antioch.
§§ 21, 22. Constantius changes his mind and recalls Athanasius with a solemn oath to defend him for the future.
§§ 23, 24. Letters of Constantius at this time.
§ 25. Return of Athanasius (346).
§ 26. Recantation of Valens and Ursacius.
§ 27. Peace and joy of the Church.

PART IV. FROM THE DEATH OF CONSTANS TO THE COUNCIL OF MILAN (351—355).

§ 28. Renewed intrigues of the Arianising party.
§§ 29, 30. Valens, Ursacius, and the Emperor return to Arianism.
§§ 31, 32. Constantius again persecutes the Church.
§ 33. Wickedness of persecution. Western bishops banished by Constantius [at Milan].
§ 34. How they diffused the truth wherever they went.

PART V. LIBERIUS (355—358).

§§ 35—37. Firmness of Liberius and rage of Constantius.
§ 38. Concerning the eunuchs at the Court.
§§ 39, 40. Liberius rebukes the Emperor and is cruelly exiled.
§ 41. After two years of exile, Liberius gives way under force.

PART VI. HOSIUS (355—358).

§ 42. Intrigues against Hosius.
§ 43. Vain attempts of Constantius to gain him over.
§ 44. Letter of Hosius remonstrating with the Emperor.
§§ 45, 46. Lapse of Hosius, his fidelity to Athanasius, recantation, and death.
§ 47. Monstrosity of the above proceedings.

---

[3] See Eichhorn, p. 61 ; Bright. p. lxxiv.

HISTORY OF THE ARIANS

PART I.

ARIAN PERSECUTION UNDER CONSTANTINE.

1. AND not long after they put in execution the designs for the sake of which they had had recourse to these artifices; for they no sooner had formed their plans, but they immediately admitted Arius and his fellows to communion. They set aside the repeated condemnations which had been passed upon them, and again pretended the imperial authority[1] in their behalf. And they were not ashamed to say in their letters, 'since Athanasius suffered, all jealousy[2] has ceased, and let us henceforward receive Arius and his fellows;' adding, in order to frighten their hearers, 'because the Emperor has commanded it.' Moreover, they were not ashamed to add, 'for these men profess orthodox opinions;' not fearing that which is written, 'Woe unto them that call bitter sweet, that put darkness for light[3];' for they are ready to undertake anything in support of their heresy. Now is it not hereby plainly proved to all men, that we both suffered heretofore, and that you now persecute us, not under the authority of an Ecclesiastical sentence[4], but on the ground of the Emperor's threats, and on account of our piety towards Christ? As also they conspired in like manner against other Bishops, fabricating charges against them also; some of whom fell asleep in the place of their exile, having attained the glory of Christian confession; and others are still banished from their country, and contend still more and more manfully against their heresy, saying, 'Nothing shall separate us from the love of Christ[5]?'

2. *Arians sacrifice morality and integrity to party.*

And hence also you may discern its character, and be able to condemn it more confidently. The man who is their friend and their associate in impiety, although he is open to ten thousand charges for other enormities which he has committed; although the evidence and proof against him are most clear; he is approved of by them, and straightway becomes the friend of the Emperor, obtaining an introduction by his impiety; and making very many pretences, he acquires confidence before the magistrates to do whatever he desires. But he who exposes their impiety, and honestly advocates the cause of Christ, though he is pure in all things, though he is conscious of no delinquencies, though he meets with no accuser; yet on the false pretences which they have framed against him, is immediately seized and sent into banishment under a sentence of the Emperor, as if he were guilty of the crimes which they wish to charge upon him, or as if, like Naboth, he had insulted the King; while he who advocates the cause of their heresy is sought for and immediately sent to take possession of the other's Church; and henceforth confiscations and insults, and all kinds of cruelty are exercised against those who do not receive him. And what is the strangest of all, the man whom the people desire, and know to be blameless[6], the Emperor takes away and banishes; but him whom they neither desire, nor know, he sends to them from a distant place with soldiers and letters from himself. And henceforward a strong necessity is laid upon them, either to hate him whom they love; who has been their teacher, and their father in godliness; and to love him whom they do not desire, and to trust their children to one of whose life and conversation and character they are ignorant; or else certainly to suffer punishment, if they disobey the Emperor.

---

[1] § 33.   [2] φθόνος.   [3] Is. v. 20.
[4] Infr. § 76.   [5] Rom. viii. 35.

[6] 1 Tim. iii. 2.

3. Recklessness of their proceedings.

In this manner the impious are now proceeding, as heretofore, against the orthodox; giving proof of their malice and impiety amongst all men everywhere. For granting that they have accused Athanasius; yet what have the other Bishops done? On what grounds can they charge them? Has there been found in their case too the dead body of an Arsenius? Is there a Presbyter Macarius, or has a cup been broken amongst them? Is there a Meletian to play the hypocrite? No: but as their proceedings against the other Bishops shew the charges which they have brought against Athanasius, in all probability, to be false; so their attacks upon Athanasius make it plain, that their accusations of the other Bishops are unfounded likewise. This heresy has come forth upon the earth like some great monster, which not only injures the innocent with its words, as with teeth[7]; but it has also hired external power to assist it in its designs. And strange it is that, as I said before, no accusation is brought against any of them; or if any be accused, he is not brought to trial; or if a shew of enquiry be made, he is acquitted against evidence, while the convicting party is plotted against, rather than the culprit put to shame. Thus the whole party of them is full of idleness; and their spies, for Bishops[8] they are not, are the vilest of them all. And if any one among them desire to become a Bishop, he is not told, 'a Bishop must be blameless[9];' but only, 'Take up opinions contrary to Christ, and care not for manners. This will be sufficient to obtain favour for you, and friendship with the Emperor.' Such is the character of those who support the tenets of Arius. And they who are zealous for the truth, however holy and pure they shew themselves, are yet, as I said before, made culprits, whenever these men choose, and on whatever pretences it may seem good to them to invent. The truth of this, as I before remarked, you may clearly gather from their proceedings.

4. Arians persecute Eustathius and others.

There was one Eustathius[1], Bishop of Antioch, a Confessor, and sound in the Faith. This man, because he was very zealous for the truth, and hated the Arian heresy, and would not receive those who adopted its tenets, is falsely accused before the Emperor Constantine, and a charge invented against him, that he had insulted his mother[2]. And immedi-

ately he is driven into banishment, and a great number of Presbyters and Deacons with him. And immediately after the banishment of the Bishop, those whom he would not admit into the clerical order on account of their impiety were not only received into the Church by them, but were even appointed the greater part of them to be Bishops, in order that they might have accomplices in their impiety. Among these was Leontius the eunuch[3], now of Antioch, and his predecessor Stephanus, George of Laodicea, and Theodosius who was of Tripolis, Eudoxius of Germanicia, and Eustathius[4], now of Sebastia.

5. Did they then stop here? No. For Eutropius[5], who was Bishop of Adrianople, a good man, and excellent in all respects, because he had often convicted Eusebius, and had advised them who came that way, not to comply with his impious dictates, suffered the same treatment as Eustathius, and was cast out of his city and his Church. Basilina[6] was the most active in the proceedings against him. And Euphration of Balanea, Kymatius of Paltus, Carterius of Antaradus[6a], Asclepas of Gaza, Cyrus of Berœa in Syria, Diodorus of Asia, Domnion of Sirmium, and Ellanicus of Tripolis, were merely known to hate the heresy; and some of them on one pretence or another, some without any, they removed under the authority of royal letters, drove them out of their cities, and appointed others whom they knew to be impious men, to occupy the Churches in their stead.

6. Case of Marcellus.

Of Marcellus[7], the Bishop of Galatia, it is perhaps superfluous for me to speak; for all men have heard how Eusebius and his fellows, who had been first accused by him of impiety, brought a counter-accusation against him, and caused the old man to be banished. He went up to Rome, and there made his defence, and being required by them, he offered a written declaration of his faith, of which the Council of Sardica approved. But Eusebius and his fellows made no defence, nor, when they were convicted of impiety out of their writings, were they put to shame, but rather assumed greater boldness against all. For

---

imputed to S. Eustathius, Constantine was likely to feel it keenly. 'Stabulariam,' says S. Ambrose, 'hanc primo fuisse asserunt, sic cognitam Constantio.' de Ob. *Theod.* 42, Stabularia, i.e. an innkeeper; so Rahab is sometimes considered to be 'cauponaria sive tabernaria et meretrix,' Cornel. à Lap. in Jos. ii. 1. ἐξ ὁμιλίας γυναικὸς οὐ σεμνῆς οὐδὲ κατὰ νόμον συνελθούσης. Zosim, *Hist.* ii. p. 78. Constantinus ex concubina Helena procreatus. Hieron. *in Chron. Euseb.* p. 773. (ed. Vallars.) Tillemont however maintains (*Empereurs*, t. 4. p. 613), and Gibbon fully admits (*Hist.* ch. 14. p. 190), the legitimacy of Constantine. The latter adds, 'Eutropius (x. 2.) expresses in a few words the real truth, and the occasion of the error, "ex *obscuriori matrimonio* ejus filius."' [Cf. *Soz.* ii. 19.] 3 Below, § 28, note. 4 *Ep. Æg.* 7. 5 *Ap. Fug.* 3. 6 Julian's mother. 6a [The text must be corrected thus; see *Apol. Fug.* 3.] 7 *Apol. Ar.* 32.

---

7 Vid. Dan. vii. 5, 7. 8 Cf. § 49. [The play on words cannot be rendered.] 9 1 Tim. iii. 2. 1 *Apol. Fug.* 3, note 9. * If the common slander of the day concerning S. Helena was

they had an introduction, to the Emperor from the women [8], and were formidable to all men.

7. *Martyrdom of Paul of Constantinople.*

And I suppose no one is ignorant of the case of Paul [9], Bishop of Constantinople ; for the more illustrious any city is, so much the more that which takes place in it is not concealed. A charge was fabricated against him also. For Macedonius his accuser, who has now become Bishop in his stead (I was present myself at the accusation), afterwards held communion with him, and was a Presbyter under Paul himself. And yet when Eusebius with an evil eye wished to seize upon the Bishopric of that city (he had been translated in the same manner from Berytus to Nicomedia), the charge was revived against Paul ; and they did not give up their plot, but persisted in the calumny. And he was banished first into Pontus by Constantine, and a second time by Constantius he was sent bound with iron chains to Singara in Mesopotamia, and from thence transferred to Emesa, and a fourth time he was banished to Cucusus in Cappadocia, near the deserts of Mount Taurus ; where, as those who were with him have declared, he died by strangulation at their hands. And yet these men who never speak the truth, though guilty of this, were not ashamed after his death to invent another story, representing that he had died from illness ; although all who live in that place know the circumstances. And even Philagrius [1], who was then Deputy-Governor [2] of those parts, and represented all their proceedings in such manner as they desired, was yet astonished at this ; and being grieved perhaps that another, and not himself, had done the evil deed, he informed Serapion the Bishop, as well as many other of our friends, that Paul was shut up by them in a very confined and dark place, and left to perish of hunger ; and when after six days they went in and found him still alive, they immediately set upon the man, and strangled him. This was the end of his life ; and they said that Philip who was Prefect was their agent in the perpetration of this murder. Divine Justice, however, did not overlook this ; for not a year passed, when Philip was deprived of his office in great disgrace, so that being reduced to a private station, he became the mockery of those whom he least desired to be the witnesses of his fall. For in extreme

distress of mind, groaning and trembling like Cain [3], and expecting every day that some one would destroy him, far from his country and his friends, he died, like one astounded at his misfortunes, in a manner that he least desired. Moreover these men spare not even after death those against whom they have invented charges whilst living. They are so eager to shew themselves formidable to all, that they banish the living, and shew no mercy on the dead ; but alone of all the world they manifest their hatred to them that are departed, and conspire against their friends, truly inhuman as they are, and haters of that which is good, savage in temper beyond mere enemies, in behalf of their impiety, who eagerly plot the ruin of me and of all the rest, with no regard to truth, but by false charges.

8. *Restoration of the Catholics.*

Perceiving this to be the case, the three brothers, Constantine, Constantius, and Constans, caused all after the death of their father to return to their own country and Church ; and while they wrote letters concerning the rest to their respective Churches, concerning Athanasius they wrote the following ; which likewise shews the violence of the whole proceedings, and proves the murderous disposition of Eusebius and his fellows.

A copy of the Letter of Constantine Cæsar to the people of the Catholic Church in the city of the Alexandrians.

I suppose that it has not escaped the knowledge of your pious minds [4], &c.

This is his letter ; and what more credible witness of their conspiracy could there be than he, who knowing these circumstances has thus written of them ?

PART II.

FIRST ARIAN PERSECUTION UNDER CONSTANTIUS.

9. Eusebius and his fellows, however, seeing the declension of their heresy, wrote to Rome, as well as to the Emperors Constantine and Constans, to accuse [1] Athanasius : but when the persons who were sent by Athanasius disproved the statements which they had written, they were put to shame by the Emperors ; and Julius, Bishop of Rome, wrote to say [2] that a Council ought to be held, wherever we should desire, in order that they might exhibit the charges which they had to make, and might also freely defend themselves concerning those things of which they too were accused. The Presbyters also who were sent by

---

[8] i.e. Constantia, Constantine's sister.
[9] *Ap. Fug.* 3. [For the presence of Ath. at CP. in 337, see Prolegg. ii. § 5 fin.]
[1] [Cf. Prolegg. ch. ii. § 6(1) note 3.]
[2] Vicarius, i.e. 'vicarius Præfecti, agens vicem Præfecti ;' Gothofred in *Cod. Theod.* i. tit. 6. vid. their office, &c., drawn out at length, ibid. t. 6, p. 334.

[3] Gen. iv. 12, LXX. supr. p. 241.   [4] Given above, *Apol. contr. Arian.* § 87.   [1] *Apol. c. Ar.* 3.   [2] Ib. 20.

them, when they saw themselves making an exposure, requested that this might be done. Whereupon these men, whose conduct is suspicious in all that they do, when they see that they are not likely to get the better in an Ecclesiastical trial, betake themselves to Constantius alone, and thenceforth bewail themselves, as to the patron of their heresy. 'Spare,' they say, 'the heresy; you see that all men have withdrawn from us; and very few of us are now left. Begin to persecute, for we are being deserted even of those few, and are left destitute. Those persons whom we forced over to our side, when these men were banished, they now by their return have persuaded again to take part against us. Write letters therefore against them all, and send out Philagrius a second time[3] as Prefect of Egypt, for he is able to carry on a persecution favourably for us, as he has already shewn upon trial, and the more so, as he is an apostate. Send also Gregory as Bishop to Alexandria, for he too is able to strengthen our heresy.'

10. *Violent Intrusion of Gregory.*

Accordingly Constantius at once writes letters, and commences a persecution against all, and sends Philagrius as Prefect with one Arsacius an eunuch; he sends also Gregory with a military force. And the same consequences followed as before[4]. For gathering together a multitude of herdsmen and shepherds, and other dissolute youths belonging to the town, armed with swords and clubs, they attacked in a body the Church which is called the Church of Quirinus[5]; and some they slew, some they trampled under foot, others they beat with stripes and cast into prison or banished. They haled away many women also, and dragged them openly into the court, and insulted them, dragging them by the hair. Some they proscribed; from some they took away their bread[6] for no other reason, but that they might be induced to join the Arians, and receive Gregory, who had been sent by the Emperor.

11. *The Easterns decline the Council at Rome.*

Athanasius, however, before these things happened[6a], at the first report of their proceedings, sailed to Rome, knowing the rage of the heretics, and for the purpose of having the Council held as had been determined. And Julius wrote letters to them, and sent the Presbyters Elpidius and Philoxenus, appointing a day[7], that they might either come, or consider them-

selves as altogether suspected persons. But as soon as Eusebius and his fellows heard that the trial was to be an Ecclesiastical one, at which no Count would be present, nor soldiers stationed before the doors, and that the proceedings would not be regulated by royal order (for they have always depended upon these things to support them against the Bishops, and without them they have no boldness even to speak); they were so alarmed that they detained the Presbyters till after the appointed time, and pretended an unseemly excuse, that they were not able to come now on account of the war which was begun by the Persians[8]. But this was not the true cause of their delay, but the fears of their own consciences. For what have Bishops to do with war? Or if they were unable on account of the Persians to come to Rome, although it is at a distance and beyond sea, why did they like lions[9] go about the parts of the East and those which are near the Persians, seeking who was opposed to them, that they might falsely accuse and banish them?

12. At any rate, when they had dismissed the Presbyters with this improbable excuse, they said to one another, 'Since we are unable to get the advantage in an Ecclesiastical trial, let us exhibit our usual audacity.' Accordingly they write to Philagrius, and cause him after a while to go out with Gregory into Egypt. Whereupon the Bishops are severely scourged and cast into chains[1]. Sarapammon, for instance, Bishop and Confessor, they drive into banishment; Potammon, Bishop and Confessor, who had lost an eye in the persecution, they beat with stripes on the neck so cruelly, that he appeared to be dead before they came to an end. In which condition he was cast aside, and hardly after some hours, being carefully attended and fanned, he revived, God granting him his life; but a short time after he died of the sufferings caused by the stripes, and attained in Christ to the glory of a second martyrdom. And besides these, how many monks were scourged, while Gregory sat by with Balacius the 'Duke!' how many Bishops were wounded! how many virgins were beaten!

13. *Cruelties of Gregory at Alexandria.*

After this the wretched Gregory called upon all men to have communion with him. But if thou didst demand of them communion, they were not worthy of stripes: and if thou didst scourge them as if evil persons, why didst thou ask it of them as if holy? But he had no other end in view, except to fulfil the designs of them

---

3 § 7, note 1, *Encycl.* 3.   4 Upon the Commission, *Apol. Ar.* 15.   5 'Cyrinus.   6 Vid. infr. § 63.
6a [A misstatement, cf. supra pp. 91, 95, note 1.]
7 προθεσμίαν, *Apol. Ar.* 25, note 6 [A.D. 340].

8 *Apol. Ar.* 25, note 8.   9 1 Pet. v. 8.   1 *Apol. Ar.* 30 and foll.

that sent him, and to establish the heresy. Wherefore he became in his folly a murderer and an executioner, injurious, crafty, and profane; in one word, an enemy of Christ. He so cruelly persecuted the Bishop's aunt, that even when she died he would not suffer her to be buried [2]. And this would have been her lot; she would have been cast away without burial, had not they who attended on the corpse carried her out as one of their own kindred. Thus even in such things he shewed his profane temper. And again when the widows and other mendicants [3] had received alms, he commanded what had been given them to be seized, and the vessels in which they carried their oil and wine to be broken, that he might not only shew impiety by robbery, but in his deeds dishonour the Lord; from whom very shortly [4] he will hear those words, 'Inasmuch as thou hast dishonoured these, thou hast dishonoured Me [5].'

14. *Profaneness of Gregory and death of Balacius.*

And many other things he did, which exceed the power of language to describe, and which whoever should hear would think to be incredible. And the reason why he acted thus was, because he had not received his ordination according to ecclesiastical rule, nor had been called to be a Bishop by apostolical tradition [6]; but had been sent out from court with military power and pomp, as one entrusted with a secular government. Wherefore he boasted rather to be the friend of Governors, than of Bishops and Monks. Whenever, therefore, our Father Antony wrote to him from the mountains, as godliness is an abomination to a sinner, so he abhorred the letters of the holy man. But whenever the Emperor, or a General, or other magistrate, sent him a letter, he was as much overjoyed as those in the Proverbs, of whom the Word has said indignantly, 'Woe unto them who leave the path of uprightness; who rejoice to do evil, and delight in the frowardness of the wicked [7].' And so he honoured with presents the bearers of these letters; but once when Antony wrote to him he caused Duke Balacius to spit upon the letter, and to cast it from him. But Divine Justice did not overlook this; for no long time after, when the Duke was on horseback, and on his way to the first halt [8], the horse turned

his head, and biting him on the thigh, threw him off; and within three days he died.

PART III.

RESTORATION OF THE CATHOLICS ON THE COUNCIL OF SARDICA.

15. While they were proceeding in like measures towards all, at Rome about fifty Bishops assembled [1], and denounced Eusebius and his fellows as persons suspected, afraid to come, and also condemned as unworthy of credit the written statement they had sent; but us they received, and gladly embraced our communion. While these things were taking place, a report of the Council held at Rome, and of the proceedings against the Churches at Alexandria, and through all the East, came to the hearing of the Emperor Constans [2]. He writes to his brother Constantius, and immediately they both determine [3] that a Council shall be called, and matters be brought to a settlement, so that those who had been injured may be released from further suffering, and the injurious be no longer able to perpetrate such outrages. Accordingly there assemble at the city of Sardica both from the East and West to the number of one hundred and seventy Bishops [4], more or less; those who came from the West were Bishops only, having Hosius for their father, but those from the East brought with them instructors of youth and advocates, Count Musonianus, and Hesychius [5] the Castrensian; on whose account they came with great alacrity, thinking that everything would be again managed by their authority. For thus by means of these persons they have always shewn themselves formidable to any whom they wished to intimidate, and have prosecuted their designs against whomsoever they chose. But when they arrived and saw that the cause was to be conducted as simply an ecclesiastical one, without the interference of the Count or of soldiers; when they saw the accusers who came from every church and city, and the evidence which was brought against them, when they saw the venerable Bishops Arius and Asterius [6], who came up in their company, withdrawing from them and siding with us [6a], and giving an account of their cunning, and how suspicious their conduct was, and that they were fearing the consequences of a trial, lest they should be con-

---

[2] Cf. *Apol. Const.* § 27 fin.
[3] ἀνεξόδων, vid. infr. § 60. Tillemont translates it, prisoners. Montfaucon has been here followed; vid. Collect. Nov. t. 2. p. xliii.
[4] ὅσον οὐδέπω, as § 32. George was pulled to pieces by the populace, A.D. 362. This was written A.D. 358, or later. [There is the common confusion in this note between Gregory and George. Gregory had died June 26, 345.]   [5] Vid. Matt. xxv. 45.
[6] [Prolegg. ch. iv. § 4.]   [7] Prov. ii. 13, 14, LXX.
[8] μονήν. vid. supr. *Ap. Ar.* 29, note 2. This halt or station which lay up the Nile was called Cereu (*V. Ant.* § 86), or Chæreu,

or the land or property of Chæreas, vid. Naz. *Orat.* 21, 29, who says it was the place where the people met Athanasius on his return from exile on Constantius's death. [The incident is related differently in *Vit. Ant. ubi supra*: see note there.]
[1] *Apol. Ar.* 1, note 1.   [2] *Apol. Const.* 4, note 8.
[3] Below, § 50.
[4] Vid. supr. pp. 127, note 10, and 147.
[5] *Apol. Ar.* 36, notes 8, 9.
[6] Below, § 18.   [6a] [Cf. § 21, note 5.]

victed by us of being false informers, and it should be discovered by those whom they produced in the character of accusers, that they had themselves suggested all they were to say, and were the contrivers of the plot. Perceiving this to be the case, although they had come with great zeal, as thinking that we should be afraid to meet them, yet now when they saw our alacrity, they shut themselves up in the Palace[7] (for they had their abode there), and proceeded to confer with one another in the following manner: 'We came hither for one result; and we see another; we arrived in company with Counts, and the trial is proceeding without them. We are certainly condemned. You all know the orders that have been given. Athanasius and his fellows have the reports of the proceedings in the Mareotis[8], by which he is cleared, and we are covered with disgrace. Why then do we delay? why are we so slow? Let us invent some excuse and be gone, or we shall be condemned if we remain. It is better to suffer the shame of fleeing, than the disgrace of being convicted as false accusers. If we flee, we shall find some means of defending our heresy; and even if they condemn us for our flight, still we have the Emperor as our patron, who will not suffer the people to expel us from the Churches.'

16. Secession of the Easterns at Sardica.

Thus then they reasoned with themselves: and Hosius and all the other Bishops repeatedly signified to them the alacrity of Athanasius and his fellows, saying, 'They are ready with their defence, and pledge themselves to prove you false accusers.' They said also, 'If you fear the trial, why did you come to meet us? either you ought not to have come, or now that you have come, not to flee.' When they heard this, being still more alarmed, they had recourse to an excuse even more unseemly than that they pretended at Antioch, viz. that they betook themselves to flight because the Emperor had written to them the news of his victory over the Persians. And this excuse they were not ashamed to send by Eustathius a Presbyter of the Sardican Church. But even thus their flight did not succeed according to their wishes; for immediately the holy Council, of which the great Hosius was president, wrote to them plainly, saying, 'Either come forward and

answer the charges which are brought against you, for the false accusations which you have made against others, or know that the Council will condemn you as guilty, and declare Athanasius and his fellows free and clear from all blame.' Whereupon they were rather impelled to flight by the alarms of conscience, than to compliance with the proposals of the letter; for when they saw those who had been injured by them, they did not even turn their faces to listen to their words, but fled with greater speed.

17. Proceedings of the Council of Sardica.

Under these disgraceful and unseemly circumstances their flight took place. And the holy Council, which had been assembled out of more than five and thirty provinces, perceiving the malice of the Arians, admitted Athanasius and his fellows to answer to the charges which the others had brought against them, and to declare the sufferings which they had undergone. And when they had thus made their defence, as we said before, they approved and so highly admired their conduct that they gladly embraced their communion, and wrote letters to all quarters, to the diocese of each, and especially to Alexandria and Egypt, and the Libyas, declaring Athanasius and his friends to be innocent, and free from all blame, and their opponents to be calumniators, evil-doers, and everything rather than Christians. Accordingly they dismissed them in peace; but deposed Stephanus and Menophantus, Acacius and George of Laodicea, Ursacius and Valens, Theodorus and Narcissus. For against Gregory, who had been sent to Alexandria by the Emperor, they put forth a proclamation to the effect that he had never been made a Bishop, and that he ought not to be called a Christian. They therefore declared the ordinations which he professed to have conferred to be void, and commanded that they should not be even named in the Church, on account of their novel and illegal nature. Thus Athanasius and his friends were dismissed in peace (the letters concerning them are inserted at the end on account of their length[9]), and the Council was dissolved.

18. Arian Persecution after Sardica.

But the deposed persons, who ought now to have remained quiet, with those who had separated after so disgraceful a flight, were guilty of such conduct, that their former proceedings appear trifling in comparison of these. For when the people of Adrianople would not have communion with them, as men who had fled

---

7 The word Palatium sometimes stands for the space or limits set apart in cities for the Emperor, Cod. Theod. XV. i. 47. sometimes for the buildings upon it, ibid. VII. x. 2, which were one of the four public works mentioned in the Laws. ibid. XV. i. 35. and 36. None but great officers of state were admitted into it. XV. i. 47. Even the judges might not lodge in it, except there was no Prætorium, VII. x. 2. Gothofr. in VII. x. 1. enumerates (with references) the Palatia in Antioch, Daphne, Constantinople, Hereclea, Milan, Treves, &c. It was a great mark then of imperial favour that the Eastern bishops were accommodated in the Palatium at Sardica.　　8 Apol. Ar. § 83, &c.

9 Not found there, but in Apol. contr. Ar. §§ 37, foll.

from the Council, and had proved culprits, they carried their complaints to the Emperor Constantius, and succeeded in causing ten of the laity to be beheaded, belonging to the Manufactory of arms[1] there, Philagrius, who was there again as Count, assisting their designs in this matter also. The tombs of these persons, which we have seen in passing[1a] by, are in front of the city. Then as if they had been quite successful, because they had fled lest they should be convicted of false accusation, they prevailed with the Emperor to command whatsoever they wished to be done. Thus they caused two Presbyters and three Deacons to be banished from Alexandria into Armenia. As to Arius and Asterius, the one Bishop of Petræ[2] in Palestine, the other Bishop in Arabia, who had withdrawn from their party, they not only banished into upper Libya, but also caused them to be treated with insult.

19. *Tyrannical measures against the Alexandrians.*

And as to Lucius[3], Bishop of Adrianople, when they saw that he used great boldness of speech against them, and exposed their impiety, they again, as they had done before, caused him to be bound with iron chains on the neck and hands, and so drove him into banishment, where he died, as they know. And Diodorus a Bishop[4] they remove ; but against Olympius of Æni, and Theodulus of Trajanople[5], both Bishops of Thrace, good and orthodox men, when they perceived their hatred of the heresy, they brought false charges. This Eusebius and his fellows had done first of all, and the Emperor Constantius wrote letters on the subject; and next these men[6] revived the accusation. The purport of the letter was, that they should not only be expelled from their cities and churches, but should also suffer capital punishment, wherever they were discovered. However surprising this conduct may be, it is only in accordance with their principles; for as being instructed by Eusebius and his fellows in such proceedings, and as heirs of their impiety and evil principles, they wished to shew themselves formidable at Alexandria, as their fathers had done in Thrace. They caused an order to be written, that the ports and gates of the cities should be watched, lest availing themselves of the permission granted by the Council, the ban-

ished persons should return to their churches. They also cause orders to be sent to the magistrates at Alexandria, respecting Athanasius and certain Presbyters, named therein, that if either the Bishop[7], or any of the others, should be found coming to the city or its borders, the magistrate should have power to behead those who were so discovered. Thus this new Jewish heresy does not only deny the Lord, but has also learnt to commit murder.

20. *Plot against the Catholic Legates at Antioch.*

Yet even after this they did not rest ; but as the father of their heresy goeth about like a lion, seeking whom he may devour, so these obtaining the use of the public posts[8] went about, and whenever they found any that reproached them with their flight, and that hated the Arian heresy, they scourged them, cast them into chains, and caused them to be banished from their country ; and they rendered themselves so formidable, as to induce many to dissemble, many to fly into the deserts, rather than willingly even to have any dealings with them. Such were the enormities which their madness prompted them to commit after their flight. Moreover they perpetrate another outrageous act, which is indeed in accordance with the character of their heresy, but is such as we never heard of before, nor is likely soon to take place again, even among the more dissolute of the Gentiles, much less among Christians. The holy Council had sent as Legates the Bishops Vincentius[9] of Capua (this is the Metropolis of Campania), and Euphrates of Agrippina[10] (this is the Metropolis of Upper Gaul), that they might obtain the Emperor's consent to the decision of the Council, that the Bishops should return to their Churches, inasmuch as he was the author of their expulsion. The most religious Constans had also written to his brother[1], and supported the cause of the Bishops. But these admirable men, who are equal to any act of audacity, when they saw the two Legates at Antioch, consulted together and formed a plot, which Stephanus[2] undertook by himself to execute, as being a suitable instrument for such purposes. Accordingly they hire a common harlot, even at the season of the most holy Easter, and stripping her introduce her by night into the apartment of the Bishop Euphrates. The harlot who thought that it was a young man who had sent to invite her, at first willingly accompanied them ; but when

---

[1] De Fabricis, vid. Gothofr. in *Cod. Theod.* x. 21.
[1a] [Apparently on his way from Treveri (see 21, n. 3) back to Alexandria in 346.]
[2] [See pp. 148, 128 note, and *infr., Tom. ad Ant.* § 8. In the text Petræ is wrongly placed in Palestine. The slip is one of many in this tract ; see Introd. above.]
[3] *Apol. Ar.* 45, *Apol. Fug.* 3.
[4] Of Tenedos, vid. *Apol. Ar.* 50, supr. § 5.
[5] *Apol. Ar.* 45, note 2.   [6] Acacius, &c.

[7] This accounts for Ath.'s caution, *Apol. Ar.* 51, and below § 21.
[8] *Apol. Ar.* 70, note 5.
[9] *Ap. Const.* 3, note 3.   [10] Cologne.   [1] Infr. § 50.
[2] Bishop of Antioch, cf. § 4, above.

they thrust her in, and she saw the man asleep and unconscious of what was going on, and when presently she distinguished his features, and beheld the face of an old man, and the array of a Bishop, she immediately cried aloud, and declared that violence was used towards her. They desired her to be silent, and to lay a false charge against the Bishop; and so when it was day, the matter was noised abroad, and all the city ran together; and those who came from the Palace were in great commotion, wondering at the report which had been spread abroad, and demanding that it should not be passed by in silence. An enquiry, therefore, was made, and her master gave information concerning those who came to fetch the harlot, and these informed against Stephanus; for they were his Clergy. Stephanus, therefore, is deposed [2a], and Leontius the eunuch appointed in his place, only that the Arian heresy may not want a supporter.

21. *Constantius' change of mind.*

And now the Emperor Constantius, feeling some compunctions, returned to himself; and concluding from their conduct towards Euphrates, that their attacks upon the others were of the same kind, he gives orders that the Presbyters and Deacons who had been banished from Alexandria into Armenia should immediately be released. He also writes publicly to Alexandria [3], commanding that the clergy and laity who were friends of Athanasius should suffer no further persecution. And when Gregory died about ten months [3a] after, he sends for Athanasius with every mark of honour, writing to him no less than three times a very friendly letter [4], in which he exhorted him to take courage and come. He sends also a Presbyter and a Deacon, that he may be still further encouraged to return; for he thought that, through alarm at what had taken place before, I [5] did not care to return. Moreover he writes to his brother Constans, that he also would exhort me to return. And he affirmed that he had been expecting Athanasius a whole year, and that he would not permit any change to be made, or any ordination to take place, as he was preserving the Churches for Athanasius their Bishop.

22. *Athanasius visits Constantius.*

When therefore he wrote in this strain, and encouraged him by means of many (for he caused Polemius, Datianus, Bardion, Thalassus [6], Taurus [7], and Florentius, his Counts, in whom Athanasius could best confide, to write also): Athanasius committing the whole matter to God, who had stirred the conscience of Constantius to do this, came with his friends to him; and he gave him a favourable audience [7a], and sent him away to go to his country and his Churches, writing at the same time to the magistrates in the several places, that whereas he had before commanded the ways to be guarded, they should now grant him a free passage. Then when the Bishop complained of the sufferings he had undergone, and of the letters which the Emperor had written against him, and besought him that the false accusations against him might not be revived by his enemies after his departure, saying [8], 'If you please, summon these persons; for as far as we are concerned they are at liberty to stand forth, and we will expose their conduct;' he would not do this, but commanded that whatever had been before slanderously written against him should all be destroyed and obliterated, affirming that he would never again listen to any such accusations, and that his purpose was fixed and unalterable. This he did not simply say, but sealed his words with oaths, calling upon God to be witness of them. And so encouraging him with many other words, and desiring him to be of good courage, he sends the following letters to the Bishops and Magistrates.

23. **Constantius Augustus, the Great, the Conqueror, to the Bishops and Clergy of the Catholic Church.**

The most Reverend Athanasius has not been deserted by the grace of God [9], &c.

Another Letter.

From Constantius to the people of Alexandria.

Desiring as we do your welfare in all respects [10], &c.

Another Letter.

Constantius Augustus, the Conqueror, to Nestorius, Prefect of Egypt.

It is well known that an order was heretofore given by us, and that certain documents are to be found prejudicial to the estimation of

---

2a [Between Easter and Midsummer 344.]
3 [Probably about August 344.]
3a [June 26, 345. Athanasius received some at least of the letters at Aquileia, where he spent Easter, 345 (*Apol. Ar.* 51, *Fest. Ind.* xvii.). He then went to see Constans at Treveri, apparently in May, 346 (*Apol. Const.* 4, Gwatkin, *Stud.* 127, n.). This compels us to assume that the first invitation to Ath. to return must have been wrung (*infr.* 49, 50) from Constantius *before* the death of Gregory. The statement in the text is therefore so far inexact, but the long illness of Gregory must have made his death a matter of daily expectation, cf. Prolegg. ch. ii. § 6 (3) fin.]
4 *Apol. Ar.* 51.
5 [Here for once Ath. speaks in the first person, cf. §§ 15, 26, 64, 69, and 51, note 2a.]

6 *Apol. Const.* 3.   7 At Ariminum.
7a *Apol. Ar.* 54; *Apol. Const.* 5.   8 Below, § 44.
9 Vid. *Apol. contr. Arian.* § 54.   10 Ib. § 55.

the most reverend Bishop Athanasius; and that these exist among the Orders[1] of your worship. Now we desire your Sobriety, of which we have good proof, to transmit to our Court, in compliance with this our order, all the letters respecting the fore-mentioned person, which are found in your Order-book.

24. The following is the letter which he wrote after the death of the blessed Constans. It was written in Latin, and is here translated into Greek[2].

Constantius Augustus, the Conqueror, to Athanasius.

It is not unknown to your Prudence, that it was my constant prayer, that prosperity might attend my late brother Constans in all his undertakings; and your wisdom may therefore imagine how greatly I was afflicted when I learnt that he had been taken off by most unhallowed hands. Now whereas there are certain persons who at the present truly mournful time are endeavouring to alarm you, I have therefore thought it right to address this letter to your Constancy, to exhort you that, as becomes a Bishop, you would teach the people those things which pertain to the divine religion, and that, as you are accustomed to do, you would employ your time in prayers together with them, and not give credit to vain rumours, whatever they may be. For our fixed determination is, that you should continue, agreeably to our desire, to perform the office of a Bishop in your own place. May Divine Providence preserve you, most beloved parent, many years.

25. *Return of Athanasius from second exile.*

Under these circumstances, when they had at length taken their leave, and begun their journey, those who were friendly rejoiced to see a friend; but of the other party, some were confounded at the sight of him; others not having the confidence to appear, hid themselves; and others repented of what they had written against the Bishop. Thus all the Bishops of Palestine[3], except some two or three, and those men of suspected character, so willingly received Athanasius, and embraced communion with him, that they wrote to excuse themselves, on the ground that in what they had formerly written, they had acted, not according to their own wishes, but by compulsion. Of the Bishops of Egypt and the Libyan provinces, of the laity both of those countries and of Alexandria, it is superfluous for me to speak. They all ran[4] together, and were possessed with unspeakable delight, that

they had not only received their friends alive contrary to their hopes; but that they were also delivered from the heretics who were as tyrants and as raging dogs towards them. Accordingly great was their joy[5], the people in the congregations encouraging one another in virtue. How many unmarried women, who were before ready to enter upon marriage, now remained virgins to Christ! How many young men, seeing the examples of others, embraced the monastic life! How many fathers persuaded their children, and how many were urged by their children, not to be hindered from Christian asceticism! How many wives persuaded their husbands, and how many were persuaded by their husbands, to give themselves to prayer[6], as the Apostle has spoken! How many widows and how many orphans, who were before hungry and naked, now through the great zeal of the people, were no longer hungry, and went forth clothed! In a word, so great was their emulation in virtue, that you would have thought every family and every house a Church, by reason of the goodness of its inmates, and the prayers which were offered to God. And in the Churches there was a profound and wonderful peace, while the Bishops wrote from all quarters, and received from Athanasius the customary letters of peace.

26. *Recantation of Ursacius and Valens.*

Moreover Ursacius and Valens, as if suffering the scourge of conscience, came to another mind, and wrote to the Bishop himself a friendly and peaceable letter[7], although they had received no communication from him. And going up to Rome they repented, and confessed that all their proceedings and assertions against him were founded in falsehood and mere calumny. And they not only voluntarily did this, but also anathematized the Arian heresy, and presented a written declaration of their repentance, addressing to the Bishop Julius the following letter in Latin, which has been translated into Greek. The copy was sent to us in Latin by Paul[8], Bishop of Treveri.

Translation from the Latin.

Ursacius and Valens to my Lord the most blessed Pope Julius.

Whereas it is well known that we[9], &c.

Translation from the Latin.

The Bishops Ursacius and Valens to my Lord and Brother, the Bishop Athanasius.

Having an opportunity of sending[10], &c.

---

[1] Or Acta Publica, vid. supr. *Ap. Ar.* 56.   [2] Another translation, *Apol. Const.* 23.   [3] *Apol. Ar.* 57.   [4] Oct. 21, 346.

[5] *Apol. Ar.* 53.   [6] 1 Cor. vii. 5.   [7] *Apol. Ar.* 58 [A.D. 347].   [8] Paulinus, supr. pp. 130, 227.   [9] Vid. *Apol. contr. Ar.* § 58.   [10] Ibid.

After writing these, they also subscribed the letters of peace which were presented to them by Peter and Irenæus, Presbyters of Athanasius, and by Ammonius a layman, who were passing that way, although Athanasius had sent no communication to them even by these persons.

27. *Triumph of Athanasius.*

Now who was not filled with admiration at witnessing these things, and the great peace that prevailed in the Churches? who did not rejoice to see the concord of so many Bishops? who did not glorify the Lord, beholding the delight of the people in their assemblies? How many enemies repented! How many excused themselves who had formerly accused him falsely! How many who formerly hated him, now shewed affection for him! How many of those who had written against him, recanted their assertions? Many also who had sided with the Arians, not through choice but by necessity, came by night and excused themselves. They anathematized the heresy, and besought him to pardon them, because, although through the plots and calumnies of these men they appeared bodily on their side, yet in their hearts they held communion with Athanasius, and were always with him. Believe me, this is true.

PART IV.

SECOND ARIAN PERSECUTION UNDER CONSTANTIUS.

28. But the inheritors of the opinions and impiety of Eusebius and his fellows, the eunuch Leontius[1], who ought not to remain in communion even as a layman[2], because he mutilated himself that he might henceforward be at liberty to sleep with one Eustolium, who is a wife as far as he is concerned, but is called a virgin; and George and Acacius, and Theodorus, and Narcissus, who are deposed by the Council; when they heard and saw these things, were greatly ashamed. And when they perceived the unanimity and peace that existed between Athanasius and the Bishops (they were more than four hundred[3], from great Rome, and all Italy, from Calabria, Apulia, Campania, Bruttia, Sicily, Sardinia, Corsica, and the whole of Africa; and those from Gaul, Britain, and Spain, with the great Confessor Hosius; and also those from Pannonia, Noricum, Siscia, Dalmatia, Dardania, Dacia, Mœsia, Macedonia, Thessaly, and all Achaia, and from Crete, Cyprus, and Lycia, with most of those from Palestine, Isauria, Egypt, the Thebais, the whole of Libya, and Pentapolis); when I say they perceived these things, they were possessed with envy and fear; with envy, on account of the communion of so many together; and with fear, lest those who had been entrapped by them should be brought over by the unanimity of so great a number, and henceforth their heresy should be triumphantly exposed, and everywhere proscribed.

29. *Relapse of Ursacius and Valens.*

First of all they persuade Ursacius, Valens and their fellows to change sides again, and like dogs[4] to return to their own vomit, and like swine to wallow again in the former mire of their impiety; and they make this excuse for their retractation, that they did it through fear of the most religious Constans. And yet even had there been cause for fear, yet if they had confidence in what they had done, they ought not to have become traitors to their friends. But when there was no cause for fear, and yet they were guilty of a lie, are they not deserving of utter condemnation? For no soldier was present, no Palatine or Notary[5] had been sent, as they now send them, nor yet was the Emperor there, nor had they been invited by any one, when they wrote their recantation. But they voluntarily went up to Rome, and of their own accord recanted and wrote it down in the Church, where there was no fear from without, where the only fear is the fear of God, and where every one has liberty of conscience. And yet although they have a second time become Arians, and then have devised this unseemly excuse for their conduct, they are still without shame.

30. *Constantius changes sides again.*

In the next place they went in a body to the Emperor Constantius, and besought him, saying, 'When we first made our request to you, we were not believed; for we told you, when you sent for Athanasius, that by inviting him to come forward, you are expelling our heresy. For he has been opposed to it from the very first, and never ceases to anathematize it. He has already written letters against us into all parts of the world, and the majority of men have embraced communion with him; and

---

[1] On the συνείσακται, vid. [D. C. A. 1939 sqq. Bright, *Notes on Canons*, p. 839], Mosheim *de Rebus Ante Const.* p. 599, Routh, *Reliqu. Sacr.* t. 2. p. 606. t. 3. p. 445. Basnag. *Diss.* vii. 19. in *Ann. Eccles.* t. 2. Muratori, *Anecdot. Græc.* p. 218. Dodwell, *Dissert. Cyprian.* iii. Bevereg. in *Can. Nic.* 3. Suicer. *Thesaur. in voc.* &c. &c. It is conjectured by Beveridge, Dodwell, Van Espen, &c., that Leontius gave occasion to the first Canon of the Nicene Council, περὶ τῶν τολμώντων ἑαυτοὺς ἐκτέμνειν.

[2] Can. *Ap.* 17. but vid. Morin. *de Pæn.* p. 185.

[3] After Sardica, vid. *Apol. Ar.* 50, note 10.

[4] [351 A.D.] Cf. 2 Pet. ii. 22. [5] *Apol. Const.* 19.

even of those who seemed to be on our side, some have been gained over by him, and others are likely to be. And we are left alone, so that the fear is, lest the character of our heresy become known, and henceforth both we and you gain the name of heretics. And if this come to pass, you must take care that we be not classed with the Manichæans. Therefore begin again to persecute, and support the heresy, for it accounts you its king.' Such was the language of their iniquity. And the Emperor, when in his passage through the country on his hasty march against Magnentius [6], he saw the communion of the Bishops with Athanasius, like one set on fire, suddenly changed his mind, and no longer remembered his oaths, but was alike forgetful of what he had written, and regardless of the duty he owed his brother. For in his letters to him, as well as in his interview with Athanasius, he took oaths that he would not act otherwise than as the people should wish, and as should be agreeable to the Bishops. But his zeal for impiety caused him at once to forget all these things. And yet one ought not to wonder that after so many letters and so many oaths Constantius had altered his mind, when we remember that Pharaoh of old, the tyrant of Egypt, after frequently promising and by that means obtaining a remission of his punishments, likewise changed, until he at last perished together with his associates.

31. *Constantius begins to persecute.*

He compelled then the people in every city to change their party; and on arriving at Arles and Milan [7], he proceeded to act entirely in accordance with the designs and suggestions of the heretics; or rather they acted themselves, and receiving authority from him, furiously attacked every one. Letters and orders were immediately sent hither to the Prefect, that for the future the corn should be taken from Athanasius and given to those who favoured the Arian doctrines, and that whoever pleased might freely insult them that held communion with him; and the magistrates were threatened if they did not hold communion with the Arians. These things were but the prelude to what afterwards took place under the direction of the Duke Syrianus. Orders were sent also to the more distant parts, and Notaries despatched to every city, and Palatines, with threats to the Bishops and Magistrates, directing the Magistrates to urge on the Bishops, and informing the Bishops that either they must subscribe against Athanasius, and hold communion with the Arians, or themselves undergo the punishment of exile, while

the people who took part with them were to understand that chains, and insults, and scourgings, and the loss of their possessions, would be their portion. These orders were not neglected, for the commissioners had in their company the Clergy of Ursacius and Valens, to inspire them with zeal, and to inform the Emperor if the Magistrates neglected their duty. The other heresies, as younger sisters of their own [8], they permitted to blaspheme the Lord, and only conspired against the Christians, not enduring to hear orthodox language concerning Christ. How many Bishops in consequence, according to the words of Scripture, were brought before rulers and kings [9], and received this sentence from magistrates, 'Subscribe, or withdraw from your churches, for the Emperor has commanded you to be deposed!' How many in every city were roughly handled, lest they should accuse them as friends of the Bishops! Moreover letters were sent to the city authorities, and a threat of a fine was held out to them, if they did not compel the Bishops of their respective cities to subscribe. In short, every place and every city was full of fear and confusion, while the Bishops were dragged along to trial, and the magistrates witnessed the lamentations and groans of the people.

32. *Persecution by Constantius.*

Such were the proceedings of the Palatine commissioners; on the other hand, those admirable persons, confident in the patronage which they had obtained, display great zeal, and cause some of the Bishops to be summoned before the Emperor, while they persecute others by letters, inventing charges against them; to the intent that the one might be overawed by the presence of Constantius, and the other, through fear of the commissioners and the threats held out to them in these pretended accusations, might be brought to renounce their orthodox and pious opinions. In this manner it was that the Emperor forced so great a multitude of Bishops, partly by threats, and partly by promises, to declare, 'We will no longer hold communion with Athanasius.' For those who came for an interview, were not admitted to his presence, nor allowed any relaxation, not so much as to go out of their dwellings, until they had either subscribed, or refused and incurred banishment thereupon. And this he did because he saw that the heresy was hateful to all men. For this reason especially he compelled so many to add their names to the small number [1] of the Arians, his earnest desire being to collect together a crowd of names, both from

---

8 *De Syn.* 12, note 11.
9 Mark xiii. 9.   1 Cf. *de Syn.* 5, note, and above *Ep. Æg.* 7.

envy of the Bishop, and for the sake of making a shew in favour of the Arian impiety, of which he is the patron ; supposing that he will be able to alter the truth, as easily as he can influence the minds of men. He knows not, nor has ever read, how that the Sadducees and the Herodians, taking unto them the Pharisees, were not able to obscure the truth ; rather it shines out thereby more brightly every day, while they crying out, 'We have no king but Cæsar[2],' and obtaining the judgment of Pilate in their favour, are nevertheless left destitute, and wait in utter shame, expecting shortly[3] to become bereft, like the partridge[4], when they shall see their patron near his death.

33. *Persecution is from the Devil.*

Now if it was altogether unseemly in any of the Bishops to change their opinions merely from fear of these things, yet it was much more so, and not the part of men who have confidence in what they believe, to force and compel the unwilling. In this manner it is that the Devil, when he has no truth on his side[5], attacks and breaks down the doors of them that admit him with axes and hammers[6]. But our Saviour is so gentle that He teaches thus, 'If any man wills to come after Me,' and, 'Whoever wills to be My disciple[7] ;' and coming to each He does not force them, but knocks at the door and says, ' Open unto Me, My sister, My spouse[8];' and if they open to Him, He enters in, but if they delay and will not, He departs from them. For the truth is not preached with swords or with darts, nor by means of soldiers ; but by persuasion and counsel. But what persuasion is there where fear of the Emperor prevails? or what counsel is there, when he who withstands them receives at last banishment and death? Even David, although he was a king, and had his enemy in his power, prevented not the soldiers by an exercise of authority when they wished to kill his enemy, but, as the Scripture says, David persuaded his men by arguments, and suffered them not to rise up and put Saul to death[1]. But he, being without arguments of reason, forces all men by his power, that it may be shewn to all, that their wisdom is not according to God, but merely human, and that they who favour the Arian doctrines have indeed no king but Cæsar; for by his means it is that these enemies of Christ accomplish whatsoever they wish to do. But while they thought that they were carrying on their designs against many by his means, they knew not that they were making many to be confessors, of whom are those who have lately[2] made so glorious a confession, religious men, and excellent Bishops, Paulinus[3] Bishop of Treveri, the metropolis of the Gauls, Lucifer, Bishop of the metropolis of Sardinia, Eusebius of Vercelli in Italy, and Dionysius of Milan, which is the metropolis of Italy. These the Emperor summoned before him, and commanded them to subscribe against Athanasius, and to hold communion with the heretics ; and when they were astonished at this novel procedure, and said that there was no Ecclesiastical Canon to this effect, he immediately said, 'Whatever I will, be that esteemed a Canon ; the "Bishops" of Syria let me thus speak. Either then obey, or go into banishment.'

34. *Banishment of the Western Bishops spread the knowledge of the truth.*

When the Bishops heard this they were utterly amazed, and stretching forth their hands to God, they used great boldness of speech against him, teaching him that the kingdom was not his, but God's, who had given it to him, Whom also they bid him fear, lest He should suddenly take it away from him. And they threatened him with the day of judgment, and warned him against infringing Ecclesiastical order, and mingling Roman sovereignty with the constitution[4] of the Church, and against introducing the Arian heresy into the Church of God. But he would not listen to them, nor permit them to speak further, but threatened them so much the more, and drew his sword against them, and gave orders for some of them to be led to execution; although afterwards, like Pharaoh, he repented. The holy men therefore shaking off the dust, and looking up to God, neither feared the threats of the Emperor, nor betrayed their cause before his drawn sword; but received their banishment, as a service pertaining to their ministry. And as they passed along, they preached the Gospel in every place and city[5], although they were in bonds, proclaiming the orthodox faith, anathematizing the Arian heresy, and stigmatizing the recantation of Ursacius and Valens. But this was contrary to the intention of their enemies; for the greater was the distance of their place of banishment, so much the more was the hatred against them increased, while the wanderings of these men were but the heralding of their impiety. For who that saw them as they passed along, did not greatly admire them

---

[2] John xix. 15, and *Orat.* i. 8, note. [3] ὅσον οὐδέπω, above, 13; Const. died Nov. 3, 361, aged 45. [4] Jer. xvii. 11, LXX. [5] Vid. note on § 67 [and Bright, *Hist. Writings of Ath.* p. lxviii. note 9]. [6] Vid. Ps. lxxiv. 6. [7] Matt. xvi. 24. [8] Cant. v. 2. [1] 1 Sam. xxvi. 9.

[2] *Apol. Const.* 27; *Apol. Fug.* 4, and below, § 76. [3] § 26, and references there. [4] διαταγῇ, cf. § 36. [5] Infr. § 40, vid. Acts viii. 4 ; Phil. i. 13.

as Confessors, and renounce and abominate the others, calling them not only impious men, but executioners and murderers, and everything rather than Christians?

PART V.

PERSECUTION AND LAPSE OF LIBERIUS.

35. Now it had been better if from the first Constantius had never become connected with this heresy at all; or being connected with it, if he had not yielded so much to those impious men; or having yielded to them, if he had stood by them only thus far, so that judgment might come upon them all for these atrocities alone. But as it would seem, like madmen, having fixed themselves in the bonds of impiety, they are drawing down upon their own heads a more severe judgment. Thus from the first[1] they spared not even Liberius, Bishop of Rome, but extended[2] their fury even to those parts; they respected not his bishopric, because it was an Apostolical throne; they felt no reverence for Rome, because she is the Metropolis of Romania[3]; they remembered not that formerly in their letters they had spoken of her Bishops as Apostolical men. But confounding all things together, they at once forgot everything, and cared only to shew their zeal in behalf of impiety. When they perceived that he was an orthodox man and hated the Arian heresy, and earnestly endeavoured to persuade all persons to renounce and withdraw from it, these impious men reasoned thus with themselves: 'If we can persuade Liberius, we shall soon prevail over all.' Accordingly they accused him falsely before the Emperor; and he, expecting easily to draw over all men to his side by means of Liberius, writes to him, and sends a certain eunuch called Eusebius with letters and offerings, to cajole him with the presents, and to threaten him with the letters. The eunuch accordingly went to Rome, and first proposed to Liberius to subscribe against Athanasius, and to hold communion with the Arians, saying, 'The Emperor wishes it, and commands you to do so.' And then shewing him the offerings, he took him by the hand, and again besought him saying, 'Obey the Emperor, and receive these.'

36. *The Eunuch Eusebius attempts Liberius in vain.*

But the Bishop endeavoured to convince him, reasoning with him thus: 'How is it possible for me to do this against Athanasius? how can we condemn a man, whom not one[4] Council only, but a second[5] assembled from all parts of the world, has fairly acquitted, and whom the Church of the Romans dismissed in peace? who will approve of our conduct, if we reject in his absence one, whose presence[6] amongst us we gladly welcomed, and admitted him to our communion? This is no Ecclesiastical Canon; nor have we had transmitted to us any such tradition[7] from the Fathers, who in their turn received from the great and blessed Apostle Peter[8]. But if the Emperor is really concerned for the peace of the Church, if he requires our letters respecting Athanasius to be reversed, let their proceedings both against him and against all the others be reversed also; and then let an Ecclesiastical Council be called at a distance from the Court, at which the Emperor shall not be present, nor any Count be admitted, nor magistrate to threaten us, but where only the fear of God and the Apostolical rule[9] shall prevail; that so in the first place, the faith of the Church may be secure, as the Fathers defined it in the Council of Nicæa, and the supporters of the Arian doctrines may be cast out, and their heresy anathematized. And then after that, an enquiry being made into the charges brought against Athanasius, and any other besides, as well as into those things of which the other party is accused, let the culprits be cast out, and the innocent receive encouragement and support. For it is impossible that they who maintain an impious creed can be admitted as members of a Council: nor is it fit that an enquiry into matters of conduct should precede the enquiry concerning the faith[1]; but all diversity of opinions on points of faith ought first to be eradicated, and then the enquiry made into matters of conduct. Our Lord Jesus Christ did not heal them that were afflicted, until they shewed and declared what faith they had in Him. These things we have received from the Fathers; these report to the Emperor; for they are both profitable for him and edifying to the Church. But let not Ursacius and Valens be listened to, for they have retracted their former assertions, and in what they now say they are not to be trusted.'

---

[1] In contrast to date of his fall.
[2] τὴν μανίαν ἐξέτειναν; vid. ἐκτεῖναι τὴν μανίαν, § 42. And so in the letter of the Council of Chalcedon to Pope Leo: which says that Dioscorus, κατ' αὐτοῦ τῆς ἀμπέλου τὴν φυλακὴν παρὰ τοῦ σωτῆρος ἐπιτετραμμένου τὴν μανίαν ἐξέτεινε, λέγομεν δὴ τῆς σῆς ὁσιότητος. Hard. *Conc.* t. 2. p. 656. [Cf. Prolegg. ch. iv. § 4.]
[3] By Romania is meant the Roman Empire, according to Montfaucon after Nannius. vid. Præfat. xxxiv. xxxv. And so Epiph. *Hær.* lxvi. 1 fin. p. 618. and lxviii. 2 init. p. 728. Nil. *Ep.* i. 75. vid. Du Cange *Gloss. Græc. in voc.*

[4] At Alexandria.   [5] At Sardica.
[6] Vid. *Apol. Ar.* 29.   [7] παράδοσις, vid. § 14.
[8] *Apol. Ar.* § 35.   [9] τῶν ἀποστόλων διάταξις, cf. § 34.
[1] Vid. Pallavicin. *Conc. Trid.* vi. 7. Sarpi. *Hist.* ii. 37.

37. *Liberius refuses the Emperor's offering.*

These were the words of the Bishop Liberius. And the eunuch, who was vexed, not so much because he would not subscribe, as because he found him an enemy to the heresy, forgetting that he was in the presence of a Bishop, after threatening him severely, went away with the offerings; and next commits an offence, which is foreign to a Christian, and too audacious for a eunuch. In imitation of the transgression of Saul, he went to the Martyry[2] of the Apostle Peter, and then presented the offerings. But Liberius having notice of it, was very angry with the person who kept the place, that he had not prevented him, and cast out the offerings as an unlawful sacrifice, which increased the anger of the mutilated creature against him. Consequently he exasperates the Emperor against him, saying, 'The matter that concerns us is no longer the obtaining the subscription of Liberius, but the fact that he is so resolutely opposed to the heresy, that he anathematizes the Arians by name.' He also stirs up the other eunuchs to say the same; for many of those who were about Constantius, or rather the whole number of them, are eunuchs[3], who engross all the influence with him, and it is impossible to do anything there without them. The Emperor accordingly writes to Rome, and again Palatines, and Notaries, and Counts are sent off with letters to the Prefect, in order that either they may inveigle Liberius by stratagem away from Rome and send him to the Court to him, or else persecute him by violence.

38. *The evil influence of Eunuchs at Court.*

Such being the tenor of the letters, there also fear and treachery forthwith became rife throughout the whole city. How many were the families against which threats were held out! How many received great promises on condition of their acting against Liberius! How many Bishops hid themselves when they saw these things! How many noble women retired to country places in consequence of the calumnies of the enemies of Christ! How many ascetics were made the objects of their plots! How many who were sojourning there, and had made that place their home, did they cause to be persecuted! How often and how strictly did they guard the harbour[4] and the approaches to the gates, lest any orthodox person should enter and visit Liberius! Rome also had trial of the enemies of Christ, and now experienced what before she would not believe, when she heard how the other Churches in every city were ravaged by them. It was the eunuchs who instigated these proceedings against all. And the most remarkable circumstance in the matter is this; that the Arian heresy which denies the Son of God, receives its support from eunuchs, who, as both their bodies are fruitless, and their souls barren of virtue, cannot bear even to hear the name of son. The Eunuch of Ethiopia indeed, though he understood not what he read[5], believed the words of Philip, when he taught him concerning the Saviour; but the eunuchs of Constantius cannot endure the confession of Peter[6], nay, they turn away when the Father manifests the Son, and madly rage against those who say, that the Son of God is His genuine Son, thus claiming as a heresy of eunuchs, that there is no genuine and true offspring of the Father. On these grounds it is that the law forbids such persons to be admitted into any ecclesiastical Council[7]; notwithstanding which they have now regarded these as competent judges of ecclesiastical causes, and whatever seems good to them, that Constantius decrees, while men with the name of Bishops dissemble with them. Oh! who shall be their historian? who shall transmit the record of these things to another generation? who indeed would believe it, were he to hear it, that eunuchs who are scarcely entrusted with household services (for theirs is a pleasure-loving race, that has no serious concern but that of hindering in others what nature has taken from them); that these, I say, now exercise authority in ecclesiastical matters, and that Constantius in submission to their will treacherously conspired against all, and banished Liberius!

39. *Liberius's speech to Constantius.*

For after the Emperor had frequently written to Rome, had threatened, sent commissioners, devised schemes, on the persecution[7a] subsequently breaking out at Alexandria, Liberius is dragged before him, and uses great boldness of speech towards him. 'Cease,' he said, 'to persecute the Christians; attempt not by my means to introduce impiety into the Church. We are ready to suffer anything rather than to be called Arian madmen. We are Christians; compel us not to become enemies of Christ. We also give you this counsel: fight not against Him who gave you this empire, nor shew impiety towards Him instead of thankful-

---

[2] [1 Sam. xiii. 9. cf. D.C.A. 1132, s.v. Martyrium.]
[3] Vid. Gibbon, *Hist.* ch. 19 init.
[4] Ostia, vid. Gibbon, *Hist.* ch. 31, p. 303.

[5] Acts viii. 27.   [6] Matt. xvi. 16, allusion to Liberius? vid. Hard. *Conc.* t. 2. p. 305 E.   [7] *Can. Nic.* i.   [7a] [356 A.D.]

ness[8]; persecute not them that believe in Him, lest you also hear the words, 'It is hard for thee to kick against the pricks[9].' Nay, I would that you might hear them, that you might obey, as the holy Paul did. Behold, here we are; we are come, before they fabricate charges. For this cause we hastened hither, knowing that banishment awaits us at your hands, that we might suffer before a charge encounters us, and that all may clearly see that all the others too have suffered as we shall suffer, and that the charges brought against them were fabrications of their enemies, and all their proceedings were mere calumny and falsehood.'

40. *Banishment of Liberius and others.*

These were the words of Liberius at that time, and he was admired by all men for them. But the Emperor instead of answering[9a], only gave orders for their banishment, separating each of them from the rest, as he had done in the former cases. For he had himself devised this plan in the banishments which he inflicted, that so the severity of his punishments might be greater than that of former tyrants and persecutors[1]. In the former persecution Maximian, who was then Emperor, commanded a number of Confessors to be banished together[2], and thus lightened their punishment by the consolation which he gave them in each other's society. But this man was more savage than he; he separated those who had spoken boldly and confessed together, he put asunder those who were united by the bond of faith, that when they came to die they might not see one another; thinking that bodily separation can disunite also the affections of the mind, and that being severed from each other, they would forget the concord and unanimity which existed among them. He knew not that however each one may remain[3] apart from the rest, he has nevertheless with him that Lord, whom they confessed in one body together, who will also provide (as he did in the case of the Prophet Elisha[4]) that more shall be with each of them, than there are soldiers with Constantius. Of a truth iniquity is blind; for in that they thought to afflict the Confessors, by separating them from one another, they rather brought thereby a great injury upon themselves. For had they continued in each other's company, and abode together, the pollutions of those impious men would have been proclaimed from one place only; but now by putting them asunder, they have made their

impious heresy and wickedness to spread abroad and become known in every place[5].

41. *Lapse of Liberius.*

Who that shall hear what they did in the course of these proceedings will not think them to be anything rather than Christians? When Liberius sent Eutropius, a Presbyter, and Hilarius, a Deacon, with letters to the Emperor, at the time that Lucifer and his fellows made their confession, they banished the Presbyter on the spot, and after stripping Hilarius[6] the Deacon and scourging him on the back, they banished him too, clamouring at him, 'Why didst thou not resist Liberius instead of being the bearer of letters from him.' Ursacius and Valens, with the eunuchs who sided with them, were the authors of this outrage. The Deacon, while he was being scourged, praised the Lord, remembering His words, 'I gave My back to the smiters[7];' but they while they scourged him laughed and mocked him, feeling no shame that they were insulting a Levite. Indeed they acted but consistently in laughing while he continued to praise God; for it is the part of Christians to endure stripes, but to scourge Christians is the outrage of a Pilate or a Caiaphas. Thus they endeavoured at the first to corrupt the Church of the Romans, wishing to introduce impiety into it as well as others. But Liberius after he had been in banishment two years gave way, and from fear of threatened death subscribed. Yet even this only shews their violent conduct, and the hatred of Liberius against the heresy, and his support of Athanasius, so long as he was suffered to exercise a free choice. For that which men are forced by torture to do contrary to their first judgment, ought not to be considered the willing deed of those who are in fear, but rather of their tormentors. They however attempted everything in support of their heresy, while the people in every Church, preserving the faith which they had learnt, waited for the return of their teachers, and condemned the Antichristian heresy, and all avoid it, as they would a serpent.

PART VI.

PERSECUTION AND LAPSE OF HOSIUS.

42. But although they had done all this, yet these impious men thought they had accomplished nothing, so long as the great Hosius escaped their wicked machinations. And now

---

8 Cf. § 34.   9 Acts ix. 5.
9a [But see Theodoret, *Hist.* ii. 16.]   1 Cf. infr. § 60.
2 § 64 [A.D. 355].   3 Cf. § 47.   4 2 Kings vi. 16.

5 Cf. § 34.
6 This Hilary afterwards followed Lucifer of Calaris in his schism. He is supposed to be the author of the Comments on S. Paul's Epistles attributed to S. Ambrose, who goes under the name of Ambrosiaster.   7 Isa. l. 6.

they undertook to extend their fury[1] to that great old man. They felt no shame at the thought that he is the father[2] of the Bishops; they regarded not that he had been a Confessor[3]; they reverenced not the length of his Episcopate, in which he had continued more than sixty years; but they set aside everything, and looked only to the interests of their heresy, as being of a truth such as neither fear God, nor regard man[4]. Accordingly they went to Constantius, and again employed such arguments as the following: 'We have done everything; we have banished the Bishop of the Romans; and before him a very great number of other Bishops, and have filled every place with alarm. But these strong measures of yours are as nothing to us, nor is our success at all more secure, so long as Hosius remains. While he is in his own place, the rest also continue in their Churches, for he is able by his arguments and his faith to persuade all men against us. He is the president of Councils[5], and his letters are everywhere attended to. He it was who put forth the Nicene Confession, and proclaimed everywhere that the Arians were heretics. If therefore he is suffered to remain, the banishment of the rest is of no avail, for our heresy will be destroyed. Begin then to persecute him also and spare him not, ancient as he is. Our heresy knows not to honour even the hoary hairs of the aged.'

43. *Brave resistance of Hosius.*

Upon hearing this, the Emperor no longer delayed, but knowing the man, and the dignity of his years, wrote to summon him. This was when he first[6] began his attempt upon Liberius. Upon his arrival he desired him, and urged him with the usual arguments, with which he thought also to deceive the others, that he would subscribe against us, and hold communion with the Arians. But the old man, scarcely bearing to hear the words, and grieved that he had even ventured to utter such a proposal, severely rebuked him, and after gaining his consent, withdrew to his own country and Church. But the heretics still complaining, and instigating him to proceed (he had the eunuchs also to remind him and to urge him further), the Emperor again wrote in threatening terms; but still Hosius, while he endured their insults, was unmoved by any fear of their designs against him, and remaining firm to his purpose, as one who had built the house of his faith upon the rock, he spake boldly against the heresy, regarding the threats held out to

him in the letters but as drops of rain and blasts of wind. And although Constantius wrote frequently, sometimes flattering him with the title of Father, and sometimes threatening and recounting the names of those who had been banished, and saying, 'Will you continue the only person to oppose the heresy? Be persuaded and subscribe against Athanasius; for whoever subscribes against him thereby embraces with us the Arian cause;' still Hosius remained fearless, and while suffering these insults, wrote an answer in such terms as these. We have read the letter, which is placed at the end[7].

44. 'Hosius to Constantius the Emperor sends health in the Lord.

I was a Confessor at the first, when a persecution arose in the time of your grandfather Maximian; and if you shall persecute me, I am ready now, too, to endure anything rather than to shed innocent blood and to betray the truth. But I cannot approve of your conduct in writing after this threatening manner. Cease to write thus; adopt not the cause of Arius, nor listen to those in the East, nor give credit to Ursacius, Valens and their fellows. For whatever they assert, it is not on account of Athanasius, but for the sake of their own heresy. Believe my statement, O Constantius, who am of an age to be your grandfather. I was present at the Council of Sardica, when you and your brother Constans of blessed memory assembled us all together; and on my own account I challenged the enemies of Athanasius, when they came to the church where I abode[8], that if they had anything against him they might declare it; desiring them to have confidence, and not to expect otherwise than that a right judgment would be passed in all things. This I did once and again, requesting them, if they were unwilling to appear before the whole Council, yet to appear before me alone; promising them also, that if he should be proved guilty, he should certainly be rejected by us; but if he should be found to be blameless, and should prove them to be calumniators, that if they should then refuse to hold communion with him, I would persuade him to go with me into the Spains. Athanasius was willing to comply with these conditions, and made no objection to my proposal; but they, altogether distrusting their cause, would not consent. And on another occasion Athanasius came to your Court[9], when you wrote for him, and his enemies being at the time in Antioch, he requested that they might be summoned either altogether or separately, in order that they might either con-

---

[1] ἐκτεῖναι τὴν μανίαν. [2] *Ap. Fug.* 5. [3] Under Maximian.
[4] Luke xviii. 2. [5] Of Nicæa and Sardica (*Ap. Fug.* 5).
[6] i.e. two years before his fall.

[7] Transferred by copyists hither.
[8] [i.e. at Sardica, cf. *Apol. Ar.* 36.] [9] Cf. § 22.

vict him, or be convicted[10], and might either in his presence prove him to be what they represented, or cease to accuse him when absent. To this proposal also you would not listen, and they equally rejected it. Why then do you still give ear to them that speak evil of him? How can you endure Valens and Ursacius, although they have retracted, and made a written confession of their calumnies[1]? For it is not true, as they pretend, that they were forced to confess; there were no soldiers at hand to influence them; your brother was not cognizant of the matter[2]. No, such things were not done under his government, as are done now; God forbid. But they voluntarily went up to Rome, and in the presence of the Bishop and Presbyters wrote their recantation, having previously addressed to Athanasius a friendly and peaceable letter. And if they pretend that force was employed towards them, and acknowledge that this is an evil thing, which you also disapprove of; then do you cease to use force; write no letters, send no Counts; but release those that have been banished, lest while you are complaining of violence, they do but exercise greater violence. When was any such thing done by Constans? What Bishop suffered banishment? When did he appear as arbiter of an Ecclesiastical trial? When did any Palatine of his compel men to subscribe against any one, that Valens and his fellows should be able to affirm this? Cease these proceedings, I beseech you, and remember that you are a mortal man. Be afraid of the day of judgment, and keep yourself pure thereunto. Intrude not yourself into Ecclesiastical matters, neither give commands unto us concerning them; but learn them from us. God has put into your hands the kingdom; to us He has entrusted the affairs of His Church; and as he who would steal the empire from you would resist the ordinance of God, so likewise fear on your part lest by taking upon yourself the government of the Church, you become guilty of a great offence. It is written, "Render unto Cæsar the things that are Cæsar's, and unto God the things that are God's[3]." Neither therefore is it permitted unto us to exercise an earthly rule, nor have you, Sire, any authority to burn incense[4]. These things I write unto you out of a concern for your salvation. With regard to the subject of your letters, this is my determination; I will not unite myself to the Arians; I anathematize their heresy. Neither will I subscribe against

Athanasius, whom both we and the Church of the Romans and the whole Council pronounced to be guiltless. And yourself also, when you understood this, sent for the man, and gave him permission to return with honour to his country and his Church. What reason then can there be for so great a change in your conduct? The same persons who were his enemies before, are so now also; and the things they now whisper to his prejudice (for they do not declare them openly in his presence), the same they spoke against him, before you sent for him; the same they spread abroad concerning him when they come to the Council. And when I required them to come forward, as I have before said, they were unable to produce their proofs; had they possessed any, they would not have fled so disgracefully. Who then persuaded you so long after to forget your own letters and declarations? Forbear, and be not influenced by evil men, lest while you act for the mutual advantage of yourself and them, you render yourself responsible. For here you comply with their desires, hereafter in the judgment you will have to answer for doing so alone. These men desire by your means to injure their enemy, and wish to make you the minister of their wickedness, in order that through your help they may sow the seeds[5] of their accursed heresy in the Church. Now it is not a prudent thing to cast one's self into manifest danger for the pleasure of others. Cease then, I beseech you, O Constantius, and be persuaded by me. These things it becomes me to write, and you not to despise.'

45. *Lapse of Hosius, due to cruel persecution.*

Such were the sentiments, and such the letter, of the Abraham-like old man, Hosius, truly so called[6]. But the Emperor desisted not from his designs, nor ceased to seek an occasion against him; but continued to threaten him severely, with a view either to bring him over by force, or to banish him if he refused to comply. And as the Officers and Satraps of Babylon[7], seeking an occasion against Daniel, found none except in the law of his God; so likewise these present Satraps of impiety were unable to invent any charge against the old man (for this true Hosius, and his blameless life were known to all), except the charge of hatred to their heresy. They

---

10 *Apol. Const.* 5.   1 *Apol. Ar.* 58.
2 § 29.   3 Matt. xxii. 21.
4 [The language of Hosius is figurative. The first mention of incense as a rite in Christian worship is in ps.-Dionys., about A.D. 500, cf. D.C.A. p. 830 *sq.*]

5 Vid. *de Decr.* 2, note 6. It is remarkable, this letter having so much its own character, and being so unlike Athanasius's writings in style, that a phrase characteristic of him should here occur in it. Did Athan. translate it from Latin?
6 ὁ ἀληθῶς Ὅσιος. κατάσκοποι, οὐ γὰρ ἐπίσκοποι, supr. § 3. infr. §§ 48, 76 fin. and so ἀληθῶς Εὐσέβιε, Theod. *Hist.* i. 4. Ὀνήσιμον, τόν ποτέ σοι ἄχρηστον, νυνὶ δὲ εὔχρηστον, Philem. 10. *De Syn.* 26, note 6.   7 Dan. vi. 5.

therefore proceeded to accuse him; though not under the same circumstances as those others accused Daniel to Darius, for Darius was grieved to hear the charge, but as Jezebel accused Naboth, and as the Jews applied themselves to Herod. And they said, 'He not only will not subscribe against Athanasius, but also on his account condemns us; and his hatred to the heresy is so great, that he also writes to others, that they should rather suffer death, than become traitors to the truth. For, he says, our beloved Athanasius also is persecuted for the Truth's sake, and Liberius, Bishop of Rome, and all the rest, are treacherously assailed.' When this patron of impiety, and Emperor of heresy[8], Constantius, heard this, and especially that there were others also in the Spains of the same mind as Hosius, after he had tempted them also to subscribe, and was unable to compel them to do so, he sent for Hosius, and instead of banishing him, detained him a whole year in Sirmium. Godless, unholy, without natural affection, he feared not God, he regarded not his father's affection for Hosius, he reverenced not his great age, for he was now a hundred years old[9]; but all these things this modern Ahab, this second Belshazzar of our times, disregarded for the sake of impiety. He used such violence towards the old man, and confined him so straitly, that at last, broken by suffering, he was brought, though hardly, to hold communion with Valens, Ursacius, and their fellows, though he would not subscribe against Athanasius. Yet even thus he forgot not his duty, for at the approach of death, as it were by his last testament, he bore witness to the force which had been used towards him, and anathematized the Arian heresy, and gave strict charge that no one should receive it.

46. *Arbitrary expulsion of so many bishops.*

Who that witnessed these things, or that has merely heard of them, will not be greatly amazed, and cry aloud unto the Lord, saying, 'Wilt Thou make a full end of Israel[10]?' Who that is acquainted with these proceedings, will not with good reason cry out and say, 'A wonderful and horrible thing is done in the land;' and, 'The heavens are astonished at this, and the earth is even more horribly afraid[11].' The fathers of the people and the teachers of the faith are taken away, and the impious are brought into the Churches? Who that saw when Liberius, Bishop of Rome, was banished, and when the great Hosius, the father[12] of the Bishops, suf-

fered these things, or who that saw so many Bishops banished out of Spain and the other parts, could fail to perceive, however little sense he might possess, that the charges[13] against Athanasius also and the rest were false, and altogether mere calumny? For this reason those others also endured all suffering, because they saw plainly that the conspiracies laid against these were founded in falsehood. For what charge was there against Liberius? or what accusation against the aged Hosius? who bore even a false witness against Paulinus, and Lucifer, and Dionysius, and Eusebius? or what sin could be lain to the account of the rest of the banished Bishops, and Presbyters, and Deacons? None whatever; God forbid. There were no charges against them on which a plot for their ruin might be formed; nor was it on the ground of any accusation that they were severally banished. It was an insurrection of impiety against godliness; it was zeal for the Arian heresy, and a prelude to the coming of Antichrist, for whom Constantius is thus preparing the way.

PART VII.

PERSECUTION AT ALEXANDRIA.

47. AFTER he had accomplished all that he desired against the Churches in Italy, and the other parts; after he had banished some, and violently oppressed others, and filled every place with fear, he at last turned his fury, as it had been some pestilential disorder, against Alexandria. This was artfully contrived by the enemies of Christ; for in order that they might have a show of the signatures of many Bishops, and that Athanasius might not have a single Bishop in his persecution to whom he could even complain, they therefore anticipated his proceedings, and filled every place with terror, which they kept up to second them in the prosecution of their designs. But herein they perceived not through their folly that they were not exhibiting the deliberate choice of the Bishops, but rather the violence which themselves had employed; and that, although his brethren should desert him, and his friends and acquaintance stand afar off, and no one be found to sympathise with him and console him, yet far above all these, a refuge with God was sufficient for him. For Elijah also was alone in his persecution, and God was all in all to the holy man. And the Saviour has given us an example herein, who also was left alone, and exposed to the designs of His enemies, to teach us, that when we are persecuted and deserted by men, we must not faint,

8 §§ 9, 30, 54.
9 οὔτε τὸν Θεὸν φοβηθεὶς ὁ ἄθεος, οὔτε τοῦ πατρὸς τὴν διάθεσιν αἰδεσθεὶς ὁ ἀνόσιος, οὔτε τὸ γῆρας αἰσχυνθεὶς ὁ ἄστοργος.
10 Ez. xi. 13.   11 Jer. v. 30; ii. 12.   12 Cf § 15.

13 Vid. in *Apol. contr. Ar.* and *ad Const.*

but place our hope in Him, and not betray the Truth. For although at first truth may seem to be afflicted, yet even they who persecute shall afterwards acknowledge it.

48. Attacks upon the Alexandrian Church.

Accordingly they urge on the Emperor, who first writes a menacing letter, which he sends to the Duke and the soldiers. The Notaries Diogenius and Hilarius[2], and certain Palatines with them, were the bearers of it; upon whose arrival those terrible and cruel outrages were committed against the Church, which I have briefly related a little above[3], and which are known to all men from the protests put forth by the people, which are inserted at the end of this history, so that any one may read them. Then after these proceedings on the part of Syrianus, after these enormities had been perpetrated, and violence offered to the Virgins, as approving of such conduct and the infliction of these evils upon us, he writes again to the senate and people of Alexandria, instigating the younger men, and requiring them to assemble together, and either to persecute Athanasius, or consider themselves as his enemies. He however had withdrawn before these instructions reached them, and from the time when Syrianus broke into the Church; for he remembered that which was written, 'Hide thyself as it were for a little moment, until the indignation be overpast[4].' One Heraclius, by rank a Count, was the bearer of this letter, and the precursor of a certain George that was despatched by the Emperor as a spy, for one that was sent from him cannot be a Bishop[5]; God forbid. And so indeed his conduct and the circumstances which preceded his entrance sufficiently prove.

49 and 50. Hypocrisy of the pretended respect of Constantius for his brother's memory.

Heraclius then published the letter, which reflected great disgrace upon the writer. For whereas, when the great Hosius wrote to Constantius, he had been unable to make out any plausible pretext for his change of conduct, he now invented an excuse much more discreditable to himself and his advisers. He said, 'From regard to the affection I entertained towards my brother of divine and pious memory, I endured for a time the coming of Athanasius among you.' This proves that he has both broken his promise, and behaved ungratefully to his brother after his death. He then declares him to be, as indeed he is, 'deserving of divine and pious remembrance;'

yet as regards a command of his, or to use his own language, the 'affection' he bore him, even though he complied merely 'for the sake' of the blessed Constans, he ought to deal fairly by his brother, and make himself heir to his sentiments as well as to the Empire. But, although, when seeking to obtain his just rights, he deposed Vetranio, with the question, 'To whom does the inheritance belong after a brother's death[6]?' yet for the sake of the accursed heresy of the enemies of Christ, he disregards the claims of justice, and behaves undutifully towards his brethren. Nay, for the sake of this heresy, he would not consent to observe even his father's wishes without infringement; but, in what he may gratify these impious men, he pretends to adopt his intention, while in order to distress the others, he cares not to shew the reverence which is due unto a father. For in consequence of the calumnies of Eusebius and his fellows, his father sent the Bishop for a time into Gaul to avoid the cruelty of his persecutors (this was shewn by the blessed Constantine, the brother of the former, after their father's death, as appears by his letters[7]), but he would not be persuaded by Eusebius and his fellows to send the person whom they desired for a Bishop, but prevented the accomplishment of their wishes, and put a stop to their attempts with severe threats.

51. How Constantius shews his respect for his father and brother.

If therefore, as he declares in his letters, he desired to observe his sire's practice, why did he first send out Gregory, and now this George, the eater of stores[8]? Why does he endeavour so earnestly to introduce into the Church these Arians, whom his father named Porphyrians[9], and banish others while he patronises them? Although his father admitted Arius to his presence, yet when Arius perjured himself and burst asunder[10] he lost the compassion of his father; who, on learning the truth, condemned him as an heretic. Why moreover, while pretending to respect the Canon of the Church, has he ordered the whole course of his conduct in opposition to them? For where is there a Canon that a Bishop should be appointed from Court? Where is there a Canon[1] that permits soldiers to invade Churches? What tradition is there allowing counts and ignorant

2 Ap. Const. 22, 24, below, § 81.   3 § 31, &c.
4 Is. xxvi. 20.   5 κατασκόπου, οὐκ ἐπίσκοπος, vid. § 45, note 6.

6 [A.D. 350, cf. Gibbon Hist. ch. xviii. vol. ii. p. 378.]
7 Apol. Ar. 87.
8 George had been pork-contractor to the army, and had been detected in peculation. vid. de Syn. 37, note 3.
9 Constantine called the Arians by this title after the philosopher Porphyry, the great enemy of Christianity. Socrates has preserved the Edict. Hist. i. 9.
10 De Morte Arii 3, &c.   1 Encycl. 2; Apol. Ar. 36.

eunuchs to exercise authority in Ecclesiastical matters, and to make known by their edicts the decisions of those who bear the name of Bishops? He is guilty of all manner of falsehood for the sake of this unholy heresy. At a former time he sent out Philagrius as Prefect a second time[2], in opposition to the opinion of his father, and we see what has taken place now. Nor 'for his brother's sake' does he speak the truth. For after his death he wrote not once nor twice, but three times to the Bishop, and repeatedly promised him that he would not change his behaviour towards him, but exhorted him to be of good courage, and not suffer any one to alarm him, but to continue to abide in his Church in perfect security. He also sent his commands by Count Asterius, and Palladius the Notary, to Felicissimus, who was then Duke, and to the Prefect Nestorius, that if either Philip the Prefect, or any other should venture to form any plot against Athanasius, they should prevent it.

52. *The Emperor has no right to rule the Church.*

Wherefore when Diogenes came, and Syrianus laid in wait for us, both he and we[2a] and the people demanded to see the Emperor's letters, supposing that, as it is written, 'Let not a falsehood be spoken before the king[3];' so when a king has made a promise, he will not lie, nor change. If then 'for his brother's sake he complied,' why did he also write those letters upon his death? And if he wrote them for 'his memory's sake,' why did he afterwards behave so very unkindly towards him, and persecute the man, and write what he did, alleging a judgment of Bishops, while in truth he acted only to please himself? Nevertheless his craft has not escaped detection, but we have the proof of it ready at hand. For if a judgment had been passed by Bishops, what concern had the Emperor with it? Or if it was only a threat of the Emperor, what need in that case was there of the so-named Bishops? When was such a thing heard of before from the beginning of the world? When did a judgment of the Church receive its validity from the Emperor? or rather when was his decree ever recognised by the Church? There have been many Councils held heretofore; and many judgments passed by the Church; but the Fathers never sought the consent of the Emperor thereto, nor did the Emperor busy

himself with the affairs of the Church[3a]. The Apostle Paul had friends among them of Cæsar's household, and in his Epistle to the Philippians he sent salutations from them; but he never took them as his associates in Ecclesiastical judgments. Now however we have witnessed a novel spectacle, which is a discovery of the Arian heresy. Heretics have assembled together with the Emperor Constantius, in order that he, alleging the authority of the Bishops, may exercise his power against whomsoever he pleases, and while he persecutes may avoid the name of persecutor; and that they, supported by the Emperor's government, may conspire the ruin of whomsoever they will[4] and these are all such as are not as impious as themselves. One might look upon their proceedings as a comedy which they are performing on the stage, in which the pretended Bishops are actors, and Constantius the performer of their behests, who makes promises to them, as Herod did to the daughter of Herodias, and they dancing before him accomplish through false accusations the banishment and death of the true believers in the Lord.

53. *Despotic interference of Constantius.*

Who indeed has not been injured by their calumnies? Whom have not these enemies of Christ conspired to destroy? Whom has Constantius failed to banish upon charges which they have brought against them? When did he refuse to hear them willingly? And what is most strange, when did he permit any one to speak against them, and did not more readily receive their testimony, of whatever kind it might be? Where is there a Church which now enjoys the privilege of worshipping Christ freely? If a Church be a maintainer of true piety, it is in danger; if it dissemble, it abides in fear. Every place is full of hypocrisy and impiety, so far as he is concerned; and wherever there is a pious person and a lover of Christ (and there are many such everywhere, as were the prophets and the great Elijah) they hide themselves, if so be that they can find a faithful friend like Obadiah, and either they withdraw into caves and dens of the earth, or pass their lives in wandering about in the deserts. These men in their madness prefer such calumnies against them

---

[3a] [This may well be taken as a statement of what *ought* to be; but in view of the history of the fourth century it can only be called a rhetorical exaggeration. See supr. § 15, *Apol. Ar.* 36, ἐκέλευσαν, Prolegg. ch. ii. § 6 (1) *init.*, and D.C.A. p. 475, with reff. there given.]

[4] οἷς ἂν ἐθέλωσι, and just before ὧν ἂν ἐθέλοι. [And more strikingly just below, § 53 fin. ἃ θέλουσι πράττει, ἐπεὶ καὶ αὐτὸς ἅπερ ἤθελεν ἤκουσε παρ' αὐτῶν.] This is a very familiar phrase with Athan. i.e. ὡς ἐθέλησεν, ἅπερ ἐθέλησαν, ὅταν θέλωσιν, οὓς ἐθέλησαν, &c. &c. Some instances are given supr. *Apol. Ar.* 2, note 3, and *de Syn.* 13, note 6.

---

[2] § 7, note 1.
[2a] The amanuensis here appears to speak for himself: but the Benedictines, with great probability, conjecture τότε καὶ for αὐτός τε καί.   [3] Ecclus. vii. 5 [*Apol. Const.* 2].

as Jezebel invented against Naboth, and the Jews against the Saviour; while the Emperor, who is the patron of the heresy, and wishes to pervert the truth, as Ahab wished to change the vineyard into a garden of herbs, does whatever they desire him to do, for the suggestions he receives from them are agreeable to his own wishes.

54. Constantius gives up the Alexandrian Churches to the heretics.

Accordingly he banished, as I said before, the genuine Bishops, because they would not profess impious doctrines, to suit his own pleasure; and so he now sent Count Heraclius to proceed against Athanasius, who has publicly made known his decrees, and announced the command of the Emperor to be, that unless they complied with the instructions contained in his letters, their bread[5] should be taken away, their idols overthrown, and the persons of many of the city-magistrates and people delivered over to certain slavery. After threatening them in this manner, he was not ashamed to declare publicly with a loud voice, 'The Emperor disclaims Athanasius, and has commanded that the Churches be given up to the Arians.' And when all wondered to hear this, and made signs to one another, exclaiming, 'What! has Constantius become a heretic?' instead of blushing as he ought, the man all the more obliged the senators and heathen magistrates and wardens[6] of the idol temples to subscribe to these conditions, and to agree to receive as their Bishop whomsoever[7] the Emperor should send them. Of course Constantius was strictly upholding the Canon of the Church, when he caused this to be done; when instead of requiring letters from the Church, he demanded them of the market-place, and instead of the people he asked them of the wardens of the temples. He was conscious that he was not sending a Bishop to preside over Christians, but a certain intruder for those who subscribed to his terms.

55. Irruption into the great Church.

The Gentiles accordingly, as purchasing by their compliance the safety of their idols, and certain of the trades[8], subscribed, though unwillingly, from fear of the threats which he had held out to them; just as if the matter had been the appointment of a general, or other magistrate. Indeed what, as heathen, were they likely to do, except whatever was pleasing to the Emperor? But the people having assembled in the great Church (for it was the fourth day of the week), Count Heraclius on the following day[9] takes with him Cataphronius the Prefect of Egypt, and Faustinus the Receiver-General[10], and Bithynus a heretic; and together they stir up the younger men of the common multitude[11] who worshipped idols, to attack the Church, and stone the people, saying that such was the Emperor's command. As the time of dismissal however had arrived, the greater part had already left the Church, but there being a few women still remaining, they did as the men had charged them, whereupon a piteous spectacle ensued. The few women had just risen from prayer and had sat down when the youths suddenly came upon them naked with stones and clubs. Some of them the godless wretches stoned to death; they scourged with stripes the holy persons of the Virgins, tore off their veils and exposed their heads, and when they resisted the insult, the cowards kicked them with their feet. This was dreadful, exceedingly dreadful; but what ensued was worse, and more intolerable than any outrage. Knowing the holy character of the virgins, and that their ears were unaccustomed to pollution, and that they were better able to bear stones and swords than expressions of obscenity, they assailed them with such language. This the Arians suggested to the young men, and laughed at all they said and did; while the holy Virgins and other godly women fled from such words as they would from the bite of asps, but the enemies of Christ assisted them in the work, nay even, it may be, gave utterance to the same; for they were well-pleased with the obscenities which the youths vented upon them.

56. The great Church pillaged.

After this, that they might fully execute the orders they had received (for this was what they earnestly desired, and what the Count and the Receiver-General instructed them to do), they seized upon the seats, the throne, and

---

5 Cf. §§ 31, 63, note 6.   6 Encycl. § 5.
7 [Observe that George has not yet arrived. Heraclius arrived 'as his precursor' (supr. § 48) along with Cataphronius the new Prefect, on June 10, 356; see § 55.]
8 τῶν ἐργασιῶν,—trades, or workmen. vid. supr. Apol. Ar. 15 Montfaucon has a note upon the word in the Collect. Nov. t. 2. p. xxvi. where he corrects his Latin in loc. of the former passage very nearly in conformity to the rendering given of it above, p. 108. 'In Onomastico monuimus, hic ἐργασίας "officinarum operas" commodius exprimere.' And he quotes an inscription [C.I.G. i. 3924] τοῦτο τὸ ἡρῷον στεφανοῖ ἡ ἐργασία τῶν βαφέων.

9 [i.e. Thursday, June 13, 356, three days after the arrival of Heraclius and Cataphronius. The church in question was apparently that of Theonas, or the Cæsareum (p. 298). According to Hist. Aceph. the churches were formally handed over to the Arians on June 15, i.e. on the Saturday. The Hist. Aceph. here fits minutely the scattered notices of Athan.: see Prolegg. ch. ii. § 8 (1).]   10 Catholicus, ib. 10, note 4.
11 τῶν ἀγοραίων, vid. Acts xvii. 5. ἀγορὰ has been used just above. vid. Suicer. Thesaur. in voc.

the table which was of wood[1], and the curtains[2] of the Church, and whatever else they were able, and carrying them out burnt them before the doors in the great street, and cast frankincense upon the flame. Alas! who will not weep to hear of these things, and, it may be, close his ears, that he may not have to endure the recital, esteeming it hurtful merely to listen to the account of such enormities? Moreover they sang the praises of their idols, and said, 'Constantius hath become a heathen, and the Arians have acknowledged our customs;' for indeed they scruple not even to pretend heathenism, if only their heresy may be established. They even were ready to sacrifice a heifer which drew the water for the gardens in the Cæsareum[3]; and would have sacrificed it, had it not been a female[4]; for they said that it was unlawful for such to be offered among them.

57. Thus acted the impious[5] Arians in conjunction with the heathens, thinking that these things tended to our dishonour. But Divine justice reproved their iniquity, and wrought a great and remarkable sign, thereby plainly shewing to all men, that as in their acts of impiety they had dared to attack none other but the Lord, so in these proceedings also they were again attempting to do dishonour unto Him. This was more manifestly proved by the marvellous event which now came to pass. One of these licentious youths ran into the Church, and ventured to sit down upon the throne; and as he sat there the wretched man uttered with a nasal sound some lascivious song. Then rising up he attempted to pull away the throne, and to drag it towards him; he knew not that he was drawing down vengeance upon himself. For as of old the inhabitants of Azotus, when they ventured to touch[6] the Ark, which it was not lawful for them even to look upon, were immediately destroyed by it, being first grievously tormented by emerods; so this unhappy person who presumed to drag the throne, drew it upon himself, and, as if Divine justice had sent the wood to punish him, he struck it into his own bowels; and

instead of carrying out the throne, he brought out by his blow his own entrails; so that the throne took away his life, instead of his taking it away. For, as it is[7] written of Judas, his bowels gushed out; and he fell down and was carried away, and the day after he died. Another also entered the Church with boughs of trees[7a], and, as in the Gentile manner he waved them in his hands and mocked, he was immediately struck with blindness, so as straightway to lose his sight, and to know no longer where he was; but as he was about to fall, he was taken by the hand and supported by his companions out of the place, and when on the following day he was with difficulty brought to his senses, he knew not either what he had done or suffered in consequence of his audacity.

58. General Persecution at Alexandria.

The Gentiles, when they beheld these things, were seized with fear, and ventured on no further outrage; but the Arians were not even yet touched with shame, but, like the Jews when they saw the miracles, were faithless and would not believe, nay, like Pharaoh, they were hardened; they too having placed their hopes below, on the Emperor and his eunuchs. They permitted the Gentiles, or rather the more abandoned of the Gentiles, to act in the manner before described; for they found that Faustinus, who is the Receiver-General by style, but is a vulgar[8] person in habits, and profligate in heart, was ready to play his part with them in these proceedings, and to stir up the heathen. Nay, they undertook to do the like themselves, that as they had modelled their heresy upon all other heresies together[9], so they might share their wickedness with the more depraved of mankind. What they did through the instrumentality of others I described above; the enormities they committed themselves surpass the bounds of all wickedness; and they exceed the malice of any hangman. Where is there a house which they did not ravage? where is there a family they did not plunder on pretence of searching for their opponents? where is there a garden they did not trample under foot? what tomb[10] did they not open, pretending they were seeking for Athanasius, though their sole object was to plunder and spoil all that came in their way? How many men's houses were sealed up[1]! The contents of how many persons' lodgings did they give away to the soldiers who assis-

---

[1] Vid. Fleury's *Church History*, xxii. 7. p. 129, note k. [Oxf. tr. 1843.] By specifying the material, Athan. implies that altars were sometimes not of wood. [cf. D.C.A. 61 *sq.*]

[2] Curtains were at the entrance, and before the chancel. vid. Bingh. *Antiqu.* viii. 6. § 8. Hofman. *Lex. in voc. velum.* also Chrysost. *Hom.* iii. in Eph.

[3] The royal quarter in Alexandria, vid. *Apol. Const.* 15. In other Palatia an aqueduct was necessary, e.g. vid. Cod. *Theod.* xv. 2. even at Daphne, though it abounded in springs, ibid. 1, 2.

[4] Vid. *Herodot.* ii. 41. who says that cows and heifers were sacred to Isis. vid. Jablonski Pantheon *Æg.* i. 1. § 15. who says that Isis was worshipped in the shape of a cow, and therefore the cows received divine honours. Yet bulls were sacrificed to Apis, ibid. iv. 2. § 9. vid. also Schweighæuser *in loc.* Herod.

[5] Vid note on *de Decr.* § 1. This is a remarkable instance of the special and technical sense of the words, εὐσέβεια, ἀσεβοῦντες, &c., being here contrasted with pagan blasphemy, &c.

[6] 1 Sam. 5, 6.

[7] Acts i. 18.

[7a] [μετὰ θαλλῶν; φαλλῶν 'pro vera lectione probabiliter haberi posse arbitror.' Montf. *Coll. Nov.* t. ii.]

[8] ἀγοραίου, see § 55, note 11, above.

[9] Cf. *Ep. Æg.* 17, and § 31, note 8. [10] Vid. Socr. *Hist.* iv. 13.

[1] *Apol. Fug.* 6.

ted them! Who had not experience of their wickedness? Who that met them but was obliged to hide himself in the market-place? Did not many an one leave his house from fear of them, and pass the night in the desert? Did not many an one, while anxious to preserve his property from them, lose the greater part of it? And who, however inexperienced of the sea, did not choose rather to commit himself to it, and to risk all its dangers, than to witness their threatenings? Many also changed their residences, and removed from street to street, and from the city to the suburbs. And many submitted to severe fines, and when they were unable to pay, borrowed of others, merely that they might escape their machinations.

59. *Violence of Sebastianus.*

For they made themselves formidable to all men, and treated all with great arrogance, using the name of the Emperor, and threatening them with his displeasure. They had to assist them in their wickedness the Duke Sebastianus, a Manichee, and a profligate young man; the[2] Prefect, the Count, and the Receiver-General as a dissembler. Many Virgins who condemned their impiety, and professed the truth, they brought out from the houses; others they insulted as they walked along the streets, and caused their heads to be uncovered by their young men. They also gave permission to the females of their party to insult whom they chose; and although the holy and faithful women withdrew on one side, and gave them the way, yet they gathered round them like Bacchanals and Furies[3], and esteemed it a misfortune if they found no means to injure them, and spent that day sorrowfully on which they were unable to do them some mischief. In a word, so cruel and bitter were they against all, that all men called them hangmen, murderers, lawless, intruders, evil-doers, and by any other name rather than that of Christians.

60. *Martyrdom of Eutychius.*

Moreover, imitating the savage practices of Scythians, they seized upon Eutychius a Subdeacon, a man who had served the Church honourably, and causing him to be scourged on the back with a leather whip, till he was at the point of death, they demanded that he should be sent away to the mines; and not simply to any mine, but to that of Phæno[4],

where even a condemned murderer is hardly able to live a few days. And what was most unreasonable in their conduct, they would not permit him even a few hours to have his wounds dressed, but caused him to be sent off immediately, saying, 'If this is done, all men will be afraid, and henceforward will be on our side.' After a short interval, however, being unable to accomplish his journey to the mine on account of the pain of his stripes, he died on the way. He perished rejoicing, having obtained the glory of martyrdom. But the miscreants were not even yet ashamed, but in the words of Scripture, 'having bowels without mercy[5],' they acted accordingly, and now again perpetrated a satanic deed. When the people prayed them to spare Eutychius and besought them for him, they caused four honourable and free citizens to be seized, one of whom was Hermias who washed the beggars' feet[6]; and after scourging them very severely, the Duke cast them into the prison. But the Arians, who are more cruel even than Scythians, when they had seen that they did not die from the stripes they had received, complained of the Duke and threatened, saying, 'We will write and tell the eunuchs[7], that he does not flog as we wish.' Hearing this he was afraid, and was obliged to beat the men a second time; and they being beaten, and knowing for what cause they suffered and by whom they had been accused, said only, 'We are beaten for the sake of the Truth, but we will not hold communion with the heretics: beat us now as thou wilt; God will judge thee for this.' The impious men wished to expose them to danger in the prison, that they might die there; but the people of God observing their time, besought him for them, and after seven days or more they were set at liberty.

61. *Ill-treatment of the Poor.*

But the Arians, as being grieved at this, again devised another yet more cruel and unholy deed; cruel in the eyes of all men, but well suited to their antichristian heresy. The Lord commanded that we should remember the poor; He said, 'Sell that ye have, and give alms;' and again, 'I was a hungred, and ye gave Me meat; I was thirsty, and ye gave Me drink; for inasmuch as ye have done it unto

---

2 Cf. § 55.
3 Vid. *de Syn.* 31, note 4, also Greg. *Naz. Orat.* 35. 3. Epiph. *Hær.* 69. 3. Theod. *Hist.* i. 3. (p. 730. ed. Schulze).
4 The mines of Phæno lie almost in a direct line between Petræ and Zoar, which is at the southern extremity of the Dead Sea. They formed the place of punishment of Confessors in the Maximinian Persecution, Euseb. *de Mart. Pal.* 7, and in the Arian Persecution at Alexandria after Athan. Theod. *H. E.* iv. 19, p. 996.

Phæno was once the seat of a Bishopric, which sent a Bishop to the Councils at Ephesus, the Ecumenical, and the Latrocinium. vid. Reland. *Palestine*, pp. 951, 952. Montfaucon *in loc.* Athan. *Le Quien. Or. Christ.* t. 3. p. 745.　　　5 Prov. xii. 10.
6 Ἑρμείαν λούοντα τοὺς ἀνεξόδους, Inauspicato verterat Hermantius, 'qui angiportos non pervios lavabat;' Montfaucon, *Coll. Nov.* t. 2. p. xliii. who translates as above, yet not satisfactorily, especially as there is no article before λούοντα. Tillemont says, 'qui avait "quelle charge" dans la police de la ville,' understanding by ἀνεξόδους, 'inclusi sive incarcerati homines;' whereas they are 'ii qui ἀνὰ τὰς ἐξόδους in exitibus viarum, stipem cogunt.' Montf. ibid. For the custom of washing the feet vid. Bingh. *Antiqu.* xii. 4. § 10.　　　7 Cf. § 38.

one of these little ones, ye have done it unto Me[8].' But these men, as being in truth opposed to Christ, have presumed to act contrary to His will in this respect also. For when the Duke gave up the Churches to the Arians, and the destitute persons and widows were unable to continue any longer in them, the widows sat down in places which the Clergy entrusted with the care of them appointed. And when the Arians saw that the brethren readily ministered unto them and supported them, they persecuted the widows also, beating them on the feet, and accused those who gave to them before the Duke. This was done by means of a certain soldier named Dynamius. And it was well-pleasing to Sebastian[9], for there is no mercy in the Manichæans ; nay, it is considered a hateful thing among them to shew mercy to a poor man[9a]. Here then was a novel subject of complaint; and a new kind of court now first invented by the Arians. Persons were brought to trial for acts of kindness which they had performed ; he who shewed mercy was accused, and he who had received a benefit was beaten ; and they wished rather that a poor man should suffer hunger, than that he who was willing to shew mercy should give to him. Such sentiments these modern Jews, for such they are, have learned from the Jews of old, who when they saw him who had been blind from his birth recover his sight, and him who had been a long time sick of the palsy made whole, accused[1] the Lord who had bestowed these benefits upon them, and judged them to be transgressors who had experienced His goodness[2].

62. Ill-treatment of the poor.

Who was not struck with astonishment at these proceedings ? Who did not execrate both the heresy, and its defenders ? Who failed to perceive that the Arians are indeed more cruel than wild beasts ? For they had no prospect of gain[3] from their iniquity, for the sake of which they might have acted in this manner; but they rather increased the hatred of all men against themselves. They thought by treachery and terror to force certain persons into their heresy, so that they might be brought to communicate with them ; but the event turned out quite the contrary. The sufferers endured as martyrdom whatever they inflicted upon them, and neither betrayed nor denied the true faith in Christ. And those who were without and witnessed their conduct, and at last even the heathen, when they saw these things, execrated them as antichristian, as cruel executioners ; for human nature is prone to pity and sympathise with the poor. But these men have lost even the common sentiments of humanity ; and that kindness which they would have desired to meet with at the hands of others, had themselves been sufferers, they would not permit others to receive, but employed against them the severity and authority of the magistrates, and especially of the Duke.

63. Ill-treatment of the Presbyters and Deacons.

What they have done to the Presbyters and Deacons ; how they drove them into banishment under sentence passed upon them by the Duke and the magistrates, causing the soldiers to bring out their kinsfolk from the houses[4], and Gorgonius, the commander of the police[5] to beat them with stripes ; and how (most cruel act of all) with much insolence they plundered the loaves[6] of these and of those who were now dead ; these things it is impossible for words to describe, for their cruelty surpasses all the powers of language. What terms could one employ which might seem equal to the subject ? What circumstances could one mention first, so that those next recorded would not be found more dreadful, and the next more dreadful still ? All their attempts and iniquities[7] were full of murder and impiety ; and so unscrupulous and artful are they, that they endeavour to deceive by promises of protection, and by bribing with money[8], that so, since they cannot recommend themselves by fair means, they may thereby make some display to impose on the simple.

PART VIII.

PERSECUTION IN EGYPT.

64. Who would call them even by the name of Gentiles ; much less by that of Christians ? Would any one regard their habits and feelings as human, and not rather those of wild beasts, seeing their cruel and savage conduct ? They are more worthless than public hangmen ; more audacious than all other heretics. To the Gentiles they are much inferior, and stand far apart and separate from them[1]. I have heard from our fathers, and I believe their report to be a faithful one, that long ago, when

---

[8] Luke xii. 33 : Matt. xxv. 35, 40.   [9] Cf. § 81.
[9a] [They would give money, but thought it wrong to give food. Ath. was possibly unaware of this distinction. See Bright, Introd. to *Hist. Tracts*, p. lxxi. note 7.]   [1] Joh. ix. ; Matt. ix. 3.
[2] Vid. *de Decr.* § 1.   [3] Cf. note on *Orat.* i. § 8.

[4] § 59.   [5] στρατηγοῦ, infr. § 81, note.
[6] τοὺς ἄρτους [i.e. their stated allowance : see also *Apol. Ar* 18], the word occurs *Encycl.* 4, *Apol. Fug.* 6, supr. §§ 31, 54, in this sense ; but Nannius, Hermant, and Tillemont, with some plausibility understand it as a Latin term naturalized, and translate 'most cruel of all, with much insolence they tore the "limbs" of the dead,' alleging that merely to take away 'loaves' was not so 'cruel' as to take away 'lives,' which the Arians had done [the parallels refute this, apart from linguistic grounds].
[7] ἀσεβήματα.   [8] p. 227, note 8, infr. § 73.   [9] §§ 20, 20.

a persecution arose in the time[2] of Maximian, the grandfather of Constantius, the Gentiles concealed our brethren the Christians, who were sought after, and frequently suffered the loss of their own substance, and had trial of imprisonment, solely that they might not betray the fugitives. They protected those who fled to them for refuge, as they would have done their own persons, and were determined to run all risks on their behalf. But now these admirable persons, the inventors of a new heresy, act altogether the contrary part; and are distinguished for nothing but their treachery. They have appointed themselves as executioners, and seek to betray all alike, and make those who conceal others the objects of their plots, esteeming equally as their enemy both him that conceals and him that is concealed. So murderous are they; so emulous in their evil-doings of the wickedness of Judas.

65. *Martyrdom of Secundus of Barka.*

The crimes these men have committed cannot adequately be described. I would only say, that as I write and wish to enumerate all their deeds of iniquity, the thought enters my mind, whether this heresy be not the fourth daughter of the horse-leach[3] in the Proverbs, since after so many acts of injustice, so many murders, it hath not yet said, 'It is enough.' No; it still rages, and goes about[4] seeking after those whom it has not yet discovered, while those whom it has already injured, it is eager to injure anew. After the night attack, after the evils committed in consequence of it, after the persecution brought about by Heraclius, they cease not yet to accuse us falsely before the Emperor (and they are confident that as impious persons they will obtain a hearing), desiring that something more than banishment may be inflicted upon us, and that hereafter those who do not consent to their impieties may be destroyed. Accordingly, being now emboldened in an extreme degree, that most abandoned Secundus[5] of Pentapolis, and Stephanus[6] his accomplice, conscious that their heresy was a defence of any injustice they might commit, on discovering a Presbyter at Barka who would not comply with their desires (he was called Secundus, being of the same name, but not of the same faith with the heretic), they kicked him till he died[7]. While he was thus suffering he imitated the Saint, and said, 'Let no one avenge my cause before human judges; I have the Lord for my avenger,

for whose sake I suffer these things at their hands.' They however were not moved with pity at these words, nor did they feel any awe of the sacred season; for it was during the time of Lent[8] that they thus kicked the man to death.

66. *Persecution the weapon of Arianism.*

O new heresy, that hast put on the whole devil in impiety and wicked deeds! For in truth it is but a lately invented evil; and although certain heretofore appear to have adopted its doctrines, yet they concealed them, and were not known to hold them. But Eusebius and Arius, like serpents coming out of their holes, have vomited forth the poison of this impiety; Arius daring to blaspheme openly, and[9] Eusebius defending his blasphemy. He was not however able to support the heresy, until, as I said before, he found a patron[1] for it in the Emperor. Our fathers called an Ecumenical Council, when three hundred of them, more or less[2], met together and condemned the Arian heresy, and all declared that it was alien and strange to the faith of the Church. Upon this its supporters, perceiving that they were dishonoured, and had now no good ground of argument to insist upon, devised a different method, and attempted to vindicate it by means of external power. And herein one may especially admire the novelty as well as wickedness of their device, and how they go beyond all other heresies. For these support their madness by persuasive arguments calculated to deceive the simple; the Greeks, as the Apostle has said, make their attack with excellency and persuasiveness of speech, and with plausible fallacies; the Jews, leaving the divine Scriptures, now, as the Apostle again has said, contend about 'fables and endless genealogies[3];' and the Manichees and Valentinians with them, and others, corrupting the divine Scriptures, put forth fables in terms of their own inventions. But the Arians are bolder than them all, and have shewn that the other heresies are but their younger sisters[4], whom, as I have said, they surpass in impiety, emulating them all, and especially the Jews in their iniquity. For as the Jews, when they were unable to prove the charges which they pretended to allege against Paul, straightway led him to the chief captain and the governor; so likewise these men, who surpass the Jews in their devices, make use only of the power of the judges; and if any one so much as speaks against them, he is dragged before the Governor or the General.

---

2 [303 A.D.]   3 Prov. xxx. 15.
4 περιέρχεται, 1 Pet. v. 8. supr. § 20, and *ad Adelph.* § 2 fin.
5 *Ep. Æg.* 7.   6 Cf. *Hist. Aceph.* ix., *de Syn.* 12, Thdt. *H.E.* ii. 28.
7 In like manner the party of Dioscorus at the Latrocinium, or Eutychian Council of Ephesus, A.D. 449, kicked to death Flavian, Patriarch of Constantinople.

8 *Encyc.* 4.   9 *Apol. Ar.* 59.   1 § 45.
2 *Apol. Ar.* 23.   3 1 Tim. i. 4.   4 Cf. § 31

67. Arianism worse than other heresies, because of Persecution.

The other heresies also, when the very Truth has refuted them on the clearest evidence, are wont to be silent, being simply confounded by their conviction. But this modern and accursed heresy, when it is overthrown by argument, when it is cast down and covered with shame by the very Truth, forthwith endeavours to coerce by violence and stripes and imprisonment those whom it has been unable to persuade by argument, thereby acknowledging itself to be anything rather than godly. For it is the part of true godliness not to compel [5], but to persuade, as I said before. Thus our Lord Himself, not as employing force, but as offering to their free choice, has said to all, 'If any man will follow after Me [6];' and to His disciples, 'Will ye also go away [7]?' This heresy, however, is altogether alien from godliness; and therefore how otherwise should it act, than contrary to our Saviour, seeing also that it has enlisted that enemy of Christ, Constantius, as it were Antichrist himself [8], to be its leader in impiety? He for its sake has earnestly endeavoured to emulate Saul in savage cruelty. For when the priests gave victuals to David, Saul commanded, and they were all destroyed, in number three hundred and five [9]; and this man, now that all avoid the heresy, and confess a sound faith in the Lord, annuls a Council of full three hundred Bishops, banishes the Bishops themselves, and hinders the people from the practice of piety, and from their prayers to God, preventing their public assemblies. And as Saul overthrew Nob, the city of the priests, so this man, advancing even further in wickedness, has given up the Churches to the impious. And as he honoured Doeg the accuser before the true priests, and persecuted David, giving ear to the Ziphites; so this man prefers heretics to the godly, and still persecutes them that flee from him, giving ear to his own eunuchs, who falsely accuse the orthodox. He does not perceive that whatever he does or writes in behalf of the heresy of the Arians, involves an attack [1] upon the Saviour.

68. Constantius worse than Saul, Ahab, and Pilate. His past conduct to his own relations.

Ahab himself did not act so cruelly towards the priests of God, as this man has acted towards the Bishops. For he was at least pricked in his conscience, when Naboth had been murdered, and was afraid at the sight [2] of Elijah, but this man neither reverenced the great Hosius, nor was wearied or pricked in conscience, after banishing so many Bishops; but like another Pharaoh, the more he is afflicted, the more he is hardened, and imagines greater wickedness day by day. And the most extraordinary instance of his iniquity was the following. It happened that when the Bishops were condemned to banishment, certain other persons also received their sentence on charges of murder or sedition or theft, each according to the quality of his offence. These men after a few months he released, on being requested to do so, as Pilate did Barabbas; but the servants of Christ he not only refused to set at liberty, but even sentenced them to more unmerciful punishment in the place of their exile, proving himself 'an undying evil [2a]' to them. To the others through congeniality of disposition he became a friend; but to the orthodox he was an enemy on account of their true faith in Christ. Is it not clear to all men from hence, that the Jews of old when they demanded Barabbas, and crucified the Lord, acted but the part which these present enemies of Christ are acting together with Constantius? nay, that he is even more bitter than Pilate. For Pilate, when he perceived [3] the injustice of the deed, washed his hands; but this man, while he banishes the saints, gnashes his teeth against them more and more.

69. But what wonder is it if, after he has been led into impious errors, he is so cruel towards the Bishops, since the common feelings of humanity could not induce him to spare

---

[5] The early theory about persecution seems to have been this,—that that was a bad cause which 'depended' upon it, but that, when a 'cause' was good, there was nothing wrong in using force in due 'subordination' to argument [so Pius IX. in *Encycl.* 'Quanta cura,' speaks of the 'officium coercendi sancitis poenis violatores catholicæ religionis]; that there was as little impropriety in the civil magistrate's inducing 'individuals' by force, when they were incapable of higher motives, as by those secular blessings which follow on Christianity. Our Lord's kingdom was not of this world, that is, it did not depend on this world; but, as subduing, engrossing, and swaying this world, it at times condescended to make use of this world's weapons against itself. The simple question was 'whether a cause depended on force for its existence.' S. Athanasius declared and the event proved, that Arianism was so dependent. When Emperors ceased to persecute, Arianism ceased to be; it had no life in itself. Again, all cruel persecution, or long continued, or on a large scale, was wrong, as arguing 'an absence' of moral and rational grounds in the 'cause' so maintained. Again, there was an evident 'impropriety' in ecclesiastical functionaries using secular weapons, as there would be in their engaging in a secular pursuit, or forming secular connections; whereas the soldier might as suitably, and should as dutifully, defend religion with the sword, as the scholar with his pen. And further there was an abhorrence of cruelty natural to us, which it was a duty to cherish and maintain. All this being considered, there is no inconsistency in S. Athanasius denouncing persecution, and in Theodosius decreeing that 'the heretical teachers, who usurped the sacred titles of Bishops or Presbyters,' should be 'exposed to the heavy penalties of exile and confiscation.' Gibbon, *Hist.* ch. 27. For a list of passages from the Fathers on the subject, vid. Limborch on the Inquisition, vol. 1. Bellarmin. *de Laicis*, c. 21, 22, and of authors in favour of persecution, vid. Gerhard *de Magistr. Polit.* p. 741, &c. [But vide supr., *Apol. Fug.* 23: 'persecution is a device of the devil;' see also *Socr.* vii. 3.]   [6] Matt. xvi. 24.   [7] John vi. 67.
[8] Cf. *De Syn.* 5, note 10.   [9] 1 Sam. xxii. 18, LXX.

[1] *Apol. Ar.* 23.   [2] 1 Kings xxi. 20.
[2a] A quotation from Homer, *Od.* xii. 118.   [3] Matt. xxvii. 24.

even his own kindred. His uncles [4] he slew; his cousins he put out of the way; he commiserated not the sufferings of his father-in-law, though he had married his daughter, or of his kinsmen; but he has ever been a transgressor of his oaths towards all. So likewise he treated his brother in an unholy manner; and now he pretends to build his sepulchre, although he delivered up to the barbarians his betrothed wife Olympias, whom his brother had protected till his death, and had brought up as his intended consort. Moreover he attempted to set aside his wishes, although he boasts to be his heir [5]; for so he writes, in terms which any one possessed of but a small measure of sense would be ashamed of. But when I compare his letters, I find that he does not possess common understanding, but that his mind is solely regulated by the suggestions of others, and that he has no mind of his own at all. Now Solomon says, 'If a ruler hearken to lies, all his servants are wicked [6].' This man proves by his actions that he is such an unjust one, and that those about him are wicked.

70. Inconstancy of Constantius.

How then, being such an one, and taking pleasure in such associates, can he ever design anything just or reasonable, entangled as he is in the iniquity of his followers, men who verily bewitch him, or rather who have trampled his brains under their heels? Wherefore he now writes letters [6a], and then repents that he has written them, and after repenting is again stirred up to anger, and then again laments his fate, and being undetermined what to do, he shews a soul destitute of understanding. Being then of such a character, one must fairly pity him, because that under the semblance and name of freedom he is the slave of those who drag him on to gratify their own impious pleasure. In a word, while through his folly and inconstancy, as the Scripture saith [7], he is willing to comply with the desires. of others, he has given himself up to condemnation, to be consumed by fire in the future judgment; at once consenting to do whatever they wish, and gratifying them in their designs against the Bishops, and in their exertion of authority over the Churches. For behold, he has now again thrown into disorder all the Churches of Alexandria [8] and of Egypt and Libya, and has publicly given orders, that the Bishops of the Catholic Church and faith be cast out of their churches, and that they be all given up to the professors of the Arian

doctrines [9]. The General began to carry this order into execution; and straightway Bishops were sent off in chains, and Presbyters and Monks bound with iron, after being almost beaten to death with stripes. Disorder prevails in every place; all Egypt and Libya are in danger, the people being indignant at this unjust command, and seeing in it the preparation for the coming of Antichrist, and beholding their property plundered by others, and given up into the hands of the heretics.

71. This wickedness unprecedented.

When was ever such iniquity heard of? when was such an evil deed ever perpetrated, even in times of persecution? They were heathens who persecuted formerly; but they did not bring their idols into the Churches. Zenobia [9a] was a Jewess, and a supporter of Paul of Samosata; but she did not give up the Churches to the Jews for Synagogues. This is a new piece of iniquity. It is not simply persecution, but more than persecution, it is a prelude and preparation [10] for the coming of Antichrist. Even if it be admitted that they invented false charges against Athanasius and the rest of the Bishops whom they banished, yet what is this to their later practices? What charges have they to allege against the whole of Egypt and Libya and Pentapolis [1]? For they have begun no longer to lay their plots against individuals, in which case they might be able to frame a lie against them; but they have set upon all in a body, so that if they merely choose to invent accusations against them, they must be condemned. Thus their wickedness has blinded their understanding [2]; and they have required, without any reason assigned, that the whole body of the Bishops shall be expelled, and thereby they shew that the charges they framed against Athanasius and the rest of the Bishops whom they banished were false, and invented for no other purpose than to support the accursed heresy of the Arian enemies of Christ. This is now no longer concealed, but has become most manifest to all men. He commanded Athanasius to be expelled out of the city, and gave up the Churches to them. And the Presbyters and Deacons that were with him, who had been appointed by Peter and Alexander, were also expelled and driven into banishment; and the real Arians, who not through any suspicions arising from circumstances, but on account of the heresy had been expelled at first together with Arius himself by

---

4 [See above, p. 134, note 8, and ref. there; also Gibbon, ch. xviii. vol. ii. p. 364 sqq.]
  5 Cf. § 60, note 6.   6 Prov. xxix. 12.   6a Cf. § 51.
  7 Prov. vii. 22, LXX.   8 Apol. Const. 27.

9 § 54.
  9a [This is 'certainly false,' see Encyclop. Brit., art. PALMYRA, p. 201, note 4.]   10 § 67, note 8.
  1 Cf. § 3.   2 Wisd. ii. 21.

the Bishop Alexander,—Secundus in Libya, in Alexandria Euzöius[3] the Chananæan, Julius, Ammon, Marcus, Irenæus, Zosimus, and Sarapion surnamed Pelycon, and in Libya Sisinnius, and the younger men with him, associates in his impiety; these have obtained possession of the Churches.

72. Banishment of Egyptian Bishops.

And the General Sebastian wrote to the governors and military authorities in every place; and the true Bishops were persecuted, and those who professed impious doctrines were brought in in their stead. They banished Bishops who had grown old in orders, and had been many years in the Episcopate, having been ordained by the Bishop Alexander; Ammonius[4], Hermes, Anagamphus, and Marcus, they sent to the Upper Oasis; Muis, Psenosiris, Nilammon, Plenes, Marcus, and Athenodorus to Ammoniaca, with no other intention than that they should perish in their passage through the deserts. They had no pity on them though they were suffering from illness, and indeed proceeded on their journey with so much difficulty on account of their weakness, that they were obliged to be carried in litters, and their sickness was so dangerous that the materials for their burial accompanied them. One of them indeed died, but they would not even permit the body to be given up to his friends for interment. With the same purpose they banished also the Bishop Dracontius to the desert places about Clysma, Philo to Babylon, Adelphius to Psinabla in the Thebais, and the Presbyters Hierax and Dioscorus to Syene. They likewise drove into exile Ammonius, Agathus, Agathodæmon, Apollonius, Eulogius, Apollos, Paphnutius, Gaius, and Flavius, ancient Bishops, as also the Bishops Dioscorus, Ammonius, Heraclides, and Psais; some of whom they gave up to work in the stone-quarries, others they persecuted with an intention to destroy, and many others they plundered. They banished also forty of the laity, with certain virgins whom they had before exposed to the fire[5]; beating them so severely with rods taken from palm-trees, that after lingering five days some of them died, and others had recourse to surgical treatment on account of the thorns left in their limbs, from which they suffered torments worse than death[6]. But what is most dreadful to the mind of any man of sound understanding, though characteristic of these miscreants, is this: When the virgins during the scourging called upon the Name

of Christ, they gnashed their teeth against them with increased fury. Nay more, they would not give up the bodies of the dead to their friends for burial, but concealed them that they might appear to be ignorant of the murder. They did not however escape detection; the whole city perceived it, and all men withdrew from them as executioners, as malefactors and robbers. Moreover they overthrew monasteries, and endeavoured to cast monks into the fire; they plundered houses, and breaking into the house of certain free citizens where the Bishop had deposited a treasure, they plundered and took it away. They scourged the widows on the soles of their feet, and hindered them from receiving their alms.

73. Character of Arian nominees.

Such were the iniquities practised by the Arians; and as to their further deeds of impiety, who could hear the account of them without shuddering? They had caused these venerable old men and aged Bishops to be sent into banishment; they now appointed in their stead profligate heathen youths, whom they thought to raise at once to the highest dignity, though they were not even Catechumens[7]. And others who were accused of bigamy[8], and even of worse crimes, they nominated Bishops on account of the wealth and civil power which they possessed, and sent them out as it were from a market, upon their giving them gold. And now more dreadful calamities befel the people. For when they rejected these mercenary dependents of the Arians, so alien from themselves, they were scourged, they were proscribed, they were shut up in prison by the General (who did all this readily, being a Manichee), in order that they might no longer seek after their own Bishops, but be forced to accept those whom they abominated, men who were now guilty of the same mockeries as they had before practised among their idols.

74. The Episcopal appointments of Constantius a mark of Antichrist.

Will not every just person break forth into lamentations at the sight or hearing of these things, at perceiving the arrogance and extreme injustice of these impious men? 'The righteous lament in the place of the impious[9].' After all these things, and now that the impiety has reached such a pitch of audacity, who will any longer venture to call this

---

3 Cf. *Dep. Ar.*   4 Cf. *Ap. Fug. 7.*
5 *Ap. Fug. 6.*   6 Ib. 7.

7 Vid. Hallier, *de Ordin.* part 2. i. 1, art. 2.
8 διγυναίοις, not διγάμοις. On the latter, vid. Suicer, *Thess. in voc.* διγαμία. Tertull. *de Monogam.*
9 Prov. xxviii. 28, LXX.

Costyllius[10] a Christian, and not rather the image of Antichrist? For what mark of Antichrist is yet wanting? How can he in any way fail to be regarded as that one? or how can the latter fail to be supposed such a one as he is? Did not the Arians and the Gentiles offer those sacrifices in the great Church in the Cæsareum[11], and utter their blasphemies against Christ as by His command? And does not the vision of Daniel thus describe[1] Antichrist; that he shall make war with the saints, and prevail against them, and exceed all that have been before him in evil deeds, and shall humble three kings, and speak words against the Most High, and shall think to change times and laws? Now what other person besides Constantius has ever attempted to do these things? He is surely such a one as Antichrist would be. He speaks words against the Most High by supporting this impious heresy: he makes war against the saints by banishing the Bishops; although indeed he exercises this power but for a little while[2] to his own destruction. Moreover he has surpassed those before him in wickedness, having devised a new mode of persecution; and after he had overthrown three kings, namely Vetranio, Magnentius, and Gallus, he straightway undertook the patronage of impiety; and like a giant[3] he has dared in his pride to set himself up against the Most High. He has thought to change laws, by transgressing the ordinance of the Lord given us through His Apostles, by altering the customs of the Church, and inventing a new kind of appointments. For he sends from strange places, distant a fifty days' journey[4], Bishops attended by soldiers to people unwilling to receive them; and instead of an introduction to the acquaintance of their people, they bring with them threatening messages and letters to the magistrates. Thus he sent Gregory from Cappadocia[5] to Alexandria; he transferred Germinius from Cyzicus to Sirmium; he removed Cecropius from Laodicea to Nicomedia.

75. Arrival of George at Alexandria, and proceedings of Constantius in Italy.

Again he transferred from Cappadocia to Milan one Auxentius[6], an intruder rather than a Christian, whom he commanded to stay there, after he had banished for his piety towards Christ Dionysius the Bishop of the place, a godly man. But this person was as yet even ignorant of the Latin language, and unskilful in everything except impiety. And now one George, a Cappadocian, who was contractor of stores[7] at Constantinople, and having embezzled all monies that he received, was obliged to fly, he commanded to enter Alexandria with military pomp, and supported by the authority of the General. Next, finding one Epictetus[8] a novice, a bold young man, he loved him[9], perceiving that he was ready for wickedness; and by his means he carries on his designs against those of the Bishops whom he desires to ruin. For he is prepared to do everything that the Emperor wishes; who accordingly availing himself of his assistance, has committed at Rome a strange act, but one truly resembling the malice of Antichrist. Having made preparations in the Palace instead of the Church, and caused some three of his own eunuchs to attend instead of the people, he then compelled three[1] ill-conditioned spies[2] (for one cannot call them Bishops), to ordain forsooth as Bishop one Felix[3], a man worthy of them, then in the Palace. For the people perceiving the iniquitous proceedings of the heretics would not allow them to enter the Churches[4], and withdrew themselves far from them.

76. Tyrannous banishment of Bishops by Constantius.

Now what is yet wanting to make him Antichrist? or what more could Antichrist do at his coming than this man has done? Will he not find when he comes that the way has been already prepared for him by this man easily to deceive the people? Again[5], he claims to himself the right of deciding causes, which he refers to the Court instead of the Church, and presides at them in person. And strange it is to say, when he perceives the accusers at a

---

7 Cf. supr. § 56, note 8.
8 Epictetus above, p. 226, is called ὑποκρίτης, which Montfaucon translated 'stage-player.' It is a question whether more than 'actor' is meant by it, alluding to the mockery of an ordination in which he seems to have taken part. Though an Asiatic apparently by birth, he was made Bishop of Civita Vecchia. We hear of him at the conference between Constantius and Liberius. Theod. H. E. ii. 13. Then he assists in the ordination of Felix. Afterwards he made a martyr of S. Ruffinian by making him run before his carriage; and he ends his historical career by taking a chief part among the Arians at Ariminum. vid. Tillem. t. vi. p. 380, &c. Ughell. Ital. t. 10. p. 56.
9 The Greek is Ἐπικτητόν τινα . . . νεώτερον . . . ἠγάπησεν, ὁρῶν, κ.τ.λ. So in the account of the νεανίσκος, Ὁ δὲ Ἰησοῦς ἐμβλέψας αὐτῷ, ἠγάπησεν αὐτόν. Mark x. 21.
1 i.e. to keep up the canonical number; and cf. the case of Novatian, in Euseb. H. E. vi. 43. On the custom, vid. Bingh. Antiqu. ii. 11, § 4.   2 § 48, note 5.
3 Cf. Tillemont, Mem. t. 6. p. 778. Bolland. Catal. Pontif. ch. 21. p. 390. [Döllinger, ' Fables respecting the Popes;' D.C.B. ii. 480. Felix figures in the middle ages as the orthodox rival of the 'Arian' Liberius.]
4 Cf. Theod. Hist. ii. 17.   5 §§ 44, 52.

---

10 An irregularly formed diminutive, or a quasi diminutive from Constantius, as Agathyllus from Agathocles, Heryllus from Heracles, &c. vid. Matth. Gr. Gramm. § 102. ed. 1820. [Curtius, § 347.]   11 Ap. Const. 14, supr. § 55.   1 Dan. vii. 25.
2 Constantius died at 45, having openly apostatized for about six years. Julian died at 32, after a reign of a year and a half. vid. supr. § 32. vid. also Bellarmin. de Notis Eccl. 17 and 18.
3 Vid. de Decr. § 32, note 8, Orat. ii. § 32. Naz. Orat. 43, 26. Socr. Hist. v. 10, p. 268.   4 Ep. Æg. 7.
5 Encycl. 2.   6 Cf. de Syn. §§ 1, 8, and Ep. Æg. 7.

loss, he takes up the accusation himself, so that the injured party may no longer be able to defend himself on account of the violence which he displays. This he did in the proceedings against Athanasius. For when he saw the boldness of the Bishops Paulinus, Lucifer, Eusebius, and Dionysius, and how out of the recantation of Ursacius and Valens [6] they confuted those who spoke against the Bishop, and advised that Valens and his fellows should no longer be believed, since they had already retracted what they now asserted, he immediately stood up [7] and said, 'I am now the accuser of Athanasius; on my account you must believe what these assert.' And then, when they said,—' But how can you be an accuser, when the accused person is not present? for if you are his accuser, yet he is not present, and therefore cannot be tried. And the cause is not one that concerns Rome, so that you should be believed as being the Emperor; but it is a matter that concerns a Bishop; for the trial ought to be conducted on equal terms both to the accuser and the accused. And besides, how can you accuse him? for you could not be present to witness the conduct of one who lived at so great a distance from you; and if you speak but what you have heard from these, you ought also to give credit to what he says; but if you will not believe him, while you do believe them, it is plain that they assert these things for your sake, and accuse Athanasius only to gratify you?'—when he heard this, thinking that what they had so truly spoken was an insult to himself, he sent them into banishment; and being exasperated against Athanasius, he wrote in a more savage strain, requiring that he should suffer what has now befallen him, and that the Churches should be given up to the Arians, and that they should be allowed to do whatever they pleased.

77. *Constantius the precursor of Antichrist.*

Terrible indeed, and worse than terrible are such proceedings; yet conduct suitable to him who assumes the character of Antichrist. Who that beheld him taking the lead of his pretended Bishops, and presiding in Ecclesiastical causes, would not justly exclaim that this was ' the abomination of desolation [8]' spoken of by Daniel? For having put on the profession of Christianity, and entering into the holy places, and standing therein, he lays waste the Churches, transgressing their Canons, and enforcing the observance of his own decrees. Will any one now venture to say that this is a peaceful time

with Christians, and not a time of persecution? A persecution indeed, such as never arose before, and such as no one perhaps will again stir up, except 'the son of lawlessness [9],' do these enemies of Christ exhibit, who already present a picture of him in their own persons. Wherefore it especially behoves us to be sober, lest this heresy which has reached such a height of impudence, and has diffused itself abroad like the 'poison of an adder [10],' as it is written in the Proverbs, and which teaches doctrines contrary to the Saviour; lest, I say, this be that 'falling away [11],' after which He shall be revealed, of whom Constantius is surely the forerunner [1]. Else wherefore is he so mad against the godly? wherefore does he contend for it as his own heresy, and call every one his enemy who will not comply with the madness of Arius, and admit gladly the allegations of the enemies of Christ, and dishonour so many venerable Councils? why did he command that the Churches should be given up to the Arians? was it not that, when that other comes, he may thus find a way to enter into them, and may take to himself him who has prepared those places for him? For the ancient Bishops who were ordained by Alexander, and by his predecessor Achillas, and by Peter before him, have been cast out; and those introduced whom the companions of soldiers nominated; and they nominated only such as promised to adopt their doctrines.

78. *Alliance of Meletians with Arians.*

This was an easy proposition for the Meletians to comply with; for the greater part, or rather the whole of them, have never had a religious education, nor are they acquainted with the 'sound faith [2]' in Christ, nor do they know at all what Christianity is, or what writings we Christians possess. For having come out, some of them from the worship of idols, and others from the senate, or from the first civil offices, for the sake of the miserable exemption [3] from duty and for the patronage they gained, and having bribed [4] the Meletians who preceded them, they have been advanced to this dignity even before they had been under instruction. And even if they pretended to have been such, yet what kind of instruction is to be obtained among the Meletians? But indeed without even pretending to be under instruction, they came at once, and immediately were called Bishops, just as children receive a name. Being then persons of this description, they thought the thing of no great consequence, nor even supposed that piety was different from

---

6 Cf. *Apol. Ar.* 58.　　7 § 33.　　8 Dan. **ix. 27.**

9 2 Thess. ii. **8.**　　10 Prov. xxiii. 32.
11 2 Thess. ii. 3.　　1 *De Syn.* 5, note 10.　　2 Cf. Tit. **i. 13,**
ii. 2.　　3 Cf. *Ap. Ar.* 56.　　4 Ib. 59, *Ep. Æg.* 22.

impiety.   Accordingly from being Meletians they readily and speedily became Arians; and if the Emperor should command them to adopt any other profession, they are ready to change again to that also.   Their ignorance of true godliness quickly brings them to submit to the prevailing folly, and that which happens to be first taught them.   For it is nothing to them to be carried about by every wind [5] and tempest, so long as they are only exempt from duty, and obtain the patronage of men ; nor would they scruple probably to change again [6] to what they were before, even to become such as they were when they were heathens.   Any how, being men of such an easy temper, and considering the Church as a civil senate, and like heathen, being idolatrously minded, they put on the honourable name [7] of the Saviour, under which they polluted the whole of Egypt, by causing so much as the name of the Arian heresy to be known therein.   For Egypt has heretofore been the only country, throughout which the profession of the orthodox faith was boldly maintained [8] ; and therefore these misbelievers have striven to introduce jealousy there also, or rather not they, but the devil who has stirred them up, in order that when his herald Antichrist shall come, he may find that the Churches in Egypt also are his own, and that the Meletians have already been instructed in his principles, and may recognise himself as already formed [9] in them.

79. Behaviour of the Meletians contrasted with that of the Alexandrian Christians.

Such is the effect of that iniquitous order which was issued by Constantius.   On the part of the people there was displayed a ready alacrity to submit to martyrdom, and an increased hatred of this most impious heresy ; and yet lamentations for their Churches, and groans burst from all, while they cried unto the Lord, ' Spare Thy people, O Lord, and give not Thine heritage unto Thine enemies to reproach [1] ;' but make haste to deliver us out of the hand of the lawless [2].   For behold, they have not spared Thy servants, but are preparing the way for Antichrist.'   For the Meletians will never resist him, nor will they care for the truth, nor will they esteem it an evil thing to deny Christ.   They are men who have not approached the word with sincerity ; like the chameleon [3] they assume every various appearance ; they are hirelings of any who will make use of them.   They make not the truth their aim, but prefer before it their present pleasure ; they say only, ' Let us eat and drink, for to-

morrow we die [4].'   Such a profession and faithless temper is more worthy of Epicritian [5] players than of Meletians.   But the faithful servants of our Saviour, and the true Bishops who believe with sincerity, and live not for themselves, but for the Lord ; these faithfully believing in our Lord Jesus Christ, and knowing, as I said before, that the charges which were alleged against the truth were false, and plainly fabricated for the sake of the Arian heresy (for by the recantation [6] of Ursacius and Valens they detected the calumnies which were devised against Athanasius, for the purpose of removing him out of the way, and of introducing into the Churches the impieties of the enemies of Christ) ; these, I say, perceiving all this, as defenders and preachers of the truth, chose rather, and endured to be insulted and driven into banishment, than to subscribe against him, and to hold communion with the Arian madmen.   They forgot not the lessons they had taught to others ; yea, they know well that great dishonour remains for the traitors, but for them which confess the truth, the kingdom of heaven ; and that to the careless and such as fear Constantius will happen no good thing ; but for them that endure tribulations here, as sailors reach a quiet haven after a storm, as wrestlers receive a crown after the combat, so these shall obtain great and eternal joy and delight in heaven ;—such as Joseph obtained after those tribulations; such as the great Daniel had after his temptations and the manifold conspiracies of the courtiers against him ; such as Paul now enjoys, being crowned by the Saviour ; such as the people of God everywhere expect.   They, seeing these things, were not infirm of purpose, but waxed strong in faith [7], and increased in their zeal more and more.   Being fully persuaded of the calumnies and impieties of the heretics, they condemn the persecutor, and in heart and mind run together the same course with them that are persecuted, that they also may obtain the crown of Confession.

80. Duty of separating from heretics.

One might say much more against this detestable and antichristian heresy, and might demonstrate by many arguments that the practices of Constantius are a prelude to the coming of Antichrist.   But seeing that, as the Prophet [8] has said, from the feet even to the head there is no reasonableness in it, but it is full of all filthiness and all impiety, so that the very name of it ought to be avoided as a dog's vomit or the

---

5 Cf. Eph. iv. 14.   6 Ap. Ar. 59. 63.   7 Cf. James ii. 7.
8 Cf. Apol. Ar. 52.   9 Ctr. Gal. iv. 19.   1 Joel ii. 17.
2 ἀνόμων, Cf. 2 Thess. ii. 8.   3 de Decr. 1, note 2.

4 1 Cor. xv. 32.   5 Histrionum genus, Montf. [The allusion is obscure.   Epicrates was a comedian of the 4th. cent. B.C.]   6 Apol. Ar. 58.
7 Cf. Rom. iv. 20.   8 Isa. i. 6.

poison of serpents; and seeing that Costyllius openly exhibits the image of the adversary[9]; in order that our words may not be too many, it will be well to content ourselves with the divine Scripture, and that we all obey the precept which it has given us both in regard to other heresies, and especially respecting this. That precept is as follows; 'Depart ye, depart ye, go ye out from thence, touch no unclean thing; go ye out of the midst of them, and be ye separate, that bear the vessels of the Lord[10].' This may suffice[11] to instruct us all, so that if any one has been deceived by them, he may go out from them, as out of Sodom, and not return again unto them, lest he suffer the fate of Lot's wife; and if any one has continued from the beginning pure from this impious heresy, he may glory in Christ and say, 'We have not stretched out our hands to a strange god[12]; neither have we worshipped the works of our own hands, nor served the creature[13] more than Thee, the God that hast created all things through Thy word, the Only-Begotten Son our Lord Jesus Christ, through whom to Thee the Father together with the same Word in the Holy Spirit be glory and power for ever and ever. Amen.'

The Second Protest[1].

81. The people of the Catholic Church in Alexandria, which is under the government of the most Reverend Bishop Athanasius, make this public protest by those whose names are under-written.

We have already protested against the nocturnal assault which was committed upon ourselves and the Lord's house; although in truth there needed no protest in respect to proceedings with which the whole city has been already made acquainted. For the bodies of the slain which were discovered were exposed in public, and the bows and arrows and other arms found in the Lord's house loudly proclaim the iniquity. But whereas after our Protest already made, the most illustrious Duke Syrianus endeavours to force all men to agree with him, as though no tumult had been made, nor any had perished (wherein is no small proof that these things were not done according to the wishes of the most gracious Emperor Augustus Constantius; for he would not have been so much afraid of

the consequences of this transaction, had he acted therein by command); and whereas also, when we went to him, and requested him not to do violence to any, nor to deny what had taken place, he ordered us, being Christians, to be beaten with clubs; thereby again giving proof of the nocturnal assault which has been directed against the Church:—

We therefore make also this present Protest, certain of us being now about to travel to the most religious Emperor Augustus: and we adjure Maximus the Prefect of Egypt, and the Controllers[2], in the name of Almighty God, and for the sake of the salvation of the most religious Augustus Constantius, to relate all these things to the piety of Augustus, and to the authority of the most illustrious Prefects[3]. We adjure also the masters of vessels, to publish these things everywhere, and to carry them to the ears of the most religious Augustus, and to the Prefects and the Magistrates in every place, in order that it may be known that a war has been waged against the Church, and that, in the times of Augustus Constantius, Syrianus has caused virgins and many others to become martyrs.

As it dawned upon the fifth before the Ides of February[4], that is to say, the fourteenth of the month Mechir, while we were keeping vigil[5] in the Lord's house, and engaged in our prayers (for there was to be a communion on the Preparation[6]); suddenly about midnight, the most illustrious Duke Syrianus attacked us and the Church with many legions of soldiers[7] armed with naked swords and javelins and other warlike instruments, and wearing helmets on their heads; and actually while we were praying, and while the lessons were being read, they broke down the doors. And when the doors were burst open by the violence of the multitude, he gave command, and some of them were shooting; others shouting, their arms rattling, and their swords flashing in the light of the lamps; and forthwith virgins were being slain, many men trampled down, and falling over one another as the soldiers came upon them, and several were pierced with arrows and perished. Some of the soldiers also were betaking themselves to plunder, and were stripping the virgins, who were more afraid of being even touched by them than they were of death. The Bishop continued sitting upon his throne, and exhorted all to pray. The Duke led on the attack, having with him Hilarius the notary, whose part in the proceedings was shewn in the

---

9 Cf. 2 Thess. ii. 4.　　　　10 Is. lii. 11.
11 [A somewhat characteristic phrase of Athanasius.]
12 Ps. xliv. 20.　　　13 Ep. Æg. 13 note 1.
1 Of the two Protests referred to supr. § 48, the first was omitted by the copyists, as being already contained, as Montfaucon seems to say, in the Apology against the Arians; yet if it be the one to which allusion is made in the beginning of the Protest which follows, it is not found there, nor does it appear what document of A.D. 356 could properly have a place in a set of papers which end with A.D. 350.

2 Ap. Ar. 73, note.　　　3 i.e. Prætorian.
4 Febr. 9.　　5 Ap. Const. 25; Ap. Fug. 24.　　6 Friday
vid. Encyc. 4, note 9.　　7 i.e. more than 5,000, Ap. Fug. 24.

sequel. The Bishop was seized, and barely escaped being torn to pieces ; and having fallen into a state of insensibility, and appearing as one dead, he disappeared from among them, and has gone we know not whither. They were eager to kill him. And when they saw that many had perished, they gave orders to the soldiers to remove out of sight the bodies of the dead. But the most holy virgins who were left behind were buried in the tombs, having attained the glory of martyrdom in the times of the most religious Constantius. Deacons also were beaten with stripes even in the Lord's house, and were shut up there.

Nor did matters stop even here : for after all this had happened, whosoever pleased broke open any door that he could, and searched, and plundered what was within. They entered even into those places which not even all Christians are allowed to enter. Gorgonius, the commander of the city force [8], knows this, for he was present. And no unimportant evidence of the nature of this hostile assault is afforded by the circumstance, that the armour and javelins and swords borne by those who entered were left in the Lord's house. They have been hung up in the Church until this time, that they might not be able to deny it : and although they sent several times Dynamius the soldier [8], as well as the Commander [9] of the city police, desiring to take them away, we would not allow it, until the circumstance was known to all.

Now if an order has been given that we should be persecuted we are all ready to suffer martyrdom. But if it be not by order of Augustus, we desire Maximus the Prefect of Egypt and all the city magistrates to request of him that they may not again be suffered thus to assail us. And we desire also that this our petition may be presented to him, that they may not attempt to bring in hither any other Bishop : for • we have resisted unto death [10], desiring to have the most Reverend Athanasius, whom God gave us at the beginning, according to the succession of our fathers; whom also the most religious Augustus Constantius himself sent to us with letters and oaths. And we believe that when his Piety is informed of what has taken place, he will be greatly displeased, and will do nothing contrary to his oaths, but will again give orders that our Bishop Athanasius shall remain with us.

To the Consuls to be elected [11] after the Consulship of the most illustrious Arbæthion and Collianus [12], on the seventeenth Mechir [13], which is the day before the Ides of February.

---

[8] στρατηγοῦ. There were two στρατηγοὶ or duumvirs at the head of the police force at Alexandria ; they are mentioned in the plural in Euseb. vii. 11, where S. Dionysius speaks of their seizing him. vid. Du Cange, *Gloss. Græc. in voc.*

[9] τὸν τῆς τάξεως, supr. § 61, στρατιώτου.

[10] *Apol. Ar.* 38.

[11] Since the Consuls came into office on the first of January, and were proclaimed in each city, it is strange that the Alexandrians here speak in February as if ignorant of their names. The phrase, however, is found elsewhere. Thus in this very year the *Chron. Aceph.* dates Jan. 5 as 'post Consulatum Arbitionis et Loliani.' And in Socr. *Hist.* ii. 29, in the instance of the year 351, when there were no Consuls, and in 346, when there was a difference on the subject between the Emperors who were eventually themselves Consuls, the first months are dated in like manner from the Consuls of the foregoing year.

[12] Lollianus. [13] Feb. 12, Leap year ; see note below, at the end of Introd. to *Letters.*

FOUR DISCOURSES AGAINST
THE ARIANS

Written between 356 and 360.

There is no absolutely conclusive evidence as to the date of these Discourses, in fact they would appear from the language of ii. 1 to have been issued at intervals. The best judges, however, are agreed in assigning them to the fruitful period of the 'third exile.' The Discourses cannot indeed be identified with the lost account of the Arian heresy addressed to certain Egyptian monks (see Introd. to Arian Hist. *supra*); but the demand for such a treatise may have set Athanasius upon the composition of a more comprehensive refutation of the heresy. It was only at this period ('Blasphemy' of Sirmium, 357) that the doctrinal controversy began to emerge from the mass of personalities and intrigues which had encumbered it for the first generation after the great Council; only now that the various parties were beginning to formulate their position; only now that the great mass of Eastern 'Conservatism' was beginning to see the nature of the issue as between the Nicene doctrine and the essential Arianism of its more resolute opponents. The situation seemed to clear, the time had come for gathering up the issues of the combat and striking a decisive blow. To this situation of affairs the treatise before us exactly corresponds. Characteristic of this period is the anxiety to conciliate and win over the so-called semi-Arians (of the type of Basil of Ancyra) who stumbled at the ὁμοούσιον, but whose fundamental agreement with Athanasius was daily becoming more clear. Accordingly we find that Athanasius pointedly avoids the famous test word in these Discourses[1] (with the exception of the fourth : see *Orat.* i. 20, note 5, 58, note 10 : it only occurs i. 9, note 12, but see *Orat.* iv. 9, 12), and even adopts (not as fully adequate *de Syn.* 53, but as true so far as it goes), the 'semi-Arian' formula 'like in essence' (*Or.* i. 21, note 8, 20, 26, iii. 26, he does not use the single compound word ὁμοιούσιος : see further, Introd. to *de Synodis*). Although, therefore, demonstrative proof is lacking, there is tolerable certainty as to the date of our Discourses. And their purpose is no less manifest : they are a decisive blow of the kind described above, aimed at the very centre of the question, and calculated to sever the abnormal alliance between conservatives who really thought with Athanasius and men like Valens or Eudoxius, whose real convictions, so far as they had any, were Arian. Moreover they gather up all the threads of controversy against Arianism proper, refute its appeal to Scripture, and leave on record for all time the issues of the great doctrinal contest of the fourth century. They have naturally become, as Montfaucon observes, the mine whence subsequent defenders of the Divinity of our Redeemer have drawn their material. There are doubtless arguments which a modern writer would scarcely adopt (e.g. ii. 63, iii. 65 *init.*, &c.), and the repeated labelling of the Arians as madmen ('fanatics' in this translation), enemies of Christ, disciples of Satan, &c., &c., is at once tedious and by its very frequency unimpressive (see ii. 43 note 8 for Newman's famous list of animal nicknames). But the serious reader will pass *sicco pede* over such features, and will appreciate 'the richness, fulness, and versatility' of the use of Scripture, 'the steady grasp of certain primary truths, especially of the Divine Unity and of Christ's real or genuine natural and Divine Sonship (i. 15, ii. 2—5, 22, 23, 73, iii. 62), the keen penetration with which Arian objections are analysed (i. 14, 27, 29, ii. 26, iii. 59), Arian imputations disclaimed, Arian statements old and new, the bolder and the more cautious, compared, Arian evasions pointed out, Arian logic traced to its conclusions, and Arianism shewn to be inconsistent, irreverent' (Bright, Introd. p. lxviii.). Above all, we see in

---

[1] Not that he was willing to suppress the term and surrender the Nicene cause, far from it ; but he sees the relative importance of things and words. This shews the absurdity of the taunt, that the Nicene theologians fought ferociously over a single 'iota.'

these Discourses what strikes us in all the writings of Athanasius from the *de Incarnatione* to the end, his firm hold of the Soteriological aspect of the question at issue, of its vital importance to the reality of Redemption and Grace, to the reality of the knowledge of God vouchsafed to sinful man in Christ (ii. 69, 70, cf. i. 35, 49, 50, ii. 67, &c., &c). The Theology and Christology of Athanasius is rooted in the idea of Redemption : our fellowship with God, our adoption as sons of God, would be unaccomplished, had not Christ imparted to us what was HIS OWN to give (i. 12, 16, cf. Harnack, *Dogmengesch.*, 2. 205). Among other points of interest we may observe the anticipatory rejection of the later heresies of Macedonius (i. 48, iii. 24), Nestorius (ii. 8 note 3, &c., and the frequent application of θεοτόκος to the B.M.V. iii. 14, 29, &c.), and Eutyches (ii. 10 note 6, &c.), the emphatic vindication of worship as the exclusive prerogative of Divinity (ii. 23, iii. 32, 'we *invoke* no creature') and of the *unique* sinless conception of Christ (iii. 33), lastly the cautious and reasonable discussion (iii. 42 *sqq.*) of our Saviour's human knowledge.

Although apparently composed at different times (see above) the four ' Discourses ' form a single work. The fourth alone ends with the usual doxology, thus announcing itself as the conclusion of the four-fold treatise. At the same time, the relation of the fourth Discourse to the others is by no means clear. It is largely occupied with a polemic against a heresy at the opposite extreme from Arianism, Monarchianism in one or other of its forms. Newman, in his introductory excursus, expresses the opinion that it consists of a series of fragmentary notes against several heresies, which for some unknown reason came to be incorporated, possibly by Athanasius himself or by his secretaries, in the great anti-Arian Manifesto. Zahn *Marcell.* pp. 198—208 shews convincingly that the system of Marcellus, either in itself or in its supposed logical consequences, is the main object of criticism all along. If we trace throughout the Discourses the purpose of conciliating the ' Conservative ' and Semi-Arian party, we can well understand that Athanasius may have appended to them a section directed against Monarchianism, which, in the persons of Marcellus and Photinus (whose names, however, are characteristically absent), must have been felt by him to be a legitimate stumbling-block in their path toward peace. At any rate the fourth oration has always been associated with the others as forming part of one work.

There is, however, some confusion in early citations, in MSS., and in early editions as to the number of ' Orations ' against the Arians. The confusion is due to the frequent practice of reckoning the *Ep. Æg.* as the first (or in one or two cases as the fourth; the Basel MS. counts *de Incar. c. Ar.* as the fifth, and our fourth as the sixth). Montfaucon (*Monitum* Migne xxvi. p. 10) ascribes this to the arrangement in many MSS. by which the *Ep. Æg.* comes immediately before the ' Orations ' Being itself directed against the Arians it has come to be labelled λόγος πρῶτος.

The title ' Orations ' is consecrated by long use, and cannot be displaced, but it is unfortunate as implying, to our ears, oratorical delivery, for which the Discourses were never meant. The original Greek term (λόγος) is common to these Discourses with the *c. Gentes, de Incarnatione, &c., &c.*

A full analysis of these Discourses is given by Bishop Kaye (*Council of Nicæa,* in 'Works,' vol. v.) ; his strictures on Newman's notes are occasionally very just. The Discourses are more concisely analysed by Ceillier (vol. v., pp. 218, *sqq.*) See also Dorner, *Doctr. of Person of Christ,* Part I., Div. 3, i. 3. The headings of Newman, prefixed to the ' chapters,' will supply the place of an analysis for readers of this volume.

The translation which follows is that of Cardinal Newman, published in 1844 (the year before his secession), in the Oxford ' Library of the Fathers.' The copious and elaborate notes and discussions which accompany it have always been acknowledged to be a masterpiece of their illustrious author. The modern reader sits down to study Athanasius, and rises from his task filled with Newman. Like all the work of Newman included in this volume, translation and notes alike have been touched by the present editor with a reverent and a sparing hand. The translation, which shews great care and fidelity, coupled with remarkable ingenuity and close study of characteristic phrases and idioms, has been, with two main exceptions, but little altered. These exceptions are (1) the substitution throughout of ' essence ' for ' substance,' (2) an attempt to remedy the most unfortunate, though not unconsidered, confusion of γεννητός and γενητός under the single rendering ' generate.' A good rendering for the latter word and its cognates is indeed not easy to find (see above, p. 149) ; but it was felt impossible, even in deference to so great a name, after the note in Lightfoot's *Ignatius,* to leave the matter as it stood.

With regard to the notes, the historical matter and the abundant cross-references have been thoroughly overhauled and in some cases modified without indication of the change. Moreover, some theological notes of minor importance have been expunged to economise space, while, for the same reason, mere references have in many cases been reluctantly substituted for the extensive patristic quotations. The notes to *Orat.* iv., which are less important theologically, have been very much curtailed. With these exceptions, all doctrinal notes proper have been left exactly as they first appeared, even where they maintain views which appear untenable : any additions or explanations by the present editor are enclosed in square brackets, which also in a very few cases denote additional or corrected references made under Dr. Pusey's authority in the reprint of 1877.

It is unnecessary to apologise to the reader for the hesitation which has been felt in touching, even to this slight extent, the work of John Henry Newman. The only apology which the editor of this volume cares to offer is for having done the little that seemed absolutely needed.

It may be added that the Cardinal published in 1881 (4th ed., 1888) a ' free translation' of the first three Discourses, based upon the Oxford translation, but of a totally different kind, amounting to a somewhat highly condensed paraphrase of the original in the luminous English of the Cardinal himself, rather than bound, as the older translation is, to the style of Athanasius. The new rendering includes the *de Decretis* and the *de Synodis;* almost all the notes are in a second volume.

The most convenient edition of the Greek text is that of Dr. Bright (Oxford, 1872), with an Introduction on the Life and Writings of Athanasius (rewritten for D. C. B., vol. i., pp. 179 *sqq.*).

TABLE OF CONTENTS OF THE FOUR DISCOURSES.

The following Table of Contents of *Orat.* i.—iii. (the contents of *Orat.* iv. will be tabulated at the end of *Exc. C.*) must be supplemented by the fuller headings prefixed to Newman's ' chapters.'

DISCOURSE I

CHAPTER I.

INTRODUCTION.

Reason for writing; certain persons indifferent about Arianism; Arians not Christians, because sectaries always take the name of their founder.

1. OF all other heresies which have departed from the truth it is acknowledged that they have but devised[1] a madness, and their irreligiousness has long since become notorious to all men. For that[2] their authors went out from us, it plainly follows, as the blessed John has written, that they never thought nor now think with us. Wherefore, as saith the Saviour, in that they gather not with us, they scatter with the devil, and keep an eye on those who slumber, that, by this second sowing of their own mortal poison, they may have companions in death. But, whereas one heresy, and that the last, which has now risen as harbinger[3] of Antichrist, the Arian, as it is called, considering that other heresies, her elder sisters, have been openly proscribed, in her craft and cunning, affects to array herself in Scripture language[4], like her father

the devil, and is forcing her way back into the Church's paradise,—that with the pretence of Christianity, her smooth sophistry (for reason she has none) may deceive men into wrong thoughts of Christ,—nay, since she has already seduced certain of the foolish, not only to corrupt their ears, but even to take and eat with Eve, till in their ignorance which ensues they think bitter sweet, and admire this loathsome heresy, on this account I have thought it necessary, at your request, to unrip 'the folds of its breast-plate[5],' and to shew the ill savour of its folly. So while those who are far from it may continue to shun it, those whom it has deceived may repent; and, opening the eyes of their heart, may understand that darkness is not light, nor falsehood truth, nor Arianism good; nay, that those[6] who call these men Christians are in great and grievous error, as neither having studied Scripture, nor understanding Christianity at all, and the faith which it contains.

2. For what have they discovered in this heresy like to the religious Faith, that they vainly talk as if its supporters said no evil? This in truth is to call even Caiaphas[7] a Christian, and to reckon the traitor Judas still

---

[1] ἐπινοήσασαι. This is almost a technical word, and has occurred again and again already, as descriptive of heretical teaching in opposition to the received traditionary doctrine. It is also found *passim* in other writers. Thus Socrates, speaking of the decree of the Council of Alexandria, 362, against Apollinaris; 'for not originating, ἐπινοήσαντες, any *novel* devotion, did they introduce it into the Church, but what from the beginning the *Ecclesiastical Tradition* declared.' *Hist.* iii. 7. The sense of the word ἐπίνοια which will come into consideration below, is akin to this, being the view taken by the mind of an object independent of (whether or not correspondent to) the object itself. [But see Bigg. *B. L.* p. 168, *sq.*]

[2] τὸ γὰρ ἐξελθεῖν . . . . δῆλον ἂν εἴη, i.e. τῷ and so infr. § 43. τὸ δὲ καὶ προσκυνεῖσθαι . . . . δῆλον ἂν εἴη.

[3] de Syn. 5.

[4] Vid. infr. § 4 fin. That heresies before the Arian appealed to Scripture we learn from Tertullian, *de Præscr.* 42, who warns Catholics against indulging themselves in their own view of isolated texts against the voice of the Catholic Church. vid. also Vincentius, who specifies *obiter* Sabellius and Novatian. *Commonit.* 2. Still Arianism was contrasted with other heresies on this point, as in these two respects; (1.) they appealed to a *secret tradition*, unknown, even to most of the Apostles, as the Gnostics, Iren. *Hær.* iii. 1 or they professed a gift of prophecy introducing fresh *revelations*, as Montanists, *de Syn.* 4, and Manichees, Aug. *contr. Faust.* xxxii. 6. (2.) The Arians availed themselves of certain texts as objections, argued keenly and plausibly from them, and would not be driven from them. *Orat.* ii. § 18. c. Epiph. *Hær.* 69. 15. Or rather they took some words of Scripture, and made their own deductions from them; viz. 'Son,' 'made,' 'exalted,' &c. 'Making their private irreligiousness as if a rule, they misinterpret all the divine oracles by it.' *Orat.* i.

[5] § 52. vid. also Epiph. *Hær.* 76. 5 fin. Hence we hear so much of their θρυλλῆται φωναί, λέξεις, ἔπη, ῥητά, sayings in general circulation, which were commonly founded on some particular text. e.g. infr., § 22, 'amply providing themselves with words of craft, they used to go about,' &c. Also ἄνω καὶ κάτω περιφέροντες, *de Decr.* § 13. τῷ ῥητῷ τεθρυλλήκασι τὰ πανταχοῦ. *Orat.* 2. § 18. τὸ πολυθρύλλητον σόφισμα, Basil. *contr. Eunom.* ii. 14. τὴν πολυθρύλλητον διαλεκτικήν, Nyssen. *contr. Eun.* iii. p. 125. τὴν θρυλλουμένην ἀπορροήν, Cyril. *Dial.* iv. p. 505. τὴν πολυθρύλλητον φώνην, Socr. ii. 43.   5 Job xli. 13 (v. 4. LXX).

[6] These Orations and Discourses seem written to shew the vital importance of the point in controversy, and the unchristian character of the heresy, without reference to the word ὁμοούσιον. He has [elsewhere] insisted that the enforcement of the symbol was but the rejection of the heresy, and accordingly he is here content to bring out the Catholic sense, as feeling that, if persons understood and embraced it, they would not scruple at the word. He seems to allude to what may be called the liberal or indifferent feeling as swaying the person for whom he writes. also infr. § 7 fin. § 9. § 10 init. § 15 fin. § 17. § 21. § 23. He mentions *in Apollin.* i. 6. one Rhetorius, who was an Egyptian, whose opinion, he says, it was 'fearful to mention.' S. Augustine tells us that this man taught that 'all heresies were in the right path, and spoke truth,' 'which,' he adds, 'is so absurd as to seem to me incredible.' *Hær.* 72. vid. also Philastr. *Hær.* 91.

[7] de Decr. §§ 2, 24, 27.

among the Apostles, and to say that they who asked Barabbas instead of the Saviour did no evil, and to recommend Hymenæus and Alexander as right-minded men, and as if the Apostle slandered them. But neither can a Christian bear to hear this, nor can he consider the man who dared to say it sane in his understanding. For with them for Christ is Arius, as with the Manichees Manichæus ; and for Moses and the other saints they have made the discovery of one Sotades[8], a man whom even Gentiles laugh at, and of the daughter of Herodias. For of the one has Arius imitated the dissolute and effeminate tone, in writing Thaliæ on his model ; and the other he has rivalled in her dance, reeling and frolicking in his blasphemies against the Saviour ; till the victims of his heresy lose their wits and go foolish, and change the Name of the Lord of glory into the likeness of the 'image of corruptible man[9],' and for Christians come to be called Arians, bearing this badge of their irreligion. For let them not excuse themselves ; nor retort their disgrace on those who are not as they, calling Christians after the names of their teachers[10], that they themselves may appear to have that Name in the same way. Nor let them make a jest of it, when they feel shame at their disgraceful appellation ; rather, if they be ashamed, let them hide their faces, or let them recoil from their own irreligion. For never at any time did Christian people take their title from the Bishops among them, but from the Lord, on whom we rest our faith. Thus, though the blessed Apostles have become our teachers, and have ministered the Saviour's Gospel, yet not from them have we our title, but from Christ we are and are named Christians. But for those who derive the faith which they profess from others, good reason is it they should bear their name, whose property they have become[1].

3. Yes surely ; while all of us are and are called Christians after Christ, Marcion broached a heresy a long time since and was cast out ; and those who continued with him who ejected him remained Christians ; but those who followed Marcion were called Christians no more, but henceforth Marcionites. Thus Valentinus also, and Basilides, and Manichæus, and Simon Magus, have imparted their own name to their followers ; and some are accosted as Valentinians, or as Basilidians, or as Manichees, or as Simonians ; and others, Cataphrygians from Phrygia, and from Novatus Novatians. So too Meletius, when ejected by Peter the Bishop and Martyr, called his party no longer Christians, but Meletians[2], and so in consequence when Alexander of blessed memory had cast out Arius, those who remained with Alexander, remained Christians ; but those who went out with Arius, left the Saviour's Name to us who were with Alexander, and as to them they were henceforward denominated Arians. Behold then, after Alexander's death too, those who communicate with his successor Athanasius, and those with whom the said Athanasius communicates, are instances of the same rule ; none of them bear his name, nor is he named from them, but all in like manner, and as is usual, are called Christians. For though we have a succession of teachers and become their disciples, yet, because we are taught by them the things of Christ, we both are, and are called, Christians all the same. But those who follow the heretics, though they have innumerable successors in their heresy, yet anyhow bear the name of him who devised it. Thus, though Arius be dead, and many of his party have succeeded him, yet those who think with him, as being known from Arius, are called Arians. And, what is a remarkable

---

8 *de Syn.* § 1.   9 Vid. Hil. *de Trin.*viii. 28 ; Rom. i. 25.
10 He seems to allude to Catholics being called Athanasians ; vid. however next ?. Two distinctions are drawn between such a title as applied to Catholics, and again to heretics, when they are taken by Catholics as a *note* against them. S. Augustine says, '*Arians* call Catholics Athanasians or Homoüsians, *not other heretics* too. But ye not only by Catholics *but also by heretics*, those who agree with you and those who disagree, are called Pelagians ; as *even by heresies* are Arians called Arians. But ye, and ye only, call us Traducianists, as Arians call us Homoüsians, as Donatists Macarians, as Manichees Pharisees, and as the other heretics use various titles.' *Op. imp.* i. 75. It may be added that the heretical name *adheres*, the Catholic dies away. S. Chrysostom draws a second distinction, 'Are we divided from the Church? have we heresiarchs? are we called from man? is there any leader to us, as to one there is Marcion, to another Manichæus, to another Arius, to another some other author of heresy? for if we too have the name of any, still it is not those who began the heresy, *but our superiors and governors of the Church.* We have not "teachers upon earth,"' &c. in Act. *Ap. Hom.* 33 fin.
1 Vid. foregoing note. Also, 'Let us become His disciples, and learn to live according to Christianity ; for whoso is called by other name besides this, is not of God.' Ignat *ad Magn.* 10. Hegesippus speaks of 'Menandrians, and Marcionites, and Carpocratians, and Valentinians, and Basilidians, and Saturnilians,'

who 'each in his own way and that a different one brought in his own doctrine.' Euseb. *Hist.* iv. 22. 'There are, and there have been, my friends, many who have taught atheistic and blasphemous words and deeds, coming in the name of Jesus ; and they are called by us from the appellation of the men, whence each doctrine and opinion began. . . . Some are called Marcians, others Valentinians, others Basilidians, others Saturnilians,' &c. Justin. *Tryph.* 35. Iren. *Hær.* i. 23. 'When men are called Phrygians, or Novatians, or Valentinians, or Marcionites, or Anthropians, or by any other name, they cease to be Christians ; for they have lost Christ's Name, and clothe themselves in human and foreign titles.' Lact. *Inst.* iv. 30. 'A. How are you a Christian, to whom it is not even granted to bear the name of Christian? for you are not called Christian but Marcionite. M. And you are called of the Catholic Church ; therefore ye are not Christians either. A. Did we profess man's name, you would have spoken to the point ; but if we are called from being all over the world, what is there bad in this?' Adamant. *Dial.* § 1, p. 809. Epiph. *Hær.* 42. p. 366, ibid. 70. 15. vid. also *Hær.* 75. 6 fin. Cyril *Cat.* xviii. 26. 'Christian is my name, Catholic my surname.' Pacian. *Ep.* 1. 'If you ever hear those who are called Christians, named, not from the Lord Jesus Christ, but from some one else, say Marcionites, Valentinians, Mountaineers, Campestrians, know that it is not Christ's Church, but the synagogue of Antichrist.' Jerom. *adv. Lucif.* fin.
2 Vid. *de Syn.* 12. [Prolegg. ch. ii. § 2.]

evidence of this, those of the Greeks who even at this time come into the Church, on giving up the superstition of idols, take the name, not of their catechists, but of the Saviour, and begin to be called Christians instead of Greeks; while those of them who go off to the heretics, and again all who from the Church change to this heresy, abandon Christ's name, and henceforth are called Arians, as no longer holding Christ's faith, but having inherited Arius's madness.

4. How then can they be Christians, who for Christians are Ario-maniacs [3]? or how are they of the Catholic Church, who have shaken off the Apostolical faith, and become authors of fresh evils? who, after abandoning the oracles of divine Scripture, call Arius's Thaliæ a new wisdom? and with reason too, for they are announcing a new heresy. And hence a man may marvel, that, whereas many have written many treatises and abundant homilies upon the Old Testament and the New, yet in none of them is a Thalia found; nay nor among the more respectable of the Gentiles, but among those only who sing such strains over their cups, amid cheers and jokes, when men are merry, that the rest may laugh; till this marvellous Arius, taking no grave pattern, and ignorant even of what is respectable, while he stole largely from other heresies, would be original in the ludicrous, with none but Sotades for his rival. For what beseemed him more, when he would dance forth against the Saviour, than to throw his wretched words of irreligion into dissolute and loose metres? that, while 'a man,' as Wisdom says, 'is known from the utterance of his word [4],' so from those numbers should be seen the writer's effeminate soul and corruption of thought [5]. In truth, that crafty one did not escape detection; but, for all his many writhings to and fro, like the serpent, he did but fall into the error of the Pharisees. They, that they might transgress the Law, pretended to be anxious for the words of the Law, and that they might deny the expected and then present Lord, were hypocritical with God's name, and were convicted

of blaspheming when they said, 'Why dost Thou, being a man, make Thyself God,' and sayest, 'I and the Father are one [6]?' And so too, this counterfeit and Sotadean Arius, feigns to speak of God, introducing Scripture language [7], but is on all sides recognised as godless [8] Arius, denying the Son, and reckoning Him among the creatures.

CHAPTER II.

EXTRACTS FROM THE THALIA OF ARIUS.

Arius maintains that God became a Father, and the Son was not always; the Son out of nothing; once He was not; He was not before his generation; He was created; named Wisdom and Word after God's attributes; made that He might make us; one out of many powers of God; alterable; exalted on God's foreknowledge of what He was to be; not very God; but called so as others by participation; foreign in essence from the Father; does not know or see the Father; does not know Himself.

5. Now the commencement of Arius's Thalia and flippancy, effeminate in tune and nature, runs thus:—

'According to faith of God's elect, God's prudent ones,
Holy children, rightly dividing, God's Holy Spirit receiving,
Have I learned this from the partakers of wisdom,
Accomplished, divinely taught, and wise in all things.
Along their track, have I been walking, with like opinions,
I the very famous, the much suffering for God's glory;
And taught of God, I have acquired wisdom and knowledge.'

And the mockeries which he utters in it, repulsive and most irreligious, are such as these [1]:—'God was not always a Father;' but 'once God was alone, and not yet a Father, but afterwards He became a Father.' 'The Son was not always;' for, whereas all things were made out of nothing, and all existing creatures and works were made, so the Word of God Himself was 'made out of nothing,' and 'once He was not,' and 'He was not before His

---

[3] *de Syn.* 13, note 4. Manes also was called mad; 'Thou must hate all heretics, but especially him who even in name is a maniac.' Cyril. *Catech.* vi. 20, vid. also ibid. 24 fin.—a play upon the name, vid. *de Syn.* 26, 'Scotinus.'

[4] Vid. Ecclus. iv. 24.

[5] It is very difficult to gain a clear idea of the character of Arius. [Prolegg. ch. ii. § 2.] Epiphanius's account of Arius is as follows:—' From elation of mind the old man swerved from the mark. He was in stature very tall, downcast in visage, with manners like wily serpent, captivitating to every guileless heart by that same crafty bearing. For ever habited in cloke and vest, he was pleasant of address, ever persuading souls and flattering; wherefore what was his very first work but to withdraw from the Church in one body as many as seven hundred women who professed virginity?' *Hær.* 69. 3, cf. ib. § 9 for a strange description of Arius attributed to Constantine, also printed in the collections of councils: Hard. i. 457.

[6] John x. 30.   [7] § 1, note 4.

[8] And so godless or atheist Aetius, *de Syn.* 6, note 3, cf. note on *de Decr.* 1, for an explanation of the word. In like manner Athan. says, *ad Serap.* iii. 2, that if a man says 'that the Son is a creature, who is Word and Wisdom, and the Expression, and the Radiance, whom whoso seeth seeth the Father,' he falls under the text, 'Whoso denieth the Son, the same hath not the Father.' 'Such a one,' he continues, 'will in no long time say, *as the fool, There is no God.*' In like manner he speaks of those who think the Son to be the Spirit as 'without (ἔξω) the Holy Trinity, and atheists' (*Serap.* iv. 6), because they really do not believe in the God *that is,* and there is none other but He. Cf. also *Serap.* i. 30. Eustathius speaks of the Arians as ἀνθρώπους ἀθέους, who were attempting κρατῆσαι τοῦ θείου. ap. Theod. *Hist.* i. 7. p. 760. Naz. speaks of the heathen πολύθεος ἀθεία. *Orat.* 25. 15. and he calls faith and regeneration 'a denial of atheism, ἀθείας, and a confession of godhead, θεότητος,' *Orat.* 23. 12. He calls Lucius, the Alexandrian Anti-pope, on account of his *cruelties,* 'this second Arius, the more copious river of the atheistic spring, τῆς ἀθέου πηγῆς.' *Orat.* 25. 11. Palladius, the Imperial officer, is ἀνὴρ ἀθεος. ibid. 12.

[1] *de Syn.* § 15. [where the metre of the Thalia is discussed in a note.]

origination,' but He as others 'had an origin of creation.' ' For God,' he says, ·was alone, and the Word as yet was not, nor the Wisdom. Then, wishing to form us, thereupon He made a certain one, and named Him Word and Wisdom and Son, that He might form us by means of Him.' Accordingly, he says that there are two wisdoms, first, the attribute co-existent with God, and next, that in this wisdom the Son was originated, and was only named Wisdom and Word as partaking of it. ' For Wisdom,' saith he, ' by the will of the wise God, had its existence in Wisdom.' In like manner, he says, that there is another Word in God besides the Son, and that the Son again, as partaking of it, is named Word and Son according to grace. And this too is an idea proper to their heresy, as shewn in other works of theirs, that there are many powers ; one of which is God's own by nature and eternal ; but that Christ, on the other hand, is not the true power of God ; but, as others, one of the so-called powers, one of which, namely, the locust and the caterpillar [2], is called in Scripture, not merely the power, but the ' great power.' The others are many and are like the Son, and of them David speaks in the Psalms, when he says, ' The Lord of hosts ' or ' powers [3].' And by nature, as all others, so the Word Himself is alterable, and remains good by His own free will, while He chooseth ; when, however, He wills, He can alter as we can, as being of an alterable nature. For 'therefore,' saith he, ' as foreknowing that He would be good, did God by anticipation bestow on Him this glory, which afterwards, as man, He attained from virtue. Thus in consequence of His works fore-known [4], did God bring it to pass that He, being such, should come to be.'

6. Moreover he has dared to say, that ' the Word is not the very God ;' 'though He is called God, yet He is not very God,' but ' by participation of grace, He, as others, is God only in name.' And, whereas all beings are foreign and different from God in essence, so too is ' the Word alien and unlike in all things to the Father's essence and propriety,' but belongs to things originated and created, and is one of these. Afterwards, as though he had succeeded to the devil's recklessness, he has stated in his Thalia, that ' even to the Son the Father is invisible,' and ' the Word cannot perfectly and exactly either see or know His own Father;' but even what He knows and what He sees, He knows and sees ' in proportion to His own measure,' as we also know according to our own power. For the Son, too, he says,

not only knows not the Father exactly, for He fails in comprehension [5], but ' He knows not even His own essence ;'—and that ' the essences of the Father and the Son and the Holy Ghost, are separate in nature, and estranged, and disconnected, and alien [6], and without participation of each other [7];' and, in his own words, ' utterly unlike from each other in essence and glory, unto infinity.' Thus as to ' likeness of glory and essence,' he says that the Word is entirely diverse from both the Father and the Holy Ghost. With such words hath the irreligious spoken; maintaining that the Son is distinct by Himself, and in no respect partaker of the Father. These are portions of Arius's fables as they occur in that jocose composition.

7. Who is there that hears all this, nay, the tune of the Thalia, but must hate, and justly hate, this Arius jesting on such matters as on a stage [8]? who but must regard him, when he pretends to name God and speak of God, but as the serpent counselling the woman? who, on reading what follows in his work, but must discern in his irreligious doctrine that error, into which by his sophistries the serpent in the sequel seduced the woman? who at such blasphemies is not transported? ' The heaven,' as the Prophet says, ' was astonished, and the earth shuddered [9]' at the transgression of the Law. But the sun, with greater horror, impatient of the bodily contumelies, which the common Lord of all voluntarily endured for us, turned away, and recalling his rays made that day sunless. And shall not all human kind at Arius's blasphemies be struck speech-less, and stop their ears, and shut their eyes, to escape hearing them or seeing their author? Rather, will not the Lord Himself have reason to denounce men so irreligious, nay, so un-thankful, in the words which He has already uttered by the prophet Hosea, 'Woe unto them, for they have fled from Me ; destruction upon

<hr/>

5 Vid. *de Syn.* 15, note 6. καταληψις was originally a Stoic word, and even when considered perfect, was, properly speaking, attributable only to an imperfect being. For it is used in contrast to the Platonic doctrine of ιδεαι, to express the hold of things obtained by the mind through the senses; it being a Stoical maxim, nihil esse in intellectu quod non fuerit in sensu. In this sense it is also used by the Fathers, to mean real and certain knowledge after inquiry, though it is also ascribed to Almighty God. As to the position of Arius, since we are told in Scripture that none 'knoweth the things of a man save the spirit of man which is in him,' if καταληψις be an exact and complete knowledge of the object of contemplation, to deny that the Son comprehended the Father, was to deny that He was in the Father, i.e. the doctrine of the περιχωρησις, *de Syn.* 15, ανεπιμικτοι, or to maintain that He was a distinct, and therefore a created, being. On the o her hand Scripture asserts that, as the Holy Spirit which is in God, 'searcheth all things, yea, the deep things of God,' so the Son, as being 'in the bosom of the Father,' alone 'hath declared Him.' vid. Clement. *Strom.* v. 12. And thus Athan. speaking of Mark xiii. 32, 'If the Son is in the Father and the Father in the Son, and the Father knows the day and the hour, it is plain that the Son too, being in the Father, and knowing the things in the Father, Himself also knows the day and the hour." *Orat.* iii. 44.
6 *de Decr.* 25, note 2. 7 *de Syn.* 15.
8 Ep. *Encycl.* 6; Epiph. *Hær.* 73. 1. 9 Jer. ii. 12.

<hr/>

2 *de Syn.* § 18; Joel ii. 25. 3 Ps. xxiv. 10.
4 *de Syn.* 26, note 7, *de Decr.* 6, note 8.

them, for they have transgressed against Me; though I have redeemed them, yet they have spoken lies against Me[10].' And soon after, 'They imagine mischief against Me; they turn away to nothing[11].' For to turn away from the Word of God, which is, and to fashion to themselves one that is not, is to fall to what is nothing. For this was why the Ecumenical[1] Council, when Arius thus spoke, cast him from the Church, and anathematized him, as impatient of such irreligion. And ever since has Arius's error been reckoned for a heresy more than ordinary, being known as Christ's foe, and harbinger[2] of Antichrist. Though then so great a condemnation be itself of special weight to make men flee from that irreligious heresy[3], as I said above, yet since certain persons called Christian, either in ignorance or pretence, think it, as I then said, little different from the Truth, and call its professors Christians; proceed we to put some questions to them, according to our powers, thereby to expose the unscrupulousness of the heresy. Perhaps, when thus caught, they will be silenced, and flee from it, as from the sight of a serpent.

CHAPTER III.

THE IMPORTANCE OF THE SUBJECT.

The Arians affect Scripture language, but their doctrine new, as well as unscriptural. Statement of the Catholic doctrine, that the Son is proper to the Father's substance, and eternal. Restatement of Arianism in contrast, that He is a creature with a beginning: the controversy comes to this issue, whether one whom we are to believe in as God, can be so in name only, and is merely a creature. What pretence then for being indifferent in the controversy? The Arians rely on state patronage, and dare not avow their tenets.

8. If then the use of certain phrases of divine Scripture changes, in their opinion, the blasphemy of the Thalia into reverent language, of course they ought also to deny Christ with the present Jews, when they see how they study the Law and the Prophets; perhaps too they will deny the Law[1] and the Prophets like Manichees[2], because the latter read some portions of the Gospels. If such bewilderment and empty speaking be from ignorance, Scripture will teach them, that the devil, the author of heresies, because of the ill savour which attaches to

evil, borrows Scripture language, as a cloak wherewith to sow the ground with his own poison also, and to seduce the simple. Thus he deceived Eve; thus he framed former heresies; thus he persuaded Arius at this time to make a show of speaking against those former ones, that he might introduce his own without observation. And yet, after all, the man of craft did not escape. For being irreligious towards the Word of God, he lost his all at once[2a], and betrayed to all men his ignorance of other heresies too[3]; and having not a particle of truth in his belief, does but pretend to it. For how can he speak truth concerning the Father, who denies the Son, that reveals concerning Him? or how can he be orthodox concerning the Spirit, while he speaks profanely of the Word that supplies the Spirit? and who will trust him concerning the Resurrection, denying, as he does, Christ for us the first-begotten from the dead? and how shall he not err in respect to His incarnate presence, who is simply ignorant of the Son's genuine and true generation from the Father? For thus, the former Jews also, denying the Word, and saying, 'We have no king but Cæsar[4],' were forthwith stripped of all they had, and forfeited the light of the Lamp, the odour of ointment, knowledge of prophecy, and the Truth itself; till now they understand nothing, but are walking as in darkness. For who was ever yet a hearer of such a doctrine[5]? or whence or from whom did the abettors and hirelings[6] of the heresy gain it? who thus expounded to them when they were at school[7]? who told them, 'Abandon the worship of the creation, and then draw near and worship a creature and a work[8]?' But if they themselves own that they have heard it now for the first time, how can they deny that this heresy is foreign, and not from our fathers[9]? But wha is not from our fathers, but has come to light in this day, how can it be but that of which the blessed Paul[10] has foretold, that 'in the latter times some shall depart from the sound faith,

---

[10] Hos. vii. 13.   [11] Ib. 15. lxx.
[1] de Decr. 27, note 1.   [2] Ib. 3, note 1, § 1, note 3.
[3] And so Vigilius of the heresies about the Incarnation, Etiamsi in erroris eorum destructionem nulli conderentur libri, hoc ipsum solum, quod hæretici sunt pronunciati, orthodoxorum securitati sufficeret. contr. Eutych. i. p. 494.   [1] de Syn. 33.
[2] Faustus, in August. contr. Faust. ii. 1. admits the Gospels (vid. Beausobre Manich. t. i. p. 291, &c.), but denies that they were written by the reputed authors. ibid. xxxii. 2. but nescio quibus Semi-judæis. ibid. xxxiii. 3. Accordingly they thought themselves at liberty to reject or correct parts of them. They rejected many of the facts, e.g. our Lord's nativity, circumcision, baptism, temptation, &c. ibid. xxxii. 6.

[2a] de Decr. 1, note 6.
[3] [A note on the intimate mutual connexion of all heresies is omitted here.]
[4] Joh. xix. 15.   [5] de Decr. 7, note 2.
[6] δωροδόκοι, and so κέρδος τῆς φιλοχρηματίας, infr. §53. He mentions προστασίας φίλων, § 10. And so S. Hilary speaks of the exemptions from taxes which Constantius granted the Clergy as a bribe to Arianize; contr. Const. 10. And again, of resisting Constantius as hostem blandientem, qui non dorsa cædit, sed ventrem palpat, non proscribit ad vitam, sed ditat in mortem, non caput gladio desecat, sed animum auro occidit. ibid. 5. vid. Coustant. in loc. Liberius says the same, Theod H. E. ii. 13. And S. Gregory Naz. speaks of φιλοχρύσους μᾶλλον ἢ φιλοχρίστους. Orat. 21. 21. On the other hand, Ep. Æg. 22, Athan. contrasts the Arians with the Meletians, as not influenced by secular views. [Prolegg. ch. ii. § 3 (2) c. (2).]
[7] de Syn. § 3 and 9.
[8] Vid. de Decr. 1. note. This consideration, as might be expected, is insisted on by the Fathers. vid. Cyril. Dial. iv. p. 511, &c. v. p. 566. Greg. Naz. 40, 42; Hil. Trin. viii. 28½ Ambros. de fid. i. n. 69 and 104.
[9] Ib. 4, note 8.   [10] 1 Tim. iv. 1, 2; Tit. i. 14.

giving heed to seducing spirits and doctrines of devils, in the hypocrisy of liars ; cauterized in their own conscience, and turning from the truth [11]?'

9. For, behold, we take divine Scripture, and thence discourse with freedom of the religious Faith, and set it up as a light upon its candlestick, saying :—Very Son of the Father, natural and genuine, proper to His essence, Wisdom Only-begotten, and Very and Only Word of God is He ; not a creature or work, but an offspring proper to the Father's essence. Wherefore He is very God, existing one[12] in essence with the very Father; while other beings, to whom He said, ' I said ye are Gods[1],' had this grace from the Father, only by participation[2] of the Word, through the Spirit. For He is the expression of the Father's Person, and Light from Light, and Power, and very Image of the Father's essence. For this too the Lord has said, 'He that hath seen Me, hath seen the Father[3].' And He ever was and is, and never was not. For the Father being everlasting, His Word and His Wisdom must be everlasting[4]. On the other hand, what have these persons to shew us from the infamous Thalia? Or, first of all, let them read it themselves, and copy the tone of the writer ; at least the mockery which they will encounter from others may instruct them how low they have fallen ; and then let them proceed to explain themselves. For what can they say from it, but that ' God was not always a Father, but became so afterwards ; the Son was not always, for He was not before His generation ; He is not from the Father, but He, as others, has come into subsistence out of nothing ; He is not proper to the Father's essence, for He is a creature and work?' And ' Christ is not very God, but He, as others, was made God by participation ; the Son has not exact knowledge of the Father, nor does the Word see the Father perfectly ; and neither exactly understands nor knows the Father. He is not the very and only Word of the Father, but is in name only called Word

and Wisdom, and is called by grace Son and Power. He is not unalterable, as the Father is, but alterable in nature, as the creatures, and He comes short of apprehending the perfect knowledge of the Father.' Wonderful this heresy, not plausible even, but making speculations against Him that is, that He be not, and everywhere putting forward blasphemy for reverent language ! Were any one, after inquiring into both sides, to be asked, whether of the two he would follow in faith, or whether of the two spoke fitly of God,— or rather let them say themselves, these abettors of irreligion, what, if a man be asked concerning God (for ' the Word was God '), it were fit to answer[5]. For from this one question the whole case on both sides may be determined, what is fitting to say,—He was, or He was not; always, or before His birth ; eternal, or from this and from then ; true, or by adoption, and from participation and in idea[6] ; to call Him one of things originated, or to unite Him to the Father ; to consider Him unlike the Father in essence, or like and proper to Him ; a creature, or Him through whom the creatures were originated ; that He is the Father's Word, or that there is another word beside Him, and that by this other He was originated, and by another wisdom ; and that He is only named Wisdom and Word, and is become a partaker of this wisdom, and second to it?

10. Which of the two theologies sets forth our Lord Jesus Christ as God and Son of the Father, this which you vomited forth, or that which we have spoken and maintain from the Scriptures? If the Saviour be not God, nor Word, nor Son, you shall have leave to say what you will, and so shall the Gentiles, and the present Jews. But if He be Word of the Father and true Son, and God from God, and ' over all blessed for ever[7],' is it not becoming to obliterate and blot out those other phrases and that Arian Thalia, as but a pattern of evil, a store of all irreligion, into which, whoso falls, 'knoweth not that giants perish with her, and reacheth the depths of Hades[8]?' This they know themselves, and in their craft they conceal it, not having the courage to speak out, but uttering something else[9]. For if they speak, a condemnation will follow ; and if they be suspected, proofs from Scripture will be cast[10] at them from every side. Wherefore, in their craft, as children of this world, after feeding their

---

[11] This passage is commonly taken by the Fathers to refer to the Oriental sects of the early centuries, who fulfilled one or other of those conditions which it specifies. It is quoted against the Marcionists by Clement. *Strom.* iii. 6. Of the Carpocratians apparently, Iren. *Hær.* i. 25 ; Epiph. *Hær.* 27. 5. Of the Valentinians, Epiph. *Hær.* 31. 34. Of the Montanists and others, ibid. 48. 8. Of the Saturnilians (according to Huet.) Origen in Matt. xx. 16. Of apostolic heresies, Cyril. *Cat.* iv. 27. Oi Marcionites, Valentinians, and Manichees, Chrysost. *de Virg.* 5. Of Gnostics and Manichees, Theod. *Hær.* ii. præf. Of Encratites, ibid. v. fin. Of Eutyches, *Ep. Anon.* 190 (apud Garner. *Diss. v. Theod.* p.901). Pseudo-Justin seems to consider it fulfilled in the Catholics of the fifth century, as being Anti-Pelagians. *Quæst.* 22. vid. Bened. note *in loc.* Besides Athanasius, no early author occurs to the writer of this, by whom it is referred to the Arians, cf. *Depos. Ar.* supr. p. 71, note 29.

[12] [This is the only occurrence of the word ὁμοούσιος in these three Discourses.]   [1] Ps. lxxxii. 6.

[2] *de Decr.* § 14 fin. ; *de Syn.* § 51.   [3] John xiv. 9.
[4] *de Decr.* 15, note 6.

[5] That is, ' Let them tell us, is it right to predicate this or to predicate that of God (of one who is God), for such is the Word, viz. that He was from eternity or was created,' &c., &c.
[6] κατ' ἐπίνοιαν, vid. *Orat.* ii. § 38.
[7] Rom. ix. 5.   [8] Prov. ix. 18. LXX.   [9] *de Decr.* 6. note 5 ; *de Syn.* 32.   [10] *de Decr.* 26, note 6.

so-called lamp from the wild olive, and fearing lest it should soon be quenched (for it is said, 'the light of the wicked shall be put out [1],') they hide it under the bushel [2] of their hypocrisy, and make a different profession, and boast of patronage of friends and authority of Constantius, that what with their hypocrisy and their professions, those who come to them may be kept from seeing how foul their heresy is. Is it not detestable even in this, that it dares not speak out, but is kept hid by its own friends, and fostered as serpents are? for from what sources have they got together these words? or from whom have they received what they venture to say [3]? Not any one man can they specify who has supplied it. For who is there in all mankind, Greek or Barbarian, who ventures to rank among creatures One whom he confesses the while to be God, and says, that He was not till He was made? or who is there, who to the God in whom he has put faith, refuses to give credit, when He says, 'This is My beloved Son [4],' on the pretence that He is not a Son, but a creature? rather, such madness would rouse an universal indignation. Nor does Scripture afford them any pretext; for it has been often shewn, and it shall be shewn now, that their doctrine is alien to the divine oracles. Therefore, since all that remains is to say that from the devil came their mania (for of such opinions he alone is sower [5]), proceed we to resist him ;— for with him is our real conflict, and they are but instruments ;—that, the Lord aiding us, and the enemy, as he is wont, being overcome with arguments, they may be put to shame, when they see him without resource who sowed this heresy in them, and may learn, though late, that, as being Arians, they are not Christians.

CHAPTER IV.

That the Son is Eternal and Increate.

These attributes, being the points in dispute, are first proved by direct texts of Scripture. Concerning the 'eternal power' of God in Rom. i. 20, which is shewn to mean the Son. Remarks on the Arian formula, 'Once the Son was not,' its supporters not daring to speak of 'a time when the Son was not.'

11. At his suggestion then ye have maintained and ye think, that 'there was once when the Son was not ;' this is the first cloke of your views of doctrine which has to be stripped off Say then what was once when the Son was not, O slanderous and irreligious men [1]? If ye say the Father, your blasphemy is but greater ; for it is impious to say that He was 'once,' or to signify Him by the word 'once.' For He is ever, and is now, and as the Son is, so is He, and is Himself He that is, and Father of the Son. But if ye say that the Son was once, when He Himself was not, the answer is foolish and unmeaning. For how could He both be and not be? In this difficulty, you can but answer, that there was a time when the Word was not ; for your very adverb 'once' naturally signifies this. And your other, 'The Son was not before His generation,' is equivalent to saying, 'There was once when He was not,' for both the one and the other signify that there is a time before the Word. Whence then this your discovery? Why do ye, as 'the heathen, rage, and imagine vain phrases against the Lord [2] and against His Christ?' for no holy Scripture has used such language of the Saviour, but rather 'always' and 'eternal' and 'coexistent always with the Father.' For, 'In the beginning was the Word, and the Word was with God, and the Word was God [3].' And in the Apocalypse he thus speaks [4]; 'Who is and who was and who is to come.' Now who can rob 'who is' and 'who was' of eternity? This too in confutation of the Jews hath Paul written in his Epistle to the Romans, 'Of whom as concerning the flesh is Christ, who is over all, God blessed for ever [5];' while silencing the Greeks, he has said, 'The visible things of Him from the creation of the world are clearly seen, being understood by the things that are made, even His eternal Power and Godhead [6];' and what the Power of God is, he teaches us elsewhere himself, 'Christ the Power of God and the Wisdom of God [7].' Surely in these words he does not designate the Father, as ye often whisper one to another, affirming that the Father is 'His eternal power.' This is not so; for he says not, 'God Himself is the power,' but 'His is the power.' Very plain is it to all that 'His' is not 'He ;' yet not something alien but rather proper to Him. Study too the context and 'turn to the Lord ;' now 'the Lord is that Spirit [8] ;' and you will see that it is the Son who is signified.

---

note 5. Thus, if 'when' be a word of time, He it is who *was* 'when' He *was not*, which is absurd. Did they mean, however, that it was the Father who 'was' before the Son? This was true, if 'before' was taken, not to imply time, but origination or beginning. And in this sense the first verse of S. John's Gospel may be interpreted 'In the Beginning,' or Origin, i.e. in the Father 'was the Word.' Thus Athan. himself understands that text, *Orat.* iv. § 1. vid. also *Orat.* iii. § 9; Nyssen. *contr. Eunom.* iii. p. 106; Cyril. *Thesaur.* 32. p. 312.   2 Ps. ii. 1.

3 John i. 1.

4 Rev. i. 4. τάδε λέγει. [On λέγει, &c., in citations, see Lightf. on Gal. iii. 16, Winer, *Gram.* § 58, 9 γ, Grimm-Thayer, *s.v.* II. 1. e.]   5 Rom. ix. 5.   6 Ib. i. 20.

7 1 Cor. i. 24. Athan. has so interpreted this text supr. *de Decr.* 15. It was either a received interpretation, or had been adduced at Nicæa, for Asterius had some years before these Discourses replied to it, vid. *de Syn.* 18, and *Orat.* ii. § 37.

8 2 Cor. iii. 16, 17. S. Athanasius observes, *Serap.* i. 4—7.

---

1 Job xviii. 5.   2 *Ep. Æg.* 18.   3 § 8, note 5.
4 Matt. iii. 17.   5 *de Decr.* 2, note 6.
1 Athan. observes that this formula of the Arians is a mere evasion to escape using the word 'time.' vid. also Cyril. *Thesaur.* iv. pp. 19, 20. Else let them explain,—'There was,' *what* 'when the Son was not?' or *what* was before the Son? since He Himself was before all times and ages, which He created, *de Decr.* 18,

12. For after making mention of the creation, he naturally speaks of the Framer's Power as seen in it, which Power, I say, is the Word of God, by whom all things have been made. If indeed the creation is sufficient of itself alone, without the Son, to make God known, see that you fall not, from thinking that without the Son it has come to be. But if through the Son it has come to be, and 'in Him all things consist[9],' it must follow that he who contemplates the creation rightly, is contemplating also the Word who framed it, and through Him begins to apprehend the Father[10]. And if, as the Saviour also says, 'No one knoweth the Father, save the Son, and he to whom the Son shall reveal Him[11],' and if on Philip's asking, 'Shew us the Father,' He said not, 'Behold the creation,' but, 'He that hath seen Me, hath seen the Father[12],' reasonably doth Paul,—while accusing the Greeks of contemplating the harmony and order of the creation without reflecting on the Framing Word within it (for the creatures witness to their own Framer) so as through the creation to apprehend the true God, and abandon their worship of it,—reasonably hath he said, 'His Eternal Power and Godhead[13],' thereby signifying the Son. And where the sacred writers say, 'Who exists before the ages,' and 'By whom He made the ages[1],' they thereby as clearly preach the eternal and everlasting being of the Son, even while they are designating God Himself. Thus, if Isaiah says, 'The Everlasting God, the Creator of the ends of the earth[2];' and Susanna said, 'O Everlasting God[3];' and

Baruch wrote, 'I will cry unto the Everlasting in my days,' and shortly after, 'My hope is in the Everlasting, that He will save you, and joy is come unto me from the Holy One[4];' yet forasmuch as the Apostle, writing to the Hebrews, says, 'Who being the radiance of His glory and the Expression of His Person[5];' and David too in the eighty-ninth Psalm, 'And the brightness of the Lord be upon us,' and, 'In Thy Light shall we see Light[6],' who has so little sense as to doubt of the eternity of the Son[7]? for when did man see light without the brightness of its radiance, that he may say of the Son, 'There was once, when He was not,' or 'Before His generation He was not.' And the words addressed to the Son in the hundred and forty-fourth Psalm, 'Thy kingdom is a kingdom of all ages[8],' forbid any one to imagine any interval at all in which the Word did not exist. For if every interval in the ages is measured, and of all the ages the Word is King and Maker, therefore, whereas no interval at all exists prior to Him[9], it were madness to say, 'There was once when the Everlasting was not,' and 'From nothing is the Son.' And whereas the Lord Himself says, 'I am the Truth[10],' not 'I became the Truth;' but always, 'I am,—I am the Shepherd,—I am the Light,'—and again, 'Call ye Me not, Lord and Master? and ye call Me well, for so I am,' who, hearing such language from God, and the Wisdom, and Word of the Father, speaking of Himself, will any longer hesitate about the truth, and not forthwith believe that in the phrase 'I am,' is signified that the Son is eternal and without beginning?

13. It is plain then from the above that the Scriptures declare the Son's eternity; it is equally plain from what follows that the Arian phrases 'He was not,' and 'before' and 'when,' are in the same Scriptures predicated of creatures. Moses, for instance, in his account of the generation of our system, says, 'And every plant of the field, before it was in the earth, and every herb of the field before it grew; for the Lord God had not caused it to rain upon the earth, and there was not a man to till the ground[1].' And in Deuteronomy, 'When the Most High divided to the nations[2].' And the Lord said in His own Person, 'If ye loved Me, ye would rejoice

that the Holy Ghost is never in Scripture called simply 'Spirit' without the addition 'of God' or 'of the Father' or 'from Me' or of the article, or of 'Holy,' or 'Comforter,' or 'of truth,' or unless He has been spoken of just before. Accordingly this text is understood of the third Person in the Holy Trinity by Origen, *contr. Cels.* vi. 70; Basil *de Sp. S.* n. 92; Psendo-Athan. *de comm. ess.* 6. On the other hand, the word πνεῦμα, 'Spirit, is used more or less distinctly for our Lord's Divine Nature whether in itself or as incarnate, in Rom. i. 4, 1 Cor. xv. 45, 1 Tim. iii. 16, Hebr. ix. 14, 1 Pet. iii. 18, John vi. 63, &c. [But cf. also Milligan *Resurr.* 238 sq.] Indeed the early Fathers speak as if the 'Holy Spirit,' which came down upon S. Mary might be considered the Word. E.g. Tertullian against the Valentinians, 'If the Spirit of God did not descend into the womb "to partake in flesh from the womb," why did He descend at all?' *de Carn. Chr.* 19. vid. also ibid. 5 and 14. *contr. Prax.* 26, Just. *Apol.* i. 33. Iren. *Hær.* v. 1. Cypr. *Idol. Van.* 6. Lactant. *Instit.* iv. 12. vid. also Hilar. *Trin.* ii. 27; Athan. λόγος ἐν τῷ πνεύματι ἔπλαττε τὸ σῶμα. *Serap.* i. 31 fin. ἐν τῷ λόγῳ ἦν τὸ πνεῦμα. ibid. iii. 6. And more distinctly even as late as S. Maximus, αὐτὸν ἀντὶ σπορᾶς συλλαβοῦσα τὸν λόγον, κεκύηκε, t. 2. p. 309. The earliest ecclesiastical authorities are S. Ignatius *ad Smyrn.* init. and S. Hermas (even though his date were A.D. 150), who also says plainly: Filius autem Spiritus Sanctus est. *Sim.* v. 5, 2, cf. ix. 1. The same use of 'Spirit' for the Word or Godhead of the Word, is also found in Tatian. *adv. Grœc.* 7. Athenag. *Leg.* 10. Theoph. *ad Autol.* ii. 10. Iren. *Hær.* iv. 36. Tertull. *Apol.* 23. Lact. *Inst.* iv. 6, 8. Hilar. *Trin.* ix. 3, and 14. Eustath. *apud* Theod. *Eran.* iii. p. 235. Athan. *contr. Apoll.* i. 8. Apollinar. *ap.* Theod. *Eran.* i. p. 71, and the Apollinarists *passim.* Greg. Naz. *Ep.* 101. *ad Cledon.* p. 85. Ambros. *Incarn.* 63. Severian. *ap.* Theod. *Eran.* ii. p. 167. Vid. Grot. *ad Marc.* ii. 8; Bull, *Def. F. N.* i. 2, § 5; Coustant. *Præf. in Hilar.* 57, &c. Montfaucon in Athan. *Serap.* iv. 19. [see also Tertullian, *de Orat.* init.]

9 Col. i. 17. 10 Vid. *contr. Gent.* 45—47. 11 Matt. xi. 27.
12 John xiv. 8, 9. 13 Rom. i. 20. 1 Heb. i. 2.
2 Is. xl. 28. 3 *Hist. Sus.* 42.

4 Bar. iv. 20, 22. 5 Heb. i. 3. 6 Ps. xc. 17; xxxvi. 9.
7 *de Decr.* 12, 27. 8 Ps. cxlv. 13.
9 Vid. *de Decr.* 18, note 5. The subject is treated at length in Greg. Nyss. *contr. Eunom.* i. t. 2. Append. p. 93—101. vid. also Ambros. *de Fid.* i. 8—11. As time measures the material creation, 'ages' were considered to measure the immaterial, as the duration of Angels. This had been a philosophical distinction, Timæus says εἰκών ἐστι χρόνος τῷ ἀγεννάτῳ χρόνῳ, ὃν αἰῶνα ποταγορεύομες. vid. also Philon. *Quod Deus Immut.* 6. Euseb. *Laud. C.* 1 prope fin., p. 501. Naz. *Or.* 38. 8.
10 John xiv. 6; x. 14; viii. 12; xiii. 13.
1 Gen. ii. 5. 2 Deut. xxxii. 8.

because I said, I go unto the Father, for My Father is greater than I. And now I have told you before it come to pass, that when it is come to pass, ye might believe[3].' And concerning the creation He says by Solomon, 'Or ever the earth was, when there were no depths, I was brought forth; when there were no fountains abounding with water. Before the mountains were settled, before the hills, was I brought forth[4].' And, 'Before Abraham was, I am[5].' And concerning Jeremiah He says, 'Before I formed thee in the womb, I knew thee[6].' And David in the Psalm says, 'Before the mountains were brought forth, or ever the earth and the world were made, Thou art God from everlasting and world without end[7].' And in Daniel, 'Susanna cried out with a loud voice and said, O everlasting God, that knowest the secrets, and knowest all things before they be[8].' Thus it appears that the phrases 'once was not,' and 'before it came to be,' and 'when,' and the like, belong to things originate and creatures, which come out of nothing, but are alien to the Word. But if such terms are used in Scripture of things originate, but 'ever' of the Word, it follows, O ye enemies of God, that the Son did not come out of nothing, nor is in the number of originated things at all, but is the Father's Image and Word eternal, never having not been, but being ever, as the eternal Radiance[9] of a Light which is eternal. Why imagine then times before the Son? or wherefore blaspheme the Word as after times, by whom even the ages were made? for how did time or age at all subsist when the Word, as you say, had not appeared, 'through' whom 'all things have been made and without' whom 'not one thing was made[10]?' Or why, when you mean time, do you not plainly say, 'a time was when the Word was not?' But while you drop the word 'time' to deceive the simple, you do not at all conceal your own feeling, nor, even if you did, could you escape discovery. For you still simply mean times, when you say, ' There was when He was not,' and ' He was not before His generation.'

CHAPTER V.

SUBJECT CONTINUED.

Objection, that the Son's eternity makes Him co-ordinate with the Father, introduces the subject of His Divine Sonship, as a second proof of His eternity. The word Son is introduced in a secondary, but is to be understood in real sense. Since all things partake of the Father in partaking of the Son, He is the whole participation of the Father, that is, He is the Son by nature; for to be wholly participated is to beget.

14. WHEN these points are thus proved, their profaneness goes further. 'If there never was, when the Son was not,' say they, 'but He is eternal, and coexists with the Father, you call Him no more the Father's Son, but brother[1].' O insensate and contentious! For if we said only that He was eternally with the Father, and not His Son, their pretended scruple would have some plausibility; but if, while we say that He is eternal, we also confess Him to be Son from the Father, how can He that is begotten be considered brother of Him who begets? And if our faith is in Father and Son, what brotherhood is there between them? and how can the Word be called brother of Him whose Word He is? This is not an objection of men really ignorant, for they comprehend how the truth lies; but it is a Jewish pretence, and that from those who, in Solomon's words, 'through desire separate themselves[2]' from the truth. For the Father and the Son were not generated from some pre-existing origin[3], that we may account Them brothers, but the Father is the Origin of the Son and begat Him; and the Father is Father, and not born the Son of any; and the Son is Son, and not brother. Further, if He is called the eternal offspring[4] of the Father, He is rightly so called. For never was the essence of the Father imperfect, that what is proper to it should be added afterwards[5]; nor, as man from man,

[1] This was an objection urged by Eunomius, cf. *de Syn.* 51, note 8. It is implied also in the Apology of the former, § 24, and in Basil. *contr. Eunom.* i. Aetius was in Alexandria with George of Cappadocia, A.D. 356-8, and Athan. wrote these Discourses in the latter year, as the *de Syn.* at the end of the next. It is probable then that he is alluding to the Anomœan arguments as he heard them reported, vid. *de Syn.* l.c. where he says, 'they say, "as you have written,"' § 51. Ἀνόμοιος κατ' οὐσίαν is mentioned infr. § 17. As the Arians here object that the First and Second Persons of the Holy Trinity are ἀδελφοί, so did they say the same in the course of the controversy of the Second and Third. vid. *Serap.* i. 15. iv. 2.
[2] Prov. xviii. 1.   [3] Vid. *de Syn.* § 51.
[4] In other words, by the Divine γέννησις is not meant an act but an eternal and unchangeable fact, in the Divine Essence. Arius. not admitting this, objected at the outset of the controversy to the phrase 'always Father, always Son,' Theod. *H. E.* i. 4. p. 749, and Eunomius argues that, 'if the Son is co-eternal with the Father, the Father was never such in act, ἐνεργὸς, but was ἀργός.' Cyril. *Thesaur.* v. p. 41. S. Cyril answers that 'works, ἔργα, are made ἔξωθεν, 'from without;' but that our Lord, as S. Athanasius here says, is neither a 'work' nor 'from without.' And hence he says elsewhere that, while men are fathers first in posse then in act, God is δυνάμει τε καὶ ἐνεργείᾳ πατήρ. *Dial.* 2. p.458. (vid. supr. p. 65. note m). Victorinus in like manner, says, that God is potentia et actione Deus sed in æterna, *Adv. Ar.* i. p. 202; and he quotes S. Alexander, speaking apparently in answer to Arius, of a semper generans generatio. And Arius scoffs at ἀειγεννής and ἀγεννητογενής. Theod. *Hist.* i. 4. p. 749. And Origen had said, ὁ σωτὴρ ἀεὶ γεννᾶται. ap. Routh. *Reliq.* t. 4. p. 304, and S. Dionysius calls Him the Radiance, ἄναρχον καὶ ἀειγενές. *Sent. Dion.* 15. S. Augustine too says, Semper gignit Pater, et semper nascitur Filius. *Ep.* 238. n. 4. Petav. *de Trin* ii. 5. n. 7, quotes the following passage from Theodorus Abucara, 'Since the Son's generation does but signify His having His existence from the Father, which He has ever, therefore He is ever begotten. For it became Him, who is properly (κυρίως) the Son, ever to be deriving His existence from the Father, and not as we who derive its commencement only. In us generation is a way to existence; in the Son of God it denotes the existence itself; in Him it has not existence for its end, but it is itself an end, τέλος, and is perfect, τέλειον.' *Opusc.* 26.
[5] *de Decr.* 22, note 9.

[3] John xiv. 28, 29.   [4] Prov. viii. 23.
[5] John viii. 58.   [6] Jer. i. 5.   [7] Ps. xc. 2.
[8] Hist. Sus. 42.   [9] de Decr. 23, note 4.   [10] John i. 3.

has the Son been begotten, so as to be later than His Father's existence, but He is God's offspring, and as being proper Son of God, who is ever, He exists eternally. For, whereas it is proper to men to beget in time, from the imperfection of their nature[6], God's offspring is eternal, for His nature is ever perfect[7]. If then He is not a Son, but a work made out of nothing, they have but to prove it; and then they are at liberty, as if imagining about a creature, to cry out, 'There was once when He was not;' for things which are originated were not, and have come to be. But if He is Son, as the Father says, and the Scriptures proclaim, and 'Son' is nothing else than what is generated from the Father; and what is generated from the Father is His Word, and Wisdom, and Radiance; what is to be said but that, in maintaining 'Once the Son was not,' they rob God of His Word, like plunderers, and openly predicate of Him that He was once without His proper Word and Wisdom, and that the Light was once without radiance, and the Fountain was once barren and dry[8]? For though they pretend alarm at the name of time, because of those who reproach them with it, and say, that He was before times, yet whereas they assign certain intervals, in which they imagine He was not, they are most irreligious still, as equally suggesting times, and imputing to God an absence of Reason[9].

15. But if on the other hand, while they acknowledge with us the name of 'Son,' from an unwillingness to be publicly and generally condemned, they deny that the Son is the proper offspring of the Father's essence, on the ground that this must imply parts and divisions[1]; what is this but to deny that He is very Son, and only in name to call Him Son at all? And is it not a grievous error, to have material thoughts about what is immaterial, and because of the weakness of their proper nature to deny what is natural and proper to the Father? It does but remain, that they should deny Him also, because they understand not how God is[2], and what the

Father is, now that, foolish men, they measure by themselves the Offspring of the Father. And persons in such a state of mind as to consider that there cannot be a Son of God, demand our pity; but they must be interrogated and exposed for the chance of bringing them to their senses. If then, as you say, 'the Son is from nothing,' and 'was not before His generation,' He, of course, as well as others, must be called Son and God and Wisdom only by participation; for thus all other creatures consist, and by sanctification are glorified. You have to tell us then, of what He is partaker[3]. All other things partake of the Spirit, but He, according to you, of what is He partaker? of the Spirit? Nay, rather the Spirit Himself takes from the Son, as He Himself says; and it is not reasonable to say that the latter is sanctified by the former. Therefore it is the Father that He partakes; for this only remains to say. But this, which is participated, what is it or whence[4]? If it be something external provided by the Father, He will not now be partaker of the Father, but of what is external to Him; and no longer will He be even second after the Father, since He has before Him this other; nor can He be called Son of the Father, but of that, as partaking which He has been called Son and God. And if this be unseemly and irreligious, when the Father says, 'This is My Beloved Son[5],' and when the Son says that God is His own Father, it follows that what is partaken is not external, but from the essence of the Father. And as to this again, if it be other than the essence of the Son, an equal extravagance will meet us; there being in that case something between this that is from the Father and the essence of the Son, whatever that be[6].

16. Such thoughts then being evidently unseemly and untrue, we are driven to say that what is from the essence of the Father, and proper to Him, is entirely the Son; for it is all one to say that God is wholly participated, and that He

---

6 Infr. § 26 fin., and de Decr. 12, note 2.

7 Vid. supr. note 4. A similar passage is found in Cyril. Thesaur. v. p. 42, Dial. ii. fin. This was retorting the objection; the Arians said, 'How can God be ever perfect, who added to Himself a Son?' Athan. answers, 'How can the Son not be eternal, since God is ever perfect?' vid. Greg. Nyssen. contr. Eunom. Append. p. 142. Cyril. Theasaur. x. p. 78. As to the Son's perfection, Aetius objects ap. Epiph. Hær. 76. pp. 925, 6, that growth and consequent accession from without were essentially involved in the idea of Sonship; whereas S. Greg. Naz. speaks of the Son as not ἀτελὴ πρότερον, εἶτα τέλειον, ὥσπερ νόμος τῆς ἡμετέρας γενέσεως, Orat. 20. 9 fin. In like manner, S. Basil argues against Eunomius, that the Son is τέλ_ος, because He is the Image, not as if copied, which is a gradual work, but as a χαρακτὴρ, or impression of a seal, or as the knowledge communicated from master to scholar, which comes to the latter and exists in him perfect, without being lost to the former. contr. Eunom. ii. 16 fin.

8 de Decr. 12, 15.

1 De Decr. §§ 10, 11.

9 Ib. 22, note 1, infr. § 19.

2 Infr. § 23.

3 De Syn. §§ 45, 51.

4 Nic. Def. 9, note 4.

5 Matt. iii. 17.

6 Here is taught us the strict unity of the Divine Essence. When it is said that the First Person of the Holy Trinity communicates divinity to the Second, it is meant that that one Essence which is the Father, also is the Son. Hence the force of the word ὁμοούσιον, which was in consequence accused of Sabellianism, but was distinguished from it by the particle ὁμοῦ, 'together,' which implied a difference as well as unity; whereas ταυτοούσιον or συνουσιον implied, with the Sabellians, an identity or a confusion. The Arians, on the other hand, as in the instance of Eusebius, &c., supr. p. 75, note 7; de Syn. 26, note 3; considered the Father and the Son two οὐσίαι. The Catholic doctrine is that, though the Divine Essence is both the Father Ingenerate and also the Only-begotten Son, it is not itself ἀγέννητος or γεννητή; which was the objection urged against the Catholics by Aetius, Epiph. Hær. 76. 10. Cf. de Decr. § 30, Orat. iii. § 36 fin., Expos. Fid. 2. vid. de Syn. 45, note 1. 'Vera et æterna substantia in se tota permanens, totam se coæternæ veritati nativitatis indulsit.' Fulgent. Resp. 7. And S. Hilary, 'Filius in Patre est et in Filio Pater, non per transfusionem. refusionemque mutuam, sed per viventis naturæ perfectam nativitatem.' Trin. vii. 31.

begets; and what does begetting signify but a Son? And thus of the Son Himself, all things partake according to the grace of the Spirit coming from Him [7]; and this shews that the Son Himself partakes of nothing, but what is partaken from the Father, is the Son; for, as partaking of the Son Himself, we are said to partake of God; and this is what Peter said, 'that ye may be partakers in a divine nature [8];' as says too the Apostle, 'Know ye not, that ye are a temple of God?' and, 'We are the temple of a living God [9].' And beholding the Son, we see the Father; for the thought [10] and comprehension of the Son, is knowledge concerning the Father, because He is His proper offspring from His essence. And since to be partaken no one of us would ever call affection or division of God's essence (for it has been shewn and acknowledged that God is participated, and to be participated is the same thing as to beget); therefore that which is begotten is neither affection nor division of that blessed essence. Hence it is not incredible that God should have a Son, the Offspring of His own essence; nor do we imply affection or division of God's essence, when we speak of 'Son' and 'Offspring;' but rather, as acknowledging the genuine, and true, and Only-begotten of God, so we believe. If then, as we have stated and are shewing, what is the Offspring of the Father's essence be the Son, we cannot hesitate, rather we must be certain, that the same [11] is the Wisdom and Word of the Father, in and through whom He creates and makes all things; and His Brightness too, in whom He enlightens all things, and is revealed to whom He will; and His Expression and Image also, in whom He is contemplated and known, wherefore 'He and His Father are one [1],' and whoso looketh on Him, looketh on the Father; and the Christ, in whom all things are redeemed, and the new creation wrought afresh. And on the other hand, the Son being such Offspring, it is not fitting, rather it is full of peril, to say, that He is a work out of nothing, or that He was not before His generation. For he who thus speaks of that which is proper to the Father's essence, already blasphemes the Father Himself [2]; since he really thinks of Him what he falsely imagines of His offspring.

CHAPTER VI.

SUBJECT CONTINUED.

Third proof of the Son's eternity, viz. from other titles indicative of His coessentiality; as the Creator; as

One of the Blessed Trinity; as Wisdom; as Word; as Image. If the Son is a perfect Image of the Father, why is He not a Father also? because God, being perfect, is not the origin of a race. Only the Father a Father because the Only Father, only the Son a Son because the Only Son. Men are not really fathers and really sons, but shadows of the True. The Son does not become a Father, because He has received from the Father to be immutable and ever the same.

17. This is of itself a sufficient refutation of the Arian heresy; however, its heterodoxy will appear also from the following:—If God be Maker and Creator, and create His works through the Son, and we cannot regard things which come to be, except as being through the Word, is it not blasphemous, God being Maker, to say, that His Framing Word and His Wisdom once was not? it is the same as saying, that God is not Maker, if He had not His proper Framing Word which is from Him, but that That by which He frames, accrues to Him from without [3], and is alien from Him, and unlike in essence. Next, let them tell us this,—or rather learn from it how irreligious they are in saying, 'Once He was not,' and, 'He was not before His generation;'—for if the Word is not with the Father from everlasting, the Triad is not everlasting; but a Monad was first, and afterwards by addition it became a Triad; and so as time went on, it seems what we know concerning God grew and took shape [4]. And further, if the Son is not proper offspring of the Father's essence, but of nothing has come to be, then of nothing the Triad consists, and once there was not a Triad, but a Monad; and a Triad once with deficiency, and then complete; deficient, before the Son was originated, complete when He had come to be; and henceforth a thing originated is reckoned with the Creator, and what once was not has divine worship and glory with Him who was ever [5]. Nay, what is more serious still, the Triad is discovered to be unlike Itself, consisting of strange and alien natures and essences. And this, in other words, is saying, that the Triad has an originated consistence. What sort of a religion then is this, which is not even like itself, but is in process of completion as time goes on, and is now not thus, and then again thus? For probably it will receive some fresh accession, and so on without limit, since at first and at starting it took its consistence by way of accessions. And so undoubtedly it may decrease on the contrary, for what is added plainly admits of being subtracted.

18. But this is not so: perish the thought; the Triad is not originated; but there is an eternal and one Godhead in a Triad, and

---

[7] *De Decr.* § 31.   [8] 2 Pet. i. 4.
[9] 1 Cor. iii. 16; 2 Cor. vi. 16.   [10] ἔννοια, vid. *de Syn.* § 48 fin.   [11] *de Decr.* 17, 24.   [1] John x. 30.   [2] *de Decr.* 1, note.

[3] *de Decr.* 25, note 2.   [4] Vid. *Orat.* iv. § 13.   [5] § 8, note 8.

there is one Glory of the Holy Triad. And you presume to divide it into different natures; the Father being eternal, yet you say of the Word which is seated by Him, 'Once He was not;' and, whereas the Son is seated by the Father, yet you think to place Him far from Him. The Triad is Creator and Framer, and you fear not to degrade It to things which are from nothing; you scruple not to equal servile beings to the nobility of the Triad, and to rank the King, the Lord of Sabaoth, with subjects[6]. Cease this confusion of things unassociable, or rather of things which are not with Him who is. Such statements do not glorify and honour the Lord, but the reverse; for he who dishonours the Son, dishonours also the Father. For if the doctrine of God is now perfect in a Triad, and this is the true and only Religion, and this is the good and the truth, it must have been always so, unless the good and the truth be something that came after, and the doctrine of God is completed by additions. I say, it must have been eternally so; but if not eternally, not so at present either, but at present so, as you suppose it was from the beginning,—I mean, not a Triad now. But such heretics no Christian would bear; it belongs to Greeks, to introduce an originated Triad, and to level It with things originate: for these do admit of deficiencies and additions; but the faith of Christians acknowledges the blessed Triad as unalterable and perfect and ever what It was, neither adding to It what is more, nor imputing to It any loss (for both ideas are irreligious), and therefore it dissociates It from all things generated, and it guards as indivisible and worships the unity of the Godhead Itself; and shuns the Arian blasphemies, and confesses and acknowledges that the Son was ever; for He is eternal, as is the Father, of whom He is the Eternal Word,—to which subject let us now return again.

19. If God be, and be called, the Fountain of wisdom and life—as He says by Jeremiah, 'They have forsaken Me the Fountain of living waters[7];' and again, 'A glorious high throne from the beginning, is the place of our sanctuary; O Lord, the Hope of Israel, all that forsake Thee shall be ashamed, and they that depart from Me shall be written in the earth, because they have forsaken the Lord, the Fountain of living waters[8];' and in the book of Baruch it is written, 'Thou hast forsaken the Fountain of wisdom[9],'—this implies that life and wisdom are not foreign to the Essence of the Fountain, but are proper to It,

nor were at any time without existence, but were always. Now the Son is all this, who says, 'I am the Life[10],' and, 'I Wisdom dwell with prudence[11].' Is it not then irreligious to say, 'Once the Son was not?' for it is all one with saying, 'Once the Fountain was dry, destitute of Life and Wisdom.' But a fountain it would then cease to be; for what begetteth not from itself, is not a fountain[1]. What a load of extravagance! for God promises that those who do His will shall be as a fountain which the water fails not, saying by Isaiah the prophet, 'And the Lord shall satisfy thy soul in drought, and make thy bones fat; and thou shalt be like a watered garden, and like a spring of water, whose waters fail not[2].' And yet these, whereas God is called and is a Fountain of wisdom, dare to insult Him as barren and void of His proper Wisdom. But their doctrine is false; truth witnessing that God is the eternal Fountain of His proper Wisdom; and, if the Fountain be eternal, the Wisdom also must needs be eternal. For in It were all things made, as David says in the Psalm, 'In Wisdom hast Thou made them all[3];' and Solomon says, 'The Lord by Wisdom hath formed the earth, by understanding hath He established the heavens[4].' And this Wisdom is the Word, and by Him, as John says, 'all things were made,' and 'without Him was made not one thing[5].' And this Word is Christ; for 'there is One God, the Father, from whom are all things, and we for Him; and One Lord Jesus Christ, through whom are all things, and we through Him[6].' And if all things are through Him, He Himself is not to be reckoned with that 'all' For he who dares[7] to call Him, through whom are all things, one of that 'all,' surely will have like speculations concerning God, from whom are all. But if he shrinks from this as unseemly, and excludes God from that all, it is but consistent that he should also exclude from that all the Only-Begotten Son, as being proper to the Father's essence. And, if He be not one of the all[8], it is sin to say concerning Him, 'He was not,' and 'He was not before His generation.' Such words may be used of the creatures; but as to the Son, He is such as the Father is, of whose essence He is proper Offspring, Word, and Wisdom[9]. For this is proper to the Son, as regards the Father, and this shews that the Father is proper to the Son; that we may neither say that God was ever without Word[10], nor that the Son

---

6 *De Decr.* § 31.   7 Jer. ii. 13.   8 Ib. xvii. 12, 13.
9 Bar. iii. 12.

10 John xiv. 6.   11 Prov. viii. **12.**   1 Supr. § 15.
2 Isa. lviii. 11.   3 Ps. civ. 24.   4 Prov. iii. 19.
5 John i. 3.   [See Westcott's *additional note* on the passage.]
6 1 Cor. viii. 6.   7 Vid. Petav. *de Trin.* ii. 12, § 4.
9 *De Decr.* § 17.
8 *De Decr.* § 30.
10 ἄλογον.   Vid. note on *de Decr.* §§ 1, 15, where other in-

was non-existent. For wherefore a Son, if not from Him? or wherefore Word and Wisdom, if not ever proper to Him?

20. When then was God without that which is proper to Him? or how can a man consider that which is proper, as foreign and alien in essence? for other things, according to the nature of things originate, are without likeness in essence with the Maker; but are external to Him, made by the Word at His grace and will, and thus admit of ceasing to be, if it so pleases Him who made them [1]; for such is the nature of things originate [2]. But as to what is proper to the Father's essence (for this we have already found to be the Son), what daring is it in irreligion to say that 'This comes from nothing,' and that 'It was not before generation,' but was adventitious [3], and can at some time cease to be again? Let a person only dwell upon this thought, and he will discern how the perfection and the plenitude of the Father's essence is impaired by this heresy; however, he will see its unseemliness still more clearly, if he considers that the Son is the Image and Radiance of the Father, and Expression, and Truth. For if, when Light exists, there be withal its Image, viz. Radiance, and, a Subsistence existing, there be of it the entire Expression, and, a Father existing, there be His Truth (viz. the Son); let them consider what depths of irreligion they fall into, who make time the measure of the Image and Form of the Godhead. For if the Son was not before His generation,

Truth was not always in God, which it were a sin to say; for, since the Father was, there was ever in Him the Truth, which is the Son, who says, 'I am the Truth [4].' And the Subsistence existing, of course there was forthwith its Expression and Image; for God's Image is not delineated from without [5], but God Himself hath begotten it; in which seeing Himself, He has delight, as the Son Himself says, 'I was His delight [6].' When then did the Father not see Himself in His own Image? or when had He not delight, that a man should dare to say, 'the Image is out of nothing,' and 'The Father had not delight before the Image was originated?' and how should the Maker and Creator see Himself in a created and originated essence? for such as is the Father, such must be the Image.

21. Proceed we then to consider the attributes of the Father, and we shall come to know whether this Image is really His. The Father is eternal, immortal, powerful, light, King, Sovereign, God, Lord, Creator, and Maker. These attributes must be in the Image, to make it true that he 'that hath seen' the Son 'hath seen the Father [7].' If the Son be not all this, but, as the Arians consider, originate, and not eternal, this is not a true Image of the Father, unless indeed they give up shame, and go on to say, that the title of Image, given to the Son, is not a token of a similar essence [8], but His name [9] only. But this, on the other hand, O ye enemies of Christ, is not an Image, nor is it an Expression. For what is the likeness of what is out of nothing to Him who brought what was nothing into being? or how can that which is not, be like Him that is, being short of Him in once not being, and in its having its place among things originate? However, such the Arians wishing Him to be, devised for themselves arguments such as this;—'If the Son is the Father's offspring and Image, and is like in all things [10] to the Father, then it neces-

---

stances are given from Athan. and Dionysius of Rome; vid. also *Orat.* iv. 2, 4. *Sent. D.* 23. Origen, supr. p. 48. Athenag. *Leg.* 10. Tat. *contr. Græc.* 5. Theoph. *ad Autol.* ii. 10. Hipp. *contr. Noet.* 10. Nyssen. *contr. Eunom.* vii. p. 215. viii. pp. 230, 240. Orat. *Catech.* 1. Naz. *Orat.* 29. 17 fin. Cyril. *Thesaur.* xiv. p. 145 (vid. Petav. *de Trin.* vi. 9). It must not be supposed from these instances that the Fathers meant that our Lord was literally what is called the *attribute* of reason or wisdom in the Divine Essence, or in other words, that He was God merely viewed as He is wise: which would be a kind of Sabellianism. But, whereas their opponents said that He was but *called* Word and Wisdom *after* the attribute (vid. *de Syn.* 15, note), they said that such titles marked, not only a typical resemblance to the attribute, but so full a correspondence and (as it were) coincidence in *nature* with it, that whatever relation that attribute had to God, such in kind had the Son;—that the attribute was His symbol, and not His mere archetype; that our Lord was eternal and proper to God, because that attribute was, which was His title, vid. *Ep. Æg.* 14, that our Lord was that Essential Reason and Wisdom,—not *by* which the Father *is* wise, but *without* which the Father was *not* wise;—not, that is, in the way of a formal cause, but in *fact.* Or, whereas the Father Himself is Reason and Wisdom, the Son is the necessary result of that Reason and Wisdom, so that, to say that there was no Word, would imply there was no Divine Reason; just as a radiance implies a light; or, as Petavius remarks, l.c. quoting the words which follow shortly after in the text, the eternity of the Original implies the eternity of the Image; τῆς ὑποστάσεως ὑπαρχούσης, πάντως εὐθὺς εἶναι δεῖ τὸν χαρακτῆρα καὶ τὴν εἰκόνα ταύτης, § 20. vid. also infr. § 31, *de Decr.* § 13, p. 21, §§ 20, 23, pp. 35, 40. Theod. *H. E.* i. 3. p. 737.

[1] This was but the opposite aspect of the tenet of our Lord's consubstantiality or eternal generation. For if He came into being at the will of God, by the same will He might cease to be; but if His existence is unconditional and necessary, as God's attributes might be, then as He had no beginning, so can He have no end; for He is in, and one with, the Father, who has neither beginning nor end. On the question of the 'will of God' as it affects the doctrine, vid. *Orat.* iii. § 59, &c.

[2] § 29, note.   [3] *De Decr.* 22, note 9.

[4] John xiv. 6.
[5] Athan. argues from the very name Image for our Lord's eternity. An Image, to be really such, must be an expression from the Original, not an external and detached imitation. vid. supr. note 10, infr. § 26. Hence S. Basil, 'He is an Image not made with the hand, or a work of art, but a living Image,' &c. vid. also *contr. Eunom.* ii. 16, 17. Epiph. *Hær.* 76. 3. Hilar. *Trin.* vii. 41 fin. Origen observes that man, on the contrary, is an example of an external or improper image of God. *Periarch.* i. 2. § 6. It might have been more direct to have argued from the name of Image to our Lord's consubstantiality rather than eternity, as, e.g. S. Gregory Naz. 'He is Image as one in essence, ὁμοούσιον, . . . for this is the nature of an image, to be a copy of the archetype.' *Orat.* 30. 20. vid. also *de Decr.* §§ 20, 23, but for whatever reason Athan. avoids the word ὁμοούσιον in these Discourses. S. Chrys. on Col. i. 15.
[6] Prov. viii 30.   [7] John xiv. 9.
[8] ὁμοίας οὐσίας. And so § 20 init. ὅμοιον κατ' οὐσίαν, and ὁμοιος τῆς οὐσίας, § 26. ὅμοιος κατ' οὐσίαν, iii. 26. and ὅμοιος κατὰ τὴν οὐσίαν τοῦ πατρός. *Ep. Æg.* 17. Also Alex. *Ep. Encycl.* 2. Considering what he says in the *de Syn.* § 38, &c., in controversy with the semi-Arians a year or two later, this use of their formula, in preference to the ὁμοούσιον (vid. foregoing note). deserves our attention.   [9] *De Decr.* § 16.   [10] *De Syn.* 27 (5) note 1, and infr. § 40.

sarily holds that as He is begotten, so He begets, and He too becomes father of a son. And again, he who is begotten from Him, begets in his turn, and so on without limit; for this is to make the Begotten like Him that begat Him.' Authors of blasphemy, verily, are these foes of God! who, sooner than confess that the Son is the Father's Image[1], conceive material and earthly ideas concerning the Father Himself, ascribing to Him severings and [2] efiluences and influences. If then God be as man, let Him become also a parent as man, so that His Son should be father of another, and so in succession one from another, till the series they imagine grows into a multitude of gods. But if God be not as man, as He is not, we must not impute to Him the attributes of man. For brutes and men, after a Creator has begun them, are begotten by succession; and the son, having been begotten of a father who was a son, becomes accordingly in his turn a father to a son, in inheriting from his father that by which he himself has come to be. Hence in such instances there is not, properly speaking, either father or son, nor do the father and the son stay in their respective characters, for the son himself becomes a father, being son of his father, but father of his son. But it is not so in the Godhead; for not as man is God; for the Father is not from a father; therefore doth He not beget one who shall become a father; nor is the Son from effluence of the Father, nor is He begotten from a father that was begotten; therefore neither is He begotten so as to beget. Thus it belongs to the Godhead alone, that the Father is properly[3] father, and the Son properly son, and in Them, and Them only, does it hold that the Father is ever Father and the Son ever Son.

22. Therefore he who asks why the Son is not to beget a son, must inquire why the Father had not a father. But both suppositions are unseemly and full of impiety. For as the Father is ever Father and never could become Son, so the Son is ever Son and never could become Father. For in this rather is He shewn to be the Father's Expression and Image, remaining what He is and not changing, but thus receiving from the Father to be one and the same. If then the Father change, let the Image change; for so is the Image and Radiance in its relation towards Him who begat It. But if the Father is unalterable, and what He is that He continues, necessarily does the Image also continue what He is, and will not alter. Now He is Son from the Father; therefore He will not become other than is proper to the Father's essence. Idly then have the foolish ones devised this objection also, wishing to separate the Image from the Father, that they might level the Son with things originated.

CHAPTER VII.

OBJECTIONS TO THE FOREGOING PROOF.

Whether, in the generation of the Son, God made One that was already, or One that was not.

22 (continued). RANKING Him among these, according to the teaching of Eusebius, and accounting Him such as the things which come into being through Him, Arius and his fellows revolted from the truth, and used, when they commenced this heresy, to go about with dishonest phrases which they had got together; nay, up to this time some of them[1], when they fall in

---

[1] The objection is this, that, if our Lord be the Father's Image, He ought to resemble Him in being a Father. S. Athanasius answers that God is not as man; with us a son becomes a father because our nature is ῥευστὴ, transitive and without stay, ever shifting and passing on into new forms and relations; but that God is perfect and ever the same, what He is once that He continues to be; God the Father remains Father, and God the Son remains Son. Moreover men become fathers by detachment and transmission, and what is received is handed on in a succession; whereas the Father, by imparting Himself wholly, begets the Son: and a perfect nativity finds its termination in itself. The Son has not a Son, because the Father has not a Father. Thus the Father is the only true Father, and the Son alone true Son; the Father only a Father, the Son only a Son; being really in their Persons what human fathers are but by office, character, accident, and name; vid. *De Decr.* 11, note 6. And since the Father is unchangeable as Father, in nothing does the Son more fulfil the idea of a perfect Image than in being unchangeable too. Thus S. Cyril also, *Thesaur.* 10. p. 124. And this perhaps may illustrate a strong and almost startling implication of some of the Greek Fathers, that the First Person in the Holy Trinity, is not God [*in virtue* of His Fatherhood]. E.g. εἰ δὲ θεὸς ὁ υἱός, οὐκ ἐπεὶ υἱός· ὁμοίως καὶ ὁ πατήρ, οὐκ ἐπεὶ πατήρ, θεός· ἀλλ᾽ ἐπεὶ οὐσία τοιάδε, εἷς ἐστι πατὴρ καὶ ὁ υἱὸς θεός. *Nyssen.* t. i. p. 915. vid. Petav. *de Deo* i. 9. § 13. Should it be asked, 'What is the Father if not God?' it is enough to answer, 'the Father.' Men differ from each other as being individuals, but the characteristic difference between Father and Son is, not that they are individuals, but that they *are* Father and Son. In these extreme statements it must be ever borne in mind that we are contemplating divine things according to *our notions.* not *in fact*: i.e. speaking of the Almighty Father, *as such*; there being no real separation between His Person and His Substance. It may be added, that, though theologians differ in their decisions, it would appear that our Lord is not the Image of the Father's person, but of the Father's substance; in other words, not of the Father considered as Father, but considered as God. That is, God the Son is like and equal to God the Father, because they are both the same God. *De Syn.* 49. note 4, also next note

[2] *Ep. Eus.* 7, *de Decr.* 11, note 8.

---

[3] κυρίως, *de Decr.* 11, note 6. Elsewhere Athan. says, 'The Father being one and only is Father of a Son one and only: and in the instance of Godhead only have the names Father and Son stay, and are ever; for of men if any one be called father, yet he has been son of another; and if he be called son, yet is he called father of another; so that in the case of men the names father and son do not properly, κυρίως, hold.' *ad Serap.* i. 16. also ibid. iv. 4 fin. and vi. vid. also κυρίως, Greg. Naz. *Orat.* 29. 5. ἀληθῶς, *Orat.* 25, 16. ὄντως. Basil. *contr. Eunom.* i. 5. p. 215.

[1] This miserable procedure, of making sacred and mysterious subjects a matter of popular talk and debate, which is a sure mark of heresy, had received a great stimulus about this time by the rise of the Anomœans. Eusebius's testimony to the profaneness which attended Arianism upon its rise will be given *de Syn.* 2, note 1. The Thalia is another instance of it. S. Alexander speaks of the interference, even judicial, in its behalf against himself, of disobedient women, δι᾽ ἐντυχίας γυναικαρίων ἀτάκτων ἃ ἠπάτησαν, and of the busy and indecent gadding about of the younger, ἐκ τοῦ περιτροχάζειν πᾶσαν ἀγυιὰν ἀσέμνως. ap. Theod. *H.E.* i. 3. p. 730, also p. 747; also of the men's buffoon conversation, p. 731. Socrates says that 'in the Imperial Court, the officers of the bedchamber held disputes with the women, and in the city in every house there was a war of dialectics.' *Hist.* ii. 2. This mania raged especially in Constantinople, and S. Gregory Naz. speaks of 'Jezebels in as thick a crop as hemlock in a field.' *Orat.* 35. 3, cf. *de Syn.* 13, n. 4. He speaks of the heretics as 'aiming at one thing only, how to make good or refute points of argument,' making 'every market-place resound with their

with boys in the market-place, question them, not out of divine Scripture, but thus, as if bursting with 'the abundance of their heart[2];' —'He who is, did He make him who was not, from that which was [not], or him who was? therefore did He make the Son, whereas He was, or whereas He was not[3]?' And again, 'Is the Unoriginate one or two?' and 'Has He free will, and yet does not alter at His own choice, as being of an alterable nature? for He is not as a stone to remain by Himself unmoveable.' Next they turn to silly women, and address them in turn in this womanish language; 'Hadst thou a son before bearing? now, as thou hadst not, so neither was the Son of God before His generation.' In such language do the disgraceful men sport and revel, and liken God to men, pretending to be Christians, but changing God's glory 'into an image made like to corruptible man[4].'

23. Words so senseless and dull deserved no answer at all; however, lest their heresy appear to have any foundation, it may be right, though we go out of the way for it, to refute them even here, especially on account of the silly women who are so readily deceived by them When they thus speak, they should have inquired of an architect, whether he can build without materials; and if he cannot, whether it follows that God could not make the universe without materials[5]. Or they should have asked every man, whether he can be without place; and if he cannot, whether it follows that God is in place, that so they may be brought to shame even by their audience. Or why is it that, on hearing that God has a Son, they deny Him by the parallel of themselves; whereas, if they hear that He creates and makes, no longer do they object their human ideas? they ought in creation also to entertain the same, and to supply God with materials, and so deny Him to be Creator, till they end in grovelling with

Manichees. But if the bare idea of God transcends such thoughts and, on very first hearing, a man believes and knows that He is in being, not as we are, and yet in being as God, and creates not as man creates, but yet creates as God, it is plain that He begets also not as men beget, but begets as God. For God does not make man His pattern; but rather we men, for that God is properly, and alone truly[6], Father of His Son, are also called fathers of our own children; for of Him 'is every fatherhood in heaven and earth named[7].' And their positions, while unscrutinized, have a shew of sense; but if any one scrutinize them by reason, they will be found to incur much derision and mockery.

24. For first of all, as to their first question, which is such as this, how dull and vague it is! they do not explain who it is they ask about, so as to allow of an answer, but they say abstractedly, 'He who is,' 'him who is not.' Who then 'is,' and what 'are not,' O Arians? or who 'is,' and who 'is not?' what are said 'to be,' what 'not to be?' for He that is, can make things which are not, and which are, and which were before. For instance, carpenter, and goldsmith, and potter, each, according to his own art, works upon materials previously existing, making what vessels he pleases; and the God of all Himself, having taken the dust of the earth existing and already brought to be, fashions man; that very earth, however, whereas it was not once, He has at one time made by His own Word. If then this is the meaning of their question, the creature on the one hand plainly was not before its origination, and men, on the other, work the existing material; and thus their reasoning is inconsequent, since both 'what is' becomes, and 'what is not' becomes, as these instances shew. But if they speak concerning God and His Word, let them complete their question and then ask, Was the God, 'who is,' ever without Reason? and, whereas He is Light, was He ray-less? or was He always Father of the Word? Or again in this manner, Has the Father 'who is' made the Word 'who is not,' or has He ever with Him His Word, as the proper offspring of His substance? This will shew them that they do but presume and venture on sophisms about God and Him who is from Him. Who indeed can bear to hear them say that God was ever without Reason? this is what they fall into a second time, though endeavouring in vain to escape it and to hide it with their sophisms. Nay, one would fain not hear them disputing at all, that God was not always

---

words, and spoiling every entertainment with their trifling and offensive talk.' *Orat. 27. 2.* The most remarkable testimony of the kind though not concerning Constantinople, is given by S. Gregory Nyssen, and often quoted, 'Men of yesterday and the day before, mere mechanics, off-hand dogmatists in theology, servants too and slaves that have been flogged, runaways from servile work, are solemn with us and philosophical about things incomprehensible.... With such the whole city is full; its smaller gates, forums, squares, thoroughfares; the clothes-venders, the money-lenders, the victuallers. Ask about pence, and he will discuss the Generate and Ingenerate; inquire the price of bread, he answers, Greater is the Father, and the Son is subject; say that a bath would suit you, and he defines that the Son is out of nothing.' t. 2. p. 898.   [2] Matt. xii. 34.

[3] This objection is found in Alex. *Ep. Encycl.* 2. ὁ ὢν θεὸς τὸν μὴ ὄντα ἐκ τοῦ μὴ ὄντος. Again, ὄντα γεγέννηκε ἢ οὐκ ὄντα. Greg. *Orat.* 29. 9. who answers it. Pseudo-Basil. *contr. Eunom.* iv. p. 281. 2. Basil calls the question πολυθρύλλητον, *contr. Eunom.* ii. 14. It will be seen to be but the Arian formula of 'He was not before His generation,' in another shape; being but this, that the very fact of His being begotten or a Son, implies a beginning, that is, a time when He was not: it being by the very force of the words absurd to say that 'God begat Him that *was*,' or to deny that 'God begat Him that was *not*.' For the symbol, οὐκ ἦν πρὶν γεννήθη, vid. *Excursus* B. at the end of this Discourse.

[4] Rom. i. 23, and § 2.   [5] *De Decr.* § 11, esp. note 6.   [6] *De Decr.* 31, note 5.   [7] Eph. iii. 15.

Father, but became so afterwards (which is necessary for their fantasy, that His Word once was not), considering the number of the proofs already adduced against them; while John besides says, 'The Word was [7a],' and Paul again writes, 'Who being the brightness of His glory [8],' and, 'Who is over all, God blessed for ever. Amen [9].'

25. They had best have been silent; but since it is otherwise, it remains to meet their shameless question with a bold retort [1]. Perhaps on seeing the counter absurdities which beset themselves, they may cease to fight against the truth. After many prayers [2] then that God would be gracious to us, thus we might ask them in turn; God who is, has He so become, whereas He was not? or is He also before His coming into being? whereas He is, did He make Himself, or is He of nothing, and being nothing before, did He suddenly appear Himself? Unseemly is such an enquiry, both unseemly and very blasphemous, yet parallel with theirs; for the answer they make abounds in irreligion. But if it be blasphemous and utterly irreligious thus to inquire about God, it will be blasphemous too to make the like inquiries about His Word. However, by way of exposing a question so senseless and so dull, it is necessary to answer thus:—whereas God is, He was eternally; since then the Father is ever, His Radiance ever is, which is His Word. And again, God who is, hath from Himself His Word who also is; and neither hath the Word been added, whereas He was not before, nor was the Father once without Reason. For this assault upon the Son makes the blasphemy recoil upon the Father; as if He devised for Himself a Wisdom, and Word, and Son from without [3]; for whichever of these titles you use, you denote the offspring from the Father, as has been said. So that this their objection does not hold; and naturally; for denying the Logos they in consequence ask questions which are illogical. As then if a person saw the sun, and then inquired concerning its radiance, and said, 'Did that which is make that which was, or that which was not,' he would be held not to reason sensibly, but to be utterly mazed, because he fancied what is from the Light to be external to it, and was raising questions, when and where and whether it were made; in like manner, thus to speculate concerning the Son and the Father and thus to inquire, is far

greater madness, for it is to conceive of the Word of the Father as external to Him, and to idly call the natural offspring a work, with the avowal, 'He was not before His generation.' Nay, let them over and above take this answer to their question;—The Father who was, made the Son who was, for 'the Word was made flesh [4];' and, whereas He was Son of God, He made Him in consummation of the ages also Son of Man, unless forsooth, after the Samosatene, they affirm that He did not even exist at all, till He became man.

26. This is sufficient from us in answer to their first question. And now on your part, O Arians, remembering your own words, tell us whether He who was needed one who was not for the framing of the universe, or one who was? You said that He made for Himself His Son out of nothing, as an instrument whereby to make the universe. Which then is superior, that which needs or that which supplies the need? or does not each supply the deficiency of the other? You rather prove the weakness of the Maker, if He had not power of Himself to make the universe, but provided for Himself an instrument from without [5], as carpenter might do or shipwright, unable to work anything without adze and saw! Can anything be more irreligious? yet why should one dwell on its heinousness, when enough has gone before to shew that their doctrine is a mere fantasy?

CHAPTER VIII.

OBJECTIONS CONTINUED.

Whether we may decide the question by the parallel of human sons, which are born later than their parents. No, for the force of the analogy lies in the idea of connaturality. Time is not involved in the idea of Son, but is adventitious to it, and does not attach to God, because He is without parts and passions. The titles Word and Wisdom guard our thoughts of Him and His Son from this misconception. God not a Father, as a Creator, *in posse* from eternity, because creation does not relate to the essence of God, as generation does.

26. (*continued*). NOR is answer needful to their other very simple and foolish inquiry, which they put to silly women; or none besides that which has been already given, namely, that it is not suitable to measure divine generation by the nature of men. However, that as before they may pass judgment on themselves, it is well to meet them on the same ground, thus:—Plainly, if they inquire of parents concerning their son, let them consider whence is the child which is begotten. For, granting

---

[7a] John i. 1.   [8] Heb. i. 3.   [9] Rom. ix. 5.
[1] Vid. Basil, *contr. Eunom.* ii. 17.
[2] This cautious and reverent way of speaking is a characteristic of S. Athanasius, *ad Serap.* i. 1. vid. ii. init. *ad Epict.* 13 fin. *ad Max.* init. *contr. Apoll.* i. init. 'I must ask another question, bolder, yet with a religious intention; be propitious, O Lord, &c.' *Orat.* iii. 63, cf. *de Decr.* 12, note 8, 15, note 6, *de Syn.* 51, note 4.
[3] *De Decr.* 25, note 2.

[4] John i. 14.
[5] ὀργανον, *de Decr.* 7, n. 6, *de Syn.* 27, note 11. This was alleged by Arius, *Socr.* i. 6. and by Eusebius, *Eccles. Theol.* i. 8. supr. *Ep. Eus.*, and by the Anomœans, supr. *de Decr.* 7, note 1.

the parent had not a son before his begetting, still, after having him, he had him, not as external or as foreign, but as from himself, and proper to his essence and his exact image, so that the former is beheld in the latter, and the latter is contemplated in the former. If then they assume from human examples that generation implies time, why not from the same infer that it implies the Natural and the Proper[1], instead of extracting serpent-like from the earth only what turns to poison? Those who ask of parents, and say, 'Had you a son before you begot him?' should add, 'And if you had a son, did you purchase him from without as a house or any other possession?' And then you would be answered, 'He is not from without, but from myself. For things which are from without are possessions, and pass from one to another; but my son is from me, proper and similar to my essence, not become mine from another, but begotten of me; wherefore I too am wholly in him, while I remain myself what I am[2].' For so it is; though the parent be distinct in time, as being man, who himself has come to be in time, yet he too would have had his child ever coexistent with him, but that his nature was a restraint and made it impossible. For Levi too was already in the loins of his great-grandfather, before his own actual generation, or that of his grandfather. When then the man comes to that age at which nature supplies the power, immediately, with nature unrestrained, he becomes father of the son from himself.

27. Therefore, if on asking parents about children, they get for answer, that children which are by nature are not from without, but from their parents, let them confess in like manner concerning the Word of God, that He is simply from the Father. And if they make a question of the time, let them say what is to restrain God—for it is necessary to prove their irreligion on the very ground on which their scoff is made—let them tell us, what is there to restrain God from being always Father of the Son; for that what is begotten must be from its father is undeniable. Moreover, they will pass judgment on themselves in attributing[3] such things to God, if, as they questioned women on the subject of time, so they inquire of the sun concerning its radiance, and of the fountain concerning its issue. They will find that these, though an offspring, always exist with those things from which they are. And if parents, such as these, have in common with their children nature and duration, why, if they suppose God inferior to things that come to be[4], do they not openly say out their own irreligion? But if they do not dare to say this openly, and the Son is confessed to be, not from without, but a natural offspring from the Father, and that there is nothing which is a restraint to God (for not as man is He, but more than the sun, or rather the God of the sun), it follows that the Word is from Him and is ever co-existent with Him, through whom also the Father caused that all things which were not should be. That then the Son comes not of nothing but is eternal and from the Father, is certain even from the nature of the case; and the question of the heretics to parents exposes their perverseness; for they confess the point of nature, and now have been put to shame on the point of time.

28. As we said above, so now we repeat, that the divine generation must not be compared to the nature of men, nor the Son considered to be part of God, nor the generation to imply any passion whatever; God is not as man; for men beget passibly, having a transitive nature, which waits for periods by reason of its weakness. But with God this cannot be; for He is not composed of parts, but being impassible and simple, He is impassibly and indivisibly Father of the Son. This again is strongly evidenced and proved by divine Scripture. For the Word of God is His Son, and the Son is the Father's Word and Wisdom; and Word and Wisdom is neither creature nor part of Him whose Word He is, nor an offspring passibly begotten. Uniting then the two titles, Scripture speaks

---

[1] Supr. *de Decr.* 6. The question was, *What* was that sense of Son which would apply to the Divine Nature? The Catholics said that its essential meaning *could* apply, viz. consubstantiality, whereas the point of posteriority to the Father depended on a condition, *time*, which could not exist in the instance of God. ib. 10. The Arians on the other hand said, that to suppose a true Son, was to think of God irreverently, as implying division, change, &c. The Catholics replied that the notion of materiality was quite as foreign from the Divine Essence as time, and as the Divine Sonship was eternal, so was it also clear both of imperfection or extension.

[2] It is from expressions such as this that the Greek Fathers have been accused of tritheism. The truth is, every illustration, as being incomplete on one or other side of it, taken by itself, tends to heresy. The title Son by itself suggests a second God, as the title Word a mere attribute, and the title Instrument a creature. All heresies are partial views of the truth, and are wrong, not so much in what they say, as in what they deny. The truth, on the other hand, is a positive and comprehensive doctrine, and in consequence necessarily mysterious and open to misconception. vid. *de Syn.* 41, note 1. When Athan. implies that the Eternal Father is in the Son, though remaining what He is, as a man in his child, he is intent only upon the point of the Son's connaturality and equality, which the Arians denied. Cf. *Orat.* iii. § 5; Ps.-Ath. *Dial.* i. (Migne xxviii. 1144 C.). S. Cyril even seems to deny that each individual man may be considered a separate substance except as the Three Persons are such (*Dial.* i. p. 409); and S. Gregory Nyssen is led to say that, strictly speaking, the abstract *man*, which is predicated of separate individuals, is still one, and this with a view of illustrating the Divine Unity. *ad Ablab.* t. 2. p. 449. vid. Petav. *de Trin.* iv. 9.

[3] [But see *Or.* iii. 65, note 2.]

[4] S. Athanasius's doctrine is, that, God containing in Himself all perfection, whatever is excellent in one created thing above another, is found in its perfection in Him. If then such generation as radiance from light is more perfect than that of children from parents, that belongs, and transcendently, to the All-perfect God.

of 'Son,' in order to herald the natural and true offspring of His essence; and, on the other hand, that none may think of the Offspring humanly, while signifying His essence, it also calls Him Word, Wisdom, and Radiance; to teach us that the generation was impassible, and eternal, and worthy of God[5]. What affection then, or what part of the Father is the Word and the Wisdom and the Radiance? So much may be impressed even on these men of folly; for as they asked women concerning God's Son, so[6] let them inquire of men concerning the Word, and they will find that the word which they put forth is neither an affection of them nor a part of their mind. But if such be the word of men, who are passible and partitive, why speculate they about passions and parts in the instance of the immaterial and indivisible God, that under pretence of reverence[7] they may deny the true and natural generation of the Son? Enough was said above to shew that the offspring from God is not an affection; and now it has been shewn in particular that the Word is not begotten according to affection. The same may be said of Wisdom; God is not as man; nor must they here think humanly of Him. For, whereas men are capable of wisdom, God partakes in nothing, but is Himself the Father of His own Wisdom, of which whoso partake are given the name of wise. And this Wisdom too is not a passion, nor a part, but an Offspring proper to the Father. Wherefore He is ever Father, nor is the character of Father adventitious to God, lest He seem alterable; for if it is good that He be Father, but has not ever been Father, then good has not ever been in Him.

29. But, observe, say they, God was always a Maker, nor is the power of framing adventitious to Him; does it follow then, that, because He is the Framer of all, therefore His works also are eternal, and is it wicked to say of them too, that they were not before origination? Senseless are these Arians; for what likeness is there between Son and work, that they should parallel a father's with a maker's function? How is it that, with that difference between offspring and work, which has been shewn, they remain so ill-instructed? Let it be repeated then, that a work is external to the nature, but a son is the proper offspring of the essence; it follows that a work need not have been always, for the workman frames it when he will; but an offspring is not subject to will, but is proper to the essence[8]. And a man may be and may be called Maker, though the works are not as yet; but father he cannot be called, nor can he be, unless a son exist. And if they curiously inquire why God, though always with the power to make, does not always make (though this also be the presumption of madmen, for 'who hath known the mind of the Lord, or who hath been His Counsellor?' or how 'shall the thing formed say to' the potter, 'why didst thou make me thus[9]?' however, not to leave even a weak argument unnoticed), they must be told, that although God always had the power to make, yet the things originated had not the power of being eternal[10]. For they are out of nothing, and therefore were not before their origination; but things which were not before their origination, how could these coexist with the ever-existing God? Wherefore God, looking to what was good for them, then made them all when He saw that, when originated, they were able to abide. And as, though He was able, even from the beginning in the time of Adam, or Noah, or Moses, to send His own Word, yet He sent Him not until the consummation of the ages (for this He saw to be good for the whole creation), so also things originated did He make when He would, and as was good for them. But the Son, not being

---

5 This is a view familiar to the Fathers, viz. that in this consists our Lord's Sonship, that He is the Word, or as S Augustine says, Christum ideo Filium quia Verbum. Aug. *Ep.* 120. 11. Cf. *de Decr.* § 17. 'If I speak of Wisdom, I speak of His offspring;' Theoph. *ad Autolyc.* i. 3. 'The Word, the genuine Son of Mind;' Clem. *Protrept.* p. 58. Petavius discusses this subject accurately with reference to the distinction between Divine Generation and Divine Procession. *de Trin.* vii. 14.

6 *Orat.* iii. 67.

7 Heretics have frequently assigned reverence as the cause of their opposition to the Church; and if even Arius affected it, the plea may be expected in any other. 'O stultos et impios metus,' says S. Hilary, 'et irreligiosam de Deo sollicitudinem.' *de Trin.* iv. 6. It was still more commonly professed in regard to the Catholic doctrine of the Incarnation. Cf. *Acta Archelai* [Routh. *Rell.* v. 169]. August. *contr. Secund.* 9, *contr. Faust.* xi. 3. As the Manichees denied our Lord a body, so the Apollinarians denied Him a rational soul, still under pretence of reverence. because, as they said, the soul was necessarily sinful. Leontius makes this their main argument, ὁ νοῦς ἁμαρτητικός ἐστι. *de Sect.* iv. p. 507. vid. also Greg. Naz. *Ep.* 101. *ad Cledon.* p. 89; Athan. *in Apoll.* i. 2. 14. Epiph. *Ancor.* 79. 80. Athan., &c., call the Apollinarian doctrine Manichean in consequence. vid. in *Apoll.* ii. 8. 9. &c. Again, the Eranistes in Theodoret, who advocates a similar doctrine, will not call our Lord *man*. *Eranist.* ii. p. 83. Eutyches, on the other hand, would call our Lord *man*, but refused to admit His human *nature*, and still with the same profession. Leon. *Ep.* 21. 1 fin. 'Forbid it,' he says at Constantinople, 'that I should say that the Christ was of two natures, or should discuss the nature, φυσιολογεῖν, of my God.' *Concil.* t. 2. p. 157 [Act. *prima conc. Chalc.* t. iv. 1001 ed. Col.] A modern argument for Universal Restitution takes a like form; 'Do not *we* shrink from the notion of another's being sentenced to eternal punishment; and are we more merciful than God?' vid. Matt. xvi. 22, 23.

8 Vid. *Orat.* iii. § 59, &c. 9 Rom. xi. 34; ib. ix. 20.

10 Athan.'s argument is as follows: that, as it *is* of the essence of a son to be 'connatural' with the father, so is it of the essence of a creature to be of 'nothing,' ἐξ οὐκ ὄντων; therefore, while it was *not* impossible 'from the nature of the case,' for Almighty God to be always Father, it *was* impossible for the same reason that He should be always a Creator. vid. infr. § 58: where he takes, 'They shall perish,' in the Psalm, not as a fact but as the definition of the *nature* of a creature. Also ii. § 1, where he says, 'It is proper to creatures and works to have said of them, ἐξ οὐκ ὄντων and οὐκ ἦν πρὶν γεννηθῇ.' vid. Cyril. *Thesaur.* 9. p. 67. *Dial.* ii. p. 460. on the question of being a Creator *in posse*, vid. supra, *Ep. Eus.* 11 note 3.

a work, but proper to the Father's offspring, always is; for, whereas the Father always is, so what is proper to His essence must always be; and this is His Word and His Wisdom. And that creatures should not be in existence, does not disparage the Maker; for He hath the power of framing them, when He wills; but for the offspring not to be ever with the Father, is a disparagement of the perfection of His essence. Wherefore His works were framed, when He would, through His Word; but the Son is ever the proper offspring of the Father's essence.

CHAPTER IX.

OBJECTIONS CONTINUED.

Whether is the Unoriginate one or two? Inconsistent in Arians to use an unscriptural word; necessary to define its meaning. Different senses of the word. If it means 'without Father,' there is but One Unoriginate; if 'without beginning or creation,' there are two. Inconsistency of Asterius. 'Unoriginate' a title of God, not in contrast with the Son, but with creatures, as is 'Almighty,' or 'Lord of powers.' 'Father' is the truer title, as not only Scriptural, but implying a Son, and our adoption as sons.

30. THESE considerations encourage the faithful, and distress the heretical, perceiving, as they do, their heresy overthrown thereby. Moreover, their further question, 'whether the Unoriginate be one or two[1],' shews how false are their views, how treacherous and full of guile. Not for the Father's honour ask they this, but for the dishonour of the Word. Accordingly, should any one, not aware of their craft, answer, 'the Unoriginated is one,' forthwith they spirt out their own venom, saying, 'Therefore the Son is among things originated,' and well have we said, 'He was not before His generation.' Thus they make any kind of disturbance and confusion, provided they can but separate the Son from the Father, and reckon the Framer of all among His

[1] The word ἀγγέν[ν]ητον was in the philosophical schools synonymous with 'God;' hence by asking whether there were two Unoriginates, the Arians implied that there were two Gods, if Christ was God in the sense in which the Father was. Hence Athan. retorts, φάσκοντες, οὐ λέγομεν δύο ἀγένητα, λέγουσι δύο θεούς. Orat. iii. 16, also ii. 38. Plato used ἀγένητον of the Supreme God [not so; he used ἀγένητον, see note 2 on de Decr. 28]; the Valentinians, Tertull. contr. Val. 7; and Basilides, Epiph. Hær. 31. 10. S. Clement uses it, see de Syn. 47, note 7. [The earlier Arians apparently argued mainly, like Asterius, from ἀγένητος (cf. Epiph. 64. 8), the later (καινοί, Epiph. Hær. 73. 19) Anomœans rather from ἀγέννητος]; viz. that ἡ ἀγεννησία is the very οὐσία of God, not an attribute. So Aetius in Epiph. Hær. 76. S. Athanasius does not go into this question, but rather confines himself to the more popular form of it, viz. the Son is by His very name not ἀγένητος, but γεννητὸς, but all γεννητὰ are creatures; which he answers, as de Decr. § 28, by saying that Christianity had brought in a new idea into theology, viz. the sacred doctrine of a true Son, ἐκ τῆς οὐσίας. This was what the Arians had originally denied, ἐν τὸ ἀγέννητον ἐν δὲ τὸ ὑπ' αὐτοῦ ἀληθῶς, καὶ οὐκ ἐκ τῆς οὐσίας αὐτοῦ γεγονός. Euseb. Nic. ap. Theod. H.E. i. 6. When they were urged what according to them was the middle idea to which the Son answered, if they would not accept the Catholic, they would not define but merely said, γέννημα, ἀλλ' οὐκ ὡς ἐν τῶν γεννημάτων. [See pp. 149, 169, and the reference there to Lightfoot.]

works. Now first they may be convicted on this score, that, while blaming the Nicene Bishops for their use of phrases not in Scripture, though these not injurious, but subversive of their irreligion, they themselves went off upon the same fault, that is, using words not in Scripture[2], and those in contumely of the Lord, knowing 'neither what they say nor whereof they affirm[3].' For instance, let them ask the Greeks, who have been their instructors (for it is a word of their invention, not Scripture), and when they have been instructed in its various significations, then they will discover that they cannot even question properly, on the subject which they have undertaken. For they have led me to ascertain[4] that by 'unoriginate' is meant what has not yet come to be, but is possible to be, as wood which is not yet become, but is capable of becoming, a vessel; and again what neither has nor ever can come to be, as a triangle quadrangular, and an even number odd. For a triangle neither has nor ever can become quadrangular; nor has even ever, nor can ever, become odd. Moreover, by 'unoriginate' is meant, what exists, but has not come into being from any, nor having a father at all. Further, Asterius, the unprincipled sophist, the patron too of this heresy, has added in his own treatise, that what is not made, but is ever, is 'unoriginate[5].' They ought then, when they ask the question, to add in what sense they take the word 'unoriginate,' and then the parties questioned would be able to answer to the point.

31. But if they still are satisfied with merely asking, 'Is the Unoriginate one or two?' they must be told first of all, as ill-educated men, that many are such and nothing is such, many, which are capable of origination, and nothing, which is not capable, as has been said. But if they ask according as Asterius ruled it, as if 'what is not a work but was always' were unoriginate, then they must constantly be told that the Son as well as the Father must in this sense be called unoriginate. For He is neither in the number of things originated, nor a work, but has ever been with the Father, as has already been shewn, in spite of their many variations for the sole sake of speaking against the Lord,

[2] De Decr. 18.   [3] 1 Tim. i. 7.   [4] De Decr. 28, note 4.
[5] The two first senses here given answer to the two first mentioned, de Decr. § 28. and, as he there says, are plainly irrelevant. The third in the de Decr. which, as he there observes, is ambiguous and used for a sophistical purpose, is here divided into third and fourth, answering to the two senses which alone are assigned in the de Syn. § 46 [where see note 5], and on them the question turns. This is an instance, of which many occur, how Athan. used his former writings and worked over again his former ground, and simplified or cleared what he had said. In the de Decr. after 350, we have three senses of ἀγένητον, two irrelevant and the third ambiguous; here in Orat. i. (358), he divides the third into two; in the de Syn. (359), he rejects and omits the two first, leaving the two last, which are the critical senses.

'He is of nothing' and 'He was not before His generation.' When then, after failing at every turn, they betake themselves to the other sense of the question, 'existing but not generated of any nor having a father,' we shall tell them that the unoriginate in this sense is only one, namely the Father; and they will gain nothing by their question[6]. For to say that God is in this sense Unoriginate, does not shew that the Son is a thing originated, it being evident from the above proofs that the Word is such as He is who begat Him. Therefore if God be unoriginate, His Image is not originated, but an Offspring[7], which is His Word and His Wisdom. For what likeness has the originated to the unoriginate? (one must not weary of using repetition;) for if they will have it that the one is like the other, so that he who sees the one beholds the other, they are like to say that the Unoriginate is the image of creatures; the end of which is a confusion of the whole subject, an equalling of things originated with the Unoriginate, and a denial of the Unoriginate by measuring Him with the works; and all to reduce the Son into their number.

32. However, I suppose even they will be unwilling to proceed to such lengths, if they follow Asterius the sophist. For he, earnest as he is in his advocacy of the Arian heresy, and maintaining that the Unoriginate is one, runs counter to them in saying, that the Wisdom of God is unoriginate and without beginning also. The following is a passage out of his work[8]: 'The Blessed Paul said not that he preached Christ the power of God or the wisdom of God, but, without the article, 'God's power and God's wisdom[9];' thus preaching that the proper power of God Himself, which is natural to Him and co-existent with Him unoriginatedly, is something besides.' And again, soon after: 'However, His eternal power and wisdom, which truth argues to be without beginning and unoriginate; this must surely be one.' For though, misunderstanding the Apostle's words, he considered that there were two wisdoms; yet, by speaking still of a wisdom coexistent with Him, he declares that the Unoriginate is not simply one, but that there is another Unoriginate with Him. For what is coexistent, coexists not with itself, but with another. If then they agree with Asterius, let them never ask again, 'Is the Unoriginate one or two,' or they will have to contest the point with him; if, on the other hand, they differ even from him,

let them not rely upon his treatise, lest, 'biting one another, they be consumed one of another[10].' So much on the point of their ignorance; but who can say enough on their crafty character? who but would justly hate them while possessed by such a madness? for when they were no longer allowed to say 'out of nothing' and 'He was not before His generation,' they hit upon this word 'unoriginate,' that, by saying among the simple that the Son was 'originate,' they might imply the very same phrases 'out of nothing,' and 'He once was not;' for in such phrases things originated and creatures are implied.

33. If they have confidence in their own positions, they should stand to them, and not change about so variously[1]; but this they will not, from an idea that success is easy, if they do but shelter their heresy under colour of the word 'unoriginate.' Yet after all, this term is not used in contrast with the Son, clamour as they may, but with things originated; and the like may be found in the words 'Almighty,' and 'Lord of the Powers[2].' For if we say that the Father has power and mastery over all things by the Word, and the Son rules the Father's kingdom, and has the power of all, as His Word, and as the Image of the Father, it is quite plain that neither here is the Son reckoned among that all, nor is God called Almighty and Lord with reference to Him, but to those things which through the Son come to be, and over which He exercises power and mastery through the Word. And therefore the Unoriginate is specified not by contrast to the Son, but to the things which through the Son come to be. And excellently: since God is not as things originated, but is their Creator and Framer through the Son. And as the word 'Unoriginate' is specified relatively to things originated, so the word 'Father' is indicative of the Son. And he who names God Maker and Framer and Unoriginate, regards and apprehends things created and made; and he who calls God Father, thereby conceives and contemplates the Son. And hence one might marvel at the obstinacy which is added to their irreligion, that, whereas the term 'unoriginate' has the aforesaid good sense, and admits of being used religiously[3], they, in their own heresy, bring it forth for the dishonour of the Son, not having read that he who honoureth the Son honoureth the Father,

6 These two senses of ἀγέννητον unbegotten and unmade were afterwards [but see notes on de Decr. 28] expressed by the distinction of νν and ν, ἀγέννητον and ἀγένητον. vid. Damasc. F. O. i. 8. p. 135. and Le Quien's note.
7 § 20, note 5.   8 De Syn. § 18, infr. ii. 37.   9. 1 Cor. i. 24.

10 Gal. v. 15.   1 De Syn. 9, note 2.
2 The passage which follows is written with his de Decr. before him. At first he but uses the same topics, but presently he incorporates into this Discourse an actual portion of his former work, with only such alterations as an author commonly makes in transcribing. This, which is not unfrequent with Athan., shews us the care with which he made his doctrinal statements, though they seem at first sight written off. It also accounts for the diffuseness and repetition which might be imputed to his composition, what seems superfluous being often only the insertion of an extract from a former work.   3 De Syn. § 47.

and he who dishonoureth the Son, dishonoureth the Father [4]. If they had any concern at all [5] for reverent speaking and the honour due to the Father, it became them rather, and this were better and higher, to acknowledge and call God Father, than to give Him this name. For, in calling God unoriginate, they are, as I said before, calling Him from His works, and as Maker only and Framer, supposing that hence they may signify that the Word is a work after their own pleasure. But that he who calls God Father, signifies Him from the Son being well aware that if there be a Son, of necessity through that Son all things originate were created. And they, when they call Him Unoriginate, name Him only from His works, and know not the Son any more than the Greeks; but he who calls God Father, names Him from the Word; and knowing the Word, he acknowledges Him to be Framer of all, and understands that through Him all things have been made.

34. Therefore it is more pious and more accurate to signify God from the Son and call Him Father, than to name Him from His works only and call Him Unoriginate [6]. For the latter title, as I have said, does nothing more than signify all the works, individually and collectively, which have come to be at the will of God through the Word; but the title Father has its significance and its bearing only from the Son. And, whereas the Word surpasses things originated, by so much and more doth calling God Father surpass the calling Him Unoriginate. For the latter is unscriptural and suspicious, because it has various senses; so that, when a man is asked concerning it, his mind is carried about to many ideas; but the word Father is simple and scriptural, and more accurate, and only implies the Son. And 'Unoriginate' is a word of the Greeks, who know not the Son; but 'Father' has been acknowledged and vouchsafed by our Lord. For He, knowing Himself whose Son He was, said, 'I am in the Father, and the Father is in Me;' and, 'He that hath seen Me, hath seen the Father,' and 'I and the Father are One [7];' but nowhere is He found to call the Father Unoriginate. Moreover, when He teaches us to pray, He says not, 'When ye pray, say, O God Unoriginate,' but rather, 'When ye pray, say, Our Father, which art in heaven [8].' And it was His will that the Summary [9] of our faith should have the same bearing, in bidding us be baptized, not into the name of Unoriginate and originate, nor into the name of Creator and creature, but into the Name of Father, Son, and Holy Ghost. For with such an initiation we too, being numbered among works, are made sons, and using the name of the Father, acknowledge from that name the Word also in the Father Himself [10]. A vain thing then is their argument about the term 'Unoriginate,' as is now proved, and nothing more than a fantasy.

CHAPTER X.

OBJECTIONS CONTINUED.

How the Word has free will, yet without being alterable. He is unalterable because the Image of the Father, proved from texts.

35. As to their question whether the Word is alterable [1], it is superfluous to examine it; it is enough simply to write down what they say, and so to shew its daring irreligion. How they trifle, appears from the following questions:—'Has He free will, or has He not? is He good from choice according to free will, and can He, if He will, alter, being of an alterable nature? or, as wood or stone, has He not His choice free to be moved and incline hither and thither?' It is but agreeable to their heresy thus to speak and think; for, when once they have framed to themselves a God out of nothing and a created Son, of course they also adopt such terms, as being suitable to a creature. However, when in their controversies with Churchmen they hear from them of the real and only Word of the Father, and yet venture thus to speak of Him, does not their doctrine then become the most loathsome that can be found? is it not enough to distract a man on mere hearing, though unable to reply, and to make him stop his ears, from astonishment at the novelty of what he hears them say, which even to mention is to blaspheme? For if the Word be alterable and changing, where will He stay, and what will be the end of His development? how shall the alterable possibly be like the Unalterable? How should he who has seen the alterable, be considered to have seen the Unalterable? At what state must He arrive, for us to be able to behold in Him the Father? for it is plain

---

4 John v. 23.
5 Here he begins a close transcript of the de Decr. § 30, the last sentence, however, of the paragraph being an addition.
6 For analogous arguments against the word ἀγέννητον, see Basil, contr. Eunom. i. 5. p. 215. Greg. Naz. Orat. 31. 23. Epiph. Hær. 76. p. 941. Greg. Nyss. contr. Eunom. vi. p. 192, &c. Cyril. Dial. ii. Pseudo-Basil. contr. Eunom. iv. p. 283.
7 John xiv. 11 ; xiv. 9; x. 30. These three texts are found together frequently in Athan. particularly in Orat. iii. where he considers the doctrines of the 'Image' and the περιχώρησις. vid. Index of Texts, also Epiph. Hær. 64. 9. Basil. Hexaem. ix. fin. Cyr. Thes. xii. p. 111. [add in S. Joan. 168, 847] Potam. Ep. ap. Dacher. t. 3. p. 299. Hil. Trin. vii. 41. et supr.

8 Luke xi. 2.　　9 De Syn. 28, note 5.
10 Here ends the extract from the de Decretis. The sentence following is added as a close.
1 τρεπτὸς, i.e. not 'changeable' but of a moral nature capable of improvement. Arius maintained this in the strongest terms at starting. 'On being asked whether the Word of God is capable of altering as the devil altered, they scrupled not to say, "Yea, He is capable."' Alex. ap. Socr. i. 6. p. 11.

that not at all times shall we see the Father in the Son, because the Son is ever altering, and is of changing nature. For the Father is unalterable and unchangeable, and is always in the same state and the same; but if, as they hold, the Son is alterable, and not always the same, but of an ever-changing nature, how can such a one be the Father's Image, not having the likeness of His unalterableness[2]? how can He be really in the Father, if His purpose is indeterminate? Nay, perhaps, as being alterable, and advancing daily, He is not perfect yet. But away with such madness of the Arians, and let the truth shine out, and shew that they are foolish. For must not He be perfect who is equal to God? and must not He be unalterable, who is one with the Father, and His Son proper to His essence? and the Father's essence being unalterable, unalterable must be also the proper Offspring from it. And if they slanderously impute alteration to the Word, let them learn how much their own reason is in peril; for from the fruit is the tree known. For this is why he who hath seen the Son hath seen the Father; and why the knowledge of the Son is knowledge of the Father.

36. Therefore the Image of the unalterable God must be unchangeable; for 'Jesus Christ is the same yesterday, to-day, and for ever[3].' And David in the Psalm says of Him, 'Thou, Lord, in the beginning hast laid the foundation of the earth, and the heavens are the work of Thine hands. They shall perish, but Thou remainest; and they all shall wax old as doth a garment. And as a vesture shalt Thou fold them up, and they shall be changed, but Thou art the same, and Thy years shall not fail[4].' And the Lord Himself says of Himself through the Prophet, 'See now that I, even I am He,' and 'I change not[5].' It may be said indeed that what is here signified relates to the Father; yet it suits the Son also to say this, specially because, when made man, He manifests His own identity and unalterableness to such as suppose that by reason of the flesh He is changed and become other than He was. More trustworthy are the saints, or rather the Lord, than the perversity of the irreligious. For Scripture, as in the above-cited passage of the Psalter, signifying under the name of heaven and earth, that the nature of all things originate and created is alterable and changeable, yet excepting the Son from these, shews us thereby that He is no wise a thing originate; nay teaches that He changes everything else, and is Himself not changed, in saying, 'Thou

art the same, and Thy years shall not fail[6].' And with reason; for things originate, being from nothing[7], and not being before their origination, because, in truth, they come to be after not being, have a nature which is changeable; but the Son, being from the Father, and proper to His essence, is unchangeable and unalterable as the Father Himself. For it were sin to say that from that essence which is unalterable was begotten an alterable word and a changeable wisdom. For how is He longer the Word, if He be alterable? or can that be Wisdom which is changeable? unless perhaps, as accident in essence[8], so they would have it, viz. as in any particular essence, a certain grace and habit of virtue exists accidentally, which is called Word and Son and Wisdom, and admits of being taken from it and added to it. For they have often expressed this sentiment, but it is not the faith of Christians; as not declaring that He is truly Word and Son of God, or that the wisdom intended is true Wisdom. For what alters and changes, and has no stay in one and the same condition, how can that be true? whereas the Lord says, 'I am the Truth[9].' If then the Lord Himself speaks thus concerning Himself, and declares His unalterableness, and the Saints have learned and testify this, nay and our notions of God acknowledge it as religious, whence did these men of irreligion draw this novelty? From their heart as from a seat of corruption did they vomit it forth[10].

CHAPTER XI.

Texts Explained; and First, Phil. ii. 9, 10.

Various texts which are alleged against the Catholic doctrine: e.g. Phil. ii. 9, 10. Whether the words 'Wherefore God hath highly exalted' prove moral probation and advancement. Argued against, first, from the force of the word 'Son;' which is inconsistent with such an interpretation. Next, the passage examined. Ecclesiastical sense of 'highly exalted,' and 'gave,' and 'wherefore;' viz. as being spoken with reference to our Lord's manhood. Secondary sense; viz. as implying the Word's 'exaltation' through the resurrection in the same sense in which Scripture speaks of His descent in the Incarnation; how the phrase does not derogate from the nature of the Word.

37. But since they allege the divine oracles and force on them a misinterpretation, according to their private sense[1], it becomes necessary to meet them just so far as to vindicate these passages, and to shew that they

---

[2] Supr. § 22. init.   [3] Heb. xiii. 8.
[4] Ps. cii. 26—28.   [5] Deut. xxxii. 39; Mal. iii. 6.

[6] Heb. i. 12.   [7] § 29, note.   [8] *Nic. Def.* 21, note 9.
[9] John xiv. 6.   [10] *De Syn.* § 16 fin.
[1] Vid. *de Syn.* 4, note 6. and cf. Tertull. *de Præscr.* 19. Rufinus *H. E.* ii. 9. Vincent. *Comm.* 2. Hippolytus has a passage very much to the same purpose, *contr. Noet.* 9 fin.

bear an orthodox sense, and that our opponents are in error. They say then, that the Apostle writes, 'Wherefore God also hath highly exalted Him, and given Him a Name which is above every name; that in the Name of Jesus every knee should bow, of things in heaven and things in earth and things under the earth[2]:' and David, 'Wherefore God, even Thy God, hath anointed Thee with the oil of gladness above Thy fellows[3].' Then they urge, as something acute: 'If He was exalted and received grace, on a 'wherefore,' and on a 'wherefore' He was anointed, He received a reward of His purpose; but having acted from purpose, He is altogether of an alterable nature.' This is what Eusebius[4] and Arius have dared to say, nay to write; while their partizans do not shrink from conversing about it in full market-place, not seeing how mad an argument they use. For if He received what He had as a reward of His purpose, and would not have had it, unless He had needed it, and had His work to shew for it, then having gained it from virtue and promotion, with reason had He 'therefore' been called Son and God, without being very Son. For what is from another by nature, is a real offspring, as Isaac was to Abraham, and Joseph to Jacob, and the radiance to the sun; but the so-called sons from virtue and grace, have but in place of nature a grace by acquisition, and are something else besides[5] the gift itself; as the men who have received the Spirit by participation, concerning whom Scripture saith, 'I begat and exalted children, and they rebelled against Me[6].' And of course, since they were not sons by nature, therefore, when they altered, the Spirit was taken away and they were disinherited; and again on their repentance that God who thus at the beginning gave them grace, will receive them, and give light, and call them sons again.

38. But if they say this of the Saviour also, it follows that He is neither very God nor very Son, nor like the Father, nor in any wise has God for a Father of His being according to essence, but of the mere grace given to Him, and for a Creator of His being according to essence, after the similitude of all others. And being such, as they maintain, it will be manifest further that He had not the name 'Son' from the first, if so be it was the prize of works done and of that very same advance which He made when He became man, and took the form of the servant; but then, when, after becoming 'obedient unto death,' He

was, as the text says, 'highly exalted,' and received that 'Name' as a grace, 'that in the Name of Jesus every knee should bow[7].' What then was before this, if then He was exalted, and then began to be worshipped, and then was called Son, when He became man? For He seems Himself not to have promoted the flesh at all, but rather to have been Himself promoted through it, if, according to their perverseness, He was then exalted and called Son, when He became man. What then was before this? One must urge the question on them again, to make it understood what their irreligious doctrine results in[8]. For if the Lord be God, Son, Word, yet was not all these before He became man, either He was something else beside these, and afterwards became partaker of them for His virtue's sake, as we have said; or they must adopt the alternative (may it return upon their heads!) that He was not before that time, but is wholly man by nature and nothing more. But this is no sentiment of the Church, but of the Samosatene and of the present Jews. Why then, if they think as Jews, are they not circumcised with them too, instead of pretending Christianity, while they are its foes? For if He was not, or was indeed, but afterwards was promoted, how were all things made by Him, or how in Him, were He not perfect, did the Father delight[9]? And He, on the other hand, if now promoted, how did He before rejoice in the presence of the Father? And, if He received His worship after dying, how is Abraham seen to worship Him in the tent[10], and Moses in the bush? and, as Daniel saw, myriads of myriads, and thousands of thousands were ministering unto Him? And if, as they say, He had His promotion now, how did the Son Himself make mention of that His glory before and above the world, when He said, 'Glorify Thou Me, O Father, with the glory which I had with Thee before the world was[11].' If, as they say, He was then exalted, how did He before that 'bow the heavens and come down;' and again, 'The Highest gave His thunder[12]?' Therefore, if, even before the world was made, the Son had

<hr />

7 Phil. ii. 8.
8 The Arians perhaps more than other heretics were remarkable for bringing objections against the received view, rather than forming a consistent theory of their own. Indeed the very vigour and success of their assault upon the truth lay in its being a mere assault, not a positive and substantive teaching. They therefore, even more than others, might fairly be urged on to the consequences of their positions. Now the text in question, as it must be interpreted if it is to serve as an objection, was an objection also to the received doctrine of the Arians. They considered that our Lord was above and before all creatures from the first, and their Creator; how then could He be exalted above all? They surely, as much as Catholics, were obliged to explain it of our Lord's manhood. They could not then use it as a weapon against the Church, until they took the ground of Paul of Samosata.
9 Prov. viii. 30.   10 De Syn. 27 (15).   11 John xvii. 5.
12 Ps. xviii. 9, 13

<hr />

2 Phil. ii. 9, 10.   3 Ps. xlv. 7.
4 Of Nicomedia. vid. Theod. H. E. i. 5.
5 § 39 end.   6 Is. i. 2. LXX.

that glory, and was Lord of glory and the Highest, and descended from heaven, and is ever to be worshipped, it follows that He had not promotion from His descent, but rather Himself promoted the things which needed promotion ; and if He descended to effect their promotion, therefore He did not receive in reward the name of the Son and God, but rather He Himself has made us sons of the Father, and deifed men by becoming Himself man.

39. Therefore He was not man, and then became God, but He was God, and then became man, and that to deify us[1]. Since, if when He became man, only then He was called Son and God, but before He became man, God called the ancient people sons, and made Moses a god of Pharaoh (and Scripture says of many, 'God standeth in the congregation of Gods[2]'), it is plain that He is called Son and God later than they. How then are all things through Him, and He before all? or how is He 'first-born of the whole creation[3],' if He has others before Him who are called sons and gods? And how is it that those first partakers[4] do not partake of the Word? This opinion is not true; it is a device of our present Judaizers. For how in that case can any at all know God as their Father? for adoption there could not be apart from the real Son, who says, 'No one knoweth the Father, save the Son, and he to whomsoever the Son will reveal Him[4a].' And how can there be deifying apart from the Word and before Him? yet, saith He to their brethren the Jews, 'If He called them gods, unto whom the Word of God came[5].' And if all that are called sons and gods, whether in earth or in heaven, were adopted and deified through the Word, and the Son Himself is the Word, it is plain that through Him are they all, and He Himself before all, or rather He Himself only is very Son[6], and He alone is very God from the very God, not receiving these prerogatives as a reward for His virtue, nor being another beside them, but being all these by nature and according to essence. For He is Offspring of the Father's essence, so that one cannot doubt that after the resemblance of the unalterable Father, the Word also is unalterable.

40. Hitherto we have met their irrational conceits with the true conceptions[1] implied in the Word 'Son,' as the Lord Himself has given us. But it will be well next to cite the divine oracles, that the unalterableness of the Son and His unchangeable nature, which is the Father's, as well as their perverseness, may be still more fully proved. The Apostle then, writing to the Philippians, says, 'Have this mind in you, which was also in Christ Jesus ; who, being in the form of God, thought it not a prize to be equal with God; but emptied Himself, taking the form of a servant, being made in the likeness of men. And, being found in fashion as a man, He humbled Himself, becoming obedient to death, even the death of the cross. Wherefore God also highly exalted Him, and gave Him a Name which is above every name ; that in the Name of Jesus every knee should bow, of things in heaven, and things in earth, and things under the earth, and that every tongue should confess that Jesus Christ is Lord, to the glory of God the Father[2].' Can anything be plainer and more express than this? He was not from a lower state promoted ; but rather, existing as God, He took the form of a servant, and in taking it, was not promoted but humbled Himself. Where then is there here any reward of virtue, or what advancement and promotion in humiliation? For if, being God, He became man, and descending from on high He is still said to be exalted, where is He exalted, being God? this withal being plain, that, since God is highest of all, His Word must necessarily be highest also. Where then could He be exalted higher, who is in the Father and like the Father in all things[3]? Therefore He is beyond the need of any addition ; nor is such as the Arians think Him. For though the Word has descended in order to be exalted, and so it is written, yet what need was there that He should humble Himself, as if to seek that which He had already? And what grace did He receive who is the Giver of grace[4]? or how did He receive that Name for worship, who is always worshipped by His Name? Nay, certainly before He became man, the sacred writers invoke Him, 'Save me, O God, for Thy Name's sake[5];' and again, 'Some put their trust in chariots, and some in horses, but we will remember the Name of the Lord our God[6].' And while He was wor-

---

1 [De Incar. 54, and note.]
2 Ps. lxxxii. 1 ; Heb. LXX.   3 Col. i. 15. vid. infr. ii. § 62.
4 In this passage Athan. considers that the participation of the Word is deification, as communion with the Son is adoption : also that the old Saints, inasmuch as they are called 'gods' and 'sons,' did partake of the Divine Word and Son, or in other words were gifted with the Spirit. He asserts the same doctrine very strongly in Orat. iv. § 22. On the other hand, infr. 47, he says expressly that Christ received the Spirit in Baptism 'that He might give it to man.' There is no real contradiction in such statements : what was given in one way under the Law, was given in another and fuller under the Gospel.
4a Matt. xi. 27.
5 John x. 35.   6 p. 157, note 6.

1 ταῖς ἐννοίαις χρώμενοι, πρὸς τὰς ἐπινοίας ἀπηντήσαμεν. cf. οὐχὶ ἐπίνοια, παράνοια δ᾽ μᾶλλον, &c. Basil. contr. Eunom. i. 6. init.   2 Phil ii. 5—11.
3 ὅμοιος κατὰ πάντα, de Syn. 21, note 10.
4 p. 162, note 3.   5 Ps. liv. 1.   6 Ib. xx. 7.

shipped by the Patriarchs, concerning the Angels it is written, ' Let all the Angels of God worship Him[7].'

41. And if, as David says in the 71st Psalm, ' His Name remaineth before the sun, and before the moon, from one generation to another[8],' how did He receive what He had always, even before He now received it? or how is He exalted, being before His exaltation the Most High? or how did He receive the right of being worshipped, who before He now received it, was ever worshipped? It is not a dark saying but a divine mystery[9]. ' In the beginning was the Word, and the Word was with God, and the Word was God;' but for our sakes afterwards the ' Word was made flesh[10].' And the term in question, ' highly exalted,' does not signify that the essence of the Word was exalted, for He was ever and is ' equal to God [1],' but the exaltation is of the manhood. Accordingly this is not said before the Word became flesh; that it might be plain that ' humbled' and ' exalted' are spoken of His human nature; for where there is humble estate, there too may be exaltation; and if because of His taking flesh ' humbled' is written, it is clear that ' highly exalted' is also said because of it. For of this was man's nature in want, because of the humble estate of the flesh and of death. Since then the Word, being the Image of the Father and immortal, took the form of the servant, and as man underwent for us death in His flesh, that thereby He might offer Himself for us through death to the Father; therefore also, as man, He is said because of us and for us to be highly exalted, that as by His death we all died in Christ, so again in the Christ Himself we might be highly exalted, being raised from the dead, and ascending into heaven, ' whither the forerunner Jesus is for us entered, not into the figures of the true, but into heaven itself, now to appear in the presence of God for us[2].' But if now for us the Christ is entered into heaven itself, though He was even before and always Lord and Framer of the heavens, for us therefore is that present exaltation written. And as He Himself, who sanctifies all, says also that He sanctifies Himself to the Father for our sakes, not that the Word may become holy, but that He Himself may in Himself sanctify

all of us, in like manner we must take the present phrase, ' He highly exalted Him,' not that He Himself should be exalted, for He is the highest, but that He may become righteousness for us [3], and we may be exalted in Him, and that we may enter the gates of heaven, which He has also opened for us, the forerunners saying, ' Lift up your gates, O ye rulers, and be ye lift up, ye everlasting doors, and the King of Glory shall come in [4].' For here also not on Him were shut the gates, as being Lord and Maker of all, but because of us is this too written, to whom the door of paradise was shut. And therefore in a human relation, because of the flesh which He bore, it is said of Him, ' Lift up your gates,' and ' shall come in,' as if a man were entering; but in a divine relation on the other hand it is said of Him, since ' the Word was God,' that He is the ' Lord' and the ' King of Glory.' Such our exaltation the Spirit foreannounced in the eighty-ninth Psalm, saying, ' And in Thy righteousness shall they be exalted, for Thou art the glory of their strength [5].' And if the Son be Righteousness, then He is not exalted as being Himself in need, but it is we who are exalted in that Righteousness, which is He [6].

42. And so too the words 'gave Him' are not written because of the Word Himself; for even before He became man He was worshipped, as we have said, by the Angels and the whole creation in virtue of being proper to the Father; but because of us and for us this too is written of Him. For as Christ died and was exalted as man, so, as man, is He said to take what, as God, He ever had, that even such a grant of grace might reach to us. For the Word was not impaired in receiving a body, that He should seek to receive a grace, but rather He deified that which He put on, and more than that, ' gave' it graciously to the race of man. For as He was ever worshipped as being the Word and existing in the form of God, so being what He ever was, though become man and called Jesus, He none the less has the whole creation under foot, and bending their knees to Him in this Name, and confessing that the Word's becoming flesh, and undergoing death in flesh, has not happened against the glory of His Godhead, but ' to the glory of God the Father.' For it is the Father's glory that man, made and then lost, should

7 Heb. i. 6.   8 Ps. lxxii. 17, 5, LXX.
9 Scripture is full of mysteries, but they are mysteries of *fact*, not of words. Its dark sayings or ænigmata are such, because in the nature of things they cannot be expressed clearly. Hence contrariwise, *Orat* ii. § 77 fin. he calls Prov. viii. 22. an enigma, with an allusion to Prov. i. 6. Sept. In like manner S. Ambrose says, Mare est scriptura divina, habens in se sensus profundos, et altitudinem propheticorum *ænigmatum*, &c. *Ep*. ii. 3. What is commonly called ' explaining away' Scripture, is this transference of the obscurity from the subject to the words used.
10 John i. 1, 14.   1 Phil. ii. 6.   2 Heb. vi. 20; ix. 24.

3 When Scripture says that our Lord was exalted, it means in that sense in which He could be exalted; just as, in saying that a man walks or eats, we speak of him not as a spirit, but as in that system of things to which the ideas of walking and eating belong. Exaltation is not a word which can belong to God; it is unmeaning, and *therefore* is *not* applied to Him in the text in question. Thus, e.g. S. Ambrose: ' Ubi humiliatus, ibi obediens. Ex eo enim nascitur obedientia, ex quo humilitas, *et in eo desinit*,' &c. *Ap. Dav. alt*. n. 39.   4 Ps. xxiv. 7.
5 Ps. lxxxix. 17, 18, LXX.   6 1 Cor. i. 30.

be found again; and, when dead, that he should be made alive, and should become God's temple. For whereas the powers in heaven, both Angels and Archangels, were ever worshipping the Lord, as they are now worshipping Him in the Name of Jesus, this is our grace and high exaltation, that even when He became man, the Son of God is worshipped, and the heavenly powers will not be astonished at seeing all of us, who are of one body with Him[7], introduced into their realms. And this had not been, unless He who existed in the form of God had taken on Him a servant's form, and had humbled Himself, yielding His body to come unto death.

43. Behold then what men considered the foolishness of God because of the Cross, has become of all things most honoured. For our resurrection is stored up in it; and no longer Israel alone, but henceforth all the nations, as the Prophet hath foretold, leave their idols and acknowledge the true God, the Father of the Christ. And the illusion of demons is come to nought, and He only who is really God is worshipped in the Name of our Lord Jesus Christ[8]. For the fact that the Lord, even when come in human body and called Jesus, was worshipped and believed to be God's Son, and that through Him the Father was known, shows, as has been said, that not the Word, considered as the Word, received this so great grace, but we. For because of our relationship to His Body we too have become God's temple, and in consequence are made God's sons, so that even in us the Lord is now worshipped, and beholders report, as the Apostle says, that God is in them of a truth[9]. As also John says in the Gospel, 'As many as received Him, to them gave He power to become children of God[10];' and in his Epistle he writes, 'By this we know that He abideth in us by His Spirit which He hath given us[11].' And this too is an evidence of His goodness towards us that, while we were exalted because that the Highest Lord is in us, and on our account grace was given to Him, because that the Lord who supplies the grace has become a man like us, He on the other hand, the Saviour, humbled Himself in taking 'our body of humiliation[1],' and took a servant's

form, putting on that flesh which was enslaved to sin[2]. And He indeed has gained nothing from us for His own promotion: for the Word of God is without want and full; but rather we were promoted from Him; for He is the 'Light, which lighteneth every man, coming into the world[3].' And in vain do the Arians lay stress upon the conjunction 'wherefore,' because Paul has said, 'Wherefore hath God highly exalted Him.' For in saying this he did not imply any prize of virtue, nor promotion from advance[4], but the cause why the exaltation was bestowed upon us. And what is this but that He who existed in form of God, the Son of a noble[5] Father, humbled Himself and became a servant instead of us and in our behalf? For if the Lord had not become man, we had not been redeemed from sins, not raised from the dead, but remaining dead under the earth; not exalted into heaven, but lying in Hades. Because of us then and in our behalf are the words, 'highly exalted' and 'given.'

44. This then I consider the sense of this passage, and that, a very ecclesiastical sense[6].

---

[2] It was usual to say against the Apollinarians, that, unless our Lord took on Him our nature, *as it is*, He had not purified and changed it, as it is, but another nature; 'The Lord came not to save Adam as free from sin, that He should become like unto him; but as, in the net of sin and now fallen, that God's mercy might raise him up with Christ.' Leont. *contr. Nestor.* &c. ii. p. 996. Accordingly, Athan. says elsewhere, 'Had not sinlessness appeared [cf. Rom. viii. 3, πέμψας] "in the nature which had sinned," how was sin condemned in the flesh?' in *Apoll.* ii. 6. 'It was necessary for our salvation,' says S. Cyril, 'that the Word of God should become man, that human flesh "subject to corruption" and "sick with the lust of pleasures," He might make His own; and, "whereas He is life and lifegiving," He might "destroy the corruption," &c. . . . . For by this means, might sin in our flesh become dead.' Ep. *ad Success.* i. p. 138. And S. Leo, 'Non alterius naturæ erat ejus caro quam nostra, nec alio illi quam cæteris hominibus anima est inspirata principio, quæ excelleret, non diversitate generis, sed sublimitate virtutis.' *Ep.* 35 fin. vid. also *Ep.* 28. 3. *Ep.* 31. 2. *Ep.* 165. 9. *Serm.* 22. 2. and 25. 5. It may be asked whether this doctrine does not interfere with that of the immaculate conception [i.e. that *Christ* was conceived sinless]; but that miracle was wrought in order that our Lord might not be born in original sin, and does not affect, or rather includes, His taking flesh of the substance of the Virgin, i.e. of a fallen nature. If indeed sin were 'of the substance' of our fallen nature, as some heretics have said, then He could not have taken our nature without partaking our sinfulness; but if sin be, as it is, a fault of the *will*, then the Divine Power of the Word could sanctify the human will, and keep it from swerving in the direction of evil. Hence 'We say not that Christ by the felicity of a flesh separated from sense *could not* feel the desire of sin, but that by perfection of virtue, and by a flesh not begotten through concupiscence of the flesh, He *had not* the desire of sin;' Aug. *Op. Imperf.* iv. 48. On the other hand, S. Athanasius expressly calls it Manichean doctrine to consider τὴν φύσιν of the flesh ἁμαρτίαν, καὶ οὐ τὴν πρᾶξιν. *contr. Apoll.* i. 12 fin. or φυσικὴν εἶναι τὴν ἁμαρτίαν. ibid. i. 14 fin. His argument in the next ch. is on the ground that all *natures* are from God, but God made man upright nor is the author of evil (vid. also *Vit. Anton.* 20): 'not as if,' he says, 'the devil wrought in man a nature (God forbid !) for of a nature the evil cannot be maker (δημιουργὸς) as is the impiety of the Manichees, but he wrought a bias of nature by transgression, and 'so death reigned over all men.' Wherefore, saith he, 'the Son of God came to destroy the works of the devil;' what works? that nature, which God made sinless, and the devil biassed to the transgression of God's command and the finding out of sin which is death, did God the Word raise again, so as to be secure from the devil's bias and the finding out of sin. And therefore the Lord said, "The prince of this world cometh and findeth nothing in Me."' vid. also § 19. Ibid. ii. 6. he speaks of the devil having 'introduced the *law* of sin.' vid. also ὅ 9.

---

[7] Infr. § 43.   [8] [*De Incar.* §§ 46, 51, &c.]
[9] ὄντως ἐν ὑμῖν ὁ θεός. 1 Cor. xiv. 25. Athan. interprets ἐν *in* not *among*; as also in 1 John iii. 24, just afterwards. Vid. ἐν ἐμοί. Gal. i. 24. ἐντὸς ὑμῶν, Luke xvii. 21, ἐσκήνωσεν ἐν ἡμῖν, John i. 14, on which text Hooker says, 'It pleased not the Word or Wisdom of God to take to itself some one person among men, for then should that one have been advanced which was assumed and no more, but Wisdom, to the end she might save many, built her house of that Nature which is common unto all; she made not this or that man her habitation, but dwelt in us.' *Eccl. Pol.* v. 52. § 3. S. Basil in his proof of the divinity of the Holy Spirit has a somewhat similar passage to the text, *de Sp. S.* c. 24.
[10] John i. 12.   [11] 1 John iii. 24.   [1] Phil. iii. 21.

[3] John i. 9.   [4] προκοπῆς 'internal advance,' Luke ii. 52.
[5] εὐγενοῦς.   [6] ἐκκλησιαστικὸς, vid. *Serap.* iv. 15. *contr. Gent.* 6. 7. 33.

However, there is another way in which one might remark upon it, giving the same sense in a parallel way; viz. that, though it does not speak of the exaltation of the Word Himself, so far as He is Word[7] (for He is, as was just now said, most high and like His Father), yet by reason of His becoming man it indicates His resurrection from the dead. For after saying, 'He hath humbled Himself even unto death,' He immediately added, 'Wherefore He hath highly exalted Him;' wishing to shew, that, although as man He is said to have died, yet, as being Life, He was exalted on the resurrection; for 'He who descended, is the same also who rose again[8].' He descended in body, and He rose again because He was God Himself in the body. And this again is the reason why according to this meaning he brought in the conjunction 'Wherefore;' not as a reward of virtue nor of advancement, but to signify the cause why the resurrection took place; and why, while all other men from Adam down to this time have died and remained dead, He only rose in integrity from the dead. The cause is this, which He Himself has already taught us, that, being God, He has become man. For all other men, being merely born of Adam, died, and death reigned over them; but He, the Second Man, is from heaven, for 'the Word was made flesh[9],' and this Man is said to be from heaven and heavenly[10], because the Word descended from heaven; wherefore He was not held under death. For though He humbled Himself, yielding His own Body to come unto death, in that it was capable of death[11], yet He was highly exalted from earth, because He was God's Son in a body. Accordingly what is here said, 'Wherefore God also hath highly exalted Him,' answers to Peter's words in the Acts, 'Whom God raised up, having loosed the bonds of death, because it was not possible that He should be holden of it[12].' For as Paul has written, 'Since being in form of God He became man, and

humbled Himself unto death, therefore God also hath highly exalted Him,' so also Peter says, 'Since, being God, He became man, and signs and wonders proved Him to beholders to be God, therefore it was not possible that He should be holden of death.' To man it was not possible to succeed in this; for death belongs to man; wherefore, the Word, being God, became flesh, that, being put to death in the flesh, He might quicken all men by His own power.

45. But since He Himself is said to be 'exalted,' and God 'gave' Him, and the heretics think this a defect[1] or affection in the essence[2] of the Word, it becomes necessary to explain how these words are used. He is said to be exalted from the lower parts of the earth, because death is ascribed even to Him. Both events are reckoned His, since it was His Body[3], and none other's, that was exalted from the dead and taken up into heaven. And again, the Body being His, and the Word not being external to it, it is natural that when the Body was exalted, He, as man, should, because of the body, be spoken of as exalted. If then He did not become man, let this not be said of Him; but if the Word became flesh, of necessity the resurrection and exaltation, as in the case of a man, must be ascribed to Him, that the death which is ascribed to Him may be a redemption of the sin of men and an abolition of death, and that the resurrection and exaltation may for His sake remain secure for us. In both respects he hath said of Him, 'God hath highly exalted Him,' and 'God hath given to Him;' that herein moreover he may shew that it is not the Father that hath become flesh, but it is His Word, who has become man, and receives after the manner of men from the Father, and is exalted by Him, as has been said. And it is plain, nor would any one

---

7 *Orat.* ii. § 8.   8 Eph. iv. 10, but ἀναστάς for ἀναβάς.
9 John i. 14.   10 In *Apoll.* i. 2.
11 It was a point in controversy with the extreme Monophysites, that is, the Eutychians, whether our Lord's body was naturally subject to death, the Catholics maintaining the affirmative, as Athanasius here. Eutyches asserted that our Lord had not a human nature, by which he meant among other things that His manhood was not subject to the *laws* of a body, but so far as He submitted to them, He did so by an act of will in each particular case; and this, lest it should seem that He was moved by the πάθη against His will ἀκουσίως; and consequently that His manhood was not subject to death. But the Catholics maintained that He had voluntarily placed Himself *under* those laws, and died *naturally*, vid. Athan. *contr. Apol.* i. 17, and that after the resurrection His body became incorruptible, not according to nature, but by grace. Leont. *de Sect.* x. p. 530. Anast. *Hodeg.* c. 23. To express their doctrine of the ὑπερφυές of our Lord's manhood the Eutychians made use of the Catholic expression 'ut voluit.' vid. Athan. l.c. Eutyches *ap.* Leon. *Ep.* 21. 'quomodo voluit et scit,' twice. vid. also *Eranist.* i. p. 11. ii. p. 105. Leont. *contr. Nest.* i. p. 967. Pseudo-Athan. Serm. *adv. Div. Hær.* § 8. (t. 2. p. 570.)   12 Acts ii. 24.

1 ἐλάττωμα, *ad Adelph.* 4.
2 At first sight it would seem as if S. Athanasius here used οὐσία *essence* for subsistence, or person; but this is not true except with an explanation. Its *direct* meaning is here, as usual, essence, though *indirectly* it comes to imply subsistence. He is speaking of that Divine Essence which, though also the Almighty Father's, is as simply and entirely the Word's as if it were only His. Nay, even when the Essence of the Father is spoken of in a sort of contrast to that of the Son, as in the phrase οὐσία ἐξ οὐσίας, harsh as such expressions are, it is not accurate to say, that οὐσία is used for subsistence or person, or that two οὐσίαι are spoken of (vid. *de Syn.* 52, note 8), except, that is, by Arians, as Eusebius, supr. *Ep. Eus.* § 6 [or by Origen, Prolegg. ii. § 3 (2) a.] Just below we find φύσις τοῦ λόγου, § 51 init.
3 This was the question which came into discussion in the Nestorian controversy, when, as it was then expressed, all that took place in respect to the Eternal Word as man, belonged to His *Person*, and therefore might be predicated of Him; so that it was heretical not to confess the Word's body (or the body of God in the Person of the Word), the Word's death (as Athan. in the text), the Word's exaltation, and the Word's, or God's, Mother, who was in consequence called θεοτόκος, which was the expression on which the controversy mainly turned. Cf. *Orat.* iii. 31, a passage as precise as if it had been written after the Nestorian and Eutychian controversies, though without the technical words then adopted.

dispute it, that what the Father gives, He gives through the Son. And it is marvellous and overwhelming verily ; for the grace which the Son gives from the Father, that the Son Himself is said to receive ; and the exaltation, which the Son bestows from the Father, with that the Son is Himself exalted. For He who is the Son of God, became Himself the Son of Man ; and, as Word, He gives from the Father, for all things which the Father does and gives, He does and supplies through Him ; and as the Son of Man, He Himself is said after the manner of men to receive what proceeds from Him, because His Body is none other than His, and is a natural recipient of grace, as has been said. For He received it as far as His man's nature[4] was exalted ; which exaltation was its being deified. But such an exaltation the Word Himself always had according to the Father's Godhead and perfection, which was His[5].

CHAPTER XII.

Texts Explained ; Secondly, Psalm xlv. 7, 8.

Whether the words 'therefore,' 'anointed,' &c., imply that the Word has been rewarded. Argued against first from the word 'fellows' or 'partakers.' He is anointed with the Spirit in His manhood to sanctify human nature. Therefore the Spirit descended on Him in Jordan, when in the flesh. And He is said to sanctify Himself for us, and give us the glory He has received. The word 'wherefore' implies His divinity. 'Thou hast loved righteousness,' &c., do not imply trial or choice.

46. Such an explanation of the Apostle's words confutes the irreligious men ; and what the sacred poet says admits also the same orthodox sense, which they misinterpret, but which in the Psalmist is manifestly religious. He says then, 'Thy throne, O God, is for ever and ever ; a sceptre of righteousness is the sceptre of Thy Kingdom. Thou hast loved righteousness, and hated iniquity, therefore God, even Thy God, hath anointed Thee with the oil of gladness above Thy fellows[1].' Behold, O ye Arians, and acknowledge even hence the truth. The Singer speaks of us all as 'fellows' or 'partakers' of the Lord ; but were He one of things which come out of nothing and of things originate, He Himself had been one of those who partake. But, since he hymned Him as the eternal God, saying, 'Thy throne, O God, is for ever and ever,' and has declared that all other things partake of Him, what conclusion must we draw, but that He is distinct from originated things, and He only the Father's veritable Word, Radiance, and Wisdom, which all

things originate partake[2], being sanctified by Him in the Spirit[3]? And therefore He is here 'anointed,' not that He may become God, for He was so even before ; nor that He may become King, for He had the Kingdom eternally, existing as God's Image, as the sacred Oracle shews ; but in our behalf is this written, as before. For the Israelitish kings, upon their being anointed, then became kings, not being so before, as David, as Hezekiah, as Josiah, and the rest ; but the Saviour on the contrary, being God, and ever ruling in the Father's Kingdom, and being Himself He that supplies the Holy Ghost, nevertheless is here said to be anointed, that, as before, being said as man to be anointed with the Spirit, He might provide for us men, not only exaltation and resurrection, but the indwelling and intimacy of the Spirit. And signifying this the Lord Himself hath said by His own mouth in the Gospel according to John, ' I have sent them into the world, and for their sakes do I sanctify Myself, that they may be sanctified in the truth[4].' In saying this He has shewn that He is not the sanctified, but the Sanctifier ; for He is not sanctified by other, but Himself sanctifies Himself, that we may be sanctified in the truth. He who sanctifies Himself is Lord of sanctification. How then does this take place ? What does He mean but this ? ' I, being the Father's Word, I give to Myself, when becoming man, the Spirit ; and Myself, become man, do I sanctify in Him, that henceforth in Me, who am Truth (for " Thy Word is Truth "), all may be sanctified.'

47. If then for our sake He sanctifies Himself, and does this when He is become man, it is very plain that the Spirit's descent on Him in Jordan was a descent upon us, because of His bearing our body. And it did not take place for promotion to the Word, but again for our sanctification, that we might share His anointing, and of us it might be said, ' Know ye not that ye are God's Temple, and the Spirit of God dwelleth in you[5]?' For when the Lord, as man, was washed in Jordan, it was we who were washed in Him and by Him[6]. And when He received the Spirit, we it was who by Him were made recipients of It. And moreover for this reason, not as Aaron or

---

4 τὸν ἄνθρωπον. de Syn. 45, note 1.

5 τὴν πατρικὴν ἑαυτοῦ θεότητα, cf. 1 Ps. xlv. 7, 8.

2 p. 156, note 4.
3 It is here said that all things 'originate' partake the Son and are 'sanctified' by the Spirit. How a γέννησις or adoption through the Son is necessary for every creature in order to its consistence, life, or preservation, has been explained, p. 162, note 3. Sometimes the Son was considered as the special Principle of reason, as by Origen, ap. Athan. Serap. iv. 9. vid. himself. de Incarn. 11. These offices of the Son and the Spirit are contrasted by S. Basil, in his de Sp. S. τὸν προστάττοντα κύριον, τὸν δημιουργοῦντα λόγον, τὸ στερεοῦν πνεῦμα, &c. c. 16. n. 38.
4 John xvii. 18, 19, vid. Cyril, Thesaur. 20.
5 1 Cor. iii. 16.   6 Pusey on Baptism, 2nd Ed. pp. 275—293.

David or the rest, was He anointed with oil, but in another way above all His fellows, 'with the oil of gladness;' which He Himself interprets to be the Spirit, saying by the Prophet, 'The Spirit of the Lord is upon Me, because the Lord hath anointed Me[7];' as also the Apostle has said, 'How God anointed Him with the Holy Ghost[8].' When then were these things spoken of Him but when He came in the flesh and was baptized in Jordan, and the Spirit descended on Him? And indeed the Lord Himself said, 'The Spirit shall take of Mine;' and 'I will send Him;' and to His disciples, 'Receive ye the Holy Ghost[9].' And notwithstanding, He who, as the Word and Radiance of the Father, gives to others, now is said to be sanctified, because now He has become man, and the Body that is sanctified is His. From Him then we have begun to receive the unction and the seal, John saying, 'And ye have an unction from the Holy One;' and the Apostle, 'And ye were sealed with the Holy Spirit of promise[10].' Therefore because of us and for us are these words. What advance then of promotion, and reward of virtue or generally of conduct, is proved from this in our Lord's instance? For if He was not God, and then had become God, if not being King He was preferred to the Kingdom, your reasoning would have had some faint plausibility. But if He is God and the throne of His kingdom is everlasting, in what way could God advance? or what was there wanting to Him who was sitting on His Father's throne? And if, as the Lord Himself has said, the Spirit is His, and takes of His, and He sends It, it is not the Word, considered as the Word and Wisdom, who is anointed with the Spirit which He Himself gives, but the flesh assumed by Him which is anointed in Him and by Him[11]; that the sanctification coming to the Lord as man, may come to all men from Him. For not of Itself, saith He, doth the Spirit speak, but the Word is He who gives It to the worthy. For this is like the passage considered above; for as the Apostle has written, 'Who existing in form of God thought it not a prize to be equal with God, but

emptied Himself, and took a servant's form,' so David celebrates the Lord, as the everlasting God and King, but sent to us and assuming our body which is mortal. For this is his meaning in the Psalm, 'All thy garments[12] smell of myrrh, aloes, and cassia;' and it is represented by Nicodemus and by Mary's company, when the one came bringing 'a mixture of myrrh and aloes, about an hundred pounds weight;' and the others[13] 'the spices which they had prepared' for the burial of the Lord's body.

48. What advancement then was it to the Immortal to have assumed the mortal? or what promotion is it to the Everlasting to have put on the temporal? what reward can be great to the Everlasting God and King in the bosom of the Father? See ye not, that this too was done and written because of us and for us, that us who are mortal and temporal, the Lord, become man, might make immortal, and bring into the everlasting kingdom of heaven? Blush ye not, speaking lies against the divine oracles? For when our Lord Jesus Christ had been among us, we indeed were promoted, as rescued from sin; but He is the same[1]: nor did He alter, when He became man (to repeat what I have said), but, as has been written, 'The Word of God abideth for ever[2].' Surely as, before His becoming man, He, the Word, dispensed to the saints the Spirit as His own[3], so also when made man, He sanctifies all by the Spirit and says to His Disciples, 'Receive ye the. Holy Ghost.' And He gave to Moses and the other seventy; and through Him David prayed to the Father, saying, 'Take not Thy Holy Spirit from me[4].' On the other hand, when made man, He said, 'I will send to you the Paraclete, the Spirit of truth[5];' and He sent Him, He, the Word of God, as being faithful. Therefore 'Jesus Christ is the same yesterday, to-day, and for ever[6],' remaining unalterable, and at once gives and receives, giving as God's Word, receiving as man. It is not the Word then, viewed as the Word, that is promoted; for He had all things and has them always; but men, who have in Him and through Him their origin[7] of receiving them.

---

7 Isai. lxi. 1. 8 Acts x. 38. 9 John xvi. 14, 7; xx. 22.
10 1 John ii. 20; Eph. i. 13.
11 Elsewhere Athan. says that our Lord's Godhead was the immediate anointing or chrism of the manhood He assumed, *in Apollin.* ii. 3, *Orat.* iv. § 36. vid. Origen. *Periarch.* ii. 6. n. 4. And S. Greg. Naz. still more expressly, and from the same text as Athan. *Orat.* x. fin. Again, 'This [the Godhead] is the anointing of the manhood, not sanctifying by an energy as the other Christs [anointed] but by a presence of Him whole who anointed, ὅλου τοῦ χρίοντος; whence it came to pass that what anointed was called man and what was anointed was made God.' *Orat.* xxx. 20. Damasc. *F. O.* iii. 3. Dei Filius, sicut pluvia in vellus, toto divinitatis unguento nostram se fudit in carnem. Chrysolog. *Serm.* 60. It is more common, however, to consider that the anointing was the descent of the Spirit, as Athan. says at the beginning of this section, according to Luke iv. 18; Acts x. 38.

12 Ps. xlv. 8. Our Lord's manhood is spoken of as a garment; more distinctly afterwards, 'As Aaron was himself, and did not change on putting round him the high priest's garment, but remaining the same, was but clothed,' &c. *Orat.* ii. 8. On the Apollinarian abuse of the idea, vid. note *in loc.*
13 John xix. 39; Luke xxiv. 1.
1 p. 159, note 8.   2 Isai. xl. 8. λόγος but ῥῆμα. LXX.
3 § 39, note 4.   4 Ps. li. 11.   5 John xv. 26.
6 Heb. xiii. 8.
7 The word origin, ἀρχή, implies the doctrine, more fully brought out in other passages of the Fathers, that our Lord has deigned to become an instrumental cause, as it may be called, of the life of each individual Christian. For at first sight it may be objected to the whole course of Athan.'s argument thus;— What connection is there between the sanctification of Christ's

For, when He is now said to be anointed in a human respect, we it is who in Him are anointed; since also, when He is baptized, we it is who in Him are baptized. But on all these things the Saviour throws much light, when He says to the Father, 'And the glory which Thou gavest Me, I have given to them, that they may be one, even as We are one[8].' Because of us then He asked for glory, and the words occur, 'took' and 'gave' and 'highly exalted,' that we might take, and to us might be given, and we might be exalted, in Him; as also for us He sanctifies Himself, that we might be sanctified in Him[9].

49. But if they take advantage of the word 'wherefore,' as connected with the passage in the Psalm, 'Wherefore God, even Thy God, hath anointed Thee,' for their own purposes, let these novices in Scripture and masters in irreligion know, that, as before, the word 'wherefore' does not imply reward of virtue or conduct in the Word, but the reason why He came down to us, and of the Spirit's anointing which took place in Him for our sakes. For He says not, 'Wherefore He anointed Thee in order to Thy being God or King or Son or Word;' for so He was before and is for ever, as has been shewn; but rather, 'Since Thou art God and King, therefore Thou wast anointed, since none but Thou couldest unite man to the Holy Ghost, Thou the Image of the Father, in which[10] we were made in the beginning; for Thine is even the Spirit.' For the nature of things originate could give no warranty for this, Angels having transgressed, and men disobeyed[11]. Wherefore there was need of God;

and the Word is God; that those who had become under a curse, He Himself might set free. If then He was of nothing, He would not have been the Christ or Anointed, being one among others and having fellowship as the rest[12]. But, whereas He is God, as being Son of God, and is everlasting King, and exists as Radiance and Expression[13] of the Father, therefore fitly is He the expected Christ, whom the Father announces to mankind, by revelation to His holy Prophets; that as through Him we have come to be, so also in Him all men might be redeemed from their sins, and by Him all things might be ruled[1]. And this is the cause of the anointing which took place in Him, and of the incarnate presence of the Word[2], which the Psalmist foreseeing, celebrates, first His Godhead and kingdom, which is the Father's, in these tones, 'Thy throne, O God, is for ever and ever; a sceptre of righteousness is the sceptre of Thy Kingdom[3];' then announces His descent to us thus, 'Wherefore God, even Thy God, hath anointed Thee with the oil of gladness above Thy fellows[4].'

50. What is there to wonder at, what to disbelieve, if the Lord who gives the Spirit, is here said Himself to be anointed with the Spirit, at a time when, necessity requiring it, He did not refuse in respect of His manhood to call Himself inferior to the Spirit? For the Jews saying that He cast out devils in Beelzebub, He answered and said to them, for the exposure of their blasphemy, 'But if I through the Spirit of God cast out demons[5].' Behold, the Giver of the Spirit here says that He cast out demons in the Spirit; but this is not said, except because of His flesh. For since man's nature is not equal of itself to casting out demons, but only in power of the Spirit, therefore as man He said, 'But if I through the Spirit of God cast out demons.' Of course too He signified that the blasphemy offered to the Holy Ghost is greater than that against His humanity, when He said, 'Whosoever shall speak a word against the Son of man, it shall be forgiven him;' such as were those who said, 'Is

---

manhood and ours? how does it prove that human nature is sanctified because a particular specimen of it was sanctified in Him? S. Chrysostom explains, *Hom. in Matt.* lxxxii. 5. And just before, 'It sufficed not for Him to be made man, to be scourged, to be sacrificed; but He assimilates us to Him (ἀναφύρει ἑαυτὸν ἡμῖν), nor merely by faith, but really, has He made us His body.' Again, 'That we are commingled (ἀνακερασθῶμεν) into that flesh, not merely through love, but really, is brought about by means of that food which He has bestowed upon us.' *Hom. in Joann.* 46. 3. And so S. Cyril writes against Nestorius: 'Since we have proved that Christ is the Vine, and we branches as adhering to a communion with Him, not spiritual merely but bodily, why clamours he against us thus bootlessly, saying that, since we adhere to Him, not in a bodily way, but rather by faith and the affection of love according to the Law, therefore He has called, not His own flesh the vine, but rather the Godhead?' in *Joann.* lib. 10. Cap. 2. pp. 863, 4. And Nyssen, *Orat. Catech.* 37. Decoctâ quasi per ollam carnis nostræ cruditate, sanctificavit in æternum nobis cibum carnem suam. Paulin. *Ep.* 23. Of course in such statements nothing *material* is implied; Hooker says, 'The mixture of His bodily substance with ours is a thing which the ancient Fathers disclaim. Yet the mixture of His flesh with ours they speak of, to signify what our very bodies through mystical conjunction receive from that vital efficacy which we know to be in His, and from bodily mixtures they borrow divers similitudes rather to declare the truth than the manner of coherence between His sacred and the sanctified bodies of saints.' *Eccl. Pol.* v. 56. § 10. But without some explanation of this nature, language such as S Athanasius's in the text seems a mere matter of words. vid. infr. § 50 fin.

8 John xvii. 22.   9 Cyril, *Thesaur.* 20. p. 197.
10 § 51, note 1.
11 ἀγγέλων μὲν παραβάντων, ἀνθρώπων δὲ παρακουσάντων. vid. infr. § 51. init. Cf. *ad Afr.* 7. vid. *de Decr.* 19, note 3.

---

infr. *Orat.* ii. iii. Cyril. in *Joann.* lib. v. 2. On the subject of the sins of Angels, vid. Huet. *Origen.* ii. 5. § 16. Petav. *Dogm.* t. 3. p. 87. Dissert. Bened. in Cyril. Hier. iii. 5. Natal. Alex. *Hist. Æt.* i. *Diss.* 7.   12 *De Decr.* 10, note 4.
13 Heb. i. 3.
1 The word *wherefore* is here declared to denote the *fitness* why the Son of God should become the Son of man. His Throne, as God, is for ever; He has loved righteousness; *therefore* He is *equal* to the anointing of the Spirit, as man. And so S Cyril on the same text, as in l. c. in the foregoing note. Cf. Leon *Ep.* 64. 2. vid. *de Incarn.* 7 fin. 10. *In illud Omn.* 2. Cyril. *in Gen.* i. p. 13.
2 ἔνσαρκος παρουσία. This phrase which has occurred above, § 8. is very frequent with Athan. vid. also Cyril. *Catech.* iii. 11. xii. 15. xiv. 27, 30, Epiph. *Hær.* 77. 17. The Eutychians avail themselves of it at the Council of Constantinople, vid. Hard. *Conc.* t. 2. pp. 164. 236.
3 Ps. xlv. 6.   4 Ib. 7.   5 Matt. xii. 28.

not this the carpenter's son [6]?' but they who blaspheme against the Holy Ghost, and ascribe the deeds of the Word to the devil, shall have inevitable punishment [7]. This is what the Lord spoke to the Jews, as man; but to the disciples shewing His Godhead and His majesty, and intimating that He was not inferior but equal to the Spirit, He gave the Spirit and said, 'Receive ye the Holy Ghost,' and 'I send Him,' and 'He shall glorify Me,' and 'Whatsoever He heareth, that He shall speak [8].' As then in this place the Lord Himself, the Giver of the Spirit, does not refuse to say that through the Spirit He casts out demons, as man; in like manner He the same, the Giver of the Spirit, refused not to say, 'The Spirit of the Lord is upon Me, because He hath anointed Me [9],' in respect of His having become flesh, as John hath said; that it might be shewn in both these particulars, that we are they who need the Spirit's grace in our sanctification, and again who are unable to cast out demons without the Spirit's power. Through whom then and from whom behoved it that the Spirit should be given but through the Son, whose also the Spirit is? and when were we enabled to receive It, except when the Word became man? and, as the passage of the Apostle shews, that we had not been redeemed and highly exalted, had not He who exists in form of God taken a servant's form. so David also shews, that no otherwise should we have partaken the Spirit and been sanctified, but that the Giver of the Spirit, the Word Himself, had spoken of Himself as anointed with the Spirit for us. And therefore have we securely received it, He being said to be anointed in the flesh; for the flesh being first sanctified in Him [10], and He being said, as man, to have received for its sake, we have the sequel of the Spirit's grace, receiving 'out of His fulness [11].'

51. Nor do the words, 'Thou hast loved righteousness and hated iniquity,' which are added in the Psalm, shew, as again you suppose, that the Nature of the Word is alterable, but rather by their very force signify His unalterableness. For since of things originate the nature is alterable, and the one portion had transgressed and the other disobeyed, as has been said, and it is not certain how they will act, but it often happens that he who is now good afterwards alters and becomes different, so that one who was but now righteous, soon is found unrighteous, wherefore there was here also need of one unalterable, that men might have the immutability of the

righteousness of the Word as an image and type for virtue [1]. And this thought commends itself strongly to the right-minded. For since the first man Adam altered, and through sin death came into the world, therefore it became the second Adam to be unalterable; that, should the Serpent again assault, even the Serpent's deceit might be baffled, and, the Lord being unalterable and unchangeable, the Serpent might become powerless in his assaults against all. For as when Adam had transgressed, his sin reached unto all men, so, when the Lord had become man and had overthrown the Serpent, that so great strength of His is to extend through all men, so that each of us may say, 'For we are not ignorant of his devices [2].' Good reason then that the Lord, who ever is in nature unalterable, loving righteousness and hating iniquity, should be anointed and Himself sent, that, He, being and remaining the same [3], by taking this alterable flesh, 'might condemn sin in it [4],' and might secure its freedom, and its ability [5] henceforth 'to fulfil the righteousness of the law' in itself, so as to be able to say, 'But we are not in the flesh but in the Spirit, if so be that the Spirit of God dwelleth in us [6].'

52. Vainly then, here again, O Arians, have ye made this conjecture, and vainly alleged the words of Scripture; for God's Word is unalterable, and is ever in one state, not as it may happen [1], but as the Father is; since how is He like the Father, unless He be thus? or how is all that is the Father's the Son's also, if He has not the unalterableness and unchangeableness of the Father [2]? Not as being subject to laws [2a], and biassed to one side, does He love the one and hate the other, lest, if from fear of falling away He chooses the one, we admit that He is alterable otherwise also; but, as being God and the Father's Word, He is a just judge and lover of virtue, or rather its dispenser. Therefore being just and holy by nature, on this account He is said to love righteousness and to hate iniquity; as much as to say, that He loves and chooses the virtuous, and rejects and hates the unrighteous. And divine Scripture

---

[1] Vid. *de Incarn.* 13. 14. vid. also *Gent.* 41 fin. and *Nic. Def.* 17, note 5. Cum justitia nulla esset in terra doctorem misit, quasi vivam legem. Lactant. *Instit.* iv. 25. 'The Only-begotten was made man like us, ... as if lending us His own stedfastness.' Cyril. *in Joann.* lib. v. 2. p. 473; vid. also *Thesaur.* 20. p. 198. August. *de Corr. et Grat.* 10—12. Damasc. *F. O.* iv. 4. But the words of Athan. embrace too many subjects to illustrate distinctly in a note.
[2] 2 Cor. ii. 11.   [3] § 48, note 1.   [4] Rom. viii. 3; ib. 4.
[5] Cf. *de Incarn.* 7, *Orat.* ii. 68.   [6] Rom. viii. 9.
[1] ἁπλῶς, οὐκ ἁπλῶς ὡρίσθη, ἀλλ' ἀκριβῶς ἐξητάσθη. Socr. i. 9. p. 31.   [2] John xvii. 10, § 35, note 2.
[2a] Eunomius said that our Lord was utterly separate from the Father, 'by natural law,' νόμῳ φύσεως; S. Basil observes, 'as if the God of all had not power over Himself, ἑαυτοῦ κύριος, but were in bondage under the decrees of necessity.' *contr. Eunom.* ii. 30.

---

[6] Matt. xii. 32; xiii. 55.   [7] [Cf. Prolegg. ch. iii. § 1 (22).].
[8] John xx. 22; xvi. 13, 14.   [9] Is. lxi. 1.
[10] § 48, note 7.   [11] John i. 16.

says the same of the Father; 'The Righteous Lord loveth righteousness; Thou hatest all them that work iniquity[3],' and 'The Lord loveth the gates of Sion, more than all the dwellings of Jacob[4];' and, 'Jacob have I loved, but Esau have I hated[5];' and in Isaiah there is the voice of God again saying, 'I the Lord love righteousness, and hate robbery of unrighteousness[6].' Let them then expound those former words as these latter; for the former also are written of the Image of God: else, misinterpreting these as those, they will conceive that the Father too is alterable. But, since the very hearing others say this is not without peril, we do well to think that God is said to love righteousness and to hate robbery of unrighteousness, not as if biassed to one side, and capable of the contrary, so as to select the latter and not choose the former, for this belongs to things originated, but that, as a judge, He loves and takes to Him the righteous and withdraws from the bad. It follows then to think the same concerning the Image of God also, that He loves and hates no otherwise than thus. For such must be the nature of the Image as is Its Father, though the Arians in their blindness fail to see either that Image or any other truth of the divine oracles. For being forced from the conceptions or rather misconceptions[7] of their own hearts, they fall back upon passages of divine Scripture, and here too from want of understanding, according to their wont, they discern not their meaning; but laying down their own irreligion as a sort of canon of interpretation[8], they wrest the whole of the divine oracles into accordance with it. And so on the bare mention of such doctrine, they deserve nothing but the reply, 'Ye do err, not knowing the Scriptures nor the power of God[9];' and if they persist in it, they must be put to silence, by the words, 'Render to' man 'the things that are' man's, 'and to God the things that are' God's[10].

CHAPTER XIII.

Texts Explained; Thirdly, Hebrews i. 4.

Additional texts brought as objections; e.g. Heb. i. 4; vii. 22. Whether the word 'better' implies likeness to the Angels; and 'made' or 'become' implies creation. Necessary to consider the circumstances under which Scripture speaks. Difference between 'better' and 'greater;' texts in proof. 'Made' or

'become' a general word. Contrast in Heb. i. 4, between the Son and the Works in point of nature. The difference of the punishments under the two Covenants shews the difference of the natures of the Son and the Angels. 'Become' relates not to the nature of the Word, but to His manhood and office and relation towards us. Parallel passages in which the term is applied to the Eternal Father.

53. But it is written, say they, in the Proverbs, 'The Lord created me the beginning of His ways, for His Works[1];' and in the Epistle to the Hebrews the Apostle says, 'Being made so much better than the Angels, as He hath by inheritance obtained a more excellent Name than they[2].' And soon after, 'Wherefore, holy brethren, partakers of the heavenly calling, consider the Apostle and High Priest of our profession, Christ Jesus, who was faithful to Him that made Him[3].' And in the Acts, 'Therefore let all the house of Israel know assuredly, that God hath made that same Jesus whom ye have crucified both Lord and Christ[4].' These passages they brought forward at every turn, mistaking their sense, under the idea that they proved that the Word of God was a creature and work and one of things originate; and thus they deceive the thoughtless, making the language of Scripture their pretence, but instead of the true sense sowing upon it the poison of their own heresy. For had they known, they would not have been irreligious against 'the Lord of glory[5],' nor have wrested the good words of Scripture. If then henceforward openly adopting Caiaphas's way, they have determined on judaizing, and are ignorant of the text, that verily God shall dwell upon the earth[6], let them not inquire into the Apostolical sayings; for this is not the manner of Jews. But if, mixing themselves up with the godless Manichees[7], they deny that 'the Word was made flesh,' and His Incarnate presence, then let them not bring forward the Proverbs, for this is out of place with the Manichees. But if for preferment-sake, and the lucre of avarice which follows[8], and the desire for good repute, they venture not on denying the text, 'The Word was made flesh,' since so it is written, either let them rightly interpret the words of Scripture, of the embodied presence of the Saviour, or, if they deny their sense, let them deny that the Lord became man at all. For it is unseemly, while confessing that 'the Word became flesh,' yet to be ashamed at what is written of Him, and on that account to corrupt the sense.

54. For it is written, 'So much better than

---

[3] Ps. xi. 7; v. 5.   [4] Ib. lxxxvii. 2.   [5] Mal. i. 2, 3.
[6] Is. lxi. 8
[7] ἐννοιῶν μᾶλλον δὲ παρανοιῶν, vid. § 40, note 1.
[8] Instead of professing to examine Scripture or to acquiesce in what they had been taught, the Arians were remarkable for insisting on certain abstract positions or inferences on which they make the whole controversy turn. Vid. Socrates' account of Arius's commencement, 'If God has a Son, he must have a beginning of existence,' &c. &c., and so the word ἀγένητόν.
[9] Matt. xxii. 29.   [10] Ib. xxii. 21.

---

[1] Prov. viii. 22. vid. *Orat.* ii. §§ 19—72.   [2] Heb. i. 4; iii. 1.
[3] Vid. *Orat.* ii. §§ 2—11.   [4] Acts ii. 36. vid. *Orat.* ii. §§ 11—18.   [5] 1 Cor. ii. 8.   [6] Zech. ii. 10; vid. 1 Kings viii. 27; Bar. iii. 37.   [7] Vid. the same contrast, *de Syn.* § 33; supr. § 8; *Orat.* iv. § 23.   [8] § 8, note 6.

the Angels;' let us then first examine this. Now it is right and necessary, as in all divine Scripture, so here, faithfully to expound the time of which the Apostle wrote, and the person [1], and the point; lest the reader, from ignorance missing either these or any similar particular, may be wide of the true sense. This understood that inquiring eunuch, when he thus besought Philip, 'I pray thee, of whom doth the Prophet speak this? of himself, or of some other man [2]?' for he feared lest, expounding the lesson unsuitably to the person, he should wander from the right sense. And the disciples, wishing to learn the time of what was foretold, besought the Lord, 'Tell us,' said they, 'when shall these things be? and what is the sign of Thy coming [3]?' And again, hearing from the Saviour the events of the end, they desired to learn the time of it, that they might be kept from error themselves, and might be able to teach others; as, for instance, when they had learned, they set right the Thessalonians [4], who were going wrong. When then one knows properly these points, his understanding of the faith is right and healthy; but if he mistakes any such points, forthwith he falls into heresy. Thus Hymenæus and Alexander and their fellows [5] were beside the time, when they said that the resurrection had already been; and the Galatians were after the time, in making much of circumcision now. And to miss the person was the lot of the Jews, and is still, who think that of one of themselves is said, 'Behold, the Virgin shall conceive, and bear a Son, and they shall call his Name Emmanuel, which is being interpreted, God with us [6];' and that, 'A prophet shall the Lord your God raise up to you [7],' is spoken of one of the Prophets; and who, as to the words, 'He was led as a sheep to the slaughter [8],' instead of learning from Philip, conjecture them spoken of Isaiah or some other of the former Prophets [9].

55. (3.) Such has been the state of mind under which Christ's enemies have fallen into their execrable heresy. For had they known the person, and the subject, and the season of the Apostle's words, they would not have expounded of Christ's divinity what belongs to His manhood, nor in their folly have committed so great an act of irreligion. Now this

will be readily seen, if one expounds properly the beginning of this lection. For the Apostle says, 'God who at sundry times and divers manners spake in times past unto the fathers by the prophets, hath in these last days spoken unto us by His Son [1];' then again shortly after he says, 'when He had by Himself purged our sins, He sat down on the right hand of the Majesty on high, having become so much better than the Angels, as He hath by inheritance obtained a more excellent Name than they [2].' It appears then that the Apostle's words make mention of that time, when God spoke unto us by His Son, and when a purging of sins took place. Now when did He speak unto us by His Son, and when did purging of sins take place? and when did He become man? when, but subsequently to the Prophets in the last days? Next, proceeding with his account of the economy in which we were concerned, and speaking of the last times, he is naturally led to observe that not even in the former times was God silent with men, but spoke to them by the Prophets. And, whereas the Prophets ministered, and the Law was spoken by Angels, while the Son too came on earth, and that in order to minister, he was forced to add, 'Become so much better than the Angels,' wishing to shew that, as much as the son excels a servant, so much also the ministry of the Son is better than the ministry of servants. Contrasting then the old ministry and the new, the Apostle deals freely with the Jews, writing and saying, 'Become so much better than the Angels.' This is why throughout he uses no comparison, such as 'become greater,' or 'more honourable,' lest we should think of Him and them as one in kind, but 'better' is his word, by way of marking the difference of the Son's nature from things originated. And of this we have proof from divine Scripture; David, for instance, saying in the Psalm, 'One day in Thy courts is better than a thousand [3]:' and Solomon crying out, 'Receive my instruction and not silver, and knowledge rather than choice gold. For wisdom is better than rubies; and all the things that may be desired are not to be compared to it [4].' Are not wisdom and stones of the earth different in essence and separate in nature? Are heavenly courts at all akin to earthly houses? Or is there any similarity between things eternal and spiritual, and things temporal and mortal? And this is what Isaiah says, 'Thus saith the Lord unto the eunuchs that keep My sabbaths, and choose the things that please Me, and take hold of My Covenant; even unto them will I

---

[1] *De Decr.* 14, note 2. [2] Acts viii. 34.
[3] Matt. xxiv. 3. [4] Vid. 1 Thess. iv. 13; 2 Thess. ii. 1, &c.
[5] 2 Tim. ii. 17, 18; 1 Tim. i. 20. [6] Is. vii. 14; Matt. i. 23.
[7] Deut. xviii. 15. [8] Is. liii. 7.
[9] The more common evasion on the part of the Jews was to interpret the prophecy of their own sufferings in captivity. It was an idea of Grotius that the prophecy received a first fulfilment in Jeremiah. vid. Justin *Tryph.* 72 et al., Iren. *Hær.* iv. 33. Tertull. in *Jud.* 9, Cyprian. *Testim. in Jud.* ii. 13, Euseb. *Dem.* iii. 2, &c. [cf. Driver and Neubauer Jewish commentaries on Is. lii. and liii. and Introduction to English Translation of these pp. xxxvii. sq.]

[1] Heb. i. 1, 2. [2] Ib. 3, 4.
[3] Ps. lxxxiv. 10. [4] Prov. viii. 10, 11.

give in Mine house, and within My walls, a place and a name better than of sons and of daughters : I will give them an everlasting name that shall not be cut off [5].' In like manner there is nought akin between the Son and the Angels ; so that the word 'better' is not used to compare but to contrast, because of the difference of His nature from them. And therefore the Apostle also himself, when he interprets the word 'better,' places its force in nothing short of the Son's excellence over things originated, calling the one Son, the other servants ; the one, as a Son with the Father, sitting on the right ; and the others, as servants, standing before Him, ard being sent, and fulfilling offices.

56. Scripture, in speaking thus, implies, O Arians, not that the Son is originate, but rather other than things originate, and proper to the Father, being in His bosom. (4.) Nor [5a] does even the expression 'become,' which here occurs, shew that the Son is originate, as ye suppose. If indeed it were simply 'become' and no more, a case might stand for the Arians ; but, whereas they are forestalled with the word 'Son' throughout the passage, shewing that He is other than things originate, so again not even the word 'become' occurs absolutely [6], but ' better' is immediately subjoined. For the writer thought the expression immaterial, knowing that in the case of one who was confessedly a genuine Son, to say ' become' is the same with saying that He had been made, and is, 'better.' For it matters not even if we speak of what is generate, as ' become' or ' made ;' but on the contrary, things originate cannot be called generate, God's handiwork as they are, except so far as after their making they partake of the generate Son, and are therefore said to have been generated also, not at all in their own nature, but because of their participation of the Son in the Spirit [7]. And this again divine Scripture recognises ; for it says in the case of things originate, 'All things came to be through Him, and without Him nothing came to be [8],' and,

'In wisdom hast Thou made them all [9] ;' but in the case of sons which are generate, 'To Job there came to be seven sons and three daughters [10],' and, 'Abraham was an hundred years old when there came to be to him Isaac his son [11] ;' and Moses said [12], 'If to any one there come to be sons.' Therefore since the Son is other than things originate, alone the proper offspring of the Father's essence, this plea of the Arians about the word 'become' is worth nothing.

(5.) If moreover, baffled so far, they should still violently insist that the language is that of comparison, and that comparison in consequence implies oneness of kind, so that the Son is of the nature of Angels, they will in the first place incur the disgrace of rivalling and repeating what Valentinus held, and Carpocrates, and those other heretics, of whom the former said that the Angels were one in kind with the Christ, and Carpocrates that Angels are framers of the world [1]. Perchance it is under the instruction of these masters that they compare the Word of God with the Angels.

57. Though surely amid such speculations, they will be moved by the sacred poet, saying, 'Who is he among the gods that shall be like unto the Lord [2],' and, ' Among the gods there is none like unto Thee, O Lord [3].' However, they must be answered, with the chance of their profiting by it, that comparison confessedly does belong to subjects one in kind, not to those which differ. No one, for instance, would compare God with man, or again man with brutes, nor wood with stone, because their natures are unlike ; but God is beyond comparison, and man is compared to man, and wood to wood, and stone to stone. Now in such cases we should not speak of ' better,' but of ' rather' and ' more ;' thus Joseph was comely rather than his brethren, and Rachel than Leah ; star [4] is not better than star, but is the rather excellent in glory ; whereas in bringing together things which differ in kind, then ' better' is used to mark the difference, as has been said in the case of wisdom and jewels. Had then the Apostle said, 'by so much has the Son precedence of the Angels,' or ' by so much greater,' you would have had a plea, as if the Son were compared with the Angels ; but, as it is, in saying that He is 'better,' and differs as far as Son from servants, the Apostle shews that He is other than the Angels in nature.

---

5 Is. lvi. 4, 5.

5a There is apparently much confusion in the arrangement of the paragraphs that follow ; though the appearance may perhaps arise from Athan.'s incorporating some passage from a former work into his text, cf. note on § 32. It is easy to suggest alterations, but not anything satisfactory. The same ideas are scattered about. Thus συγκριτικῶς occurs in (3) and (5). The Son's seat on the right, and Angels in ministry, (3) fin. (10) (11). ' Become' interpreted as 'is originated and is,' (4) and (11). The explanation of ' become,' (4) (9) (11) (14). The Word's ἐπιδημία is introduced in (7) and (8) παρουσία being the more common word ; ἐπιδημία occurs Orat. ii. § 67 init. Serap. i. 9. Vid. however, § 61, notes. If a change must be suggested, it would be to transfer (4) after (8) and (10) after (3).

6 ἀπολελυμένως. vid. also Orat. ii. 54. 62. iii. 22. Basil. contr. Eunom. i. p. 244. Cyril. Thesaur. 25, p. 236. διαλελυμένως. Orat. iv. 1.

7 [The note, referred to above, p. 169, in which Newman defends the treatment of γενητὸν and γεννητὸν as synonymous, while yet admitting that they are expressly distinguished by Ath. in the text, is omitted for lack of space.] 8 John i. 3.

9 Ps. civ. 24. 10 Job i. 2. 11 Gen. xxi. 5.
12 Cf. Deut. xxi. 15.
1 These tenets and similar ones were common to many branches of the Gnostics, who paid worship to the Angels, or ascribed to them the creation ; the doctrine of their consubstantiality with our Lord arose from their belief in emanation. S. Athanasius here uses the word ὁμογενής, not ὁμοούσιος which was usual with them (vid Bull. D. F N. ii. 1, § 2) as with the Manichees after them, Beausobre, Manich. iii. 8. 2 Ps. lxxxix. 7. 3 Ib. lxxxvi 8.
4 Orat. ii. § 20.

(6.) Moreover by saying that He it is who has 'laid the foundation of all things [5],' he shews that He is other than all things originate. But if He be other and different in essence from their nature, what comparison of His essence can [6] there be, or what likeness to them? though, even if they have any such thoughts, Paul shall refute them, who speaks to the very point, 'For unto which of the Angels said He at any time, Thou art My Son, this day have I begotten Thee? And of the Angels He saith, Who maketh His Angels spirits, and His ministers a flame of fire [7].'

58. Observe here, the word 'made' belongs to things originate, and he calls them things made; but to the Son he speaks not of making, nor of becoming, but of eternity and kingship, and a Framer's office, exclaiming, 'Thy Throne, O God, is for ever and ever;' and, 'Thou, Lord, in the beginning hast laid the foundation of the earth, and the heavens are the works of Thine hands; they shall perish, but Thou remainest.' From which words even they, were they but willing, might perceive that the Framer is other than things framed, the former God, the latter things originate, made out of nothing. For what has been said, 'They shall perish,' is said, not as if the creation were destined for destruction, but to express the nature of things originate by the issue to which they tend [8]. For things which admit of perishing, though through the grace [9] of their Maker they perish not, yet have come out of nothing, and themselves witness that they once were not. And on this account, since their nature is such, it is said of the Son, 'Thou remainest,' to shew His eternity; for not having the capacity of perishing, as things originate have, but having eternal duration, it is foreign to Him to have it said, 'He was not before His generation,' but proper to Him to be always, and to endure together with the Father. And though the Apostle had not thus written in his Epistle to the Hebrews, still his other Epistles, and the whole of Scripture, would certainly forbid their entertaining such notions concerning the Word. But since he has here expressly written it, and, as has been above shewn, the Son is Offspring of the Father's essence, and He is Framer, and other things are framed by Him, and He is the Radiance and Word and Image and Wisdom of the Father, and things originate stand and serve in their place below the Triad, therefore the Son is different in kind and different in essence from things originate, and on the contrary is proper to the Father's essence and one in nature with it [10].' And hence

it is that the Son too says not, 'My Father is better than I [11],' lest we should conceive Him to be foreign to His Nature, but 'greater,' not indeed in greatness, nor in time, but because of His generation from the Father Himself [12], nay, in saying 'greater' He again shews that He is proper to His essence.

59. (7). And the Apostle's own reason for saying, 'so much better than the Angels,' was not any wish in the first instance to compare the essence [1] of the Word to things originate (for He cannot be compared, rather they are incommeasurable), but regarding the Word's visitation in the flesh, and the Economy which He then sustained, he wished to shew that He was not like those who had gone before Him; so that, as much as He excelled in nature those who were sent afore by Him, by so much also the grace which came from and through Him was better than the ministry through Angels [2]. For it is the function of servants, to demand the fruits and no more; but of the Son and Master to forgive the debts and to transfer the vineyard.

(8.) Certainly what the Apostle proceeds to say shews the excellence of the Son over things originate; 'Therefore we ought to give the more earnest heed to the things which we have heard, lest at any time we should let them slip. For if the word spoken by Angels was stedfast, and every transgression and disobedience received a just recompense of reward; how shall we escape, if we neglect so great salvation; which at the first began to be spoken by the Lord, and was confirmed unto us by them that heard Him [3].' But if the Son were in the number of things originate, He was not better than they, nor did disobedience involve increase of punishment because of Him; any more than in the Ministry of Angels there was not, according to each Angel, greater or less guilt in the transgressors, but the Law was one, and one was its vengeance on transgressors. But, whereas the Word is not in the number of originate things, but is Son of the Father, therefore, as He Himself is better and His acts better and transcendent, so also the punishment is worse. Let them contemplate then the grace which is through the Son, and let them acknowledge the witness which He gives even from His works, that He is other than things originated, and alone the very Son in the Father and the Father in Him.

He says that the Son is ἑτερογενὴς καὶ ἑτεροούσιος τῶν γενητῶν, καὶ τῆς τοῦ πατρὸς οὐσίας ἴδιος καὶ ὁμοφυής. vid. §§ 20, 21, notes.
[11] John xiv. 28.
[12] Athan. otherwise explains this text, *Incarn. contr. Arian.* 4. if it be his. This text is thus taken by Basil. *contr. Eun.* iv. p. 289. Naz. *Orat.* 30. 7, &c. &c. [1] §§ 60. 62. 64. ii. § 18.
[2] He also applies this text to our Lord's economy and ministry *de Sent. D.* 11. *in Apoll.* ii. 15. [3] Heb. ii. 1—3.

---

[5] Heb. i. 10. [6] *De Syn.* 45, note 9. [7] Heb. i. 7.
[8] § 29, note 10. [9] *De Decr.* 19, note 3.
[10] Here again is a remarkable avoidance of the word ὁμοούσιον.

And the Law [4] was spoken by Angels, and perfected no one [5], needing the visitation of the Word, as Paul hath said; but that visitation has perfected the work of the Father. And then, from Adam unto Moses death reigned [6]; but the presence of the Word abolished death [7]. And no longer in Adam are we all dying [8]; but in Christ we are all reviving. And then, from Dan to Beersheba was the Law proclaimed, and in Judæa only was God known; but now, unto all the earth has gone forth their voice, and all the earth has been filled with the knowledge of God [9], and the disciples have made disciples of all the nations [10], and now is fulfilled what is written, 'They shall be all taught of God [11].' And then what was revealed was but a type; but now the truth has been manifested. And this again the Apostle himself describes afterwards more clearly, saying, 'By so much was Jesus made a surety of a better testament;' and again, 'But now hath He obtained a more excellent ministry, by how much also He is the Mediator of a better covenant, which was established upon better promises.' And, 'For the Law made nothing perfect, but the bringing in of a better hope did.' And again he says, 'It was therefore necessary that the patterns of things in the heavens should be purified with these; but the heavenly things themselves with better sacrifices than these [12].' Both in the verse before us, then, and throughout, does he ascribe the word 'better' to the Lord, who is better and other than originated things. For better is the sacrifice through Him, better the hope in Him; and also the promises through Him, not merely as great compared with small, but the one differing from the other in nature, because He who conducts this economy, is 'better' than things originated.

60. (9.) Moreover the words 'He is become surety' denote the pledge in our behalf which He has provided. For as, being the 'Word,' He 'became flesh [1],' and 'become' we ascribe to the flesh, for it is originated and created, so do we here the expression 'He is become,' expounding it according to a second sense, viz. because He has become man. And let these contentious men know, that they fail in this their perverse purpose; let them know that Paul does not signify that His essence [2] has become, knowing, as he did, that He is

Son and Wisdom and Radiance and Image of the Father; but here too he refers the word 'become' to the ministry of that covenant, in which death which once ruled is abolished. Since here also the ministry through Him has become better, in that 'what the Law could not do in that it was weak through the flesh, God sending His own Son in the likeness of sinful flesh, and for sin condemned sin in the flesh [3],' ridding it of the trespass, in which, being continually held captive, it admitted not the Divine mind. And having rendered the flesh capable of the Word, He made us walk, no longer according to the flesh, but according to the Spirit, and say again and again, 'But we are not in the flesh but in the Spirit,' and, 'For the Son of God came into the world, not to judge the world, but to redeem all men, and that the world might be saved through Him [4].' Formerly the world, as guilty, was under judgment from the Law; but now the Word has taken on Himself the judgment, and having suffered in the body for all, has bestowed salvation to all [5]. With a view to this has John exclaimed, 'The law was given by Moses, but grace and truth came by Jesus Christ [6].' Better is grace than the Law, and truth than the shadow.

61. (10.) 'Better' then, as has been said, could not have been brought to pass by any other than the Son, who sits on the right hand of the Father. And what does this denote but the Son's genuineness, and that the Godhead of the Father is the same as the Son's [7]? For in that the Son reigns in His Father's kingdom, is seated upon the same throne as the Father, and is contemplated in the Father's Godhead, therefore is the Word God, and whoso beholds the Son, beholds the Father; and thus there is one God. Sitting then on the right, yet He does not place His Father on the left [8]; but whatever is right [9] and precious in the Father, that also the Son has, and says, 'All things that the Father hath are Mine [10].' Wherefore also the Son, though sitting on the right, also sees the Father on the right, though it be as become man that He says, 'I saw the Lord always before My face, for He is on My right hand, therefore I shall not fall [11].' This shews moreover that the Son is in the Father

---

4 Part of this chapter, as for instance (7) (8) is much more finished in point of style than the general course of his Orations. It may be indeed only the natural consequence of his warming with his subject, but this beautiful passage looks very much like an insertion. Some words of it are found in *Sent. D.* 11. written a few years sooner [cf. *supr.* 33, note 2.]
5 Heb. vii. 19. 6 Rom. v. 14. 7 2 Tim. i. 10.
8 1 Cor. xv. 22. 9 Is. xi. 9; vid. Ps. lxxvi. 1, and xix. 4.
10 Matt. xxviii. 19. 11 John vi. 45; Is. liv. 13.
12 Heb. vii. 22; viii. 6; vii. 19; ix. 23. 1 John i. 14.
2 § 45, note.

3 Rom. viii. 3. 4 John iii. 17.
5 Vid. *Incarn.* passim. Theod. *Eranist.* iii. pp. 196—198, &c. &c. It was the tendency of all the heresies concerning the Person of Christ to explain away or deny the Atonement. The Arians, after the Platonists, insisted on the pre-existing Priesthood, as if the incarnation and crucifixion were not of its essence. The Apollinarians resolved the Incarnation into a manifestation, Theod. *Eran.* i. The Nestorians denied the Atonement, *Procl. ad Armen.* p. 615. And the Eutychians, Leont. *Ep.* 28, 5.
6 John i. 17. 7 *De Syn.* 45, note 1.
8 Cf. August. *de Fid. et Symb.* 14. Does this passage of Athan.'s shew that the Anthropomorphites were stirring in Egypt already? δεξιόν
10 John xvi. 15. 11 Ps. xvi. 8.

and the Father in the Son; for the Father being on the right, the Son is on the right; and while the Son sits on the right of the Father, the Father is in the Son. And the Angels indeed minister ascending and descending; but concerning the Son he saith, 'And let all the Angels of God worship Him [12].' And when Angels minister, they say, 'I am sent unto thee,' and, 'The Lord has commanded;' but the Son, though He say in human fashion, 'I am sent [13],' and comes to finish the work and to minister, nevertheless says, as being Word and Image, 'I am in the Father, and the Father in Me;' and, 'He that hath seen Me, hath seen the Father;' and, 'The Father that abideth in Me. He doeth the works [14];' for what we behold in that Image are the Father's works.

(11.) What has been already said ought to shame those persons who are fighting against the very truth; however, if, because it is written, 'become better,' they refuse to understand 'become,' as used of the Son, as 'has been and is [1];' or again as referring to the better covenant having come to be [2], as we have said, but consider from this expression that the Word is called originate, let them hear the same again in a concise form, since they have forgotten what has been said.

62. If the Son be in the number of the Angels, then let the word 'become' apply to Him as to them, and let Him not differ at all from them in nature; but be they either sons with Him, or be He an Angel with them; sit they one and all together on the right hand of the Father, or be the Son standing with them all as a ministering Spirit, sent forth to minister Himself as they are. But if on the other hand Paul distinguishes the Son from things originate, saying, 'To which of the Angels said He at any time, Thou art My Son?' and the one frames heaven and earth, but they are made by Him; and He sitteth with the Father, but they stand by ministering, who does not see that he has not used the word 'become' of the essence of the Word, but of the ministration come through Him? For as, being the 'Word,' He 'became flesh,' so when become man, He became by so much better in His ministry than the ministry which came by the Angels, as Son excels servants and Framer things framed. Let them cease therefore to take the word 'become' of the substance of the Son, for He is not one of originated things; and let them acknowledge that it is indicative of His ministry and the Economy which came to pass.

(12.) But how He became better in His ministry, being better in nature than things originate, appears from what has been said before, which, I consider, is sufficient in itself to put them to shame. But if they carry on the contest, it will be proper upon their rash daring to close with them, and to oppose to them those similar expressions which are used concerning the Father Himself. This may serve to shame them to refrain their tongue from evil, or may teach them the depth of their folly. Now it is written, 'Become my strong rock and house of defence, that Thou mayest save me [3].' And again, 'The Lord became a defence for the oppressed [4],' and the like which are found in divine Scripture. If then they apply these passages to the Son, which perhaps is nearest to the truth, then let them acknowledge that the sacred writers ask Him, as not being originate, to become to them 'a strong rock and house of defence;' and for the future let them understand 'become,' and 'He made,' and 'He created,' of His incarnate presence. For then did He become 'a strong rock and house of defence,' when He bore our sins in His own body upon the tree, and said, 'Come unto Me, all ye that labour and are heavy laden, and I will give you rest [5].'

63. But if they refer these passages to the Father, will they, when it is here also written, 'Become' and 'He became,' venture so far as to affirm that God is originate? Yea, they will dare, as they thus argue concerning His Word; for the course of their argument carries them on to conjecture the same things concerning the Father, as they devise concerning His Word. But far be such a notion ever from the thoughts of all the faithful! for neither is the Son in the number of things originated, nor do the words of Scripture in question, 'Become,' and 'He became,' denote beginning of being, but that succour which was given to the needy. For God is always, and one and the same; but men have come to be afterwards through the Word, when the Father Himself willed it; and God is invisible and inaccessible to originated things, and especially to men upon earth. When then men in infirmity invoke Him, when in persecution they ask help, when under injuries they pray, then the Invisible, being a lover of man, shines forth upon them with His beneficence, which He exercises through and in His proper Word. And forthwith the divine manifestation is made to every one according to his need, and is made to the weak health, and to the persecuted a 'refuge' and 'house of defence;' and to the injured He says, 'While thou speakest I

---

[12] Heb. i. 6.
[13] Vid. John xvii. 3; Mark x. 45. [14] John xiv. 10, 9.
[1] Of His divine nature, (4) (8). [2] Of His human nature, and (10).

[3] Ps. xxx 3. Ib. ix. 9. [5] Matt. xi. 28.

will say, Here I am[6].' Whatever defence then comes to each through the Son, that each says that God has come to be to himself, since succour comes from God Himself through the Word. Moreover the usage of men recognises this, and every one will confess its propriety. Often succour comes from man to man; one has undertaken toil for the injured, as Abraham for Lot; and another has opened his home to the persecuted, as Obadiah to the sons of the prophets; and another has entertained a stranger, as Lot the Angels; and another has supplied the needy, as Job those who begged of him. And then, should one and the other of these benefited persons say, 'Such a one became an assistance to me,' and another 'and to me a refuge,' and 'to another a supply,' yet in so saying would not be speaking of the original becoming or of the essence of their benefactors, but of the beneficence coming to themselves from them; so also when the saints say concerning God, 'He became' and 'become Thou,' they do not denote any original becoming, for God is without beginning and unoriginate, but the salvation which is made to be unto men from Him.

64. This being so understood, it is parallel also respecting the Son, that whatever, and however often, is said, such as, 'He became' and 'become,' should ever have the same sense: so that as, when we hear the words in question, 'become better than the Angels' and 'He became,' we should not conceive any original becoming of the Word, nor in any way fancy from such terms that He is originate; but should understand Paul's words of His ministry and Economy when He became man. For when 'the Word became flesh and dwelt among us[7]' and came to minister and to grant salvation to all, then He became to us salvation, and became life, and became propitiation; then His economy in our behalf became much better than the Angels, and He became the Way and became the Resurrection. And as the words 'Become my strong rock' do not denote that the essence of God Himself became, but His lovingkindness, as has been said, so also here the 'having become better than the Angels,' and, 'He became,' and, 'by so much is Jesus become a better surety,' do not signify that the essence of the Word is originate (perish the thought!), but the beneficence which towards us came to be through His becoming Man; unthankful though the heretics be, and obstinate in behalf of their irreligion.

---

6 Is. lviii. 9.

John i. 14.

EXCURSUS B. ON § 22 (Note 3).

On the meaning of the formula πρὶν γεννηθῆναι οὐκ ἦν, in the Nicene Anathema.

IT was observed on p. 75, note 4[b], that there were two clauses in the Nicene Anathema which required explanation. One of them, ἐξ ἑτέρας ὑποστάσεως ἢ οὐσίας, has been discussed in the Excursus, pp. 77—82; the other, πρὶν γεννηθῆναι οὐκ ἦν, shall be considered now.

Bishop Bull has suggested a very ingenious interpretation of it, which is not obvious, but which, when stated, has much plausibility, as going to explain, or rather to sanction, certain modes of speech in some early Fathers of venerable authority, which have been urged by heterodox writers, and given up by Catholics of the Roman School, as savouring of Arianism. The foregoing pages have made it abundantly evident that the point of controversy between Catholics and Arians was, not whether our Lord was God, but whether He was Son of God; the solution of the former question being involved in that of the latter. The Arians maintained that the very word 'Son' implied a 'beginning,' or that our Lord was not Very God; the Catholics said that it implied 'connaturality,' or that He was Very God as one with God. Now five early writers, Athenagoras, Tatian, Theophilus, Hippolytus, and Novatian, of whom the authority of Hippolytus is very great, not to speak of Theophilus and Athenagoras, whatever be thought of Tatian and of Novatian, seem to speak of the divine generation as taking place immediately before the creation of the world, that is, as if not eternal, though at the same time they teach that our Lord existed before that generation. In other words they seem to teach that He was the Word from eternity, and became the Son at the beginning of all things ; some of them expressly considering Him, first as the λόγος ἐνδιάθετος, or Reason, in the Father, or (as may be speciously represented) a mere attribute ; next, as the λόγος προφορικὸς, or Word, terms which are explained, note on *de Syn.* 26 (5). This doctrine, when divested of figure and put into literal statement, might appear nothing more or less than this,— that at the beginning of the world the Son was created after the likeness of the Divine attribute of Reason, as its image or expression, and thereby became the Divine Word ; was made the instrument of creation, called the Son from that ineffable favour and adoption which God had bestowed on Him, and in due time sent into the world to manifest God's perfections to mankind ;—which, it is scarcely necessary to say, is the doctrine of Arianism.

Thus S. Hippolytus says,—

Τῶν δὲ γινομένων ἀρχηγὸν καὶ σύμβουλον καὶ ἐργάτην ἐγέννα λόγον, ὃν λόγον ἔχων ἐν ἑαυτῷ ἀόρατόν τε ὄντα τῷ κτιζομένῳ κόσμῳ, ὁρατὸν ποιεῖ· προτέραν φωνὴν φθεγγόμενος, καὶ φῶς ἐκ φωτὸς γεννῶν, προῆκεν τῇ κτίσει κύριον. *contr. Noet.* 10.

And S. Theophilus :—

Ἔχων οὖν ὁ θεὸς τὸν ἑαυτοῦ λόγον ἐνδιάθετον ἐν τοῖς ἰδίοις σπλάγχνοις, ἐγέννησεν αὐτὸν μετὰ τῆς ἑαυτοῦ σοφίας ἐξερευξάμενος πρὸ τῶν ὅλων . . . . ὁπότε δὲ ἠθέλησεν ὁ θεὸς ποιῆσαι ὅσα ἐβουλεύσατο, τοῦτον τὸν λόγον ἐγέννησε προφορικόν. πρωτότοκον πάσης κτίσεως. *ad Autol.* ii. 10—22.

Bishop Bull, *Defens. F. N.* iii. 5—8, meets this representation by maintaining that the γέννησις which S. Hippolytus and other writers spoke of, was but a metaphorical generation, the real and eternal truth being shadowed out by a succession of events in the economy of time, such as is the Resurrection (Acts xiii. 33), nay, the Nativity ; and that of these His going forth to create the worlds was one. And he maintains (ibid. iii. 9) that such is the mode of speaking adopted by the Fathers after the Nicene Council as well as before. And then he adds (which is our present point), that it is even alluded to and recognised in the Creed of the Council, which anathematizes those who say that ' the Son was not before His generation,' i.e. who deny that 'the Son *was* before His *generation*,' which statement accordingly becomes indirectly a Catholic truth.

I am not aware whether any writer has preceded or followed this great authority in this view[1]. The more obvious mode of understanding the Arian formula is this, that it is an argument *ex absurdo*, drawn from the force of the word Son, in behalf of the Arian doctrine ; it being, as they would say, a truism, that, 'whereas He was begotten, He was not *before* He was begotten,' and the denial of it a contradiction in terms. This certainly does seem to myself the true force of the formula ; so much so, that if Bishop Bull's explanation be admissible, it must, in order to its being so, first be shewn to be reducible to this sense, and to be included under it.

The point at issue between the two interpretations is this ; whether the clause πρὶν γεννηθῆναι οὐκ ἦν is intended for a *denial* of the *contrary* proposition, 'He was before His generation,' as Bishop Bull says ; or whether it is what Aristotle calls an enthymematic sentence, *assuming* the falsity, as confessed on all hands, of that contrary proposition, as self-contradictory, and directly denying, not it, but 'He was from everlasting.' Or, in other words, whether it opposes the position of the five writers, or the great Catholic doctrine itself ; and whether in consequence the Nicene Fathers are in their anathema indirectly sanctioning that position, or stating that doctrine. Bull considers that both sides *contemplated* the proposition, 'He was before His generation,'—and that the Catholics asserted or defended it ; some reasons shall here be given for the contrary view.

1. Now first, let me repeat, what was just now observed by the way, that the formula in question, when taken as an enthymematic sentence, or *reductio ad absurdum*, exactly expresses the main argument of the Arians, which they brought forward in so many shapes, as feeling that their cause turned upon it, ' He is a son, *therefore* He had a beginning.' Thus Socrates records Arius's words in the beginning of the controversy, (1) ' If the Father begat the Son, He who is begotten has a beginning of existence ; (2) therefore once the Son was not, ἦν ὅτε οὐκ ἦν ; (3) therefore He has His subsistence from nothing, ἐξ οὐκ ὄντων ἔχει τὴν ὑπόστασιν.' *H. E.* i. 5. The first of these propositions exactly answers to the οὐκ ἦν πρὶν γεννηθῆναι taken enthymematically ; and it may be added that when so taken, the three propositions will just answer to the three first formulæ anathematized at Nicæa, two of which are indisputably the same as two of them ; viz. ὅτι ἦν ποτε

---

[1] Waterland expresses the view here taken, and not Bishop Bull's ; vol. i. p. 114. Bull's language, on the other hand, is very strong : ' Sæpe olim, ut verum ingenue fatear, animum meum subiit admiratio, quid effato isto, ' Filius priusquam nasceretur, non erat,' sibi voluerint Ariani. De nativitate Christi ex beatissima Virgine dictum non esse exponendum constat: . . . Itaque de nativitate Filii loquuntur, quæ hujus universi creationem ante-

cessit. *Quis* vero, inquam, *sensus* dicti hujus " Filius non erat, sive non existebat, priusquam nasceretur ex Patre ante conditum mundum?" Ego sane nullus dubito, quin hoc pronunciatum Arianorum oppositum fuerit Catholicorum istorum sententiæ, qui docerent, Filium quidem paulo ante conditum mundum inexplicabili quodam modo ex Patre progressum fuisse ad constituendum universa, &c. *D. F. N.* iii. 9. § 2.

ὅτε οὐκ ἦν· ὅτι ποὶν γεννηθῆναι οὐκ ἦν· ὅτι ἐξ οὐκ ὄντων ἐγένετο. On the other hand, we hear nothing in the controversy of the position which Bull conceives to be opposed by Arius ('He *was* before His generation'), that is, supposing the formula in question does not allude to it ; unless indeed it is worth while to except the statement reprobated in the Letter of the Arians to Alexander, ὄντα πρότερον, γεννηθέντα εἰς υἱόν, which is explained, *de Syn.* 16, note 12.

2. Next, it should be observed that the other formulæ here, as elsewhere, mentioned, are enthymematic also, or carry their argument with them, and that, an argument resolvable often into the original argument derived from the word 'Son.' Such are ὁ ὢν τὸν μὴ ὄντα ἐκ τοῦ ὄντος ἢ τὸν ὄντα ; and ἐν τὸ ἀγένητον ἢ δύο ; and in like manner as regards the question of the τρεπτόν ; 'Has He free will' (thus Athanasius states the Arian objection) 'or has He not? is He good from choice according to free will, and can He, if He will, alter, being of an alterable nature? as wood or stone, has He not His choice free to be moved, and incline hither and thither?' supr. § 35. That is, they wished the word τρεπτὸς to carry with it its own self-evident application to our Lord, with the alternative of an absurdity ; and so to prove His created nature.

3. In § 32, S. Athanasius observes that the formula of the ἀγένητον was the later substitute for the original formulæ of Arius ; 'when they were no longer allowed to say, "out of nothing," and "He was not before His generation,"' they hit upon this word Unoriginate, that, by saying among the simple that the Son was originate, *they might imply the very same phrases* "out of nothing" and "He once was not."' Here he does not in so many words say that the argument from the ἀγένητον was a *substitute* for the οὐκ ἦν πρὶν γεννηθῆναι, yet surely it is not unfair so to understand him. But it is plain that the ἀγένητον was brought forward merely to express by an appeal to philosophy and earlier Fathers, that to be a Son was to have a beginning and a creation, and not to be God. This therefore will be the sense of the οὐκ ἦν πρὶν γεννηθῆναι. Nay, when the Arians asked, 'Is the ἀγένητον one or two,' they actually did assume that it was granted by their opponents that the Father only was ἀγένητος ; which it was not, if the latter held, nay, if they had sanctioned at Nicæa, as Bull says, that our Lord ἦν πρὶν γεννηθῇ ; and moreover which they knew and confessed was not granted, if their own formula οὐκ ἦν πρὶν γεννηθῆναι was directed against this statement.

4. Again, it is plain that the οὐκ ἦν πριν γεννηθῆναι is used by S. Athanasius as the *same* objection with ὁ ὢν τὸν μὴ ὄντα ἐκ τοῦ ὄντος, &c. E.g. he says, 'We might ask them in turn, God who is, has He so become, whereas He was not? or is He also before His generation? whereas He is, did He make Himself, or is He of nothing, &c., § 25. Now the ὁ ὢν τὸν μὴ ὄντα, &c., is evidently an *argument*, and that, grounded on the absurdity of saying ὁ ὢν τὸν ὄντα. S. Alexander's Encyclical Letter (vid. Socr. i. 6), compared with Arius's original positions and the Nicene Anathemas as referred to above, is a strong confirmation. In these three documents the formulæ agree together, except one ; and that one, which in Arius's language is 'he who is begotten has a beginning of existence,' is in the Nicene Anathema, οὐκ ἦν πρὶν γεννηθῆναι, but in S. Alexander's circular, ὁ ὢν θεὸς τὸν μὴ ὄντα ἐκ τοῦ μὴ ὄντος πεποίηκεν. The absence of the οὐκ ἦν πρὶν, &c., in S. Alexander is certainly remarkable. Moreover the two formulæ are treated as synonymous by Greg. Naz. *Orat.* 29. 9. Cyril, *Thesaur.* 4. p. 29 fin., and by Basil as quoted below. But indeed there is an internal correspondence between them, shewing that they have but one meaning. They are really but the same sentence in the active and in the passive voice.

5. A number of scattered passages in Athanasius lead us to the same conclusion. For instance, if the Arian formula had the sense which is here maintained, of being an argument against our Lord's eternity, the Catholic answer would be, 'He could not be *before* His generation because His generation is *eternal*, as being from the Father.' Now this is precisely the language Athanasius uses, when it occurs to him to introduce the words in question. Thus in *Orat.* ii. § 57 he says, 'The creatures began to come to be (γίνεσθαι) ; but the Word of God, not having beginning (ἀρχὴν) of being, surely did not begin to be, nor begin to come to be, but was always. And the works have a beginning (ἀρχὴν) in the making, and the beginning precedes things which come to be ; but the Word not being of such, rather Himself becomes the Framer of those things which have a beginning. And the being of things originate is measured by their becoming (ἐν τῷ γίνεσθαι), and at some beginning (origin) doth God begin to make them through the Word, that it may be known that they were not before their origination (πρὶν γενεσθαι) ; but the Word hath His being in no other origin than the Father' (vid. supr. § 11, note 1), 'whom they themselves allow to be unoriginate, so that He too exists unoriginately in the Father, being His offspring not His creature.' We shall find that other Fathers say just the same. Again, we have already come to a passage where for 'His generation,' he substitutes 'making,' a word which Bull would not say that either the Nicene Council or S. Hippolytus would use ; clearly shewing that the Arians were not quoting and denying a Catholic statement in the οὐκ ἦν πρὶν, &c., but laying down one of their own. 'Who is there in all mankind, Greek or Barbarian, who ventures to rank among creatures One whom he confesses the while to be God, and says that "He was not 'before He was made,' πρὶν ποιηθῇ."' *Orat.* i. § 10. Arius, who is surely the best explainer of his own words, says the same ; that is, he interprets 'generation' by 'making,' or confesses that he is bringing forward an argument, not opposing a dogma ; 'Before His generation,' he says, 'or creation, or destination (ὁρισθῇ), Rom. i. 4), or founding (vid. Prov. viii. 23), He was not ; for He was not ingenerate.' Theod. *Hist.* i. 4. Eusebius of Nicomedia also, in a passage which has already come before us, says distinctly, '"It is plain to any one," that what has been made was not before its *generation ;* but what came to be has an origin of being.' *De Syn.* § 17.

6. If there are passages in Athanasius which seem to favour the opposite interpretation, that is, to imply that the Catholics held or allowed, as Bp. Bull considers, that 'before His generation, He was,' they admit of an explanation. E.g. "How is He not in the number of the creatures, if, as they say, He was not before His generation? for it is proper to the creatures and works, not to be before their generation.' *Orat.* ii. § 22. This might be taken to imply that the Arians said, 'He was not,' and Catholics 'He was.' But the real meaning is this, 'How is He not a creature, if the *formula be true*, which they use, "He was not before His generation?"' for it may indeed properly be *said* of creatures that "they were not before their generation."' And so again when he says, 'if the Son was not before His generation, Truth was not always in God,' supr. § 20, he does not thereby imply that the Son *was* before His generation, but he means, 'if it be *true* that, &c.,' 'if the *formula holds*,' 'if it can be *said* of the Son, "He was not, &c."' Accordingly, shortly afterwards, in a passage already cited, he says the same of the Almighty Father in the way of parallel ; 'God who is, hath He so become, whereas He was not, or "is He too before His generation?"' (§ 25), not implying here any generation at all, but urging

that the question is *idle* and *irrelevant*, that the formula is *unmeaning* and does not *apply to*, cannot be *said* of, Father or Son.

7. Such an explanation of these passages, as well as the view here taken of the formula itself, receive abundant confirmation from S. Gregory Nazianzen and S. Hilary. What has been maintained is, that when S. Athanasius says, 'if the Son *is* not before His generation, then, &c.,' he does but mean, 'if it can be said,' 'if the words can be *used or applied* in this case.' Now the two Fathers just mentioned both decide that it is not true, *either* that the Son *was* before His generation, *or* that He was not; in other words, that the question is unmeaning and irrelevant, which is just the interpretation which has been here given to Athanasius. But again, in thus speaking, they thereby assert also that they did *not* hold, that they do *not* allow, that formula which Bull considers the Nicene Fathers defended and sanctioned, as being Catholic and in use both before the Council and after, viz. 'He *was* before His generation.' Thus S. Gregory in the passage in which he speaks of 'did He that is make Him that is not, &c.,' and 'before His generation, &c.,' as one and the same, expressly says, 'In His case, to be begotten *is concurrent* with existence and is from the beginning,' and that *in contrast* to the instance of men; who he says, do fulfil in a manner 'He who is, &c.' (Levi being in the loins of Abraham), i.e. fulfil Bull's proposition, 'He was before generation.' He proceeds, 'I say that *the question is irrelevant*, not the answer difficult.' And presently after, mentioning some idle inquiries by way of parallel, he adds, 'more ill-instructed, be sure, is it to decide whether what was generated *from the beginning* was or was not *before* generation, πρὸ τῆς γεννήσεως.' *Orat.* 29. 9.

8. S. Hilary, on the other hand, is so full on the subject in his *de Trin.* xii., and so entirely to the point for which I would adduce him, that but a few extracts of what might be made are either necessary or practicable. He states and argues on the formula expressly as an *objection;* Adjiciant hæc *arguta* satis atque *auditu placentia;* Si, inquit, natus est, cœpit; et cum cœpit, non fuit; et cum non fuit, non patitur ut fuerit. Atque *idcirco* piæ intelligentiæ sermonem esse contendant, Non fuit ante quam nasceretur, *quia* ut esset, qui non erat, natus est.' n. 18. He answers the objection in the same way, 'Unigenitus Deus neque non fuit aliquando non filius, neque fuit aliquid ante quam filius, neque quidquam aliquid ipse nisi filius,' n. 15, which is in express words to *deny*, 'He was before His generation.' Again, as Gregory, 'Ubi pater auctor est, ibi et nativitas est; et vero ubi auctor æternus est, ibi et nativitatis æternitas est,' n. 21. And he substitutes 'being always born' for 'being before birth;' 'Numquid ante tempora æterna esse, id ipsum sit quod est, eum qui erat nasci? quia nasci quod erat, jam non nasci est, sed se ipsum demutare nascendo. . . . Non est itaque id ipsum, natum ante tempora æterna semper esse, et esse antequam nasci.' n. 30. And he concludes, in accordance with the above explanation of the passages of Athanasius which I brought as if objections, thus: 'Cum itaque natum semper esse, nihil aliud sit confitendum esse, quam natum, id sensui, antequam nascitur *vel fuisse, vel non fuisse* non subjacet. n. 31.'

9. It may seem superfluous to proceed, but as Bishop Bull is an authority not lightly to be set aside, a passage from S. Basil shall be added. Eunomius objects, 'God begat the Son either being or not being, &c. . . . to him that is, there needs not generation.' He replies that Eunomius, '*because* animals first are not. and then are generated, and he who is born to-day, yesterday did not exist, *transfers* this conception to the subsistence of the Only-begotten; and says, *since* He has been generated, He was not before His generation, πρὸ τῆς γεννήσεως,' *contr. Eunom.* ii. 14. And he solves the objection as the other Fathers, by saying that our Lord is from everlasting, speaking of S. John, in the first words of his Gospel, as τῇ ἀϊδιότητι τοῦ πατρὸς τοῦ μονογενοῦς συνάπτων τὴν γέννησιν. § 15.

These then being the explanations which the contemporary and next following Fathers give of the Arian formula which was anathematized at Nicæa, it must be observed that the line of argument which Bishop Bull is pursuing, does not lead him to assign any direct reasons for the substitution of a different interpretation in their place. He is engaged, not in commenting on the Nicene Anathema, but in proving that the Post-Nicene Fathers admitted that view or statement of doctrine which he conceives *also* implied in that anathema; and thus the sense of the anathema, instead of being the subject of proof, is, as he believes, one of the proofs of the point which he is establishing. However, since these other collateral evidences which he adduces, may be taken to be some sort of indirect comment upon the words of the Anathema, the principal of them in point of authority, and that which most concerns us, shall here be noticed: it is a passage from the second Oration of Athanasius.

While commenting on the words, ἀρχὴ ὁδῶν εἰς τὰ ἔργα in the text, 'The Lord has created me the beginning of His ways unto the works,' S. Athanasius is led to consider the text 'first born of every creature,' πρωτότοκος πάσης κτίσεως: and he says that He who was μονογενὴς from eternity, became by a συγκατάβασις at the creation of the world πρωτότοκος. This doctrine Bp. Bull considers declaratory of a going forth, προέλευσις, or figurative *birth* from the Father, at the beginning of all things.

It will be observed that the very point to be proved is this, viz. not that there was a συγκατάβασις merely, but that according to Athanasius there was a γέννησις or proceeding from the Father, and that the word πρωτότοκος marks it. Bull's words are, that 'Catholici quidam Doctores, qui post exortam controversiam Arianam vixerunt, . . . illam τοῦ λόγου . . . . ex Patre *progressionem* (quod et συγκατάβασιν, hoc est, condescensionem eorum nonnulli appellarunt), ad condendum hæc universa agnovere; atque ejus etiam *progressionis respectu* ipsum τὸν λόγον a Deo Patre quasi *natum* fuisse et omnis creaturæ *primogenitum* in Scripturis dici confessi sunt.' *D. F. N.* iii. 9. § 1. Now I consider that S. Athanasius does not, as this sentence says, understand by primogenitus that our Lord was 'progressionis respectu a Deo Patre *quasi natus.*' He does not seem to me to speak of a generation or birth of the Son at all, though figurative, but of the birth of *all things*, and that *in* Him.

That Athanasius does not call the συγκατάβασις of the Word a birth, as denoted by the term πρωτότοκος, is plain from his own avowal in the passage to which Bull refers. 'Nowhere in the Scriptures,' he says, 'is He called πρωτότοκος τοῦ Θεοῦ, first-born *of God*, nor creature of God, but Only-begotten, Word, Wisdom, have their relation to the Father, and are proper to Him.' ii. 62. Here surely he expressly denies Bull's statement that 'first-born' means 'a Deo natus,' 'born of God.' Such additions as παρὰ τοῦ πατρὸς, he says, are reserved for μονογενὴς and λόγος.

He goes on to say *what* the term πρωτότοκος does mean : viz. instead of having any reference to a προέλευσις from the Father, it refers solely to the creatures ; our Lord is not called πρωτότοκος, because His προέλευσις is a 'type of His eternal generation,' but because by that προέλευσις He became the 'Prototype of all creation.' He, as it were, stamped His image, His Sonship, upon creation, and became the first-born in the sense of being the Archetypal Son. If this is borne out by the passage, Athanasius, it is plain, does not speak of any γέννησις whatever at the era of creation, though figurative ; πρωτότοκος does but mean μονογενὴς πρωτεύων ἐν τῇ κτίσει, or ἀρχὴ τῆς κτίσεως, or πρωτότυπον γέννημα, or μόνος γεννητὸς ἐν τοῖς γενητοῖς ; and no warrant is given, however indirect, to the idea that in the Nicene Anathema, the Fathers implied an allowance of the proposition, 'He was before His generation.'

As the whole passage occurs in the Discourse which immediately follows, it is not necessary to enter formally into the proof of this view of it, when the reader will soon be able to judge of it for himself. But it may be well to add two passages, one from Athenagoras, the other from S. Cyril, not in elucidation of the words of Athanasius, but of the meaning which I would put upon them.

The passage from Athenagoras is quoted by Bull himself, who of course is far from denying the doctrine of our Lord's Archetypal office ; and does but wish in addition to find in Athanasius the doctrine of a γέννησις. Athenagoras says that the Son is 'the first offspring, πρῶτον γέννημα, of the Father, not as come to be, γενόμενον (for God being Eternal Mind had from the beginning in Himself the Word, as having Reason eternally, λογικὸς ὢν), but that while as regards matter heavy and light were mixed together' (the passage is corrupt here), 'He went forth, προελθὼν, as an *idea* and *energy*,' i.e. as an Agent to create, and a Form and Rule to create by. And then he goes on to quote the very text on which Athanasius is employed when he explains πρωτότοκος. 'And the Prophetic Spirit confirms this doctrine, saying, The Lord hath created me a beginning (origin) of His ways, for His works.' *Leg.* 10.

And so S. Cyril, 'He is Only-begotten according to nature, as being alone from the Father, God from God, Light kindled from Light ; and He is First-born for our sakes, that, *as if to some immortal root* the whole creation might be ingrafted and might bud forth from the Everlasting. For all things were made by Him, and *consist* for ever and are *preserved in Him*.' *Thesaur.* 25 p. 238.

In conclusion it may be suggested whether the same explanation which has here been given of Athanasius's use of πρωτότοκος does not avail more exactly to the defence of two of the five writers from the charge of inaccurate doctrine, than that which Bull has preferred.

As to Athenagoras, we have already seen that he does not speak of a γέννησις at all in his account of creation, but simply calls the Son πρῶτον γέννημα, i.e. πρωτότυπον γέννημα.

Nor does Tatian approach nearer to the doctrine of a γέννησις. He says that at the creation the Word ἔργον πρωτότοκον τοῦ πατρὸς γίνεται. τοῦτον ἴσμεν τοῦ κόσμου τὴν ἀρχήν. *ad Graec.* 5. Here the word ἔργον, which at first sight promises a difficulty, does in fact explain both himself and Athenagoras. He says that at creation the Word became, γίνεται, not a *Son* (figuratively), as Bull would grant to the parties whom he is opposing, but a *work*. It was His great condescension, συγκατάβασις, to be accounted the first of the works, as being their *type* ; that as they were to be raised to an adoption and *called* sons, so He for that purpose might stoop to creation, and be *called* a work. As Tatian uses the word ἀρχὴ in the concluding clause, there is great reason to think that he is alluding to the very text which Athanasius and Athenagoras expressly quote, in which Wisdom is said to be 'created a beginning, ἀρχὴ, of ways, unto the *works*, εἰς τὰ ἔργα.'

As to Novatian, Bishop Bull himself observes that it is a question whether he need be understood to speak of any generation but that which is eternal ; nor does Pamelius otherwise explain him.

DISCOURSE II

CHAPTER XIV.

TEXTS EXPLAINED; FOURTHLY, HEBREWS iii. 2.

Introduction; the *Regula Fidei* counter to an Arian sense of the text; which is not supported by the word 'servant,' nor by 'made' which occurs in it; (how can the Judge be among the 'works' which 'God will bring into judgment?') nor by 'faithful;' and is confuted by the immediate context, which is about Priesthood; and by the foregoing passage, which explains the word 'faithful' as meaning trustworthy, as do 1 Pet. iv. fin. and other texts. On the whole *made* may safely be understood either of the divine generation or the human creation.

1. I DID indeed think that enough had been said already against the hollow professors of Arius's madness, whether for their refutation or in the truth's behalf, to insure a cessation and repentance of their evil thoughts and words about the Saviour. They, however, for whatever reason, still do not succumb; but, as swine and dogs wallow[1] in their own vomit and their own mire, rather invent new expedients for their irreligion. Thus they misunderstand the passage in the Proverbs, 'The Lord hath created me a beginning of His ways for His works[2],' and the words of the Apostle, 'Who was faithful to Him that made Him[3],' and straightway argue, that the Son of God is a work and a creature. But although they might have learned from what is said above, had they not utterly lost their power of apprehension, that the Son is not from nothing nor in the number of things originate at all, the Truth witnessing[4] it (for, being God, He cannot be a work, and it is impious to call Him a creature, and it is of creatures and works that we say, 'out of nothing,' and 'it was not before its generation'), yet since, as if dreading to desert their own fiction, they are accustomed to allege the aforesaid passages of divine Scripture, which have a good meaning, but are by them practised on, let us

proceed afresh to take up the question of the sense of these, to remind the faithful, and to shew from each of these passages that they have no knowledge at all of Christianity. Were it otherwise, they would not have shut themselves up in the unbelief[5] of the present Jews[6], but would have inquired and learned[6a] that, whereas 'In the beginning was the Word, and the Word was with God, and the Word was God,' in consequence, it was when at the good pleasure of the Father the Word became man, that it was said of Him, as by John, 'The Word became flesh[7];' so by Peter, 'He hath made Him Lord and Christ[8];'—as by means of Solomon in the Person of the Lord Himself, 'The Lord created me a beginning of His ways for His works[9];' so by Paul, 'Become so much better than the Angels[10];' and again, 'He emptied Himself, and took upon Him the form of a servant[11];' and again, 'Wherefore, holy brethren, partakers of the heavenly calling, consider the Apostle and High Priest of our profession, Jesus, who was faithful to Him that made Him[12].' For all these texts have the same force and meaning, a religious one, declarative of the divinity of the Word, even those of them which speak humanly concerning Him, as having become the Son of man. But, though this distinction is sufficient for their refutation, still, since from a misconception of the Apostle's words (to mention them first), they consider the Word of God to be one of the works, because of its being written, 'Who was faithful to Him that made Him,' I have thought it needful to silence this further argument of theirs, taking in hand[13], as before, their statement.

---

[5] Cf. Rom. xi. 32.
[6] τῶν νῦν Ἰουδαίων, means literally 'the Jews of this day,' as here and *Orat.* i. 8. 10. 38. *Orat.* ii. 1. b. iii. 28. c. But elsewhere this and similar phrases as distinctly mean the Arians, being used in contrast to the Jews. Their likeness to the Jews is drawn out, *Orat.* iii. 27. de Decr. i.
[6a] ἐρωτῶντες ἐμανθάνον; and so μαθὼν ἐδιδάσκεν, *Orat.* iii. 9. *de Decr.* 7. *supr.* p. 13, note a.　　[7] John i. 14.
[8] Acts ii. 36.　　[9] Prov. viii. 22.　　[10] Heb. i. 4.
[11] Phil. ii. 7.　　[12] Heb. iii. 1, 2; *Sent. D.* 11.
[13] By λαμβάνοντες παρ' αὐτῶν τὸ λῆμμα, 'accepting the proposition they offer,' he means that he is engaged in going through

---

[1] κυλιόμενοι, *Orat.* iii. 16. and *infr.* 19—72.　　[3] Heb. iii. 2.
[2] Prov. viii. 22. Cf. i. 53
[4] Vid. *infr.* note on 35.

2. If then He be not a Son, let Him be called a work, and let all that is said of works be said of Him, nor let Him and Him alone be called Son, nor Word, nor Wisdom; neither let God be called Father, but only Framer and Creator of things which by Him come to be; and let the creature be Image and Expression of His framing will, and let Him, as they would have it, be without generative nature, so that there be neither Word, nor Wisdom, no, nor Image, of His proper substance. For if He be not Son [1], neither is He Image [2]. But if there be not a Son, how then say you that God is a Creator? since all things that come to be are through the Word and in Wisdom, and without This nothing can be, whereas you say He hath not That in and through which He makes all things. For if the Divine Essence be not fruitful itself [3], but barren, as they hold, as a light that lightens not, and a dry fountain, are they not ashamed to speak of His possessing framing energy? and whereas they deny what is by nature, do they not blush to place before it what is by will [4]? But if He frames things that are external to Him and before were not, by willing them to be, and becomes their Maker, much more will He first be Father of an Offspring from His proper Essence. For if they attribute to God the willing about things which are not, why recognise they not that in God which lies above the will? now it is a something that surpasses will, that He should be by nature, and should be Father of His proper Word. If then that which comes first, which is according to nature, did not exist, as they would have it in their folly, how could that which is second come to be, which is according to will? for the Word is first, and then the crea-tion. On the contrary the Word exists, whatever they affirm, those irreligious ones; for through Him did creation come to be, and God, as being Maker, plainly has also His framing Word, not external, but proper to Him;—for this must be repeated. If He has the power of will, and His will is effective, and suffices for the consistence of the things that come to be, and His Word is effective, and a Framer, that Word must surely be the living Will [5] of the Father, and an essential [6] energy, and a real Word, in whom all things both consist and are excellently governed. No one can even doubt, that He who disposes is prior to the disposition and the things disposed. And thus, as I said, God's creating is second to His begetting; for Son implies something proper to Him and truly from that blessed and everlasting Essence; but what is from His will, comes into consistence from without, and is framed through His proper Offspring who is from It.

3. As we have shewn then they are guilty of great extravagance who say that the Lord is not Son of God, but a work, and it follows that we all of necessity confess that He is Son. And if He be Son, as indeed He is, and a son is confessed to be not external to his father but from him, let them not question about the terms, as I said before, which the sacred writers use of the Word Himself, viz. not 'to Him that begat Him,' but 'to Him that made Him;' for while it is confessed what His nature is, what word is used in such instances need raise no question [7]. For terms do not disparage His Nature; rather that Nature draws to Itself those terms and changes them. For terms are not prior to essences, but essences are first, and terms second. Wherefore also when the essence is a work or creature, then the words 'He made,' and 'He became,' and 'He created,' are used of it properly, and designate the work. But when the Essence is an Offspring and Son, then 'He made,' and 'He became,' and 'He created,' no longer properly belong to it, nor designate a work; but 'He made' we use without question for 'He begat.' Thus fathers often call the sons born of them their servants, yet without denying the genuineness of their nature; and often they affectionately call their own servants children, yet without putting out of sight their purchase of them originally; for they use the one appellation from their authority as being fathers, but in the other they speak from affection. Thus Sara called Abraham lord, though not a servant but a wife; and while to

certain texts brought against the Catholic view, instead of bringing his own proofs, vid. *Orat.* i. 37. Yet after all it is commonly his way, as here, to start with some general exposition of the Catholic doctrine which the Arian sense of the text in question opposes, and thus to create a prejudice or proof against the latter. vid. *Orat.* i. 10. 38. 40. init. 53. d. ii. 5. 12. init. 32—34. 35. 44. init. which refers to the whole discussion, 18—43. 73. 77. iii 18. init. 36. init. 42. 54. 51. init. &c. On the other hand he makes the ecclesiastical sense the rule of interpretation, τούτῳ [τῷ σκοπῷ, the general drift of Scripture doctrine] ὥσπερ κανόνι χρησάμενοι προσέχωμεν τῇ ἀναγνώσει τῆς θεοπνεύστου γραφῆς, iii. 28. fin. This illustrates what he means when he says that certain texts have a 'good,' 'pious,' 'orthodox' sense, i.e. they can be interpreted (in spite, if so be, of appearances) in harmony with the *Regula Fidei.* vid. *infr.* § 43, note; also notes on 35. and iii. 58.

[1] § 22, note.

[2] i.e. in any true sense of the word 'image;' or, so that He may be accounted the ἀπαράλλακτος εἰκων of the Father, vid. *de Syn.* i. The ancient Fathers consider, that the Divine Sonship is the very consequence (so to speak) of the necessity that exists. that One who is Infinite Perfection should subsist again in a Perfect Image of Himself, which is the doctrine to which Athan. goes on to allude, and the idea of which (he says) is prior to that of creation. A redundatio in imaginem is synonymous with a generatio Filii. Cf. Thomassin, *de Trin.* 19. 1.

[3] For καρπογόνος ἡ οὐσία, *de Decr.* 15. n. 9. γεννητικὸς, *Orat.* iii. 66. iv. 4. fin. ἄγονος, i. 14. fin. *Sent. Dion.* 15. 19. ἡ φυσικὴ γονιμότης, *Damasc. F. O.* i. 8 p. 133. ἄκαρπος, *Cyr. Thes.* p. 45. Epiph. *Hær.* 65 p. 609. b. Vid. the γέννησις and the κτίσις contrasted together *Orat.* i. 29. *de Decr.* 11, n. 6, *de Syn.* 51, n. 4. The doctrine in the text is shortly expressed, *infr. Orat.* iv. 4 fin. εἰ ἄγονος καὶ ἀνενέργητος. [4] *Orat.* iii. 59, &c.

[5] *Orat.* iii. 63. c.   [6] ἐνούσιος, *infr.* 28.
[7] § 1, note 13.

Philemon the master the Apostle joined Onesimus the servant as a brother, Bathsheba, although mother, called her son servant, saying to his father, 'Thy servant Solomon[8];'—afterwards also Nathan the Prophet came in and repeated her words to David, 'Solomon thy servant[9].' Nor did they mind calling the son a servant, for while David heard it, he recognised the 'nature,' and while they spoke it, they forgot not the 'genuineness,' praying that he might be made his father's heir, to whom they gave the name of servant; for to David he was son by nature.

4. As then, when we read this, we interpret it fairly, without accounting Solomon a servant because we hear him so called, but a son natural and genuine, so also, if, concerning the Saviour, who is confessed to be in truth the Son, and to be the Word by nature, the saints say, 'Who was faithful to Him that made Him,' or if He say of Himself, 'The Lord created me,' and, 'I am Thy servant and the Son of Thine handmaid[1],' and the like, let not any on this account deny that He is proper to the Father and from Him; but, as in the case of Solomon and David, let them have a right idea of the Father and the Son. For if, though they hear Solomon called a servant, they acknowledge him to be a son, are they not deserving of many deaths[2], who, instead of preserving the same explanation in the instance of the Lord, whenever they hear 'Offspring,' and 'Word,' and 'Wisdom,' forcibly misinterpret and deny the generation, natural and genuine, of the Son from the Father; but on hearing words and terms proper to a work, forthwith drop down to the notion of His being by nature a work, and deny the Word; and this, though it is possible, from His having been made man, to refer all these terms to His humanity? And are they not proved to be ·an abomination' also 'unto the Lord,' as having 'diverse weights[3]' with them, and with this estimating those other instances, and with that blaspheming the Lord? But perhaps they grant that the word 'servant' is used under a certain understanding, but lay stress upon 'Who made' as some great support of their heresy. But this stay of theirs also is but a broken reed; for if they are aware of the style of Scripture, they must at once give sentence against[4] themselves. For as Solomon, though a son, is called a servant, so, to repeat what was said above, although parents call the sons springing from themselves 'made' and 'created' and 'becoming,' for all this they do not deny their

nature. Thus Hezekiah, as it is written in Isaiah, said in his prayer, 'From this day I will make children, who shall declare Thy righteousness, O God of my salvation[5].' He then said, 'I will make;' but the Prophet in that very book and the Fourth of Kings, thus speaks, 'And the sons who shall come forth of thee[6].' He uses then 'make' for 'beget,' and he calls them who were to spring from him, 'made,' and no one questions whether the term has reference to a natural offspring. Again, Eve on bearing Cain said, 'I have gotten a man from the Lord[7];' thus she too used 'gotten' for 'brought forth.' For, first she saw the child, yet next she said, ' I have gotten.' Nor would any one consider, because of 'I have gotten,' that Cain was purchased from without, instead of being born of her. Again, the Patriarch Jacob said to Joseph, 'And now thy two sons, Ephraim and Manasseh, which became thine in Egypt, before I came unto thee into Egypt, are mine[8].' And Scripture says about Job, 'And there came to him seven sons and three daughters[9].' As Moses too has said in the Law, 'If sons become to any one,' and ' If he make a son[10].' Here again they speak of those who are begotten, as 'become' and 'made,' knowing that, while they are acknowledged to be sons, we need not make a question of 'they became,' or 'I have gotten,' or 'I made[11].' For nature and truth draw the meaning to themselves.

5. This being so[1], when persons ask whether the Lord is a creature or work, it is proper to ask of them this first, whether He is Son and Word and Wisdom. For if this is shewn, the surmise about work and creation falls to the ground at once and is ended. For a work could never be Son and Word; nor could the Son be a work. And again, this being the state of the case, the proof is plain to all, that the phrase, 'To Him who made Him' does not serve their heresy, but rather condemns it. For it has been shewn that the expression 'He made' is applied in divine Scripture even to children genuine and natural; whence, the Lord being proved to be the Father's Son naturally and genuinely, and Word, and Wisdom, though 'He made' be used concerning Him, or 'He became,' this is not said of Him as if a work, but the saints make no question about using the expression,—for instance in the case of Solomon, and Heze-

[8] 1 Kings i. 19.   [9] ver. 26.   [1] Ps. cxvi. 16.
[2] πολλάκις ἀπολωλέναι δίκαιοι, vid. *infr.* § 28.
[3] Prov. xx. 23   [4] *Apol. c. Ar.* 36.

[5] Is. xxxviii. 19, LXX.   [6] 2 Kings xx. 18; Is. xxxix. 7.
[7] Gen. iv. 1, and *infr.* 44. note on Qanâ.   [8] Gen. xlviii. 5,
LXX.   [9] Job i. 2, LXX.   [10] Cf. Deut. xxi. 15;
vid. Lev. xxv. 21, LXX.   [11] *Serap.* ii. 6. b.
[1] That is, while the style of Scripture *justifies* us in thus interpreting the word 'made,' doctrinal truth *obliges* us to do so. He considers the Regula Fidei the principle of interpretation, and accordingly he goes on at once to apply it. vid. *supr.* § 1, note 13.

kiah's children. For though the fathers had begotten them from themselves, still it is written, 'I have made,' and 'I have gotten,' and 'He became.' Therefore God's enemies, in spite of their repeated allegation of such phrases[2], ought now, though late in the day, after what has been said, to disown their irreligious thoughts, and think of the Lord as of a true Son, Word, and Wisdom of the Father, not a work, not a creature. For if the Son be a creature, by what word then and by what wisdom was He made Himself[3]? for all the works were made through the Word and the Wisdom, as it is written, 'In wisdom hast Thou made them all,' and, 'All things were made by Him, and without Him was not anything made[4].' But if it be He who is the Word and the Wisdom, by which all things come to be, it follows that He is not in the number of works, nor in short of things originate, but the Offspring of the Father.

6. For consider how grave an error it is, to call God's Word a work. Solomon says in one place in Ecclesiastes, that 'God shall bring every work into judgment, with every secret thing, whether it be good or whether it be evil[1].' If then the Word be a work, do you mean that He as well as others will be brought into judgment? and what room is there for judgment, when the Judge is on trial? who will give to the just their blessing, who to the unworthy their punishment, the Lord, as you must suppose, standing on trial with the rest? by what law shall He, the Lawgiver, Himself be judged? These things are proper to the works, to be on trial, to be blessed and to be punished by the Son. Now then fear the Judge, and let Solomon's words convince you. For if God shall bring the works one and all into judgment, but the Son is not in the number of things put on trial, but rather is Himself the Judge of works one and all, is not the proof clearer than the sun, that the Son is not a work but the Father's Word, in whom all the works both come to be and come into judgment? Further, if the expression, 'Who was faithful,' is a difficulty to them, from the thought that 'faithful' is used of Him as of others, as if He exercises faith and so receives the reward of faith, they must proceed at this rate to find fault with Moses for saying, 'God faithful and true[2],' and with St. Paul for writing, 'God is faithful, who will not suffer you to be tempted above that ye are able[3].' But when the saints spoke thus, they were not thinking of God

in a human way, but they acknowledged two senses of the word 'faithful' in Scripture, first 'believing,' then 'trustworthy,' of which the former belongs to man, the latter to God. Thus Abraham was faithful, because He believed God's word; and God faithful, for, as David says in the Psalm, 'The Lord is faithful in all His words[4],' or is trustworthy, and cannot lie. Again, 'If any faithful woman have widows[5],' she is so called for her right faith; but, 'It is a faithful saying[6],' because what He hath spoken has a claim on our faith, for it is true, and is not otherwise. Accordingly the words, 'Who is faithful to Him that made Him,' implies no parallel with others, nor means that by having faith He became well-pleasing; but that, being Son of the True God, He too is faithful, and ought to be believed in all He says and does, Himself remaining unalterable and not changed[7] in His human Economy and fleshly presence.

7. Thus then we may meet these men who are shameless, and from the single expression 'He made,' may shew that they err in thinking that the Word of God is a work. But further, since the drift also of the context is orthodox, shewing the time and the relation to which this expression points, I ought to shew from it also how the heretics lack reason; viz. by considering, as we have done above, the occasion when it was used and for what purpose. Now the Apostle is not discussing things before the creation when he thus speaks, but when 'the Word became flesh;' for thus it is written, 'Wherefore, holy brethren, partakers of the heavenly calling, consider the Apostle and High Priest of our profession Jesus, who was faithful to Him that made Him.' Now when became He 'Apostle,' but when He put on our flesh? and when became He 'High Priest of our profession,' but when, after offering Himself for us, He raised His Body from the dead, and, as now, Himself brings near and offers to the Father those who in faith approach Him, redeeming all, and for all propitiating God? Not then as wishing to signify the Essence of the Word nor His natural generation from the Father, did the Apostle say, 'Who was faithful to Him that made Him'—(perish the thought! for the Word is not made, but makes)—but as signifying His

---

[2] λεξείδια, Orat. iii. 59. a Sent. D. 4. c.
[3] Orat. iii. 62 init. infr. § 22, note. [4] Ps. civ. 24; John i. 3.
[1] Eccles. xii. 14. [2] Combines Greek of Deut. xxxii. 4 and Ex. xxxiv. 6; cf. Rev. iii. 14. [3] 1 Cor. x. 13.

[4] Ps. cxlv. 14. LXX. [5] 1 Tim. v. 16. [6] Tit. iii. 8, &c.
[7] ἄτρεπτος καὶ μὴ ἀλλοιούμενος; vid. supr. de Decr. 14. it was the tendency of Arianism to consider that in the Incarnation some such change actually was undergone by the Word, as they had from the first maintained in the abstract was possible; that whereas He was in nature τρεπτὸς, He was in fact ἀλλοιούμενος. This was implied in the doctrine that His superhuman nature supplied the place of a soul in His manhood. Hence the semi-Arian Sirmian Creed anathematizes those who said, τὸν λόγον τροπὴν ὑπομεμενηκότα, vid. De Syn. 27. 12). This doctrine connected them with the Apollinarian and Eutychian Schools, to the former of which Athan. compares them, contr. Apoll. i. 12. while, as opposing the latter, Theodoret entitles his first Dialogue Ἄτρεπτος.

descent to mankind and High-priesthood which did 'become'—as one may easily see from the account given of the Law and of Aaron. I mean, Aaron was not born a high-priest, but a man; and in process of time, when God willed, he became a high-priest; yet became so, not simply, nor as betokened by his ordinary garments, but putting over them the ephod, the breastplate [1], the robe, which the women wrought at God's command, and going in them into the holy place, he offered the sacrifice for the people; and in them, as it were, mediated between the vision of God and the sacrifices of men. Thus then the Lord also, 'In the beginning was the Word, and the Word was with God, and the Word was God;' but when the Father willed that ransoms should be paid for all and to all, grace should be given, then truly the Word, as Aaron his robe, so did He take earthly flesh, having Mary for the Mother of His Body as if virgin earth [2], that, as a High Priest, having He as others an offering, He might offer Himself to the Father, and cleanse us all from sins in His own blood, and might rise from the dead.

8. For what happened of old was a shadow of this; and what the Saviour did on His coming, this Aaron shadowed out according to the Law. As then Aaron was the same and did not change by putting on the high-priestly dress [3], but remaining the same was only robed, so that, had any one seen him offering, and had said, 'Lo, Aaron has this day become high-priest,' he had not implied that he then had been born man, for man he was even before he became high-priest, but that he had been made high-priest in his ministry, on putting on the garments made and prepared for the high-priesthood; in the same way it is possible in the Lord's instance also to understand aright, that He did not become other than Himself on taking the flesh, but, being the same as before, He was robed in it; and the expressions 'He became' and 'He was made,' must not be understood as if the Word,

considered as the Word [3a], were made, but that the Word, being Framer of all, afterwards [4] was made High Priest, by putting on a body which was originate and made, and such as He can offer for us; wherefore He is said to be made. If then indeed the Lord did not become man [5], that is a point for the Arians to battle; but if the 'Word became flesh,' what ought to have been said concerning Him when become man, but 'Who was faithful to Him that made Him?' for as it is proper to the Word to have it said of Him, 'In the beginning was the Word,' so it is proper to man to 'become' and to be 'made.' Who then, on seeing the Lord as a man walking about, and yet appearing to be God from His works, would not have asked, Who made Him man? and who again, on such a question, would not have answered, that the Father made Him man, and sent Him to us as High Priest? And this meaning, and time, and character, the Apostle himself, the writer of the words, 'Who is faithful to Him that made Him,' will best make plain to us, if we attend to what goes before them. For there is one train of thought, and the lection is all about One and the Same. He writes then in the Epistle to the Hebrews thus; 'Forasmuch then as the children are partakers of flesh and blood, He also Himself likewise took part of the same; that through death He might destroy him that had the power of death, that is, the devil; and deliver them who through fear of death were all their lifetime subject to bondage. For verily He took not on Him the nature of Angels; but He took on Him the seed of Abraham. Wherefore in all things it behoved

---

[3a] ᾗ λόγος ἐστι. cf. i. 43. Orat. ii. 74. e. iii. 38 init. 39. b. 41 init. 45 init. 52. b. iv. 23. f.

[4] The Arians considered that our Lord's Priesthood preceded His Incarnation, and belonged to His Divine Nature, and was in consequence the token of an inferior divinity. The notice of it therefore in this text did but confirm them in their interpretation of the words made, &c. For the Arians, vid. Epiph. Hær. 69, 37. Eusebius too had distinctly declared, Qui videbatur, erat agnus Dei: qui occultabatur sacerdos Dei. advers. Sabell. i. p. 2. b. vid. also Demonst. i. 10. p. 38. iv. 16. p. 193. v. 3. p. 223. contr. Marc. pp. 8 and 9. 66. 74. 95. Even S. Cyril of Jerusalem makes a similar admission, Catech. x. 14. Nay S. Ambrose calls the Word, plenum justitiæ sacerdotalis, de fug. sæc. 3. 14. S. Clement Alex. before them speaks once or twice of the λόγος ἀρχιερεὺς, e.g. Strom. ii. 9 fin. and Philo still earlier uses similar language, de Profug. p. 466. (whom S. Ambrose follows), de Somniis p. 597. vid. Thomassin. de Incarn. x. 9. Nestorius on the other hand maintained that the Man Christ Jesus was the Priest, relying on the text which has given rise to this note; Cyril, adv. Nest. p. 64. and Augustine and Fulgentius may be taken to countenance him, de Consens. and Evang. i. 6. ad Thrasim. iii. 30. The Catholic doctrine is, that the Divine Word is Priest in and according to His manhood. vid. the parallel use of πρωτότοκος, infr. 62—64. 'As He is called Prophet and even Apostle for His humanity,' says S. Cyril Alex. 'so also Priest.' Glaph. ii. p. 58. and so Epiph. loc. cit. Thomassin loc. cit. makes a distinction between a divine Priesthood or Mediatorship, such as the Word may be said to sustain between the Father and all creatures, and an earthly one for the sake of sinners. vid. also Huet Origenian. ii. 3. § 4, 5. For the history of the controversy among Protestants as to the Nature to which His Mediatorship belongs, vid. Petav. Incarn. xii. 3. 4. [Herzog-Plitt Art. Stancar.]

[5] [One of the few passages in which Ath. glances at the Arian Christology. A long note is omitted here on the subject of Or. i. 8, note 3.]

---

[1] Exod. xxix. 5.

[2] ἀνεργάστου γῆς is an allusion to Adam's formation from the ground; and so Irenæus, Hær. iii. 21. fin. and many later fathers.

[3] This is one of those distinct and luminous protests by anticipation against Nestorianism, which in consequence may be abused to the purpose of the opposite heresy. Such expressions as περιτιθέμενος τὴν ἐσθῆτα, ἐκαλύπτετο, ἐνδυσάμενος σῶμα, were familiar with the Apollinarians, against whom S. Athanasius is, if possible, even more decided. Theodoret objects Hær. v. 11. p. 422. to the word προκάλυμμα, as applied to our Lord's manhood, as implying that He had no soul; vid. also Naz. Ep. 102. fin. (ed. 1840). In Naz. Ep. 101. p. 90. παραπέτασμα is used to denote an Apollinarian idea. Such expressions were taken to imply that Christ was not in nature man, only in some sense human; not a substance, but an appearance; yet pseudo-Athan. contr. Sabell. Greg. 4. has παραπεπετασμένην and κάλυμμα, ibid. init. S. Cyril. Hieros. καταπέτασμα, Catech. xii. 26. xiii. 32. after Hebr. x. 20. and Athan. ad Adelph. 5. e. Theodor. παραπέτασμα, Eran. i. p. 22. and προκάλυμμα, ibid. p. 23. and adv. Gent. vi. p. 877. and στολῇ, Eran. l. c. S. Leo has caro Christi velamen, Ep. 59. p. 979. vid. also Serm. 22. p. 70. Serm. 25. p. 84.

Him to be made like unto His brethren, that He might be a merciful and faithful High Priest in things pertaining to God, to make reconciliation for the sins of the people. For in that He Himself hath suffered being tempted, He is able to succour them that are tempted. Wherefore, holy brethren, partakers of a heavenly calling, consider the Apostle and High Priest of our profession, Jesus ; who was faithful to Him that made Him [6].'

9. Who can read this whole passage without condemning the Arians, and admiring the blessed Apostle, who has spoken well? for when was Christ 'made,' when became He 'Apostle,' except when, like us, He 'took part in flesh and blood?' And when became He 'a merciful and faithful High Priest,' except when 'in all things He was made like unto His brethren?' And then was He 'made like,' when He became man, having put upon Him our flesh. Wherefore Paul was writing concerning the Word's human Economy, when he said, 'Who was faithful to Him that made Him,' and not concerning His Essence. Have not therefore any more the madness to say that the Word of God is a work; whereas He is Son by nature Only-begotten, and then had 'brethren,' when He took on Him flesh like ours ; which moreover, by Himself offering Himself, He was named and became 'merciful and faithful,'—merciful, because in mercy to us He offered Himself for us, and faithful, not as sharing faith with us, nor as having faith in any one as we have, but as deserving to receive faith in all He says and does, and as offering a faithful sacrifice, one which remains and does not come to nought. For those which were offered according to the Law, had not this faithfulness, passing away with the day and needing a further cleansing ; but the Saviour's sacrifice, taking place once, has perfected everything, and is become faithful as remaining for ever. And Aaron had successors, and in a word the priesthood under the Law exchanged its first ministers as time and death went on ; but the Lord having a high priesthood without transition and without succession, has become a 'faithful High Priest,' as continuing for ever ; and faithful too by promise, that He may hear[7] and not mislead those who come to Him. This may be also learned from the Epistle of the great Peter, who says, 'Let them that suffer according to the will of God, commit their souls to a faithful Creator[8].' For He is faithful as not changing, but abiding ever, and rendering what He has promised.

10. Now the so-called gods of the Greeks, unworthy the name, are faithful neither in their essence nor in their promises ; for the same are not everywhere, nay, the local deities come to nought in course of time, and undergo a natural dissolution ; wherefore the Word cries out against them, that 'faith is not strong in them,' but they are 'waters that fail,' and 'there is no faith in them.' But the God of all, being one really and indeed and true, is faithful, who is ever the same, and says, 'See now, that I, even I am He,' and I 'change not[1] ;' and therefore His Son is 'faithful,' being ever the same and unchanging, deceiving neither in His essence nor in His promise ;— as again says the Apostle writing to the Thessalonians, 'Faithful is He who calleth you, who also will do it[2] ;' for in doing what He promises, He is faithful to His words. And he thus writes to the Hebrews as to the word's meaning 'unchangeable ;' 'If we believe not, yet He abideth faithful ; He cannot deny Himself[3].' Therefore reasonably the Apostle, discoursing concerning the bodily presence of the Word, says, an 'Apostle and faithful to Him that made Him,' shewing us that, even when made man, 'Jesus Christ' is 'the same yesterday, and to-day, and for ever[4]' is unchangeable. And as the Apostle makes mention in his Epistle of His being made man when mentioning His High Priesthood, so too he kept no long silence about His Godhead, but rather mentions it forthwith, furnishing to us a safeguard on every side, and most of all when he speaks of His humility, that we may forthwith know His loftiness and His majesty which is the Father's. For instance, he says, 'Moses as a servant, but Christ as a Son[5] ;' and the former 'faithful in his house,' and the latter 'over the house,' as having Himself built it, and being its Lord and Framer, and as God sanctifying it. For Moses, a man by nature, became faithful, in believing God who spoke to Him by His Word; but[6] the Word was not as one of things originate in a body, nor as creature in creature, but as God in flesh[7], and Framer of all and Builder in that which was built by Him. And men are clothed in flesh in order to be and to subsist ; but the Word of God was made man in order to sanctify the flesh, and, though He was Lord, was in the form of a servant ; for the whole creature is the

---

[1] Vid. Jer. ix. 3. and xv. 18 ; Deut. xxxii. 20, LXX. ; ib. xxxii. 39 ; Mal. iii. 6.   [2] 1 Thess. v. 24.   [3] 2 Tim. ii. 13. [4] Heb. xiii. 8.   [5] Heb. iii. 5, 6.
[6] Here is a protest beforehand against the Monophysite doctrine, but such anticipations of various heresies are too frequent, as we proceed, to require or bear notice.
[7] θεὸς ἐν σαρκὶ, vid. λόγος ἐν σ. iii. 54. a. θ. ἐν σώματι, ii. 12. c. 15. a. λ. ἐν σώμ. Sent. D. 8 fin.

---

[6] Heb. ii. 14—18 ; iii. 2.   [7] Or, answer, vid. infr. iii. 27.
[8] 1 Pet. iv. 19.

Word's servant, which by Him came to be, and was made.

11. Hence it holds that the Apostle's expression, 'He made,' does not prove that the Word is made, but that body, which He took like ours; and in consequence He is called our brother, as having become man. But if it has been shewn, that, even though the word 'made' be referred to the Very Word, it is used for 'begat,' what further perverse expedient will they be able to fall upon, now that the present discussion has cleared up the word in every point of view, and shewn that the Son is not a work, but in Essence indeed the Father's offspring, while in the Economy, according to the good pleasure[8] of the Father, He was on our behalf made, and consists as man? For this reason then it is said by the Apostle, 'Who was faithful to Him that made Him;' and in the Proverbs, even creation is spoken of. For so long as we are confessing that He became man, there is no question about saying, as was observed before, whether 'He became,' or 'He has been made,' or 'created,' or 'formed,' or 'servant,' or 'son of an handmaid,' or 'son of man,' or 'was constituted,' or 'took His journey,' or 'bridegroom,' or 'brother's son,' or 'brother.' All these terms happen to be proper to man's constitution; and such as these do not designate the Essence of the Word, but that He has become man.

CHAPTER XV.

Texts Explained ; Fifthly, Acts ii. 36.

The *Regula Fidei* must be observed ; *made* applies to our Lord's manhood ; and to His manifestation ; and to His office relative to us ; and is relative to the Jews. Parallel instance in Gen. xxvii. 29, 37. The context contradicts the Arian interpretation.

11 (*continued*). THE same is the meaning of the passage in the Acts which they also allege, that in which Peter says, that 'He hath made both Lord and Christ that same Jesus whom ye have crucified.' For here too it is not written, 'He made for Himself a Son,' or 'He made Himself a Word,' that they should have such notions. If then it has not escaped their memory, that they speak concerning the Son of God, let them make search whether it is anywhere written. 'God made Himself a Son,' or 'He created for Himself a Word;' or again, whether it is anywhere written in plain terms, 'The Word is a work or creation;' and then let them proceed to make their case, the insensate men, that here too they may receive their answer. But if they can produce nothing

of the kind, and only catch at such stray expressions as 'He made' and 'He has been made,' I fear lest, from hearing, 'In the beginning God made the heaven and the earth,' and 'He made the sun and the moon,' and 'He made the sea,' they should come in time to call the Word the heaven, and the Light which took place on the first day, and the earth, and each particular thing that has been made, so as to end in resembling the Stoics, as they are called, the one drawing out their God into all things[1], the other ranking God's Word with each work in particular ; which they have well nigh done already, saying that He is one of His works.

12. But here they must have the same answer as before, and first be told that the Word is a Son, as has been said above[2], and not a work, and that such terms are not to be understood of His Godhead, but the reason and manner of them investigated. To persons who so inquire, the human Economy will plainly present itself, which He undertook for our sake. For Peter, after saying, 'He hath made Lord and Christ,' straightway added, 'this Jesus whom ye crucified;' which makes it plain to any one, even, if so be, to them, provided they attend to the context, that not the Essence of the Word, but He according to His manhood is said to have been made. For what was crucified but the body? and how could be signified what was bodily in the Word, except by saying 'He made?' Especially has that phrase, 'He made,' a meaning consistent with orthodoxy; in that he has not said, as I observed before, 'He made Him Word,' but 'He made Him Lord,' nor that in general terms[3], but 'towards' us, and 'in the midst of' us, as much as to say, 'He manifested Him.' And this Peter himself, when he began this primary teaching, carefully[4] expressed, when he said to them, 'Ye men of Israel, hear these words: Jesus of Nazareth, a man manifested of God towards you by miracles, and wonders, and signs, which God did by Him in the midst of you, as ye yourselves know[5].' Consequently the term which he uses in the end, 'made,' this He has explained in the beginning by 'manifested,' for by the signs and wonders which the Lord did, He was manifested to be not merely man, but God in a body and Lord also, the Christ. Such also is the passage in the Gospel according to John, 'Therefore the more did the Jews persecute Him, because He not only broke the Sabbath, but said also that God was His own Father, making Himself

---

[8] κατ᾽ εὐδοκίαν *Orat.* iii. 64. init.

[1] Brucker *de Zenon.* § 7. n. 14.   [2] § 1, note 13.   [3] ἁπλῶς.
[4] μετὰ παρατηρήσεως. vid. infr. 44. e. 59. b. 71. e. *Orat.* iii. 52. b.
[5] Acts ii. 22.

equal with God [6].' For the Lord did not then fashion Himself to be God, nor indeed is a made God conceivable, but He manifested it by the works, saying, 'Though ye believe not Me, believe My works, that ye may know that I am in the Father, and the Father in Me [7].' Thus then the Father has 'made' Him Lord and King in the midst of us, and towards us who were once disobedient; and it is plain that He who is now displayed as Lord and King, does not then begin to be King and Lord, but begins to shew His Lordship, and to extend it even over the disobedient.

13. If then they suppose that the Saviour was not Lord and King, even before He became man and endured the Cross, but then began to be Lord, let them know that they are openly reviving the statements of the Samosatene. But if, as we have quoted and declared above, He is Lord and King everlasting, seeing that Abraham worships Him as Lord, and Moses says, 'Then the Lord rained upon Sodom and upon Gomorrah brimstone and fire from the Lord out of heaven [8];' and David in the Psalms, 'The Lord said unto my Lord, Sit Thou on My right hand [9];' and, 'Thy Throne, O God, is for ever and ever; a sceptre of righteousness is the sceptre of Thy Kingdom [10];' and, 'Thy Kingdom is an everlasting Kingdom [11];' it is plain that even before He became man, He was King and Lord everlasting, being Image and Word of the Father. And the Word being everlasting Lord and King, it is very plain again that Peter said not that the Essence of the Son was made, but spoke of His Lordship over us, which 'became' when He became man, and, redeeming all by the Cross, became Lord of all and King. But if they continue the argument on the ground of its being written, 'He made,' not willing that 'He made' should be taken in the sense of 'He manifested,' either from want of apprehension, or from their Christ-opposing purpose, let them attend to another sound exposition of Peter's words. For he who becomes Lord of others, comes into the possession of beings already in existence; but if the Lord is Framer of all and everlasting King, and when He became man, then gained possession of us, here too is a way in which Peter's language evidently does not signify that the Essence of the Word is a work, but the after-subjection of all things, and the Saviour's Lordship which came to be over all. And this coincides with what we said before [11a]; for as we then introduced the words, 'Become my God and defence,' and 'the Lord became a refuge for the oppressed [12],' and it stood to reason that these expressions do not shew that God is originate, but that His beneficence 'becomes' towards each individual, the same sense has the expression of Peter also.

14. For the Son of God indeed, being Himself the Word, is Lord of all; but we once were subject from the first to the slavery of corruption and the curse of the Law, then by degrees fashioning for ourselves things that were not, we served, as says the blessed Apostle, 'them which by nature are no Gods [1],' and, ignorant of the true God, we preferred things that were not to the truth; but afterwards, as the ancient people when oppressed in Egypt groaned, so, when we too had the Law 'engrafted [2]' in us, and according to the unutterable sighings [3] of the Spirit made our intercession, 'O Lord our God, take possession of us [4],' then, as 'He became for a house of refuge' and a 'God and defence,' so also He became our Lord. Nor did He then begin to be, but we began to have Him for our Lord. For upon this, God being good and Father of the Lord, in pity, and desiring to be known by all, makes His own Son put on Him a human body and become man, and be called Jesus, that in this body offering Himself for all, He might deliver all from false worship and corruption, and might Himself become of all Lord and King. His becoming therefore in this way Lord and King, this it is that Peter means by, 'He hath made Him Lord,' and 'hath sent Christ;' as much as to say, that the Father in making Him man (for to be made belongs to man), did not simply make Him man, but has made Him in order to His being Lord of all men, and to His hallowing all through the Anointing. For though the Word existing in the form of God took a servant's form, yet the assumption of the flesh did not make a servant [5] of the Word, who was by nature Lord; but rather, not only was it that emancipation of all humanity which takes place by the Word, but that very Word who was by nature Lord, and was then made man, hath by means of a servant's form been made Lord of all and Christ, that is, in order to hallow all by the Spirit. And as God, when 'becoming a God and defence,' and saying, 'I will be a God to them,' does not then become God more than before, nor then begins to become God, but, what He ever is, that He then becomes to those who need Him, when it

---

12 Ps. lxxi. 3. *stony rock*, E. V. Ps. ix. 9. *defence*.
1 Gal. iv. 8. 2 James i. 21.
3 Rom. viii. 26. 4 Is. xxvi. 13. LXX.
5 οὐκ ἐδούλου τὸν λόγον· though, as he said *sup.* § 10, the Word became a servant, as far as He was man. He says the same thing *Ep. Æg* 17. So say Naz. *Orat.* 32. 18. Nyssen. *ad Simpl.* (t. 2. p. 471.) Cyril. Alex. *adv. Theodor.* p. 223. Hilar. *de Trin.* xi. Ambros. 1. *Epp.* 46, 3.

---

6 John v. 16, 18. 7 John x. 38. not to the letter.
8 Gen. xix. 24. 9 Ps. cx. 1. 10 Ps. xlv. 6.
11 Ps. cxlv. 13. 11a § 62, cf. Serm. Maj. de Fid. 1.

pleaseth Him, so Christ also being by nature Lord and King everlasting, does not become Lord more than He was at the time He is sent forth, nor then begins to be Lord and King, but what He is ever, that He then is made according to the flesh; and, having redeemed all, He becomes thereby again Lord of quick and dead. For Him henceforth do all things serve, and this is David's meaning in the Psalm, 'The Lord said unto my Lord, Sit Thou on My right hand, until I make Thine enemies Thy footstool [6].' For it was fitting that the redemption should take place through none other than Him who is the Lord by nature, lest, though created by the Son, we should name another Lord, and fall into the Arian and Greek folly, serving the creature beyond the all-creating God [7].

15. This, at least according to my nothingness, is the meaning of this passage; moreover, a true and a good meaning have these words of Peter as regards the Jews. For Jews, astray from the truth, expect indeed the Christ as coming, but do not reckon that He undergoes a passion, saying what they understand not; 'We know that, when the Christ cometh, He abideth for ever, and how sayest Thou, that He must be lifted up [8]?' Next they suppose Him, not the Word coming in flesh, but a mere man, as were all the kings. The Lord then, admonishing Cleopas and the other, taught them that the Christ must first suffer; and the rest of the Jews that God was come among them, saying, 'If He called them gods to whom the word of God came, and the Scripture cannot be broken, say ye of Him whom the Father hath sanctified and sent into the world, Thou blasphemest, because I said, I am the Son of God [9]?'

16. Peter then, having learned this from the Saviour, in both points set the Jews right, saying, "O Jews, the divine Scriptures announce that Christ cometh, and you consider Him a mere man as one of David's descendants, whereas what is written of Him shews Him to be not such as you say, but rather announces Him as Lord and God, and immortal, and dispenser of life. For Moses has said, 'Ye shall see your Life hanging before your eyes [1].' And David in the hundred and ninth Psalm, 'The Lord said unto My Lord, Sit Thou on My right hand, till I make Thine enemies Thy footstool [2];' and in the fifteenth, 'Thou shalt not leave my soul in hades, neither

shalt Thou suffer Thy Holy One to see corruption [3].' Now that these passages have not David for their scope he himself witnesses, avowing that He who was coming was His own Lord. Nay you yourselves know that He is dead, and His remains are with you. That the Christ then must be such as the Scriptures say, you will plainly confess yourselves. For those announcements come from God, and in them falsehood cannot be. If then ye can state that such a one has come before, and can prove him God from the signs and wonders which he did, ye have reason for maintaining the contest, but if ye are not able to prove His coming, but are expecting such an one still, recognise the true season from Daniel, for his words relate to the present time. But if this present season be that which was of old afore-announced, and ye have seen what has taken place among us, be sure that this Jesus, whom ye crucified, this is the expected Christ. For David and all the Prophets died, and the sepulchres of all are with you, but that Resurrection which has now taken place, has shewn that the scope of these passages is Jesus. For the crucifixion is denoted by 'Ye shall see your Life hanging,' and the wound in the side by the spear answers to 'He was led as a sheep to the slaughter [4],' and the resurrection, nay more, the rising of the ancient dead from out their sepulchres (for these most of you have seen), this is, 'Thou shalt not leave My soul in hades,' and 'He swallowed up death in strength [5],' and again, 'God will wipe away.' For the signs which actually took place shew that He who was in a body was God, and also the Life and Lord of death. For it became the Christ, when giving life to others, Himself not to be detained by death; but this could not have happened, had He, as you suppose, been a mere man. But in truth He is the Son of God, for men are all subject to death. Let no one therefore doubt, but the whole house of Israel know assuredly that this Jesus, whom ye saw in shape a man, doing signs and such works, as no one ever yet had done, is Himself the Christ and Lord of all. For though made man, and called JESUS, as we said before, He received no loss by that human passion, but rather, in being made man, He is manifested as Lord of quick and dead. For since, as the Apostle said, 'in the wisdom of God the world by wisdom knew not God, it pleased God by the foolishness of preaching to save them that believe [6].' And so, since we men would not acknowledge God through His Word, nor serve the Word of God our

---

[6] Ps. cx. 1.
[7] Vid. Rom. i. 25. and so both text and application very frequently, e.g. *Ep. Æg.* 4. e. 13. c. Vid. supr. i. 8, note 8, infr. iii. 16. note   [8] John xii. 34, not to the letter.
[9] John x. 36.
[1] Deut. xxviii. 66. Vid. [*de Incar.* 35. The text is frequently thus explained by the Fathers].   [2] Ps. cx. 1.

[3] Ps. xvi. 10.   [4] Is. liii. 7.   [5] Is. xxv. 8.
[6] 1 Cor. i. 21.

natural Master, it pleased God to shew in man His own Lordship, and so to draw all men to Himself. But to do this by a mere man beseemed not[7]; lest, having man for our Lord, we should become worshippers of man[8]. Therefore the Word Himself became flesh, and the Father called His Name Jesus, and so 'made' Him Lord and Christ, as much as to say, 'He made Him to rule and to reign;' that while in the Name of Jesus, whom ye crucified, every knee bows, we may acknowledge as Lord and King both the Son and through Him the Father."

17. The Jews then, most of them[1], hearing this, came to themselves and forthwith acknowledged the Christ, as it is written in the Acts. But, the Ario-maniacs on the contrary choose to remain Jews, and to contend with Peter; so let us proceed to place before them some parallel phrases; perhaps it may have some effect upon them, to find what the usage is of divine Scripture. Now that Christ is everlasting Lord and King, has become plain by what has gone before, nor is there a man to doubt about it; for being Son of God, He must be like Him[2], and being like, He is certainly both Lord and King, for He says Himself, 'He that hath seen Me, hath seen the Father.' On the other hand, that Peter's mere words, 'He hath made Him both Lord and Christ,' do not imply the Son to be a creature, may be seen from Isaac's blessing, though this illustration is but a faint one for our subject. Now he said to Jacob, 'Become thou lord over thy brother;' and to Esau, 'Behold, I have made him thy lord[3].' Now though the word 'made' had implied Jacob's essence and the coming into being, even then it would not be right in them as much as to imagine the same of the Word of God, for the Son of God is no creature as Jacob was; besides, they might inquire and so rid themselves of that extravagance. But if they do not understand it of his essence nor of his coming into being, though Jacob was by nature creature and work, is not their madness worse than the Devil's[4], if what they dare not ascribe in consequence of a like phrase even to things by nature originate, that they attach to the Son of God, saying that He is a creature? For Isaac said 'Become' and 'I have made,' signifying neither the coming into being nor the essence of Jacob (for after thirty years and

more from his birth he said this); but his authority over his brother, which came to pass subsequently.

18. Much more then did Peter say this without meaning that the Essence of the Word was a work; for he knew Him to be God's Son, confessing, 'Thou art the Christ, the Son of the Living God[5];' but he meant His Kingdom and Lordship which was formed and came to be according to grace, and was relatively to us. For while saying this, he was not silent about the Son of God's everlasting Godhead which is the Father's; but He had said already, that He had poured the Spirit on us; now to give the Spirit with authority, is not in the power of creature or work, but the Spirit is God's Gift[6]. For the creatures are hallowed by the Holy Spirit; but the Son, in that He is not hallowed by the Spirit, but on the contrary Himself the Giver of it to all[7], is therefore no creature, but true Son of the Father. And yet He who gives the Spirit, the same is said also to be made; that is, to be made among us Lord because of His manhood, while giving the Spirit because He is God's Word. For He ever was and is, as Son, so also Lord and Sovereign of all, being like in all things[8] to the Father, and having all that is the Father's[9], as He Himself has said[10].

CHAPTER XVI.

INTRODUCTORY TO PROVERBS viii. 22, THAT THE SON IS NOT A CREATURE.

Arian formula, a creature but not as one of the creatures; but each creature is unlike all other creatures; and no creature can create. The Word then differs from all creatures in that in which they, though otherwise differing, all agree together, as creatures; viz. in being an efficient cause; in being the one medium or instrumental agent in creation; moreover in being the revealer of the Father; and in being the object of worship.

18. (continued). Now in the next place let us consider the passage in the Proverbs, 'The Lord created me a beginning of His ways for His works[1];' although in shewing that the Word is no work, it has been also shewn that He is no creature. For it is the same

---

7 In the text the Mediatorial Lordship is made an office of God the Word; still, not as God, but as man. Cf. Augustine, *Trin.* i. 27. 28. In like manner the Priesthood is the office of God in the form of man, supr. 8, note 4. And so again none but the Eternal Son could be πρωτότοκος, yet He is so called when sent as Creator and as incarnate. infr. 64.   8 Infr. iii. 32 fin.
1 οἱ πλεῖστοι. [An exaggeration, cf. Rom. xi. 7, &c.]
2 § 22, note.   3 Gen. xxvii. 29, 37.   4 Alluding to the temptation.

5 Matt. xvi. 16.
6 θεοῦ δῶρον. And so more distinctly S. Basil, δῶρον τοῦ θεοῦ τὸ πνεῦμα. *de Sp. S.* 57, and more frequently the later Latins, as in the Hymn, 'Altissimi Donum Dei;' and the earlier, e.g. Hil. *de Trin.* ii. 29. and August. *Trin.* xv. 29. v. 15, Petav. *Trin.* vii. 13. § 20.   7 Supr. ch. xii.   8 ὅμοιος κατὰ πάντα. vid. infr. § 22, note 4.   9 Vid. infr. note on *Orat.* iii. 1.   10 Vid. John xvi. 15.
1 Prov. viii. 22. [This text, which had been immemorially applied to the Λόγος (*supr.* p. 168, note 7), and which in the false rendering of the LXX. strongly favoured the Arian side], is presently explained at greater length than any other of the texts he handles, forming the chief subject of the Oration henceforth, after an introduction which extends down to 44.

to say work or creature, so that the proof that He is no work is a proof also that He is no creature. Whereas one may marvel at these men, thus devising excuses to be irreligious, and nothing daunted at the refutations which meet them upon every point. For first they set about deceiving the simple by their questions [2], 'Did He who is make from that which was not one that was not or one that was [3]?' and, 'Had you a son before begetting him [4]?' And when this had been proved worthless, next they invented the question, 'Is the Unoriginate one or two [5]?' Then, when in this they had been confuted, straightway they formed another, 'Has He free-will and an alterable nature [6]?' But being forced to give up this, next they set about saying, 'Being made so much better than the Angels [7];' and when the truth exposed this pretence, now again, collecting them all together, they think to recommend their heresy by 'work' and 'creature [8].' For they mean those very things over again, and are true to their own perverseness, putting into various shapes and turning to and fro the same errors, if so be to deceive some by that variousness. Although then abundant proof has been given above of this their reckless expedient, yet, since they make all places sound with this passage from the Proverbs, and to many who are ignorant of the faith of Christians, seem to say somewhat, it is necessary to examine separately, 'He created' as well as 'Who was faithful to Him that made Him [9];' that, as in all others, so in this text also, they may be proved to have got no further than a fantasy.

19. And first let us see the answers, which they returned to Alexander of blessed memory, in the outset, while their heresy was in course of formation. They wrote thus: 'He is a creature, but not as one of the creatures; a work, but not as one of the works; an offspring, but not as one of the offsprings [1].' Let every one consider the profligacy and craft of this heresy; for knowing the bitterness of its own malignity, it makes an effort to trick itself out with fair words, and says, what indeed it means, that He is a creature, yet thinks to be able to screen itself by adding, 'but not as one of the creatures.' However, in thus writing, they rather convict themselves of irreligion; for if, in your opinion, He is simply

a creature, why add the pretence [2], 'but not as one of the creatures?' And if He is simply a work, how 'not as one of the works?' In which we may see the poison of the heresy. For by saying, 'offspring, but not as one of the offsprings,' they reckon many sons, and one of these they pronounce to be the Lord; so that according to them He is no more Only-begotten, but one out of many brethren, and is called [3] offspring and son. What use then is this pretence of saying that He is a creature and not a creature? for though ye shall say, Not as 'one of the creatures,' I will prove this sophism of yours to be foolish. For still ye pronounce Him to be one of the creatures; and whatever a man might say of the other creatures, such ye hold concerning the Son, ye truly 'fools and blind [4].' For is any one of the creatures just what another is [5], that ye should predicate this of the Son as some prerogative [6]? And all the visible creation was made in six days:—in the first, the light which He called day; in the second the firmament; in the third, gathering together the waters, He bared the dry land, and brought out the various fruits that are in it; and in the fourth, He made the sun and the moon and all the host of the stars; and on the fifth, He created the race of living things in the sea, and of birds in the air; and on the sixth, He made the quadrupeds on the earth, and at length man. And 'the invisible things of Him from the creation of the world are clearly seen, being understood by the things that are made [7]; and neither the light is as the night, nor the sun as the moon; nor the irrational as rational man; nor the Angels as the Thrones, nor the Thrones as the Authorities, yet they are all creatures, but each of the things made according to its kind

---

[2] From the methodical manner in which the successive portions of his foregoing Oration are here referred to, it would almost seem as if he were answering in course some Arian work. vid. also *supr. Orat.* i. 37, 53. *infr. Orat.* iii. 26. He does not seem to be tracing the controversy historically.   3 Supr. ch. vii.   4 Ch. viii.
5 Ch. ix.   6 Ch. x.   7 Ch. xiii.   8 Ch. xiv. and xv.
9 Ch. xiv. Heb. iii. 2.
1 Vid. Arius's letter, *de Syn.* 16. This was the sophism by means of which Valens succeeded with the Fathers of Arminium. vid. S. Jerome *in Luciferian.* 18. vid. also in Eusebius, *supr. Ep. Eus.* 6.

[2] *De Syn.* 32.
3 υἱὸν χρηματίζειν. The question between Catholics and Arians was whether our Lord was a true Son, or only *called* Son. 'Since they whisper something about Word and Wisdom as only *names* of the Son, &c." ὀνόματα μόνον, *supr.* i. 26, note 1, and *de Decr.* 16, note 10. And so 'the title of Image is not a token of a similar substance, but His *name* only,' *supr.* i. 21, and so *infr.* 38. where τοῖς ὀνόμασι is synonymous with κατ' ἐπίνοιαν, as *Sent. D.* 22. f. a. Vid. also 39. *Orat.* iii. 11. 18. 'not named Son, but ever Son,' iv. 24. fin. *Ep. Æg.* 16. 'We call Him so, and mean truly what we say; they say it, but do not confess it.' Chrysost. in *Act. Hom.* 33. 4. vid. also νόθοις ὥσπερ ὀνόμασι, Cyril. *de Trin.* ii. p. 418. Non hæc nuda nomina, Ambros. *de Fid.* i. 17. Yet, since the Sabellians equally failed here, also considering the Sonship as only a notion or title, vid. *Orat.* iv. 2. (where in contrast, 'The Father is Father, and the Son Son,' vid. supr. p. 319, note 1.) 12. 23. 25. the word 'real' was used as against *them*, and in opposition to ἀνυπόστατος λόγος, by the Arians, and in consequence failed as a test of orthodox teaching; e.g. by Arius, *supr.* p. 97. by Euseb. *in Marc.* pp. 19, d. 35, b. 161, c. by Asterius, *infr.* 37. by Palladius and Secundus in the Council of Aquileia ap. Ambros. *Opp.* t. 2. p. 791. (ed. Bened.) by Maximinus ap. August. *contr. Max.* i. 6.   4 Matt. xxiii. 19.
5 And so S. Ambrose, Quæ enim creatura non sicut alia creatura non est? Homo non ut Angelus, terra non ut cœlum. *de Fid.* i. n. 130. and a similar passage in Nyss. *contr. Eun.* iii. p. 132, 3.
6 ἐξαίρετον. vid. *infr. Orat.* iii. 3. init. iv. 28. init. Euseb. *Eccl. Theol.* pp. 47. b. 73. b. 89. b. 124. a. 129. c. Theodor. *H. E.* p. 732. Nyss. *contr. Eunom.* iii. p. 133. a. Epiph. *Hær.* 76. p. 970. Cyril. *Thes.* p. 160.   7 Rom. i. 20.

exists and remains in its own essence, as it was made.

20. Let the Word then be excepted from the works, and as Creator be restored to the Father, and be confessed to be Son by nature; or if simply He be a creature, then let Him be assigned the same condition as the rest one with another, and let them as well as He be said every one of them to be 'a creature, but not as one of the creatures, offspring or work, but not as one of the works or offsprings.' For ye say that an offspring is the same as a work, writing 'generated or made[1].' For though the Son excel the rest on a comparison, still a creature He is nevertheless, as they are; since in those which are by nature creatures one may find some excelling others. Star, for instance, differs from star in glory, and the rest have all of them their mutual differences when compared together; yet it follows not for all this that some are lords, and others servants to the superior, nor that some are efficient causes[2], others by them come into being, but all have a nature which comes to be and is created, confessing in their own selves their Framer: as David says in the Psalms, 'The heavens declare the glory of God, and the firmament sheweth His handy work[3];' and as Zorobabel the wise says, 'All the earth calleth upon the Truth, and the heaven blesseth it: all works shake and tremble at it[4].' But if the whole earth hymns the Framer and the Truth, and blesses, and fears it, and its Framer is the Word, and He Himself says, 'I am the Truth[5],' it follows that the Word is not a creature, but alone proper to the Father, in whom all things are disposed, and He is celebrated by all, as Framer; for 'I was by Him disposing[6];' and 'My Father worketh hitherto, and I work[7].' And the word 'hitherto' shews His eternal existence in the Father as the Word; for it is proper to the Word to work the Father's works and not to be external to Him.

21. But if what the Father worketh, that the Son worketh also[1], and what the Son createth, that is the creation of the Father, and yet the Son be the Father's work or creature, then either He will work His own self, and will be His own creator (since what the Father worketh is the Son's work also), which is absurd and impossible; or, in that He creates and worketh the things of the Father, He Himself is not a work nor a creature; for else being Himself an efficient cause[2], He may cause that to be in the case of things caused, which He Himself has become, or rather He may have no power to cause at all.

For how, if, as you hold, He is come of nothing, is He able to frame things that are nothing into being? or if He, a creature, withal frames a creature, the same will be conceivable in the case of every creature, viz. the power to frame others. And if this pleases you, what is the need of the Word, seeing that things inferior can be brought to be by things superior? or at all events, every thing that is brought to be could have heard in the beginning God's words, 'Become' and 'be made,' and so would have been framed. But this is not so written, nor could it be. For none of things which are brought to be is an efficient cause, but all things were made through the Word: who would not have wrought all things, were He Himself in the number of the creatures. For neither would the Angels be able to frame, since they too are creatures, though Valentinus, and Marcion, and Basilides think so, and you are their copyists; nor will the sun, as being a creature, ever make what is not into what is; nor will man fashion man, nor stone devise stone, nor wood give growth to wood. But God is He who fashions man in the womb, and fixes the mountains, and makes wood grow; whereas man, as being capable of science, puts together and arranges that material, and works things that are, as he has learned; and is satisfied if they are but brought to be, and being conscious of what his nature is, if he needs aught, knows to ask[3] it of God.

22. If then God also wrought and compounded out of materials, this indeed is a gentile thought, according to which God is an artificer and not a Maker, but yet even in that case let the Word work the materials, at the bidding and in the service of God[1]. But if He

---

1 γεννηθέντα ἢ ποιηθέντα; as if they were synonymous; in opposition to which the Nicene Creed says, γεννηθέντα οὐ ποιηθέντα. In like manner Arius in his letter to Eusebius uses the words, πρὶν γεννηθῇ ἤτοι κτισθῇ, ἢ ὁρισθῇ, ἢ θεμελιωθῇ, Theodor. H. E. p. 750. And to Alexander, ἀχρόνως γεννηθεὶς καὶ πρὸ αἰώνων κτισθεὶς καὶ θεμελιωθείς· de Syn. 16. And Eusebius to Paulinus, κτιστὸν καὶ θεμελιωτὸν καὶ γεννητόν Theod. p. 752. The different words profess to be Scriptural, and to explain each other; 'created' being in Prov. viii. 22. 'made' in the passages considered in the last two chapters, 'appointed' or 'declared' in Rom. i. 4. and 'founded' or 'established' in Prov. viii. 23. which is discussed *infr.* 22, &c. vid. also 52. ² 21, note 2.
3 Ps. xix. 1. ⁴ 1 Esdr. iv. 36. 5 John xiv. 6.
⁶ Prov. viii. 30, LXX. 7 John v. 17. ¹ *Orat.* iii. 11. note.

2 ποιητικὸν αἴτιον, also, *infr.* 27. and *Orat.* iii. 14. and *contr. Gent.* 9 init. No creature can create, vid. e.g. about Angels, August. *de Civ. Dei* xii. 24. *de Trin.* iii. 13—18. Damasc. *F. O.* ii. 3. Cyril *in Julian,* ii. p. 62. 'Our reason rejects the idea that the Creator should be a creature, for creation is by the Creator.' Hil. *Trin.* xii. 5. πῶς δύναται τὸ κτιζόμενον κτίζειν; ἢ πῶς ὁ κτίζων κτίζεται; Athan. *ad Afros.* 4 fin. Vid. also *Serap.* i. 24, 6. iii. 4, e. The Gnostics who attributed creation to Angels are alluded to *infr.* *Orat.* iii. 12. Epiph. *Hær.* 52. 53, 163, &c. Theodor. *Hær.* i. 1 and 3. 3 *De Decr.* 11.
¹ προσταττόμενος καὶ ὑπουργῶν. It is not quite clear that Athan. accepts these words in his own person, as has been assumed *de Decr.* 9. note 2, *de Syn.* 27 (3). Vid. *de Decr.* 7. and *infr.* 24. and 31, which, as far as they go, are against the use of the word. Also S. Basil objects to ὑπουργὸς *contr. Eunom.* ii. 21. and S. Cyril in *Joan.* p. 48. though S. Basil speaks of τὸν προστάττοντα κύριον. i. 46, note 3. and S. Cyril of the Son's ὑποταγή, *Thesaur.* p. 255.

calls into existence things which existed not by His proper Word, then the Word is not in the number of things non-existing and called ; or we have to seek another Word[2], through whom He too was called ; for by the Word the things which were not have come to be. And if through Him He creates and makes, He is not Himself of things created and made ; but rather He is the Word of the Creator God, and is known from the Father's works which He Himself worketh, to be 'in the Father and the Father in Him,' and ' He that hath seen Him hath seen the Father[3],' because the Son's Essence is proper to the Father, and He in all points like Him[4]. How then does He create through Him, unless it be His Word and His Wisdom? and how can He be Word and Wisdom, unless He be the proper offspring of His Essence[5], and did not come to be, as others, out of nothing? And whereas all things are from nothing, and are creatures, and the Son, as they say, is one of the creatures too, and of things which once were not, how does He alone reveal the Father, and none else but He know the Father? For could He, a work, possibly know the Father, then must the Father be also known by all according to the proportion of the measures of each : for all of them are works as He is. But if it be impossible for things originate either to see or to know, for the sight and the knowledge of Him surpasses all (since God Himself says, ' No one shall see My face and live[6]'), yet the Son has declared, 'No one knoweth the Father, save the Son[7],' therefore the Word is different from all things originate, in that He alone knows and alone sees the Father, as He says, ' Not that any one hath seen the Father, save He that is from the Father,' and ' no one knoweth the Father save

the Son[8],' though Arius think otherwise. How then did He alone know, except that He alone was proper to Him? and how proper, if He were a creature, and not a true Son from Him? (For one must not mind saying often the same thing for religion's sake.) Therefore it is irreligious to think that the Son is one of all things ; and blasphemous and unmeaning to call Him ' a creature, but not as one of the creatures, and a work, but not as one of the works, an offspring, but not as one of the offsprings ;' for how not as one of these, if, as they say, He was not before His generation[9]? for it is proper to the creatures and works not to be before their origination, and to subsist out of nothing, even though they excel other creatures in glory; for this difference of one with another will be found in all creatures, which appears in those which are visible[10].

23. Moreover if, as the heretics hold, the Son were creature or work, but not as one of the creatures, because of His excelling them in glory, it were natural that Scripture should describe and display Him by a comparison in His favour with the other works ; for instance, that it should say that He is greater than Archangels, and more honourable than the Thrones, and both brighter than sun and moon, and greater than the heavens. But he is not in fact thus referred to ; but the Father shews Him to be His own proper and only Son, saying, 'Thou art My Son,' and ' This is My beloved Son, in whom I am well pleased[1] ' Accordingly the Angels ministered unto Him, as being one beyond themselves ; and they worship Him, not as being greater in glory, but as being some one beyond all the creatures, and beyond themselves, and alone the Father's proper Son according to essence[2]. For if He was worshipped as excelling them in glory, each of things subservient ought to worship what excels itself. But this is not the case[3] ; for creature does not worship creature, but servant Lord, and creature God. Thus Peter the Apostle hinders Cornelius who would worship him, saying, ' I myself also am a man[4].' And an Angel, when John would worship him in the Apocalypse, hinders him, saying, ' See thou do it not ; for I am thy fellow-servant, and of thy brethren the Prophets, and of them that keep the sayings of this book : worship God[5].' Therefore to God alone appertains worship, and this the very Angels know, that though they excel other beings in glory, yet they are all creatures and not to be worshipped[6], but worship the Lord. Thus Manoah, the father of

---

Vid. ' ministering, ὑπηρετοῦντα, to the Father of all.' Just. *Tryph.* p. 72. 'The Word become minister, ὑπηρέτης, of the Creator,' Origen *Hom. in Joan.* p. 61. also *Constit. Ap.* viii. 12. but Pseudo-Athan. objects to ὑπηρετῶν, *de Comm. Essent.* 30. and Athan. apparently, *infr.* 28. Again, 'Whom did He order, præcepit?' Iren. *Hær.* iii. 8. n. 3. 'The Father bids, ἐντέλλεται (allusion to Ps. xxxiii. 9. vid. *infr.* 31), the Word accomplishes. . . . He who commands, κελεύων, is the Father, He who obeys, ὑπακούων, the Son. . . . The Father willed, ἠθέλησεν, the Son did it.' Hippol. *contr. Noet.* 14. on which Fabricius's note. S. Hilary speaks of the Son as ' subditus per obedientiæ obsequelam.' *de Syn.* 51. Vid. below, on § 31. In note 8 there the principle is laid down for the use of these expressions. [*Supr.* p. 87, note 2.]

[2] Cf. *Ep. Æg.* 14. vid. also *supr.* p. 155. and *Orat.* iii. 2. 64. Aug. *in Joan. Tract.* i. 11. Vid. a parallel argument with reference to the Holy Spirit. *Serap.* i. 25. b.

[3] Vid. John xiv. 9, 10.

[4] τὴν κατὰ πάντα ὁμοιότητα: vid. parallel instances, *de Syn.* 26 (5) note 1, which add, ὅμοιος κατὰ πάντα, *Orat.* i. 40. κατὰ πάντα καὶ ἐν πᾶσι, *Ep. Æg.* 17, c. τοῦ πατρὸς ὅμοιος, *Orat.* ii. 17. *Orat.* iii. 20, a. ' not ὅμοιος, as the Church preaches, but ὡς αὐτοὶ θέλουσι' (vid. p. 289, note 4), also *de Syn.* 53, note 9.

[5] As Sonship is implied in ' Image' (*supr.* § 2, note 2), so it is implied in ' Word' and ' Wisdom.' *Orat.* iv. 15. *Orat.* iii. 29 init. *de Decr.* 17. And still more pointedly, *Orat.* iv. 24 fin. vid. also *supr.* i. 28, note 5. And so ' Image' is implied in Sonship : ' being Son of God He must be like Him,' *supr.* 17. And so ' Image' is implied in Word ;' ἐν τῇ ἰδίᾳ εἰκόνι, ἥτις ἐστὶν ὁ λόγος αὐτοῦ, *infr.* 82, d. also 34, c. On the contrary, the very root of heretical error was the denial that these titles implied each other, vid. *supr.* 27, *de Decr.* 17, 24, notes.   [6] Vid. Ex. xxxiii. 20.

[7] Matt. xi. 27.

[8] John vi. 46, not to the letter.   [9] Vid. *supr.* 1. and *Exc. B.*
[10] Greek text dislocated.   [1] Ps. ii. 7 ; Matt. iii. 17.
[2] *De Decr.* 10.   [3] Vid. *Orat.* iii. 12.   [4] Acts x. 26
[5] Rev. xxii. 9.   [6] [A note, to the effect that ' worship' i an ambiguous term, is omitted here.]

Samson, wishing to offer sacrifice to the Angel, was thereupon hindered by him, saying, 'Offer not to me, but to God[7].' On the other hand, the Lord is worshipped even by the Angels; for it is written, 'Let all the Angels of God worship Him[8];' and by all the Gentiles, as Isaiah says, 'The labour of Egypt and merchandize of Ethiopia and of the Sabeans, men of stature, shall come over unto thee, and they shall be thy servants;' and then, 'they shall fall down unto thee, and shall make supplication unto thee, saying, Surely God is in thee, and there is none else, there is no God[9].' And He accepts His disciples' worship, and certifies them who He is, saying, 'Call ye Me not Lord and Master? and ye say well, for so I am.' And when Thomas said to Him, 'My Lord and my God[10],' He allows his words, or rather accepts him instead of hindering him. For He is, as the other Prophets declare, and David says in the Psalm, 'the Lord of hosts, the Lord of Sabaoth,' which is interpreted, 'the Lord of Armies,' and God True and Almighty, though the Arians burst[11] at the tidings.

24. But He had not been thus worshipped, nor been thus spoken of, were He a creature merely. But now since He is not a creature, but the proper offspring of the Essence of that God who is worshipped, and His Son by nature, therefore He is worshipped and is believed to be God, and is Lord of armies, and in authority, and Almighty, as the Father is; for He has said Himself, 'All things that the Father hath, are Mine[1].' For it is proper to the Son, to have the things of the Father, and to be such that the Father is seen in Him, and that through Him all things were made, and that the salvation of all comes to pass and consists in Him.

CHAPTER XVII.

INTRODUCTION TO PROVERBS viii. 22
CONTINUED.

Absurdity of supposing a Son or Word created in order to the creation of other creatures; as to the creation being unable to bear God's immediate hand, God condescends to the lowest. Moreover, if the Son a creature, He too could not bear God's hand, and an infinite series of media will be necessary. Objected, that, as Moses who led out the Israelites was a man, so our Lord; but Moses was not the Agent in creation:—again, that unity is found in created ministrations, but all such ministrations are defective and dependent:—again, that He learned to create, yet

could God's Wisdom need teaching? and why should He learn, if the Father worketh hitherto? If the Son was created to create us, He is for our sake, not we for His.

24 (*continued*). AND here it were well to ask them also this question[1], for a still clearer refutation of their heresy;—Wherefore, when all things are creatures, and all are brought into consistence from nothing, and the Son Himself, according to you, is creature and work, and once was not, wherefore has He made 'all things through Him' alone, 'and without Him was made not one thing[2]?' or why is it, when 'all things' are spoken of, that no one thinks the Son is signified in the number, but only things originate; whereas when Scripture speaks of the Word, it does not understand Him as being in the number of 'all,' but places Him with the Father, as Him in whom Providence and salvation for 'all' are wrought and effected by the Father, though all things surely might at the same command have come to be, at which He was brought into being by God alone? For God is not wearied by commanding[3], nor is His strength unequal to the making of all things, that He should alone create the only Son[4], and need His ministry and aid for the framing of the rest. For He lets nothing stand over, which He wills to be done; but He willed only[5], and all things subsisted, and no one 'hath resisted His will[6].' Why then were not all things brought into being by God alone at that same command, at which the Son came into being? Or let them tell us, why did all things through Him come to be, who was Himself but originate? How void of reason! however, they say concerning Him, that 'God willing to create originate nature, when He saw that it could not endure the untempered hand of the Father, and to be created by Him, makes and creates first and alone one only, and calls Him Son and Word, that, through Him as a medium, all things might thereupon be brought to be[6a].' This they not only have said, but they have dared to put it into writing, namely, Eusebius, Arius, and Asterius who sacrificed[7].

25. Is not this a full proof of that irreligion,

---

7 Vid. Judg. xiii. 16.   8 Heb. i. 6.   9 Is. xlv. 14.
10 John xiii. 13; xx. 28.
11 διαρρηγνύωσιν ἑαυτούς· also *ad Adelph.* 8. and vid. *supr.* note on *de Decr.* 17. vid. also διαρρηγνύωνται, *de Syn.* 54. καὶ διαρραγοῖεν, Marcell. ap. Euseb. *Eccl. Theol.* p. 116. also p. 40 τρίζωσι τοὺς ὀδόντως, *de Fug.* 26. init. τρίζετωσαν, *ad Adelph.* 8. *Hist. Ar.* 68. fin. and literally 72. a. κόπτουσιν ἑαυτούς. *In illud Omnia* 5.   1 John xvi. 15.

1 These sections 24—26 are very similar to *de Decr.* 7, 8, yet not in wording or order, as is the case with other passages.
2 John i. 3.   3 *De Decr.* 7.
4 μόνος μόνον, also *infr.* 30. this phrase is synonymous with 'not as one of the creatures,' vid. μόνος ὑπὸ μόνου, *supr.* p. 12. also p. 75. note 6. vid. μόνως, *de Syn.* 26. fin. note 2, though that term is somewhat otherwise explained by S. Greg. Naz. μόνως οὐχ ὡς τὰ σώματα, *Orat.* 25, 16. Eunomius understood by μονογενής, not μόνος γεννηθεὶς but παρὰ μόνου. It should be observed, however, that this is a sense in which some of the Greek Fathers understand the term, thus contrasting generation with procession. vid. Petav. *Trin.* vii. 11. § 3.   5 §§ 29, 31.   6 Rom. ix. 19.
6a Vid. *de Decr.* § 8. *supr.* p. 2. also Cyril. *Thesaur.* pp. 150, 241. *de Trin.* p. 523. Basil *contr. Eunom.* ii. 21. vid. also *infr.* 29. *Orat.* iv. 11, 12.   7 *De Decr.* 8.

with which they have drugged themselves with much madness, till they blush not to be intoxicate against the truth? For if they shall assign the toil of making all things as the reason why God made the Son only, the whole creation will cry out against them as saying unworthy things of God; and Isaiah too who has said in Scripture, 'The Everlasting God, the Lord, the Creator of the ends of the earth, fainteth not, neither is weary: there is no searching of His understanding [1].' And if God made the Son alone, as not deigning to make the rest, but committed them to the Son as an assistant, this on the other hand is unworthy of God, for in Him there is no pride. Nay the Lord reproves the thought, when He says, 'Are not two sparrows sold for a farthing?' and 'one of them shall not fall on the ground without your Father which is in heaven.' And again, 'Take no thought for your life, what ye shall eat, nor yet for your body, what ye shall put on. Is not the life more than meat, and the body than raiment? Behold the fowls of the air, for they sow not, neither do they reap, nor gather into barns; yet your heavenly Father feedeth them; are ye not much better than they? Which of you by taking thought, can add one cubit unto his stature? And why take ye thought for raiment? Consider the lilies of the field, how they grow; they toil not, neither do they spin: and yet I say unto you, that even Solomon in all his glory was not arrayed like one of these. Wherefore if God so clothe the grass of the field which to-day is, and to-morrow is cast into the oven, shall He not much more clothe you, O ye of little faith [2]?' If then it be not unworthy of God to exercise His Providence, even down to things so small, a hair of the head, and a sparrow, and the grass of the field, also it was not unworthy of Him to make them. For what things are the subjects of His Providence, of those He is Maker through His proper Word. Nay a worse absurdity lies before the men who thus speak; for they distinguish [3] between the creatures and the framing; and consider the latter the work of the Father, the creatures the work of the Son; whereas either all things must be brought to be by the Father with the Son, or if all that is originate comes to be through the Son, we must not call Him one of the originated things.

26. Next, their folly may be exposed thus:— if even the Word be of originated nature, how, whereas this nature is too feeble to be God's own handywork, could He alone of all endure to be made by the unoriginate and unmitigated Essence of God, as ye say? for it follows either that, if He could endure it, all could endure it, or, it being endurable by none, it was not endurable by the Word, for you say that He is one of originate things. And again, if because originate nature could not endure to be God's own handywork, there arose need of a mediator [4], it must follow, that, the Word being originate and a creature, there is need of medium in His framing also, since He too is of that originate nature which endures not to be made of God, but needs a medium. But if some being as a medium be found for Him, then again a fresh mediator is needed for that second, and thus tracing back and following out, we shall invent a vast crowd of accumulating mediators; and thus it will be impossible that the creation should subsist, as ever wanting a mediator, and that medium not coming into being without another mediator; for all of them will be of that originate nature which endures not to be made of God alone, as ye say. How abundant is that folly, which obliges them to hold that what has already come into being, admits not of coming! Or perhaps they opine that they have not even come to be, as still seeking their mediator; for, on the ground of their so irreligious and futile notion [5], what is would not have subsistence, for want of the medium.

27. But again they allege this:—'Behold, through Moses too did He lead the people from Egypt, and through him He gave the Law, yet he was a man; so that it is possible for like to be brought into being by like.' They should veil their face when they say this, to save their much shame. For Moses was not sent to frame the world, nor to call into being things which were not, or to fashion men like himself, but only to be the minister of words to the people, and to King Pharaoh. And this is a very different thing, for to minister is of things originate as of servants, but to frame and to create is of God alone, and of His proper Word and His Wisdom. Wherefore, in the matter of framing, we shall find none but God's Word; for 'all things are made in Wisdom,' and 'without the Word was made not one thing.' But as regards ministrations there are, not one only, but many out of their whole number, whomever the Lord will send. For there are many Archangels, many Thrones, and Authorities, and Dominions, thousands of thousands, and myriads of myriads, standing before Him [1], minis-

---

[1] Is. xl. 28.　　[2] Matt. x. 29; vi. 25—30.
[3] διαιροῦσιν, as *supr. de Decr.* 7.

[4] Vid. ib. 8. vid. also a similar argument in Epiphanius *Hær.* 76. p. 951. but the arguments of Ath. in these Orations are so generally adopted by the succeeding Fathers, that it is impossible and needless to enumerate the instances of agreement.
[5] And so *de Decr.* 8.　　[1] i. 62. and Ambros. *de Fid.* iii. 106.

tering and ready to be sent. And many Prophets, and twelve Apostles, and Paul. And Moses himself was not alone, but Aaron with him, and next other seventy were filled with the Holy Ghost. And Moses was succeeded by Joshua the son of Nun, and he by the Judges, and they not by one, but by a number of Kings. If then the Son were a creature and one of things originate, there must have been many such sons, that God might have many such ministers, just as there is a multitude of those others. But if this is not to be seen, but while the creatures are many, the Word is one, any one will collect from this, that the Son differs from all, and is not on a level with the creatures, but proper to the Father. Hence there are not many Words, but one only Word of the one Father, and one Image of the one God[2]. 'But behold,' they say, 'there is one sun only[3], and one earth.' Let them maintain, senseless as they are, that there is one water and one fire, and then they may be told that everything that is brought to be, is one in its own essence; but for the ministry and service committed to it, by itself it is not adequate nor sufficient alone. For God said, 'Let there be lights in the firmament of heaven, to give light upon the earth, and to divide the day from the night; and let them be for signs and for seasons and for days and years.' And then he says, 'And God made two great lights, the greater light to rule the day, and the lesser light to rule the night: He made the stars also. And God set them in the firmament of the heaven, to give light upon the earth, and to rule over the day and over the night[4].'

28. Behold there are many lights, and not the sun only, nor the moon only, but each is one in essence, and yet the service of all is one and common; and what each lacks, is supplied by the other, and the office of lighting is performed by all[5]. Thus the sun has authority to shine throughout the day and no more; and the moon through the night; and the stars together with them accomplish the seasons and years, and become for signs, each according to the need that calls for it. Thus too the earth is not for all things, but for the fruits only, and to be a ground to tread on for the living things that inhabit it. And the firmament is to divide between waters and waters, and to be a place to set the stars in. So also fire and water, with other things, have been brought into being to be the constituent parts of bodies; and in short no one thing is alone, but all things that are made, as if members

of each other, make up as it were one body, namely, the world. If then they thus conceive of the Son, let all men throw stones[6] at them, considering the Word to be a part of this universe, and a part insufficient without the rest for the service committed to Him. But if this be manifestly irreligious, let them acknowledge that the Word is not in the number of things originate, but the sole and proper Word of the Father, and their Framer. 'But,' say they, 'though He is a creature and of things originate; yet as from a master and artificer has He[7] learned to frame, and thus ministered[8] to God who taught Him.' For thus the Sophist Asterius, on the strength of having learned to deny the Lord, has dared to write, not observing the absurdity which follows. For if framing be a thing to be taught, let them beware lest they say that God Himself be a Framer not by nature but by science, so as to admit of His losing the power. Besides, if the Wisdom of God attained to frame by teaching, how is He still Wisdom, when He needs to learn? and what was He before He learned? For it was not Wisdom, if it needed teaching; it was surely but some empty thing, and not essential Wisdom[9], but from advancement it had the name of Wisdom, and will be only so long Wisdom as it can keep what it has learned. For what has accrued not by any nature, but from learning, admits of being one time unlearned. But to speak thus of the Word of God, is not the part of Christians but of Greeks.

29. For if the power of framing accrues to any one from teaching, these insensate men are ascribing jealousy and weakness[1] to God;— jealousy, in that He has not taught many how to frame, so that there may be around Him, as Archangels and Angels many, so framers many; and weakness, in that He could not make by Himself, but needed a fellow-worker, or under-worker; and that, though it has been already shewn that created nature admits of being made by God alone, since they consider the Son to be of such a nature and so made. But God is deficient in nothing: perish the thought! for He has said Himself, 'I am full[2].' Nor did the Word become Framer of all from teaching; but being the Image and Wisdom of the Father, He does the things of the Father. Nor hath He made the Son for the making of things created; for behold, though the Son exists, still[3] the Father is seen to work, as the Lord Himself says, 'My Father worketh hitherto and I work[4].' If

---

2 § 36, note 4.
4 Gen. i. 14—18.

3 Vid. Euseb. *Demon.* iv. 5 fin.
5 § 48.

6 § 4, note 2.
8 § 22, note 1.
1 i. 27.   2 Is. i. 11.
4 John v. 17.

7 Cyril. *in Joan.* p. 47, c.
9 οὐσιώδης σοφια. vid. *Orat.* iv. 1.
3 vid. p. 315, note 6. *Serap.* ii. 2. fin.

however, as you say, the Son came into being for the purpose of making the things after Him, and yet the Father is seen to work even after the Son, you must hold even in this light the making of such a Son to be superfluous. Besides, why, when He would create us, does He seek for a mediator at all, as if His will did not suffice to constitute whatever seemed good to Him? Yet the Scriptures say, 'He hath done whatsoever pleased Him[5],' and 'Who hath resisted His will[6]?' And if His mere will[7] is sufficient for the framing of all things, you make the office of a mediator superfluous; for your instance of Moses, and the sun and the moon has been shewn not to hold. And here again is an argument to silence you. You say that God, willing the creation of originated nature, and deliberating concerning it, designs and creates the Son, that through Him He may frame us; now, if so, consider how great an irreligion[8] you have dared to utter.

30. First, the Son appears rather to have been for us brought to be, than we for Him; for we were not created for Him, but He is made for us[9]; so that He owes thanks to us, not we to Him, as the woman to the man. 'For the man,' says Scripture, 'was not created for the woman, but the woman for the man.' Therefore, as 'the man is the image and glory of God, and the woman the glory of the man[10],' so we are made God's image and to His glory; but the Son is our image, and exists for our glory. And we were brought into being that we might be; but God's Word was made, as you must hold, not that He might be[1]; but as an instrument[2] for our need, so that not we from Him, but He is constituted from our need. Are not men who even conceive such thoughts, more than insensate? For if for us the Word was made, He has not precedence[3] of us with God; for He did not take counsel about us having Him within Him, but having us in Himself, counselled, as they say, concerning His own Word. But if so, perchance the Father had not even a will for the Son at all; for not as having a will for Him, did He create Him, but with a will for us, He formed Him for our sake; for He designed Him after designing us; so that, according to these irreligious men, henceforth the Son, who was made as an instrument, is superfluous, now that they are made for whom He was created. But if the Son alone was made by God alone, because He could endure it, but we, because we could not,

were made by the Word, why does He not first take counsel about the Word, who could endure His making, instead of taking counsel about us? or why does He not make more of Him who was strong, than of us who were weak? or why making Him first, does He not counsel about Him first? or why counselling about us first, does He not make us first, His will being sufficient for the constitution of all things? But He creates Him first, yet counsels first about us; and He wills us before the Mediator; and when He wills to create us, and counsels about us, He calls us creatures; but Him, whom He frames for us, He calls Son and proper Heir. But we, for whose sake He made Him, ought rather to be called sons; or certainly He, who is His Son, is rather the object of His previous thoughts and of His will, for whom He makes all us. Such the sickness, such the vomit[4] of the heretics.

CHAPTER XVIII.

INTRODUCTION TO PROVERBS viii. 22
CONTINUED.

Contrast between the Father's operations immediately and naturally in the Son, instrumentally by the creatures; Scripture terms illustrative of this. Explanation of these illustrations; which should be interpreted by the doctrine of the Church; perverse sense put on them by the Arians, refuted. Mystery of Divine Generation. Contrast between God's Word and man's word drawn out at length. Asterius betrayed into holding two Unoriginates; his inconsistency. Baptism how by the Son as well as by the Father. On the Baptism of heretics. Why Arian worse than other heresies.

31. BUT the sentiment of Truth[1] in this matter must not be hidden, but must have high utterance. For the Word of God was not made for us, but rather we for Him, and 'in Him all things were created[2].' Nor for that we were weak, was He strong and made by the Father alone, that He might frame us by means of Him as an instrument; perish the thought! it is not so. For though it had seemed good to God not to make things originate, still had the Word been no less with God, and the Father in Him. At the same time, things originate could not without the Word be brought to be; hence they were made through Him,—and reasonably. For since the Word is the Son of God by nature proper to His essence, and is from Him, and in Him[3], as He said Himself, the creatures could not have come to be, except through Him. For as the light enlightens all things by its radiance, and without its radiance nothing would be illuminated, so also the Father, as by

5 Ps. cxv. 3.   6 Rom. ix. 19.
7 § 24, note 5.   8 Notes on § 58, and *de Decr.* 1.
9 Vid. *Orat.* iv. 11.   10 1 Cor. xi. 7, 9.
1 Cf. *infr.* ch. 20.   2 ὄργανον, *supr.* i. 26, n. 5.
3 πρῶτος ἡμῶν, § 63, note

4 ἔμετοι καὶ ναυτίαι; ναυτίαι sea-sickness; Epictetus, in a somewhat similar sense, 'There is great danger of pouring forth straightway, what one has not digested.' *Enchirid.* 46.
    1 § 35, note 2.   2 Col. i. 16.   3 *De Syn.* 42, note 1.

a hand [4], in the Word wrought all things, and without Him makes nothing. For instance, God said, as Moses relates, 'Let there be light,' and 'Let the waters be gathered together,' and 'let the dry land appear,' and 'Let Us make man [5];' as also Holy David in the Psalm, 'He spake and they were made; He commanded and they were created [6].' And He spoke [7], not that, as in the case of men, some under-worker might hear, and learning the will of Him who spoke might go away and do it; for this is what is proper to creatures, but it is unseemly so to think or speak of the Word. For the Word of God is Framer and Maker, and He is the Father's Will [8]. Hence it is that divine Scripture says not that one heard and answered, as to the manner or nature of the things which He wished made; but God only said, 'Let it become,' and he adds, 'And it became;' for what He thought good and counselled, that forthwith the Word began to do and to finish. For when God commands others, whether the Angels, or converses with Moses, or commands Abraham, then the hearer answers; and the one says, 'Whereby shall I know [9]?' and the other, 'Send some one else [10];' and again, 'If they ask me, what is His Name, what shall I say to them [11]?' and the Angel said to Zacharias, 'Thus saith the Lord [12];' and he asked the Lord, 'O Lord of hosts, how long wilt Thou not have mercy on Jerusalem?' and waits to hear good words and comfortable. For each of these has the Mediator [13] Word, and the Wisdom of God which makes known the will of the Father. But when that Word Himself works and creates, then there is no questioning and answer, for the Father is in Him and the Word in the Father; but it suffices to will, and the work is done; so that the word 'He said' is a token of the will for our sake, and 'It was so,' denotes the work which

is done through the Word and the Wisdom, in which Wisdom also is the Will of the Father. And 'God said' is explained in 'the Word,' for, he says, 'Thou hast made all things in Wisdom;' and 'By the Word of the Lord were the heavens made fast;' and 'There is one Lord Jesus Christ, by whom are all things, and we by Him [1].'

32. It is plain from this that the Arians are not fighting with us about their heresy; but while they pretend us, their real fight is against the Godhead Itself. For if the voice were ours which says, 'This is My Son [2],' small were our complaint of them; but if it is the Father's voice, and the disciples heard it, and the Son too says of Himself, 'Before all the mountains He begat me [3],' are they not fighting against God, as the giants [4] in story, having their tongue, as the Psalmist says, a sharp sword [5] for irreligion? For they neither feared the voice of the Father, nor reverenced the Saviour's words, nor trusted the Saints, one of whom writes, 'Who being the Brightness of His glory and the Expression of His subsistence,' and 'Christ the power of God and the Wisdom of God [6];' and another says in the Psalm, 'With Thee is the well of life, and in Thy Light shall we see light,' and 'Thou madest all things in Wisdom [7];' and the Prophets say, 'And the Word of the Lord came to me [8];' and John, 'In the beginning was the Word;' and Luke, 'As they delivered them unto us which from the beginning were eye-witnesses and ministers of the Word [9];' and as David again says, 'He sent His Word and healed them [10].' All these passages proscribe in every light the Arian heresy, and signify the eternity of the Word, and that He is not foreign but proper to the Father's Essence. For when saw any one light without radiance? or who dares to say that the expression can be different from the subsistence? or has not a man himself lost his mind [11] who even entertains the thought that God was ever without Reason and without Wisdom? For such illustrations and such images has Scripture proposed, that, considering the inability of human nature to comprehend God, we might be able to form ideas even from these however poorly and dimly, and as far as is attainable [12]. And as the creation contains

---

4 ὡς διὰ χειρός. vid. *supr.* p. 155, note 6 And so in *Orat.* iv. 26, a. *de Incarn. contr. Arian.* 12. a. κραταιὰ χεὶρ τοῦ πατρός. Method. *de Creat.* ap. Phot. cod. 235. p. 937. Iren. *Hær.* iv. 20. n. 1. v. 1 fin. and. 5. n. 2. and 6. n. 1. Clement. *Protrept.* p. 93. (ed. Potter.) Tertull. *contr. Hermog.* 45. Cypr. *Testim.* ii. 4. Euseb. *in Psalm* cviii. 27. Clement. *Recogn.* viii. 43. Clement. *Hom.* xvi. 12. Cyril. Alex. frequently, e.g. *in Joan.* pp. 876, 7. *Thesaur.* p. 154. Pseudo-Basil. χεὶρ δημιουργική, *contr. Eunom.* v. p. 297. Job. ap. Phot. 222. p. 582. and August. *in Joann.* 48, 7. though he prefers another use of the word.

5 Gen. i. 3, 9, 26. 6 Ps. clxviii. 5.

7 Vid. *de Decr.* 9. *contr. Gent.* 46. Iren. *Hær.* iii. 8. n. 3. Origen *contr. Cels.* ii. 9. Tertull. *adv. Prax.* 12. fin. Patres Antioch. *ap.* Routh t. 2. p. 468. Prosper *in Psalm.* 148. (149.) Basil. *de Sp. S.* n. 20. Hilar. *Trin.* iv. 16. vid. *supr.* § 22, note. Didym. *de Sp. S.* 36. August. *de Trin.* i. 26. On this mystery vid. Petav. *Trin.* vi. 4.

8 βουλή. And so βούλησις presently; and ζῶσα βουλή, *supr.* 2. and *Orat.* iii. 63. fin. and so Cyril *Thes.* p. 54, who uses it expressly (as it is always used by implication), in contrast to the κατὰ βούλησιν of the Arians, though Athan. uses κατὰ τὸ βούλημα, e.g. *Orat.* iii. 31. where vid. note; αὐτὸς τοῦ πατρὸς θέλημα, Nyss. *contr. Eunom.* xii. p. 345. The principle to be observed in the use of such words is this; that we must ever speak of the Father's will, command, &c., and the Son's fulfilment, assent, &c., as one act. vid. notes on *Orat.* iii. 11 and 15. *infr.* [Cf. p. 87. note 2.]

9 Gen. xv. 8.   10 Ex. iv. 13.   11 Ib. iii. 13.

12 Zech. i. 3, 12.   13 § 16, note 7.

---

1 Ps. civ. 24; xxxiii. 6; 1 Cor. viii. 6.   2 Vid. Matt. xvii. 5.   3 Prov. viii. 25, LXX.

4 τοὺς μυθευομένους γίγαντας, vid. *supr. de Decr.* fin. Also ὡς τοὺς γίγαντας, *Orat.* iii. 42. In *Hist. Arian.* 74. he calls Constantius a γίγας. The same idea is implied in the word θεομάχος so frequently applied to Arianism, as in this sentence.

5 Ps. lvii. 4.   6 Heb. i. 3; 1 Cor. i. 24.   7 Ps. xxxvi. 9; civ. 24.   8 Jer. ii. 1.   9 John i. 1; Luke i. 2.   10 Ps. cvii. 20.

11 Vid. p. 150, n. 6, also *Gent.* 40 fin. where what is here, as commonly, applied to the Arians, is, before the rise of Arianism, applied to unbelievers.

12 Vid. *de Decr.* 12, 16, notes i. 26, n. 2, ii. 36, n. 1. *de Syn.*

abundant matter for the knowledge of the being of a God and a Providence ('for by the greatness and beauty of the creatures proportionably the Maker of them is seen [13]'), and we learn from them without asking for voices, but hearing the Scriptures we believe, and surveying the very order and the harmony of all things, we acknowledge that He is Maker and Lord and God of all, and apprehend His marvellous Providence and governance over all things; so in like manner about the Son's Godhead, what has been above said is sufficient, and it becomes superfluous, or rather it is very mad to dispute about it, or to ask in an heretical way, How can the Son be from eternity? or how can He be from the Father's Essence, yet not a part? since what is said to be of another, is a part of him; and what is divided, is not whole.

33. These are the evil sophistries of the heterodox; yet, though we have already shewn their shallowness, the exact sense of these passages themselves and the force of these illustrations will serve to shew the baseless nature of their loathsome tenet. For we see that reason is ever, and is from him and proper to his essence, whose reason it is, and does not admit a before and an after. So again we see that the radiance from the sun is proper to it, and the sun's essence is not divided or impaired; but its essence is whole and its radiance perfect and whole [1], yet without impairing the essence of light, but as a true offspring from it. We understand in like manner that the Son is begotten not from without but from the Father, and while the Father remains whole, the Expression of His Subsistence is ever, and preserves the Father's likeness and unvarying Image, so that he who sees Him, sees in Him the Subsistence too, of which He is the Expression. And from the operation of the Expression we understand the true Godhead of the Subsistence, as the Saviour Himself teaches when He says, 'The Father who dwelleth in Me, He doeth the works [2]' which I do; and 'I and the Father are one,' and 'I in the Father and the Father in Me [3].' Therefore let this Christ-opposing heresy attempt

first to divide [4] the examples found in things originate, and say, 'Once the sun was without his radiance,' or, 'Radiance is not proper to the essence of light,' or 'It is indeed proper, but it is a part of light by division; and then let it divide Reason, and pronounce that it is foreign to mind, or that once it was not, or that it was not proper to its essence, or that it is by division a part of mind. And so of His Expression and the Light and the Power, let it do violence to these as in the case of Reason and Radiance; and instead let it imagine what it will [5]. But if such extravagance be impossible for them, are they not greatly beside themselves, presumptuously intruding into what is higher than things originate and their own nature, and essaying impossibilities [6]?

34. For if in the case of these originate and irrational things offsprings are found which are not parts of the essences from which they are, nor subsist with passion, nor impair the essences of their originals, are they not mad again in seeking and conjecturing parts and passions in the instance of the immaterial and true God, and ascribing divisions to Him who is beyond passion and change, thereby to perplex the ears of the simple [1] and to pervert them from the Truth? for who hears of a son but conceives of that which is proper to the father's essence? who heard, in his first catechising [2], that God has a Son and has made all things by His proper Word, but understood it in that sense in which we now mean it? who on the rise of this odious heresy of the Arians, was not at once startled at what he heard, as strange [3], and a second sowing, besides that Word which had been sown from the beginning? For what is sown in every soul from the beginning is that God has a Son, the Word, the Wisdom, the Power, that is, His Image and Radiance; from which it at once follows that He is always; that He is from the Father; that He is like; that He is the eternal offspring of His essence; and there is no idea involved in these of creature or work. But when the man who is an enemy, while men slept, made a second sowing [4], of 'He is a creature,' and 'There was once when He was not,' and 'How can it be?' thenceforth the wicked heresy of Christ's enemies rose as tares, and forthwith, as bereft of every

---

41, n. 1. *In illud Omnia* 3 fin. vid. also 6. Aug. *Confess.* xiii. 11. And again, *Trin.* xv. 39. And S. Basil *contr. Eunom.* ii. 17.
[13] Wisd. xiii. 5.
[1] The Second Person in the Holy Trinity is not a quality or attribute or relation, but the One Eternal Substance; not a part of the First Person, but whole or entire God; nor does the generation impair the Father's Substance, which is, antecedently to it, whole and entire God. Thus there are two Persons, in Each Other ineffably, Each being wholly one and the same Divine Substance, yet not being merely separate aspects of the Same, Each being God as absolutely as if there were no other Divine Person but Himself. Such a statement indeed is not only a contradiction in the terms used, but in our ideas, yet not therefore a contradiction in fact; unless indeed any one will say that human words can express in one formula, or human thought embrace in one idea, the unknown and infinite God. Basil. *contr. Eun.* i. 10. vid. *infr.* § 38, n. 3.   [2] John xiv. 10.   [3] John x. 30.

[4] διελεῖν, vid. § 25, note 3.
[5] *Hist. Ar.* 52, n. 4.   [6] *In illud Omn.* 6. init.
[1] Cf. p. 69, notes 7 and 8.   [2] *De Decr.* 7, n. 2; *De Syn.* 3, n. 2; *Or.* i. 8.
[3] He here makes the test of the truth of explicit doctrinal statements to lie in their not shocking, or their answering to the religious sense of the Christian.
[4] Vid. *supr. de Decr.* 2. n. 6. Tertullian *de Carn. Christ.* 17. S. Leo, as Athan. makes 'seed' in the parable apply peculiarly to *faith* in distinction to *obedience. Serm.* 69. 5 init.

right thought, they meddle [5] like robbers, and venture to say, 'How can the Son always exist with the Father?' for men come of men and are sons, after a time; and the father is thirty years old, when the son begins to be, being begotten; and in short of every son of man, it is true that he was not before his generation. And again they whisper, 'How can the Son be Word, or the Word be God's Image? for the word of men is composed of syllables [6], and only signifies the speaker's will, and then is over [7] and is lost.'

35. They then afresh, as if forgetting the proofs which have been already urged against them, 'pierce themselves through [1]' with these bonds of irreligion, and thus argue. But the word of truth [2] confutes them as follows:—if they were disputing concerning any man, then let them exercise reason in this human way, both concerning His Word and His Son; but if of God who created man, no longer let them entertain human thoughts, but others which are above human nature. For such as he that begets, such of necessity is the offspring; and such as is the Word's Father, such must be also His Word. Now man, begotten in time, in time [3] also himself begets the child; and whereas from nothing he came to be, therefore his word [4] also is over and continues not. But God is not as man, as Scripture has said; but is existing and is ever; therefore also His Word is existing [5] and is everlastingly with the Father, as radiance of light. And man's word is composed of syllables, and neither lives nor operates anything, but is only significant of the speaker's intention, and does but go forth and go by, no more to appear, since it was not at all before it was spoken; wherefore the word of man neither lives nor operates anything, nor in short is man. And this happens to it, as I said before, because man who begets it, has his nature out of nothing. But God's Word is not merely pronounced, as one may say, nor a sound of accents, nor by His Son is meant His command [6]; but as radiance of light, so is He perfect offspring from perfect [7]. Hence He is God also, as being God's Image; for 'the Word was God [8],' says Scripture. And man's

words avail not for operation; hence man works not by means of words but of hands, for they have being, and man's word subsists not. But the 'Word of God,' as the Apostle says, 'is living and powerful and sharper than any two-edged sword, piercing even to the dividing asunder of soul and spirit, and of the joints and marrow, and is a discerner of the thoughts and intents of the heart. Neither is there any creature that is not manifest in His sight; but all things are naked and opened unto the eyes of Him with whom we have to do [9].' He is then Framer of all, 'and without Him was made not one thing [10],' nor can anything be made without Him.

36. Nor must we ask why the Word of God is not such as our word, considering God is not such as we, as has been before said; nor again is it right to seek how the word is from God, or how He is God's radiance, or how God begets, and what is the manner of His begetting [1]. For a man must be beside himself to venture on such points; since a thing ineffable and proper to God's nature, and known to Him alone and to the Son, this he demands to be explained in words. It is all one as if they sought where God is, and how God is, and of what nature the Father is. But as to ask such questions is irreligious, and argues an ignorance of God, so it is not holy to venture such questions concerning the generation of the Son of God, nor to measure God and His Wisdom by our own nature and infirmity. Nor is a person at liberty on that account to swerve in his thoughts from the truth, nor, if any one is perplexed in such inquiries, ought he to disbelieve what is written. For it is better in perplexity to be silent and believe, than to disbelieve on account of the perplexity: for he who is perplexed may in some way obtain mercy [2], because, though he has questioned, he has yet kept quiet; but when a man is led by his perplexity into forming for himself doctrines which beseem not, and utters what is unworthy of God, such daring incurs a sentence without mercy. For in such perplexities divine Scripture is able to afford him some relief, so as to take rightly what is written, and to dwell upon our word as an illustration; that as it is proper to us and is from us, and not a work external to us, so also God's Word is proper to Him and from Him, and is not a work; and yet is not like the word

---

5 περιεργάζονται. This can scarcely be, as Newman suggests, an error of the press for περιέρχονται. The Latin translates 'circumire cœperunt.'
6 *Orat.* iv. 1.   7 πέπαυται, *Orat.* iv. 2.   1 Vid. 1 Tim. vi. 10.
2 ὁ τῆς ἀληθείας λόγος ἐλέγχει. This and the like are usual forms of speech with Athan. and others. In some instances the words ἀλήθεια, λόγος, &c., are almost synonymous with the *Regula Fidei*; vid. παρὰ τὴν ἀλήθειαν, *infr.* 36. and Origen *de Princ. Præf.* 1. and 2.   3 *Orat.* i. 21.
4 For this contrast between the Divine Word and the human which is Its shadow, vid. also *Orat.* iv. 1. circ. fin. Iren. *Hær.* ii. 13. n. 8. Origen. *in Joan.* i. p. 25. e. Euseb. *Demonstr* v. 5. p. 230. Cyril, *Cat.* xi. 10. Basil, *Hom.* xvi. 3. Nyssen *contr. Eunom.* xii p. 350. Orat. *Cat.* i. p. 478. Damasc. *F. O.* i. 6. August. *in Psalm* xliv. 5.   5 Vid. *Serap.* i. 28, a   6 § 31, n. 7.
7 *De Syn.* 24, n. 9; *infr.* 26. note   8 John i. 1.

9 Heb. iv. 12, 13.   10 John i. 3.
1 Eusebius has some forcible remarks on this subject. As, he says, we do not know how God can create out of nothing, so we are utterly ignorant of the Divine Generation. It is written, He who believes, not he who knows, has eternal life. The sun's radiance itself is but an earthly image, and gives us no true idea of that which is above all images. *Eccl. Theol.* i. 12. So has S. Greg. Naz. *Orat.* 29. 8. vid. also Hippol. *in Noet.* 16. Cyril, *Cat.* xi. 11. and 19. and Origen, according to Mosheim, *Ante Const.* p 619. And instances in Petav. *de Trin.* v. 6. § 2. and 3.
2 Cf. August. *Ep.* 43. init. vid. also *de Bapt. contr. Don.* iv. 23.

of man, or else we must suppose God to be man. For observe, many and various are men's words which pass away day by day; because those that come before others continue not, but vanish. Now this happens because their authors are men, and have seasons which pass away, and ideas which are successive; and what strikes them first and second, that they utter; so that they have many words, and yet after them all nothing at all remaining; for the speaker ceases, and his word forthwith is spent. But God's Word is one and the same, and, as it is written, 'The Word of God endureth for ever[3],' not changed, not before or after other, but existing the same always. For it was fitting, whereas God is One, that His Image should be One also, and His Word One, and One His Wisdom[4].

37. Wherefore I am in wonder how, whereas God is One, these men introduce, after their private notions, many images and wisdoms and words[5], and say that the Father's proper and natural Word is other than the Son, by whom He even made the Son[6], and that He who is really Son is but notionally[7] called Word, as vine, and way, and door, and tree of life; and that He is called Wisdom also in name, the proper and true Wisdom of the Father, which coexist ingenerately[8] with Him, being other than the Son, by which He even made the Son, and named Him Wisdom as partaking of it. This they have not confined to words, but Arius composed in his Thalia, and the Sophist Asterius wrote, what we have stated above, as follows: 'Blessed Paul said not that he preached Christ, the Power of God or the Wisdom of God, but without the addition of the article, 'God's power' and 'God's wisdom[9],' thus preaching that the proper Power of God Himself which is natural to Him, and co-existent in Him ingenerately, is something besides, generative indeed of Christ, and creative of the whole world, concerning which he teaches in his Epistle to the Romans thus,—'The invisible

things of Him from the creation of the world are clearly seen, being understood by the things that are made, even His eternal Power and Godhead[10].' For as no one would say that the Godhead there mentioned was Christ, but the Father Himself, so, as I think, 'His eternal Power and Godhead also is not the Only Begotten Son, but the Father who begat Him[11].' And he teaches that there is another power and wisdom of God, manifested through Christ. And shortly after the same Asterius says, 'However His eternal power and wisdom, which truth argues to be without beginning and ingenerate, the same must surely be one. For there are many wisdoms which are one by one created by Him, of whom Christ is the first-born and only-begotten; all however equally depend on their Possessor. And all the powers are rightly called His who created and uses them:—as the Prophet says that the locust, which came to be a divine punishment of human sins, was called by God Himself not only a power, but a great power; and blessed David in most of the Psalms invites, not the Angels alone, but the Powers to praise God.'

38. Now are they not worthy of all hatred for merely uttering this? for if, as they hold, He is Son, not because He is begotten of the Father and proper to His Essence, but that He is called Word only because of things rational[1], and Wisdom because of things gifted with wisdom, and Power because of things gifted with power, surely He must be named a Son because of those who are made sons: and perhaps because there are things existing, He has even His existence[2], in our notions only[3]. And then after all what is He? for He is none of these Himself, if they are but His names[4]: and He has but a semblance of being, and is decorated with these names

---

3 Vid. Ps. cxix. 89.
4 Vid. *supr.* 35. *Orat.* iv. 1. also presently, ' He is likeness and image of the sole and true God, being Himself also,' 49. μόνος ἐν μόνῳ, *Orat.* iii. 21. ὅλος ὅλου εἰκών. *Serap.* i. 16, a. 'The Offspring of the Ingenerate,' says S. Hilary, 'is One from One, True from True, Living from Living, Perfect from Perfect, Power of Power, Wisdom of Wisdom, Glory of Glory.' *de Trin.* ii. 8. τέλειος τέλειον γεγέννηκεν, πνεῦμα πνεῦμα. Epiph. *Hær.* p. 495. ' As Light from Light, and Life from Life, and Good from Good'; so from Eternal Eternal. Nyss. *contr. Eunom.* i. p. 164. App.
5 πολλοὶ λόγοι, vid. *de Decr.* 16, n. 4. *infr.* 39 init. and οὐδ' ἐκ πολλῶν εἷς, *Sent. D.* 25. a. also *Ep. Æg.* 14. c. Origen *in Joan.* tom. ii. 3. Euseb. *Demonstr.* v. 5. p. 229 fin. *contr. Marc.* p. 4 fin. *contr. Sabell.* init. August. *in Joan.* Tract. i. 8. also vid. Philo's use of λόγοι for Angels as commented on by Burton, *Bampt. Lect.* p. 556. The heathens called Mercury by the name of λόγος. vid. Benedictine note f. in Justin, *Ap.* i. 21.
6 This was the point in which Arians and [Marcellus] agreed, vid. *infr.* n. 9, and *de Decr.* 24, n. 9, also *Sent D.* 25. *Ep. Æg.* 14 fin. Epiph. *Hær.* 72. p. 835. b.
7 That is, they allowed Him to be 'really Son,' and argued that He was but 'notionally Word. vid. § 19, n. 3.
8 ἀγεννήτως, vid. Euseb. *Eccl. Theol.* p. 106. d.
9 1 Cor. i. 24.

10 Rom. i. 20.
11 *Or.* i. 11, n. 7.   1 λογικά, vid. *Ep. Æg.* 13 fin.
2 Of course this line of thought consistently followed, leads to a kind of Pantheism; for what is the Supreme Being, according to it, but an ideal standard of perfection, the sum total of all that we see excellent in the world in the highest degree, a creation of our minds, without real objective existence? The true view of our Lord's titles, on the other hand, is that He is That properly and in perfection, of which in measure and degree the creatures partake from and in Him. Vid. *supr. de Decr.* 17, n. 5.
3 κατ' ἐπίνοιαν, in idea or notion. This is a phrase of very frequent occurrence, both in Athan. and other writers. We have found it already just above, and *de Syn.* 15. *Or.* i. 9, also *Orat.* iv. 2, 3. *de Sent. D.* 2, *Ep. Æg.* 12, 13, 14. It denotes our idea or conception of a thing in contrast to the thing itself. Thus, the sun is to a savage a bright circle in the sky; a man is a 'rational animal,' according to a certain process of abstraction; a herb may be medicine upon one division, food in another; virtue may be called a mean; and faith is to one man an argumentative conclusion, to another a moral peculiarity, good or bad. In like manner, the Almighty is in reality most simple and uncompounded, without parts, passions, attributes, or properties; yet we speak of Him as good or holy, or as angry or pleased, denoting some particular aspect in which our infirmity views, in which also it can view, what is infinite and incomprehensible. That is, He is κατ' ἐπίνοιαν holy or merciful, being in reality a Unity which is all mercifulness and also all holiness, not in the way of qualities but as one indivisible perfection; which is too great for us to conceive as It is.   4 § 19.

from us. Rather this is some recklessness of the devil, or worse, if they are not unwilling that they should truly subsist themselves, but think that God's Word is but in name. Is not this portentous, to say that Wisdom co-exists with the Father, yet not to say that this is the Christ, but that there are many created powers and wisdoms, of which one is the Lord whom they go on to compare to the caterpillar and locust? and are they not profligate, who, when they hear us say that the Word coexists with the Father, forthwith murmur out, 'Are you not speaking of two Unoriginates?' yet in speaking themselves of ' His Unoriginate Wisdom,' do not see that they have already incurred themselves the charge which they so rashly urge against us[5]? Moreover, what folly is there in that thought of theirs, that the Unoriginate Wisdom coexisting with God is God Himself! for what ·coexists does not co-exist with itself, but with some one else, as the Evangelists say of the Lord, that He was together with His disciples ; for He was not together with Himself, but with His disciples;— unless indeed they would say that God is of a compound nature, having wisdom a constituent or complement of His Essence, un-originate as well as Himself[6], which moreover they pretend to be the framer of the world, that so they may deprive the Son of the framing of it. For there is nothing they would not maintain, sooner than hold the truth concerning the Lord.

39. For where at all have they found in divine Scripture, or from whom have they heard, that there is another Word and another Wisdom besides this Son, that they should frame to themselves such a doctrine? True, indeed, it is written, 'Are not My words like fire, and like a hammer that breaketh the rock in pieces[1]?' and in the Proverbs, 'I will make known My words unto you[2];' but these are precepts and commands, which God has spoken to the saints through His proper and only true Word, concerning which the Psalmist

said, 'I have refrained my feet from every evil way, that I may keep Thy words[3].' Such words accordingly the Saviour signifies to be distinct from Himself, when He says in His own person, 'The words which I have spoken unto you[4].' For certainly such words are not off-springs or sons, nor are there so many words that frame the world, nor so many images of the One God, nor so many who have become men for us, nor as if from many such there were one who has become flesh, as John says; but as being the only Word of God was He preached by John, 'The Word was made flesh,' and 'all things were made by Him[5].' Wherefore of Him alone, our Lord Jesus Christ, and of His oneness with the Father, are written and set forth the testimonies, both of the Father signifying that the Son is One, and of the saints, aware of this and saying that the Word is One, and that He is Only-Begotten. And His works also are set forth ; for all things, visible and invisible, have been brought to be through Him, and 'without Him was made not one thing[6].' But concerning another or any one else they have not a thought, nor frame to themselves words or wisdoms, of which neither name nor deed are signified by Scripture, but are named by these only. For it is their invention and Christ-opposing surmise, and they make the most[7] of the name of the Word and the Wisdom ; and framing to themselves others, they deny the true Word of God, and the real and only Wisdom of the Father, and thereby, miserable men, rival the Manichees. For they too, when they behold the works of God, deny Him the only and true God, and frame to themselves another, whom they can shew neither by work, nor in any testimony drawn from the divine oracles.

40. Therefore, if neither in the divine oracles is found another wisdom besides this Son, nor from the fathers[1] have we heard of any such, yet they have confessed and written of the Wisdom coexisting with the Father unoriginately, proper to Him, and the Framer of the world, this must be the Son who even according to them is eternally coexistent with the Father. For He is Framer of all, as it is written, 'In Wisdom hast Thou made them all[2].' Nay, Asterius himself, as if forgetting what he wrote before, afterwards, in Caiaphas's[3] fashion, involuntarily, when urging the Greeks, instead of naming many wisdoms, or the caterpillar, confesses but one, in these words;— 'God the Word is one, but many are the

---

5 The Anomœan in Max. *Dial.* i. a. urges against the Catholic that, if the Son exists in the Father, God is compound. Athan. here retorts that Asterius speaks of Wisdom as a really existing thing in the Divine Mind. Vid. next note.

6 On this subject vid. *Orat.* iv. n. 2. Nothing is more remarkable than the confident tone in which Athan. accuses Arians as here, and [Marcellus] in *Orat.* iv. 2. of considering the Divine Nature as compound, as if the Catholics were in no respect open to such a charge. Nor are they ; though in avoiding it, they are led to enunciate the most profound and ineffable mystery. Vid. *supr.* § 33, n. 1. The Father is the One Simple Entire Divine Being, and so is the Son ; They do in no sense share identity between Them ; Each is ὅλος Θεός. This is not ditheism or tritheism, for they are the same God ; nor is it Sabellianism, for They are eternally distinct and substantive Persons ; but it is a depth and height beyond our intellect, how what is Two in so full a sense can also in so full a sense be One, or how the Divine Nature does not come under number. vid. notes on *Orat.* iii. 27 and 36. Thus, ' being uncompounded in nature,' says Athan. ' He is Father of One Only Son.' *de Decr.* 11. In truth the distinction into Persons, as Petavius remarks, ' avails especially towards the unity and simplicity of God.' vid. *de Deo*, ii. 4, 8.

1 Jer. xxiii. 29.　　2 Prov. i. 23.

3 Ps. cxix. 101.　　　　4 Joh. vi. 63.
5 John i. 14, 3.　　　6 Cf. *Orat.* i. 19, note 5.
7 καταχρῶνται, vid. *supr.* p. 154, note 3.　　1 Ib. note 2.
2 Ps. civ. 24.　　　　3 Vid. John xi. 50.

things rational; and one is the essence and nature of Wisdom, but many are the things wise and beautiful.' And soon afterwards he says again:—'Who are they whom they honour with the title of God's children? for they will not say that they too are words, nor maintain that there are many wisdoms. For it is not possible, whereas the Word is one, and Wisdom has been set forth as one, to dispense to the multitude of children the Essence of the Word, and to bestow on them the appellation of Wisdom.' It is not then at all wonderful, that the Arians should battle with the truth, when they have collisions with their own principles and conflict with each other, at one time saying that there are many wisdoms, at another maintaining one; at one time classing wisdom with the caterpillar, at another saying that it coexists with the Father and is proper to Him; now that the Father alone is unoriginate, and then again that His Wisdom and His Power are unoriginate also. And they battle with us for saying that the Word of God is ever, yet forget their own doctrines, and say themselves that Wisdom coexists with God unoriginately[4]. So dizzied[5] are they in all these matters, denying the true Wisdom, and inventing one which is not, as the Manichees who make to themselves another God, after denying Him that is.

41. But let the other heresies and the Manichees also know that the Father of the Christ is One, and is Lord and Maker of the creation through His proper Word. And let the Ariomaniacs know in particular, that the Word of God is One, being the only Son proper and genuine from His Essence, and having with His Father the oneness of Godhead indivisible, as we said many times, being taught it by the Saviour Himself. Since, were it not so, wherefore through Him does the Father create, and in Him reveal Himself to whom He will, and illuminate them? or why too in the baptismal consecration is the Son named together with the Father? For if they say that the Father is not all-sufficient, then their answer is irreligious[6], but if He be, for this it is right to say, what is the need of the Son for framing the worlds, or for the holy laver? For what fellowship is there between creature and Creator? or why is a thing made classed with the Maker in the consecration of all of us? or why, as you hold, is faith in one Creator and in one creature delivered to us? for if it was that we might be joined to the Godhead, what need of the creature? but if that we might be united to the Son a creature, superfluous, according to you, is this naming of the Son in Baptism, for God who made Him a Son is able to make us sons also. Besides, if the Son be a creature, the nature of rational creatures being one, no help will come to creatures from a creature[7], since all[8] need grace from God. We said a few words just now on the fitness that all things should be made by Him; but since the course of the discussion has led us also to mention holy Baptism, it is necessary to state, as I think and believe, that the Son is named with the Father, not as if the Father were not all-sufficient, not without meaning, and by accident; but, since He is God's Word and own Wisdom, and being His Radiance, is ever with the Father, therefore it is impossible, if the Father bestows grace, that He should not give it in the Son, for the Son is in the Father as the radiance in the light. For, not as if in need, but as a Father in His own Wisdom hath God founded the earth, and made all things in the Word which is from Him, and in the Son confirms the Holy Laver. For where the Father is, there is the Son, and where the light, there the radiance; and as what the Father worketh, He worketh through the Son[9], and the Lord Himself says, 'What I see the Father do, that do I also;' so also when baptism is given, whom the Father baptizes, him the Son baptizes; and whom the Son baptizes, he is consecrated in the Holy Ghost[10]. And again as when the sun shines, one might say that the radiance illuminates, for the light is one and indivisible, nor can be detached, so where the Father is or is named, there plainly is the Son also; and is the Father named in Baptism? then must the Son be named with Him[11].

---

[4] Asterius held, 1. that there was an Attribute called Wisdom; 2. that the Son was created by and called after that Attribute; or 1. that Wisdom was ingenerate and eternal, 2. that there were created wisdoms, words, powers many, of which the Son was one.
[5] σκοτοδινιῶσι, *Orat.* iii. 42. init.
[6] He says that it is contrary to all our notions of religion that Almighty God cannot create, enlighten, address, and unite Himself to His creatures immediately. This seems to be implied in saying that the Son was created for creation, illumination, &c.; whereas in the Catholic view the Son is but that Divine Person who in the Economy of grace is creator, enlightener, &c. God is represented all-perfect but acting according to a certain divine order. This is explained just below. Here the remark is in point about the right and wrong sense of the words 'commanding,' 'obeying,' &c. *supr.* § 31, note 7.

[7] § 16, note 7.   [8] *Supr.* p. 162, note 3.
[9] Vid. notes on *Orat.* iii. 1—15. e.g. and 11 and 15.
[10] *Orat.* iii. 15. note.
[11] Vid. *supr.* 33, note 1. and notes on iii. 3—6. 'When the Father is mentioned, His Word is with Him, and the Spirit who is in the Son. And if the Son be named, in the Son is the Father, and the Spirit is not external to the Word.' *ad Serap.* i. 14. and vid. Hil. *Trin.* vii. 31. Passages like these are distinct from such as the one quoted from Athan. *supr.* p. 76, note 3, where it is said that in 'Father' is *implied* 'Son,' i.e. argumentatively as a correlative. vid. *Sent. D.* 17. *de Decr.* 19, n. 6. The latter accordingly Eusebius does not scruple to admit *in Sabell.* i. ap. Sirm. t. i. p. 8, a. 'Pater statim, ut dictus fuit pater, *requirit ista vox* filium, &c.;' for here no περιχώρησις is implied, which *is* the doctrine of the text, and is *not* the doctrine of an Arian who considered the Son an instrument. Yet Petavius observes as to the very *word* περιχ. that one of its first senses in ecclesiastical writers was this which Arians would not disclaim; its use to express the Catholic doctrine here spoken of was later. vid. *de Trin.* iv. 16.

42. Therefore, when He made His promise to the Father, He thus spoke; 'I and the Father will come, and make Our abode in him;' and again, 'that, as I and Thou are One, so they may be one in Us.' And the grace given is one, given from the Father in the Son, as Paul writes in every Epistle, 'Grace unto you, and peace from God our Father and the Lord Jesus Christ [1].' For the light must be with the ray, and the radiance must be contemplated together with its own light. Whence the Jews, as denying the Son as well as they, have not the Father either; for, as having left the 'Fountain of Wisdom [2],' as Baruch reproaches them, they put from them the Wisdom springing from it, our Lord Jesus Christ (for 'Christ,' says the Apostle, is 'God's power and God's wisdom [3]),' when they said, 'We have no king but Cæsar [4].' The Jews then have the penal award of their denial; for their city as well as their reasoning came to nought. And these too hazard the fulness of the mystery, I mean Baptism; for if the consecration is given to us into the Name of Father and Son, and they do not confess a true Father, because they deny what is from Him and like His Essence, and deny also the true Son, and name another of their own framing as created out of nothing, is not the rite administered by them altogether empty and unprofitable, making a show, but in reality being no help towards religion? For the Arians do not baptize into Father and Son, but into Creator and creature, and into Maker and work [5]. And as a creature is other than the Son, so the Baptism, which is supposed to be given by them, is other than the truth, though they pretend to name the Name of the Father and the Son, because of the words of Scripture, For not he who simply says, 'O Lord,' gives Baptism; but he who with the Name has also the right faith [6]. On this account therefore our Saviour also did not simply command to baptize, but first says, 'Teach;' then thus: 'Baptize into the Name of Father, and Son, and Holy Ghost;' that the right faith might follow upon learning, and together with faith might come the consecration of Baptism.

43. There are many other heresies too, which use the words only, but not in a right sense, as I have said, nor with sound faith [1], and in consequence the water which they administer is unprofitable, as deficient in piety, so that he who is sprinkled [2] by them is rather polluted [3] by irreligion than redeemed. So Gentiles also, though the name of God is on their lips, incur the charge of Atheism [4], because they know not the real and very God, the Father of our Lord Jesus Christ. So Manichees and Phrygians [5], and the disciples of the Samosatene, though using the Names, nevertheless are heretics, and the Arians follow in the same course, though they read the words of Scripture, and use the Names, yet they too mock those who receive the rite from them, being more irreligious than the other heresies, and advancing beyond them, and making them seem innocent by their own recklessness of speech. For these other heresies lie against the truth in some certain respect, either erring concerning the Lord's Body, as if He did not take flesh of Mary, or as if He has not died at all, nor become man, but only appeared, and was not truly, and seemed to have a body when He had not, and seemed to have the shape of man, as visions in a dream; but the Arians are without disguise irreligious against the Father Himself. For hearing from the Scriptures that His Godhead is represented in the Son as in an image, they blaspheme, saying, that it is a creature, and everywhere concerning that Image, they carry about [6] with them the phrase, 'He was not,' as mud in a wallet [7], and spit it forth as serpents [8] their venom. Then, whereas their doctrine is nauseous to all men, forthwith, as a support against its fall, they prop up the heresy with human [9] patronage, that the simple, at the sight or even by the fear may overlook the mischief of their perversity. Right indeed is it to pity their dupes; well is it to weep over them, for that they sacrifice their own interest for that immediate phantasy which pleasures furnish, and forfeit their future hope. In thinking to be baptized into the name of one who exists not, they will receive nothing; and ranking themselves with a creature, from the creation they will have no help, and believing in one unlike [10] and foreign to the Father in essence, to the

---

[1] Vid. John xiv. 23, and John xvii. 21; Rom. i. 7, &c.
[2] Bar. iii. 12.   [3] 1 Cor. i. 24.   [4] John xix. 15.
[5] De Decr. 31; Or. i. 34.
[6] The *prima facie* sense of this passage is certainly unfavourable to the validity of heretical baptism; vid. Coust. *Pont. Rom. Ep.* p. 227. Voss. *de Bapt. Disp.* 19 and 20. Forbes *Instruct. Theol.* x. 2, 3, and 12. Hooker's *Eccl. Pol.* v. 62. § 5—11. On Arian Baptism in particular vid. Jablonski's *Diss. Opusc.* t. iv. p. 113. [And, in violent contrast to Athan., Siricius (bishop of Rome) *letter to Himerius,* A.D 385. (Coust. 623.)]
[1] τὴν π. ὑγιαινοῦσαν. *Dep. Ar.* 5, note 6.

[2] ῥαντιζόμενον, Bingh. *Antiqu.* xi. 11. § 5.   [3] Cf. Cyprian, *Ep.* 76 fin. (ed. Ben.) and *Ep.* 71 cir. init. Optatus *ad Parmen.* i. 12.   [4] ἀθεότητος. vid. *supr. de Decr.* 1, note 1, *Or.* i. 4, note 1. 'Atheist' or rather 'godless' was the title given by pagans to those who denied, and by the Fathers to those who professed, polytheism. Thus Julian says that Christians preferred 'atheism to godliness.' vid. Suicer *Thes. in voc.*   [5] Montanists.
[6] περιφέρουσι, § 34. n. 5.   [7] Instead of provisions.
[8] Cf. *Ep. Æg.* 19. *Hist. Ar.* 66. and so Arians are dogs (with allusion to 2 Pet. ii. 22.), *de Decr.* 4. *Hist. Ar.* 29. lions, *Hist. Ar.* 11. wolves, *Ap. c. Arian.* 49. hares, *de Fug.* 10. chameleons, *de Decr.* init. hydras, *Orat.* iii. 58 fin. eels, *Ep. Æg.* 7 fin. cuttlefish, *Orat.* iii. 59. gnats, *de Decr.* 14 init. *Orat.* iii. 59. init. beetles, *Orat.* iii. fin. leeches, *Hist. Ar.* 65 init. *de Fug.* 4. [swine, *Or.* ii. 1.] In many of these instances the allusion is to Scripture. On names given to heretics in general, vid. the Alphabetum bestialitatis hereticæ ex Patrum Symbolis, in the Calvinismus bestiarum religio attributed to Raynaudus and printed in the Apopompæus of his works. Vid. on the principle of such applications *infr. Orat.* iii. 18.   [9] *Orat.* i. 9.   [10] *Orat.* iii. 4. note.

Father they will not be joined, not having His own Son by nature, who is from Him, who is in the Father, and in whom the Father is, as He Himself has said; but being led astray by them, the wretched men henceforth remain destitute and stripped of the Godhead. For this phantasy of earthly goods will not follow them upon their death; nor when they see the Lord whom they have denied, sitting on His Father's throne, and judging quick and dead, will they be able to call to their help any one of those who have now deceived them; for they shall see them also at the judgment-seat, repenting for their deeds of sin and irreligion.

CHAPTER XIX.

Texts Explained; Sixthly, Proverbs viii. 22.

Proverbs are of a figurative nature, and must be interpreted as such. We must interpret them, and in particular this passage, by the *Regula Fidei*. 'He created me' not equivalent to 'I am a creature.' Wisdom a creature so far forth as Its human body. Again, if He is a creature, it is as 'a beginning of ways,' an office which, though not an attribute, is a consequence, of a higher and divine nature. And it is 'for the works,' which implied the works existed, and therefore much more He, before He was created. Also 'the Lord' not the Father 'created' Him, which implies the creation was that of a servant.

44. We have gone through thus much before the passage in the Proverbs, resisting the insensate fables which their hearts have invented, that they may know that the Son of God ought not to be called a creature, and may learn lightly to read what admits in truth of a right[1] explanation. For it is written, 'The Lord created me a beginning of His ways, for His works[2];' since, however, these are proverbs, and it is expressed in the way of proverbs, we must not expound them nakedly in their first sense, but we must inquire into the person, and thus religiously put the sense on it. For what is said in proverbs, is not said plainly, but is put forth latently[3], as the Lord Himself has taught us in the Gospel according to John, saying, 'These things have I spoken unto you in proverbs, but the time cometh when I shall no more speak unto you in proverbs, but openly[4].' Therefore it is necessary to unfold the sense[5] of what is

said, and to seek it as something hidden, and not nakedly to expound as if the meaning were spoken 'plainly,' lest by a false interpretation we wander from the truth. If then what is written be about Angel, or any other of things originate, as concerning one of us who are works, let it be said, 'created me;' but if it be the Wisdom of God, in whom all things originate have been framed, that speaks concerning Itself, what ought we to understand but that 'He created' means nothing contrary to 'He begat?' Nor, as forgetting that It is Creator and Framer, or ignorant of the difference between the Creator and the creatures, does It number Itself among the creatures; but It signifies a certain sense, as in proverbs, not 'plainly,' but latent; which It inspired the saints to use in prophecy, while soon after It doth Itself give the meaning of 'He created' in other but parallel expressions, saying, 'Wisdom made herself a house[6].' Now it is plain that our body is Wisdom's house[7], which It took on Itself to become man; hence consistently does John say, 'The Word was made flesh[8];' and by Solomon Wisdom says of Itself with cautious exactness[9], not 'I am a creature,' but only 'The Lord created me a beginning of His ways for His works[10],' yet not 'created me that I might have being,' nor 'because I have a creature's beginning and origin.'

45. For in this passage, not as signifying the Essence of His Godhead, nor His own everlasting and genuine generation from the Father, has the Word spoken by Solomon, but on the other hand His manhood and Economy towards us. And, as I said before, He has not said 'I am a creature,' or 'I became a creature,' but only 'He created[1].' For the creatures, having a created essence, are

---

6 Prov. ix. 1.
7 Ut intra intemerata viscera ædificante sibi Sapientia domum, Verbum caro fieret. Leon. *Ep.* 31, 2. Didym. *de Trin.* iii. 3. p. 337. (ed. 1769.) August. *Civ. D.* xvii. 20. Cyril *in Joann.* p. 384, 5. Max. *Dial.* iii. p. 1029. (ap. Theodor. ed. Schutz.) vid. *supr. Or.* i. 11, note 8. Hence S. Clement. Alex. ὁ λόγος ἑαυτὸν γεννᾷ. *Strom.* v. 3.　　8 John i. 14.　　9 § 12, n. 4.
10 The passage is in like manner interpreted of our Lord's human nature by Epiph. *Hær.* 69, 20—25. Basil. *Ep.* viii. 8. Naz. *Orat.* 30, 2. Nyss. *contr. Eunom.* i. p. 34. et al. Cyril. *Thesaur.* p. 154. Hilar. *de Trin.* xii. 36—49. Ambros. *de Fid.* i. 15. August. *de Fid. et Symb.* 6.
1 He seems here to say that it is both true that 'The Lord created,' and yet that the Son was not created. Creatures alone are created, and He was not a creature. Rather something belonging or relating to Him, something short of His substance or nature, was created. However, it is a question in controversy whether even His Manhood can be called a creature, though many of the Fathers (including Athan. in several places) seem so to call it. On the whole it would appear, (1.) that if 'create,' like 'Son,' be a *personal* term, He is not a creature; but if it be a word of *nature*, He is a creature; (2.) that our Lord is a creature in respect to the flesh (vid. *infr.* 47); (3.) that since the flesh is infinitely beneath His divinity, it is neither natural nor safe to call Him a creature (cf. Thom. Aq. *Sum. Th.* iii. xvi. 8, 'non dicimus, quod Æthiops est albus, sed quod est albus secundum dentes') and (4.) that, if the flesh is worshipped, still it is worshipped as in the Person of the Son, not by a separate act of worship. Cf. *infr. Letter* 60. *ad Adelph.* 3. Epiph. has imitated this passage, *Ancor.* 51. introducing the illustration of a king and his robe, &c.

---

1 καλῶς ἀναγινώσκειν. . . . ὀρθὴν ἔχον τὴν διάνοιαν, i.e. the text admits of an interpretation consistent with the analogy of faith, and so μετ' εὐσεβείας just below. vid. § 1. n. 13. Such phrases are frequent in Athan.
2 Prov. viii. 22. Athanasius follows the Sept. rendering of the Hebrew Qanâ by ἔκτισε. The Hebrew sense is appealed to by Eusebius, *Eccles. Theol.* iii. 2, 3. S. Epiphanius, *Hær.* 69. 25. and S. Jerome *in Isai.* 26. 13. Cf. Bas. *c. Eun.* ii. 20, and Greg. Nyss. *c. Eun.* i. p. 34.
3 This passage of Athan. has been used by many later fathers.
4 John xvi. 25.
5 Here, as in so many other places, he is explaining what is obscure or latent in Scripture by means of the *Regula Fidei*. Cf. Vincentius, *Commonit.* 2. Vid. especially the first sentence of the following paragraph, τί δεῖ νοεῖν κ.τ.λ. vid. *supr.* note 1.

originate, and are said to be created, and of course the creature is created : but this mere term 'He created' does not necessarily signify the essence or the generation, but indicates something else as coming to pass in Him of whom it speaks, and not simply that He who is said to be created, is at once in His Nature and Essence a creature[2]. And this difference divine Scripture recognises, saying concerning the creatures, 'The earth is full of Thy creation,' and 'the creation itself groaneth together and travaileth together[3];' and in the Apocalypse it says, 'And the third part of the creatures in the sea died which had life;' as also Paul says, 'Every creature of God is good, and nothing is to be refused if it be received with thanksgiving[4];' and in the book of Wisdom it is written, 'Having ordained man through Thy wisdom, that he should have dominion over the creatures which Thou hast made[5].' And these, being creatures, are also said to be created, as we may further hear from the Lord, who says, 'He who created them, made them male and female[6];' and from Moses in the Song, who writes, 'Ask now of the days that are past, which were before thee since the day that God created man upon the earth, and from the one side of heaven unto the other[7].' And Paul in Colossians, 'Who is the Image of the Invisible God, the Firstborn of every creature, for in Him were all things created that are in heaven, and that are on earth, visible and invisible, whether they be thrones, or dominions, or principalities, or powers ; all things were created through Him, and for Him, and He is before all[8].'

---

[2] τὸ λεγόμενον κτίζεσθαι τῇ φύσει καὶ τῇ οὐσίᾳ κτίσμα. also *infr.* 60. Without meaning that the respective terms are synonymous, is it not plain that in a later phraseology this would have been, 'not simply that He is in His Person a creature,' or 'that His Person is created?' Athan.'s use of the phrase οὐσία τοῦ λόγου has already been noticed, *supr.* i. 45, and passages from this Oration are given in another connexion, *supr.* p. 70, note 15. The term is synonymous with the Divine Nature as existing in the Person of the Word. [Cf. Prolegg. ch. ii. § 3 (2) b.] In the passage in the text the οὐσία of the Word is contrasted to the οὐσία of creatures ; and it is observable that it is implied that our Lord has not taken on Him a created οὐσία. 'He said not, Athan. remarks, 'I became a creature, for the creatures have a created essence ;' he adds that 'He created' signifies, *not* essence, but something taking place in Him περὶ ἐκεῖνον, i.e. some adjunct or accident (e.g. notes on *de Decr.* 22), or as he says *supr.* § 8, envelopment or dress. And *infr.* § 51, he contrasts the οὐσία and the ἀνθρώπινον of the Word; as in *Orat.* i. 41. οὐσία and ἡ ἀνθρωπότης; and φύσις and σάρξ, iii. 34. init. and λόγος and σάρξ, 38. init. And He speaks of the Son 'taking on Him the *economy,*' *infr.* 76, and of the ὑπόστασις.τοῦ λόγου being one with ὁ ἄνθρωπος, iv. 25, c. It is observed, § 8, note, how this line of teaching might be wrested to the purposes of the Apollinarian and Eutychian heresies ; and, considering Athan.'s most emphatic protests against their errors in his later works, as well as his strong statements in *Orat.* iii. there is no hazard in this admission. His ordinary use of ἄνθρωπος for the manhood might quite as plausibly be perverted on the other hand into a defence of Nestorianism. Vid. also the Ed. Ben. on S. Hilary, præf. p. xliii. who uses *natura* absolutely for our Lord's Divinity, as contrasted to the *dispensatio*, and divides His titles into *naturalia* and *assumpta.*   [3] Ps. civ. 24. LXX. ; Rom. viii. 22.
[4] Rev. viii. 9 ; 1 Tim. iv. 4.   [5] Wisd. ix. 2.
[6] Matt. xix. 4. (ὁ κτίσας).   [7] Deut. iv. 32.
[8] Col. i. 15—17.

---

46. That to be called creatures, then, and to be created belongs to things which have by nature a created essence, these passages are sufficient to remind us, though Scripture is full of the like ; on the other hand that the single word 'He created' does not simply denote the essence and mode of generation, David shews in the Psalm, 'This shall be written for another generation, and the people that is created shall praise the Lord[1];' and again, 'Create in me a clean heart, O God[2];' and Paul in Ephesians says, 'Having abolished the law of commandments contained in ordinances, for to create in Himself of two one new man[3]; and again, 'Put ye on the new man, which after God is created in righteousness and true holiness[4].' For neither David spoke of any people created in essence, nor prayed to have another heart than that he had, but meant renovation according to God and renewal ; nor did Paul signify two persons created in essence in the Lord, nor again did he counsel us to put on any other man ; but he called the life according to virtue the 'man after God,' and by the 'created' in Christ he meant the two people who are renewed in Him. Such too is the language of the book of Jeremiah ; 'The Lord created a new salvation for a planting, in which salvation men shall walk to and fro[5];' and in thus speaking, he does not mean any essence of a creature, but prophesies of the renewal of salvation among men, which has taken place in Christ for us. Such then being the difference between 'the creatures' and the single word 'He created,' if you find anywhere in divine Scripture the Lord called 'creature,' produce it and fight ; but if it is nowhere written that He is a creature, only He Himself says about Himself in the Proverbs, 'The Lord created me,' shame upon you, both on the ground of the distinction aforesaid and for that the diction is like that of proverbs ; and accordingly let 'He created' be understood, not of His being a creature, but of that human nature which became His, for to this belongs creation. Indeed is it not evidently unfair in you, when David and Paul say 'He created,' then indeed not to understand it of the essence and the generation, but the renewal ; yet, when the Lord says 'He created' to number His essence with the creatures? and again when Scripture says, 'Wisdom built her an house, she set it upon seven pillars[6],' to understand 'house'

---

[1] Ps. cii. 18. LXX.   [2] Ps. li. 12.   [3] Eph. ii. 15.
[4] Eph. iv. 22 ; vid. Cyr. *Thes.* p. 156.
[5] Jer. xxxi. 22. vid. also *supr.* p. 85, where he notices that this is the version of the Septuagint, Aquila's being 'The Lord created a new thing in woman.' Athan. has preserved Aquila's version in three other places, in Psalm xxx. 12. lix. 5. lxv. 18.
[6] Prov. ix. 1.

allegorically, but to take 'He created' as it stands, and to fasten on it the idea of creature? and neither His being Framer of all has had any weight with you, nor have you feared His being the sole and proper Offspring of the Father, but recklessly, as if you had enlisted against Him, do ye fight, and think less of Him than of men.

47. For the very passage proves that it is only an invention of your own to call the Lord creature For the Lord, knowing His own Essence to be the Only-begotten Wisdom and Offspring of the Father, and other than things originate and natural creatures, says in love to man, 'The Lord created me a beginning of His ways,' as if to say, 'My Father hath prepared for Me a body, and has created Me for men in behalf of their salvation.' For, as when John says, 'The Word was made flesh[1], we do not conceive the whole Word Himself to be flesh[2], but to have put on flesh and become man, and on hearing, 'Christ hath become a curse for us,' and 'He hath made Him sin for us who knew no sin[3],' we do not simply conceive this, that whole Christ has become curse and sin, but that He has taken on Him the curse which lay against us (as the Apostle has said, 'Has redeemed us from the curse,' and 'has carried,' as Isaiah has said, ' our sins,' and as Peter has written, ' has borne them in the body on the wood[4]); so, if it is said in the Proverbs 'He created,' we must not conceive that the whole Word is in nature a creature, but that He put on the created body[5] and that God created Him for our sakes, preparing for Him the created body, as it is written, for us, that in Him we might be capable of being renewed and deified. What then deceived you, O senseless, to call the Creator a creature? or whence did you purchase for you this new thought, to parade it[6]? For the Proverbs say 'He created,' but they call not the Son creature, but Offspring; and, according to the distinction in Scripture aforesaid of ' He created' and ' creature,' they acknowledge, what is

by nature proper to the Son, that He is the Only-begotten Wisdom and Framer of the creatures, and when they say 'He created,' they say it not in respect of His Essence, but signify that He was becoming a beginning of many ways; so that 'He created' is in contrast to 'Offspring,' and His being called the ' Beginning of ways[7]' to His being the Only-begotten Word.

48. For if He is Offspring, how call ye Him creature? for no one says that He begets what He creates, nor calls His proper offspring creatures; and again, if He is Only-begotten, how becomes He ' beginning of the ways?' for of necessity, if He was created a beginning of all things, He is no longer alone, as having those who came into being after Him. For Reuben, when he became a beginning of the children[1], was not only-begotten, but in time indeed first, but in nature and relationship one among those who came after him. Therefore if the Word also is 'a beginning of the ways,' He must be such as the ways are, and the ways must be such as the Word, though in point of time He be created first of them. For the beginning or initiative of a city is such as the other parts of the city are, and the members too being joined to it, make the city whole and one, as the many members of one body; nor does one part of it make, and another come to be, and is subject to the former, but all the city equally has its government and constitution from its maker. If then the Lord is in such sense created as a ' beginning' of all things, it would follow that He and all other things together make up the unity of the creation, and He neither differs from all others, though He become the ' beginning' of all, nor is He Lord of them, though older in point of time; but He has the same manner of framing and the same Lord as the rest. Nay, if He be a creature, as you hold, how can He be created sole and first at all, so as to be beginning of all? when it is plain from what has been said, that among the creatures not any is of a constant[2] nature and of prior formation, but each has its origination with all the rest, however it may excel others in glory. For as to the separate stars or the great lights, not this appeared first, and that second, but in one day and by the same command, they were all called into being. And such was the original formation of the quadrupeds, and of birds, and fishes, and cattle, and plants; thus too has the race

---

[1] John i. 14.   [2] § 10. n. 6.   [3] Gal. iii. 13; 2 Cor. v. 21.
[4] Gal. iii. 13; Is. liii. 4; 1 Pet. ii. 24.
[5] Here he says that, though our Lord's flesh is created or He is created as to the flesh, it is not right to call Him a creature. This is very much what S. Thomas says, as referred to in § 45, note 1, in the words of the Schools, that Æthiops, albus secundum dentes, non est albus. But why may not our Lord be so called upon the principle of the *communicatio Idiomatum* (*infr.* note on iii. 31.) as He is said to be born of a Virgin, to have suffered, &c.? The reason is this:—birth, passion, &c., confessedly belong to His human nature, without adding ' according to the flesh;' but ' creature' not implying humanity, might appear a simple attribute of His Person, if used without limitation. Thus, as S. Thomas adds, though we may not absolutely say Æthiops est albus, we may say 'crispus est,' or in like manner, 'calvus est.' Since crispus, or calvus, can but refer to the hair. Still more does this remark apply in the case of 'Sonship,' which is a personal attribute altogether; as is proved, says Petav. *de Incarn.* vii. 6 fin. by the instance of Adam, who was in all respects a man like Seth, yet not a son. Accordingly, we may not call our Lord, even according to the manhood, an adopted Son.   [6] πομπεύετε, *infr.* 82.

[7] ἀρχὴν ὁδῶν· and so in Justin's *Tryph.* 61. The Bened. Ed. *in loc.* refers to a similar application of the word to our Lord in Tatian *contr. Gent.* 5. Athenag. *Ap.* 10. Iren. *Hær.* iv. 20. n. 3. Origen. *in Joan.* tom. 1. 39. Tertull. *adv. Prax.* 6. and Ambros. *de Fid.* iii. 7.   [1] ἀρχὴ τέκνων, Gen. xlix. 3.
[2] Cf. p. 157, note 7.

made after God's Image come to be, namely men; for though Adam only was formed out of earth, yet in him was involved the succession of the whole race.

49. And from the visible creation, we clearly discern that His invisible things also, 'being perceived by the things that are made[3],' are not independent of each other; for it was not first one and then another, but all at once were constituted after their kind. For the Apostle did not number individually, so as to say 'whether Angel, or Throne, or Dominion, or Authority,' but he mentions together all according to their kind, 'whether Angels, or Archangels, or Principalities[4]:' for in this way is the origination of the creatures. If then, as I have said, the Word were creature, He must have been brought into being, not first of them, but with all the other Powers, though in glory He excel the rest ever so much. For so we find it to be in their case, that at once they came to be, with neither first nor second, and they differ from each other in glory, some on the right of the throne, some all around, and some on the left, but one and all praising and standing in service before the Lord[5]. Therefore if the Word be creature, He would not be first or beginning of the rest; yet if He be before all, as indeed He is, and is Himself alone First and Son, it does not follow that He is beginning of all things as to His Essence[6], for what is the beginning of all is in the number of all. And if He is not such a beginning, then neither is He a creature, but it is very plain that He differs in essence and nature from the creatures, and is other than they, and is Likeness and Image of the sole and true God, being Himself sole also. Hence He is not classed with creatures in Scripture, but David rebukes those who dare even to think of Him as such, saying, 'Who among the gods is like unto the Lord[7]?' and 'Who is like unto the Lord among the sons of God?' and Baruch, 'This is our God, and another shall not be reckoned with Him[8].' For the One creates, and the rest are created; and the One is the own Word and Wisdom of the Father's Essence, and through this Word things which came to be, which before existed not, were made.

50. Your famous assertion then, that the Son is a creature, is not true, but is your fantasy only; nay Solomon convicts you of having many times slandered him. For he has not called Him creature, but God's Offspring and Wisdom, saying, 'God in Wisdom established the earth,' and 'Wisdom built her an house[1].' And the very passage in question proves your irreligious spirit; for it is written, 'The Lord created me a beginning of His ways for His works.' Therefore if He is before all things, yet says 'He created me' (not 'that I might make the works,' but) 'for the works,' unless 'He created' relates to something later than Himself, He will seem later than the works, finding them on His creation already in existence before Him, for the sake of which He is also brought into being. And if so, how is He before all things notwithstanding? and how were all things made through Him and consist in Him? for behold, you say that the works consisted before Him, for which He is created and sent. But it is not so; perish the thought! false is the supposition of the heretics. For the Word of God is not creature but Creator; and says in the manner of proverbs, 'He created me' when He put on created flesh. And something besides may be understood from the passage itself; for, being Son and having God for His Father, for He is His proper Offspring, yet here He names the Father Lord; not that He was servant, but because He took the servant's form. For it became Him, on the one hand being the Word from the Father, to call God Father: for this is proper to son towards father; on the other, having come to finish the work, and taken a servant's form, to name the Father Lord. And this difference He Himself has taught by an apt distinction, saying in the Gospels, 'I thank Thee, O Father,' and then, 'Lord of heaven and earth[2].' For He calls God His Father, but of the creatures He names Him Lord; as shewing clearly from these words, that, when He put on the creature[3], then it was He called the Father Lord. For in the prayer of David the Holy Spirit marks the same distinction, saying in the Psalms, 'Give Thy strength unto Thy Child, and help the Son of Thine handmaid[4].' For the natural and true child of God is one, and the sons of the handmaid, that is, of the nature of things originate, are other. Wherefore the One, as Son, has the Father's might; but the rest are in need of salvation.

51. (But if, because He was called child,

---

3 Rom. i. 20.   4 Vid. Col. i. 16.   5 i. 61; ii. 27.
6 He says that, though none could be 'a beginning' of creation, who was a creature, yet still that such a title belongs not to His essence. It is the name of an *office* which the Eternal Word alone can fill. His Divine Sonship is both superior and necessary to that office of a 'Beginning.' Hence it is both true (as he says) that 'if the Word is a creature, He is not a beginning;' and yet that that 'beginning' is 'in the number of the creatures.' Though He becomes the 'beginning,' He is not 'a beginning as to His *essence*,' vid. *supr.* i. 49, and *infr.* § 60. where he says, 'He who is *before all*, cannot be a *beginning of all*, but is other than all,' which implies that the beginning of all is not other than all. vid. § 8, note 4, on the Priesthood, and § 16, n. 7.
7 Ps. lxxxix. 6.   8 Bar. iii. 35.

1 Vid. Prov. iii. 19; ix. 1.   2 Matt. xi. 25.
3 τὸ κτιστὸν, i.e. σῶμα, § 47.   4 Ps lxxxvi. 16.

they idly talk, let them know that both Isaac was named Abraham's child, and the son of the Shunamite was called young child.) Reasonably then, we being servants, when He became as we, He too calls the Father Lord, as we do ; and this He has so done from love to man, that we too, being servants by nature, and receiving the Spirit of the Son, might have confidence to call Him by grace Father, who is by nature our Lord. But as we, in calling the Lord Father, do not deny our servitude by nature (for we are His works, and it is ' He that hath made us, and not we ourselves[1] '), so when the Son, on taking the servant's form, says, ' The Lord created me a beginning of His ways,' let them not deny the eternity of His Godhead, and that ' in the beginning was the Word,' and ' all things were made by Him,' and ' in Him all things were created[2].'

CHAPTER XX.

TEXTS EXPLAINED ; SIXTHLY, PROVERBS viii. 22 CONTINUED.

Our Lord is said to be created ' for the works,' i.e. with a particular purpose, which no mere creatures are ever said to be. Parallel of Isai. xlix. 5, &c. When His manhood is spoken of, a reason for it is added ; not so when His Divine Nature ; Texts in proof.

51 (continued). FOR the passage in the Proverbs, as I have said before, signifies, not the Essence, but the manhood of the Word ; for if He says that He was created ' for the works,' He shews His intention of signifying, not His Essence, but the Economy which took place ' for His works,' which comes second to being. For things which are in formation and creation are made specially that they may be and exist[3], and next they have to do whatever the Word bids them, as may be seen in the case of all things. For Adam was created, not that He might work, but that first He might be man ; for it was after this that he received the command to work. And Noah was created, not because of the ark, but that first he might exist and be a man ; for after this he received commandment to prepare the ark. And the like will be found in every case on inquiring into it ;—thus the great Moses first was made a man, and next was entrusted with the government of the people. Therefore here too we must suppose the like ; for thou seest, that the Word is not created into existence, but, ' In the beginning was the Word,' and He is afterwards sent ' for the works' and the Economy towards them. For

before the works were made, the Son was ever, nor was there yet need that He should be created ; but when the works were created and need arose afterwards of the Economy for their restoration, then it was that the Word took upon Himself this condescension and assimilation to the works; which He has shewn us by the word ' He created.' And through the Prophet Isaiah willing to signify the like, He says again : ' And now thus saith the Lord, who formed me from the womb to be His servant, to gather together Jacob unto Him and Israel, I shall be brought together and be glorified before the Lord[4].'

52. See here too, He is formed, not into existence, but in order to gather together the tribes, which were in existence before He was formed. For as in the former passage stands ' He created,' so in this ' He formed ;' and as there ' for the works,' so here ' to gather together ;' so that in every point of view it appears that ' He created ' and ' He formed ' are said after ' the Word was.' For as before His forming the tribes existed, for whose sake He was formed, so does it appear that the works exist, for which He was created. And when ' in the beginning was the Word,' not yet were the works, as I have said before ; but when the works were made and the need required, then ' He created ' was said ; and as if some son, when the servants were lost, and in the hands of the enemy by their own carelessness, and need was urgent, were sent by his father to succour and recover them, and on setting out were to put over him the like dress[1] with them, and should fashion himself as they, lest the capturers, recognising him[2] as the master, should take to flight and prevent his descending to those who were hidden under the earth by them ; and then were any one to inquire of him, why he did so, were to make answer, ' My Father thus formed and prepared me for his works,' while in thus speaking, he neither implies that he is a servant nor one of the works, nor speaks of the beginning of His origination, but of the subsequent charge given him over the works,—in the same way the Lord also, having put over Him our flesh, and ' being found in fashion as a man,' if He were questioned by those who saw Him thus and marvelled, would say, ' The Lord created Me the beginning of His ways for His works,' and ' He formed Me to gather together Israel.' This again the Spirit[3] foretells in the Psalms, saying, ' Thou didst set Him over the works of Thine hands[4];' which elsewhere the Lord signified of Himself, ' I am set as King by Him upon His

---

[1] Ps. c. 3. [2] John i. 1, 3 ; Col. i. 16.
[3] He says in effect, ' Before the generation of the works, they were not ; but Christ on the contrary ' (not, 'was before His generation,' as Bull's hypothesis, supr. Exc. B. would require, but) ' is from everlasting,' vid. § 57, note.

[4] Isai. xlix. 5. LXX.   [1] § 7
[2] Vid. the well-known passage in S. Ignatius, ad Eph. 19 [and Lightfoot's note].   [3] Supr. 20.   [4] Heb. ii. 7.

holy hill of Sion [5].' And as, when He shone [6] in the body upon Sion, He had not His beginning of existence or of reign, but being God's Word and everlasting King, He vouchsafed that His kingdom should shine in a human way in Sion, that redeeming them and us from the sin which reigned in them, He might bring them under His Father's Kingdom, so, on being set 'for the works,' He is not set for things which did not yet exist, but for such as already were and needed restoration.

53. 'He created' then and 'He formed' and 'He set,' having the same meaning, do not denote the beginning of His being, or of His essence as created, but His beneficent renovation which came to pass for us. Accordingly, though He thus speaks, yet He taught also that He Himself existed before this, when He said, 'Before Abraham came to be, I am [1];' and 'when He prepared the heavens, I was present with Him;' and 'I was with Him disposing things [2].' And as He Himself was before Abraham came to be, and Israel had come into being after Abraham, and plainly He exists first and is formed afterwards, and His forming signifies not His beginning of being but His taking manhood, wherein also He collects together the tribes of Israel; so, as 'being always with the Father,' He Himself is Framer of the creation, and His works are evidently later than Himself, and 'He created' signifies, not His beginning of being, but the Economy which took place for the works, which He effected in the flesh. For it became Him, being other than the works, nay rather their Framer, to take upon Himself their renovation [3], that, whereas He is created for us, all things may be now created in Him. For when He said 'He created,' He forthwith added the reason, naming 'the works,' that His creation for the works might signify His becoming man for their renovation. And this is usual with divine Scripture [4]; for when it signifies the fleshly origination of the Son, it adds also the cause [5] for which He became man; but when he speaks or His servants declare anything of His Godhead, all is said in simple diction, and with an absolute sense, and without reason being added. For He is the Father's Radiance; and as the Father is, but not for any reason, neither must we seek the reason of that Radiance. Thus it is written, 'In the beginning was the Word, and the Word was with God, and the Word was God [6];' and the wherefore it assigns not [7]; but when 'the

Word was made flesh [8],' then it adds the reason why, saying, 'And dwelt among us.' And again the Apostle saying, 'Who being in the form of God,' has not introduced the reason, till 'He took on Him the form of a servant;' for then he continues, 'He humbled Himself unto death, even the death of the cross [9];' for it was for this that He both became flesh and took the form of a servant.

54. And the Lord Himself has spoken many things in proverbs; but when giving us notices about Himself, He has spoken absolutely [1]; 'I in the Father and the Father in Me,' and 'I and the Father are one,' and 'He that hath seen Me, hath seen the Father,' and 'I am the Light of the world,' and, 'I am the Truth [2];' not setting down in every case the reason, nor the wherefore, lest He should seem second to those things for which He was made. For that reason would needs take precedence of Him, without which not even He Himself had come into being. Paul, for instance, 'separated an Apostle for the Gospel, which the Lord had promised afore by the Prophets [3],' was thereby made subordinate to the Gospel, of which he was made minister, and John, being chosen to prepare the Lord's way, was made subordinate to the Lord; but the Lord, not being made subordinate to any reason why He should be Word, save only that He is the Father's Offspring and Only-begotten Wisdom, when He becomes man, then assigns the reason why He is about to take flesh. For the need of man preceded His becoming man, apart from which He had not put on flesh [4]. And what the need was for which He became man, He Himself thus signifies, 'I came down from heaven, not to do Mine own will, but the will of Him that sent Me. And this is the will of Him which hath sent Me, that of all which He hath given Me, I should lose nothing, but should raise it up again at the last day. And this is the will of My Father, that every one which seeth the Son and believeth on Him may have everlasting life, and I will raise him up at the last day [5].' And again; 'I am come a light into the world, that whosoever believeth on Me, should not abide in darkness [6].' And again he says; 'To this end was I born, and for this cause came I into the world, that I should bear witness unto the truth [7].' And John has written: 'For this was manifested the Son of God, that He might destroy the works of the devil [8].'

---

[5] Ps. ii. 6. LXX.   [6] ἐπέλαμψε, vid. of the Holy Spirit, *Serap.* i. 20, c.   [1] John viii. 58.
[2] Prov. viii. 27, 30, LXX.   [3] p. 335, note 1.
[4] ἔθος ἐστὶ τῇ θείᾳ γραφῇ· and so *Orat.* iii. 18, b. And τῆς γραφῆς ἔθος ἐχούσης, ibid. 30, d.   [5] Vid. Naz. *Orat.* 30. 2.
[6] John i. 1.   [7] Naz. ibid.

[8] John i. 14.   [9] Phil. ii. 6—8.   [1] *Infr.* 62.
[2] John xiv. 6, 9, 10; x. 30; viii. 12.   [3] Rom. i. 1, 2.
[4] It is the general teaching of the Fathers that our Lord would not have been incarnate had not man sinned. [But see Prolegg. ch. iv. § 3, c.] Cf. *de Incarn.* 4. vid. Thomassin. at great length *de Incarn.* ii. 5—11. also Petav. *de Incarn.* ii. 17, 7—12. Vasquez. *in* 3 *Thom. Disp.* x. 4 and 5.   [5] John vi. 38—40.
[6] Ib. xii. 46.   [7] Ib. xviii. 37.   [8] 1 John iii. 8.

55. To give a witness then, and for our sakes to undergo death, to raise man up and destroy the works of the devil[1], the Saviour came, and this is the reason of His incarnate presence. For otherwise a resurrection had not been, unless there had been death; and how had death been, unless He had had a mortal body? This the Apostle, learning from Him, thus sets forth, 'Forasmuch then as the children are partakers of flesh and blood, He also Himself likewise took part of the same; that through death He might bring to nought him that had the power of death, that is, the devil, and deliver them who through fear of death were all their lifetime subject to bondage[2].' And, 'Since by man came death, by man came also the resurrection of the dead[3].' And again, 'For what the Law could not do, in that it was weak through the flesh, God, sending His own Son in the likeness of sinful flesh, and for sin, condemned sin in the flesh; that the ordinance of the Law might be fulfilled in us, who walk not after the flesh but after the Spirit[4].' And John says, 'For God sent not His Son into the world to condemn the world, but that the world through Him might be saved[5].' And again, the Saviour has spoken in His own person, 'For judgment am I come into this world, that they who see not might see, and that they which see might become blind[6].' Not for Himself then, but for our salvation, and to abolish death, and to condemn sin, and to give sight to the blind, and to raise up all from the dead, has He come; but if not for Himself, but for us, by consequence not for Himself but for us is He created. But if not for Himself is He created, but for us, then He is not Himself a creature, but, as having put on our flesh, He uses such language. And that this is the sense of the Scriptures, we may learn from the Apostle, who says in Ephesians, 'Having broken down the middle wall of partition between us, having abolished in His flesh the enmity, even the law of commandments contained in ordinances, to create in Himself of twain one new

man, so making peace[7].' But if in Him the twain are created, and these are in His body, reasonably then, bearing the twain in Himself, He is as if Himself created; for those who were created in Himself He made one, and He was in them, as they. And thus, the two being created in Him, He may say suitably, 'The Lord created me.' For as by receiving our infirmities, He is said to be infirm Himself, though not Himself infirm, for He is the Power of God, and He became sin for us and a curse, though not having sinned Himself, but because He Himself bare our sins and our curse, so[8], by creating us in Him, let Him say, 'He created me for the works,' though not Himself a creature.

56. For if, as they hold, the Essence of the Word being of created nature, therefore He says, 'The Lord created me,' being a creature, He was not created for us; but if He was not created for us, we are not created in Him; and, if not created in Him, we have Him not in ourselves but externally; as, for instance, as receiving instruction from Him as from a teacher[1]. And it being so with us, sin has not lost its reign over the flesh, being inherent and not cast out of it. But the Apostle opposes such a doctrine a little before, when he says, 'For we are His workmanship, created in Christ Jesus[2];' and if in Christ we are created, then it is not He who is created, but we in Him; and thus the words 'He created' are for our sake. For because of our need, the Word, though being Creator, endured words which are used of creatures; which are not proper to Him, as being the Word, but are ours who are created in Him. And as, since the Father is always, so is His Word, and always being, always says 'I was daily His delight, rejoicing always before Him[3],' and 'I am in the Father and the Father in Me[4];' so, when for our need He became man, consistently does He use language, as ourselves, 'The Lord hath created Me,' that, by His dwelling in the flesh, sin might perfectly be expelled from the flesh, and we might have a free mind[5]. For what ought He, when made

---

[1] Two ends of our Lord's Incarnation are here mentioned; that He might die for us, and that He might renew us, answering nearly to those specified in Rom. iv. 25. 'who was delivered for our offences and raised again for our justification.' The general object of His coming, including both of these, is treated of in *Incarn.* esp. §§ 4—20. and in the two books against Apollinaris. Vid. *supr.* § 8. § 9. Also *infr. Orat.* iv. 6. And Theodoret, *Eran.* iii. p. 196, 7. Vigil. Thaps. *contr. Eutych.* i. p. 496. (B. P. ed. 1624.) and S. Leo speaks of the whole course of redemption, i.e. incarnation, atonement, regeneration, justification, &c., as one sacrament, not drawing the line distinctly between the several agents, elements, or stages in it, but considering it to lie in the intercommunion of Christ's and our persons. *Serm.* 63. 14. He speaks of His fortifying us against our passions and infirmities, both *sacramento susceptionis* and exemplo. *Serm.* 65, 2. and of a duplex remedium cujus aliud in *sacramento*, aliud in exemplo. *Serm.* 67, 5. also 69, 5. The tone of his teaching is throughout characteristic of the Fathers, and very like that of S. Athanasius.

[2] Heb. ii. 14, 15.   [3] 1 Cor. xv. 21.   [4] Rom. viii. 3, 4.
[5] John iii. 17.   [6] Ib. ix. 39.

[7] Eph. ii. 14, 15.
[8] The word αὐτὸς, 'Himself,' is all along used, where a later writer would have said 'His Person;' vid. *supr.* § 45, n. 2; still there is more to be explained in this passage, which, taken in the letter, would speak a language very different from Athan.'s, as if the infirmities or the created nature of the Word were not more real than His imputed sinfulness. (vid. on the other hand *infr.* iii. 31—35). But nothing is more common in theology than comparisons which are only parallel to a certain point as regards the matter in hand, especially since many doctrines do not admit of exact illustrations. Our Lord's real manhood and imputed sinfulness were alike adjuncts to His Divine Person, which was of an Eternal and Infinite Nature; and therefore His Manhood may be compared to an Attribute, or to an accident, without meaning that it really was either.   [1] Note on iii. 19.
[2] Eph. ii. 10.   [3] Prov. viii. 30.   [4] John xiv. 10.
[5] ἐλεύθερον τὸ φρόνημα. vid. also beginning of the paragraph, where sanctification is contrasted to teaching. vid. also note on 79, *infr. Contr. Apoll.* i. 20. fin. ibid. ii. 6. also *Orat.* iii. 33, where vid.

man, to say? 'In the beginning I was man?' this were neither suitable to Him nor true; and as it beseemed not to say this, so it is natural and proper in the case of man to say, 'He created' and 'He made' Him. On this account then the reason of 'He created' is added, namely, the need of the works; and where the reason is added, surely the reason rightly explains the lection. Thus here, when He says 'He created,' He sets down the cause, 'the works;' on the other hand, when He signifies absolutely the generation from the Father, straightway He adds, 'Before all the hills He begets me[6];' but He does not add the 'wherefore,' as in the case of 'He created,' saying, 'for the works,' but absolutely, 'He begets me,' as in the text, 'In the beginning was the Word[7].' For, though no works had been created, still 'the Word' of God 'was,' and 'the Word was God.' And His becoming man would not have taken place, had not the need of men become a cause. The Son then is not a creature.

CHAPTER XXI.

Texts Explained; Sixthly, Proverbs viii. 22, continued.

Our Lord not said in Scripture to be 'created,' or the works to be 'begotten.' 'In the beginning' means in the case of the works 'from the beginning.' Scripture passages explained. We are made by God first, begotten next; creatures by nature, sons by grace. Christ begotten first, made or created afterwards. Sense of 'First-born of the dead;' of 'First-born among many brethren;' of 'First-born of all creation,' contrasted with 'Only-begotten.' Further interpretation of 'beginning of ways,' and 'for the works.' Why a creature could not redeem; why redemption was necessary at all. Texts which contrast the Word and the works.

57. For had He been a creature, He had not said, 'He begets me,' for the creatures are from without, and are works of the Maker; but the Offspring is not from without nor a work, but from the Father, and proper to His Essence. Wherefore they are creatures; this God's Word and Only-begotten Son. For instance, Moses did not say of the creation, 'In the beginning He begat;' nor 'In the beginning was,' but 'In the beginning God created the heaven and the earth[1].' Nor did David say in the Psalm, 'Thy hands have "begotten me,"' but 'made me and fashioned

me[2],' everywhere applying the word 'made' to the creatures. But to the Son contrariwise; for he has not said 'I made,' but 'I begat[3],' and 'He begets me,' and 'My heart uttered a good Word[4].' And in the instance of the creation, 'In the beginning He made;' but in the instance of the Son, 'In the beginning was the Word[5].' And there is this difference, that the creatures are made upon the beginning, and have a beginning of existence connected with an interval; wherefore also what is said of them, 'In the beginning He made,' is as much as saying of them, 'From the beginning He made:'—as the Lord, knowing that which He had made, taught, when He silenced the Pharisees, with the words, 'He which made them from the beginning, made them male and female[6];' for from some beginning, when they were not yet, were originate things brought into being and created. This too the Holy Spirit has signified in the Psalms, saying, 'Thou, Lord, at the beginning hast laid the foundation of the earth[7];' and again, 'O think upon Thy congregation which Thou hast purchased from the beginning[8];' now it is plain that what takes place at the beginning, has a beginning of creation, and that from some beginning God purchased His congregation. And that 'In the beginning He made,' from his saying 'made,' means 'began to make,' Moses himself shews by saying, after the completion of all things, 'And God blessed the seventh day and sanctified it, because that in it He had rested from all His work which God began to make[9].' Therefore the creatures began to be made; but the Word of God, not having beginning of being, certainly did not begin to be, nor begin to come to be, but was ever. And the works have their beginning in their making, and their beginning precedes their coming to be; but the Word, not being of things which come to be, rather comes to be Himself the Framer of those which have a beginning. And the being of things originate is measured by their becoming[10], and from some beginning does God begin to make them through the Word, that it may be known that they were not before their origination; but the Word has His being, in no other beginning[11] than the Father, whom[12] they allow to be without beginning, so that He too exists without beginning in the Father, being His Offspring, not His creature.

---

note, and 34. vid. for ἀρχή, *Orat.* i. 48, note 7. Also vid. *infr. Orat.* iii. 56. a. iv. 33, a. Naz. *Epp. ad Cled.* 1. and 2. (101, 102. Ed. Ben.) Nyssen. *ad Theoph. in Apoll.* p. 696. Leo, *Serm.* 26, 2. *Serm.* 72, 2. vid. *Serm.* 22, 2. ut corpus regenerati fiat caro Crucifixi. *Serm.* 63, 6. Hæc est nativitas nova dum homo nascitur in Deo; in quo homine Deus natus est, carne antiqui seminis suscepta, sine semine antiquo, ut illam novo semine, id est, spiritualiter, reformaret, exclusis antiquitatis sordibus expiatam. Tertull. *de Carn. Christ.* 17. vid. *supr.* i. 51, note 5. and note on 64 *infr.* 65 and 70. and on iii. 34.

6 Prov. viii. 25.   7 John i. 1.   1 Gen. i. 1.

2 Ps. cxix. 73.   3 Ps. ii. 7.   4 Ps. xlv. 1.
5 John i. 1.   6 Matt. xix. 4.   7 Ps. cii. 25.
8 Ps. lxxiv. 2.   9 Gen. ii. 3.   10 *Supr.* i. 29, n. 10.
11 ἀρχῇ, vid. *Orat.* iv. 1.
12 In this passage 'was from the beginning' is made equivalent with 'was not before generation,' and both are contrasted with 'without beginning' or 'eternal;' vid. the bearing of this on Bishop Bull's explanation of the Nicene Anathema, *supr. Exc. B*, where this passage is quoted.

58. Thus does divine Scripture recognise the difference between the Offspring and things made, and shew that the Offspring is a Son, not begun from any beginning, but eternal; but that the thing made, as an external work of the Maker, began to come into being. John therefore delivering divine doctrine[1] about the Son, and knowing the difference of the phrases, said not, 'In the beginning has become' or 'been made,' but 'In the beginning was the Word;' that we might understand 'Offspring' by 'was,' and not account of Him by intervals, but believe the Son always and eternally to exist. And with these proofs, how, O Arians, misunderstanding the passage in Deuteronomy, did you venture a fresh act of irreligion[2] against the Lord, saying that 'He is a work,' or 'creature,' or indeed 'offspring?' for offspring and work you take to mean the same thing; but here too you shall be shewn to be as unlearned as you are irreligious. Your first passage is this, 'Is not He thy Father that bought thee? did He not make thee and create thee[3]? And shortly after in the same Song he says, 'God that begat thee thou didst desert, and forgattest God that nourished thee[4].' Now the meaning conveyed in these passages is very remarkable; for he says not first 'He begat,' lest that term should be taken as indiscriminate with 'He made,' and these men should have a pretence for saying, 'Moses tells us indeed that God said from the beginning, "Let Us make man[5]," but he soon after says himself, 'God that begat thee thou didst desert,' as if the terms were indifferent; for offspring and work are the same. But after the words 'bought' and 'made,' he has added last of all 'begat,' that the sentence might carry its own interpretation; for in the word 'made' he accurately denotes what belongs to men by nature, to be works and things made; but in the word 'begat' he shews God's lovingkindness exercised towards men after He had created them. And since they have proved ungrateful upon this, thereupon Moses reproaches them, saying first, 'Do ye thus requite the Lord?' and then adds, 'Is not He thy Father that bought thee? Did He not make thee and create thee[6]?' And next he says, 'They sacrificed unto devils, not to God, to gods whom they knew not. New gods and strange came up, whom your fathers knew not; the God that begat thee thou didst desert[7].'

59. For God not only created them to be men, but called them to be sons, as having begotten them. For the term 'begat' is here as elsewhere expressive of a Son, as He says by the Prophet, 'I begat sons and exalted them;' and generally, when Scripture wishes to signify a son, it does so, not by the term 'created,' but undoubtedly by that of 'begat.' And this John seems to say, 'He gave to them power to become children of God, even to them that believe on His Name; which were begotten not of blood, nor of the will of the flesh, nor of the will of man, but of God[1].' And here too the cautious distinction[2] is well kept up, for first he says 'become,' because they are not called sons by nature but by adoption; then he says 'were begotten,' because they too had received at any rate the name of son. But the People, as says the Prophet, 'despised' their Benefactor. But this is God's kindness to man, that of whom He is Maker, of them according to grace He afterwards becomes Father also; becomes, that is, when men, His creatures, receive into their hearts, as the Apostle says, 'the Spirit of His Son, crying, Abba, Father[3].' And these are they who, having received the Word, gained power from Him to become sons of God; for they could not become sons, being by nature creatures, otherwise than by receiving the Spirit of the natural and true Son. Wherefore, that this might be, 'The Word became flesh,' that He might make man capable of Godhead. This same meaning may be gained also from the Prophet Malachi, who says, 'Hath not One God created us? Have we not all one Father[4]?' for first he puts 'created,' next 'Father,' to shew, as the other writers, that from the beginning we were creatures by nature, and God is our Creator through the Word; but afterwards we were made sons, and thenceforward God the Creator becomes our Father also. Therefore 'Father' is proper to the Son; and not 'creature,' but 'Son' is proper to the Father. Accordingly this passage also proves, that we are not sons by nature, but the Son who is in us[5]; and again, that God is not our Father by nature, but of that Word in us, in whom and because of whom we 'cry, Abba, Father[6].' And so in like manner, the Father calls them sons in whomsoever He sees His own Son, and says, 'I begat;' since begetting is significant of a Son, and making is indicative of the works. And thus it is that we are not

[1] θεολογῶν, vid. § 71, note.
[2] The technical sense of εὐσέβεια, ἀσέβεια, pietas, impietas, for 'orthodoxy, heterodoxy,' has been noticed *supr.* p. 150, and derived from 1 Tim. iii. 16. The word is contrasted ch. iv. 8. with the (perhaps Gnostic) 'profane and old-wives fables,' and with 'bodily exercise.'   [3] Deut. xxxii. 6. LXX.   [4] Ibid. 18.
[5] Gen. i. 26.   [6] Deut. xxxii. 6.   [7] Ibid. 17.

[1] John i. 12, 13.   [2] παρατηρήσεως, § 12, note.
[3] De Decr. 31 fin.   [4] Mal. ii. 10.
[5] τὸν ἐν ἡμῖν υἱόν. vid. also *supr.* 10. circ. fin. 56. init. and τὸν ἐν αὐτοῖς οἰκοῦντα λόγον. 61. init. Also *Orat.* i. 50 fin. iii. 23—25. and *de Decr.* 31 fin. *Or.* i. 48, note 7, § 56, n. 5. *infr.* notes on 79.
[6] Gal. iv. 6.

begotten first, but made; for it is written, 'Let Us make man[7];' but afterwards, on receiving the grace of the Spirit, we are said thenceforth to be begotten also; just as the great Moses in his Song with an apposite meaning says first 'He bought,' and afterwards 'He begat;' lest, hearing 'He begat,' they might forget their own original nature; but that they might know that from the beginning they are creatures, but when according to grace they are said to be begotten, as sons, still no less than before are men works according to nature.

60. And that creature and offspring are not the same, but differ from each other in nature and the signification of the words, the Lord Himself shews even in the Proverbs. For having said, 'The Lord created me a beginning of His ways;' He has added, 'But before all the hills He begat me.' If then the Word were by nature and in His Essence[1] a creature, and there were no difference between offspring and creature, He would not have added, 'He begat me,' but had been satisfied with 'He created,' as if that term implied 'He begat;' but, as it is, after saying, 'He created me a beginning of His ways for His works,' He has added, not simply 'begat me,' but with the connection of the conjunction 'But,' as guarding thereby the term 'created,' when he says, 'But before all the hills He begat me.' For 'begat me' succeeding in such close connection to 'created me,' makes the meaning one, and shews that 'created' is said with an object[2], but that 'begat me' is prior to 'created me.' For as, if He had said the reverse, 'The Lord begat me,' and went on, 'But before the hills He created me,' 'created' would certainly precede 'begat,' so having said first 'created,' and then added 'But before all the hills He begat me,' He necessarily shews that 'begat' preceded 'created.' For in saying, 'Before all He begat me,' He intimates that He is other than all things; it having been shewn to be true[3] in an earlier part of this book, that no one creature was made before another, but all things originate subsisted at once together upon one and the same command[4]. Therefore neither do the words which follow 'created,' also follow 'begat me;' but in the case of 'created' is added 'beginning of ways,' but of 'begat me,' He says not, 'He begat me as a beginning,' but 'before all He begat me.' But He who is before all is not a beginning of all, but is other than all[5]; but if other than all (in which 'all' the beginning of all is included), it follows that He is other than the creatures;

and it becomes a clear point, that the Word, being other than all things and before all, afterwards is created 'a beginning of the ways for works,' because He became man, that, as the Apostle has said, He who is the 'Beginning' and 'First-born from the dead, in all things might have the preeminence[6].'

61. Such then being the difference between 'created' and 'begat me,' and between 'beginning of ways' and 'before all,' God, being first Creator, next, as has been said, becomes Father of men, because of His Word dwelling in them. But in the case of the Word the reverse; for God, being His Father by nature, becomes afterwards both His Creator and Maker, when the Word puts on that flesh which was created and made, and becomes man. For, as men, receiving the Spirit of the Son, become children through Him, so the Word of God, when He Himself puts on the flesh of man, then is said both to be created and to have been made. If then we are by nature sons, then is He by nature creature and work; but if we become sons by adoption and grace, then has the Word also, when in grace towards us He became man, said, 'The Lord created me.' And in the next place, when He put on a created nature and became like us in body, reasonably was He therefore called both our Brother and 'First-born[1].' For though it was after us[2] that He was made man for us, and our brother by similitude of body, still He is therefore called and is the 'First-born' of us, because, all men being lost, according to the transgression of Adam, His flesh before all others was saved and liberated, as being the Word's body[3]; and henceforth we, becoming incorporate with It, are saved after Its pattern. For in It the Lord becomes our guide to the Kingdom of Heaven and to His own Father, saying, 'I am the way' and 'the door[4],' and 'through Me all must enter.' Whence also is He said to be 'First-born from the dead[5],' not that He died before us, for we had died first; but because having undergone death for us and abolished it, He was the first to rise, as man, for our sakes raising His own Body. Henceforth He having risen, we too from Him and because of Him rise in due course from the dead.

---

6 Col. i. 18.
1 Rom. viii. 29. Bishop Bull's hypothesis about the sense of πρωτότοκος τῆς κτίσεως has been commented on *supr.* p. 347. As far as Athan.'s discussion proceeds in this section, it only relates to πρωτότοκος of *men* (i.e. from the dead), and is equivalent to the 'beginning of ways.'
2 Marcellus seems to have argued against Asterius from the same texts (Euseb. *in Marc.* p. 12), that, since Christ is called 'first-born from the dead,' though others had been recalled to life before Him, therefore He is called 'first-born of creation,' not in point of time, but of dignity. vid. Montacut. *Not.* p. 11. Yet Athan. argues contrariwise. *Orat.* iv. 29. *Orat.* iii. 31. note.   4 John xiv. 6; x. 9.   5 Rev. i. 5.

---

7 Gen. i. 26.   1 § 45, note 2.   2 Ch. 20.
3 pp. 367, 374.   4 § 48.   5 § 6, note 49.

62. But if He is also called 'First-born of the creation [1],' still this is not as if He were levelled to the creatures, and only first of them in point of time (for how should that be, since He is 'Only-begotten?'), but it is because of the Word's condescension [2] to the creatures, according to which He has become the 'Brother' of 'many.' For the term 'Only-begotten' is used where there are no brethren, but 'First-born [3]' because of brethren. Accordingly it is nowhere written in the Scriptures, 'the first-born of God,' nor 'the creature of God;' but 'Only-begotten' and 'Son' and 'Word' and 'Wisdom,' refer to Him as proper to the Father [4]. Thus, 'We have seen His glory, the glory as of the Only-begotten of the Father [5];' and 'God sent His Only-begotten Son [6];' and 'O Lord, Thy Word endureth for ever [7];' and 'In the beginning was the Word, and the Word was with God;' and 'Christ the Power of God and the Wisdom of God [8];' and 'This is My beloved Son;' and 'Thou art the Christ, the Son of the Living God [9].' But 'first-born' implied the descent to the creation [10]; for of it has He been called first-born; and 'He created' implies His grace towards the works, for for them is He created. If then He is Only-begotten, as indeed He is, 'First-born' needs some explanation; but if He be really First-born, then He is not Only-begotten [10]. For the same cannot be both Only-begotten and First-born, except in different relations;— that is, Only-begotten, because of His generation from the Father, as has been said; and First-born, because of His condescension to the creation and His making the many His brethren. Certainly, those two terms being inconsistent with each other, one should say that the attribute of being Only-begotten has justly the preference in the instance of

the Word, in that there is no other Word, or other Wisdom, but He alone is very Son of the Father. Moreover [11], as was before [12] said, not in connection with any reason, but absolutely [13] it is said of Him, 'The Only-begotten Son which is in the bosom of the Father [14];' but the word 'First-born' has again the creation as a reason in connection with it, which Paul proceeds to say, 'for in Him all things were created [15].' But if all the creatures were created in Him, He is other than the creatures, and is not a creature, but the Creator of the creatures.

63. Not then because He was from the Father was He called 'First-born,' but because in Him the creation came to be ; and as before the creation He was the Son, through whom was the creation, so also before He was called the First-born of the whole creation, not the less was the Word Himself with God and the Word was God. But this also not understanding, these irreligious men go about saying, 'If He is First-born of all creation, it is plain that He too is one of the creation.' Senseless men ! if He is simply 'First-born [1]' of the whole creation,' then He is other than the whole creation ; for he says not, 'He is First-born above the rest of the creatures,' lest He be reckoned to be as one of the creatures, but it is written, 'of the whole creation,' that He may appear other than the creation [2]. Reuben, for instance, is not said to be first-born of all the children of Jacob [3], but of Jacob himself and his brethren ; lest he should be thought to be some other beside the children of Jacob. Nay, even concerning the Lord Himself the Apostle says not, 'that He may become First-born of

---

[1] Here again, though speaking of the 'first-born of creation,' Athan. simply views the phrase as equivalent to 'first-born of the *new* creation or "*brother*" *of many*;' and so *infr.* 'first-born because of the brotherhood He has made with many.'

[2] Bp. Bull considers συγκατάβασις as equivalent to a figurative γέννησις, an idea which (vid. *supr.* p. 346 *sq.*) seems quite foreign from Athan.'s meaning. In Bull's sense of the word, Athan. could not have said that the senses of Only-begotten and First-born were contrary to each other, *Or.* i. 28. Συγκαταβῆναι occurs *supr.* 51 fin. of the Incarnation. What is meant by it will be found *infr.* 78—81. viz. that our Lord came 'to implant in the creatures a type and semblance of His Image ;' which is just what is here maintained against Bull. The whole passage referred to is a comment on the word συγκατάβασις, and begins and ends with an introduction of that word. Vid. also *c. Gent.* 47.

[3] Vid. Rom. viii. 29.

[4] This passage has been urged against Bull *supr. Exc. B.* All the words (says Athan.) which are proper to the Son, and describe Him fitly, are expressive of what is 'internal' to the Divine Nature, as Begotten, Word, Wisdom, Hand, &c., but (as he adds presently) the 'first-born,' like 'beginning of ways,' is relative to creation ; and therefore cannot denote our Lord's essence or Divine subsistence, but something temporal, an office, character, or the like. [5] John i. 14.

[6] 1 John iv. 9. [7] Ps. ⸴xix. 89. [8] 1 Cor. i. 24.

[9] Matt. iii. 17 ; xvi. 16.

[10] This passage is imitated by Theodoret. *in Coloss.* i. 15, but the passages from the Fathers referable to these Orations are too many to enumerate.

[11] We now come to a third and wider sense of πρωτότοκος, as found (not in Rom. viii. 29, and Col. i. 18, but) in Col. i. 15, where by 'creation' Athan. understands 'all things visible and invisible.' As then 'for the works' was just now taken to argue that 'created' was used in a relative and restricted sense, the same is shewn as regards 'first-born by the words 'for in Him all things were created.' [12] i. 52.

[13] ἀπολελυμένως; *supr.* i. 56, note 6, and §§ 53, 56, and so ἀπολύτως Theophylact to express the same distinction *in loc. Coloss.* [14] John i. 18. [15] Col. i. 16.

[1] It would be perhaps better to translate 'first-born *to* the creature,' to give Bull's idea ; τῆς κτίσεως not being a partitive genitive, or πρωτότοκος a superlative (though he presently so considers it), but a simple appellative and τῆς κτ. a common genitive of relation, as 'the king of a country,' 'the owner of a house.' 'First-born of creation' is like 'author, type, life of creation.' Hence S. Paul goes on at once to say, 'for *in* Him all things were made,' not simply 'by and for,' as at the end of the verse ; or as Athan. says here, 'because in Him the creation came to be.' On the distinction of διὰ and ἐν, referring respectively to the first and second creations, vid. *In illud Omn.* 2. (*Supr.* p. 88.)

[2] To understand this passage, the Greek idiom must be kept in view. Cf. Milton's imitation 'the fairest of her daughters Eve.' Vid. as regards the very word πρῶτος, John i. 15 ; and *supr.* § 30, note 3, also πλείστην ἢ ἔμπροσθεν ἐξουσίαν 3 *Maccab.* 7, 21. Accordingly as in the comparative to obviate this exclusion, we put in the word 'other.' (ante 'alios immanior omnes), so too in the Greek superlative, 'Socrates is wisest of "other" heathen.' Athanasius then says in this passage, that 'first-born of creatures' implies that our Lord was not a creature ; whereas it is not said of Him 'first-born of brethren,' lest He should be excluded from men, but first-born "among" brethren,' where 'among' is equivalent to 'other.'

[3] Gen. xlix. 3, LXX. Vid. also *contr. Gent.* 41 sq. where the text Col. i. 15 is quoted.

all,' lest He be thought to bear a body other than ours, but 'among many brethren[4],' because of the likeness of the flesh. If then the Word also were one of the creatures, Scripture would have said of Him also that He was First-born of other creatures ; but in fact, the saints saying that He is 'First-born of the whole creation[5],' the Son of God is plainly shewn to be other than the whole creation and not a creature. For if He is a creature, He will be First-born of Himself. How then is it possible, O Arians, for Him to be before and after Himself? next, if He is a creature, and the whole creation through Him came to be, and in Him consists, how can He both create the creation and be one of the things which consist in Him? Since then such a notion is in itself unseemly, it is proved against them by the truth, that He is called 'First-born among many brethren' because of the relationship of the flesh, and 'First-born from the dead,' because the resurrection of the dead is from Him and after Him ; and 'First-born of the whole creation,' because of the Father's love to man, which brought it to pass that in His Word not only 'all things consist[6],' but the creation itself, of which the Apostle speaks, 'waiting for the manifestation of the sons of God, shall be delivered' one time 'from the bondage of corruption into the glorious liberty of the children of God[7].' Of this creation thus delivered, the Lord will be First-born, both of it and of all those who are made children, that by His being called first, those that come after Him may abide[8], as depending on the Word as a beginning[9].

64. And I think that the irreligious men themselves will be shamed from such a thought ; for if the case stands not as we have said, but they will rule it that He is 'First-born of the whole creation' as in essence—a creature among creatures, let them reflect that they will be conceiving Him as brother and fellow of the things without reason and life. For of the whole creation these also are parts ; and the 'First-born' must be first indeed in point of time but only thus, and in kind and similitude[1] must be the same with all. How then can they say this without exceeding all measures of irreligion? or who will endure them, if this is their language? or who can but hate them even imagining such things? For it is evident to all, that neither for Himself, as being a creature, nor as having any connection according to essence with the whole creation, has He been called 'First-

born' of it : but because the Word, when at the beginning He framed the creatures, condescended to things originate, that it might be possible for them to come to be. For they could not have endured His nature, which was untempered splendour, even that of the Father, unless condescending by the Father's love for man He had supported them and taken hold of them and brought them into existence[2] ; and next, because, by this condescension of the Word, the creation too is made a son[3] through Him, that He might be in all respects 'First-born' of it, as has been said, both in creating, and also in being brought for the sake of all into this very world. For so it is written, 'When He bringeth the First-born into the world, He saith, Let all the Angels of God worship Him[4].' Let Christ's enemies hear and tear themselves to pieces, because His coming into the world is what makes Him called 'First-born' of all ; and thus the Son is the Father's 'Only-begotten,' because He alone is from Him, and He is the 'First-born of creation,' because of this adoption of all as sons[5]. And as He is First-born among brethren and rose from the dead 'the first fruits of them that slept[6];' so, since it became Him 'in all things to have the preeminence[7],' therefore He is created 'a beginning of ways,' that we, walking along it and entering through Him who says, 'I am the Way' and 'the Door,' and partaking of the knowledge of the Father, may also hear the words, 'Blessed are the undefiled in the Way,' and 'Blessed are the pure in heart, for they shall see God[8].'

65. And thus since the truth declares that the Word is not by nature a creature, it is fitting now to say, in what sense He is 'beginning of

---

[2] He does not here say with Asterius that God could not create man immediately, for the Word is God, but that He did not create him without at the same time infusing a grace or presence from Himself into his created nature to enable it to endure His external plastic hand ; in other words, that he was created *in Him*, not as something external to Him (in spite of the διὰ *supr.* 63, n. 1. vid. *supr. de Decr.* 19. 3. and *Gent.* 47. where the συγκατάβασις is spoken of.

[3] As God *created* Him, in that He created human nature in Him, so is He *first-born*, in that human nature is adopted in Him. Leo *Serm.* 63. 3.   [4] Heb. i. 6.

[5] Thus he considers that 'first-born' is mainly a title, connected with the Incarnation. and also connected with our Lord's office at the creation (vid. parallel of Priesthood, § 8, n. 4). In each economy it has the same meaning ; it belongs to Him as the type, idea, or rule on which the creature was made or new-made, and the life by which it is sustained. Both economies are mentioned *Incarn.* 13, 14. *Orat.* i. 51. iii. 20. *infr.* 76. init. He came τὴν τοῦ ἀρχετύπου πλάσιν ἀναστήσασθαι ἑαυτῷ *contr. Apoll.* ii. 5. And so again, ἡ ἰδέα ὅπερ λόγον εἰρήκασι. Clem. *Strom.* v. 3. ἰδέαν ἰδεῶν καὶ ἀρχὴν λεκτέον τὸν πρωτότοκον πάσης κτίσεως Origen. *contr. Cels.* vi. 64. fin. 'Whatever God was about to make in the creature, was already in the Word, nor would be in the things, were it not in the Word.' August. in Psalm xliv. 5. He elsewhere calls the Son, 'ars quædam omnipotentis atque sapientis Dei, plena omnium rationum viventium incommutabilium.' *de Trin.* vi. 11. And so Athan. *infr.* iii. 9. fin. Eusebius, in commenting on the very passage which Athan. is discussing (Prov. viii. 22), presents a remarkable contrast to these passages, as making the Son, not the ἰδέα, but the external minister of the Father's ἰδέα. *de Eccl. Theol.* pp. 164, 5. vid. *supr.* § 31, n. 7.
[6] 1 Cor. xv. 20.   [7] Col. i. 18.
[8] Ps. cxix. 1 ; Matt. v. 8.

---

[4] Rom. viii 29.   [5] Col. i. 15.   [6] Ib. i. 17.
[7] Rom. viii. 19, 21. Thus there are two senses in which our Lord is 'first-born to the creation ;' viz. in its first origin, and in its restoration after man's fall ; as he says more clearly in the next section.   [8] *De Decr.* 19, n. 3.   [9] i. 48, n. 7.   [1] § 20.

ways.' For when the first way, which was through Adam, was lost, and in place of paradise we deviated unto death, and heard the words, 'Dust thou art, and unto dust [1] shalt thou return,' therefore the Word of God, who loves man, puts on Him created flesh at the Father's will [2], that whereas the first man had made it dead through the transgression, He Himself might quicken it in the blood of His own body [3], and might open 'for us a way new and living,' as the Apostle says, 'through the veil, that is to say, His flesh [4];' which he signifies elsewhere thus, 'Wherefore, if any man be in Christ, he is a new creation; old things are passed away, behold all things are become new [5].' But if a new creation has come to pass, some one must be first of this creation; now a man, made of earth only, such as we are become from the transgression, he could not be. For in the first creation, men had become unfaithful, and through them that first creation had been lost; and there was need of some one else to renew the first creation, and preserve the new which had come to be. Therefore from love to man none other than the Lord, the 'beginning' of the new creation, is created as 'the Way,' and consistently says, 'The Lord created me a beginning of ways for His works;' that man might walk no longer according to that first creation, but there being as it were a beginning of a new creation, and with the Christ 'a beginning of its ways,' we might follow Him henceforth, who says to us, 'I am the Way:'—as the blessed Apostle teaches in Colossians, saying, 'He is the Head of the body, the Church, who is the Beginning, the First-born from the dead, that in all things He might have the preeminence.'

66. For if, as has been said, because of the resurrection from the dead He is called a beginning, and then a resurrection took place when He, bearing our flesh, had given Himself to death for us, it is evident that His words, 'He created me a beginning of ways,' is indicative not of His essence [6], but of His bodily presence. For to the body death was proper [7]; and in like manner to the bodily presence are the words proper, 'The Lord created me a

beginning of His ways.' For since the Saviour was thus created according to the flesh, and had become a beginning of things new created, and had our first fruits, viz. that human flesh which He took to Himself, therefore after Him, as is fit, is created also the people to come, David saying, 'Let this be written for another generation, and the people that shall be created shall praise the Lord [2].' And again in the twenty-first Psalm, 'The generation to come shall declare unto the Lord, and they shall declare His righteousness, unto a people that shall be born whom the Lord made [3].' For we shall no more hear, 'In the day that thou eatest thereof, thou shalt surely die [4];' but 'Where I am, there ye' shall 'be also;' so that we may say, 'We are His workmanship, created unto good works [5].' And again, since God's work, that is, man, though created perfect, has become wanting through the transgression, and dead by sin, and it was unbecoming that the work of God should remain imperfect (wherefore all the saints were praying concerning this, for instance in the hundred and thirty-seventh Psalm, saying, 'Lord, Thou shalt requite for me; despise not then the works of Thine hands [6]'); therefore the perfect [7] Word of God puts around Him an imperfect body, and is said to be created 'for the works;' that, paying the debt [8] in our stead, He might, by Himself, perfect. what was wanting to man. Now immortality was wanting to him, and the way to paradise. This then is what the Saviour says, 'I glorified Thee on the earth, I perfected the work which Thou hast given Me to do [9];' and again, 'The works which the Father hath given Me to perfect, the same works that I do, bear witness of Me;' but 'the works [10]' He here says that the Father had given Him to perfect, are those for which He is created, saying in the Proverbs, 'The Lord created me a beginning of His ways, for His works;' for it is all one to say, 'The Father hath given me the works,' and 'The Lord created me for the works.'

67. When then received He the works to perfect, O God's enemies? for from this also 'He created' will be understood. If ye say, 'At the beginning when He brought them into being out of what was not,' it is an untruth; for they were not yet made; whereas He appears to speak as taking what was already in being. Nor is it pious to refer to the time

---

[1] Gen. iii. 19.　　[2] § 31, n. 8.
[3] Vid. *Or.* i. § 48, 7, i. 51, 5, *supr.* 56, 5. Irenæus, *Hær.* iii. 19, n. 1. Cyril. *in Joan.* lib. ix. cir. fin. This is the doctrine of S. Athanasius and S. Cyril, one may say, *passim.*
[4] Heb. x. 20.　　[5] 2 Cor. v. 17.　　[6] § 45, n. 2.
[7] Athanasius here says that our Lord's body was subject to death; and so *Incarn.* 20, c. also 8, b. 18. init. *Orat.* iii. 56. And so τὸν ἄνθρωπον σαθρωθέντα. *Orat.* iv. 33. And so S. Leo in his Tome lays down that in the Incarnation, suscepta est ab æternitate mortalitas. *Ep.* 28. 3. And S. Austin, Utique vulnerabile atque mortale corpus habuit [Christus] *contr. Faust.* xiv. 2. A Eutychian sect denied this doctrine (the Aphthartodocetæ), and held that our Lord's manhood was naturally indeed corrupt, but became from its union with the Word incorrupt from the moment of conception; and in consequence it held that our Lord did not suffer and die, except by miracle. vid. Leont. *c. Nest.* ii. (Canis. t. i. pp. 563, 4, 8.) vid. *supr.* i. 43 and 44, notes; also *infr.* 76, note. And further, note on iii. 57.

[2] Ps. cii. 18.　　[3] Ib. xxii. 32.　　[4] Gen. ii. 17.
[5] John xiv. 3; Eph. ii. 10.　　[6] Ps. cxxxviii. 8.
[7] Cf. *Orat.* iv. 11.
[8] ἀνθ' ἡμῶν τὴν ὀφειλὴν ἀποδιδούς, and so the Lord's death λύτρον πάντων. *Incarn. V.D.* 25. λύτρον καθάρσιον. Naz. *Orat.* 30, 20. fin. also *supr.* 9, 13, 14, 47, 55, 67. *In Illud. Omn.* 2 fin.
[9] John xvii. 4.　　[10] Ib. v. 36.

which preceded the Word's becoming flesh, lest His coming should thereupon seem superfluous, since for the sake of these works that coming took place. Therefore it remains for us to say that when He has become man, then He took the works. For then He perfected them, by healing our wounds and vouchsafing to us the resurrection from the dead. But if, when the Word became flesh, then were given to Him the works, plainly when He became man, then also is He created for the works. Not of His essence then is 'He created' indicative, as has many times been said, but of His bodily generation. For then, because the works were become imperfect and mutilated from the transgression, He is said in respect to the body to be created; that by perfecting them and making them whole, He might present the Church unto the Father, as the Apostle says, 'not having spot or wrinkle or any such thing, but holy and without blemish[1].' Mankind then is perfected in Him and restored, as it was made at the beginning, nay, with greater grace. For, on rising from the dead, we shall no longer fear death, but shall ever reign in Christ in the heavens. And this has been done, since the own Word of God Himself, who is from the Father, has put on the flesh, and become man. For if, being a creature, He had become man, man had remained just what he was, not joined to God; for how had a work been joined to the Creator by a work[2]? or what succour had come from like to like, when one as well as other needed it[3]? And how, were the Word a creature, had He power to undo God's sentence, and to remit sin, whereas it is written in the Prophets, that this is God's doing? For 'who is a God like unto Thee, that pardoneth iniquity, and passeth by transgression[4]?' For whereas God has said, 'Dust thou art, and unto dust shalt thou return[5],' men have become mortal; how then could things originate undo sin? but the Lord is He who has undone it, as He says Himself, 'Unless the Son shall make you free[6];' and the Son, who made free, has shewn in truth that He is no creature, nor one of things originate, but the proper Word and Image of the Father's Essence, who at the beginning sentenced, and alone remitteth sins. For since it is said in the Word, 'Dust thou art, and unto dust thou shalt return,' suitably through the Word Himself and in Him the

freedom and the undoing of the condemnation has come to pass.

68. 'Yet,' they say, 'though the Saviour were a creature, God was able to speak the word only and undo the curse.' And so another will tell them in like manner, 'Without His coming among us at all, God was able just to speak and undo the curse;' but we must consider what was expedient for mankind, and not what simply is possible with God[1]. He could have destroyed, before the ark of Noah, the then transgressors; but He did it after the ark. He could too, without Moses, have spoken the word only and have brought the people out of Egypt; but it profited to do it through Moses. And God was able without the judges to save His people; but it was profitable for the people that for a season judges should be raised up to them. The Saviour too might have come among us from the beginning, or on His coming might not have been delivered to Pilate; but He came 'at the fulness of the ages[2],' and when sought for said, 'I am He[3].' For what He does, that is profitable for men, and was not fitting in any other way; and what is profitable and fitting, for that He provides[4]. Accordingly He came, not 'that He might be ministered unto, but that He might minister[5],' and might work our salvation. Certainly He was able to speak the Law from heaven, but He saw that it was expedient to men for Him to speak from Sinai; and that He has done, that it might be possible for Moses to go up, and for them hearing the word near them the rather to believe. Moreover, the good reason of what He did may be seen thus; if God had but spoken, because it was in His power, and so the curse had been undone, the power had been shewn of Him who gave the word, but man had become such as Adam was before the transgression, having received grace from without[6], and not having it united to the body; (for he was such when he was placed in Paradise) nay, perhaps had become worse,

---

[1] Vid. also *Incarn.* 44. In this statement Athan. is supported by Naz. *Orat.* 19, 13. Theodor. *adv. Gent.* vi. p. 876, 7. August. *de Trin.* xiii. 13. It is denied in a later age by S. Anselm, but S. Thomas and the schoolmen side with the Fathers. vid. Petav. *Incarn.* ii. 13. However, it will be observed from what follows that Athan. thought the Incarnation still absolutely *essential* for the renewal of human nature in holiness. Cf. *de Incarn.* 7. That is, we might have been pardoned, we could not have been new-made, without the Incarnation; and so *supr.* 67.

[2] Gal. iv. 4.   [3] John xviii. 5.

[4] 'Was it not in His power, had He wished it, even in a day to bring on the whole rain [of the deluge]? in a day, nay in a moment?' Chrysost. *in Gen. Hom.* 24, 7. He proceeds to apply this principle to the pardon of sin. On the subject of God's power as contrasted with His acts, Petavius brings together the statements of the Fathers, *de Deo*, v. 6.   [5] Vid. Matt. xx. 28.

[6] Athan. here seems to say that Adam in a state of innocence had but an external divine assistance, not an habitual grace; this, however, is contrary to his own statements already referred to, and the general doctrine of the fathers. vid. e.g. Cyril. *in Joan.* v. 2. August. *de Corr. et Grat.* 31. vid also *infr.* § 76, note

---

[1] Eph. v. 27.
[2] Vid. *de Decr.* 10, 2. 4; *Or.* i. 49, § 16, n. 7. Iren. *Hær.* iii. 20.
[3] Cf. *infr. Orat.* iv. 6. vid. also iii. 33 init. August. *Trin.* xiii. 18. Id. *in Psalm* 129, n. 12. Leon. *Serm.* 28, n. 3. Basil. *in Psalm* 48, n. 4. Cyril. *de rect. fid.* p. 132. vid. also Procl. *Orat.* i. p. 63. (ed. 1630.) Vigil. *contr. Eutych.* v. p. 529, e. Greg. *Moral.* xxiv. init. Job. *ap.* Phot. 222. p. 583.
[4] Mic. vii. 18.   [5] Gen. iii. 19.   [6] Vid. John viii. 36.

because he had learned to transgress. Such then being his condition, had he been seduced by the serpent, there had been fresh need for God to give command and undo the curse; and thus the need had become interminable[7], and men had remained under guilt not less than before, as being enslaved to sin; and, ever sinning, would have ever needed one to pardon them, and had never become free, being in themselves flesh, and ever worsted by the Law because of the infirmity of the flesh.

69. Again, if the Son were a creature, man had remained mortal as before, not being joined to God; for a creature had not joined creatures to God, as seeking itself one to join it[1]; nor would a portion of the creation have been the creation's salvation, as needing salvation itself. To provide against this also, He sends His own Son, and He becomes Son of Man, by taking created flesh; that, since all were under sentence of death, He, being other than them all, might Himself for all offer to death His own body; and that henceforth, as if all had died through Him, the word of that sentence might be accomplished (for 'all died[2]' in Christ), and all through Him might thereupon become free from sin and from the curse which came upon it, and might truly abide[3] for ever, risen from the dead and clothed in immortality and incorruption. For, the Word being clothed in the flesh, as has many times been explained, every bite of the serpent began to be utterly staunched from out it; and whatever evil sprung from the motions of the flesh, to be cut away, and with these death also was abolished, the companion of sin, as the Lord Himself says[4], 'The prince of this world cometh, and findeth nothing in Me;' and 'For this end was He manifested,' as John has written, 'that He might destroy the works of the devil[5].' And these being destroyed from the flesh, we all were thus liberated by the kinship of the flesh, and for the future were joined, even we, to the Word. And being joined to God, no longer do we abide upon earth; but, as He Himself has said, where He is, there shall we be also; and henceforward we shall fear no longer the serpent, for he was brought to nought when he was assailed by the Saviour in the flesh, and heard Him say, 'Get thee behind Me, Satan[6],' and thus he is cast out of paradise into the eternal fire. Nor shall we have to watch against woman beguiling us, for 'in the resurrection they neither marry nor

are given in marriage, but are as the Angels[7];' and in Christ Jesus it shall be 'a new creation,' and 'neither male nor female, but all and in all Christ[8];' and where Christ is, what fear, what danger can still happen?

70. But this would not have come to pass, had the Word been a creature; for with a creature, the devil, himself a creature, would have ever continued the battle, and man, being between the two, had been ever in peril of death, having none in whom and through whom he might be joined to God and delivered from all fear. Whence the truth shews us that the Word is not of things originate, but rather Himself their Framer. For therefore did He assume the body originate and human, that having renewed it as its Framer, He might deify it[1] in Himself, and thus might introduce us all into the kingdom of heaven after His likeness. For man had not been deified if joined to a creature, or unless the Son were very God; nor had man been brought into the Father's presence, unless He had been His natural and true Word who had put on the body. And as we had not been delivered from sin and the curse, unless it had been by nature human flesh, which the Word put on (for we should have had nothing common with what was foreign), so also the man had not been deified, unless the Word who became flesh had been by nature from the Father and true and proper to Him. For therefore the union was of this kind, that He might unite what is man by nature to Him who is in the nature of the Godhead, and his salvation and deification might be sure. Therefore let those who deny that the Son is from the Father by nature and proper to His Essence, deny also that He took true human flesh[2] of Mary Ever-Virgin[3]; for in neither case had it been of profit to us men, whether the Word were not true and naturally Son

---

7 Mark xii. 25.　　8 Gal. vi. 15; iii. 28.
1 ἐν ἑαυτῷ θεοποιήσῃ. supr. p. 65, note 5. vid. also ad Adelph. 4. a. Serap. i. 24, e. and § 56, note 5. and iii. 33. De Decr. 14. Orat. i. 42. vid. also Orat. iii. 23. fin. 33. init. 34. fin. 38, b. 39, d. 48. fin. 53. For our becoming θεοὶ vid. Orat. iii. 25. θεοὶ κατὰ χάριν. Cyr. in Joan. p. 74. θεοφορούμεθα. Orat. iii. 23, c. 41, a. 45 init. χριστόφοροι. ibid. θεούμεθα. iii. 48 fin. 53. Theodor. H.E. i. p. 846. init.　　2 § 45, n. 2.
3 Vid. also Athan. in Luc. (Migne xxvii. 1393 c). This title, which is commonly applied to S. Mary by later writers, is found Epiph. Hær. 78, 5. Didym. Trin. i. 27. p. 84. Rufin. Fid. i. 43. Lepor. ap Cassian. Incarn. i. 5. Leon. Ep. 28, 2. Cæsarius has ἀειπαῖς. Qu. 20. On the doctrine itself vid. a letter of S. Ambrose and his brethren to Siricius, and the Pope's letter in response. (Coust. Ep. Pont. p. 669—682.) Also Pearson On the Creed, Art. 3. [§§ 9, 10, p. 267 in Bohn's ed.] He replies to the argument from 'until' in Matt. i. 25, by referring to Gen. xxviii 15. Deut. xxxiv. 6. 1 Sam. xv. 35. 2 Sam. vi. 23. Matt. xxviii 20. He might also have referred to Psalm cx. 1. 1 Cor. xv. 25. which are the more remarkable, because they were urged by the school of Marcellus as a proof that our Lord's kingdom would have an end, and are explained by Euseb. Eccl. Theol. iii. 13, 14. Vid. also Cyr. Cat. 15, 29; where the true meaning of 'until' (which may be transferred to Matt. i. 25), is well brought out. 'He who is King before He subdued His enemies, how shall He not the rather be King, after He has got the mastery over them?'

---

7 εἰς ἄπειρον, de Decr. 8.　　1 De Decr. 10.
2 2 Cor. v. 14.　　3 διαμείνωσιν, § 63, n. 8; § 73, Gent. 41, Serm. Maj. de Fid. 5.　　4 John xiv. 30. ἔχει t. rec. εὑρίσκει Ath et al.　　5 1 John iii. 8.　　6 Matt. xvi. 23.

of God, or the flesh not true which He assumed. But surely He took true flesh, though Valentinus rave; yea the Word was by nature Very God, though Ariomaniacs rave[4]; and in that flesh has come to pass the beginning[5] of our new creation, He being created man for our sake, and having made for us that new way, as has been said.

71. The Word then is neither creature nor work; for creature, thing made, work, are all one; and were He creature and thing made, He would also be work. Accordingly He has not said, 'He created Me a work,' nor 'He made Me with the works,' lest He should appear to be in nature and essence[6] a creature; nor, 'He created Me to make works,' lest, on the other hand, according to the perverseness of the irreligious, He should seem as an instrument[7] made for our sake. Nor again has He declared, 'He created Me before the works,' lest, as He really is before all, as an Offspring, so, if created also before the works, He should give 'Offspring' and 'He created' the same meaning. But He has said with exact discrimination[8], 'for the works;' as much as to say, 'The Father has made Me into flesh, that I might be man,' which again shews that He is not a work but an offspring. For as he who comes into a house, is not part of the house, but is other than the house, so He who is created for the works, must be by nature other than the works. But if otherwise, as you hold, O Arians, the Word of God be a work, by what[9] Hand and Wisdom did He Himself come into being? for all things that came to be, came by the Hand and Wisdom of God, who Himself says, 'My hand hath made all these things[1];' and David says in the Psalm, 'And Thou, Lord, in the beginning hast laid the foundations of the earth, and the heavens are the work of Thy hands[2];' and again, in the hundred and forty-second Psalm, 'I do remember the time past, I muse upon all Thy works, yea I exercise myself in the works of Thy hands[3].' Therefore if by the Hand of God the works are wrought, and it is written that 'all things were made through the Word,' and 'without Him was not made one thing[4],' and again, 'One Lord Jesus, through whom are all things[5],' and 'in Him all things consist[6],' it is very plain that the Son cannot be a work, but He is the Hand[7] of God and the Wisdom. This knowing, the martyrs in Babylon, Ananias, Azarias, and Misael, arraign the Arian irreligion. For

when they say, 'O all ye works of the Lord, bless ye the Lord,' they recount things in heaven, things on earth, and the whole creation, as works; but the Son they name not. For they say not, 'Bless, O Word, and praise, O Wisdom;' to shew that all other things are both praising and are works; but the Word is not a work nor of those that praise, but is praised with the Father and worshipped and confessed as God[8], being His Word and Wisdom, and of the works the Framer. This too the Spirit has declared in the Psalms with a most apposite distinction, 'the Word of the Lord is true, and all His works are faithful[9];' as in another Psalm too He says, 'O Lord, how manifold are Thy works! in Wisdom hast Thou made them all[10].'

72. But if the Word were a work, then certainly He as others had been made in Wisdom; nor would Scripture distinguish Him from the works, nor while it named them works, preach Him as Word and own Wisdom of God. But, as it is, distinguishing Him from the works, He shews that Wisdom is Framer of the works, and not a work. This distinction Paul also observes, writing to the Hebrews, 'The Word of God is quick and powerful, and sharper than any two-edged sword, reaching even to the dividing of soul and spirit, joints and marrow, and a discerner of the thoughts and intents of the heart, neither is there any creature hidden before Him, but all things are naked and open unto the eyes of Him with whom is our account[1].' For behold he calls things originate 'creature;' but the Son he recognises as the Word of God, as if He were other than the creatures. And again saying, 'All things are naked and open to the eyes of Him with whom is our account,' he signifies that He is other than all of them. For hence it is that He judges, but each of all things originate is bound to give account to Him. And so also, when the whole creation is groaning together with us in order to be set free from the bondage of corruption, the Son is thereby shewn to be other than the creatures. For if He were creature, He too would be one of those who groan, and would need one who should bring adoption and deliverance to Himself as well as others. But if the whole creation groans together, for the sake of freedom from the bondage of corruption, whereas the Son is not of those that groan nor of those who need freedom, but He it is who gives sonship and freedom to all, saying to the Jews of His

4 *De Syn.* 13, n. 4.   5 i. 48, n. 7.   6 § 45, note 2.
7 ὄργανον, note on iii. 31.   8 § 12, note.   9 § 22, n. 2.
1 Is. lxvi. 2.   2 Ps. cii. 25.   3 Ib. cxliii. 5.
4 John i. 3   5 1 Cor. viii. 9.   6 Col. i. 17.
      7 § 31, n. 4.

8 θεολογούμενος. vid. *de Decr.* 31, n. 5. also *Incarn. c. Ar.* 3. 19, *Serap.* i. 28. 29. 31. *contr. Sab. Greg.* and *passim ap. Euseb. contr. Marcell.* e.g. p. 42, d. 86, a. 99, d. 122. c. 124, b. &c. κυριολογεῖν, *In Illud. Omn.* 6, *contr. Sab. Greg.* § 4, f.
      9 Ps. xxxiii. 4.   10 Ib. civ. 24.   1 Heb. iv. 12, 13.

time [2], 'The servant remains not in the house for ever, but the Son remaineth for ever ; if then the Son shall make you free, ye shall be free indeed [3] ;' it is clearer than the light from these considerations also, that the Word of God is not a creature but true Son, and by nature genuine, of the Father. Concerning then ' The Lord hath created me a beginning of the ways,' this is sufficient, as I think, though in few words, to afford matter to the learned to frame more ample refutations of the Arian heresy.

CHAPTER XXII.

TEXTS EXPLAINED; SIXTHLY, THE CONTEXT OF PROVERBS viii. 22, VIZ. 22—30.

It is right to interpret this passage by the *Regula Fidei*. 'Founded' is used in contrast to superstructure ; and it implies, as in the case of stones in building, previous existence. 'Before the world' signifies the divine intention and purpose. Recurrence to Prov. viii. 22, and application of it to created Wisdom as seen in the works. The Son reveals the Father, first by the works, then by the Incarnation.

BUT since the heretics, reading the next verse, take a perverse view of that also, because it is written, 'He founded me before the world [4],' namely, that this is said of the Godhead of the Word and not of His incarnate Presence [5], it is necessary, explaining this verse also, to shew their error.

73. It is written, 'The Lord in Wisdom founded the earth [1] ;' if then by Wisdom the earth is founded, how can He who founds be founded ? nay, this too is said after the manner of proverbs [2], and we must in like manner investigate its sense ; that we may know that, while by Wisdom the Father frames and founds the earth to be firm and steadfast [3], Wisdom Itself is founded for us, that It may become beginning and foundation of our new creation and renewal. Accordingly here as before, He says not, ' Before the world He hath made me Word or Son,' lest there should be as it were a beginning of His making. For this we must seek before all things, whether He is Son [4], and on this point specially search the Scriptures [5] ;' for

this it was, when the Apostles were questioned, that Peter answered, saying, ' Thou art the Christ, the Son of the Living God [6].' This also the father [7] of the Arian heresy asked as one of his first questions ; ' If Thou be the Son of God [8] ;' for he knew that this is the truth and the sovereign principle of our faith ; and that, if He were Himself the Son, the tyranny of the devil would have its end ; but if He were a creature, He too was one of those descended from that Adam whom he deceived, and he had no cause for anxiety. For the same reason the Jews of the day [9] were angered, because the Lord said that He was Son of God, and that God was His proper Father. For had He called Himself one of the creatures, or said, ' I am a work,' they had not been startled at the intelligence, nor thought such words blasphemy, knowing, as they did, that even Angels had come among their fathers ; but since He called Himself Son, they perceived that such was not the note of a creature, but of Godhead and of the Father's nature [10]. The Arians then ought, even in imitation of their own father the devil, to take some special pains [11] on this point ; and if He has said, ' He founded me to be Word or Son,' then to think as they do ; but if He has not so spoken, not to invent for themselves what is not.

74. For He says not, ' Before the world He founded me as Word or Son,' but simply, ' He founded me,' to shew again, as I have said, that not for His own sake [1] but for those who are built upon Him does He here also speak, after the way of proverbs. For this knowing, the Apostle also writes, ' Other foundation can no man lay than that is laid, which is Jesus Christ ; but let every man take heed how he buildeth thereupon [2].' And it must be that the foundation should be such as the things built on it, that they may admit of being well compacted together. Being then the Word, He has not, as Word [3], any such as Himself, who may be compacted with Him ; for He is Only-begotten ; but having become man, He has the like of Him, those namely the likeness of whose flesh He has put on. Therefore according to His manhood He is founded, that we, as precious stones, may admit of building upon Him, and may become a temple of the Holy Ghost who dwelleth in us. And as He is a foundation, and we stones built upon Him, so again He is a Vine and we knit to Him as branches,—not according to the Essence of the Godhead ; for this surely is impossible ; but according to His manhood, for the branches

---

[2] § 1, n. 6.   [3] John viii. 35, 36.   [4] Prov. viii. 23.
[5] *Or.* i. 49, **n. 2.**   [1] Prov. iii. 19.   [2] Cf. 44, n. 3.
[3] § 69. 3.   [4] *Serap.* ii. 7, 8.
[5] Vid. *supr.* pp. 74, 172, and notes. vid. also *Serap.* i. 32 init. iv. fin. *contr. Apoll.* i. 6, 8, 9, 11, 22 ; ii. 8, 9, 13, 14, 17—19. 'The doctrine of the Church should be proved, not announced (ἀποδεικτικῶς οὐκ ἀποφαντικῶς) ; therefore shew that Scripture thus teaches.' Theod. *Eran.* p. 199. Ambros. *de Incarn.* 14. Non recipio quod extra Scripturam de tuo infers. Tertull. *Carn. Christ.* 7. vid. also 6. Max. *dial.* v. 29. Heretics in particular professed to be guided by Scripture. Tertull. *Praescr.* 8. For Gnostics vid. Tertullian's grave sarcasm : 'Utantur hæretici omnes scripturis ejus, cujus utuntur etiam mundo.' *Carn. Christ.* 6. For Arians, vid. *supr. Or.* i. 1, n. 4. And so Marcellus, 'We consider it unsafe to lay down doctrine concerning things which we have not learned with exactness from the divine Scriptures.' (leg. περὶ ὧν . . παρὰ τῶν). Euseb. *Eccl. Theol.* p. 177, d. And Macedonians, vid. Leont. *de Sect.* iv. init. And Monophysites, 'I have not learned this from Scripture ; and I have a great fear of saying what it is silent about.' Theod. *Eran.* p. 215 ; also Hilar. *ad Const.* ii. 9. Hieron. *c. Lucif.* 27. August. *Ep.* 120, 13.

[6] Matt. xvi. 16.   [7] *Ep. Æg.* 4. *Sent. D.* 3. c. *infr.* 59 init. 67. fin. note *infr.* on iii. 8.   [8] Matt. iv. 3.   [9] § 1, n. 6. [10] πατρικήν, vid. *de Syn.* 45, n. 1.   [11] περιεργάζεσθαι, vid. iii. 18.   [1] § 60, n. 2.   [2] 1 Cor. iii. 10, 11 ; Didym. *Trin.* iii. 3. p. 341.   [3] § 8, note 3ᵃ.

must be like the vine, since we are like Him according to the flesh. Moreover, since the heretics have such human notions, we may suitably confute them with human resemblances contained in the very matter they urge. Thus He saith not, 'He made me a foundation,' lest He might seem to be made and to have a beginning of being, and they might thence find a shameless occasion of irreligion ; but, 'He founded me.' Now what is founded is founded for the sake of the stones which are raised upon it ; it is not a random process, but a stone is first transported from the mountain and set down in the depth of the earth. And while a stone is in the mountain, it is not yet founded ; but when need demands, and it is transported, and laid in the depth of the earth, then forthwith if the stone could speak, it would say, 'He now founded me, who brought me hither from the mountain.' Therefore the Lord also did not when founded take a beginning of existence ; for He was the Word before that ; but when He put on our body, which He severed and took from Mary, then He says 'He hath founded me ;' as much as to say, 'Me, being the Word, He hath enveloped in a body of earth.' For so He is founded for our sakes, taking on Him what is ours [4], that we, as incorporated and compacted and bound together in Him through the likeness of the flesh, may attain unto a perfect man, and abide [5] immortal and incorruptible.

75. Nor let the words 'before the world' and 'before He made the earth' and 'before the mountains were settled' disturb any one ; for they very well accord with 'founded' and 'created ;' for here again allusion is made to the Economy according to the flesh. For though the grace which came to us from the Saviour appeared, as the Apostle says, just now, and has come when He sojourned among us ; yet this grace had been prepared even before we came into being, nay, before the foundation of the world, and the reason why is kindly and wonderful. It beseemed not that God should counsel concerning us afterwards, lest He should appear ignorant of our fate. The God of all then,—creating us by His own Word, and knowing our destinies better than we, and foreseeing that, being made 'good [1],' we should in the event be transgressors of the commandment, and be thrust out of paradise for disobedience,—being loving and kind, prepared beforehand in His own Word, by whom also He created us [2], the Economy of our salvation ; that though by the serpent's deceit we fell from Him, we might not remain quite dead, but

having in the Word the redemption and salvation which was afore prepared for us, we might rise again and abide immortal, what time He should have been created for us 'a beginning of the ways,' and He who was the 'First-born of creation' should become 'first-born' of the 'brethren,' and again should rise 'first-fruits of the dead.' This Paul the blessed Apostle teaches in his writings ; for, as interpreting the words of the Proverbs 'before the world' and 'before the earth was,' he thus speaks to Timothy [3] ; 'Be partaker of the afflictions of the Gospel according to the power of God, who hath saved us and called us with a holy calling, not according to our works, but according to His own purpose and grace, which was given us in Christ Jesus before the world began, but is now made manifest by the appearing of our Saviour Jesus Christ, who hath abolished death, and brought to light life [4].' And to the Ephesians ; 'Blessed be God even the Father of our Lord Jesus Christ, who hath blessed us with all spiritual blessing in heavenly places in Christ Jesus, according as He hath chosen us in Him before the foundation of the world, that we should be holy and without blame before Him in love, having predestinated us to the adoption of children by Jesus Christ to Himself [5].'

76. How then has He chosen us, before we came into existence, but that, as he says himself, in Him we were represented [6] beforehand ? and how at all, before men were created, did He predestinate us unto adoption, but that the Son Himself was 'founded before the world,' taking on Him that economy which was for our sake ? or how, as the Apostle goes on to say, have we 'an inheritance being predestinated,' but that the Lord Himself was founded 'before the world,' inasmuch as He had a purpose, for our sakes, to take on Him through the flesh all that inheritance of judgment which lay against us, and we henceforth were made sons in Him ? and how did we receive it 'before the world was,' when we were not yet in being, but afterwards in time, but that in Christ was stored the grace which has reached us ? Wherefore also in the Judgment, when every one shall receive according to his conduct, He says, 'Come, ye blessed of My Father, inherit the kingdom prepared for you from the foundation of the world [1].' How then, or in whom, was it prepared before we came to be, save in the Lord who 'before the world' was founded for this purpose ; that we, as built upon Him, might partake, as well-compacted stones, the life and grace which is from Him ? And this took place, as natur-

---

4 *Letter* 59. 6. Leon. *Ep.* 28. 3.   5 διαμείνωμεν, 69, n. 3.   3 Didym. *Trin.* iii. 3. p. 342.   4 2 Tim. i. 8—10.
      1 Gen. i. 31.   2 i. 49, n. 10.   5 Eph. i. 3—5.   6 Cf. 64, notes 3, 5.   1 Matt. xxv. 34.

ally suggests itself to the religious mind, that, as I said, we, rising after our brief death, may be capable of an eternal life, of which we had not been capable[2], men as we are, formed of earth, but that 'before the world' there had been prepared for us in Christ the hope of life and salvation. Therefore reason is there that the Word, on coming into our flesh, and being created in it as ' a beginning of ways for His works,' is laid as a foundation according as the Father's will[3] was in Him before the world, as has been said, and before land was, and before the mountains were settled, and before the fountains burst forth ; that, though the earth and the mountains and the shapes of visible nature pass away in the fulness of the present age, we on the contrary may not grow old after their pattern, but may be able to live after them, having the spiritual life and blessing which before these things have been prepared for us in the Word Himself according to election. For thus we shall be capable of a life not temporary, but ever afterwards abide[4] and live in Christ ; since even before this our life had been founded and prepared in Christ Jesus.

77. Nor in any other way was it fitting that our life should be founded, but in the Lord who is before the ages, and through whom the ages were brought to be ; that, since it was in Him, we too might be able to inherit that everlasting life. For God is good ; and being good always, He willed this, as knowing that our weak nature needed the succour and salvation which is from Him. And as a wise architect, proposing to build a house, consults also about repairing it, should it at any time become dilapidated after building, and, as counselling about this, makes preparation and gives to the workmen materials for a repair ; and thus the means of the repair are provided before the house ; in the same way prior to us is the repair of our salvation founded in Christ, that in Him we might even be new-created. And the will and the purpose were made ready 'before the world,' but have taken effect when the need required, and the Saviour came among us. For the Lord Himself will stand us in place of all things in the heavens, when He receives us into everlasting life. This then suffices to prove that the Word of God is not a creature, but that the sense of the passage is right[5]. But since that

passage, when scrutinized, has a right sense in every point of view, it may be well to state what it is ; perhaps many words may bring these senseless men to shame. Now here I must recur to what has been said before, for what I have to say relates to the same proverb and the same Wisdom. The Word has not called Himself a creature by nature, but has said in proverbs, 'The Lord created me;' and He plainly indicates a sense not spoken 'plainly' but latent[6], such as we shall be able to find by taking away the veil from the proverb. For who, on hearing from the Framing Wisdom, 'The Lord created me a beginning of His ways,' does not at once question the meaning, reflecting how that creative Wisdom can be created? who on hearing the Only-begotten Son of God say, that He was created ' a beginning of ways,' does not investigate the sense, wondering how the Only-begotten Son can become a Beginning of many others? for it is a dark saying[7]; but 'a man of understanding,' says he, 'shall understand a proverb and the interpretation, the words of the wise and their dark sayings[8].'

78. Now the Only-begotten and very Wisdom[1] of God is Creator and Framer of all things; for 'in Wisdom hast Thou made them all[2],' he says, and 'the earth is full of Thy creation.' But that what came into being might not only be, but be good[3], it pleased God that His own Wisdom should condescend[4] to the creatures, so as to introduce an impress and semblance of Its Image on all in common and on each, that what was made might be manifestly wise works and worthy of God[5]. For as of the Son of God, considered as the Word, our word is an image, so of the same Son considered as Wisdom is the wisdom which is implanted in us as an image ; in which wisdom we, having the power of knowledge and thought, become recipients of the All-framing Wisdom ; and through It we are able to know Its Father. ' For he who hath the Son,' saith He, 'hath the Father also ;' and 'he that receiveth Me, receiveth Him that sent Me[6].' Such an impress then of Wisdom being created in us, and being in all the works, with reason does the true and framing Wisdom take to Itself what belongs to its own impress, and say, ' The Lord created me for His works ;' for what the wisdom in us says, that

---

[2] The Catholic doctrine seems to be, that Adam innocent was mortal, yet would not in fact have died ; that he had no principle of eternal life within him, but was sustained continually by divine power, till such time as immortality should have been given him. vid. *Incarn.* 4. Cf. Augustine, *de pecc. mer.* i. 3. *Gen. ad lit.* vi. 20. Pope Pius V. condemned the assertion of Baius, Immortalitas primi hominis non erat gratiæ beneficium sed naturalis conditio. His decision of course is here referred to only historically.

[3] Cf. 31. n. 8.　　　[4] 74, n. 5.　　　[5] § 44, n. 1.

[6] Cf. 73, n. 2. and reff.
[7] αἴνιγμα, *supr.* i. 41, n. 9.　　　[8] Prov. i. 5, 6.
[1] αὐτοσοφία vid. *infr.* note on iv. 2.　　[2] Ps. civ. 24. Sept.
[3] *supr. de Decr.* 19, n. 3.　　　[4] Cf. 64, notes 2 and 5.
[5] Didymus argues in favour of interpreting the passage of created wisdom at length, *Trin.* iii. 3. He says that the context makes this interpretation necessary.
[6] 1 John ii. 23 ; Matt. x. 40.

the Lord Himself speaks as if it were His own ; and, whereas He is not Himself created, being Creator, yet because of the image of Him created in the works[7], He says this as if of Himself. And as the Lord Himself has said, 'He that receiveth you, receiveth Me[8],' because His impress is in us, so, though He be not among the creatures, yet because His image and impress is created in the works, He says, as if in His own person, 'The Lord created me a beginning of His ways for His works.' And therefore has this impress of Wisdom in the works been brought into being, that, as I said before, the world might recognise in it its own Creator the Word, and through Him the Father. And this is what Paul said, 'Because that which may be known of God is manifest in them, for God has shewed it unto them : for the invisible things of Him from the creation of the world are clearly seen, being understood by the things that are made[9].' But if so, the Word is not a creature in essence[10]; but the wisdom which is in us and so called, is spoken of in this passage in the Proverbs.

79. But if this too fails to persuade them, let them tell us themselves, whether there is any wisdom in the creatures or not[1]? If not, how is it that the Apostle complains, 'For after that in the Wisdom of God the world by wisdom knew not God[2]?' or how is it if there is no wisdom, that a 'multitude of wise men[3]' are found in Scripture? for 'a wise man feareth and departeth from evil[4];' and 'through wisdom is a house builded[5];' and the Preacher says, 'A man's wisdom maketh his face to shine;' and he blames those who are headstrong thus, 'Say not thou, what is the cause that the former days were better than these? for thou dost not inquire in wisdom concerning this[6].' But if, as the Son of Sirach says, 'He poured her out upon all His works ; she is with all flesh according to His gift, and He hath given her to them that love Him[7],' and this outpouring is a note, not of the Essence of the Very[8] Wisdom and Only-begotten, but of that wisdom which is imaged in the world, how is it incredible that the All-framing and true Wisdom Itself, whose impress is the wisdom and knowledge poured out in the

world, should say, as I have already explained, as if of Itself, 'The Lord created me for His works?' For the wisdom in the world is not creative, but is that which is created in the works, according to which 'the heavens declare the glory of God, and the firmament sheweth His handywork[9].' This if men have within them[10], they will acknowledge the true Wisdom of God ; and will know that they are made really[11] after God's Image. And, as some son of a king, when the father wished to build a city[12], might cause his own name to be printed upon each of the works that were rising, both to give security to them of the works remaining, by reason of the show of his name on everything, and also to make them remember him and his father from the name, and having finished the city might be asked concerning it, how it was made, and then would answer, 'It is made securely, for according to the will of my father, I am imaged in each work, for my name was made in the works ;' but saying this, he does not signify that his own essence is created, but the impress of himself by means of his name ; in the same manner, to apply the illustration, to those who admire the wisdom in the creatures, the true Wisdom makes answer, 'The Lord created me for the works,' for my impress is in them ; and I have thus condescended for the framing of all things.

80. Moreover, that the Son should be speaking of the impress that is within us as if it were Himself, should not startle any one, considering (for we must not shrink from repetition[1]) that, when Saul was persecuting the Church, in which was His impress and image, He said, as if He were Himself under persecution, 'Saul, why persecutest thou Me[2]?' Therefore (as has been said), as, supposing the impress itself of Wisdom which is in the works had said, 'The Lord created me for the works,' no one would have been startled, so, if He, the True and Framing Wisdom, the Only-begotten Word of God, should use what belongs to His image as about Himself, namely, 'The Lord created me for the works,' let no one, overlooking the wisdom created in the world and

7 Athan. here considers wisdom as the image of the Creator in the Universe. He explains it of the Church, de Incarn. contr. Ar. 6. if it be his [but see Prolegg. ch. iii. § 1 (36)]; (and so Didym. Trin. iii. 3 fin.) Cf. Jerome, in Eph. iv. 23, 24. Naz. Orat. 30, 2. Epiphanius says, 'Scripture has nowhere confirmed this passage (Prov. viii. 22), nor has any Apostle referred it to Christ.' (vid. also Basil. contr. Eunom. ii. 20.) Hær. 69. pp. 743—745. He proceeds to shew how it may apply to Him.
8 Matt. x. 40.   9 Rom. i. 19, 20.   10 Cf. 45, n. 2.
1 Vid. Epiph. Hær. 69.   2 1 Cor. i. 21.
3 Vid. Wisd. vi. 24.   4 Prov. xiv. 16.   5 Ib. xxiv.
6 Eccles. viii. 1 ; vii. 10.   7 Ecclus. i. 9, 10.
8 Cf. 78, n. 1.

9 Ps. xix. 1.
10 Cf. contr. Gent. 2, 30, 40, &c. vid. also Basil. de Sp. S. n. 19. Cyril. in Joan. p. 75.
11 De Decr. 31, n. 5.
12 This is drawn out somewhat differently, and very strikingly in contr. Gent. 43. The Word indeed is regarded more as the Governor than the Life of the world, but shortly before he spoke of the Word as the Principle of permanence. 41 fin.
1 τὸ αὐτὸ γὰρ λέγειν οὐκ ὀκνητέον : where Petavius, de Trin. ii. 1. § 8. ingeniously but without any authority reads οὐκ ὀκνεῖ θεόν. It is quite a peculiarity of Athan. to repeat and to apologize for doing so. The very same words occur supr. 22, c. Orat. iii. 54, a. Serap. i. 19, b. 27, e. Vid. also 2, c. 41, d. 67, a. 69, b. iii. 39 init. vid. especially supr. p. 47, note 6.   2 Acts ix. 4.

in the works, think that 'He created' is said of the Substance of the Very[3] Wisdom, lest, diluting the wine with water[3a], he be judged a defrauder of the truth. For It is Creative and Framer; but Its impress is created in the works, as the copy of the image. And He says, 'Beginning of ways,' since such wisdom becomes a sort of beginning. and, as it were, rudiments of the knowledge of God; for a man entering, as it were, upon this way first, and keeping it in the fear of God (as Solomon says[4], 'The fear of the Lord is the beginning of wisdom'), then advancing upwards in his thoughts and perceiving the Framing Wisdom which is in the creation, will perceive in It also Its Father[5], as the Lord Himself has said, 'He that hath seen Me, hath seen the Father,' and as John writes, 'He who acknowledgeth the Son, hath the Father also[6].' And He says, 'Before the world He founded me[7],' since in Its impress the works remain settled and eternal. Then, lest any, hearing concerning the wisdom thus created in the works, should think the true Wisdom, God's Son, to be by nature a creature, He has found it necessary to add, 'Before the mountains, and before the earth, and before the waters, and before all hills He begets me,' that in saying, 'before every creature' (for He includes all the creation under these heads), He may shew that He is not created together with the works according to Essence. For if He was created 'for the works,' yet is before them, it follows that He is in being before He was created. He is not then a creature by nature and essence, but as He Himself has added, an Offspring. But in what differs a creature from an offspring, and how it is distinct by nature, has been shewn in what has gone before.

81. But since He proceeds to say, 'When He prepared the heaven, I was present with Him[8],' we ought to know that He says not this as if without Wisdom the Father prepared the heaven or the clouds above (for there is no room to doubt that all things are created in Wisdom, and without It was made not even one[1] thing); but this is what He says, 'All things took place in Me and through Me, and when there was need that Wisdom should be created in the works, in My Essence indeed I was with the Father, but by a condescension[2]

to things originate, I was disposing over the works My own impress, so that the whole world as being in one body, might not be at variance but in concord with itself.' All those then who with an upright understanding, according to the wisdom given unto them, come to contemplate the creatures, are able to say for themselves, 'By Thy appointment all things continue[3];' but they who make light of this must be told, 'Professing themselves to be wise, they became fools;' for 'that which may be known of God is manifest in them; for God has revealed it unto them; for the invisible things of Him from the creation of the world are clearly seen, being perceived by the things that are made, even His eternal Power and Godhead, so that they are without excuse. Because that when they knew God, they glorified Him not as God, but served the creature more than the Creator of all, who is blessed for ever. Amen[4].' And they will surely be shamed at hearing, 'For, after that in the wisdom of God (in the mode we have explained above), the world by wisdom knew not God, it pleased God by the foolishness of the preaching to save them that believe[5].' For no longer, as in the former times, God has willed to be known by an image and shadow of wisdom, that namely which is in the creatures, but He has made the true Wisdom Itself to take flesh, and to become man, and to undergo the death of the cross; that by the faith in Him, henceforth all that believe may obtain salvation. However, it is the same Wisdom of God, which through Its own Image in the creatures (whence also It is said to be created), first manifested Itself, and through Itself Its own Father; and afterwards, being Itself the Word, has 'become flesh[6],' as John says, and after abolishing death and saving our race, still more revealed Himself and through Him His own Father, saying, 'Grant unto them that they may know Thee the only true God, and Jesus Christ whom Thou hast sent[7].'

82. Hence the whole earth is filled with the knowledge of Him; for the knowledge of Father through Son and of Son from Father is one and the same, and the Father delights in Him, and in the same joy the Son rejoices in the Father, saying, 'I was by Him, daily His delight, rejoicing always before Him[1].' And this again proves that the Son is not foreign, but proper to the Father's Essence. For behold, not because of us has He come to be,

---

3 Cf. above, 79, n. 8.
3a Isa. i. 22. *Infr.* iii. 35. *Ep. Æg.* § 17. *Ambros. de Fid.* iii. 65. p. 157. note 4. 4 Prov. i. 7, LXX.
5 The whole of this passage might be illustrated at great length from the *contr. Gent.* and the *Incarn. V. D.* vid. *supr.* notes on 79. Cf. *c. Gent.* 34, and *Incarn.* 11, 41, 42, &c. Vid. also Basil. *contr. Eunom.* ii. 16.
6 John xiv. 9; 1 John ii. 23. and so Cyril *in Joan.* p. 864. vid. Wetstein *in loc.* 7 Vid. Prov. viii. 24—26. 8 Ib. viii. 27.
1 John . 3.
2 Here again the συγκατάβασις has no reference whatever to a

figurative γέννησις, as Bishop Bull contends, but to His impressing the image of Wisdom on the works, or what He above calls the Son's image, on which account He is πρωτότοκος.
3 Vid. Ps. cxix. 91. 4 Rom. i. 19—25. 5 1 Cor. i. 21.
6 John i. 14. 7 Vid. ib. xvii. 3. 1 Prov. viii. 30.

as the irreligious men say, nor is He out of nothing (for not from without did God procure for Himself a cause of rejoicing), but the words denote what is His own and like. When then was it, when the Father rejoiced not? but if He ever rejoiced, He was ever, in whom He rejoiced. And in whom does the Father rejoice, except as seeing Himself in His own Image, which is His Word? And though in sons of men also He had delight, on finishing the world, as it is written in these same Proverbs[2], yet this too has a consistent sense. For even thus He had delight, not because joy was added to Him, but again on seeing the works made after His own Image; so that even this rejoicing of God is on account of His Image. And how too has the Son delight, except as seeing Himself in the Father? for this is the same as saying, ' He that hath seen Me, hath seen the Father,' and ' I am in the Father and the Father in Me[3].' Vain then is your vaunt as is on all sides shewn, O Christ's enemies, and vainly did ye parade[4] and circulate everywhere your text, ' The Lord created me a beginning of His ways,' perverting its sense, and publishing, not Solomon's meaning, but your own comment[5]. For behold your sense is proved to be but a fantasy; but the passage in the Proverbs, as well as all that is above said, proves that the Son is not a creature in nature and essence, but the proper Offspring of the Father, true Wisdom and Word, by whom ' all things were made,' and ' without Him was made not one thing[6].'

---

[2] Prov. viii. 31.

[3] John xiv. 9, 10.
[4] ἐνεπομπεύσατε. 'The ancients said πομπεύειν "to use bad language," and the coarse language of the procession, πομπεία. This arose from the custom of persons in the Bacchanalian cars using bad language towards by-standers, and their retorting it.' Erasm. *Adag.* p. 1158. He quotes Menander,
ἐπὶ τῶν ἁμαξῶν εἰσὶ πομπεῖαί τινες
σφόδρα λοίδοροι.
[5] διάνοιαν, ἐπίνοιαν, *supr. Or.* i. 52, n. 7. [6] John i. 3.

DISCOURSE III

CHAPTER XXIII.

TEXTS EXPLAINED; SEVENTHLY, JOHN xiv. 10.

Introduction. The doctrine of the coinherence. The Father and the Son Each whole and perfect God. They are in Each Other, because their Essence is One and the Same. They are Each Perfect and have One Essence, because the Second Person is the Son of the First. Asterius's evasive explanation of the text under review; refuted. Since the Son has all that the Father has, He is His Image; and the Father is the One God, because the Son is in the Father.

1. THE Ario-maniacs, as it appears, having once made up their minds to transgress and revolt from the Truth, are strenuous in appropriating the words of Scripture, ' When the impious cometh into a depth of evils, he despiseth[1];' for refutation does not stop them, nor perplexity abash them; but, as having ' a whore's forehead,' they ' refuse to be ashamed[2]' before all men in their irreligion. For whereas the passages which they alleged, ' The Lord created me[3],' and ' Made better than the Angels[4],' and ' First-born[5],' and ' Faithful to Him that made Him[6],' have a right sense[7], and inculcate religiousness towards Christ, so it is that these men still, as if bedewed with the serpent's poison, not seeing what they ought to see, nor understanding what they read, as if in vomit from the depth of their irreligious heart, have next proceeded to disparage our Lord's words, ' I in the Father and the Father in Me[8];' saying, ' How can the One be contained in the Other and the Other in the One?' or ' How at all can the Father who is the greater be contained in the Son who is the less?' or ' What wonder, if the Son is in the Father, considering it is written even of us, ' In Him we live and move and have our being[9]?' And this state of mind is consistent with their perverseness, who think God to be material, and understand not what

---

[1] Prov. xviii. 3, LXX. [2] Jer. iii. 3. [3] *Supr.* ch. xix.
[4] Ch. xiii. [5] Ch. xxi. [6] Ch. xiv. [7] ii. 44, n. 1.

[8] John xiv. 10.
[9] Acts xvii. 28. Vid. *supr.* ii. 41, note 11. The doctrine of the περιχώρησις, which this objection introduces, is the test of orthodoxy opposed to Arianism. Cf. *de Syn.* 15, n. 4. This is seen clearly in the case of Eusebius, whose language approaches to Catholic more nearly than Arians in general. After all his strong assertions, the question recurs, is our Lord a distinct being from God, as we are, or not? he answers in the affirmative, vid. *supr.* p. 75, n. 7, whereas we believe that He is literally and numerically one with the Father, and therefore His Person dwells in the Father's Person by an ineffable union. And hence the language of Dionysius [of Rome] *supr. de Decr.* 26. 'the Holy Ghost must repose and habitate in God,' ἐμφιλοχωρεῖν τῷ θεῷ καὶ ἐνδιαιτᾶσθαι. And hence the strong figure of S. Jerome (in which he is followed by S. Cyril, *Thesaur.* p. 51), 'Filius locus est Patris, sicut et Pater locus est Filii.' in Ezek. iii. 12. So Athan. contrasts the creatures who are ἐν μεμερισμένοις τόποις and the Son. *Serap.* iii. 4. Cf. even in the Macrostich Creed, language of this character, viz. 'All the Father embosoming the Son, and all the Son hanging and adhering to the Father, and alone resting on the Father's breast continually.' *De Syn.* 26 (7), where vid. note 3.

is 'True Father' and 'True Son,' nor 'Light Invisible' and 'Eternal,' and Its 'Radiance Invisible,' nor 'Invisible Subsistence,' and 'Immaterial Expression' and 'Immaterial Image.' For did they know, they would not dishonour and ridicule the Lord of glory, nor interpreting things immaterial after a material manner, pervert good words. It were sufficient indeed, on hearing only words which are the Lord's, at once to believe, since the faith of simplicity is better than an elaborate process of persuasion; but since they have endeavoured to profane even this passage to their own heresy, it becomes necessary to expose their perverseness and to shew the mind of the truth, at least for the security of the faithful. For when it is said, 'I in the Father and the Father in Me,' They are not therefore, as these suppose, discharged into Each Other, filling the One the Other, as in the case of empty vessels, so that the Son fills the emptiness of the Father and the Father that of the Son[10], and Each of Them by Himself is not complete and perfect (for this is proper to bodies, and therefore the mere assertion of it is full of irreligion), for the Father is full and perfect, and the Son is the Fulness of Godhead. Nor again, as God, by coming into the Saints, strengthens them, thus is He also in the Son. For He is Himself the Father's Power and Wisdom, and by partaking of Him things originate are sanctified in the Spirit; but the Son Himself is not Son by participation, but is the Father's own Offspring[11]. Nor again is the Son in the Father, in the sense of the passage, 'In Him we live and move and have our being;' for, He as being from the Fount[12] of the Father is the Life, in which all things are both quickened and consist; for the Life does not live in life[13], else it would not be Life, but rather He gives life to all things.

2. But now let us see what Asterius the Sophist says, the retained pleader[1] for the heresy. In imitation then of the Jews so far, he writes as follows; 'It is very plain that He has said, that He is in the Father and the Father again in Him, for this reason, that neither the word on which He was discoursing is, as He says, His own, but the Father's, nor the works belong to Him, but to the Father who gave Him the power.' Now this, if uttered at random by a little child, had been excused from his age; but when one who bears the title of Sophist, and professes universal knowledge[2], is the writer, what a serious condemnation does he deserve! And does he not shew himself a stranger to the Apostle[3], as being puffed up with persuasive words of wisdom, and thinking thereby to succeed in deceiving, not understanding himself what he says nor whereof he affirms[4]? For what the Son has said as proper and suitable to a Son only, who is Word and Wisdom and Image of the Father's Essence, that he levels to all the creatures, and makes common to the Son and to them; and he says, lawless[5] man, that the Power of the Father receives power, that from this his irreligion it may follow to say that in a son[6] the Son was made a son, and the Word received a word's authority; and, far from granting that He spoke this as a Son, He ranks Him with all things made as having learned it as they have. For if the Son said, 'I am in the Father and the Father in Me,' because His discourses were not His own words but the Father's, and so of His works, then,—since David says, 'I will hear what the Lord God shall say in me[7],' and again Solomon[8], 'My words are spoken by God,' and since Moses was minister of words which were from God, and each of the Prophets spoke not what was his own but what was from God, 'Thus saith the Lord,' and since the works of the Saints, as they professed, were not their own but God's who gave the power, Elijah for instance and Elisha invoking God that He Himself would raise the dead, and Elisha saying to Naaman, on cleansing him from the

---

10 This is not inconsistent with S. Jerome as quoted in the foregoing note. Athan. merely means that such illustrations cannot be taken literally, as if spoken of natural subjects. The Father is the τόπος or locus of the Son, because when we contemplate the Son in His fulness as ὅλος θεός, we merely view the Father as that Person in whom God the Son is; our mind abstracts His Essence which is the Son for the moment from Him, and regards Him merely as Father. Thus *in Illud. Omn.* 4, *supr.* p. 89. It is, however, but an operation of the mind, and not a real emptying of Godhead from the Father, if such words may be used. Father and Son are both the same God, though really and eternally distinct from each other; and Each is full of the Other, that is, their Essence is one and the same. This is insisted on by S. Cyril, *in Joan.* p. 28. And by S. Hilary, *Trin.* vii. fin. vid. also iii. 23. Cf. the quotation from S. Anselm made by Petavius, *de Trin.* iv. 16 fin. [Cf. D.C.B. *s.v.* METANGISMONITAE.]

11 Vid. *de Decr.* 10, n. 4, 19, n. 3; *Or.* i. 15, n. 6. On the other hand Eusebius considers the Son, like a creature, ἐξ αὐτῆς τῆς πατρικῆς [not οὐσίας, but] μετουσίας, ὥσπερ ἀπὸ πηγῆς, ἐπ' αὐτὸν προχεομένης πληρούμενον. *Eccl. Theol.* i. 2. words which are the more observable, the nearer they approach to the language of Athan. in the text and elsewhere. Vid. *infr.* by way of contrast, οὐδὲ κατὰ μετουσίαν αὐτοῦ, ἀλλ' ὅλον ἴδιον αὐτοῦ γέννημα. 4.

12 *De Decr.* 15, n. 9.

13 i.e. Son does not live by the *gift* of life, for He *is* life, and does but give it, not receive. S. Hilary uses different language with the same meaning, *de Trin.* ii. 11. Other modes of expression for the same mystery are found *infr.* 3. also 6 fin. Vid. *de Syn.* 45, n. 1. and Didymus ἡ πατρικὴ θεότης. p. 82. and S. Basil,

---

ἐξ οὗ ἔχει τὸ εἶναι. contr. *Eunom.* ii. 12 fin. Just above Athan. says that 'the Son is the fulness of the Godhead.' Thus the Father is the Son's life because the Son is from Him, and the Son the Father's because the Son is in Him. All these are but different ways of signifying the περιχώρησις.

1 συνηγόρου, *infr.* § 60.

2 πάντα γινώσκειν ἐπαγγελλόμενος. Gorgias, according to Cicero *de fin.* ii. init. was the first who ventured in public to say προβάλλετε, 'give me a question.' This was the ἐπάγγελμα of the Sophists; of which Aristotle speaks. *Rhet.* ii. 24 fin. Vid. Cressol. *Theatr. Rhet.* iii. 11.

3 1 Cor. ii. 4.   4 1 Tim. i. 7.

5 παράνομος. *infr.* 47, c. *Hist. Ar.* 71, 75, 79. *Ep. Æg.* 16, d. Vid. ἄνομος. 2 Thess. ii. 8.

6 ἐν υἱῷ, but ἐν τῷ υἱῷ. *Ep. Æg.* 14 fin vid. *Or.* ii. 22, note 2.

7 Ps. lxxxv. 8, LXX.   8 1 Kings viii. 59, *or* x. 24?

leprosy, 'that thou mayest know that there is a God in Israel[9],' and Samuel too in the days of the harvest praying to God to grant rain, and the Apostles saying that not in their own power they did miracles but in the Lord's grace—it is plain that, according to Asterius, such a statement must be common to all, so that each of them is able to say, 'I in the Father and the Father in me;' and as a consequence that He is no longer one Son of God and Word and Wisdom, but, as others, is only one out of many.

3. But if the Lord said this, His words would not rightly have been, 'I in the Father and the Father in Me,' but rather, 'I too am in the Father, and the Father is in Me too,' that He may have nothing of His own and by prerogative[1], relatively to the Father, as a Son, but the same grace in common with all. But it is not so, as they think; for not understanding that He is genuine Son from the Father, they belie Him who is such, whom alone it befits to say, 'I in the Father and the Father in Me.' For the Son is in the Father, as it is allowed us to know, because the whole Being of the Son is proper to the Father's essence[2], as radiance from light, and stream from fountain; so that whoso sees the Son, sees what is proper to the Father, and knows that the Son's Being, because from the Father, is therefore in the Father. For the Father is in the Son, since the Son is what is from the Father and proper to Him, as in the radiance the sun, and in the word the thought, and in the stream the fountain: for whoso thus contemplates the Son, contemplates what is proper to the Father's Essence, and knows that the Father is in the Son. For whereas the Form[3] and Godhead of the Father is the Being of the Son, it follows that the Son is in the Father and the Father in the Son[4].

4. On this account and reasonably, having

said before, 'I and the Father are One,' He added, 'I in the Father and the Father in Me,[5]' by way of shewing the identity[6] of Godhead and the unity of Essence. For they are one, not[7] as one thing divided into two parts, and these nothing but one, nor as one thing twice named, so that the Same becomes at one time Father, at another His own Son, for this Sabellius holding was judged an heretic. But They are two, because the Father is Father and is not also Son, and the Son is Son and not also Father[8]; but the nature is one; (for the offspring is not unlike[9] its parent, for it is his image), and all that is the Father's, is the Son's[10]. Wherefore neither is the Son another God, for He was not procured from without, else were there many, if a godhead be procured foreign from the Father's[1]; for if the Son be other, as an Offspring, still He is the Same as God; and He and the Father are one in propriety and peculiarity of nature, and in the identity of the one Godhead, as has been said. For the radiance also is light, not second to the sun, nor a different light, nor from participation of it, but a whole and proper offspring of it. And such an offspring is necessarily one light; and no one would say that they are two lights[2], but sun and radiance two, yet one the light from the sun enlightening in its radiance all things. So also the Godhead of the Son is the Father's; whence also it is indivisible; and thus there is one God and none other but He. And so, since they are one, and the Godhead itself one, the same things are said of the Son, which are said of the Father, except His being said to be Father[3]:—for instance[4], that He is God, 'And the Word was God[5];' Almighty, 'Thus saith He which was and is and is to come, the Almighty[6];' Lord, 'One Lord Jesus Christ[7];' that He is Light, 'I am the Light[8];' that He wipes out sins, 'that ye may know,' He says, 'that the Son of man hath power upon earth to forgive sins[9];' and so with other attributes. For 'all things,' says the Son Himself, 'whatsoever the Father hath, are Mine[10];' and again, 'And Mine are Thine.'

5. And on hearing the attributes of the Father spoken of a Son, we shall thereby see the Father in the Son; and we shall contemplate the Son in the Father, when what is said of the Son is said of the Father also.

---

9 2 Kings v. 8, 15.   1 Or. ii. 19, n. 6.

2 Since the Father and the Son are the numerically One God, it is but expressing this in other words to say that the Father is in the Son and the Son in the Father, for all They have and all They are is common to Each, excepting Their being Father and Son. A περιχώρησις of Persons is implied in the Unity of Essence. This is the connexion of the two texts so often quoted; 'the Son is in the Father and the Father in the Son,' because 'the Son and the Father are one.' And the cause of this unity and περιχώρησις is the Divine γέννησις. Thus S. Hilary, Trin. ii. 4. vid. Or. ii. 33, n. 1.

3 εἴδους. Petavius here prefers the reading ἰδίου; θεότης and τὸ ἴδιον occur together infr. 6. and 56. εἶδος occurs Orat. i. 20, a. de Syn. 52. vid. de Syn. 52, n. 6. infr. 6, 16, Ep. Æg. 17, contr. Sabell. Greg. 8, c. 12, vid. infr. §§ 6, 16, notes.

4 In accordance with § 1, note 10, Thomassin observes that by the mutual coinherence or indwelling of the Three Blessed Persons is meant 'not a commingling as of material liquids, nor as of soul with body, nor as the union of our Lord's Godhead and humanity, but it is such that the whole power, life, substance, wisdom, essence, of the Father, should be the very essence, substance, wisdom, life, and power of the Son.' de Trin. xxviii. 1. S. Cyril adopts Athan.'s language to express this doctrine in Joan. p. 105. de Trin. vi. p. 621, in Joan. p. 168. Vid. infr. ταὐτότης οὐσίας, 21. πατρικὴ θεότης τοῦ υἱοῦ, 26. and 41. and de Syn. 45, n. 1. vid. also Damasc. F. O. i. 8. pp. 139, 140.

5 John x. 30.   6 De Syn. 45, n. 1.   7 Infr. Orat. iv. 9.
8 Infr. 11.

9 ἀνόμοιον; and so ἀνόμοιος κατὰ πάντα. Orat. i. 6. κατ' οὐσίαν. 17. Orat. ii. 43. τῆς οὐσίας. infr. 14. vid. ἀνομοιότης. infr. 8, c.

10 Cf. in illud. Omn. 4. 'As the Father is I am (ὁ ὢν) so His Word is I Am and God over all.' Serap. i. 28, a; ib. ii. 2.

1 Cf. i. 6.   2 Doctrine of the Una Res, de Syn. 45, n. 1.
3 Ib. 49, n. 4.   4 Parallel to de Syn. 49.   5 John i. 1.
6 Rev. i. 8.   7 1 Cor. viii. 6.   8 John viii. 12.
9 Luke v. 24.   10 John xvi. 15; xvii. 10.

And why are the attributes of the Father ascribed to the Son, except that the Son is an Offspring from Him? and why are the Son's attributes proper to the Father, except again because the Son is the proper Offspring of His Essence? And the Son, being the proper Offspring of the Father's Essence, reasonably says that the Father's attributes are His own also; whence suitably and consistently with saying, 'I and the Father are One,' He adds, 'that ye may know that I am in the Father and the Father in Me[1].' Moreover, He has added this again, 'He that hath seen Me, hath seen the Father[2];' and there is one and the same sense in these three[3] passages. For he who in this sense understands that the Son and the Father are one, knows that He is in the Father and the Father in the Son; for the Godhead of the Son is the Father's, and it is in the Son; and whoso enters into this, is convinced that 'He that hath seen the Son, hath seen the Father;' for in the Son is contemplated the Father's Godhead. And we may perceive this at once from the illustration of the Emperor's image. For in the image is the shape and form of the Emperor, and in the Emperor is that shape which is in the image. For the likeness of the Emperor in the image is exact[4]; so that a person who looks at the image, sees in it the Emperor; and he again who sees the Emperor, recognises that it is he who is in the image[5]. And from the likeness not differing, to one who after the image wished to view the Emperor, the image might say, 'I and the Emperor are one; for I am in him, and he in me; and what thou seest in me, that thou beholdest in him, and what thou hast seen in him, that thou beholdest in me[6].' Accordingly he who wor-ships the image, in it worships the Emperor also; for the image is his form and appearance. Since then the Son too is the Father's Image, it must necessarily be understood that Godhead and propriety of the Father is the Being of the Son.

6. And this is what is said, 'Who being in the form of God[1],' and 'the Father in Me.' Nor is this Form[2] of the Godhead partial merely, but the fulness of the Father's Godhead is the Being of the Son, and the Son is whole God. Therefore also, being equal to God, He 'thought it not a prize to be equal to God;' and again since the Godhead and the Form of the Son is none other's than the Father's[3], this is what He says, 'I in Father.' Thus 'God was in Christ reconciling the world unto Himself[4];' for the propriety of the Father's Essence is that Son, in whom the creation was then reconciled with God. Thus what things the Son then wrought are the Father's works, for the Son is the Form of that Godhead of the Father, which wrought the works. And thus he who looks at the Son, sees the Father; for in the Father's Godhead is and is contemplated the Son; and the Father's Form which is in Him shews in Him the Father; and thus the Father is in the Son. And that propriety and Godhead which is from the Father in the Son, shews the Son in the Father, and His inseparability from Him; and whoso hears and beholds that what is said of the Father is also said of the Son, not as accruing to His Essence by grace or participation, but because the very Being of the Son is the proper Offspring of the Father's Essence, will fitly understand the words, as I said before, 'I in the Father, and the Father in Me;' and 'I and the Father are One[5].' For the Son is such as the Father is, because He has all that is the Father's. Wherefore also is He implied together with the Father. For, a son not being, one cannot say father; whereas when we call God a Maker, we do not of necessity intimate the things which have come to be; for a maker is before his works[6].

---

[1] John x. 30, 38; xiv. 10.   [2] Ib. xiv. 9.
[3] Here these three texts, which so often occur together, are recognized as 'three;' so are they by Eusebius *Eccl. Theol.* iii. 19; and he says that Marcellus and 'those who Sabellianize with him,' among whom he included Catholics, were in the practice of adducing them, θρυλλοῦντες; which bears incidental testimony to the fact that the doctrine of the περιχώρησις was the great criterion between orthodox and Arian. Many instances of the joint use of the three are given *supr.* i. 34, n. 7. to which may be added *Orat.* ii. 54 init. iii. 16 fin. 67 fin. iv. 17, a. *Serap.* ii. 9, c. Serm. *Maj. de fid.* 29. Cyril. *de Trin.* p. 554. *in Joann.* p. 168. Origen *Periarch.* p. 56. Hil. *Trin.* ix. 1. Ambros. *Hexaem.* 6. August. *de Cons. Ev.* i. 7.   [4] ἀπαράλλακτος, *de Syn.* 23, n. 1.
[5] Vid. Basil. *Hom. contr. Sab.* p. 192. The honour paid to the Imperial Statues is well known. Ambros. *in Psalm* cxviii. x. 25. vid. also Chrysost. *Hom. on Statues, passim, fragm. in Act. Conc.* vii. (t. 4, p. 89. Hard.) Socr. vi. 18. The Seventh Council speaks of the images sent by the Emperors into provinces instead of their coming in person; Ducange in v. Lauratum. Vid. a description of the imperial statutes and their honours in Gothofred, *Cod. Theod.* t. 5, pp. 346, 7. and in Philostorg. xii. 12. vid. also Molanus *de Imaginibus* ed. Paquot, p. 197.
[6] Athanasius guards against what is defective in this illustration in the next chapter, but independent of such explanation a mistake as to his meaning would be impossible; and the passage affords a good instance of the imperfect and partial character of all illustration; of the Divine Mystery. What it is taken to symbolize is the unity of the Father and Son, for the Image is not a Second Emperor but the same. vid. *Sabell. Greg.* 6. But no one, who bowed before the Emperor's Statue can be supposed to have really worshipped it; whereas our Lord is the Object of supreme worship, which terminates in Him, as being really one with Him whose Image He is. From the custom of paying honour to the Imperial Statues, the Cultus Imaginum was introduced into the Eastern Church. The Western Church, not having had the civil custom, resisted. vid. Döllinger, *Church History*, vol. 3. p. 55. E. Tr. The Fathers, e.g. S. Jerome, set themselves against the civil custom, as idolatrous, comparing it to that paid to Nebuchadnezzar's statue. vid. Hieron. in Dan. iii. 18. Incense was burnt before those of the Emperors; as afterwards before the Images of the Saints.
[1] Phil. ii. 6.   [2] εἶδος, vid. *infr.* 16, note.
[3] Here first the Son's εἶδος is the εἶδος of the Father, then the Son is the εἶδος of the Father's Godhead, and then in the Son is the εἶδος of the Father. These expressions are equivalent, if Father and Son are, each separately, ὅλος θεός. vid. *infr.* § 16, note. S. Greg. Naz. uses the word ὀπίσθια (Exod. xxxiii. 23), which forms a contrast to εἶδος, for the Divine Works. *Orat.* 28, 3.
[4] 2 Cor. v. 19.   [5] John xiv. 10; x. 30.
[6] Vid. *supr. de Decr.* 30; *Or.* i. 33. This is in opposition to the Arians, who said that the title Father implied priority of ex-

But when we call God Father, at once with the Father we signify the Son's existence. Therefore also he who believes in the Son, believes also in the Father: for he believes in what is proper to the Father's Essence; and thus the faith is one in one God. And he who worships and honours the Son, in the Son worships and honours the Father; for one is the Godhead; and therefore one [7] the honour and one the worship which is paid to the Father in and through the Son. And he who thus worships, worships one God; for there is one God and none other than He. Accordingly when the Father is called the only God, and we read that there is one God [8], and 'I am,' and 'beside Me there is no God,' and 'I the first and I the last [9],' this has a fit meaning. For God is One and Only and First; but this is not said to the denial of the Son [10], perish the thought; for He is in that One, and First and Only, as being of that One and Only and First the Only Word and Wisdom and Radiance. And He too is the First, as the Fulness of the Godhead of the First and Only, being whole and full God [11]. This then is not said on His account, but to deny that there is other such as the Father and His Word.

CHAPTER XXIV.

TEXTS EXPLAINED; EIGHTHLY, JOHN xvii. 3. AND THE LIKE.

Our Lord's divinity cannot interfere with His Father's prerogatives, as the One God, which were so earnestly upheld by the Son. 'One' is used in contrast to false gods and idols, not to the Son, through whom the Father spoke. Our Lord adds His Name to the Father's, as included in Him. The Father the First, not as if the Son were not First too, but as Origin.

7. Now that this is the sense of the Prophet is clear and manifest to all; but since the irreligious men, alleging such passages also, dishonour the Lord and reproach us, saying, 'Behold God is said to be One and Only and First; how say ye that the Son is God? for if He were God, He had not said, "I Alone," nor "God is One [1];"' it is necessary to declare the sense of these phrases in addition, as far as we can, that all may know from this also that the Arians are really contending with God [2]. If there then is rivalry of the Son towards the

Father, then be such words uttered against Him; and if according to what is said to David concerning Adonijah and Absalom [3], so also the Father looks upon the Son, then let Him utter and urge such words against Himself, lest He the Son, calling Himself God, make any to revolt from the Father. But if he who knows the Son, on the contrary, knows the Father, the Son Himself revealing Him to him, and in the Word he shall rather see the Father, as has been said, and if the Son on coming, glorified not Himself but the Father, saying to one who came to Him, 'Why callest thou Me good? none is good save One, that is, God [4];' and to one who asked, what was the great commandment in the Law, answering, 'Hear, O Israel, the Lord our God is One Lord [5];' and saying to the multitudes, 'I came down from heaven, not to do My own will, but the will of Him that sent Me [6];' and teaching the disciples, 'My Father is greater than I,' and 'He that honoureth Me, honoureth Him that sent Me [7];' if the Son is such towards His own Father, what is the difficulty [8], that one must need take such a view of such passages? and on the other hand, if the Son is the Father's Word, who is so wild, besides these Christ-opposers, as to think that God has thus spoken, as traducing and denying His own Word? This is not the mind of Christians; perish the thought; for not with reference to the Son is it thus written, but for the denial of those falsely called gods, invented by men.

8. And this account of the meaning of such passages is satisfactory; for since those who are devoted to gods falsely so called, revolt from the True God, therefore God, being good and careful for mankind, recalling the wanderers, says, 'I am Only God,' and 'I Am,' and 'Besides Me there is no God,' and the like; that He may condemn things which are not, and may convert all men to Himself. And as, supposing in the daytime when the sun was shining, a man were rudely to paint a piece of wood, which had not even the appearance of light, and call that image the cause of light, and if the sun with regard to it were to say, 'I alone am the light of the day, and there is no other light of the day but I,' he would say this, with regard, not to his own radiance, but to the error arising from the wooden image and the dissimilitude of that vain representation; so it is with 'I am,' and 'I am Only God,' and 'There is none other besides Me,' viz. that He may make men renounce falsely called gods, and that they may recognise Him the true God

---

istence. Athan. says that the title 'Maker' does, but that the title 'father' does not. vid. *supr.* p. 76, n. 3; *Or.* i. 29, n. 10: ii. 41, n. 11.
[7] Athan. *de Incarn. c. Ar.* 19, c. vid. Ambros. *de fid.* iii. cap. 12, 13. Naz. *Orat.* 23, 8. Basil. *de Sp. S.* n. 64.
[8] Mark xii. 29.   [9] Ex. iii. 14; Deut. xxxii. 39, LXX.; Is. xliv. 6.   [10] *De Decr.* 19, n. 6.
[11] Vid. *supr.* 1, note 10; ii. 41 fin. also *infr.* iv. 1. Pseudo-Ath. *c. Sab. Greg.* 5—12. Naz. *Orat.* 40, 41. Synes. *Hymn.* iii. pp. 328, 9. Ambros. *de Fid.* i. n. 18. August. *Ep.* 170, 5. vid. *Or.* ii. 38, n. 6. and *infr.* note on 36 fin.
[1] Deut. xxxii. 39; vi. 4, &c.   [2] θεομάχοι. vid. Acts v. 39.

[3] 2 Sam. xv. 13; 1 Kings i. 11.
[4] Luke xviii. 19, and vid. Basil. *Ep.* 236, 1.   [5] Mark xii. 29.
[6] John vi. 38; xiv. 28.   [7] John v. 23, cf. xiii. 20.
[8] § 58, note.

instead.   Indeed when God said this, He said it through His own Word, unless forsooth the modern[9] Jews add this too, that He has not said this through His Word; but so hath He spoken, though they rave, these followers of the devil[10].   For the Word of the Lord came to the Prophet, and this was what was heard ; nor is there a thing which God says or does, but He says and does it in the Word.   Not then with reference to Him is this said, O Christ's enemies, but to things foreign to Him and not from[11] Him.   For according to the aforesaid illustration, if the sun had spoken those words, he would have been setting right the error and have so spoken, not as having his radiance without him, but in the radiance shewing his own light.   Therefore not for the denial of the Son, nor with reference to Him, are such passages, but to the overthrow of falsehood. Accordingly God spoke not such words to Adam at the beginning, though His Word was with Him, by whom all things came to be ; for there was no need, before idols came in ; but when men made insurrection against the truth, and named for themselves gods such as they would[12], then it was that need arose of such words, for the denial of gods that were not. Nay I would add, that they were said even in anticipation of the folly of these Christ-opposers[13], that they might know, that what-soever god they devise external to the Father's Essence, he is not True God, nor Image and Son of the Only and First.

9.   If then the Father be called the only true God, this is said not to the denial of Him who said, 'I am the Truth[1],' but of those on the other hand who by nature are not true, as the Father and His Word are.   And hence the Lord Himself added at once, 'And Jesus Christ whom Thou didst send[2].'   Now had He been a creature, He would not have added this, and ranked Himself with His Creator (for what fellowship is there between the True and the not true ?) ; but as it is, by adding Himself to the Father, He has shewn that He is of the Father's nature ; and He has given us to know that of the True Father He is True Offspring.   And John too, as he had learned[3], so he teaches

this, writing in his Epistle, 'And we are in the True, even in His Son Jesus Christ ; This is the True God and eternal life[4].'   And when the Prophet says concerning the creation, 'That stretcheth forth the heavens alone[5],' and when God says, 'I only stretch out the heavens,' it is made plain to every one, that in the Only is signified also the Word of the Only, in whom 'all things were made,' and without whom 'was made not one thing.'   Therefore, if they were made through the Word, and yet He says, 'I Only,' and together with that Only is under-stood the Son, through whom the heavens were made, so also then, if it be said, 'One God,' and 'I Only,' and 'I the First,' in that One and Only and First is understood the Word coexist-ing, as in the Light the Radiance.   And this can be understood of no other than the Word alone.   For all other things subsisted out of nothing through the Son, and are greatly differ-ent in nature ; but the Son Himself is natural and true Offspring from the Father ; and thus the very passage which these insensates have thought fit to adduce, 'I the First,' in defence of their heresy, doth rather expose their per-verse spirit.   For God says, 'I the First and I the Last;' if then, as though ranked with the things after Him, He is said to be first of them, so that they come next to Him, then certainly you will have shewn that He Himself precedes the works in time only[6] ; which, to go no further, is extreme irreligion ; but if it is in order to prove that He is not from any, nor any before Him, but that He is Origin and Cause of all things, and to destroy the Gentile fables, that He has said 'I the First,' it is plain also, that when the Son is called First-born, this is done not for the sake of ranking Him with the creation, but to prove the framing and adoption of all things[7] through the Son.   For as the Father is First, so also is He both First[8], as

---

4 1 John v. 20.   5 Isai. xliv. 24.
6 He says that in 'I the first' the question of time does not come in, else creatures would come 'second' to the Creator, as if His and their duration admitted of a common measure. 'First' then does not imply succession, but is equivalent to ἀρχή; a word which, as 'Father,' does not imply that the Son is not from eter-nity.   7 ii. 62, n. 2.
8 It is no inconsistency to say that the Father is first, and the Son first also, for comparison or number does not enter into mys-tery. Since Each is ὅλος θεὸς, Each, as contemplated by our finite reason, at the moment of contemplation excludes the Other. Though we 'say' Three Persons, Person hardly denotes one abstract 'idea,' certainly not as containing under it three indi-vidual subjects, but it is a 'term' applied to the One God in three ways. It is the doctrine of the Fathers, that, though we use words expressive of a Trinity, yet that God is beyond number, and that Father, Son, and Holy Ghost, though eternally distinct from each other, can scarcely be viewed together in common, except as 'One' substance, as if they could not be generalized into Three Any whatever; and as if it were, strictly speaking, incorrect to speak of 'a' Person, or otherwise than of 'the' Person, whether of Father, or of Son, or of Spirit. The question has almost been admitted by S. Austin, whether it is not possible to say that God is 'One' Person (Trin. vii. 8), for He is wholly and entirely Father, and at the same time wholly and entirely Son, and wholly and entirely Holy Ghost. Some references to the Fathers shall be given on that subject, infr. 36 fin. vid. also supr. § 6, n. 11. Meanwhile the doctrine here stated will account for such expressions as 'God from God,' i.e. the One

---

9 οἱ νῦν, cf. Or. ii. 1, note 6, and Hist. Ar. 61, fin.
10 διαβολικοί. vid. supr. p. 187, and de Decr. 5, note 2. vid. also Orat. ii. 38, a. 73, a. 74 init. Ep. Æg. 4 and 6. In the passage before us there seems an allusion to false accusation or lying, which is the proper meaning of the word ; διαβάλλων occurs shortly before. And so in Apol. ad Const. when he calls Magnentius διάβολος, it is as being a traitor, 7. and soon after he says that his accuser was τὸν διαβόλου πρῶτον ἀναλαβών, where the word has no article, and διαβέβλημαι and διεβλήθην have preceded. vid. also Hist. Ar. 52 fin. And so in Sent. D. his speaking of the Arians' 'father the devil,' 3, c. is explained 4, b. by τοὺς πατέρας διαβαλλόντων and τῆς εἰς τὸν ἐπίσκοπον διαβολῆς.
11 παρά, vid. § 24 end, and John xv. 26.   12 οὓς ἤθελον, infr. § 10, n. 1.
13 Who worship one whom they themselves call a creature, vid. supr. i. 8, n. 8, & ii. 14, n. 7, 21, n. 2, and below, § 16 notes.
1 John xiv. 6.   2 Ib. xvii. 3.   3 μαθὼν ἐδίδαξε, de Decr. 7, n. 8 ; Or. ii. 1, note 6ᵃ.

Image of the First, and because the First is in Him, and also Offspring from the Father, in whom the whole creation is created and adopted into sonship.

CHAPTER XXV.

TEXTS EXPLAINED; NINTHLY, JOHN x. 30; xvii. 11, &c.

Arian explanation, that the Son is one with the Father in will and judgment; but so are all good men, nay things inanimate; contrast of the Son. Oneness between Them is in nature, because oneness in operation. Angels not objects of prayer, because they do not work together with God, but the Son; texts quoted. Seeing an Angel, is not seeing God. Arians in fact hold two Gods, and tend to Gentile polytheism. Arian explanation that the Father and Son are one, *as* we are one with Christ, is put aside by the *Regula Fidei*, and shewn invalid by the usage of Scripture in illustrations; the true force of the comparison; force of the terms used. Force of 'in us;' force of 'as;' confirmed by S. John. In what sense we are 'in God' and His 'sons.'

10. HOWEVER here too they introduce their private fictions, and contend that the Son and the Father are not in such wise ' one,' or ' like,' as the Church preaches, but, as they themselves would have it[1]. For they say, since what the Father wills, the Son wills also, and is not contrary either in what He thinks or in what He judges, but is in all respects concordant[2] with Him, declaring doctrines which are the same, and a word consistent and united with the Father's teaching, therefore it is that He and the Father are One; and some of them have dared to write as well as say this[3]. Now what can be more unseemly or irrational than this? for if therefore the Son and the Father are One, and if in this way the Word is like the Father, it follows forthwith[4] that the Angels[5] too, and the other beings above us, Powers and Authorities, and Thrones and Dominions, and what we see, Sun and Moon, and the Stars, should be sons also, as the Son; and that it should be

said of them too, that they and the Father are one, and that each is God's Image and Word. For what God wills, that will they; and neither in judging nor in doctrine are they discordant, but in all things are obedient to their Maker. For they would not have remained in their own glory, unless what the Father willed, that they had willed also. He, for instance, who did not remain, but went astray, heard the words, 'How art thou fallen from heaven, O Lucifer, son of the morning[6]?' But if this be so, how is only He Only-begotten Son and Word and Wisdom? or how, whereas so many are like the Father, is He only an Image? for among men too will be found many like the Father, numbers, for instance, of martyrs, and before them the Apostles and Prophets, and again before them the Patriarchs. And many now too keep the Saviour's command, being merciful ' as their Father which is in heaven[7],' and observing the exhortation, ' Be ye therefore followers of God as dear children, and walk in love, as Christ also hath loved us[8];' many too have become followers of Paul as he also of Christ[8a]. And yet no one of these is Word or Wisdom or Only-begotten Son or Image; nor did any one of them make bold to say, 'I and the Father are One,' or, 'I in the Father, and the Father in Me[9];' but it is said of all of them, ' Who is like unto Thee among the gods, O Lord? and who shall be likened to the Lord among the sons of God[10]?' and of Him on the contrary that He only is Image true and natural of the Father. For though we have been made after the Image[11], and called both image and glory of God, yet not on our own account still, but for that Image and true Glory of God inhabiting us, which is His Word, who was for us afterwards made flesh, have we this grace of our designation.

11. This their notion then being evidently unseemly and irrational as well as the rest, the likeness and the oneness must be referred to the very Essence of the Son; for unless it be so taken, He will not be shewn to have anything beyond things originate, as has been said, nor will He be like the Father, but He will be like the Father's doctrines; and He differs from the Father, in that the Father is Father[1], but the

---

God (who is the Son) from the One God (who is the Father); vid. *supr. de Syn.* 52, note 8. Again, ἡ οὐσία αὕτη τῆς οὐσίας τῆς πατρικῆς ἐστι γέννημα. *de Syn.* 48, b. Vid. also *infr. Orat.* iv. 1 and 2.

[1] ὡς αὐτοὶ θέλουσι. vid. § 8, n. 12. 'not as you say, but as we will.' This is a common phrase with Athan. vid. *supr. Or.* i. 13, n. 6. and especially *Hist. Ar.* 52, n. 4. (vid. also *Sent. Dion.* 4, 14). It is here contrasted to the Church's doctrine, and connected with the word ἴδιος· tor which *de Syn.* 3, n. 6; *Or.* i. 37, n. 1. Vid. also *Letter* 54. fin. Also *contr. Apoll.* ii. 5 init. in contrast with the εὐαγγελικὸς ὅρος.

[2] σύμφωνος. vid. *infr.* 23, *de Syn.* 48, and 53, n. 9. the Arian συμφωνία is touched on *de Syn.* 23, n. 3. Besides Origen, Novatian, the Creed of Lucian, and (if so) S. Hilary, as mentioned in the former of these notes, 'one' is explained as oneness of will by S. Hippolytus, *contr. Noet.* 7, where he explains John x. 30. by xvii. 22. like the Arians; and, as might be expected, by Eusebius *Eccl. Theol.* iii. p. 193. and by Asterius ap. Euseb. *contr. Marc.* pp. 28, 37. The passages of the Fathers in which this text is adduced are collected by Maldonat. *in loc.*

[3] Asterius, § 2, init.

[4] ὥρα. vid. *de Syn.* 34, n. 4. also *Orat.* ii. 6, b. iv. 19, c. d. Euseb. *contr. Marc.* p. 47, b. p. 91, b. Cyril. *Dial.* p. 456. *Thesaur.* p. 255 fin.

[5] This argument is found *de Syn.* 48. vid. also Cyril. *de Trin.* i. p 407.

---

[6] Is. xiv. 12.   [7] Luke vi. 36 (cf. Tisch. *in loc.*)
[8] Eph. v. 1, 2.   [8a] 1 Cor. xi. 1.   [9] John x. 30; xiv. 10.
[10] Vid. Ps lxxxvi. 8; lxxxix. 6.   [11] Aug. *de Trin.* vii. fin.
[1] Cf. *Serap.* i. 16. *de Syn.* 51. and *infr.* § 19, note. And so S. Cyril, cf. *Or.* i. 21—24, *de Decr.* 11, n. 6, *Thesaur.* p. 133, Naz. *Orat.* 29, 5. vid. also 23, 6 fin. 25, 16. vid. also the whole of Basil, *adv. Eun.* ii. 23. 'One must not say,' he observes, 'that these names properly and primarily, κυρίως καὶ πρώτως belong to men, and are given by us but by a figure καταχρηστικῶς (ii. 39, n. 7) to God. For our Lord Jesus Christ, referring us back to the Origin of all and True Cause of beings says, "Call no one your father upon earth, for One is your Father, which is in heaven."' He adds, that if He is properly and not metaphorically even our Father (*de Decr.* 31, n. 5), much more is He the πατὴρ τοῦ κατὰ φύσιν υἱοῦ. Vid. also Euseb. *contr. Marc.* p. 22, c. *Eccl. Theol.* i.

doctrines and teaching are the Father's. If then in respect to the doctrines and the teaching the Son is like the Father, then the Father according to them will be Father in name only, and the Son will not be an exact Image, or rather will be seen to have no propriety at all or likeness of the Father; for what likeness or propriety has he who is so utterly different from the Father? for Paul taught like the Saviour, yet was not like Him in essence[2].' Having then such notions, they speak falsely; whereas the Son and the Father are one in such wise as has been said, and in such wise is the Son like the Father Himself and from Him, as we may see and understand son to be towards father, and as we may see the radiance towards the sun. Such then being the Son, therefore when the Son works, the Father is the Worker[3], and the Son coming to the Saints, the Father is He who cometh in the Son[4], as He promised when He said, ' I and My Father will come, and will make Our abode with him[5];' for in the Image is contemplated the Father, and in the Radiance is the Light. Therefore also, as we said just now, when the Father gives grace and peace, the Son also gives it, as Paul signifies in every Epistle, writing, ' Grace to you and peace from God our Father and the Lord Jesus Christ.' For one and the same grace is from the Father in the Son, as the light of the sun and of the radiance is one, and as the sun's illumination is effected through the radiance; and so too when he prays for the Thessalonians, in saying, ' Now God Himself even our Father, and the Lord Jesus Christ, may He direct our way unto you[6],' he has guarded the unity of the Father and of the Son. For he has not said, ' May they direct,' as if a double grace were given from two Sources, This and That, but ' May He direct,' to shew that the Father gives it through the Son;—at which these irreligious ones will not blush, though they well might.

12. For if there were no unity, nor the Word the own Offspring of the Father's Essence, as the radiance of the light, but the Son were divided in nature from the Father, it were sufficient that the Father alone should give, since none of originate things is a partner with his Maker in His givings; but, as it is, such a mode of giving shews the oneness of the Father and the Son. No one, for instance, would pray to receive from God and the Angels[1], or from any other creature, nor would any one say, ' May God and the Angel give thee;' but from Father and the Son, because of Their oneness and the oneness of Their giving. For through the Son is given what is given; and there is nothing but the Father operates it through the Son; for thus is grace secure to him who receives it. And if the Patriarch Jacob, blessing his grandchildren Ephraim and Manasses, said, ' God which fed me all my life long unto this day, the Angel which delivered me from all evil, bless the lads[2],' yet none of created and natural Angels did he join to God their Creator, nor rejecting God that fed him, did he from Angel ask the blessing on his grandsons; but in saying, ' Who delivered me from all evil,' he shewed that it was no created Angel, but the Word of God, whom he joined to the Father in his prayer, through whom, whomsoever He will, God doth deliver. For knowing that He is also called the Father's ' Angel of great Counsel[3],' he said that none other than He was the Giver of blessing, and Deliverer from evil. Nor was it that he desired a blessing for himself from God but for his grandchildren from the Angel, but whom He Himself had besought saying, ' I will not let Thee go except Thou bless me[4]' (for that was God, as he says himself, ' I have seen God face to face'), Him he prayed to bless also the sons of Joseph. It is proper then to an Angel to minister at the command of God, and often does he go forth to cast out the Amorite, and is sent to guard the people in the way; but these are not his doings, but of God who commanded and sent him, whose also it is to deliver, whom He will deliver. There-

12. fin. ii. 6. Marcellus, on the other hand, said that our Lord was κυρίως λόγος, not κυρίως υἱός. ibid. ii. 10 fin. vid. supr. ii. 19, note 3.

[2] κατ' οὐσίαν ὅμοιος, Or. i. 21, n. 8.   [3] Supr. § 6.

[4] And so ἐργαζομένου τοῦ πατρὸς, ἐργάζεσθαι καὶ τὸν υἱόν. In illud Omn. 1, d. Cum luce nobis prodeat, In Patre totus Filius, et totus in Verbo Pater. Hymn. Brev. in fer. 2. Ath. argues from this oneness of operation the oneness of substance. And thus S. Chrysostom on the text under review argues that if the Father and Son are one κατὰ τὴν δύναμιν, they are one also in οὐσία. in Joan. Hom. 61, 2, d. Tertullian in Prax. 22. and S. Epiphanius, Hær. 57. p. 488. seem to say the same on the same text. vid. Lampe in loc. And so S. Athan. τριὰς ἀδιαίρετος τῇ φύσει, καὶ μία ταύτης ἡ ἐνέργεια. Serap. i. 28, f. ἐν θελήμα πατρὸς καὶ υἱοῦ καὶ βούλημα, ἐπεὶ καὶ ἡ φύσις μία. In illud Omn. 5. Various passages of the Fathers to the same effect (e.g. of S. Ambrose, si unius voluntatis et operationis, unius est essentiæ, de Sp. ii. 12. fin. and of S. Basil, ὧν μία ἐνέργεια, τούτων καὶ οὐσία μία, of Greg. Nyss. and Cyril. Alex.) are brought together in the Lateran Council. Concil. Hard. t. 3, p. 859, &c. The subject is treated at length by Petavius Trin. iv. 15.

[5] John xiv. 23.   [6] 1 Thess. iii. 11.

[1] Vid. Basil de Sp. S. c. 13. Chrysostom on Col. 2. And Theodoret on Col. iii. 17. says, ' Following this rule, the Synod of Laodicea, with a view to cure this ancient disorder, passed a decree against the praying to Angels, and leaving our Lord Jesus Christ.' ' All supplication, prayer, intercession, and thanksgiving is to be addressed to the Supreme God, through the High Priest who is above all Angels, the Living Word and God. . . . But angels we may not fitly call upon, since we have not obtained a knowledge of them which is above men.' Origen contr. Cels. v. 4, 5. vid. also for similar statements Voss. de Idololatr. i. 9. The doctrine of the Gnostics, who worshipped Angels, is referred to supr. Orat. i. 56, fin. note 1.

[2] Gen. xlviii. 15, 16. vid. Serap. i. 14. And on the doctrine vid. de Syn. 27 (15, 16). Infr. § 14, he shews that his doctrine, when fully explained, does not differ from S. Augustine, for he says, ' what was seen was an Angel, but God spoke in him,' i.e. sometimes the Son is called an Angel, but when an Angel was seen, it was not the Son; and if he called himself God, it was not he who spoke, but the Son was the unseen speaker. vid. Benedictine Monitum in Hil, Trin. iv. For passages vid. Tertull. de Præscr. p. 447, note f. Oxf. Transl.

[3] Is. ix. 6, LXX.   [4] Gen. xxxii. 26, 30.

fore it was no other than the Lord God Himself whom he had seen, who said to him, 'And behold I am with thee, to guard thee in all the way whither thou[5] goest;' and it was no other than God whom He had seen, who kept Laban from his treachery, ordering him not to speak evil words to Jacob; and none other than God did he himself beseech, saying, 'Rescue me from the hand of my brother Esau, for I fear him[6];' for in conversation too with his wives he said, 'God hath not suffered Laban to injure me.'

13. Therefore it was none other than God Himself that David too besought concerning his deliverance, 'When I was in trouble, I called upon the Lord, and He heard me; deliver my soul, O Lord, from lying lips and from a deceitful tongue[1].' To Him also giving thanks he spoke the words of the Song in the seventeenth Psalm, in the day in which the Lord delivered him from the hand of all his enemies and from the hand of Saul, saying, 'I will love Thee, O Lord my strength; the Lord is my strong rock and my defence and deliverer[2].' And Paul, after enduring many persecutions, to none other than God gave thanks, saying, 'Out of them all the Lord delivered me; and He will deliver in Whom we trust[3].' And none other than God blessed Abraham and Isaac; and Isaac praying for Jacob, said, 'May God bless thee and increase thee and multiply thee, and thou shalt be for many companies of nations, and may He give thee the blessing of Abraham my father[4].' But if it belong to none other than God to bless and to deliver, and none other was the deliverer of Jacob than the Lord Himself, and Him that delivered him the Patriarch besought for his grandsons, evidently none other did he join to God in his prayer, than God's Word, whom therefore he called Angel, because it is He alone who reveals the Father. Which the Apostle also did when he said, 'Grace unto you and peace from God our Father and the Lord Jesus Christ[4a].' For thus the blessing was secure, because of the Son's indivisibility from the Father, and for that the grace given by Them is one and the same. For though the Father gives it, through the Son is the gift; and though the Son be said to vouchsafe it, it is the Father who supplies it through and in the Son; for 'I thank my God,' says the Apostle writing to the Corinthians, 'always on your behalf, for the grace of God which is given you in Christ Jesus[5].' And this one may see in the instance of light and radiance; for what the light enlightens,

that the radiance irradiates; and what the radiance irradiates, from the light is its enlightenment. So also when the Son is beheld, so is the Father, for He is the Father's radiance; and thus the Father and the Son are one.

14. But this is not so with things originate and creatures; for when the Father works, it is not that any Angel works, or any other creature; for none of these is an efficient cause[1], but they are of things which come to be; and moreover being separate and divided from the only God, and other in nature, and being works, they can neither work what God works, nor, as I said before, when God gives grace, can they give grace with Him. Nor, on seeing an Angel would a man say that he had seen the Father; for Angels, as it is written, are 'ministering spirits sent forth to minister[2],' and are heralds of gifts given by Him through the Word to those who receive them. And the Angel on his appearance, himself confesses that he has been sent by his Lord; as Gabriel confessed in the case of Zacharias, and also in the case of Mary, bearer of God[3]. And he who beholds a vision of Angels, knows that he has seen the Angel and not God. For Zacharias saw an Angel; and Isaiah saw the Lord. Manoah, the father of Samson, saw an Angel; but Moses beheld God. Gideon saw an Angel, but to Abraham appeared God. And neither he who saw God, beheld an Angel, nor he who saw an Angel, considered that he saw God; for greatly, or rather wholly, do things by nature originate differ from God the Creator. But if at any time, when the Angel was seen, he who saw it heard God's voice, as took place at the bush; for 'the Angel of the Lord was seen in a flame of fire out of the bush, and the Lord called Moses out of the bush, saying, I am the God of thy father, the God of Abraham and the God of Isaac and the God of Jacob[4],' yet was not

---

[1] *Or.* ii. 21, n. 2.   [2] Heb. i. 14.

[3] τῆς θεοτόκου Μαρίας. [Prolegg. ch. iv. § 5.] vid. also *infr.* 29, 33. *Orat.* iv. 32. *Incarn. c. Ar.* 8, 22. *supr. Or.* i. 45, n. 3. As to the history of this title, Theodoret, who from his party would rather be disinclined towards it, says that the most ancient (τῶν πάλαι καὶ προπαλαι) heralds of the orthodox faith taught to name and believe the Mother of the Lord θεοτόκον, according to 'the Apostolical tradition.' *Hær.* iv. 12. And John of Antioch, whose championship of Nestorius and quarrel with S. Cyril are well known, writes to the former. 'This title no ecclesiastical teacher has put aside; those who have used it are many and eminent, and those who have not used it have not attacked those who used it.' *Concil. Eph.* part i. c. 25 (Labb.). Socrates *Hist.* vii. 32. says that Origen, in the first tome of his Comment on the Romans (vid. de la Rue in Rom. lib. i. 5. the original is lost), treated largely of the word; which implies that it was already in use. 'Interpreting,' he says, ' *how* θεοτόκος is used, he discussed the question at length.' Constantine implies the same in a passage which divines, e.g. Pearson (On the Creed, notes on *Art.* 3.), have not dwelt upon (or rather have apparently overlooked, in arguing from Ephrem. *ap.* Phot. *Cod.* 228, p. 776. that the literal phrase 'Mother of God' originated in S. Leo). [See vol. 1, p. 569 of this Series.]   [4] Vid. Ex. iii. 2—6.

---

[5] Gen. xxviii. 15, LXX.   [6] Ib. xxxi. 7; xxxii. 11.   [1] Ps. cxx.
[1,2]   [2] Ps. xviii. 1, 2.   [3] Vid. 2 Tim. iii. 11; 2 Cor. i. 10.
[4] Gen. xxviii. 3, 4, LXX.   [4a] Rom. i. 7, &c.   [5] 1 Cor. i. 4.

the Angel the God of Abraham, but in the Angel God spoke. And what was seen was an Angel; but God spoke in him[5]. For as He spoke to Moses in the pillar of a cloud in the tabernacle, so also God appears and speaks in Angels. So again to the son of Nun He spake by an Angel. But what God speaks, it is very plain He speaks through the Word, and not through another. And the Word, as being not separate from the Father, nor unlike and foreign to the Father's Essence, what He works, those are the Father's works, and His framing of all things is one with His; and what the Son gives, that is the Father's gift. And he who hath seen the Son, knows that, in seeing Him, he has seen, not Angel, nor one merely greater than Angels, nor in short any creature, but the Father Himself. And he who hears the Word, knows that he hears the Father; as he who is irradiated by the radiance, knows that he is enlightened by the sun.

15. For divine Scripture wishing us thus to understand the matter, has given such illustrations, as we have said above, from which we are able both to press the traitorous Jews, and to refute the allegation of Gentiles who maintain and think, on account of the Trinity, that we profess many gods[6]. For, as the illustration shews, we do not introduce three Origins or three Fathers, as the followers of Marcion and Manichæus; since we have not suggested the image of three suns, but sun and radiance. And one is the light from the sun in the radiance; and so we know of but one origin; and the All-framing Word we profess to have no other manner of godhead, than that of the Only God, because He is born from Him. Rather then will the Ario-maniacs with reason incur the charge of polytheism or else of atheism[7], because they idly talk of the Son as external and a creature, and again the Spirit as from nothing. For either they will say that the Word is not God; or saying that He is God[8], because it is so written, but not proper to the Father's Essence, they will introduce many because of their difference of kind (unless forsooth they shall dare to say that by participation only, He, as all things else, is called God; though, if this be their sentiment, their irreligion is the same, since they consider the Word as one among all things). But let this never even come into our mind. For there is but one form[9] of Godhead, which is also in the Word; and one God, the Father, existing by Himself according as He is above

all, and appearing in the Son according as He pervades all things, and in the Spirit according as in Him He acts in all things through the Word[10]. For thus we confess God to be one through the Triad, and we say that it is much more religious than the godhead of the heretics with its many kinds[11], and many parts, to entertain a belief of the One Godhead in a Triad.

16. For if it be not so, but the Word is a creature and a work out of nothing, either He is not True God because He is Himself one of the creatures, or if they name Him God from regard for the Scriptures, they must of necessity say that there are two Gods[1], one Creator, the other creature, and must serve two Lords, one Unoriginate, and the other originate and a creature; and must have two faiths, one in the True God, and the other in one who is made and fashioned by themselves and called God. And it follows of necessity in so great blindness, that, when they worship the Unoriginate, they renounce the originate, and when they come to the creature, they turn from the Creator. For they cannot see the One in the Other, because their natures and operations are foreign and distinct[2]. And with such sentiments, they will certainly be going on to more gods, for this will be the essay[3] of those who revolt from the One God. Wherefore then, when the Arians have these speculations and views, do they not rank themselves with the Gentiles? for they too, as these, worship the creature rather than God the Creator of all[4], and though they shrink from the Gentile name, in order to deceive the unskilful, yet they secretly hold a like sentiment with them. For their subtle saying which they are accustomed to urge, ' We say not two Unoriginates[5],' they plainly say to deceive the simple; for in their very professing 'We say not two Unoriginates,' they imply two Gods, and these with different natures, one originate and one Unoriginate. And though the Greeks worship one Unoriginate and many originate, but these one Unoriginate and one originate, this is no differ-

---

[5] § 12, note 2.
[6] Serap. i. 28 fin. Naz. Orat. 23, 8. Basil. Hom. 24 init. Nyssen. Orat. Catech. 3. p. 481.
[7] Infr. § 64. Ep. Æg. 14.　　[8] Infr. § 16, notes.　　[9] εἶδος.

[10] And so infr. 25, 36 fin. Serap. i. 20, b. vid. also ibid. 28, f. a. 30, a. 31, d. iii. 1, b. 5 init. et fin. Eulogius ap. Phot. cod. p. 865. Damascen. F. O. i. 7. Basil de Sp. S. 47, e. Cyr. Cat. xvi. 4. ibid. 24. Pseudo-Dion. de Div. Nom. i. p. 403. Pseudo-Athan. c. Sab. Greg. 10, e.　　[11] πολυειδοῦς.
[1] Vid. p. 75, note 7; de Syn. 27 (2), and 50, note 5. The Arians were in the dilemma of holding two gods or worshipping the creature, unless they denied to our Lord both divinity and worship. vid. de Decr. 6, note 1; Or. i. 30, n. 1. But ' every substance,' says S. Austin, ' which is not God, is a creature, and which is not a creature, is God.' de Trin. i 6. And so S. Cyril in Joan. p. 52. vid. also Naz. Orat. 31, 6. Basil. contr. Eunom. ii. 31.
[2] § 11, n. 4.　　[3] ἐπιχείρημα, de Decr. 1, note.
[4] Vid. supr. ii. 14, n. 7. Petavius gives a large collection of passages, de Trin. ii. 12. § 5. from the Fathers in proof of the worship of Our Lord evidencing His Godhead. On the Arians as idolaters vid. supr. Or. i. 8, n. 8. also Ep. Æg. 4, 13. and Adelph. 3 init. Serap. i. 29, d. Theodoret in Rom. i. 25.　　[5] Or. i. 30, n. 1.

ence from them; for the God whom they call originate is one out of many, and again the many gods of the Greeks have the same nature with this one, for both he and they are creatures. Unhappy are they, and the more for that their hurt is from thinking against Christ; for they have fallen from the truth, and are greater traitors than the Jews in denying the Christ, and they wallow[6] with the Gentiles, hateful[7] as they are to God, worshipping the creature and many deities. For there is One God, and not many, and One is His Word, and not many; for the Word is God, and He alone has the Form[8] of the Father. Being then such, the Saviour Himself troubled the Jews with these words, 'The Father Himself which hath sent Me, hath borne witness of Me; ye have neither heard His voice at any time nor seen His Form; and ye have not His Word abiding in you; for whom He hath sent, Him ye believe not[9].' Suitably has He joined the 'Word' to the 'Form,' to shew that the Word of God is Himself Image and Expression and Form of His Father; and that the Jews who did not receive Him who spoke to them, thereby did not receive the Word, which is the Form of God. This too it was that the Patriarch Jacob having seen, received a blessing from Him and the name of Israel instead of Jacob, as divine Scripture witnesses, saying, 'And as he passed by the Form of God, the Sun rose upon him[10].' And This it was who said, 'He that hath seen Me hath seen the Father,' and, 'I in the Father and the Father in Me,' and, 'I and the Father are one[11];' for thus God is One, and one the faith in the Father and Son; for, though the Word be God, the Lord our God is one Lord; for the Son is proper to

that One, and inseparable according to the propriety and peculiarity of His Essence.

17. The Arians, however, not even thus abashed, reply, 'Not as you say, but as we will[1];' for, whereas you have overthrown our former expedients, we have invented a new one, and it is this:—So are the Son and the Father One, and so is the Father in the Son and the Son in the Father, as we too may become one in Him. For this is written in the Gospel according to John, and Christ desired it for us in these words, 'Holy Father, keep through Thine own Name, those whom Thou hast given Me, that they may be one, as We are[2].' And shortly after; 'Neither pray I for these alone, but for them also which shall believe on Me through their Word; that they all may be one, as Thou, Father, art in Me, and I in Thee, that they also may be one in Us, that the world may believe that Thou hast sent Me. And the glory which Thou gavest Me I have given them, that they may be one, even as We are one; I in them, and Thou in Me, that they may be made perfect in one, and that the world may know that Thou didst send Me[3].' Then, as having found an evasion, these men of craft[4] add, 'If, as we become one in the Father, so also He and the Father are one, and thus He too is in the Father, how pretend you from His saying, "I and the Father are One," and "I in the Father and the Father in Me," that He is proper and like[5] the Father's Essence? for it follows either that we too are proper to the Father's Essence, or He foreign to it, as we are foreign.' Thus they idly babble; but in this their perverseness I see nothing but unreasoning audacity and recklessness from the devil[6], since it is saying after his pattern, 'We will ascend to heaven, we will be like the Most High.' For what is given to man by grace, this they would make equal to the Godhead of the Giver. Thus hearing that men are called sons, they thought themselves equal to the True Son by nature such[7]. And now again hearing from the Saviour, 'that they may be one as We are[8],' they deceive themselves, and are arrogant enough to think that they may be such as the Son is in the Father and the Father in the Son; not considering the fall of their 'father the devil[9],' which happened upon such an imagination.

18. If then, as we have many times said, the Word of God is the same with us, and nothing differs from us except in time, let Him be like us, and have the same place with the

---

6 συγκυλίονται, vid. *Orat.* i. 23. ii. 1 init.; *Decr.* 9 fin.; *Gent.* 19, c. cf. 2 Pet. ii. 22.   7 θεοστυγεῖς, *infr.* Letter 54. 1 fin.
8 εἶδος· also in Gen. xxxii. 30. 31. Sept. [a substitute for Heb. 'face.'] vid. Justin *Tryph.* 126. and *supr. de Syn.* 56, n. 6. for the meaning of the word. It was just now used for 'kind.' Athan. says, *de Syn. ubi supr.* 'there is but one form of Godhead;' yet the word is used of the Son as synonymous with · image.' It would seem as if there are a certain class of words, all expressive of the One Divine Substance, which admit of more appropriate application either ordinarily or under circumstances, to This or That Divine Person who is also that One Substance. Thus 'Being' is more descriptive of the Father as the πηγὴ θεότητος, and He is said to be 'the Being of the Son;' yet the Son is really the One Supreme Being also. On the other hand the words μορφή and εἶδος [on them see Lightfoot, *Philipp.* p. 128] are rather descriptive of the Divine Substance in the Person of the Son, and He is called 'the form of the Father,' yet there is but one Form and Face of Divinity, who is at once Each of Three Persons; while 'Spirit' is appropriated to the Third Person, though God is a Spirit. Thus again S. Hippolytus says ἐκ [τοῦ πατρὸς] δύναμις λόγος, yet shortly before, after mentioning the Two Persons, he adds, δύναμιν δὲ μίαν, contr. *Noet.* 7 and 11. And thus the word 'Subsistence,' ὑπόστασις, which expresses the One Divine Substance, has been found more appropriate to express that Substance viewed personally. Other words may be used correlatively of either Father or Son; thus the Father is the Life of the Son, the Son the Life of the Father; or, again, the Father is in the Son and the Son in the Father. Others in common, as 'the Father's Godhead is the Son's,' ἡ πατρικὴ υἱοῦ θεότης, as indeed the word οὐσία itself. Other words on the contrary express the Substance in This or That Person only, as 'Word,' 'Image,' &c.   9 John v. 37.
10 Gen. xxxii. 31, LXX.   11 John xiv. 9, 10; x. 30.

1 § 10, n. 1.   2 John xvii. 11.   3 Ib. 20—23.
4 οἱ δόλιοι. crafty as they are, also *infr.* 59.   5 *Or.* i. 21, n. 8, cf. *infr.* § 67.   6 διαβολικήν vid. § 8, n. 10, cf. Isa. xiv. 14.
7 *Supr.* p. 171, note 5.   8 John viii. 44.   9 ii. 73, n. 7.

Father as we have; nor let Him be called Only-begotten, nor Only Word or Wisdom of the Father; but let the same name be of common application to all us who are like Him. For it is right, that they who have one nature, should have their name in common, though they differ from each other in point of time. For Adam was a man, and Paul a man, and he who is now born is a man, and time is not that which alters the nature of the race [1]. If then the Word also differs from us only in time, then we must be as He. But in truth neither we are Word or Wisdom, nor is He creature or work; else why are we all sprung from one, and He the Only Word? but though it be suitable in them thus to speak, in us at least it is unsuitable to entertain their blasphemies. And yet, needless [2] though it be to refine upon [3] these passages, considering their so clear and religious sense, and our own orthodox belief, yet that their irreligion may be shewn here also, come let us shortly, as we have received from the fathers, expose their heterodoxy from the passage. It is a custom [4] with divine Scripture to take the things of nature as images and illustrations for mankind; and this it does, that from these physical objects the moral impulses of man may be explained; and thus their conduct shewn to be either bad or righteous. For instance, in the case of the bad, as when it charges, 'Be ye not like to horse and mule which have no understanding [5].' Or as when it says, complaining of those who have become such, 'Man, being in honour, hath no understanding, but is compared unto the beasts that perish.' And again, 'They were as wanton horses [6].' And the Saviour to expose Herod said, 'Tell that fox [7];' but, on the other hand, charged His disciples, 'Behold I send you forth as sheep in the midst of wolves; be ye therefore wise as serpents and harmless as doves [8].' And He said this, not that we may become in nature beasts of burden, or become serpents and doves; for He hath not so made us Himself, and therefore nature does not allow of it; but that we might eschew the irrational motions of the one, and being aware of the wisdom of that other animal, might not be deceived by it, and might take on us the meekness of the dove.

19. Again, taking patterns for man from divine subjects, the Saviour says; 'Be ye merciful, as your Father which is in heaven is merciful [1];' and, 'Be ye perfect, as your heavenly Father is perfect [2].' And He said this too, not that we might become such as the Father; for to become as the Father, is impossible for us creatures, who have been brought to be out of nothing; but as He charged us, 'Be ye not like to horse,' not lest we should become as draught animals, but that we should not imitate their want of reason, so, not that we might become as God, did He say, 'Be ye merciful as your Father,' but that looking at His beneficent acts, what we do well, we might do, not for men's sake, but for His sake, so that from Him and not from men we may have the reward. For as, although there be one Son by nature, True and Only-begotten, we too become sons, not as He in nature and truth, but according to the grace of Him that calleth, and though we are men from the earth, are yet called gods [3], not as the True God or His Word, but as has pleased God who has given us that grace; so also, as God do we become merciful, not by being made equal to God, nor becoming in nature and truth benefactors (for it is not our gift to benefit but belongs to God), but in order that what has accrued to us from God Himself by grace, these things we may impart to others, without making distinctions, but largely towards all extending our kind service. For only in this way can we anyhow become imitators, and in no other, when we minister to others what comes from Him. And as we put a fair and right [4] sense upon these texts, such again is the sense of the lection in John. For he does not say, that, as the Son is in the Father, such we must become:—whence could it be? when He is God's Word and Wisdom, and we were fashioned out of the earth, and He is by nature and essence Word and true God (for thus speaks John, 'We know that the Son of God is come, and He hath given us an understanding to know Him that is true, and we are in Him that is true, even in His Son Jesus Christ; this is the true God and eternal life [5]), and we are made sons through Him by adoption and grace, as partaking of His Spirit (for 'as many as received Him,' he says, 'to them gave He power to become children of God, even to them that believe on His Name [6]), and therefore also He is the Truth (saying, 'I am the Truth,' and in His address to His Father, He said, 'Sanctify them through Thy Truth, Thy Word is Truth [7]'); but we by imitation [8] become virtuous [9] and sons:—therefore

---

[1] De Decr. 10; Or. i. 26, n. 1.　[2] Cf. Hist. Ar. 80, n. 11.
[3] περιεργάζεσθαι· vid. Or. ii. 34, n. 5.　[4] Orat. ii. 53, n. 4; Orat. iv. 33 init.　[5] Ps. xxxii. 9; xlix. 20.　[6] Jer. v. 8.
[7] Luke xiii. 32.　[8] Matt. x. 16.　[1] Luke vi. 36.
[2] Matt. v. 48.

[3] θεοί, §§ 23 end, 25, and ii. 70, n. 1.　[4] ii. 44, n. 1.
[5] 1 John v. 20.　[6] John i. 12.　[7] Ib. xiv. 6; xvii. 17.
[8] κατὰ μίμησιν. Clem. Alex. Pædag. i. 3. p. 102. ed. Pott. Naz. Ep. 102. p. 95. (Ed. Ben.) Leo in various places, supr. ii. 55, n. 1. Iren. Hær. v. 1. August. Serm. 101, 6. August. Trin. iv. 17. also ix. 21. and Eusebius, κατὰ τὴν αὐτοῦ μίμησιν. Eccl. Theol. iii. 19, a. For inward grace as opposed to teaching, vid. supr. Orat. ii. 56, n. 5, and 79, n. 10.
[9] ἐνάρετοι so πανάρετος Clem. Rom. Ep. i.

not that we might become such as He, did He say 'that they may be one as We are;' but that as He, being the Word, is in His own Father, so that we too, taking an examplar and looking at Him, might become one towards each other in concord and oneness of spirit, nor be at variance as the Corinthians, but mind the same thing, as those five thousand in the Acts [10], who were as one.

20. For it is as 'sons,' not as the Son; as 'gods,' not as He Himself; and not as the Father, but 'merciful as the Father.' And, as has been said, by so becoming one, as the Father and the Son, we shall be such, not as the Father is by nature in the Son and the Son in the Father, but according to our own nature, and as it is possible for us thence to be moulded and to learn how we ought to be one, just as we learned also to be merciful. For like things are naturally one with like; thus all flesh is ranked together in kind [1]; but the Word is unlike us and like the Father. And therefore, while He is in nature and truth one with His own Father, we, as being of one kind with each other (for from one were all made, and one is the nature of all men), become one with each other in good disposition [2], having as our copy the Son's natural unity with the Father. For as He taught us meekness from Himself, saying, 'Learn of Me, for I am meek and lowly in heart [3],' not that we may become equal to Him, which is impossible, but that looking towards Him, we may remain meek continually, so also here, wishing that our good disposition towards each other should be true and firm and indissoluble, from Himself taking the pattern, He says, 'that they may be one as We are,' whose oneness is indivisible; that is, that they learning from us of that indivisible Nature, may preserve in like manner agreement one with another. And this imitation of natural conditions is especially safe for man, as has been said; for, since they remain and never change, whereas the conduct of men is very changeable, one may look to what is unchangeable by nature, and avoid what is bad and remodel himself on what is best.

21. And for this reason also the words, 'that they may be one in Us,' have a right sense. If, for instance, it were possible for us to become as the Son in the Father, the words ought to run, 'that they may be one in Thee,' as the Son is in the Father; but, as it is, He has not said this; but by saying 'in Us' He has pointed out the distance and difference; that He indeed is alone in the Father alone, as Only Word and Wisdom; but we in the Son, and through Him in the Father. And thus speaking, He meant this only, 'By Our unity may they also be so one with each other, as We are one in nature and truth; for otherwise they could not be one, except by learning unity in Us.' And that 'in Us' has this signification, we may learn from Paul, who says, 'These things I have in a figure transferred to myself and to Apollos, that ye may learn in us not to be puffed up above that is written [1].' The words 'in Us' then, are not 'in the Father,' as the Son is in Him; but imply an example and image, instead of saying, 'Let them learn of Us.' For as Paul to the Corinthians, so is the oneness of the Son and the Father a pattern and lesson to all, by which they may learn, looking to that natural unity of the Father and the Son, how they themselves ought to be one in spirit towards each other. Or if it needs to account for the phrase otherwise, the words 'in Us' may mean the same as saying, that in the power of the Father and the Son they may be one, speaking the same things [2]; for without God this is impossible. And this mode of speech also we may find in the divine writings, as 'In God will we do great acts;' and 'In God I shall leap over the wall [3];' and 'In Thee will we tread down our enemies [4].' Therefore it is plain, that in the Name of Father and Son we shall be able, becoming one, to hold firm the bond of charity. For, dwelling still on the same thought, the Lord says, 'And the glory which Thou gavest Me, I have given to them, that they may be one as We are one.' Suitably has He here too said, not, 'that they may be in Thee as I am,' but 'as We are;' now he who says 'as' [5], signifies not identity, but an image and example of the matter in hand.

22. The Word then has the real and true identity of nature with the Father; but to us it is given to imitate it, as has been said; for He immediately adds, 'I in them and Thou in Me; that they may be made perfect in one.' Here at length the Lord asks something greater and more perfect for us; for it is plain that the Word has come to be in us [6], for He has put on our body. 'And Thou Father in Me;' 'for I am Thy Word, and since Thou art in Me, because I am Thy Word, and I in them because of the body, and because of Thee the salvation of men is perfected in Me, therefore I ask that they also may become one, according to the body that is in Me and according to its perfection; that they too may

---

[10] Acts iv. 4, 32.　　[1] Cf. ii. 23, 42.　　[2] διαθέσει, de Decr. 2, note 5; Ep. ad Mon. (1) init. Hipp. c. Noet. 7.　　[3] Matt. xi. 29.

[1] 1 Cor. iv. 6.　　[2] Vid. 1 Cor. i. 10.　　[3] Ps. lx. 12; xviii. 29. [4] Ps. xliv. 5.　Vid. Olear. de Styl. N. T. p. 4. (ed. 1702.) [Winer. xlviii. a.]
[5] This remark which comes in abruptly is pursued presently, vid. § 23.　　[6] Cf. de Decr. 31, fin.

become perfect, having oneness with It, and having become one in It; that, as if all were carried by Me, all may be one body and one spirit, and may grow up unto a perfect man[7].' For we all, partaking of the Same, become one body, having the one Lord in ourselves. The passage then having this meaning, still more plainly is refuted the heterodoxy of Christ's enemies. I repeat it; if He had said simply and absolutely[8] 'that they may be one in Thee,' or 'that they and I may be one in Thee,' God's enemies had had some plea, though a shameless one; but in fact He has not spoken simply, but, 'As Thou, Father, in Me, and I in Thee, that they may be all one.' Moreover, using the word 'as,' He signifies those who become distantly as He is in the Father; distantly not in place but in nature; for in place nothing is far from God[9], but in nature only all things are far from Him. And, as I said before, whoso uses the particle 'as' implies, not identity, nor equality, but a pattern of the matter in question, viewed in a certain respect[10].

23. Indeed we may learn also from the Saviour Himself, when He says, 'For as Jonah was three days and three nights in the whale's belly, so shall the Son of man be three days and three nights in the heart of the earth[1].' For Jonah was not as the Saviour, nor did Jonah go down to hades; nor was the whale hades; nor did Jonah, when swallowed up, bring up those who had before been swallowed by the whale, but he alone came forth, when the whale was bidden. Therefore there is no identity nor equality signified in the term 'as,' but one thing and another; and it shews a certain kind[2] of parallel in the case of Jonah, on account of the three days. In like manner then we too, when the Lord says 'as,' neither become as the Son in the Father, nor as the Father is in the Son. For we become one as the Father and the Son in mind and agreement[3] of spirit, and the Saviour will be as Jonah in the earth; but as the Saviour is not Jonah, nor, as he was swallowed up, so did the Saviour descend into hades, but it is but a parallel, in like manner, if we too become one, as the Son in the Father, we shall not be as

the Son, nor equal to Him; for He and we are but parallel. For on this account is the word 'as' applied to us; since things differing from others in nature, become as they, when viewed in a certain relation[5]. Wherefore the Son Himself, simply and without any condition is in the Father; for this attribute He has by nature; but for us, to whom it is not natural, there is needed an image and example, that He may say of us, 'As Thou in Me, and I in Thee.' 'And when they shall be so perfected,' He says, 'then the world knows that Thou hast sent Me, for unless I had come and borne this their body, no one of them had been perfected, but one and all had remained corruptible[6] Work Thou then in them, O Father, and as Thou hast given to Me to bear this, grant to them Thy Spirit, that they too in It may become one, and may be perfected in Me. For their perfecting shews that Thy Word has sojourned among them; and the world seeing them perfect and full of God[7], will believe altogether that Thou hast sent Me, and I have sojourned here. For whence is this their perfecting, but that I, Thy Word, having borne their body, and become man, have perfected the work, which Thou gavest Me, O Father? And the work is perfected, because men, redeemed from sin, no longer remain dead; but being deified[8], have in each other, by looking at Me, the bond of charity[9].'

24. We then, by way of giving a rude view of the expressions in this passage, have been led into many words, but blessed John will shew from his Epistle the sense of the words, concisely and much more perfectly than we can. And he will both disprove the interpretation of these irreligious men, and will teach how we become in God and God in us; and how again we become One in Him, and how far the Son differs in nature from us, and will stop the Arians from any longer thinking that they shall be as the Son, lest they hear it said to them, 'Thou art a man and not God,' and 'Stretch not thyself, being poor, beside a rich man[1].' John then thus writes; 'Hereby know we that we dwell in Him and He in us, because He hath given us of His Spirit[2].' Therefore because of the grace of the Spirit which has been given to us, in Him we come to be, and He in us[3]; and since it is the Spirit of God, therefore through His becoming in us, reasonably are we, as having the Spirit, considered to be in God, and thus is God in us. Not then as the Son in the Father, so

---

7 Vid. Eph. iv. 13.   8 Cf. ii. 62, n. 13.

9 Vid. de Decr. 11, n. 5, which is explained by the present passage. When Ath. there says, 'without all in nature,' he must mean as here, 'far from all things in nature.' S. Clement loc. cit. gives the same explanation, as there noticed. It is observable that the contr. Sab. Greg. 10 (which the Benedictines consider not Athan.'s) speaks as de Decr. supr. Eusebius says the same thing, de Incorpor. i. init. ap. Sirm. Op. p. 68. vid. S. Ambros. Quomodo creatura in Deo esse potest, &c. de Fid. i. 106. and supr. § 1, n. 10.

10 Vid. Glass. Phil. Sacr. iii. 5. can. 27. and Dettmars, de Theol. Orig. ap. Lumper. Hist. Patr. t. 10, p. 212. Vid. also supr. ii. 55, n. 8.   1 Matt. xii. 40.

2 ὁμοιότητά πως, and so at the end of 22. κατά τι θεωρούμενον. [A note, discussing certain views of Coplestone, Toplady, and Blanco White, is omitted here.]   3 συμφωνία, 10, n. 2.

5 Cyril in Joan. p. 227, &c.   6 Cf. ii. 65, n. 3.
7 θεοφορουμένους, ii. 70, n. 1.   8 § 19. n. 3.
9 σύνδεσμον τῆς ἀγαπῆς, 21. circ. fin.   1 Ez. xxviii. 2;
Prov. xxiii. 4, LXX.   2 1 John iv. 13.   3 Cf. 22, n. 6.

also we become in the Father; for the Son does not merely partake the Spirit, that therefore He too may be in the Father; nor does He receive the Spirit, but rather He supplies It Himself to all; and the Spirit does not unite the Word to the Father [4], but rather the Spirit receives from the Word. And the Son is in the Father, as His own Word and Radiance; but we, apart from the Spirit, are strange and distant from God, and by the participation of the Spirit we are knit into the Godhead; so that our being in the Father is not ours, but is the Spirit's which is in us and abides in us, while by the true confession we preserve it in us, John again saying, 'Whosoever shall confess that Jesus is the Son of God, God dwelleth in him and he in God [5].' What then is our likeness and equality to the Son? rather, are not the Arians confuted on every side? and especially by John, that the Son is in the Father in one way, and we become in Him in another, and that neither we shall ever be as He, nor is the Word as we; except they shall dare, as commonly, so now to say, that the Son also by participation of the Spirit and by improvement of conduct [6] came to be Himself also in the Father. But here again is an excess of irreligion, even in admitting the thought. For He, as has been said, gives to the Spirit, and whatever the Spirit hath, He hath from [7] the Word.

25. The Saviour, then, saying of us, 'As Thou, Father, art in Me, and I in Thee, that they too may be one in Us,' does not signify that we were to have identity with Him; for this was shewn from the instance of Jonah; but it is a request to the Father, as John has written, that the Spirit should be vouchsafed through Him to those who believe, through whom we are found to be in God, and in this respect to be conjoined in Him. For since the Word is in the Father, and the Spirit is given from [1] the Word, He wills that we should receive the Spirit, that, when we receive It, thus having the Spirit of the Word which is in the Father, we too may be found on account of the Spirit to become One in the Word, and through Him in the Father. And if He say, 'as we,' this again is only a request that such grace of the Spirit as is given to the disciples may be without failure or revocation [2]. For what the Word has by nature [3], as I said, in the Father, that He wishes to be given to us through the

Spirit irrevocably; which the Apostle knowing, said, 'Who shall separate us from the love of Christ?' for 'the gifts of God' and 'grace of His calling are without repentance [4].' It is the Spirit then which is in God, and not we viewed in our own selves; and as we are sons and gods [5] because of the Word in us [6], so we shall be in the Son and in the Father, and we shall be accounted to have become one in Son and in Father, because that that Spirit is in us, which is in the Word which is in the Father. When then a man falls from the Spirit for any wickedness, if he repent upon his fall, the grace remains irrevocably to such as are willing [7]; otherwise he who has fallen is no longer in God (because that Holy Spirit and Paraclete which is in God has deserted him), but the sinner shall be in him to whom he has subjected himself, as took place in Saul's instance; for the Spirit of God departed from him and an evil spirit was afflicting him [8]. God's enemies hearing this ought to be henceforth abashed, and no longer to feign themselves equal to God. But they neither understand (for 'the irreligious,' he saith, ' does not understand knowledge' [9]) nor endure religious words, but find them heavy even to hear.

CHAPTER XXVI.

INTRODUCTORY TO TEXTS FROM THE GOSPELS ON THE INCARNATION.

Enumeration of texts still to be explained. Arians compared to the Jews. We must recur to the *Regula Fidei*. Our Lord did not come into, but became, man, and therefore had the acts and affections of the flesh. The same works divine and human. Thus the flesh was purified, and men were made immortal. Reference to 1 Pet. iv. 1.

26. FOR behold, as if not wearied in their words of irreligion, but hardened with Pharaoh, while they hear and see the Saviour's human attributes in the Gospels [1], they have utterly forgotten, like the Samosatene, the Son's paternal Godhead [2], and with arrogant and audacious tongue they say, 'How can the Son be from the Father by nature, and be like Him in essence, who says, 'All power is given unto Me;' and 'The Father judgeth no man, but hath committed all judgment unto the Son;' and 'The Father loveth the Son, and hath given all things into His hand; he that believeth in the Son hath everlasting life;' and again, 'All things were delivered unto Me of My Father,

---

4 [i.e. not by grace] Vid. the end of this section and 25 init. *supr. Or.* i. 15. also Cyril *Hier. Cat.* xvi. 24. Epiph. *Ancor.* 67 init. Cyril *in Joan.* pp. 929, 930.   5 1 John iv. 15.
6 βελτιώσει πράξεως, and so *ad Afros.* τρόπων βελτίωσις. 8. *Supr. Or.* i. 37, 43. it is rather some external advance.
7 § 8, note 11.   1 ἐκ.   2 Cf. ii. 63, n. 8.
3 κατὰ φύσιν, *supr. de Decr.* 31, n. 5.

4 Rom. viii. 35; vid. xi. 29.   5 θεοί, *Or.* ii. 70, n. 1.
6 Cf. ii. 59; n. 5.   7 Cf. *Or.* i. 37, end.   8 1 Sam. xvi. 14.
9 Prov. xxix. 7. νοεῖ, Ath. συνήσει.
1 This Oration alone, and this entirely, treats of texts from the Gospels; hitherto from the Gospel according to St. John, and now chiefly from the first three. Hence they lead Athan. to treat more distinctly of the doctrine of the Incarnation, and to anticipate a refutation of both Nestorius and Eutyches.   2 § 1, n. 13.

and no one knoweth the Father save the Son, and he to whomsoever the Son will reveal Him;' and again, 'All that the Father hath given unto Me, shall come to Me[3].' On this they observe, 'If He was, as ye say, Son by nature, He had no need to receive, but He had by nature as a Son.' "Or how can He be the natural and true Power of the Father, who near upon the season of the passion says, 'Now is My soul troubled, and what shall I say? Father, save Me from this hour; but for this came I unto this hour. Father, glorify Thy Name. Then came there a voice from heaven, saying, I have both glorified it, and will glorify it again[4].' And He said the same another time; 'Father, if it be possible, let this cup pass from Me;' and 'When Jesus had thus said, He was troubled in spirit and testified and said, Verily, verily, I say unto you, that one of you shall betray Me[5].'" Then these perverse men argue; 'If He were Power, He had not feared, but rather He had supplied power to others.' Further they say; 'If He were by nature the true and own Wisdom of the Father, how is it written, 'And Jesus increased in wisdom and stature, and in favour with God and man[6]?' In like manner, when He had come into the parts of Cæsarea Philippi, He asked the disciples whom men said that He was; and when He was at Bethany He asked where Lazarus lay; and He said besides to His disciples, 'How many loaves have ye[7]? How then,' say they, 'is He Wisdom, who increased in wisdom, and was ignorant of what He asked of others?' This too they urge; "How can He be the own Word of the Father, without whom the Father never was, through whom He makes all things, as ye think, who said upon the Cross, 'My God, My God, why hast Thou forsaken Me?' and before that had prayed, 'Glorify Thy Name,' and, 'O Father, glorify Thou Me with the glory which I had with Thee before the world was.' And He used to pray in the deserts and charge His disciples to pray lest they should enter into temptation; and, 'The spirit indeed is willing,' He said, 'but the flesh is weak.' And, 'Of that day and that hour knoweth no man, no, nor the Angels, neither the Son[8].'" Upon this again say the miserable men, "If the Son were, according to your interpretation[9], eternally existent with God, He had not been ignorant of the Day, but had known as Word; nor had been forsaken as

being co-existent; nor had asked to receive glory, as having it in the Father; nor would have prayed at all; for, being the Word, He had needed nothing; but since He is a creature and one of things originate, therefore He thus spoke, and needed what He had not; for it is proper to creatures to require and to need what they have not."

27. This then is what the irreligious men allege in their discourses; and if they thus argue, they might consistently speak yet more daringly; 'Why did the Word become flesh at all?' and they might add; 'For how could He, being God, become man?' or, 'How could the Immaterial bear a body?' or they might speak with Caiaphas still more Judaically, 'Wherefore at all did Christ, being a man, make Himself God[1]?' for this and the like the Jews then muttered when they saw, and now the Ario-maniacs disbelieve when they read, and have fallen away into blasphemies. If then a man should carefully parallel the words of these and those, he will of a certainty find them both arriving at the same unbelief, and the daring of their irreligion equal, and their dispute with us a common one. For the Jews said; 'How, being a man, can He be God?' And the Arians, 'If He were very God from God, how could He become man?' And the Jews were offended then and mocked, saying, 'Had He been Son of God, He had not endured the Cross;' and the Arians standing over against them, urge upon us, 'How dare ye say that He is the Word proper to the Father's Essence, who had a body, so as to endure all this?' Next, while the Jews sought to kill the Lord, because He said that God was His own Father and made Himself equal to Him, as working what the Father works, the Arians also, not only have learned to deny, both that He is equal to God and that God is the own and natural Father of the Word, but those who hold this they seek to kill. Again, whereas the Jews said, 'Is not this the Son of Joseph, whose father and mother we know? how then is it that He saith, Before Abraham was, I am, and I came down from heaven[2]?' the Arians on the other hand make response[3] and say conformably, 'How can He be Word or God who slept as man, and wept, and inquired?' Thus both parties deny the Eternity and Godhead of the Word in consequence of those human attributes which the Saviour took on Him by reason of that flesh which He bore.

28. Such error then being Judaic, and Judaic after the mind of Judas the traitor,

---

[3] Matt. xxviii. 18; John v. 22; iii. 35, 36; Matt. **xi. 27**; John **vi. 37**; *infr.* §§ 35—41.   [4] John xii. 27, 28.
[5] Matt. xxvi. 39; John xiii. 21; *infr.* §§ 53—58.
[6] Luke ii. 52; *infr.* §§ 50—53.   [7] Matt. xvi. 13; John xi. 34; Mark vi. 38; *infr.* § 27.   [8] Matt. xxvii. 46; John xii. 28; xvii. 5; Matt. xxvi. 41; Mark xiii. 32; *infr.* §§ 42—50.
[9] διάνοιαν, ii. 44, a. 53, c.; iv. 17, d. &c.

[1] *De Decr.* 1; *Or.* i. 4.   [2] John vi. 42; viii. 58.
[3] ἐπακούουσιν. Montfaucon (Onomasticon in t. 2 fin.) so interprets this word. vid. *Apol. contr. Ar.* 88. note 7.

let them openly confess themselves scholars of Caiaphas and Herod, instead of cloking Judaism with the name of Christianity, and let them deny outright, as we have said before, the Saviour's appearance in the flesh, for this doctrine is akin to their heresy; or if they fear openly to Judaize and be circumcised[4], from servility towards Constantius and for their sake whom they have beguiled, then let them not say what the Jews say; for if they disown the name, let them in fairness renounce the doctrine. For we are Christians, O Arians, Christians we; our privilege is it well to know the Gospels concerning the Saviour, and neither with Jews to stone Him, if we hear of His Godhead and Eternity, nor with you to stumble at such lowly sayings as He may speak for our sakes as man. If then you would become Christians[5], put off Arius's madness, and cleanse[6] with the words of religion those ears of yours which blaspheming has defiled; knowing that, by ceasing to be Arians, you will cease also from the malevolence of the present Jews. Then at once will truth shine on you out of darkness, and ye will no longer reproach us with holding two Eternals[7], but ye will yourselves acknowledge that the Lord is God's true Son by nature, and not as merely eternal[8], but revealed as co-existing in the Father's eternity. For there are things called eternal of which He is Framer; for in the twenty-third Psalm it is written, 'Lift up your gates, O ye rulers, and be ye lift up, ye everlasting gates[9];' and it is plain that through Him these things were made; but if even of

things everlasting He is the Framer, who of us shall be able henceforth to dispute that He is anterior to those things eternal, and in consequence is proved to be Lord not so much from His eternity, as in that He is God's Son; for being the Son, He is inseparable from the Father, and never was there when He was not, but He was always; and being the Father's Image and Radiance, He has the Father's eternity. Now what has been briefly said above may suffice to shew their misunderstanding of the passages they then alleged; and that of what they now allege from the Gospels they certainly give an unsound interpretation[10], we may easily see, if we now consider the scope[11] of that faith which we Christians hold, and using it as a rule, apply ourselves, as the Apostle teaches, to the reading of inspired Scripture. For Christ's enemies, being ignorant of this scope, have wandered from the way of truth, and have stumbled[12] on a stone of stumbling, thinking otherwise than they should think.

29. Now the scope and character of Holy Scripture, as we have often said, is this,—it contains a double account of the Saviour; that He was ever God, and is the Son, being the Father's Word and Radiance and Wisdom[1]; and that afterwards for us He took flesh of a Virgin, Mary Bearer of God[2], and was made man. And this scope is to be found throughout inspired Scripture, as the Lord Himself has said, 'Search the Scriptures, for they are they which testify of Me[3].' But lest I should exceed in writing, by bringing together all the passages on the subject, let it suffice to mention as a specimen, first John saying, 'In the beginning was the Word, and the Word was with God, and the Word was God. The same was in the beginning with God. All things were made by Him, and without Him was made not one thing[4];' next, 'And the Word was made flesh and dwelt among us, and we beheld His glory, the glory as of one Only-begotten from the Father[5];' and next Paul writing, 'Who being in the form of God, thought it not a prize to be equal with God, but emptied Himself, taking the form of a servant, being made in the likeness of men, and being found in fashion like a man, He humbled Himself, becoming obedient unto death, even the death of the Cross[6].' Any one, beginning with these passages and going through the

---

4 *Or.* i. 38.   5 *Apol. Fug.* 27, n. 10.   6 *De Decr.* 2, n. 9, c. *Sab. Greg.* 6 fin.

7 Cf. *de Decr.* 25, n. 4. The peculiarity of the Catholic doctrine, as contrasted with the heresies on the subject of the Trinity, is that it professes a mystery. It involves, not merely a contradiction in the terms used, which would be little, for we might solve it by assigning different senses to the same word, or by adding some limitation (e.g. if it were said that Satan was an Angel and not an Angel, or man was mortal and immortal), but an incongruity in the ideas which it introduces. To say that the Father is wholly and absolutely the one infinitely-simple God, and then that the Son is also, and yet that the Father is eternally distinct from the Son, is to propose ideas which we cannot harmonize together; and our reason is reconciled to this state of the case only by the consideration (though fully by means of it) that no idea of ours can embrace the simple truth, so that we are obliged to separate it into portions, and view it in aspects, and adumbrate it under many ideas, if we are to make any approximation towards it at all; as in mathematics we approximate to a circle by means of a polygon, great as is the dissimilitude between the two figures. [Cf. Prolegg. ch. ii. § 3 (2) b.]

8 οὐχ ἁπλῶς ἀΐδιος, i.e. ἀΐδιος is not one of our Lord's highest titles, for things have it which the Son Himself has created, and whom of course He precedes. Instead of two ἀΐδια then, as the Arians say, there are many ἀΐδια; and our Lord's high title is not this, but that He is 'the Son,' and thereby 'eternal in the Father's eternity,' or there was not ever when He was not, and 'Image' and 'Radiance.' The same line of thought is implied throughout his proof of our Lord's eternity in *Orat.* i. ch. 4-6. This is worth remarking, as constituting a special distinction between ancient and modern Scripture proofs of the doctrine, and as coinciding with what was said *supr. Or.* ii. 1, n. 13, 44, n. 1. His mode of proof is still more brought out by what he proceeds to say about the σκοπός, or general bearing or drift of the Christian faith, and its availableness as a κανὼν or rule of interpretation.

9 Ps. xxiv. 7.

---

10 Cf. 26, n. 9.   11 σκοπὸς, vid. 58. fin.   12 Rom. ix. 32.
1 *Or.* i. 28, n. 5.
2 θεοτόκου. vid. *supr.* 14, n. 3. Vid. S. Cyril's quotations in his *de Recta Fide*, p. 49, &c.; and Cyril himself. *Adv. Nest.* i. p. 18. Procl. *Hom.* i. p. 60. Theodor. *ap. Conc. Eph.* (p. 1529. Labbe.) Cassian. *Incarn.* iv. 2. Hil. *Trin.* ii. 25. Ambros. *Virgin.* i. n. 47. Chrysost. ap. Cassian. *Incarn.* vii. 30. Jerom. in Ezek. 44 init. Capreolus of Carthage, ap. Sirm. *Opp.* t. i. p. 216. August. *Serm.* 291, 6. Hippolytus, ap. Theod. *Eran.* i. p. 55, &c. Ignatius, *Ep. ad Eph.* 7.   3 John v. 39.   4 Ib. i. 1—3.   5 *v.* 14.
6 Phil. ii. 6—8.

whole of the Scripture upon the interpretation [7] which they suggest, will perceive how in the beginning the Father said to Him, ' Let there be light,' and ' Let there be a firmament,' and ' Let us make man [8];' but in fulness of the ages, He sent Him into the world, not that He might judge the world, but that the world by Him might be saved, and how it is written, ' Behold, the Virgin shall be with child, and shall bring forth a Son, and they shall call his Name Emmanuel, which, being interpreted, is God with us [9].'

30. The reader then of divine Scripture may acquaint himself with these passages from the ancient books; and from the Gospels on the other hand he will perceive that the Lord became man; for ' the Word,' he says, ' became flesh, and dwelt among us [1].' And He became man, and did not come into man; for this it is necessary to know, lest perchance these irreligious men fall into this notion also, and beguile any into thinking, that, as in former times the Word was used to come into each of the Saints, so now He sojourned in a man, hallowing him also, and manifesting [10] Himself as in the others. For if it were so, and He only appeared in a man, it were nothing strange, nor had those who saw Him been startled, saying, Whence is He? and wherefore dost Thou, being a man, make Thyself God? for they were familiar with the idea, from the words, ' And the Word of the Lord came ' to this or that of the Prophets [2]. But now, since the Word of God, by whom all things came to be, endured to become also Son of man, and humbled Himself, taking a servant's form, therefore to the Jews the Cross of Christ is a scandal, but to us Christ is ' God's power' and ' God's wisdom [3];' for ' the Word,' as John says, ' became flesh ' (it being the custom [4] of Scripture to call man by the name of ' flesh,' as it says by Joel the Prophet, ' I will pour out My Spirit upon all flesh;' and as Daniel said to Astyages, ' I do not worship idols made with hands, but the Living God, who hath created the heaven and the earth, and hath sovereignty over all flesh [5];' for both he and Joel call mankind flesh).

31. Of old time He was wont to come to the Saints individually, and to hallow those who rightly [6] received Him; but neither, when they were begotten was it said that He had become man, nor, when they suffered, was it said that He Himself suffered. But when He came among us from Mary once at the end of the ages for the abolition of sin (for so it was pleasing to the Father, to send His own Son ' made of a woman, made under the Law '), then it is said, that He took flesh and became man, and in that flesh He suffered for us (as Peter says, ' Christ therefore having suffered for us in the flesh [7]'), that it might be shewn, and that all might believe, that whereas He was ever God, and hallowed those to whom He came, and ordered all things according to the Father's will [8], afterwards for our sakes He became man, and ' bodily [9],' as the Apostle says, the Godhead dwelt in the flesh; as much as to say, ' Being God, He had His own body, and using this as an instrument [10], He became man for our sakes.' And on account of this, the properties of the flesh are said to be His, since He was in it, such as to hunger, to thirst, to suffer, to weary, and the like, of which the flesh is capable; while on the other hand the works proper to the Word Himself, such as to raise the dead, to restore sight to the blind, and to cure the woman with an issue of blood, He did through His own body [11]. And the Word bore the infirmities of the flesh, as His own, for His was the flesh; and the flesh ministered to the works of the Godhead, because the Godhead was in it, for the body was God's [12]. And well has

---

7 Gal. iv. 4; 1 Pet. iv. 1.
8 κατὰ τὸ βούλημα. vid. *Orat.* i. 63. *infr.* § 63, notes. Cf. *supr.* ii. 31, n. 7, for passages in which Ps. xxxiii. 9. is taken to shew the unity of Father and Son from the instantaneousness of the accomplishment upon the willing, as well as the Son's existence before creation. Hence the Son not only works κατὰ τὸ βούλημα, but is the βουλὴ of the Father. ibid. note 8. For the contrary Arian view, even when it is highest, vid Euseb. *Eccl. Theol.* iii. 3. quoted ii. 64, n. 5. In that passage the Father's νεύματα are spoken of, a word common with the Arians. Euseb. ibid. p. 75, a. *de Laud. Const.* p. 528, Eunom. *Apol.* 20 fin. The word is used of the Son's command given to the creation, in Athan. *contr. Gent.* e.g. 42, 44, 46. S. Cyril. Hier. frequently as the Arians, uses it of the Father. *Catech.* x. 5, xi. *passim*, xv. 25, &c. The difference between the orthodox and Arian views on this point is clearly drawn out by S. Basil *contr. Eunom.* i. 21.
9 Col. ii. 9.
10 τούτῳ χρώμενος ὀργάνῳ *infr.* 42. and ὄργανον πρὸς τὴν ἐνέργειαν καὶ τὴν ἔκλαμψιν τῆς θεότητος. 53. This was a word much used afterwards by the Apollinarians, who looked on our Lord's manhood as merely a *manifestation* of God. vid. *Or.* ii. 8, n. 3. vid. σχῆμα ὀργανικὸν in *Apoll.* i. 2, 15. vid. a parallel in Euseb. *Laud. Const.* p. 536. However, it is used freely by Athan. e.g. *infr.* 35, 53. *Incarn.* 8, 9, 41, 43, 44. This use of ὄργανον must not be confused with its heretical application to our Lord's Divine Nature, vid. Basil *de Sp. S.* n. 19 fin. of which *de Syn.* 27 (3). It may be added that φανέρωσις is a Nestorian as well as a Eutychian idea; Facund. *Tr. Cap.* ix. 2, 3. and the Syrian use of *parsopa* Asseman. *B. O.* t. 4. p. 219. Thus both parties really denied the Atonement. vid. *supr. Or.* i. 60, n. 5; ii. 8, n. 4.
11 *Orat.* iv. 6. and *fragm. ex Euthym.* p. 1275. ed. Ben. This interchange [of language] is called theologically the ἀντίδοσις or communicatio ἰδιωμάτων. Nyssen. *in Apoll.* t. 2. pp. 697, 8. Leon. *Ep.* 28, 51. Ambros. *de fid.* ii. 58. Nyssen. *de Beat.* p. 767. Cassian. *Incarn.* vi. 22. Aug. *contr. Serm. Ar. c.* 8 init. Plain and easy as such statements seem, they are of the utmost importance in the Nestorian and Eutychian controversies.
12 θεοῦ ἦν σῶμα. also *ad Adelph.* 3. *ad Max.* 2. and so τὴν πτωχεύσασαν φύσιν θεοῦ ὅλην γενομένην. c. *Apoll.* ii. 11. τὸ πάθος τοῦ λόγου. ibid. 16, c. σὰρξ τοῦ λόγου. *infr.* 34. σῶμα σοφίας *infr.* 53. also *Or.* ii. 10, n. 7. πάθος Χριστοῦ τοῦ θεοῦ μου. Ignat. *Rom.* 6. ὁ θεὸς πέπονθεν. Melit. *ap. Anast. Hodeg.* 12. Dei passiones. Tertull. *de Carn. Christ.* 5. Dei interemptores. ibid. caro Deitatis. Leon. *Serm.* 65 fin. Deus mortuus et sepultus. Vigil. *c. Eut.* ii. p. 502. vid. *supr. Or.* i. 45, n. 3. Yet Athan. objects to the phrase, ' God suffered in the flesh,' i.e. as used by the Apollinarians. vid.

---

7 Cf. 26, n. 9.   8 Gen. i. 3, 6, 26; *de Syn.* 28 (14).
9 Matt. i. 23.   1 John i. 14.   2 *Ad Epict.* 11, *ad Max.* 2.
3 1 Cor. i. 24.   4 *Infr.* iv. 33 init.   5 Joel ii. 28; Bel
and Dr. 5.   6 *Or.* i. 39, n. 4.

the Prophet said 'carried[13];' and has not said, 'He remedied our infirmities,' lest, as being external to the body, and only healing it, as He has always done, He should leave men subject still to death; but He carries our infirmities, and He Himself bears our sins, that it might be shewn that He has become man for us, and that the body which in Him bore them, was His own body; and, while He received no hurt[14] Himself by 'bearing our sins in His body on the tree,' as Peter speaks, we men were redeemed from our own affections[15], and were filled with the righteousness[16] of the Word.

32. Whence it was that, when the flesh suffered, the Word was not external to it; and therefore is the passion said to be His: and when He did divinely His Father's works, the flesh was not external to Him, but in the body itself did the Lord do them. Hence, when made man, He said[1], 'If I do not the works of the Father, believe Me not; but if I do, though ye believe not Me, believe the works, that ye may know that the Father is in He and I in Him.' And thus when there was need to raise Peter's wife's mother, who was sick of a fever, He stretched forth His hand humanly, but He stopped the illness divinely. And in the case of the man blind from the birth, human was the spittle which He gave forth from the flesh, but divinely did He open the eyes through the clay. And in the case of Lazarus, He gave forth a human voice, as man; but divinely, as God, did He raise Lazarus from the dead[2]. These things were so done, were so manifested, because He had a body, not in appearance, but in truth[3]; and it became the Lord, in putting on human flesh, to put it on whole with the affections proper to it; that, as we say that the body was His own, so also we may say that the affections of the body were proper to

Him alone, though they did not touch Him according to His Godhead. If then the body had been another's, to him too had been the affections attributed; but if the flesh is the Word's (for 'the Word became flesh'), of necessity then the affections also of the flesh are ascribed to Him, whose the flesh is. And to whom the affections are ascribed, such namely as to be condemned, to be scourged, to thirst, and the cross, and death, and the other infirmities of the body, of Him too is the triumph and the grace. For this cause then, consistently and fittingly such affections are ascribed not to another[4], but to the Lord; that the grace also may be from Him[5], and that we may become, not worshippers of any other, but truly devout towards God, because we invoke no originate thing, no ordinary[6] man, but the natural and true Son from God, who has become man, yet is not the less Lord and God and Saviour.

33. Who will not admire this? or who will not agree that such a thing is truly divine? for if the works of the Word's Godhead had not taken place through the body, man had not been deified; and again, had not the properties of the flesh been ascribed to the Word, man had not been thoroughly delivered from them[1]; but though they had ceased for a little while, as I said before, still sin had remained in him and corruption, as was the case with mankind before Him; and for this reason:—Many for instance have been made holy and clean from all sin; nay, Jeremiah was hallowed[2] even from the womb, and John, while yet in the womb, leapt for joy at the voice of Mary Bearer of God[3]; nevertheless 'death reigned from Adam to Moses, even over those that had not sinned after the similitude of Adam's transgression[4];' and thus man remained mortal and corruptible as before, liable to the affections proper to their nature. But now the Word having become man and having appropriated[5] what

---

contr. Apoll. ii. 13 fin. [Cf. Harnack, Dogmg. ed. 1. vol. i. pp. 131, 628. notes.]   13 Is. liii. 4.

14 οὐδὲν ἐβλάπτετο. (1 Pet. ii. 24.) Cf. de Incarn. 17, 54, 34.; Euseb. de Laud. Const. p. 536. and 538. also Dem. Evang. vii. p. 348. Vigil. contr. Eutych. ii. p. 503. (B. P. ed. 1624.) Anast. Hodeg. c. 12. p. 220 (ed. 1606.) also p. 222. Vid. also the beautiful passage in Pseudo-Basil: Hom. in Sanct. Christ. Gen. (t. 2. p. 596. ed. Ben.) also Rufin. in Symb. 12. Cyril. Quod unus est Christus. p. 776. Damasc. F. O. iii. 6 fin. August. Serm. 7. p. 26 init. ed. 1842. Suppl. 1.   15 παθῶν, vid. § 33, n. 2.

16 Orat. i. 51.

1 John x. 37, 38. vid. Incarn. 18. Cf. Leo, Serm. 54, 2. 'Suscepit nos in suam proprietatem illa natura, quæ nec nostris sua, nec suis nostra consumeret, &c.' Serm. 72, p. 286. vid. also Ep. 165, 6. Serm. 30, 5. Cyril Cat. iv. 9. Amphiloch. ap. Theod. Eran. i. p. 66. also pp. 30, 87, 8. ed. 16.4.

2 Cf. Leo's Tome (Ep. 28.) 4. 'When He touched the leper, it was the man that was seen; but something beyond man, when He cleansed him, &c.' Ambros. Epist. i. 46. n. 7. Hil. Trin. x. 23 fin. vid. infr. 56 note, and S. Leo's extracts in his Ep. 165. Chrysol. Serm. 34 and 35. Paul. ap. Conc. Eph. (p. 1620. Labbe.) These are instances of what is theologically called the θεανδρικὴ ἐνέργεια [a condemned formula], i.e. the union of the energies of both Natures in one act.

3 μὴ φαντασίᾳ ἀλλ' ἀληθῶς. vid. Incarn. 18, d. ad Epict. 7, c. The passage is quoted by S. Cyril. Apol. adv. Orient. p. 194.

4 οὐκ ἄλλου, ἀλλὰ τοῦ κυρίου· and so οὐκ ἑτέρου τινός, Incarn. 18; also Orat. i. 45. supr. p. 244. and Orat. iv. 35. Cyril Thes. p. 197. and Anathem. 11. who defends the phrase against the Orientals.   5 Cf. Procl. ad Armen. p. 615, ed. 1630.

6 κοινόν opposed to ἴδιον. vid. infr. § 51, Cyril Epp. p. 23, c. communem, Ambros. de Fid. i. 94.

2 Vid. Jer. i. 5. And so S. Jerome, S. Leo, &c., as mentioned in Corn. a Lap. in loc. S. Jerome implies a similar gift in the case of Asella, ad Marcell. (Ep. xxiv. 2.) And so S. John Baptist, Maldon. in Luc. i. 16. It is remarkable that no ancient writer (unless indeed we except S. Austin), [Patrol. Lat. xlvii. 1144?] refers to the instance of S. Mary;—perhaps from the circumstance of its not being mentioned in Scripture.

3 θεοτόκου. For instances of this word vid. Alexandr. Ep. ad Alex. ap. Theodor. H. E. i. 4. p. 745. (al. 20). Athan. (supra); Cyril. Cat. x. 19. Julian Imper. ap. Cyril c. Jul. viii. p. 262. Amphiloch. Orat. 4. p. 41. (if Amphil.) ed. 1644. Nyssen. Ep. ad Eustath. p. 1093. Chrysost. apud. Suicer Symb. p. 240. Greg. Naz. Orat 29, 4 Ep. 181. p. 85. ed. Ben. Antiochus and Ammon. ap. Cyril. de Recta Fid. pp. 49, 50. Pseudo-Dion. contr. Samos. 5. Pseudo-Basil. Hom. t. 2. p. 600 ed. Ben.   4 Rom. v. 14.

5 ἰδιοποιουμένου. vid. also [Incar. 8.] infr. § 38. ad Epict. 6, c. fragm. ex Euthym. (t. i p. 1275. ed. Ben.) Cyril. in Joann. p. 151, a.

pertains to the flesh, no longer do these things touch the body, because of the Word who has come in it, but they are destroyed[6] by Him, and henceforth men no longer remain sinners and dead according to their proper affections, but having risen according to the Word's power, they abide[7] ever immortal and incorruptible. Whence also, whereas the flesh is born of Mary Bearer of God[8], He Himself is said to have been born, who furnishes to others an origin of being; in order that He may transfer our origin into Himself, and we may no longer, as mere earth, return to earth, but as being knit into the Word from heaven, may be carried to heaven by Him. Therefore in like manner not without reason has He transferred to Himself the other affections of the body also; that we, no longer as being men, but as proper to the Word, may have share in eternal life. For no longer according to our former origin in Adam do we die; but henceforward our origin and all infirmity of flesh being transferred to the Word, we rise from the earth, the curse from sin being removed, because of Him who is in us[9], and who has become a curse for us. And with reason; for as we are all from earth and die in Adam, so being regenerated from above of water and Spirit, in the Christ we are all quickened; the flesh being no longer earthly, but being henceforth made Word[10], by reason of God's Word who for our sake 'became flesh.'

34. And that one may attain to a more exact knowledge of the impassibility of the Word's nature and of the infirmities ascribed to Him because of the flesh, it will be well to listen to the blessed Peter; for he will be a trustworthy witness concerning the Saviour. He writes then in his Epistle thus; 'Christ then having suffered for us in the flesh[1].' Therefore also when He is said to hunger and

thirst and to toil and not to know, and to sleep, and to weep, and to ask, and to flee, and to be born, and to deprecate the cup, and in a word to undergo all that belongs to the flesh[2], let it be said, as is congruous, in each case, 'Christ then hungering and thirsting "for us in the flesh;"' and 'saying He did not know, and being buffeted, and toiling "for us in the flesh;"' and 'being exalted too, and born, and growing "in the flesh;"' and 'fearing and hiding "in the flesh;"' and 'saying, "If it be possible let this cup pass from Me[3]," and being beaten, and receiving, "for us in the flesh;"' and in a word all such things 'for us in the flesh.' For on this account has the Apostle himself said, 'Christ then having suffered,' not in His Godhead, but 'for us in the flesh,' that these affections may be acknowledged as, not proper to the very Word by nature, but proper by nature to the very flesh.

Let no one then stumble at what belongs to man, but rather let a man know that in nature the Word Himself is impassible, and yet because of that flesh which He put on, these things are ascribed to Him, since they are proper to the flesh, and the body itself is proper to the Saviour. And while He Himself, being impassible in nature, remains as He is, not harmed[4] by these affections, but rather obliterating and destroying them, men, their passions as if changed and abolished[5] in the Impassible, henceforth become themselves also impassible and free[6] from them for ever, as John taught, saying, 'And ye know that He was manifested to take away our sins, and in Him is no sin[7].' And this being so, no heretic shall object, 'Wherefore rises the flesh, being by nature mortal? and if it rises, why not hunger too and thirst, and suffer, and remain mortal? for it came from the earth, and how can its natural condition pass from it?' since the flesh is able now to make answer to this so contentious heretic, 'I am from earth, being by nature mortal, but afterwards I have become the Word's flesh, and He 'carried' my affections, though He is without them; and so I became free from them, being no more abandoned to their service because of the Lord who has made me free from them. For if you object to my being rid of that corruption which is by nature, see that you object not to God's Word having taken my form

---

For ἴδιον, which occurs so frequently here, vid. Cyril. *Anathem.* 11. And οἰκείωται. *contr. Apoll.* ii. 16, e. Cyril. *Schol. de Incarn.* p. 782, d. Concil. *Eph.* pp. 1644, d. 1697, b. (Hard.) Damasc. *F. O.* iii. 3. p. 208. ed. Ven. Vid. Petav. *de Incarn.* iv. 15.

[6] Vid. *Or.* i. §§ 45, 46, ii. 65, note. Vid. also iv. 33. *Incarn. c. Arian.* 12. *contr. Apoll.* i. 17. ii. 6. 'Since God the Word willed to annul the passions, whose end is death, and His deathless nature was not capable of them . . . He is made flesh of the Virgin, in the way He knoweth, &c.' Procl. *ad Armen.* p. 616. also Leo. *Serm.* 22. pp. 69. 71. *Serm.* 26. p. 88. Nyssen *contr. Apoll.* t. 2 p. 696. Cyril. *Epp.* p. 138, 9. *in Joan.* p. 95. Chrysol. *Serm.* 148.

[7] ii. 69, n. 3, &c.

[8] θεοτόκου. *supr.* 14, n. 3. For 'mater Dei' vid. before S. Leo, Ambros. *de Virg.* ii. 7. Cassian. *Incarn.* ii. 5. vii. 25. Vincent. Lir. *Commonit.* 21. It is obvious that θεοτόκος, though framed as a test against Nestorians, was equally effective against Apollinarians [?] and Eutychians, who denied that our Lord had taken human flesh at all, as is observed by Facundus *Def. Trium. Cap.* i. 4. Cf. Cyril. *Epp.* pp. 106, 7. Yet these sects, as the Arians, maintained the term. vid. *supr. Or.* ii. 8, n. 5.

[9] ii. 59. n. 5.

[10] λογωθείσης τῆς σαρκός. This strong term is here applied to human nature generally; Damascene speaks of the λόγωσις of the flesh, but he means especially our Lord's flesh. *F. O.* iv. 18. p. 286. (Ed. Ven.) for the words θεοῦσθαι, &c. vid. *supr.* ii. 70, n. 1.

[1] 1 Pet. iv. 1.

[2] Cf. Chrysost. *in Joann. Hom.* 67. 1 and 2. Cyril *de Rect. Fid.* p. 18. 'As a man He doubts, as a man He is troubled; it is not His Power (virtus) that is troubled, not His Godhead, but His soul, &c.' Ambros. *de Fid.* ii. n. 56. vid. a beautiful passage in S. Basil's *Hom.* iv. 5. in which he insists on our Lord's having wept to shew us how to weep neither too much nor too little.

[3] Mat. xxvi. 39.

[4] βλαπτόμενος, § 31, n. 15.　　　　　　　[5] Cf. 33, n. 6.

[6] Vid. *Or.* ii. 56, n. 5. Cf. Cyril. *de Rect. Fid.* p. 18.

[7] 1 John iii. 5.

of servitude; for as the Lord, putting on the body, became man, so we men are deified by the Word as being taken to Him through His flesh, and henceforward inherit life everlasting.'

35. These points we have found it necessary first to examine, that, when we see Him doing or saying aught divinely through the instrument[1] of His own body, we may know that He so works, being God, and also, if we see Him speaking or suffering humanly, we may not be ignorant that He bore flesh and became man, and hence He so acts and so speaks. For if we recognise what is proper to each, and see and understand that both these things and those are done by One[2], we are right in our faith, and shall never stray. But if a man looking at what is done divinely by the Word, deny the body, or looking at what is proper to the body, deny the Word's presence in the flesh, or from what is human entertain low thoughts concerning the Word, such a one, as a Jewish vintner[3], mixing water with the wine, shall account the Cross an offence, or as a Gentile, will deem the preaching folly. This then is what happens to God's enemies the Arians; for looking at what is human in the Saviour, they have judged Him a creature. Therefore they ought, looking also at the divine works of the Word, to deny[4] the origination of His body, and henceforth to rank themselves with Manichees[5]. But for them, learn they, however tardily, that 'the Word became flesh;' and let us, retaining the general scope[6] of the faith, acknowledge that what they interpret ill, has a right interpretation[7].

CHAPTER XXVII.

TEXTS EXPLAINED; TENTHLY, MATTHEW xi. 27: JOHN iii. 35, &c.

These texts intended to preclude the Sabellian notion of the Son; they fall in with the Catholic doctrine concerning the Son; they are explained by 'so' in John v. 26. (Anticipation of the next chapter.) Again they are used with reference to our Lord's human nature; for our sake, that we might receive and not lose, as receiving in Him. And consistently with other parts of Scripture, which shew that He had the power, &c., before He received it. He was God and man, and His actions are often at once divine and human.

35 (*continued*). FOR, 'The Father loveth the Son, and hath given all things into His hand;' and, 'All things were given unto Me of My Father;' and, 'I can do nothing of Myself, but as I hear, I judge[8];' and the like passages do not shew that the Son once had not these prerogatives—(for had not He eternally what the Father has, who is the Only Word and Wisdom of the Father in essence, who also says, 'All that the Father hath are Mine[1],' and what are Mine, are the Father's? for if the things of the Father are the Son's and the Father hath them ever, it is plain that what the Son hath, being the Father's, were ever in the Son),—not then because once He had them not, did He say this, but because, whereas the Son hath eternally what He hath, yet He hath them from the Father.

36. For lest a man, perceiving that the Son has all that the Father hath, from the exact likeness and identity of that He hath, should wander into the irreligion of Sabellius, considering Him to be the Father, therefore He has said 'Was given unto Me,' and 'I received,' and 'Were delivered to Me[2],' only to shew that He is not the Father, but the Father's Word, and the Eternal Son, who because of His likeness to the Father, has eternally what He has from Him, and because He is the Son, has from the Father what He has eternally. Moreover that 'Was given' and 'Were delivered,' and the like, do not impair[3] the Godhead of the Son, but rather shew Him to be truly[4] Son, we may learn from the passages themselves. For if all things are delivered unto Him, first, He is other than that all which He has received; next, being Heir of all things, He alone is the Son and proper according to the Essence of the Father. For if He were one of all, then He were not 'heir of all[5],' but every one had received according as the Father willed and gave. But now, as receiving all things, He is other than them all, and alone proper to the Father. Moreover that 'Was given' and 'Were delivered' do not shew that once He had them not, we may conclude from a similar passage, and in like manner concerning them all; for the Saviour Himself says, 'As the Father hath life in Himself, so hath He given also to the Son to have life in Himself[6].' Now from the words 'Hath given,' He signifies that He is not the Father; but in saying 'so,' He shews the Son's natural likeness and propriety towards the Father. If then once the Father had not, plainly the Son once had not; for as

---

[1] Cf. 31, n. 10.
[2] Vid. *infr.* 39—41. and 56, n. 7. Cf. Procl. *ad Armen.* p. 615. Leo's Tome (*Ep.* 28, 3) also Hil. *Trin.* ix. 11 fin. 'Vagit infans, sed in cœlo est, &c.' ibid. x. 54. Ambros. *de Fid.* ii. 77. Erat vermis in cruce sed dimittebat peccata. Non habebat speciem, sed plenitudinem divinitatis, &c. Id. *Epist.* i. 46, n. 5. Theoph. *Ep. Pasch.* 6. ap. *Conc. Ephes.* p. 1404. Hard.
[3] Vid. Is. i. 22, LXX.; *Or.* ii. 80; *de Decr.* 10.
[4] Thus heresies are *partial* views of the truth, starting from some truth which they exaggerate, and disowning and protesting against other truth, which they fancy inconsistent with it. vid. *supr. Or.* i. 26, n. 2. [5] *De Syn.* 33; *Or.* i. 8.
[6] Cf. § 28, n. 11. [7] Cf. § 30, n. 7.

[8] John iii. 35; Matt. xi. 27; John v. 30.
[1] John xvi. 15; xvii. 10.
[2] John x. 18; Mat. xxviii. 18. [3] *Or.* i. 45; *ad Adelph.* 4
[4] *Or.* ii. 19, n. 3. [5] Heb. i. 2. [6] John v. 26.

the Father, 'so' also the Son has. But if this is irreligious to say, and religious on the contrary to say that the Father had ever, is it not unseemly in them when the Son says that, 'as' the Father has, 'so' also the Son has, to say that He has not 'so[7],' but otherwise? Rather then is the Word faithful, and all things which He says that He has received, He has always, yet has from the Father; and the Father indeed not from any, but the Son from the Father. For as in the instance of the radiance, if the radiance itself should say, 'All places the light hath given me to enlighten, and I do not enlighten from myself, but as the light wills,' yet, in saying this, it does not imply that it once had not, but it means, 'I am proper to the light, and all things of the light are mine;' so, and much more, must we understand in the instance of the Son. For the Father, having given all things to the Son, in the Son still[8] hath all things; and the Son having, still the Father hath them; for the Son's Godhead is the Father's Godhead, and thus the Father in the Son exercises His Providence[9] over all things.

37. And while such is the sense of expressions like these, those which speak humanly concerning the Saviour admit of a religious meaning also. For with this end have we examined them beforehand, that, if we should hear Him asking where Lazarus is laid[1], or when He asks on coming into the parts of Cæsarea, 'Whom do men say that I am?' or, 'How many loaves have ye?' and, 'What will ye that I shall do unto you[2]?' we may know, from what has been already said, the right[3]

sense of the passages, and may not stumble as Christ's enemies the Arians. First then we must put this question to the irreligious, why they consider Him ignorant? for one who asks, does not for certain ask from ignorance; but it is possible for one who knows, still to ask concerning what He knows. Thus John was aware that Christ, when asking, 'How many loaves have ye?' was not ignorant, for he says, 'And this He said to prove him, for He Himself knew what He would do[4].' But if He knew what He was doing, therefore not in ignorance, but with knowledge did He ask. From this instance we may understand similar ones; that, when the Lord asks, He does not ask in ignorance, where Lazarus lies, nor again, whom men do say that He is; but knowing the thing which He was asking, aware what He was about to do. And thus with ease is their clever point exploded; but if they still persist[5] on account of His asking, then they must be told that in the Godhead indeed ignorance is not, but to the flesh ignorance is proper, as has been said. And that this is really so, observe how the Lord who inquired where Lazarus lay, Himself said, when He was not on the spot but a great way off, 'Lazarus is dead[6],' and where he was dead; and how that He who is considered by them as ignorant, is He Himself who foreknew the reasonings of the disciples, and was aware of what was in the heart of each, and of 'what was in man,' and, what is greater, alone knows the Father and says, 'I in the Father and the Father in Me[7].'

38. Therefore this is plain to every one, that the flesh indeed is ignorant, but the Word Himself, considered as the Word, knows all things even before they come to be. For He did not, when He became man, cease to be God[1]; nor, whereas He is God does He shrink from what is man's; perish the thought; but rather, being God, He has taken to Him the flesh, and being in the flesh deifies the flesh. For as He asked questions in it, so also in it did He raise the dead; and He shewed to all that He who quickens the dead and recalls the soul, much more discerns the secret of all. And He knew where Lazarus lay, and yet He asked; for the All-holy Word of God, who endured all things for our sakes, did this, that so carrying our ignorance, He might vouchsafe to us the knowledge of His own only and true Father, and of Himself, sent because of us for the salvation of all, than which no grace could be greater.

---

7 Or. ii. 55, n. 8.

8 πάλιν. vid. Or. i. 15, n. 6. Thus iteration is not duplication in respect to God; though *how* this is, is the inscrutable Mystery of the Trinity in Unity. Nothing can be named which the Son is in Himself, as distinct from the Father; we are but told His *relation* towards the Father, and thus the sole meaning we are able to attach to Person is a relation of the Son towards the Father; and distinct from and beyond that relation, He is but the One God, who is also the Father. This sacred subject has been touched upon *supr. Or.* iii. 9, n. 8. In other words, there is an indestructible essential relation existing in the One Indivisible infinitely simple God, such as to constitute Him, viewed on each side of that relation (what in human language we call) Two (and in like manner Three), yet without the notion of number really coming in. When we speak of 'Person,' we mean nothing more than the One God in substance, viewed relatively to Him the One God, as viewed in that Correlative which we therefore call another Person. These various statements are not here intended to explain, but to bring home to the mind *what* it is which faith receives. We say 'Father, Son, and Spirit,' but when we would abstract a general idea of Them in order to number Them, our abstraction really does hardly more than carry us back to the One Substance. Such seems the meaning of such passages as Basil. *Ep.* 8, 2; *de Sp. S.* c. 18; Chrysost. *in Joan. Hom.* ii. 3 fin. 'In respect of the Adorable and most Royal Trinity, 'first' and 'second' have no place; for the Godhead is higher than number and times.' Isid. *Pel. Ep.* 3, 18. Eulog. *ap.* Phot. 230. p. 864. August. *in Joan.* 39, 3 and 4; *de Trin.* v. 10. 'Unity is not number, but is itself the principle of all things.' Ambros. *de Fid.* i. n. 19. 'A trine numeration then does not make number, which they rather run into, who make some difference between the Three.' Boeth. *Trin. unus Deus.* p. 959. The last remark is found in Naz. *Orat.* 31, 18. Many of these references are taken from Thomassin *de Trin.* 17.   9 §§ 11, n. 4, 15, n. 11.

1 Vid. *infr.* 46; John xi. 34.

2 Matt. xvi. 13; Mark vi. 38; Matt. xx. 32.   3 ii. 44, n. 1.

4 John vi. 6.

5 Petavius refers to this passage in proof that S. Athanasius did not in his real judgment consider our Lord ignorant, but went on to admit it in argument after having first given his own real opinion. vid. § 45, n. 2.   6 John xi. 14.

7 John ii. 25; xiv. 11.   1 Or. ii. 8, n. 3.

When then the Saviour uses the words which they allege in their defence, ' Power is given to Me,' and, 'Glorify Thy Son,' and Peter says, ' Power is given unto Him,' we understand all these passages in the same sense, that humanly because of the body He says all this. For though He had no need, nevertheless He is said to have received what He received humanly, that on the other hand, inasmuch as the Lord has received, and the grant is lodged with Him, the grace may remain sure. For while mere man receives, he is liable to lose again (as was shewn in the case of Adam, for he received and he lost [2]), but that the grace may be irrevocable, and may be kept sure [3] by men, therefore He Himself appropriates [4] the gift ; and He says that He has received power, as man, which He ever had as God, and He says, ' Glorify Me,' who glorifies others, to shew that He hath a flesh which has need of these things. Wherefore, when the flesh receives, since that which receives is in Him, and by taking it He hath become man, therefore He is said Himself to have received.

39. If then (as has many times been said) the Word has not become man, then ascribe to the Word, as you would have it, to receive, and to need glory, and to be ignorant ; but if He has become man (and He has become), and it is man's to receive, and to need, and to be ignorant, wherefore do we consider the Giver as receiver, and the Dispenser to others do we suspect to be in need, and divide the Word from the Father as imperfect and needy, while we strip human nature of grace ? For if the Word Himself, considered as Word, has received and been glorified for His own sake, and if He according to His Godhead is He who is hallowed and has risen again, what hope is there for men ? for they remain as they were, naked, and wretched, and dead, having no interest in the things given to the Son. Why too did the Word come among us, and become flesh ? if that He might receive these things, which He says that He has received, He was without them before that, and of necessity will rather owe thanks Himself to the body [1], because, when He came into it, then He receives these things from the Father, which He had not before His descent into the flesh. For on this shewing He seems rather to be Himself promoted because of the body [2], than the body promoted because of Him. But this notion is Judaic. But if that He might redeem mankind [3], the Word did come among us ; and that He might hallow and deify them, the Word became flesh (and for this He did become), who does not

see that it follows, that what He says that He received, when He became flesh, that He mentions, not for His own sake, but for the flesh ? for to it, in which He was speaking, pertained the gifts given through Him from the Father. But let us see what He asked, and what the things altogether were which He said that He had received, that in this way also they may be brought to feeling. He asked then glory, yet He had said, ' All things were delivered unto Me [4].' And after the resurrection, He says that He has received all power ; but even before that He had said, ' All things were delivered unto Me,' He was Lord of all, for ' all things were made by Him ; ' and ' there is One Lord by whom are all things [5].' And when He asked glory, He was as He is, the Lord of glory ; as Paul says, ' If they had known it, they would not have crucified the Lord of glory [6] ; ' for He had that glory which He asked when He said, ' the glory which I had with Thee before the world was [7].'

40. Also the power which He said He received after the resurrection, that He had before He received it, and before the resurrection. For He of Himself rebuked Satan, saying, ' Get thee behind Me, Satan [1] ; ' and to the disciples He gave the power against him, when on their return He said, ' I beheld Satan, as lightning, fall from heaven [2].' And again, that what He said that He had received, that He possessed before receiving it, appears from His driving away the demons, and from His unbinding what Satan had bound, as He did in the case of the daughter of Abraham ; and from His remitting sins, saying to the paralytic, and to the woman who washed His feet, ' Thy sins be forgiven thee [3] ; ' and from His both raising the dead, and repairing the first nature of the blind, granting to him to see. And all this He did, not waiting till He should receive, but being ' possessed of power [4].' From all this it is plain that what He had as Word, that when He had become man and was risen again, He says that He received humanly [5] ; that for His sake men might henceforward upon earth have power against demons, as having become partakers of a divine nature ; and in heaven, as being delivered from corruption, might reign everlastingly. Thus we must acknowledge this once for all, that nothing which He says that He received, did He receive as not possessing before ; for the Word, as being God, had them always ; but in these passages He is said humanly to have received, that, whereas the flesh received in Him, henceforth from it the

---

2 *Or.* ii. 68.   3 ii. 69, n. 3.   4 ἰδιοποιεῖται, cf. 33, n. 5.
1 *Infr.* 51.   2 *Or.* i. 38.
3 Redemption an *internal* work. vid. *supr.* ii. 55, n. 1.

4 Luke x. 22.   5 1 Cor. viii. 6.
6 1 Cor. ii. 8.   7 Joh. xvii. 5.   1 Luke iv. 8.
2 Luke x. 18, 19.   3 Vid. ib. xiii. 16 ; Matt. ix. 5 ; Luke
vii. 48.   4 Is. ix. 6, LXX.   5 *Or.* i. 45.

gift might abide [6] surely for us. For what is said by Peter, 'receiving from God honour and glory, Angels being made subject unto Him [7],' has this meaning. As He inquired humanly, and raised Lazarus divinely, so 'He received' is spoken of Him humanly, but the subjection of the Angels marks the Word's Godhead.

41. Cease then, O abhorred of God [8], and degrade not the Word; nor detract from His Godhead, which is the Father's [9], as though He needed or were ignorant; lest ye be casting your own arguments against the Christ, as the Jews who once stoned Him. For these belong not to the Word, as the Word; but are proper to men; and, as when He spat, and stretched forth the hand, and called Lazarus, we did not say that the triumphs were human, though they were done through the body, but were God's, so, on the other hand, though human things are ascribed to the Saviour in the Gospel, let us, considering the nature of what is said and that they are foreign to God, not impute them to the Word's Godhead, but to His manhood. For though 'the Word became flesh,' yet to the flesh are the affections proper; and though the flesh is possessed by God in the Word, yet to the Word belong the grace and the power. He did then the Father's works through the flesh; and as truly contrariwise were the affections of the flesh displayed in Him; for instance, He inquired and He raised Lazarus, He chid [10] His Mother, saying, 'My hour is not yet come,' and then at once He made the water wine. For He was Very God in the flesh, and He was true flesh in the Word. Therefore from His works He revealed both Himself as Son of God, and His own Father, and from the affections of the flesh He shewed that He bore a true body, and that it was His own.

CHAPTER XXVIII.

TEXTS EXPLAINED; ELEVENTHLY, MARK xiii. 32 AND LUKE ii. 52.

Arian explanation of the former text is against the *Regula Fidei*; and against the context. Our Lord said He was ignorant of the Day, by reason of His human nature. If the Holy Spirit knows the Day, therefore the Son knows; if the Son knows the

Father, therefore He knows the Day; if He has all that is the Father's, therefore knowledge of the Day; if in the Father, He knows the Day in the Father; if He created and upholds all things, He knows when they will cease to be. He knows not as Man, argued from Matt. xxiv. 42. As He asked about Lazarus's grave, &c., yet knew, so He knows; as S. Paul says, 'whether in the body I know not,' &c., yet knew, so He knows. He said He knew not for our profit, that we be not curious (as in Acts i. 7, where on the contrary He did not say He knew not). As the Almighty asks of Adam and of Cain, yet knew, so the Son knows [as God]. Again, He advanced in wisdom also as man, else He made Angels perfect before Himself. He advanced, in that the Godhead was manifested in Him more fully as time went on.

42. THESE things being so, come let us now examine into 'But of that day and that hour knoweth no man, neither the Angels of God, nor the Son [1];' for being in great ignorance as regards these words, and being stupified [2] about them, they think they have in them an important argument for their heresy. But I, when the heretics allege it and prepare themselves with it, see in them the giants [3] again fighting against God. For the Lord of heaven and earth, by whom all things were made, has to litigate before them about day and hour; and the Word who knows all things is accused by them of ignorance about a day; and the Son who knows the Father is said to be ignorant of an hour of a day; now what can be spoken more contrary to sense, or what madness can be likened to this? Through the Word all things have been made, times and seasons and night and day and the whole creation; and is the Framer of all said to be ignorant of His work? And the very context of the lection shews that the Son of God knows that hour and that day, though the Arians fall headlong in their ignorance. For after saying, 'nor the Son,' He relates to the disciples what precedes the day, saying, 'This and that shall be, and then the end.' But He who speaks of what precedes the day, knows certainly the day also, which shall be manifested subsequently to the things foretold. But if He had not known the hour, He had not signified the events before it, as not knowing when it should be. And as any one, who, by way of pointing out a house or city to those who were ignorant of it, gave an

---

[6] διαμείνῃ, *Or.* ii. 69, 3.   [7] 2 Pet. i. 17; 1 Pet. iii. 22.
[8] θεοστυγεῖς, *supr.* § 16, n. 7. *infr.* § 58, *de Mort. Ar.* 1. *In illud Omn.* 6.   [9] § 1, n. 11.
[10] John ii. 4. ἐπέπληττε; and so ἐπετίμησε, Chrysost. *in loc.* Joan. and Theophyl. ὡς δεσπότης ἐπιτιμᾷ, Theodor. *Eran.* ii. p. 106. ἐντρέπει, Anon. ap. Corder. *Cat. in loc.* μέμφεται, Alter Anon. ibid. ἐπιτιμᾷ οὐκ ἀτιμάζων ἀλλὰ διορθούμενος, Euthym. *in loc.* οὐκ ἐπέπληξεν, Pseudo-Justin. *Quæst. ad Orthod.* 136. It is remarkable that Athan. dwells on these words as implying our Lord's humanity (i.e. because Christ appeared to *decline* a miracle), when one reason assigned for them by the Fathers is that He wished, in the words τί μοι καί σοι, to remind S. Mary that He was the Son of God and must be 'about His Father's business.' 'Repellens ejus intempestivam festinationem,' Iren. *Hær.* iii. 16, n. 7. It is observable that ἐπιπλήττει and ἐπιτιμᾷ are the words used by Cyril, &c. (*infr.* § 54, note 4), for our Lord's treatment of His own sacred body. But they are very vague words, and have a strong meaning or not, as the case may be.

[1] Mark xiii. 32. S. Basil takes the words οὐδ' ὁ υἱός, εἰ μὴ ὁ πατήρ, to mean, 'nor does the Son know, except the Father knows,' or 'nor would the Son but for, &c.' or 'nor does the Son know, except as the Father knows.' 'The cause of the Son's knowing is from the Father.' *Ep.* 236, 2. S. Gregory alludes to the same interpretation, οὐδ' ὁ υἱὸς ἢ ὡς ὅτι ὁ πατήρ. 'Since the Father knows, therefore the Son.' Naz. *Orat.* 30, 16. S. Irenæus seems to adopt the same when he says, 'The Son was not ashamed to *refer* the knowledge of that day to the Father;' *Hær.* ii. 28, n. 6. as Naz, *supr.* uses the words ἐπὶ τὴν αἰτίαν ἀναφερέσθω. And so Photius distinctly, εἰς ἀρχὴν ἀναφέρεται. 'Not the Son, but the Father, that is, whence knowledge comes to the Son as from a fountain.' *Epp.* p. 342. ed. 1651.
[2] σκοτοδινιῶντες, *de Decr.* § 18 init.; *Or.* ii. 40, n. 5.
[3] γίγαντας θεομαχοῦντας, ii. 32, n. 4.

account of what comes before the house or city, and having described all, said, 'Then immediately comes the city or the house,' would know of course where the house or the city was (for had he not known, he had not described what comes before lest from ignorance he should throw his hearers far out of the way, or in speaking he should unawares go beyond the object), so the Lord saying what precedes that day and that hour, knows exactly, nor is ignorant, when the hour and the day are at hand.

43. Now why it was that, though He knew, He did not tell His disciples plainly at that time, no one may be curious[1] where He has been silent; for 'Who hath known the mind of the Lord, or who hath been His counsellor[2]?' but why, though He knew, He said, 'no, not the Son knows,' this I think none of the faithful is ignorant, viz. that He made this as those other declarations as man by reason of the flesh. For this as before is not the Word's deficiency[3], but of that human nature[4] whose property it is to be ignorant. And this again will be well seen by honestly examining into the occasion, when and to whom the Saviour spoke thus. Not then when the heaven was made by Him, nor when He was with the Father Himself, the Word 'disposing all things[5],' nor before He became man did He say it, but when 'the Word became flesh[6].' On this account it is reasonable to ascribe to His manhood everything which, after He became man, He speaks humanly. For it is proper to the Word to know what was made, nor be ignorant either of the beginning or of the end of these (for the works are His), and He knows how many things He wrought, and the limit of their consistence. And knowing of each the beginning and the end, He knows surely the general and common end of all. Certainly when He says in the Gospel concerning Himself in His human character, 'Father, the hour is come, glorify Thy Son[7],' it is plain that He knows also the hour of the end of all things, as the Word, though as man He is ignorant of it, for ignorance is proper to man[8], and especially

ignorance of these things. Moreover this is proper to the Saviour's love of man; for since He was made man, He is not ashamed, because of the flesh which is ignorant[9], to say 'I know not,' that He may shew that knowing as God, He is but ignorant according to the flesh[10]. And therefore He said not, 'no, not the Son of God knows,' lest the Godhead should seem ignorant, but simply, 'no, not the Son,' that the ignorance might be the Son's as born from among men.

44. On this account, He alludes to the Angels, but He did not go further and say, 'not the Holy Ghost;' but He was silent, with a double intimation; first that if the Spirit knew, much more must the Word know, considered as the Word, from whom the Spirit receives[1]; and next by His silence about the Spirit, He made it clear, that He said of His human ministry, 'no, not the Son.' And a proof of it is this; that, when He had spoken humanly[2] 'No, not the Son knows,'

---

the Word, it never was ignorant really, but knew all things which human soul can know. vid. Eulog. *ap. Phot.* 230. p. 884. As Pope Gregory expresses it, 'Novit in natura, non ex natura humanitatis.' *Epp.* x. 39. However, this view of the sacred subject was received by the Church only after S. Athanasius's day, and it cannot be denied that others of the most eminent Fathers seem to impute ignorance to our Lord as man, as Athan. in this passage. Of course it is not meant that our Lord's soul has the same perfect knowledge as He has as God. This was the assertion of a General of the Hermits of S. Austin at the time of the Council of Basel, when the proposition was formally condemned, animam Christi Deum videre tam clare et intense quam clare et intense Deus videt seipsum. vid. Berti *Opp.* t. 3. p. 42. Yet Fulgentius had said, 'I think that in no respect was full knowledge of the Godhead wanting to that Soul, whose Person is one with the Word: whom Wisdom so assumed that it is itself that same Wisdom.' *ad Ferrand.* iii. p. 223. ed. 1639. Yet, *ad Trasmund.* i. 7. he speaks of ignorance attaching to our Lord's human nature.
9 Cf. § 48.
10 And so Athan. *ad Serap.* ii. 9. S. Basil on the question being asked him by S. Amphilochius, says that he shall give him the answer he had 'heard from a boy from the fathers,' but which was more fitted for pious Christians than for cavillers, and that is, that 'our Lord says many things to men in His human aspect; as "Give me to drink,"... yet He who asked was not flesh without a soul, but Godhead using flesh which had one.' *Ep.* 236, 1. He goes on to suggest another explanation which has been mentioned § 42, note 1. Cf. Cyril *Trin.* pp. 623, 4. vid. also *Thes.* p. 220. 'As he submitted as man to hunger and thirst, so .... to be ignorant.' p. 221. vid. also Greg. Naz. *Orat.* 30, 15. Theodoret expresses the same opinion very strongly, speaking of a gradual revelation to the manhood from the Godhead, but in an argument where it was to his point to do so; in *Anath.* 4. t. v. p. 23. ed. Schulze. Theodore of Mopsuestia also speaks of a revelation made by the Word. ap. Leont. *c. Nest.* (Canis. i. p. 579.)
1 *Or.* i. 47; *Serap.* i. 20 fin.
2 Leporius, in his Retractation, which S. Augustine subscribed, writes, 'That I may in this respect also leave nothing to be cause of suspicion to any one, I then said, nay I answered when it was put to me, that our Lord Jesus Christ was ignorant as He was man, (secundum hominem). But now not only do I not presume to say so, but I even anathematize my former opinion expressed on this point,' *ap. Sirm.* t. i. p. 210. A subdivision also of the Eutychians were called by the name of Agnoetæ from their holding that our Lord was ignorant of the day of judgment. 'They said,' says Leontius, 'that He was ignorant of it, as we say that He underwent toil.' *de Sect.* 5. circ. fin. Felix of Urgela held the same doctrine according to Agobard's testimony, see § 46, n. 2. Montfaucon observes on the text, that the assertion of our Lord's ignorance 'seems to have been condemned in no one in ancient times, unless joined to other error.' And Petavius, after drawing out the authorities for and against it, says, 'Of these two opinions, the latter, which is now received both by custom and by the agreement of divines, is deservedly preferred to the former. For it is more agreeable to Christ's dignity, and more befitting His character and office of Mediator and Head, that is, Fountain of all grace and wisdom, and moreover of Judge, who is concerned in knowing the time fixed for exercising that function.

---

1 Cf. § 18, n. 3.   * Rom. xi. 34.   3 *Or.* i. 45.
4 Cf. ii. 45, n. 2.   5 Prov. viii. 27, LXX.
6 John i. 14.   7 Ib. xvii. 1.
8 Though our Lord, as having two natures, had a human as well as a divine knowledge, and though that human knowledge was not only limited because human, but liable to ignorance in matters in which greater knowledge was possible; yet it is the doctrine of the [later] Church, that *in fact* He was not ignorant even in His human nature, according to its capacity, since it was from the first taken out of its original and natural condition, and 'deified' by its union with the Word. As then (*supr.* ii. 45, note 1) His manhood was created, yet He may not be called a creature even in His manhood, and as (*supr.* ii. 14, note 5) His flesh was in its abstract nature a servant, yet He is not a servant in fact, even as regards the flesh; so, though He took on Him a soul which left to itself had been partially ignorant, as other human souls, yet as ever enjoying the beatific vision from its oneness with

VOL. IV.   E e

He yet shews that divinely He knew all things. For that Son whom He declares not to know the day, Him He declares to know the Father; for 'No one,' He says, 'knoweth the Father save the Son[3].' And all men but the Arians would join in confessing, that He who knows the Father, much more knows the whole of the creation; and in that whole, its end. And if already the day and the hour be determined by the Father, it is plain that through the Son are they determined, and He knows Himself what through Him has been determined[4], for there is nothing but has come to be and has been determined through the Son. Therefore He, being the Framer of the universe, knows of what nature, and of what magnitude, and with what limits, the Father has willed it to be made; and in the how much and how far is included its period. And again, if all that is the Father's, is the Son's (and this He Himself has[5] said), and it is the Father's attribute to know the day, it is plain that the Son too knows it, having this proper to Him from the Father. And again, if the Son be in the Father and the Father in the Son, and the Father knows the day and the hour, it is clear that the Son, being in the Father and knowing the things of the Father, knows Himself also the day and the hour. And if the Son is also the Father's Very Image, and the Father knows the day and the hour, it is plain that the Son has this likeness[6] also to the Father of knowing them. And it is not wonderful if He, through whom all things were made, and in whom the universe consists, Himself knows what has been brought to be, and when the end will be of each and of all together; rather is it wonderful that this audacity, suitable as it is to the madness of the Ario-maniacs, should have forced us to have recourse to so long a defence. For ranking the Son of God, the Eternal Word, among things originate, they are not far from venturing to maintain that the Father Himself is second to the creation; for if He who knows the Father knows not the day nor the hour, I fear lest the knowledge of the creation, or rather of the lower portion of it, be greater, as they in their madness would say, than knowledge concerning the Father.

45. But for them, when they thus blaspheme the Spirit, they must expect no remission ever of such irreligion, as the Lord has said[1]; but

let us, who love Christ and bear Christ within us, know that the Word, not as ignorant, considered as Word, has said 'I know not,' for He knows, but as shewing His manhood[2], in that to be ignorant is proper to man, and that He had put on flesh that was ignorant[3], being in which, He said according to the flesh, 'I know not.' And for this reason, after saying, 'No not the Son knows,' and mentioning the ignorance of the men in Noah's day, immediately He added, 'Watch therefore, for ye know not in what hour your Lord doth come,' and again, 'In such an hour as ye think not, the Son of man cometh[4].' For I too, having become as you for you, said 'no, not the Son.' For, had He been ignorant divinely, He must have said, 'Watch therefore, for I know not,' and, 'In an hour when I think not;' but in fact this hath He not said; but by saying 'Ye know not' and 'When ye think not,' He has signified that it belongs to man to be ignorant; for whose sake He too having a flesh like theirs and having become man, said 'No, not the Son knows,' for He knew not in flesh, though knowing as Word. And again the

<hr>

[2] It is a question to be decided, whether our Lord speaks of actual ignorance in His human Mind, or of the natural ignorance of that Mind considered as human; ignorance *in* or *ex* natura; or, which comes to the same thing, whether He spoke of a real ignorance, or of an economical or professed ignorance, in a certain view of His incarnation or office, as when He asked, 'How many loaves have ye?' when 'He Himself knew what He would do,' or as He is called sin, though sinless. Thus it has been noticed, *supr.* ii. 55, n. 7, that Ath. seems to make His infirmities altogether only imputative, not real, as if shewing that the subject had not in his day been thoroughly worked out. In like manner S. Hilary, who, if the passage be genuine, states so clearly our Lord's ignorance, *de Trin.* ix. fin. yet, as Petavius observes, seems elsewhere to deny to Him those very affections of the flesh to which he has there paralleled it. And this view of Athan.'s meaning is favoured by the turn of his expressions. He says such a defect belongs to '*that human nature* whose property it is to be ignorant;' § 43. that '*since* He was made man, He is not *ashamed*, because of the flesh which is ignorant, *to say*, "I know not;"' ibid. and, as here, that 'as *shewing* His manhood, in that to be ignorant is *proper* to man, and that He had *put on* a flesh *that was ignorant*, being in which, He *said* according to the flesh, "I know not;"' 'that He might *shew* that as man He knows not;' § 46. that '*as* man' (i.e. on the *ground* of being man, not in the *capacity* of man), 'He knows not;' ibid. and that, 'He *asks* about Lazarus humanly,' even when 'He was *on His way* to raise him,' which implied surely knowledge in His human nature. The reference to the parallel of S. Paul's professed ignorance when he really knew, § 47. leads us to the same suspicion. And so 'for *our profit* as I think, did He this.' §§ 48—50. The natural want of precision on such questions in the early ages was shewn or fostered by such words as οἰκονομικῶς, which, in respect of this very text, is used by S. Basil to denote both our Lord's Incarnation, *Ep.* 236, 1 fin. and His gracious accommodation of Himself and His truth, *Ep.* 8, 6. and with the like variety of meaning, with reference to the same text, by Cyril. *Trin.* p. 623. and *Thesaur.* p. 224. (And the word *dispensatio* in like manner, Ben. note on *Hil.* x. 8.) In the latter *Ep.* S. Basil suggests that our Lord 'economizes by a feigned ignorance.' § 6. And S. Cyril. *Thesaur.* p. 224. And even in *de Trin.* vi. he seems to recognise the distinction laid down just now between the natural and actual state of our Lord's humanity; and so Hilary, *Trin.* ix. 62. And he gives reasons why He professed ignorance, n. 67. viz. as S. Austin words it, Christum se dixisse nescientem, in quo alios facit occultando nescientes. *Ep.* 180, 3. S. Austin follows him, saying, Hoc nescit quod nescienter facit. *Trin.* i. 23. Pope Gregory says that the text 'is most certainly to be referred to the Son not as He is Head, but as to His body which we are.' *Ep* x. 39. And S. Ambrose *de fid.* v. 222. And so Cæsarius, Qu. 20. and Photius *Epp.* p. 366. Chrysost. in Matt. *Hom.* 77, 3. Theodoret, however, but in controversy, is very severe on the principle of Economy. 'If He knew the day, and wishing to conceal it, said He was ignorant, see what a blasphemy is the result. Truth tells an untruth.' l. c. pp. 23, 4.   3 § 48.   4 Matt. xxiv. 42, 44.

<hr>

In consequence, the former opinion, though formerly it received the countenance of some men of high eminence, was afterwards marked as a heresy.' *Incarn.* xi. 1. § 15.
3 Mat. xi. 27.   4 *Or.* ii. 41, iii. 9, 46.   5 John xvi. 15.
6 Basil. *Ep.* 236, 1. Cyril. *Thes.* p. 220. Ambros. *de fid.* v. 197. Hence the force of the word 'living' commonly joined to such words as εἴκων, σφραγίς, βουλή. ἐνέργεια, when speaking of our Lord, e.g. Naz. *Orat.* 30, 20, c. Vid. § 63, *fin.* note.
1 *Or.* i. 50, n. 7.

example from Noah exposes the shamelessness of Christ's enemies; for there too He said, not, 'I knew not,' but 'They knew not until the flood came [5].' For men did not know, but He who brought the flood (and it was the Saviour Himself) knew the day and the hour in which He opened the cataracts of heaven, and broke up the great deep, and said to Noah, 'Come thou and all thy house into the ark [6].' For were He ignorant, He had not foretold to Noah, 'Yet seven days and I will bring a flood upon the earth.' But if in describing the day He makes use of the parallel of Noah's time, and He did know the day of the flood, therefore He knows also the day of His own coming.

46. Moreover, after narrating the parable of the Virgins, again He shews more clearly who they are who are ignorant of the day and the hour, saying, 'Watch therefore, for ye know neither the day nor the hour [1].' He who said shortly before, 'No one knoweth, no not the Son,' now says not 'I know not,' but 'ye know not.' In like manner then, when His disciples asked about the end, suitably said He then, 'no, nor the Son,' according to the flesh because of the body; that He might shew that, as man, He knows not; for ignorance is proper to man [2]. If however He is the Word, if it is He who is to come, He to be Judge, He to be the Bridegroom, He knoweth when and in what hour He cometh, and when He is to say, 'Awake, thou that sleepest, and arise from the dead, and Christ shall give thee light [3].' For as, on becoming man, He hungers and thirsts and suffers with men, so with men, as man He knows not; though divinely, being in the Father Word and Wisdom, He knows, and there is nothing which He knows not. In like manner also about Lazarus [4] He asks humanly, who was on His way to raise him, and knew whence He should recall Lazarus's soul; and it was a greater thing to know where the soul was, than to know where the body lay; but He asked humanly, that He might raise divinely. So too He asks of the disciples, on coming into the parts of Cæsarea,

though knowing even before Peter made answer. For if the Father revealed to Peter the answer to the Lord's question, it is plain that through the Son [5] was the revelation, for 'No one knoweth the Son,' saith He, 'save the Father, neither the Father save the Son, and he to whomsoever the Son will reveal Him [6].' But if through the Son is revealed the knowledge both of the Father and the Son, there is no room for doubting that the Lord who asked, having first revealed it to Peter from the Father, next asked humanly; in order to shew, that asking after the flesh, He knew divinely what Peter was about to say. The Son then knew, as knowing all things, and knowing His own Father, than which knowledge nothing can be greater or more perfect.

47. This is sufficient to confute them; but to shew still further that they are hostile to the truth and Christ's enemies, I could wish to ask them a question. The Apostle in the Second Epistle to the Corinthians writes, 'I knew a man in Christ, above fourteen years ago, whether in the body I do not know, or whether out of the body I do not know; God knoweth [1].' What now say ye? Knew the Apostle what had happened to him in the vision, though he says 'I know not,' or knew he not? If he knew not, see to it, lest, being familiar with error, ye err in the trespass [2] of the Phrygians [3], who say that the Prophets and the other ministers of the Word know neither what they do nor concerning what they announce. But if he knew when he said 'I know not,' for he had Christ within him revealing to him all things, is not the heart of God's enemies indeed perverted and 'self-condemned?' for when the Apostle says, 'I know not,' they say that he knows; but when the Lord says, 'I know not,' they say that He does not know. For if since Christ was within him, Paul knew that of which he says, 'I know not,' does not much more Christ Himself know, though He say, 'I know not?' The Apostle then, the Lord revealing it to him, knew what happened to him; for on this account he says, 'I knew a man in Christ;' and knowing the man, he knew also how the man was caught away. Thus Elisha, who beheld Elijah, knew

---

5 Matt. xxiv. 39.   6 Gen. vii. 1.   1 Matt. xxv. 13.
2 The mode in which Athan. here expresses himself, is as if he did not ascribe ignorance literally, but apparent ignorance, to our Lord's soul, vid. *supr.* 45. n. 2 ; not certainly in the broad sense in which heretics have done so. As Leontius, e.g. reports of Theodore of Mopsuestia, that he considered Christ 'to be ignorant so far, as not to know, when He was tempted, who tempted Him ;' *contr. Nest.* iii. (Canis. t. i. p. 579.) and Agobard of Felix the Adoptionist that he held 'Our Lord Jesus Christ according to the flesh *truly* to have been ignorant of the sepulchre of Lazarus, when He said to his sisters, 'Where have ye laid him?' and was *truly* ignorant of the day of judgment ; and was *truly* ignorant what the two disciples were saying, as they walked by the way, of what had been done at Jerusalem ; and was *truly* ignorant whether He was more loved by Peter than by the other disciples, when He said, 'Simon Peter, Lovest thou Me more than these?' *B. P.* t. 9. p. 1177. [Cf. *Prolegg.* ch. iv. § 5.]
3 Eph. v. 14.   4 § 37.

5 Cf. 44, n. 4.   6 Luke x. 22.
1 2 Cor. xii. 2. S. Augustine understands the passage differently, i.e. that S. Paul really did not know whether or not he was in the body. Gen. *ad lit.* xii. 14.
2 παρανομίαν, § 2, n 5.
3 Cf. Jerome, 'He speaks not in ecstasy, as Montanus, Prisca, and Maximilla rave;' *Præf. in Naum.* In like manner Tertullian speaks of 'amentia, as the spiritalis vis qua constat prophetia ;' *de Anim.* 21. Cf. Eusebius, *Hist.* v. 16. Epiphanius too, noticing the failure of Maximilla's prophecies, says, 'Whatever the prophets have said, they spoke with understanding, following the sense.' *Hær.* 48. p. 403. In the *de Syn.* 4. Athan. speaks of the Montanists as making a fresh beginning of Christianity ; i.e. they were the first heretics who professed to prophesy and to introduce a new or additional revelation.

also how he was taken up; but though knowing, yet when the sons of the Prophets thought that Elijah was cast upon one of the mountains by the Spirit, he knowing from the first what he had seen, tried to persuade them; but when they urged it, he was silent, and suffered them to go after him. Did he then not know, because he was silent? he knew indeed, but as if not knowing, he suffered them, that they being convinced, might no more doubt about the taking up of Elijah. Therefore much more Paul, himself being the person caught away, knew also how he was caught; for Elijah knew; and had any one asked, he would have said how. And yet Paul says 'I know not,' for these two reasons, as I think at least; one, as he has said himself, lest because of the abundance of the revelations any one should think of him beyond what he saw; the other, because, our Saviour having said 'I know not,' it became him also to say 'I know not,' lest the servant should appear above his Lord, and the disciple above his Master.

48. Therefore He who gave to Paul to know, much rather knew Himself; for since He spoke of the antecedents of the day, He also knew, as I said before, when the Day and when the Hour, and yet though knowing, He says, 'No, not the Son knoweth.' Why then said He at that time 'I know not,' what He, as Lord[1], knew? as we may by searching conjecture, for our profit[2], as I think at least, did He this; and may He grant to what we are now proposing a true meaning! On both sides did the Saviour secure our advantage; for He has made known what comes before the end, that, as He said Himself, we might not be startled nor scared, when they happen, but from them may expect the end after them. And concerning the day and the hour He was not willing to say according to His divine nature, 'I know,' but after the flesh, 'I know not,' for the sake of the flesh which was ignorant[3], as I have said before; lest they should ask Him further, and then either He should have to pain the disciples by not speaking, or by speaking might act to the prejudice of them and us all. For whatever He does, that altogether He does for our sakes, since also for us 'the Word became flesh.' For us therefore He said 'No, not the Son knoweth;' and neither was He untrue in thus saying (for He said humanly, as man, 'I know not'), nor did He suffer the disciples to force Him to speak, for by saying 'I know

not' He stopped their inquiries. And so in the Acts of the Apostles it is written, when He went upon the Angels, ascending as man, and carrying up to heaven the flesh which He bore, on the disciples seeing this, and again asking, 'When shall the end be, and when wilt Thou be present?' He said to them more clearly, 'It is not for you to know the times or the seasons which the Father hath put in His own power[4].' And He did not then say, 'No, not the Son,' as He said before humanly, but, 'It is not for you to know.' For now the flesh had risen and put off its mortality and been deified; and no longer did it become Him to answer after the flesh when He was going into the heavens; but henceforth to teach after a divine manner, 'It is not for you to know times or seasons which the Father hath put in His own power; but ye shall receive Power[5].' And what is that Power of the Father but the Son? for Christ is 'God's Power and God's Wisdom.'

49. The Son then did know, as being the Word; for He implied this in what He said,—'I know, but it is not for you to know; for it was for your sakes that sitting also on the mount I said according to the flesh, 'No, not the Son knoweth,' for the profit of you and all. For it is profitable to you to hear so much both of the Angels and of the Son, because of the deceivers which shall be afterwards; that though demons should be transfigured as Angels, and should attempt to speak concerning the end, you should not believe, since they are ignorant; and that, if Antichrist too, disguising himself, should say, 'I am Christ,' and should try in his turn to speak of that day and end, to deceive the hearers, ye, having these words from Me, 'No, not the Son,' may disbelieve him also. And further, not to know when the end is, or when the day of the end, is expedient for man, lest knowing, they might become negligent of the time between, awaiting the days near the end; for they will argue that then only must they attend to themselves[1]. Therefore also has He been silent of the time when each shall die, lest men, being elated on the ground of knowledge, should forthwith neglect themselves for the greater part of their time. Both then, the end of all things and the limit of each of us hath the Word concealed from us (for in the end of all is the end of each, and in the end of each the end of all is comprehended), that, whereas it is uncertain and

[1] δεσπότης, § 56, 6.
[2] This expression, which repeatedly occurs in this and the following sections, surely implies that there was something economical in our Lord's profession of ignorance. He said with a purpose, not as a mere plain fact or doctrine. [But see Prolegg. ch. iv. § 5.]   [3] 43, n. 9; 45, n. 3.

[4] Acts i. 7.
[5] Vid. Basil. Ep. 8, 6. Cyril. Thes. p. 222. Ambros. de fid. v. 212. Chrysost. and Hieron. in loc. Matt.
[1] Vid. Hilar. in Matt. Comment. 26, 4; de Trin. ix. 67; Ambros. de Fid. v. c. 17. Isidor. Pelus. Epp. i. 117. Chrysost. in Matt. Hom. 77, 2 and 3.

always in prospect, we may advance day by day as if summoned, reaching forward to the things before us and forgetting the things behind[2]. For who, knowing the day of the end, would not be dilatory with the interval? but, if ignorant, would not be ready day by day? It was on this account that the Saviour added, 'Watch therefore, for ye know not what hour your Lord doth come;' and, 'In such an hour as ye think not, the Son of man cometh[3].' For the advantage then which comes of ignorance has He said this; for in saying it, He wishes that we should always be prepared; 'for you,' He says, 'know not; but I, the Lord, know when I come, though the Arians do not wait for Me, who am the Word of the Father.'

50. The Lord then, knowing what is good for us beyond ourselves, thus secured the disciples; and they, being thus taught, set right those of Thessalonica[4] when likely on this point to run into error. However, since Christ's enemies do not yield even to these considerations, I wish, though knowing that they have a heart harder than Pharaoh, to ask them again concerning this. In Paradise God asks, 'Adam, where art Thou[5]?' and He inquires of Cain also, 'Where is Abel thy brother[6]?' What then say you to this? for if you think Him ignorant and therefore to have asked, you are already of the party of the Manichees, for this is their bold thought; but if, fearing the open name, ye force yourselves to say, that He asks knowing, what is there extravagant or strange in the doctrine, that ye should thus fall, on finding that the Son, in whom God then inquired, that same Son who now is clad in flesh, inquires of the disciples as man? unless forsooth, having become Manichees, you are willing to blame[7] the question then put to Adam and all that you may give full play[8] to your perverseness. For being exposed on all sides, you still make a whispering[9] from the words of Luke, which are rightly said, but ill understood by you.

And what this is, we must state, that so also their corrupt[10] meaning may be shewn.

51. Now Luke says, 'And Jesus advanced in wisdom and stature, and in grace with God and man[1].' This then is the passage, and since they stumble in it, we are compelled to ask them, like the Pharisees and the Sadducees, of the person concerning whom Luke speaks. And the case stands thus. Is Jesus Christ man, as all other men, or is He God bearing flesh? If then He is an ordinary[2] man as the rest, then let Him, as a man, advance; this however is the sentiment of the Samosatene, which virtually indeed you entertain also, though in name you deny it because of men. But if He be God bearing flesh, as He truly is, and 'the Word became flesh,' and being God descended upon earth, what advance had He who existed equal to God? or how had the Son increase, being ever in the Father? For if He who was ever in the Father, advanced, what, I ask, is there beyond the Father from which His advance might be made? Next it is suitable here to repeat what was said upon the point of His receiving and being glorified. If He advanced[3] when He became man, it is plain that, before He became man, He was imperfect; and rather the flesh became to Him a cause of perfection, than He to the flesh. And again, if, as being the Word, He advances, what has He more to become than Word and Wisdom and Son and God's Power? For the Word is all these, of which if one can anyhow partake as it were one ray, such a man becomes all-perfect among men, and equal to Angels. For Angels, and Archangels, and Dominions, and all the Powers, and Thrones, as partaking the Word, behold always the face of His Father. How then does He who to others supplies perfection, Himself advance later than they? For Angels even ministered to His human birth, and the passage from Luke comes later than the ministration of the Angels. How then at all can it even come into thought of man? or how did Wisdom advance in wisdom? or how did He who to others gives grace (as Paul says in every Epistle, knowing that through Him grace is given, 'The grace of our Lord Jesus Christ be with you all'), how did He advance in grace? for either let them say that the Apostle is untrue, and presume to say that the Son is not Wisdom, or else if He is Wisdom as Solomon said, and if Paul wrote, 'Christ God's Power and God's Wisdom,' of what advance did Wisdom admit further?

52. For men, creatures as they are, are

[2] Vid. Phil. iii. 13.   [3] Matt. xxiv. 42; Luke xii. 40.
[4] Vid. 2 Thess. ii. 1, 2.
[5] Gen. iii. 9; iv. 9. This seems taken from Origen, *in Matt.* t. 10. § 14. vid. also Pope Gregory and Chrysost. *infr.*
[6] S. Chrysostom, S. Ambrose, and Pope Gregory, in addition to the instances in the text, refer to 'I will go down now, and *see whether* they have done, &c., and if not, I will *know*.' Gen. xviii. 21. 'The Lord came down *to see* the city and the tower, &c.' Gen. xi. 5. 'God looked down from heaven upon the children of men *to see*, &c.' Ps. liii. 3. '*It may be* they will reverence My Son.' Matt. xxi. 37; Luke xx. 13. 'Seeing a fig-tree afar off, having leaves, He came, *if haply* He *might find*, &c.' Mark xi. 13. 'Simon, lovest thou Me?' John xxi. 15. vid. Ambros. *de Fid.* v. c. 17. Chrys. *in Matt. Hom.* 77, 3. Greg. *Epp.* x. 39. Vid. also the instances, *supr.* § 37. Other passages may be added, such as Gen xxii. 12. vid. Berti *Opp.* t. 3. p. 42. But the difficulty of the passage lies in its signifying that there is a sense in which the Father knows what the Son knows not.
[7] *Or.* i. 8, n. 2.   [8] νεανιεύησθε, vid. *Decr.*18 init. *de Fug.* 4. b.   [9] τονθορύζετε, vid. *Decr.* 16.

[10] διεφθαρμένη, § 58 fin.   [1] Luke ii. 52.   [2] § 32, n. 7.
[3] *De Syn.* 24, n. 9, vid. *supr.* § 39; *Orat.* iv. 11.

capable in a certain way of reaching forward and advancing in virtue[1]. Enoch, for instance, was thus translated, and Moses increased and was perfected; and Isaac 'by advancing became great[2];' and the Apostle said that he 'reached forth[3]' day by day to what was before him. For each had room for advancing, looking to the step before him. But the Son of God, who is One and Only, what room had He for reaching forward? for all things advance by looking at Him; and He, being One and Only, is in the Only Father, from whom again He does not reach forward, but in Him abideth ever[3a]. To men then belongs advance; but the Son of God, since He could not advance, being perfect in the Father, humbled Himself for us, that in His humbling we on the other hand might be able to increase. And our increase is no other than the renouncing things sensible, and coming to the Word Himself; since His humbling is nothing else than His taking our flesh. It was not then the Word, considered as the Word, who advanced; who is perfect from the perfect Father[4], who needs nothing, nay brings forward others to an advance; but humanly is He here also said to advance, since advance belongs to man[5]. Hence the Evangelist, speaking with cautious exactness[6], has mentioned stature in the advance; but being Word and God He is not measured by stature, which belongs to bodies. Of the body then is the advance; for, it advancing, in it advanced also the manifestation[7] of the Godhead to those who saw it. And, as the Godhead was more and more revealed, by so much more did His grace as man increase before all men. For as a child He was carried to the Temple; and when He became a boy, He remained there, and questioned the priests about the Law. And by degrees His body increasing, and the Word manifesting Himself[8] in it, He is confessed henceforth by Peter first, then also by all, 'Truly this is the Son of God[9];' however wilfully the Jews, both the ancient and these modern[10], shut fast their eyes, lest they see that to advance in wisdom is not the advance of Wisdom Itself, but rather the manhood's advance in It. For 'Jesus advanced in wisdom and grace;' and, if we may speak what is explanatory as well as true, He advanced in Himself; for 'Wisdom builded herself an house,' and in herself she gave the house advancement.

53. (What moreover is this advance that is spoken of, but, as I said before, the deifying and grace imparted from Wisdom to men, sin being obliterated in them and their inward corruption, according to their likeness and relationship to the flesh of the Word?) For thus, the body increasing in stature, there developed in it the manifestation of the Godhead also, and to all was it displayed that the body was God's Temple[1], and that God was in the body. And if they urge, that 'The Word become flesh' is called Jesus, and refer to Him the term 'advanced,' they must be told that neither does this impair[2] the Father's Light[3], which is the Son, but that it still shews that the Word has become man, and bore true flesh. And as we said[4] that He suffered in the flesh, and hungered in the flesh, and was fatigued in the flesh, so also reasonably may He be said to have advanced in the flesh; for neither did the advance, such as we have described it, take place with the Word external to the flesh, for in Him was the flesh which advanced and His is it called, and that as before, that man's advance might abide[5] and fail not, because of the Word which is with it. Neither then was the advance the Word's, nor was the flesh Wisdom, but the flesh became the body of Wisdom[6]. Therefore, as we have already said, not Wisdom, as Wisdom, advanced in respect of Itself; but the manhood advanced in Wisdom, transcending by degrees human nature, and being deified, and becoming and appearing to all as the organ[7] of Wisdom for the operation and the shining forth[8] of the Godhead. Wherefore neither said he, 'The Word advanced,' but Jesus, by which Name the Lord was called when He became man; so that the advance is of the human nature in such wise as we explained above.

CHAPTER XXIX.

TEXTS EXPLAINED; TWELFTHLY, MATTHEW. xxvi. 39; JOHN xii. 27, &c.

Arian inferences are against the *Regula Fidei*, as before.

---

[1] It is the doctrine of the [medieval and modern] Church that Christ, as man, was perfect in knowledge from the first, as if ignorance were hardly separable from sin, and were the direct consequence or accompaniment of original sin. Cf. Aug. *de Pecc. Mer.* ii. 48. As to the limits of Christ's perfect knowledge as man, Petavius observes, that we must consider 'that the soul of Christ knew all things that are or ever will be or ever have been, but not what are only *in posse*, not in fact.' *Incarn.* xi. 3, 6.
[2] Vid. Gen. xxvi. 13.   [3] Phil. iii. 13.   [3a] § 4, n. 10.
[4] *Or.* ii. 36, n. 4.   [5] Vid. Serm. *Maj. de Fid.* 18.
[6] *Or.* ii. 12, n. 4.   [7] § 31, n. 10.
[8] It is remarkable, considering the tone of his statements in the present chapter, that here and in what follows Athan. should resolve our Lord's advance in wisdom merely to its gradual manifestation through the flesh [but he says expressly 'the Manhood advanced in wisdom!'] and it increases the proof that his statements are not to be taken in the letter, and as if fully brought out and settled. Naz. says the same, *Ep. ad Cled.* 101. p. 86. which is the more remarkable since he is chiefly writing against the Apollinarians, who considered a φανέρωσις the great end of our Lord's coming; and Cyril. *c. Nest.* iii. p. 87. Theod. *Hor.* v. 13. On the other hand, S. Epiphanius speaks of Him as growing in wisdom as man. *Hær.* 77. p. 1019—24. and S. Ambrose, *Incarn.* 71—14. Vid. however Ambr. *de fid.* as quoted *subr.* § 45, n. 2.

[9] Matt. xvi. 16; xxvii. 54.   [10] *Or.* ii. 1, n. 6.
[1] *Or.* ii. 10, n. 7; iii. 58.   [2] i. 45.   [3] iii. 16, n. 8.
[4] § 34.   [5] ii. 69, n. 3.   [6] § 31, n. 12.
[7] 31, n. 10.   [8] *Or.* ii. 52, n. 6.

He wept and the like, as man. Other texts prove Him God. God could not fear. He feared because His flesh feared.

54. THEREFORE as, when the flesh advanced, He is said to have advanced, because the body was His own, so also what is said at the season of His death, that He was troubled, that He wept, must be taken in the same sense[1]. For they, going up and down[2], as if thereby recommending their heresy anew, allege; "Behold, 'He wept,' and said, 'Now is My soul troubled,' and He besought that the cup might pass away; how then, if He so spoke, is He God, and Word of the Father?" Yea, it is written that He wept, O God's enemies, and that He said, 'I am troubled,' and on the Cross He said, 'Eloi, Eloi, lama sabachthani,' that is, 'My God, My God, why hast Thou forsaken Me?' and He besought that the cup might pass away[3]. Thus certainly it is written; but again I would ask you (for the same rejoinder must of necessity be made to each of your objections[4]), If the speaker is mere man, let him weep and fear death, as being man; but if He is the Word in flesh[5] (for one must not be reluctant to repeat), whom had He to fear being God? or wherefore should He fear death, who was Himself Life, and was rescuing others from death? or how, whereas He said, 'Fear not him that kills the body[6],' should He Himself fear? And how should He who said to Abraham, 'Fear not, for I am with thee,' and encouraged Moses against Pharaoh, and said to the son of Nun, 'Be strong, and of a good courage[7],' Himself feel terror before Herod and Pilate? Further, He who succours others against fear (for 'the Lord,' says Scripture, 'is on my side, I will not fear what man shall do unto me[8]'), did He fear governors, mortal men? did He who Himself was come against death, feel terror of death? Is it not both unseemly and irreligious to say that He was terrified at death or hades, whom the keepers of the gates of hades[9] saw and shuddered? But if, as you would hold, the Word was in terror, wherefore, when He spoke long before of the conspiracy of the Jews, did He not flee, nay said when actually sought, 'I am He?' for He could have avoided death, as He said, 'I have power to lay down My life, and I have power to take it again;' and 'No one taketh it from Me[10].'

55. But these affections were not proper to the nature of the Word, as far as He was Word; but in the flesh which was thus affected was the Word, O Christ's enemies and unthankful Jews! For He said not all this prior to the flesh; but when the 'Word became flesh,' and has become man, then is it written that He said this, that is, humanly. Surely He of whom this is written was He who raised Lazarus from the dead, and made the water wine, and vouchsafed sight to the man born blind, and said, 'I and My Father are one[1].' If then they make His human attributes a ground for low thoughts concerning the Son of God, nay consider Him altogether man from the earth, and not[2] from heaven, wherefore not from His divine works recognise the Word who is in the Father, and henceforward renounce their self-willed[3] irreligion? For they are given to see, how He who did the works is the same as He who shewed that His body was passible by His permitting[4] it to weep and hunger, and to shew other properties of a body. For while by means of such He made it known that, though God impassible, He had taken a passible flesh; yet from the works He shewed Himself the Word of God, who had afterwards become man, saying, 'Though ye believe not Me, beholding Me clad in a human body, yet believe the works, that ye may know that "I am in the Father, and the Father in Me[5]"' And Christ's enemies seem to me to shew plain shamelessness and blasphemy; for, when they hear 'I and the Father are one[6],' they violently distort the sense, and separate the unity of the Father and the Son; but reading of His tears or sweat or sufferings, they do not advert to His body, but on account of these rank in the creation Him by whom the creation was made. What then is left for them to differ from the Jews in? for as the Jews blasphemously ascribed God's works to Beelzebub, so also will these, ranking with creatures the Lord who wrought those works, undergo the same condemnation as theirs without mercy.

56. But they ought, when they hear 'I and the Father are one,' to see in Him the oneness of the Godhead and the propriety of the Father's Essence; and again when they hear, 'He wept' and the like, to say that these are proper to the body; especially since on each side they have an intelligible ground, viz. that this is written as of God and that with reference

---

[1] διανοίᾳ, § 26 et passim.   [2] ἄνω καὶ κάτω, vid. de Decr. 14, n. 1; Or. ii. 34, n. 5.   [3] John xi. 35; xii. 27; Matt. xxvi. 39; Mark xv. 34.   [4] Cf. ii. 80.   [5] § 53, n. 2.   [6] Luke xii. 4.   [7] Gen. xv. 1; xxvi. 24; Exod. iv. 12, &c.; Josh. i. 6.   [8] Ps. cxviii. 6.   [9] Job xxxviii. 17. LXX.; De Syn. 8, below, § 56.   [10] John xviii. 5; x. 18.

[1] Ib. x. 30.   [2] ἄνθρωπον ὅλον, Orat. iv. 35 fin.   [3] ἰδίαν, Orat. i. 52 fin.   [4] This our Lord's suspense or permission, at His will, of the operations of His manhood is a great principle in the doctrine of the Incarnation. Cf. Theophylact, in Joh. xi. 34. And Cyril, fragm. in Joan. p. 685. Leon. Ep. 35, 3. Aug. in Joan. xlix. 18. vid. note on § 57, sub. fin. The Eutychians perverted this doctrine, as if it implied that our Lord was not subject to the laws of human nature, and that He suffered merely 'by permission of the Word.' Leont. ap. Canis. t. i. p. 563. In like manner Marcion or Manes said that His 'flesh appeared from heaven in resemblance, ὡς ἠθέλησεν.' Athan. contr. Apoll. ii. 3.   [5] John x. 38; xiv. 10.   [6] Ib. x. 30.

to His manhood. For in the incorporeal, the properties of body had not been, unless He had taken a body corruptible and mortal[1]; for mortal was Holy Mary, from whom was His body. Wherefore of necessity when He was in a body suffering, and weeping, and toiling, these things which are proper to the flesh, are ascribed to Him together with the body. If then He wept and was troubled, it was not the Word, considered as the Word, who wept and was troubled, but it was proper to the flesh; and if too He besought that the cup might pass away, it was not the Godhead that was in terror, but this affection too was proper to the manhood. And that the words 'Why hast Thou forsaken Me?' are His, according to the foregoing explanations (though He suffered nothing, for the Word was impassible), is notwithstanding declared by the Evangelists; since the Lord became man, and these things are done and said as from a man, that He might Himself lighten[2] these very sufferings of the flesh, and free it from them[3]. Whence neither can the Lord be forsaken by the Father, who is ever in the Father, both before He spoke, and when He uttered this cry. Nor is it lawful to say that the Lord was in terror, at whom the keepers of hell's gates shuddered[4] and set open hell, and the graves did gape, and many bodies of the saints arose and appeared to their own people[5]. Therefore be every heretic dumb, nor dare to ascribe terror to the Lord whom death, as a serpent, flees, at whom demons tremble, and the sea is in alarm; for whom the heavens are rent and all the powers are shaken. For behold when He says, 'Why hast Thou forsaken Me?' the Father shewed that He was ever and even then in Him; for the earth knowing its Lord[6] who spoke, straightway trembled, and the vail was rent, and the sun was hidden, and the rocks were torn asunder, and the graves, as I have said, did gape, and the dead in them arose; and, what is wonderful, they who were then present and had before denied Him, then seeing these signs, confessed that 'truly He was the Son of God[7].'

57. And as to His saying, 'If it be possible, let the cup pass,' observe how, though He thus spake, He rebuked[1] Peter, saying, 'Thou savourest not the things that be of God, but those that be of men.' For He willed[2] what

He deprecated, for therefore had He come; but His was the willing (for for it He came), but the terror belonged to the flesh. Wherefore as man He utters this speech also, and yet both were said by the Same, to shew that He was God, willing in Himself, but when He had become man, having a flesh that was in terror. For the sake of this flesh He combined His own will with human weakness[3], that destroying this affection He might in turn make man undaunted in face of death. Behold then a thing strange indeed! He to whom Christ's enemies impute words of terror, He by that so-called[4] terror renders men undaunted and fearless. And so the Blessed Apostles after Him from such words of His conceived so great a contempt of death, as not even to care for those who questioned them, but to answer, 'We ought to obey God rather than men[5].' And the other Holy Martyrs were so bold, as to think that they were rather passing to life than undergoing death. Is it not extravagant then, to admire the courage of the servants of the Word, yet to say that the Word Himself was in terror, through whom they despised death? But from that most enduring purpose and courage of the Holy Martyrs is shewn, that the Godhead was not in terror, but the Saviour took away our terror. For as He abolished death by death, and by human means all human evils, so by this so-called terror did He remove our terror, and brought about that never more should men fear death. His word and deed go together. For human were the sayings, 'Let the cup pass,' and 'Why hast Thou forsaken Me?' and divine the act whereby the Same did cause the sun to fail and the dead to rise. Again He said humanly, 'Now is My soul troubled;' and He said divinely, 'I have power to lay down My life, and power to take it again[6].' For to be troubled was proper

---

the Divine, though psychologically distinct.] Cf. Anast. *Hodeg.* i. p. 12.

[3] It is observable that, as elsewhere we have seen Athan. speak of the *nature* of the Word, and of, not the *nature* of man as united to Him, but of *flesh, humanity,* &c. (vid. *Or.* ii. 45, n. 2.) so here, instead of speaking of two wills, he speaks of the Word's *willing* and human *weakness, terror,* &c. In another place he says still more pointedly, 'The *will* was of the Godhead alone; since the whole *nature* of the Word was manifested in the second Adam's *human form* and visible *flesh.*' *contr. Apoll.* ii. 10. Cf. S. Leo on the same passage: 'The first request is one of infirmity, the second of power; the first He asked in our [character], the second in His own. . . . The inferior will give way to the superior,' &c. *Serm.* 56, 2. vid. a similar passage in Nyssen. *Antirrh. adv. Apol.* 32. vid. also 31. An obvious objection may be drawn from such passages, as if the will 'of the flesh' were represented as contrary (vid. foregoing note) to the will of the Word. The whole of our Lord's prayer is offered by Him as man, because it is a prayer; the first part is not from Him as man, but the second, which corrects it, from Him as God [i.e. the first part is not human *as contrasted* with the second]; but the former part is from the sinless infirmity of our nature, the latter from His human will expressing its acquiescence in His Father's, that is, in His Divine Will. 'His Will,' says S. Greg. Naz. 'was not contrary to God, being all deified, θεωθὲν ὅλον.'

[4] νομιζομένῃ, vid. *Orat.* i. 10.   [5] Acts v. 29.
[6] John xii. 27; x. 18.

---

[1] *Or.* i. 43, 44. notes; ii. 66, n. 7. *Serm. Maj. de Fid.* 9. Tertull. *de Carn. Chr.* 6.   [2] § 44, nn. 2, 6.   [3] ii. 56, n. 5.
[4] Job xxxviii. 17, LXX.   [5] Vid. Matt. xxvii. 52, 53, similar passage *supr.* p. 88.   [6] δεσποτὴν, § 14, &c.
[7] Vid. Matt. xxvii. 54. Vid. *Or.* ii. 16; 35, n. 2. Cf. Leo's Tome (*Ep.* 28.) 4. Nyssen. *contr. Eunom.* iv. p. 161. Ambros. *Epist.* i. 46. n. 7. vid. Hil. *Trin.* x. 48. Also vid. Athan. *Sent. D.* nn. *Serm. Maj. de Fid.* 24.
[1] Matt. xvi. 23, cf. §§ 40, 41.
[2] [The human will of the Saviour is in absolute harmony with

to the flesh, and to have power to lay down His life[7] and take it again, when He will, was no property of men but of the Word's power. For man dies, not by his own power, but by necessity of nature and against his will; but the Lord, being Himself immortal, but having a mortal flesh, had power, as God, to become separate from the body and to take it again, when He would. Concerning this too speaks David in the Psalm, 'Thou shalt not leave My soul in hades, neither shalt Thou suffer Thy Holy One to see corruption[8].' For it beseemed, that the flesh, corruptible as it was, should no longer after its own nature remain mortal, but because of the Word who had put it on, should abide incorruptible. For as He, having come in our body, was conformed to our condition, so we, receiving Him, partake of the immortality that is from Him.

58. Idle then is the excuse for stumbling, and petty the notions concerning the Word, of these Ario-maniacs, because it is written, ' He was troubled,' and ' He wept.' For they seem not even to have human feeling, if they are thus ignorant of man's nature and properties; which do but make it the greater wonder, that the Word should be in such a suffering flesh, and neither prevented those who were conspiring against Him, nor took vengeance of those who were putting Him to death, though He was able, He who hindered some from dying, and raised others from the dead. And He let His own body suffer, for therefore did He come, as I said before, that in the flesh He might suffer, and thenceforth the flesh might be made impassible and immortal[9], and that, as we have many times said, contumely and other troubles might determine upon Him and come short of others after Him, being by Him annulled utterly; and that henceforth men might for ever abide[10] incorruptible, as a temple of the Word[11]. Had Christ's enemies thus dwelt on these thoughts, and recognised the ecclesiastical scope as an anchor for the faith, they would not have made shipwreck of the faith, nor been so shameless as to resist those who would fain recover them from their fall, and to deem those as enemies who are admonishing them to be religious[12].

CHAPTER XXX.

OBJECTIONS CONTINUED, AS IN CHAPTERS vii.—x.

Whether the Son is begotten of the Father's will? This virtually the same as whether once He was not? and used by the Arians to introduce the latter question. The *Regula Fidei* answers it at once in the negative by contrary texts. The Arians follow the Valentinians in maintaining a precedent will; which really is only exercised by God towards creatures. Instances from Scripture. Inconsistency of Asterius. If the Son by will, there must be another Word before Him. If God is good, or exist, by His will, then is the Son by His will. If He willed to have reason or wisdom, then is His Word and Wisdom at His will. The Son is the Living Will, and has all titles which denote connaturality. That will which the Father has to the Son, the Son has to the Father. The Father wills the Son and the Son wills the Father.

58. (*continued*). BUT[1], as it seems, a heretic is a wicked thing in truth, and in every respect his heart is depraved[2] and irreligious. For behold, though convicted on all points, and shewn to be utterly bereft of understanding, they feel no shame; but as the hydra of Gentile fable, when its former serpents were destroyed, gave birth to fresh ones, contending against the slayer of the old by the production of new, so also they, hostile[3] and hateful to God[4], as hydras[5], losing their life in the objections which they advance, invent for themselves other questions Judaic and foolish, and new expedients, as if Truth were their enemy, thereby to shew the rather that they are Christ's opponents in all things.

59. After so many proofs against them, at which even the devil who is their father[6] had himself been abashed and gone back, again as from their perverse heart they mutter forth other expedients, sometimes in whispers, sometimes with the drone[7] of gnats; ' Be it so,' say they; 'interpret these places thus, and gain the victory in reasonings and proofs; still you must say that the Son has received being from the Father at His will and pleasure;' for thus they deceive many, putting forward the will and the pleasure of God. Now if any of those who believe aright[8] were to say this in

---

[7] This might be taken as an illustration of the ut voluit *supr.* Or. i. 44, n. 11. And so the expressions in the Evangelists, ' Into Thy hands I *commend* My Spirit,' ' He *bowed the head*,' ' He *gave up* the ghost,' are taken to imply that His death was His free act. vid. Ambros. *in loc. Luc.* Hieron. *in loc. Matt.* also Athan. *Serm. Maj. de Fid.* 4. It is Catholic doctrine that our Lord, as man, submitted to death of His free will, and not as obeying an express command of the Father. Cf. S. Chrysostom on john x. 18. Theophylact. *in Hebr.* xii. 2; Aug. *de Trin.* iv. 16.
[8] Ps. xvi. 10.   [9] Or. ii. 65, n. 3.   [10] Ib. 69, n. 3.   [11] § 53.
[12] Thus ends the exposition of texts, which forms the body of these Orations. It is remarkable that he ends as he began, with reference to the ecclesiastical scope, or *Regula Fidei*, which has so often come under our notice, vid. Or. ii. 35. n. 2. 44, n. 1, as if distinctly to tell us, that Scripture did not so force its meaning

on the individual as to dispense with an interpreter, and as if his own deductions were not to be viewed merely in their own logical power, great as that power often is, but as under the authority of the Catholic doctrines which they subserve. Vid. *Or.* iii. 18, n. 3.
[1] This chapter is in a very different style from the foregoing portions of this Book, and much more resembles the former two; not only in its subject and the mode of treating it, but in the words introduced, e.g. ἐπισπείρουσι, ἐπινοοῦσι, γογγύζουσι, καθ' ὑμᾶς, ἄτοπον, λεξείδιον, εἰς τῶν πάντων, &c. And the references are to the former Orations.   [2] See 50, n. 10 ; *Serap.* i. 18.
[3] θεομάχοι, *de Decr.* 3. n. 1 ; *Or.* ii. 32, n. 4. Vid. Dissert. by Bucher on the word in Acts v. 39. *ap. Thesaur. Theol. Phil. N. T.* t. 2.
[4] θεοστυγεῖς, § 40.   [5] § 64, note.   [6] *Or.* i. 73, n. 7.
[7] περιβομβοῦσι. *De Decr.* 14, n. 1 ; also *de Fug.* 2, 6. Naz. *Orat.* 27, 2. c.
[8] S. Ignatius speaks of our Lord as ' Son of God according to the will (θέλημα) and power of God.' *ad Smyrn.* 1. S. Justin as

simplicity, there would be no cause to be suspicious of the expression, the right intention[9] prevailing over that somewhat simple use of words[10]. But since the phrase is from the heretics[11], and the words of heretics are suspicious, and, as it is written, 'The wicked are deceitful,' and 'The words of the wicked are deceit[12],' even though they but make signs[13], for their heart is depraved, come let us examine this phrase also, lest, though convicted on all sides, still, as hydras, they invent a fresh word, and by such clever language and specious evasion, they sow again that irreligion of theirs in another way. For he who says, 'The Son came to be at the Divine will,' has the same meaning as another who says, 'Once He was not,' and 'The Son came to be out of nothing,' and 'He is a creature.' But since they are now ashamed of these phrases, these crafty ones have endeavoured to convey their meaning in another way, putting forth the word 'will,' as cuttlefish their blackness, thereby to blind the simple[14], and to keep in mind their peculiar heresy. For whence[15] bring they 'by will and pleasure?' or from what Scripture? let them say, who are so suspicious in their words and so inventive of irreligion. For the Father who revealed from heaven His own Word, declared, 'This is My beloved Son;' and by David He said, 'My heart uttered a good Word;' and John He bade say, 'In the beginning was the Word;' and David says in the Psalm, 'With Thee is the well of life, and in Thy light shall we see light;' and the Apostle writes, 'Who being the Radiance of Glory,' and again, 'Who being in the form of God,' and, 'Who is the Image of the invisible God[16].'

60. All everywhere tell us of the being of the Word, but none of His being 'by will,' nor at all of His making; but they, where, I ask, did they find will or pleasure 'precedent[1]' to the Word of God, unless forsooth, leaving the Scriptures, they simulate the perverseness of Valentinus? For Ptolemy the Valentinian said that the Unoriginate had a pair of attributes, Thought and Will, and first He thought and then He willed; and what He thought, He could not put forth[2], unless when the power of the Will was added. Thence the Arians taking a lesson, wish will and pleasure to precede the Word. For them then, let them rival the doctrine of Valentinus; but we, when we read the divine discourses, found 'He was' applied to the Son, but of Him only did' we hear as being in the Father and the Father's Image; while in the case of things originate only, since also by nature these things once were not, but afterwards came to be[3], did we recognise a precedent will and pleasure, David saying in the hundred and thirteenth Psalm, 'As for our God He is in heaven, He hath done whatsoever pleased Him,' and in the hundred and tenth, 'The works of the Lord are great, sought out unto all His good pleasure;' and again, in the hundred and thirty-fourth, 'Whatsoever the Lord pleased, that did He in heaven, and in earth, and in the sea, and in all deep places[4].' If then He be work and thing made, and one among others, let Him, as others, be said 'by will' to have come to be, and Scripture shews that these are thus brought into being. And Asterius, the advocate[5] for the heresy, acquiesces, when he thus writes, 'For if it be unworthy of

---

'God and Son according to His will, βουλήν.' *Tryph.* **127**, and 'begotten from the Father at His will, θελήσει.' ibid. **61**. and he says, δυνάμει καὶ βουλῇ αὐτοῦ. ibid. **128**. S. Clement 'issuing from the Father's will itself quicker than light.' *Gent.* **10** fin. S. Hippolytus, 'Whom God the Father, willing, βουληθείς, begat as He willed, ὡς ἠθέλησεν. contr.* Noet. **16**. Origen, ἐκ θελήματος. ap. Justin. *ad. Menn.* vid. also cum filius charitatis etiam voluntatis. *Periarch.* iv. **28**.

9 διανοίας interpretation, § **26**, n. **9**.
10 Cf. *Ep. Æg.* **8**. and *supr.* ii. **3**. Also *Letter* **54** fin. Vid. *supr. de Decr.* **10**, n. **3**. And vid. Leont. *contr. Nest.* iii. **41**. (p. **581**. Canis.) He here seems alluding to the Semi-Arians, Origen, and perhaps the earlier Fathers.
11 Tatian had said θελήματι προπηδᾷ ὁ λόγος. *Gent.* **5**. Tertullian had said, 'Ut primum voluit Deus ea edere, ipsum primum protulit sermonem. *adv. Prax.* **6**. Novatian, Ex quo, quando ipse voluit, Sermo filius natus est. *de Trin.* **31**. And Constit. Apost. τὸν πρὸ αἰώνων εὐδοκίᾳ τοῦ πατρὸς γεννηθέντα. vii. **41**. Pseudo-Clem. Genuit Deus voluntate præcedente. *Recognit.* iii. **10**. Eusebius, κατὰ γνώμην καὶ προαίρεσιν βουληθεὶς ὁ θεός· ἐκ τῆς τοῦ πατρὸς βουλῆς καὶ δυνάμεως. *Dem.* iv. **3**. Arius, θελήματι καὶ βουλῇ ὑπέστη. ap. Theod. *H.E.* i. **4**. p. **750**. vid. also *de Syn.* **16**.　　12 Prov. xii. **5**, **6**. LXX.
13 *De Decr.* **20**.　　14 p. **69**. n. **8**.
15 And so *supr. de Decr.* **18**, 'by what Saint have they been taught "at will?"' That is, no one ever taught it in the sense in which *they* explained it ; that he has just said, 'He who says "at will" has the same meaning as he who says "Once He was not."' Cf. below §§ **61**, **64**, **66**. Certainly as the earlier Fathers had used the phrase, so those who came after Arius. Thus Nyssen in the passage in *contr. Eun.* vii. referred to in the next note. And Hilar. *Syn.* **37**. The same father says, unitate Patris et virtute. Psalm xci. **8**. and ut voluit, ut potuit, ut scit qui genuit. *Trin.* iii. **4**. And he addresses Him as non invidum bonorum tuorum in Unigeniti tui nativitate. ibid. vi. **21**. S. Basil too speaks of our Lord as αὐτοζωὴν καὶ αὐτοάγαθον, 'from the quickening Fountain, the Father's goodness, ἀγαθότητος.' *contr. Eun.* ii. **25**. And Cæsarius calls Him ἀγάπην πατρός. *Quæst.* **39**. Vid. Ephrem. Syr. *adv. Scrut. R.* vi. **1**. *Oxf. Tra.* and note there. Maximus Taurin. says, that God is per omnipotentiam Pater. *Hom. de trad. Symb.* p. **270**. ed. **1784**, vid. also Chrysol. *Serm.* **61**. Ambros. *de Fid.* iv. **8**. Petavius refers in addition to such passages as one just quoted from S. Hilary, which speak of God as not invidus, so as not to communicate Himself, since He was able. Si non potuit, infirmus ; si non voluit, invidus. August. *contr. Maxim.* iii. **7**.

16 Matt. iii. **17** ; Ps. xlv. **1** ; John i. **1** ; Ps. xxxvi. **9** ; Heb. i. **3** ; Phil. ii. **26** ; Col. i. **15**.
1 προηγουμένη and **61** fin. The antecedens voluntas has been mentioned in *Recogn. Clem. supr.* note **11**. For Ptolemy vid. Epiph. *Hær.* p. **215**. The Catholics, who allowed that our Lord was θελήσει, explained it as a σύνδρομος θέλησις, and not a προηγουμένη ; as Cyril. *Trin.* ii. p. **56**. And with the same meaning S. Ambrose, nec voluntas ante Filium nec potestas. *de Fid.* v. **224**. And S. Gregory Nyssen, 'His immediate union, ἄμεσος συνάφεια, does not exclude the Father's will, βούλησιν, nor does that will separate the Son from the Father.' *contr. Eunom.* vii. p. **206**, **7**. vid. the whole passage. The alternative which these words, σύνδρομος and προηγουμένη, expressed was this ; whether an act of Divine Purpose or Will took place *before* the Generation of the Son, or whether both the Will and the Generation were eternal, as the Divine Nature was eternal. Hence Bull says, with the view of exculpating Novatian, Cum Filius dicitur ex Patre, quando ipse voluit, nasci, Velle illud Patris æternum fuisse intelligendum.' *Defens. F. N.* iii. **8**. § **8**.
2 προβάλλειν, *de Syn.* **16**, n. **8**.　　3 ἐπιγέγονε, *Or.* i. **25**, **28** fin.
iii. **6**.　　4 Ps. cxv. **3** ; cxi. **2**. LXX. ; cxxxv. **6**.　　5 Cf. ii. n. **1**.

the Framer of all, to make at pleasure, let His being pleased be removed equally in the case of all, that His Majesty be preserved unimpaired. Or if it be befitting God to will, then let this better way obtain in the case of the first Offspring. For it is not possible that it should be fitting for one and the same God to make things at His pleasure, and not at His will also. In spite of the Sophist having introduced abundant irreligion in his words, namely, that the Offspring and the thing made are the same, and that the Son is one offspring out of all offsprings that are, He ends with the conclusion that it is fitting to say that the works are by will and pleasure.

61. Therefore if He be other than all things, as has been above shewn[1], and through Him the works rather came to be, let not 'by will' be applied to Him, or He has similarly come to be as the things consist which through Him come to be. For Paul, whereas he was not before, became afterwards an Apostle 'by the will of God[2];' and our own calling, as itself once not being, but now taking place afterwards, is preceded by will, and, as Paul himself says again, has been made 'according to the good pleasure of His will[3].' And what Moses relates, 'Let there be light,' and 'Let the earth appear,' and 'Let Us make man,' is, I think, according to what has gone before[3a], significant of the will of the Agent. For things which once were not but happened afterwards from external causes, these the Framer counsels to make; but His own Word begotten from Him by nature, concerning Him He did not counsel beforehand; for in Him the Father makes, in Him frames, other things whatever He counsels; as also James the Apostle teaches, saying, 'Of His own will begat He us with the Word of truth[4].' Therefore the Will of God concerning all things, whether they be begotten again or are brought into being at the first, is in His Word, in whom He both makes and begets again what seems right to Him; as the Apostle[5] again signifies, writing to Thessalonica; 'for this is the will of God in Christ Jesus concerning you.' But if, in whom He makes, in Him also is the will, and in Christ is the pleasure of the Father, how can He, as others, come into being by will and pleasure? For if He too came to be as you maintain, by will, it follows that the will concerning Him consists in some other Word, through whom He in turn comes to be; for it has been shewn that God's will is not in the things which He brings into being, but in Him through whom and in whom all

things made are brought to be. Next, since it is all one to say 'By will' and Once He was not,' let them make up their minds to say, 'Once He was not,' that, perceiving with shame that times are signified by the latter, they may understand that to say 'by will' is to place times before the Son; for counselling goes before things which once were not, as in the case of all creatures. But if the Word is the Framer of the creatures, and He coexists with the Father, how can to counsel precede the Everlasting as if He were not? for if counsel precedes, how through Him are all things? For rather He too, as one among others is by will begotten to be a Son, as we too were made sons by the Word of Truth; and it rests, as was said, to seek another Word, through whom He too has come to be, and was begotten together with all things, which were according to God's pleasure.

62. If then there is another Word of God, then be the Son originated by a word; but if there be not, as is the case, but all things by Him have come to be, which the Father has willed, does not this expose the many-headed[1] craftiness of these men? that feeling shame at saying 'work,' and 'creature,' and 'God's Word was not before His generation,' yet in another way they assert that He is a creature, putting forward 'will,' and saying, 'Unless He has by will come to be, therefore God had a Son by necessity and against His good pleasure.' And who is it then who imposes necessity on Him, O men most wicked, who draw everything to the purpose of your heresy? for what is contrary to will they see; but what is greater and transcends it has escaped their perception. For as what is beside purpose is contrary to will, so what is according to nature transcends and precedes counselling[2]. A man by counsel builds a house, but by nature he begets a son; and what is in building began to come into being at will, and is external to the maker; but the son is proper offspring of the father's essence, and is not external to him; wherefore neither does he counsel concerning him, lest he appear to counsel about himself. As far then as the Son transcends the creature, by so much does what is by nature transcend the will[3]. And they, on hearing of Him, ought

<hr/>

[1] 64, note 4.
[2] Thus he makes the question a nugatory one, as if it did not go to the point, and could not be answered, or might be answered either way, as the case might be. Really Nature and Will go together in the Divine Being, but in order, as we regard Him, Nature is first, Will second, and the generation belongs to Nature, not to Will. And so *supr. Or.* i. 29; ii. 2. In like manner S. Epiphanius, *Hær.* 69, 26. vid. also *Ancor.* 51. vid. also Ambros. *de Fid.* iv. 4. vid. others, as collected in Petav. *Trin.* vi. 8. §§ 14—16.
[3] Two distinct meanings may be attached to 'by will' (as Dr. Clark observes, *Script. Doct.* p. 142. ed. 1738), either a concurrence or acquiescence, or a positive act. S. Cyril uses it in the

<hr/>

[1] Cf. ii. 18—43.   [2] 1 Cor. i. 1, &c.   [3] Eph. i. 5.
[3a] ii. 31 seqq.   [4] James i. 18.   [5] 1 Thess. v. 18.

not to measure by will what is by nature; forgetting however that they are hearing about God's Son, they dare to apply human contrarieties in the instance of God, 'necessity' and 'beside purpose,' to be able thereby to deny that there is a true Son of God. For let them tell us themselves,—that God is good and merciful, does this attach to Him by will or not? if by will, we must consider that He began to be good, and that His not being good is possible; for to counsel and choose implies an inclination two ways, and is incidental to a rational nature. But if it be too unseemly that He should be called good and merciful upon will, then what they have said themselves must be retorted on them,— 'therefore by necessity and not at His pleasure He is good;' and, 'who is it that imposes this necessity on Him?' But if it be unseemly to speak of necessity in the case of God, and therefore it is by nature that He is good, much more is He, and more truly, Father of the Son by nature and not by will.

63. Moreover let them answer us this:—(for against their shamelessness I wish to urge a further question, bold indeed, but with a religious intent; be propitious, O Lord [1]!)—the Father Himself, does He exist, first having counselled, then being pleased, or before counselling? For since they are so bold in the instance of the Word, they must receive the like answer, that they may know that this their presumption reaches even to the Father Himself. If then they shall themselves take counsel about will, and say that even He is from will, what then was He before He counselled, or what gained He, as ye consider, after counselling? But if such a question be unseemly and self-destructive, and shocking even to ask (for it is enough only to hear God's Name for us to know and understand that He is He that Is), will it not also be against reason to have parallel thoughts concerning the Word of God, and to make pre-

tences of will and pleasure? for it is enough in like manner only to hear the Name of the Word, to know and understand that He who is God not by will, has not by will but by nature His own Word. And does it not surpass all conceivable madness, to entertain the thought only, that God Himself counsels and considers and chooses and proceeds to have a good pleasure, that He be not without Word and without Wisdom, but have both? for He seems to be considering about Himself, who counsels about what is proper to His Essence. There being then much blasphemy in such a thought, it will be religious to say that things originate have come to be 'by favour and will,' but the Son is not a work of will, nor has come after [2], as the creation, but is by nature the own Offspring of God's Essence. For being the own Word of the Father, He allows us not to account [3] of will as before Himself, since He is Himself the Father's Living Counsel [4], and Power, and Framer of the things which seemed good to the Father. And this is what He says of Himself in the Proverbs; 'Counsel is mine and security, mine is understanding, and mine strength [5].' For as, although Himself the 'Understanding,' in which He prepared the heavens, and Himself 'Strength and Power' (for Christ is 'God's Power and God's Wisdom [6]'), He here has altered the terms and said, 'Mine is understanding' and 'Mine strength,' so while He says, 'Mine is counsel,' He must Himself be the Living [7] Counsel of the Father; as we have learned from the Prophet also, that He becomes 'the Angel of great Counsel [8],' and was called the good pleasure of the Father; for thus we must refute them, using human illustrations [9] concerning God.

64. Therefore if the works subsist 'by will and favour,' and the whole creature is made 'at God's good pleasure,' and Paul was called to be an Apostle 'by the will of God,' and our calling has come about 'by His good pleasure and will,' and all things have come into being through the Word, He is external to the things which have come to be by will, but rather is Himself the Living

---

former sense, when he calls it σύνδρομος, as quoted § 60, n. 1; and when he says (with Athan. *infr.*) that 'the Father wills His own subsistence, θελητής ἐστι, but is not what He is from any will, ἐκ βουλήσεως τινός,' *Thes.* p. 56; Dr. Clark would understand it in the latter sense, with a view of inferring that the Son was subsequent to a Divine act, i.e. not eternal; but what Athan. says leads to the conclusion, that it does not matter which sense is taken. He does not meet the Arian objection, 'if not by will therefore by necessity,' by speaking of a concomitant will, or merely saying that the Almighty exists or is good, by will, with S. Cyril, but he says that 'nature *transcends* will and necessity also.' Accordingly, Petavius is even willing to allow that the ἐκ βουλῆς is to be ascribed to the γέννησις in the sense which Dr. Clark wishes, i.e. he grants that it may precede the γέννησις, i.e. in *order*, not in time, in the succession of our ideas, *Trin.* vi. 8, §§ 20, 21; and follows S. Austin, *Trin.* xv. 20. in preferring to speak of our Lord rather as voluntas de voluntate, than, as Athan. is led to do, as the voluntas Dei.

1 Vid. *Or.* i. 25, n. 2. Also *Serap.* i. 15, 16 init. 17, 20; iv. 8, 14. *Ep. Æg.* 11 fin. Didym. *Trin.* iii. 3. p. 341. Ephr. Syr. *adv. Hær. Serm.* 55 init. (t. 2. p. 557.) Facund. *Tr. Cap.* iii. 3 init.

2 ἐπιγεγονώς, § 60, n. 3.   3 λογίσασθαί τινα βούλησιν, as § 66 (Latin version inexact).

4 ἀγαθοῦ πατρὸς ἀγαθὸν βούλημα. Clem. *Ped.* iii. circ. fin. σοφία, χρηστότης, δύναμις, θέλημα παντοκρατορικόν. *Strom.* v. p. 547. Voluntas et potestas patris. Tertull. *Orat.* 4. Natus ex Patri quasi voluntas ex mente procedens. Origen. *Periarch.* i. 2. § 6. S. Jerome notices the same interpretation of 'by the will of God' in the beginning of Comment. in *Ephes.* But cf. Aug. *Trin.* xv. 20. And so Cæsarius, ἀγάπη ἐξ ἀγάπης. *Qu.* 39.

5 Prov. viii. 14.   6 1 Cor. i. 24.

7 ζῶσα βουλή. *supr. Or.* ii. 2. Cyril *in Joan.* p. 213. ζῶσα δύναμις. Sabell. *Greg.* 5. c. ζῶσα εἰκών. Naz. *Orat.* 30, 20. c. ζῶσα ἐνέργεια. Syn. Antioch. *ap. Routh. Reliqu.* t. 2. p. 469. ζῶσα ἰσχύς. Cyril. *in Joan.* p. 951. ζῶσα σοφία. Origen. *contr. Cels.* iii. fin. ζῶν λόγος. Origen. ibid. ζῶν ὄργανον (heretically) Euseb. *Dem.* iv. 2.

8 Is. ix. 6.   9 *Or.* ii. 33, n. 12.

Counsel of the Father, by which all these things have come to be; by which David also gives thanks in the seventy-second Psalm. 'Thou hast holden me by my right hand; Thou shalt guide me with Thy Counsel[1].' How then can the Word, being the Counsel and Good Pleasure of the Father, come into being Himself ' by good pleasure and will,' like every one else? unless, as I said before, in their madness they repeat that He has come into being through Himself, or through some other[2]. Who then is it through whom He has come to be? let them fashion another Word; and let them name another Christ, rivalling the doctrine of Valentinus[3]; for Scripture it is not. And though they fashion another, yet assuredly he too comes into being through some one; and so, while we are thus reckoning up and investigating the succession of them, the many-headed[4] heresy of the Atheists[5] is discovered to issue in polytheism[6] and madness unlimited; in the which, wishing the Son to be a creature and from nothing, they imply the same thing in other words ·by pretending the words will and pleasure, which rightly belong to things originate and creatures. Is it not irreligious then to impute the characteristics of things originate to the Framer of all? and is it not blasphemous to say that will was in the Father before the Word? for if will precedes in the Father, the Son's words are not true, 'I in the Father;' or even if He is in the Father, yet He will hold but a second place, and it became Him not to say 'I in the Father,' since will was before Him, in which all things were brought into being and He Himself subsisted, as you hold. For though He excel in glory, He is not the less one of the things which by will come into being. And, as we have said before, if it be so, how is He Lord and they servants[7]? but He is Lord of all, because He is one with the Father's Lordship; and the creation is all in bondage, since it is external to the Oneness of the Father, and, whereas it once was not, was brought to be.

65. Moreover, if they say that the Son is by will, they should say also that He came to be by understanding; for I consider understanding and will to be the same. For what a man counsels, about that also he has understanding; and what he has in understanding, that also he

counsels. Certainly the Saviour Himself has made them correspond, as being cognate, when He says, 'Counsel is mine and security; mine is understanding, and mine strength[1].' For as strength and security are the same (for they mean one attribute), so we may say that Understanding and Counsel are the same, which is the Lord. But these irreligious men are unwilling that the Son should be Word and Living Counsel; but they fable that there is with God[2], as if a habit[3], coming and going[4], after the manner of men, understanding, counsel, wisdom; and they leave nothing undone, and they put forward the 'Thought' and 'Will' of Valentinus, so that they may but separate the Son from the Father, and may call Him a creature instead of the proper Word of the Father. To them then must be said what was said to Simon Magus; 'the irreligion of Valentinus perish with you[5];' and let every one rather trust to Solomon, who says, that the Word is Wisdom and Understanding. For he says, 'The Lord by Wisdom founded the earth, by Understanding He established the heavens.' And as here by Understanding, so in the Psalms, 'By the Word of the Lord were the heavens made.' And as by the Word the heavens, so 'He hath done whatsoever pleased Him.' And as the Apostle writes to Thessalonians, 'the will of God is in Christ Jesus[6].' The Son of God then, He is the 'Word' and the 'Wisdom;' He the 'Understanding' and the Living 'Counsel;' and in Him is the 'Good Pleasure of the Father;' He is 'Truth' and 'Light' and 'Power' of the Father. But if the Will of God is Wisdom and Understanding, and the Son is Wisdom, he who says that the Son is 'by will,' says virtually that Wisdom has come into being in wisdom, and the Son is made in a son, and the Word created through the Word[7]; which is incompatible with God and is opposed to His Scriptures. For the Apostle proclaims the Son to be the own Radiance and Expression, not of the Father's will[8], but of His Essence[9] Itself, saying, 'Who being the Radiance of His glory and the Expression of His

---

[1] Ps. lxxiii. 23, 24.
[2] δι' ἑτέρου τινός. This idea has been urged against the Arians again and again, as just above, § 61; e.g. de Decr. 8, 24; Or. i. 15, below 65, sub. fin. vid. also Epiph. Hær. 76. p. 951. Basil. contr. Eunom. ii. 11. c. 17, a. &c.
[3] § 60.
[4] πολυκέφαλος αἵρεσις. And so πολυκ. πανουργία, § 62. The allusion is to the hydra, with its ever-springing heads, as introduced § 58, n. 5. and with a special allusion to Asterius who is mentioned, § 60, and in de Syn. 18. is called πολυκ. σοφιστής.
[5] Or. ii. 43, n. 4.   [6] § 16, n. 4.   [7] Or. i. 57; ii. 23.

[1] Prov. viii. 14.
[2] περὶ τὸν θεόν. vid. de Decr. 22, n. 1; Or. i. 15. Also Orat. i. 27, where (n. 2 a.), it is mistranslated. Euseb. Eccl. Theol. iii. p. 150. vid. de Syn. 34, n. 7.
[3] ἕξιν. vid. Or. ii. 38, n. 6; iv. 2, n. 2.
[4] συμβαινούσαν καὶ ἀποσυμβαινούσαν, vid. de Decr. 11, n. 7, and 22, n. 9, σύμβαμα, Euseb. Eccl. Theol. iii. p. 150. in the same, though a technical sense. vid. also Serap. i. 26; Naz. Orat. 31, 15 fin.   [5] Acts viii. 20.   [6] Prov. iii. 19; Ps. xxxiii. 6; cxxxv. 6, cxv. 3; 1 Thess. v. 18.   [7] Read 'a word,' cf. p. 394, n. 6.   [8] De Syn. 53, n. 9.
[9] οὐσία and ὑπόστασις are in these passages made synonymous; and so infr. Orat. iv. 1, f. And in iv. 33 fin. to the Son is attributed ἡ πατρικὴ ὑπόστασις. Vid. also ad Afros. 4. quoted supr. Exc. A, pp. 77, sqq. Ὑπ. might have been expected too in the discussion in the beginning of Orat. iii. did Athan. distinguish between them. It is remarkable how seldom it occurs at all in

Subsistence [10].' But if, as we have said before, the Father's Essence and Subsistence be not from will, neither, as is very plain, is what is proper to the Father's Subsistence from will; for such as, and so as, that Blessed Subsistence, must also be the proper Offspring from It. And accordingly the Father Himself said not, 'This is the Son originated at My will,' nor 'the Son whom I have by My favour,' but simply 'My Son;' and more than that, 'in whom I am well pleased;' meaning by this, This is the Son by nature; and 'in Him is lodged My will about what pleases Me.'

66. Since then the Son is by nature and not by will, is He without the pleasure of the Father and not with the Father's will? No, verily; but the Son is with the pleasure of the Father, and, as He says Himself, 'The Father loveth the Son, and sheweth Him all things [1].' For as not 'from will' did He begin to be good, nor yet is good without will and pleasure (for what He is, that also is His pleasure), so also that the Son should be, though it came not 'from will,' yet it is not without His pleasure or against His purpose. For as His own Subsistence is by His pleasure, so also the Son, being proper to His Essence, is not without His pleasure. Be then the Son the object of the Father's pleasure and love; and thus let every one religiously account of [2] the pleasure and the not-unwillingness of God. For by that good pleasure wherewith the Son is the object of the Father's pleasure, is the Father the object of the Son's love, pleasure, and honour; and one is the good pleasure which is from Father in Son, so that here too we may contemplate the Son in the Father and the Father in the Son. Let no one then, with Valentinus, introduce a precedent will; nor let any one, by this pretence of 'counsel,' intrude between the Only Father and the Only Word; for it were madness to place will and consideration between them. For it is one thing to say, 'Of will He came to be,' and another, that the Father has love and good pleasure towards His Son who is His own by nature. For to say, 'Of will He came to be,' in the first place implies that once He was not; and next it implies an inclination two ways, as has been said, so that one might suppose that the Father could even not will the Son. But to say of the Son, 'He might not have been,' is an irreligious presumption reaching even to the Essence of the Father, as if what is His own might

not have been. For it is the same as saying, 'The Father might not have been good.' And as the Father is always good by nature, so He is always generative [3] by nature; and to say, 'The Father's good pleasure is the Son,' and 'The Word's good pleasure is the Father,' implies, not a precedent will, but genuineness of nature, and propriety and likeness of Essence. For as in the case of the radiance and light one might say, that there is no will preceding radiance in the light, but it is its natural offspring, at the pleasure of the light which begat it, not by will and consideration, but in nature and truth, so also in the instance of the Father and the Son, one might rightly say, that the Father has love and good pleasure towards the Son, and the Son has love and good pleasure towards the Father.

67. Therefore call not the Son a work of good pleasure; nor bring in the doctrine of Valentinus into the Church; but be He the Living Counsel, and Offspring in truth and nature, as the Radiance from the Light. For thus has the Father spoken, 'My heart uttered a good Word;' and the Son conformably, 'I in the Father and the Father in Me [4].' But if the Word be in the heart, where is will? and if the Son in the Father, where is good pleasure? and if He be Will Himself, how is counsel in Will? it is unseemly; lest the Word come into being in a word, and the Son in a son, and Wisdom in a wisdom, as has been repeatedly [5] said. For the Son is the Father's All; and nothing was in the Father before the Word; but in the Word is will also, and through Him the objects of will are carried into effect, as holy Scriptures have shewn. And I could wish that the irreligious men, having fallen into such want of reason [6] as to be considering about will, would now ask their childbearing women no more, whom they used to ask, 'Hadst thou a son before conceiving him [7]?' but the father, 'Do ye become fathers by counsel, or by the natural law of your will?' or 'Are your children like your nature and essence [8]?' that, even from fathers they may learn shame, from whom they assumed this proposition [9] about birth, and from whom they hoped to gain knowledge in point. For they will reply to them, 'What we beget, is like, not our good pleasure [10], but like ourselves; nor become we parents by previous counsel, but to beget is proper to our nature; since we too are images of our fathers.' Either

---

these Orations, except as contained in Heb. i. 3. Vid. also p. 70, note 13. Yet the phrase τρεῖς ὑποστάσεις is certainly found in *Illud Omn.* fin. and in *Incarn. c. Arian.* 10. (if genuine) and apparently in *Expos..Fid.* 2. Vid. also *Orat.* iv. 25 init.
[10] Heb. i. 3.   [1] John iii. 35; v. 20.   [2] 63, n. 3.

[3] *Or.* i. 14, n. 4; ii. 2, n. 3.   [4] Ps. xlv. 1; John xiv. 10.
[5] § 2, n. 6, &c.   [6] *De Decr.* i. n. 6.   [7] *Or.* i. 26.
[8] τῆς οὐσίας ὅμοια, vid. *Or.* i. 21, n. 8. Also ii. 42, b. iii. 11,
14 *sub. fin.*, 17, n. 5.   [9] *Or.* ii. 1, n. 13.   [10] 65, n. 8.

then let them condemn themselves[11], and cease asking women about the Son of God, or let them learn from them, that the Son is begotten not by will, but in nature and truth. Becoming and suitable to them is a refutation from human instances[12], since the perverse-minded men dispute in a human way concerning the Godhead. Why then are Christ's enemies still mad? for this, as well as their other pretences, is shewn and proved to be mere fantasy and fable; and on this account, they ought, however late, contemplating the precipice of folly down which they have fallen, to rise again from the depth and to flee the snare of the devil, as we admonish them. For Truth is loving unto men and cries continually, 'If because of My clothing of the body ye believe Me not, yet believe the works, that ye may know tha'. "I am in the Father and the Father in Me," and "I and the Father are one," and "He that hath seen Me hath seen the Father[13]."' But the Lord according to His wont is loving to man, and would fain 'help them that are fallen,' as the praise of David[14] says; but the irreligious men, not desirous to hear the Lord's voice, nor bearing to see Him acknowledged by all as God and God's Son, go about, miserable men, as beetles, seeking with their father the devil pretexts for irreligion. What pretexts then, and whence will they be able next to find? unless they borrow blasphemies of Jews and Caiaphas, and take atheism from Gentiles? for the divine Scriptures are closed to them, and from every part of them they are refuted as insensate and Christ's enemies.

[11] De Decr. 3, n. 2; Orat. i. 27, ii. 4; Apol. c. Ar. 36. [12] Cf. 63, n. 9.

[13] John x. 38, 30; xiv. 9; cf. § 5, n. 3. [14] Ps. cxlvi. 8.

EXCURSUS C

INTRODUCTORY[1] TO THE FOURTH DISCOURSE AGAINST THE ARIANS

THE fourth Discourse, as has been already observed (p. 304), stands on a footing of its own. To begin with, it is not quoted in antiquity, as the first three are, as part of the work of Ath. against the Arians (details in Newman, p. 499). Again, the fact that not only the *Ep. Æg.*, but even the dubious *de Incar. c. Arian.*, are in some MSS. included in the *Orationes*, while our present oration appears sometimes as the 'fifth' sometimes as the 'sixth,' cast a shade of doubt upon its claim to be included in the 'Pentabiblus against the Arians' referred to by Photius. In addition to these external considerations, Newman lays stress on the apparent want of continuity in its argument; on its non-conformity to the structural plan of *Orat.* i.—iii., on the use of the term ὁμοούσιον (§§ 10, 22, contrast *Orat.* i. § 9, p. 311, note 12); on certain peculiarities of style which seem characteristic of disjointed notes rather than of a systematic treatise; on the reference to 'Eusebius' (of Cæsarea) as apparently still living (§ 8); and on the general absence of personal reference to opponents, while yet a definite and extant system seems to be combated.

Now a comparison with the works of Eusebius against Marcellus leaves little doubt that the system combated by Athan. is that of the latter (described briefly *Prolegg.* ch. ii. § 3 (2) c).

After laying down as a thesis (§ 1) the substantive existence of the divine Word or Wisdom, Athan. proceeds to combat the idea that the Word has no personality distinct from that of the Father. Setting aside the alternative errors of Sabellius (§ 2) and Arius (§ 3), he taxes with the consequence of involving two Ἀρχαί a view that the Word had a substantive existence and was then united to the Father (cf. Euseb. *c. Marcell.* 32 A, 108 A, 106 C, D). This consequence can only be avoided by falling into the Sabellian alternative of a Θεὸς διφυής (cf.

[1] The above *Excursus* is substituted for the longer introduction of Newman (republished in Latin in his *Tracts, Theological and Ecclesiastical*, 1872), and is in the main a condensation of the more recent and final discussion of Zahn (*Marcellus*, 1867, pp. 198 *seqq.*). The result of the latter is to confirm the main contention of Newman, viz. that the system, rather than the person, of Marcellus is throughout in view. Earlier discussions pointing the same way are cited: 'In Eusebii contra Marcellum libros Observationes, auctore K.S.C.,' Lips. 1787 (cited by Newman); Rettberg, *Marcelliana*, Præf. p. 7; Kuhn, *Kathol. Dogm.* ii. p. 344, note 1 (by Zahn).

Tertullian's 'Deum versipellem'), unless the true solution, that of the eternal divine γέννησις, be accepted (§ 3 worked out in 4, 5). The argument, apparently interrupted by an anti-Arian digression §§ 6, 7, is resumed § 8, whence it proceeds without break to § 24. Eusebius, insisting against Marcellus on the eternity of Christ's Kingdom, inconsistently defends those who deny the eternity of His Person. But if so, how inconsistent are those who deny the Son any pre-existence, while yet repelling the Arian formulæ with indignation! In §§ 9—12, taking Joh. x. 30 as his text, Athan. asks his opponents *in what sense* Christ and the Father 'are one,' distinguishing from his own answer that of Sabellius (9, 10), and that of Marcellus (11, 12), whom he presses with the paradoxical character of his explanation of the divine γέννησις. In §§ 13, 14, he examines the (Marcellian, *not Sabellian*) doctrine of πλατυσμὸς and συστολή, charging it with Sabellianism *as its consequence*. Next (§§ 15—24) Ath. turns upon the radically weak point of the system of Marcellus (*Prolegg. ubi supra*), and asks What do his followers mean by 'the Son?' Do they mean merely (*a*) the man, Christ (§ 20, Photinus), or (*b*) the union of Word and Man, or (*c*) the Word regarded as Incarnate? The latter was the answer (§ 22) of Marcellus himself. This last point leads to a discussion (§ 24) of those O. T. passages on which Marcellus notoriously relied. § 25, which Zahn understands as a direct polemic against Sabellius, is far more probably, as Newman maintains in his note, a supplemental argument against Marcellianism, for the view combated is said to *lead* inevitably to Sabellianism. The concluding portion, §§ 26—36, turns the argument of § 24, that Scripture declares the identity of Son and Word, against those who (adopting alternative (*a*) *supra*) drift from Marcellianism toward the Samosatene rather than toward the Sabellian position (on the connection of the two see *Prolegg.* ch. ii. § 3 (2) a and c). Even here, the name of Photinus, to whose position the section specially applies, is significantly withheld.

Such is the course of the argument in the Fourth Oration; and with the exception of §§ 6, 7, and again possibly § 25, it forms a homogeneous, if not a finished and elaborated piece of argument. Its date and composition may be left an open question; but its purpose as an appendix to *Orat.* i.—iii., is we think open to little doubt (*supr.* p. 304). Of Sabellius, who left no writings[2], the age of Athanasius knew little, except that he identified Father and Son (υἱοπατώρ), and denied the Trinity of Persons. Most that is told us of Sabellius from the fourth century onwards requires careful sifting, in order to eliminate what really belongs to Marcellus, Photinus, or others who were taxed with Sabellianism, and combated as 'Sabellians.' But with the simple patri-passianism which is the one undoubted element in the teaching of Sabellius, Marcellus had little or nothing in common. The criticism of Marcellus that Sabellius 'knew not the Word' reveals the true difference between them. To Sabellius, creation and redemption were the work of the one God under successive changes of manifestation; to Marcellus, they were the realisation of a process eternally latent in God; but both Marcellus and apparently Sabellius referred to the divine Nature what the theology of the Church has consistently referred to the divine Will.

The following table will make the foregoing scheme clear.

§ 1.　　　　Introductory. Thesis : the co-eternal personality of the Son or Word.

§§ 2—5.　　Those who, while rejecting Arianism, would avoid Sabellianism, must accept the eternal divine Generation of the Son.

§§ 6, 7.　　[Digression : the humiliation of the Word explained against the Arians.]

§ 8.　　　　The eternity of Christ's Kingdom and of His Person implied each in the other.

§§ 9—12.　　In what sense Christ and the Father are, and are not, one. The divine γέννησις.

§§ 13, 14.　The doctrine of divine dilatation and contraction denies true personal distinctions in the Godhead.

§§ 15—24. The Son and the Word identical. Refutation of the three alternative suppositions, and of the argument alleged from the O. T. in support of them.

§ 25.　　　Final refutation of the doctrine of dilatation.

§§ 26—36. The Scriptural identification of Son and Word refutes the restriction of the former title to the man Jesus.

---

[2] The Articles SABELLIANISM and SABELLIUS (both *sub. fin.*) in D.C.B. vol. iv., state the contrary, but the present writer follows the standard discussion of Zahn, of which the learned articles in question do not seem to take account.

DISCOURSE IV

1. THE Word is God from God; for 'the Word was God[1],' and again, ' Of whom are the Fathers, and of whom Christ, who is God over all, blessed for ever. Amen[2].' And since Christ is God from God, and God's Word, Wisdom, Son, and Power, therefore but One God is declared in the divine Scriptures. For the Word, being Son of the One God, is referred to Him of whom also He is; so that Father and Son are two, yet the Monad of the Godhead is indivisible and inseparable. And thus too we preserve One Beginning of Godhead and not two Beginnings, whence there is strictly a Monarchy. And of this very Beginning the Word is by nature Son, not as if another beginning, subsisting by Himself, nor having come into being externally to that Beginning, lest from that diversity a Dyarchy and Polyarchy should ensue; but of the one Beginning He is own Son, own Wisdom, own Word, existing from It. For, according to John, 'in' that ' Beginning was the Word, and the Word was with God,' for the Beginning was God; and since He is from It, therefore also ' the Word was God.' And as there is one Beginning and therefore one God, so one is that Essence and Subsistence which indeed and truly and really is, and which said ' I am that I am[3],' and not two, that there be not two Beginnings; and from the One, a Son in nature and truth, is Its own Word, Its Wisdom, Its Power, and inseparable from It. And as there is not another essence, lest there be two Beginnings, so the Word which is from that One Essence has no dissolution, nor is a sound significative, but is an essential Word and essential Wisdom, which is the true Son.

For were He not essential, God will be speaking into the air[3a], and having a body, in nothing differently from men; but since He is not man, neither is His Word according to the infirmity of man[4]. For as the Beginning is one Essence, so Its Word is one, essential, and subsisting, and Its Wisdom. For as He is God from God, and Wisdom from the Wise, and Word from the Rational, and Son from Father, so is He from Subsistence Subsistent, and from Essence Essential and Substantive, and Being from Being.

2. Since were He not essential Wisdom and substantive Word, and Son existing, but simply Wisdom and Word and Son in the Father, then the Father Himself would have a nature compounded of Wisdom and Word. But if so, the forementioned absurdities would follow; and He will be His own Father, and the Son begetting and begotten by Himself; or Word, Wisdom, Son, is a name only, and He does not subsist who owns, or rather who is, these titles. If then He does not subsist, the names are idle and empty, unless we say that God is Very Wisdom[5] and Very Word. But if so, He is His own Father and Son; Father, when Wise, Son, when Wisdom; but these things are not in God as a certain quality; away with the dishonourable[6] thought; for it will issue in this, that God is compounded of essence and quality[7]. For whereas all quality is in essence, it will clearly follow that the Divine Monad, indivisible as it is, must be compound, being severed into essence and accident[8]. We must ask then these headstrong men; The Son was proclaimed as God's Wisdom and Word; how then is He such? if as a quality, the absurdity has been shewn; but if God is that Very Wisdom, then it is the absurdity of Sabellius; therefore He is so, as an Offspring in a proper sense from the Father

---

[3a] 1 Cor. xiv. 9.   [4] Or. ii. 7.
[5] Or. ii. 19, n. 3, and below, § 4.
[6] § 9.   [7] Cf. ad Afros. 8.   [8] Cf. Euseb. Eccl.
Theol. p. 121. His opinion was misstated supr., p. 164 sq., note 9.

---

[1] John i. 1.   [2] Rom. ix. 5.   [3] Exod. iii. 14.

Himself, according to the illustration of light. For as there is light from fire, so from God is there a Word, and Wisdom from the Wise, and from the Father a Son. For in this way the Monad remains undivided and entire, and Its Son, Word not unessential, nor not subsisting, but essential truly. For were it not so, all that is said would be said notionally[1] and verbally[2]. But if we must avoid that absurdity, then is a true Word essential. For as there is a Father truly, so Wisdom truly. In this respect then they are two; not because, as Sabellius said, Father and Son are the same, but because the Father is Father and the Son Son, and they are one, because He is Son of the Essence of the Father by nature, existing as His own Word. This the Lord said, viz. 'I and the Father are One[3];' for neither is the Word separated from the Father, nor was or is the Father ever Wordless; on this account He says, 'I in the Father and the Father in Me[4].'

3. And again, Christ is the Word of God. Did He then subsist by Himself, and subsisting, has He become joined to the Father, or did God make Him or call Him His Word? If the former, I mean if He subsisted by Himself and is God, then there are two Beginnings; and moreover, as is plain, He is not the Father's own, as being not of the Father, but of Himself. But if on the contrary He be made externally, then is He a creature. It remains then to say that He is from God Himself; but if so, that which is from another is one thing, and that from which it is, is a second; according to this then there are two. But if they be not two, but the names belong to the same, cause and effect will be the same, and begotten and begetting, which has been shewn absurd in the instance of Sabellius. But if He be from Him, yet not another, He will be both begetting and not begetting; begetting because He produces from Himself, and not begetting, because it is nothing other than Himself. But if so, the same is called Father and Son notionally. But if it be unseemly so to say, Father and Son must be two; and they are one, because the Son is not from without, but begotten of God. But if any one shrinks from saying 'Offspring,' and only says that the Word exists with God, let such a one fear lest, shrinking from what is said in Scripture, he fall into absurdity, making God a being of double nature. For not granting that the Word is from the Monad, but simply as if He were joined to the Father, he introduces a twofold essence, and neither of them Father of the other. And the same of Power. And

we may see this more clearly, if we consider it with reference to the Father; for there is One Father, and not two, but from that One the Son. As then there are not two Fathers, but One, so not two Beginnings, but One, and from that One the Son essential.

4. But the Arians we must ask contrariwise: (for the Sabellianisers must be confuted from the notion of a Son, and the Arians from that of a Father:) let us say then—Is God wise and not word-less: or on the contrary, is He wisdom-less and word-less[1]? if the latter, there is an absurdity at once; if the former, we must ask, how is He wise and not word-less? does He possess the Word and the Wisdom from without, or from Himself? If from without, there must be one who first gave to Him, and before He received He was wisdom-less and word-less. But if from Himself, it is plain that the Word is not from nothing, nor once was not; for He was ever; since He of whom He is the Image, exists ever. But if they say that He is indeed wise and not word-less, but that He has in Himself His own wisdom and own word, and that, not Christ, but that by which He made Christ, we must answer that, if Christ in that word was brought to be, plainly so were all things; and it must be He of whom John says, 'All things were made by Him,' and the Psalmist, 'In Wisdom hast Thou made them all[2].' And Christ will be found to speak untruly, 'I in the Father,' there being another in the Father. And 'the Word became flesh[3]' is not true according to them. For if He in whom 'all things came to be,' Himself became flesh, but Christ is not in the Father, as Word 'by whom all things came to be,' then Christ has not become flesh, but perhaps Christ was named Word. But if so, first, there will be another besides the name, next, all things were not by Him brought to be, but in that other, in whom Christ also was made. But if they say that Wisdom is in the Father as a quality or that He is Very Wisdom[4], the absurdities will follow already mentioned. For He will be compound[5], and will prove His own Son and Father[6]. Moreover, we must confute and silence them on the ground, that the Word which is in God cannot be a creature nor out of nothing; but if once a Word be in God, then He must be Christ who says, 'I am in the Father and the Father in Me[7],' who also is therefore the Only-begotten, since no other was begotten from Him. This is One Son, who is Word, Wisdom, Power; for God is not compounded of these,

---

[1] Cf. ii. 38, n. 2.   [2] Cf. i. 52, n. 1.   3 John x. 30.
[4] Ib. xiv. 10.

[1] Or. i. 19, n. 5.   [2] John i. 3; Ps. civ. 24.   3 John i. 14
[4] § 2.   5 § 9, fin.   6 § 10.   7 John xiv. 10.

but is generative [8] of them. For as He frames the creatures by the Word, so according to the nature of His own Essence has He the Word as an Offspring, through whom He frames and creates and dispenses all things. For by the Word and the Wisdom all things have come to be, and all things together remain according to His ordinance [9]. And the same concerning the word 'Son;' if God be without Son [10], then is He without Work; for the Son is His Offspring through whom He works [11]; but if not, the same questions and the same absurdities will follow their audacity.

5. From Deuteronomy; 'But ye that did attach yourselves unto the Lord your God are alive every one of you this day [1].' From this we may see the difference, and know that the Son of God is not a creature. For the Son says, 'I and the Father are One,' and, 'I in the Father, and the Father in Me;' but things originate, when they make advance, are attached unto the Lord. The Word then is in the Father as being His own; but things originate, being external, are attached, as being by nature foreign, and attached by free choice. For a son which is by nature, is one [2] with him who begat him; but he who is from without, and is made a son, will be attached to the family. Therefore he immediately adds, 'What nation is there so great who hath God drawing nigh unto them [3]?' and elsewhere, 'I a God drawing nigh [4];' for to things originate He draws nigh, as being strange to Him, but to the Son, as being His own, He does not draw nigh, but He is in Him. And the Son is not attached to the Father, but co-exists with Him; whence also Moses says again in the same Deuteronomy, 'Ye shall obey His voice, and apply yourselves unto Him [5];' but what is applied, is applied from without.

§§ 6, 7. When the Word and Son hungered, wept, and was wearied, He acted as our Mediator, taking on Him what was ours, that He might impart to us what was His.

6. But in answer to the weak and human notion of the Arians, their supposing that the Lord is in want, when He says, 'Is given unto Me,' and 'I received,' and if Paul says, 'Wherefore He highly exalted Him,' and 'He set Him at the right hand [1],' and the like, we must say that our Lord, being Word and Son of God, bore a body, and became Son of Man, that, having become Mediator between God and men, He might minister the things of God to us, and ours to God. When then He

is said to hunger and weep and weary, and to cry Eloi, Eloi, which are our human affections, He receives them from us and offers to the Father [2], interceding for us, that in Him they may be annulled [3]. And when it is said, 'All power is given unto Me,' and 'I received,' and 'Wherefore God highly exalted Him,' these are gifts given from God to us through Him. For the Word was never in want [4], nor has come into being [5]; nor again were men sufficient to minister these things for themselves, but through the Word they are given to us; therefore, as if given to Him, they are imparted to us. For this was the reason of His becoming man, that, as being given to Him, they might pass on to us [6]. For of such gifts mere man had not become worthy; and again the mere Word had not needed them [7]; the Word then was united to us, and then imparted to us power, and highly exalted us [8]. For the Word being in man, highly exalted man himself; and, when the Word was in man, man himself received. Since then, the Word being in flesh, man himself was exalted, and received power, therefore these things are referred to the Word, since they were given on His account; for on account of the Word in man were these gifts given. And as 'the Word became flesh [9],' so also man himself received the gifts which came through the Word. For all that man himself has received, the Word is said to have received [10]; that it might be shewn, that man himself, being unworthy to receive, as far as his own nature is concerned, yet has received because of the Word become flesh. Wherefore if anything be said to be given to the Lord, or the like, we must consider that it is given, not to Him as needing it, but to man himself through the Word. For every one interceding for another, receives the gift in his own person, not as needing, but on his account for whom he intercedes.

7. For as He takes our infirmities, not being infirm [1], and hungers not hungering, but sends up what is ours that it may be abolished, so the gifts which come from God instead of our infirmities, doth He too Himself receive, that man, being united to Him, may be able to partake them. Hence it is that the Lord says, 'All things whatsoever Thou hast given Me, I have given them,' and again, 'I pray for them [2].' For He prayed for us, taking on Him what is ours, and He was giving what He received. Since then, the Word being united to man himself, the Father, regarding Him,

---

8 iii. 66, n. 3.   9 Ps. cxix. 91.   10 Or. ii. 2, n. 3.   11 Or. ii. 41; iii. 11, n. 4.   1 Deut. iv. 4.   2 i. 26, n. 2.   3 Deut. iv. 7, LXX.   4 Jer. xxiii. 23, LXX.   5 Deut. xiii. 4.   1 Matt. xxviii. 18; John x. 18; Phil. ii. 9; Eph. i. 20.

2 De Decr. 14; Or. ii. 8, 9.   3 Or. iii. 33, n. 6, and 34. 4 Or. i. 43.   5 Or. i. 43; ii. 65, 67.   6 Or. i. 42, 45. 7 Or. i. 48; iii. 38.   8 Or. i. 41, 42.   9 John i. 14. 10 iii. 38.   1 Or. ii. 60; iii. 37.   2 John xvii. 7—9.

vouchsafed to man to be exalted, to have all power and the like; therefore are referred to the Word Himself, and are as if given to Him, all things which through Him we receive. For as He for our sake became man, so we for His sake are exalted. It is no absurdity then, if, as for our sake He humbled Himself, so also for our sake He is said to be highly exalted. So 'He gave to Him,' that is, 'to us for His sake ;' 'and He highly exalted Him 3,' that is, 'us in Him.' And the Word Himself, when we are exalted, and receive, and are succoured, as if He Himself were exalted and received and were succoured, gives thanks to the Father, referring what is ours to Himself, and saying, ' All things, whatsoever Thou hast given Me, I have given unto them 4.'

§ 8. Arians date the Son's beginning earlier than Marcellus, &c.

8. Eusebius and his fellows, that is, the Ario-maniacs, ascribing a beginning of being to the Son, yet pretend not to wish Him to have a beginning of kingship 5. But this is ridiculous; for he who ascribes to the Son a beginning of being, very plainly ascribes to Him also a beginning of reigning ; so blind are they, confessing what they deny. Again, those who say that the Son is only a name, and that the Son of God, that is, the Word of the Father, is unessential and non-subsistent, pretend to be angry with those who say, ' Once He was not.' This is ridiculous also ; for they who give Him no being at all, are angry with those who at least grant Him to be in time. Thus these also confess what they deny, in the act of censuring the others. And again Eusebius and his fellows, confessing a Son, deny that He is the Word by nature, and would have the Son called Word notionally ; and the others confessing Him to be Word, deny Him to be Son, and would have the Word called Son notionally, equally void of footing.

§§ 9, 10. Unless Father and Son are two in name only, or as parts and so each imperfect, or two gods, they are coessential, one in Godhead, and the Son from the Father.

9. 'I and the Father are One 1.' You say that the two things are one, or that the one has two names, or again that the one is divided into two. Now if the one is divided into two, that which is divided must need be a body, and neither part perfect, for each is a part and not a whole. But if again the one have two names, this is the expedient of Sabellius, who said that Son and

Father were the same, and did away with either, the Father when there is a Son, and the Son when there is a Father. But if the two are one, then of necessity they are two, but one according to the God-head, and according to the Son's coessentiality with the Father, and the Word's being from the Father Himself ; so that there are two, because there is Father, and Son, namely the Word ; and one because one God. For if not, He would have said, 'I am the Father,' or 'I and the Father am ;' but, in fact, in the 'I' He signifies the Son, and in the 'And the Father,' Him who begat Him ; and in the 'One' the one Godhead and His coessentiality 2. For the Same is not, as the Gentiles hold, Wise and Wisdom, or the Same Father and Word ; for it were unfit for Him to be His own Father, but the divine teaching knows Father and Son, and Wise and Wisdom, and God and Word ; while it ever guards Him indivisible and inseparable and indissoluble in all respects.

10. But if any one, on hearing that the Father and the Son are two, misrepresent us as preaching two Gods (for this is what some feign to themselves, and forthwith mock, saying, 'You hold two Gods'), we must answer to such, If to acknowledge Father and Son, is to hold two Gods, it instantly 3 follows that to confess but one we must deny the Son and Sabellianise. For if to speak of two is to fall into Gentilism, therefore if we speak of one, we must fall into Sabellianism. But this is not so ; perish the thought ! but, as when we say that Father and Son are two, we still confess one God, so when we say that there is one God, let us consider Father and Son two, while they are one in the Godhead, and in the Father's Word being indissoluble and indivisible and inseparable from Him. And let the fire and the radiance from it be a simili-tude of man, which are two in being and in appearance, but one in that its radiance is from it indivisibly.

§§ 11, 12. Marcellus and his disciples, like Arians, say that the Word was, not indeed created, but issued, to create us, as if the Divine silence were a state of inaction, and when God spake by the Word, He acted ; or that there was a going forth and return of the Word ; a doctrine which implies change and imperfection in Father and Son.

11. They fall into the same folly with the Arians ; for Arians also say that He was created for us, that He might create us, as if God waited till our creation for His issue, as the one party say, or His creation, as the

---

3 Phil. ii. 9.   4 John xvii. 7, 8.
5 Euseb. c. Marcell. pp. 6, 32, 49, &c. &c.   1 John x. 30.

2 Here again is the word ὁμοούσιον. Contrast the language of *Orat.* iii. when commenting on the same text, in the same way ; e.g. ἐν τῇ ἰδιότητι καὶ οἰκειότητι τῆς φύσεως, καὶ τῇ ταυτότητι τῆς μιᾶς θεότητος, § 4.   3 Cf. *Or.* iii. 10, note 4.

other. Arians then are more bountiful to us than to the Son; for they say, not we for His sake, but He for ours, came to be; that is, if He was therefore created, and subsisted, that God through Him might create us. And these, as irreligious or more so, give to God less than to us. For we oftentimes, even when silent, yet are active in thinking, so as to form the results of our thoughts into images; but God they would have inactive when silent, and when He speaks then to exert strength; if, that is, when silent He could not make, and when speaking He began to create. For it is just to ask them, whether the Word, when He was in God, was perfect, so as to be able to make. If on the one hand He was imperfect, when in God, but by being begotten became perfect [1], we are the cause of His perfection, that is, if He has been begotten for us; for on our behalf He has received the power of making. But if He was perfect in God, so as to be able to make, His generation is superfluous; for He, even when in the Father, could frame the world; so that either He has not been begotten, or He was begotten, not for us, but because He is ever from the Father. For His generation evidences, not that we were created, but that He is from God; for He was even before our creation.

12. And the same presumption will be proved against them concerning the Father; for if, when silent, He could not make, of necessity He has gained power by begetting, that is, by speaking. And whence has He gained it? and wherefore? If, when He had the Word within Him, He could make, He begets needlessly, being able to make even in silence. Next, if the Word was in God before He was begotten, then being begotten He is without and external to Him. But if so, how says He now, 'I in the Father and the Father in Me [2]?' but if He is now in the Father, then always was He in the Father, as He is now, and needless is it to say, 'For us was He begotten, and He reverts after we are formed, that He may be as He was.' For He was not anything which He is not now, nor is He what He was not; but He is as He ever was, and in the same state and in the same respects; otherwise He will seem to be imperfect and alterable. For if, what He was, that He shall be afterwards, as if now He were not so, it is plain, He is not now what He was and shall be. I mean, if He was before in God, and afterwards shall be again, it follows that now the Word is not in God. But the Lord refutes such persons when He says, 'I in the Father and the Father in Me;' for so is

He now as He ever was. But if so He now is, as He was ever, it follows, not that at one time He was begotten and not at another, nor that once there was silence with God, and then He spake, but there is ever a Father[3], and a Son who is His Word, not in name[4] alone a Word, nor the Word in notion only a Son, but existing coessential[5] with the Father, not begotten for us, for we are brought into being for Him. For, if He were begotten for us, and in His begetting we were created, and in His generation the creature consists, and then He returns that He may be what He was before, first, He that was begotten will be again not begotten. For if His progression be generation, His return will be the close[6] of that generation, for when He has come to be in God, God will be silent again. But if He shall be silent, there will be what there was when He was silent, stillness and not creation, for the creation will cease to be. For, as on the Word's outgoing, the creation came to be, and existed, so on the Word's retiring, the creation will not exist. What use then for it to come into being, if it is to cease? or why did God speak, that then He should be silent? and why did He issue One whom He recalls? and why did He beget One whose generation He willed to cease? Again it is uncertain what He shall be. For either He will ever be silent, or He will again beget, and will devise a different creation (for He will not make the same, else that which was made would have remained, but another); and in due course He will bring that also to a close, and will devise another, and so on without end[7].

§§ 13, 14. *Such a doctrine precludes all real distinctions of personality in the Divine Nature. Illustration of the Scripture doctrine from 2 Cor. vi. 11, &c.*

13. This perhaps he[1] borrowed from the Stoics, who maintain that their God contracts and again expands with the creation, and then rests without end. For what is dilated is first straitened; and what is expanded is at first contracted; and it is what it was, and does but undergo an affection. If then the Monad being dilated became a Triad, and the Monad was the Father[1a], and the Triad is Father, Son, and Holy Ghost, first the Monad being dilated, underwent an affection and became what it was not; for it was dilated, whereas it had not been dilate. Next, if the Monad itself was dilated into a Triad, and that, Father and Son and Holy Ghost, then Father and Son and Spirit prove the same, as Sabellius held, unless the Monad which he speaks of is some-

---

[1] *De Syn.* 24, n. 9; *Or.* i. 14, n. 7.   [2] John xiv. 10.

[3] i. 21, n. 1.   [4] ii. 19, n. 3.   [5] ὁμοούσιος, 9, n. 2.
[6] παῦλα, cf. ii. 34, 35.   [7] εἰς ἄπειρον, ii. 68.
[1] i.e. Marcellus, cf. §§ 14, 25, &c.   [1a] Cf. § 25.

thing besides the Father, and then he ought not to speak of dilatation, since the Monad was to make Three, so that there was a Monad, and then Father, Son, and Spirit. For if the Monad were dilated, and expanded itself, it must itself be that which was expanded. And a Triad when dilated is no longer a Monad, and when a Monad it is not yet a Triad. And so, He that was Father was not yet Son and Spirit; but, when become These, is no longer only Father. And a man who thus should lie, must ascribe a body to God, and represent Him as passible; for what is dilatation, but an affection of that which is dilated? or what the dilated, but what before was not so, but was strait indeed; for it is the same, in time only differing from itself.

14. And this the divine Apostle knows, when he writes to the Corinthians, 'Be ye not straitened in us, but be ye yourselves dilated, O Corinthians[2];' for he advises identical persons to change from straitness to dilatation. And as, supposing the Corinthians being straitened were in turn dilated, they had not been others, but still Corinthians, so if the Father was dilated into a Triad, the Triad again is the Father alone. And he says again the same thing, ' Our heart is dilated[3];' and Noah says, 'May God dilate for Japheth[4],' for the same heart and the same Japheth is in the dilatation. If then the Monad dilated, it would dilate for others; but if it dilated for itself, then it would be that which was dilated; and what is that but the Son and Holy Spirit? And it is well to ask him, when thus speaking, what was the action[5] of this dilatation? or, in very truth, wherefore at all it took place? for what does not remain the same, but is in course of time dilated, must necessarily have a cause of dilatation. If then it was in order that Word and Spirit should be with Him, it is beside the purpose to say, 'First Monad, and then dilated;' for Word and Spirit were not afterwards, but ever, or God would be wordless[6], as the Arians hold. So that if Word and Spirit were ever, ever was it dilated, and not at first a Monad; but if it were dilated afterwards, then afterwards is there a Word. But if for the Incarnation it was dilated, and then became a Triad, then before the Incarnation there was not yet a Triad. And it will seem even that the Father became flesh, if, that is, He be the Monad, and was dilated in the Man; and thus perhaps there will only be a Monad, and flesh, and thirdly Spirit; if, that is, He was Himself dilated; and there will be in name only a Triad. It is absurd

too to say that it was dilated for creating; for it were possible for it, remaining a Monad, to make all; for the Monad did not need dilatation, nor was wanting in power before being dilated; it is absurd surely and impious, to think or speak thus in the case of God. Another absurdity too will follow. For if it was dilated for the sake of the creation, and while it was a Monad the creation was not, but upon the Consummation it will be again a Monad after dilatation, then the creation too will come to nought. For as for the sake of creating it was dilated, so, the dilatation ceasing, the creation will cease also.

§§ 15—24. Since the Word is from God, He must be Son. Since the Son is from everlasting, He must be the Word; else either He is superior to the Word, or the Word is the Father. Texts of the New Testament which state the unity of the Son with the Father; therefore the Son is the Word. Three hypotheses refuted—1. That the Man is the Son; 2. That the Word and Man together are the Son; 3. That the Word became Son on His incarnation. Texts of the Old Testament which speak of the Son. If they are merely prophetical, then those concerning the Word may be such also.

15. Such absurdities will be the consequence of saying that the Monad is dilated into a Triad. But since those who say so venture to separate Word and Son, and to say that the Word is one and the Son another, and that first was the Word and then the Son, come let us consider this doctrine also. Now their presumption takes various forms; for some say that the man whom the Saviour assumed is the Son[1]; and others both that the man and the Word then became Son, when they were united[2]. And others say that the Word Himself then became Son when He became man[3]; for from being Word, they say, He has become Son, not being Son before, but only Word. Now both are Stoic[4] doctrines, whether to say that God was dilated or to deny the Son, but especially is it absurd to name the Word, yet deny Him to be Son. For if the Word be not from God, reasonably might they deny Him to be Son; but if He is from God, how see they not that what exists from anything is son of him from whom it is? Next, if God is Father of the Word, why is not the Word Son of His own Father? for one is and is called father, whose is the son; and one is and is called son of another, whose is the father. If then God is not Father of Christ, neither is the Word Son; but if God be Father, then reasonably also the Word is Son. But if afterwards there is Father, and first God, this is an Arian thought[4a]. Next, it is absurd

² 2 Cor. vi. 12, 13.   3 Ib. vi. 11.   4 Gen. ix. 27, LXX.
5 ἐνέργεια [Prolegg. ch. ii. § 3 (2) c.]   6 Or. i. 19.

1 Vid. § 20.   2 Vid. § 21.   3 Vid. § 22 fin.
4 Cf. Ritt. and Prell. (Ed. 5) § 398 (?).   4a §§ 8, 13.

that God should change; for that belongs to bodies; but if they argue that in the instance of creation He became afterwards a Maker, let them know that the change is in the things [5] which afterwards came to be, and not in God.

16. If then the Son too were a work, well might God begin to be a Father towards Him as others; but if the Son is not a work, then ever was the Father and ever the Son [1]. But if the Son was ever, He must be the Word; for if the Word be not Son, and this is what a man waxes bold to say, either he holds that Word to be Father or the Son superior to the Word. For the Son being 'in the bosom of the Father [2],' of necessity either the Word is not before the Son (for nothing is before Him who is in the Father), or if the Word be other than the Son, the Word must be the Father in whom is the Son. But if the Word is not Father but Word, the Word must be external to the Father, since it is the Son who is 'in the bosom of the Father.' For not both the Word and the Son are in the bosom, but one must be, and He the Son, who is Only-begotten. And it follows for another reason, if the Word is one, and the Son another, that the Son is superior to the Word; for 'no one knoweth the Father save the Son [3],' not the Word. Either then the Word does not know, or if He knows, it is not true that 'no one knows.' And the same of 'He that hath seen Me, hath seen the Father,' and 'I and the Father are One,' for this is uttered by the Son, not the Word, as they would have it, as is plain from the Gospel; for according to John when the Lord said, 'I and the Father are One,' the Jews took up stones to stone Him. 'Jesus [4] answered them, Many good works have I shewed you from My Father, for which of those works do ye stone Me? The Jews answered Him, saying, For a good work we stone Thee not, but for blasphemy, and because that Thou, being a man, makest Thyself God. Jesus answered them, Is it not written in your law, I said, Ye are gods? If he called them gods unto whom the Word of God came, and the Scripture cannot be broken, say ye of Him, whom the Father hath sanctified and sent into the world, Thou blasphemest, because I said, I am the Son of God? If I do not the works of My Father, believe Me not. But if I do, though ye believe not Me, believe the works, that ye may know and believe that the Father is in Me, and I in the Father.' And yet, as far as the surface of the words intimated, He said neither 'I am God,' nor 'I am Son of God,' but 'I and the Father are One.'

17. The Jews then, when they heard 'One,' thought like Sabellius that He said that He was the Father, but our Saviour shews their sin by this argument: 'Though I had said "God," you should have remembered what is written, " I said, Ye are gods;" ' then to clear up 'I and the Father are One,' He has explained the Son's oneness with the Father in the words, 'Because I said, I am the Son of God.' For if He did not say it in words, still He has referred the sense of 'are One' to the Son. For nothing is one with the Father, but what is from Him. What is that which is from Him but the Son? And therefore He adds, 'that ye may know that I am in the Father, and the Father in Me.' For, when expounding the 'One,' He said that the union and the inseparability lay, not in This being That, with which It was One, but in His being in the Father and the Father in the Son. For thus He overthrows both Sabellius, in saying, 'I am ' not, "the Father," but, 'the Son of God;' and Arius, in saying, 'are One.' If then the Son and the Word are not the same, it is not that the Word is one with the Father, but the Son; nor he that hath seen the Word 'hath seen the Father,' but 'he that hath seen' the Son. And from this it follows, either that the Son is greater than the Word, or the Word has nothing beyond the Son. For what can be greater or more perfect than 'One,' and 'I in the Father and the Father in Me,' and 'He that hath seen Me, hath seen the Father?' for these utterances also belong to the Son. And hence the same John says, 'He that hath seen Me, hath seen Him that sent Me,' and, 'He that receiveth Me, receiveth Him that sent Me;' and, 'I am come a light into the world, that whosoever believeth in Me, should not abide in darkness. And, if any one hear My words and observe them not, I judge him not; for I came not to judge the world, but to save the world. The word which he shall hear, the same shall judge him in the last day, because I go unto the Father [5].' The preaching, He says, judges him who has not observed the commandment; ' for if,' He says, 'I had not come and spoken unto them, they had not had sin; but now they shall have no cloke [6],' He says, having heard My words, through which those who observe them shall reap salvation.

18. Perhaps they will have so little shame as to say, that this utterance belongs not to the Son but to the Word; but from what preceded it appeared plainly that the speaker was the Son.

5 Cf. i. 29.   1 Or. i. 14, n. 4.
2 John i. 18.   3 Matt. xi. 27.   4 John x. 32—38.   5 John xii. 45; Matt. x. 40; John xii. 46—48.   6 John xv. 22.

For He who here says, 'I came not to judge the world but to save[1],' is shewn to be no other than the Only-begotten Son of God, by the same John's saying before[2], 'For God so loved the world that He gave His Only-begotten Son, that whosoever believeth on Him should not perish, but have everlasting life. For God sent not His Son into the world to condemn the world, but that the world through Him might be saved. He that believeth on Him is not condemned, but he that believeth not is condemned already, because he hath not believed in the Name of the Only-begotten Son of God. And this is the condemnation, that light is come into the world, and men loved darkness rather than light, because their deeds are evil[3].' If He who says, 'For I came not to judge the world, but that I might save it,' is the Same as says, 'He that seeth Me, seeth Him that sent Me[4],' and if He who came to save the world and not judge it is the Only-begotten Son of God, it is plain that it is the same Son who says, 'He that seeth Me, seeth Him that sent Me.' For He who said, 'He that believeth on Me,' and, 'If any one hear My words, I judge him not,' is the Son Himself, of whom Scripture says, 'He that believeth on Him is not condemned, but He that believeth not is condemned already, because He hath not believed in the Name of the Only-begotten Son of God.' And again : 'And this is the condemnation' of him who believeth not on the Son, 'that light hath come into the world,' and they believed not in Him, that is, in the Son ; for He must be 'the Light which lighteth every man that cometh into the world[5].' And as long as He was upon earth according to the Incarnation, He was Light in the world, as He said Himself, 'While ye have light, believe in the light, that ye may be the children of light ;' for 'I,' says He, 'am come a light into the world[6].'

19. This then being shewn, it follows that the Word is the Son. But if the Son is the Light, which has come into the world, beyond all dispute the world was made by the Son. For in the beginning of the Gospel, the Evangelist, speaking of John the Baptist, says, 'He was not that Light, but that he might bear witness concerning that Light[1].' For Christ Himself was, as we have said before, the True Light that lighteth every man that cometh into the world. For if 'He was in the world, and the world was made by Him[2],' of necessity He is the Word of God, concerning whom also the Evangelist witnesses that all things were made by Him. For either they will be compelled to speak of two worlds, that the one may have

come into being by the Son and the other by the Word, or, if the world is one and the creation one, it follows that Son and Word are one and the same before all creation, for by Him it came into being. Therefore if as by the Word, so by the Son also all things came to be, it will not be contradictory, but even identical to say, for instance, 'In the beginning was the Word,' or, 'In the beginning was the Son.' But if because John did not say, 'In the beginning was the Son,' they shall maintain that the attributes of the Word do not suit with the Son, it at once follows that the attributes of the Son do not suit with the Word. But it was shewn that to the Son belongs, 'I and the Father are One,' and that it is He 'Who is in the bosom of the Father,' and, 'He that seeth Me, seeth Him that sent Me[3];' and that 'the world was brought into being by Him,' is common to the Word and the Son ; so that from this the Son is shewn to be before the world ; for of necessity the Framer is before the things brought into being. And what is said to Philip must belong, according to them, not to the Word, but to the Son. For, 'Jesus said,' says Scripture, 'Have I been so long time with you, and yet thou hast not known Me, Philip ? He that hath seen Me, hath seen the Father. And how sayest thou then, Shew us the Father ? Believest thou not, that I am in the Father and the Father in Me ? the words that I speak unto you, I speak not of Myself, but the Father that dwelleth in Me, He doeth the works. Believe Me that I am in the Father and the Father in Me, or else, believe Me for the very works' sake. Verily, verily, I say unto you, he that believeth on Me, the works that I do shall he do also, and greater works than these shall he do, because I go unto the Father. And whatsoever ye shall ask in My Name, that will I do, that the Father may be glorified in the Son[4].' Therefore if the Father be glorified in the Son, the Son must be He who said, 'I in the Father and the Father in Me ;' and He who said, 'He that hath seen Me, hath seen the Father ;' for He, the same who thus spoke, shews Himself to be the Son, by adding, 'that the Father may be glorified in the Son.'

20. If then they say that the Man whom the Word wore, and not the Word, is the Son of God the Only-begotten, the Man must be by consequence He who is in the Father, in whom also the Father is ; and the Man must be He who is One with the Father, and who is in the bosom of the Father, and the True Light. And they will be compelled to say that through the Man Himself the world came into being, and that the Man was He who came not to judge the

---

[1] John xii. 47.   [2] Ib. iii. 16—19.   [3] Ib. iii. 18, 19.
[4] Ib. xii. 45.   [5] Ib. i. 9.   Ib. xii. 36, 46.   [1] Ib. i. 8.
[2] Ib. i. 10.

[3] John x. 30 ; i. 18 ; xii. 45.   [4] Ib. xiv. 9—13.

world but to save it; and that He it was who was in being before Abraham came to be. For, says Scripture, Jesus said to them, 'Verily, verily, I say unto you, before Abraham was, I am[5].' And is it not absurd to say, as they do, that one who came of the seed of Abraham after two and forty generations[6], should exist before Abraham came to be? is it not absurd, if the flesh, which the Word bore, itself is the Son, to say that the flesh from Mary is that by which the world was made? and how will they retain 'He was in the world?' for the Evangelist, by way of signifying the Son's antecedence to the birth according to the flesh, goes on to say, 'He was in the world.' And how, if not the Word but the Man is the Son, can He save the world, being Himself one of the world? And if this does not shame them, where shall be the Word, the Man being in the Father? And where will the Word stand to the Father, the Man and the Father being One? But if the Man be Only-begotten, what will be the place of the Word? Either one must say that He comes second, or, if He be above the Only-begotten, He must be the Father Himself. For as the Father is One, so also the Only-begotten from Him is One; and what has the Word above the Man, if the Word is not the Son? For, while Scripture says that through the Son and the Word the world was brought to be, and it is common to the Word and to the Son to frame the world, yet Scripture proceeds to place the sight of the Father, not in the Word but in the Son, and to attribute the saving of the world, not to the Word, but to the Only-begotten Son. For, saith it, Jesus said, 'Have I been so long while with you, and yet hast thou not known Me, Philip? He that hath seen Me, hath seen the Father.' Nor does Scripture say that the Word knows the Father, but the Son; and that not the Word sees the Father, but the Only-begotten Son who is in the bosom of the Father.

21. And what more does the Word contribute to our salvation than the Son, if, as they hold, the Son is one, and the Word another? for the command is that we should believe, not in the Word, but in the Son. For John says, 'He that believeth on the Son, hath everlasting life; but he that believeth not the Son, shall not see life[1].' And Holy Baptism, in which the substance of the whole faith is lodged, is administered not in the Word, but in Father, Son, and Holy Ghost. If then, as they hold, the Word is one and the Son another, and the Word is not the Son, Baptism has no connection with the Word. How then are they able to hold that the Word is with the Father, when

He is not with Him in the giving of Baptism? But perhaps they will say, that in the Father's Name the Word is included? Wherefore then not the Spirit also? or is the Spirit external to the Father? and the Man indeed (if the Word is not Son) is named after the Father, but the Spirit after the Man? and then the Monad, instead of dilating into a Triad, dilates according to them into a Tetrad, Father, Word, Son, and Holy Ghost. Being brought to shame on this ground, they have recourse to another, and say that not the Man by Himself whom the Lord bore, but both together, the Word and the Man, are the Son; for both joined together are named Son, as they say. Which then is cause of which? and which has made which a Son? or, to speak more clearly, is the Word a Son because of the flesh? or is the flesh called Son because of the Word? or is neither the cause, but the concurrence of the two? If then the Word be a Son because of the flesh, of necessity the flesh is Son, and all those absurdities follow which have been already drawn from saying that the Man is Son. But if the flesh is called Son because of the Word, then even before the flesh the Word certainly, being such, was Son. For how could a being make other sons, not being himself a son, especially when there was a father[2]? If then He makes sons for Himself, then is He Himself Father; but if for the Father, then must He be Son, or rather that Son, by reason of Whom the rest are made sons.

22. For if, while He is not Son, we are sons, God is our Father and not His. How then does He appropriate the name instead, saying, 'My Father,' and 'I from the Father[3]?' for if He be common Father of all, He is not His Father only, nor did He alone come out from the Father. But he says, that He is sometimes called our Father also, because He has Himself become partaker in our flesh. For on this account the Word has become flesh, that, since the Word is Son, therefore, because of the Son dwelling in us[4], He may be called our Father also; for 'He sent forth,' says Scripture, 'the Spirit of His Son into our hearts, crying, Abba, Father[5].' Therefore the Son in us, calling upon His own Father, causes Him to be named our Father also. Surely in whose hearts the Son is not, of them neither can God be called Father. But if because of the Word the Man is called Son, it follows necessarily, since the ancients[6] are called sons even before the Incarnation, that the Word is Son even before His sojourn among us; for 'I begat sons,' saith Scripture; and in

5 John viii. 58.   6 Vid. Matt. i. 17.   1 John iii. 36.

2 Cf. iii. 11, n. 1.   3 John v. 17; xvi. 28.   4 Or. ii. 60. n. 5.   5 Gal. iv. 6.   6 Below, § 29.

the time of Noah, 'When the sons of God saw,' and in the Song, 'Is not He thy Father7?' Therefore there was also that True Son, for whose sake they too were sons. But if, as they say again, neither of the two is Son, but it depends on the concurrence of the two, it follows that neither is Son; I say, neither the Word nor the Man, but some cause, on account of which they were united; and accordingly that cause which makes the Son will precede the uniting. Therefore in this way also the Son was before the flesh. When this then is urged, they will take refuge in another pretext, saying, neither that the Man is Son, nor both together, but that the Word was Word indeed simply in the beginning, but when He became Man, then He was named 7a Son; for before His appearing He was not Son but Word only; and as the 'Word became flesh,' not being flesh before, so the Word became Son, not being Son before. Such are their idle words; but they admit of an obvious refutation.

23. For if simply, when made Man, He has become Son, the becoming Man is the cause. And if the Man is cause of His being Son, or both together, then the same absurdities result. Next, if He is first Word and then Son, it will appear that He knew the Father afterwards, not before; for not as being Word does He know Him, but as Son. For 'No one knoweth the Father but the Son.' And this too will result, that He has come afterwards to be 'in the bosom of the Father1,' and afterwards He and the Father have become One; and afterwards is, 'He that hath seen Me, hath seen the Father2.' For all these things are said of the Son. Hence they will be forced to say, The Word was nothing but a name. For neither is it He who is in us with the Father, nor whoso has seen the Word, hath seen the Father, nor was the Father known to any one at all, for through the Son is the Father known (for so it is written, 'And he to whomsoever the Son will reveal Him'), and, the Word not being yet Son, not yet did any know the Father. How then was He seen by Moses, how by the fathers? for He says Himself in the Kingdoms, 'Was I not plainly revealed to the house of thy father3?' But if God was revealed, there must have been a Son to reveal, as He says Himself, 'And he to whomsoever the Son will reveal Him.' It is irreligious then and foolish to say that the Word is one and the Son another, and whence they gained such an idea it were well to ask them. They answer, Because no mention is made in the

Old Testament of the Son, but of the Word; and for this reason they are positive in their opinion that the Son came later than the Word, because not in the Old, but in the New only, is He spoken of. This is what they irreligiously say; for first to separate between the Testaments, so that the one does not hold with the other, is the device of Manichees and Jews, the one of whom oppose the Old, and the other the New4. Next, on their shewing, if what is contained in the Old is of older date, and what in the New of later, and times depend upon the writing, it follows that 'I and the Father are One,' and 'Only-begotten,' and 'He that hath seen Me hath seen the Father5,' are later, for these testimonies are adduced not from the Old but from the New.

24. But it is not so; for in truth much is said in the Old also about the Son, as in the second Psalm, 'Thou art My Son, this day have I begotten Thee1;' and in the ninth the title2, Unto the 'end concerning the hidden things of the Son, a Psalm of David;' and in the forty-fourth, 'Unto the end, concerning the things that shall be changed to the Sons of Korah for understanding, a song about the Well-beloved;' and in Isaiah, 'I will sing to my Well-beloved a song of my Well-beloved touching my vineyard. My Well-beloved hath a vineyard3;' Who is this 'Well-beloved' but the Only-begotten Son? as also in the hundred and ninth, 'From the womb I begat Thee before the morning star4,' concerning which I shall speak afterwards; and in the Proverbs, 'Before the hills He begat me;' and in Daniel, 'And the form of the Fourth is like the Son of God5;' and many others. If then from the Old be ancientness, ancient must be the Son, who is clearly described in the Old Testament in many places. 'Yes,' they say, 'so it is, but it must be taken prophetically.' Therefore also the Word must be said to be spoken of prophetically; for this is not to be taken one way, that another. For if 'Thou art My Son' refer to the future, so does 'By the Word of the Lord were the heavens established;' for it is not said 'were brought to be,' nor 'He made.' But that 'established' refers to the future, it states elsewhere: 'The Lord reigned5a,' followed by 'He so established the earth that it can never be moved.' And if the words in the forty-fourth Psalm 'for My Well-beloved' refer to the future, so does what follows upon them, 'My heart uttered a good Word.' And if 'From the womb' relates to a man, therefore

---

7 Is. i. 2, LXX.; Gen. vi. 2; Deut. xxxii. 6.
7a Or. ii. 19, n. 3.　　1 Matt. xi. 27; John i. 18.
− a John xiv. 9.　　3 1 Sam. ii. 27, LXX.

4 Cf. i. 53, n. 7; iii. 35, n. 5.　　5 John x. 30; i. 18; xiv. 9.
1 Ps. ii. 7.　　2 Ib. ix. title xlv. title.　　3 Is. v. 1.
4 Ps. cx. 3, LXX.　　5 Prov. viii. 25, LXX.; Dan. iii. 25.
5a Cf. Exp. in Ps. xcii.

also ' From the heart.' For if the womb is human, so is the heart corporeal. But if what is from the heart is eternal, then what is 'From the womb' is eternal. And if the ' Only-begotten ' is ' in the bosom,' therefore the ' Well-beloved ' is ' in the bosom.' For ' Only-begotten ' and ' Well-beloved ' are the same, as in the words ' This is My Well-beloved Son [6].' For not as wishing to signify His love towards Him did He say ' Well-beloved,' as if it might appear that He hated others, but He made plain thereby His being Only-begotten, that He might shew that He alone was from Him. And hence the Word, with a view of conveying to Abraham the idea of ' Only-begotten,' says, ' Offer thy son thy well-beloved [7];' but it is plain to any one that Isaac was the only son from Sara. The Word then is Son, not lately come to be, or named Son, but always Son. For if not Son, neither is He Word; and if not Word, neither is He Son. For that which is from the father is a son; and what is from the Father, but that Word that went forth from the heart, and was born from the womb? for the Father is not Word, nor the Word Father, but the one is Father, and the other Son; and one begets, and the other is begotten.

§ 25. Marcellian illustration from 1 Cor. xii. 4, refuted.

25. Arius then raves in saying that the Son is from nothing, and that once He was not, while Sabellius also raves in saying that the Father is Son, and again, the Son Father [1], in subsistence [2] One, in name Two; and he [3] raves also in using as an example the grace of the Spirit. For he says, ' As there are "diversities of gifts, but the same Spirit," so also the Father is the same [4], but is dilated into Son and Spirit.' Now this is full of absurdity; for if as with the Spirit, so it is with God, the Father will be Word and Holy Spirit, to one becoming Father, to another Son, to another Spirit, accommodating himself to the need of each, and in name indeed Son and Spirit, but in reality Father only; having a beginning in that He becomes a Son, and then ceasing to be called Father, and made man in name, but in truth not even coming among us; and untrue in saying ' I and the Father,' but in reality being Himself the Father, and the other absurdities which result in the instance of Sabellius. And the name of the Son and the Spirit will necessarily cease, when the need has been supplied; and what happens will altogether be but make-belief, because it has been dis-

played, not in truth, but in name. And the Name of Son ceasing, as they hold, then the grace of Baptism will cease too; for it was given in the Son [5]. Nay, what will follow but the annihilation of the creation? for if the Word came forth that we might be created [6], and when He was come forth, we were, it is plain that when He retires into the Father, as they say, we shall be no longer. For He will be as He was; so also we shall not be, as then we were not; for when He is no more gone forth, there will be no more a creation. This then is absurd.

§§ 26—36. That the Son is the Co-existing Word, argued from the New Testament. Texts from the Old Testament continued; especially Ps. cx. 3. Besides, the Word in Old Testament may be Son in New, as Spirit in Old Testament is Paraclete in New. Objection from Acts x. 36; answered by parallels, such as 1 Cor. i. 5. Lev. ix. 7. &c. Necessity of the Word's taking flesh, viz. to sanctify, yet without destroying, the flesh.

26. But that the Son has no beginning of being, but before He was made man was ever with the Father, John makes clear in his first Epistle, writing thus : ' That which was from the beginning, which we have heard, which we have seen with our eyes, which we have looked upon, and our hands have handled of the Word of Life; and the Life was manifested, and we have seen it; and we bear witness and declare unto you that Eternal Life, which was with the Father, and was manifested unto us [1].' While he says here that ' the Life,' not ' became,' but ' was with the Father,' in the end of his Epistle he says the Son is the Life, writing, ' And we are in Him that is True, even in His Son, Jesus Christ; this is the True God and Eternal Life [2].' But if the Son is the Life, and the Life was with the Father, and if the Son was with the Father, and the same Evangelist says, ' And the Word was with God [3],' the Son must be the Word, which is ever with the Father. And as the ' Son ' is ' Word,' so ' God ' must be ' the Father.' Moreover, the Son, according to John, is not merely ' God ' but ' True God;' for according to the same Evangelist, ' And the Word was God;' and the Son said, ' I am the Life [4].' Therefore the Son is the Word and Life which is with the Father. And again, what is said in the same John, ' The Only-begotten Son which is in the bosom of the Father [5],' shews that the Son was ever. For whom John calls Son, Him David mentions in the Psalm as God's Hand [6], saying, ' Why stretchest Thou not forth Thy Right Hand out of Thy bosom [7]?' Therefore if the Hand is in

---

6 Ps. xxxiii. 6; xciii. 1; xlv. 1; Matt. iii. 17.   7 Gen. xxii. 2.
§ 13.   2 ὑποστάσει, iii. 65, n. 9.   3 i.e. Marcellus.
4 (1 Cor. xii. 4.) So Marcellus, § 13.

5 § 21.   6 ii. 24, n. 6; iv. 11, n. 4.   1 1 John i. 1, 2.
2 Ib. v. 20.   3 John i. 1.   4 Ib. xiv. 6.
5 Ib. i. 18.   6 ii. 31, n. 4.   7 Ps. lxxiv. 11, LXX.

the bosom, and the Son in the bosom, the Son will be the Hand, and the Hand will be the Son, through whom the Father made all things; for it is written, 'Thy Hand made all these things,' and 'He led out His people with His Hand [8];' therefore through the Son. And if 'this is the changing of the Right Hand of the Most Highest,' and again, 'Unto the end, concerning the things that shall be changed, a song for My Well-beloved [9];' the Well-beloved then is the Hand that was changed; concerning whom the Divine Voice also says, 'This is My Beloved Son.' This 'My Hand' then is equivalent to 'This My Son.'

27. But since there are ill-instructed men who, while resisting the doctrine of a Son, think little of the words, 'From the womb before the morning star I begat Thee [1];' as if this referred to His relation to Mary, alleging that He was born of Mary 'before the morning star,' for that to say 'womb' could not refer to His relation towards God, we must say a few words here. If then, because the 'womb' is human, therefore it is foreign to God, plainly 'heart' too has a human meaning [2], for that which has heart has womb also. Since then both are human, we must deny both, or seek to explain both. Now as a word is from the heart, so is an offspring from the womb; and as when the heart of God is spoken of, we do not conceive of it as human, so if Scripture says 'from the womb,' we must not take it in a corporeal sense. For it is usual with divine Scripture to speak and signify in the way of man what is above man. Thus speaking of the creation it says, 'Thy hands made me and fashioned me,' and, 'Thy hand made all these things,' and, 'He commanded and they were created [3].' Suitable then is its language about everything; attributing to the Son 'propriety' and 'genuineness,' and to the creation 'the beginning of being.' For the one God makes and creates; but Him He begets from Himself, Word or Wisdom. Now 'womb' and 'heart' plainly declare the proper and the genuine; for we too have this from the womb; but our works we make by the hand.

28. What means then, say they, 'Before the morning star?' I would answer, that if 'Before the morning star' shews that His birth from Mary was wonderful, many others besides have been born before the rising of the star. What then is said so wonderful in His instance, that He should record it as some choice prerogative [4], when it is common to many? Next, to

beget differs from bringing forth; for begetting involves the primary foundation, but to bring forth is nothing else than the production of what exists. If then the term belongs to the body, let it be observed that He did not then receive a beginning of coming to be when he was evangelized to the shepherds by night, but when the Angel spoke to the Virgin. And that was not night, for this is not said; on the contrary, it was night when He issued from the womb. This difference Scripture makes, and says on the one hand that He was begotten before the morning star, and on the other speaks of His proceeding from the womb, as in the twenty-first Psalm, 'Thou art he that drew Me from the womb [5].' Besides, He did not say, 'before the rising of the morning star,' but simply 'before the morning star.' If then the phrase must be taken of the body, then either the body must be before Adam, for the stars were before Adam, or we have to investigate the sense of the letter. And this John enables us to do, who says in the Apocalypse, 'I am Alpha and Omega, the first and the last, the beginning and the end. Blessed are they who make broad their robes, that they may have right to the tree of life, and may enter in through the gates into the city. For without are dogs, and sorcerers, and whoremongers, and murderers, and idolaters, and whosoever maketh and loveth a lie. I Jesus have sent My Angel, to testify these things in the Churches. I am the Root and the Offspring of David, the Bright and Morning Star. And the Spirit and the Bride say, Come; and let him that heareth say, Come; and let him that is athirst, Come; and whosoever will, let him take of the water of life freely [6].' If then 'the Offspring of David' be the 'Bright and Morning Star,' it is plain that the flesh of the Saviour is called 'the Morning Star,' which the Offspring from God preceded; so that the sense of the Psalm is this, 'I have begotten Thee from Myself before Thy appearance in the flesh;' for 'before the Morning Star' is equivalent to 'before the Incarnation of the Word.'

29. Thus in the Old also, statements are plainly made concerning the Son; at the same time it is superfluous to argue the point; for if what is not stated in the Old is of later date, let them who are thus disputatious, say where in the Old is mention made of the Spirit, the Paraclete? for of the Holy Spirit there is mention, but nowhere of the Paraclete. Is then the Holy Spirit one, and the Paraclete another, and the Paraclete the later, as not mentioned in the Old? but far be it to say that the Spirit is later, or to

---

8 Vid. Is. lxvi. 2; Deut. vii. 8.   9 Ps. lxxvii. 10, LXX.;
xlv. title.   1 Ib. cx. 3, LXX.   2 § 24.   3 Ps. cxix. 73;
cxlviii. 5.   4 ἐξαιρέτου, ii. 19, n. 6.   5 Ps. xxii. 9.   6 Rev. xxii. 13—17.

distinguish the Holy Ghost as one and the Paraclete as another; for the Spirit is one and the same, then and now hallowing and comforting those who are His recipients; as one and the same Word and Son led even then to adoption of sons those who were worthy [1]. For sons under the Old were made such through no other than the Son. For unless even before Mary there were a Son who was of God, how is He before all, when they are sons before Him? and how also 'First-born,' if He comes second after many? But neither is the Paraclete second, for He was before all, nor the Son later; for 'in the beginning was the Word [2].' And as the Spirit and Paraclete are the same, so the Son and Word are the same; and as the Saviour says concerning the Spirit, 'But the Paraclete which is the Holy Ghost, whom the Father will send in My Name [3],' speaking of One and Same, and not distinguishing, so John describes similarly when he says, 'And the Word became flesh, and dwelt among us, and we beheld His glory, glory as of one Only-begotten from the Father [4].' For here too he does not distinguish but witnesses the identity. And as the Paraclete is not one and the Holy Ghost another, but one and the same, so Word is not one, and Son another, but the Word is Only-Begotten; for He says not the glory of the flesh itself, but of the Word. He then who dares distinguish between Word and Son, let him distinguish between Spirit and Paraclete; but if the Spirit cannot be distinguished, so neither can the Word, being also Son and Wisdom and Power. Moreover, the word 'Well-beloved' even the Greeks who are skilful in phrases know to be equivalent with 'Only-begotten.' For Homer speaks thus of Telemachus, who was the only-begotten of Ulysses, in the second book of the Odyssey:

O'er the wide earth, dear youth, why seek to run,
An only child, a well-beloved [5] son?
He whom you mourn, divine Ulysses, fell
Far from his country, where the strangers dwell.

Therefore he who is the only son of his father is called well-beloved.

30. Some of the followers of the Samosatene, distinguishing the Word from the Son, pretend that the Son is Christ, and the Word another; and they ground this upon Peter's words in the Acts, which he spoke well, but they explain badly [6]. It is this: 'The Word He sent to the children of Israel, preaching peace by Jesus Christ; this is Lord of all [7].' For they say that since the Word spoke through Christ, as in the instance of the Prophets, 'Thus saith the Lord,' the prophet was one and the Lord another. But to this it is parallel to oppose the words in the first to the Corinthians, 'waiting for the revelation of our Lord Jesus Christ, who shall also confirm you unto the end unblameable in the day of our Lord Jesus Christ [8].' For as one Christ does not confirm the day of another Christ, but He Himself confirms in His own day those who wait for Him, so the Father sent the Word made flesh, that being made man He might preach by means of Himself. And therefore he straightway adds, 'This is Lord of all;' but Lord of all is the Word.

31. 'And Moses said unto Aaron, Go unto the altar and offer thy sin-offering, and thy burnt-offering, and make an atonement for thyself and for the people; and offer the offering of the people, and make an atonement for them, as the Lord commanded Moses [1].' See now here, though Moses be one, Moses himself speaks as if about another Moses, 'as the Lord commanded Moses.' In like manner then, if the blessed Peter speak of the Divine Word also, as sent to the children of Israel by Jesus Christ, it is not necessary to understand that the Word is one and Christ another, but that they were one and the same by reason of the uniting which took place in His divine and loving condescension and becoming man. And even if He be considered in two ways [2], still it is without any division of the Word, as when the inspired John says, 'And the Word became flesh, and dwelt among us [3].' What then is said well and rightly [4] by the blessed Peter, the followers of the Samosatene, understanding badly and wrongly, stand not in the truth. For Christ is understood in both ways in Divine Scripture, as when it says Christ 'God's power and God's wisdom [5].' If then Peter says that the Word was sent through Jesus Christ unto the children of Israel, let him be understood to mean, that the Word incarnate has appeared to the children of Israel, so that it may correspond to 'And the Word became flesh.' But if they understand it otherwise, and, while confessing the Word to be divine, as He is, separate from Him the Man that He has taken, with which also we believe that He is made one, saying that He has been sent through Jesus Christ, they are, without knowing it, contradicting themselves. For those who in this place separate the divine Word from the divine Incarnation, have, it seems, a degraded notion of the doctrine of His having become flesh, and entertain Gentile thoughts, as they do, conceiving that the divine Incarnation is an alteration of the Word. But it is not so; perish the thought.

32. For in the same way that John here preaches that incomprehensible union, 'the

[1] Cf. i. 39, n. 4.   [2] John i. 1.   [3] Ib. xiv. 26.
[4] Ib. i. 14.   [5] μοῦνος ἐὼν ἀγαπητός, line 365.
[6] Cf. ii. 1, n. 13.   [7] Acts x. 36.

[8] 1 Cor. i. 7, 8.   [1] Lev. ix. 7.   [2] Cf. iii. 29, init.
[3] John i. 14.   [4] ii. 44, n. 1.   [5] 1 Cor. i. 24.

mortal being swallowed up of life [1],' nay, of Him who is Very Life (as the Lord said to Martha, 'I am the Life [2]'), so when the blessed Peter says that through Jesus Christ the Word was sent, he implies the divine union also. For as when a man heard ' The Word became flesh,' he would not think that the Word ceased to be, which is absurd, as has been said before, so also hearing of the Word which has been united to the flesh, let him understand the divine mystery one and simple. More clearly however and indisputably than all reasoning does what was said by the Archangel to the Bearer of God herself, shew the oneness of the Divine Word and Man. For he says, ' The Holy Ghost shall come upon thee, and the Power of the Highest shall overshadow thee: therefore also that Holy Thing which shall be born of thee, shall be called the Son of God [3].' Irrationally then do the followers of the Samosatene separate the Word who is clearly declared to be made one with the Man from Mary. He is not therefore sent through that Man; but He rather in Him sent, saying, ' Go ye, teach all nations [4].'

33. And this is usual with Scripture [5], to express itself in inartificial and simple phrases. For so also in Numbers we shall find, Moses said to Raguel the Midianite, the father-in-law of Moses; for there was not one Moses who spoke, and another whose father-in-law was Raguel, but Moses was one. And if in like manner the Word of God is called Wisdom and Power and Right-Hand and Arm and the like, and if in His love to man He has become one with us, putting on our first-fruits and blended with it, therefore the other titles also have, as was natural, become the Word's portions. For that John has said, that in the beginning was the Word, and He with God and Himself God, and all things through Him, and without Him nothing made, shews clearly that even man is the formation of God the Word. If then after taking him, when enfeebled [6], into Himself, He renews him again through that sure renewal unto endless permanence, and therefore is made one with him in order to raise him to a diviner lot, how can we possibly say that the Word was sent through the Man who was from Mary, and reckon Him, the Lord of Apostles, with the other Apostles, I mean prophets, who were sent by Him? And how can Christ be called a mere man? on the contrary, being made one with the Word, He is with reason called Christ and Son of God, the prophet having long since loudly and clearly ascribed the Father's subsistence to Him, and

said, ' And I will send My Son Christ [7],' and in the Jordan, 'This is My Well-beloved Son.' For when He had fulfilled His promise, He shewed, as was suitable, that He was He whom He said He had sent.

34. Let us then consider Christ in both ways, the divine Word made one in Mary with Him which is from Mary. For in her womb the Word fashioned for Himself His house, as at the beginning He formed Adam from the earth; or rather more divinely, concerning whom Solomon too says openly, knowing that the Word was also called Wisdom, 'Wisdom builded herself an house [1];' which the Apostle interprets when he says, ' Which house are we [2],' and elsewhere calls us a temple, as far as it is fitting to God to inhabit a temple, of which the image, made of stones, He by Solomon commanded the ancient people to build; whence, on the appearance of the Truth, the image ceased. For when the ruthless men wished to prove the image to be the truth, and to destroy that true habitation which we surely believe His union with us to be, He threatened them not; but knowing that their crime was against themselves, He says to them, ' Destroy this Temple, and in three days I will raise it up [3],' He, our Saviour, surely shewing thereby that the things about which men busy themselves, carry their dissolution with them. For unless the Lord had built the house, and kept the city, in vain did the builders toil, and the keepers watch [4]. And so the works of the Jews are undone, for they were a shadow; but the Church is firmly established; it is 'founded on the rock,' and ' the gates of hades shall not prevail against it [5].' Theirs [6] it was to say, ' Why dost Thou, being a man, make Thyself God [7]?' and their disciple is the Samosatene; whence to his followers with reason does he teach his heresy. But ' we did not so learn Christ, if so be that we heard' Him, and were taught from Him, ' putting off the old man, which is corrupt according to the deceitful lusts,' and taking up ' the new, which after God is created in righteousness and true holiness [8].' Let Christ then in both ways be religiously considered.

35. But if Scripture often calls even the body by the name of Christ, as in the blessed Peter's words to Cornelius, when he teaches him of ' Jesus of Nazareth, whom God anointed with the Holy Ghost,' and again to the Jews, ' Jesus of Nazareth, a Man approved of God for you [1],' and again the blessed Paul to the Athenians, ' By that Man, whom He

---

[1] 2 Cor. v. 4.   [2] John xi. 25.   [3] Luke i. 35.
[4] Matt. xxviii. 19.   [5] Cf. ii. 53, n. 4.
[6] σταθρωθέντα, cf. ii. 66, n. 7.

[7] Vid. 2 Esdr. vii. 28, 29; Acts iii. 20.   [1] Prov. ix. 1.
[2] Heb. iii. 6.   [3] John ii. 19.   [4] Vid. Ps. cxxvii. 1.
[5] Vid. Matt. vii. 25; xvi. 18.   [6] ἐκείνων, John x. 33.
[7] De Decr. 1; Or. i. 4, iii. 27; de Syn. 50.   [8] Eph. iv. 20—24.
[1] Acts x. 38; ii. 22.

ordained, giving assurance to all men, in that He raised Him from the dead [2]' (for we find the appointment and the mission often synonymous with the anointing; from which any one who will may learn, that there is no discordance in the words of the sacred writers, but that they but give various names to the union of God the Word with the Man from Mary, sometimes as anointing, sometimes as mission, sometimes as appointment), it follows that what the blessed Peter says is right [3], and he proclaims in purity the Godhead of the Only-begotten, without separating the subsistence of God the Word from the Man from Mary (perish the thought! for how should he, who had heard in so many ways, 'I and the Father are one,' and 'He that hath seen Me, hath seen the Father [4]?)' In which Man, after the resurrection also, when the doors were shut, we know of His coming to the whole band [4a] of the Apostles, and dispersing all that was hard to believe in it by His words, 'Handle Me and see, for a spirit hath not flesh and bones, as ye see Me have [5].' And He did not say, 'This,' or 'this Man which I have taken to Me,' but 'Me.' Wherefore the Samosatene will gain no allowance, being refuted by so many arguments for the union of God the Word, nay by God the Word Himself, who now brings the news to all, and assures them by eating, and permitting to them that handling of Him which then took place. For certainly he who gives food to others, and they who give him, touch hands. For 'they gave Him,' Scripture says, 'a piece of a broiled fish and of an honey-comb, and' when He had 'eaten before them, He took the remains and gave to them [6].' See now, though not as Thomas was allowed, yet by another way, He afforded to them full assurance, in being touched by them; but if you would now see the scars, learn from Thomas. 'Reach hither thy hand and thrust it into My side, and reach hither thy finger and behold My hands [7];' so says God the Word, speaking of His own [8] side and hands, and of Himself as whole man and God to-

gether, first affording to the Saints even perception of the Word through the body [9], as we may consider, by entering when the doors were shut; and next standing near them in the body and affording full assurance. So much may be conveniently said for confirmation of the faithful, and correction of the unbelieving.

36. And so let Paul of Samosata also stand corrected on hearing the divine voice of Him who said 'My body,' not 'Christ besides Me who am the Word,' but 'Him [1] with Me, and Me with Him.' For I the Word am the chrism, and that which has the chrism from Me is the Man [2]; not then without Me could He be called Christ, but being with Me and I in Him. Therefore the mention of the mission of the Word shews the uniting which took place with Jesus, born of Mary, Whose Name means Saviour, not by reason of anything else, but from the Man's being made one with God the Word. This passage has the same meaning as 'the Father that sent Me,' and 'I came not of Myself, but the Father sent Me [3].' For he has given the name of mission [4] to the uniting with the Man, with Whom the Invisible nature might be known to men, through the visible. For God changes not place, like us who are hidden in places, when in the fashion of our littleness He displays Himself in His existence in the flesh; for how should He, who fills the heaven and the earth? but on account of the presence in the flesh the just have spoken of His mission. Therefore God the Word Himself is Christ from Mary, God and Man; not some other Christ but One and the Same; He before ages from the Father, He too in the last times from the Virgin; invisible [5] before even to the holy powers of heaven, visible now because of His being one with the Man who is visible; seen, I say, not in His invisible Godhead but in the operation [6] of the Godhead through the human body and whole Man, which He has renewed by its appropriation to Himself. To Him be the adoration and the worship, who was before, and now is, and ever shall be, even to all ages. Amen.

[2] Acts xvii. 31.   [3] ii. 44, n. 1.   [4] John x. 30; xiv. 9.   [9] Vid. 1 John i. 1.   [1] i.e. τὸν Χρ. vid. Matt. xxvi. 26.
[4a] ξυνωρίς.   [5] Luke xxiv. 39.   [6] Ib. xxiv. 42,   [2] Or. i. 47, n. 11.   [3] John vi. 44, viii. 42.   [4] § 35, line 8.
43, vid. Wetstein in loc.   [7] John xx. 27.   [8] Cf. iii. 33, n. 5.   [5] De Syn. 27 (15).   [6] ἐνεργεία, § 14, n. 5.

DE SYNODIS

(WRITTEN 359, ADDED TO AFTER 361.)

THE *de Synodis* is the last of the great and important group of writings of the third exile. With the exception of §§ 30, 31, which were inserted at a later recension after the death of Constantius (cf. *Hist. Ar.* 32 end), the work was all written in 359, the year of the 'dated' creed (§ 4 ἀπὸ τῆς νῦν ὑπατείας) and of the fateful assemblies of Rimini and Seleucia. It was written moreover after the latter council had broken up (Oct. 1), but before the news had reached Athanasius of the Emperor's chilling reception of the Ariminian deputies, and of the protest of the bishops against their long detention at that place. The documents connected with the last named episode reached him only in time for his postscript (§ 55). Still less had he heard of the melancholy surrender of the deputies of Ariminum at Niké on Oct. 10, or of the final catastrophe (cf. the allusion in the inserted § 30, also *Prolegg.* ch. ii. § 8 (2) *fin.*).

The first part only (see Table *infra*) of the letter is devoted to the history[1] of the twin councils. Athanasius is probably mistaken in ascribing the movement for a great council to the Acacian or Homœan anxiety to eclipse and finally set aside the Council of Nicæa. The Semi-Arians, who were ill at ease and anxious to dissociate themselves from the growing danger of Anomœanism, and who at this time had the ear of Constantius, were the persons who desired a doctrinal settlement. It was the last effort of Eastern 'Conservatism' (yet see Gwatkin, *Studies*, p. 163) to formulate a position which without admitting the obnoxious ὁμοούσιον should yet condemn Arianism, conciliate the West, and restore peace to the Christian world. The failure of the attempt, gloomy and ignominious as it was, was yet the beginning of the end, the necessary precursor of the downfall of Arianism as a power within the Church. The cause of this failure is to be found in the intrigues of the Homœans, Valens in the West, Eudoxius and Acacius in the East. Nicæa was chosen by Constantius for the *venue* of the great Synod. But Basil, then in high favour, suggested Nicomedia, and thither the bishops were summoned. Before they could meet, the city was destroyed by an earthquake, and the *venue* was changed to Nicæa again. Now the Homœans saw their opportunity. Their one chance of escaping disaster was in the principle 'divide et impera.' The Council was divided into two : the Westerns were to meet at Ariminum, the Easterns at Seleucia in Cilicia, a place with nothing to recommend it excepting the presence of a strong military force. Hence also the conference of Homœan and Semi-Arian bishops at Sirmium, who drew up in the presence of Constantius, on Whitsun-Eve, the famous 'dated' or 'third Sirmian' Creed. Its wording (ὅμοιον κατὰ πάντα) shews the predominant influence of the Semi-Arians, in spite of the efforts of Valens to get rid of the test words, upon which the Emperor insisted. Basil moreover issued a separate memorandum to explain the sense in which he signed the creed, emphasising the absolute likeness of the Son to the Father (Bright, *Introd.*, lxxxiii., Gwatkin, pp. 168 *sq.*), and accepting the Nicene doctrine in everything but the name. But for all Basil might say, the Dated Creed by the use of the word ὅμοιον had opened the door to any evasion that an Arian could desire : for ὅμοιον is a relative term admitting of degrees : what is only 'like' is *ipso facto* to some extent *un*like (see below, § 53). The party of Basil, then, entered upon the decisive contest already outmanœuvred, and doomed to failure. The events which followed are described by Athanasius (§§ 8—12). At Ariminum the Nicene, at Seleucia the Semi-Arian cause carried all before it. The Dated Creed, rejected with scorn at Ariminum, was unsuccessfully propounded in an altered form by Acacius at Seleucia. The rupture between Homœans and Semi-Arians was complete. So far only does Athanasius carry his account of the Synods : at this point he steps in with a fresh blow at the link which united Eastern Conservatism with the mixed multitude of original Arians like Euzoius and Valens, ultra Arians like Aetius and

---

[1] He undertakes to tell ἅπερ ἑώρακα καὶ ἔγνων ἀκριβῶς, words which have given rise to the romantic but ill-founded tradition that, ubiquitous and untiring in his exile, he was a secret spectator of the proceedings of his enemies at these distant gatherings. (So Gibbon and, as far as Seleucia is concerned, Tillemont. Montfaucon, as usual, takes the more sober and likely view.)

Eunomius, and Arianising opportunists like Acacius, Eudoxius, and their tribe.   In the latter he recognises deadly foes who are to be confuted and exposed without any thought of compromise ; in the former, brethren who misunderstand their own position, and whom explanation will surely bring round to their natural allies.   In this twofold aim the *de Synodis* stands in the lines of the great anti-Arian discourses (*supra*, p. 304).   But with the eye of a general Athanasius suits his attack to the new position.   With the Arians, he has done with theological argument ; he points indignantly to their intrigues and their brow-beating, to their lack of consistent principle, their endless synods and formularies (§§ 21—32) ; concisely he exposes the hollowness of their objection to the Nicene formula, the real logical basis upon which their position rests (§§ 33—40, see Bright, xc.—xcii.).   But to the Semi-Arians he turns with a serious and carefully stated vindication of the ὁμοούσιον.   The time has come to press it earnestly upon them as the only adequate expression of what they really mean, as the only rampart which can withstand the Arian invasion.   This, the last portion (§§ 41 —54) of the letter, is the *raison d'être* of the whole : the account of the Synods is merely a means to this end, not his main purpose ; the exposure of Arian principles and of Arian variations subserves the ultimate aim of detaching from them those of whom Athanasius was now hoping better things.   It may be said that he over-rated the hopefulness of affairs as far as the immediate future was concerned.   The weak acceptance by the Seleucian majority (or rather by their delegates) of the Arian creed of Niké, the triumph of Acacius, Eudoxius and their party as Constantius drifted in the last two years of his life nearer and nearer to ultra-Arianism (*de Syn.* 30, 31, his rupture with Basil, *Theodt.* ii. 27), the ascendancy of Arianism under Valens, and the eventual consolidation of a Semi-Arian sect under the name of Macedonius, all this at the first glance is a sad commentary upon the hopefulness of the *de Synodis*.   But (1) even if this were all the truth, Athanasius was right : he was acting a noble part.   In the *de Synodis* 'even Athanasius rises above himself.'   Driven to bay by the pertinacity of his enemies, exasperated as we see him in the *de Fuga* and *Arian History*, 'yet no sooner is he cheered with the news of hope than the importunate jealousies of forty years are hushed (contrast *Ep. Æg.* 7) in a moment, as though the Lord had spoken peace to the tumult of the grey old exile's troubled soul' (Gwatkin, *Studies*, p. 176, *Arian Controv.*, p. 98).   The charity that hopeth all things is always justified of her works.   (2) Athanasius, however, was right in his estimate of the position.   Not only did many of the Semi-Arians (e.g. the fifty-nine in 365) accept the ὁμοούσιον, but it was from the ranks of the Semi-Arians that the men arose who led the cause of Nicæa to its ultimate victory in the East.   There accompanied Basil of Ancyra from the Seleucian Synod to Constantinople a young deacon and ascetic, who read and welcomed the appeal of Athanasius.   Writing a few months later, this young theologian, Basil of Cæsarea, adopts the words of the *de Synodis:* 'one God we confess, one in nature not in number, for number belongs to the category of quantity, . . . neither Like nor Unlike, for these terms belong to the category of quality (cf. below, § 53) . . . He that is essentially God is Co-essential with Him that is essentially God . . . . If I am to state my own opinion, I accept "Like in essence" with the addition of "exactly" as identical in sense with "Coessential". . . but "exactly like" [without "essence"] I suspect. . . . Accordingly since "Coessential" is the term less open to abuse, on this ground I too adopt it' (*Epp.* 8, 9, the Greek in Gwatkin, *Studies*, p. 242)[2].   Basil the Great is, not indeed the only, but the conspicuous and abundant justification of the insight of Athanasius in the *de Synodis*.

Turning to subordinate parts of the Letter, we may note the somewhat unfair use made of the unlucky blunder of the Dated Creed, as though its compilers thereby admitted that their faith had no earlier origin.   The dating of the creed was doubtless 'an offence against good taste as well as ecclesiastical propriety' (as sad a blunder in its way as Macaulay's celebrated letter to his constituents from 'Windsor Castle'), and it was only in human nature to make the most of it.   More serious is the objection taken to the revolting title Αὐγούστου τοῦ αἰωνίου (which set a bad precedent for later times, Bright, lxxxiv, note 4) in contrast to the denial of the eternity of the Son.   At any rate, lending itself as it did to such obvious criticisms, we are not surprised to read (§ 29) that the copies of the creed were hastily called in and a fresh recension substituted for it.

Lastly it must be remembered that Athanasius does not aim at giving a complete catalogue of Arian or Arianising creeds, any more than at giving a full history of the double council.   Accordingly we miss (1) the confession of Arius and Euzoius, presented to Constantine in 330 ; (2) The confession 'colourless in wording, but heterodox in aim,' drawn up at Sirmium[3] against Photinus in 347 (Hil. *Fragm.* 2. 21 sq. Hefele, vol. i. p. 192) ; (3) The formulary propounded by the Emperor at Milan in 355 (Hil. *Syn.* 78) ; (4) The confession of the council of Ancyra[4], 358, alluded to § 41, see n. 9) ; (5) The Anomœan Ecthesis of Eudoxius and Aetius, Constantinople 359 (Thdt. *H.E.* ii. 27).

---

[2] Observe also that the Semi-Arian document of reconciliation in 363 (Socr. iii. 25) adopts the point pressed in *de Syn.* 41.
[3] This is, strictly speaking, the 'first' Sirmian creed, but in the Table below that of 351 is counted as such.
[4] The 'Semi-Arian digest of three confessions,' number 5 in Newman's list of Sirmian creeds, is left out of the reckoning here, as the confused statement of *Soz.* iv. 15, is the sole evidence for its existence.   It cannot be the confession referred to in Hil. *Fragm.* vi. 6, 7.   But see Newman, *Arians*, Appendix iii. note 5 ; Gwatkin, *Studies*, pp. 162, 189, *sub fin.*

In the *de Synodis* we have a worthy conclusion of the anti-Arian writings which are the legacy and the record of the most stirring and eventful period of the noble life of our great bishop.

The translation of this tract by Newman has been more closely revised than those of the 'de Decretis' and the first three 'Discourses,' as it appeared somewhat less exact in places. In §§ 10, 11, the Athanasian version has been followed, as, inaccurate as the version certainly is in places, this seemed more suitable to an edition of Athanasius; moreover, it appears to preserve some more original readings than the Hilarian text. The notes have been curtailed to some extent, especially those containing purely historical matter.

TABLE OF CONTENTS.

COUNCILS OF ARIMINUM AND SELEUCIA

PART I.

HISTORY OF THE COUNCILS.

Reason why two Councils were called. Inconsistency and folly of calling any; and of the style of the Arian formularies; occasion of the Nicene Council; proceedings at Ariminum; Letter of the Council to Constantius; its decree. Proceedings at Seleucia; reflections on the conduct of the Arians.

1. PERHAPS news has reached even yourselves concerning the Council, which is at this time the subject of general conversation; for letters both from the Emperor and the Prefects[1] were circulated far and wide for its convocation. However, you take that interest in the events which have occurred, that I have determined upon giving you an account of what I have seen myself, and accurately ascertained, which may save you from the suspense attendant on the reports of others; and this the more, because there are parties who are in the habit of misrepresenting what has happened. At Nicæa then, which had been fixed upon, the Council has not met, but a second edict was issued, convening the Western Bishops at Ariminum in Italy, and the Eastern at Seleucia the Rugged, as it is called, in Isauria. The professed reason of such a meeting was to treat of the faith touching our Lord Jesus Christ; and those who alleged it, were Ursacius, Valens, and one Germinius[2] from Pannonia; and from Syria, Acacius, Eudoxius, and Patrophilus[3] of Scythopolis. These men who had always been of the Arian party, and 'understood neither how they believe or whereof they affirm,' and were silently deceiving first one and then another, and scattering the second sowing[4] of their heresy, influenced some who seemed to be somewhat, and the Emperor Constantius among them, being a heretic[5], on some pretence about the Faith, to call a Council; under the idea that

they should be able to put into the shade the Nicene Council, and prevail upon all to turn round, and to establish irreligion everywhere instead of the Truth.

2. Now here I marvel first, and think that I shall carry every sensible man whatever with me, that, whereas a General Council had been fixed, and all were looking forward to it, it was all of a sudden divided into two, so that one part met here, and the other there. However, this was surely the doing of Providence, in order in the respective Councils to exhibit the faith without guile or corruption of the one party, and to expose the dishonesty and duplicity of the other. Next, this too was on the mind of myself and my true brethren here, and made us anxious, the impropriety of this great gathering which we saw in progress; for what pressed so much, that the whole world was to be put in confusion, and those who at the time bore the profession of clergy, should run about far and near, seeking how best to learn to believe in our Lord Jesus Christ? Certainly if they were believers already, they would not have been seeking, as though they were not. And to the catechumens, this was no small scandal; but to the heathen, it was something more than common, and even furnished broad merriment[1], that Christians, as if waking out of sleep at this time of day, should be enquiring how they were to believe concerning Christ; while their professed clergy, though claiming deference from their flocks, as teachers, were unbelievers on their own shewing, in that they were seeking what they had not. And the party of Ursacius, who were at the bottom of all this, did not understand what wrath they were storing up (Rom. ii. 5) against themselves, as our Lord says by His saints, 'Woe unto them, through whom My Name is blasphemed among the Gentiles' (Is. lii. 5; Rom. ii. 24); and by His own mouth in the Gospels (Matt. xviii. 6), 'Whoso shall offend one of these little ones, it were better for him

---

[1] [On the Prefects, see Gibbon, ch. xvii., and Gwatkin, pp. 272–281.]
[2] [Cf. *Hist. Ar.* 74, D.C.B. ii. 661.] At a later date he approached very nearly to Catholicism.
[3] [See *Prolegg.* ch. ii. § 3 (1), and, on the Arian leaders at this time, § 8 (2).]   [4] Cf. *de Decr.* § 2.   [5] *Infr.* § 12, note.

[1] Cf. Ammianus, *Hist.* xxi. 16. Eusebius, *Vit. Const.* ii. 61.

that a millstone were hanged about his neck, and that he were drowned in the depth of the sea, than,' as Luke adds, 'that he should offend one of these little ones' (Luke xvii. 2).

3. What defect of teaching was there for religious truth in the Catholic Church[2], that they should enquire concerning faith now, and should prefix this year's Consulate to their profession of faith? For Ursacius and Valens and Germinius and their friends have done what never took place, never was heard of among Christians. After putting into writing what it pleased them to believe, they prefix to it the Consulate, and the month and the day of the current year[3]; thereby to shew all sensible men, that their faith dates, not from of old, but now, from the reign of Constantius[4]; for whatever they write has a view to their own heresy. Moreover, though pretending to write about the Lord, they nominate another master for themselves, Constantius, who has bestowed on them this reign of irreligion[5]; and they who deny that the Son is everlasting, have called him Eternal Emperor; such foes of Christ are they in addition to irreligion. But perhaps the dates in the holy Prophets form their excuse for the Consulate; so bold a pretence, however, will serve but to publish more fully their ignorance of the subject. For the prophecies of the saints do indeed specify their times (for instance, Isaiah and Hosea lived in the days of Uzziah, Jotham, Ahaz, and Hezekiah; Jeremiah in the days of Josiah; Ezekiel and Daniel prophesied under Cyrus and Darius; and others in other times); yet they were not laying the foundations of divine religion; it was before them, and was always, for before the foundation of the world God prepared it for us in Christ. Nor were they signifying the respective dates of their own faith; for they had been believers before these dates. But the dates did but belong to their own preaching. And this preaching spoke beforehand of the Saviour's coming, but directly of what was to happen to Israel and the nations; and the dates denoted not the commencement of faith, as I said before, but of the prophets themselves, that is, when it was they thus prophesied. But our modern sages, not in historical narration, nor in prediction of the future, but, after writing, 'The Catholic Faith was published,' immediately add the Consulate and the month and the

day, that, as the saints specified the dates of their histories, and of their own ministries, so these may mark the date of their own faith. And would that they had written, touching 'their own[6]' (for it does date from to-day); and had not made their essay as touching 'the Catholic,' for they did not write, 'Thus we believe,' but 'the Catholic Faith was published.'

4. The boldness then of their design shews how little they understand the subject; while the novelty of their phrase matches the Arian heresy. For thus they shew, when it was they began their own faith, and that from that same time present they would have it proclaimed. And as according to the Evangelist Luke, there 'was made a decree' (Luke ii. 1) concerning the taxing, and this decree before was not, but began from those days in which it was made by its framer, they also in like manner, by writing, 'The Faith is now published,' shewed that the sentiments of their heresy are novel, and were not before. But if they add 'of the Catholic Faith,' they fall before they know it into the extravagance of the Phrygians, and say with them, 'To us first was revealed,' and 'from us dates the Faith of Christians.' And as those inscribe it with the names of Maximilla and Montanus[7], so do these with 'Constantius, Master,' instead of Christ. If, however, as they would have it, the faith dates from the present Consulate, what will the Fathers do, and the blessed Martyrs? nay, what will they themselves do with their own catechumens, who departed to rest before this Consulate? how will they wake them up, that so they may obliterate their former lessons, and may sow in turn the seeming discoveries which they have now put into writing[8]? So ignorant they are on the subject; with no knowledge but that of making excuses, and those unbecoming and unplausible, and carrying with them their own refutation.

5. As to the Nicene Council, it was not a common meeting, but convened upon a pressing necessity, and for a reasonable object. The Syrians, Cilicians, and Mesopotamians, were out of order in celebrating the Feast, and kept Easter with the Jews[9]; on the other hand, the Arian heresy had risen up against the Catholic Church, and found supporters in Eusebius and his fellows, who were both zealous

---

[2] Cf. *Orat.* ii. § 34. And Hilary *de Syn.* 91; *ad Const.* ii. 7.
[3] Cf. Hil. *ad Const.* ii. 4, 5.
[4] Cf. Tertull. *de Præscr.* 37; Hil. *de Trin.* vi. 21; Vincent. Lir. *Commonit.* 24; Jerom. *in Lucif.* 27; August. *de Bapt. contr. Don.* iii. 3.
[5] [Cf. *Hist. Ar.* §§ 52 66, 76, 44, and Prolegg. ch. ii. § 3 (2), c. 2, and § 6 (1).]

[6] 'He who speaketh of his own, ἐκ τῶν ἰδίων, speaketh a lie.' Athan. *contr. Apoll.* i. fin. . . . The Simonists, Dositheans, &c. . . . each privately (ἰδίως) and separately has brought in a private opinion.' Hegesippus, ap Euseb. *Hist.* iv. 22. Sophronius at Seleucia cried out, 'If to publish day after day our own private (ἰδίαν) will, be a profession of faith, accuracy of truth will fail us.' Socr. ii. 40.   [7] Vid. *supr. Orat.* iii. § 47.
[8] Cf. Tertull. *Præscr.* 29; Vincent, *Comm.* 24; Greg. Naz. *ad Cledon Ep.* 102, p. 97.   [9] Cf. D.C.A. i. 588 *sqq.*

for the heresy, and conducted the attack upon religious people. This gave occasion for an Ecumenical Council, that the feast might be everywhere celebrated on one day, and that the heresy which was springing up might be anathematized. It took place then; and the Syrians submitted, and the Fathers pronounced the Arian heresy to be the forerunner of Antichrist [10], and drew up a suitable formula against it. And yet in this, many as they are, they ventured on nothing like the proceedings [11] of these three or four men [12]. Without prefixing Consulate, month, and day, they wrote concerning Easter, 'It seemed good as follows,' for it did then seem good that there should be a general compliance; but about the faith they wrote not, 'It seemed good,' but, 'Thus believes the Catholic Church;' and thereupon they confessed how they believed, in order to shew that their own sentiments were not novel, but Apostolical; and what they wrote down was no discovery of theirs, but is the same as was taught by the Apostles [13].

6. But the Councils which they are now setting in motion, what colourable pretext have they [1]? If any new heresy has risen since the Arian, let them tell us the positions which it has devised, and who are its inventors? and in their own formula, let them anathematize the heresies antecedent to this Council of theirs, among which is the Arian, as the Nicene Fathers did, that it may appear that they too have some cogent reason for saying what is novel. But if no such event has happened, and they have it not to shew, but rather they themselves are uttering heresies, as holding Arius's irreligion, and are exposed day by day, and day by day shift their ground [2], what need is there of Councils, when the Nicene is sufficient, as against the Arian heresy, so against the rest, which it has condemned one and all by means of the sound faith? For even the notorious Aetius, who was surnamed godless [3], vaunts not of the discovering of any mania of his own, but under stress of weather has been wrecked upon Arianism, himself and the

persons whom he has beguiled. Vainly then do they run about with the pretext that they have demanded Councils for the faith's sake; for divine Scripture is sufficient above all things; but if a Council be needed on the point, there are the proceedings of the Fathers, for the Nicene Bishops did not neglect this matter, but stated the doctrine so exactly, that persons reading their words honestly, cannot but be reminded by them of the religion towards Christ announced in divine Scripture [4].

7. Having therefore no reason on their side, but being in difficulty whichever way they turn, in spite of their pretences, they have nothing left but to say; 'Forasmuch as we contradict our predecessors, and transgress the traditions of the Fathers, therefore we have thought good that a Council should meet [5]; but again, whereas we fear lest, should it meet at one place, our pains will be thrown away, therefore we have thought good that it be divided into two; that so when we put forth our documents to these separate portions, we may overreach with more effect, with the threat of Constantius the patron of this irreligion, and may supersede the acts of Nicæa, under pretence of the simplicity of our own documents.' If they have not put this into words, yet this is the meaning of their deeds and their disturbances. Certainly, many and frequent as have been their speeches and writings in various Councils, never yet have they made mention of the Arian heresy as objectionable; but, if any present happened to accuse the heresies, they always took up the defence of the Arian, which the Nicene Council had anathematized; nay, rather, they cordially welcomed the professors of Arianism. This then is in itself a strong argument, that the aim of the present Councils was not truth, but the annulling of the acts of Nicæa; but the proceedings of them and their friends in the Councils themselves, make it equally clear that this was the case:—For now we must relate everything as it occurred.

8. When all were in expectation that they were to assemble in one place, whom the Emperor's letters convoked, and to form one Council, they were divided into two; and, while some betook themselves to Seleucia called the Rugged, the others met at Ariminum, to the number of those four hundred bishops and more, among whom were Germinius, Auxentius, Valens, Ursacius, Demophilus, and Gaius [6]. And, while the whole assembly was discussing the matter from the

---

[10] πρόδρομος, præcursor, is almost a received word for the predicted apostasy or apostate (vid. note on S. Cyril's *Cat.* xv. 9), but the distinction was not always carefully drawn between the apostate and the Antichrist. [Cf. both terms applied to Constantius, *Hist. Ar. passim,* and by Hilary and Lucifer.]

[11] At Seleucia Acacius said, 'If the Nicene faith has been altered once and many times since, no reason why we should not dictate another faith now.' Eleusius the Semi-Arian answered, 'This Council is called, not to learn what it does not know, nor to receive a faith which it does not possess, but walking in the faith of the fathers' (meaning the Council of the Dedication. A.D. 341. vid. *infr.* § 22), 'it swerves not from it in life or death.' On this Socrates (*Hist.* ii. 40) observes, 'How call you those who met at Antioch Fathers, O Eleusius, you who deny *their* Fathers,' &c.

[12] ὀλίγοι τινές, says Pope Julius, *supr.* p. 118, cf. τινές, p. 225.

[13] *Infr.* § 9, note.   [1] Ad *Ep. Æg.* 10.

[2] Vid. *de Decr.* init. and § 4. We shall have abundant instances of the Arian changes as this Treatise proceeds. Cf. Hilary *contr. Constant.* 23. Vincent. *Comm.* 20.

[3] Vid. *de Decr.* 1. note.

[4] Vid. *de Decr.* 32, note.

[5] Cf. the opinion of Nectarius and Sisinnius, Socr. v. 10.

[6] [On Demophilus and Gaius see D.C.B. i. 812, 387 (20); on Auxentius, *ad Afr.* note q.]

Divine Scriptures, these men produced [7] a paper, and, reading out the Consulate, they demanded that it should be preferred to every Council, and that no questions should be put to the heretics beyond it, nor inquiry made into their meaning, but that it should be sufficient by itself;—and what they had written ran as follows :—

The Catholic Faith [8] was published in the presence of our Master the most religious and gloriously victorious Emperor, Constantius, Augustus, the eternal and august, in the Consulate of the most illustrious Flavii, Eusebius and Hypatius, in Sirmium on the 11th of the Calends of June [9].

We believe in one Only and True God, the Father Almighty, Creator and Framer of all things :

And in one Only-begotten Son of God, who, before all ages, and before all origin, and before all conceivable time, and before all comprehensible essence, was begotten impassibly from God : through whom the ages were disposed and all things were made ; and Him begotten as the Only-begotten, Only from the Only Father, God from God, like to the Father who begat Him, according to the Scriptures ; whose origin no one knoweth save the Father alone who begat Him. We know that He, the Only-begotten Son of God, at the Father's bidding came from the heavens for the abolishment of sin, and was born of the Virgin Mary, and conversed with the disciples, and fulfilled the Economy according to the Father's will, and was crucified, and died and descended into the parts beneath the earth, and regulated the things there, Whom the gate-keepers of hell saw (Job xxxviii. 17, LXX.) and shuddered ; and He rose from the dead the third day, and conversed with the disciples, and fulfilled all the Economy, and when the forty days were full, ascended into the heavens, and sitteth on the right hand of the Father, and is coming in the last day of the resurrection in the glory of the Father, to render to every one according to his works.

And in the Holy Ghost, whom the Only-begotten of God Himself, Jesus Christ, had promised to send to the race of men, the Paraclete, as it is written, 'I go to My Father, and I will ask the Father, and He shall send unto you another Paraclete, even the Spirit of Truth He shall take of Mine and shall teach and bring to your remembrance all things' (Joh. xiv. 16, 17, 26 ; xvi. 14).

But whereas the term 'essence,' has been adopted by the Fathers in simplicity, and gives offence as being misconceived by the people, and is not contained in the Scriptures, it has seemed good to remove it, that it be never in any case used of God again, because the divine Scriptures nowhere use it of Father and Son. But we say that the Son is like the Father in all things, as also the Holy Scriptures say and teach [1].

9. When this had been read, the dishonesty of its framers was soon apparent. For on the Bishops proposing that the Arian heresy should be anathematized together with the other heresies too, and all assenting, Ursacius and Valens and those with them refused; till in the event the Fathers condemned them, on the ground that their confession had been written, not in sincerity, but for the annulling of the acts of

Nicæa, and the introduction instead of their unhappy heresy. Marvelling then at the deceitfulness of their language and their unprincipled intentions, the Bishops said : ' Not as if in need of faith have we come hither ; for we have within us faith, and that in soundness : but that we may put to shame those who gainsay the truth and attempt novelties. If then ye have drawn up this formula, as if now beginning to believe, ye are not so much as clergy, but are starting with school ; but if you meet us with the same views with which we have come hither, let there be a general unanimity, and let us anathematize the heresies, and preserve the teaching of the Fathers. Thus pleas for Councils will not longer circulate about, the Bishops at Nicæa having anticipated them once for all, and done all that was needful for the Catholic Church [2].' However, even then, in spite of this general agreement of the Bishops, still the above-mentioned refused. So at length the whole Council, condemning them as ignorant and deceitful men, or rather as heretics, gave their suffrages in behalf of the Nicene Council, and gave judgment all of them that it was enough ; but as to the forenamed Ursacius and Valens, Germinius, Auxentius, Gaius, and Demophilus, they pronounced them to be heretics, deposed them as not really Christians, but Arians, and wrote against them in Latin what has been translated in its substance into Greek, thus :—

10. Copy of an Epistle from the Council to Constantius Augustus [3].

We believe that what was formerly decreed was brought about both by God's command and by order of your piety. For we the bishops, from all the Western cities, assembled together at Ariminum, both that the Faith of the Catholic Church might be made known, and that gainsayers might be detected. For, as we have found after long deliberation, it appeared desirable to adhere to and maintain to the end, that faith which, enduring from antiquity, we have received as preached by the prophets, the Gospels, and the Apostles through our Lord Jesus Christ, Who is Keeper of your Kingdom and Patron of your power. For it appeared wrong and unlawful to make any change in what was rightly and justly defined, and what was resolved upon in common at Nicæa along with the Emperor your father, the most glorious Constantine,—the doctrine and spirit of which [definition] went abroad and was proclaimed in the hearing and understanding of all men. For it alone was the conqueror and destroyer of the heresy of Arius, by which not that only but the other heresies [4] also were destroyed, to which of a truth it is perilous to add, and full of danger to minish aught from it, since if either be done, our enemies will be able with impunity to do whatever they will.

Accordingly Ursacius and Valens, since they had been

---

[7] [See Prolegg. ch. ii. § 8 (2), and Introd. to this Tract.]
[8] 8th Confession, or 3rd Sirmian, of 359, vid. § 29, *infr.*
[9] May 22, 359, Whitsun-Eve.
[1] On the last clause, see Prolegg. *ubi supra.*

[2] [Cf. *Tom. ad Ant.* 5, Soz. iii. 12.]
[3] Cf. Socr. ii. 39 ; Soz. iv. 10 ; Theod. *H.E.* ii. 19 ; Niceph. i. 40. The Latin original is preserved by Hilary, *Fragm.* viii., but the Greek is followed here, as stated *supr. Introd.*
[4] The Hilarian Latin is much briefer here.

from of old abettors and sympathisers of the Arian dogma, were properly declared separate from our communion, to be admitted to which they asked to be allowed a place of repentance and pardon for the transgressions of which they were conscious, as the documents drawn up by them testify. By which means forgiveness and pardon on all charges has been obtained. Now the time of these transactions was when the council was assembled at Milan [4a], the presbyters of the Roman Church being also present. But knowing at the same time that Constantine of worthy memory had with all accuracy and deliberation published the Faith then drawn up ; when he had been baptized by the hands of men, and had departed to the place which was his due, [we think it] unseemly to make a subsequent innovation and to despise so many saints, confessors, martyrs, who compiled and drew up this decree; who moreover have continued to hold in all matters according to the ancient law of the Church ; whose faith God has imparted even to the times of your reign through our Master Jesus Christ, through whom also it is yours to reign and rule over the world in our day [5]. Once more then the pitiful men of wretched mind with lawless daring have announced themselves as the heralds of an impious opinion, and are attempting to upset every summary of truth. For when according to your command the synod met, those men laid bare the design of their own deceitfulness. For they attempted in a certain unscrupulous and disorderly manner to propose to us an innovation, having found as accomplices in this plot Germinius, Auxentius [5a], and Gaius, the stirrers up of strife and discord, whose teaching by itself has gone beyond every pitch of blasphemy. But when they perceived that we did not share their purpose, nor agree with their evil mind, they transferred themselves to our council, alleging that it might be advisable to compile something instead. But a short time was enough to expose their plans. And lest the Churches should have a recurrence of these disturbances, and a whirl of discord and confusion throw everything into disorder, it seemed good to keep undisturbed the ancient and reasonable institutions, and that the above persons should be separated from our communion. For the information therefore of your clemency, we have instructed our legates to acquaint you with the judgment of the Council by our letter, to whom we have given this special direction, to establish the truth by resting their case upon the ancient and just decrees ; and they will also assure your piety that peace would not be accomplished by the removal of those decrees as Valens and Ursacius alleged. For how is it possible for peace-breakers to bring peace ? on the contrary, by their means strife and confusion will arise not only in the other cities, but also in the Church of the Romans. On this account we ask your clemency to regard our legates with favourable ears and a serene countenance, and not to suffer aught to be abrogated to the dishonour of the dead; but allow us to abide by what has been defined and laid down by our forefathers, who, we venture to say, we trust in all things acted with prudence and wisdom and the Holy Spirit; because by these novelties not only are the faithful made to disbelieve, but the infidels also are embittered [5b]. We pray also that you should give orders that so many Bishops who are detained abroad, among whom are numbers who are broken with age and poverty, may be enabled to return to their own country, lest the Churches suffer, as being

deprived of their Bishops. This, however, we ask with earnestness, that nothing be innovated upon existing creeds, nothing withdrawn ; but that all remain incorrupt which has continued in the times of your Father's piety and to the present time ; and that you will not permit us to be harassed, and estranged from our sees ; but that the Bishops may in quiet give themselves always to prayers and worship, which they do always offer for your own safety and for your reign, and for peace, which may the Divinity bestow on you for ever. But our legates are conveying the subscriptions and titles of the Bishops, and will also inform your piety from the Holy Scriptures themselves.

11. *Decree of the Council* [6].

As far as it was fitting and possible, dearest brethren, the general Council and the holy Church have had patience, and have generously displayed the Church's forbearance towards Ursacius and Valens, Gaius, Germinius, and Auxentius ; who by so often changing what they had believed, have troubled all the Churches, and still are endeavouring to foist their heretical spirit upon the faith of the orthodox. For they wish to annul the formulary passed at Nicæa, which was framed against the Arian heresy. They have presented to us besides a creed drawn up by themselves from without, and utterly alien to the most holy Church ; which we could not lawfully receive. Even before this, and now, have they been pronounced heretics and gainsayers by us, whom we have not admitted to our communion, but condemned and deposed them in their presence by our voices. Now then, what seems good to you, again declare, that each one's vote may be ratified by his subscription.

The Bishops answered with one accord, It seems good that the aforenamed heretics should be condemned, that the Catholic faith may remain in peace.

Matters at Ariminum then had this speedy issue ; for there was no disagreement there, but all of them with one accord both put into writing what they decided upon, and deposed the Arians [7].

12. Meanwhile the transactions in Seleucia the Rugged were as follows : it was in the month called by the Romans September, by the Egyptians Thoth, and by the Macedonians Gorpiæus, and the day of the month according to the Egyptians the 16th [8], upon which all the members of the Council assembled together. And there were present about a hundred and sixty ; and whereas there were many who were accused among them, and their accusers were crying out against them, Acacius, and Patrophilus, and Uranius of Tyre, and Eudoxius, who usurped the Church of Antioch, and Leontius [8a], and Theodotus [8b], and Evagrius, and

---

4a 347.
5 The whole passage is either much expanded by Athan., or much condensed by Hilary.
5a Auxentius, omitted in Hilary's copy. A few words are wanting in the Latin in the commencement of one of the sentences which follow. [See above, note 3.]
5b The Greek here mistranslates 'credulitatem' as though it were 'crudelitatem.' The original sense is the heathen are kept back from believing.

6 This Decree is also preserved in Hilary, who has besides preserved the 'Catholic Definition' of the Council, in which it professes its adherence to the Creed of Nicæa, and, in opposition to the Sirmian Confession which the Arians had proposed, acknowledges in particular both the word and the meaning of 'substance:' 'substantiæ nomen et rem, a multis sanctis Scripturis insinuatam mentibus nostris, obtinere debere sui firmitatem.' *Fragm.* vii. 3. [The decree is now re-translated from the Greek.]
7 [On the subsequent events at Ariminum, see Prolegg. *ubi supra.*]
8 i.e. Sep. 14, 359 (Egyptian leap-year.) Gorpiæus was the first month of the Syro-Macedonic year among the Greeks, dating according to the era of the Seleucidæ. The original transactions at Ariminum had at this time been finished as much as two months, and its deputies were waiting for Constantius at Constantinople.
8a [Of Tripolis, D.C.B. iii. 688 (3).]   8b ['Theodosius' *infr.*]

Theodulus, and George who has been driven from the whole world[9], adopt an unprincipled course. Fearing the proofs which their accusers had to shew against them, they coalesced with the rest of the Arian party (who were mercenaries in the cause of irreligion for this purpose, and were ordained by Secundus, who had been deposed by the great Council), the Libyan Stephen, and Seras, and Polydeuces, who were under accusation upon various charges, next Pancratius, and one Ptolemy a Meletian[10]. And they made a pretence[11] of entering upon the question of faith, but it was clear they were doing so from fear of their accusers ; and they took the part of the heresy, till at length they were divided among themselves. For, whereas those with Acacius and his fellows lay under suspicion and were very few, the others were the majority ; therefore Acacius and his fellows, acting with the boldness of desperation, altogether denied the Nicene formula, and censured the Council, while the others, who were the majority, accepted the whole proceedings of the Council, except that they complained of the word 'Coessential,' as obscure and so open to suspicion. When then time passed, and the accusers pressed, and the accused put in pleas, and thereby were led on further by their irreligion and blasphemed the Lord, thereupon the majority of Bishops became indignant[12], and deposed Acacius, Patrophilus, Uranius, Eudoxius, and George the contractor[1], and others from Asia, Leontius, and Theodosius, Evagrius and Theodulus, and excommunicated Asterius, Eusebius, Augarus, Basilicus, Phœbus, Fidelius, Eutychius, and Magnus. And this they did on their non-appearance, when summoned to defend themselves on charges which numbers preferred against them. And they decreed that so they should remain, until they made their defence and cleared themselves of the offences imputed to them. And after despatching the sentence pronounced against them to the diocese of each, they pro-

ceeded to Constantius, the most irreligious[2] Augustus, to report to him their proceedings, as they had been ordered. And this was the termination of the Council in Seleucia.

13. Who then but must approve of the conscientious conduct of the Bishops at Ariminum? who endured such labour of journey and perils of sea, that by a sacred and canonical resolution they might depose the Arians, and guard inviolate the definitions of the Fathers. For each of them deemed that, if they undid the acts of their predecessors, they were affording a pretext to their successors to undo what they themselves then were enacting[3]. And who but must condemn the fickleness of Eudoxius, Acacius, and their fellows, who sacrifice the honour due to their own fathers to partizanship and patronage of the Ario-maniacs[4]? for what confidence can be placed in their acts, if the acts of their fathers be undone? or how call they them fathers and themselves successors, if they set about impeaching their judgment? and especially what can Acacius say of his own master, Eusebius, who not only gave his subscription in the Nicene Council, but even in a letter[5] signified to his flock, that that was true faith, which the Council had declared? for, if he explained himself in that letter in his own way[6], yet he did not contradict the Council's terms, but even charged it upon the Arians, that their position that the Son was not before His generation, was not even consistent with His being before Mary. What then will they proceed to teach the people who are under their teaching? that the Fathers erred? and how are they themselves to be trusted by those, whom they teach to disobey their Teachers? and with what eyes too will they look upon the sepulchres of the Fathers whom they now name heretics? And why do they defame the Valentinians, Phrygians, and Manichees, yet give the name of saint to those whom they themselves suspect of making parallel statements? or how can they any longer be Bishops, if they were ordained by persons whom they accuse of heresy[7]? But if their sentiments were wrong and their writings se-

---

[9] There is little to observe of these Acacian Bishops in addition to [the names and sees in Epiph. *Hær.* lxxiii. 26] except that George is the Cappadocian, the notorious intruder into the see of S. Athanasius. [For his expulsion see Fest. *Ind.* xxx, and on the composition of the council, see Gwatkin, note G, p. 190.]

[10] The Meletian schismatics of Egypt had formed an alliance with the Arians from the first. Cf. *Ep. Æg.* 22. vid. also *Hist. Arian.* 31, 78. After Sardica the Arians attempted a coalition with the Donatists of Africa. Aug. *contr. Cresc.* iii. 38.

[11] Acacius had written to the Semi-Arian Macedonius of Constantinople in favour of the κατὰ πάντα ὅμοιον, and of the Son's being τῆς αὐτῆς οὐσίας, and this the Council was aware of. Soz. iv. 22. Acacius made answer that no one ancient or modern was ever judged by his writings. Socr. ii. 40.

[12] They also confirmed the Semi-Arian Confession of the Dedication, 341. of which *infr.* § 22. After this the Acacians drew up another Confession, which Athan. has preserved, *infr.* § 29. in which they persist in their rejection of all but Scripture terms. This the Semi-Arian majority rejected, and proceeded to depose its authors.

[1] Pork contractor to the troops, ὑποδέκτην, *Hist. Arian.* 75. vid. Naz. *Orat.* 21. 16.

[2] [Cf. *supr.* pp. 237, 267.]   [3] *Supr.* § 5, note 1.

[4] On the word 'Ἀρειομανίται, Gibbon observes, 'The ordinary appellation with which Athanasius and his followers chose to compliment the Arians, was that of Ariomanites,' ch. xxi. note 61. Rather, the name originally was a state title. injoined by Constantine, vid. Petav. *de Trin.* i. 8 fin. Naz. *Orat.* p. 794. note e. [Petavius states this, but without proof.] Several meanings are implied in this title ; the real reason for it was the fanatical fury with which it spread and maintained itself ; and hence the strange paronomasia of Constantine, 'Ἀρὲς ἄρειε, with an allusion to Hom. *Il.* v. 31. A second reason, or rather sense, of the appellation was that, denying the Word, they have forfeited the gift of reason, e.g. τῶν 'Ἀρειομανιτῶν τὴν ἀλογίαν. *de Sent. Dion.* init. 24 fin. *Orat.* ii. § 32, iii. § 63. [The note, which is here much condensed, gives profuse illustrations of this figure of speech.]

[5] Vid. *supr.* pp. 152, 74.

[6] ὡς ἠθέλησεν. vid. also *de Decr.* § 3. ὡς ἠθέλησαν. *ad Ep. Æg.* 5.   [7] § 5, note 1.

duced the world, then let their memory perish altogether; when, however, you cast out their books, go and cast out their remains too from the cemeteries, so that one and all may know that they are seducers, and that you are parricides.

14. The blessed Apostle approves of the Corinthians because, he says, 'ye remember me in all things, and keep the traditions as I delivered them to you' (1 Cor. xi. 2); but they, as entertaining such views of their predecessors, will have the daring to say just the reverse to their flocks: 'We praise you not for remembering your fathers, but rather we make much of you, when you hold not their traditions.' And let them go on to accuse their own unfortunate birth, and say, 'We are sprung not of religious men but of heretics.' For such language, as I said before, is consistent in those who barter their Fathers' fame and their own salvation for Arianism, and fear not the words of the divine proverb, 'There is a generation that curseth their father' (Prov. xxx. 11; Ex. xxi. 17), and the threat lying in the Law against such. They then, from zeal for the heresy, are of this obstinate temper; you, however, be not troubled at it, nor take their audacity for truth. For they dissent from each other, and, whereas they have revolted from their Fathers, are not of one and the same mind, but float about with various and discordant changes. And, as quarrelling with the Council of Nicæa, they have held many Councils themselves, and have published a faith in each of them, and have stood to none[8], nay, they will never do otherwise, for perversely seeking, they will never find that Wisdom which they hate. I have accordingly subjoined portions both of Arius's writings and of whatever else I could collect, of their publications in different Councils; whereby you will learn to your surprise with what object they stand out against an Ecumenical Council and their own Fathers without blushing.

PART II.

HISTORY OF ARIAN OPINIONS.

Arius's own sentiments; his Thalia and Letter to S. Alexander; corrections by Eusebius and others; extracts from the works of Asterius; letter of the Council of Jerusalem; first Creed of Arians at the Dedication of Antioch; second, Lucian's on the same occasion; third, by Theophronius; fourth, sent to Constans in Gaul; fifth, the Macrostich sent into Italy; sixth, at Sirmium; seventh, at the same place; and eighth also, as given above in § 8; ninth, at Seleucia; tenth, at Constantinople; eleventh, at Antioch.

15. Arius and those with him thought and

professed thus: 'God made the Son out of nothing, and called Him His Son;' 'The Word of God is one of the creatures;' and 'Once He was not;' and 'He is alterable; capable, when it is His Will, of altering.' Accordingly they were expelled from the Church by the blessed Alexander. However, after his expulsion, when he was with Eusebius and his fellows, he drew up his heresy upon paper, and imitating in the Thalia no grave writer, but the Egyptian Sotades, in the dissolute tone of his metre[1], he writes at great length, for instance as follows:—

Blasphemies of Arius.

God Himself then, in His own nature, is ineffable by all men. Equal or like Himself He alone has none, or one in glory. And Ingenerate we call Him, because of Him who is generate by nature. We praise Him as without beginning because of Him who has a beginning. And adore Him as everlasting, because of Him who in time has come to be. The Unbegun made the Son a beginning of things originated; and advanced Him as a Son to Himself by adoption. He ·has nothing proper to God in proper subsistence. For He is not equal, no, nor one in essence[2] with Him. Wise is God, for He is the teacher of Wisdom[3]. There is full proof that God is invisible to all beings; both to things which are through the Son, and to the Son He is invisible. I will say it expressly, how by the Son is seen the Invisible; by that power by which God sees, and in His own measure, the Son endures to see the Father, as is lawful. Thus there is a Triad, not in equal glories. Not intermingling with each other[4] are their subsistences. One more glorious than the other in their glories unto immensity. Foreign from the Son in essence is the Father, for He is without beginning. Understand that the Monad was; but the Dyad was not, before it was in existence. It follows at once that, though the Son was not, the Father was God. Hence the Son, not being (for He existed at the will of the Father), is God Only-begotten[4a], and He is alien from either. Wisdom existed as Wisdom by the will of the Wise God.

---

1 Cf. *Orat.* i. §§ 2—5; *de Sent. D.* 6; Socr. i. 9. The Arian Philostorgius tells us that 'Arius wrote songs for the sea and for the mill and for the road, and then set them to suitable music,' *Hist.* ii. 2. It is remarkable that Athanasius should say the *Egyptian* Sotades, and again in *Sent. D.* 6. There were two Poets of the name; one a writer of the Middle Comedy, *Athen. Deipn.* vii. 11; but the other, who is here spoken of, was a native of Maronea in Crete, according to Suidas (*in voc.*), under the successors of Alexander, *Athen.* xiv. 4. He wrote in Ionic metre, which was of infamous name from the subjects to which he and others applied it. vid. *Suid.* ibid. Horace's Ode, 'Miserarum est neque amori, &c.' is a specimen of this metre, and some have called it Sotadic; but Bentley shews *in loc.* that Sotades wrote in the Ionic *a majore.* Athenæus implies that all Ionic metres were called Sotadic, or that Sotades wrote in various Ionic metres. The Church adopted the Doric music, and forbade the Ionic and Lydian. The name 'Thalia' commonly belonged to convivial songs; Martial contrasts the 'lasciva Thalia' with 'carmina sanctiora,' *Epigr.* vii. 17. vid. Thaliarchus, 'the master of the feast,' Horat. *Od.* i. 9. [The metre of the fragments of the 'Thalia' is obscure, there are no traces of the Ionic foot, but very distinct anapæstic cadences. In fact the lines resemble ill-constructed or very corrupt anapæstic tetrameters catalectic, as in a comic *Parabasis.* For Sotades, the Greek text here reads corruptly Sosates.]

2 This passage ought to have been added *supr.* p. 163, note 8, as containing a more direct denial of the ὁμοούσιον.

3 That is, Wisdom, or the Son, is but the *disciple* of Him who is Wise, and not the *attribute* by which He is Wise, which is what the Sabellians said, vid. *Orat.* iv. § 2, and what Arius imputed to the Church.

4 ἀνεπίμικτοί, that is, he denied the περιχώρησις, vid. *supr. Orat.* iii. 3, &c.

4a [John i. 18, best MSS., and cf. Hort, *Two Diss.* p. 26.]

8 *Ad Ep. Æg.* 6.

Hence He is conceived in numberless conceptions[5]: Spirit, Power, Wisdom, God's glory, Truth, Image, and Word. Understand that He is conceived to be Radiance and Light. One equal to the Son, the Superior is able to beget; but one more excellent, or superior, or greater, He is not able. At God's will the Son is what and whatsoever He is. And when and since He was, from that time He has subsisted from God. He, being a strong God, praises in His degree the Superior. To speak in brief, God is ineffable to His Son. For He is to Himself what He is, that is, unspeakable. So that nothing which is called comprehensible[6] does the Son know to speak about; for it is impossible for Him to investigate the Father, who is by Himself. For the Son does not know His own essence, For, being Son, He really existed, at the will of the Father. What argument then allows, that He who is from the Father should know His own parent by comprehension? For it is plain that for that which hath a beginning to conceive how the Unbegun is, or to grasp the idea, is not possible.

16. And what they wrote by letter to the blessed Alexander, the Bishop, runs as follows:—

To Our Blessed Pope[7] and Bishop, Alexander, the Presbyters and Deacons send health in the Lord.

Our faith from our forefathers, which also we have learned from thee, Blessed Pope, is this:—We acknowledge One God, alone Ingenerate, alone Everlasting, alone Unbegun, alone True, alone having Immortality, alone Wise, alone Good, alone Sovereign; Judge, Governor, and Providence of all, unalterable and unchangeable, just and good, God of Law and Prophets and New Testament; who begat an Only-begotten Son before eternal times, through whom He has made both the ages and the universe; and begat Him, not in semblance, but in truth; and that He made Him subsist at His own will, unalterable and unchangeable; perfect creature of God, but not as one of the creatures; offspring, but not as one of things begotten; nor as Valentinus pronounced that the offspring of the Father was an issue[8]; nor as Manichæus taught that the offspring was a portion of the Father, one in essence[9]; nor as Sabellius, dividing the Monad, speaks of a Son-and-Father[10]; nor as Hieracas, of one torch from another,

or as a lamp divided into two[11]; nor that He who was before, was afterwards generated or new-created into a Son[12], as thou too thyself, Blessed Pope, in the midst of the Church and in session hast often condemned; but, as we say, at the will of God, created before times and before ages, and gaining life and being from the Father, who gave subsistence to His glories together with Him. For the Father did not, in giving to Him the inheritance of all things, deprive Himself of what He has ingenerately in Himself; for He is the Fountain of all things. Thus there are Three Subsistences. And God, being the cause of all things, is Unbegun and altogether Sole, but the Son being begotten apart from time by the Father, and being created and founded before ages, was not before His generation, but being begotten apart from time before all things, alone was made to subsist by the Father. For He is not eternal or co-eternal or co-unoriginate with the Father, nor has He His being together with the Father, as some speak of relations[1], introducing two ingenerate beginnings, but God is before all things as being Monad and Beginning of all. Wherefore also He is before the Son; as we have learned also from thy preaching in the midst of the Church. So far then as from God He has being, and glories, and life, and all things are delivered unto Him, in such sense is God His origin. For He is above Him, as being His God and before Him. But if the terms 'from Him,' and 'from the womb,' and 'I came forth from the Father, and I am come[2]' (Rom. xi. 36; Ps. cx. 3; John xvi. 28), be understood by some to mean as if a part of Him, one in essence or as an issue, then the Father is according to them compounded and divisible and alterable and material, and, as far as their belief goes, has the circumstances of a body, Who is the Incorporeal God.

This is a part of what Arius and his fellows vomited from their heretical hearts.

17. And before the Nicene Council took place, similar statements were made by Eusebius and his fellows, Narcissus, Patrophilus, Maris, Paulinus, Theodotus, and Athanasius of [A]nazarba[3]. And Eusebius of Nicomedia

---

5 ἐπινοίαις, that is, our Lord's titles are but *names*, or *figures*, not properly belonging to Him, but [cf. Bigg. *B.L.* p. 168 *sq.*]

6 κατὰ κατάληψιν, that is, there is nothing comprehensible in the Father for the Son to know and declare. On the other hand the doctrine of the Anomœans was, that all men could know Almighty God perfectly.

7 The ordinary title of eminent bishops, especially of the bishop of Alexandria.]

8 What the Valentinian προβολὴ was is described in Epiph. *Hær.* 31, 13 [but see D.C.B. iv. 1086 *sqq.*] Origen protests against the notion of προβολή, *Periarch.* iv. p. 190, and Athanasius *Expos.* § 1. The Arian Asterius too considers προβολὴ to introduce the notion of τεκνογονία, Euseb. *contr. Marc.* i. 4. p. 20. vid. also Epiph. *Hær.* 72. 7. Yet Eusebius uses the word προβάλλεσθαι. *Eccl. Theol.* i. 8. On the other hand Tertullian uses it with a protest against the Valentinian sense. Justin has προβληθὲν γέννημα, *Tryph.* 62. And Nazianzen calls the Almighty Father προβολεὺς of the Holy Spirit. *Orat.* 29. 2. Arius introduces the word here as an *argumentum ad invidiam*. Hil. *de Trin.* vi. 9.

9 The Manichees adopting a material notion of the divine substance, considered that it was divisible, and that a portion of it was absorbed by the power of darkness.

10 υἱοπατόρα. The term is ascribed to Sabellius, Ammon. *in Caten. Joan.* i. 1. p. 14: to Sabellius and [invidiously to] Marcellus, Euseb. *Eccl. Theol.* ii. 5: Cf., as to Marcellus, Cyr. Hier. *Catech.* xv. 9. also viv. 8. xi. 16; Epiph. *Hær.* 73. 11 fin. : to Sabellians, Athan. *Expos. Fid.* 2. and 7, and Greg. Nyssen. *contr. Eun.* xii. p. 733: to certain heretics, Cyril. Alex. *in Joann.* p. 243: to Praxeas and Montanus, *Mar. Merc.* p. 128: to Sabellius, Cæsar. *Dial.* i. p. 550: to Noetus, Damasc. *Hær.* 57.

11 [On Hieracas, see D.C.B. iii. 24; also Epiph. *Hær.* 67; Hil. *Trin.* vi. 12.]

12 Bull considers that the doctrine of such Fathers is here spoken of as held that our Lord's συγκατάβασις to create the world was a γένησις, and certainly such language as that of Hippol. *contr. Noet.* § 15. favours the supposition. But one class of [Monarchians] may more probably be intended, who held that the Word became the Son upon His incarnation, such as Marcellus, vid. Euseb. *Eccles. Theol.* i. 1. *contr. Marc.* ii. 3. vid. also *Eccles. Theol.* ii. 9. p. 114 b. μηδ' ἄλλοτε ἄλλην κ.τ.λ. Also the Macrostich says, 'We anathematize those who call Him the mere Word of God, not allowing Him to be Christ and Son of God before all ages, and but from the time He took on Him our flesh: such are the followers of Marcellus and Photinus, &c.' *infr.* § 26. Again, Athanasius, *Orat.* iv. 15, says that, of those who divide the Word from the Son, some called our Lord's manhood the Son, some the two Natures together, and some said 'that the Word Himself became the Son when He was made man.' It makes it more likely that Marcellus is meant, that Asterius seems to have written against him before the Nicene Council, and that Arius in other of his writings borrowed from Asterius. vid. *de Decret.* § 8.

1 Eusebius's letter to Euphration, which is mentioned just after, expresses this more distinctly—'If they coexist, how shall the Father be Father and the Son Son? or how the One first, the Other second? and the One ingenerate and the other generate?' *Acta Conc.* 7. p. 301. The phrase τὰ πρός τι Bull well explains to refer to the Catholic truth that the Father or Son being named; the Other is therein implied without naming. *Defens. F. N.* iii. 9. § 4. Hence Arius, in his Letter to Eusebius, complains that Alexander says, ἀεὶ ὁ θεός, ἀεὶ ὁ υἱός· ἅμα πατήρ, ἅμα υἱός. Theod. *H. E.* i. 4.

2 ἥκω, and so Chrys. *Hom.* 3. *Hebr.* init. Epiph. *Hær.* 73. 31, and 36.

3 Most of these original Arians were attacked in a work of Marcellus's which Eusebius answers. 'Now he replies to Asterius,' says Eusebius, 'now to the great Eusebius' [of Nicomedia], 'and then he turns upon that man of God, that indeed

wrote over and above to Arius, to this effect, 'Since your sentiments are good, pray that all may adopt them ; for it is plain to any one, that what has been made was not before its origination ; but what came to be has a beginning of being.' And Eusebius of Cæsarea in Palestine, in a letter to Euphration the Bishop [3a], did not scruple to say plainly that Christ was not true God [4]. And Athanasius of [A]nazarba uncloked the heresy still further, saying that the Son of God was one of the hundred sheep. For writing to Alexander the Bishop, he had the extreme audacity to say : 'Why complain of Arius and his fellows, for saying, The Son of God is made as a creature out of nothing, and one among others ? For all that are made being represented in parable by the hundred sheep, the Son is one of them. If then the hundred are not created and originate, or if there be beings beside that hundred, then may the Son be not a creature nor one among others ; but if those hundred are all originate, and there is nothing besides the hundred save God alone, what absurdity do Arius and his fellows utter, when, as comprehending and reckoning Christ in the hundred, they say that He is one among others ? ' And George who now is in Laodicea, and then was presbyter of Alexandria, and was staying at Antioch, wrote to Alexander the Bishop ; 'Do not complain of Arius and his fellows, for saying, "Once the Son of God was not," for Isaiah came to be son of Amos, and, whereas Amos was before Isaiah came to be, Isaiah was not before him, but came to be afterwards.' And he wrote to the Arians, ' Why complain of Alexander the Pope, saying, that the Son is from the Father ? for you too need not fear to say that the Son was from God. For if the Apostle wrote (1 Cor. xi. 12), 'All things are from God,' and it is plain that all things are made of nothing, though the Son too is a creature and one of things made, still He may be said to be from God in that sense in which all things are said to be 'from God.' From him then those who hold with Arius learned to simulate the phrase 'from God,' and to use it indeed, but not in a good meaning. And George himself was deposed by Alexander for certain reasons, and among them for manifest irreligion ; for he was himself a presbyter, as has been said before.

18. On the whole then such were their statements, as if they all were in dispute and rivalry with each other, which should make the heresy more irreligious, and display it in a more naked form. And as for their letters I had them not at hand, to dispatch them to you ; else I would have sent you copies ; but, if the Lord will, this too I will do, when I get possession of them. And one Asterius [5] from Cappadocia, a many-headed Sophist, one of the fellows of Eusebius, whom they could not advance into the Clergy, as having done sacrifice in the former persecution in the time of Constantius's grandfather, writes, with the countenance of Eusebius and his fellows, a small treatise, which was on a par with the crime of his sacrifice, yet answered their wishes ; for in it, after comparing, or rather preferring, the locust and the caterpillar to Christ, and saying that Wisdom in God was other than Christ, and was the Framer as well of Christ as of the world, he went round the Churches in Syria and elsewhere, with introductions from Eusebius and his fellows, that as he once made trial of denying, so now he might boldly oppose the truth. The bold man intruded himself into forbidden places, and seating himself in the place of Clergy [6], he used to read publicly this treatise of his, in spite of the general indignation. The treatise is written at great length, but portions of it are as follows :—

For the Blessed Paul said not that he preached Christ, His, that is, God's, 'own Power' or 'Wisdom,' but without the article, ' God's Power and God's Wisdom' (1 Cor. i. 24), preaching that the own power of God Himself was distinct, which was connatural and co-existent with Him unoriginately, generative indeed of Christ, creative of the whole world ; concerning which he teaches in his Epistle to the Romans, thus, 'The invisible things of Him from the creation of the world are clearly seen, being understood by the things which are made, even His eternal power and divinity' (Rom. i. 20). For as no one would say that the Deity there mentioned was Christ, but the Father Himself, so, as I think, His eternal power is also not the Only-begotten God (Joh. i. 18), but the Father who begat Him. And he tells us of another Power and Wisdom of God, namely, that which is manifested through Christ, and made known through the works themselves of His Ministry.

And again :—

Although His eternal Power and Wisdom, which

---

thrice blessed person Paulinus [of Tyre]. Then he goes to war with Origen. . . . Next he marches out against Narcissus, and pursues the other Eusebius,' [himself]. ' In a word, he counts for nothing all the Ecclesiastical Fathers, being satisfied with no one but himself.' *contr. Marc.* i. 4. [On Maris (who was *not* at Ariminum, and scarcely at Antioch in 363) see D.C.B. *s.v.* (2). On Theodotus see vol. i. of this series, p. 320, note 37. On Paulinus, *ib.* p. 369.]

[3a] [Of Balaneæ, see *Ap. Fug.* 3 ; *Hist. Ar.* 5.]

[4] Quoted, among other passages from Eusebius, in the 7th General Council, Act. 6. p. 409. [Mansi. xiii. 701 D]. ' The Son Himself is God, but not Very God.' [But see Prolegg. *ubi supr.* note 5].

[5] Asterius has been mentioned above, p. 155, note 2, &c. Philostorgius speaks of him as adopting Semi-Arian terms ; and Acacius gives an extract from him containing them, ap. Epiph. *Hær.* 72. 6. He seems to be called many-headed with an allusion to the Hydra, and to his activity in the Arian cause and his fertility in writing. He wrote comments on Scripture. [See Prolegg. ii. § 3 (2) a, *sub. fin.*]

[6] None but the clergy might enter the Chancel, i.e. in Service time. Hence Theodosius was made to retire by S. Ambrose. *Theod.* v. 17. The Council of Laodicea, said to be held A.D. 372, forbids any but persons in orders, ἱερατικοί, to enter the Chancel and then communicate. Can. 19. vid. also 44. *Conc.* t. 1. pp. 788, 789. It is doubtful what orders the word ἱερατικοί is intended to include. vid. Bingham, *Antiqu.* viii. 6. § 7.

truth argues to be Unbegun and Ingenerate, would appear certainly to be one and the same, yet many are those powers which are one by one created by Him, of which Christ is the First-born and Only-begotten. All however equally depend upon their Possessor, and all His powers are rightly called His, who created and uses them; for instance, the Prophet says that the locust, which became a divine punishment of human sin, was called by God Himself, not only a power of God, but a great power (Joel ii. 25). And the blessed David too in several of the Psalms, invites, not Angels alone, but Powers also to praise God. And while he invites them all to the hymn, he presents before us their multitude, and is not unwilling to call them ministers of God, and teaches them to do His will.

19. These bold words against the Saviour did not content him, but he went further in his blasphemies, as follows:

The Son is one among others; for He is first of things originate, and one among intellectual natures; and as in things visible the sun is one among phenomena, and it shines upon the whole world according to the command of its Maker, so the Son, being one of the intellectual natures, also enlightens and shines upon all that are in the intellectual world.

And again he says, Once He was not, writing thus:—'And before the Son's origination, the Father had pre-existing knowledge how to generate; since a physician too, before he cured, had the science of curing[7].' And he says again: 'The Son was created by God's beneficent earnestness; and the Father made Him by the superabundance of His Power' And again: 'If the will of God has pervaded all the works in succession, certainly the Son too, being a work, has at His will come to be and been made.' Now though Asterius was the only person to write all this, Eusebius and his fellows felt the like in common with him.

20. These are the doctrines for which they are contending; for these they assail the ancient Council, because its members did not propound the like, but anathematized the Arian heresy instead, which they were so eager to recommend. This was why they put forward, as an advocate of their irreligion, Asterius who sacrificed, a sophist too, that he might not spare to speak against the Lord, or by a show of reason to mislead the simple. And they were ignorant, the shallow men, that they were doing harm to their own cause. For the ill savour of their advocate's idolatrous sacrifice betrayed still more plainly that the heresy is Christ's foe. And now again, the general agitations and troubles which they are exciting, are in consequence of their belief, that by their numerous murders and their monthly Councils, at length they will undo the sentence which has been passed against the Arian heresy[8]. But here too they seem ignorant, or

to pretend ignorance, that even before Nicæa that heresy was held in detestation, when Artemas[9] was laying its foundations, and before him Caiaphas's assembly and that of the Pharisees his contemporaries. And at all times is this gang of Christ's foes detestable, and will not cease to be hateful, the Lord's Name being full of love, and the whole creation bending the knee, and confessing 'that Jesus Christ is Lord, to the glory of God the Father' (Phil. ii. 11).

21. Yet so it is, they have convened successive Councils against that Ecumenical One, and are not yet tired. After the Nicene, Eusebius and his fellows had been deposed; however, in course of time they intruded themselves without shame upon the Churches, and began to plot against the Bishops who withstood them, and to substitute in the Church men of their own heresy. Thus they thought to hold Councils at their pleasure, as having those who concurred with them, whom they had ordained on purpose for this very object. Accordingly, they assemble at Jerusalem, and there they write thus:—

The Holy Council assembled in Jerusalem[1] by the grace of God, &c. . . . . their orthodox teaching in writing[2], which we all confessed to be sound and ecclesiastical. And he reasonably recommended that they should be received and united to the Church of God, as you will know yourselves from the transcript of the same Epistle, which we have transmitted to your reverences. We believe that yourselves also, as if recovering the very members of your own body, will experience great joy and gladness, in acknowledging and recovering your own bowels, your own brethren and fathers; since not only the Presbyters, Arius and his fellows, are given back to you, but also the whole Christian people and the entire multitude, which on occasion of the aforesaid men have a long time been in dissension among you. Moreover it were fitting, now that you know for certain what has passed, and that the men have communicated with us and have been received by so great a Holy Council, that you should with all readiness hail this your coalition and peace with your own members, specially since the articles of the faith which they have published preserve indisputable the universally confessed apostolical tradition and teaching.

22. This was the beginning of their Councils, and in it they were speedy in divulging their views, and could not conceal them. For when they said that they had banished all jealousy, and, after the expulsion of Athanasius, Bishop of Alexandria, recommended the reception of Arius and his friends, they shewed that their measures against Athanasius himself then, and before against all the other Bishops who withstood them, had for their object their receiving

---

[7] Ep. Æg. 13.   [8] Vid. infr. § 32.

[9] [On Artemas or Artemon and Theodotus, see Prolegg. ii. § 3 (2) a.]

[1] [See Apol. Ar. 84; Hist. Ar. 1; Prolegg. ii. § 5. The first part of the letter will be found supr. Apol. Ar. p. 144.]

[2] This is supposed to be the same Confession which is preserved by Socr. i. 26. and Soz. ii. 27. and was presented to Constantine by Arius in 330.

Arius and his fellows, and introducing the heresy into the Church. But although they had approved in this Council all Arius's malignity, and had ordered to receive his party into communion, as they had set the example, yet feeling that even now they were short of their wishes, they assembled a Council at Antioch under colour of the so-called Dedication[3]; and, since they were in general and lasting odium for their heresy, they publish different letters, some of this sort, and some of that; and what they wrote in one letter was as follows:—

We have not been followers of Arius,—how could Bishops, such as we, follow a Presbyter?—nor did we receive any other faith beside that which has been handed down from the beginning. But, after taking on ourselves to examine and to verify his faith, we admitted him rather than followed him; as you will understand from our present avowals.

For we have been taught from the first, to believe[4] in one God, the God of the Universe, the Framer and Preserver of all things both intellectual and sensible.

And in One Son of God, Only-begotten, who existed before all ages, and was with the Father who had begotten Him, by whom all things were made, both visible and invisible, who in the last days according to the good pleasure of the Father came down; and has taken flesh of the Virgin, and jointly fulfilled all His Father's will, and suffered and risen again, and ascended into heaven, and sitteth on the right hand of the Father, and cometh again to judge quick and dead, and remaineth King and God unto all ages.

And we believe also in the Holy Ghost; and if it be necessary to add, we believe concerning the resurrection of the flesh, and the life everlasting.

23. Here follows what they published next at the same Dedication in another Epistle, being dissatisfied with the first, and devising something newer and fuller:

We believe[5], conformably to the evangelical and apostolical tradition, in One God, the Father Almighty, the Framer, and Maker, and Provider of the Universe, from whom are all things.

And in One Lord Jesus Christ, His Son, Only-begotten God (Joh. i. 18), by whom are all things, who was begotten before all ages from the Father, God from God, whole from whole, sole from sole[6], perfect from perfect, King from King, Lord from Lord, Living Word, Living Wisdom, true Light, Way, Truth, Resurrection, Shepherd, Door, both unalterable and[7] unchangeable; exact Image[1] of the Godhead, Essence, Will, Power and

Glory of the Father; the first born of every creature, who was in the beginning with God, God the Word, as it is written in the Gospel, 'and the Word was God' (John i. 1); by whom all things were made, and in whom all things consist; who in the last days descended from above, and was born of a Virgin according to the Scriptures, and was made Man, Mediator[2] between God and man, and Apostle of our faith, and Prince of life, as He says, 'I came down from heaven, not to do Mine own will, but the will of Him that sent Me' (John vi. 38); who suffered for us and rose again on the third day, and ascended into heaven, and sat down on the right hand of the Father, and is coming again with glory and power, to judge quick and dead.

And in the Holy Ghost, who is given to those who believe for comfort, and sanctification, and initiation, as also our Lord Jesus Christ enjoined His disciples, saying, 'Go ye, teach all nations, baptizing them in the Name of the Father, and the Son, and the Holy Ghost' (Matt. xxviii. 19); namely of a Father who is truly Father, and a Son who is truly Son, and of the Holy Ghost who is truly Holy Ghost, the names not being given without meaning or effect, but denoting accurately the peculiar subsistence, rank, and glory of each that is named, so that they are three in subsistence, and in agreement one[3].

Holding then this faith, and holding it in the presence of God and Christ, from begnining to end, we anathematize every heretical heterodoxy[4]. And if any teaches, beside the sound and right faith of the Scriptures, that time, or season, or age[5], either is or has been before the generation of the Son, be he anathema. Or if any one says, that the Son is a creature as one of the creatures, or an offspring as one of the offsprings, or a work as one of the works, and not the aforesaid articles one after another, as the divine Scriptures have delivered, or if he teaches or preaches beside what we received, be he anathema. For all that has been delivered in the divine Scriptures, whether by Prophets or Apostles, do we truly and reverentially both believe and follow[6].

24. And one Theophronius[7], Bishop of Tyana, put forth before them all the following statement of his personal faith. And they subscribed it, accepting the faith of this man:—

God[8] knows, whom I call as a witness upon my soul, that so I believe:—in God the Father Almighty, the Creator and Maker of the Universe, from whom are all things.

And in His Only-begotten Son, Word, Power, and Wisdom, our Lord Jesus Christ, through whom are all things; who has been begotten from the Father before the ages, perfect God from perfect God[9], and was with

---

3 [Prolegg. ch. ii. § 6 (2).]

4 1st Confession or 1st of Antioch. A.D. 341. [See Socr. ii. 10.]

5 2nd Confession or 2nd of Antioch, A.D. 341. This formulary is that known as *the* Formulary of the Dedication. It is quoted as such by Socr. ii. 39, 40. Soz. iv. 15. and *infr.* § 29. [On its attribution to Lucian, see Prolegg. *ubi supr.*, and Caspari *Alte. u. Neue Q.* p. 42 note.] 6 Vid. 10th Confession, *infr.* § 30.

7 These strong words and those which follow, whether Lucian's or not, mark the great difference between this confession and the foregoing. The words 'unalterable and unchangeable' are formal anti-Arian symbols, as the τρεπτὸν or alterable was one of the most characteristic parts of Arius's creed. vid. *Orat.* i. § 35, &c.

1 On ἀπαράλλακτος εἰκὼν κατ' οὐσίαν, which was synonymous with ὁμοιούσιος, vid. *infr.* § 38. *supr.* p. 163, note 9. It was in order to secure the true sense of ἀπαράλλακτον that the Council adopted the word ὁμοούσιον. 'Απαράλλακτον is accordingly used as a familiar word by Athan. *de Decr.* §§ 20, 24. *Orat.* iii. § 36. *contr. Gent.* 41. 46. fin. Philostorgius ascribing it to Asterius, and Acacius quotes a passage from his writings containing

it; cf. S. Alexander τὴν κατὰ πάντα ὁμοιότητα αὐτοῦ ἐκ φύσεως ἀπομαξάμενος, in Theod. *H.E.* i. 4. Χαρακτήρ, Hebr. i. 3. contains the same idea. Basil. *contr. Eunom.* i. 18.

2 This statement perhaps is the most Catholic in the Creed; not that the former are not more explicit in themselves, or that in a certain true sense our Lord may not be called a Mediator before He became incarnate, but because the Arians, even Eusebius, like Philo and the Platonists, consider Him as made in the beginning the 'Eternal Priest of the Father,' *Demonst.* v. 3. *de Laud. C.* 3, 11, 'an intermediate divine power,' §§ 26, 27, and notes.

3 On this phrase, which is justified by S. Hilary, *de Syn.* 32, and is protested against in the Sardican Confession, Theod. *H.E.* ii. 6 [see Prolegg. *ubi supr.*]

4 The whole of these anathemas are [a compromise]. The Council anathematizes '*every* heretical heterodoxy;' *not*, as Athanasius observes, *supr.*, § 7, the Arian.

5 Our Lord was, as they held, *before* time, but still created.

6 This emphatic mention of Scripture is also virtually an Arian evasion, admitting of a silent reference to themselves as interpreters of Scripture. 7 On this Creed see Prolegg. *ubi supr.*

8 3rd Confession or 3rd of Antioch, A.D. 341.

9 It need scarcely be said, that 'perfect from perfect' is symbol on which the Catholics laid stress, Athan. *Orat.* ii. 35.

God in subsistence, and in the last days descended, and was born of the Virgin according to the Scriptures, and was made man, and suffered, and rose again from the dead, and ascended into the heavens, and sat down on the right hand of His Father, and cometh again with glory and power to judge quick and dead, and remaineth for ever:

And in the Holy Ghost, the Paraclete, the Spirit of truth (Joh. xv. 26), which also God promised by His Prophet to pour out (Joel ii. 28) upon His servants, and the Lord promised to send to His disciples: which also He sent, as the Acts of the Apostles witness.

But if any one teaches, or holds in his mind, aught beside this faith, be he anathema; or with Marcellus of Ancyra[10], or Sabellius, or Paul of Samosata, be he anathema, both himself and those who communicate with him.

25. Ninety Bishops met at the Dedication under the Consulate of Marcellinus and Probinus, in the 14th of the Indiction[1], Constantius the most irreligious being present. Having thus conducted matters at Antioch at the Dedication, thinking that their composition was deficient still, and fluctuating moreover in their own opinions, again they draw up afresh another formulary, after a few months, professedly concerning the faith, and despatch Narcissus, Maris, Theodorus, and Mark into Gaul[2]. And they, as being sent from the Council, deliver the following document to Constans Augustus of blessed memory, and to all who were there:

We believe[3] in One God, the Father Almighty, Creator and Maker of all things; from whom all fatherhood in heaven and on earth is named. (Eph. iii. 15.)

And in His Only-begotten Son, our Lord Jesus Christ, who before all ages was begotten from the Father, God from God, Light from Light, by whom all things were made in the heavens and on the earth, visible and invisible, being Word, and Wisdom, and Power, and Life, and True Light; who in the last days was made man for us, and was born of the Holy Virgin; who was crucified, and dead, and buried, and rose again from the dead the third day, and was taken up into heaven, and sat down on the right hand of the Father; and is coming at the consummation of the age, to judge quick and dead, and to render to every one according to his works; whose Kingdom endures indissolubly into the infinite ages[4]; for He shall be seated on the right hand of the Father, not only in this age but in that which is to come.

And in the Holy Ghost, that is, the Paraclete; which, having promised to the Apostles, He sent forth after His ascension into heaven, to teach them and to remind of all things; through whom also shall be sanctified the souls of those who sincerely believe in Him.

But those who say, that the Son was from nothing, or from other subsistence and not from God, and, there was time when He was not, the Catholic Church regards as aliens[5].

26. As if dissatisfied with this, they hold their meeting again after three years, and dispatch Eudoxius, Martyrius, and Macedonius of Cilicia[6], and some others with them, to the parts of Italy, to carry with them a faith written at great length, with numerous additions over and above those which have gone before. They went abroad with these, as if they had devised something new.

We believe[7] in one God the Father Almighty, the Creator and Maker of all things, from whom all fatherhood in heaven and on earth is named.

And in His Only-begotten Son our Lord Jesus Christ, who before all ages was begotten from the Father, God from God, Light from Light, by whom all things were made, in heaven and on the earth, visible and invisible, being Word and Wisdom and Power and Life and True Light, who in the last days was made man for us, and was born of the Holy Virgin, crucified and dead and buried, and rose again from the dead the third day, and was taken up into heaven, and sat down on the right hand of the Father, and is coming at the consummation of the age to judge quick and dead, and to render to every one according to his works, whose Kingdom endures unceasingly unto the infinite ages; for He sitteth on the right hand of the Father not only in this age, but also in that which is to come.

And we believe in the Holy Ghost, that is, the Paraclete, which, having promised to the Apostles, He sent forth after the ascension into heaven, to teach them and to remind of all things: through whom also shall be sanctified the souls of those who sincerely believe in Him.

Epiph. *Hær.* 76. p. 945. but it admitted of an evasion. An especial reason for insisting on it in the previous centuries had been the Sabellian doctrine, which considered the title 'Word' when applied to our Lord to be adequately explained by the ordinary sense of the term, as a word spoken by us. In consequence they insisted on His τὸ τέλειον, perfection, which became almost synonymous with His personality. (Thus the Apollinarians, e.g. denied that our Lord was *perfect* man, because His *person* was not human. Athan. *contr. Apoll.* i. 2.) And Athan. condemns the notion of 'the λόγος ἐν τῷ θεῷ ἀτελὴς, γεννηθεὶς τέλειος, *Orat.* iv. 11. The Arians then, as being the especial opponents of the Sabellians, insisted on nothing so much as our Lord's being a real, living, substantial, Word. vid. Eusebius *passim.* 'The Father,' says Acacius against Marcellus, 'begat the Only-begotten, alone alone, and perfect perfect; for there is nothing imperfect in the Father, wherefore neither is there in the Son, but the Son's perfection is the genuine offspring of His perfection, and superperfection.' *ap. Epiph. Hær.* 72. 7. Τέλειος then was a relative word, varying with the subject matter, vid. *Damasc. F. O.* i. 8. p. 138. and when the Arians said that our Lord was perfect God, they meant, 'perfect, *in that sense in which* He is God'—i.e. as a secondary divinity.—Nay, in one point of view, holding as they did no real condescension or assumption of a really new state, they would use the term of His divine Nature more freely than the Catholics sometimes had. 'Nor was the Word,' says Hippolytus, 'before the flesh and by Himself, perfect Son, though being perfect Word, Only-begotten; nor could the flesh subsist by itself without the Word, because that in the Word it has its consistence: thus then He was manifested One perfect Son of God.' *contr. Noet.* 15.

[10] [See Prolegg.] Marcellus wrote his work against Asterius in 335, the year of the Arian Council of Jerusalem, which at once took cognisance of it, and cited Marcellus to appear before them. The next year a Council held at Constantinople condemned and deposed him.   [1] A.D. 341.

[2] [Cf. Prolegg. ii. § 6 (3) *init.*]

[3] 4th Confession, or 4th of Antioch, A.D. 342. The fourth, fifth, and sixth Confessions are the same, and with them agree the Creed of Philippopolis [A.D. 343, see Gwatkin, *Stud.* p. 119, espec. note 2].

[4] These words, which answer to those [of our present 'Nicene' Creed], are directed against the doctrine of Marcellus [on which see Prolegg. ii. § 3 (2) c, 3]. Cf. Eusebius, *de Eccl. Theol.* iii. 8. 17. *cont. Marc.* ii. 4.

[5] S. Hilary, as we have seen above, p. 78, by implication calls this the Nicene Anathema; but it omits many of the Nicene clauses, and evades our Lord's eternal existence, substituting for 'once He was not,' 'there was *time* when He was not.' It seems to have been considered sufficient for Gaul, as used now, for Italy as in the 5th Confession or Macrostich, and for Africa as in the creed of Philippopolis.

[6] Little is known of Macedonius who was Bishop of Mopsuestia, or of Martyrius; and too much of Eudoxius. This Long Confession, or Macrostich, which follows, is remarkable.; [see *Prolegg.* ch. ii. § 6 (3), Gwatkin, p. 125 *sq.*]

[7] 5th Confession or Macrostich, A.D. 344. [Published by the Council which deposed Stephen and elected Leontius bishop of Antioch.]

But those who say, (1) that the Son was from nothing, or from other subsistence and not from God; (2) and that there was a time or age when He was not, the Catholic and Holy Church regards as aliens. Likewise those who say, (3) that there are three Gods: (4) or that Christ is not God; (5) or that before the ages He was neither Christ nor Son of God; (6) or that Father and Son, or Holy Ghost, are the same; (7) or that the Son is Ingenerate; or that the Father begat the Son, not by choice or will; the Holy and Catholic Church anathematizes.

(1.) For neither is safe to say that the Son is from nothing, (since this is no where spoken of Him in divinely inspired Scripture,) nor again of any other subsistence before existing beside the Father, but from God alone do we define Him genuinely to be generated. For the divine Word teaches that the Ingenerate and Unbegun, the Father of Christ, is One[8].

(2.) Nor may we, adopting the hazardous position, 'There was once when He was not,' from unscriptural sources, imagine any interval of time before Him, but only the God who has generated Him apart from time; for through Him both times and ages came to be. Yet we must not consider the Son to be co-unbegun and co-ingenerate with the Father; for no one can be properly called Father or Son of one who is co-unbegun and co-ingenerate with Him[9]. But we acknowledge[10] that the Father who alone is Unbegun and Ingenerate, hath generated inconceivably and incomprehensibly to all: and that the Son hath been generated before ages, and in no wise to be ingenerate Himself like the Father, but to have the Father who generated Him as His beginning; for 'the Head of Christ is God.' (1 Cor. xi. 3.)

(3.) Nor again, in confessing three realities and three Persons, of the Father and the Son and the Holy Ghost according to the Scriptures, do we therefore make Gods three; since we acknowledge the Self-complete and Ingenerate and Unbegun and Invisible God to be one only[1], the God and Father (Joh. xx. 17) of the Only-begotten, who alone hath being from Himself, and alone vouchsafes this to all others bountifully.

(4.) Nor again, in saying that the Father of our Lord Jesus Christ is one only God, the only Ingenerate, do we therefore deny that Christ also is God before ages: as the disciples of Paul of Samosata, who say that after the incarnation He was by advance[2] made God, from being made by nature a mere man. For we acknowledge, that though He be subordinate to His Father and God, yet, being before ages begotten of God, He is God perfect according to nature and true[3], and not first man and then God, but first God and then becoming man for us, and never having been deprived of being.

(5.) We abhor besides, and anathematize those who make a pretence of saying that He is but the mere word of God and unexisting, having His being in another,— now as if pronounced, as some speak, now as mental[4],—

holding that He was not Christ or Son of God or mediator or image of God before ages; but that He first became Christ and Son of God, when He took our flesh from the Virgin, not quite four hundred years since. For they will have it that then Christ began His Kingdom, and that it will have an end after the consummation of all and the judgment[5]. Such are the disciples of Marcellus and Scotinus[6] of Galatian Ancyra, who, equally with Jews, negative Christ's existence before ages, and His Godhead, and unending Kingdom, upon pretence of supporting the divine Monarchy. We, on the contrary, regard Him not as simply God's pronounced word or mental, but as Living God and Word, existing in Himself, and Son of God and Christ; being and abiding with His Father before ages, and that not in foreknowledge only[7], and ministering to Him for the whole framing whether of things visible or invisible. For He it is, to whom the Father said, 'Let Us make man in Our image, after Our likeness[8]' (Gen. i. 26), who also was seen in His own Person[9] by the patriarchs, gave the law, spoke by the prophets, and at last, became man, and manifested His own Father to all men, and reigns to never-ending ages. For Christ has taken no recent dignity, but we have believed Him to be perfect from the first, and like in all things to the Father[1].

(6.) And those who say that the Father and Son and Holy Ghost are the same, and irreligiously take the Three Names of one and the same Reality and Person, we justly proscribe from the Church, because they suppose the illimitable and impassible Father to be limitable withal and passible through His becoming man: for such are they whom Romans call Patripassians, and we Sabellians[2]. For we acknowledge that the Father who sent, remained in the peculiar state of His unchangeable Godhead, and that Christ who was sent fulfilled the economy of the Incarnation.

(7.) And at the same time those who irreverently say that the Son has been generated not by choice or will, thus encompassing God with a necessity which excludes choice and purpose, so that He begat the Son unwillingly, we account as most irreligious and alien to the Church; in that they have dared to define such things concerning God, beside the common notions concerning Him, nay, beside the purport of divinely inspired Scripture. For

---

Damasc. *F. O.* ii. 21. To use either absolutely and to the exclusion of the other would have involved some form of Sabellianism, or Arianism as the case might be; but each might correct the defective sense of either S. Theophilus speaks of our Lord as at once ἐνδιάθετος and προφορικός. *ad Autol.* ii. 10 and 22, S. Cyril as ἐνδιάθετος, *in Joann.* p. 39. but see also *Thesaur.* p. 47. When the Fathers deny that our Lord is the προφορικὸς λόγος, they only mean that that title is not, even as far as its philosophical idea went, an adequate representative of Him, a word spoken being insubstantive, vid. *Orat.* ii. 35; Hil. *de Syn.* 46; Cyr. *Catech.* xi. 10; Damas. *Ep.* ii. p. 203; Cyril *in Joann.* p. 31; Iren. *Hær.* ii. 12. n. 5. Marcellus is said by Eusebius to have considered our Lord as first the one and then the other. *Eccl. Theol.* ii. 15.

[5] This passage seems taken from Eusebius, and partly from Marcellus's own words. S. Cyril speaks of his doctrine in like terms. *Catech.* xv. 27.

[6] i.e. Photinus. [A note illustrating the frequency of similar nicknames is omitted. On Photinus, see Prolegg. ch. ii. § 3. *ad fin.*] [7] Cf. Euseb. *contr. Marc.* i. 2. [8] Cf. § 27, notes.

[9] αὐτοπροσωπῶς and so Cyril Hier. *Catech.* xv. 14 and 17 (It means, 'not in personation'), and Philo contrasting divine appearances with those of Angels. *Leg. Alleg.* iii. 62. On the other hand, Theophilus on the text, 'The voice of the Lord God walking in the garden,' speaks of the Word, 'assuming the person, πρόσωπον, of the Father,' and 'in the person of God,' *ad Autol.* ii. 22. the word not then having its theological sense.

[1] ὅμοιον κατὰ πάντα. Here again we have a strong Semi-Arian or almost Catholic formula introduced by the bye. Of course it admitted of evasion, but in its fulness it included 'essence.' [See above § 8, note 1, and Introd.]

[2] See vol. i. of this series, p. 295, note 1. In the reason which the Confession alleges against that heretical doctrine it is almost implied that the divine nature of the Son suffered on the Cross. They would naturally fall into this notion directly they gave up our Lord's absolute divinity. It would naturally follow that our Lord had no human soul, but that His pre-existent nature stood in the place of it:—also that His Mediatorship was no peculiarity of His Incarnation. vid. § 23, note 2. § 27, *Anath.* 12, note.

---

[8] It is observable that here and in the next paragraph the only reasons they give against using the only two Arian formulas which they condemns is that they are not found in Scripture. Here, in their explanation of the ἐξ οὐκ ὄντων, or from nothing, they do but deny it with Eusebius's evasion, *supr.* p. 75, note 5.

[9] They argue after the usual Arian manner, that the term 'Son' essentially implies beginning, and excludes the title 'co-unoriginate;' but see *supr.* § 16, note 1, and p. 154, note 5.

[10] [The four lines which follow are cited by Lightfoot, *Ign.* p. 91. ed. 2, as from *de Syn.* § 3.]

[1] Cf. § 28, end. [2] ἐκ προκοπῆς, *de Decr.* § 10, note 10.

[3] These strong words, θεὸν κατὰ φύσιν τέλειον καὶ ἀληθῆ are of a different character from any which have occurred in the Arian Confessions. They can only be explained away by considering them used *in contrast* to the Samosatene doctrine; so that 'perfect according to nature' and 'true,' will not be directly connected with 'God' so much as opposed to, 'by advance,' 'by adoption,' &c.

[4] The use of the words ἐνδιάθετος and προφορικὸς, *mental* and *pronounced*, to distinguish the two senses of λόγος, *reason* and *word*, came from the school of the Stoics, and is found in Philo, and was under certain limitations allowed in Catholic theology,

we, knowing that God is absolute and sovereign over Himself, have a religious judgment that He generated the Son voluntarily and freely ; yet, as we have a reverent belief in the Son's words concerning Himself (Prov. viii. 22), 'The Lord created me a beginning of His ways for His works,' we do not understand Him to have been originated like the creatures or works which through Him came to be. For it is irreligious and alien to the ecclesiastical faith, to compare the Creator with handiworks created by Him, and to think that He has the same manner of origination with the rest. For divine Scripture teaches us really and truly that the Only-begotten Son was generated sole and solely [2a]. Yet[3], in saying that the Son is in Himself, and both lives and exists like the Father, we do not on that account separate Him from the Father, imagining place and interval between their union in the way of bodies. For we believe that they are united with each other without mediation or distance [4], and that they exist inseparable ; all the Father embosoming the Son, and all the Son hanging and adhering to the Father, and alone resting on the Father's breast continually [4a]. Believing then in the All-perfect Triad, the most Holy, that is, in the Father, and the Son, and the Holy Ghost, and calling the Father God, and the Son God, yet we confess in them, not two Gods, but one dignity of Godhead, and one exact harmony of dominion, the Father alone being Head over the whole universe wholly, and over the Son Himself, and the Son subordinated to the Father ; but, excepting Him, ruling over all things after Him which through Himself have come to be, and granting the grace of the Holy Ghost unsparingly to the saints at the Father's will. For that such is the account of the Divine Monarchy towards Christ, the sacred oracles have delivered to us.

Thus much, in addition to the faith before published in epitome, we have been compelled to draw forth at length, not in any officious display, but to clear away all unjust suspicion concerning our opinions, among those who are ignorant of our affairs : and that all in the West may know, both the audacity of the slanders of the heterodox, and as to the Orientals, their ecclesiastical mind in the Lord, to which the divinely inspired Scriptures bear witness without violence, where men are not perverse.

27. However they did not stand even to this ; for again at Sirmium [5] they met together [5a] against Photinus [6] and there composed a faith again,

not drawn out into such length, not so full in words ; but subtracting the greater part and adding in its place, as if they had listened to the suggestions of others, they wrote as follows :—

We believe[7] in One God, the Father Almighty, the Creator and Maker of all things, 'from whom all fatherhood in heaven and earth is named [8].'

And in His Only-begotten Son, our Lord Jesus the Christ, who before all the ages was begotten from the Father, God from God, Light from Light, by whom all things were made, in heaven and on the earth, visible and invisible, being Word and Wisdom and True Light and Life, who in the last of days was made man for us, and was born of the Holy Virgin, and crucified and dead and buried, and rose again from the dead the third day, and was taken up into heaven, and sat down on the right hand of the Father, and is coming at the consummation of the age, to judge quick and dead, and to render to every one according to his works ; whose Kingdom being unceasing endures unto the infinite ages ; for He shall sit on the right hand of the Father, not only in this age, but also in that which is to come.

And in the Holy Ghost, that is, the Paraclete ; which, having promised to the Apostles to send forth after His ascension into heaven, to teach and to remind them of all things, He did send ; through whom also are sanctified the souls of those who sincerely believe in Him.

(1.) But those who say that the Son was from nothing or from other subsistence [9] and not from God, and that there was time or age when He was not, the Holy and Catholic Church regards as aliens.

(2.) Again we say, Whosoever says that the Father and the Son are two Gods, be he anathema [10].

(3.) And whosoever, saying that Christ is God, before ages Son of God, does not confess that He has subserved the Father for the framing of the universe, be he anathema [11].

39—63. Philastrius and Vigilius call the Council a meeting ol 'holy bishops' and a 'Catholic Council,' de Hær. 65. in Eutych. v. init. What gave a character and weight to this Council was, that it met to set right a real evil, and was not a mere pretence with Arian objects.

7 6th Confession, or 1st Sirmian, A.D. 351.
8 Eph. iii. 15. 9 Vid. p. 77, sqq.
10 This Anathema which has occurred in substance in the Macrostich, and again infr. Anath. 18 and 23. is a disclaimer of their in fact holding a supreme and a secondary God. In the Macrostich it is disclaimed upon a simple Arian basis. The Semi-Arians were more open to this imputation ; Eusebius, as we have seen above, distinctly calling our Lord a second and another God. vid. p. 75, note 7. It will be observed that this Anathema contradicts the one which immediately follows, and the 11th, in which Christ is called God ; except, on the one hand, the Father and Son are One God, which was the Catholic doctrine, or, on the other, the Son is God in name only, which was the pure Arian or Anomœan.

11 The language of Catholics and heretics is very much the same on this point of the Son's ministration, with this essential difference of sense, that Catholic writers mean a ministration internal to the divine substance and an instrument connatural with the Father, and Arius meant an external and created medium of operation. Thus S. Clement calls our Lord 'the All-harmonious Instrument (ὄργανον) of God.' Protrept. p. 6 ; Eusebius 'an animated and living instrument (ὄργανον ἔμψυχον), nay, rather divine and vivific of every substance and nature.' Demonstr. iv. 4. S. Basil, on the other hand, insists that the Arians reduced our Lord to 'an inanimate instrument,' ὄργανον ἄψυχον, though they called Him ὑπουργὸν τελειότατον, most perfect minister or underworker. adv. Eunom. ii. 21. Elsewhere he makes them say, 'the nature of a cause is one, and the nature of an instrument, ὀργάνου, another ; . . . . foreign then in nature is the Son from the Father, since such is an instrument from a workman.' De Sp. S. n. 6 fin. vid. also n. 4 fin. 19, and 20. And so S. Gregory, 'The Father signifies, the Word accomplishes, not servilely, nor ignorantly, but with knowledge and sovereignty, and to speak more suitably, in a father's way, πατρικῶς. Orat. 30. 11. Cf. S. Cyril, in Joann. p. 48. Explanations such as these secure for the Catholic writers some freedom in their modes of speaking, e.g. Athan. speaks oi the Son, as 'enjoined and ministering,' προσταττόμενος, καὶ ὑπουργῶν, Orat. ii. § 22. Thus S. Irenæus speaks of the Father being

---

[2a] The Confession still insists upon the unscripturalness of the Catholic positions. On the main subject of this paragraph the θελήσει γεννηθὲν, cf. Orat. iii. 59, &c. The doctrine of the μονογενὲς has already partially come before us in de Decr. §§ 7—9. pp. 154 sq. Μόνως, not as the creatures. vid. p. 75, note 6.

3 The following passage is in its very form an interpolation or appendix, while its doctrine bears distinctive characters of something higher than the old absolute separation between the Father and the Son. [Eusebius of Cæs. had] considered Them as two οὐσίαι, ὅμοιαι like, but not as ὁμοούσιοι ; his very explanation of the word τέλειος was 'independent' and 'distinct.' Language then, such as that in the text, was the nearest assignable approach to the reception of the ὁμοούσιον ; [and in fact, to] the doctrine of the περιχώρησις, of which supr. Orat. iii.

4 De Decr. § 8. 4a De Decr. § 26.

5 Sirmium [Mitrowitz on the Save] was a city of lower Pannonia, not far from the Danube, and was the great bulwark of the Illyrian provinces of the Empire. There Vetranio assumed the purple ; and there Constantius was born. The frontier war caused it to be from time to time the Imperial residence. We hear of Constantius at Sirmium in the summer of 357. Ammian. xvi. 10. He also passed there the ensuing winter. ibid. xvii. 12. In October, 358, after the Sarmatian war, he entered Sirmium in triumph, and passed the winter there. xvii. 13 fin. and with a short absence in the spring, remained there till the end of May, 359.

5a [Cf. Prolegg. ch. ii. § 7]. The leading person in this Council was Basil of Ancyra. Basil held a disputation with Photinus. Silvanus too of Tarsus now appears for the first time : while, according to Socrates, Mark of Arethusa drew up the Anathemas ; the Confession used was the same as that sent to Constans, of the Council of Philippopolis, and the Macrostich.

6 S. Hilary treats their creed as a Catholic composition. de Syn.

(4.) Whosoever presumes to say that the Ingenerate, or a part of Him, was born of Mary, be he anathema.

(5.) Whosoever says that according to foreknowledge[1] the Son is before Mary and not that, generated from the Father before ages, He was with God, and that through Him all things were originated, be he anathema.

(6.) Whosoever shall pretend that the essence of God is dilated or contracted[2], be he anathema.

(7.) Whosoever shall say that the essence of God being dilated made the Son, or shall name the dilation of His essence Son, be he anathema.

(8.) Whosoever calls the Son of God the mental or pronounced Word[3], be he anathema.

(9.) Whosoever says that the Son from Mary is man only, be he anathema.

(10.) Whosoever, speaking of Him who is from Mary God and man, thereby means God the Ingenerate[4], be he anathema.

(11.) Whosoever shall explain 'I God the First and I the Last, and besides Me there is no God,' (Is. xliv. 6), which is said for the denial of idols and of gods that are not, to the denial of the Only-begotten, before ages God, as Jews do, be he anathema.

(12.) Whosoever hearing 'The Word was made flesh,' (John i. 14), shall consider that the Word has changed into flesh, or shall say that He has undergone alteration by taking flesh, be he anathema[5].

(13.) Whosoever hearing the Only-begotten Son of God to have been crucified, shall say that His Godhead has undergone corruption, or passion, or alteration, or diminution, or destruction, be he anathema.

(14.) Whosoever shall say that 'Let Us make man' (Gen. i. 26), was not said by the Father to the Son, but by God to Himself, be he anathema[6].

(15.) Whosoever shall say that Abraham saw, not the Son, but the Ingenerate God or part of Him, be he anathema[7].

(16.) Whosoever shall say that with Jacob, not the

Son as man, but the Ingenerate God or part of Him, has wrestled, be he anathema[8].

(17.) Whosoever shall explain, 'The Lord rained fire from the Lord' (Gen. xix. 24), not of the Father and the Son, and says that He rained from Himself, be he anathema. For the Son, being Lord, rained from the Father Who is Lord.

(18.) Whosoever, hearing that the Father is Lord and the Son Lord and the Father and Son Lord, for there is Lord from Lord, says there are two Gods, be he anathema. For we do not place the Son in the Father's order, but as subordinate to the Father; for He did not descend upon Sodom without the Father's will, nor did He rain from Himself, but from the Lord, that is, the Father authorising it. Nor is He of Himself set down on the right hand, but He hears the Father saying, 'Sit Thou on My right hand' (Ps. cx. 1).

(19.) Whosoever says that the Father and the Son and the Holy Ghost are one Person, be he anathema.

(20.) Whosoever, speaking of the Holy Ghost as Paraclete, shall mean the Ingenerate God, be he anathema[9].

(21.) Whosoever shall deny, what the Lord taught us, that the Paraclete is other than the Son, for He hath said, 'And another Paraclete shall the Father send to you, whom I will ask,' (John xiv. 16) be he anathema.

(22.) Whosoever shall say that the Holy Ghost is part of the Father or of the Son[1], be he anathema.

(23.) Whosoever shall say that the Father and the Son and the Holy Ghost are three Gods, be he anathema.

(24.) Whosoever shall say that the Son of God at the will of God has come to be, as one of the works, be he anathema.

(25.) Whosoever shall say that the Son has been generated, the Father not wishing it[2], be he anathema. For not by compulsion, led by physical necessity, did the Father, as He wished not, generate the Son, but He at once willed, and, after generating Him from Himself apart from time and passion, manifested Him.

(26.) Whosoever shall say that the Son is without beginning and ingenerate, as if speaking of two unbegun and two ingenerate, and making two Gods, be he anathema. For the Son is the Head, namely the beginning of all: and God is the Head, namely the beginning of Christ; for thus to one unbegun beginning of the universe do we religiously refer all things through the Son.

(27.) And in accurate delineation of the idea of Christianity we say this again; Whosoever shall not say that Christ is God, Son of God, as being before ages, and having subserved the Father in the framing of the Universe, but that from the time that He was born of Mary, from thence He was called Christ and Son, and took an origin of being God, be he anathema.

28. Casting aside the whole of this, as if they had discovered something better, they

---

well-pleased and commanding, κελεύοντος, and the Son doing and framing. *Hær.* iv. 75. S. Basil too, in the same treatise in which are some of the foregoing protests, speaks of 'the Lord ordering, προστάσσοντα, and the Word framing.' *de Sp. S.* n. 38, S. Cyril of Jerusalem, of 'Him who bids, ἐντέλλεται, bidding to one who is present with Him,' *Cat.* xi. 16. vid. also ὑπηρετῶν τῇ βουλῇ, Justin. *Tryph.* 126, and ὑπουργόν, Theoph. *ad Autol.* ii. 10. ἐξυπηρετῶν θελήματι, Clem. *Strom.* vii. p. 832.

1 § 26, n. 7.   2 *Orat.* iv. § 13.
3 § 26, n. 4.   4 § 26 (2) n. (2).
5 The 12th and 13th Anathemas are intended to meet the charge which is alluded to § 26 (6), note 2, that Arianism involved the doctrine that our Lord's divine nature suffered. [But see Gwatkin, p. 147.] Athanasius brings this accusation against them distinctly in his work against Apollinaris. *contr. Apoll.* i. 15. vid. also Ambros. *de Fide*, iii. 31. Salig in his *de Eutychianismo ant. Eutychen* takes notice of none of the passages in the text.
6 This Anathema is directed against Marcellus, who held the very opinion which it denounces, that the Almighty spake with Himself. Euseb. *Eccles. Theol.* ii. 15. The Jews said that Almighty God spoke to the Angels. Basil. *Hexaem.* fin. Others that the plural was used as authorities on earth use it in way of dignity. Theod. *in Gen.* 19. As to the Catholic Fathers, as is well known, they interpreted the text in the sense here given. See Petav.
7 This again, in spite of the wording, which is directed against the Catholic doctrine [or Marcellus?] is a Catholic interpretation. vid. (besides Philo *de Somniis.* i. 12.) Justin. *Tryph.* 56. and 126. Iren. *Hær.* iv. 10. n. 1. Tertull. *de carn. Christ.* 6. *adv. Marc.* iii. 9. *adv. Prax.* 16. Novat. *de Trin.* 18. Origen. *in Gen. Hom.* iv. 5. Cyprian. *adv. Jud.* ii. 5. Antioch. Syn. *contr. Paul. apud Routh. Rell.* t. 2. p. 469. Athan. *Orat.* ii. 13. Epiph. *Ancor.* 29 and 39. *Hær.* 71. 5. Chrysost. *in Gen. Hom.* 41. 7. These references are principally from Petavius; also from Dorscheus, who has written an elaborate commentary on this Council, &c. The Catholic doctrine is that the Son has condescended to become visible by means of material appearances. Augustine seems to have been the first who changed the mode of viewing the texts in question, and considered the divine appearance, not God the Son, but a created Angel. Vid. *de Trin.* ii. *passim.* Jansenius considers that he did so from a suggestion of S. Ambrose, that the hitherto received view had been the origo hæresis Arianæ, vid. his *Augustinus, lib. proœm.* c. 12. t. 2. p. 12.

8 This and the following Canon are Catholic in their main doctrine, and might be illustrated, if necessary, as the foregoing.
9 It was an expedient of the later Macedonians to deny that the Holy Spirit was God because it was not usual to call Him Ingenerate. They asked the Catholics whether the Holy Spirit was *Ingenerate, generate,* or *created,* for into these three they divided all things. vid. Basil. *in Sabell. et Ar. Hom.* xxiv. 6. But, as the Arians had first made the alternative only between *Ingenerate* and *created,* and Athan. *de Decr.* § 28. shews that *generate* is a third idea really distinct from one and the other, so S. Greg. Naz. adds, *processive,* ἐκπορευτὸν, as an intermediate idea, contrasted with *Ingenerate,* yet distinct from *generate. Orat.* xxxi. 8. In other words, *Ingenerate* means, not only *not generate,* but *not from any origin.* vid. August. *de Trin.* xv. 26.
1 *Supra* (16).   2 § 26 (7).

propound another faith, and write at Sirmium in Latin what is here translated into Greek [3].

Whereas[4] it seemed good that there should be some discussion concerning faith, all points were carefully investigated and discussed at Sirmium in the presence of Valens, and Ursacius, and Germinius, and the rest.

It is held for certain that there is one God, the Father Almighty, as also is preached in all the world.

And His One Only-begotten Son, our Lord Jesus Christ, generated from Him before the ages ; and that we may not speak of two Gods, since the Lord Himself has said, 'I go to My Father and your Father, and My God and your God' (John xx. 17). On this account He is God of all, as also the Apostle taught : 'Is He God of the Jews only, is He not also of the Gentiles? yea of the Gentiles also : since there is one God who shall justify the circumcision from faith, and the uncircumcision through faith' (Rom. iii. 29, 30) ; and every thing else agrees, and has no ambiguity.

But since many persons are disturbed by questions concerning what is called in Latin 'Substantia,' but in Greek 'Usia,' that is, to make it understood more exactly, as to 'Coessential,' or what is called, 'Like-in-Essence,' there ought to be no mention of any of these at all, nor exposition of them in the Church, for this reason and for this consideration, that in divine Scripture nothing is written about them, and that they are above men's knowledge and above men's understanding ; and because no one can declare the Son's generation, as it is written, 'Who shall declare His generation' (Is. liii. 8)? for it is plain that the Father only knows how He generated the Son, and again the Son how He has been generated by the Father. And to none can it be a question that the Father is greater : for no one can doubt that the Father is greater in honour and dignity and Godhead, and in the very name of Father, the Son Himself testifying, 'The Father that sent Me is greater than I' (John x. 29, Ib. xiv. 28). And no one is ignorant, that it is Catholic doctrine, that there are two Persons of Father and Son, and that the Father is greater, and the Son subordinated to the Father together with all things which the Father has subordinated to Him, and that the Father has no beginning, and is invisible, and immortal, and impassible ; but that the Son has been generated from the Father, God from God, Light from Light, and that His origin, as aforesaid, no one knows, but the Father only. And that the Son Himself and our Lord and God, took flesh, that is, a body, that is, man, from Mary the Virgin, as the Angel preached beforehand ; and as all the Scriptures teach, and especially the Apostle himself, the doctor of the Gentiles, Christ took man of Mary the Virgin, through which He has suffered. And the whole faith is summed up[5], and secured in this, that a Trinity should ever be preserved, as we read in the Gospel, 'Go ye and baptize all the nations in the Name of the Father and of the Son and of the Holy Ghost' (Matt. xxviii. 19). And entire and perfect is the number of the Trinity ; but the Paraclete, the Holy Ghost, sent forth through the Son, came according to the promise, that He might teach and sanctify the Apostles and all believers[6].

29. After drawing up this, and then becoming dissatisfied, they composed the faith which to their shame they paraded with 'the Consulate.' And, as is their wont, condemning this also, they caused Martinian the notary to seize it from the parties who had the copies of it[7]. And having got the Emperor Constantius to put forth an edict against it, they form another dogma afresh, and with the addition of certain expressions, according to their wont, they write thus in Isauria.

We decline[8] not to bring forward the authentic faith published at the Dedication at Antioch[9] ; though certainly our fathers at the time met together for a particular subject under investigation. But since 'Coessential' and 'Like-in-essence,' have troubled many persons in times past and up to this day, and since moreover some are said recently to have devised the Son's 'Unlikeness' to the Father, on their account we reject 'Coessential' and 'Like-in-essence,' as alien to the Scriptures, but 'Unlike' we anathematize, and account all who profess it as aliens from the Church. And we distinctly confess the 'Likeness' of the Son to the Father, according to the Apostle, who says of the Son, 'Who is the Image of the Invisible God' (Col. i. 15).

And we confess and believe in one God, the Father Almighty, the Maker of heaven and earth, of all things visible and invisible.

And we believe also in our Lord Jesus Christ, His Son, generated from Him impassibly before all the ages, God the Word, God from God, Only-begotten, light, life, truth, wisdom, power, through whom all things were made, in the heavens and on the earth, whether visible or invisible. He, as we believe, at the end of the world, for the abolishment of sin, took flesh of the Holy Virgin, and was made man, and suffered for our sins, and rose again, and was taken up into heaven, and sitteth on the right hand of the Father, and is coming again in glory, to judge quick and dead.

We believe also in the Holy Ghost, which our Saviour and Lord named Paraclete, having promised to send Him to the disciples after His own departure, as He did send ; through whom He sanctifieth those in the Church who believe, and are baptized in the Name of Father and Son and Holy Ghost.

But those who preach aught beside this faith the Catholic Church regards as aliens. And that to this faith that is equivalent which was published lately at Sirmium, under sanction of his religiousness the Emperor, is plain to all who read it.

30. Having written thus in Isauria, they

---

3 [The 'blasphemia' of Potamius, bishop of Lisbon ; see *Prolegg.* ch. ii. § 8 (2), Hil. *de Syn.* 11 ; Socr. ii. 30].

4 7th Confession, or 2nd Sirmian, A.D. 357.

5 κεφάλαιον. vid. *de Decr.* § 31. p. 56 ; *Orat.* i. § 34 ; Epiph. *Hær.* 73. 11.

6 It will be observed that this Confession ; 1. by denying 'two Gods,' and declaring that the One God is the God of Christ, implies that our Lord is not God. 2. It says that the word ' substance,' and its compounds, ought not to be used as being unscriptural, mysterious, and leading to disturbance ; 3. it holds that the Father is greater than the Son 'in honour, dignity, and godhead ;' 4. that the Son is subordinate to the Father *with* all other things ; 5. that it is the Father's characteristic to be invisible and impassible. They also say that our Lord, hominem suscepisse per

quem *compassus* est, a word which Phœbadius condemns in his remarks on this Confession ; where, by the way, he uses the word 'spiritus' in the sense of Hilary and the Ante-Nicene Fathers, in a connection which at once explains the obscure words of the suppositious Sardican Confession (vid. above, § 9, note 3), and turns them into another evidence of this additional heresy involved in Arianism. 'Impassibilis Deus,' says Phœbadius, 'quia Deus *Spiritus* . . . non ergo passibilis Dei Spiritus, licet in homine suo passus.' Now the Sardican Confession is thought ignorant, as well as unauthoritative, e.g. by Natalis Alex. *Sæc.* 4. *Diss.* 29, because it imputes to Valens and Ursacius the following belief, which he supposes to be Patripassianism, but which exactly answers to this aspect and representation of Arianism : ὅτι ὁ λόγος καὶ ὅτι τὸ πνεῦμα καὶ ἐσταυρώθη καὶ ἐσφάγη καὶ ἀπέθανεν καὶ ἀνέστη. Theod. *H.E.* ii. 6. p. 844.

7 Socrates [wrongly] connects this with the 'blasphemia.' *Hist.* ii. 30. 8 9th Confession, at Seleucia A.D. 359.

9 The Semi-Arian majority in the Council had just before been confirming the Creed of the Dedication ; hence this beginning. vid. *supr.* § 11. The present creed, as if to propitiate the Semi-Arian majority, adds an anathema upon the Anomœan as well as on the Homoūsion and Homœusion.

went up to Constantinople [1], and there, as if dissatisfied, they changed it, as is their wont, and with some small additions against using even 'Subsistence' of Father, Son, and Holy Ghost, they transmitted it to those at Ariminum, and compelled even those in the said parts to subscribe, and those who contradicted them they got banished by Constantius. And it runs thus:—

We believe [2] in One God, Father Almighty, from whom are all things;

And in the Only-begotten Son of God, begotten from God before all ages and before every beginning, by whom all things were made, visible and invisible, and begotten as only-begotten, only from the Father only [3], God from God, like to the Father that begat Him according to the Scriptures; whose origin no one knows, except the Father alone who begat Him. He as we acknowledge, the Only-begotten Son of God, the Father sending Him, came hither from the heavens, as it is written, for the undoing of sin and death, and was born of the Holy Ghost, of Mary the Virgin according to the flesh, as it is written, and conversed with the disciples, and having fulfilled the whole Economy according to the Father's will, was crucified and dead and buried and descended to the parts below the earth; at whom hades itself shuddered: who also rose from the dead on the third day, and abode with the disciples, and, forty days being fulfilled, was taken up into the heavens, and sitteth on the right hand of the Father, to come in the last day of the resurrection in the Father's glory, that He may render to every man according to his works.

And in the Holy Ghost, whom the Only-begotten Son of God Himself, Christ, our Lord and God, promised to send to the race of man, as Paraclete, as it is written, 'the Spirit of truth' (Joh. xvi. 13), which He sent unto them when He had ascended into the heavens.

But the name of 'Essence,' which was set down by the Fathers in simplicity, and, being unknown by the people, caused offence, because the Scriptures contain it not, it has seemed good to abolish, and for the future to make no mention of it at all; since the divine Scriptures have made no mention of the Essence of Father and Son. For neither ought Subsistence to be named concerning Father, Son, and Holy Ghost. But we say that the Son is Like the Father, as the divine Scriptures say and teach; and all the heresies, both those which have been afore condemned already, and whatever are of modern date, being contrary to this published statement, be they anathema [4].

31. However, they did not stand even to this; for coming down from Constantinople to Antioch, they were dissatisfied that they had written at all that the Son was 'Like the Father, as the Scriptures say;' and putting their ideas upon paper [5], they began reverting to their first doctrines, and said that 'the Son is altogether unlike the Father,' and that the 'Son is in no manner like the Father,' and so much did they change, as to admit those who spoke the Arian doctrine nakedly and to deliver to them the Churches with licence to bring forward the words of blasphemy with impunity [6]. Because then of the extreme shamelessness of their blasphemy they were called by all Anomœans, having also the name of Exucontian [7], and the heretical Constantius for the patron of their irreligion, who persisting up to the end in irreligion, and on the point of death, thought good to be baptized [8]; not however by religious men, but by Euzoius [9], who for his Arianism had been deposed, not once, but often, both when he was a deacon, and when he was in the see of Antioch.

32. The forementioned parties then had proceeded thus far, when they were stopped and deposed. But well I know, not even under these circumstances will they stop, as many as have now dissembled [10], but they will always be making parties against the truth, until they return to themselves and say, 'Let us rise and go to our fathers, and we will say unto them, We anathematize the Arian heresy, and we acknowledge the Nicene Council;' for against this is their quarrel. Who then, with ever so little understanding, will bear them any longer? who, on hearing in every Council some things taken away and others added, but perceives that their mind is shifty and treacherous against Christ? who on seeing them embodying to so great a length both their professions of faith, and their own exculpation, but sees that they are giving sentence against themselves, and studiously writing much which may be likely by their officious display and abundance of words to seduce the simple and

---

[1] These two sections seem to have been inserted by Athanafter his Letter was finished, and contain later occurrences in the history of Ariminum, than were contemplated when he wrote *supr.* § 11. vid. note 7 *in loc.* It should be added that at this Council Ulfilas the Apostle of the Goths, who had hitherto followed the Council of Nicæa, conformed, and thus became the means of spreading through his countrymen the Creed of Ariminum.

[2] 10th Confession at Niké and Constantinople, A.D. 359, 360.

[3] μόνος ἐκ μόνου. This phrase may be considered a symptom of Anomœan influence; μόνος παρά, or ὑπό, μόνου being one special formula adopted by Eunomius, explanatory of μονογενὴς, in accordance with the original Arian theory, mentioned *de Decr.* § 7. *supr.* p. 154, that the Son was the one instrument of creation. Eunomius said that He alone was created by the Father alone; all other things being created by the Father, not alone, but *through* Him whom alone He had first created. vid. Cyril. *Thesaur.* 25. Basil *contr. Eunom.* ii. 21. Acacius ap. Epiph. *Hær.* 72. 7. p. 839.

[4] Here as before, instead of speaking of Arianism, the Confession anathematizes *all* heresies, vid. *supr.* § 23, n. 4.

[5] 11th Confession at Antioch, A.D. 361. [Socr. ii. 45. The occasion was the installation of Euzoius in place of Meletius.]

[6] Acacius, Eudoxius, and the rest, after ratifying at Constantinople the Creed framed at Niké and subscribed at Ariminum, appear next at Antioch a year and a half later, when they throw off the mask, and, avowing the Anomœan Creed, 'revert,' as S. Athanasius says, 'to their first doctrines,' i.e. those with which Arius started.

[7] From ἐξ οὐκ ὄντων, 'out of nothing,' one of the original Arian positions concerning the Son. Theodoret says that they were also called Hexakionitæ, from the nature of their place of meeting, *Hær.* iv. 3. and Du Cange confirms it so far as to shew that there was a place or quarter of Constantinople Hexakionium. [Cf. Soph. *Lex. s.v.*]

[8] This passage shews that Athanasius did not insert these sections till two years after the composition of the work itself; for Constantine died A.D. 361.

[9] Euzoius, now Arian Bishop of Antioch, was excommunicated with Arius in Egypt and at Nicæa, and was restored with him to the Church at the Council of Jerusalem.

[10] ὑπεκρίναντο. *Hypocrites* is almost a title of the Arians (with an apparent allusion to 1 Tim. iv. 2. vid. Socr. i. p. 5, *Orat.* i. § 8).

hide what they are in point of heresy? But as the heathen, as the Lord said, using vain words in their prayers (Mat. vi. 7), are nothing profited; so they too, after all this out-pouring, were not able to quench the judgment pronounced against the Arian heresy, but were convicted and deposed instead; and rightly; for which of their formularies is to be accepted by the hearer? or with what confidence shall they be catechists to those who come to them? for if they all have one and the same meaning, what is the need of many? But if need has arisen of so many, it follows that each by itself is deficient, not complete; and they establish this point better than we can, by their innovating on them all and re-making them. And the number of their Councils, and the difference of their statements is a proof that those who were present at them, while at variance with the Nicene, are yet too feeble to harm the Truth.

PART III.

ON THE SYMBOLS 'OF THE ESSENCE AND 'COESSENTIAL.'

We must look at the sense not the wording. The offence excited is at the sense; meaning of the Symbols; the question of their not being in Scripture. Those who hesitate only at 'coessential,' not to be considered Arians. Reasons why 'coessential' is better than 'like-in-essence,' yet the latter may be interpreted in a good sense. Explanation of the rejection of 'coessential' by the Council which condemned the Samosatene; use of the word by Dionysius of Alexandria; parallel variation in the use of Unoriginate; quotation from Ignatius and another; reasons for using 'coessential;' objections to it; examination of the word itself; further documents of the Council of Ariminum.

33. BUT since they are thus minded both towards each other and towards those who preceded them, proceed we to ascertain from them what absurdity they have seen, or what they complain of in the received phrases, that they have proved 'disobedient to parents' (Rom. i. 30), and contend against an Ecumenical Council[1]? 'The phrases "of the essence" and "co-essential,"' say they, 'do not please us, for they are an offence to some and a trouble to many.' This then is what they allege in their writings; but one may reasonably answer them thus: If the very words were by themselves a cause of offence to them, it must have followed, not that some only should have been offended, and many troubled, but that we also and all the rest should have been affected by them in the same way; but

if on the contrary all men are well content with the words, and they who wrote them were no ordinary persons but men who came together from the whole world, and to these testify in addition the 400 Bishops and more who now met at Ariminum, does not this plainly prove against those who accuse the Council, that the terms are not in fault, but the perverseness of those who misinterpret them? How many men read divine Scripture wrongly, and as thus conceiving it, find fault with the Saints? such were the former Jews, who rejected the Lord, and the present Manichees who blaspheme the Law[3]; yet are not the Scriptures the cause to them, but their own evil humours. If then ye can shew the terms to be actually unsound, do so and let the proof proceed, and drop the pretence of offence created, lest you come into the condition of the Pharisees of old. For when they pretended offence at the Lord's teaching, He said, 'Every plant, which My heavenly Father hath not planted, shall be rooted up' (Matt. xv. 13). By which He shewed that not the words of the Father planted by Him were really an offence to them, but that they mis-interpreted what was well said, and offended themselves. And in like manner they who at that time blamed the Epistles of the Apostle, impeached, not Paul, but their own deficient learning and distorted minds.

34. For answer, what is much to the purpose, Who are they whom you pretend are offended and troubled at these terms? of those who are religious towards Christ not one; on the contrary they defend and maintain them. But if they are Arians who thus feel, what wonder they should be distressed at words which destroy their heresy? for it is not the terms which offend them, but the proscription of their irreligion which afflicts them. Therefore let us have no more murmuring against the Fathers, nor pretence of this kind; or next[4] you will be making complaints of the Lord's Cross, because it is 'to Jews an offence and to Gentiles foolishness,' as said the Apostle[5] (1 Cor. i. 23, 24). But as the Cross is not faulty, for to us who believe it is 'Christ the power of God and the wisdom of God,' though Jews rave, so neither are the terms of the Fathers faulty, but profitable to those who honestly read, and subversive of all irreligion, though the Arians so often burst with rage as being condemned by them. Since then the pretence that persons are offended does not hold, tell us yourselves, why is it you are

---

[1] The subject before us, naturally rises out of what has gone before. The Anomœan creed was hopeless; but with the Semi-Arians all that remained was the adjustment of phrases. Accordingly, Athan. goes on to propose such *explanations* as might clear the way for a re-union of Christendom. § 47, note.

[3] Vid. *Orat.* i. 8; iv. 23.
[4] ὥρα. vid. *Orat.* i. §15; iv. §10; *Serap.* ii. 1. καίρος. *de Decr.* § 15. init.
[5] 'The Apostle' is a common title of S. Paul in antiquity. Cf. August. *ad Bonifac.* iii. 3.

not pleased with the phrase 'of the essence' (this must first be enquired about), when you yourselves have written that the Son is generated from the Father? If when you name the Father, or use the word 'God,' you do not signify essence, or understand Him according to essence, who is that He is, but signify something else about Him[6], not to say inferior, then you should not have written that the Son was from the Father, but from what is about Him or in Him[7]; and so, shrinking from saying that God is truly Father, and making Him compound who is simple, in a material way, you will be authors of a newer blasphemy. And, with such ideas, you must needs consider the Word, and the title 'Son,' not as an essence but as a name[7a] only, and in consequence hold your own views as far as names only, and be talking, not of what you believe to exist, but of what you think not to exist.

35. But this is more like the crime of the Sadducees, and of those among the Greeks who had the name of Atheists. It follows that you will deny that even creation is the handywork of God Himself that is; at least, if 'Father' and 'God' do not signify the very essence of Him that is, but something else, which you imagine: which is irreligious, and most shocking even to think of. But if, when we hear it said, 'I am that I am,' and, 'In the beginning God created the heaven and the earth,' and, 'Hear, O Israel, the Lord our God is one Lord,' and, 'Thus saith the Lord Almighty' (Ex. iii. 14; Gen. i. 1; Deut. vi. 4), we understand nothing else than the very simple, and blessed, and incomprehensible essence itself of Him that is, (for though we be unable to master what He is, yet hearing 'Father,' and 'God,' and 'Almighty,' we understand nothing else to be meant than the very essence of Him that is[8]); and if ye too have said, that the Son is from God, it follows that you have said that He is from the 'essence' of the Father. And since the Scriptures precede you which say, that the Lord is Son of the Father, and the Father Himself precedes them, who says, 'This is My beloved Son' (Matt. iii. 17), and a son is no other than the offspring from his father, is it not evident that the Fathers have suitably said that the Son is from the Father's essence? considering that it is all one to say rightly 'from God,' and to say 'from the essence.' For all the creatures, though they be said to have come into being from God, yet are not from God

as the Son is; for they are not offsprings in their nature, but works. Thus, it is said, 'in the beginning God,' not 'generated,' but 'made the heaven and the earth, and all that is in them' (Gen. i. 1). And not, 'who generates,' but 'who maketh His angels spirits, and His ministers a flame of fire' (Ps. civ. 4). And though the Apostle has said, 'One God, from whom all things' (1 Cor. viii. 6), yet he says not this, as reckoning the Son with other things; but, whereas some of the Greeks consider that the creation was held together by chance, and from the combination of atoms[9]; and spontaneously from elements of similar structure[10], and has no cause; and others consider that it came from a cause, but not through the Word; and each heretic has imagined things at his will, and tells his fables about the creation; on this account the Apostle was obliged to introduce 'from God,' that he might thereby certify the Maker, and shew that the universe was framed at His will. And accordingly he straightway proceeds: 'And one Lord Jesus Christ, through whom all things' (1 Cor. viii. 6), by way of excepting the Son from that 'all' (for what is called God's work, is all done through the Son; and it is not possible that the things framed should have one origin with their Framer), and by way of teaching that the phrase 'of God,' which occurs in the passage, has a different sense in the case of the works, from what it bears when used of the Son; for He is offspring, and they are works: and therefore He, the Son, is the proper offspring of His essence, but they are the handywork of his will.

36. The Council, then, comprehending this[1], and aware of the different senses of the same word, that none should suppose, that the Son was said to be 'from God' like the creation, wrote with greater explicitness, that the Son was 'from the essence.' For this betokens the true genuineness of the Son towards the Father; whereas, by the simple phrase 'from God,' only the Creator's will in framing is signified. If then they too had this meaning, when they wrote that the Word was 'from the Father,' they had nothing to complain of in the Council; but if they meant 'of God,' in the instance of the Son, as it is used of the creation, then as understanding it of the creation, they should not name the Son, or they will be manifestly mingling blasphemy with religiousness; but either they have to cease reckoning the Lord with the creatures, or at least to refrain from unworthy and unbecoming statements about

---

6 Cf. *de Decr.* 22, note 1.   7 *De Decr.* 24, note 9.
7a Vid. supr. *Orat.* i. § 15; *de Decr.* § 22, note 1.
8 *De Decr.* 29, note 7.

9 Democritus, or Epicurus.   10 Anaxagoras.
1 *De Decr.* § 19.

the Son. For if He is a Son, He is not a creature; but if a creature, then not a Son. Since these are their views, perhaps they will be denying the Holy Laver also, because it is administered into Father and into Son; and not into Creator and Creature, as they account it. 'But,' they say, 'all this is not written: and we reject these words as un-scriptural.' But this, again, is an unblushing excuse in their mouths. For if they think everything must be rejected which is not writ-ten, wherefore, when the Arian party invent such a heap of phrases, not from Scripture[2], 'Out of nothing,' and 'the Son was not before His generation,' and 'Once He was not,' and 'He is alterable,' and 'the Father is ineffable and invisible to the Son,' and 'the Son knows not even His own essence;' and all that Arius has vomited in his light and irreligious Thalia, why do not they speak against these, but rather take their part, and on that account contend with their own Fathers? And, in what Scripture did they on their part find 'Unoriginate,' and 'the term essence,' and 'there are three subsistences,' and 'Christ is not very God,' and 'He is one of the hundred sheep,' and 'God's Wisdom is ingenerate and without beginning, but the created powers are many, of which Christ is one?' Or how, when in the so-called Dedication, Acacius and Euse-bius and their fellows used expressions not in Scripture, and said that 'the First-born of the creation' was 'the exact Image of the es-sence and power and will ,and glory,' do they complain of the Fathers, for making mention of unscriptural expressions, and especially of essence? For they ought either to complain of themselves, or to find no fault with the Fathers.

37. Now, if certain others made excuses of the expressions of the Council, it might per-haps have been set down, either to ignorance or to caution. There is no question, for instance, about George of Cappadocia[3], who was expelled from Alexandria; a man, with-out character in years past, nor a Christian in any respect; but only pretending to the name to suit the times, and thinking 'religion to be a' means of 'gain' (1 Tim. vi. 5). And there-fore there is no reason to complain of his making mistakes about the faith, considering he knows neither what he says, nor whereof he affirms; but, according to the text, 'goeth after all, as a bird' (1 Tim. i. 7; Prov. vii. 22, 23, not LXX. ?) But when Acacius, and Eudoxius, and Patrophilus say this, do not they deserve the strongest reprobation? for while they write what is unscriptural themselves, and have accepted

many times the term 'essence' as suitable, especially on the ground of the letter[3a] of Eu-sebius, they now blame their predecessors for using terms of the same kind. Nay, though they say themselves, that the Son is 'God from God,' and 'Living Word,' 'Exact Image of the Father's essence;' they accuse the Nicene Bishops of saying, that He who was begotten is 'of the essence' of Him who begat Him, and 'Coessential' with Him. But what marvel if they conflict with their pre-decessors and their own Fathers, when they are inconsistent with themselves, and fall foul of each other? For after publishing, in the so-called Dedication at Antioch, that the Son is exact Image of the Father's essence, and swearing that so they held and anathematizing those who held otherwise, nay, in Isauria, writing down, 'We do not decline the authentic faith published in the Dedication at Antioch[4],' where the term 'essence' was introduced, as if forgetting all this, shortly after, in the same Isauria, they put into writing the very contrary, saying, We reject the words 'coessential,' and 'like-in-essence,' as alien to the Scriptures, and abolish the term 'essence,' as not con-tained therein[4a].

38. Can we then any more account such men Christians? or what sort of faith have they who stand neither to word nor writing, but alter and change every thing according to the times? For if, O Acacius and Eudoxius, you 'do not decline the faith published at the Dedication,' and in it is written that the Son is 'Exact Image of God's essence,' why is it ye write in Isauria, 'we reject the Like in essence?' for if the Son is not like the Fa-ther according to essence, how is He 'exact image of the essence?' But if you are dis-satisfied at having written 'Exact Image of the essence,' how is it that ye 'anathematize those who say that the Son is Unlike?' for if He be not according to essence like, He is surely unlike: and the Unlike cannot be an Image. And if so, then it does not hold that 'he that hath seen the Son, hath seen the Father' (John xiv. 9), there being then the greatest possible difference between Them, or rather the One being wholly Unlike the Other. And Unlike cannot possibly be called Like. By what artifice then do you call Unlike like, and consider Like to be unlike, and pretend to say that the Son is the Father's Image? for if the Son be not like the Father in essence, something is wanting to the Image, and it is not a complete Image, nor a perfect radiance[5].

[3a] Supr. p. 73.   [4] Supr. § 29.   [4a] Supr. § 8.
[5] It must not be supposed from this that he approves [as ade-quate] the phrase ὅμοιος κατ' οὐσίαν or ὁμοιούσιος, in this Treatise, for infr. § 53. he rejects it on the ground that when we speak of

How then read you, 'In Him dwelleth all the fulness of the Godhead bodily?' and, 'from His fulness all we received' (Coloss. ii. 9; John i. 16)? how is it that you expel the Arian Aetius as an heretic, though ye say the same with him? for he is your companion, O Acacius, and he became Eudoxius's master in this so great irreligion[6]; which was the reason why Leontius the Bishop made him deacon, that using the name of the diaconate as sheep's clothing, he might be able with impunity to pour forth the words of blasphemy.

39. What then has persuaded you to contradict each other, and to procure to yourselves so great a disgrace? You cannot give any good account of it; this supposition only remains, that all you do is but outward profession and pretence, to secure the patronage of Constantius and the gain from thence accruing. And ye make nothing of accusing the Fathers, and ye complain outright of the expressions as being unscriptural; and, as it is written, 'opened your legs to every one that passed by' (Ez. xvi. 25); so as to change as often as they wish, in whose pay and keep you are. Yet, though a man use terms not in Scripture, it makes no difference, so that his meaning be religious[6a]. But the heretic, though he use scriptural terms, yet, as being equally dangerous and depraved, shall be asked in the words of the Spirit, 'Why dost thou preach My laws, and takest My covenant in thy mouth' (Ps. l. 16)? Thus whereas the devil, though speaking from the Scriptures, is silenced by the Saviour, the blessed Paul, though he speaks from profane writers, 'The Cretans are always liars,' and, 'For we are His offspring,' and, 'Evil communications corrupt good manners,' yet has a religious meaning, as being holy,—is 'doctor of the nations, in faith and verity,' as having 'the mind of Christ' (Tit. i. 12; Acts xvii. 28; 1 Cor. xv. 33; 1 Tim. ii. 7; 1 Cor. ii. 16), and what he speaks, he utters religiously. What then is there even plausible, in the Arian terms, in which the 'caterpillar' (Joel ii. 25) and the 'locust' are preferred to the Saviour, and He is reviled with 'Once Thou wast not.' and 'Thou wast created,' and 'Thou art foreign to God in essence,' and, in a word, no irreverence is unused among them? But what did the Fathers omit in the way of reverence? or rather, have they not a lofty view and a Christ-loving religiousness? And yet these, they wrote, 'We reject;' while those others they endure in their insults towards the Lord, and betray to all men, that for no other cause do they resist that great Council but that it condemned the Arian heresy. For it is on this account again that they speak against the term Coessential, about which they also entertain wrong sentiments. For if their faith was right, and they confessed the Father as truly Father, believed the Son to be genuine Son, and by nature true Word and Wisdom of the Father, and as to saying that the Son is 'from God,' if they did not use the words of Him as of themselves, but understood Him to be the proper offspring of the Father's essence, as the radiance is from light, they would not every one of them have found fault with the Fathers; but would have been confident that the Council wrote suitably; and that this is the right faith concerning our Lord Jesus Christ.

40. 'But,' say they, 'the sense of such expressions is obscure to us;' for this is another of their pretences,—'We reject them[7],' say they, 'because we cannot master their meaning.' But if they were true in this profession, instead of saying, 'We reject them,' they should ask instruction from the well informed; else ought they to reject whatever they cannot understand in divine Scripture, and to find fault with the writers. But this were the venture of heretics rather than of us Christians; for what we do not understand in the sacred oracles, instead of rejecting, we seek 'from persons to whom the Lord has revealed it, and from them we ask for instruction. But since they thus make a pretence of the obscurity of such expressions, let them at least confess what is annexed to the Creed, and anathematize those who hold that 'the Son is from nothing,' and 'He was not before His generation,' and 'the Word of God is a creature and work,' and 'He is alterable by nature,' and 'from another subsistence;' and in a word let them anathematize the Arian heresy, which has originated such irreligion. Nor let them say any more, 'We reject the terms,' but that 'we do not yet understand them;' by way of having some reason to shew for declining them. But I know well, and am sure, and they know it too, that if they could confess all this and anathematize the Arian heresy, they would no longer deny those terms of the Council. For on this account it was that the Fathers, after declaring that the Son was begotten from the Father's essence, and Coessential with Him, thereupon added, 'But those who say'—what has just been quoted,

---

'like,' we imply qualities, not essence. Yet he himself frequently uses it, as other Fathers, and *Orat.* i. § 26. uses ὅμοιος τῆς οὐσίας.
6 [Prolegg. ch. ii. § 8 (2) a.]
6a Vid. p. 162, note 8. Cf. Greg. Naz. *Orat.* 31. 24. vid. also Hil. *contr. Constant.* 16. August. *Ep.* 238. n. 4—6. Cyril. *Dial.* i. p. 391. Petavius refers to other passages. *de Trin.* v. 5. § 6.

7 § 8.

the symbols of the Arian heresy,—'we anathematize;' I mean, in order to shew that the statements are parallel, and that the terms in the Creed imply the disclaimers subjoined, and that all who confess the terms, will certainly understand the disclaimers. But those who both dissent from the latter and impugn the former, such men are proved on every side to be foes of Christ.

41. Those who deny the Council altogether, are sufficiently exposed by these brief remarks; those, however, who accept everything else that was defined at Nicæa, and doubt only about the Coessential, must not be treated as enemies; nor do we here attack them as Ariomaniacs, nor as opponents of the Fathers, but we discuss the matter with them as brothers with brothers[8], who mean what we mean, and dispute only about the word. For, confessing that the Son is from the essence of the Father, and not from other subsistence, and that He is not a creature nor work, but His genuine and natural offspring, and that He is eternally with the Father as being His Word and Wisdom, they are not far from accepting even the phrase, 'Coessential.' Now such is Basil, who wrote from Ancyra concerning the faith[9]. For only to say 'like according to essence,' is very far from signifying 'of the essence,' by which, rather, as they say themselves, the genuineness of the Son to the Father is signified. Thus tin is only like to silver, a wolf to a dog, and gilt brass to the true metal; but tin is not from silver, nor could a wolf be accounted the offspring of a dog[10]. But since they say that He is 'of the essence' and 'Like-in-essence,' what do they signify by these but 'Coessential[11]?' For, while to say only 'Like-in-essence,' does not necessarily convey 'of the essence,' on the contrary, to say 'Coessential,' is to signify the meaning of both terms, 'Like-in-essence,' and 'of the essence.' And accordingly they themselves in controversy with those who say that the Word is a creature, instead of allowing Him to be genuine Son, have taken their proofs against them from human illustrations of son and father[12], with this exception that God is not as man, nor the generation of the Son as issue of man, but such as may be ascribed to God, and is fit for us to think. Thus they have called the Father the Fount of Wisdom and Life, and the Son the Radiance of the Eternal Light, and the Offspring from the Fountain, as He says, 'I am the Life,' and, 'I Wisdom dwell with Prudence' (John xiv. 6; Prov. viii. 12). But the Radiance from the Light, and Offspring from Fountain, and Son from Father, how can these be so fitly expressed as by 'Coessential?' And is there any cause of fear, lest, because the offspring from men are coessential, the Son, by being called Coessential, be Himself considered as a human offspring too? perish the thought! not so; but the explanation is easy. For the Son is the Father's Word and Wisdom; whence we learn the impassibility and indivisibility of such a generation from the Father[1]. For not even man's word is part of him, nor proceeds from him according to passion[2]; much less God's Word; whom the Father has declared to be His own Son, lest, on the other hand, if we merely heard of 'Word,' we should suppose Him, such as is the word of man, impersonal; but that, hearing that He is Son, we may acknowledge Him to be living Word and substantive Wisdom.

42. Accordingly, as in saying 'offspring,' we have no human thoughts, and, though we know God to be a Father, we entertain no material ideas concerning Him, but while we listen to these illustrations and terms, we think suitably of God, for He is not as man, so in like manner, when we hear of 'coessential,' we ought to transcend all sense, and, according to the Proverb, 'understand by the understanding what is set before us' (Prov. xxiii. 1); so as to know, that not by will, but in truth, is He genuine from the Father, as Life from Fountain, and Radiance from Light. Else[3] why should we understand 'offspring' and 'son,' in no corporeal way, while we conceive of 'coessential' as after the manner of bodies? especially since these terms are not here used about different subjects, but of whom 'offspring' is predicated, of Him is 'coessential' also.

---

8 [See Prolegg. ch. ii. § 8 (2) c.]

9 [Ath. is referring to the Council of Ancyra, 358.]

10 So also *de Decr.* § 23. p. 40. Pseudo-Ath. *Hyp. Mel. et Euseb.* Hil. *de Syn.* 89. The illustration runs into this position, 'Things that are like, [need] not be the same.' vid. § 39. note 5. On the other hand, Athan. himself contends for the ταυτὸν τῇ ὁμοιώσει, 'the *same* in likeness.' *de Decr.* § 20.

11 Vid. Socr. iii. 25. p. 204. a.b. *Una substantia* religiose prædicabitur quæ ex *nativitatis* proprietate et ex naturæ *similitudine* ita indifferens sit, ut una dicatur. Hil. *de Syn.* 67.

12 Here at last Athan. alludes to the Ancyrene Synodal Letter, vid. Epiph. *Hær.* 73. 5 and 7. about which he has kept a pointed silence above, when tracing the course of the Arian confessions. That is, he treats the Semi-Arians as tenderly as S. Hilary, *as soon as* they break company with the Arians. The Ancyrene Council of 358 was a protest against the 'blasphemia' or second Sirmian Confession

---

1 It is usual with the Fathers to use the two terms 'Son' and 'Word,' to guard and complete the ordinary sense of each other, vid. p. 157, note 6; and p. 167, note 4. The term Son, used by itself, was abused into Arianism; and the term Word into Sabellianism; again the term Son might be accused of introducing material notions, and the term Word of imperfection and transitoriness. Each of them corrected the other. *Orat.* i. § 28. iv. § 8. Euseb. *contr. Marc.* ii. 4. p. 54. Isid. Pel. *Ep.* iv. 141. So S. Cyril says that we learn 'from His being called Son that He is from Him, τὸ ἐξ αὐτοῦ; from His being called Wisdom and Word, that He is in Him,' τὸ ἐν αὐτῷ. *Thesaur.* iv. p. 31. However, S Athanasius observes, that properly speaking the one term implies the other, i.e. in its fulness. *Orat.* iii. § 3. iv. § 24 fin. On the other hand the heretics accused Catholics of inconsistency, or of a union of opposite errors, because they accepted all the Scripture images together. Vigilius of Thapsus, *contr. Eutych.* ii. init. vid. also i. init. and Eulogius, *ap. Phot.* 225, p. 759.

2 *De Decr.* § 10.　　　3 Vid. Epiph. *Hær.* 73. 3, &c.

And it is but consistent to attach the same sense to both expressions as applied to the Saviour, and not to interpret 'offspring' in a good sense, and 'coessential' otherwise; since to be consistent, ye who are thus minded and who say that the Son is Word and Wisdom of the Father, should entertain a different view of these terms also, and understand Word in another sense, and Wisdom in yet another. But, as this would be absurd (for the Son is the Father's Word and Wisdom, and the Offspring from the Father is one and proper to His essence), so the sense of 'Offspring' and 'Coessential' is one, and whoso considers the Son an offspring, rightly considers Him also as 'coessential.'

43. This is sufficient to shew that the meaning of the beloved ones [4] is not foreign nor far from the 'Coessential.' But since, as they allege [5] (for I have not the Epistle in question), the Bishops who condemned the Samosatene [6] have said in writing that the Son is not coessential with the Father, and so it comes to pass that they, for caution and honour towards those who have so said, thus feel about that expression, it will be to the purpose cautiously to argue with them this point also. Certainly it is unbecoming to make the one conflict with the others; for all are fathers; nor is it religious to settle, that these have spoken well, and those ill; for all of them fell asleep in Christ. Nor is it right to be disputatious, and to compare the respective numbers of those who met in the Councils, lest the three hundred seem to throw the lesser into the shade; nor to compare the dates, lest those who preceded seem to eclipse those that came after. For all, I say, are fathers; and yet not even the three hundred laid down nothing new, nor was it in any self-confidence that they became champions of words not in Scripture, but they fell back upon fathers, as did the others, and used their words. For there have been two of the name of Dionysius, much older than the seventy who deposed the Samosatene, of whom one was of Rome, and the other of Alexandria. But a charge had been laid by some persons against the Bishop of Alexandria before the Bishop of Rome, as if he had said that the Son was made, and not coessential with the Father. And, the synod at Rome being indignant, the Bishop of Rome expressed their united sentiments in a letter to his namesake. And so the latter, in defence, wrote a book with the title

'of Refutation and Defence;' and thus he writes to the other:

44. And[7] I wrote in another Letter a refutation of the false charge which they bring against me, that I deny that Christ is coessential with God. For though I say that I have not found or read this term anywhere in holy Scripture, yet my remarks which follow, and which they have not noticed, are not inconsistent with that belief. For I instanced a human production, which is evidently homogeneous, and I observed that undeniably fathers differed from their children, only in not being the same individuals; otherwise there could be neither parents nor children. And my Letter, as I said before, owing to present circumstances, I am unable to produce, or I would have sent you the very words I used, or rather a copy of it all; which, if I have an opportunity, I will do still. But I am sure from recollection, that I adduced many parallels of things kindred with each other, for instance, that a plant grown from seed or from root, was other than that from which it sprang, and yet altogether one in nature with it; and that a stream flowing from a fountain, changed its appearance and its name, for that neither the fountain was called stream, nor the stream fountain, but both existed, and that the fountain was as it were father, but the stream was what was generated from the fountain.

45. Thus the Bishop. If then any one finds fault with those who met at Nicæa, as if they contradicted the decisions of their predecessors, he might reasonably find fault also with the seventy, because they did not keep to the statements of their own predecessors; but such were the Dionysii and the Bishops assembled on that occasion at Rome. But neither these nor those is it pious to blame; for all were charged with the embassy of Christ, and all have given diligence against the heretics, and the one party condemned the Samosatene, while the other condemned the Arian heresy. And rightly have both these and those written, and suitably to the matter in hand. And as the blessed Apostle, writing to the Romans, said, 'The Law is spiritual, the Law is holy, and the commandment holy and just and good' (Rom. vii. 14, 12); and soon after, 'What the Law could not do, in that it was weak' (Ib. viii. 3), but wrote to the Hebrews, 'The Law has made no one perfect' (Heb. vii. 19); and to the Galatians, 'By the Law no one is justified' (Gal. iii. 11), but to Timothy, 'The Law is good, if a man use it lawfully' (1 Tim. i. 8); and no one would accuse the Saint of inconsistency and variation in writing, but rather would admire how suitably he wrote to each, to teach the Romans and the others to turn from the letter to the spirit, but to instruct the Hebrews and Galatians to place their hopes, not in the Law, but in the Lord who had given the Law; —so, if the Fathers of the two Councils made different mention of the Coessential, we ought not in any respect to differ from them, but to investigate their meaning, and this will fully

---

4 § 54, note 2. 5 Vid. Hilar. *de Syn.* 81 init.; Epiph. *Hær.* 73. 12.
6 There were three Councils held against Paul of Samosata, of the dates of 264, 269, and an intermediate year. The third is spoken of in the text, which contrary to the opinion of Pagi, S. Basnage, and Tillemont, Pearson fixes at 265 or 266.

7 Vid. p. 167, and a different translation, p. 182

shew us the agreement of both the Councils. For they who deposed the Samosatene, took Coessential in a bodily sense, because Paul had attempted sophistry and said, 'Unless Christ has of man become God, it follows that He is Coessential with the Father; and if so, of necessity there are three essences, one the previous essence, and the other two from it;' and therefore guarding against this they said with good reason, that Christ was not Coessential[8]. For the Son is not related to the Father as he imagined. But the Bishops who anathematized the Arian heresy, understanding Paul's craft, and reflecting that the word 'Coessential,' has not this meaning when used of things immaterial[9], and especially of God, and acknowledging that the Word was not a creature, but an offspring from the essence, and that the Father's essence was the origin and root and fountain of the Son, and that he was of very truth His Father's likeness, and not of different nature, as we are, and separate from the Father, but that, as being from Him, He exists as Son indivisible, as radiance is with respect to Light, and knowing too the illustrations used in Dionysius's case, the 'fountain,' and the defence of 'Coessential,' and before this the Saviour's saying, symbolical of unity[10], 'I and the Father are one,' and 'he that hath seen Me hath seen the Father' (John x. 30, Ib. xiv. 9), on these grounds reasonably asserted on their part, that the Son was Coessential. And as, according to a former remark, no one would blame the Apostle, if he wrote to the Romans about the Law in one way, and to the Hebrews in another; in like manner, neither would the present Bishops find fault with the ancient, having regard to their interpretation, nor again in view of theirs and of the need of their so writing about the Lord, would the ancient censure their successors. Yes surely, each Council has a sufficient reason for its own language; for since the Samosatene held that the Son was not before

Mary, but received from her the origin of His being, therefore those who then met deposed him and pronounced him heretic; but concerning the Son's Godhead writing in simplicity, they arrived not at accuracy concerning the Coessential, but, as they understood the word, so spoke they about it. For they directed all their thoughts to destroy the device of the Samosatene, and to shew that the Son was before all things, and that, instead of becoming God from man, He, being God, had put on a servant's form, and being Word, had become flesh, as John says (Phil. ii. 7; Joh. i. 14). This is how they dealt with the blasphemies of Paul; but when Eusebius, Arius, and their fellows said that though the Son was before time, yet was He made and one of the creatures, and as to the phrase 'from God,' they did not believe it in the sense of His being genuine Son from Father, but maintained it as it is said of the creatures, and as to the oneness[1] of likeness[2] between the Son and the Father, did not confess that the Son is like the Father according to essence, or according to nature as a son resembles his father, but because of Their agreement of doctrines and of teaching[3]; nay, when they drew a line and an utter distinction between the Son's essence and the Father, ascribing to Him an origin of being, other than the Father, and degrading Him to the creatures, on this account the Bishops assembled at Nicæa, with a view to the craft of the parties so thinking, and as bringing together the sense from the Scriptures, cleared up the point, by affirming the 'Coessential;' that both the true genuineness of the Son might thereby be known, and that to things originate might be ascribed nothing in common with Him. For the precision of this phrase detects their pretence, whenever they use the phrase 'from God,' and gets rid of all the subtleties with which they seduce the simple. For whereas they contrive to put a sophistical construction on all other words at their will, this phrase only, as detecting their heresy, do they dread; which the Fathers set down as a bulwark[4] against their irreligious notions one and all.

46. Let then all contention cease, nor

---

[8] This is in fact the objection which Arius urges against the Coessential, *supr.* § 16, when he calls it the doctrine of Manichæus and Hieracas, vid. § 16, note 11. The same objection is protested against by S. Basil, *contr. Eunom.* i. 19. Hilar. *de Trin.* iv. 4. Yet, while S. Basil agrees with Athan. in his account of the reason of the Council's rejection of the word, S. Hilary on the contrary reports that Paul himself accepted it, i.e. in a Sabellian sense, and therefore the Council rejected it. 'Male homoüsion Samosatenus confessus est, sed numquid melius Arii negaverunt.' *de Syn.* 86.

[9] Cf. Soz. iii. 18. The heretical party, starting with the notion in which their heresy in all its shades consisted, that the Son was a distinct being from the Father, concluded that '*like* in essence' was the only term which would express the relation of the Son to the Father. Here then the word 'coessential' did just enable the Catholics to join issue with them, as exactly expressing what the Catholics wished to express, viz. that there was no such distinction between Them as made the term 'like' necessary, but that as material parent and offspring are individuals under one common *species*, so the Eternal Father and Son are Persons under one common *individual essence*. [10] § 49.

[1] τὴν τῆς ὁμοιώσεως ἑνότητα: and so pp. 163, note 9, 165, 166. And Basil. ταὐτότητα τῆς φύσεως, *Ep.* 8. 3: [but] ταὐτότητα τῆς οὐσίας, Cyril *in Joan.* lib. iii. c. v. p. 302. [cf. ταὐτοούσιον, p. 315, note 6.] It is uniformly asserted by the Catholics that the Father's godhead, θεότης, is the Son's; e.g. *infr.* § 52; *supr.* p. 329 b, line 8; p 333, note 5; *Orat.* i. 49 fin. ii. § 18. § 73. fin. iii. § 26; iii. § 5 fin. iii. § 53; μίαν τὴν θεότητα καὶ τὸ ἴδιον τῆς οὐσίας τοῦ πατρός. § 56 *supr.* p. 84 fin. vid. § 52. note. This is an approach to the doctrine of the Una Res, defined in the fourth Lateran Council [in 1215, see Harnack *Dogmg.* iii. 447, note, and on the doctrine of the Greek Fathers, *Prolegg.* ch. ii. § 3 (2) b.]
[2] Vid. Epiph. *Hær.* 73. 9 fin. [3] § 23, note 3.
[4] ἐπιτείχισμα; in like manner σύνδεσμον πίστεως. Epiph. *Ancor.* 6; cf. *Hær.* 69. 70; Ambros. *de Fid.* iii. 15.

let us any longer conflict, though the Councils have differently taken the phrase 'Coessential,' for we have already assigned a sufficient defence of them; and to it the following may be added:—We have not derived the word 'Unoriginate' from Scripture, (for no where does Scripture call God Unoriginate,) yet since it has many authorities in its favour, I was curious about the term, and found that it too has different senses [5]. Some, for instance, call what is, but is neither generated, nor has any personal cause at all, unoriginate; and others, the uncreate. As then a person, having in view the former of these senses, viz. 'that which has no personal cause,' might say that the Son was not unoriginate, yet would not blame any one whom he perceived to have in view the other meaning, 'not a work or creature but an eternal offspring,' and to affirm accordingly that the Son was unoriginate, (for both speak suitably with a view to their own object); so, even granting that the Fathers have spoken variously concerning the Coessential, let us not dispute about it, but take what they deliver to us in a religious way, when especially their anxiety was directed in behalf of religion.

47. Ignatius, for instance, who was appointed Bishop in Antioch after the Apostles, and became a martyr of Christ, writes concerning the Lord thus : ' There is one physician, fleshly and spiritual, originate and unoriginate [6], God in man, true life in death, both from Mary and from God ;' whereas some teachers who followed Ignatius, write in their turn, ' One is the Unoriginate, the Father, and one the genuine Son from Him, true offspring, Word and Wisdom of the Father [7].' If therefore we have hostile feelings towards these writers, then have we right to quarrel with the Councils; but if, knowing their faith in Christ, we are persuaded that the blessed Ignatius was right in writing that Christ was originate on account of the flesh (for He became flesh), yet unoriginate, because He is not in the number of things made and originated, but Son from Father ; and if we are aware too that those who have said that the Unoriginate is One, meaning the Father, did not mean to lay down that the Word was originated and made, but that the Father has no personal cause, but rather is Himself Father of Wisdom, and in Wisdom has made all things that are originated ; why do we not combine all our Fathers in religious belief, those who deposed the Samosatene as well as those who proscribed the Arian heresy, instead of making distinctions between them and refusing to entertain a right opinion of them ? I repeat, that those, in view of the sophistical explanation of the Samosatene, wrote, ' He is not coessential [8] ;' and these, with an apposite meaning, said that He was. For myself, I have written these brief remarks, from my feeling towards persons who were religious to Christ-ward ; but were it possible to come by the Epistle which we are told that the former wrote, I consider we should find further grounds for the aforesaid proceeding of those blessed men. For it is right and meet thus to feel, and to maintain a good conscience toward the Fathers, if we be not spurious children, but have received the traditions from them, and the lessons of religion at their hands.

48. Such then, as we confess and believe, being the sense of the Fathers, proceed we even in their company to examine once more the matter, calmly and with a kindly sympathy, with reference to what has been said before, viz. whether the Bishops collected at Nicæa do not really prove to have thought aright. For if the Word be a work and foreign to the Father's essence, so that He is separated from the Father by the difference of nature, He cannot be one in essence with Him, but rather He is homogeneous by nature with the works, though He surpass them in grace [9]. On the other hand, if we confess that He is not a work but the genuine offspring of the Father's essence, it would follow that He is inseparable from the Father, being connatural, because He is begotten from Him. And being such, good reason He should be called Coessential.

---

5 [In this passage the difficulties and confusion which surround the terms ἀγένητος and ἀγέννητος (supr. p. 149, &c.) come to a head. The question is (assuming, as proved by Lightfoot, the validity of the distinction of the two in Athan.) which word is to be read here. The MSS. are divided throughout between the two readings, but it is clear (so Lightf. and Zahn on Ign. Eph. 7) that one word alone is in view throughout the present passage. That word, then, is pronounced by Lightf., partly on the strength of the quotation from the unnamed teachers (infr. note 7), partly on the ground of a reference to § 26 (see note 10 there), to be ἀγέννητος. With all deference to so great an authority, I cannot hesitate to pronounce for ἀγένητος. (1.) The parallelism of the two senses with the third and fourth senses of ἀγέν. Orat. i. 30. is almost decisive by itself. (2.) Ath.'s explanation of Ignatius. viz. that Christ is γένητος on account of the flesh (he would have referred γέννητος to His Essence, Orat. i. 56, certainly not to the flesh), while as Son and Word He is distinct from γέννητα and ποιήματα, is even more decisive. (3.) His explanation § 46, sub fin. that the Son is ἀγένητος because He is ἀίδιον γέννημα would lose all sense if ἀγέννητος were read. As a matter of fact, ἀγέννητος is the specific, ἀγένητος the generic term : the former was not applicable to the Eternal Son ; the latter was, except in the first of the two senses distinguished in the text : a sense, however, more properly coming under the specific idea of ἀγέννητος. This was the ambiguity which made the similarity of the two words so dangerous a weapon in Arian hands. The above note does not of course affect the true reading of Ign. Eph. 7, as to which Lightfoot and Zahn speak with authority : but it seems clear that Athan., however mistakenly, quotes Ign. with the reading ἀγένητος.]

6 Ign. ad Eph. [Lightf. Ign. p. 90, Zahn Patr. Apost. ii. p. 338.]

7 Not known, but cf. Clement. Strom. vi. 7. p. 769. ἐν μὲν τὸ

ἀγέννητον, ὁ παντοκράτωρ θεὸς, ἐν δὲ καὶ τὸ προγεννηθὲν δι' οὗ τὰ πάντα ἐγένετο, καὶ χωρὶς αὐτοῦ ἐγένετο οὐδὲ ἕν.

8 [On the subject of the rejection of the ὁμοούσιον at this Council of Antioch, see Prolegg. ch. ii. § 3 (2) b.]

9 De Decr. § 1.

Next, if the Son be not such from participation, but is in His essence the Father's Word and Wisdom, and this essence is the offspring of the Father's essence [10], and its likeness as the radiance is of the light, and the Son says, 'I and the Father are One,' and, 'he that hath seen Me, hath seen the Father' (John x. 30; xiv. 9), how must we understand these words? or how shall we so explain them as to preserve the oneness of the Father and the Son? Now as to its consisting in agreement [1] of doctrines, and in the Son's not disagreeing with the Father, as the Arians say, such an interpretation is a sorry one; for both the Saints, and still more Angels and Archangels, have such an agreement with God, and there is no disagreement among them. For he who disagreed, the devil, was beheld to fall from the heavens, as the Lord said. Therefore if by reason of agreement the Father and the Son are one, there would be things originated which had this agreement with God, and each of these might say, 'I and the Father are One.' But if this be absurd, and so it truly is, it follows of necessity that we must conceive of Son's and Father's oneness in the way of essence. For things originate, though they have an agreement with their Maker, yet possess it only by influence [2], and by participation, and through the mind; the transgression of which forfeits heaven. But the Son, being an offspring from the essence, is one by essence, Himself and the Father that begat Him.

49. This is why He has equality with the Father by titles expressive of unity [3], and what is said of the Father, is said in Scripture of the Son also, all but His being called Father [4]. For the Son Himself said, 'All things that the Father hath are Mine' (John xvi. 15); and He says to the Father, 'All Mine are Thine, and Thine are Mine' (John xvii. 10),—as for instance [4a], the name God; for 'the Word was God;'—Almighty, 'Thus saith He that is, and that was, and that is to come, the Almighty' (John i. 1; Apoc. i. 8):—the being Light, 'I am,' He says, 'the Light' (John viii. 12):—the Operative Cause, 'All things were made by Him,' and, 'whatsoever I see the Father do, I do also' (John i. 3; v. 19):—the being

Everlasting, 'His eternal power and godhead,' and, 'In the beginning was the Word,' and, 'He was the true Light, which lighteth every man that cometh into the world;'—the being Lord, for, 'The Lord rained fire and brimstone from the Lord,' and the Father says, 'I am the Lord,' and, 'Thus saith the Lord, the Almighty God;' and of the Son Paul speaks thus, 'One Lord Jesus Christ, through whom all things' (Rom. i. 20; John i. 1; ib. 9; Gen. xix. 24; Isa. xlv. 5; Am. v. 16; 1 Cor. viii. 6). And on the Father Angels wait, and again the Son too is worshipped by them, 'And let all the Angels of God worship Him;' and He is said to be Lord of Angels, for 'the Angels ministered unto Him,' and 'the Son of Man shall send His Angels.' The being honoured as the Father, for 'that they may honour the Son,' He says, 'as they honour the Father;' —being equal to God, 'He counted it not a prize to be equal with God' (Heb. i. 6; Matt. iv. 11; xxiv. 31; John v. 23; Phil. ii. 6):— the being Truth from the True, and Life from the Living, as being truly from the Fountain, even the Father;—the quickening and raising the dead as the Father, for so it is written in the Gospel. And of the Father it is written, 'The Lord thy God is One Lord,' and, 'The God of gods, the Lord, hath spoken, and hath called the earth;' and of the Son, 'The Lord God hath shined upon us,' and, 'The God of gods shall be seen in Sion.' And again of God, Isaiah says, 'Who is a God like unto Thee, taking away iniquities and passing over unrighteousness?' (Deut. vi. 4; Ps. l. 1; cxviii. 27; lxxxiv. 7, LXX.; Mic. vii. 18). But the Son said to whom He would, 'Thy sins are forgiven thee;' for instance, when, on the Jews murmuring, He manifested the remission by His act, saying to the paralytic, 'Rise, take up thy bed, and go unto thy house.' And of God Paul says, 'To the King eternal;' and again of the Son, David in the Psalm, 'Lift up your gates, O ye rulers, and be ye lift up ye everlasting doors, and the King of glory shall come in.' And Daniel heard it said, 'His Kingdom is an everlasting Kingdom, and His Kingdom shall not be destroyed' (Matt. ix. 5; Mark ii. 11; 1 Tim. i. 17; Ps. xxiv. 7; Dan. iv. 3; vii. 14). And in a word, all that you find said of the Father, so much will you find said of the Son, all but His being Father, as has been said.

50. If then any think of other beginning, and other Father, considering the equality of these attributes, it is a mad thought. But if, since the Son is from the Father, all that is the Father's is the Son's as in an Image and Expression, let it be considered dispassionately, whether an essence foreign from the

---

[10] § 51, note.   [1] § 23, note 3, yet vid. Hipp. *contr. Noet.* 7.
[2] κινήσει vid. Cyril. *contr. Jul.* viii. p. 274. Greg. Nyss. *de Hom. Op.* p. 87.   [3] § 45.
[4] By 'the Son being *equal* to the Father,' is but meant that He is His 'exact image;' it does not imply any distinction of essence. Cf. Hil. *de Syn.* 73. But this implies some exception, for else He would not be like or equal, but the same. *ibid.* 72. Hence He is the Father's image in all things except in being the Father. πλὴν τῆς ἀγεννησίας καὶ τῆς πατρότητος. Damasc. *de Imag.* iii. 18. p. 354. vid. also Basil. *contr. Eun.* ii. 28; Theod. *Inconfus.* p. 91; Basil. *Ep.* 38. 7 fin. [Through missing this point the] Arians asked why the Son was not the beginning of a θεογονία. *Supr.* p. 319 a, note 1. vid. *infr.* note 8.
[4a] Vid. *Orat.* iii. § 4.

Father's essence admit of such attributes; and whether such a one be other in nature and alien in essence, and not coessential with the Father. For we must take reverent heed, lest transferring what is proper to the Father to what is unlike Him in essence, and expressing the Father's godhead by what is unlike in kind and alien in essence, we introduce another essence foreign to Him, yet capable of the properties of the first essence [5], and lest we be silenced by God Himself, saying, 'My glory I will not give to another,' and be discovered worshipping this alien God, and be accounted such as were the Jews of that day, who said, 'Wherefore dost Thou, being a man, make Thyself God?' referring, the while, to another source the things of the Spirit, and blasphemously saying, 'He casteth out devils through Beelzebub' (Isa. xlii. 8; John x. 33; Luke xi. 15). But if this is shocking, plainly the Son is not unlike in essence, but coessential with the Father; for if what the Father has is by nature the Son's, and the Son Himself is from the Father, and because of this oneness of godhead and of nature He and the Father are one, and He that hath seen the Son hath seen the Father, reasonably is He called by the Fathers 'Coessential;' for to what is other in essence, it belongs not to possess such prerogatives.

51. And again, if, as we have said before, the Son is not such by participation, but, while all things originated have by participation the grace of God, He is the Father's Wisdom and Word of which all things partake [6], it follows that He, being the deifying and enlightening power of the Father, in which all things are deified and quickened, is not alien in essence from the Father, but coessential. For by partaking of Him, we partake of the Father; because that the Word is the Father's own. Whence, if He was Himself too from participation, and not from the Father His essential Godhead and Image, He would not deify [7], being deified Himself. For it is not possible that He, who merely possesses from participation, should impart of that partaking to others, since what He has is not His own, but the Giver's; and what He has received, is barely the grace sufficient for Himself. However, let us fairly examine the reason why some, as is said, decline the 'Coessential,' whether it does not rather shew that

the Son is coessential with the Father. They say then, as you have written, that it is not right to say that the Son is coessential with the Father, because he who speaks of 'coessential' speaks of three, one essence pre-existing, and that those who are generated from it are coessential: and they add, 'If then the Son be coessential with the Father, then an essence must be previously supposed, from which they have been generated; and that the One is not Father and the Other Son, but they are brothers together [8].' As to all this, though it be a Greek interpretation, and what comes from them does not bind us [9], still let us see whether those things which are called coessential and are collateral, as derived from one essence presupposed, are coessential with each other, or with the essence from which they are generated. For if only with each other, then are they other in essence and unlike, when referred to that essence which generated them; for other in essence is opposed to coessential; but if each be coessential with the essence which generated them, it is thereby confessed that what is generated from any thing, is coessential with that which generated it; and there is no need of seeking for three essences, but merely to seek whether it be true that this is from that [10]. For should it happen that there were not two brothers, but that only one had come of that essence, he that was generated would not be called alien in essence, merely because there was no other from the essence than he; but though alone, he must be coessential with him that begat him. For what shall we say about Jephtha's daughter; because she was only-begotten, and 'he had not,' says Scripture, 'other child' (Jud. xi. 34); and again, concerning the widow's son, whom the Lord raised from the dead, because he too had no brother, but was only-begotten, was on that account neither of these coessential with him that begat? Surely they were, for they were children, and this is a property of children with reference to their parents. And

---

5 Arianism was in the dilemma of denying Christ's divinity, or introducing a second God. The Arians proper went off on the former side of the alternative, the Semi-Arians on the latter; and Athan., as here addressing the Semi Arians, insists on the greatness of the latter error. This of course was *the* objection which attached to the words ὁμοιούσιον, ἀπαράλλακτος εἰκων, &c., when disjoined from the ὁμοούσιον; and Eusebius's language, *supr.* p. 75, note 7, shews us that it is not an imaginary one.

6 *De Decr.* § 10. p. 15, note 4.　　7 ἐθεοποίησε *Orat.* ii. § 70. de Decr. § 14.

8 Cf. *supr.* p. 314, note 1, Cyr. *Thesaur.* pp. 22, 23.
9 Cf. p. 169, note 4[a] [and on οὐσία as a philosophical and theological term, *Prolegg.* ch. ii. § 3 (2) b. On the divergence of its theological use from its philosophical sense, see] Anastasius, *Hodeg.* 6. and Theorian, *Legat. ad Arm.* pp. 441, 2. Socr. iii. 25. Damascene, speaking of the Jacobite use of φύσις and ὑπόστασις says, ' Who of holy men ever thus spoke? unless ye introduce to us your S. Aristotle, as a thirteenth Apostle, and prefer the idolater to the divinely inspired.' *cont. Jacob.* 10. p. 399. and so again Leontius, speaking of Philoponus, who from the Monophysite confusion of nature and hypostasis was led into Tritheism. ' He thus argued, taking his start from Aristotelic principles; for Aristotle says that there are of individuals particular substances as well as one common.' *De Sect.* v. fin.
10 The argument, when drawn out, is virtually this : if, because two subjects are coessential, a third is pre-supposed of which they partake, then, since either of these two is coessential with that of which both partake, a new third must be supposed in which it and the pre-existing substance partake. and thus an infinite series of things coessential must be supposed. Vid. Basil. *Ep.* 52. n. 2. [Cf. Aristot. *Frag.* 183, p. 1509 b 23.]

in like manner also, when the Fathers said that the Son of God was from His essence, reasonably have they spoken of Him as co-essential. For the like property has the radiance compared with the light. Else it follows that not even the creation came out of nothing. For whereas men beget with passion[1], so again they work upon an existing subject matter, and otherwise cannot make. But if we do not understand creation in a human way[2], when we attribute it to God, much less seemly is it to understand generation in a human way, or to give a corporeal sense to Coessential; instead of receding from things originate, casting away human images, nay, all things sensible, and ascending[3] to the Father[4], lest we rob the Father of the Son in ignorance, and rank Him among His own creatures.

52. Further, if, in confessing Father and Son, we spoke of two beginnings or two Gods, as Marcion and Valentinus[5], or said that the Son had any other mode of godhead, and was not the Image and Expression of the Father, as being by nature born from Him, then He might be considered unlike; for such essences are altogether unlike each other. But if we acknowledge that the Father's godhead is one and sole, and that of Him the Son is the Word and Wisdom; and, as thus believing, are far from speaking of two Gods, but understand the oneness of the Son with the Father to be, not in likeness of their teaching, but according to essence and in truth, and hence speak not of two Gods but of one God; there being but one Form[6] of Godhead, as the Light is one and the Radiance; (for this was seen by the Patriarch Jacob, as Scripture says, 'The sun rose upon him when the Form of God passed by,' Gen. xxxii. 31, LXX.); and be holding this, and understanding of whom He was Son and Image, the holy Prophets say, 'The Word of the Lord came to me;' and recognising the Father, who was beheld and revealed in Him, they made bold to say, 'The God of our fathers

hath appeared unto me, the God of Abraham, and Isaac, and Jacob' (Exod. iii. 16); this being so, wherefore scruple we to call Him coessential who is one with the Father, and appears as doth the Father, according to likeness and oneness of godhead? For if, as has been many times said, He has it not to be proper to the Father's essence, nor to resemble, as a Son, we may well scruple: but if this be the illuminating and creative Power, specially proper to the Father, without Whom He neither frames nor is known (for all things consist through Him and in Him); wherefore, perceiving the fact, do we decline to use the phrase conveying it? For what is it to be thus connatural with the Father, but to be one in essence with Him? for God attached not to Him the Son from without[7], as needing a servant; nor are the works on a level with the Creator, and honoured as He is, or to be thought one with the Father. Or let a man venture to make the distinction, that the sun and the radiance are two lights, or different essences; or to say that the radiance accrued to it over and above, and is not a simple and pure offspring from the sun; such, that sun and radiance are two, but the light one, because the radiance is an off-spring from the Sun. But, whereas not more divisible, nay less divisible is the nature[8] of the Son towards the Father, and the godhead not accruing to the Son, but the Father's godhead being in the Son, so that he that hath seen the Son hath seen the Father in Him; wherefore should not such a one be called Coessential?

53. Even this is sufficient to dissuade you from blaming those who have said that the Son was coessential with the Father, and yet let us examine the very term 'Coessential,' in itself, by way of seeing whether we ought to use it at all, and whether it be a proper term, and is suitable to apply to the Son. For you know yourselves, and no one can dispute it, that Like is not predicated of essence, but of habits, and qualities; for in the case of essences we speak, not of likeness, but of identity. Man, for instance, is said to be like man, not in essence, but according to habit and character; for in essence men are of one nature. And again, man is not said to be unlike dog, but to be of different nature.

---

[1] Orat. i. § 28.

[2] Vid. de Decr. § 11, note 6: also Cyril, Thesaur. iv. p. 29: Basil. contr. Eun. ii. 23: Hil. de Syn. 17.   [3] Naz. Orat. 28. 2.

[4] S. Basil says in like manner that, though God is Father κυρίως properly, supr. p. 156, note 1, 157, note 6, 171, note 5, 319, note 3), yet it comes to the same thing if we were to say that He is τροπικῶς and ἐκ μεταφορᾶς, figuratively, such, contr. Eun. ii. 24; γέννησις implies two things,—passion and relationship, οἰκείωσις φύσεως; accordingly we must take the latter as an indication of the divine sense of the term. Cf. also supr. p. 158, note 7, p. 322, Orat. ii. 32, iii. 18, 67, and Basil. contr. Eunom. ii. 17; Hil. de Trin. iv. 2. Vid. also Athan. ad Serap. i. 20. and Basil. Ep. 38. n. 5. and what is said of the office of faith in each of these.

[5] Supr. p. 167, note 7, and p. 307.

[6] ἑνὸς ὄντος εἴδους θεότητος: for the word εἶδος, cf. Orat. iii. 16 is generally applied to the Son, as in what follows, and is synonymous [?] with hypostasis; but it is remarkable that here it is almost synonymous with οὐσία or φύσις. Indeed in one sense nature, substance, and hypostasis, are all synonymous, i.e. as one and all denoting the Una Res, which is Almighty God. The apparent confusion is useful as reminding us of this great truth; vid. note 8, infr.

[7] De Decr. § 31.

[8] [φύσις is here (as the apodosis of the clause shows) as well as in the next section, used as a somewhat more vague equivalent for οὐσία, not, as Newman contends in an omitted note, for 'person,' a use which is scarcely borne out by the (no doubt somewhat fluctuating) senses of φύσις in the passages quoted by him from Alexander (in Theod. H.E. i. 4, cf. Origen's use of οὐσία, Prolegg. ch. ii. § 3 (2) a) and Cyril c. Nest. iii. p. 91. φύσις and οὐσία are nearly equivalent in the manifesto of Basil of Ancyra, whom Ath. has in view here, see Epiph. Hær. 73. 12—22.]

Accordingly while the former are of one nature and coessential, the latter are different in both. Therefore, in speaking of Like according to essence, we mean like by participation ; (for Likeness is a quality, which may attach to essence), and this would be proper to creatures, for they, by partaking, are made like to God. For 'when He shall appear,' says Scripture, 'we shall be like Him' (1 John iii. 2), like, that is, not in essence but in sonship, which we shall partake from Him. If then ye speak of the Son as being by participation, then indeed call Him Like-in-essence ; but thus spoken of, He is not Truth, nor Light at all, nor in nature God. For things which are from participation, are called like, not in reality, but from resemblance to reality ; so that they may swerve, or be taken from those who share them. And this, again, is proper to creatures and works. Therefore, if this be out of place, He must be, not by participation, but in nature and truth Son, Light, Wisdom, God ; and being by nature, and not by sharing, He would properly be called, not Like-in-essence, but Coessential. But what would not be asserted, even in the case of others (for the Like has been shewn to be inapplicable to essences), is it not folly, not to say violence, to put forward in the case of the Son, instead of the ' Coessential ? '

54. This is why the Nicene Council was correct in writing, what it was becoming to say, that the Son, begotten from the Father's essence, is coessential with Him. And if we too have been taught the same thing, let us not fight with shadows, especially as knowing, that they who have so defined, have made this confession of faith, not to misrepresent the truth, but as vindicating the truth and religiousness towards Christ, and also as destroying the blasphemies against Him of the Ario-maniacs. For this must be considered and noted carefully, that, in using unlike-in-essence, and other-in-essence, we signify not the true Son, but some one of the creatures, and an introduced and adopted Son, which pleases the heretics ; but when we speak uncontroversially of the Coessential, we signify a genuine Son born of the Father ; though at this Christ's enemies often burst with rage[9]. What then I have learned myself, and have heard men of judgment say, I have written in few words ; but do you, remaining on the foundation of the Apostles, and holding fast the traditions of the Fathers, pray that now at length all strife and rivalry may cease, and the futile questions of the heretics may be

condemned, and all logomachy[1] ; and the guilty and murderous heresy of the Arians may disappear, and the truth may shine again in the hearts of all, so that all every where may 'say the same thing' (1 Cor. i. 10), and think the same thing[2], and that, no Arian contumelies remaining, it may be said and confessed in every Church, 'One Lord, one faith, one baptism' (Eph. iv. 5), in Christ Jesus our Lord, through whom to the Father be the glory and the strength, unto ages of ages. Amen.

Postscript.

55. After I had written my account of the Councils[3], I had information that the most irreligious[4] Constantius had sent Letters to the Bishops remaining in Ariminum ; and I have taken pains to get copies of them from true brethren and to send them to you, and also what the Bishops answered ; that you may know the irreligious craft of the Emperor, and the firm and unswerving purpose of the Bishops towards the truth.

Interpretation of the Letter[5].

Constantius, Victorious and Triumphant, Augustus, to all Bishops who are assembled at Ariminum.

That the divine and adorable Law is our chief care, your excellencies are not ignorant ; but as yet we have been unable to receive the twenty Bishops sent by your wisdom, and charged with the legation from you, for we are pressed by a necessary expedition against the Barbarians ; and as ye know, it beseems to have the soul clear from every care, when one handles the matters of the Divine Law. Therefore we have ordered the Bishops to await our return at Adrianople ; that, when all public affairs are well arranged, then at length we may hear and weigh their suggestions. Let it not then be grievous to your constancy to await their return, that, when they come back with our answer to you, ye may be able to bring matters to a close which so deeply affect the well-being of the Catholic Church.

This was what the Bishops received at the hands of three emissaries.

Reply of the Bishops.

The letter of your humanity we have received, most God-beloved Lord Emperor, which reports that, on account of stress of public affairs, as yet you have been unable to attend to our deputies ; and in which you com-

---

1 And so ταῖς λογομαχίαις, Basil de Sp. S. n. 16. It is used with an allusion to the fight against the Word, as χριστομαχεῖν and θεομαχεῖν. Thus λογομαχεῖν μελετήσαντες, καὶ λοιπὸν πνευματομαχοῦντες, ἔσονται μετ᾽ ὀλίγον νεκροὶ τῇ ἀλογίᾳ. Serap. iv. 1.
2 Cf. Hil. de Syn. 77, and appendix, note 3, also supr. p. 303, and note. The ὁμοούσιον was not imposed upon Ursacius and Valens, A.D. 347, by Pope Julius ; nor in the Council of Aquileia in 381, was it offered by S. Ambrose to Palladius and Secundianus. S. Jerome's account of the apology made by the Fathers of Ariminum is of the same kind. ' We thought,' they said, 'the sense corresponded to the words, nor in the Church of God, where there is simplicity, and a pure confession, did we fear that one thing would be concealed in the heart, another uttered by the lips. We were deceived by our good opinion of the bad.' ad Lucif. 19.
3 § 11, note 7.   4 § 12, note 2.
5 These two Letters are both in Socr. ii. 37. And the latter is in Theod. H. E. ii. 15. p. 878. in a different version from the Latin original.

---

9 p. 171, note 6.

mand us to await their return, until your godliness shall be advised by them of what we have defined conformably to our ancestors. However, we now profess and aver at once by these presents, that we shall not recede from our purpose, as we also instructed our deputies. We ask then that you will with serene countenance command these letters of our mediocrity to be read; but also that you will graciously receive those, with which we charged our deputies. This however your gentleness comprehends as well as we, that great grief and sadness at present prevail, because that, in these your most happy days, so many Churches are without Bishops. And on this account we again request your humanity, most God-beloved Lord Emperor, that, if it please your religiousness, you would command us, before the severe winter weather sets in, to return to our Churches, that so we may be able, unto God Almighty and our Lord and Saviour Christ, His Only-begotten Son, to fulfil together with our flocks our wonted prayers in behalf of your imperial sway, as indeed we have ever performed them, and at this time make them.

ADDITIONAL NOTE.

[The 'list of Sirmian confessions' published by Newman as an *Excursus* to the *de Synodis* is omitted here. It will be found printed as 'Appendix iii.' to his *Arians of the Fourth Century*.

The *Excursus* on a Creed ascribed (at the Council of Ephesus, see Hard. *Conc.* i. 1640, Hahn. § 83 ; Routh *Rell.* iii. 367) to the 70 bishops who condemned Paul of Samosata, at Antioch A.D. 269, and containing the formula ὁμοούσιον (against this, *supr.* §§ 43—47), is also omitted, as bearing only very indirectly on the *de Synodis*. Caspari *Alte und Neue Quellen* (xi), p. 161, has thoroughly investigated the Confession since Newman wrote, and has proved (what Newman half suspected) that the document is of Apollinarian origin. As Caspari was unaware of Newman's discussion, this result comes as the result of two independent investigations pursued on very different lines.]

TOMUS AD ANTIOCHENOS

THE word 'tome' (τόμος) means either a section, or, in the case of such a document as that before us, a concise statement. It is commonly applied to synodical letters (cf. the 'Tome' of Leo, A.D. 450, to Flavian).

Upon the accession of Julian (November, 361) the Homœan ascendancy which had marked the last six years of Constantius collapsed. A few weeks after his accession (Feb. 362) an edict recalled all the exiled Bishops. On Feb. 21 Athanasius re-appeared in Alexandria. He was joined there by Lucifer of Cagliari and Eusebius of Vercellæ, who were in exile in Upper Egypt. Once more free, he took up the work of peace which had busied him in the last years of his exile (see Prolegg. ch. ii. § 9). With a heathen once more on the throne of the Cæsars, there was everything to sober Christian party spirit, and to promise success to the council which met under Athanasius during the ensuing summer. Among the twenty-one bishops who formed the assembly the most notable are Eusebius of Vercellæ, Asterius of Petra, and Dracontius of Lesser Hermopolis and Adelphius of Onuphis, the friends and correspondents of Athanasius. The rest, with the exception of Anatolius of Eubœa, were all from Egypt and Marmarica, and (probably three only) from S.W. Asia. The council (Newman, *Arians*, v. i.; Gwatkin, *Stud.* p. 205, Krüger, *Lucif.* 45—53, was occupied with four problems : (1) The terms on which communion should be vouchsafed to those Arians who desired to re-unite (§§ 3, 8). They were to be asked for nothing beyond the Nicene test, and an express anathema against Arianism, including the doctrine that the Holy Spirit is a Creature. The latter point had been rising into prominence of late, and had called forth from Athanasius his four Discourses to Serapion of Thmuis. The emphatic way in which the point is pressed in § 3, implies that an attempt was being made in some quarter to subscribe the Nicene Creed, while maintaining the Arian position with regard to the Holy Spirit. The language of § 3 cannot be reconciled with the hypothesis (Gwatkin, *Studies*, 233), that no formal requirement was made by this council on the subject. The person aimed at was possibly Acacius, who (*Serap.* iv. 7) had treated the subject with levity, and yet was now disposed to come to terms (as he did a year later, Socr. iii. 25). It is true that we find the names of Macedonius and his followers (N.B. not Eleusius) in the number of the 59 who betook themselves to Liberius (Socr. iv. 12), and neither in their letter nor in his reply is there any allusion to the doctrine of the Holy Spirit ; and that Basil (*Ep.* 204), with the sanction of Athanasius (cf. below, *Letters* 62, 63), did not press the test upon those who were otherwise orthodox. But the council of 362 has Syrian circumstances specially in view ; and however we may explain it, its language is too clear to be mistaken. (On the *general* subject, cf. *Letter* 55.) (2) The Arian Christology also occupied the council (§ 7). The integrity of Christ's human nature on the one hand, its perfect Union with the Word on the other, are clearly emphasised. This question had begun to come into prominent discussion in several parts of the Christian world (e.g. at Corinth, see *infr. Letter* 59), and was soon to give rise to the system of Apollinarius, who, however, it is interesting to note, was a party, by his legates, to the present decision. (3) The state of the Church at Antioch was the most practical problem before the council. Meletius was returning to the presidency of the main body of the Antiochene church, whose chief place of worship was the 'Palaea' (§ 3). Since the deposition of Eustathius (*c.* 330), the intransigent or 'protestant' body had been without a bishop, and were headed by the respected presbyter Paulinus. Small in numbers, and dependent for a church upon the good will of the Arians, they were yet strong in the unsullied orthodoxy of their antecedents, in the sympathy of the West and of Athanasius himself, who had given offence at Antioch in 346 by worshipping with them alone. Clearly the right course was that they should reunite with the main body under Meletius, and this was what the council recommended (§ 3), although, perhaps in deference to the more uncompromising spirits, the union is treated (*ib.* and 4) as a return of the larger body to the smaller, instead of *vice versa*. (For the sequel, see Prolegg. *ubi supra*.) (4) With the rivalry of parties at Antioch, a weighty question of theological terminology was indirectly involved. The word ὑπόστασις had been used in the Nicene anathema as a synonym of οὐσία (see *Excursus A*, pp. 77 *sqq.* above), and in this sense it was commonly used by Athanasius in agreement with the New Testament use of the word

(Westcott on Heb. i. 3), with Dionysius of Rome, and with the West, to whom ὑπόστασις was etymologically identified with 'Substantia' their (perhaps imperfect) equivalent for οὐσία. On the other hand, the general tendency of Eastern Theology had been to use ὑπόστασις in the sense of Subject or Person, for which purpose it expressed the idea of individual essence less ambiguously than πρόσωπον. This was the use of the word adopted by Origen, Dionysius Alex. (*supr. de Sent. Dionys.*), Alexander of Alexandria (in his letter Thdt. *H.E.* i. 4. p. 16, l. 19), and by Athanasius himself in an earlier work (p. 90, *supr.*) At Antioch the Eustathians appear to have followed the Nicene and Western usage, using the word to emphasise the Individual Unity of God as against Arian or Subordinationist views, while the Meletians protested against the Marcellian monarchianism by insisting on *three* Hypostases in the Godhead. The contradiction was mainly verbal, the two parties being substantially at one as to the doctrine, but varying in its expression. Hence the wise and charitable decision of the council, which came naturally from one who, like Athanasius, could use either expression, though he had come to prefer the Western to the Eastern use[1].

The Tome was carried to Antioch by the five bishops named at the beginning of § 1, and there subscribed by Paulinus and Karterius of Antaradus. As to its effect among the friends of Meletius our information is only inferential (see Gwatkin, *Studies*, p. 208). On the supposed disciplinary legislation of this council in relation to the *Syntagma Doctrinæ*, see Prolegg. ch. ii. §§ 9.

N.B. The translation of the present tract as well as that of the *ad Afros* and of *Letters* 56, 59, 60, 61, was made independently of that by Dr. Bright in his *Later Treatises of S. Athanasius* (see Prolegg. ch. i. § 2), but has been carefully collated with it, and in not a few cases improved by its aid. For a fuller commentary on these pieces than has been possible in this volume, the reader is referred to Dr. Bright's work.

---

[1] It may be well to trace briefly the sense of these technical terms, the history and significance of which is a forcible reminder of the inability of Theology to bring the Infinite within the categories of the Finite, to do more than guard our Faith by pointing out the paths which experience has shewn to lead to some false limitation of the fulness of the Revelation of God in Christ.

The distinction (drawn out Prolegg. ch. ii. § 3 (2) b) between the primary and secondary sense of οὐσία in Greek metaphysics does not easily fit the doctrine of the Holy Trinity. The οὐσία common to Father and Son is not the name of a *Species*, as 'Man' applies to Peter and Paul. But neither can the idea of πρώτη οὐσία be reconciled with inherence in three distinct personal existences. (Cf. *supr.* p. 409, note 7.)

But here the word ὑπόστασις comes in to help our imagination. The word (see Socr. *H.E.* iii. 7. Westcott, *ubi supr.* and Newman, *Arians*, *App.* 4), from various literal senses came to be transferred to the philosophical vocabulary, doing duty as verbal substantive not only for ὑφεστάναι but for ὑποκεῖσθαι. Like the concrete ὑποκείμενον it was applied (a) to matter as underlying form, (b) to substance as underlying attributes. In this latter use it served to distinguish πρώτη from δευτέρα οὐσία, expressing moreover a complete self-contained existence in a way that οὐσία did not. When therefore the idea of personal individuality has to be expressed, ὑπόστασις is more suitable than οὐσία. But the ambiguity of the latter word remains. Those who preferred to speak of μία ὑπόστασις thought of the Divine Essence rather as πρώτη οὐσία, and of One Personal God, with whom Father, Son, and Spirit were each absolutely and fully identified (περιχώρησις), while with those who preferred τρεῖς ὑποστάσεις the idea of the Divine οὐσία approximated to δευτέρα οὐσία, and guarded against Tritheism solely by holding fast to the Monarchia of the Father. The corrective to each position lay in the recognition of the other, i.e. of its own incompleteness. (See further Prolegg. *ubi supr.* and Zahn, *Marcell.* p. 87, *sq.*)

TOME OR SYNODAL LETTER
TO THE PEOPLE OF ANTIOCH

To our beloved and much-desired fellow-ministers Eusebius [1], Lucifer [2], Asterius [3], Kymatius, and Anatolius, Athanasius and the bishops present in Alexandria from Italy and Arabia, Egypt and Libya ; Eusebius, Asterius, Gaius, Agathus, Ammonius, Agathodæmon, Dracontius, Adelphius, Hermæon, Marcus, Theodorus, Andreas, Paphnutius, another Marcus, Zoilus, Menas, George, Lucius, Macarius and the rest, all greeting in Christ.

We are persuaded that being ministers of God and good stewards ye are sufficient to order the affairs of the Church in every respect. But since it has come to us, that many who were formerly separated from us by jealousy now wish for peace, while many also having severed their connection with the Arian madmen are desiring our communion, we think it well to write to your courtesy what ourselves and the beloved Eusebius and Asterius have drawn up : yourselves being our beloved and truly most-desired fellow-ministers. We rejoice at the said tidings, and pray that even if any be left still far from us, and if any appear to be in agreement with the Arians, he may promptly leave their madness, so that for the future all men everywhere may say, ' One Lord, one faith [4].' For as the psalmist says, what is so good or pleasant as for brethren to dwell in unity [5]. But our dwelling is the Church, and our mind ought to be the same. For thus we believe that the Lord also will dwell with us, who says, ' I will dwell with them and walk in them [6],' and ' Here will I dwell for I have a delight therein [7].' But by 'here' what is meant but there where one faith and religion is preached ?

2. Mission of Eusebius and Asterius.

We then of Egypt truly wished to go to you along with our beloved Eusebius and Asterius, for many reasons, but chiefly that we might embrace your affection and together enjoy the said peace and concord. But since, as we declared in our other letters, and as ye may learn from our fellow-ministers, the needs of the church detain us, with much regret we begged the same fellow-ministers of ours, Eusebius and Asterius, to go to you in our stead. And we thank their piety in that although they might have gone at once to their dioceses, they preferred to go to you at all costs, on account of the pressing need of the Church. They therefore having consented, we consoled ourselves with the consideration that you and they being there, we all were present with you in mind.

3. The ' Meletians' to be acknowledged, and all who renounce heresy, especially as to the Holy Spirit.

As many then as desire peace with us, and specially those who assemble in the Old [Church] [8] and those again who are seceding

---

[1] Eusebius of Vercellæ, exiled (*Hist. Ar.* 33; *Ap. Fug.* 4) after Milan 355. See D.C.B. ii. 374 (93).

[2] Lucifer of Calaris : cf. *Letters* 50, 51, below, and *Hist. Ar.* 33 ; *Apol. Fug.* 4.

[3] The following are all the details that can be collected with regard to the bishops named in the text. Asterius (*Hist. Ar.* 18 note) ; Kymatius of Paltus in Syria Prima (*Apol. Fug.* 3 ; *Hist. Ar.* 5) ; Anatolius of Eubœa (not in D.C.B.) ; Gaius (*Apol. Fug.* 7 ; *Hist. Ar.* 72, D.C.B. i. 387, No. 19??) ; Agathus, *Hist. Ar.* 72 (not in D.C.B.) ; Ammonius (see *Hist. Ar.* 72 *sub-fin.* ; *Ap. Fug.* 7, *Letter* 49. 7, and *infr.* Appendix, note 1 as to names in D.C.B.) ; Agathodæmon (*Hist. Ar.* ibid.) ; Dracontius and Adelphius (*Letters* 49, 60) ; Hermæon (Hermion in § 10) unknown, unless the 'Hermes' of *Hist. Ar.* 72 ; Marcus (2), (cf. D.C.B. iii. 825 (7) for works ascribed to one or the other) ; Paphnutius, (*Hist. Ar.* 72 ; D.C B. iv. 184 (4)) ; Zoilus of Andropolis (Harduin, &c., *suo jure*, identify him with the bishop of the Syrian Larissa, who signs at Antioch in 363, *Conc.* i. 742 ; D.C.B. iv. 1220) ; Andreas, George, Lucius, Macarius, Menas, and Theodore, are unknown and not in D.C.B. The names all recur (excepting those of George, Lucius, Macarius), in § 10, where the sees are specified.

[4] Eph. iv. 5.   [5] See Ps. cxxxiii. 1.
[6] 2 Cor. vi. 16, and Lev. xxvi. 12.   [7] Ps. cxxxii. 14.
[8] Ἐν τῇ παλαιᾷ, cf. Theodt. *H.E.* i. 3 : possibly the old Town is meant, viz. the main part of Antioch on the left bank of the Orontes, so called in distinction from the 'New' town of Seleucu

from the Arians, do ye call to yourselves, and receive them as parents their sons, and welcome them as tutors and guardians ; and unite them to our beloved Paulinus and his people, without requiring more from them than to anathematise the Arian heresy and confess the faith confessed by the holy fathers at Nicæa, and to anathematise also those who say that the Holy Spirit is a Creature and separate from the Essence of Christ. For this is in truth a complete renunciation of the abominable heresy of the Arians, to refuse to divide the Holy Trinity, or to say that any part of it is a creature. For those who, while pretending to cite the faith confessed at Nicæa, venture to blaspheme the Holy Spirit, do nothing more than in words deny the Arian heresy while they retain it in thought. But let the impiety of Sabellius and of Paul of Samosata also be anathematised by all, and the madness of Valentinian and Basilides, and the folly of the Manichæans. For if this be done, all evil suspicion will be removed on all hands, and the faith of the Catholic Church alone be exhibited in purity.

4. *The parties at Antioch to unite.*

But that we, and they who have ever remained in communion with us, hold this faith, we think no one of yourselves nor any one else is ignorant. But since we rejoice with all those who desire re-union, but especially with those that assemble in the Old [church], and as we glorify the Lord exceedingly, as for all things so especially for the good purpose of these men, we exhort you that concord be established with them on these terms, and, as we said above, without further conditions, without namely any further demand upon yourselves on the part of those who assemble in the Old [church], or Paulinus and his fellows propounding anything else, or aught beyond the Nicene definition.

5. *The creed of Sardica not an authorised formula. Question of 'hypostasis.'*

And prohibit even the reading or publication of the paper, much talked of by some, as having been drawn up concerning the Faith at the synod of Sardica. For the synod made no definition of the kind. For whereas some demanded, on the ground that the Nicene synod was defective, the drafting of a creed, and in their haste even attempted it [8a], the holy synod

assembled in Sardica was indignant, and decreed that no statement of faith should be drafted, but that they should be content with the Faith confessed by the fathers at Nicæa, inasmuch as it lacked nothing but was full of piety, and that it was undesirable for a second creed to be promulged, lest that drafted at Nicæa should be deemed imperfect, and a pretext be given to those who were often wishing to draft and define a creed. So that if a man propound the above or any other paper, stop them, and persuade them rather to keep the peace. For in such men we perceive no motive save only contentiousness. For as to those whom some were blaming for speaking of three Subsistences [9], on the ground that the phrase is unscriptural and therefore suspicious, we thought it right indeed to require nothing beyond the confession of Nicæa, but on account of the contention we made enquiry of them, whether they meant, like the Arian madmen, subsistences foreign and strange, and alien in essence from one another, and that each Subsistence was divided apart by itself, as is the case with creatures in general and in particular with those begotten of men, or like different substances, such as gold, silver, or brass ;—or whether, like other heretics, they meant three Beginnings and three Gods, by speaking of three Subsistences.

They assured us in reply that they neither meant this nor had ever held it. But upon our asking them 'what then do you mean by it, or why do you use such expressions ?' they replied, Because they believed in a Holy Trinity, not a trinity in name only, but existing and subsisting in truth, 'both a Father truly existing and subsisting, and a Son truly substantial and subsisting, and a Holy Spirit subsisting and really existing do we acknowledge,' and that neither had they said there were three Gods or three beginnings, nor would they at all tolerate such as said or held so, but that they acknowledged a Holy Trinity but One Godhead, and one Beginning, and that the Son is coessential with the Father, as the fathers said ; while the Holy Spirit is not a creature, nor external, but proper to and inseparable from the Essence of the Father and the Son.

6. *The question of one Subsistence (Hypostasis) or three, not to be pressed.*

Having accepted then these men's interpretation and defence of their language, we made enquiry of those blamed by them for speaking of One Subsistence, whether they use the expression in the sense of Sabellius, to the nega-

---

Callinicus which occupied the Island in the river. The 'Old' *Church*, or Church of the Apostles, was situated in the Old Town, and was at present occupied by the orthodox party of Meletius. The old orthodox party of Paulinus had only one small church in the New Town, granted for their use out of respect for Paulinus by the Arian bishop Euzoius (Socr. *H.E.* iii. 9).

[8a] The draft is given by Theodt. *H.E.* ii. 8; it insists vehemently on the '(J)ne Hypostasis.'

[9] ὑποστάσεις.

tion of the Son and the Holy Spirit, or as though the Son were non-substantial, or the Holy Spirit impersonal [10]. But they in their turn assured us that they neither meant this nor had ever held it, but 'we use the word Subsistence thinking it the same thing to say Subsistence or Essence;' 'But we hold that there is One, because the Son is of the Essence of the Father, and because of the identity of nature. For we believe that there is one Godhead, and that it has one nature, and not that there is one nature of the Father, from which that of the Son and of the Holy Spirit are distinct.' Well, thereupon they who had been blamed for saying there were three Subsistences agreed with the others, while those who had spoken of One Essence, also confessed the doctrine of the former as interpreted by them. And by both sides Arius was anathematised as an adversary of Christ, and Sabellius, and Paul of Samosata, as impious men, and Valentinus and Basilides as aliens from the truth, and Manichæus as an inventor of mischief. And all, by God's grace, and after the above explanations, agree together that the faith confessed by the fathers at Nicæa is better than the said phrases, and that for the future they would prefer to be content to use its language.

7. The human Nature of Christ complete, not Body only.

But since also certain seemed to be contending together concerning the fleshly Economy of the Saviour, we enquired of both parties. And what the one confessed, the others also agreed to, that the Word did not, as it came to the prophets, so dwell in a holy man at the consummation of the ages, but that the Word Himself was made flesh, and being in the Form of God, took the form of a servant [11], and from Mary after the flesh became man for us, and that thus in Him the human race is perfectly and wholly delivered from sin and quickened from the dead, and given access to the kingdom of the heavens. For they confessed also that the Saviour had not a body without a soul, nor without sense or intelligence; for it was not possible, when the Lord had become man for us, that His body should be without intelligence: nor was the salvation effected in the Word Himself a salvation of body only, but of soul also. And being Son of God in truth, He became also Son of Man, and being God's Only-begotten Son, He became also at the same time 'firstborn among many

brethren [12].' Wherefore neither was there one Son of God before Abraham, another after Abraham [1]: nor was there one that raised up Lazarus, another that asked concerning him; but the same it was that said as man, 'Where does Lazarus lie [2];' and as God raised him up: the same that as man and in the body spat, but divinely as Son of God opened the eyes of the man blind from his birth [3]; and while, as Peter says [4], in the flesh He suffered, as God opened the tomb and raised the dead. For which reasons, thus understanding all that is said in the Gospel, they assured us that they held the same truth about the Word's Incarnation and becoming Man.

8. Questions of words must not be suffered to divide those who think alike.

These things then being thus confessed, we exhort you not hastily to condemn those who so confess, and so explain the phrases they use, nor to reject them, but rather to accept them as they desire peace and defend themselves, while you check and rebuke, as of suspicious views, those who refuse so to confess and to explain their language. But while you refuse toleration to the latter, counsel the others also who explain and hold aright, not to enquire further into each other's opinions, nor to fight about words to no useful purpose, nor to go on contending with the above phrases, but to agree in the mind of piety. For they who are not thus minded, but only stir up strife with such petty phrases, and seek something beyond what was drawn up at Nicæa, do nothing except 'give their neighbour turbid confusion to drink [5],' like men who grudge peace and love dissensions. But do ye, as good men and faithful servants and stewards of the Lord, stop and check what gives offence and is strange, and value above all things peace of that kind, faith being sound. Perhaps God will have pity on us, and unite what is divided, and, there being once more one flock [6], we shall all have one leader, even our Lord Jesus Christ.

9. The above terms unanimously agreed upon.

These things, albeit there was no need to require anything beyond the synod of Nicæa, nor to tolerate the language of contention, yet for the sake of peace, and to prevent the rejection of men who wish to believe aright, we enquired into. And what they confessed, we put briefly into writing, we namely who are left in Alexandria, in common

---

[10] ἀνουσίου, ἀνυποστάτου, the words are rendered 'unessential' and 'not subsisting' in another connection, supr. p. 434, &c.
[11] Phil. ii. 7, &c.

[12] Rom. viii. 29. [1] John viii. 58.
[2] Ib. xi. 34. [3] Mark viii. 22, &c. [4] 1 Pet. iv. 1.
[5] Hab. ii. 15. [6] John x. 16.

with our fellow-ministers, Asterius and Eusebius. For most of us had gone away to our dioceses. But do you on your part read this in public where you are wont to assemble, and be pleased to invite all to you thither. For it is right that the letter should be there first read, and that there those who desire and strive for peace should be re-united. And then, when they are re-united, in the spot where all the laity think best, in the presence of your courtesy, the public assemblies should be held, and the Lord be glorified by all together. The brethren who are with me greet you. I pray that you may be well, and remember us to the Lord; both I, Athanasius, and likewise the other bishops assembled, sign, and those sent by Lucifer, bishop of the island of Sardinia, two deacons, Herennius and Agapetus; and from Paulinus, Maximus and Calemerus, deacons also. And there were present certain monks of Apolinarius[7] the bishop, sent from him for the purpose.

10. *Signatures.*

The names of the several bishops to whom the letter is addressed are: Eusebius of the city of Virgilli in Gaul[8], Lucifer of the island of Sardinia, Asterius of Petra, Arabia, Kymatius of Paltus, Cœle-Syria, Anatolius of Eubœa.

Senders: the Pope Athanasius, and those present with him in Alexandria, viz.: Eusebius, Asterius, and the others above-mentioned, Gaius of Paratonium[9] in Hither Libya, Agathus of Phragonis and part of Elearchia in Egypt, Ammonius of Pachnemunis[10] and the rest of Elearchia, Agathodæmon of Schedia[11] and Menelaitas, Dracontius of Lesser Hermupolis, Adelphius of Onuphis[12] in Lychni, Hermion of Tanes[13], Marcus of Zygra[16], Hither Libya, Theodorus of Athribis[14], Andreas of Arsenoe, Paphnutius of Sais, Marcus of Philæ, Zoilus of Andrôs[15], Menas of Antiphra[16].

Eusebius also signs the following in Latin, of which the translation is:

I Eusebius, according to your exact confession made on either side by agreement concerning the Subsistences, also add my agreement; further concerning the Incarnation of our Saviour, namely that the Son of God has become Man, taking everything upon Himself without sin, like the composition of our old man, I ratify the text of the letter. And whereas the Sardican paper is ruled out, to avoid the appearance of issuing anything beyond the creed of Nicæa, I also add my consent, in order that the creed of Nicæa may not seem by it to be excluded, and [I agree] that it should not be published. I pray for your health in the Lord.

I Asterius agree to what is above written, and pray for your health in the Lord.

11. *The 'Tome' signed at Antioch.*

And after this Tome was sent off from Alexandria, thus signed by the aforesaid, [the recipients] in their turn signed it:

I Paulinus hold thus, as I received from the fathers, that the Father perfectly exists and subsists, and that the Son perfectly subsists, and that the Holy Spirit perfectly subsists. Wherefore also I accept the above explanation concerning the Three Subsistences, and the one Subsistence, or rather Essence, and those who hold thus. For it is pious to hold and confess the Holy Trinity in one Godhead. And concerning the Word of the Father becoming Man for us, I hold as it is written, that, as John says, the Word was made Flesh, not in the sense of those most impious persons who say that He has undergone a change, but that He has become Man for us, being born of the holy Virgin Mary and of the Holy Spirit. For the Saviour had a body neither without soul, nor without sense, nor without intelligence. For it were impossible, the Lord being made Man for us, that His body should be without intelligence. Wherefore I anathematise those who set aside the Faith confessed at Nicæa, and who do not say that the Son is of the Father's Essence, and coessential with the Father. Moreover I anathematise those who say that the Holy Spirit is a Creature made through the Son. Once more I anathematise the heresy of Sabellius and of Photinus[17], and every heresy, walking in the Faith of Nicæa, and in all that is above written. I Karterius[18] pray for your health.

---

7 Of Laodicea, the later heresiarch.　　8 i.e. Vercellæ, in 'Cisalpine' Gaul, or Lombardy.

9 In Marmarica or 'Libya Siccior' near the *Ras el Harzeit.*

10 Capital of the Sebennytic nome, near *Handahur.*

11 A town and custom-house near Andropolis, between Alxa. and the Canopic arm of the Nile.

12 Chief town of a nome in the Delta.　　13 'Zoan.'

14 A very important town near the head of the Tanite arm. See Amm. Marc. xxii. 16. 6, who calls it one of the four largest cities in Egypt proper.　　15 i.e. Andropolis (above, note 11).

16 West of Alxa. toward the Libyan dessert, and not far from Zygra in Marmarica.

17 See Prolegg. ch. ii. § 3 (2) *ad fin.* This is remarkable as the first Eastern condemnation of Photinus by name from the Nicene side. He had been condemned at Sirmium in 347, and under pressure from the East apparently at Milan in 345 and 347, as well as in the Councils of Antioch in 344, and Sirmium in 351 (*supr.* pp. 463, 464). On the document of Paulinus, see Epiph. *Hær.* lxxvii. 20, 21, also Dr. Bright's note.

18 Bishop of Antaradus on the Syrian coast (D.C.B. i. 410 (3)); see *de Fuga,* 3, and *Hist. Ar.* 5. note 6a.

THE fragment which follows, containing an interesting report of a story told by Athanasius to Ammonius, Bishop of Pachnemunis, is inserted here as furnishing undesignedly important details as to the movements of Athanasius in 363. See Prolegg. ch. v. § 3 h, also ch. ii. § 9. It is excerpted by Montfaucon from an account of the Abbat Theodore, written for Theophilus, Bishop of Alexandria (385—412) by a certain Ammon (*Acta SS. Maii,* Tom. iii. Append., pp. 63—71). The writer was at that time a bishop (see unknown) : he was born about 335, as he was seventeen years old when he embraced the monastic life a year 'and more' after the proclamation of Gallus as Cæsar (Mar. 15, 351). About the time of the expulsion of Athanasius by Syrianus he retired to Nitria, where he remained many years, and finally returned to Alexandria, where he appears (*infra*) as one of the clergy ; the date of his elevation to the Episcopate cannot be fixed, but it obviously cannot be as early as 356-7 (so D.C.B. i. 102 (2), and probably is much later even than 362, in which year he would still be hardly twenty-eight. (He mentions the objections to the election of Athanasius, who was probably 30 in 328, on the ground of his youth.) Accordingly (apart from the different form of his name) he cannot [1] be identified with either of the Ammonii referred to in *Tom. ad Ant.* 1, note 3 ; *Hist. Ar.* 72, &c. The elder of the two does not concern us here : the younger (*supr.* pp. 483, 486), is the Ammonius to whom Athanasius told the story in the hearing of Ammon, and was now dead. Of Hermon, bishop of Bubastis, mentioned as present along with Ammonius, Theophilus, and Ammon when the story was told, nothing is known (except that the date D.C.B. iii. 4 (2) is over 25 years too early). As he is not 'of blessed memory,' he was possibly still living during the Episcopate of Theophilus and Ammon. (There is nothing to identify him with the bishop of *Tanes* in *Tom. Ant.* 1, 10.)

The story itself is given at second-hand, from Ammon's recollection of a statement by Athanasius some 12 to 15 years (at least) before he wrote. The prophetic details about Jovian may therefore be put down to natural accretion (*Letter* 56, note 2). But (apart from the fact that Julian's death must have been rumoured long before the tardy official announcement of it, Tillem. *Emp.* iv. 449 *sqq.*, Prolegg. *ubi supr.*) that Athanasius told of the φήμη of Julian's death among the monks of the Thebaid need not be doubted. The story is one of a very large class, many of which are fairly authenticated. To say nothing of the φήμη at the battle of Mycale ; we have in recent times the authority of Mr. R. Stuart Poole, of the British Museum, for the fact that on the night of the death of the Duke of Cambridge (July 9, 1850), Mr. Poole's brother 'suddenly took out his watch and said, "Note the time, the Duke of Cambridge is dead," and that the time proved to be correct ;' also the case of a Mr. Edmonds who saw at Leicester, early in the morning of Nov. 4, 1837, an irruption of water into the works of the Thames tunnel, by which a workman was drowned ; (other curious cases in 'Phantasms of the Living' vol. 2., pp. 367 *sqq.*). The letter or memoir from which this 'Narratio' is taken, was published by the Bollandists from a Medicean MS., and it bears every internal mark of genuineness. In what way it is integrally connected with the *Vita Antonii* (Gwatkin, *Studies,* p. 101), except by the fact that it happens to mention Antony, I fail to see. On the subject of Theodore of Tabenne, the main subject of the memoir, see Amélineau's *S. Pakhôme* (*ut supra,* p. 188), also *infr. Letter* 58, note 3.

"As I think your holiness was present and heard, when his blessedness Pope Athanasius, in the presence of other clergy of Alexandria and of my insignificance, formerly related in the Great Church something about Theodorus [2], to Ammonius of blessed memory, bishop of Elearchia [3], and to Hermon, bishop of the city of Bumastica [4]; I write only what is necessary to put your reverence in mind of what he said. When the famous bishops were wondering at the blessed Antony, Pope Athanasius—for Antony was often with him—said to them :

I saw also at that season great men of God, who are lately dead, Theodorus chief of the Tabennesian monks, and the father of the monks around [5] Antinoopolis, called Abbas Pammon. For when I was pursued by Julian, and was expecting to be slain by him—for this news was shewn me by good friends—these two came to me on the same day at Antinoopolis. And having planned to hide with Theodorus, I embarked on his vessel, which was completely covered in, while Abbas Pammon accompanied us. And when the wind was unfavourable, I was very anxious and prayed ; and the monks with Theodore got out and towed the boat. And as Abbas Pammon was encouraging me in my anxiety, I said, 'Believe me when I say that my heart is never so trustful in time of peace as in time of persecution. For I have good confidence that suffering for Christ, and strengthened by His mercy, even though I am slain, I shall find mercy with Him.' And while I was still saying this, Theodorus fixed his eyes on Abbas Pammon and smiled, while the other nearly laughed. So I said to them, 'Why have you laughed at my words, do you convict me of cowardice ?' and Theodorus said to Abbas Pammon, 'Tell him why we smiled.' At which the latter said, 'You ought to tell him.' So Theodorus said, 'in this very hour Julian has been slain in Persia,' for so God had declared beforehand concerning him : 'the haughty man, the despiser and the boaster, shall finish nothing [6]. But a Christian Emperor shall arise who shall be illustrious, but shall live only a short time [7]. Wherefore you ought not to harass yourselves by departing into the Thebaid, but secretly to go to the Court, for you will meet him by the way, and having been kindly received by him, will return to your Church. And he soon shall be taken by God.' And so it happened. From which cause I believe, that many who are well pleasing to God live unnoticed, especially among the monks. For those men were unnoticed also, such as the blessed Amun and the holy Theodorus [8] in the mountain of Nitria, and the servant of God, the happy old man, Pammon."

---

[1] The Articles in D.C.B. i. 102 (2) and (3), combine variously data belonging to three distinct persons. (1) The old bishop ordained by Alexander (see unknown, see *Hist. Ar.* 72 init.). Signs the synodal letter of the Sardican Council ; is one of the infirm prelates cruelly expelled by George, along with coffins to bury them in case of the journey being fatal (see also *Apol. Fug.* 7). (2) Another Ammonius, probably not a signatory of Sardica (cf. *Apol. Ar.* 50, with *Ep. Fest.* for 347), but a contemporary of Serapion, sent by Athanasius with Serap. to Constantius in 353. He had been a monk, but was then (*Dracont.* 7) bishop of Pachnemunis and part of Elearchia (*Tom.* 10), in which capacity, along with other exiles of 356-7 (*Hist. Ar.* 72 ; *Ap. Fug.* 7), he attends

the Council of 362. He is the 'Ammonius of blessed memory in the text. (3) Ammon, born 335, baptized 352, monk at Tabenne and Nitria 352—367(?), then at Alexandria, and finally (about 390) bishop of an unknown see in Egypt : wrote a short account of S. Theodore for Pope Theophilus.

[2] Cf. *Vit. Ant.* 60, and see below, letters 57, 58, and *Acta SS. Maii,* vol. iii. pp. 334—357, and *Appx.* ; also D.C.B. iv. 954 (53). [3] *Tom. Ant.* 4. [4] i.e. Bubastis. [5] Opposite Hermupolis Magna in Upper Egypt. [6] Habak. ii. 5. [7] Cf *Letter* 56, note 2. [8] On *this* Theodore, see D.C.B. *s.v.* no. (67).

AD AFROS EPISTOLA SYNODICA

(WRITTEN ABOUT 369.)

THE synodical letter which follows was written after the accession of Damasus to the Roman see (366). Whether it was written before any Western synod had formally condemned Auxentius of Milan (see *Letter* 59. 1) may be doubted : the complaint (§ 10) is rather that he still retains possession of his see, which in fact he did until 374, the year after the death of Athanasius. At any rate, Damasus had had time to hold a large synod, the letter of which had reached Athanasius. The history of the synods held by Damasus seems hopelessly obscure, and the date of our encyclical is correspondingly doubtful. Damasus certainly held at one time a synod of some 90 bishops from Italy and the Gauls, the letter of which was sent to Illyricum and to the East (Thdt. *H. E.* ii. 22 ; Soz. vi. 23 ; Hard. *Conc.* i. 771 : the Latin of the copy sent to Illyricum is dated 'Siricio et Ardabure vv. cl. coss.,' an additional element of confusion). The name of Sabinus at the end of the Latin copy sent to the East seems to fix the date of this synod (D.C.B. i. 294) to 372. Thus the synod referred to § 1 below must have been an earlier one, the acts of which are lost. It cannot have been held before the end of 367 or beginning of 368 (Montf. *Vit. Ath.*), as the earlier period of the episcopate of Damasus was fully occupied by different matters. Accordingly our encyclical falls between 368 and 372, probably as soon as Damasus had been able to assemble so large a synod, and Athanasius to write in reply (§ 10). It may be added that the letter of the Damasine synod of 372 refers in ambiguous terms to the condemnation of Auxentius as having already taken place, ('damnatum esse liquet:' was this because they felt unable to dislodge him? see Tillem. viii. 400).

The occasion of the letter is two-fold : principally to counteract the efforts that were being made in the West, and especially in Africa (still later in the time of S. Augustine, see *Collat. cum Maximin.* 4; and for earlier Arian troubles in Africa, *Nicene Lib.* vol. i. p. 287), to represent the council of Ariminum as a final settlement of the Faith, and so to set aside the authority of the Nicene definition. The second object is involved in the first. The head and centre of the dying efforts of Arianism in the Roman West was apparently Auxentius, 'one of the last survivors of the victory of Ariminum.' That he should be still undisturbed in his see, while working far and wide to the damage of the Catholic cause, was to Athanasius a distressing surprise, and he was urging the Western bishops to put an end to such an anomaly.

In the encyclical before us he begins (1—3) by contrasting the synod of Nicæa with that of Ariminum, and pointing out the real history of the latter, going over again to some extent the ground of the earlier sections of the *de Synodis*. He touches (3. end) on the disastrous termination of the Council. He then proceeds to vindicate the Nicene creed (4—8) as essentially Scriptural, i.e. as the only possible bar to the unscriptural formulæ of the Arians. This he illustrates (5, 6) by an account, substantially identical with that in the *de Decretis*, of the evasions of every other test by the Arian bishops at Nicæa. He repeatedly urges that the formula was no invention of the Nicene Fathers (6, 9), appealing to the admission of Eusebius to this effect. He attacks the Homœan position, shewing that its characteristic watchword merely dissembles the alternative between Anomœanism and the true co-essentiality of the Son (7). The most novel argument in the Letter is that of § 4, where he refutes the repudiation of οὐσία and ὑπόστασις in the creed of Niké by an argument from Scripture, starting from Ex. iii. 14 (as *de Decr.* 22 and *de Syn.* 29), and turning upon the equivalence of the two terms in question. This would appeal to Westerns, and expresses the usual view of Ath. himself (*Tom. ad Ant. Introd.*) but would not have much force with those who were accustomed to the Eastern terminology.

The insistence (in § 11) that the Nicene formula involves the Godhead of the Spirit should be noted. It seems to imply that, as a rule, such an explicit assurance as is insisted upon in *Tom ad Ant.* 3, would be superfluous.

The completeness of the work of Athanasius, now very near his end, in winning over all Egypt to unanimity in faith and in personal attachment to himself, is quaintly reflected in the naive assurance (§ 10) that the bishops of Egypt and the Libyas 'are all of one mind, and we always sign for one another if any chance not to be present.'

The translation has been carefully compared with that of Dr. Bright (*supr.* p. 482).

TO THE BISHOPS OF AFRICA

LETTER OF NINETY BISHOPS OF EGYPT AND LIBYA INCLUDING ATHANASIUS

---

1. Pre-eminence of the Council of Nicæa. Efforts to exalt that of Ariminum at its expense.

The letters are sufficient which were written by our beloved fellow-minister Damasus, bishop of the Great Rome, and the large number of bishops who assembled along with him ; and equally so are those of the other synods which were held, both in Gaul and in Italy, concerning the sound Faith which Christ gave us, the Apostles preached, and the Fathers, who met at Nicæa from all this world of ours, have handed down. For so great a stir was made at that time about the Arian heresy, in order that they who had fallen into it might be reclaimed, while its inventors might be made manifest. To that council, accordingly, the whole world has long ago agreed, and now, many synods having been held, all men have been put in mind, both in Dalmatia and Dardania, Macedonia, Epirus and Greece, Crete, and the other islands, Sicily, Cyprus, Pamphylia, Lycia, and Isauria, all Egypt and the Libyas, and most of the Arabians have come to know it, and marvelled at those who signed it, inasmuch as even if there were left among them any bitterness springing up from the root of the Arians ; we mean Auxentius, Ursacius, Valens and their fellows, by these letters they have been cut off and isolated. The confession arrived at at Nicæa was, we say once more, sufficient and enough by itself, for the subversion of all irreligious heresy, and for the security and furtherance of the doctrine of the Church. But since we have heard that certain wishing to oppose it are attempting to cite a synod supposed to have been held at Ariminum, and are eagerly striving that it should prevail rather than the other, we think it right to write and put you in mind, not to endure anything of the sort : for this is nothing else but a second growth of the Arian heresy. For what else do they wish for who reject the synod held against it, namely the Nicene, if not that the cause of Arius should prevail ?

What then do such men deserve, but to be called Arians, and to share the punishment of the Arians ? For they were not afraid of God, who says, ' Remove not the eternal boundaries which thy fathers placed [1],' and ' He that speaketh against father or mother, let him die the death [2] :' they were not in awe of their fathers, who enjoined that they who hold the opposite of their confession should be anathema.

2. The Synod of Nicæa contrasted with the local Synods held since.

For this was why an ecumenical synod has been held at Nicæa, 318 bishops assembling to discuss the faith on account of the Arian heresy, namely, in order that local synods should no more be held on the subject of the Faith, but that, even if held, they should not hold good. For what does that Council lack, that any one should seek to innovate ? It is full of piety, beloved ; and has filled the whole world with it. Indians have acknowledged it, and all Christians of other barbarous nations. Vain then is the labour of those who have often made attempts against it. For already the men we refer to have held ten or more synods, changing their ground at each, and while taking away some things from earlier decisions, in later ones make changes and additions. And so far they have gained nothing by writing, erasing, and using force, not knowing that ' every plant that the Heavenly Father hath not planted shall be plucked up [3].' But the word of the Lord which came through the ecumenical Synod at Nicæa, abides for ever [3a]. For if one compare number with number, these who met at Nicæa are more than those at local synods, inasmuch as the whole is greater than the part. But if a man wishes to discern the reason of the Synod at Nicæa, and that of the large number subsequently held by

---

[1] Prov. xxii. 28.   [2] Ex. xxi. 17.   [3] Matt. xv. 13.
[3a] 1 Pet. i. 25.

these men, he will find that while there was a reasonable cause for the former, the others were got together by force, by reason of hatred and contention. For the former council was summoned because of the Arian heresy, and because of Easter, in that they of Syria, Cilicia and Mesopotamia differed from us, and kept the feast at the same season as the Jews. But thanks to the Lord, harmony has resulted not only as to the Faith, but also as to the Sacred Feast. And that was the reason of the synod at Nicæa. But the subsequent ones were without number, all however planned in opposition to the ecumenical.

3. The true nature of the proceedings at Ariminum.

This being pointed out, who will accept those who cite the synod of Ariminum, or any other, against the Nicene? or who could help hating men who set at nought their fathers' decisions, and put above them the newer ones, drawn up at Ariminum with contention and violence? or who would wish to agree with these men, who do not accept even their own? For in their own ten or more synods, as I said above, they wrote now one thing, now another, and so came out clearly as themselves the accusers of each one. Their case is not unlike that of the Jewish traitors in old times. For just as they left the one well of the living water, and hewed for themselves broken cisterns, which cannot hold water, as the prophet Jeremiah has it[4], so these men, fighting against the one ecumenical synod, 'hewed for themselves' many synods, and all appeared empty, like 'a sheaf without strength[5].' Let us not then tolerate those who cite the Ariminian or any other synod against that of Nicæa. For even they who cite that of Ariminum appear not to know what was done there, for else they would have said nothing about it. For ye know, beloved, from those who went from you to Ariminum, how Ursacius and Valens, Eudoxius[5a] and Auxentius[5b] (and there Demophilus[5c] also was with them), were deposed, after wishing to write something to supersede the Nicene decisions. For on being requested to anathematise the Arian heresy, they refused, and preferred to be its ringleaders. So the bishops, like genuine servants of the Lord and orthodox believers (and there were nearly 200[6]), wrote that they were

satisfied with the Nicene alone, and desired and held nothing more or less than that. This they also reported to Constantius, who had ordered the assembling of the synod. But the men who had been deposed at Ariminum went off to Constantius, and caused those who had reported against them to be insulted, and threatened with not being allowed to return to their dioceses, and to be treated with violence in Thrace that very winter, to compel them to tolerate their innovations.

4. The Nicene formula in accordance with Scripture.

If then any cite the synod of Ariminum, firstly let them point out the deposition of the above persons, and what the bishops wrote, namely that none should seek anything beyond what had been agreed upon by the fathers at Nicæa, nor cite any synod save that one. But this they suppress, but make much of what was done by violence in Thrace[6a]; thus shewing that they are dissemblers of the Arian heresy, and aliens from the sound Faith. And again, if a man were to examine and compare the great synod itself, and those held by these people, he would discover the piety of the one and the folly of the others. They who assembled at Nicæa did so not after being deposed: and secondly, they confessed that the Son was of the Essence of the Father. But the others, after being deposed again and again, and once more at Ariminum itself, ventured to write that it ought not to be said that the Son had Essence or Subsistence. This enables us to see, brethren, that they of Nicæa breathe the spirit of Scripture, in that God says in Exodus[6b], 'I am that I am,' and through Jeremiah, 'Who is in His substance[7] and hath seen His word;' and just below, 'if they had stood in My subsistence[8] and heard My words:' now subsistence is essence, and means nothing else but very being, which Jeremiah calls existence, in the words, 'and they heard not the voice of existence[9].' For subsistence, and essence, is existence: for it is, or in other words exists. This Paul also perceiving wrote to the Hebrews, 'who being the brightness of his glory, and the express Image of his subsistence[10].' But the others, who think they know the Scriptures and call themselves wise, and do not choose to speak of subsistence in God (for thus they wrote at Ariminum and at other synods of theirs), were surely with justice deposed, saying as they did,

---

4 ii. 13.   5 Hos. viii. 7, LXX.
5a Eudoxius was at Seleucia, not at Ariminum.
5b See note on § 10 *infr.*
5c Bishop of Berœa in Macedonia Tertia, and from 370—380 successor of Eudoxius as Arian bishop of CP.
6 There were some 400 in all, so that the orthodox majority must have been far more than 200 (see *de Syn.* 8, 33). But Gwatkin (*Stud.* 170, note 3), inclines to accept the statement in the text.

6a i.e. at Niké, 359.   6b Ex. iii. 14.   7 ὑποστήματι, Jer. xxiii. 18, LXX.   8 ὑποστάσει, *v.* 22.   9 ὕπαρξις, Jer. ix. 10, LXX.   10 Heb. i. 3.

like the fool did in his heart[1], 'God is not.' And again the fathers taught at Nicæa that the Son and Word is not a creature, nor made, having read 'all things were made through Him[2],' and 'in Him were all things created, and consist[3];' while these men, Arians rather than Christians, in their other synods have ventured to call Him a creature, and one of the things that are made, things of which He Himself is the Artificer and Maker. For if 'through Him all things were made' and He too is a creature, He would be the creator of Himself. And how can what is being created create? or He that is creating be created?

5. *How the test 'Coessential' came to be adopted at Nicæa.*

But not even thus are they ashamed, although they say such things as cause them to be hated by all; citing the Synod of Ariminum, only to shew that there also they were deposed. And as to the actual definition of Nicæa, that the Son is coessential with the Father, on account of which they ostensibly oppose the synod, and buzz around everywhere like gnats about the phrase, either they stumble at it from ignorance, like those who stumble at the stone of stumbling that was laid in Sion[4]; or else they know, but for that very reason are constantly opposing and murmuring, because it is an accurate declaration and full in the face of their heresy. For it is not the phrases that vex them, but the condemnation of themselves which the definition contains. And of this, once again, they are themselves the cause, even if they wish to conceal the fact of which they are perfectly aware, —But we must now mention it, in order that hence also the accuracy of the great synod may be shewn. For[5] the assembled bishops wished to put away the impious phrases devised by the Arians, namely 'made of nothing,' and that the Son was 'a thing made,' and a 'creature,' and that 'there was a time when He was not,' and that 'He is of mutable nature.' And they wished to set down in writing the acknowledged language of Scripture, namely that the Word is of God by nature Only-begotten, Power, Wisdom of the Father, Very God, as John says, and as Paul wrote, brightness of the Father's glory and express image of His person[1]. But Eusebius and his fellows, drawn on by their own error, kept conferring together as follows: 'Let us assent. For we also are of God: for "there is one God of whom are all things[2]," and "old

things are passed away, behold all things are made new, but all things are of God[3]."' And they considered what is written in the Shepherd[4], 'Before all things believe that God is one, who created and set all things in order, and made them to exist out of nothing.' But the Bishops, beholding their craftiness, and the cunning of their impiety, expressed more plainly the sense of the words 'of God,' by writing that the Son is of the Essence of God, so that whereas the Creatures, since they do not exist of themselves without a cause, but have a beginning of their existence, are said to be 'of God,' the Son alone might be deemed proper to the Essence of the Father. For this is peculiar to one who is Only-begotten and true Word in relation to a Father, and this was the reason why the words 'of the essence' were adopted. Again[4a], upon the bishops asking the dissembling minority if they agreed that the Son was not a Creature, but the Power and only Wisdom of the Father, and the Eternal Image, in all respects exact, of the Father, and true God, Eusebius and his fellows were observed exchanging nods with one another, as much as to say 'this applies to us men also, for we too are called "the image and glory of God[5]," and of us it is said, "For we which live are alway[6]," and there are many Powers, and "all the power[7] of the Lord went out of the land of Egypt," while the caterpillar and the locust are called His "great power[8]." And "the Lord of powers[9] is with us, the God of Jacob is our help." For we hold that we are proper[1] to God, and not merely so, but insomuch that He has even called us brethren. Nor does it vex us, even if they call the Son Very God. For when made He exists in verity.'

6. *The Nicene test not unscriptural in sense, nor a novelty.*

Such was the corrupt mind of the Arians. But here too the Bishops, beholding their craftiness, collected from the Scriptures the figures of brightness, of the river and the well, and of the relation of the express Image to the Subsistence, and the texts, 'in thy light shall we see light[2],' and 'I and the Father are one[3].' And lastly they wrote more plainly, and concisely, that the Son was coessential with the Father; for all the above passages signify this. And their murmuring, that the phrases are unscriptural, is exposed as vain by themselves, for they have uttered their impieties in unscriptural terms: (for such are 'of

---

[1] Ps. xiv. 1. [2] John i. 3. [3] Col. i. 16. [4] Rom. ix. 33.
[5] This passage repeats in substance the account in *de Decr.* 19.
[1] ὑπόστασις. [2] 1 Cor. viii. 6.

[3] 2 Cor. v. 17, 18. [4] Herm. *Mand.* 1. [4a] Cf. *de Decr.* § 20, *ubi supr.* [5] 1 Cor. xi. 7. [6] Ps. cxv. 18 (*v.* 26, LXX.); cf. 2 Cor. iv. 11. [7] δύναμις, Ex. xii. 41. [8] Joel ii. 25. [9] δυνάμεων, Ps. xlvi. 7. [1] ἰδίους. [2] Ps. xxxvi. 9. [3] John x. 30.

nothing' and 'there was a time when He was not'), while yet they find fault because they were condemned by unscriptural terms pious in meaning. While they, like men sprung from a dunghill, verily 'spoke of the earth⁴,' the Bishops, not having invented their phrases for themselves, but having testimony from their Fathers, wrote as they did. For ancient bishops, of the Great Rome and of our city, some 130 years ago, wrote⁵ and censured those who said that the Son was a creature and not coessential with the Father. And Eusebius knew this, who was bishop of Cæsarea, and at first an accomplice⁶ of the Arian heresy; but afterwards, having signed at the Council of Nicæa, wrote to his own people affirming as follows: 'we know that certain eloquent and distinguished bishops and writers even of ancient date used the word "coessential" with reference to the Godhead of the Father and the Son.'

7. *The position that the Son is a Creature inconsistent and untenable.*

Why then do they go on citing the Synod of Ariminum, at which they were deposed? Why do they reject that of Nicæa, at which their Fathers signed the confession that the Son is of the Father's Essence and coessential with Him? Why do they run about? For now they are at war not only with the bishops who met at Nicæa, but with their own great bishops and their own friends. Whose heirs or successors then are they? How can they call men fathers, whose confession, well and apostolically drawn up, they will not accept? For if they think they can object to it, let them speak, or rather answer, that they may be convicted of falling foul of themselves, whether they believe the Son when He says, 'I and my Father are one,' and 'he that hath seen Me hath seen the Father⁶ᵃ.' 'Yes,' they must answer, 'since it is written we believe it.' But if they are asked how they are one, and how he that hath seen the Son hath seen the Father, of course, we suppose they will say, 'by reason of resemblance,' unless they have quite come to agree with those who hold the brother-opinion to theirs, and are called⁷ Anomœans. But if once more they are asked, 'how is He like?' they brasen it out and say, 'by perfect virtue and harmony, by having the same will with the Father, by not willing what the Father wills not.' But let them

understand that one assimilated to God by virtue and will is liable also to the purpose of changing; but the Word is not thus, unless He is 'like' in part, and as we are, because He is not like [God] in essence also. But these characteristics belong to us, who are originate, and of a created nature. For we too, albeit we cannot become like God in essence, yet by progress in virtue imitate God, the Lord granting us this grace, in the words, 'Be ye merciful as your Father is merciful:' 'be ye perfect as your heavenly Father is perfect⁸.' But that originate things are changeable, no one can deny, seeing that angels transgressed, Adam disobeyed, and all stand in need of the grace of the Word. But a mutable thing cannot be like God who is truly unchangeable, any more than what is created can be like its creator. This is why, with regard to us, the holy man said, 'Lord, who shall be likened unto thee⁹,' and 'who among the gods is like unto thee, Lord¹;' meaning by gods those who, while created, had yet become partakers of the Word, as He Himself said, 'If he called them gods to whom the word of God came².' But things which partake cannot be identical or similar to that whereof they partake. For example, He said of Himself, 'I and the Father are one³,' implying that things originate are not so. For we would ask those who allege the Ariminian Synod, whether a created essence can say, 'what things I see my Father make, those I make also⁴.' For things originate are made and do not make; or else they made even themselves. Why, if, as they say, the Son is a Creature and the Father is His Maker, surely the Son would be His own maker, as He is able to make what the Father makes, as He said. But such a supposition is absurd and utterly untenable, for none can make himself.

8. *The Son's relation to the Father essential, not merely ethical.*

Once more, let them say whether things originate could say⁵, 'all things whatsoever the Father hath are Mine.' Now, He has the prerogative of creating and making, of Eternity, of omnipotence, of immutability. But things originate cannot have the power of making, for they are creatures; nor eternity, for their existence has a beginning; nor of omnipotence and immutability, for they are under sway, and of changeable nature, as the Scriptures say. Well then, if these prerogatives belong to the Son, they clearly do so, not on account of His virtue, as said above, but essentially, even as

---

4 John iii. 31.   5 See *de Syn.* § 43, and *de Sent. Dionys.* 18, 19, also *supr.* p. 76.
6 But see Socrates, ii. 21, and D.C.B. ii. p. 347.
6ᵃ John x. 30, and xiv. 9.
7 Cf. *de Syn.* § 31 (a chapter added after the death of Constantius). The Anomœan sect, headed by Eunomius, and deriving its intellectual impetus from Aetius, belongs to the second generation of the Arian movement (their watchword is characterised as recent in the creed of Niké, 359 A.D.), and was comparatively unfamiliar *to* Athanasius. Cf. Prolegg. ch. ii. § 8.

8 Luke vi. 36; Matt. v. 48.   9 Ps. lxxxiii. 1, LXX.
1 Ps. lxxxvi. 8.   2 John x. 35.   3 Ib. x. 30.
4 Ib. v. 19: the word ποίεω is taken in the sense of *making*.
5 John xvi. 15.

the synod said, 'He is of no other essence' but of the Father's, to whom these prerogatives are proper. But what can that be which is proper to the Father's essence, and an off-spring from it, or what name can we give it, save 'coessential?' For that which a man sees in the Father, that sees he also in the Son; and that not by participation, but essentially. And this is [the meaning of] 'I and the Father are one,' and 'he that hath seen Me hath seen the Father.' Here especially once more it is easy to shew their folly. If it is from virtue, the antecedent of willing and not willing, and of moral progress, that you hold the Son to be like the Father; while these things fall under the category of quality; clearly you call God compound of quality and essence. But who will tolerate you when you say this? For God, who compounded all things to give them being, is not compound, nor of similar nature to the things made by Him through the Word. Far be the thought. For He is simple essence, in which quality is not, nor, as James says, 'any variableness or shadow of turning[6].' Accordingly, if it is shewn that it is not from virtue (for in God there is no quality, neither is there in the Son), then He must be proper to God's essence. And this you will certainly admit if mental apprehension is not utterly destroyed in you. But what is that which is proper to and identical with the essence of God, and an Offspring from it by nature, if not by this very fact coessential with Him that begat it? For this is the distinctive relation of a Son to a Father, and he who denies this, does not hold that the Word is Son in nature and in truth.

9. *The honest repudiation of Arianism involves the acceptance of the Nicene test.*

This then the Fathers perceived when they wrote that the Son was coessential with the Father, and anathematised those who say that the Son is of a different Subsistence[7]: not inventing phrases for themselves, but learning in their turn, as we said, from the Fathers who had been before them. But after the above proof, their Ariminian Synod is superfluous, as well as any[7a] other synod cited by them as touching the Faith. For that of Nicæa is sufficient, agreeing as it does with the ancient bishops also, in which too their fathers signed, whom they ought to respect, on pain of being thought anything but Christians. But if even after such proofs, and after the testimony of the ancient bishops, and the signature of their own Fathers, they pretend as if in ignorance to be alarmed at the phrase

'coessential,' then let them say and hold, in simpler terms and truly, that the Son is Son by nature, and anathematise as the synod enjoined those who say that the Son of God is a Creature or a thing made, or of nothing, or that there was once a time when He was not, and that He is mutable and liable to change, and of another Subsistence. And so let them escape the Arian heresy. And we are confident that in sincerely anathematising these views, they *ipso facto* confess that the Son is of the Father's Essence, and coessential with Him. For this is why the Fathers, having said that the Son was coessential, straightway added, 'but those who say that He is a creature, or made, or of nothing, or that there was once a time when He was not,' the Catholic Church anathematises: namely in order that by this means they might make it known that these things are meant by the word 'coessential.' And the meaning 'Coessential' is known from the Son not being a Creature or thing made: and because he that says 'coessential' does not hold that the Word is a Creature: and he that anathematises the above views, at the same time holds that the Son is coessential with the Father; and he that calls Him 'coessential,' calls the Son of God genuinely and truly so; and he that calls Him genuinely Son understands the texts, 'I and the Father are one,' and 'he that hath seen Me hath seen the Father[8].'

10. *Purpose of this Letter; warning against Auxentius of Milan.*

Now it would be proper to write this at greater length. But since we write to you who know, we have dictated it concisely, praying that among all the bond of peace might be preserved, and that all in the Catholic Church should say and hold the same thing. And we are not meaning to teach, but to put you in mind. Nor is it only ourselves that write, but all the bishops of Egypt and the Libyas, some ninety in number. For we all are of one mind in this, and we always sign for one another if any chance not to be present. Such being our state of mind, since we happened to be assembled, we wrote, both to our beloved Damasus, bishop of the Great Rome, giving an account of Auxentius[9] who has in-

---

6 James i. 17   7 ὑπόστασις.   7a Omit ἡ with most MSS.

8 John x. 30, and xiv. 9.
9 Auxentius (not in D.C.B.) was a native of Cappadocia (*Hist. Ar.* 75), and had been ordained presbyter at Alexandria by Gregory (next note). Upon the expulsion of the somewhat weak-kneed Dionysius after the council at Milan (355) he was appointed to that see by Constantius, although according to Athanasius (*ubi supr.*) he knew no Latin, nor any thing else except irreligion ('a busybody rather than a Christian'). He took a leading part along with Valens and others at the Council of Ariminum (*de Syn.* 8, 10) and was included in the deposition of Arian leaders by that synod. Under the orthodox Valentinian he maintained his see in

truded upon the church at Milan; namely that he not only shares the Arian heresy, but is also accused of many offences, which he committed with Gregory[10], the sharer of his impiety; and while expressing our surprise that so far he has not been deposed and expelled from the Church, we thanked [Damasus] for his piety and that of those who assembled at the Great Rome, in that by expelling Ursacius and Valens, and those who hold with them, they preserved the harmony of the Catholic Church. Which we pray may be preserved also among you, and therefore entreat you not to tolerate, as we said above, those who put forward a host of synods held concerning the Faith, at Ariminum, at Sirmium, in Isauria, in Thrace, those in Constantinople, and the many irregular ones in Antioch. But let the Faith confessed by the Fathers at Nicæa alone hold good among you, at which all the fathers, including those of the men who now are fighting

---

spite of the efforts of Philaster, Evagrius, and Eusebius of Vercellæ, and in spite of the condemnations passed upon him by various Western synods (362—371, see *ad Epict*. 1). In 364, Hilary travelled to Milan on purpose to expose him before Valentinian. In a discussion ordered by the latter, Hilary extorted from Auxentius a confession which satisfied the Emperor, but not Hilary himself, whose persistent denunciation of its insincerity caused his dismissal from the town. Auxentius seems after this to have intrigued to obtain Illyrian signatures to the creed of (Niké or) Ariminum (Hard. *Conc*. 1. pp. 771, 773). Upon his death (374) Ambrose was elected bishop of Milan, but was confronted by the Arian party with a rival bishop in the person of a second Auxentius, said to have been a pupil of Ulfilas.

[10] The intrusive bishop of Alexandria, 339—346. He had ordained his fellow-countryman Auxentius (Hilar. *in Aux*. 8).

against it, were present, as we said above, and signed: in order that of us too the Apostle may say, 'Now I praise you that ye remember me in all things, and as I handed the traditions to you, so ye hold them fast[11].'

11. *Godhead of the Spirit also involved in the Nicene Creed.*

For this Synod of Nicæa is in truth a proscription of every heresy. It also upsets those who blaspheme the Holy Spirit, and call Him a Creature. For the Fathers, after speaking of the faith in the Son, straightway added, 'And we believe in the Holy Ghost,' in order that by confessing perfectly and fully the faith in the Holy Trinity they might make known the exact form of the Faith of Christ, and the teaching of the Catholic Church. For it is made clear both among you and among all, and no Christian can have a doubtful mind on the point, that our faith is not in the Creature, but in one God, Father Almighty, maker of all things visible and invisible: and in one Lord Jesus Christ His Only-begotten Son, and in one Holy Ghost; one God, known in the holy and perfect Trinity, baptized into which, and in it united to the Deity, we believe that we have also inherited the kingdom of the heavens, in Christ Jesus our Lord, through whom to the Father be the glory and the power for ever and ever. Amen.

---

[11] 1 Cor. xi. 2.

LETTERS OF ATHANASIUS
WITH TWO ANCIENT CHRONICLES OF HIS LIFE

THE Letters cannot be arranged in strict sequence of time without breaking into the homogeneity of the *corpus* of Easter Letters. Accordingly we divide them into two parts: (1) all that remain of the Easter or Festal Epistles: (2) Personal Letters. From the latter class we exclude synodical or encyclical documents, or treatises merely inscribed to a friend, such as those printed above pp. 91, 149, 173, 222, &c., &c., the *ad Serapionem, ad Marcellinum*, &c. There remain a number of highly interesting letters, the survivals of what must have been a large correspondence, all of which, excepting six (Nos. 52, 54, 56, 59, 60, 61), now appear in English for the first time. They are arranged as nearly as possible in strict chronological order, though this is in some cases open to doubt (e.g. 60, 64, &c.). They mostly belong to the later half of the episcopate of Athanasius, and are therefore placed after the Festal Collection, which however itself extends to the end of the Bishop's life. The immemorial numbering of the latter collection is of course retained, although many of the forty-five are no longer to be found.

Prefixed to the Letters are two almost contemporary chronicles, the one preserved in the same MS. as Letters 46, 47, the other prefixed to the Syriac MS., which is our sole channel for the bulk of the Easter Letters. A memorandum appended to Letter 64 specifies certain fragments not included in this volume. The striking fragment *Filiis suis* has been conjecturally placed among the remains of *Letter* 29.

For the arrangement of the Letters, the reader is referred to the general Table of Contents to this volume. We now give

A. The *Historia Acephala* or Maffeian fragment, with short introduction.

B. The Chronicon Prævium or *Festal Index*, with introduction to it and to the Festal Letters.

A.

The *Historia Acephala*. This most important document was brought to light in 1738 by the Marchese F. Scipio Maffei († 1755), from a Latin MS. (uncial parchment) in the Chapter Library at Verona. It was reprinted from Maffei's *Osservazioni Letterarie* in the Padua edition of Athanasius; also in 1769 by Gallandi (*Bibl. Patr.* v. 222), from which edition (the reprint in Migne, xxvi. 1443 *sqq.* being full of serious misprints) the following version has been made. The Latin text (including letters 46, 47, and a Letter of the Council of Sardica) is very imperfect, but the annalist is so careful in his reckonings, and so often repeats himself, that the careful reader can nearly always use the document to make good its own gaps or wrong readings. Beyond this (except the insertion of the consuls for 372, § 17 *ad fin.*) the present editor has not ventured [1] to go. The importance and value of the fragment must now be shewn.

The annalist evidently writes under the episcopate of Theophilus, to which he hurriedly brings down his chronology after the death of Athanasius (§ 19). At the fortieth anniversary of the episcopate of Athanasius, June 8, 368, he makes a pause (§ 17) in order to reckon up his dates. This passage is the key of the whole of his chronological data. He accounts for the period of forty years (thus placing the accession of Ath. at June 8, 328, in agreement with the Index), shewing how it is exactly made up by the periods of 'exile' and of 'quiet' previously mentioned. To 'quiet' he assigns 'xxii years v months and x days,' to 'exile' xvii years vi months xx days; total xl years. He then shews how the latter is made up by the several exiles he has chronicled. As the text stands we have the following sum:

TABLE A.	Exiles (1)				xc months	iii days
	[(2)]	.	.	.	.	.
	(3)	.	.	.	lxxii ,,	xiv ,,
	(4)	.	.	.	xv ,,	xxii ,,
	(5)	.	.	.	iv ,,	
	'exact result'	xvii years	vi months	xx days.		

Now the exact result of the figures as they stand is 182 months, 9 days, *i.e.* 15 years 2 months and 9 days, or 2 years 4 months and 11 days too little. Moreover of the well-known 'five exiles,' only four are accounted for. An exile has thus dropped out, and an item of 2 years 4 months 11 days. Now this corresponds exactly with the interval from Epiphi 17 (July 11), 335 (departure for Tyre, *Fest. Ind.* viii), to Athyr 27 (Nov. 23), 337

---

[1] The corrections were made before he could obtain the essay and text of Sievers (*Zeitsch. Hist. Theol.* 1868), where he now finds them nearly all anticipated. Sievers' discussion has been carefully and gratefully used, but his text is defective, especially from the accidental omission of one of the key-clauses of the whole (§ 17).

(return to Alexandria *F. I.* x). The annalist then (followed apparently by Theodt. *H. E.* ii. 1) reckoned the *first* exile at the above figure. But what of the first figure in our table, xc months iii days? It again exactly coincides with the interval from Pharm. 21 (Apr. 16, Easter Monday), 339 to Paophi 24 (Oct. 21), 346, on which day (§ 1) Athan. returned from his *second* exile. This double coincidence cannot be an accident. It demonstrates beyond all dispute that the missing item of 'ann. ii, mens. iv, d. xii' has dropped out after ' Treveris in Galliis,' and that 'mens. xc, dies iii' *relates to the second exile,* so that, in § 1 also, the annalist wrote not ' annos vi' but 'annos *vii menses* vi *dies iii,*' which he repeats § 17 by its equivalent 'mens. xc, d. iii,' while words have dropped out in § 1 to the effect of what is supplied in brackets. (Hefele, ii. 50, Eng. Tr., is therefore in error here).

I would add that the same obvious principle of correcting a clearly corrupt figure by the writer's own subsequent reference to it, enables us also to correct the last figures of § 2 by those of § 5, to correct the items by the sum total of §§ 6, 7, and lastly to correct the corrupt readings ' Gregorius' for Georgius, and 'Constans' for Constantius, by the many uncorrupt places which shew that the annalist himself was perfectly aware of the right names.

In one passage alone (§ 13 'Athyr' twice for Mechir, cf. *Fest. Ind.* viii) is conjecture really needed ; but even here the consuls are correctly given, and support the right date.

We are now in a position to construct tables of 'exiles' and 'quiet' periods from the *Historia* as corrected by itself.

TABLE B. *Exiles, &c., of Athanasius.*

Exiles lasted			beginning	Quiet periods begin	lasting		
No. Years Mo.		Days		No.	Years Mo.		Days
1 (a) ii iv		xi	(b) Epiphi 17, 335 (July 11)	1 Payni 14, 328 (June 8)	vii	i	iii (b)
2 vii vi		iii	(b) Pharmuthi 21, 339 (Apr. 16)	2 (b) Athyr 27, 337 (Nov. 23)	i	iv	xxiv (b)
3 vi		xiv	Mechir 13, 356 (Feb. 8)	3 Paophi 24, 346 (Oct. 21)	ix	iii	xix(§5)
4 i iii		xxii	Paophi 27, 362 (Oct. 24)	4 Mechir 27, 362 (Feb. 21)	viii		(§10)
5 iv			Paophi 8, 365 (Oct. 5)	5 (c) Mechir 19, 364 (Feb. 14)	i	vii	xvii (b)
				6 Mechir 7, 366 (Feb. 1)	ii	iv	vii (a)
xvii vi		xx	Total Exiles	Total ' quiet' (to June 8, 368)	xxii	v	x

N.B. In the above Table, (a) denotes dates or figures *directly implied* in the existing text, (b) those implied by it *in combination* with other sources, (c) those based on *conjectural* emendation of the existing text. All unmarked data are expressly given.

Table B shews the deliberate and careful calculation which runs through the system of our annalist. Once or twice he indulges in a round figure, exiles 1 and 5 are each a day too long by the Egyptian calendar, and this is set off by his apparently reckoning the fifth quiet period as two days too short. But the writer clearly knew his own mind. In fact, the one just ground on which we might distrust his chronology is its systematic character. He has a thorough scheme of his own, which he carries out to a nicety. Now such a chronology is not necessarily untrustworthy. Its consistency *may* be artificial ; on the other hand, it may be due to accurate knowledge of the facts. Whether this is so or not must be ascertained partly from a writer's known opportunities and capacity, partly from his agreement or discrepancy with other sources of knowledge. Now our annalist wrote in the time of Theophilus (385—412), and may therefore rank as a contemporary of Athanasius (cf. Prolegg. ch. v.) His opportunities therefore were excellent. As to his capacity, his work bears every trace of care and skill. He is no historian, nor a stylist, but as an annalist he understood what he was doing. As to agreement with other data, we remark to begin with that it was the publication of this fragment in the 18th century that first shed a ray of light on the Erebus and Chaos of the chronology of the Council of Sardica and its adjacent events ; that it at once justified the critical genius of Montfaucon, Tillemont and others, against the objections with which their date for the death of Athanasius [2] was assailed, and here again upset the confused chronological statements of the fifth-century historians in favour of the incidental evidence of many more primary authorities [3]. But most important of all is its confirmation by the evidence of the *Festal Letters* discovered in 1842, and especially by their *Index,* the so-called 'Chronicon Athanasianum.' It is evident at a glance that our annalist is quite independent of the *Index,* as he gives many details which it does not contain. But neither can the *Index* be a compilation from the annalist. Each writer had access to information not embodied in the other, and there is no positive evidence that either used the other in any way. When they agree, therefore, their evidence has the greatest possible weight. Their main heads of agreement are indicated in the Chronological Table, Prolegg. *sub fin.*

It remains to notice shortly the two digressions on the doings of Eudoxius and the Anomœans (§§ 2, 12 of Migne, paragraphs II, IX of Gallandi). Here the annalist is off his own ground, and evidently less well informed. In § 2 we learn nothing of interest : but the ' Ecthesis' of the Anomœans in par. IX is of importance, and only too evidently authentic. It still awaits a critical examination, and it is not easy to give it its exact place in the history of the later Arianism. Apparently it belongs to the period 360—364, when the Anomœans were organising their schism (Gwatkin, pp. 226, 180) the names being those of the ultra-Arians condemned by the Homœans in 360 (Prolegg. ch. ii. § 8 *fin.*).

The contrast between the vagueness of statement in these digressions, and the writer's firmness of touch in dealing with Alexandrian affairs is most significant.

The fragment runs as follows :

HISTORIA ACEPHALA.

I. 1. The Emperor Constantius also wrote concerning the return of Athanasius, and among the Emperor's letters this one too is to be found.

2. And it came to pass after the death of Gregory that Athanasius returned from the city of Rome and the parts of Italy, and entered Alexandria Paophi xxiv, Coss. Constantius IV, Constans III (October 21, 346) ; that is after [vii] years vi [months and iii days,] and

---

[2] But our annalist gives May 3, while *Fest. Ind.* gives May 2, the day solemnised in the Coptic Martyrologies (Mai, *Script. Vett.* vol. 4, part 2, pp. 29, 114), and doubtless the right one. Perhaps,

if Athanasius died in the night of May 2-3, the former day might be chosen for his commemoration, while our annalist may still be literally exact.   [3] See Tillem. viii. 719 *sqq.*

remained quiet at Alexandria ix[1] years iii[2] months [and xix days].

II. Now after his return, Coss. Limenius[3] and Catulinus (349), Theodore[3a], Narcissus[3b], and George, with others, came to Constantinople, wishing to persuade Paul to communicate with them, who received them not even with a word, and answered their greeting with an anathema. So they took to themselves Eusebius of Nicomedia[3c], and laid snares for the most blessed Paul, and lodging a calumny against him concerning Constans and Magnentius, expelled him from CP. that they might have room there, and sow the Arian heresy. Now the people of CP., desiring the most blessed Paul, raised continual riots to prevent his being taken from the city, for they loved his sound doctrine. The Emperor, however, was angry, and sent Count Hermogenes to cast him out; but the people, hearing this, dragged forth Hermogenes through the midst of the town. From which matter they obtained a pretext against the Bishop, and exiled him to Armenia. Theodore and the rest wishing to place in the See of that Town Eudoxius, an ally and partisan of the Arian heresy, ordained [Bishop] of Germanicia, while the people were stirred to riot, and would not allow any one to sit in the See of blessed Paul,—they took Macedonius, a presbyter of Paul, and ordained him bishop of the town of CP., whom the whole assembly of bishops condemned, since against his own father he had disloyally received laying on of hands from heretics.

However, after Macedonius had communicated with them and signed, they brought in pretexts of no importance, and removing him from the Church, they instal the aforesaid Eudoxius of Antioch[3d], whence [the partakers] in this secession are called Macedonians, making shipwreck concerning the Holy Spirit.

III. 3. After this time Athanasius, hearing that there was to be disturbance against him, the Emperor Constantius[4] being in residence at Milan (353), sent to court a vessel with v Bishops, Serapion of Thmuis, Triadelphus of Nicotas, Apollo of Upper Cynopolis, Ammonius of Pachemmon, . . . and iii Presbyters of Alexandria, Peter the Physician, Astericus, and Phileas. After their setting sail from Alexandria, Coss. Constantius VI Augustus, and Constantius[4] Cæsar II, Pachom xxiv (May 19, 353), presently four days after Montanus of the Palace entered Alexandria Pachom xxviii, and gave a letter of the same Constantius[4] Augustus to the bishop Athanasius, forbidding him to come to court, on which account the bishop was exceedingly desolate, and the whole people much troubled[5]. So Montanus, accomplishing nothing, set forth, leaving the bishop at Alexandria.

4. Now after a while Diogenes, Imperial Notary, came to Alexandria in the month of Mensor (August, 355) Coss. Arbetion and Lollianus: that is ii years and v months[5a] from when Montanus left Alexandria. And Diogenes pressed every one urgently to compel the bishop to leave the town, and afflicted all not a little. Now on the vi day of the month Thoth, he made a sharp attempt to besiege the church, and he spent iv months in his efforts, that is from the month Mensor, or from the [first] day of those intercalated until the xxvi day of Choiac (Dec. 23). But as the people and the judges strongly resisted Diogenes, Diogenes returned without success on the xxvi day of the

said month Choiac, Coss. Arbetion and Lollianus, after iv months as aforesaid.

IV. 5. Now Duke Syrianus, and Hilary the Notary, came from Egypt to Alexandria on the tenth day of Tybi (Jan. 6, 356) after Coss. Arbetion and Lollianus. And sending in front all the legions of soldiers throughout Egypt and Libya, the Duke and the Notary entered the Church of Theonas with their whole force of soldiers by night, on the xiii day of Mechir, during the night preceding the xiv. And breaking the doors of the Church of Theonas, they entered with an infinite force of soldiers. But bishop Athanasius escaped their hands, and was saved, on the aforesaid xiv of Mechir[6]. Now this happened ix years iii months and xix days from the Bishop's return from Italy. But when the Bishop was delivered, his presbyters and people remained in possession of the Churches, and holding communion iv months, until there entered Alexandria the prefect Cataphronius and Count Heraclius in the month Pahyni xvi day, Coss. Constantius[4] VIII and Julianus Cæsar I (June 10, 356).

V. 6. And four days after they entered[6a] the Athanasians were ejected from the Churches, and they were handed over to those who belonged to George[7], and were expecting him as Bishop. So they received the Churches on the xxi day of Pahyni. Moreover George[7] arrived at Alexandria, Coss. Constantius[4] IX, and Julianus Cæsar II, Mechir xxx (Feb. 24, 357), that is, eight months and xi days from when his party received the Churches. So George[7] entered Alexandria, and kept the Churches xviii whole months: and then the common people attacked him in the Church of Dionysius, and he was hardly delivered with danger and a great struggle on the i day of the month Thoth, Coss. Tatianus and Cerealis (Aug. 29, 358). Now George[7] was ejected from Alexandria on the x[8] day after the riot, namely v of Paophi (Oct. 2). But they who belonged to Bishop Athanasius, ix days after the departure of George[7], that is on the xiv of Pa[ophi], cast out the men of George[7], and held the Churches two months and xiv days; until there came Duke Sebastian from Egypt and cast them out, and again assigned the Churches to the party of George on the xxviii day of the month Choiac (Dec. 24).

7. Now ix whole months after the departure of George from Alexandria, Paulus the Notary arrived Pahyni xxix, Coss. Eusebius, Hypatius (June 23, 359), and published an Imperial Order on behalf of George, and coerced many in vengeance for him. And [ii years and] v months after, George came to Alexandria Athyr xxx (Coss. Taurus, and Florentius) from court (Nov. 26, 361), that is iii years and two months after he had fled. And at Antioch they of the Arian heresy, casting out the Paulinians from the Church, appointed Meletius. When he would not consent to their evil mind, they ordained Euzoius a presbyter of George[7] of Alexandria in his stead.

VI. 8. Now George, having entered Alexandria as aforesaid on the xxx Athyr, remained safely in the town iii days, that is [till] iii Choiac. For, on the iv day of that same month, the prefect Gerontius announced the death of the Emperor Constantius, and that Julianus alone held the whole Empire. Upon which news, the citizens of Alexandria and all shouted against George, and with one accord placed him under custody. And he was in prison bound with iron from the aforesaid iv day of Choiac, up to the xxvii of the same month, xxiv days. For on the xxviii day of the same month early in the morning, nearly all the people of that town led forth George from prison, and also the Count who was with him, the Superintendent of the building of the

---

[1] Corrected from §§ 5, 17, *infr.*; text 'xvi.' [2] Corrected from § 5; text '6 months.' [3] Text 'Hypatius.' [3a] Of Heraclea.
[3b] Cf. *Apol. Fug.* 1, &c., &c.
[3c] Bishop of CP. 338—341. On his death Paul was restored, but Macedonius appointed by the Arians. This was in 341-2. The final expulsion and death of Paul was about the date given in the text; but the events of several years are lumped together without clear distinction. [3d] In 360.
[4] Text 'Constans.' This passage (3—5), is used by Soz. iv. 9.
[5] Fatigatus,' Soz. ἐταράχθησαν. [5a] Cf. *Apol. Const.* 22; read ii years ii months.

[6] Text throughout 'Methir.' [6a] *Supr.* p. 290.
[7] Text 'Gregory;' §§ 6, 7 are used by Soz. iv. 10, § 8 by Soz. v. 7.
[8] Read '34th.'

Church which is called Cæsareum, and killed them both, and carried their bodies round through the midst of the town, that of George on a camel, but that of Dracontius, men dragging it by ropes; and so having insulted them, at about the vii hour of the day, they burnt the bodies of each.

VII. 9. Now in the next . . . . day of Mechir the x day of the month, after Coss. Taurus and Florentius (Feb. 4, 362), an order of the Emperor Julian was published commanding those things to be restored to the idols and temple attendants and the public account, which in former times had been taken away from them.

10. But after iii days, Mechir xiv, an order was given of the same Emperor Julian, also of the Vicar Modestus, to Gerontius prefect, ordering all Bishops hitherto defeated by factions and exiled to return to their towns and provinces. Now this letter was published on the following day Mechir xv, while subsequently an edict also of the prefect Gerontius was published, by which the Bishop Athanasius was ordered to return to his Church. And xii days after the publication of this Edict Athanasius was seen at Alexandria, and entered the Church in the same month Mechir, xxvii day, so that there is from his flight which took place in the times of Syrianus and Hilary till his return, when Julianus . . . . Mechir xxvii. He remained in the Church until Paophi xxvi, Coss. Mamertinus and Nevitta (Oct. 23, 362), viii whole months.

11. Now on the aforesaid day, Paophi xxvii, he [the prefect] published an Edict of the Emperor Julianus, that Athanasius, Bishop, should retire from Alexandria, and no sooner was the Edict published, than the Bishop left the town and abode round about Thereu[9]. Soon after his departure Olympus the prefect, in obedience to the same[10] Pythiodorus, and those who were with him, most difficult persons, sent into exile Paulus and Astericius, presbyters of Alexandria, and directed them to live at the town of Andropolis.

VIII. 12. Now Olympus the same prefect, in the month Mensor, xxvi day, Coss. Julianus Augustus IV. and Sallustius (Aug. 20, 363), announced that Julian the Emperor was dead, and that Jovianus a Christian was Emperor. And in the following month, Thoth xviii, a letter of the Emperor Jovianus came to Olympus the prefect that only the most high God should be worshipped, and Christ, and that the peoples, holding communion in the Churches, should practise religion. Moreover Paulus and Astericius, the aforesaid presbyters, returned from exile at the town of Andropolis, and entered Alexandria, on the x day of Thoth, after x months.

13. Now Bishop Athanasius, having tarried as aforesaid at Thereon, went up to the higher parts of Egypt as far as Upper Hermopolis in the Thebaid, and as far as Antinoopolis. And while he was staying in these places, it was learned that the Emperor Julian was dead, and that Jovian a Christian was Emperor. So the Bishop entered Alexandria secretly, his arrival not being known to many, and went by sea to meet the Emperor Jovian, and afterwards, Church affairs being settled[10a], received a letter, and came to Alexandria and entered into the Church on the xix day of Athyr[11] Coss. Jovianus and Varronianus. From his leaving Alexandria according to the order of Julian until he arrived on the aforesaid xix day of Athyr[11] after one year and iii months, and xxii days.

IX. Now at CP. Eudoxius of Germanicia held the Church, and there was a division between him and Macedonius; but by means of Eudoxius there went forth another worse heresy from the spurious [teaching] of the Arians, Aetius and Patricius[11a] of Nicæa, who communicated with Eunomius, Heliodorus, and Stephen. And Eudoxius adopting this, communicated with Euzoius, Bishop at Antioch, of the Arian sect, and they deposed on a pretext Seleucius[11b] and Macedonius, and Hypatian[11c], and other xv Bishops belonging to them, since they would not receive 'Unlike' nor 'Creature of the Uncreated.' Now their Exposition is as follows:—

Exposition of Patricius[11a] and Aetius, who communicated with Eunomius, Heliodorus, and Stephen.

These are the attributes of God, Unbegotten, without origin, Eternal, not to be commanded, Immutable, All-seeing, Infinite, Incomparable, Almighty, knowing the future without foresight; without beginning[12]. These do not belong to the Son, for He is commanded, is under command, is made from nothing, has an end, is not compared [with the Father], the Father surpasses Him . . . of Christ is found: as pertaining to the Father, He is ignorant of the future. He was not God, but Son of God; God of those who are after Him: and in this He possesses invariable likeness with the Father, namely He sees all things because all things . . . because He is not changed in goodness; [but] not like in the quality of Godhead, nor in nature. But if we said that He was born of the quality of Godhead, we say that He resembles the offspring of serpents[12a], and that is an impious saying: and like as a statue produces rust from itself, and will be consumed by the rust itself, so also the Son, if He is produced from the nature of the Father, will consume the Father. But from the work, and the newness of work, the Son is naturally God, and not from the Nature, but from another nature like as the Father, but not from Him. For He was made the image of God, and we are out of God, and from God. Inasmuch as all things are from God, and the Son also, as if from something [else]. Like as iron if it has rust will be diminished, like as a body if it produces worms is eaten up, like as a wound if it produce discharges will be consumed by them, so [thinks] he who says that the Son is from the Nature of the Father; now let him who does not say that the Son is like the Father be put outside the Church and be anathema. If we shall say that the Son of God is God, we bring in Two without beginning: we call Him Image of God; he who calls Him 'out from God' Sabellianises. And he who says that he is ignorant of the nativity of God Manicheanizes: if any one shall say that the Essence of the Son is like the Essence of the Father unbegotten, he blasphemes. For just as snow and white lead are similar in whiteness but dissimilar in kind, so also the Essence of the Son is other than the Essence of the Father. But snow has a different whiteness[13] . . .

Be pleased to hear that the Son is like the Father in His operations; like as Angels cannot comprehend the Nature of Archangels, let them please to understand, nor Archangels the Nature of a Cherubin, nor Cherubins the Nature of the Holy Spirit, nor the Holy Spirit the Nature of the Only-begotten, nor the Only-begotten the nature of the Unbegotten God.

14. Now when the Bishop Athanasius was about coming from Antioch to Alexandria, the Arians Eudoxius, Theodore, Sophronius, Euzoius and Hilary took counsel and appointed Lucius, a presbyter of George, to seek audience of the Emperor Jovian at the Palace, and to say what is contained in the copies[13a]. *Now here we have omitted some less necessary matter.*

[11a] Can this be the Hypatius of Philst. ix. 19? For Heliodorus and Stephen, see *Hist. Ar.* p. 294; *de Syn.* 12; Theod. *H.E.* ii. 28, and Gwatkin, *Studies,* pp. 226, 180 note.
[11b] i.e. Eleusius.
[11c] i.e. Eustathius.　　　[12] Lat. 'dominio' for ἀρχή.
[12a] Cf. Matt. iii. 7.　　[13] Text imperfect, 'Externo autem conniventes oculos egressi.'
　　　　　　　　　　　　　　　[13] i.e. the memoranda printed as Appendix to *Letter* 56. § 14 is used, but badly, by Soz. vi. 5.

---

9 Compare 'Chereu' in *Vit. Ant.* 86.　　10 The previous reference to him has dropped out; see *Fest. Ind.* xxxv.
10a Used by Soz. vi. 5.　　11 Read Mechir, i.e. Feb. 14, 364.

X. 15. Now after Jovian, Valentinian and Valens having been somewhat rapidly summoned to the throne, a decree of theirs, circulated everywhere, which also was delivered at Alexandria on Pachon x, Coss. Valentinian and Valens (May 5, 365), to the effect that the Bishops deposed and expelled from their Churches under Constantius,.who had in the time of Julian's reign reclaimed for themselves and taken back their Bishopric, should now be cast out anew from the Churches, a penalty being laid on the courts of a fine of ccc pounds of gold, unless that is they should have [ba]nished the Bishops from the Churches and towns. On which account at Alexandria great confusion and riot arose, insomuch that the whole Church was troubled, since also the officials were few in number with the prefect Flavian and his staff: and on account of the imperial order and the fine of gold they were urgent that the Bishops should leave the town; the Christian multitude resisting and gainsaying the officials and the judge, and maintaining that the Bishop Athanasius did not come under this definition nor under the Imperial order, because neither did Constantius banish him, but even restored him. Likewise also Julian persecuted him; he recalled all, and him for the sake of idolatry he cast out anew, but Jovian brought him back. This opposition and riot went on until the next month Payni, on the xiv day; for on this day the prefect Flavian made a report, declaring that he had consulted the Emperors on this very point which was stirred at Alexandria, and so they all became quiet in a short time[13b].

XI. 16. iv months and xxiv days after, that is on Paophi viii, the Bishop Athanasius left the Church secretly by night, and retired to a villa near the New River[13c]. But the prefect Flavian and Duke Victorinus not knowing that he had retired, on the same night arrived at the Church of Dionysius with a force of soldiers: and having broken the back door, and entered the upper parts of the house in search of the Bishop's apartment, they did not find him, for, not long before he had retired, and he remained, staying at the aforesaid property from the above day, Paophi viii, till Mechir vi, that is iv whole months (Oct. 5 –Jan. 31). After this, the Imperial notary Bresidas, in the same month Mechir came to Alexandria with an Imperial letter, ordering the said Bishop Athanasius to return to Town, and hold the Churches as usual; and on the vii day of the month Mechir, after Coss. Valentinian and Valens, that is Coss. Gratian and Degalaifus, the said notary Bresidas with Duke Victorinus and Flavian the Prefect assembled at the palace and announced to the officers of the courts who were present, and the people, that the Emperors had ordered the Bishop to return to town, and straightway the said Bresidas the notary went forth with the officers of the courts, and a multitude of the people of the Christians to the aforesaid villa, and taking the Bishop Athanasius with the Imperial order, led him in to the Church which is called that of Dionysius on the vii day of the month Mechir.

XII. 17. From Coss. Gratian and Dagalaifus (366) to the next consulships of Lupicinus and Jovinus (367) and that of [Valentinian II. and] Valens II. on Payni xiv (June 8, 368) in [this] Consulship xl [years of the Bishopric] of Athanasius are finished. Out of which [years] he abode at Treveri in Gaul [ii years iv months

xi days[14], and in Italy and the West] xc months and iii days. At Alexandria [and] in uncertain places in hiding, when he was being harassed by Hilary the notary and the Duke, lxxii months and xiv days. In Egypt and Antioch upon journeys xv months and xxii days: upon the property near the new river iv months. The result will be exactly vi[1] months and xvii years and[2] xx days. Moreover, he remained in quiet at Alexandria xxii years and v months x days. But also, he twice stayed a little time outside Alexandria in his last journey and at Tyre and at CP. Accordingly, the result will be as I have stated above, xl years of the episcopate of Athanasius until Payni [x]iv, Coss. Valentinian and Valens. And in the following consulate of Valentinian and Victor, Payni xiv, i year, and in the following consulships of Valentinian [III] and Valens III Payni xiv, and in the following Consulships of Gratian and Probus, [and the next of Modestus and Arintheus], and another consulship of Valentinian [IV] and Valens IV, on Pachon viii he falls asleep (May 3, 373).

XIII. 18. Now in the aforesaid consulship of Lupicinus and Jovinus, Lucius being specially desirous to claim for himself the episcopate of the Arians a long time after he had left Alexandria, arrived in the aforesaid consulship, and entered the town secretly by night on the xxvi day of the month Thoth (Sept. 24, 367): and as it is said, abode in a certain small house, keeping in hiding for that day. But next day he went to a house where his mother was staying; and his arrival being known at once all over the town, the whole people assembled and blamed his entry. And Duke Trajanus and the Prefect were extremely displeased at his irrational and bold arrival, and sent officials to cast him out of the town. So the officials came to Lucius, and considering all of them that the people were angry and very riotous against him they feared to bring him out of the house by themselves, lest he should be killed by the multitude. And they reported this to the judges. And presently the judges themselves, Duke Trajan, and the Prefect Tatianus [came] to the place with many soldiers, entered the house and brought out Lucius themselves at the vii hour of the day, on the xxvii day of Thoth. Now while Lucius was following the judges, and the whole people of the town after them, Christians and Pagans, and of divers religions, all alike with one breath, and with one mind, and of one accord, did not cease, from the house whence he was led, through the middle of the town, as far as the house of the Duke, from shouting, and hurling at him withal insults and criminal charges, and from crying, ' Let him be taken out of the town.' However, the Duke took him into his house, and he stayed with him for the remaining hours of the day, and the whole night, and on the following the xxviii of the same month, the Duke early in the morning, and taking him in charge as far as Nicopolis[3], handed him over to soldiers to be escorted from Egypt.

19. Now whereas Athanasius died on the viii of the month Pachon, the v day before he fell asleep, he ordained Peter, one of the ancient presbyters, Bishop, who carried on the Episcopate, following him in all things. After whom Timothy his B[rother] succeeded to the Episcopate for iv years. After him Theophilus from [being] deacon was ordained Bishop (385). The End.

13[h] §§ 15, 16 are used by Soz. vi. 18. suburb.   13[c] i.e. in the western

14 i.e. July 11, 335, to Nov. 23, 337, see above, p. 496.
1 Migne xi. (misprint).   2 The following 14 words are left out by an error in Sievers.   3 A short distance east of Alexandria, see *Dict. Gr. and Rom. Geog. s.v.*

THE FESTAL LETTERS, AND THEIR INDEX

Or Chronicon Athanasianum

THE latter document is from the hand, it would seem, of the original collector of the Easter Letters of Athanasius (yet see *infr.* note 6ᵃ). He gives, in a paragraph corresponding to each Easter in the episcopate of Athanasius, a summary of the calendar data for the year, a notice of the most important events, and especially particulars as to the Letter for the Easter in question, viz., Whether any peculiar circumstances attended its publication, and whether for some reason the ordinary Letter was omitted.

The variations of practice which had rendered the Paschal Feast a subject of controversy from very early times (see *Dict. Christ. Antiq.* EASTER) had given rise to the custom of the announcement of Easter at a convenient interval beforehand by circular letters. In the third century the Bishops of Alexandria issued such letters (e.g. Dionysius in Eus. *H.E.* vii. 20), and at the Council of Nicæa, where the Easter question was dealt with (*ad Afros.* 2), the Alexandrian see was requested to undertake the duty of announcing the correct date to the principal foreign Churches as well as to its own suffragan sees. (This is doubted in the learned article PASCHAL LETTERS D.C.A. p. 1562, but the statement of Cyril. Alex. in his 'Prologus Paschalis' is express : cf. Ideler 2, 259. The only doubt is, whether the real reference is to *Sardica*, see *Index* xv. and *Ep.* 18.) This was probably due to the astronomical learning for which Alexandria was famous⁴. At any rate we have fragments of the Easter letters of Dionysius and of Theophilus, and a collection of the Letters of Cyril⁴ᵃ.

The Easter letters of Athanasius were, until 1842, only known to us by allusions in Jerome (*de V. illustr.* 87) and others, and by fragments in Cosmas Indicopleustes purporting to be taken from the 2nd, 5th, 6th, 22nd, 24th, 28th, 29th, 40th, and 45th. Cardinal Mai had also shortly before the discovery of the 'Corpus' unearthed a minute fragment of the 13th. But in 1842 Archdeacon Tattam brought home from the Monastery of the Theotokos in the desert of Skete a large number of Syriac MSS., which for over a century European scholars had been vainly endeavouring to obtain. Among these, when deposited in the British Museum, Cureton discovered a large collection of the Festal Letters of Athanasius, with the 'Index,' thus realising the suspicion of Montfaucon (Migne xxvi.) that the lost treasure might be lurking in some Eastern monastery. Another consignment of MSS. from the same source produced some further portions, which were likewise included in the translation revised for the present volume⁵.

(1) *Number of Festal Letters of Athanasius.*—This question, which is of first-rate importance for the chronology of the period, must be regarded as settled, at any rate until some discovery which shall revolutionise all existing data. The number 45, which was the maximum known to antiquity⁵ᵃ, is confirmed by the Index, and by the fact that the citations from Cosmas (see above) tally with the order of the Letters in this Syriac version in every case where the letter is preserved entire, while Letter 39, preserved by a different writer, also tallies with the reference to it in the Index. It is therefore unassailably established on our existing evidence that the last Easter letter of Ath. was his '45th,' in other words that 45 is the *full or normal* number of his festal letters. This clinches the reckoning of the *Index* and *Hist. Aceph.* that he was bishop for 45 Easters (329—373 inclusive), i.e. for parts of 46 years (328—373 inclusive). Moreover it corroborates, and is rivetted firm by, the statement of Cyril. Alex. *Ep.* 1, that Athan. graced the see of Alexandria 'fully 46 years.' ' Il le dit en voulant faire son eloge : de sorte qu'il y a tout lieu de croire qu'il n'a point passé les 46 ans : car *pour peu qu'il fust entré dans la* 47ᵐᵉ *année,* S. Cyrille auroit dû *naturellement luy donner* 47 *ans*⁶.' So Tillemont (viii. 719), whose opinion is all the more valuable from the fact that he is unable to harmonise it with his date for the accession of Ath., and accordingly forgets, p. 720 (*sub. fin.*), what he has said on the previous page.

But we observe that many of the 45 Letters are represented in the 'corpus' by blanks. This is doubtless often the result of accidental loss. But the Index informs us that in several years, owing to his adversities, 'the Pope was unable to write.' This however may be fairly understood to refer to the usual public or circular letter. Often when unable to write this, he sent a few cordial lines to some friend (*Letter* 12) or to the clergy (17, 18) or people (29 ? see notes there) of Alexandria, in order that the true Easter might be kept (cf. the Arian blunder in 340, *Ind.* xii, with the note to Serapion *Letter* 12 from Rome). But occasionally the Index is either corrupt or mistaken, e.g. No. xiii, where the Pope is stated to have written no letter, while yet the 'Corpus' contains one, apparently entire and of the usual public kind. We may therefore still hope for letters or fragments for any of the 'missing' years.

---

⁴ So Leo Magnus (*Ep. ad Marcian. Imp.*) 'apud Ægyptios huius supputationis antiquitus tradita peritia.'
⁴ᵃ We trace differences of opinion in spite of the authority of the Alexandrian Pope in 'Index' xii, xv, xxi, and *Ep.* 18.
⁵ Further details in Migne, P.G. xxvi. 1339 *sqq.* and Preface (by Williams?) to Oxford Transl. of *Fest. Epp.* (Parker, 1854.)
⁵ᵃ The very late Arabic Life of Ath. alone gives 47 (Migne

xxv. p. ccli.), a statement which we may safely ignore in view of the general character of the document which is 'crowded with incredible trivialities and follies' (Montf.), outbidding by far the 'unparalleled rubbish' (id.) of the worst of the Greek biographies (see Migne xxv. p. liv. *sq.*).
⁶ The italics are ours. Cf. Rufin. *H.E.* ii. 3, 'xlvi *anno* sacerdotii sui.'

(2) The Festal Letters are fully worthy to rank with any extant writings of Athanasius. The same warmth, vigour, and simplicity pervades them as we find elsewhere in his writings, especially in such gems as the letter to Dracontius (*Ep.* 49). Their interest, however (apart from chronology), is mainly personal and practical. Naturally the use and abuse of Fast and Festival occupy a prominent place throughout. Repeatedly he insists on the joyfulness of Christian feasts, and on the fact that they are typical of, and intended to colour, the whole period of the Christian's life. We gather from *Ep.* 12 that Lent was kept less strictly in Egypt than in some other Christian countries. He insists not only upon fasting, but upon purity and charity, especially toward the poor (*Ep.* 1. 11, cf. *Ep.* 47. 4, &c.). We trace the same ready command of Scripture, the same grave humour in the unexpected turn given to some familiar text (*Ep.* 39) as we are used to in Athanasius. The Eucharist is a feeding upon the Word (4. 3), and to be prepared for by amendment of life, repentance, and confession of sin (i.e. to God, *Ep.* 7. 10). Of special importance is the Canon of Holy Scripture in *Ep.* 39, on which see Prolegg. ch. iv § 4.

It should be observed that the interval before Easter at which notice was given varied greatly. Some letters (e.g. 1, 2, 20) by a natural figure of speech, refer to the Feast as actually come ; but others (17, 18) were certainly written as early as the preceding Easter. Letter 4 was written not long before Lent, but was (§ 1) unusually late. The statement of Cassian referred to below (note to *Ep.* 17) is therefore incorrect at any rate for our period.

(3) *The Index to the Festal Letters.*—This chronicle, so constantly referred to throughout this volume, is of uncertain date, but probably (upon internal evidence) only 'somewhat later' (Hefele, *E. Tr.* vol. ii. p. 50) than Athanasius himself. Its special value is in the points where it agrees with the *Hist. Aceph.* (*supr.* Prolegg. ch. v.), where we recognise the accredited reckoning of the Alexandrian Church as represented by Cyril and Proterius (see Tillem. *ubi supr.*). The writer undoubtedly makes occasional slips (cf. *Index* iii. with *Letter* iv. and p. 512, note 1, *Index* xiii. with *Letter* 6a xiii. !), and the text would be a miracle if it had come down to us uncorrupt (see notes *passim*) : but on the main dates he is consistent with himself, with the *Chron. Aceph.* and (so far as they come in contact) with the notices of the Alexandrian bishops above mentioned.

The writer's m e t h o d, however, must be attended to if we are to avoid a wrong impression as to his accuracy. *Firstly*, his y e a r is not the Julian but the Egyptian year (*infr.* Table C) from Aug. 29 to Aug. 28. Each year is designated by the *new* consuls who come into office in the fifth month. *Secondly*, in each year he takes a l e a d i n g e v e n t or events, round which he groups antecedent or consequent facts, which often belong to other years. Two or three examples will make this clear. (*a*) Year Aug. 30, 335—Aug. 28, 336 : leading event, exile of Athanasius (he reaches CP. Oct. 30, 335, leaves for Gaul [Feb. 7], both in the same Egyptian year). Antecedent : His departure for Tyre July 11, 335, at end of *previous Egyptian Year*. (β) The 'eventful' year Aug. 337—Aug. 338 : leading event, triumphant return of Athanasius from Gaul, Oct. 21, 337. Antecedent : death of Constantine on previous 22nd of May (i.e. 337 7). (γ) Year 342-3 : leading event, Council of Sardica (summons issued, at any rate, before end of Aug. 343). Consequent events : temporary collapse of Arian party and recantation of Ursacius and Valens (344—347 ? Further examples in Gwatkin, *Studies*, p. 105). Bearing this in mind, the discriminating student will derive most important help from the study of the Index : when its data agree with those derived from other good sources, they must be allowed first-rate authority. This is the principle followed in the Prolegomena (ch. v.) and throughout this volume. On the main points in dispute, as shewn above, we have to reckon with a compact uniform chronological system, checked and counter-checked by careful calculations (*Hist. Aceph.*), and transmitted by two independent channels ; in agreement, moreover, as concerns the prior and posterior limits, with the reckoning adopted by the successors of Athanasius in the see.

N.B.—The *translation* of the Index and Festal Letters is revised by Miss Payne Smith from that contained in the Oxford 'Library of the Fathers.' A German translation by Larsow was published at Berlin 1852. The Latin Version (from an Italian translation) of Card. Mai is in Migne, xxvi. 1351 *sqq.*

The following Tables bear specially on the Festal Index.

TABLE C.   *The Egyptian Year.*

After the final settlement of Egypt by Augustus as a province of the Roman Empire, the use of the Julian form of computation was established in Alexandria, the first day of the new Calendar being fixed to the 29th of August, the 1st of Thot of the year in which the innovation took place ; from which period, six, instead of five, supplementary days were added at the end of every fourth year; so that the form of the Alexandrian year was as follows. *The months from Phamenoth 5 (Mar. 1) onwards are unaffected by leap-year.*

			Pharmuthi		27 March
Thot	. . .	29 August	Pachon	.	26 April
Paophi	. .	28 September	Paoni (Payni)	.	26 May
Athyr	. .	28 October	Epiphi	.	25 June
Choiak	. .	27 November	Mesori	.	25 July
Tybi	. .	27 December	Epagomena	.	24 August
Mechir	. .	26 January			
Phamenoth	. .	25 February			

N.B.—In leap-years, the *Diocletian* year (see p. 503, note 4) began on the previous Aug. 30, which was accordingly the First of Thot, owing to the additional 'epagomenon' which preceded it. Accordingly all the months *to Phamenoth inclusive* begin a day late. Then, the Julian intercalary day coming in as Feb. 29, Pharmuthi and the succeeding months begin as shewn above. (See Ideler, vol. 1, pp. 161, 164, also 140, 142.)

6a Some phenomena might suggest (Hefele, ii. 88, note) that the *Index* was originally prefixed to another collection of the letters, and was copied by a collector or transcriber of our present corpus ; cf. *Index* xiii., note 17b, and p. 527, note 1.

7 Misunderstood by Hefele, vol. ii. p. 88 (*E. Tra.*).

TABLE D

OF THE CHRONOLOGICAL INFORMATION GIVEN IN THE INDEX TO THE PASCHAL LETTERS

N.B.—The Year of our Lord, the Golden Numbers, and Dominical Letter, and the date of Easter according to the Modern Reckoning, are added. The age of the Moon on Easter-day is apparently given from observations or reckoned by some lost system (see *Index* x. xxii.); in about one case out of three it varies from the modern reckoning, perhaps once or twice from corruption of text. The Epact is a day too little for 342, 344, 361, 362, 363 (see Galle in Larsow *F. B.* p. 48, *sqq.*).

Number of Letter.	Year of Diocl.	Year of our Lord.	Easter Day.			Day of Lunar Month.	Epact (age of Moon on Mar. 22).	Sunday Letter and Concurrentes.	Indictⁿ.	Golden Numbers.
			Egyptian Calendar.	Roman Calendar.	Modern Reckoning					
...	44	328	19 Pharm.	XVIII Kal. Mai	14 April	18	25	1 F	1	6
I	45	329	11 Pharm.	VIII Id. April	6 April	22	6	2 E	2	7
II	46	330	24 Pharm.	XIII Kal. Mai	19 April	15	17	3 D	3	8
III	47	331	16 Pharm.	III Id. April	11 April	18	28	4 C	4	9
IV	48	332	7 Pharm.	IV Non. April	2 April	20	9	6 A	5	10
V	49	333	20 Pharm.	XVII Kal. Mai	¹15 April	15	20	7 G	6	11
VI	50	334	12 Pharm.	VII Id. April	7 April	17	1	1 F	7	12
VII	51	335	4 Pharm.	III Kal. April	30 March	20	12	2 E	8	13
VIII	52	336	23 Pharm.	XIV Kal. Mai	18 April	20	23	4 C	9	14
IX	53	337	8 Pharm.	III Non. April	3 April	16	4	5 B	10	15
X	54	338	30 Phamᵗʰ.	VII Kal. April	26 March	18½	15	6 A	11	16
XI	55	339	20 Pharm.	XVII Kal. Mai	15 April	20	26	7 G	12	17
XII	56	340	4 Pharm.	III Kal. April	30 March	15	7	2 E	13	18
XIII	57	341	24 Pharm.	XIII Kal. Mai	19 April	16	18	3 D	14	19
XIV	58	342	16 Pharm.	III Id. April	11 April	16	29	4 C	15	1
XV	59	343	1 Pharm.	VI Kal. April	27 March	15	11	5 B	1	2
XVI	60	344	20 Pharm.	XVII Kal. Mai	15 April	19	21	7 G	2	3
XVII	61	345	12 Pharm.	VII Id. April	7 April	19	3	1 F	3	4
XVIII	62	346	4 Pharm.	III Kal. April	²30 March	21	14	2 E	4	5
XIX	63	347	17 Pharm.	Prid. Id. April	12 April	15	25	3 D	5	6
XX	64	348	8 Pharm.	III Non. April	3 April	18	6	5 B	6	7
XXI	65	349	30 Phamᵗʰ.	VII Kal. April	³26 March	19	17	6 A	7	8
XXII	66	350	13 Pharm.	VI Id. April	8 April	19	28	7 G	8	9
XXIII	67	351	5 Pharm.	Prid. Kal. April	31 March	18	9	1 F	9	10
XXIV	68	352	24 Pharm.	XIII Kal. Mai	19 April	18	20	3 D	10	11
XXV	69	353	16 Pharm.	III Id. April	11 April	21	1	4 C	11	12
XXVI	70	354	1 Pharm.	VI Kal. April	27 March	17	12	5 B	12	13
XXVII	71	355	21 Pharm.	XVI Kal. Mai	16 April	18	23	6 A	13	14
XXVIII	72	356	12 Pharm.	VII Id. April	7 April	17	4	1 F	14	15
XXIX	73	357	27 Phamᵗʰ.	X Kal. April	23 March	17	15	2 E	15	16
XXX	74	358	17 Pharm.	Prid. Id. April	12 April	17	26	3 D	1	17
XXXI	75	359	9 Pharm.	Prid. Non. April	4 April	20	7	4 C	2	18
XXXII	76	360	28 Pharm.	IX Kal. Mai	23 April	21	18	6 A	3	19
XXXIII	77	361	13 Pharm.	VI Id. April	8 April	17	29	7 G	4	1
XXXIV	78	362	5 Pharm.	Prid. Kal. April	31 March	25	⁴10	1 F	5	2
XXXV	79	363	25 Pharm.	XII Kal. Mai	20 April	20	21	2 E	6	3
XXXVI	80	364	9 Pharm.	Prid. Non. April	4 April	16	3	4 C	7	4
XXXVII	81	365	1 Pharm.	VI Kal. April	27 March	19	14	5 B	8	5
XXXVIII	82	366	21 Pharm.	XVI Kal. Mai	16 April	20	25	6 A	9	6
XXXIX	83	367	6 Pharm.	Kal. April	1 April	16	6	7 G	10	7
XL	84	368	25 Pharm.	XII Kal. Mai	20 April	16	17	2 E	11	8
XLI	85	369	17 Pharm.	Prid. Id. April	12 April	15	28	3 D	12	9
XLII	86	370	2 Pharm.	V Kal. April	28 March	15	9	4 C	13	10
XLIII	87	371	22 Pharm.	XV Kal. Mai	17 April	16	20	5 B	14	11
XLIV	88	372	13 Pharm.	VI Id. April	8 April	19	1	7 G	15	12
XLV	89	373	5 Pharm.	Prid. Kal. April	31 March	21	12	1 F	1	13

¹ According to the usual Antegregorian rule, Easter would fall on April 22.   ² According to the usual rule, Easter would fall on March 23; see *Letter* 18, note 3.   ³ According to rule, Easter would fall on April 23, which perhaps was the day really observed, as it agrees with the age of the moon; but see note on *Index No. xxi.*   ⁴ Read Moon 20, Epact 11.

INDEX.

An Index of the months of each year, and of the days, and of the Indictions, and of the Consulates, and of the Governors in Alexandria, and of all the Epacts, and of those [days] which are named 'of the Gods [1],' and the reason [any Letter] was not sent, and the returns from exile [2]—from the Festal Letters of Pope Athanasius.

The Festal Letters of Athanasius, Bishop of Alexandria, which he sent year by year, to the several cities and all the provinces subject to him; that is, from Pentapolis, and on to Libya, Ammoniaca, the greater and the lesser Oasis, Egypt, and Augustamnica, with the Heptanomis of [3] the upper and middle Thebais; [commencing] from the 44th [4] year of the Diocletian Era, in which the Paschal Festival was on xvi [5] Pharmuthi; xviii Kal. Mai; xviii Moon; when Alexander, his predecessor, having departed this life on xxii Pharmuthi [6], he [Athan.] succeeded him after the Paschal festival on xiv Pauni, Indict. i, Januarius and Justus being Consuls, the governor Zenius of Italy being the Præfect of Egypt, Epact xxv; Gods, i.

I. (Aug. 29, 328, to Aug. 28, A.D. 329.) In this year, Easter-day was on xi Pharmuthi; viii. Id. Ap.; xxii Moon; Coss. Constantinus Aug. viii, Constantinus Cæs. IV; the same governor Zenius being Præfect of Egypt; Indict. ii; Epact vi; Gods, ii. This was the first Letter he [Athan.] sent; for he was ordained Bishop in the preceding year after the Paschal feast, Alexander, as is known, having despatched one for that year, before he was released from life. This was in the 45th of the Diocletian Æra.

II. (329–330.) In this year, Easter-day was on xxiv Pharmuthi; xiii Kal. Mai; xv Moon; Coss. Gallicianus, Symmachus; the governor Magninianus the Cappadocian being Præfect of Egypt; Indict. iii; Epact xvii; Gods, iii. In this year he went through the Thebais.

III. (330–331.) In this year, Easter-day was on xvi Pharmuthi; xviii Moon; iii Id. Ap.; Coss. Annius Bassus, Ablavius; the governor Hyginus [6a] of Italy, Præfect of Egypt; Epact xxviii; Indict. iv. He sent this Letter while journeying on his return from the Imperial Court. For in this year he went to the Imperial Court to the Emperor Constantine the Great, having been summoned before him, on account of an accusation his enemies made, that he had been appointed when too young. He appeared, was thought worthy of favour and honour, and returned [6b] when the fast was half finished.

IV. (331–332.) In this year, Easter-day was on xvii [7] Pharmuthi; xx Moon; iv Non. Apr.; Epact ix; Gods, vi; Coss. Pacatianus, Hilarianus; the same governor Hyginus, Præfect of Egypt; Indict. v. In this year he went through Pentapolis, and was in Ammoniaca.

V. (332–333.) In this year, Easter-day was on xx Pharmuthi; xv Moon; xvii Kal. Mai; Epact xx; Coss. Dalmatius, Zenophilus; the governor Paternus [8], Præfect of Egypt; Indict. vi.

VI. (333–334.) In this year, Easter-day was on xii Pharmuthi; xvii Moon; vii Id. Apr.; Indict. vii; Epact i; Gods, i; Coss. Optatus, Paulinus; the same governor Paternus [8a] Præfect of Egypt. In this year

he went through the lower country. In it he was summoned to a Synod, his enemies having previously devised mischief against him in Cæsarea of Palestine; but becoming aware of the conspiracy, he excused himself from attending.

VII. (334–335.) In this year, Easter-day was on xiv [8b] Pharmuthi; xx Moon; iii Kal. Ap.; Indict. viii; Epact xii; Gods, ii; Coss. Constantius [8c], Albinus; the same governor Paternus, Præfect of Egypt.

VIII. (335–336.) In this year, Easter-day was on xxiii Pharmuthi; xx Moon; xiv Kal. Mai; Indict. ix; Epact xxiii; Gods, iii; Coss. Nepotianus, Facundus; the governor Philagrius, the Cappadocian, Præfect of Egypt. In this year he went to that Synod of his enemies which was assembled at Tyre. Now he journeyed from this place on xvii Epiphi [9], but when a discovery was made of the plot against him, he removed thence and fled in an open boat to Constantinople. Arriving there on ii Athyr [10], after eight days he presented himself before the Emperor Constantine, and spoke plainly. But his enemies, by various secret devices, influenced the Emperor, who suddenly condemned him to exile, and he set out on the tenth of Athyr [11] to Gaul, to Constans Cæsar, the son of Augustus. On this account he wrote no Festal Letter.

IX. (336–7.) In this year, Easter-day was on viii Pharmuthi; xvi Moon; iv [11a] Non. Ap.; Indict. x; Epact iv; Gods, v; Coss. Felicianus, Titianus; the governor Philagrius, the Cappadocian, Præfect of Egypt. He was in Treviri of Gaul, and on this account was unable to write a Festal Letter.

X. (337–8.) In this year, Easter-day was on xxx Phamenoth; vii Kal. Ap.; xix [11b] Moon; Indict. xi; Epact xv; Gods, vi; Coss. Ursus, Polemius; the governor Theodorus [12], of Heliopolis, Præfect of Egypt. In this year, Constantine having died on xxvii Pachon [12a], Athanasius, now liberated, returned from Gaul triumphantly on xxvii [13] Athyr. In this year, too, there were many events. Antony, the great leader, came to Alexandria, and though he remained there only two days, shewed himself wonderful in many things, and healed many. He went away on the third of Messori [14].

XI. (338–9.) In this year, Easter-day was on xx Pharmuthi; xx Moon; xvii Kal. Mai; Epact xxvi; Gods, vii; Indict. xii; Coss. Constantius II, Constans I [15]; the governor Philagrius, the Cappadocian, Præfect of Egypt. In this year, again, there were many tumults. On the xxii Phamenoth [16] he was pursued in the night, and the next day he fled from the Church of Theonas, after he had baptized many. Then, four days after, Gregorius the Cappadocian entered the city as Bishop.

XII. (339–340.) In this year, Easter-day was on xiv [17] Pharmuthi; xv Moon; iii Kal. Ap.; Epact vii; Gods, ii; Indict. xiii; Coss. Acyndinus, Proclus; the same governor Philagrius, Præfect of Egypt. Gregorius continued his acts of violence, and therefore [Ath.] wrote no Festal Letter. The Arians proclaimed [Easter] on xxvii Phamenoth, and were much ridiculed on account of this error. Then altering it in the middle of the fast, they kept it with us on iv [17] Pharmuthi, as above. He [Athanasius] gave notice of it to the presbyters of Alexandria in a short note, not being able to send a Letter as usual, on account of his flight and the treachery.

XIII. (340–341.) In this year, Easter-day was on xxiv Pharmuthi; xvi Moon; xiii. Kal. Mai; Epact xviii;

---

1 The 'Gods' correspond to the Concurrentes,' i.e. to the days of the week upon which Mar. 24 occurs in the year in question. (See Table, and Ideler, 2. 261), and so to the 'Sunday letters,' which follow the 'gods' in inverse order, 'a' corresponding to years when there were 6 'gods,' b to 5, &c.. f to 1, g to 7.
2 The meaning of these words is doubtful. Larsow renders them 'the answers from abroad.'   3 Read 'and.'
4 i.e. the year beginning Aug. 30, 327 (328 being leap-year). The 'Diocletian' era, or era 'of the martyrs,' was that used by the Egyptian Christians. It is incorrectly described in D.C.A. s.v. Era; see Ideler, *ut supr.*
5 Read xix (April 14). The corruption is easy in Syriac.
6 April 17.   6a The heading to *Ep.* 3 gives Florentius.
6b This ought to have been placed under iv; but see p. 512, note 7.   7 Read vii.   8 Vid. *Ep. Fest.* v. n. 2.
8a The headings of Letters 6, 7, give Philagrius.

8b Read iv, as below, No. xii.   8c i.e. Julius C.; the Syr. has Constantinus, by an error.   9 July 11, 335.   10 Oct. 30, 335.
11 Read 'Mechir,' Feb. 5, 336 (Gwatkin, p. 137, the correction is due to Sievers).   11a Read iii.   11b 'xviii½,' heading of *Letter* 10.
12 Superseded by Philagrius (see heading, and Prolegg. ch. ii. § 6 (1) note).   12a May 22, 337.   13 Nov. 23, 337.
14 July 27, 338, *supr.* p. 214.   15 The Syriac has erroneously Constantius I., Constans II.   16 Mar. 18, 339.   17 Read iv. as above, No. vii.

Gods, iii; Indict. xiv; Coss. Marcellinus, Probinus; the governor Longinus, of Nicæa, Præfect of Egypt. Augustamnica was separated [17a]. On account of Gregorius continuing in the city, and exercising violence, although his illness commenced, the Pope did not write a Festal Letter even this time [17b].

XIV. (341–2.) In this year, Easter-day was on xvi Pharmuthi; xx [18] Moon; iii Id.' Ap.; Epact xxix; Gods, iv; Indict. xv; Coss. Constantius III, Constans II; the governor Longinus of Nicæa, Præfect of Egypt. Because Gregorius was in the city, [though] severely ill, the Pope was unable to send [any Letter].

XV. (342–3.) In this year, Easter-day was on i Pharmuthi; xv Moon; vi Kal. Ap.; Epact xi; Gods, v; Indict. i; Coss. Placidus, Romulus; the same governor Longinus, of Nicæa, Præfect of Egypt. In this year the Synod of Sardica was held [19]; and when the Arians had arrived, they returned to Philippopolis, for Philagrius gave them this advice there. In truth, they were blamed everywhere, and were even anathematised by the Church of Rome, and having written a recantation to Pope Athanasius, Ursacius and Valens were put to shame. There was an agreement made at Sardica respecting Easter, and a decree was issued to be binding for fifty years, which the Romans and Alexandrians everywhere announced in the usual manner. Again he [Athan.] wrote a Festal Letter.

XVI. (343–4.) In this year, Easter-day was on xx Pharmuthi; xix Moon; xvii Kal. Mai; Epact xxi; Gods, vi[i], Coss. Leontius, Sallustius; the governor Palladius, of Italy, Præfect of Egypt; Indict. ii. Being at Naissus on his return from the Synod, he there celebrated Easter [20]. Of this Easter-day he gave notice in few words to the presbyters of Alexandria, but he was unable to do so to the country.

XVII. (344–5.) In this year, Easter-day was on xii Pharmuthi; xviii Moon; vii. Id. Ap.; Epact ii; Gods, i; Indict. iii; Coss. Amantius, Albinus; the governor Nestorius of Gaza, Præfect of Egypt. Having travelled to Aquileia, he kept Easter there. Of this Easter-day, he gave notice in few words to thé presbyters of Alexandria, but not to the country.

XVIII. (345–6.) In this year, Easter-day was on iv Pharmuthi; xxi [1] Moon; iii Kal. Ap.; Epact xiv; Gods, ii; Indict. iv; Coss. Constantius [2] Aug. IV, Constans Aug. III; the same governor Nestorius of Gaza, Præfect of Egypt. Gregorius having died on the second of Epiphi [3], he returned from Rome and Italy, and entered the city and the Church. Moreover he was thought worthy of a grand reception, for on the xxiv Paophi [4], the people and all those in authority met him a hundred miles distant, and he continued in honour. He had already sent the Festal Letter for this year, in few words, to the presbyters.

XIX. (346–7.) In this year, Easter-day was on xvii Pharmuthi; xv. Moon; Prid. Id. Apr.; Epact xxv; Gods, iii; Indict. v; Coss. Rufinus, Eusebius; the same governor Nestorius of Gaza, Præfect of Egypt. He wrote this Letter while residing here in Alexandria.

giving notice of some things which he had not been able to do before.

XX. (347–8.) In this year, Easter-day was on viii Pharmuthi; xviii Moon; iii Non. Ap.; Epact vi; Gods, v [4a] Indict. vi; Coss. Philippus, Salia; the same governor Nestorius of Gaza, Præfect of Egypt. This Letter also he sent while residing in Alexandria.

XXI. (348–9.) In this year, Easter-day was on xxx Phamenoth; ... xix Moon, ... vii Kal. Ap.; Epact xvii; Gods, vi; Indict. vii. But because the Romans refused, for they said they held a tradition from the Apostle Peter not to pass the twenty-sixth day of Pharmuthi, nor . . the thirtieth of Phamenoth, xxi Moon ....[5], vii Kal. Ap.; Coss. Limenius, Catullinus; the same governor Nestorius of Gaza, Præfect of Egypt. He sent this also while residing in Alexandria.

XXII. (349–50.) In this year, Easter-day was on xiii Pharmuthi; xix Moon, the second hour; vi Id. Ap.; Epact xxviii; Gods, vii; Indict. viii; Coss. Sergius, Nigrianus; the same governor Nestorius of Gaza, Præfect of Egypt. In this year, Constans was slain by Magnentius, and Constantius held the empire alone; then he wrote to the Pope [Athan.], telling him to fear nothing because of the death of Constans, but to confide in him as he had done in Constans while living.

XXIII. (350–1.) In this year, Easter-day was on v Pharmuthi; Moon xviii; Prid. Kal. Ap.; Epact ix; Gods, i; Indict. ix; the Consulship after that of Sergius and Nigrianus; the same governor Nestorius of Gaza, again Præfect of Egypt.

XXIV. (351–2.) In this year, Easter-day was on xxiv Pharmuthi; xviii Moon; xiii Kal. Mai; Epact xx; Gods, iii; Indict. x; Coss. Constantius Aug. V, Constantius Cæsar I; the same governor Nestorius of Gaza, Præfect of Egypt. Gallus was proclaimed Cæsar [6], and his name changed into Constantius.

XXV. (352–3.) In this year, Easter-day was on xvi Pharmuthi; xxi Moon; iii Id. Ap.; Epact i; Gods, iv; Indict. xi; Coss. Constantius Aug. VI, Constantius Cæsar II; the governor Sebastianus of Thrace, Præfect of Egypt. In this year, Serapion [7], Bishop of Thmuis, and Triadelphus of Nicion, and the presbyters Petrus and Astricius, with others, were sent to the emperor Constantius, through fear of mischief from the Arians. They returned, having effected nothing. In' this year, Montanus, Silentiarius of the Palace, [was sent] . . . against [the] [8] Bishop, but, a tumult having been excited, he retired, having failed to effect anything.

XXVI. (353–4.) In this year, Easter-day was on i [8a] Pharmuthi; xvii Moon; vi Kal. Ap.; Epact xii; Gods, v; Indict. xii; Coss. Constantius Aug. VII, Constantius Cæsar III.; the same governor Sebastianus of Thrace, Præfect of Egypt.

XXVII. (354–5.) In this year, Easter-day was on xxi Pharmuthi; xviii Moon; xvi Kal. Mai; Epact xxiii; Gods, vi; Indict. xiii; Coss. Arbetion, Lollianus; the governor Maximus the Elder of Nicæa, Præfect of Egypt. In this year, Diogenes, the Secretary of the Emperor, entered with the design of seizing the Bishop. But he, too, having raged in vain, went away quietly.

XXVIII. (355–6.) In this year, Easter-day was on xii Pharmuthi; xvii Moon; vii Id. Ap.; Epact iv; Gods, i; Indict. xiv; Coss. Constantius Aug. VIII, Julianus Cæsar I; the same governor Maximus the

---

[17a] i.e. 'made a separate province.' This had been known (Gothofr. *in Cod. Th.* xii. i. 34) to fall between 325 and 342; and Augustamnica is not mentioned as a province in 338-9, *supr.* p. 101.

[17b] This and the similar notice at the end of xiv are incorrect. The Index may have been written for a collection which lacked Letters 13, 14.

[18] The Syriac has xvi, which is an error

[19] The summons for the Council was issued 'in this year,' i.e. before August. 343, but the proceedings fall in the autumn and winter, i.e. in the next Egyptian year, and the sequel (about Ursac. and Valens) refers to what took place about 347.

[20] Easter, i.e. Apr. 15, 344, at Nish, or Nissa, in Servia.

[1] The Syriac in this place has xxiv. But we find **xxi in the** heading to the Letter itself.

[2] The Syriac has Constantinus.

[3] June 26 of the previous year (345).   [4] Oct. 21, 346.

[4a] Text 'iv.'

[5] The text is imperfect and apparently very corrupt; 'xix Moon' fits Pharm. 28 (Apr. 23), which was the true Easter, and probably observed at Alexandria, while the Romans, refusing to go beyond Apr. 21, kept Easter on Pham. 30 (Mar. 26), on which day the Moon was really xxi days old. See Table D, and *Letter* 18. *Letter* 21 is lost.

[6] In the previous year, Mar. 15, 351.   [7] Cf. *Letters* 49, 54.

[8] Text corrupt.   [8a] Text 'iv

Elder of Nicæa, Præfect of Egypt, who was succeeded by Cataphronius of Byblus. In this year, Syrianus Dux, having excited a tumult in the Church on the thirteenth of Mechir, on the fourteenth[9] at night entered Theonas with his soldiers; but he was unable to capture [Athanasius], for he escaped in a miraculous manner.

XXIX (356–7.) In this year, Easter-day was on xxvii Phamenoth; xvii Moon; x Kal. Ap.; Epact xv; Gods, ii; Indict. xv; Coss. Constantius Aug. IX, Julianus Cæsar II; the same governor Cataphronius, of Byblus, Præfect of Egypt, to whom succeeded Parnassius. Then Georgius entered on the thirtieth of Mechir, and acted with excessive violence. But Athanasius, the Bishop, had fled, and was sought for in the city with much oppression, many being in danger on this account. Therefore no Festal Letter was written[9a].

XXX. (357–8.) In this year, Easter-day was on xvii Pharmuthi; Prid. Id. Ap.; xvii Moon; Epact xxvi; Gods, iii; Indict. i; Coss. Tatianus, Cerealis; the governor Parius of Corinth, Præfect of Egypt. Athanasius, the Bishop, lay concealed in the city of Alexandria. But Georgius left on the fifth of Paophi[9b] being driven away by the multitude. On this account, neither this year was the Pope able to send a Festal Letter.

XXXI. (358–9.) In this year, Easter-day was on ix[9c] Pharmuthi; Prid. Non. Ap.; xx Moon; Epact vii; the same governor Parius, who was succeeded by Italicianus of Italy for three months; after him Faustinus, of Chalcedon. Neither this year did the Pope write [any Letter].

XXXII. (359–60.) In this year, Easter-day was on xxviii Pharmuthi; ix Kal. Mai; xxi Moon; Epact xviii; Gods, vi; Indict. iii; Coss. Constantius Aug. X, Julianus Cæsar III; the governor Faustinus, of Chalcedon, Præfect of Egypt. This Præfect and Artemius Dux, having entered a private house and a small cell, in search of Athanasius the Bishop, bitterly tortured Eudæmonis, a perpetual virgin. On this account no [Letter] was written this year.

XXXIII. (360–1.) In this year, Easter-day was on xiii Pharmuthi; vi Id. Ap.; xvii Moon; Epact xxix; Gods, vii; Indict. iv; Coss. Taurus, Florentius; the same governor Faustinus[10], Præfect of Egypt, who was succeeded by Gerontius the Armenian. He was unable to send [a Letter]. In this year, Constantius died[10a], and Julianus holding the empire alone, there was a cessation of the persecution against the Orthodox. For commands were issued everywhere from the emperor Julianus, that the Orthodox ecclesiastics who had been persecuted in the time of Constantius should be let alone.

XXXIV. (361–2.) In this year, Easter-day was on v[10b] Pharmuthi; Prid. Kal. Ap.; xxv Moon; Epact x; Gods, i; Indict. v; Coss. Mamertinus, Nevitta; the same governor Gerontius, who was succeeded by Olympus of Tarsus. In this year, in Mechir, Athanasius the Bishop returned to the Church, after his flight, by the command of Julianus Augustus, who pardoned all the Bishops and Clergy in exile, as was before said. This year, then, he wrote [a Letter].

XXXV. (362–3.) In this year, Easter-day was on xxv Pharmuthi; xii Kal. Mai; xx Moon; Epact xxi; Gods, ii; Indict. vi; Coss. Julianus Augustus IV, Sallustius; the same governor Olympus, Præfect of Egypt. Pythiodorus Trico of Thebes, a Philosopher, brought a decree of Julianus on the twenty-

seventh of Paophi, and set it in action against the Bishop first, and uttered many threats. So he [Athan.] left the city at once, and went up to the Thebais. And when after eight months Julianus died, and his death was announced, Athanasius returned secretly by night to Alexandria. Then on the eighth of Thoth, he embarked[10c] at the Eastern Hierapolis, and met the emperor Jovian, by whom he was dismissed with honour. He sent this Festal Letter to all the country, while being driven by persecution from Memphis to the Thebais, and it was delivered as usual.

XXXVI. (363–4). In this year, Easter-day was on ix Pharmuthi; Prid. Non. Ap.; xvi Moon; Epact iii; Gods, iv; Indict. vii; Coss. Jovianus Aug., Varronianus; the governor Aerius, of Damascus, Præfect; who was succeeded by Maximus of Rapheotis, and he again by Flavianus the Illyrian. In this year, the Pope returned to Alexandria and the Church on the twenty-fifth of Mechir. He sent the Festal Letter, according to custom, from Antioch to all the Bishops in all the province.

XXXVII. (364–5.) In this year, Easter-day was on i Pharmuthi; v[i] Kal. Ap.; xix Moon; Epact xiv; Gods, v; Indict. viii; Coss. Valentinianus Aug. I, Valens Aug.; the same Flavianus, the Illyrian, being governor. We received the Cæsareum; but again, the Pope being persecuted[11] with accusations, withdrew[12] to the garden of the new river. But a few days[13] after, Barasides, the notary, came to him with the Præfect, and obtained an entrance for him into the Church. Then, an earthquake happening on the twenty-seventh of Epiphi[13a], the sea returned from the East, and destroyed many persons, and much damage was caused.

XXXVIII. (365–6.) In this year, Easter-day was on xxi Pharmuthi; xvi Kal. Mai; xx Moon; Epact xxv; Gods, vi; Indict. ix; in the first year of the Consulship of Gratianus, the son of Augustus, and Daglaiphus; the same governor Flavianus, Præfect. On the twenty-seventh of Epiphi, the heathen made an attack, and the Cæsareum was burnt, and consequently many of the citizens suffered great distress, while the authors of the calamity were condemned and exiled. After this, Proclianus the Macedonian, became chief.

XXXIX. (366–7.) In this year, Easter-day was on vi[14] Pharmuthi; Kal. Ap.; xvi Moon; Epact vi; Gods, vii; Indict. x; Coss. Lupicinus, Jovinus; the same Proclianus being governor, who was succeeded by Tatianus of Lycia. In this year, when Lucius had attempted an entrance on the twenty-sixth of Thoth[15], and lay concealed by night in a house on the side of the enclosure of the Church; and when Tatianus the Præfect and Trajanus Dux brought him out, he left the city, and was rescued in a wonderful manner, while the multitude sought to kill him. In this year he [Ath.] wrote, forming a Canon of the Holy Scriptures.

XL. (367–8.) In this year, Easter-day was on xxv Pharmuthi; xii Kal. Mai; xvi Moon; Epact xvii; Gods, ii; Indict. xi; Coss. Valentinianus Aug. II, Valens Aug. II; the same governor Tatianus, Præfect. He [Athan.] began to build anew the Cæsareum, on the 6th of Pachon, having been honoured with an imperial command by Trajanus Dux. He also discovered the incendiaries, and immediately cleared away the rubbish of the burnt ruins, and restored the edifice in the month Pachon.

XLI. (368–9.) In this year, Easter-day was on xvii[16] Pharmuthi; Prid. Id. Ap.; xv Moon; Epact xxviii;

9 Feb. 8—9, 356.
9b Oct. 2, 358.
10 Or Pausanias. This name is written vaguely in the Syriac, varying in all the three places in which it occurs.
10a Nov. 23, 361.
9a But see *Letter* 29, note 1.
9c Text 'xix.'
10b Text 'xv.'

10c Prolegg. ch. v. § 3, h.
13 Feb. i. 366.
13a July 21, 365; so also *Chron. Pasch.* and Amm. Marc. xxvi.
15, specially mentioning Alexandria.
15 Sep. 24, 367; cf. *Hist. Aceph.*
11 May 5, 365.
12 Oct. 5, 365.
14 Text 'xvi.'
16 Text 'xxvii.'

Gods, iii ; Indict. xii ; Coss. Valentinianus (son of Augustus) I, Victor; the same Tatianus being governor. The Pope began to build that Church in Mendidium which bears his name, on the twenty-fifth [17] of the month Thoth, at the beginning of the eighty-fifth year of the Diocletian Era.

XLII. (369–70.) In this year, Easter-day was on ii Pharmuthi ; v [18] Kal. Ap. ; xv Moon; Epact ix ; Gods, iv ; Indict. xiii ; Coss. Valentinianus Aug. III, Valens Aug. III; the same Tatianus being governor, who was succeeded by Olympius Palladius, of Samosata. The Pope finished the Church, called after his name, at the close of the eighty-sixth year of the Diocletian Era ; in which also he celebrated the dedication, on the fourteenth [19] of Mesori.

XLIII. (370–1.) In this year, Easter-day was on xxii Pharmuthi ; xv Kal. Mai ; xvi Moon ; Epact xx ;

Gods, v; Indict. xiv; Coss. Gratianus Aug. II, Probus ; the same Palladius being governor ; who was succeeded as Præfect of Egypt by Ælius Palladius, of Palestine, who was called Cyrus.

XLIV. (371–2.) In this year, Easter-day was on xiii Pharmuthi ; vi Id. Ap. ; xix Moon ; Epact i ; Gods, vii [20]. Indict. xv ; Coss. Modestus, Arintheus ; the same Ælius Palladius the governor, called Cyrus, Præfect of Egypt.

XLV. (372–3.) In this year, Easter-day was on v Pharmuthi ; Prid. Kal. Ap. ; xxi Moon ; Epact xii ; Gods, i ; Indict. i ; Coss. Valentinianus IV, Valens IV; the same governor Ælius Palladius, Præfect of Egypt. At the close of this year, on the seventh of Pachon [21], he [Athan.] departed this life in a wonderful manner.

The end of the heads of the Festal Letters of holy Athanasius, Bishop of Alexandria.

---

[17] Sept. 22, 368.
[18] Text 'iv.'   [19] Aug. 7, 370.

[20] The Syr. has 'and not one,' which must be incorrect. [21] [May 2, 373.]

I. FESTAL LETTERS

LETTER I.

For 329.

Easter-day xi Pharmuthi ; viii Id. April; Ær. Dioclet. 45 ; Coss. Constantinus Aug. VIII. Constantinus Cæs. IV ; Præfect. Septimius Zenius ; Indict. II.

OF FASTING, AND TRUMPETS, AND FEASTS.

COME, my beloved, the season calls us to keep the feast. Again, 'the Sun of Righteousness [1], causing His divine beams to rise upon us, proclaims beforehand the time of the feast, in which, obeying Him, we ought to celebrate it, lest when the time has passed by, gladness likewise may pass us by. For discerning the time is one of the duties most urgent on us, for the practice of virtue ; so that the blessed Paul, when instructing his disciple, teaches him to observe the time, saying, 'Stand (ready) in season, and out of season [2]'—that knowing both the one and the other, he might do things befitting the season, and avoid the blame of unseasonableness. For thus the God of all, after the manner of wise Solomon [3], distributes everything in time and season, to the end that, in due time, the salvation of men should be everywhere spread abroad. Thus the 'Wisdom of God [4],' our Lord and Saviour Jesus Christ, not out of season, but in season, 'passed upon holy souls, fashioning the friends

of God and the prophets [5];' so that although very many were praying for Him, and saying, 'O that the salvation of God were come out of Sion [6]!'—the Spouse also, as it is written in the Song of Songs, was praying and saying, 'O that Thou wert my sister's son, that sucked the breasts of my mother [7]!' that Thou wert like the children of men, and wouldest take upon Thee human passions for our sake ! —nevertheless, the God of all, the Maker of times and seasons, Who knows our affairs better than we do, while, as a good physician, He exhorts to obedience in season —the only one in which we may be healed —so also does He send Him not unseasonably, but seasonably, saying, 'In an acceptable time have I heard Thee, and in the day of salvation I have helped Thee [8].'

2. And, on this account, the blessed Paul, urging us to note this season, wrote, saying, 'Behold, now is the accepted time ; behold, now is the day of salvation [9].' At set seasons also He called the children of Israel to the Levitical feasts by Moses, saying, 'Three times in a year ye shall keep a feast to Me [10]' (one of which, my beloved, is that now at hand), the trumpets of the priests sounding and urging its observance; as the holy Psalmist commanded, saying, 'Blow with the trumpet in the new moon, on the [solemn] day of your feast [11].' Since this sentence enjoins upon us to blow both on the new moons, and on the solemn [12]

---

[1] Mal. iv. 2.
[2] 2 Tim. iv. 2. The due celebration of the feast is spoken of as producing a permanent beneficial effect on the Christian. Cf. *Letter* 4.
[3] Eccl. iii. 7. Cf. S. Cyril. *Homil. Pasch. V.*   [4] 1 Cor. i. 24.

[5] Wisd. vii. 27.   [6] Ps. xiv. 7.   [7] Cant. viii. 1.
[8] Isa. xlix. 8.   [9] 2 Cor. vi. 2.   [10] Exod. xxiii. 14.
[11] Ps. lxxxi. 3, cf. Num. x. 8.   [12] Or *appointed*, and so *passim*.

days, He hath made a solemn day of that in which the light of the moon is perfected in the full; which was then a type, as is this of the trumpets. At one time, as has been said, they called to the feasts; at another time to fasting and to war. And this was not done without solemnity, nor by chance, but this sound of the trumpets was appointed, so that every man should come to that which was proclaimed. And this ought to be learned not merely from me, but from the divine Scriptures, when God was revealed to Moses, and said, as it is written in the book of Numbers; 'And the Lord spake unto Moses, saying, Make to thee two trumpets; of silver shalt thou make them, and they shall be for thee to call the congregation [13];'—very properly for those who here love Him. So that we may know that these things had reference to the time of Moses—yea, were to be observed so long as the shadow lasted, the whole being appointed for use, 'till the time of reformation [1].' 'For' (said He) 'if ye shall go out to battle in your land against your enemies that rise up against you [2]' (for such things as these refer to the land, and no further), 'then ye shall proclaim with the trumpets, and shall be remembered before the Lord, and be delivered from your enemies.' Not only in wars did they blow the trumpet, but under the law, there was a festal trumpet also. Hear him again, going on to say, 'And in the day of your gladness, and in your feasts, and your new moons, ye shall blow with the trumpets [3].' And let no man think it a light and contemptible matter, if he hear the law command respecting trumpets; it is a wonderful and fearful thing. For beyond any other voice or instrument, the trumpet is awakening and terrible; so Israel received instruction by these means, because he was then but a child. But in order that the proclamation should not be thought merely human, being superhuman, its sounds resembled those which were uttered when they trembled before the mount [4]; and they were reminded of the law that was then given them, and kept it.

3. For the law was admirable, and the shadow was excellent, otherwise, it would not have wrought fear, and induced reverence in those who heard; especially in those who at that time not only heard but saw these things. Now these things were typical, and done as in a shadow. But let us pass on to the meaning, and henceforth leaving the figure at a distance, come to the truth, and look upon the priestly trumpets of our Saviour, which cry out, and call us, at one time to war,

as the blessed Paul saith; 'We wrestle not with flesh and blood, but with principalities, with powers, with the rulers of this dark world, with wicked spirits in heaven [5].' At another time the call is made to virginity, and self-denial, and conjugal harmony, saying, To virgins, the things of virgins; and to those who love the way of abstinence, the things of abstinence; and to those who are married [6], the things of an honourable marriage; thus assigning to each its own virtues and an honourable recompense. Sometimes the call is made to fasting, and sometimes to a feast. Hear again the same [Apostle] blowing the trumpet, and proclaiming, 'Christ our Passover is sacrificed; therefore let us keep the feast, not with old leaven, neither with the leaven of malice and wickedness [7].' If thou wouldest listen to a trumpet much greater than all these, hear our Saviour saying; 'In that last and great day of the feast, Jesus stood and cried, saying, If any man thirst, let him come unto Me and drink [8].' For it became the Saviour not simply to call us to a feast, but to 'the great feast;' if only we will be prepared to hear, and to conform to the proclamation of every trumpet.

4. For since, as I before said, there are divers proclamations, listen, as in a figure, to the prophet blowing the trumpet; and further, having turned to the truth, be ready for the announcement of the trumpet, for he saith, 'Blow ye the trumpet in Sion: sanctify a fast [9].' This is a warning trumpet, and commands with great earnestness, that when we fast, we should hallow the fast. For not all those who call upon God, hallow God, since there are some who defile Him; yet not Him—that is impossible—but their own mind concerning Him; for He is holy, and has pleasure in the saints [10]. And therefore the blessed Paul accuses those who dishonour God; 'Transgressors of the law dishonour God [11].' So then, to make a separation from those who pollute the fast, he saith here, 'sanctify a fast.' For many, crowding to the fast, pollute themselves in the thoughts of their hearts, sometimes by doing evil against their brethren, sometimes by daring to defraud. And, to mention nothing else, there are many who exalt themselves above their neighbours, thereby causing great mischief. For the boast of fasting did no good to the Pharisee, although he fasted twice in the week [12], only because he exalted himself against the publican. In the same manner the Word blamed

---

13 Num. x. 1, 2.   1 Heb. ix. 10.   5 Eph. vi. 12.   6 Cf. 1 Cor. vii. 2, 5.   7 Ib. v. 7, 8.
2 Numb. x. 9.   3 Ib. x. 10.   4 Exod. xix. 16.   8 John vii. 37.   9 Joel ii. 15.   10 Ps. xvi. 3.
11 Rom. ii. 23.   12 Luke xviii. 12.

the children of Israel on account of such a fast as this, exhorting them by Isaiah the Prophet, and saying, 'This is not the fast and the day that I have chosen, that a man should humble his soul; not even if thou shouldest bow down thy neck like a hook, and shouldest strew sackcloth and ashes under thee; neither thus shall ye call the fast acceptable [13].' That we may be able to shew what kind of persons we should be when we fast, and of what character the fast should be, listen again to God commanding Moses, and saying, as it is written in Leviticus [14], 'And the Lord spake unto Moses, saying, In the tenth day of this seventh month, there shall be a day of atonement; a convocation, and a holy day shall it be to you; and ye shall humble your souls, and offer whole burnt-offerings unto the Lord.' And afterwards, that the law might be defined on this point, He proceeds to say; 'Every soul that shall not humble itself, shall be cut off from the people [15].'

5. Behold, my brethren, how much a fast can do, and in what manner the law commands us to fast. It is required that not only with the body should we fast, but with the soul. Now the soul is humbled when it does not follow wicked opinions, but feeds on becoming virtues. For virtues and vices are the food of the soul, and it can eat either of these two meats, and incline to either of the two, according to its own will. If it is bent toward virtue, it will be nourished by virtues, by righteousness, by temperance, by meekness, by fortitude, as Paul saith; 'Being nourished by the word of truth [16].' Such was the case with our Lord, who said, 'My meat is to do the will of My Father which is in heaven [17].' But if it is not thus with the soul, and it inclines downwards, it is then nourished by nothing but sin. For thus the Holy Ghost, describing sinners and their food, referred to the devil when He said, 'I have given him to be meat to the people of Æthiopia [18].' For this is the food of sinners. And as our Lord and Saviour Jesus Christ, being heavenly bread, is the food of the saints, according to this; 'Except ye eat My flesh, and drink My blood [1];' so is the devil the food of the impure, and of those who do nothing which is of the light, but work the deeds of darkness. Therefore, in order to withdraw and turn them from vices, He commands them to be nourished with the food of virtue; namely, humbleness of mind, lowliness to endure humiliations, the acknowledgment of God. For not only does such a fast as this obtain pardon for souls, but being kept

holy, it prepares the saints, and raises them above the earth.

6. And indeed that which I am about to say is wonderful, yea it is of those things which are very miraculous; yet not far from the truth, as ye may be able to learn from the sacred [2] writings. That great man Moses, when fasting, conversed with God, and received the law. The great and holy Elijah, when fasting, was thought worthy of divine visions, and at last was taken up like Him who ascended into heaven. And Daniel, when fasting, although a very young man, was entrusted with the mystery, and he alone understood the secret things of the king, and was thought worthy of divine visions. But because the length of the fast of these men was wonderful, and the days prolonged, let no man lightly fall into unbelief; but rather let him believe and know, that the contemplation of God, and the word which is from Him, suffice to nourish those who hear, and stand to them in place of all food. For the angels are no otherwise sustained than by beholding at all times the face of the Father, and of the Saviour who is in heaven. And thus Moses, as long as he talked with God, fasted indeed bodily, but was nourished by divine words. When he descended among men, and God was gone up from him, he suffered hunger like other men. For it is not said that he fasted longer than forty days— those in which he was conversing with God. And, generally, each one of the saints has been thought worthy of similar transcendent nourishment.

7. Wherefore, my beloved, having our souls nourished with divine food, with the Word, and according to the will of God, and fasting bodily in things external, let us keep this great and saving feast as becomes us. Even the ignorant Jews received this divine food, through the type, when they ate a lamb in the passover. But not understanding the type, even to this day they eat the lamb, erring in that they are without the city and the truth. As long as Judæa and the city existed, there were a type, and a lamb, and a shadow, since the law thus commanded [3]: These things shall not be done in another city; but in the land of Judæa, and in no place without [the land of Judæa]. And besides this, the law commanded them to offer whole burnt-offerings and sacrifices, there being no other altar than that in Jerusalem. For on this account, in that city alone was there an altar and temple built, and in no other city were they permitted

---

[13] Is. lviii. 5. [14] Levit. xxiii. 26, sq.
[15] Ib. xxiii. 29. [16] 1 Tim. iv. 6. [17] John iv. 34.
[18] Ps. lxxiv. 14, LXX. [1] John vi. 53.

[2] The word in the Syriac is 'priestly.' But in this and in other places, it appears to be for the Greek Ἱερός. Cf. τὰ ἱερὰ γραμματα. 2 Tim. iii. 15. [3] Deut. xii. 11, 13, 14.

to perform these rites, so that when that city should come to an end, then those things that were figurative might also be done away.

8. Now observe; that city, since the coming of our Saviour, has had an end, and all the land of the Jews has been laid waste; so that from the testimony of these things (and we need no further proof, being assured by our own eyes of the fact) there must, of necessity, be an end of the shadow. And not from me should these things be learned, but the sacred voice of the prophet foretold, crying; 'Behold upon the mountains the feet of Him that bringeth good tidings, and publisheth peace[4];' and what is the message he published, but that which he goes on to say to them, 'Keep thy feasts, O Judah; pay to the Lord thy vows. For they shall no more go to that which is old; it is finished; it is taken away: He is gone up who breathed upon the face, and delivered thee from affliction[5].' Now who is he that went up? a man may say to the Jews, in order that even the boast of the shadow may be done away; neither is it an idle thing to listen to the expression, 'It is finished; he is gone up who breathed.' For nothing was finished before he went up who breathed. But as soon as he went up, it was finished. Who was he then, O Jews, as I said before? If Moses, the assertion would be false; for the people were not yet come to the land in which alone they were commanded to perform these rites. But if Samuel, or any other of the prophets, even in that case there would be a perversion of the truth; for hitherto these things were done in Judæa, and the city was standing. For it was necessary that while that stood, these things should be performed. So that it was none of these, my beloved, who went up. But if thou wouldest hear the true matter, and be kept from Jewish fables, behold our Saviour who went up, and 'breathed upon the face, and said to His disciples, Receive ye the Holy Ghost[6].' For as soon as these things were done, everything was finished, for the altar was broken, and the veil of the temple was rent; and although the city was not yet laid waste, the abomination was ready to sit in the midst of the temple, and the city and those ancient ordinances to receive their final consummation.

9. Since then we have passed beyond that time of shadows, and no longer perform rites under it, but have turned, as it were, unto the Lord; 'for the Lord is the Spirit, and where the Spirit of the Lord is, there is liberty[7];'—as

we hear the sacred trumpet, no longer slaying a material lamb, but that true Lamb that was slain, even our Lord Jesus Christ; 'Who was led as a sheep to the slaughter, and was dumb as a lamb before her shearers[8];' being purified by His precious blood, which speaketh better things than that of Abel, having our feet shod with the preparation of the Gospel, holding in our hands the rod and staff of the Lord, by which that saint was comforted, who said[9], 'Thy rod and Thy staff they comfort me;' and to sum up, being in all respects prepared, and careful for nothing, because, as the blessed Paul saith, 'The Lord is at hand[10];' and as our Saviour saith, 'In an hour when we think not, the Lord cometh;—Let us keep the Feast, not with old leaven, neither with the leaven of malice and wickedness; but with the unleavened bread of sincerity and truth. Putting off the old man and his deeds, let us put on the new man[11], which is created in God,' in humbleness of mind, and a pure conscience; in meditation of the law by night and by day. And casting away all hypocrisy and fraud, putting far from us all pride and deceit, let us take upon us love towards God and towards our neighbour, that being new [creatures], and receiving the new wine, even the Holy Spirit, we may properly keep the feast, even the month of these new [fruits][12].

10. We[13] begin the holy fast on the fifth day of Pharmuthi (March 31), and adding to it according to the number of those six holy and great days, which are the symbol of the creation of this world, let us rest and cease (from fasting) on the tenth day of the same Pharmuthi (April 5), on the holy sabbath of the week. And when the first day of the holy week dawns and rises upon us, on the eleventh day of the same month (April 6), from which again we count all the seven weeks one by one, let us keep feast on the holy day of Pentecost—on that which was at one time to the Jews, typically, the feast of weeks, in which they granted forgiveness and settlement of debts; and indeed that day was one of deliverance in every respect. Let us keep the feast on the first day of the great week, as a symbol of the world to come, in which we here receive a pledge that we shall have everlasting life hereafter. Then having passed

---

4 Nah. i. 15.
6 John xx. 22.

5 Nah. i. 15; ii. 1, LXX.
7 2 Cor. iii. 17.

8 Is. liii. 7.   9 Ps. xxiii. 4.   10 Phil. iv. 5.
11 Luke xii. 40; 1 Cor. v. 8; Ephes. iv. 22—24.
12 Alluding to Deut. xvi. 1, LXX.
13 We should not have much difficulty in fixing upon many of the phrases and expressions used by S. Athan. towards the close of his Epistles, by referring to the concluding sentences in the Paschal Letters of S. Cyril, who seems herein to have closely imitated his illustrious predecessor in the Patriarchate. The Syriac translator must frequently have had before him the following expressions: ἀρχόμενοι τῆς ἁγίας τεσσαρακοστῆς—ἐπισυνάπτοντες—συνάπτοντες ἑξῆς—περιλύοντες τὰς νηστείας—καταπαύοντες τὰς νηστείας—ἑσπέρᾳ βαθείᾳ σαββάτου—τῇ ἐπιφωσκούσῃ κυριακῇ.

hence, we shall keep a perfect feast with Christ, while we cry out and say, like the saints, 'I will pass to the place of the wondrous tabernacle, to the house of God; with the voice of gladness and thanksgiving, the shouting of those who rejoice [14];' whence pain and sorrow and sighing have fled, and upon our heads gladness and joy shall have come to us! May we be judged worthy to be partakers in these things.

11. Let us remember the poor, and not forget kindness to strangers; above all, let us love God with all our soul, and might, and strength, and our neighbour as ourselves. So may we receive those things which the eye hath not seen, nor the ear heard, and which have not entered into the heart of man, which God hath prepared for those that love Him [15], through His only Son, our Lord and Saviour, Jesus Christ; through Whom, to the Father alone, by the Holy Ghost, be glory and dominion for ever and ever. Amen.

Salute one another with a kiss. All the brethren who are with me salute you.

Here endeth the first Festal Letter of holy Athanasius.

LETTER II.

For 330.

Easter-day xxiv Pharmuthi; xiii Kal. Mai; Æra Dioclet. 46; Coss. Gallicianus, Valerius Symmachus; Præfect, Magninianus; Indict. iii.

AGAIN, my brethren, is Easter come and gladness; again the Lord hath brought us to this season; so that when, according to custom, we have been nourished with His words, we may duly keep the feast. Let us celebrate it then, even heavenly joy, with those saints who formerly proclaimed a like feast, and were ensamples to us of conversation in Christ. For not only were they entrusted with the charge of preaching the Gospel, but, if we enquire, we shall see, as it is written, that its power was displayed in them. 'Be ye therefore followers of me [1],' he wrote to the Corinthians. Now the apostolic precept exhorts us all, for those commands which he sent to individuals, he at the same time enjoined upon every man in every place, for he was 'a teacher of all nations in faith and truth [2].' And, generally, the commands of all the saints urge us on similarly, as Solomon makes use of proverbs, saying, 'Hear, my children, the instruction of a father, and attend to know understanding; for I give you a good

gift, forsake ye not my word: for I was an obedient son to my father, and beloved in the sight of my mother [3].' For a just father brings up [his children] well, when he is diligent in teaching others in accordance with his own upright conduct, so that when he meets with opposition, he may not be ashamed on hearing it said, 'Thou therefore that teachest others, teachest thou not thyself [4]?' but rather, like the good servant, may both save himself and gain others; and thus, when the grace committed to him has been doubled, he may hear, 'Thou good and faithful servant, thou hast been faithful in a little, I will set thee over much: enter into the joy of thy Lord [5].'

2. Let us [6] then, as is becoming, as at all times, yet especially in the days of the feast, be not hearers only, but doers of the commandments of our Saviour; that having imitated the behaviour of the saints, we may enter together into the joy of our Lord which is in heaven, which is not transitory, but truly abides; of which evil doers having deprived themselves, there remains to them as the fruit of their ways, sorrow and affliction, and groaning with torments. Let a man see what these become like, that they bear not the likeness [7] of the conversation of the saints, nor of that right understanding, by which man at the beginning was rational, and in the image of God. But they are compared to their disgrace to beasts without understanding, and becoming like them in unlawful pleasures, they are spoken of as wanton horses [7a]; also, for their craftiness, and errors, and sin laden with death, they are called a 'generation of vipers,' as John saith [8]. Now having thus fallen, and grovelling in the dust like the serpent [9], having their minds set on nothing beyond visible things, they esteem these things good, and rejoicing in them, serve their own lusts and not God.

3. Yet even in this state, the man-loving Word, who came for this very reason, that He might seek and find that which was lost, sought to restrain them from such folly, crying and saying, 'Be ye not as the horse and the mule which have no understanding, whose cheeks ye hold in with bit and bridle [10].' Because they were careless and imitated the wicked, the prophet prays in spirit and says, 'Ye are to me like merchant-men of Phœnicia [11].' And the avenging Spirit protests against them in these words, 'Lord, in Thy city Thou wilt despise their image [12].' Thus, being changed

---

14 Ps. xlii. 4.   15 1 Cor. ii. 9; Is. lxiv. 4.
1 1 Cor. iv. 16.   2 1 Tim. ii. 7. Cf. Letter iii.

3 Prov. iv. 1.   4 Rom. ii. 21.   5 Mat. xxv. 21.
6 We have here the first fragment extant of the original Greek text. It is to be found in Cosmas Indicopleustes, p. 316.
7 Syr. εἰκών.   7a Jer. v. 8.   8 i.e. the Baptist, Matt. iii. 7; Luke iii. 7.   9 Cf. *Vit. Anton. supr.* p. 202.
10 Ps. xxxii. 9. Cf. *Orat.* iii. 18.   11 Is. xxiii. 2, LXX.
12 Ps. lxxiii. 20.

into the likeness of fools, they fell so low in their understanding, that by their excessive reasoning, they even likened the Divine Wisdom to themselves, thinking it to be like their own arts. Therefore, 'professing themselves to be wise, they became fools, and changed the glory of the incorruptible God into the likeness of the corruptible image of man, and birds, and four-footed beasts, and creeping things. Wherefore God gave them over to a reprobate mind, to do those things which are not convenient[13].' For they did not listen to the prophetic voice that reproved them (saying), 'To what have ye likened the Lord, and with what have ye compared Him[14]?' neither to David, who prayed concerning such as these, and sang, 'All those that make them are like unto them, and all those who put their trust in them[15].' Being blind to the truth, they looked upon a stone as God, and hence, like senseless creatures, they walked in darkness, and, as the prophet cried, 'They hear indeed, but they do not understand; they see indeed, but they do not perceive; for their heart is waxen fat, and with their ears they hear heavily[16].'

4. Now those who do not observe the feast, continue such as these even to the present day, feigning indeed and devising names of feasts[17], but rather introducing days of mourning than of gladness; 'For there is no peace to the wicked, saith the Lord[1].' And as Wisdom saith, 'Gladness and joy are taken from their mouth[2].' Such are the feasts of the wicked. But the wise servants of the Lord, who have truly put on the man which is created in God[3], have received gospel words, and reckon as a general commandment that given to Timothy, which saith, 'Be thou an example to the believers in word, in conversation, in love, in faith, in purity[4].' So well do they keep the Feast, that even the unbelievers, seeing their order[5], may say, 'God is with them of a truth[6].' For as he who receives an apostle receives Him who sent him[6a], so he who is a follower of the saints, makes the Lord in every respect his end and aim, even as Paul, being a follower of Him, goes on to say, 'As I also of Christ[7].' For there were first our Saviour's own words, who from the height of His divinity, when conversing with His disciples, said, 'Learn of Me, for I am meek and lowly in heart, and ye shall find rest to your souls[8].' Then too when He

poured water into a basin, and girded Himself with a towel, and washed His disciples' feet, He said to them, 'Know what I have done. Ye call Me Master and Lord, and ye say well, for so I am. If therefore I, your Lord and Master, have washed your feet, ye also ought to wash one another's feet: for I have given you an example, that as I have done to you, ye also should do[9].'

5. Oh! my brethren, how shall we admire the loving-kindness of the Saviour? With what power, and with what a trumpet should a man cry out, exalting these His benefits! That not only should we bear His image, but should receive from Him an example and pattern of heavenly conversation; that as He hath begun, we should go on, that suffering, we should not threaten, being reviled, we should not revile again, but should bless them that curse, and in everything commit ourselves to God who judgeth righteously[10]. For those who are thus disposed, and fashion themselves according to the Gospel, will be partakers of Christ, and imitators of apostolic conversation, on account of which they shall be deemed worthy of that praise from him, with which he praised the Corinthians, when he said, ' I praise you that in everything ye are mindful of me[11].' Afterwards, because there were men who used his words, but chose to hear them as suited their lusts, and dared to pervert them, as the followers of Hymenæus and Alexander, and before them the Sadducees, who as he said, 'having made shipwreck of faith,' scoffed at the mystery of the resurrection, he immediately proceeded to say, 'And as I have delivered to you traditions, hold them fast[12].' That means, indeed, that we should think not otherwise than as the teacher has delivered.

6. For not only in outward form did those wicked men dissemble, putting on as the Lord says sheep's clothing, and appearing like unto whited sepulchres; but they took those divine words in their mouth, while they inwardly cherished evil intentions. And the first to put on this appearance was the serpent, the inventor of wickedness from the beginning—the devil,—who, in disguise, conversed with Eve, and forthwith deceived her. But after him and with him are all inventors of unlawful heresies, who indeed refer to the Scriptures, but do not hold such opinions as the saints have handed down, and receiving them as the traditions of men, err, because they do not rightly know them nor their[13] power. Therefore Paul justly praises the Corinthians[11], because their opinions were in accordance with his traditions. And the

---

[13] Rom. i. 22, 28, and cf. c. Gent. 19. 2. [14] Is. xl. 18.
[15] Ps. cxv. 8. [16] Is. vi. 9.
[17] Syr. σχηματισάμενος. The allusion in this sentence is evidently to the conduct of Jeroboam, as recorded 1 Kings xii. 32, 33. The phraseology of the Syriac resembles that of the Syr. version in v. 33. [1] Is. xlviii. 22. [2] Vid. Letter iii. note.
[3] Eph. iv. 24. [4] 1 Tim. iv. 12. [5] τάξις, Syr. Cf. Col. ii. 5, βλέπων ὑμῶν τὴν τάξιν. [6] 1 Cor. xiv. 25.
[6a] Matt. x. 40. [7] 1 Cor. xi. 1. [8] Matt. xi. 29.

[9] John xiii. 12. [10] 1 Pet. ii. 21—23. [11] 1 Cor. xi 2.
[12] 1 Tim. i. 19; 2 Tim. ii. 18; 1 Cor. xi. 2. [13] Matt. xxii. 29.

Lord most righteously reproved the Jews, saying, 'Wherefore do ye also transgress the commandments of God on account of your traditions [14].' For they changed the commandments they received from God after their own understanding, preferring to observe the traditions of men. And about these, a little after, the blessed Paul again gave directions to the Galatians who were in danger thereof, writing to them, 'If any man preach to you aught else than that ye have received, let him be accursed [15].'

7. For there is no fellowship whatever between the words of the saints and the fancies of human invention; for the saints are the ministers of the truth, preaching the kingdom of heaven, but those who are borne in the opposite direction have nothing better than to eat, and think their end is that they shall cease to be, and they say, 'Let us eat and drink, for to-morrow we die [16].' Therefore blessed Luke reproves the inventions of men, and hands down the narrations of the saints, saying in the beginning of the Gospel, 'Since many have presumed to write narrations of those events of which we are assured, as those who from the beginning were witnesses and ministers of the Word have delivered to us; it hath seemed good to me also, who have adhered to them all from the first, to write correctly in order to thee, O excellent Theophilus, that thou mayest know the truth concerning the things in which thou hast been instructed [17].' For as each of the saints has received, that they impart without alteration, for the confirmation of the doctrine of the mysteries. Of these the (divine) word would have us disciples, and these should of right be our teachers, and to them only is it necessary to give heed, for of them only is 'the word faithful and worthy of all acceptation [18];' these not being disciples because they heard from others, but being eye-witnesses and ministers of the Word, that which they had heard from Him have they handed down.

Now some have related the wonderful signs performed by our Saviour, and preached His eternal Godhead. And others have written of His being born in the flesh of the Virgin, and have proclaimed the festival of the holy passover, saying, 'Christ our Passover is sacrificed [19];' so that we, individually and collectively, and all the churches in the world may remember, as it is written, 'That Christ rose from the dead, of the seed of David, according to the Gospel [20].' And let us not forget that which Paul delivered, declaring it to the Corinthians; I mean His resurrection, whereby 'He

destroyed him that had the power of death, that is, the devil [1];' and raised us up together with Him, having loosed the bands of death, and vouchsafed a blessing instead of a curse, joy instead of grief, a feast instead of mourning, in this holy joy of Easter, which being continually in our hearts, we always rejoice, as Paul commanded; 'We pray without ceasing; in everything we give thanks [2].' So we are not remiss in giving notice of its seasons, as we have received from the Fathers. Again we write, again keeping to the apostolic traditions, we remind each other when we come together for prayer; and keeping the feast in common, with one mouth we truly give thanks to the Lord. Thus giving thanks unto Him, and being followers of the saints, 'we shall make our praise in the Lord all the day [3],' as the Psalmist says. So, when we rightly keep the feast, we shall be counted worthy of that joy which is in heaven.

8. We begin the fast of forty days on the 13th of the month Phamenoth (Mar. 9). After we have given ourselves to fasting in continued succession, let us begin the holy Paschal [5] week on the 18th of the month Pharmuthi (April 13). Then resting on the 23rd of the same month Pharmuthi (April 18), and keeping the feast afterwards on the first of the week, on the 24th (April 19), let us add to these the seven weeks of the great Pentecost, wholly rejoicing and exulting in Christ Jesus our Lord, through Whom to the Father be glory and dominion in the Holy Ghost, for ever and ever. Amen.

The brethren which are with me salute you. Salute one another with a holy kiss [6].

Here endeth the second Festal Letter of the holy lord Athanasius, Bishop of Alexandria.

LETTER III.

For 331.

Easter-day xvi Pharmuthi; iii Id. April; Æra Dioclet. 47; Coss. Annius Bassus, Ablabius; Præfect, Florentius; Indict. iv.

AGAIN, my beloved brethren, the day of the feast draws near to us, which, above all others, should be devoted to prayer, which the law commands to be observed, and which it would be an unholy thing for us to pass over in silence. For although we have been held under restraint by those who afflict us, that, because of them, we should not announce to you this season; yet thanks be to 'God, who comforteth the afflicted [1],' that we have

---

[14] Matt. xv. 3.   [15] Gal. i. 9.   [16] Is. xxii. 13.
[17] Luke i. 1.   [18] 1 Tim. i. 15.   [19] 1 Cor. v. 7.
[20] 2 Tim. ii. 8.

[1] Heb. ii. 14.   [2] 1 Thess. v. 17.   [3] Ps. xxxv. 28.
[5] In Syriac there is but one word 'pescha' to express the Passover and Easter feasts, it is therefore sometimes rendered Easter, and sometimes Passover, in the following pages.
[6] The twenty-fifth Paschal Letter of S. Cyril ends with the same words. This is the usual form in which our author concludes his Paschal Letters. S. Cyril employs it but once, as above.
[1] 2 Cor. vii. 6   The historical reference is not quite certain.

not been overcome by the wickedness of our accusers and silenced; but obeying the voice of truth, we together with you cry aloud in the day of the feast. For the God of all hath commanded, saying, 'Speak [2], and the children of Israel shall keep the Passover.' And the Spirit exhorts in the Psalm; 'Blow the trumpet in the new moons [3], in the solemn day of your feast.' And the prophet cries; 'Keep thy feasts, O Judah [4].' I do not send word to you as though you were ignorant; but I publish it to those who know it, that ye may perceive that although men have separated us, yet God having made us companions, we approach the same feast, and worship the same Lord continually. And we do not keep the festival as observers of days, knowing that the Apostle reproves those who do so, in those words which he spake; 'Ye observe days, and months, and times, and years [5].' But rather do we consider the day solemn because of the feast; so that all of us, who serve God in every place, may together in our prayers be well-pleasing to God. For the blessed Paul, announcing the nearness of gladness like this, did not announce days, but the Lord, for whose sake we keep the feast, saying, 'Christ, our Passover, is sacrificed [6];' so that we all, contemplating the eternity of the Word, may draw near to do Him service.

2. For what else is the feast, but the service of the soul? And what is that service, but prolonged prayer to God, and unceasing thanksgiving [7]? The unthankful departing far from these are rightly deprived of the joy springing therefrom: for 'joy and gladness are taken from their mouth [8].' Therefore, the [divine] word doth not allow them to have peace; 'For there is no peace to the wicked, saith the Lord [9],' they labour in pain and grief. So, not even to him who owed ten thousand talents did the Gospel grant forgiveness in the sight of the Lord [10]. For even he, having received forgiveness of great things, was forgetful of kindness in little ones, so that he paid the penalty also of those former things. And justly indeed, for having himself experienced kindness, he was required to be merciful to his fellow servant. He too that received the one talent, and bound it up in a napkin, and hid it in the earth, was in conse-

quence cast out for unthankfulness, hearing the words, 'Thou wicked and slothful servant, thou knewest that I reap where I sowed not, and gather where I have not strawed; thou oughtest therefore to have put my money to the exchangers, and on my return, I should have received mine own. Take therefore the talent from him, and give it to him that hath ten talents [11].' For, of course, when he was required to deliver up to his lord that which belonged to him, he should have acknowledged the kindness of him who gave it, and the value of that which was given. For he who gave was not a hard man, had he been so, he would not have given even in the first instance; neither was that which was given unprofitable and vain, for then he had not found fault. But both he who gave was good, and that which was given was capable of bearing fruit. As therefore 'he who withholdeth corn in seed-time is cursed [12],' according to the divine proverb, so he who neglects grace, and hides it without culture, is properly cast out as a wicked and unthankful person. On this account, he praises those who increased [their talents], saying, 'Well done, good and faithful servant; thou hast been faithful in a little, I will place thee over much; enter into the joy of thy Lord [13].'

3. This was right and reasonable; for, as the Scripture declares, they had gained as much as they had received. Now, my beloved, our will ought to keep pace with the grace of God, and not fall short; lest while our will remains idle, the grace given us should begin to depart, and the enemy finding us empty and naked, should enter [into us], as was the case with him spoken of in the Gospel, from whom the devil went out; 'for having gone through dry places, he took seven other spirits more wicked than himself; and returning and finding the house empty, he dwelt there, and the last state of that man was worse than the first [14].' For the departure from virtue gives place for the entrance of the unclean spirit. There is, moreover, the apostolic injunction, that the grace given us should not be unprofitable; for those things which he wrote particularly to his disciple, he enforces on us through him [15], saying, 'Neglect not the gift that is in thee. For he who tilleth his land shall be satisfied with bread; but the paths of the slothful are strewn with thorns;' so that the Spirit forewarns a man not to fall into them, saying, 'Break up your fallow ground, sow not among thorns [16].' For when a man despises the grace given him, and forth-

---

but the *Index* iii. is clearly right in its statement that Ath. was absent at this time, as well as in 332.
2 'Εἶπον, καὶ,' as LXX. not Peshito.
3 Cf. S. Cyril. *Hom. Pasch.* xxx. near the beginning.
4 Numb. ix. 2; Ps. lxxxi. 3; Nah. i. 15.
5 Gal. iv. 10. 6 1 Cor. v. 7.
7 Cf. Clemens Alex. *Strom.* 7. 1. ἀδιάλειπτος ἀγάπη. Also 1 Thess. v. 16, 17, both in the Greek and in the Syriac vers. and *Letter* 11.
8 Apparently a quotation from Scripture, perhaps from Jer. vii. the phraseology of *v*. 28. being transferred to the sentiment of *v*. 34. The expression has already occurred, *Letter* 2. 4.
9 Is. xlviii. 22. 10 Matt. xviii. 24.

11 Matt. xxv. 26. 12 Prov. xi. 26. 13 Matt. xxv. 23.
14 Ib. xii. 43–45. 15 Cf. *Letter* 2, near beginning.
16 1 Tim. iv. 14; Prov. xii. 11; Ib. xv. 19; Jer. iv. 3.

with falls into the cares of the world, he delivers himself over to his lusts ; and thus in the time of persecution he is offended [17], and becomes altogether unfruitful. Now the prophet points out the end of such negligence, saying, 'Cursed is he who doeth the work of the Lord carelessly [18].' For a servant of the Lord should be diligent and careful, yea, moreover, burning like a flame, so that when, by an ardent spirit, he has destroyed all carnal sin, he may be able to draw near to God, who, according to the expression of the saints, is called 'a consuming fire [19].'

4. Therefore, the God of all, 'Who maketh His angels [spirits],' is a spirit, 'and His ministers a flame of fire [1].' Wherefore, in the departure from Egypt, He forbade the multitude to touch the mountain, where God was appointing them the law, because they were not of this character. But He called blessed Moses to it, as being fervent in spirit, and possessing unquenchable grace, saying, 'Let Moses alone draw near [2].' He entered into the cloud also, and when the mountain was smoking, he was not injured; but rather, through 'the words of the Lord, which are choice silver purified in the earth [3],' he descended purified. Therefore the blessed Paul, when desirous that the grace of the Spirit given to us should not grow cold, exhorts, saying, 'Quench not the Spirit [4].' For so shall we remain partakers of Christ [5], if we hold fast to the end the Spirit given at the beginning. For he said, 'Quench not;' not because the Spirit is placed in the power of men, and is able to suffer anything from them ; but because bad and unthankful men are such as manifestly wish to quench it, since they, like the impure, persecute the Spirit with unholy deeds. 'For the holy Spirit of discipline will flee deceit, nor dwell in a body that is subject unto sin ; but will remove from thoughts that are without understanding [6].' Now they being without understanding, and deceitful, and lovers of sin, walk still as in darkness, not having that 'Light which lighteth every man that cometh into the world [7].' Now a fire such as this laid hold of Jeremiah the prophet, when the word was in him as a fire, and he said, 'I pass away from every place, and am not able to endure it [8].' And our Lord Jesus Christ, being good and a lover of men, came that He might cast this upon earth, and said, 'And what? would that it were already

kindled [9]!' For He desired, as He testified in Ezekiel [10], the repentance of a man rather than his death : so that evil should be entirely consumed in all men, that the soul, being purified, might be able to bring forth fruit; for the word which is sown by Him will be productive, some thirty, some sixty, some an hundred [11]. Thus, for instance, those who were with Cleopas [12], although infirm at first from lack of knowledge, yet afterwards were inflamed with the words of the Saviour, and brought forth the fruits of the knowledge of Him. The blessed Paul also, when seized by this fire, revealed it not to flesh and blood, but having experienced the grace, he became a preacher of the Word. But not such were those nine lepers who were cleansed from their leprosy, and yet were unthankful to the Lord who healed them; nor Judas, who obtained the lot of an apostle, and was named a disciple of the Lord, but at last, 'while eating bread with the Saviour, lifted up his heel against Him, and became a traitor [13].' But such men have the due reward of their folly, since their expectation will be vain through their ingratitude; for there is no hope for the ungrateful, the last fire, prepared for the devil and his angels, awaits those who have neglected divine light. Such then is the end of the unthankful.

5. But the faithful and true servants of the Lord, knowing that the Lord loves the thankful, never cease to praise Him, ever giving thanks unto the Lord. And whether the time is one of ease or of affliction, they offer up praise to God with thanksgiving, not reckoning these things of time, but worshipping the Lord, the God of times [14]. Thus of old time, Job, who possessed fortitude above all men, thought of these things when in prosperity; and when in adversity, he patiently endured, and when he suffered, gave thanks. As also the humble David, in the very time of affliction sang praises and said, 'I will bless the Lord at all times [15].' And the blessed Paul, in all his Epistles, so to say, ceased not to thank God. In times of ease, he failed not, and in afflictions he gloried, knowing that 'tribulation worketh patience, and patience experience, and experience hope, and that hope maketh not ashamed [16].' Let us, being followers of such men, pass no season without thanksgiving, but especially now, when the time is one of tribulation, which the heretics excite against us, will we praise the Lord, uttering the words of the saints; 'All these

---

[17] σκανδαλίζεται, Matt. xiii. 21.   [18] Jer. xlviii. 10.
[19] Deut. iv. 24 ; ix. 3 ; and Heb. xii. 29.   [1] Ps. civ. 4.
[2] Exod. xxiv. 2.   [3] Ps. xii. 6.   [4] 1 Thess. v. 19.
[5] Conf. S. Athan. *Expos. in Psalmos*, t. i. p. 863. πῦρ ὥσπερ νοητόν, τὴν τοῦ ἁγίου Πνεύματος μέθεξιν ἐμβαλών.
[6] Wisd. i. 5.   [7] John i. 9.   [8] Jer. xx. 9, cf. *Letter* 49. 5.

[9] Luke xii. 49.   [10] Ezek. xviii. 23, 32.   [11] Mark iv. 20.
[12] Luke xxiv.   [13] Ps. xli. 9 ; John xiii. 18.
[14] Cf. *Letter* 1. 1, note 12.   [15] Ps. xxxiv. 1.   [16] Rom. v. 3.

things have come upon us, yet have we not forgotten Thee[17].' For as the Jews at that time, although suffering an assault from the tabernacles[17a] of the Edomites, and oppressed by the enemies of Jerusalem, did not give themselves up, but all the more sang praises to God; so we, my beloved brethren, though hindered from speaking the word of the Lord, will the more proclaim it, and being afflicted, we will sing Psalms[17b], in that we are accounted worthy to be despised, and to labour anxiously for the truth. Yea, moreover, being grievously vexed, we will give thanks. For the blessed Apostle, who gave thanks at all times, urges us in the same manner to draw near to God, saying, 'Let your requests, with thanksgiving, be made known unto God[18].' And being desirous that we should always continue in this resolution, he says, 'At all times give thanks; pray without ceasing[19].' For he knew that believers are strong while employed in thanksgiving, and that rejoicing they pass over the walls of the enemy, like those saints who said, 'Through Thee will we pierce through our enemies, and by my God I will leap over a wall[20].' At all times let us stand firm, but especially now, although many afflictions overtake us, and many heretics are furious against us. Let us then, my beloved brethren, celebrate with thanksgiving the holy feast which now draws near to us, 'girding up the loins of our minds[1],' like our Saviour Jesus Christ, of Whom it is written, 'Righteousness shall be the girdle of His loins, and faithfulness the girdle of His reins[2].' Each one of us having in his hand the staff which came out of the root of Jesse, and our feet shod with the preparation of the Gospel[3], let us keep the feast as Paul saith, 'Not with the old leaven, but with the unleavened bread of sincerity and truth[4];' reverently trusting that we are reconciled through Christ, and not departing from faith in Him, nor do we defile ourselves together with heretics, and strangers to the truth, whose conversation and whose will degrade them. But rejoicing in afflictions, we break through the furnace of iron and darkness, and pass, unharmed, over that terrible Red Sea. Thus also, when we look upon the confusion of heretics, we shall, with Moses, sing that great song of praise, and say, 'We will sing unto the Lord, for He is to be gloriously praised[5].' Thus, singing praises, and seeing that the sin which is in us has been cast into the sea, we pass over to the wilderness. And being first purified by the

fast of forty days, by prayers, and fastings, and discipline, and good works, we shall be able to eat the holy Passover in Jerusalem.

6. The beginning of the fast of forty days is on the fifth of Phamenoth (Mar. 1); and when, as I have said, we have first been purified and prepared by those days, we begin the holy week of the great Easter on the tenth of Pharmuthi (Apr. 5), in which, my beloved brethren, we should use more prolonged prayers, and fastings, and watchings, that we may be enabled to anoint our lintels with precious blood, and to escape the destroyer[6]. Let us rest then, on the fifteenth of the month Pharmuthi (Apr. 10), for on the evening of that Saturday we hear the angels' message, 'Why seek ye the living among the dead? He is risen[7].' Immediately afterwards that great Sunday receives us, I mean on the sixteenth of the same month Pharmuthi (April 11), on which our Lord having risen, gave us peace towards our neighbours. When then we have kept the feast according to His will, let us add from that first day in the holy week, the seven weeks of Pentecost, and as we then receive the grace of the Spirit, let us at all times give thanks to the Lord; through Whom to the Father be glory and dominion, in the Holy Ghost, for ever and ever. Amen.

Salute one another with a holy kiss. The brethren who are with me salute you. I pray, brethren beloved and longed for, that ye may have health, and that ye may be mindful of us in the Lord.

Here endeth the third Festal Letter of holy Athanasius.

LETTER IV.

For 332.

Easter-day vii Pharmuthi[1], iv Non. Apr.; Æra Dioclet. 48; *Coss. Fabius Pacatianus, Mæcilius Hilarianus; Præfect, Hyginus[2]; Indict. v.*

He sent this Letter from the Emperor's Court by a soldier[3].

I SEND untó you, my beloved, late and beyond the accustomed time[4]; yet I trust you will forgive the delay, on account of my protracted journey, and because I have been tried with illness. Being hindered by these two causes, and unusually severe storms having occurred,

---

[6] Exod. xii. 7, 23.   [7] Luke xxiv. 5.
[1] The Syriac text has 17th instead of 7th. There is the same error in the index. The correct day is given towards the end of the Letter.
[2] There is sometimes a difficulty, in the absence of independent testimony, in ascertaining the exact orthography of the proper names, from the loose manner in which they are written in the Syriac. Here, however, it is clearly Hyginus, as in Sozomen, lib. ii. c. 25, Larsow writes it Eugenius. He has also the 46th instead of the 48th of the Diocletian Æra. The word 'Fabius' is not clear. In Baronii *Annal. Eccles.* however, we find it Ovinius.
[3] See note 6 at the end of the Letter.
[4] In the index it is stated that the *third*, but not that the *fourth*, Letter was sent late, but see *Letter* 3, note 1.

---

[17] Ps. xliv. 17.
[17b] Cf. James v. 13.
[20] Ps. xviii. 29.
[3] Ib. xi. 1; Eph. vi. 15.

[17a] Compare Ps. lxxxiii. 6.
[18] Phil. iv. 6.   [19] 1 Thess. v. 17.
[1] 1 Pet. i. 13.   [2] Is. xi. 5.
[4] 1 Cor. v. 8.   [5] Exod. xv. 1.

I have deferred writing to you. But notwithstanding my long journeys, and my grievous sickness, I have not forgotten to give you the festal notification, and, in discharge of my duty, I now announce to you the feast. For although the date of this letter is later [4a] than that usual for this announcement, it should still be considered well-timed, since our enemies having been put to shame and reproved by the Church, because they persecuted us without a cause [5], we may now sing a festal song of praise, uttering the triumphant hymn against Pharaoh; 'We will sing unto the Lord, for He is to be gloriously praised; the horse and his rider He hath cast into the sea [6].'

2. It is well, my beloved, to proceed from feast to feast; again festal meetings, again holy vigils arouse our minds, and compel our intellect to keep vigil unto contemplation of good things. Let us not fulfil these days like those that mourn, but, by enjoying spiritual food, let us seek to silence our fleshly lusts [7]. For by these means we shall have strength to overcome our adversaries, like blessed Judith [8], when having first exercised herself in fastings and prayers, she overcame the enemies, and killed Olophernes. And blessed Esther, when destruction was about to come on all her race, and the nation of Israel was ready to perish, defeated the fury of the tyrant by no other means than by fasting and prayer to God, and changed the ruin of her people into safety [9]. Now as those days are considered feasts for Israel, so also in old time feasts were appointed when an enemy was slain, or a conspiracy against the people broken up, and Israel delivered. Therefore blessed Moses of old time ordained the great feast of the Passover, and our celebration of it, because, namely, Pharaoh was killed, and the people were delivered from bondage. For in those times it was especially, when those who tyrannized over the people had been slain, that temporal feasts and holidays were observed in Judæa [10].

3. Now, however, that the devil, that tyrant against the whole world, is slain, we do not approach a temporal feast, my beloved, but an eternal and heavenly. Not in shadows do we shew it forth, but we come to it in truth. For they being filled with the flesh of a dumb lamb, accomplished the feast, and having anointed their door-posts with the blood, implored aid against the destroyer [11]. But now we,

eating of the Word of the Father, and having the lintels of our hearts sealed with the blood of the New Testament [12], acknowledge the grace given us from the Saviour, who said, 'Behold, I have given unto you to tread upon serpents and scorpions, and over all the power of the enemy [13].' For no more does death reign; but instead of death henceforth is life, since our Lord said, 'I am the life [14];' so that everything is filled with joy and gladness; as it is written, 'The Lord reigneth, let the earth rejoice.' For when death reigned, 'sitting down by the rivers of Babylon, we wept [15],' and mourned, because we felt the bitterness of captivity; but now that death and the kingdom of the devil is abolished, everything is entirely filled with joy and gladness. And God is no longer known only in Judæa, but in all the earth, 'their voice hath gone forth, and the knowledge of Him hath filled all the earth [16].' What follows, my beloved, is obvious; that we should approach such a feast, not with filthy raiment, but having clothed our minds with pure garments. For we need in this to put on our Lord Jesus [17], that we may be able to celebrate the feast with Him. Now we are clothed with Him when we love virtue, and are enemies to wickedness, when we exercise ourselves in temperance and mortify lasciviousness, when we love righteousness before iniquity, when we honour sufficiency, and have strength of mind, when we do not forget the poor, but open our doors to all men, when we assist humble-mindedness, but hate pride.

4. By these things Israel of old, having first, as in a figure, striven for the victory, came to the feast, for these things were then foreshadowed and typified. But we, my beloved, the shadow having received its fulfilment, and the types being accomplished, should no longer consider the feast typical, neither should we go up to Jerusalem which is here below, to sacrifice the Passover, according to the unseasonable observance of the Jews, lest, while the season passes away, we should be regarded as acting unseasonably [18]; but, in accordance with the injunction of the Apostles, let us go beyond the types, and sing the new song of praise. For perceiving this, and being assembled together with the Truth [19], they drew near, and said unto our Saviour, 'Where wilt Thou that we should make ready for Thee the Passover [1]?' For no longer were these things to be done which belonged to Jerusalem which is beneath; neither there alone was the feast to be celebrated, but wherever God willed it to be. Now

---

4a i.e. too late to give notice of the beginning of Lent, *infr.* § 5, and *Letter* 5, § 6.
5 Constantine, in his letter, *supr.* p. 133, speaks of the envy of the accusers of Athan. and of their unsuccessful efforts to criminate him. 6 Exod. xv. 1.
7 τοῖς τῆς σαρκὸς ἐπιτιμῶντες πάθεσιν. S. Cyril. *Hom. Pasch.* xx. 8 Judith xiii. 8. 9 Esther iv. 16.
10 Cf. Esther ix. 20—28; Judith ix. xv.
11 Conf. S. Cyril. *Hom. Pasch.* xxiv. p. 293. Ed. Paris, 1638.

12 Matt. xxvi. 28. 13 Luke x. 19, *Vit. Ant.* 30.
14 John xiv. 6. 15 Ps. xcvii. 1; cxxxvii. 1. 16 Ib. lxxvi. 1; xix. 4. 17 Cf. Rom. xiii. 14. 18 Cf. *Letter* i. (beginning)
19 σὺν τῇ ἀληθείᾳ. I understand this as referring to Christ. Vid. John xiv. 6. 1 Matt. xxvi. 17.

He willed it to be in every place, so that 'in every place incense and a sacrifice might be offered to Him [2].' For although, as in the historical account, in no other place might the feast of the Passover be kept save only in Jerusalem, yet when the things pertaining to that time were fulfilled, and those which belonged to shadows had passed away, and the preaching of the Gospel was about to extend everywhere; when indeed the disciples were spreading the feast in all places, they asked the Saviour, 'Where wilt Thou that we shall make ready?' The Saviour also, since He was changing the typical for the spiritual, promised them that they should no longer eat the flesh of a lamb, but His own, saying, 'Take, eat and drink; this is My body, and My blood [3].' When we are thus nourished by these things, we also, my beloved, shall truly keep the feast of the Passover.

5. We begin on the first of Pharmuthi (Mar. 27), and rest on the sixth of the same month (Apr. 1), on the evening of the seventh day; and the holy first day of the week having risen upon us on the seventh of the same Pharmuthi (Apr. 2), celebrate we too the days of holy Pentecost following thereon, shewing forth through them the world to come [4], so that henceforth we may be with Christ for ever, praising God over all in Christ Jesus, and through Him, with all saints, we say unto the Lord, Amen. Salute one another with a holy kiss. All the brethren who are with me salute you. We have sent this letter from the Court, by the hand of an attendant officer [5], to whom it was given by Ablavius [6], the Præfect of the Prætorium, who fears God in truth. For I am at the Court, having been summoned by the emperor Constantine to see him. But the Meletians, who were present there, being envious, sought our ruin before the Emperor. But they were put to shame and driven away thence as calumniators, being confuted by many things. Those who were driven away were Callinicus, Ision, Eudæmon, and Gelœus [7] Hieracammon, who, on account of the shame of his name, calls himself Eulogius.

Here endeth the fourth Festal Letter of holy Athanasius.

LETTER V.

For 333.

Easter-day [1], Coss. Dalmatius and Zenophilus; Præfect, Paternus [2]; vi Indict.; xvii Kal. Maii, xx Pharmuthi; xv Moon; vii Gods; Æra Dioclet. 49.

WE duly proceed, my brethren, from feasts to feasts, duly from prayers to prayers, we advance from fasts to fasts, and join holy-days to holy-days. Again the time has arrived which brings to us a new beginning [3], even the announcement of the blessed Passover, in which the Lord was sacrificed. We eat, as it were, the food of life, and con-stantly thirsting we delight our souls at all times, as from a fountain, in His precious blood. For we continually and ardently desire; He stands ready for those who thirst; and for those who thirst there is the word of our Saviour, which, in His loving-kindness, He uttered on the day of the feast; 'If any man thirst, let him come to Me and drink [4].' Nor was it then alone when any one drew near to Him, that He cured his thirst; but whenever any one seeks, there is free access for him to the Saviour. For the grace of the feast is not limited to one time, nor does its splendid brilliancy de-cline; but it is always near, enlightening the minds of those who earnestly desire it [5]. For therein is constant virtue, for those who are illuminated in their minds, and me-ditate on the divine Scriptures day and night, like the man to whom a blessing is given, as it is written in the sacred Psalms; 'Blessed is the man who hath not walked in the counsel of the ungodly, nor stood in the way of sinners, nor sat in the seat of corrupters. But his de-light is in the law of the Lord, and in His law doth he meditate day and night [6].' For it is not the sun, or the moon, or the host of those other stars which illumines him, but he glitters with the high effulgence of God over all.

2. For it is God, my beloved, even the God Who at first established the feast for us, Who vouchsafes the celebration of it year by year. He both brought about the slaying of His Son for salvation, and gave us this reason for the holy feast, to which every year bears witness, as often as at this season the feast is pro-claimed. This also leads us on from the cross through this world to that which is before us, and God produces even now from it the

---

[2] Mal. i. 11.   [3] Matt. xxvi. 26—28.
[4] Cf. Bingham, xx. ch. 6; Cass. Coll. xxi. 11; Cyril uses the same comparison towards the end of his 26th Paschal discourse.
[5] 'Officilius.' Cureton considers this may be an error for the Latin Officialis.
[6] Ablavius, Præfect of the East, the minister and favourite of Constantine the Great, was murdered after the death of the latter. He was consul in the preceding year. Zozimus ii. 40. (Smith's *Dict. of Gr. and Rom. Biography*.)
[7] The name means 'Laughable.'

[1] See *supr.* Table D, and note. The full moon ('Moon xiv') was really on Pharm. 20, but seems to have been calculated to fall on the previous day.
[2] The Syriac seems to represent 'Paterius,' not 'Paternus' as Larsow writes it. A former præfect of Egypt was called Paterius, according to Gelas. Cyz. in Hard. *Conc.* i. 459.
[3] Cf. Rev. iii. 14, c. Apoll. i. 20.
[4] John vii. 37. The Syriac is rather obscure here.
[5] Vid. note 2, to *Letter* 1.   [6] Ps. i. 1, 2

joy of glorious salvation, bringing us to the same assembly, and in every place uniting all of us in spirit; appointing us common prayers, and a common grace proceeding from the feast. For this is the marvel of His loving-kindness, that He should gather together in the same place those who are at a distance; and make those who appear to be far off in the body, to be near together in unity of spirit.

3. Wherefore then, my beloved, do we not acknowledge the grace as becometh the feast? Wherefore do we not make a return to our Benefactor? It is indeed impossible to make an adequate return to God; still, it is a wicked thing for us who receive the gracious gift, not to acknowledge it. Nature itself manifests our inability; but our own will reproves our unthankfulness. Therefore the blessed Paul, when admiring the greatness of the gift of God, said, 'And who is sufficient for these things[7]?' For He made the world free by the blood of the Saviour; then, again, He has caused the grave to be trodden down by the Saviour's death, and furnished a way to the heavenly gates free from obstacles to those who are going up[8]. Wherefore, one of the saints, while he acknowledged the grace, but was insufficient to repay it, said, 'What shall I render unto the Lord for all He has done unto me[9]?' For instead of death he had received life, instead of bondage[10], freedom, and instead of the grave, the kingdom of heaven. For of old time, 'death reigned from Adam to Moses;' but now the divine voice hath said, 'To-day shalt thou be with Me in Paradise.' And the saints, being sensible of this, said, 'Except the Lord had helped me, my soul had almost dwelt in hell[10a].' Besides all this, being powerless to make a return, he yet acknowledged the gift, and wrote finally, saying, 'I will take the cup of salvation, and call on the name of the Lord; precious in His sight is the death of His saints[11].'

With regard to the cup, the Lord said, 'Are ye able to drink of that cup which I am about to drink of?' And when the disciples assented, the Lord said, 'Ye shall indeed drink of My cup; but that ye should sit on My right hand, and on My left, is not Mine to give; but to those for whom it is prepared[12].' Therefore, my beloved, let us be sensible of the gift,

though we are found insufficient to repay it. As we have ability, let us meet the occasion. For although nature is not able, with things unworthy of the Word, to return a recompense for such benefits, yet let us render Him thanks while we persevere in piety. And how can we more abide in piety than when we acknowledge God, Who in His love to mankind has bestowed on us such benefits? (For thus we shall obediently keep the law, and observe its commandments. And, further, we shall not, as unthankful persons, be accounted transgressors of the law, or do those things which ought to be hated, for the Lord loveth the thankful); when too we offer ourselves to the Lord, like the saints, when we subscribe ourselves entirely [as] living henceforth not to ourselves, but to the Lord Who died for us, as also the blessed Paul did, when he said, 'I am crucified with Christ, yet I live; yet not I, but Christ liveth in me[13].'

4. Now our life, my brethren, truly consists in our denying all bodily things, and continuing stedfast in those only of our Saviour. Therefore the present season requires of us, that we should not only utter such words, but should also imitate the deeds of the saints. But we imitate them, when we acknowledge Him who died, and no longer live unto ourselves, but Christ henceforth lives in us; when we render a recompense to the Lord to the utmost of our power, though when we make a return we give nothing of our own, but those things which we have before received from Him, this being especially of His grace, that He should require, as from us, His own gifts. He bears witness to this when He says, 'My offerings are My own gifts[14].' That is, those things which you give Me are yours, as having received them from Me, but they are the gifts of God. And let us offer to the Lord every virtue, and that true holiness which is in Him, and in piety let us keep the feast to Him with those things which He has hallowed for us. Let us thus engage in the holy fasts, as having been prescribed by Him, and by means of which we find the way to God. But let us not be like the heathen, or the ignorant Jews, or as the heretics and schismatics of the present time. For the heathen think the accomplishment of the feast is in the abundance of food; the Jews, erring in the type and shadow, think it still such; the schismatics keep it in separate places, and with vain imaginations. But let us, my brethren, be superior to the heathen, in keeping the feast with sincerity of soul, and purity of body; to the Jews, in no longer receiving the type and the shadow, but

---

[7] 2 Cor. ii. 17.
[8] This sentence is preserved in the original Greek in Cosmas, *Topogr. Christ.* p. 316.　　[9] Ps. cxvi. 12.
[10] Pseudo-Ath. *in Matt.* xxi. 9. (Migne xxviii. 1025), after quoting the same passage from the Epistle to the Romans, says, ἀλλ' ἐπεδήμησεν ὁ Κύριος ἡμῶν Ἰησοῦς Χριστὸς λυτρούμενος τοὺς αἰχμαλώτους, καὶ ζωοποιῶν τοὺς τεθανατωμένους.
[10a] Rom. v. 14; Luke xxiii. 43; Ps. xciv. 17.
[11] Ps. cxvi. 13, 15.　　[12] Matt. xx. 22, 23

[13] Gal. ii. 20.　　[14] Num. xxviii. 2, LXX.

as having been gloriously illumined with the light of truth, and as looking upon the Sun of Righteousness [15] ; to the schismatics, in not rending the coat of Christ, but in one house, even in the Catholic Church, let us eat the Passover of the Lord, Who, by ordaining His holy laws, guided us towards virtue, and counselled the abstinence of this feast. For the Passover is indeed abstinence from evil for exercise of virtue, and a departure from death unto life. This may be learnt even from the type of old time. For then they toiled earnestly to pass from Egypt to Jerusalem, but now we depart from death to life ; they then passed from Pharaoh to Moses, but now we rise from the devil to the Saviour. And as, at that time, the type of deliverance bore witness every year, so now we commemorate our salvation. We fast meditating on death, that we may be able to live; and we watch, not as mourners, but as they that wait for the Lord, when He shall have returned from the wedding, so that we may vie with each other in the triumph, hastening to announce the sign of victory over death.

5. Would therefore, O my beloved, that as the word requires, we might here so govern ourselves at all times and entirely, and so live, as never to forget the noble acts of God, nor to depart from the practice of virtue! As also the Apostolic voice exhorts ; ' Remember Jesus Christ, that He rose from the dead [16].' Not that any limited season of remembrance was appointed, for at all times He should be in our thoughts. But because of the slothfulness of many, we delay from day to day. Let us then begin in these days. To this end a time of remembrance is permitted, that it may show forth to the saints the reward of their calling, and may exhort the careless while reproving them [17]. Therefore in all the remaining days, let us persevere in virtuous conduct, repenting as is our duty, of all that we have neglected, whatever it may be; for there is no one free from defilement, though his course may have been but one hour on the earth, as Job, that man of surpassing fortitude, testifies. But, ' stretching forth to those things that are to come [18],' let us pray that we may not eat the Passover unworthily, lest we be exposed to dangers. For to those who keep the feast in purity, the Passover is heavenly food ; but to those who observe it profanely and contemptuously, it is a danger and reproach. For it is written, ' Whosoever

shall eat and drink unworthily, is guilty of the death of our Lord [19].' Wherefore, let us not merely proceed to perform the festal rites, but let us be prepared to draw near to the divine Lamb, and to touch heavenly food. Let us cleanse our hands, let us purify the body. Let us keep our whole mind from guile ; not giving up ourselves to excess, and to lusts, but occupying ourselves entirely with our Lord, and with divine doctrines ; so that, being altogether pure, we may be able to partake of the Word [20]

6. We begin the holy fast on the fourteenth of Pharmuthi (Apr. 9), on the [first] evening of the week [21]; and having ceased on the nineteenth of the same month Pharmuthi (Apr 14), the first day of the holy week dawns upon us on the twentieth of the same month Pharmuthi (Apr. 15), to which we join the seven weeks of Pentecost ; with prayers, and fellowship with our neighbour, and love towards one another, and that peaceable will which is above all. For so shall we be heirs of the kingdom of heaven, through our Lord Jesus Christ, through Whom to the Father be glory and dominion for ever and ever. Amen. All the brethren who are with me salute you. Salute one another with a holy kiss.

Here endeth the fifth Festal Letter of holy Athanasius.

LETTER VI.

For 334.

Easter-day, xii Pharmuth, vii Id. April: xvii Moon; Æra Dioclet. 50 ; Coss. Optatus Patricius, Anicius Paulinus ; Præfect, Philagrius [1], the Cappadocian; vii Indict.

Now again, my beloved, has God brought us to the season of the feast, and through His loving-kindness we have reached the period of assembly for it. For that God who brought Israel out of Egypt, even He at this time calls us to the feast, saying by Moses, ' Observe the month of new fruits [2], and keep the Passover to the Lord thy God [3]:' and by the prophet, ' Keep thy feasts, O Judah ; pay to the Lord thy vows [4].' If then God Himself loves the feast, and calls us to it, it is not right, my brethren, that it should be delayed, or observed carelessly ; but with alacrity and zeal we should come to it, so that having begun joyfully here, we may also receive an earnest of that heavenly feast. For if we diligently celebrate the feast here, we shall doubtless receive the perfect joy which is in heaven, as

---

[15] Mal. iv. 2.   [16] 2 Tim. ii. 8.
[17] The reasoning of Athan. is to this effect. The due observance of such festival will have its effect in quickening our *habitual* meditation on the resurrection. The same mode of reasoning might be applied to all the other Christian festivals.
[18] Job xiv. 4 (LXX.) ; Phil. iii. 13.

[19] 1 Cor. xi. 27.   [20] Cf. 2 Pet. i. 4.   [21] Syr. ' sabbath.
[1] The index gives still Paternus for Letters 6 and 7. On Philarius, see p. 93, note 2.
[2] Cf. i. 9, n. 12.   [3] Deut. xvi. 1.   [4] Nahum i. 15.

the Lord says; 'With desire I have desired to eat this Passover with you before I suffer. For I say unto you, that I will not eat it, until it is fulfilled with you in the kingdom of God[5].' Now we eat it if, understanding the reason of the feast, and acknowledging the Deliverer, we conduct ourselves in accordance with His grace, as Paul saith; 'So that we may keep the Feast, not with old leaven, neither with the leaven of wickedness; but with the unleavened bread of sincerity and truth[6].' For the Lord died in those days, that we should no longer do the deeds of death. He gave His life, that we might preserve our own from the snares of the devil. And, what is most wonderful, the Word became flesh, that we should no longer live in the flesh, but in spirit should worship God, who is Spirit. He who is not so disposed, abuses the days, and does not keep the feast, but like an unthankful person finds fault with the grace, and honours the days overmuch, while he does not supplicate the Lord who in those days redeemed him. Let him by all means hear, though fancying that he keeps the feast, the Apostolic voice reproving him; 'Ye observe days, and months, and times, and years: I fear lest I have laboured among you in vain[7].'

2. For the feast is not on account of the days; but for the Lord's sake, who then suffered for us, we celebrate it, for 'our Passover, Christ, is sacrificed[8].' Even as Moses, when teaching Israel not to consider the feast as pertaining to the days, but to the Lord, said, 'It is the Lord's Passover[9].' To the Jews, when they thought they were keeping the Passover, because they persecuted the Lord, the feast was useless; since it no longer bore the name of the Lord, even according to their own testimony. It was not the Passover of the Lord, but that of the Jews[10]. The Passover was named after the Jews, my brethren, because they denied the Lord of the Passover. On this account, the Lord, turning away His face from such a doctrine of theirs, saith, 'Your new moons and your sabbaths My soul hateth[11].'

3. So now, those who keep the Passover in like manner, the Lord again reproves, as He did those lepers who were cleansed, when He loved the one as thankful, but was angry with the others as ungrateful, because they did not acknowledge their Deliverer, but thought more of the cure of the leprosy than of Him who healed them. 'But one of them when he saw that he was healed, turned back, and

with a loud voice glorified God, and fell on his face at the feet of Jesus giving Him thanks; and he was a Samaritan. And Jesus answering said, Were there not ten cleansed? but those nine—whence are there none found who returned to give glory to God, but this stranger[12]?' And there was more given to him than to the rest; for being cleansed from his leprosy, he heard from the Lord, 'Arise, go thy way, thy faith hath saved thee[13].' For he who gives thanks, and he who glorifies, have kindred feelings, in that they bless their Helper for the benefits they have received. So the Apostle exhorts all men to this, saying, 'Glorify God with your body;' and the prophet commands, saying, 'Give glory to God.' Although testimony was borne by Caiaphas[14] against our Redeemer, and He was set at nought by the Jews, and was condemned by Pilate in those days, yet exalted exceedingly and most mighty was the voice of the Father which came to Him; 'I have glorified, and will glorify again[15].' For those things which He suffered for our sake have passed away; but those which belong to Him as the Saviour remain for ever.

4. But in our commemoration of these things, my brethren, let us not be occupied with meats, but let us glorify the Lord, let us become fools for Him who died for us, even as Paul said; 'For if we are foolish, it is to God; or if we are sober-minded, it is to you; since because one died for all men, therefore all were dead to Him; and He died for all, that we who live should not henceforth live to ourselves, but to Him who died for us, and rose again[16].' No longer then ought we to live to ourselves, but, as servants to the Lord. And not in vain should we receive the grace, as the time is especially an acceptable one[17], and the day of salvation hath dawned, even the death of our Redeemer[18]. For even for our sakes the Word came down, and being incorruptible, put on a corruptible body for the salvation of all of us. Of which Paul was confident, saying, 'This corruptible must put on incorruption[19].' The Lord too was sacrificed, that by His blood He might abolish death. Full well did He once, in a certain place, blame those who participated vainly in the shedding of His blood, while they did not delight themselves in the flesh of the Word, saying, 'What profit is there in my blood, that I go down to corruption[20]?' This does not mean that the descent of the Lord was without profit, for it gained the whole world; but rather that

5 Luke xxii. 15, 16.   6 1 Cor. v. 8.
7 Gal. iv. 10, 11.   8 1 Cor. v. 7.   9 Exod. xii. 11.
10 Cf. John vi. 4. 'And the passover, *a feast of the Jews*, was nigh.' Cf. Origenis *Comment. in Ioannem*, tom. x. § 11. p. 172. ed. 1759.   11 Is. i. 14.

12 Luke xvii. 15, &c.   13 Ib. 19.   14 1 Cor. vi. 20; Is. xlii. 12; Matt. xxvi. 65.   15 John xii. 28.   16 2 Cor. v. 13—15. 17 Ib. vi. 1, 2.   18 Cf. S. Cyril. *Hom. Pasch.* xxiv. sub init. 19 1 Cor. xv. 53.   20 Ps. xxx. 9.

after He had thus suffered, sinners would prefer to suffer loss than to profit by it. For He regarded our salvation as a delight and a peculiar gain; while on the contrary He looked upon our destruction as loss.

5. Also in the Gospel, He praises those who increased the grace twofold, both him who made ten talents of five, and him who made four talents of two, as those who had profited, and turned them to good account; but him who hid the talent He cast out as wanting, saying to him, 'Thou wicked servant! oughtest thou not to have put My money to the exchangers? then at My coming I should have received Mine own with interest. Take, therefore, from him the talent, and give it to him that hath ten talents. For to every one that hath shall be given, and he shall have more abundantly; but from him that hath not, shall be taken away even that which he hath. And cast ye the unprofitable servant into outer darkness; there shall be weeping and gnashing of teeth[21].' For it is not His will that the grace we have received should be unprofitable; but He requires us to take pains to render Him His own fruits, as the blessed Paul saith; 'The fruit of the Spirit is love, joy, and peace[1].' Having therefore this right resolution, and owing no man anything, but rather giving everything to every man, he was a teacher of the like rightness of principle, saying, 'Render to all their dues[2].' He was like those sent by the householder to receive the fruits of the vineyard from the husbandmen[3]; for he exhorted all men to render a return. But Israel despised and would not render, for their will was not right, nay moreover they killed those that were sent, and not even before the Lord of the vineyard were they ashamed, but even He was slain by them. Verily, when He came and found no fruit in them, He cursed them through the fig-tree, saying, 'Let there be henceforth no fruit from thee[4];' and the fig-tree was dead and fruitless, so that even the disciples wondered when it withered away.

6. Then was fulfilled that which was spoken by the prophet; 'I will take away from them the voice of joy and the voice of gladness, the voice of the bridegroom and the voice of the bride, the scent of myrrh, and the light of a lamp, and the whole land shall be destroyed[5].' For the whole service of the law has been abolished from them, and henceforth and for ever they remain without a feast. And they observe not the Passover; for how can they? They have no abiding place, but they wander everywhere. And they eat unleavened bread contrary to the law, since they are unable first to sacrifice the lamb, as they were commanded to do when eating unleavened bread. But in every place they transgress the law, and as the judgments of God require, they keep days of grief instead of gladness. Now the cause of this to them was the slaying of the Lord, and that they did not reverence the Only-Begotten. At this time the altogether wicked heretics and ignorant schismatics are in the same case; the one in that they slay the Word, the other in that they rend the coat. They too remain expelled from the feast, because they live without godliness and knowledge, and emulate the conduct shewn in the matter of Bar-Abbas the robber, whom the Jews desired instead of the Saviour. Therefore the Lord cursed them under the figure of the fig-tree. Yet even thus He spared them in His loving-kindness, not destroying them root and all. For He did not curse the root, but [said], that no man should eat fruit of it thenceforth. When He did this, He abolished the shadow, causing it to wither; but preserved the root, so that we might [not][6] be grafted upon it; 'they too, if they abide not in unbelief, may attain to be grafted into their own olive tree[7].' Now when the Lord had cursed them because of their negligence, He removed from them the new moons, the true lamb, and that which is truly the Passover.

7. But to us it came: there came too the solemn day, in which we ought to call to the feast with a trumpet[8], and separate ourselves to the Lord with thanksgiving, considering it as our own festival[9]. For we are bound to celebrate it, not to ourselves but to the Lord; and to rejoice, not in ourselves but in the Lord, who bore our griefs and said, 'My soul is sorrowful unto death[10].' For the heathen, and all those who are strangers to our faith, keep feasts according to their own wills, and have no peace, since they commit evil against God. But the saints, as they live to the Lord also keep the feast to Him, saying, 'I will rejoice in Thy salvation,' and, 'my soul shall be joyful in the Lord.' The commandment is common to them, 'Rejoice, ye righteous, in the Lord[11]'—so that they also may be gathered together, to sing that common and festal Psalm, 'Come, let us rejoice[12],' not in ourselves, but, 'in the Lord.'

---

6 The negative (which is here placed within brackets) is found in the Syriac text; but there is little doubt that it is an error.
7 Rom. xi. 23.
8 Cf. *Letter* i. S. Cyril, *Hom.* i. *de Festis Pasch.* vol. **v.** pt. 2, p. 6.
9 The Passover is no longer to be a feast of the Jews: it is to be celebrated by Christians as a festival of the Lord. Vid. § 2. n. 10.
10 Matt. xxvi. 38.
11 Ps. ix. 14, xxxv. 9; Ib. xxxiii. 1.
12 Ps. xcv. 1.

8. For thus the patriarch Abraham rejoiced not to see his own day, but that of the Lord; and thus looking forward ' he saw it, and was glad [13].' And when he was tried, by faith he offered up Isaac, and sacrificed his only-begotten son—he who had received the promises. And, in offering his son, he worshipped the Son of God. And, being restrained from sacrificing Isaac, he saw the Messiah in the ram [14], which was offered up instead as a sacrifice to God. The patriarch was tried, through Isaac, not however that he was sacrificed, but He who was pointed out in Isaiah; ' He shall be led as a lamb to the slaughter, and as a sheep before her shearers he shall be speechless [15];' but He took away the sin of the world. And on this account [Abraham] was restrained from laying his hand on the lad, lest the Jews, taking occasion from the sacrifice of Isaac, should reject the prophetic declarations concerning our Saviour, even all of them, but more especially those uttered by the Psalmist; ' Sacrifice and offering Thou wouldest not; a body Thou hast prepared Me [16];' and should refer all such things as these to the son of Abraham.

9. For the sacrifice was not properly the setting to rights [17] of Isaac, but of Abraham who also offered, and by that was tried. Thus God accepted the will of the offerer, but prevented that which was offered from being sacrificed. For the death of Isaac did not procure freedom to the world, but that of our Saviour alone, by whose stripes we all are healed [18]. For He raised up the falling, healed the sick, satisfied those who were hungry, and filled the poor, and, what is more wonderful, raised us all from the dead; having abolished death, He has brought us from affliction and sighing to the rest and gladness of this feast, a joy which reacheth even to heaven. For not we alone are affected by this, but because of it, even the heavens rejoice with us, and the whole church of the firstborn, written in heaven [19], is made glad together, as the prophet proclaims, saying, ' Rejoice, ye heavens, for the Lord hath had mercy upon Israel. Shout, ye foundations of the earth. Cry out with joy, ye mountains, ye high places, and all the trees which are in them, for the Lord hath redeemed Jacob, and Israel hath been glorified [20].' And again; ' Rejoice, and be glad, ye heavens; let the hills melt into gladness,

for the Lord hath had mercy on His people, and comforted the oppressed of the people [1].'

10. The whole creation keeps a feast, my brethren, and everything that hath breath praises the Lord [2], as the Psalmist [says], on account of the destruction of the enemies, and our salvation. And justly indeed; for if there is joy in heaven over one sinner that repenteth [3], what should there not be over the abolition of sin, and the resurrection of the dead? Oh what a feast and how great the gladness in heaven! how must all its hosts joy and exult, as they rejoice and watch in our assemblies, those that are held continually, and especially those at Easter? For they look on sinners while they repent; on those who have turned away their faces, when they become converted; on those who formerly persisted in lusts and excess, but who now humble themselves by fastings and temperance; and, finally, on the enemy who lies weakened, lifeless, bound hand and foot, so that we may mock at him; 'Where is thy victory, O Death? where is thy sting, O Grave [4]?' Let us then sing unto the Lord a song of victory.

11. Who then will lead us to such a company of angels as this? Who, coming with a desire for the heavenly feast, and the angelic holiday, will say like the prophet, ' I will pass to the place of the wondrous tabernacle, unto the house of God; with the voice of joy and praise, with the shouting of those who keep festival [5]?' To this course the saints also encourage us, saying, ' Come, let us go up to the mountain of the Lord, and to the house of the God of Jacob [6].' But not for the impure is this feast, nor is the ascent thereto for sinners; but it is for the virtuous and diligent; and for those who live according to the aim of the saints; for, ' Who shall ascend to the hill of the Lord? or who shall stand in His holy place, but he that hath clean hands, and a pure heart; who hath not devoted his soul to vanity, nor sworn deceitfully to his neighbour. For he,' as the Psalmist adds, when he goes up, 'shall receive a blessing from the Lord [7].' Now this clearly also refers to what the Lord gives to them at the right hand, saying, ' Come, ye blessed, inherit the kingdom prepared for you [8].' But the deceitful, and he that is not pure of heart, and possesses nothing that is pure (as the Proverb saith, 'To a deceitful man there is nothing good [9]'), shall assuredly, being a stranger, and of a different race from the saints, be accounted unworthy to eat the Passover, for ' a foreigner shall not

---

[13] John viii. 56; Heb. xi. 17.
[14] Gen. xxii. 15. The Syriac, here rendered by 'ram,' is the usual word for sheep, common gender. It is the same word that is used directly after, in the quotation from Isaiah, and rendered 'lamb.'　　　[15] Is. liii. 7.　　　[16] Ps. xl. 6.
[17] The phrase 'setting to rights' is used for want of one that would better express the meaning. The Syriac noun is that used to render διόρθωσις in Heb. ix. 10, from a verb 'to make straight, set upright, or right.'　　　[18] Is. liii. 5.
[19] Heb. xii. 23.　　　[20] Is. xliv. 23.

[1] Is. xlix. 13.　　[2] Ps. cl. 6.　　[3] Luke xv. 7.　　[4] 1 Cor. xv. 55. Cf. Incarn. 27.　　[5] Ps. xlii. 4.　　[6] Is. ii. 3.
[7] Ps. xxiv. 3.　　[8] Matt. xxv. 34.　　[9] Prov. xiii. 13, LXX.

eat of it [10].' Thus Judas, when he thought he kept the Passover, because he plotted deceit against the Saviour, was estranged from the city which is above, and from the apostolic company. For the law commanded the Passover to be eaten with due observance; but he, while eating it, was sifted of the devil [11], who had entered his soul.

12. Wherefore let us not celebrate the feast after an earthly manner, but as keeping festival in heaven with the angels. Let us glorify the Lord, by chastity, by righteousness, and other virtues. And let us rejoice, not in ourselves, but in the Lord, that we may be inheritors with the saints. Let us keep the feast then, as Moses. Let us watch like David, who rose seven times, and in the middle of the night gave thanks for the righteous judgments of God. Let us be early, as he said, ' In the morning I will stand before Thee, and Thou wilt look upon me: in the morning Thou wilt hear my voice [12].' Let us fast like Daniel; let us pray without ceasing, as Paul commanded; all of us recognising the season of prayer, but especially those who are honourably married; so that having borne witness to these things, and thus having kept the feast, we may be able to enter into the joy of Christ in the kingdom of heaven [13]. But as Israel, when going up to Jerusalem, was first purified in the wilderness, being trained to forget the customs of Egypt, the Word by this typifying to us the holy fast of forty days, let us first be purified and freed from defilement [14], so that when we depart hence, having been careful of fasting, we may be able to ascend to the upper chamber [15] with the Lord, to sup with Him ; and may be partakers of the joy which is in heaven. In no other manner is it possible to go up to Jerusalem, and to eat the Passover, except by observing the fast of forty days.

13. We begin the fast of forty days on the first day of the month Phamenoth (Feb. 25); and having prolonged it till the fifth of Pharmuthi (Mar. 31), suspending it upon the Sundays and the Saturdays [16] preceding them, we then begin again on the holy days of Easter, on the sixth of Pharmuthi (Apr. 1), and cease on the eleventh of the same month (Apr. 6), late in the evening [17] of the Saturday, whence dawns on us the holy Sunday, on the twelfth of Pharmuthi (Apr. 7), which extends its beams, with unobscured grace, to all the seven weeks of the holy Pentecost. Resting on that day, let us ever keep Easter joy in Christ Jesus our Lord, through Whom, to the Father, be glory and dominion for ever and ever. Amen. All the brethren who are with me salute you. Salute one another with a holy kiss.

Here endeth the sixth Festal Letter of the holy and God-clad Athanasius.

LETTER VII.

For 335.

Easter-day iv Pharmuthi, iii Kal. April; xx Moon; Ær. Dioclet. 51 ; Coss. Julius Constantius, the brother of Augustus, Rufinus Albinus ; Præfect, the same Philagrius ; viii Indict.

THE blessed Paul [1] wrote to the Corinthians [2] that he always bore in his body the dying of Jesus, not as though he alone should make that boast, but also they and we too, and in this let us be followers of him, my brethren. And let this be the customary boast of all of us at all times. In this David participated, saying in the Psalms, ' For thy sake we die all the day ; we are accounted as sheep for the slaughter [3].' Now this is becoming in us, especially in the days of the feast, when a commemoration of the death of our Saviour is held. For he who is made like Him in His death, is also diligent in virtuous practices, having mortified his members which are upon the earth [4], and crucifying the flesh with the affections and lusts, he lives in the Spirit, and is conformed to the Spirit [5]. He is always mindful of God, and forgets Him not, and never does the deeds of death. Now, in order that we may bear in our body the dying of Jesus, he immediately adds the way of such fellowship, saying, ' we having the same spirit of faith, as it is written, I believed, and therefore have I spoken ; we also believe, and therefore speak [6].' He adds also, speaking of the grace that arises from knowledge ; ' For He that raised up Jesus, will also raise us up with Jesus, and will present us before Him with you [7].'

2. When by such faith and knowledge the saints have embraced this true life, they receive, doubtless, the joy which is in heaven ; for which the wicked not caring, are deservedly

---

10 Exod. xii. 43.   11 Cf. Luke xxii. 31.   12 Ps. v. 3.
13 A line or two is preserved here in the original Greek in Cosmas *Topog. Christ.* p. 316.
14 Gregory Nazianzen speaks of the Lenten fast as καθαρσις προεόρτιος, vol. i. p. 715. § 30. ed. Ben. fol. Par. 1778.
15 Cf. Luke xiv. 15.
16 The Saturdays and Sundays during Lent were not observed as fasts, with the exception of the day before Easter-day. S. Ambrose says, Quadragesima tot's præter Sabbatum et Dominicam jejunatur diebus. vol. i. p. 545, § 34. ed Par. 1686-90.
17 Cf. Dionys Alex. *ad Basilid.* in Routh *Rell. Sac.* iii. 226.

1 The twentieth Letter, as far as it is extant, bears a great resemblance with this. In both, the comparison between natural and spiritual food is enlarged upon, and several of the same quotations are adduced in them, to illustrate the character of sinners and their food, as contrasted with righteous, and the nourishment they derive from God.   2 2 Cor. iv. 10.
3 Ps. xliv. 22.   4 Col. iii. 5.   5 Gal. v. 25.
6 2 Cor. iv. 13.   7 Ib. 14, reading with R.V. marg. and Vulg. against Text. Rec. and Pesh.

deprived of the blessedness arising from it. For, 'let the wicked be taken away, so that he shall not see the glory of the Lord[8].' For although, when they shall hear the universal proclamation of the promise, 'Awake, thou that sleepest, and arise from the dead[9],' they shall rise and shall come even to heaven, knocking and saying, 'Open to us[10];' nevertheless the Lord will reprove them, as those who put the knowledge of Himself far from them, saying, 'I know you not.' But the holy Spirit cries against them, 'The wicked shall be turned into hell, even all the nations that forget God[11].' Now we say that the wicked are dead, but not in an ascetic life opposed to sin; nor do they, like the saints, bear about dying in their bodies. But it is the soul which they bury in sins and follies, drawing near to the dead, and satisfying it with dead nourishment; like young eagles which, from high places, fly upon the carcases of the dead, and which the law prohibited, commanding figuratively, 'Thou shalt not eat the eagle, nor any other bird that feedeth on a dead carcase[12];' and it pronounced unclean whatsoever eateth the dead. But these kill the soul with lusts, and say nothing but, 'let us eat and drink, for to-morrow we die[13].' And the kind of fruit those have who thus love pleasures, he immediately describes, adding, 'And these things are revealed in the ears of the Lord of Hosts, that this sin shall not be forgiven you until ye die[14].' Yea, even while they live they shall be ashamed, because they consider their belly their lord; and when dead, they shall be tormented, because they have made a boast of such a death. To this effect also Paul bears witness, saying, 'Meats for the belly, and the belly for meats; but God shall destroy both it and them[15].' And the divine word declared before concerning them; 'The death of sinners is evil, and those who hate the righteous commit sin[16].' For bitter is the worm, and grievous the darkness, which wicked men inherit.

3. But the saints, and they who truly practise virtue, 'mortify their members which are upon the earth, fornication, uncleanness, passions, evil concupiscence[17];' and, as the result of this, are pure and without spot, confiding in the promise of our Saviour, who said, 'Blessed are the pure in heart, for they shall see God[18].' These, having become dead to the world, and renounced the merchandise of the world, gain an honourable death; for, 'precious in the sight of the Lord is the death of His saints[19].' They are also able, preserving the Apostolic likeness, to say, 'I am crucified with Christ, nevertheless I live; yet not I, but Christ liveth in me[20].' For that is the true life, which a man lives in Christ; for although they are dead to the world, yet they dwell as it were in heaven, minding those things which are above, as he who was a lover of such a habitation said, 'While we walk on earth, our dwelling is in heaven[21].' Now those who thus live, and are partakers in such virtue, are alone able to give glory to God, and this it is which essentially constitutes a feast and a holiday[1]. For the feast does not consist in pleasant intercourse at meals, nor splendour[2] of clothing, nor days of leisure, but in the acknowledgment of God, and the offering of thanksgiving and of praise to Him[3]. Now this belongs to the saints alone, who live in Christ; for it is written, 'The dead shall not praise Thee, O Lord, neither all those who go down into silence; but we who live will bless the Lord, from henceforth even for ever[4].' So was it with Hezekiah, who was delivered from death, and therefore praised God, saying, 'Those who are in hades cannot praise Thee; the dead cannot bless Thee; but the living shall bless Thee, as I also do[5].' For to praise and bless God belongs to those only who live in Christ, and by means of this they go up to the feast; for the Passover is not of the Gentiles, nor of those who are yet Jews in the flesh; but of those who acknowledge the truth in Christ[6], as he declares who was sent to proclaim such a feast; 'Our Passover, Christ, is sacrificed[7].'

4. Therefore, although wicked men press forward to keep the feast, and as at a feast praise God, and intrude into the Church of the saints, yet God expostulates, saying to the sinner, 'Why dost thou talk of My ordinances?' And the gentle Spirit rebukes them, saying, 'Praise is not comely in the mouth of a sinner[8].' Neither hath sin any place in common with the praise of God; for the sinner has a mouth speaking perverse things, as the Proverb saith, 'The mouth of the wicked answereth evil things[9].' For how is it possible for us to praise God with an impure mouth? since things which are contrary to each other cannot coexist. For what communion has righteousness with iniquity? or, what fellowship is there between light and darkness? So exclaims Paul, a minister of the Gospel[10].

---

8 Is. xxvi. 10 (LXX.).   9 Eph. v. 14.   10 Matt. xxv. 11.
11 Luke xiii. 25; Ps. ix. 17.   12 Lev. xi. 13.   13 Is. xxii. 13.
14 Ib. 14.   15 1 Cor. vi. 13.   16 Ps. xxxiv. 21.   17 Col. iii. 5.   18 Matt. v. 8.   19 Ps. cxvi. 15.

20 Gal. ii. 20.
21 The quotation is uncertain, but see ad Diognet. v. 9; cf. also Phil. iii. 20, with which the passage in the text is coupled, and ascribed to 'the Apostle,' in the probably spurious Homily on Matt. xxi. 2 (Migne xxviii. p. 177).
1 Cf. Letter iii. 'What else is the feast, but the service of God?'   2 Cf. 1 Tim. ii. 9. sub fin.
3 Cf. Letter vi. 3, note 14.   4 Ps. cxv. 17, 18.   5 Is. xxxviii. 18.   6 Vid. Letter vi. 2, note 10.   7 1 Cor. v. 7.   8 Ps. l. 16; Ecclus. xv. 9. These two texts are also quoted in juxtaposition, supr. p. 224.   9 Prov. xv. 28.   10 2 Cor. vi. 14.

Thus it is that sinners, and all those who are aliens from the Catholic Church, heretics, and schismatics, since they are excluded from glorifying (God) with the saints, cannot properly even continue observers of the feast. But the righteous man, although he appears dying to the world, uses boldness of speech, saying, ' I shall not die, but live, and narrate all Thy marvellous deeds[11].' For even God is not ashamed to be called the God[12] of those who truly mortify their members which are upon the earth[13], but live in Christ ; for He is the God of the living, not of the dead. And He by His living Word quickeneth all men, and gives Him to be food and life to the saints ; as the Lord declares, ' I am the bread of life[14].' The Jews, because they were weak in perception, and had not exercised the senses of the soul in virtue, and did not comprehend this discourse about bread, murmured against Him, because He said, ' I am the bread which came down from heaven, and giveth life unto men[15].'

5. For sin has her own special bread, of her death, and calling to those who are lovers of pleasure and lack understanding, she saith, ' Touch with delight secret bread, and sweet waters which are stolen[16] ;' for he who merely touches them knows not that that which is born from the earth perishes with her. For even when the sinner thinks to find pleasure, the end of that food is not pleasant, as the Wisdom of God saith again, ' Bread of deceit is pleasant to a man ; but afterwards his mouth shall be filled with gravel[17].' And, ' Honey droppeth from the lips of a whorish woman, which for a time is sweet to thy palate ; but at the last thou shalt find it more bitter than gall, and sharper than a two-edged sword[18].' Thus then he eats and rejoices for a little time ; afterwards he spurneth it when he hath removed his soul afar. For the fool knoweth not that those who depart far from God shall perish. And besides, there is the restraint of the prophetic admonition which says, ' What hast thou to do in the way of Egypt, to drink the waters of Gihon ? And what hast thou to do in the way of Asshur, to drink the waters of the rivers[19] ?' And the Wisdom of God which loves mankind forbids these things, crying, ' But depart quickly, tarry not in the place, neither fix thine eye upon it ; for thus thou shalt pass over strange waters, and depart quickly from the strange river[20].' She also calls them to herself, ' For wisdom hath builded her house, and supported it on seven pillars ; she hath killed her sacrifices, and mingled her wine in

the goblets, and prepared her table ; she hath sent forth her servants, inviting to the goblet with a loud proclamation, and saying, Whoso is foolish, let him turn in to me ; and to them that lack understanding she saith, Come, eat of my bread, and drink of the wine I have mingled for you[1].' And what hope is there instead of these things ? ' Forsake folly that ye may live, and seek understanding that ye may abide[2].' For the bread of Wisdom is living fruit, as the Lord said ; ' I am the living bread which came down from heaven : if any man eat of this bread, he shall live for ever[3].' For when Israel ate of the manna, which was indeed pleasant and wonderful, yet he died, and he who ate it did not in consequence live for ever, but all that multitude died in the wilderness. The Lord teaches, saying, I am the bread of life : your fathers did eat manna in the wilderness, and are dead. This is the bread which came down from heaven, that a man should eat thereof, and not die[4].'

6. Now wicked men hunger for bread like this, for effeminate souls will hunger ; but the righteous alone, being prepared, shall be satisfied, saying, ' I shall behold Thy face in righteousness ; I shall be satisfied when Thy glory is seen by me[5].' For he who partakes of divine bread always hungers with desire ; and he who thus hungers has a never-failing gift, as Wisdom promises, saying, ' The Lord will not slay the righteous soul with famine.' He promises too in the Psalms, ' I will abundantly bless her provision ; I will satisfy her poor with bread.' We may also hear our Saviour saying, ' Blessed are they who hunger and thirst after righteousness, for they shall be filled[6].' Well then do the saints and those who love the life which is in Christ raise themselves to a longing after this food. And one earnestly implores, saying, ' As the hart panteth after the fountains of waters, so panteth my soul after Thee, O God ! My soul thirsteth for the living God, when shall I come and see the face of God ?' And another ; ' My God, my God, I seek Thee early ; my soul thirsteth for Thee ; often does my flesh, in a dry and pathless land, and without water. So did I appear before Thee in holiness to see Thy power and Thy glory[7].'

7. Since these things are so, my brethren, let us mortify our members which are on the earth[8], and be nourished with living bread, by faith and love to God, knowing that without faith it is impossible to be partakers of such bread as this. For our Saviour, when He called all men to him, and said, ' If any man

---

[11] Ps. cxviii. 17.   [12] Cf. Heb. xi. 16.   [13] Cf. Col. iii. 5.
[14] John vi. 48.   [15] Ib. 51.   [16] Prov. ix. 17.   [17] Ib.
xx. 17.   [18] Ib. v. 3.   [19] Jer. ii. 18.   [20] Prov. ix. 18,
LXX.

[1] Prov. ix. 1—5.   [2] Ib. 6.   [3] John vi. 51.
[4] Ib. 48—51.   [5] Ps. xvii. 15.
[6] Prov. x. 3 ; Matt. v. 6 ; Ps. cxxxii. 15, he notices the various reading of the LXX. on the latter, Exp. in Ps. in loc.
[7] Ps. xlii. 1 ; lxiii. 1, 2.   [8] Col. iii. 5.

thirst, let him [come] to Me and drink [9],' immediately spoke of the faith without which a man cannot receive such food; ' He that believeth on Me, as the Scripture saith, out of his belly shall flow rivers of living water [10].' To this end He continually nourished His believing disciples with His words, and gave them life by the nearness of His divinity, but to the Canaanitish woman, because she was not yet a believer, He deigned not even a reply, although she stood greatly in need of food from Him.   He did this not from scorn, far from it (for the Lord is loving to men and good, and on that account He went into the coasts of Tyre and Sidon); but because of her unbelief, and because she was of those who had not the word.   And He did it righteously, my brethren; for there would have been nothing gained by her offering her supplication before believing, but by her faith she would support her petition; ' For He that cometh to God, must first believe that He is, and that He is a rewarder of them that seek Him;' and that ' without faith it is impossible for a man to please Him [11].'   This Paul teaches.   Now that she was hitherto an unbeliever, one of the profane, He shews, saying, ' It is not meet to take the children's bread, and to cast it to dogs [12].'   She then, being convinced by the power of the word, and having changed her ways, also gained faith; for the Lord no longer spoke to her as a dog, but conversed with her as a human being, saying, ' O woman, great is thy faith [13] !'   As therefore she believed, He forthwith granted to her the fruit of faith, and said, ' Be it to thee as thou desirest.   And her daughter was healed in the self-same hour.'

8. For the righteous man, being nurtured in faith and knowledge, and the observance of divine precepts, has his soul always in health. Wherefore it is commanded to ' receive to ourselves him who is weak in the faith [14],' and to nourish him, even if he is not yet able to eat bread, but herbs, ' for he that is weak eateth herbs.'   For even the Corinthians were not able to partake of such bread, being yet babes, and like babes they drank milk.   ' For every one that partaketh of milk is unskilful in the word of righteousness [15],' according to the words of that divine man.   The Apostle exhorts his beloved son Timothy, in his first Epistle, ' to be nourished with the word of faith, and the good doctrine whereto he had attained.'   And in the second, ' Preserve thou the form of sound words which thou hast heard of me, in faith and love which are in Christ Jesus [16].'   And not only here, my brethren, is

this bread the food of the righteous, neither are the saints on earth alone nourished by such bread and such blood; but we also eat them in heaven, for the Lord is the food even of the exalted spirits, and the angels, and He is the joy of all the heavenly host [17].   And to all He is everything, and He has pity upon all according to His loving-kindness.   Already hath the Lord given us angels' food [18], and He promises to those who continue with Him in His trials, saying, ' And I promise to you a kingdom, as My Father hath promised to Me; that ye shall eat and drink at My table in My kingdom, and sit on twelve thrones, judging the twelve tribes of Israel [1].'   O what a banquet is this, my brethren, and how great is the harmony and gladness of those who eat at this heavenly table !   For they delight themselves not with that food which is cast out, but with that which produces life everlasting.   Who then shall be deemed worthy of that assembly? Who is so blessed as to be called, and accounted worthy of that divine feast?   Truly, ' blessed is he who shall eat bread in Thy kingdom [2].'

9. Now he who has been counted worthy of the heavenly calling, and by this calling has been sanctified, if he grow negligent in it, although washed becomes defiled: ' counting the blood of the covenant by which he was sanctified a profane thing, and despising the Spirit of grace,' he hears the words, ' Friend, how camest thou in hither, not having wedding garments?'   For the banquet of the saints is spotless and pure; ' for many are called, but few chosen [3].'   Judas to wit, though he came to the supper, because he despised it went out from the presence of the Lord, and having abandoned his Life [4], hanged himself. But the disciples who continued with the Redeemer shared in the happiness of the feast. And that young man who went into a far country, and there wasted his substance, living in dissipation, if he receive a desire for this divine feast, and, coming to himself, shall say, ' How many hired servants of my father have bread to spare, while I perish here with hunger !' and shall next arise and come to his father, and confess to him, saying, ' I have sinned against heaven and before thee, and am not worthy to be called thy son; make me as one of thy hired servants [5];'—when he shall thus confess, then he shall be counted worthy of more than he prayed for.   For the father does not receive him as a hired servant, neither does he look upon him as a stranger, but he kisses him as a son, he brings him

---

9 John vii. 37.   10 Ib. 38.   11 Heb. xi. 6.   17 Cf. *Letter* i. 6.   18 Cf. Ps. lxxviii. 25.   1 Luke
12 Matt. xv. 26.   13 Ib. 28.   14 Rom. xiv. 1.   xxii. 29, 30.   2 Ib. xiv. 15.   3 Heb. x. 29; Matt. xxii. 12;
15 1 Cor. iii. 1; Heb. v. 13.   16 1 Tim. iv. 6; 2 Tim. i. 13.   Ib. 14.   4 Cf. Col. iii. 4.   5 Luke xv. 17.

back to life as from the dead, and counts him worthy of the divine feast, and gives him his former and precious robe. So that, on this account, there is singing and gladness in the paternal home.

10. For this is the work of the Father's loving-kindness and goodness, that not only should He make him alive from the dead, but that He should render His grace illustrious through the Spirit. Therefore, instead of corruption, He clothes him with an incorruptible garment; instead of hunger, He kills the fatted calf; instead of far journeys, [the Father] watched for his return, providing shoes for his feet; and, what is most wonderful, placed a divine signet-ring upon his hand; whilst by all these things He begat him afresh in the image of the glory of Christ. These are the gracious gifts of the Father, by which the Lord honours and nourishes those who abide with Him, and also those who return to Him and repent. For He promises, saying, 'I am the bread of life; he that cometh unto Me shall not hunger, and he that believeth on Me shall never thirst[6].' We too shall be counted worthy of these things, if at all times we cleave to our Saviour, and if we are pure, not only in these six days of Easter[7], but consider the whole course of our life as a feast[8], and continue near and do not go far off, saying to Him, 'Thou hast the words of eternal life, and whither shall we go[9]?' Let those of us who are far off return, confessing our iniquities, and having nothing against any man, but by the spirit mortifying the deeds of the body[10]. For thus, having first nourished the soul here, we shall partake with angels at that heavenly and spiritual table; not knocking and being repulsed like those five foolish virgins[11], but entering with the Lord, like those who were wise and loved the bridegroom; and shewing the dying of Jesus in our bodies[12], we shall receive life and the kingdom from Him.

11. We begin the fast of forty days on the twenty-third of Mechir (Feb. 17), and the holy fast of the blessed feast on the twenty-eighth of Phamenoth (Mar. 24); and having joined to these· six days after them, in fastings and watchings, as each one is able, let us rest on the third of the month Pharmuthi (Mar. 29), on the evening of the seventh day. Also that day which is holy and blessed in everything, which possesses the name of Christ, namely the

Lord's day[13], having risen upon us on the fourth of Pharmuthi (Mar. 30), let us afterwards keep the holy feast of Pentecost. Let us at all times worship the Father in Christ, through Whom to Him and with Him be glory and dominion by the Holy Ghost for ever and ever. Amen. All the brethren who are with me salute you: salute one another with a holy kiss.

There is no eighth or ninth, for he did not send them, for the reason before mentioned[1].

Here endeth the seventh Festal Letter of holy Athanasius the Patriarch.

LETTER X.

For 338.

Coss. Ursus and Polemius; Præf. the same Theodorus, of Heliopolis, and of the Catholics[2]. After him, for the second year, Philagrius; Indict. xi; Easter-day, vii Kal. Ap.[3] xxx Phamenoth; Moon 18½; Æra Dioclet. 54.

[4]ALTHOUGH I have travelled all this distance from you, my brethren, I have not forgotten the custom which obtains among you, which has been delivered to us by the fathers[5], so as to be silent without notifying to you the time of the annual holy feast, and the day for its celebration. For although I have been hindered by those afflictions of which you have doubtless heard, and severe trials have been laid upon me, and a great distance has separated us; while the enemies of the truth have followed our tracks, laying snares to discover a letter from us, so that by their accusations, they might add to the pain of our wounds; yet the Lord, strengthening and comforting us in our afflictions, we have not feared, even when held fast in the midst of such machinations and conspiracies, to indicate and make known to you our saving Easter-feast, even from the ends of the earth. Also when I wrote to the presbyters of Alexandria, I urged that these letters might be sent to you through their instrumentality, al-

---

[13] κυριώνυμος—κυριακὴ L. Vid. Suicer *Thes. sub. voc.* κυριακὴ. *Expos. in Psalm.* cxvii. 24.
[1] See the *Index.* This notice suggests that the present collection of letters has undergone a recension since its union with the *Index.*
[2] The text is difficult; possibly the Syriac translator is responsible for the difficulty. But we know from Ath. (*supr.* p. 273) that the reappointment of Philagrius was in the express interest of the Arians: it is, therefore, probable that Theodorus was not unfavourable to Athanasius. See Prolegg. ch. ii. § 6 (1), and Sievers, pp. 101, 102.
[3] In the *Chron. Pasch.* tom. ii. p. 202, Easter-day is wrongly given as falling on viii. Kal. Ap.
[4] See Prolegg. ch. v. § 3 b. The letter may have been finished (see §§ 3, 11) after Ath. had returned home, but the language of § 1 seems to be applicable only to his residence at Treveri, and § 11 may be reconciled to this supposition. In this case (§ 1 *sub. fin.*) it was probably begun as early as the Easter of 337; cf. *Letters* 17 and 18.
[5] See above, p. 500.

---

[6] John vi. 35.
[7] Vid. Suicer. *Thes. in. voc.* ἀποκρέως, and the notes of Valesius on Euseb. *Orat. in laud. Constant.* ch. ix. With us, Easter-week includes the six days *following* Easter-Sunday; with the Greeks, the ἑβδομὰς τῶν πασχῶν was applied to the *preceding* six days, as here.
[8] Vid. *supr. Letters* 5. 1, 7, 3. init.
[9] John vi. 68.
[10] Rom. viii. 13.
[11] Matt. xxv. 1—12.
[12] 2 Cor. iv. 10.

though I knew the fear imposed on them by the adversaries. Still, I exhorted them to be mindful of the apostolic boldness of speech, and to say, 'Nothing separates us from the love of Christ; neither affliction, nor distress, nor persecution, nor famine, nor nakedness, nor peril, nor sword[6].' Thus, keeping the feast myself, I was desirous that you also, my beloved, should keep it; and being conscious that an announcement like this is due from me, I have not delayed to discharge this duty, fearing to be condemned by the Apostolic counsel; 'Render to every man his due[7].'

2. While I then committed all my affairs to God, I was anxious to celebrate the feast with you, not taking into account the distance between us. For although place separate us, yet the Lord the Giver of the feast, and Who is Himself our feast[8], Who is also the Bestower of the Spirit[9], brings us together in mind, in harmony, and in the bond of peace[10]. For when we mind and think the same things, and offer up the same prayers on behalf of each other, no place can separate us, but the Lord gathers and unites us together. For if He promises, that 'when two or three are gathered together in His name, He is in the midst of them[11],' it is plain that being in the midst of those who in every place are gathered together, He unites them, and receives the prayers of all of them, as if they were near, and listens to all of them, as they cry out the same Amen[12]. I have[13] borne affliction like this, and all those trials which I mentioned, my brethren, when I wrote to you.

3. And that we may not distress you at all, I would now (only) briefly remind you of these things, because it is not becoming in a man to forget, when more at ease, the pains he experienced in tribulation; lest, like an unthankful and forgetful person, he should be excluded from the divine assembly. For at no time should a man freely praise God, more than when he has passed through afflictions; nor, again, should he at any time give thanks more than when he finds rest from toil and temptations. As Hezekiah, when the Assyrians perished, praised the Lord, and gave thanks, saying, 'The Lord is my salvation[14]; and I will not cease to bless Thee with harp all the days of my life, before the

house of the Lord[15].' And those valiant and blessed three who were tried in Babylon, Hananiah, Mishael, and Azariah, when they were in safety and the fire became to them as dew, gave thanks, praising and saying words of glory to God[16].' I too like them have written, my brethren, having these things in mind; for even in our time, God hath made possible those things which are impossible to men. And those things which could not be accomplished by man, the Lord has shewn to be easy of accomplishment, by bringing us to you. For He does not give us as a prey to those who seek to swallow us up. For it is not so much us, as the Church, and the faith and godliness which they planned to overwhelm with wickedness.

4. But God, who is good, multiplied His loving-kindness towards us, not only when He granted the common salvation of us all through His Word, but now also, when enemies have persecuted us, and have sought to seize upon us. As the blessed Paul saith in a certain place, when describing the incomprehensible riches of Christ: 'But God, being rich in mercy, for the great love wherewith He loved us, even when we were dead in follies and sins, quickened us with Christ[17].' For the might of man and of all creatures, is weak and poor; but the Might which is above man, and uncreated, is rich and incomprehensible, and has no beginning, but is eternal. He does not then possess one method only of healing, but being rich, He works in divers manners for our salvation by means of His Word, Who is not restricted or hindered in His dealings towards us; but since He is rich and manifold, He varies Himself according to the individual capacity of each soul. For He is the Word and the Power and the Wisdom of God, as Solomon testifies concerning Wisdom, that 'being one, it can do all things, and remaining in itself, it maketh all things new; and passing upon holy souls, fashioneth the friends of God and the prophets[18].' To those then who have not yet attained to the perfect way He becomes like a sheep giving milk, and this was administered by Paul: 'I have fed you with milk, not with meat[19].' To those who have advanced beyond the full stature of childhood, but still are weak as regards perfection, He is their food, according to their capacity, being again administered by Paul[20], 'Let him that is weak

---

6 Rom. viii. 35.　　　7 Rom. xiii. 7; cf. *Ep.* iii. init.
8 Cf. 1 Cor. v. 7.　　9 Cf. *Orat.* i. 50; ii. 18; Luke xi. 13.
10 Cf. Eph. iv. 3.　　11 Matt. xviii. 20.　　12 Cf. *Apol. Const.* 16.
13 Thus far Athan. has been referring to the circumstances attending his exile for the last two years. The principal subject of the remaining part consists of the duty incumbent on us to praise and thank God for deliverance from affliction, and to exercise forgiveness towards our enemies. He several times (e.g. §§ 3, 10) speaks of his restoration to the Church of Alexandria.
14 The Syriac translator must have found in the Greek copy the reading of the Codex Alex. Κύριε—the rendering of 'Jehovah,' not that of the Vatican text. Θεέ.

15 Is. xxxviii. 20.　　16 'Song of Three Children,' 25—28.
17 Eph. ii. 4, 5.　　18 Wisd. vii. 27; cf. *Ep.* i.　　19 1 Cor. iii. 2.
20 Rom. xiv. 2. The sense in the last few lines, and in those that follow, is clear, though the construction appears somewhat obscure. Milks, herbs, and meat are severally mentioned in connection with the different advances made in the Christian course. The translation of Larsow is less satisfactory.

eat herbs.' But as soon as ever a man begins to walk in the perfect way, he is no longer fed with the things before mentioned, but he has the Word for bread, and flesh for food, for it is written, 'Strong meat is for those who are of full age, for those who, by reason of their capacity, have their senses exercised[1].' And further, when the word is sown it does not yield a uniform produce of fruit in this human life, but one various and rich; for it bringeth forth, some an hundred, and some sixty, and some thirty[2], as the Saviour teaches—that Sower of grace, and Bestower of the Spirit[3]. And this is no doubtful matter, nor one that admits no confirmation; but it is in our power to behold the field which is sown by Him; for in the Church the word is manifold and the produce[4] rich. Not with virgins alone is such a field adorned; nor with monks alone, but also with honourable matrimony and the chastity of each one. For in sowing, He did not compel the will beyond the power. Nor is mercy confined to the perfect, but it is sent down also among those who occupy the middle and the third ranks, so that He might rescue all men generally to salvation. To this intent He hath prepared many mansions[5] with the Father, so that although the dwelling-place is various in proportion to the advance in moral attainment, yet all of us are within the wall, and all of us enter within the same fence, the adversary being cast out, and all his host expelled thence. For apart from light there is darkness, and apart from blessing there is a curse, the devil also is apart from the saints, and sin far from virtue. Therefore the Gospel rebukes Satan, saying, 'Get thee behind Me, Satan[6].' But us it calls to itself, saying, 'Enter ye in at the strait gate.' And again, 'Come, blessed of My Father, inherit the kingdom which is prepared for you[7].' So also the Spirit cried aforetime in the Psalms, saying, 'Enter into His gates with psalms[8].' For through virtue a man enters in unto God, as Moses did into the thick cloud where God was. But through vice a man goes out from the presence of the Lord; as Cain[9] when he had slain his brother, went out, as far as his will was concerned, from before the face of God; and the Psalmist enters, saying, 'And I will go in to the altar of God, even to the God that delighteth my youth[10].' But of the devil the

Scripture beareth witness, that the devil went out from before God, and smote Job[11] with sore boils. For this is the characteristic of those who go out from before God—to smite and to injure the men of God. And this is the characteristic of those who fall away from the faith—to injure and persecute the faithful. The saints on the other hand, take such to themselves and look upon them as friends; as also the blessed David, using openness of speech, says, 'Mine eyes are on the faithful of the earth, that they may dwell with me.' But those that are weak in the faith[12], Paul urges that we should especially take to ourselves. For virtue is philanthropic[13], just as in men of an opposite character, sin is misanthropic. So Saul, being a sinner, persecuted David, whereas David, though he had a good opportunity, did not kill Saul. Esau too persecuted Jacob, while Jacob overcame his wickedness by meekness. And those eleven sold Joseph, but Joseph, in his loving-kindness, had pity on them.

5. But what need we many words? Our Lord and Saviour, when He was persecuted by the Pharisees, wept for their destruction. He was injured, but He threatened[14] not; not when He was afflicted, not even when He was killed. But He grieved for those who dared to do such things. He, the Saviour, suffered for man, but they despised and cast from them life, and light, and grace. All these were theirs through that Saviour Who suffered in our stead. And verily for their darkness and blindness, He wept. For if they had understood the things which are written in the Psalms, they would not have been so vainly daring against the Saviour, the Spirit having said, 'Why do the heathen rage, and the people imagine a vain thing?' And if they had considered the prophecy of Moses, they would not have hanged Him Who was their Life[15]. And if they had examined with their understanding the things which were written, they would not have carefully fulfilled the prophecies which were against themselves, so as for their city to be now desolate, grace taken from them, and they themselves without the law, being no longer called children, but strangers. For thus in the Psalms was it before declared, saying, 'The strange children have acted falsely by Me.' And by Isaiah the prophet; 'I have begotten and brought up children, and they have rejected Me[16].' And they are no longer named the people of God, and a holy nation, but

---

[1] Heb. v. 14.
[2] Matt. xiii. 8. In the Syriac text, as published by Mr. Cureton, as well as in the German translation by Larsow, there is a hiatus here, the next two or three pages, as far as the words 'He wept,' (§ 5 *init.*) being wanting. Two more leaves were afterwards discovered among the fragments in the British Museum by the learned Editor. One of them belongs to this part; the other to the eleventh Letter.   [3] Vid. note 9, *supr.*
[4] Syr. 'virtue,' a letter (rish) having been inserted by mistake.
[5] John xiv. 2   [6] Matt. iv. 10.   [7] Matt. vii. 13; xxv. 34.
[8] Ps. c. 4.   [9] Gen. iv. 16; Exod. xix. 9.   [10] Ps. xliii. 4.

[11] Job ii. 7. In the MS. *Jesus* is written by mistake for *Job.*
[12] Ps. ci. 6; Rom. xiv. 1.   [13] Cf. *Letter* xi. sub. init.
[14] The Syriac is 'was persecuted'—which supplies no good sense.   [15] Ps. ii. 1; Deut. xxviii. 66.
[16] Ps. xviii. 45; Is. i. 2.

rulers of Sodom, and people of Gomorrah; having exceeded in this even the iniquity of the Sodomites, as the prophet also saith, 'Sodom is justified before thee [17].' For the Sodomites raved against angels, but these against the Lord and God and King of all, and these dared to slay the Lord of angels, not knowing that Christ, who was slain by them, liveth. But those Jews who had conspired against the Lord died, having rejoiced a very little in these temporal things, and having fallen away from those which are eternal. They were ignorant of this—that the immortal promise has not respect to temporal enjoyment, but to the hope of those things which are everlasting. For through many tribulations, and labours, and sorrows, the saint enters into the kingdom of heaven; but when he arrives where sorrow, and distress, and sighing, shall flee away, he shall thenceforward enjoy rest; as Job, who, when tried here, was afterwards the familiar friend of the Lord. But the lover of pleasures, rejoicing for a little while, afterwards passes a sorrowful life; like Esau, who had temporal food, but afterwards was condemned thereby.

6. We may take as a type of this distinction, the departure of the children of Israel and the Egyptians from Egypt. For the Egyptians, rejoicing a little while in their injustice against Israel, when they went forth, were all drowned in the deep; but the people of God, being for a time smitten and injured, by the conduct of the taskmasters, when they came out of Egypt, passed through the sea unharmed, and walked in the wilderness as an inhabited place. For although the place was unfrequented by man and desolate, yet, through the gracious gift of the law, and through converse with angels, it was no longer desert, but far more than an inhabited country. As also Elisha [1], when he thought he was alone in the wilderness, was with companies of angels; so in this case, though the people were at first afflicted and in the wilderness, yet those who remained faithful afterwards entered the land of promise. In like manner those who suffer temporal afflictions here, finally having endured, attain comfort, while those who here persecute are trodden under foot, and have no good end. For even the rich man [2], as the Gospel affirms, having indulged in pleasure here for a little while, suffered hunger there, and having drunk largely here, he there thirsted exceedingly. But Lazarus, after being afflicted in worldly things, found rest in heaven, and having hungered for bread ground from corn, he was there satisfied with that which is better than manna, even the Lord who came down and said, 'I am the bread which came down from heaven, and giveth life to mankind [3].'

7. Oh! my dearly beloved, if we shall gain comfort from afflictions, if rest from labours, if health after sickness, if from death immortality, it is not right to be distressed by the temporal ills that lay hold on mankind. It does not become us to be agitated because of the trials which befall us. It is not right to fear if the gang that contended with Christ, should conspire against godliness; but we should the more please God through these things, and should consider such matters as the probation and exercise of a virtuous life. For how shall patience be looked for, if there be not previously labours and sorrows? Or how can fortitude be tested with no assault from enemies? Or how shall magnanimity be exhibited, unless after contumely and injustice? Or how can long-suffering be proved, unless there has first been the calumny of Antichrist [4]? And, finally, how can a man behold virtue with his eyes, unless the iniquity of the very wicked has previously appeared? Thus even our Lord and Saviour Jesus Christ comes before us, when He would shew men how to suffer, Who when He was smitten bore it patiently, being reviled He reviled not again, when He suffered He threatened not, but He gave His back to the smiters, and His cheeks to buffetings, and turned not His face from spitting [5]; and at last, was willingly led to death, that we might behold in Him the image of all that is virtuous and immortal, and that we, conducting ourselves after these examples, might truly tread on serpents and scorpions, and on all the power of the enemy [6].

8. Thus too Paul, while he conducted himself after the example of the Lord, exhorted us, saying, 'Be ye followers of me, as I also am of Christ [7].' In this way he prevailed against all the divisions of the devil, writing, 'I am persuaded that neither death, nor life, nor angels, nor principalities, nor things present, nor things to come, nor powers, nor height, nor depth, nor any other creature, shall be able to separate us from the love of God which is in Jesus Christ [8].' For the enemy draws near to us in afflictions, and trials, and labours, using every endeavour to ruin us. But the man who is in Christ, combating those things that are contrary, and opposing wrath by long-suffering, contumely by meekness, and vice by virtue, obtains the victory, and exclaims, 'I can do all

[17] Ezek. xvi. 48, cf. Lam. iv. 6.
[1] The reference is to 2 Kings vi. 13—17, though 'the wilderness' agrees better with the history of Elijah, 1 Kings xix. 4—8.
[2] Luke xvi. 19.

[3] John vi. 51.   [4] i.e. Arians. See *Index* to this vol. *s.v.*
[5] 1 Pet. ii. 23; Isa. l. 6.   [6] Cf. Pseudo-Ath. *de Pass. et Cruc.* 19.   [7] 1 Cor. xi. 1.   [8] Rom. viii. 38, 39.

things through Christ Who strengtheneth me;' and, 'In all these things we are conquerors through Christ Who loved us 9.' This is the grace of the Lord, and these are the Lord's means of restoration for the children of men. For He suffered to prepare freedom from suffering for those who suffer in Him, He descended that He might raise us up, He took on Him the trial of being born, that we might love Him Who is unbegotten, He went down to corruption, that corruption might put on immortality, He became weak for us, that we might rise with power, He descended to death, that He might bestow on us immortality, and give life to the dead. Finally, He became man, that we who die as men might live again, and that death should no more reign over us; for the Apostolic word proclaims, 'Death shall not have the dominion over us 10.'

9. Now because they did not thus consider these matters, the Ario-maniacs 11, being · opponents of Christ, and heretics, smite Him who is their Helper with their tongue, and blaspheme Him who set [them] free, and hold all manner of different opinions against the Saviour. Because of His coming down, which was on behalf of man, they have denied His essential Godhead; and seeing that He came forth from the Virgin, they doubt His being truly the Son of God, and considering Him as become incarnate in time, they deny His eternity; and, looking upon Him as having suffered for us, they do not believe in Him as the incorruptible Son from the incorruptible Father. And finally, because He endured for our sakes, they deny the things which concern His essential eternity; allowing the deed of the unthankful, these despise the Saviour, and offer Him insult instead of acknowledging His grace. To them may these words justly be addressed: Oh! unthankful opponent of Christ, altogether wicked, and the slayer of his Lord, mentally blind, and a Jew in his mind, hadst thou understood the Scriptures, and listened to the saints, who said, 'Cause Thy face to shine, and we shall be saved;' or again, 'Send out Thy light and Thy truth 12;'—then wouldest thou have known that the Lord did not descend for His own sake, but for ours; and for this reason, thou wouldest the more have admired His loving-kindness. And hadst thou considered what the Father is, and what the Son, thou wouldest not have blasphemed the Son, as of a mutable nature 13. And hadst thou understood His work of loving-kindness towards us, thou wouldest not have alienated the Son

from the Father, nor have looked upon Him as a stranger 14, Who reconciled us to His Father. I know these [words] are grievous, not only to those who dispute with Christ 15, but also to the schismatics; for they are united together, as men of kindred feelings. For they have learned to rend the seamless coat 16 of God: they think it not strange to divide the indivisible Son from the Father 17.

10. I know indeed, that when these things are spoken, they will gnash their teeth upon us, with the devil who stirs them up, since they are troubled by the declaration of the true glory concerning the Redeemer. But the Lord, Who always has scoffed at the devil, does the same even now, saying, 'I am in the Father, and the Father in Me 18.' This is the Lord, Who is manifested in the Father, and in Whom also the Father is manifested; Who, being truly the Son of the Father, at last became incarnate for our sakes, that He might offer Himself to the Father in our stead, and redeem us through His oblation and sacrifice. This is He Who once brought the people of old time out of Egypt; but Who afterwards redeemed all of us, or rather the whole race of men, from death, and brought them up from the grave. This is He Who in old time was sacrificed as a lamb, He being signified in the lamb; but Who afterwards was slain for us, for 'Christ our Passover is sacrificed 19.' This is He Who delivered us from the snare of the hunters, from the opponents of Christ, I say, and from the schismatics, and again rescued us His Church. And because we were then victims of deceit, He has now delivered us by His own self.

11. What then is our duty, my brethren, for the sake of these things, but to praise and give thanks to God, the King of all? And let us first exclaim in the words of the Psalms, 'Blessed be the Lord, Who hath not given us over as a prey to their teeth 20.' Let us keep the feast in that way which He hath dedicated for us unto salvation—the holy day of Easter—so that we may celebrate the feast which is in heaven with the angels. Thus anciently, the people of the Jews, when they came out of affliction into a state of ease, kept the feast, singing a song of praise for their victory. So also the people in the time of Esther, because they were delivered from the edict of death, kept a feast to the Lord 21, reckoning it a feast, returning thanks to the

14 Cf. supr. p. 70.   15 i.e. the Arians.
16 Syr. χιτών. The words translated 'rend' and 'seamless' are cognate in the Syriac, and answer to σχίζειν and its derivatives.
17 The Arians were thence called Διατομίται. Vid. Damascen. de hæresib. apud Cotel. eccles. Gr. monum. p. 298.
18 John xiv. 11.   19 1 Cor. v. 7.   20 Ps. cxxiv. 6.
21 Cf. Esth. iii. 9; ix. 21; Letter iv. p. 32.

9 Phil. iv. 13; Rom. viii. 37.   10 Rom. vi. 9, 14, cf. de Pass. et Cruc. 11.   11 The Syriac mistranslates Arius and Manetes.
12 Ps. xliii. 3, lxxx. 7.   13 Cf. Orat. i. 35; ii. 6, and notes there.

Lord, and praising Him for having changed their condition. Therefore let us, performing our vows to the Lord, and confessing our sins, keep the feast to the Lord, in conversation, moral conduct, and manner of life; praising our Lord, Who hath chastened us a little, but hath not utterly failed nor forsaken us, nor altogether kept silence from us. For if, having brought us out of the deceitful and famous Egypt of the opponents of Christ, He hath caused us to pass through many trials and afflictions, as it were in the wilderness, to His holy Church, so that from hence, according to custom, we can send to you, as well as receive letters from you; on this account especially I both give thanks to God myself, and exhort you to thank Him with me and on my behalf, this being the Apostolic custom, which these opponents of Christ, and the schismatics, wished to put an end to, and to break off. The Lord did not permit it, but both renewed and preserved that which was ordained by Him through the Apostle, so that we may keep the feast together, and together keep holy-day, according to the tradition and commandment of the fathers.

12. We begin the fast of forty days on the nineteenth of the month Mechir (Feb. 13); and the holy Easter-fast on the twenty-fourth of the month Phamenoth (Mar. 20). We cease from the fast on the twenty-ninth of the month Phamenoth (Mar. 25), late in the evening of the seventh day. And we thus keep the feast on the first day of the week which dawns on the thirtieth of the month Phamenoth (Mar. 26); from which, to Pentecost, we keep holy-day, through seven weeks, one after the other. For when we have first meditated properly on these things, we shall attain to be counted worthy of those which are eternal, through Christ Jesus our Lord, through Whom to the Father be glory and dominion for ever and ever. Amen. Greet one another with a holy kiss, remembering us in your holy prayers. All the brethren who are with me salute you, at all times remembering you. And I pray that ye may have health in the Lord, my beloved brethren, whom we love above all.

Here endeth the tenth Letter of holy Athanasius.

LETTER XI.

For 339.

Coss. Constantius Augustus II, Constans I; Præfect, Philagrius the Cappadocian, for the second time; Indict. xii; Easter-day xvii Kal. Mai, xx Pharmuthi; Æra Dioclet. 55.

THE blessed Paul, being girt about with

every virtue [1], and called faithful of the Lord—for he was conscious of nothing in himself but what was a virtue and a praise [2], or what was in harmony with love and godliness—clave to these things more and more, and was carried up even to heavenly places, and was borne to Paradise [3]; to the end that, as he surpassed the conversation of men, he should be exalted above men. And when he descended, he preached to every man; 'We know in part, and we prophesy in part; here I know in part; but then shall I know even as also I am known [4].' For, in truth, he was known to those saints who are in heaven, as their fellow-citizen [5]. And in relation to all that is future and perfect, the things known by him here were in part; but with respect to those things which were committed and entrusted to him by the Lord, he was perfect; as he said, 'We who are perfect, should be thus minded [6].' For as the Gospel of Christ is the fulfilment and accomplishment of the ministration which was supplied by the law of Israel, so future things will be the accomplishment of such as now exist, the Gospel being then fulfilled, and the faithful receiving those things which, not seeing now, they yet hope for, as Paul saith; 'For what a man seeth, why doth he also hope for? But if we hope for those things we see [not], we then by patience wait for them [7].' Since then that blessed man was of such a character, and apostolic grace was committed to him, he wrote, wishing 'that all men should be as he was [8].' For virtue is philanthropic [9], and great is the company of the kingdom of heaven, for thousands of thousands and myriads of myriads there serve the Lord. And though a man enters it through a strait and narrow way, yet having entered, he beholds immeasurable space, and a place greater than any other, as they declare, who were eye-witnesses and heirs of these things. 'Thou didst place afflictions before us.' But afterwards, having related their afflictions, they say, 'Thou broughtest us forth into a wide place;' and again, 'In affliction Thou hast enlarged us [10].' For truly, my brethren, the course of the saints here is straitened; since they either toil painfully through longing for those things which are to come, as he who said, 'Woe is me that my pilgrimage is prolonged [11];' or they are distressed and spent for the salvation of other men, as Paul wrote to the Corinthians, saying, 'Lest, when I come to you, God should humble me, and I should bewail many of those who have sinned already, and not repented for the uncleanness and for-

---

[1] Cf. Eph. vi. 14. [2] Cf. 1 Cor. iv. 4. [3] 2 Cor. xii. 4.
[4] 1 Cor. xiii. 9, 12. [5] Cf. Eph. ii. 19. [6] Phil. iii. 15.
[7] Rom. viii. 24, 25. [8] 1 Cor. vii. 7. [9] Cf. *Letter* 10. §4.
[10] Ps. lxvi. 11, 12; iv. 1. [11] Ib. cxx. 5, LXX.

nication and lasciviousness which they have committed [12].' As Samuel bewailed the destruction of Saul, and Jeremiah wept for the captivity of the people. But after this affliction, and sorrow, and sighing, when they depart from this world, a certain divine gladness, and pleasure, and exultation receives them, from which misery and sorrow, and sighing, flee away.

2. Since we are thus circumstanced, my brethren, let us never loiter in the path of virtue; for hereto he counsels us, saying, 'Be ye followers of me, as I also am of Christ [13].' For he gave this advice not to the Corinthians only, since he was not their Apostle only, but being 'a teacher of the Gentiles in faith and verity [14],' he admonished us all through them; and in short, the things he wrote to each particular person are commandments common to all men [15]. On this account, in writing to different people, some he exhorted, as, for instance, in the Epistles to the Romans, and the Ephesians, and Philemon. Some he reproved, and was indignant with them, as in the case of the Corinthians and Galatians. To some he gave advice, as to the Colossians and Thessalonians. The Philippians he approved of, and rejoiced in them. The Hebrews he taught that the law was a shadow to them [16]. But to his elect sons, Timothy and Titus, when they were near, he gave instruction; when far away, he put them in remembrance. For he was all things to all men; and being himself a perfect man, he adapted his teaching to the need of every one, so that by all means he might rescue some of them. Therefore his word was not without fruit; but in every place it is planted and productive even to this day.

3. And wherefore, my beloved? For it is right that we should search into the apostolic mind. Not only in the beginning of the Epistles, but towards their close, and in the middle of them, he used persuasions and admonitions. I hope therefore that, by your prayers, I shall in no respect falsely represent the plan of that holy man. As he was well skilled in these divine matters, and knew the power of the divine teaching, he deemed it necessary, in the first place, to make known the word concerning Christ, and the mystery regarding Him; and then afterwards to point to the correction of habits, so that when they had learned to know the Lord, they might earnestly desire to do those things which He commanded. For when the Guide to the laws is unknown, one does not readily pass on to the observance of them. Faithful Moses,

the minister of God, adopted this method; for when he promulgated the words of the divine dispensation of laws, he first proclaimed the matters relating to the knowledge of God: 'Hear, O Israel, the Lord thy God is one Lord [17].' Afterwards, having shadowed Him forth to the people, and taught of Him in Whom they ought to believe, and informed their minds of Him Who is truly God, he proceeds to lay down the law relating to those things whereby a man may be well-pleasing to Him, saying, 'Thou shalt not commit adultery; thou shalt not steal;' together with the other commandments. For also, according to the Apostolic teaching, 'He that draweth near to God must believe that He is, and that He is a rewarder of them that seek Him [18].' Now He is sought by means of virtuous deeds, as the prophet saith; 'Seek ye the Lord, and when ye have found Him, call upon Him; when He is near to you, let the wicked forsake his ways, and the lawless man his thoughts [19].'

4. It will also be well if a man is not offended at the testimony of the Shepherd, saying in the beginning of his book, 'Before all things believe that there is one God, Who created and established all these things, and from non-existence called them into being [1].' And, further, the blessed Evangelists— who recorded the words of the Lord—in the beginning of the Gospels, wrote the things concerning our Saviour; so that, having first made known the Lord, the Creator, they might be believed when narrating the events that took place. For how could they have been believed, when writing respecting him who [was blind] from his mother's womb, and those other blind men who recovered their sight, and those who rose from the dead, and the changing of water into wine, and those lepers who were cleansed; if they had not taught of Him as the Creator, writing, 'In the beginning was the Word [2]?' Or, according to Matthew, that He Who was born of the seed of David, was Emmanuel, and the Son of the living God? He from Whom the Jews, with the Arians, turn away their faces, but Whom we acknowledge and worship. The Apostle therefore, as was meet, sent to different people, but his own son he especially reminded, 'that he should not despise the things in which he had been instructed by him,' and enjoined on him, 'Remember Jesus Christ, who rose from the dead, of the seed of David, according to my Gospel [3].' And speaking of these things being delivered to him, to be always had in remembrance, he immediately writes to him. saying, 'Meditate on these things: be engaged

[12] 2 Cor. xii. 21.   [13] 1 Cor. xi. 1.   [14] 1 Tim. ii. 7.   [17] Deut. vi. 4.   [18] Heb. xi. 6.   [19] Is. lv. 6, 7.
[15] Cf. *Letter* ii. § 1, and *Letter* iii. § 5.   [16] Vid. *Letter* vii.   [1] Herm. *Mand.* 1.   [2] John i. 1.   [3] 2 Tim. iii. 14; ii. 8.
8, note 17.

in them [4].' For constant meditation, and the remembrance of divine words, strengthens piety towards God, and produces a love to Him inseparable and not merely formal [5]; as he, being of this mind, speaks about himself and others like-minded, saying boldly, 'Who shall separate us from the love of God [6]?' For [7] such men, being confirmed in the Lord, and possessing an unshaken disposition towards Him, and being one in spirit (for [8] 'he who is joined to the Spirit is one spirit'), are sure 'as the mount Sion;' and although ten thousand trials may rage against them, they are founded upon a rock, which is Christ [9]. In Him the careless take no delight; and having no continuous purpose of good, they are sullied by temporal attacks, and esteem nothing more highly than present things, being unstable and deserving reproof as regards the faith. For 'either the care of this world, or the deceitfulness of riches, chokes them [10];' or, as Jesus said in that parable which had reference to them, since they have not established the faith that has been preached to them, but continue only for a time, immediately, in time of persecution, or when affliction ariseth through the word, they are offended. Now those who meditate evil, we say, [think] not truth, but falsehood; and not righteousness, but iniquity, for their tongue learns to speak lies. They have done evil, and have not ceased that they might repent. For, persevering with delight in wicked actions, they hasten thereto without turning back, even treading under foot the commandment with regard to neighbours, and, instead of loving them, devise evil against them, as the saint testifies, saying, 'And those who seek me evil have spoken vanity, and imagined deceit all the day [11].' But that the cause of such meditation is none other than the want of instruction, the divine proverb has already declared; 'The son that forsaketh the commandment of his father meditateth evil words [12].' But such meditation, because it is evil, the Holy Spirit blames in these words, and reproves too in other terms, saying, 'Your hands are polluted with blood, your fingers with sins; your lips have spoken lawlessness, and your tongue imagineth iniquity: no man

speaketh right things, nor is there true judgment [13].' But what the end is of such perverse imagining, He immediately declares, saying, 'They trust in vanities and speak falsehood; for they conceive mischief, and bring forth lawlessness. They have hatched the eggs of an asp, and woven a spider's web; and he who is prepared to eat of their eggs, when he breaks them finds gall, and a basilisk therein [14].' Again, what the hope of such is, He has already announced. 'Because righteousness does not overtake them, when they waited for light, they had darkness; when they waited for brightness, they walked in a thick cloud. They shall grope for the wall like the blind, and as those who have no eyes shall they grope; they shall fall at noon-day as at midnight; when dead, they shall groan. They shall roar together as a bear, or as a dove [15].'

This is the fruit of wickedness, these rewards are given to its familiars, for perverseness does not deliver its own. But in truth, against them it sets itself, and it tears them first, and on them especially it summons ruin. Woe to them against whom these are brought; for 'it is sharper than a two-edged sword [16],' slaying beforehand and very swiftly those who will lay hold of it. For their tongue, according to the testimony of the Psalmist, is a 'sharp sword, and their teeth spears and arrows [17].' But the wonderful part is that while often he against whom men imagine [harm] suffers nothing, they are pierced by their own spears: for they possess, even in themselves, before they reach others, anger, wrath, malice, guile, hatred, bitterness. Although they may not be able to bring these upon others, they forthwith return upon and against themselves, as he prays, saying, 'Let their sword enter into their own heart.' There is also such a proverb as this: 'The wicked is held fast by the chain of his sins [18].'

5. The Jews in their imaginings, and in their agreeing to act unjustly against the Lord, forgot that they were bringing wrath upon themselves. Therefore does the Word lament for them, saying, 'Why do the people exalt themselves, and the nations imagine vain things [19]?' For vain indeed was the imagination of the Jews, meditating death against the Life [1], and devising unreasonable things against the Word of the Father [2].' For who that looks upon their dispersion, and the desolation of their city, may not aptly say, 'Woe unto them,

---

4 1 Tim. iv. 15.
5 The Syriac word here rendered 'not merely formal' is one which seems to take no other meaning than 'inexpiable'—a sense scarcely admissible in this place. The Greek was probably ἀγαπὴν πρὸς αὐτὸν ἀχώριστον καὶ οὐκ ἀφοσιουμένην. This supposition would account for the Syriac misapprehension of the word.
6 Rom. viii. 35.
7 The Syriac text from here to the words, 'There is also such a proverb as this' (end of §), was discovered after Cureton's edition of the Syriac, and is absent in Larsow.
8   Cor. vi 17.   Ps. cxxv. 1; 1 Cor. x. 4; Matt. vii. 25.
10 Matt. xiii. 22.   11 Ps. xxxviii. 12.   12 Prov. xix.
27, LXX.

13 Is. lix. 3, 4.   14 Ib. lix. 4, 5.   15 Ib. lix. 9—11.
16 Heb. iv. 12.   17 Ps. lvii. 4.   18 Ib. xxxvii. 15; Prov.
v. 22.   19 Ps. ii. 1.
1 The parallel clause of this sentence would seem to determine that by 'Life' here we must understand Christ.
2 ἄλογα κατὰ τοῦ Λόγου τοῦ Πατρός. Cf. Suicer. Thes. s.v. Ἄλογος tom. i. p. 199.

for they have imagined an evil imagination, saying against their own soul, let us bind the righteous man, because he is not pleasing to us[3].' And full well is it so, my brethren ; for when they erred concerning the Scriptures, they knew not that 'he who diggeth a pit for his neighbour falleth therein ; and he who destroyeth a hedge, a serpent shall bite him[4].' And if they had not turned their faces from the Lord, they would have feared what was written before in the divine Psalms : ' The heathen are caught in the pit which they made ; in the snare which they hid is their own foot taken. The Lord is known when executing judgments : by the works of his hands is the sinner taken[5].' Let them observe this, and how that ' the snare they know not shall come upon them, and the net they hid take them[6].' But they understood not these things, for had they done so, ' they would not have crucified the Lord of glory[7].'

6. Therefore the righteous and faithful servants of the Lord, who ' are made disciples for the kingdom of heaven, and bring forth from it things new and old ;' and who ' meditate on the words of the Lord, when sitting in the house, when lying down or rising up, and when walking by the way[8] ;'—since they are of good hope because of the promise of the Spirit which said, ' Blessed is the man that hath not walked in the counsel of the ungodly, nor stood in the way of sinners, nor sat in the seat of corrupters ; but his delight is in the law of the Lord, and in His law doth he meditate day and night[9] ;'—being grounded in faith, rejoicing in hope, fervent in spirit, they have boldness to say, ' My mouth shall speak wisdom, and the meditation of my heart shall be of understanding.' And again, ' I have meditated on all Thy works, and on the work of Thy hands has been my meditation.' And, ' If I have remembered Thee on my bed, and in the morning have meditated on Thee[10].' Afterwards, advancing in boldness, they say, ' The meditation of my heart is before Thee at all times[11].' And what is the end of such an one? He cites immediately ; ' The Lord is my Helper and my Redeemer[12].' For to those who thus examine themselves, and conform their hearts to the Lord, nothing adverse shall happen ; for indeed, their heart is strengthened by confidence in the Lord, as it is written, ' They who trust in the Lord are as mount Sion : he who dwelleth in Jerusalem shall not be moved for ever[13].' For if at any time, the crafty one shall be presump-

tuously bold against them, chiefly that he may break the rank of the saints, and cause a division among brethren ; even in this the Lord is with them, not only as an avenger on their behalf, but also when they have already been beaten, as a deliverer for them. For this is the divine promise ; ' The Lord shall fight for you[14].' Henceforth, although afflictions and trials from without overtake them, yet, being fashioned after the apostolic words, and ' being stedfast in tribulations, and persevering in prayers[15]' and in meditation on the law, they stand against those things which befall them, are well-pleasing to God, and give utterance to the words which are written, ' Afflictions and distresses are come upon me ; but Thy commandments are my meditation[16].'

7. And whereas, not only in action, but also in the thoughts of the mind, men are moved to deeds of virtue, he afterwards adds, saying, ' Mine eyes prevent the dawn, that I might meditate on Thy words[17].' For it is meet that the spiritual meditations of those who are whole should precede their bodily actions. And does not our Saviour, when intending to teach this very thing begin with the thoughts of the mind? saying, 'Whosoever looketh on a woman to lust after her, hath already committed adultery:' and, 'Whosoever shall be angry with his brother, is guilty of murder[18].' For where there is no wrath, murder is prevented ; and where lust is first removed, there can be no accusation of adultery. Hence meditation on the law is necessary, my beloved, and uninterrupted converse with virtue, ' that the saint may lack nothing, but be perfect to every good work[19].' For by these things is the promise of eternal life, as Paul wrote to Timothy, calling constant meditation exercise, and saying, ' Exercise thyself unto godliness ; for bodily exercise profiteth little ; but godliness is profitable for all things, since it has the promise of the present life, and of that which is eternal[20].'

8. Worthy of admiration is the virtue of that man, my brethren ! for through Timothy he enjoins upon all[1], that they should have regard to nothing more than to godliness, but above everything to adjudge the chief place to faith in God. For what grace has the unrighteous man, though he may feign to keep the commandments? Nay rather, the unrighteous man is unable even to keep a portion of the law, for as is his mind, such of necessity must be his actions ; as the Spirit says, reproving such ; ' The fool hath said in his heart,

3 Is. iii. 9, 10, LXX. ; cf. Wisd. ii. 12.   4 Eccl. x. 8.
5 Ps. ix. 15.   6 Ib. xxxv. 8.   7 1 Cor. ii. 8.   8 Matt.
xiii. 52 ; Deut. vi. 7.   9 Ps. i. 1.   10 Ib. xlix. 3 ; cxliii. 5 ;
lxiii. 6.   11 Ib. xix. 14.   12 Ib.   13 Ib. cxxv. 1, LXX.
14 Exod. xiv. 14.   15 Rom. xii. 12.   16 Ps. cxix. 143.
17 Ib. cxix. 148.   18 Matt. v. 28, 22.   19 2 Tim. iii. 17.
20 1 Tim. iv. 7, 8.   1 Cf. Letter 3, § 3, note 17 ; Apol. Const. 26.

there is no God.' After this the Word, shew-ing that actions correspond with thoughts, says, 'They are corrupt; they are profane in their machinations[2].' The unrighteous man then, in every respect corrupts his body; stealing, committing adultery, cursing, being drunken, and doing such like things. Even as Jeremiah, the prophet, convicts Israel of these things, crying out and saying, 'Oh, that I had a lodge far off in the wilderness! then would I leave my people and depart from them: for they are all adulterers, an assembly of oppressors, who draw out their tongue as a bow; lying and not truth has prevailed upon the earth, and they proceed from iniquities to iniquities; but Me they have not known[3].' Thus, for wickedness and falsehood, and for deeds, in which they [proceed] from iniquity to iniquity, he reproves their practices; but, because they knew not the Lord, and were faithless, he charges them with unrighteous-ness.

9. For faith and godliness are allied to each other, and sisters; and he who believes in Him is godly, and he also who is godly, believes the more[4]. He therefore who is in a state of wickedness, undoubtedly also wan-ders from the faith; and he who falls from godliness, falls from the true faith. Paul, for instance, bearing testimony to the same point, advises his disciple, saying, 'Avoid profane conversations; for they increase unto more ungodliness, and their word takes hold as doth a canker, of whom are Hymenæus and Phi-letus[5].' In what their wickedness consisted he declares, saying, 'Who have erred from the faith, saying that the resurrection is al-ready past[6].' But again, desirous of shewing that faith is yoked with godliness, the Apostle says, 'And all those who will live godly in Jesus Christ shall suffer persecution[7].' After-wards, that no man should renounce godliness through persecution, he counsels them to pre-serve the faith, adding, 'Thou, therefore, con-tinue in the things thou hast learned, and hast been assured of[8].' And as when brother is helped by brother, they become as a wall to each other; so faith and godliness, being of like growth, hang together, and he who is practised in the one, of necessity is strength-ened by the other. Therefore, wishing the disciple to be exercised in godliness unto the end, and to contend for the faith, he counsels them, saying, 'Fight the good fight of faith, and lay hold on eternal life[9].' For if a man first put away the wickedness of idols, and rightly confesses Him Who is truly God, he next fights by faith with those who war against Him.

10. For of these two things we speak of—faith and godliness—the hope is the same, even everlasting life; for he saith, 'Fight the good fight of faith; lay hold on eternal life.' And, 'exercise thyself unto godliness, for it hath the promise of the life that now is, and of that which is to come[10].' For this cause, the Ario-maniacs, who now have gone out from the Church, being opponents of Christ, have digged a pit of unbelief, into which they themselves have been thrust; and, since they have advanced in ungodliness, they 'overthrow the faith of the simple[11];' blaspheming the Son of God, and saying that He is a creature, and has His being from things which are not. But as then against the adherents of Philetus and Hymenæus, so now the Apostle fore-warns all men against ungodliness like theirs, saying, 'The foundation of God standeth sure, having this seal, The Lord knoweth them that are His; and, Let every one that nameth the name of the Lord depart from iniquity[12].' For it is well that a man should depart from wickedness and deeds of iniquity, that he may be able properly to celebrate the feast; for he who is defiled with the pollutions of the wicked is not able to sacrifice the Passover to the Lord our God. Hence, the people who were then in Egypt said, 'We cannot sacrifice the Passover in Egypt to the Lord our God[13].' For God, Who is over all, willed that they should go far away from the servants of Pha-raoh, and from the furnace of iron; so that being set free from wickedness, and having carefully put away from them all strange no-tions, they might receive the knowledge of God and of virtuous actions. For He saith, 'Go far from them: depart from the midst of them, and touch not the unclean things[14].' For a man will not otherwise depart from sin, and lay hold on virtuous deeds, than by medi-tation on his acts; and when he has been practised by exercise in godliness, he will lay hold on the confession of faith[15], which also Paul, after he had fought the fight, possessed, namely, the crown of righteousness which was laid up; which the righteous Judge will give, not to him alone, but to all who are like him.

11. For such meditation and exercise in godliness, being at all times the habit of the saints, is urgent on us at the present time, when the divine word desires us to keep the feast with them if we are in this disposition. For what else is the feast, but the constant

---

[2] Ps. xiv. 1, 2.   [3] Jer. ix. 2.   [4] Cf. John vii. 17.
[5] 2 Tim. ii. 16, 17.   [6] Ib. ii. 18.   [7] Ib. iii. 12.   [8] Ib.
iii. 14.   [9] 1 Tim. iv. 7.

[10] 1 Tim. iv. 7, 8.   [11] Rom. xvi. 18.   [12] 2 Tim. ii. 19.
[13] Exod. viii. 26.   [14] 2 Cor. vi. 17.
[15] The Syriac appears to be a translation of κρατήσει τῆς ὁμο-
λογίας τῆς πίστεως (cf. Heb. iv. 14).

worship of God, and the recognition of godliness, and unceasing prayers from the whole heart with agreement? So Paul wishing us to be ever in this disposition, commands, saying, 'Rejoice evermore; pray without ceasing; in everything give thanks[16].' Not therefore separately, but unitedly and collectively, let us all keep the feast together, as the prophet exhorts, saying, 'O come, let us rejoice in the Lord; let us make a joyful noise unto God our Saviour[17].' Who then is so negligent, or who so disobedient to the divine voice, as not to leave everything, and run to the general and common assembly of the feast? which is not in one place only, for not one place alone keeps the feast; but 'into all the earth their song has gone forth, and to the ends of the world their words.' And the sacrifice is not offered in one place, but 'in every nation, incense and a pure sacrifice is offered unto God[1].' So when in like manner from all in every place, praise and prayer shall ascend to the gracious and good Father, when the whole Catholic Church which is in every place, with gladness and rejoicing, celebrates together the same worship to God, when all men in common send up a song of praise and say, Amen[2]; how blessed will it not be, my brethren! who will not, at that time, be engaged, praying rightly? For the walls of every adverse power, yea even of Jericho especially, falling down, and the gift[3] of the Holy Spirit being then richly poured upon all men, every man perceiving the coming of the Spirit shall say, 'We are all filled in the morning with Thy favour, and we rejoice and are made glad in our days[4].'

12. Since this is so, let us make a joyful noise with the saints, and let no one of us fail of his duty in these things; counting as nothing the affliction or the trials which, especially at this time, have been enviously directed against us by the party of Eusebius. Even now they wish to injure us, and by their accusations to compass our death, because of that godliness, whose helper is the Lord. But, as faithful servants of God, knowing that He is our salvation in the time of trouble:—for our Lord promised beforehand, saying, 'Blessed are ye when men revile you and persecute you, and say all manner of evil against you falsely, for My sake. Rejoice, and be exceeding glad, for your reward is great in heaven[5].' Again, it is the Redeemer's own word, that affliction shall not befall every man in this world, but only those who have a holy fear of Him:—on this account, the more the

enemies hem us in, the more let us be at liberty; although they revile us, let us come together; and the more they would turn us aside from godliness, let us the more boldly preach it, saying, 'All these things are come upon us, yet have we not forgotten Thee[6],' and we have not done evil with the Ariomaniacs, who say that Thou hast existence from those things that exist not. The Word which is eternally with the Father, is also from Him.

13. Let us therefore keep the feast, my brethren, celebrating it not at all as an occasion of distress and mourning, neither let us mingle with heretics through temporal trials brought upon us by godliness. But if anything that would promote joy and gladness should offer, let us attend to it; so that our heart may not be sad, like that of Cain; but that, like faithful and good servants of the Lord, we may hear the words, 'Enter into the joy of thy Lord[7].' For we do not institute days of mourning and sorrow, as some may consider these of Easter to be, but we keep the feast, being filled with joy and gladness. We keep it then, not regarding it after the deceitful error of the Jews, nor according to the teaching of the Arians, which takes away the Son from the Godhead, and numbers Him among creatures; but we look to the correct doctrine we derive from the Lord. For the guile of the Jews, and the unbounded impiety of the Arians, cause nothing but sad reflections, for the former at the beginning slew the Lord; but these latter take away His position of having conquered that death to which the Jews brought Him, in that they say He is not the Creator, but a creature. For if He were a creature, He would have been holden by death; but if He was not holden by death, according to the Scriptures, He is not a creature, but the Lord of the creatures, and the subject[8] of this immortal feast.

14. For the Lord of death would abolish death, and being Lord, what He would was accomplished; for we have all passed from death unto life. But the imagination of the Jews, and of those who are like them, was vain, since the result was not such as they contemplated, but turned out adverse to themselves; and 'at both of them He that sitteth in the heaven shall laugh: the Lord shall have them in derision[9].' Hence, when our Saviour was led to death, He restrained the women who followed Him weeping, saying, 'Weep not for Me[10];' meaning to shew that the Lord's death is an event, not of sorrow but of joy, and that He Who dies for us is alive. For He does not derive His being from those

16 1 Thess. v. 16—18.   17 Ps. xcv. 1.   1 Ib. xix. 4; Mal. i. 11.   2 For a parallel passage to this, vid. *Letter* x. 2.   3 Cf. *Letter* x. 2, note 9. Vid. also John vii. 39; Rom. v. 5; John xx. 22.   4 Ps. xc. 14, LXX.   5 Matt. v. 11, 12.

6 Ps. xliv. 17.   7 Matt. xxv. 21.   8 Syr. ὑπόθεσις. Cf. *Letter* x. 2, note 8.   9 Ps. ii. 4.   10 Luke xxiii. 28.

things which are not, but from the Father. It is truly a subject of joy, that we can see the signs of victory against death, even our own incorruptibility, through the body of the Lord. For since He rose gloriously, it is clear that the resurrection of all of us will take place; and since His body remained without corruption, there can be no doubt regarding our incorruption [11]. For as by one man [12], as saith Paul (and it is the truth), sin passed upon all men, so by the resurrection of our Lord Jesus Christ, we shall all rise. 'For,' he says, 'this corruptible must put on incorruption, and this mortal must put on immortality [13].' Now this came to pass in the time of the Passion, in which our Lord died for us, for 'our Passover, Christ, is sacrificed [14].' Therefore, because He was sacrificed, let each of us feed upon Him, and with alacrity and diligence partake of His sustenance; since He is given to all without grudging, and is in every one 'a well of water flowing to everlasting life [15].'

15. We begin the fast of forty days on the ninth of the month Phamenoth (Mar. 5); and having, in these days, served the Lord with abstinence, and first purified ourselves [16], we commence also the holy Easter on the fourteenth of the month Pharmuthi (April 9). Afterwards, extending the fast to the seventh day, on the seventeenth [17] of the month, let us rest late in the evening. And the light of the Lord having first dawned upon us, and the holy Sunday on which our Lord rose shining upon us, we should rejoice and be glad with the joy which arises from good works, during the seven weeks which remain—to Pentecost—giving glory to the Father, and saying, 'This is the day which the Lord hath made: we will rejoice and be glad in it [18],' through our Lord and Saviour Jesus Christ, through Whom to the same, and to His Father, be glory and dominion for ever and ever. Amen. Salute one another with a holy kiss. All the brethren who are with me salute you. That ye may have health in the Lord, I pray, brethren beloved.

Here endeth the eleventh Letter of holy Athanasius.

*XII.

(Probably for 340 A.D.)

To the Beloved Brother, and our fellow Minister Serapion [1].

THANKS be to Divine Providence for those things which, at all times, it vouchsafes to us; for it has vouchsafed to us now to come to the season of the festival. Having, therefore, according to custom, written the Letter respecting the festival, I have sent it to you, my beloved; that through you all the brethren may be able to know the day of rejoicing. But because some Meletians, being come from Syria, have boasted that they had received what does not belong to them, I mean, that they also were reckoned in the Catholic Church; on this account, I have sent to you a copy of one letter of our fellow-ministers who are of Palestine, that when it reaches you, you may know the fraud of the pretenders in this matter. For because they boasted, as I have said before, it was necessary for me to write to the Bishops who are in Syria, and immediately those of Palestine sent us a reply, having agreed in [2] the judgment against them, as you may learn from this example. That you may not have to consider the letters of all the Bishops one after the other, I have sent you one, which is of like character with the rest, in order that from it you may know the purport of all of them. I know also that when they are convicted in this matter, they will incur perfect odium at the hands of all men. And thus far concerning the pretenders. But I have further deemed it highly necessary and very urgent, to make known to your modesty—for I have written this to each one—that you should proclaim the fast of forty days to the brethren, and persuade them to fast, lest, while all the world is fasting, we who are in Egypt should be derided, as the only people who do not fast, but take our pleasure in these days. For if, on account of the Letter [not] being yet read, we do not fast, we should take away this pretext, and it should be read before the fast of forty days, so that they may not make this an excuse for neglect or fasting. Also, when it is read, they may be able to learn about the fast. But O, my beloved, whether in this way or any other, persuade and teach them to fast the forty days. For it is a disgrace that when all the world does this, those alone who are in Egypt, instead of fasting, should find their pleasure. For even I being grieved because men deride us for this, have been constrained to write to you. When therefore you receive the letters, and have read them and given the exhortation, write to me in return, my beloved, that I also may rejoice upon learning it.

2. But I have also thought it necessary to inform [3] you of the fact, that Bishops have suc-

---

[11] Cf. *de Incarn.* § 50. [12] Rom. v. 12. [13] 1 Cor. xv. 53. [14] Ib. v. 7. [15] John iv. 14. [16] Cf. *Letter* vi. II. [17] Read 'nineteenth.' [18] Ps. cxviii. 24.
[1] This Letter being introduced (as it is in the MS.) after the eleventh, with the remark at the end of it, that there is no twelfth; together with the exhortations concerning fasting contained in it, was probably written in lieu of a twelfth. Serapion was doubtless the Bishop of Thmuis (see *Letter* 54).

[2] Or, 'fulfilled the judgment.' Cureton.
[3] There is a similar notification of the appointment of fresh Bishops appended to the nineteenth Letter.

ceeded those who have fallen asleep. In Tanis, in the stead of Elias [4], is Theodorus. In Arsenoitis, Silvanus [5] instead of Calosiris. In Paralus, Nemesion is instead of Nonnus [6]. In Bucolia [7] is Heraclius. In Tentyra, Andronicus is instead of Saprion [8], his father. In Thebes, Philon instead of Philon. In Maximianopolis, Herminus instead of Atras. In the lower Apollon is Sarapion instead of Plution. In Aphroditon, Serenus is in the place of Theodorus. In Rhinocoruron, Salomon. In Stathma, Arabion, and in Marmarica. In the eastern Garyathis, Andragathius [9] in the place of Hierax. In the southern Garyathis, Quintus [9] instead of Nicon [10]. So that to these you may write, and from these receive the canonical Letters.

Salute one another with a holy kiss. All the brethren who are with me salute you.

He wrote this from Rome. There is no twelfth Letter.

LETTER XIII.

(For 341.)

Coss. Marcellinus, Probinus ; Præf. Longinus ; Indict. xiv ; Easter-day, xiii Kal. Maii, xxiv Pharmuthi ; Æra Dioclet. 57.

AGAIN, my beloved brethren, I am ready to notify to you the saving feast [1], which will take place according to annual custom. For although the opponents of Christ [2] have oppressed you together with us with afflictions and sorrows ; yet, God having comforted us by our mutual faith [3], behold, I write to you even from Rome. Keeping the feast here with the brethren, still I keep it with you also in will and in spirit, for we send up prayers in common to God, ' Who hath granted us not only to believe in Him, but also now to suffer for His sake [4].' For troubled as we are, because we are so far from you, He moves us to write, that

by a letter we might comfort ourselves, and provoke one another to good [4a]. For, indeed, numerous afflictions and bitter persecutions directed against the Church have been against us. For heretics, corrupt in their mind, untried in the faith, rising against the truth, violently persecute the Church, and of the brethren, some are scourged and others torn with stripes, and hardest of all, their insults reach even to the Bishops. Nevertheless, it is not becoming, on this account, that we should neglect the feast. But we should especially remember it, and not at all forget its commemoration from time to time. Now the unbelievers do not consider that there is a season for feasts, because they spend all their lives in revelling and follies ; and the feasts which they keep are an occasion of grief rather than of joy. But to us in this present life they are above all an uninterrupted passage [to heaven]—it is indeed our season. For such things as these serve for exercise and trial, so that, having approved ourselves zealous and chosen servants of Christ, we may be fellow-heirs with the saints [5]. For thus Job : ' The whole world is a place of trial to men upon the earth [5a].' Nevertheless, they are proved in this world by afflictions, labours, and sorrows, to the end that each one may receive of God such reward as is meet for him, as He saith by the prophet, ' I am the Lord, Who trieth the hearts, and searcheth the reins, to give to every one according to his ways [6].'

2. Not that He first knows the things of a man on his being proved (for He knows them all before they come to pass), but because He is good and philanthropic, He distributes to each a due reward according to his actions, so that every man may exclaim, Righteous is the judgment of God ! As the prophet says again, ' The Lord trieth the just, and discerneth the reins [7].' Again, for this cause He tries each one of us, either that to those who know it not, virtue may be manifested by means of those who are proved, as was said respecting Job ; ' Thinkest thou that I was revealed to thee for any other cause, than that thou shouldest be seen righteous [8] ?' or that, when men come to a sense of their deeds, they may be able to know of what manner they are, and so may either repent of their wickedness, or abide confirmed in the faith. Now the blessed Paul, when troubled by afflictions, and persecutions, and hunger and thirst, ' in everything was a conqueror, through Jesus Christ, Who loved us [9].' Through suffering he was weak indeed in body, yet, believing and hoping, he was made strong

---

4 Larsow writes ' Ilius.' Tanis is situate in Augustamnica Prima. Vid. Quatremère *Mémoires geogr. et histor. sur l'Egypte*, tom. i. p. 284, &c. (L.) The word Τάνις is the LXX. rendering of ' Zoan.' In the *Apol. c. Ar.* 50, we have a list of ninety-four Egyptian Bishops, among others, who subscribed to the letter of the Council of Sardica. A reference to this list explains some names which otherwise would have been obscure. For a list of the Egyptian Bishoprics, the reader is referred to Neale's *Hist. of the Holy Eastern Church.* Gen. Introd. vol. i. pp. 115, 116. To the list there given must be added the names of Bucolia, Stathma, the Eastern Garyathis, the Southern Garyathis. There were two Egyptian Bishops named Elias who subscribed their names to the letter of the Council of Sardica.
5 Silvanus was succeeded by Andreas, as we learn from the postscript to the nineteenth Letter.
6 An Egyptian Bishop named Nonnus was present at the Synod of Tyre. *Apol. c. Ar.* § 79.
7 For a dissertation on the situation of Bucolia, see the treatise by Quatremère, already referred to (tom. i. pp. 224—233). In p. 233, he writes ; La contrée de l'Elearchie ou des Bucolies est, si je ne me trompe, parfaitement identique avec la province de Baschmour.
8 An Egyptian Bishop of the name of Saprion was at the Synod of Tyre. *Apol. c. Ar.* § 79. He is ' Serapion' in *Vit. Pach.* 20.
9 *Apol. Ar.* 50.   10 *Apol. Ar.* 79.   1 Vid. *Letter* x. 1.
2 The Arians (οἱ χριστόμαχοι).   3 Cf. Rom. i. 12.
4 Phil.   20

4a Cf. Heb. x. 24   5 Cf. Col. i. 12.   5a Job vii. 1. not LXX.   6 Jer. xvii. 10.   7 Ib. xx. 12.   8 Job xl. 8, 9, (3, 4, LXX.).   9 Rom. viii. 37.

in spirit, and his strength was made perfect in weakness [9a].

3. The other saints also, who had a like confidence in God, accepted a like probation with gladness, as Job said, 'Blessed be the name of the Lord [10].' But the Psalmist, 'Search me, O Lord, and try me : prove my reins and my heart [11].' For since, when the strength is proved, it convinceth the foolish, they perceiving the cleansing and the advantage resulting from the divine fire, were not discouraged in trials like these, but they rather delighted in them, suffering no injury at all from the things which happened, but being seen to shine more brightly, like gold from the fire [12], as he said, who was tried in such a school of discipline as this ; 'Thou hast tried my heart, Thou hast visited me in the night-season ; Thou hast proved me, and hast not found iniquity in me, so that my mouth shall not speak of the works of men [13].' But those whose actions are not restrained by law, who know of nothing beyond eating and drinking and dying, account trials as danger. They soon stumble at them, so that, being untried in the faith, they are given over to a reprobate mind, and do those things which are not seemly [13a]. Therefore the blessed Paul, when urging us to such exercises as these, and having before measured himself by them, says, 'Therefore I take pleasure in afflictions, in infirmities.' And again, 'Exercise thyself unto godliness [14].' For since he knew the persecutions that befel those who chose to live in godliness, he wished his disciples to meditate beforehand on the difficulties connected with godliness ; that when trials should come, and affliction arise, they might be able to bear them easily, as having been exercised in these things. For in those things wherewith a man has been conversant in mind, he ordinarily experiences a hidden joy. In this way, the blessed martyrs, becoming at first conversant with difficulties, were quickly perfected in Christ, regarding as nought the injury of the body, while they contemplated the expected rest.

4. But all those who 'call their lands by their own names [15],' and have wood, and hay, and stubble [16] in their thoughts ; such as these, since they are strangers to difficulties, become aliens from the kingdom of heaven. Had they however known that 'tribulation perfecteth patience, and patience experience, and experience hope, and hope maketh not ashamed,' they would have exercised themselves, after the example of Paul, who said, 'I keep under my body and bring it into subjection, lest when I have preached to others, I myself should be a castaway [1].' They would easily have borne the afflictions which were brought upon them to prove them from time to time, if the prophetic admonition [2] had been listened to by them ; 'It is good for a man to take up Thy yoke in his youth ; he shall sit alone and shall be silent, because he hath taken Thy yoke upon him. He will give his cheek to him who smiteth him ; he will be filled with reproaches. Because the Lord does not cast away for ever ; for when He abases, He is gracious, according to the multitude of His tender mercies [3].' For though all these things should proceed from the enemies, stripes, insults, reproaches, yet shall they avail nothing against the multitude of God's tender mercies ; for we shall quickly recover from them since they are merely temporal, but God is always gracious, pouring out His tender mercies on those who please [Him]. Therefore, my beloved brethren, we should not look at these temporal things, but fix our attention on those which are eternal. Though affliction may come, it will have an end, though insult and persecution, yet are they nothing to the hope which is set [before us]. For all present matters are trifling compared with those which are future ; the sufferings of this present time not being worthy to be compared with the hope that is to come [4]. For what can be compared with the kingdom ? or what is there in comparison with life eternal ? Or what is all we could give here, to that which we shall inherit yonder ? For we are 'heirs of God, and joint-heirs with Christ [5].' Therefore it is not right, my beloved, to consider afflictions and persecutions, but the hopes which are laid up for us because of persecutions.

5. Now to this the example of Issachar, the patriarch, may persuade, as the Scripture [6] saith, 'Issachar desires that which is good, resting between the heritages ; and when he saw that the rest was good, and the land fertile [7], he bowed his shoulder to labour, and became a husbandman.' Being consumed by divine love, like the spouse in the Canticles, he gathered abundance from the holy Scriptures, for his mind was captivated not by the old alone, but by both the heritages. And hence as it were, spreading his wings, he beheld afar off 'the rest' which is in heaven, and,—

---

[1] Rom. v. 3 ; 1 Cor. ix. 27.   [2] Lam. iii. 27.
[3] Cf. Serapion *Epistola ad Monachos*, in Mai *Spicileg. Rom.* tom. iv. p. li. (L.)
[4] Cf. Rom. viii. 18 ; 2 Cor. iv. 17.   [5] Rom. viii. 17.
[6] Gen. xlix. 14.
[7] Jarchi interprets the passage figuratively of Issachar being strong to bear the yoke of the law. The Jerusalem Targum thus paraphrases the verse. 'And he saw the rest of the world to come, that it was good, and the portion of the land of Israel, that it was pleasant ; therefore he inclined his shoulders to work in the law, and his brethren brought gifts unto him.

[9a] 2 Cor. xii. 9.   [10] Job i. 21.   [11] Ps. xxvi. 2.   [12] Cf. Mal. iii. 3 ; 1 Pet. i. 7.   [13] Ps. xvii. 3, 4, LXX.   [13a] Rom. i. 28.   [14] 2 Cor. xii. 10 ; 1 Tim. iv. 7.   [15] Ps. xlix. 11 (Larsow mistakes the reference)   [16] Cf. 1 Cor. iii. 12.

since this 'land' consists of such beautiful works,—how much more truly the heavenly [country] must also [consist] of such[8] ; for the other is ever new, and grows not old. For this 'land' passes away, as the Lord said ; but that which is ready to receive the saints is immortal. Now when Issachar, the patriarch, saw these things, he joyfully made his boast of afflictions and toils, bowing his shoulders that he might labour. And he did not contend with those who smote him, neither was he disturbed by insults ; but like a strong man triumphing the more by these things, and the more earnestly tilling his land, he received profit from it. The Word scattered the seed, but he watchfully cultivated it, so that it brought forth fruit, even a hundred-fold.

6. Now what does this mean, my beloved, but that we also, when the enemies are arrayed against us, should glory in afflictions[8a], and that when we are persecuted, we should not be discouraged, but should the rather press after the crown of the high calling[9] in Christ Jesus our Lord? and that being insulted, we should not be disturbed, but should give our cheek to the smiter, and bow the shoulder? For the lovers of pleasure and the lovers of enmity are tried, as saith the blessed Apostle James, 'when they are drawn away by their own lusts and enticed[10].' But let us, knowing that we suffer for the truth, and that those who deny the Lord smite and persecute us, 'count it all joy, my brethren,' according to the words of James, 'when we fall into trials of various temptations, knowing that the trial of our faith worketh patience[11].' Let us rejoice as we keep the feast, my brethren, knowing that our salvation is ordered in the time of affliction. For our Saviour did not redeem us by inactivity, but by suffering for us He abolished death. And respecting this, He intimated to us before, saying, 'In the world ye shall have tribulation[12].' But He did not say this to every man, but to those who diligently and faithfully perform good service to Him, knowing beforehand, that they should be persecuted who would live godly toward Him.

7. 'But evil-doers and sorcerers will wax worse and worse, deceiving and being deceived[13].' If therefore, like those expounders of dreams and false prophets who professed to give signs, these ignorant men being drunk, not with wine, but with their own wickedness, make a profession of priesthood, and glory in their threats, believe them not ; but since we are tried, let us humble ourselves, not being drawn away by them. For so God warned His people by Moses, saying, 'If there shall rise up among you a prophet, or a dreamer of dreams, and shall give signs and tokens, and the sign or the token shall come to pass which he spake to thee, saying, Let us go and serve strange gods, which ye have not known ; ye shall not hearken unto the words of that prophet or that dreamer of dreams. For the Lord your God trieth you, that He may know whether you will love the Lord your God with all your heart[14].' So we, when we are tried by these things, will not separate ourselves from the love of God. But let us now keep the feast, my beloved, not as introducing a day of suffering, but of joy in Christ, by Whom we are fed every day. Let us be mindful of Him Who was sacrificed in the days of the Passover ; for we celebrate this, because Christ the Passover was sacrificed[15]. He Who once brought His people out of Egypt, and hath now abolished death, and him that had the power of death, that is the devil[16], will likewise now turn him to shame, and again grant aid to those who are troubled, and cry unto God day and night[17].

8. We begin the fast of forty days on the thirteenth of Phamenoth (9 Mar.), and the holy week of Easter on the eighteenth of Pharmuthi (Apr. 13) ; and resting on the seventh day, being the twenty-third (Apr. 18), and the first of the great week having dawned on the twenty-fourth of the same month Pharmuthi (Apr. 19), let us reckon from it till Pentecost. And at all times let us sing praises, calling on Christ, being delivered from our enemies by Christ Jesus our Lord, through Whom to the Father be glory and dominion for ever and ever. Amen. Greet one another with a holy kiss. All those who are here with me salute you. I pray, my beloved brethren, that ye may have health in the Lord.

He wrote this also from Rome. Here endeth the thirteenth Letter.

LETTER XIV.

(For 342.)

Coss. Augustus Constantius III, Constans II ; Præf. the same Longinus ; Indict. xv ; Easter-day iii Id. Apr., xvi Pharmuthi ; Æra Dioclet. 58.

THE gladness of our feast, my brethren, is always near at hand, and never fails those who wish to celebrate it[1]. For the Word is near, Who is all things on our behalf, even our Lord Jesus Christ, Who, having promised that His habitation with us should be perpetual, in

---

8 Larsow's rendering of the above is followed.　8a Rom. **v. 3.**
9 Cf. Phil. **14.** τὸ βραβεῖον τῆς ἄνω κλήσεως.　10 James i. 14.
11 Ib. i. 2.　12 John xvi. 33.　13 2 Tim. iii. 13.

14 Deut. xiii. 1—3.　15 1 Cor. **v. 7.**　16 Heb. ii. 14.
17 Luke xviii. 7.　1 Cf. *Letter* v. 1.

virtue thereof cried, saying, 'Lo, I am with you all the days of the world[2].' For as He is the Shepherd, and the High Priest, and the Way and the Door, and everything at once to us, so again, He is shewn to us as the Feast, and the Holyday, according to the blessed Apostle; 'Our Passover, Christ, is sacrificed[3].' He it was who was expected, He caused a light to shine at the prayer of the Psalmist, who said, 'My Joy, deliver me from those who surround me[4];' this being indeed true rejoicing, this being a true feast, even deliverance from wickedness, whereto a man attains by thoroughly adopting an upright conversation, and being approved in his mind of godly submission towards God[5]. For thus the saints all their lives long were like men rejoicing at a feast. One found rest in prayer to God, as blessed David[6], who rose in the night, not once but seven times. Another gave glory in songs of praise, as great Moses, who sang a song of praise for the victory over Pharaoh, and those task-masters[7]. Others performed worship with unceasing diligence, like great Samuel and blessed Elijah; who have ceased from their course, and now keep the feast in heaven, and rejoice in what they formerly learnt through shadows, and from the types recognise the truth.

2. But what sprinklings shall we now employ, while we celebrate the feast? Who will be our guide, as we haste to this festival? None can do this, my beloved, but Him Whom you will name with me, even our Lord Jesus Christ, Who said, 'I am the Way.' For it is He Who, according to the blessed John, 'taketh away the sin of the world[8].' He purifies our souls, as Jeremiah the prophet says in a certain place, 'Stand in the ways and see, and enquire, and look which is the good path, and ye shall find in it cleansing for your souls[9].' Of old time, the blood of he-goats and the ashes of a heifer, sprinkled upon those who were unclean, were fit only to purify the flesh[9a]; but now, through the grace of God the Word, every man is thoroughly cleansed. Following Him, we may, even here, as on the threshold of the Jerusalem which is above, meditate beforehand on the feast which is eternal, as also the blessed Apostles, together following the Saviour Who was their Leader, have now become teachers of a like grace, saying, 'Behold, we have left all, and followed Thee[10].' For the following of the Lord, and the feast which is of the Lord, is not accomplished by words only, but by deeds, every enactment of laws and every command involving a distinct performance. For as great Moses, when administering the holy laws, exacted a promise from the people[11], respecting the practice of them, so that having promised, they might not neglect them, and be accused as liars, thus also, the celebration of the feast of the Passover raises no question, and demands no reply; but when the word is given, the performance of it follows, for He saith, 'And the children of Israel shall keep the Passover[12];' intending that there should be a ready performance of the commandment, while the command should aid its execution. But respecting these matters, I have confidence in your wisdom, and your care for instruction. Such points as these have been touched upon by us often and in various Letters.

3. But now, which is above all things most necessary, I wish to remind you, and myself with you, how that the command would have us come to the Paschal feast not profanely and without preparation, but with sacramental and doctrinal rites, and prescribed observances, as indeed we learn from the historical account, 'A man who is of another nation, or bought with money, or uncircumcised, shall not eat the Passover[13].' Neither should it be eaten in 'any' house, but He commands it to be done in haste; inasmuch as before we groaned and were made sad by the bondage to Pharaoh, and the commands of the task-masters. For when in former time the children of Israel acted in this way, they were counted worthy to receive the type, which existed for the sake of this feast, nor is the feast now introduced on account of the type. As also the Word of God, when desirous of this, said to His disciples, 'With desire I have desired to eat this Passover with you[14].' Now that is a wonderful account, for a man might have seen them at that time girded as for a procession or a dance, and going out with staves, and sandals, and unleavened bread. These things, which took place before in shadows, were typical. But now the Truth is nigh unto us, 'the Image of the invisible God[15],' our Lord Jesus Christ, the true Light, Who instead of a staff, is our sceptre, instead of unleavened bread, is the bread which came down from heaven, Who, instead of sandals, hath furnished us with the preparation of the Gospel[16], and Who, to speak briefly, by all these hath guided us to His Father. And if enemies afflict us and persecute us, He again, instead of Moses, will encourage us with better words, saying, 'Be of

---

[2] Matt. xxviii. 20.   [3] 1 Cor. v. 7.   [4] Ps. xxxi. 7, LXX.
[5] Cf. Letter iii. 2.   [6] Ps. cxix. 62, 164.   [7] Exod. xv.
[8] John xiv. 6; i. 29.   [9] Jer. vi. 16.   [9a] Heb. ix. 13.
[10] Mark x. 28.

[11] Exod. xix. 8.   [12] Ib. xii. 47.   [13] Ib. xii. 43—48.
[14] Luke xxii. 15.   [15] Col. i. 15.   [16] Eph. vi. 15.

good cheer; I have overcome the wicked one [17].' And if after we have passed over the Red Sea heat should again vex us or some bitterness of the waters befall us, even thence again the Lord will appear to us, imparting to us of His sweetness, and His life-giving fountain, saying, 'If any man thirst, let him come to Me, and drink [18].'

4. Why therefore do we tarry, and why do we delay, and not come with all eagerness and diligence to the feast, trusting that it is Jesus who calleth us? Who is all things for us, and was laden in ten thousand ways for our salvation; Who hungered and thirsted for us, though He gives us food and drink in His saving gifts [19]. For this is His glory, this the miracle of His divinity, that He changed our sufferings for His happiness. For, being life, He died that He might make us alive, being the Word, He became flesh, that He might instruct the flesh in the Word, and being the fountain of life, He thirsted our thirst, that thereby He might urge us to the feast, saying, 'If any man thirst, let him come to Me, and drink [1].' At that time, Moses proclaimed the beginning of the feast, saying, 'This month is the beginning of months to you [2].' But the Lord, Who came down in the end of the ages [3], proclaimed a different day, not as though He would abolish the law, far from it, but that He should establish the law, and be the end of the law. 'For Christ is the end of the law to every one that believeth in righteousness;' as the blessed Paul saith, 'Do we make void the law by faith? far from it: we rather establish the law [4].' Now these things astonished even the officers who were sent by the Jews, so that wondering they said to the Pharisees, 'No man ever thus spake [5].' What was it then that astonished those officers, or what was it which so affected the men as to make them marvel? It was nothing but the boldness and authority of our Saviour. For when of old time prophets and scribes studied the Scriptures, they perceived that what they read did not refer to themselves, but to others. Moses, for instance, 'A prophet will the Lord raise up unto you of your brethren, like unto me; to him hearken in all that he commands you.' Isaiah again, 'Behold, a virgin shall conceive and bear a son, and ye shall call his name Emmanuel [6].' And others prophesied in different and various ways, concerning the Lord. But by the Lord, of Himself, and of no other, were these things prophesied; to Himself He limited them all, saying, 'If any man thirst, let him come to

Me [7]'—not to any other person, but to 'Me.' A man may indeed hear from those concerning My coming, but he must not henceforth drink from others, but from Me.

5. Therefore let us also, when we come to the feast, no longer come as to old shadows, for they are accomplished, neither as to common feasts, but let us hasten as to the Lord, Who is Himself the feast [8], not looking upon it as an indulgence and delight of the belly, but as a manifestation of virtue. For the feasts of the heathen are full of greediness, and utter indolence, since they consider they celebrate a feast when they are idle [9]; and they work the works of perdition when they feast. But our feasts consist in the exercise of virtue and the practice of temperance; as the prophetic word testifies in a certain place, saying, 'The fast of the fourth, and the fast of the fifth, and the fast of the seventh, and the fast of the tenth [month], shall be to the house of Judah for gladness, and rejoicing, and for pleasant feasts [10].' Since therefore this occasion for exercise is set before us, and such a day as this is come, and the prophetic voice has gone forth that the feast shall be celebrated, let us give all diligence to this good proclamation, and like those who contend on the race course, let us vie with each other in observing the purity of the fast [11], by watchfulness in prayers, by study of the Scriptures, by distributing to the poor, and let us be at peace with our enemies. Let us bind up those who are scattered abroad, banish pride, and return to lowliness of mind, being at peace with all men, and urging the brethren unto love. Thus also the blessed Paul was often engaged in fastings and watchings, and was willing to be accursed for his brethren. Blessed David again, having humbled himself by fastings, used boldness, saying, 'O Lord my God, if I have done this, if there is any iniquity in my hands, if I have repaid those who dealt evil with me, then may I fall from my enemies as a vain man [12].' If we do these things, we shall conquer death; and receive an earnest [13] of the kingdom of heaven.

6. We begin the holy Easter feast on the tenth of Pharmuthi (April 5), desisting from the holy fasts on the fifteenth of the same month Pharmuthi (April 10), on the evening of the seventh day. And let us keep the holy feast on the sixteenth of the same month Pharmuthi (April 11); adding one by one [the days] till the holy Pentecost, passing on to which, as through a succession of feasts, let us keep the festival to the Spirit, Who is even

---

[17] John xvi. 33; cf. 1 John ii. 13.   [18] Ib. vii. 37.   [19] Cf. supr. p. 88.   [1] John vii. 37.   [2] Exod. xii. 2.   [3] Heb. ix. 26.   [4] Rom. x. 4; iii. 31.   [5] John vii. 46.   [6] Deut. xviii. 15; Is. vii. 14. These two texts are also quoted together in *Orat.* i. § 54.

[7] John vii. 37.   [8] Cf. 1 Cor. v. 7.   [9] Cf. *Letter* vii. 3. [10] Zech. viii. 19.   [11] Cf. 1 Cor. ix. 24—27.   [12] Rom. ix. 3; Ps. vii. 3, 4, LXX.   [13] Syr. Ἀρραβων. Cf. Eph. i. 13, 14, &c.

now near us, in Jesus Christ, through Whom and with Whom to the Father be glory and dominion for ever and ever. Amen.

The fifteenth and sixteenth are wanting.

LETTER XVII.

(For 345.)

Coss. Amantius, Albinus; Præf. Nestorius of Gaza; Indict. iii; Easter-day, vii Id. Apr., xii Pharmuthi; Moon 19; Æra Dioclet. 61.

ATHANASIUS to the Presbyters and Deacons of Alexandria, and to the beloved brethren, greeting in Christ.

According to custom, I give you notice respecting Easter, my beloved, that you also may notify the same to the districts of those who are at a distance, as is usual. Therefore, after this present festival [1], I mean this which is on the twentieth of the month Pharmuthi, the Easter-day following will be on the vii Id. April, or according · to the Alexandrians, on the twelfth of Pharmuthi. Give notice therefore in all those districts, that Easter-day will be on the vii Id. April, or according to the Alexandrian reckoning on the twelfth of Pharmuthi. That you may be in health in Christ, I pray, my beloved brethren.

LETTER XVIII.

(For 346)

Coss. Augustus Constantius IV, Constans III; Præf. the same Nestorius; Indict. iv; Easter-day iii Kal. Apr., iv Pharmuthi; Moon 21; Æra Dioclet. 62.

ATHANASIUS, to the Presbyters and Deacons of Alexandria, brethren beloved in the Lord, greeting.

You have done well, dearly beloved brethren, that you have given the customary notice of the holy Easter in those districts; for I have seen and acknowledged your exactness. By other letters I have also given you notice, that when this year is finished, ye may know concerning the next. Yet now I have thought it necessary to write the same things that, when you have it exactly, you also may write with care. Therefore, after the conclusion of this feast, which is now drawing to its close, on the twelfth of the month Pharmuthi, which is on the vii Id. Apr. [2], Easter-day will be on the iii Kal. April; the fourth of Pharmuthi, according to the Alexandrians. When therefore the feast is finished, give no-

tice again in these districts, according to early custom, thus: Easter Sunday is on the iii Kal. April, which is the fourth of Pharmuthi, according to the Alexandrian reckoning. And let no man hesitate concerning the day, neither let any one contend, saying, It is requisite that Easter should be held on the twenty-seventh of the month Phamenoth; for it was discussed in the holy Synod [3], and all there settled it to be on the iii Kal. April. I say then that it is on the fourth of the month Pharmuthi; for the week before this is much too early [4]. Therefore let there be no dispute, but let us act as becometh us. For I have thus written to the Romans also. Give notice then as it has been notified to you, that it is on the iii Kal. April; the fourth of Pharmuthi, according to the Alexandrian reckoning.

That ye may have health in the Lord, I pray, my dearly beloved brethren.

LETTER XIX.

(For 347.)

Coss. Rufinus, Eusebius; Præf. the same Nestorius; Indict. v; Easter-day, Prid. Id. Apr., Pharmuthi xvii; Æra Dioclet. 63; Moon 15.

'BLESSED is God, the Father of our Lord Jesus Christ [1],' for such an introduction is fitting for an Epistle, and more especially now, when it brings thanksgiving to the Lord, in the Apostle's words, because He hath brought us from a distance, and granted us again to send openly to you, as usual, the Festal Letters. For this is the season of the feast, my brethren, and it is near; being not now proclaimed by trumpets, as the history records [2], but being made known and brought near to us by the Saviour, Who suffered on our behalf and rose again, even as Paul preached, saying, 'Our Passover, Christ, is sacrificed [3].' Henceforth the feast of the Passover is ours, not that of a stranger, nor is it any longer of the Jews [4]. For the time of shadows is abolished, and those former things have ceased, and now the month of new things [4a] is at hand, in which every man should keep the feast, in obedience to Him who said, 'Observe the

---

[1] Observe that Athan. gives notice *at Easter*, A.D. 344, upon what day Easter is to be observed in A.D. 345, and not immediately after the succeeding Epiphany, as Cassian asserts to have been the custom of the Patriarch of Alexandria. (Cassian. *Collat.* x. 1.) Cf. *Letters* 2, 4, 10, 18, &c.

[2] The number vii is omitted in the MS.

[3] Sardica, in 343.

[4] The 14th day of the Moon, reckoning from the time of *mean* New Moon, took place on Sunday the 23rd. According to the rule which obtained in later times, and continued in use until the Gregorian reformation of the Calendar, the 14th day of the *Ecclesiastical* Moon took place on Saturday the 22nd, which would make Easter-day happen on the 23rd. It would seem, therefore, that the decision of the Synod referred to, brought the Ecclesiastical Moon into closer accordance with that of the heavens, than the later Calendar would have done. In 357 Easter was apparently kept on Mar. 23.

[1] Eph. i. 3.   [2] Cf. *Letter* i. 1.   [3] 1 Cor. v. 7, cf. *Letter* i.   [4] Cf. *Letter* 6, § 2, and note.   [4a] Deut. xvi. 1, LXX.

month of new things, and keep the Passover to the Lord thy God[5].' Even the heathen fancy they keep festival, and the Jews hypocritically feign to do so. But the feast of the heathen He reproves, as the bread[6] of mourners, and He turns His face from that of the Jews, as being outcasts, saying, 'Your new moons and your sabbaths My soul hateth[7].'

2. For actions not done lawfully and piously, are not of advantage, though they may be reputed to be so, but they rather argue hypocrisy in those who venture upon them. Therefore, although such persons feign to offer sacrifices, yet they hear from the Father, 'Your whole burnt-offerings are not acceptable, and your sacrifices do not please Me; and although ye bring fine flour, it is vanity, incense also is an abomination unto Me[8].' For God does not need anything[9]; and, since nothing is unclean to Him, He is full in regard to them, as He testifies, by Isaiah, saying, 'I am full[10].' Now there was a law given about these things, for the instruction of the people, and to prefigure things to come, for Paul saith to the Galatians; 'Before faith came, we were kept guarded under the law, being shut up in the faith which should afterwards be revealed unto us; wherefore the law was our instructor in Christ, that we might be justified by faith[11].' But the Jews knew not, neither did they understand, therefore they walked in the day-time as in darkness, feeling for, but not touching, the truth we possess, which [was contained] in the law; conforming to the letter, but not submitting to the spirit. And when Moses was veiled, they looked on him, but turned away their faces from him when he was uncovered. For they knew not what they read, but erroneously substituted one thing for another. The prophet, therefore, cried against them, saying, 'Falsehood and faithlessness have prevailed among them.' The Lord also therefore said concerning them, 'The strange children have dealt falsely with Me; the strange children have waxen old[12].' But how gently does He reprove them, saying, 'Had ye believed Moses, ye would have believed Me, for he wrote of Me[13].' But being faithless, they went on to deal falsely with the law, affirming things after their own pleasure, but not understanding the Scripture; and, further, as they had hypocritically made a pretence of the plain text of Scripture, and had confidence in this, He is angry with them, saying by Isaiah, 'Who hath re-

quired these of your hands[14]?' And by Jeremiah, since they were very bold, he threatens, 'Gather together your whole burnt-offerings with your sacrifices, and eat flesh, for I spake not unto your fathers, nor commanded them in the day that I brought them out of the land of Egypt, concerning whole burnt-offerings and sacrifices[15].' For they did not act as was right, neither was their zeal according to law, but they rather sought their own pleasure in such days, as the prophet accuses them, beating down their bondsmen, and gathering themselves together for strifes and quarrels, and they smote the lowly with the fist, and did all things that tended to their own gratification. For this cause, they continue without a feast until the end, although they make a display now of eating flesh, out of place and out of season. For, instead of the legally-appointed lamb, they have learned to sacrifice to Baal; instead of the true unleavened bread, 'they collect the wood, and their fathers kindle the fire, and their wives prepare the dough, that they may make cakes to the host of heaven, and pour out libations to strange gods, that they may provoke Me to anger, saith the Lord[16].' They have the just reward of such devices, since, although they pretend to keep the Passover, yet joy and gladness is taken from their mouth, as saith Jeremiah, 'There hath been taken away from the cities of Judah, and the streets of Jerusalem, the voice of those who are glad, and the voice of those who rejoice; the voice of the bridegroom, and the voice of the bride[17].' Therefore now, 'he who among them sacrificeth an ox, is as he who smiteth a man, and he who sacrificeth a lamb is as he who killeth a dog, he that offereth fine flour, is as [if he offered] swine's blood, he that giveth frankincense for a memorial, is as a blasphemer[18].' Now these things will never please God, neither thus hath the word required of them. But He saith, 'These have chosen their own ways; and their abominations are what their soul delighteth in[19].'

3. And what does this mean my brethren? For it is right for us to investigate the saying of the prophet, and especially on account of heretics who have turned their mind against the law. By Moses then, God gave commandment respecting sacrifices, and all the book called Leviticus is entirely taken up with the arrangement of these matters, so that He might accept the offerer. So through the Prophets, He blames him who despised these things, as disobedient to the command-

5 Deut. xvi. 1, LXX., cf. *Letter* 1, § 9, and note.   6 Hos. ix. 4.   7 Is. i. 14.   8 Ib. i. 13; Jer. vi. 20.   9 *Orat.* ii. 28, 29.   10 Is. i. 11.
11 Gal. iii. 23, 24. Athan. reads into S. Paul's words the thought that the Law itself, however misunderstood by the Jews, involved the faith of Christ.   12 Ps. xviii. 44, 45, LXX.
13 John v. 46.

14 Is. i. 12.   15 Jer. vii. 21, 22.   16 Ib. vii. 18.   17 Ib. vii. 34.   18 Is. lxvi. 3.   19 Ib.

ment, saying, 'I have not required these at your hands. Neither did I speak to your fathers respecting sacrifices, nor command them concerning whole burnt-offerings[1].' Now it is the opinion of some, that the Scriptures do not agree together, or that God, Who gave the commandment, is false. But there is no disagreement whatever, far from it, neither can the Father, Who is truth, lie; 'for it is impossible that God should lie[2],' as Paul affirms. But all these things are plain to those who rightly consider them, and to those who receive with faith the writings of the law. Now it appears to me—may God grant, by your prayers, that the remarks I presume to make may not be far from the truth—that not at first were the commandment and the law concerning sacrifices, neither did the mind of God, Who gave the law, regard whole burnt-offerings, but those things which were pointed out and prefigured by them. 'For the law contained a shadow of good things to come.' And, 'Those things were appointed until the time of reformation[3].'

4. Therefore, the whole law did not treat of sacrifices, though there was in the law a commandment concerning sacrifices, that by means of them it might begin to instruct men and might withdraw them from idols, and bring them near to God, teaching them for that present time. Therefore neither at the beginning, when God brought the people out of Egypt, did He command them concerning sacrifices or whole burnt-offerings, nor even when they came to mount Sinai. For God is not as man, that He should be careful about these things beforehand; but His commandment was given, that they might know Him Who is truly God, and His Word, and might despise those which are falsely called gods, which are not, but appear in outward show. So He made Himself known to them in that He brought them out of Egypt, and caused them to pass through the Red Sea. But when they chose to serve Baal, and dared to offer sacrifices to those that have no existence, and forgat the miracles which were wrought in their behalf in Egypt, and thought of returning thither again; then indeed, after the law, that commandment concerning sacrifices was ordained as law; so that with their mind, which at one time had meditated on those which are not, they might turn to Him Who is truly God, and learn not, in the first place, to sacrifice, but to turn away their faces from idols, and conform to what God commanded. For when He saith, 'I have not spoken concerning sacrifices, neither given commandment con-

cerning whole burnt-offerings,' He immediately adds, 'But this is the thing which I commanded them, saying, Obey My voice, and I will be to you a God, and ye shall be to Me a people, and ye shall walk in all the ways that I command you[4].' Thus then, being before instructed and taught, they learned not to do service to any one but the Lord. They attained to know what time the shadow should last, and not to forget the time that was at hand, in which no longer should the bullock of the herd be a sacrifice to God, nor the ram of the flock, nor the he-goat[5], but all these things should be fulfilled in a purely spiritual manner, and by constant prayer, and upright conversation, with godly words; as David sings, 'May my meditation be pleasing to Him. Let my prayer be set forth before Thee as incense, and the lifting up of my hands as the evening sacrifice[6].' The Spirit also, who is in him, commands, saying, 'Offer unto God the sacrifice of praise, and pay to the Lord thy vows. Offer the sacrifice of righteousness, and put your trust in the Lord[7].'

5. Samuel, that great man, no less clearly reproved Saul, saying, 'Is not the word better than a gift[7a]?' For hereby a man fulfils the law, and pleases God, as He saith, 'The sacrifice of praise shall glorify Me.' Let a man 'learn what this means, I will have mercy, and not sacrifice[8],' and I will not condemn the adversaries. But this wearied them, for they were not anxious to understand, 'for had they known, they would not have crucified the Lord of glory[9].' And what their end is, the prophet foretold, crying, 'Woe unto their soul, for they have devised an evil thought, saying, let us bind the just man, because he is not pleasing to us[10]. The end of such abandonment as this can be nothing but error, as the Lord, when reproving them, saith, 'Ye do err, not knowing the Scriptures[11].' Afterwards when, being reproved, they should have come to their senses, they rather grew insolent, saying, 'We are Moses' disciples; and we know that God spake to Moses[12];' dealing the more falsely by that very expression, and accusing themselves. For had they believed him to whom they hearkened, they would not have denied the Lord, Who spake by Moses, when He was present. Not so did the eunuch in the Acts, for when he heard, 'Understandest thou what thou readest[13]?' he was not ashamed to confess his ignorance, and implored to be taught. Therefore, to him who became a learner, the grace of the Spirit was given. But as for those

---

[1] Is. i. 12; Jer. vii. 22.   [2] Heb. vi. 18.   [3] Ib. x. 1; ix. 10.

[4] Jer. vii. 22, 23.   [5] Exod. xii. 5.   [6] Ps. civ. 34; cxli. 2. [7] Ib. l. 14; iv. 5.   [7a] Ecclus. xviii. 17.   [8] Ps. l. 23; Hosea vi. 6; Matt. ix. 13.   [9] 1 Cor. ii. 8.   [10] Is. iii. 9, 10; Wisd. ii. 12.   [11] Matt. xxii. 29.   [12] John ix. 28, 29. [13] Acts viii. 30.

Jews who persisted in their ignorance; as the proverb saith, 'Death came upon them. For the fool dies in his sins [14].'

6. Like these too, are the heretics, who, having fallen from true discernment, dare to invent to themselves atheism. 'For the fool saith in his heart, There is no God. They are corrupt, and become abominable in their doings [15].' Of such as are fools in their thoughts, the actions are wicked, as He saith, 'can ye, being evil, speak good things [16];' for they were evil, because they thought wickedness. Or how can those do just acts, whose minds are set upon fraud? Or how shall he love, who is prepared beforehand to hate? How shall he be merciful, who is bent upon the love of money? How shall he be chaste, who looks upon a woman to lust after her? 'For from the heart proceed evil thoughts, fornications, adulteries, murders [17].' By them the fool is wrecked, as by the waves of the sea, being led away and enticed by his fleshly pleasures; for this stands written, 'All flesh of fools is greatly tempest-tossed [1].' While he associates with folly, he is tossed by a tempest, and perishes, as Solomon says in the Proverbs, 'The fool and he who lacketh understanding shall perish together, and shall leave their wealth to strangers [2].' Now they suffer such things, because there is not among them one sound of mind to guide them. For where there is sagacity, there the Word, who is the Pilot of souls, is with the vessel; 'for he that hath understanding shall possess guidance [3];' but they who are without guidance fall like the leaves. Who has so completely fallen away as Hymenæus and Philetus, who held evil opinions respecting the resurrection, and concerning faith in it suffered shipwreck? And Judas being a traitor, fell away from the Pilot, and perished with the Jews [4]. But the disciples since they were wise, and therefore remained with the Lord, although the sea was agitated, and the ship covered with the waves, for there was a storm, and the wind was contrary, yet fell not away. For they awoke the Word, Who was sailing with them [5], and immediately the sea became smooth at the command of its Lord, and they were saved. They became preachers and teachers at the same time; relating the miracles of our Saviour, and teaching us also to imitate their example. These things were written on our account and for our profit, so that through these signs we may acknowledge the Lord Who wrought them.

7. Let us, therefore, in the faith of the disciples, hold frequent converse with our Master. For the world is like the sea to us, my brethren, of which it is written, 'This is the great and wide sea, there go the ships; the Leviathan, which Thou hast created to play therein [6].' We float on this sea, as with the wind, through our own free-will, for every one directs his course according to his will, and either, under the pilotage of the Word, he enters into rest, or, laid hold on by pleasure, he suffers shipwreck, and is in peril by storm. For as in the ocean there are storms and waves, so in the world there are many afflictions and trials. The unbelieving therefore 'when affliction or persecution ariseth is offended [7],' as the Lord said. For not being confirmed in the faith, and having his regard towards temporal things, he cannot resist the difficulties which arise from afflictions. But like that house, built on the sand by the foolish man, so he, being without understanding [8], falls before the assault of temptations, as it were by the winds. But the saints, having their senses exercised in self-possession [9], and being strong in faith, and understanding the word, do not faint under trials; but although, from time to time, circumstances of greater trial are set against them, yet they continue faithful, and awaking the Lord Who is with them, they are delivered. So, passing through water and fire, they find relief and duly keep the feast, offering up prayers with thanksgiving to God Who has redeemed them. For either being tempted they are known, like Abraham, or suffering they are approved, like Job, or being oppressed and deceitfully treated, like Joseph, they patiently endure it, or being persecuted, they are not overtaken; but as it is written, through God they 'leap over the wall [10]' of wickedness, which divides and separates between brethren, and turns them from the truth. In this manner the blessed Paul, when he took pleasure in infirmities, in reproach, in necessities, in persecutions, and in distresses for Christ, rejoiced, and wished all of us to rejoice saying, 'Rejoice always; in everything give thanks [11].'

8. For what is so fitting for the feast, as a turning from wickedness, and a pure conversation, and prayer offered without ceasing to God, with thanksgiving? Therefore let us, my brethren, looking forward to celebrate the eternal joy in heaven, keep the feast here also, rejoicing at all times, praying incessantly, and in everything giving thanks to the Lord. I give thanks to God, for those other wonders He has done, and for the various helps that

---

14 Prov. xxiv. 9, LXX., cf. Ps. lv. 15.   15 Ps. xiv. 1.
16 Matt. xii. 34.   17 Ib. xv. 19.   1 Prov. xxvi. 10, LXX.
2 Not Proverbs, but Ps. xlix. 10.   3 Prov. i. 5, LXX.
4 Supr. Letter 7, § 9.   5 Mark iv. 37—41.

6 Ps. civ. 25, 26.   7 Mark iv. 17.   8 Luke vi. 49.
9 Heb. v. 14.   10 Ps. xviii. 29.   11 1 Thess. 5. 18.

have now been granted us, in that though He hath chastened us sore, He did not deliver us over to death, but brought us from a distance, even as from the ends of the earth, and hath united us again with you. I have been mindful, while I keep the feast, to give you also notice of the great feast of Easter, that so we may go up together, as it were, to Jerusalem, and eat the Passover, not separately but as in one house [12]; let us not as sodden in water, water down the word of God; neither let us, as having broken its bones, destroy the commands of the Gospel. But as roasted with fire, with bitterness, being fervent in spirit, in fastings and watchings, with lying on the ground, let us keep it with penitence and thanksgiving.

9. We begin the fast of forty days on the sixth day of Phamenoth (Mar. 2); and having passed through that properly, with fasting and prayers, we may be able to attain to the holy day. For he who neglects to observe the fast of forty days, as one who rashly and impurely treads on holy things, cannot celebrate the Easter festival. Further, let us put one another in remembrance, and stimulate one another not to be negligent, and especially that we should fast those days, so that fasts may receive us in succession, and we may rightly bring the feast to a close.

10. The fast of forty days begins then, as was already said, on the sixth of Phamenoth (Mar. 2), and the great week of the Passion on the eleventh of Pharmuthi (Apr. 6). And let us rest from the fast on the sixteenth of it (Apr. 11), on the seventh day, late in the evening. Let us keep the feast when the first of the week dawns upon us, on the seventeenth of the same month Pharmuthi (Apr. 12). Let us then add, one after the other, the seven holy weeks of Pentecost, rejoicing and praising God, that He hath by these things made known to us beforehand, joy and rest everlasting, prepared in heaven for us and for those who truly believe in Christ Jesus our Lord; through Whom, and with Whom, be glory and dominion to the Father, with the Holy Ghost, for ever and ever. Amen.

Salute one another with a holy kiss. The brethren who are with me salute you.

[13] I have also thought it necessary to inform you of the appointment of Bishops, which has taken place in the stead of our blessed fellow-ministers, that ye may know to whom to write, and from whom ye should receive letters. In Syene, therefore, Nilammon, instead of Nilammon of the same name. In Latopolis, Masis, instead of Am-

monius. In Coptos, Psenosiris [14], instead of Theodorus [15]. In Panopolis, because Artemidorus [16] desired it, on account of his old age, and weakness of body, Arius is appointed coadjutor. In Hypsele, Arsenius, having become reconciled to the Church. In Lycopolis, Eudæmon [17] in the stead of Plusianus [18]. In Antinoöpolis, Arion [19], instead of Ammonius and Tyrannus [20]. In Oxyrynchus, Theodorus, instead of Pelagius. In Nilopolis, instead of Theon, Amatus [1], and Isaac, who are reconciled to each other. In Arsenoitis, Andreas [2], instead of Silvanus [3]. In Prosopitis, Triadelphus, instead of Serapammon [4]. In Diosphacus, on the river side, Theodorus, instead of Serapammon. In Sais, Paphnutius, instead of Nemesion. In Xois, Theodorus, instead of Anubion; and there is also with him Isidorus, who is reconciled to the Church. In Sethroitis, Orion [5], instead of Potammon [6]. In Clysma, Tithonas [7], instead of Jacob; and there is with him Paulus, who has been reconciled to the Church.

LETTER XX.

(For 348.)

Coss. Philippus, Salia; Præfect the same Nestorius; Indict. vi; Easter-day iii Non. Apr., viii Pharmuthi; Æra Dioclet. 64; Moon 18.

LET us now keep the feast, my brethren, for as our Lord then gave notice to His disciples, so He now tells us beforehand, that 'after some days is the Passover [1],' in which the Jews indeed betrayed the Lord, but we celebrate His death as a feast, rejoicing because we then obtained rest from our afflictions. We are diligent in assembling ourselves together, for we were scattered in time past and were lost, and are found. We were far off, and are brought nigh, we were strangers, and have become His, Who suffered for us, and was nailed on the cross, Who bore our sins, as the prophet [1a] saith, and was afflicted for us, that He might put away from all of us grief, and sorrow, and sighing. When we thirst, He satisfies us on the feast-day itself, standing and crying, 'If any man thirst, let him come to Me, and drink [2].' For such is the love of the saints at all times, that they never once leave off, but offer the uninterrupted, constant sacrifice to the Lord, and continually thirst, and ask of Him to drink [3]; as David sang, 'My God, my God, early will I seek

---

[12] Exod. xii. 8, 9, 46. [13] Vid. *Letter* 2, note.

[14] *Supr.* p. 127? [15] *Supr.* p. 142. [16] *Supr.* p. 136, &c
[17] p. 127? [18] p. 136. [19] p. 127? [20] p. 142. [1] p. 127.
[2] Cf. *Tom. ad Ant.* 10. [3] *Supr. Letter* 12. [4] pp. 127, 273.
[5] p. 127. [6] p. 273. [7] Tithoes, p. 127. [1] Matt. xxvi. 2.
[1a] Isa. liii. 4. [2] John vii. 37.
[3] Cf. *Letter* vii. 5—7. The striking similarity between the seventh and the twentieth Letters has been already noticed.

Thee, my soul thirsteth for Thee; many times my heart and flesh longeth for Thee in a barren land, without a path, and without water. Thus was I seen by Thee in the sanctuary[4].' And Isaiah the prophet says, 'From the night my spirit seeketh Thee early, O God, because Thy commandments are light[5].' And another says, 'My soul fainteth for the longing it hath for Thy judgments at all times.' And again he says, 'For Thy judgments I have hoped, and Thy law will I keep at all times[6].' Another boldly cries out, saying, 'Mine eye is ever towards the Lord' And with him one says, 'The meditation of my heart is before Thee at all times.' And Paul further advises, 'At all times give thanks; pray without ceasing[7].' Those who are thus continually engaged, are waiting entirely on the Lord, and say, 'Let us follow on to know the Lord: we shall find Him ready as the morning, and He will come to us as the early and the latter rain for the earth[8].' For not only does He satisfy them in the morning; neither does He give them only as much to drink as they ask; but He gives them abundantly according to the multitude of His loving-kindness, vouchsafing to them at all times the grace of the Spirit. And what it is they thirst for He immediately adds, saying, 'He that believeth on Me.' For, 'as cold waters are pleasant to those who are thirsty[9],' according to the proverb, so to those who believe in the Lord, the coming of the Spirit is better than all refreshment and delight.

2. It becomes us then in these days of the Passover, to rise early with the saints, and approach the Lord with all our soul, with purity of body, with confession and godly faith in Him; so that when we have here first drunk, and are filled with these divine waters which [flow] from Him, we may be able to sit at table with the saints in heaven, and may share in the one voice of gladness which is there. From this sinners, because it wearied them, are rightly cast out, and hear the words, 'Friend, how camest thou in hither, not having a wedding garment[10]?' Sinners indeed thirst, but not for the grace of the Spirit; but being inflamed with wickedness, they are wholly set on fire by pleasures, as saith the Proverb, 'All day long he desires evil desires.' But the Prophet cries against them, saying, 'Wo unto those who rise up early, and follow strong drink; who continue until the evening, for wine inflameth them[11].' And since they run wild in wantonness, they dare to thirst for the

destruction of others. Having first drunk of lying and unfaithful waters, those things have come upon them, which are stated by the Prophet; 'My wound,' saith he, 'is grievous, whence shall I be healed; it hath surely been to me like deceitful waters, in which there is no trust[12].' Secondly, while they drink with their companions, they lead astray and disturb the right mind, and turn away the simple from it. And what does he cry? 'Wo unto him who causeth his neighbour to drink turbid destruction, and maketh him drunk, that he may look upon his caverns[13].' But those who dissemble, and steal away the truth, quench their hearts. Having first drunk of these things, they go on to say those things which the whore saith in the Proverbs, 'Lay hold with delight on hidden bread, and sweet stolen waters[14].' They lay snares secretly, because they have not the freedom of virtue, nor the boldness of Wisdom[15], who praises herself in the gates, and employs freedom of speech in the broad ways, preaching on high walls. For this reason, they are bidden to 'lay hold with delight[16],' because, having the choice between faith and pleasures, they steal the sweetness of truth, and disguise their own bitter waters [to escape] from the blame of their wickedness, which would have been speedy and public. On this account, the wolf puts on the skin of the sheep, sepulchres deceive by their whitened exteriors[17]. Satan, that is[18] . . .

. . . . .

. . . . .

FROM LETTER XXII[19].

(For 350.)

WHERE our Lord Jesus Christ, who took upon Him to die for all, stretched forth His hands, not somewhere on the earth beneath, but in the air itself, in order that the Salvation effected by the Cross might be shewn to be for all men everywhere: destroying the devil who was working in the air: and that He might consecrate our road up to Heaven, and make it free.

FROM LETTER XXIV[19].

(For 352.)

AND at that time when they went forth and crossed over Egypt, their enemies were the sport of the sea; but now, when we pass over

---

4 Ps. lxiii. 1, 2, LXX.   5 Is. xxvi. 9.   6 Ps. cxix. 20, 43, 44.
7 Ib. xxv. 15; xix. 14; 1 Thess. v. 17.   8 Hos. vi. 3.
9 John vii. 38; Prov. xxv. 25.   10 Matt. xxii. 12.
11 Prov. xxi. 26; Is. v. 11.

12 Jer. xv. 18.   13 Hab. ii. 15, LXX.   14 Prov. ix. 17.
15 Ib. viii. 2.   16 Cf. Letter vii. § 5.   17 Matt. vii. 15; xxiii. 27.
18 The Syriac MS. (which is imperfect) ends here. The fragments that follow are derived from different sources, mention whereof is made in the notes.
19 The above fragments are from Cosmas Indicopleustes: the Greek in Migne xxvi. 1432, sqq.

from earth to Heaven, Satan himself henceforth falls like lightning from Heaven.

FROM LETTER XXVII.

(For 355.)

From the twenty-seventh Festal Letter of Athanasius, Bishop of Alexandria and Confessor; of which the commencement is, 'Again the season of the day of the living Passover [1].'

FOR who is our joy and boast, but our Lord and Saviour Jesus Christ, Who suffered for us, and by Himself made known to us the Father? For He is no other than He Who of old time spake by the Prophets; but now He saith to every man, 'I Who speak am near [2].' Right well is this word spoken, for He does not at one time speak, at another keep silence; but continually and at all times, from the beginning without ceasing, He raises up every man, and speaks to every man in his heart.

FROM LETTER XXVIII [3].

(For 356.)

. . . IN order that while He might become a sacrifice for us all, we, nourished up in the words of truth, and partaking of His living doctrine, might be able with the saints to receive also the joy of Heaven. For thither, as He called the disciples to the upper chamber, so does the Word call us with them to the divine and incorruptible banquet; having suffered for us here, but there, preparing the heavenly tabernacles for those who most readily hearken to the summons, and unceasingly, and [gazing] at the goal, pursue the prize of their high calling; where for them who come to the banquet, and strive with those who hinder them, there is laid up both a crown, and incorruptible joy. For even though, humanly speaking, the labour of such a journey is great, yet the Saviour Himself has rendered even it light and kindly.

ANOTHER FRAGMENT.

BUT let us, brethren, who have received the vineyard from the Saviour, and are invited to the heavenly banquet, inasmuch as the Feast is now drawing nigh, take the branches of the palm [4] trees, and proving conquerors of sin, let us too like those, who on that occasion went to

meet the Saviour, make ourselves ready by our conduct, both to meet Him when He comes, and to go in with Him and partake of the immortal food, and from thenceforth live eternally in the heavens.

FROM LETTER XXIX [1].

(For 357.)

From the twenty-ninth Letter, of which the beginning is, 'Sufficient for this present time is that which we have already written.'

THE Lord proved the disciples [2], when He was asleep on the pillow, at which time a miracle was wrought, which is especially calculated to put even the wicked to shame. For when He arose, and rebuked the sea, and silenced the storm, He plainly shewed two things; that the storm of the sea was not from the winds, but from fear of its Lord Who walked upon it, and that the Lord Who rebuked it was not a creature, but rather its Creator, since a creature is not obedient to another creature. For although the Red Sea was divided before by Moses [3], yet it was not Moses who did it, for it came to pass, not because he spake, but because God commanded. And if the sun stood still in Gibeon [4], and the moon in the valley of Ajalon, yet this was the work, not of the son of Nun, but of the Lord, Who heard his prayer. He it was Who both rebuked the sea, and on the cross caused the sun to be darkened [5].

ANOTHER FRAGMENT [6].

AND whereas what is human comes to an end, what is divine does not. For which reason also when we are dead, and when our nature is tired out, he raises us up, and leads us up [though] born of earth to heaven.

ANOTHER FRAGMENT [7].

Here begins a letter of S. Athanasius, Bishop of Alexandria, to his children. May God comfort you. I know moreover that not only this thing saddens you, but also the fact that while others have obtained the churches by violence, you are meanwhile cast out from your places. For they hold the places, but you the Apostolic Faith. They are, it is true, in the places, but outside of the true Faith; while you are

---

[1] The fragment here given of the twenty-seventh Letter, as well as fragments of the twenty-ninth and forty-fourth, are from Syriac translations, discovered by Mr. Cureton as quoted by Severus Patriarch of Antioch, in his work against Johannes Grammaticus contained in the Syriac collection of the British Museum (Cod. Add. 12, 157, fol. 202), and published by him with the preceding Letters. Their style would argue them to be part of the same translation.   [2] John iv. 26.
[3] From Cosmas, see Migne xxvi. p. 1433.   [4] John xii. 13.

[1] If these fragments are authentic, the statement in the *Index*, that this year no letter could be sent, is an error.
[2] Mark iv. 37—41.   [3] Exod. xiv. 21.   [4] Josh. x. 12.
[5] Matt. xxvii. 45.   [6] From Cosmas; Migne xxvi. 1436.
[7] The following fragment (Migne, *ib.* p. 1189), was published by Montfaucon from a Colbertine Latin MS. of about 800 A.D. He conjectured that it belonged to a Festal Letter. On this hypothesis, which is, however, as Mai observes, by no means self-evident, we append it to the above fragments of *Letter* 29, since internal evidence connects it with the handing over of the churches at Alexandria to the partisans of George, June, 356. At any rate, in spite of the heading of the fragment, its beginning is clearly not preserved.

outside the places indeed, but the Faith, within you. Let us consider whether is the greater, the place or the Faith. Clearly the true Faith. Who then has lost more, or who possesses more? He who holds the place, or he who holds the Faith? Good indeed is the place, when the Apostolic Faith is preached there, holy is it if the Holy One dwell there. (*After a little:*) But ye are blessed, who by faith are in the Church, and dwell upon the foundations of the faith, and have full satisfaction, even the highest degree of faith which remains among you unshaken. For it has come down to you from Apostolic tradition, and frequently has accursed envy wished to unsettle it, but has not been able. On the contrary, they have rather been cut off by their attempts to do so. For this is it that is written, 'Thou art the Son of the Living God[8],' Peter confessing it by revelation of the Father, and being told, ' Blessed art thou Simon Barjona, for flesh and blood did not reveal it to thee, but ' My Father Who is in heaven,' and the rest. No one therefore will ever prevail against your Faith, most beloved brethren. For if ever God shall give back the churches (for we think He will) yet without[9] such restoration of the churches the Faith is sufficient for us. And lest, speaking without the Scriptures, I should [seem to] speak too strongly, it is well to bring you to the testimony of Scriptures, for recollect that the Temple indeed was at Jerusalem ; the Temple was not deserted, aliens had invaded it, whence also the Temple being at Jerusalem, those exiles went down to Babylon by the judgment of God, who was proving, or rather correcting them ; while manifesting to them in their ignorance punishment [by means] of blood-thirsty enemies[10]. And aliens indeed had held the Place, but knew not the Lord of the Place, while in that He neither gave answer nor spoke, they were deserted by the truth. What profit then is the Place to them?

For behold they that hold the Place are charged by them that love God with making it a den of thieves, and with madly making the Holy Place a house of merchandise, and a house of judicial business for themselves to whom it was unlawful to enter there. For this and worse than this is what we have heard, most beloved, from those who are come from thence. However really, then, they seem to hold the church, so much the more truly are they cast out. And they think themselves to be within the truth, but are exiled, and in captivity, and [gain] no advantage by the church alone. For the truth of things is judged ...

From LETTER XXXIX.

(For 367.)

Of the particular books and their number, which are accepted by the Church. From the thirty-ninth Letter of Holy Athanasius, Bishop of Alexandria, on the Paschal festival; wherein he defines canonically what are the divine books which are accepted by the Church.

. . . . 1. They have[1] fabricated books which they call books of tables[2], in which they shew stars, to which they give the names of Saints. And therein of a truth they have inflicted on themselves a double reproach : those who have written such books, because they have perfected themselves in a lying and contemptible science ; and as to the ignorant and simple, they have led them astray by evil thoughts concerning the right faith established in all truth and upright in the presence of God.

. . . . 2. But[2a] since we have made mention of heretics as dead, but of ourselves as possessing the Divine Scriptures for salvation ; and since I fear lest, as Paul wrote to the Corinthians[3], some few of the simple should be beguiled from their simplicity and purity, by the subtilty of certain men, and should henceforth read other books —those called apocryphal—led astray by the similarity of their names with the true books ; I beseech you to bear patiently, if I also write, by way of remembrance, of matters with which you are acquainted, influenced by the need and advantage of the Church.

3. In proceeding to make mention of these things, I shall adopt, to commend my undertaking, the pattern of Luke the Evangelist, saying on my own account : 'Forasmuch as some have taken in hand[4],' to reduce into order for themselves the books termed apocryphal, and to mix them up with the divinely inspired Scripture, concerning which we have been fully persuaded, as they who from the beginning were eyewitnesses and ministers of the Word, delivered to the fathers ; it seemed

---

[1] This section is preserved in the Coptic (Memphitic) Life of S. Theodore (Amélineau *Ann. du Musée Guimet.* xvii. p. 239). Its contents and the context in which it is quoted appear decisive for its identification as part of *Letter* 39. But the Letter from which the fragment comes is stated in the context to have been received by Theodore in the spring previous to his death. If Theodore died in 364, as seems probable on other grounds (see p. 569, note 3), the speech from which our fragment comes must have been written for him by his biographer. This is not unlikely, nor does it throw any suspicion on the genuineness of the fragment itself.
[2] Copt. ἀπογράμμων : astrological charts or tables appear to be meant.
[2a] The remainder of the thirty-ninth Letter has long been before the world, having been preserved, with the heading of the Letter, in the original Greek, by Theodorus Balsamon. It may be found in the first volume of the Benedictine edition of the works of S. Athan. tom. i. p. 767. ed. 1777. [Migne, *ubi supra*]. A Syriac translation of it was discovered by Cureton in an anonymous Commentary on the Scriptures in the collection of the British Museum (*Cod.* 12, 168). This translation commences only at the quotation from S. Luke. The Syriac is apparently the work of a different translator.   [3] 2 Cor. xi. 3.   [4] Luke i. 1.

---

[8] Matt. xvi. 16, 17.   [9] Text corrupt.   [10] Lat. somewhat obscure.

good to me also, having been urged thereto by true brethren, and having learned from the beginning, to set before you the books included in the Canon, and handed down, and accredited as Divine; to the end that any one who has fallen into error may condemn those who have led him astray; and that he who has continued stedfast in purity may again rejoice, having these things brought to his remembrance.

4. There are, then, of the Old Testament, twenty-two books in number; for, as I have heard, it is handed down that this is the number of the letters among the Hebrews; their respective order and names being as follows. The first is Genesis, then Exodus, next Leviticus, after that Numbers, and then Deuteronomy. Following these there is Joshua, the son of Nun, then Judges, then Ruth. And again, after these four books of Kings, the first and second being reckoned as one book, and so likewise the third and fourth as one book. And again, the first and second of the Chronicles are reckoned as one book. Again Ezra, the first and second[4a] are similarly one book. After these there is the book of Psalms, then the Proverbs, next Ecclesiastes, and the Song of Songs. Job follows, then the Prophets, the twelve being reckoned as one book. Then Isaiah, one book, then Jeremiah with Baruch, Lamentations, and[5] the epistle, one book; afterwards, Ezekiel and Daniel, each one book. Thus far constitutes the Old Testament.

5. Again it is not tedious to speak of the [books] of the New Testament. These are, the four Gospels, according to Matthew, Mark, Luke, and John. Afterwards, the Acts of the Apostles and Epistles (called Catholic), seven, viz. of James, one; of Peter, two; of John, three; after these, one of Jude. In addition, there are fourteen Epistles of Paul, written in this order. The first, to the Romans; then two to the Corinthians; after these, to the Galatians; next, to the Ephesians; then to the Philippians; then to the Colossians; after these, two to the Thessalonians, and that to the Hebrews; and again, two to Timothy; one to Titus; and lastly, that to Philemon. And besides, the Revelation of John.

6. These are fountains of salvation, that they who thirst may be satisfied with the living words they contain. In these alone is proclaimed the doctrine of godliness. Let no man add to these, neither let him take ought from these. For concerning these the Lord put to shame the Sadducees, and said, 'Ye do

err, not knowing the Scriptures.' And He reproved the Jews, saying, 'Search the Scriptures, for these are they that testify of Me[6].'

7. But for greater exactness I add this also, writing of necessity; that there are other books besides these not indeed included in the Canon, but appointed by the Fathers to be read by those who newly join us, and who wish for instruction in the word of godliness. The Wisdom of Solomon, and the Wisdom of Sirach, and Esther, and Judith, and Tobit, and that which is called the Teaching of the Apostles, and the Shepherd. But the former, my brethren, are included in the Canon, the latter being [merely] read; nor is there in any place a mention of apocryphal writings. But they are an invention of heretics, who write them when they choose, bestowing upon them their approbation, and assigning to them a date, that so, using them as ancient writings, they may find occasion to lead astray the simple.

FROM LETTER XL[7].
(For 368.)

'YE are they that have continued with Me in My temptations; and I appoint unto you a kingdom, as My Father hath appointed unto Me, that ye may eat and drink at My table in My kingdom[1].' Being called, then, to the great and heavenly Supper, in that upper room which has been swept, let us 'cleanse ourselves,' as the Apostle exhorted, 'from all filthiness of the flesh and spirit, perfecting holiness in the fear of God[2];' that so, being spotless within and without,—without, clothing ourselves with temperance and justice; within, by the Spirit, rightly dividing the word of truth —we may hear, 'Enter into the joy of thy Lord[3].'

FROM LETTER XLII.
(For 370.)

FOR we have been called, brethren, and are now called together, by Wisdom, and according to the Evangelical parable, to that great and heavenly Supper, and sufficient for every creature; I mean, to the Passover,—to Christ, Who is sacrificed; for 'Christ our Passover is sacrificed.' (And afterwards:) They, therefore, that are thus prepared shall hear, 'Enter into the joy of thy Lord[4].'

FROM LETTER XLIII.
(For 371.)

OF us, then, whose also is the Passover, the calling is from above, and 'our conversation

---

4a i.e. Ezra and Nehemiah.
5 i.e. Baruch vi.—The Syriac has the conjunction, which is rejected by the Benedictine editors.

6 Matt. xxii. 29; John v. 39.
7 The following fragments are, except Letter 44, preserved in the original Greek, by Cosmas (Migne xxvi. 1440 sqq.).
1 Luke xxii. 28—30.   2 2 Cor. vii. 1.   3 Matt. xxv. 21.
4 (b and 1 Cor. v. 7.

is in heaven,' as Paul says; 'For we have here no abiding city, but we seek that which is to come [5],' whereto, also, looking forward, we properly keep the feast. (*And again, afterwards :*) Heaven truly is high, and its distance from us infinite; for 'the heaven of heavens,' says he, 'is the Lord's [6].' But not, on that account, are we to be negligent or fearful, as though the way thereto were impossible; but rather should we be zealous. Yet not, as in the case of those who formerly, removing from the east and finding a plain in Senaar, began [to build a tower], is there need for us to bake bricks with fire, and to seek slime for mortar; for their tongues were confounded, and their work was destroyed. But for us the Lord has consecrated a way through His blood, and has made it easy. (*And again :*) For not only has He afforded us consolation respecting the distance, but also in that He has come and opened the door for us which was once shut. For, indeed, it was shut from the time He cast out Adam from the delight of Paradise, and set the Cherubim and the flaming sword, that turned every way, to keep the way of the tree of life—now, however, opened wide. And He that sitteth upon the Cherubim having appeared with greater grace and loving-kindness, led into Paradise with himself the thief who confessed, and having entered heaven as our forerunner, opened the gates to all. (*And again :*) Paul also, 'pressing toward the mark for the prize of the high calling [7],' by it was taken up to the third heaven, and having seen those things which are above, and then descended, he teaches us, announcing what is written to the Hebrews, and saying, 'For ye are not come unto the mount that might be touched, and that burned with fire, and clouds, and darkness, and a tempest, and to the voice of words. But ye are come unto Mount Sion, and unto the city of the living God, the heavenly Jerusalem, and to an innumerable company of angels, and to the general assembly and Church of the first-born, which are written in heaven [8].' Who would not wish to enjoy the high companionship with these! Who not desire to be enrolled with these, that he may hear with them, 'Come, ye blessed of My Father, inherit the kingdom prepared for you from the foundation of the world [9].'

From LETTER XLIV.

(For 372.)

And again, from the forty-fourth Letter, of which the commencement is, 'All that our Lord and Saviour Jesus Christ did instead of us and for us [1].'

When therefore the servants of the Chief Priests and the Scribes saw these things, and heard from Jesus, 'Whosoever is athirst, let him come to Me and drink [2];' they perceived that this was not a mere man like themselves, but that this was He Who gave water to the saints, and that it was He Who was announced by the prophet Isaiah. For He was truly the splendour of the light [3], and the Word of God. And thus as a river from the fountain he gave drink also of old to Paradise; but now to all men He gives the same gift of the Spirit, and says, 'If any man thirst, let him come to Me and drink.' Whosoever 'believeth on Me, as saith the Scripture, rivers of living water shall flow out of his belly [4].' This was not for man to say, but for the living God, Who truly vouchsafes life, and gives the Holy Spirit.

From LETTER XLV.

(For 373.)

Let us all take up our sacrifices, observing distribution to the poor, and enter into the holy place, as it is written; 'whither also our forerunner Jesus is entered for us, having obtained eternal redemption [5].' . . . (*From the same :*) . . . And this is a great proof that, whereas we were strangers, we are called friends; from being formerly aliens, we are become fellow-citizens with the saints, and are called children of the Jerusalem which is above, whereof that which Solomon built was a type. For if Moses made all things according to the pattern shewed him in the mount, it is clear that the service performed in the tabernacle was a type of the heavenly mysteries, whereto the Lord, desirous that we should enter, prepared for us the new and abiding way. And as all the old things were a type of the new, so the festival that now is, is a type of the joy which is above, to which coming with psalms and spiritual songs, let us begin the fasts [6].

---

[5] Phil. iii. 20 Heb. xiii. 14.   [6] Ps. cxv. 16.   [7] Phil. iii. 14.
[8] Heb. xii. 18—23.   [9] Matt. xxv. 34.

[1] See *Letter* 27, note 1.   [2] John vii. 37.   [3] Cf. Heb. i. 3.
[4] John vii. 37, 38.   [5] Heb. vi. 20; ix. 12.
[6] This fragment is the latest writing of Athanasius that we possess.

II. PERSONAL LETTERS

LETTER XLVI.

Letter¹ to the Mareotis from Sardica,

A.D. 343-4.

ATHANASIUS to the presbyters and deacons and the people of the Catholic Church in the Mareotis, brethren beloved and longed for, greeting in the Lord.

The holy council has praised your piety in Christ. They have all acknowledged your spirit and fortitude in all things, in that ye did not fear threats, and though you had to bear insults and persecutions against your piety you held out. Your letters when read out to all produced tears and enlisted universal sympathy. They loved you though absent, and reckoned your persecutions as their own. Their letter to you is a proof of their affection: and although it would suffice to include you along with the holy Church of Alexandria², yet the holy synod has written separately to you in order that ye may be encouraged not to give way on account of your sufferings, but to give thanks to God; because your patience shall have good fruit.

Formerly the character of the heretics was not evident. But now it is revealed and laid open to all. For the holy synod has taken cognisance of the calumnies these men have concocted against you, and has had them in abhorrence, and has deposed Theodore, Valens, Ursacius, in Alexandria³ and the Mareotis by consent of all. The same notice has been given to other Churches also. And since the cruelty and tyranny practised by them against the Churches can no longer be borne, they have been cast out from the episcopate and expelled from the communion of all. Moreover of Gregory they were unwilling even to make mention, for since the man has lacked the very name of bishop, they thought it superfluous to name him. But on account of those who are deceived by him they have mentioned his name; not because he seemed worthy of mention, but that those deceived by him might thereby recognise his infamy and blush

at the kind of man with whom they have communicated. You will learn what has been written about them from the previous document⁴: and though not all of the bishops came together to sign, yet it was drawn up by all, and they signed for all. Salute one another with a holy kiss. All the brethren salute you.

I, Protogenes⁵, bishop, desire that you may be preserved in the Lord, beloved and longed for.

I, Athenodorus*, bishop, desire that ye may be preserved in the Lord, most beloved brethren. [Other signatures] Julian, Ammonius, Aprianus, Marcellus, Gerontius*, Porphyrius*, Zosimus, Asclepius, Appian, Eulogius, Eugenius, Liodorus (26), Martyrius, Eucarpus, Lucius*, Caloes. Maximus: by letters from the Gauls I desire that ye may be preserved in the Lord, beloved. We, Arcidamus and Philoxenus, presbyters, and Leo a deacon, from Rome, desire that ye may be preserved. I, Gaudentius, bishop of Naissus, desire that ye may be preserved in the Lord. [Also] Florentius of Meria in Pannonia, Ammianus (9), of Castellum in Pannonia, Januarius of Beneventum, Prætextatus of Narcidonum in Pannonia, Hyperneris (48) of Hypata in Thessaly, Castus of Cæsaraugusta, Severus of Calcisus in Thessaly, Julian of Therae Heptapolis⁶, Lucius of Verona, Eugenius (35) of Hecleal Cycbinae⁷, Zosimus (92) of Lychni⁷ Sunosion in Apulia⁸, Hermogenes of Syceon⁹, Thryphos of Magara, Paregorius* of Caspi, Caloes (21) of Castromartis, Ireneus of Syconis, Macedonius of Lypianum, Martyrius of Naupacti, Palladius of Dius, Broseus (87) of Lu[g]dunum in Gaul, Ursacius of Brixia, Amantius of Viminacium, by the presbyter Maximus, Alexander of Gypara in Achaia, Eutychius of Mothona, Aprianus of Petavio in Pannonia, Antigonus of Pallene in Macedonia, Dometius* of Acaria Constantias, Olympius of Enorodope¹⁰, Zosimus of Oreomarga, Protasius of Milan, Mark of Siscia on the Save, Eucarpus of Opûs in Achaia, Vitalis* of Vertara in Africa, Helianus of Tyrtana, Symphorus of Herapythae in Crete, Mosinius (64) of Heracla, Eucissus of Chisamus¹¹, Cydonius of Cydonia¹².

---

¹ This and the following letters were first printed by Scipio Maffei from a Latin MS. in the Chapter Library of Verona, along with the *Historia Acephala*. They were included in Galland, *Bibl. Patr.* vol. 5, and in Justiniani's Ed. of Athanasius (Padua, 1777). The letters are printed in Migne, xxvi. 1333, *sqq.*, along with one (from the same source) addressed by the Council to the Mareotic Churches. Hefele doubts their genuineness, but without reason (ii. 166, *E. Tra.*) The list of signatures (an independent source of information, *supr.* p. 147) alone proves the contrary. The two letters may be taken as a supplement to the documents given, *Apol. c. Ar.* 37—50 (see also p. 147), with which they have many points of resemblance. The Latin is very bad and occasionally without sense; it bears clear traces of being a rendering by an unskilful hand from Greek.

² In the letter referred to in note 1.
³ i.e. has given notice to those places of their deposition

⁴ The letter of the Council.
⁵ For the probably correct names and sees, see p. 147, *sq.* The asterisk denotes signatories of the letter of the Council to the Mareotis, the numbers in brackets denote those of the list on pp. 147, *sq.*
⁶ Thera was divided into seven districts. Herod. iv. 153.
⁷ These two sees are a puzzle.
⁸ Probably Canusium, the name of Stercorius being lost, lurks in this corruption.   ⁹ In Galatia?
¹⁰ Æni in Thrace. D.C.B. iv. 75 (3).
¹¹ In Crete, near Cydonia.
¹² 59 signatures, to which add Stercorius (note 8) and Athanasius, making 61.

LETTER XLVII.

To the Church of Alexandria on the same occasion.

ATHANASIUS to all the presbyters and deacons of the holy Catholic Church at Alexandria and the Parembola, brethren most beloved, greeting.

In writing this I must begin my letter, most beloved brethren, by giving thanks to Christ. But now this is especially fitting, since both many things and great, done by the Lord, deserve our thanks[1], and those who believe in Him ought not to be ungrateful for His many benefits. We thank the Lord therefore, who always manifests us to all in the faith, who also has at this time done many wonderful things for the Church. For what the heretical party of Eusebius and heirs of Arius have maintained and spread abroad, all the bishops who assembled have pronounced false and fictitious. And the very men who are thought terrible by many, like those who are called giants, were counted as nothing, and rightly so, for just as the darkness is illuminated when light comes, so, iniquity is unveiled by the coming of the just, and when the good are present, the worthless are exposed.

For you yourselves, beloved, are not ignorant what the successors of the ill-named heresy of Eusebius did, namely Theodore, Narcissus, Valens, Ursacius, and the worst of them all, George, Stephen, Acacius, Menophantus, and their colleagues, for their madness is manifest to all; nor has it escaped your observation what they committed against the Churches. For you were the first they injured, your Church the first they tried to corrupt. But they who did so many great things, and were, as I said above, terrible to the minds of all, have been so frightened as to pass all imagination. For not only did they fear the Roman Synod, not only when invited to it did they excuse themselves, but, now also having arrived at Sardica, so conscience-stricken were they, that when they had seen the judges, they were astonished. So they fainted in their minds. Verily, one might say to them: 'Death, where is thy sting, Death, where is thy victory?' For neither did it go as they wished, for them to give judgment as they pleased; this time they could not over-reach whom they would. But they saw faithful men, that cared for justice, nay rather, they saw our Lord Himself among them, like the demons of old from the tombs; for being sons of falsehood, they could not bear to see the truth. So Theodore, Narcissus,

and Ursacius, with their friends said as follows[2]: 'Stay, what have we to do with you, men of Christ? We know that you are true, and fear to be convicted: we shrink from confessing our calumnies to your face. We have nothing to do with you; for you are Christians, while we are foes to Christ; and while with you truth is powerful, we have learned to over-reach. We thought our deeds were hid; we did not think that we were now coming to judgment; why do you expose our deeds before their time; and by exposing us vex us before the day?' and although they are of the worst character and walk in darkness, yet they have learnt at last that there is no agreement between light and darkness, and no concord between Christ and Belial. Accordingly, beloved brethren, since they knew what they had done, and saw their victims[3] ready as accusers, and the witnesses before their eyes, they followed the example of Cain and fled like him; in that they greatly wandered[4], for they imitated his flight, and so have received his condemnation. For the holy council knows their works; it has heard our blood crying aloud, heard from themselves the voices of the wounded. All the Bishops know how they have sinned, and how many things they have done against our Churches and others; and accordingly they have expelled these men from the Churches like Cain. For who did not weep when your letter was read? who did not groan to see whom those men had exiled? Who did not reckon your tribulations his own? Most beloved brethren, you suffered formerly when they were committing evil against you, and perhaps it is no long time since the war has ceased. Now, however, all the Bishops who assembled and heard what you have suffered, grieved and lamented just as you did when you suffered the injuries and[5] they shared your grief at that time . . . .

On account of these deeds then, and all the others which they have committed against the Churches, the holy general council has deposed them all, and not only has judged them aliens from the Church, but has held them

---

[1] Latin hardly translateable.

[2] Cf. *Hist. Ar.* and Introd. Fialon, p. 209, remarks on the uncritical adoption (by Fleury and his plagiarist Rohrbacher) of these satirical colloquies as an authentic account of what was actually said.

[3] Lat. 'quæcunque miserrimos videntes accusatores, testes præ oculis habentes:' apparently a barbarous rendering of ἴδοντες καὶ τοὺς παρ' αὐτῶν παθόντας, τοὺς κατηγόρους, τοὺς ἐλέγχους πρὸ ὀφθαλμῶν ἔχοντες, as in *Apol. Ar.* 45.

[4] 'Granditer erraverunt,' either for μακρὰν ἀπέφυγον, or for σφόδρα ἐπλημμέλησαν: no verb elsewhere used in this connection in Athanasius exactly corresponds to 'erraverunt,' nor is the flight to Philippopolis elsewhere compared, as here, to that of Cain. But the latter comparison is often used by Ath. in other connections.

[5] illis . . . erat dolor communis illo tempore quo processistis The Latin has quite lost the sense.

unworthy to be called Christians. For how can men be called Christians who deny Christ? And how can men be admitted to church who do evil against the Churches? Accordingly, the holy council has sent to the Churches everywhere, that they may be marked among all, so that they who were deceived by them may now return to full assurance and truth. Do not therefore fail, beloved brethren; like servants of God, and professors of the faith of Christ, be tried in the Lord, and let not tribulation cast you down, neither let troubles caused by the heretics who plot against you make you sad. For you have the sympathy of the whole world in your grief, and what is more, it bears you all in mind. Now I think that those deceived by them will, when they see the severe sentence of the Council, turn aside from them and reject their impiety. If, however, even after this their hand is lifted up, do you not be astonished, nor fear if they rage; but pray and raise your hands to God, and be sure that the Lord will not tarry but will perform all things according to your will. I could wish indeed to write you a longer letter with a detailed account of what has taken place, but since the presbyters and deacons are competent to tell you in person of all they have seen, I have refrained from writing much. One thing alone I charge you, considering it a necessity, that having the fear of the Lord before your eyes you will put Him first, and carry on all things with your wonted concord as men of wisdom and understanding. Pray for us, bearing in mind the necessities of the widows[6], especially since the enemies of truth have taken away what belongs to them. But let your love overcome the malice of the heretics. For we believe that according to your prayers the Lord will be gracious and permit me to see you speedily. Meanwhile you will learn the proceedings at the Synod by what all the Bishops have written to you, and from the appended letter you will perceive the deposition of Theodore, Narcissus, Stephen, Acacius, George, Menophantus, Ursacius and Valens. For Gregory they did not wish to mention: since they thought it superfluous to name a man who lacked the very name of bishop. Yet for the sake of those deceived by him they have mentioned his name, not that his name was worthy of mention, but in order that those deceived by him may learn his infamy and blush for the sort of man they have communicated with[7] .... I pray that

you may be preserved in the Lord, brethren most beloved and longed for.

LETTER XLVIII.
Letter to Amun[1].
Written before 354 A.D.

ALL things made by God are beautiful and pure, for the Word of God has made nothing useless or impure. For 'we are a sweet savour of Christ in them that are being saved[2],' as the Apostle says. But since the devil's darts are varied and subtle, and he contrives to trouble those who are of simpler mind, and tries to hinder the ordinary exercises of the brethren, scattering secretly among them thoughts of uncleanness and defilement; come let us briefly dispel the error of the evil one by the grace of the Saviour, and confirm the mind of the simple. For 'to the pure all things are pure,' but both the conscience and all that belongs to the unclean are defiled[3]. I marvel also at the craft of the devil, in that, although he is corruption and mischief itself, he suggests thoughts under the show of purity; but with the result of a snare rather than a test. For with the object, as I said before, of distracting ascetics from their customary and salutary meditation, and of appearing to overcome them, he stirs some such buzzing thoughts as are of no profit in life, vain questions and frivolities which one ought to put aside. For tell me, beloved and most pious friend, what sin or uncleanness there is in any natural secretion,—as though a man were minded to make a culpable matter of the cleanings of the nose or the sputa from the mouth? And we may add also the secretions of the belly, such as are a physical necessity of animal life. Moreover if we believe man to be, as the divine Scriptures say, a work of God's hands, how could any defiled work proceed from a pure Power? and if, according to the divine Acts of the Apostles[4], 'we are God's offspring,' we have nothing unclean in ourselves. For then only do we incur defilement, when we commit sin, that foulest of things. But when any bodily excretion takes place independently of will, then we experience this, like other things, by a necessity of nature. But since those whose only pleasure is to gainsay what is said aright, or rather what is made by God, pervert even a

---

6 For the φιλοπτωχία of Athanasius, cf. *Hist. Ar.* 61, *Vit. Ant.* 17, 30, and the stress laid on the hardship of the ἄρτοι (as here) in *Encycl.* 4, *Hist. Ar. ubi supr.* and 72.

7 .... 'tamen, et hoc cum illis.'

1 See Migne xxvi. 1169, *sqq.*; Prolegg. ch. ii. § 7. Amun, probably the Nitrian monk (*supr.* p. 212, and D.C.B. i. 102 init.). At any rate, Athanasius addresses his correspondent as 'elder' and 'father,' which accords well with the language of *Vit. Ant. ubi supr.* The letter states clearly Athanasius' opinion as to the relative value of the celibate and married state. It also shews the healthy good sense of the great bishop in dealing with the morbid scrupulosity which even at that early date had begun to characterise certain circles in the Monastic world.　　2 2 Cor. ii. 15

3 Tit. i. 15.　　4 Acts xvii. 28.

saying in the Gospels, alleging that 'not that which goeth in defileth a man, but that which goeth out⁵,' we are obliged to make plain this unreasonableness,—for I cannot call it a question—of theirs. For firstly, like unstable persons, they wrest the Scriptures⁶ to their own ignorance. Now the sense of the divine oracle is as follows. Certain persons, like these of to-day, were in doubt about meats. The Lord Himself, to dispel their ignorance, or it may be to unveil their deceitfulness, lays down that, not what goes in defiles the man, but what goes out. Then he adds exactly whence they go out, namely from the heart. For there, as he knows, are the evil treasures of profane thoughts and other sins. But the Apostle teaches the same thing more concisely, saying, 'But meat shall not bring us before God⁷.' Moreover, one might reasonably say no natural secretion will bring us before him for punishment. But possibly medical men (to put these people to shame even at the hands of outsiders) will support us on this point, telling us that there are certain necessary passages accorded to the animal body, to provide for the dismissal of the superfluity of what is secreted in our several parts; for example, for the superfluity of the head, the hair and the watery discharges from the head, and the purgings of the belly, and that superfluity again of the seminative channels. What sin then is there in God's name, elder most beloved of God, if the Master who made the body willed and made these parts to have such passages? But since we must grapple with the objections of evil persons, as they may say, 'If the organs have been severally fashioned by the Creator, then there is no sin in their genuine use,' let us stop them by asking this question: What do you mean by use? That lawful use which God permitted when He said, 'Increase and multiply, and replenish the earth⁸,' and which the Apostle approves in the words, 'Marriage is honourable and the bed undefiled⁹,' or that use which is public, yet carried on stealthily and in adulterous fashion? For in other matters also which go to make up life, we shall find differences according to circumstances. For example, it is not right to kill, yet in war it is lawful and praiseworthy to destroy the enemy; accordingly not only are they who have distinguished themselves in the field held worthy of great honours, but monuments are put up proclaiming their achievements. So that the same act is at one time and under some circumstances unlawful, while under others, and at the right time, it is lawful and permissible. The same reasoning applies to the relation of the sexes. He is blessed who, being freely yoked in his youth, naturally begets children. But if he uses nature licentiously, the punishment of which the Apostle¹ writes shall await whoremongers and adulterers.

For there are two ways in life, as touching these matters. The one the more moderate and ordinary, I mean marriage; the other angelic and unsurpassed, namely virginity. Now if a man choose the way of the world, namely marriage, he is not indeed to blame; yet he will not receive such great gifts as the other. For he will receive, since he too brings forth fruit, namely thirtyfold². But if a man embrace the holy and unearthly way, even though, as compared with the former, it be rugged and hard to accomplish, yet it has the more wonderful gifts: for it grows the perfect fruit, namely an hundredfold. So then their unclean and evil objections had their proper solution long since given in the divine Scriptures. Strengthen then, father, the flocks²ᵃ under you, exhorting them from the Apostolic writings, guiding them from the Evangelical, counselling them from the Psalms, and saying, 'quicken me according to Thy Word³;' but by 'Thy Word,' is meant that we should serve Him with a pure heart. For knowing this, the Prophet says, as if interpreting himself, 'Make me a clean heart, O God⁴,' lest filthy thoughts trouble me. David again, 'And stablish me with Thy free spirit⁵,' that even if ever thoughts disturb me, a certain strong power from Thee may stablish me, acting as a support. Giving then this and the like advice, say with regard to those who are slow to obey the truth, 'I will teach Thy ways unto the wicked,' and, confident in the Lord that you will persuade them to desist from such wickedness, sing 'and sinners shall be converted unto Thee⁶.' And be it granted, that they who raise malicious questions may cease from such vain labour, and that they who doubt in their simplicity may be strengthened with a 'free spirit;' while as many of you as surely know the truth, hold it unbroken and unshaken in Christ Jesus our Lord, with whom be to the Father glory and might, together with the Holy Spirit, for ever and ever. Amen.

LETTER XLIX.

*Letter to Dracontius*¹.

Written A.D. 354 or 355.

I AM at a loss how to write. Am I to blame

---

5 Matt. xv. 11.   6 2 Pet. iii. 16.   7 1 Cor. viii. 8.
8 Gen. i. 28.   9 Heb. xiii. 4.

1 Heb. xiii. 4.   2 See Mark iv. 20, &c.
2a This is a clear reference to the Monastic Societies which had now long existed in the Nitrian desert.   3 Ps. cxix. 107.
4 Ps. li. 10.   5 Ib. 12.   6 Ib. li. 13.
1 Dracontius, Bishop of Hermupolis Parva, was one of the

you for your refusal? or for having regard to the trials, and hiding for fear of the Jews[2]? In any case, however it may be, what you have done is worthy of blame, beloved Dracontius. For it was not fitting that after receiving the grace you should hide, nor that, being a wise man, you should furnish others with a pretext for flight. For many are offended when they hear it; not merely that you have done this, but that you have done it having regard to the times and to the afflictions which are weighing upon the Church. And I fear lest, in flying for your own sake, you prove to be in peril in the sight of the Lord on account of others. For if 'he that offendeth one of the little ones, should rather choose that a mill stone were hanged about his neck, and that he were drowned in the depths of the sea[2a],' what can be in store for you, if you prove an offence to so many? For the surprising unanimity about your election in the district[3] of Alexandria will of necessity be broken up by your retirement: and the episcopate of the district will be grasped at by many,—and many unfit persons, as you are well aware. And many heathen who were promising to become Christians upon your election will remain heathen, if your piety sets at nought the grace given you.

2. What defence will you offer for such conduct? With what arguments will you be able to wash away and efface such an impeachment? How will you heal those who on your account are fallen and offended? Or how will you be able to restore the broken peace? Beloved Dracontius, you have caused us grief instead of joy, groaning instead of consolation. For we expected to have you with us as a consolation; and now we behold you in flight, and that you will be convicted in judgment, and when upon your trial will repent it. And 'Who shall have pity upon thee[4],' as the Prophet says, who will turn his mind to you for peace, when he sees the brethren for whom Christ died injured on account of your flight? For you must know, and not be in doubt, that while before your election you lived to yourself, after

it, you live for your flock. And before you had received the grace of the episcopate, no one knew you; but after you became one, the laity expect you to bring them food, namely instruction from the Scriptures. When then they expect, and suffer hunger, and you are feeding yourself[5] only, and our Lord Jesus Christ comes and we stand before Him, what defence will you offer when He sees His own sheep hungering? For had you not taken the money, He would not have blamed you. But He would reasonably do so if upon taking it you dug and buried it,—in the words which God forbid that your piety should ever hear: 'Thou oughtest to have given my money to the bankers, that when I came I might demand it of them[6].'

3. I beseech you, spare yourself and us. Yourself, lest you run into peril; us, lest we be grieved because of you. Take thought of the Church, lest many of the little ones be injured on your account, and the others be given an occasion of withdrawing. Nay but if you feared the times and acted as you did from timidity, your mind is not manly; for in such a case you ought to manifest zeal for Christ, and rather meet circumstances boldly, and use the language of blessed Paul: 'in all these things we are more than conquerors[7];' and the more so in that we ought to serve not the time, but the Lord[8]. But if the organising of the Churches is distasteful to you, and you do not think the ministry of the episcopate has its reward, why, then you have brought yourself to despise the Saviour that ordered these things. I beseech you, dismiss such ideas, nor tolerate those who advise you in such a sense, for this is not worthy of Dracontius. For the order the Lord has established by the Apostles abides fair and firm; but the cowardice of the brethren shall cease[8a].

4. For if all were of the same mind as your present advisers, how would you have become a Christian, since there would be no bishops? Or if our successors are to inherit this state of mind, how will the Churches be able to hold together? Or do your advisers think that you have received nothing, that they despise it? If so surely they are wrong. For it is time for them to think that the grace of the Font is nothing, if some are found to despise it. But

---

bishops expelled from their sees, 356-7. His place of exile was the desert near 'Clysma,' i.e. the gulf of Suez (*Hist. Ar.* 75, cf. Hieron. *Vit. Hilar.* 30). We find him in 362 at the Council of Alexandria. The present letter, written to urge Dracontius not to refuse the Episcopate, was written just before Easter (§ 10), when persecution was expected (§ 3), and after the mission of Serapion, Ammonius and others to Constantius, A.D. 353. It was probably written, therefore, early either in 354 or 355. The letter is one of the masterpieces of Athanasius: its unforced warmth, vigour, and affection can fail to touch no one who reads it. It is, like the letter to Amun, one of our most important documents for the history of Egyptian Monasticism. (Migne xxv. 524 *sqq.*)

[2] Cf. Joh. iii. 2; xix. 38.   [2a] Matt. xviii. 6.

[3] Hermupolis Parva was in the nome, or department, of Alexandria (anciently called the nome of Hermupolis in the Delta), and lay on a canal 44 miles east of the Capital; it is identified with *Damanhur.* Agathammon, a Meletian bishop of this 'district,' is mentioned in the list, *Apol. Ar.* 71, where the district of 'Sais' seems to include a much wider area than the ancient Saite nome (Maspero. *Hist. Anc.* 4, p. 24).   [4] Jer xv. 5.

[5] Cf. Ezek. xxxiv. 2.
[6] See Matt. xxv. 27, and Luke xix. 23. It is not clear whether by the 'money' received by Drac. is meant his actual consecration, or merely his election.   [7] Rom. viii. 37.
[8] Rom. xii. 11, and Westcott and Hort on various reading.
[8a] It should be observed that the fear of Dracontius was, not that he would suffer *in dignity* by becoming a bishop, but lest he should deteriorate *spiritually* (§ 8, init.). Cf. the dying soliloquy of Pope Eugenius IV.: 'Gabriele, hadst thou never been Pope nor Cardinal it had been better for thy salvation.' See also S. Bernard, *de Consideratione.*

you have received it, beloved Dracontius; do not tolerate your advisers nor deceive yourself. For this will be required of you by the God who gave it. Have you not heard the Apostle say, 'Neglect not the gift that is in thee[9]?' or have you not read how he accepts the man that had doubled his money, while he condemned the one that had hidden it? But may it come to pass that you may quickly return, in order that you too may be one of those who are praised. Or tell me, whom do your advisers wish you to imitate? For we ought to walk by the standard of the saints and the fathers, and imitate them, and to be sure that if we depart from them we put ourselves also out of their fellowship. Whom then do they wish you to imitate? The one who hesitated, and while wishing to follow, delayed it and took counsel because of his family[1], or blessed Paul, who, the moment the stewardship was entrusted to him, 'straightway conferred not with flesh and blood[2]?' For although he said, 'I am not worthy to be called an Apostle[3],' yet, knowing what he had received, and being not ignorant of the giver, he wrote, 'For woe is me if I preach not the gospel[4].' But, as it was 'woe to me' if he did not preach, so, in teaching and preaching the gospel, he had his converts as his joy and crown[5]. This explains why the saint[6] was zealous to preach as far as Illyricum, and not to shrink from proceeding to Rome[7], or even going as far as the Spains[8], in order that the more he laboured, he might receive so much the greater reward for his labour. He boasted then that he had fought the good fight, and was confident that he should receive the great crown[1]. Therefore, beloved Dracontius, whom are you imitating in your present action? Paul, or men unlike him? For my part, I pray that you, and myself, may prove an imitator of all the saints.

5. Or possibly there are some who advise you to hide, because you have given your word upon oath not to accept the office if elected. For I hear that they are buzzing in your ears to this effect, and consider that they are thus acting conscientiously. But if they were truly conscientious, they would above all have feared God, Who imposed this ministry upon you. Or if they had read the divine Scriptures, they would not have advised you contrary to them. For it is time for them to blame Jeremiah also, and to impeach the great Moses, in that they did not listen to their advice, but fearing God fulfilled their ministry, and prophesying were made perfect. For they

also when they had received their mission and the grace of Prophecy, refused. But afterwards they feared, and did not set at nought Him that sent them. Whether then you be of stammering utterance, and slow of tongue, yet fear God that made you, or if you call yourself too young to preach, yet reverence Him Who knew you before you were made. Or if you have given your word (now their word was to the saints as an oath), yet read Jeremiah, how he too had said, 'I will not name the Name of the Lord[2],' yet afterwards he feared the fire kindled within him, and did not do as he had said, nor hid himself as if bound by an oath, but reverenced Him that had entrusted to him his office, and fulfilled the prophetic call. Or are you not aware, beloved, that Jonah also fled, but met with the fate that befel him, after which he returned and prophesied?

6. Do not then entertain counsels opposite to this. For the Lord knows our case better than we ourselves, and He knows to whom He is entrusting His Churches. For even if a man be not worthy, yet let him not look at his former life, but let him carry out his ministry, lest, in addition to his life he incur also the curse of negligence. I ask you, beloved Dracontius, whether knowing this, and being a wise man, you are not pricked in your soul? Do you not feel anxious lest any of those entrusted to you should perish? Do you not burn, as with a fire in your conscience? Are you not in fear of the day of judgment, in which none of your present advisers will be there to aid you? For each shall give account of those entrusted to his hands. For how did his excuse benefit the man who hid the money? Or how did it benefit Adam to say, 'The woman beguiled me[3]?' Beloved Dracontius, even if you are really weak, yet you ought to take up the charge, lest, the Church being unoccupied, the enemies injure it, taking advantage of your flight. You should gird yourself up, so as not to leave us alone in the struggle; you should labour with us, in order to receive the reward also along with all.

7. Make haste then, beloved, and tarry no longer, nor suffer those who would prevent you: but remember Him that has given, and come hither to us who love you, who give you Scriptural advice, in order that you may both be installed by ourselves, and, as you minister in the churches make remembrance of us. For you are not the only one who has been elected from among monks, nor the only one to have presided over a monastery, or to have been beloved by monks. But you know that not only was Serapion a monk, and presided

---

9 1 Tim. iv. 14.   1 Luke ii . 61.   2 Gal. i. 16.   3 1 Cor. xv. 9.   4 Ib. ix. 16.   5 1 Th. ii. 19.
6 Reading τῷ ἁγίῳ as proposed by Montf.
7 Rom. i. 15.   8 Ib. xv. 19, 28.   1 2 Tim. iv. 7, 8.

2 Jer. xx. 9.   3 Gen. iii. 12.

over that number of monks; you were not unaware of how many monks Apollos was father; you know Agathon, and are not ignorant of Ariston. You remember Ammonius who went abroad [3a] with Serapion. Perhaps you have also heard of Muitus [3aa] in the upper Thebaid, and can learn about Paul [3b] at Latopolis, and many others. And yet these, when elected, did not gainsay; but taking Elisha as an example, and knowing the story of Elijah, and having learnt all about the disciples and apostles, they grappled with the charge, and did not despise the ministry, and were not inferior to themselves, but rather look for the reward of their labour, advancing themselves, and guiding others onward. For how many have they turned away from the idols? How many have they caused to cease from their familiarity with demons by their warning? How many servants have they brought to the Lord, so as to cause those who saw such wonders to marvel at the sight? Or is it not a great wonder to make a damsel live as a virgin, and a young man live in continence, and an idolater come to know Christ?

8. Let not monks then prevent you, as though you alone had been elected from among monks; nor do you make excuses, to the effect that you will deteriorate. For you may even grow better if you imitate Paul, and follow up the actions of the Saints. For you know that men like those, when appointed stewards of the mysteries, all the more pressed forward to the mark of their high calling [4]. When did Paul meet martyrdom and expect to receive his crown, if not after being sent to teach? When did Peter make his confession, if not when he was preaching the Gospel, and had become a fisher of men [5]? When was Elijah taken up, if not after completing his prophetic career? When did Elisha gain a double share of the Spirit, if not after leaving all to follow Elijah? Or why did the Saviour choose disciples, if not to send them out as apostles?

9. So take these as an example, beloved Dracontius, and do not say, or believe those who say, that the bishop's office is an occasion of sin, nor that it gives rise to temptations to sin. For it is possible for you also as a bishop to hunger and thirst [6], as Paul did. You can drink no wine, like Timothy [7], and fast constantly too, like Paul [8], in order that thus

fasting after his example you may feast others with your words, and while thirsting for lack of drink, water others by teaching. Let not your advisers, then, allege these things. For we know both bishops who fast, and monks who eat. We know bishops who drink no wine, as well as monks who do. We know bishops who work [9] wonders, as well as monks who do not. Many also of the bishops have not even married, while monks have been [1] fathers of children; just as conversely we know bishops who are fathers of children and monks 'of the completest kind [2].' And again, we know clergy who suffer hunger, and monks who fast. For it is possible in the latter way, and not forbidden in the former. But let a man, wherever he is, strive earnestly; for the crown is given not according to position, but according to action.

10. Do not then suffer those who give contrary advice. But rather hasten and delay not; the more so as the holy festival is approaching; so that the laity may not keep the feast without you, and you bring great danger upon yourself. For who will in your absence preach them the Easter sermon? Who will announce to them the great day of the Resurrection, if you art in hiding? Who will counsel them, if you are in flight, to keep the feast fittingly? Ah, how many will be the better if you appear, how many be injured if you fly! And who will think well of you for this? and why do they advise you not to take up the bishop's office, when they themselves wish to have presbyters [3]? For if you are bad, let them not associate with you. But if they know that you are good, let them not envy the others. For if, as they say, teaching and government is an occasion of sin, let them not be taught themselves, nor have presbyters, lest they deteriorate, both they and those who teach them. But do not attend to these human sayings, nor suffer those who give such advice, as I have often already said. But rather make haste and turn to the Lord, in order that, taking thought for his sheep, you may remember us also. But to this end I have bidden our beloved Hierax, the presbyter, and Maximus the reader go, and bid you by word of mouth also, that you may be able thus to learn both with what feelings I have written, and the danger that results from gainsaying the ordinance of the Church.

[3a] In 353, see *Fest. Ind.* xxv.; Sozom. iv. 9.
[3aa] Perhaps the 'Muis' of the Sardican subscriptions (*Apol. Ar.*) and the 'Move' of *Vit. Pachom. c.* 72.
[3b] Paulus, perhaps identical with the 'Philo' of Sard. subsc. and *Vit. Pach. ubi supr.* A 'Philo' and 'Muius' also occur close together in *Apol. Fug.* 7 (note 9).
[4] Phil. iii. 14. [5] Matt. iv. 19. [6] Phil. iv. 12.
[7] 1 Tim. v. 23. [8] 2 Cor. xi. 27.

[9] σημεῖα. At the end of § 7 this word can only be rendered 'wonders.' But here it appears at least probable that it has the different sense of 'miracles.'
[1] Probably the reference is to married men who had *subsequently* become monks. Or else, as monks at this time lived in many cases in the world, not in communities, it may refer to married men leading an ascetic life. [2] ἐξ ὁλοκλήρου γένους.
[3] This is not our earliest notice of ordained ersons in monastic societies. see *Apol. Ar.* 67.

LETTER L.

First Letter to Lucifer [1].

To our lord, and most beloved brother the Bishop and Confessor Lucifer. Athanasius greeting in the Lord.

Being well in body by God's favour, we have now sent our most beloved deacon Eutyches, that your most pious holiness, as is much desired by us, may be pleased to inform us of the safety of yourself and those with you. For we believe it is by the life of you Confessors and servants of God that the state of the Catholic Church is renewed; and that what heretics have assayed to rend in pieces, our Lord Jesus Christ by your means restores whole.

For although the forerunners of Antichrist have by the power of this world done everything to put out the lantern of truth, yet the Deity by your confession shews its light all the clearer, so that none can fail to see their deceit. Heretofore perhaps they were able to dissimulate: now they are called Antichrists. For who can but execrate them, and fly from their communion like a taint, or the poison of a serpent? The whole Church everywhere is mourning, every city groans, aged bishops are suffering in exile, and heretics dissembling, who while denying Christ have made themselves publicans, sitting in the Churches and exacting revenue [2]. O new kind of men and of persecution which the devil has devised, namely to use such cruelty, and even ministers as the agents of evil. But although they act thus, and have gone all lengths in pride and blasphemy, yet your confession, your piety and wisdom, will be the very greatest comfort and solace to the brotherhood. For it has been reported to us that your holiness has written to Constantius

Augustus; and we wonder more and more that dwelling as it were among scorpions you yet preserve freedom of spirit, in order, by advice or teaching or correction, to bring those in error to the light of truth. I ask then, and all confessors join me in asking, that you will be good enough to send us a copy; so that all may perceive, not by hearsay only but by letters, the valour of your spirit, and the confidence and firmness of your faith. Those who are with me salute your holiness. I salute all those who are with you. May the deity ever keep you safe and sound and mindful of us, most beloved lord, and true man of God.

Upon receiving this letter, blessed Lucifer sent the books which he had addressed to Constantius; and when he had read them Athanasius sent the following letter:

LETTER LI.

Second Letter to Lucifer.

To the most glorious lord and deservedly much-desired fellow-Bishop Lucifer, Athanasius greeting in the Lord.

Although I believe that tidings have reached your holiness also of the persecution which the enemies of Christ have just now attempted to raise, seeking our blood, yet our own most beloved messengers can tell your piety about it. For to such a length did they dare to carry their madness by means of the soldiers, that they not only banished the Clergy of the city, but also went out to the Hermits, and laid their fatal hands upon Solitaries. Hence I also withdrew far away, lest those who entertained me should suffer trouble at their hands. For whom do Arians spare, who have spared not even their own souls? Or how can they give up their infamous actions while they persist in denying Christ our Lord the only Son of God? This is the root of their wickedness; on this foundation of sand they build up the perversity of their ways, as we find it written in the thirteenth Psalm, 'The fool said in his heart there is no God;' and presently follows, 'Corrupt are they and become abominable in their works [2a].' Hence the Jews who denied the Son of God, deserved to be called 'a sinful nation, a people laden with iniquity, a seed of evil doers, children without law [3].' Why 'without law?'—because you have deserted the Lord. And so the most blessed Paul, when he had begun not only to believe in the Son of God, but also to preach His deity, wrote, 'I know nothing against myself [4].' Accordingly we too, according to your confession of faith, desire to hold the Apostolic tradi-

---

[1] Lucifer, bishop of Calaris (Cagliäri) in Sardinia, exiled by Constantius after the Council of Milan (Prolegg. ch. ii. § 7), first to Germanicia, then to Eleutheropolis in Palestine, at both of which places he was subjected to harsh treatment, lastly to the Thebaid. The violence of his advocacy of the Nicene faith, coupled with extreme personal abusiveness, may have aggravated his sufferings. On his part in the events of 362, see Prolegg. ch. ii. § 9. The present letters exist only in Latin (Migne xxvi. 1181), and are probably a translation from the Greek. Athan. may have known Latin, but there is no evidence that he ever wrote in that language. The play on the name Lucifer in *Letter* 51 proves nothing to the contrary. Dr. Bright (in D.C.B. i. 198, note) expresses a doubt as to the genuineness of our letters which is I think unsupported by internal evidence. The main difficulty is in the reconciliation of the apparent references (51 init.) to the events of 356 as recent with the clear references to the *de Athanasio* and *Moriendum pro Filio Dei* of Lucifer, neither of which works were penned before 358, while the latter in its final form mentions the translation of Eudoxius to CP., and therefore falls as late as 360 (for proof of this, see Krüger, *Lucifer*, pp. 102–109). But on close examination, the language of *Letter* 51 is satisfied by the events of 359, the vindictive commission of Paul Catena and the search for Athanasius among the Monasteries (cf. *Letter* 53, note 1). The respectful reference to Constantius in *Letter* 50 is of a purely formal character. The reference to the parents of Athanasius as still living is of great interest as one of the very few notices of the family of the great bishop (Prolegg. ch. ii. § 1). The agitated tone of the Epistles reminds us of the *Arian History*, and they may be set down to about the year 359. On Lucifer, the monograph of Krüger is the standard authority.

[2] An exact description of George in 357 and 358.

[2a] Ps. xiv. 1.   [3] Isa. i. 4.   [4] 1 Cor. iv. 4.

tion, and to live according to the commands of the divine law, that we may be found along with you in that band in which now Patriarchs, Prophets, Apostles and Martyrs are rejoicing. So then, though the Arian madness, aided by external power, was so active that our brethren on account of their fury could not even see the open air with freedom, yet by God's favour, according to your prayers, I have been able, though with trouble and danger, to see the brother who is wont to bring me necessaries and the letters of your holiness, along with those of others. And so we have received the books of your most wise and religious soul, in which we have seen the image of an Apostle, the confidence of a Prophet, the teaching of truth, the doctrine of true faith, the way of heaven, the glory of martyrdom, the triumphs against the Arian heresy, the unimpaired tradition of our Fathers, the right rule of the Church's order. O truly Lucifer, who according to your name bring the light of truth, and have set it on a candlestick to give light to all. For who, except the Arians, does not clearly see from your teaching the true faith and the taint of the Arians. Forcibly and admirably, like light from darkness, you have separated the truth from the subtilty and dishonesty of heretics, defended the Catholic Church, proved that the arguments of the Arians are nothing but a kind of hallucination, and taught that the diabolical gnashings of the teeth are to be despised. How good and welcome are your exhortations to martyrdom ; how highly to be desired have you shewn death to be on behalf of Christ the Son of the living God [5]. What love you have shewn for the world to come and for the heavenly life. You seem to be a true temple of the Saviour, Who dwells in you and utters these exact words through you, and has given such grace to your discourses. Beloved as you were before among all, now such passionate affection for you is settled in the minds of all, that they call you the Elijah of our times; and no wonder. For if they who seem to please God are called Sons of God, much more proper is it to give that name to the associates of the Prophets, namely the Confessors, and especially to you. Believe me, Lucifer, it is not you only who has uttered this, but the Holy Spirit with you. Whence comes so great a memory for the Scriptures? Whence an unimpaired sense and understanding of them? Whence has such an order of discourse been framed? Whence did you get such exhortations to the way of heaven, whence such confidence against the devil, and such proofs against heretics, unless the Holy

Spirit had been lodged in you? Rejoice therefore to see that you are already there where also are your predecessors the martyrs, that is, among the band of angels. We also rejoice, having you as an example of valour, and patience, and liberty. For I blush to say anything of what you have written about my name [5a], lest I should appear a flatterer. But I know and believe that the Lord Himself, Who has revealed all knowledge to your holy and religious spirit, will reward you for this labour also with a reward in the kingdom of the heavens. Since then you are such a man, we ask the Lord in prayer that you may pray for us, that in His mercy He may now deign to look down upon the Catholic Church, and deliver all His servants from the hands of persecutors; in order that all they too who have fallen on account of temporal fear may at length be enabled to raise themselves and return to the way of righteousness, led away from which they are wandering, poor people, not knowing in what a pit they are. In particular I ask, if I have said anything amiss, you would be good enough to overlook it, for from so great a fountain my unskilfulness has not been able to draw what it might have done. But as to our brethren, I ask you again to overlook my not having been able to see them. For truth itself is my witness that I wished and longed to compass this, and was greatly grieved at being unable. For my eyes ceased not from tears, nor my spirit from groaning, because we are not permitted even to see the brethren. But God is my witness, that on account of their persecution I have not been able to see even the parents whom I have [6]. For what is there that the Arians leave undone? They watch the roads, observe those who enter and leave the city, search the vessels, go round the deserts, ransack houses, harass the brethren, cause unrest to everybody. But thanks be to God, in so doing they are more and more incurring the execration of all, and coming to be truly known for what your holiness has called them: slaves of Antichrist. And, poor wretches, hated as they are, they persist in their malice, until they shall be condemned to the death of their ancestor Pharaoh. Those with me salute your piety. Pray salute those who are with you. May God's divine grace preserve you, mindful of us and ever blessed, worthily called man of God, servant of Christ, partner of the Apostles, comfort of the brotherhood, master of truth, and in all things most longed for.

---

5 Lucifer had written among other books one called 'Moriendum pro Dei Filio.' His two books 'pro sancto Athanasio' are referred to below.

5a Lucifer's two books *pro Athanasio.*
6 'Parentes quos habeo.' Can this refer to liteial parents? (1) he was now over 60 years old : (2) some 6 years later, under Valens, he hid, according to the tale in Socr. iv. 13, for four months in his father's tomb (see Prolegg. ch. ii. § 9).

LETTER LII.

First Letter to Monks[1].

(Written 358—360).

1. To those in every place[2] who are living a monastic life, who are established in the faith of God, and sanctified in Christ, and who say, 'Behold, we have forsaken all, and followed Thee[2a],' brethren dearly beloved and longed for, heartiest greeting in the Lord.

1. In compliance with your affectionate request, which you have frequently urged upon me, I have written a short account of the sufferings which ourselves and the Church have undergone, refuting, according to my ability, the accursed heresy of the Arian madmen, and proving how entirely it is alien from the Truth. And I thought it needful to represent to your Piety what pains the writing of these things has cost me, in order that you may understand thereby how truly the blessed Apostle has said, 'O the depth of the riches both of the wisdom and knowledge of God[3];' and may kindly bear with a weak man such as I am by nature. For the more I desired to write, and endeavoured to force myself to understand the Divinity of the Word, so much the more did the knowledge thereof withdraw itself from me; and in proportion as I thought that I apprehended it, in so much I perceived myself to fail of doing so. Moreover also I was unable to express in writing even what I seemed to myself to understand; and that which I wrote was unequal to the imperfect shadow of the truth which existed in my conception.

2. Considering therefore how it is written in the Book of Ecclesiastes, 'I said, I will be wise, but it was far from me; That which is far off, and exceeding deep, who shall find it out[4]?' and what is said in the Psalms, 'The knowledge of Thee is too wonderful for me; it is high, I cannot attain unto it[5];' and that Solomon says, 'It is the glory of God to conceal a thing[6];' I frequently designed to stop and to cease writing; believe me, I did. But lest I should be found to disappoint you, or by my silence to lead into impiety those who have made enquiry of you, and are given to disputation, I constrained myself to write briefly, what I have now sent[6a] to your piety. For although a perfect apprehension of the truth is at present far removed from us by reason of the infirmity of the flesh, yet it is possible, as the Preacher himself has said, to perceive the madness of the impious, and having found it, to say that it is 'more bitter than death[7].' Wherefore for this reason, as perceiving this and able to find it out, I have written, knowing that to the faithful the detection of impiety is a sufficient information wherein piety consists. For although it be impossible to comprehend what God is, yet it is possible to say what He is not[8]. And we know that He is not as man; and that it is not lawful to conceive of any originated nature as existing in Him. So also respecting the Son of God, although we are by nature very far from being able to comprehend Him; yet is it possible and easy to condemn the assertions of the heretics concerning Him, and to say, that the Son of God is not such; nor is it lawful even to conceive in our minds such things as they speak, concerning His Godhead; much less to utter them with the lips.

3. Accordingly I have written as well as I was able; and you, dearly beloved, receive these communications not as containing a perfect exposition of the Godhead of the Word, but as being merely a refutation of the impiety of the enemies of Christ, and as containing and affording to those who desire it, suggestions for arriving at a pious and sound faith in Christ. And if in anything they are defective (and I think they are defective in all respects), pardon it with a pure conscience, and only receive favourably the boldness of my good intentions in support of godliness. For an utter condemnation of the heresy of the Arians, it is sufficient for you to know the judgment given by the Lord in the death of Arius, of which you have already been informed by others. 'For what the Holy God hath purposed, who shall scatter[1]?' and whom the Lord condemned who shall justify[2]? After such a sign given, who do not now acknowledge, that the heresy is hated of God, however it may have men for its patrons? Now when you have read this account, pray for me, and exhort one another so to do. And immediately send it back to me, and suffer no one whatever to take a copy of it, nor transcribe it for yourselves[3]. But like

---

[7] Eccles. vii. 26.

[8] Newman observes *in loc.* "This negative character of our knowledge, whether of the Father or of the Son, is insisted on by other writers. . . . . 'All we can know about the Divine Nature is, that it is *not* to be known; and whatever positive statements we make concerning God, relate not to His Nature, but to the accompaniments of His Nature.' Damasc. *F.O.* i. 4; S. Basil *c. Eunom.* i. 10, 'Totum ab animo rejicite; *quidquid occurrerit, negate . . . .* dicite *non est illud.*' August. *Enarrat. 2. in Psalm* xxvi. 8. Cyril, *Catech.* xi. 11: Anonym. in *Append. Aug. Oper.* t. 5. p. 383. [Patr. Lat. xxxix. 2175.]   [1] Is. xiv. 27.

[2] Rom. viii. 33, 34, so quoted *Ep. Æg.* 19.   [3] *Letter* 54, fin.

---

[1] This beautiful and striking Letter (Migne xxv. 691) formed the introduction to a work, which the Author, as he says in the course of it, thought unworthy of being preserved for posterity. Some critics have supposed it to be the Orations against the Arians; but this opinion can hardly be maintained (*supr.* p. 267). The Epistle was written in 358, or later, before the Epistle to Serapion. On its relation to the 'Arian History,' see above, pp. 267, 268.

[2] This appears inconsistent with the directions below, § 3 (note 3). The heading is, therefore, of doubtful genuineness.

[2a] Matt. xix. 27.   [3] Rom. xi. 33.   [4] Eccles. vii. 23, 24.
[5] Ps. cxxxix. 6.   [6] Prov. xxv. 2.   [6a] Probably a lost writing.

good money-changers [4] be satisfied with the reading; but read it repeatedly if you desire to do so. For it is not safe that the writings of us babblers and private persons should fall into the hands of them that shall come after. Salute one another in love, and also all that come unto you in piety and faith. For 'if any man' as the Apostle has said, 'love not the Lord, let him be anathema. The grace of our Lord Jesus Christ be with you [5]. Amen.'

LETTER LIII.

Second letter [1] to Monks.

Athanasius, Archbishop [2] of Alexandria, to the Solitaries.

Athanasius to those who practise a solitary life, and are settled in faith in God, most beloved brethren, greeting in the Lord.

I thank the Lord who hath given to you to believe in Him, that ye too may have with the saints eternal life. But because there are certain persons who hold with Arius and go about the monasteries with no other object save that under colour of visiting you, and returning from us they may deceive the simple; whereas there are certain who, while they affirm that they do not hold with Arius, yet compromise themselves and worship with his party; I have been compelled, at the instance of certain most sincere brethren, to write at once in order that keeping faithfully and without guile the pious faith which God's grace works in you, you may not give occasion of scandal to the brethren. For when any sees you, the faithful in Christ, associate and communicate with such people, [or worshipping along with

them], certainly they will think it a matter of indifference and will fall into the mire of irreligion. Lest, then, this should happen, be pleased, beloved, to shun those who hold the impiety [of Arius], and moreover to avoid those who, while they pretend not to hold with Arius, yet worship with the impious. And we are specially bound to fly from the communion of men whose opinions we hold in execration. [If then any come to you, and, as blessed John [3] says, brings with him right doctrine, say to him, All hail, and receive such an one as a brother.] But if any pretend that he confesses the right faith, but appear to communicate with those others, exhort him to abstain from such communion, and if he promise to do so, treat him as a brother, but if he persist in a contentious spirit, him avoid. [I might greatly lengthen my letter, adding from the divine Scriptures the outline of this teaching. But since, being wise men, you can anticipate those who write, and rather, being intent upon self-denial, are fit to instruct others also, I have dictated a short letter, as from one loving friend to others, in the confidence] that living as you do you will preserve a pure and sincere faith, and that those persons, seeing that you do not join with them in worship, will derive benefit, fearing lest they be accounted as impious, and as those who hold with them.

LETTER LIV.

To Serapion, concerning the death of Arius.

Athanasius to Serapion [1], a brother and fellow-minister, health in the Lord.

I have read the letters of your piety, in which you have requested me to make known to you the events of my times relating to myself, and to give an account of that most impious heresy of the Arians, in consequence of which I have endured these sufferings, and

---

[4] "On this celebrated text, as it may be called, which is cited so frequently by the Fathers, vid. Coteler. *in Const. Apol.* ii. 36. in Clement *Hom.* ii. 51. Potter in Clem. *Strom.* i. p. 425. Vales. in Euseb. *Hist.* vii. 7." [Westcott, Introd. to Study of Gospels, *Appendix C.*]

[5] 1 Cor. xvi. 22, 23.

[1] This short letter, like those to Lucifer, was printed at first in Latin, evidently the almost servile rendering of a Greek original. The latter was discovered by Montfaucon after the completion of the Benedictine edition, and printed in his 'Nova Collectio Patrum' (1706). (Migne xxvi. 1185.)

The date is fixed *a parte post* in an interesting manner. We read in the Life of Pachomius, § 88 (the story is also found in the Coptic documents in the collection of Zoega p. 36), that when Duke Artemius came to the monastery of Pabau in search of Athanasius, the steward of the community replied, 'Although Athanasius is our Father under God, we have never seen his face.' The Duke answered by a request for the prayers of the brethren before he left. The 'abbat Psarphi' replied that the 'Father' had forbidden the monks to pray with strangers who consorted with the Arians,—a clear allusion to the letter before us. Now Duke Artemius was in search of Athanasius in 359-60 (*Fest. Ind.*). Accordingly our letter was issued before that date.

The Greek text is evidently imperfect : the square brackets in the translation denote passages supplied from the Latin. The first part of the letter (down to the words 'along with'...) is preserved in a contemporary inscription (Boeckh. C.I.G. iv. 8607) on the walls of an ancient Egyptian tomb at Abd-el-Kurna, which in those later days had become a monastic cell. The remainder is effaced. (See Fialon, p. 134, who has failed to notice the identity of the inscription with our present letter.)

[2] This first heading is from the inscription mentioned above, note 1, and is important as recording a very early use of the title 'archbishop.' See also *Letter* 55, note 1, *supr.* p. 137, note 6, and *Epiph.* vol. ii. p. 188 c (Migne).

[3] 2 John 10.

[1] On this letter (Migne xxv. 686) in relation to other writings, see above, *Letter* 52, note 1, and pp. 267, 268. Serapion would seem to have been the right-hand man of Athan. among the bishops of Egypt. The dates of his birth and episcopate are not certain, but the tone of the letters to him imply that he is junior to Athanasius. The theory of Ceillier, based on a precarious inference from the words of an untrustworthy writer (Philip of Side) that *this* Serapion (the name was very common) had presided over the catechetical school before Peter, i.e. at the end of the third century, is quite out of the question. Moreover, no Serapion appears among the Egyptian bishops at Tyre in 335 (p. 142), but the name occurs among the Alexandrian *presbyterate* of the same date (pp. 139, 140), while two *bishops* of the name sign the Sardican decrees (p. 127). It is then not unlikely that Athan. selected Serapion for the very important (Amm. Marc. xxii. 16) see of Thmuis in the Delta between 337 and 339 (*supr. Letter* 12, note 1). In 353 the trusted suffragan is chosen for a difficult and perilous mission to Constantius (*supr.* pp. 497, 504). For some reason we miss his name from the list of exiles in 356-7 (pp. 257, 297), nor is he named as present at the 'Council of Confessors' in 362. During the third exile, however, Ath. addressed to him our present letter, and an important dogmatic treatise (Prolegg. ch. iii. § 1, no. 22). Serapion was a friend and legatee of S. Antony (*supr.* p. 220). The date of Serapion's death is not known, but he is said to have been living after 368 (Leont. *adv. fraud. Apoll.* in Galland. xii. 701, see Bright, *Later Treat.* p. 44). For further details, and for writings ascribed to him, see D.C.B. iv. 613 (9). On the death of Arius, see Prolegg. ch. ii. § 5.

also of the manner of the death of Arius. With two out of your three demands I have reapily undertaken to comply, and have sent to your Godliness what I wrote to the Monks; from which you will be able to learn my own history as well as that of the heresy. But with respect to the other matter, I mean the death, I debated with myself for a long time, fearing lest any one should suppose that I was exulting in the death of that man. But yet, since a disputation which has taken place amongst you concerning the heresy, has issued in this question, whether Arius died after previously communicating with the Church; I therefore was necessarily desirous of giving an account of his death, as thinking that the question would thus be set at rest, considering also that by making this known I should at the same time silence those who are fond of contention. For I conceive that when the wonderful circumstances connected with his death become known, even those who before questioned it will no longer venture to doubt that the Arian heresy is hateful in the sight of God.

2. I was not at Constantinople when he died, but Macarius the Presbyter was, and I heard the account of it from him. Arius had been invited by the Emperor Constantine, through the interest of Eusebius and his fellows; and when he entered the presence the Emperor enquired of him, whether he held the Faith of the Catholic Church? And he declared upon oath that he held the right Faith, and gave in an account of his Faith in writing, suppressing the points for which he had been cast out of the Church by the Bishop Alexander, and speciously alleging expressions out of the Scriptures. When therefore he swore that he did not profess the opinions for which Alexander had excommunicated him, [the Emperor] dismissed him, saying[2], 'If thy Faith be right, thou hast done well to swear; but if thy Faith be impious, and thou hast sworn, God judge of thee according to thy oath.' When he thus came forth from the presence of the Emperor, Eusebius and his fellows, with their accustomed violence, desired to bring him into the Church. But Alexander, the Bishop of Constantinople of blessed memory, resisted them, saying that the inventor of the heresy ought not to be admitted to communion; whereupon Eusebius and his fellows threatened, declaring, 'As we have caused him to be invited by the Emperor, in opposition to your wishes, so to-morrow, though it be contrary to your desire, Arius shall have communion with us in this Church.' It was the Sabbath when they said this.

3. When the Bishop Alexander heard this, he was greatly distressed, and entering into the church, he stretched forth his hands unto God, and bewailed himself; and casting himself upon his face in the chancel, he prayed, lying upon the pavement. Macarius also was present, and prayed with him, and heard his words. And he besought these two things, saying, 'If Arius is brought to communion to-morrow, let me Thy servant depart, and destroy not the pious with the impious; but if Thou wilt spare Thy Church (and I know that Thou wilt spare), look upon the words of Eusebius and his fellows, and give not thine inheritance to destruction and reproach[3], and take off Arius, lest if he enter into the Church, the heresy also may seem to enter with him, and henceforward impiety be accounted for piety.' When the Bishop had thus prayed, he retired in great anxiety; and a wonderful and extraordinary circumstance took place. While Eusebius and his fellows threatened, the Bishop prayed; but Arius, who had great confidence in Eusebius and his fellows, and talked very wildly, urged by the necessities of nature withdrew, and suddenly, in the language of Scripture, 'falling headlong he burst asunder in the midst[4],' and immediately expired as he lay, and was deprived both of communion and of his life together.

4. Such has been the end of Arius: and Eusebius and his fellows, overwhelmed with shame, buried their accomplice, while the blessed Alexander, amidst the rejoicings of the Church, celebrated the Communion with piety and orthodoxy, praying with all the brethren, and greatly glorifying God, not as exulting in his death (God forbid!), for 'it is appointed unto all men once to die[5],' but because this thing had been shewn forth in a manner transcending human judgments. For the Lord Himself judging between the threats of Eusebius and his fellows, and the prayer of Alexander, condemned the Arian heresy, shewing it to be unworthy of communion with the Church, and making manifest to all, that although it receive the support of the Emperor and of all mankind, yet it was condemned by the Church herself. So the antichristian gang of the Arian madmen has been shewn to be unpleasing to God and impious; and many of those who before were deceived by it changed their opinions. For none other than the Lord Himself who was blasphemed by them condemned the heresy which rose up against Him, and again shewed that howsoever the Emperor Constantius may now use violence to the Bishops in behalf of it, yet it is excluded

---

[2] Ep. Æg. 18.   [3] Joel ii. 17.   [4] Acts i. 18.   [5] Heb. ix. 27.

from the communion of the Church, and alien from the kingdom of heaven. Wherefore also let the question which has arisen among you be henceforth set at rest ; (for this was the agreement made among you), and let no one join himself to the heresy, but let even those who have been deceived repent. For who shall receive what the Lord condemned? And will not he who takes up the support of that which He has made excommunicate, be guilty of great impiety, and manifestly an enemy of Christ?

5. Now this is sufficient to confound the contentious ; read it therefore to those who before raised this question, as well as what was briefly addressed to the Monks against the heresy, in order that they may be led thereby more strongly to condemn the impiety and wickedness of the Arian madmen. Do not however consent to give a copy of these to any one, neither transcribe them for yourself (I have signified the same to the Monks also) ; but as a sincere friend, if anything is wanting in what I have written, add it, and immediately send them back to me. For you will be able to learn from the letter which I have written to the Brethren, what pains it has cost me to write it, and also to perceive that it is not safe for the writings of a private person to be published (especially if they relate to the highest and chief doctrines), for this reason ;—lest what is imperfectly expressed through infirmity or the obscurity of language, do hurt to the reader. For the majority of men do not consider the faith, or the aim of the writer, but either through envy or a spirit of contention, receive what is written as themselves choose, according to an opinion which they have previously formed, and misinterpret it to suit their pleasure. But the Lord grant that the Truth and a sound [6] faith in our Lord Jesus Christ may prevail among all, and especially among those to whom you read this. Amen.

LETTER LV.

Letter to Rufinianus.

To our lord, son, and most desired fellow-minister Rufinianus [1]. Athanasius greeting in the Lord.

You write what is proper for a beloved son to write to a father : accordingly, I embraced you when you came near me in writing, most desired Rufinianus. And I, though I might write to you as a son both in the opening and the middle and the close, refrained, lest my commendation and testimony should be made known by writing. For you are my letter, as it is written [2], known and read in the heart. That you then are in such case, believe, yea believe. I address you, and invite you to write. For by doing so you afford me the highest gratification. But since in an honourable and church-like spirit, such as becomes your piety, you ask me about those who were drawn away by necessity but not corrupted by error, and wish me to write what resolution has been come to about them, whether in synods or elsewhere ; know, most desired Lord, that to begin with [3], when violence was ceased, a synod [4] has been held, bishops from foreign parts being present ; while others have been held by our fellow-ministers resident in Greece, as well as by those in Spain and Gaul [5] : and the same decision was come to here and everywhere, namely, in the case of those who had fallen and been leaders of impiety, to pardon them upon their repentance, but not to give them the position of clergy : but in the case of men not deliberate in impiety, but drawn away by necessity and violence, that they should not only receive pardon, but should occupy the position of clergy : the more so, in that they offered a plausible defence, and what had happened seemed due to a certain special purpose [6]. For they assured us that they had not gone over to impiety ; but lest certain most impious persons should be elected and ruin the Churches they elected rather to acquiesce in the violence and to bear the burden, than to lose the people. But in saying this, they appeared to us to say what was plausible ; for they alleged in excuse Aaron the brother of Moses, who in the wilderness acquiesced in the people's transgression ; and that he had had as his excuse the danger of the people returning to Egypt and abiding in idolatry. For there was reason in the view, that if they remained

---

[6] ὑγιαινουσαν, vid. *supr.* p. 71, § 5. fin.

[1] This letter (Migne xxvi. 1180) deals with one of the questions which occupied the council of 362 (*supr.* p. 481), and was probably written not long after, although the contents furnish no precise terminus *ad quem.* The personality and see of Rufinianus are uncertain. The latter must have been distant from Alexandria : the Coptic documents call him 'Rufinus the archbishop,' which seems to place him outside Egypt. The mention of Eudoxius and Euzoius *sub. fin.* possibly points to Syria. I suspect that he is the 'Lucinianus' associated with 'Eusebius' (of Vercellæ ?) in the little fragment (4) quoted in note 7 below, which comes from a letter of Ath. dealing with the same subject. The Coptic 'Acts'

of Revillout, p. 462 (as referred to *supr.* p. 188) give part of a letter of Rufinianus himself, which shews that the correspondence of which our letter is the principal relic bore on the Christological decision of the Council of 362 : 'Sound is the idea of perfection for the Divinity, as for the Economy of the Manhood : Sound is the doctrine of the Divinity in a single essence. Pure, and wholesome for the souls of the faithful, is the Confession of the Holy Triad. Perfect then is the Economy of the Manhood of the Saviour, and Perfect is His Soul also ; nothing is lacking in Him. It is thus that It was manifested to us.'

[2] 2 Cor. iii. 2.

[3] Immediately after the death of Constantius.

[4] At Alexandria, A.D. 362, see above p. 481.

[5] These unnamed councils are all connected with the general return of the exiled orthodox bishops on Julian's accession. They are possibly the same as are referred to again in the opening of the letter to Epict. below, p. 570.　　[6] οἰκονομία.

in the wilderness they might cease from their impiety : but if they went into Egypt they would become ruined and increase the impiety in their midst. For this reason, then, they have been allowed to rank as clergy, those who had been deceived and suffered violence being pardoned. I give this information to your piety in the confidence that you will both accept[7] what has been resolved upon, and not charge those who assembled, as I have said, with remissness. But be good enough to read it to the clergy and laity under you, that they may be informed, and may not blame you for being thus minded about such persons. For it would not be fitting for me to write, when your piety is able to do so, and to announce our mind with regard to them, and carry out all that remains to be done. Thanks to the Lord that filled you[8] with all utterance and with all knowledge. Let then those that repent openly anathematise by name the error of Eudoxius and Euzoius. For they blasphemed still, and wrote that He was a creature, ringleaders of the Arian heresy. But let them confess the faith confessed by the fathers at Nicæa, and that they put no other synod before that one. Greet the brotherhood with you. That with us greets you in the Lord.

LETTER LVI.

To the Emperor Jovian.

COPY of a letter of the Emperor Jovian, sent to Athanasius, the most holy Archbishop of Alexandria.

To the most religious and friend of God, Athanasius, Jovian.

Admiring exceedingly the achievements of your most honourable life, and of your likeness to the God of all, and of your affection toward our Saviour Christ, we accept you, most honoured bishop. And inasmuch as you have not flinched from all labour, nor from the fear of your persecutors, and, regarding dangers and threats of the sword as dung, holding the rudder of the orthodox faith which is dear to you, are contending even until now for the truth, and continue to exhibit yourself as a pattern to all the people of the faithful, and an example of virtue :—our imperial Majesty recalls you, and desires that you should return to the office of the teaching of salvation. Return then to the holy Churches, and tend the people of God, and send up to God with zeal your prayers for our clemency. For we know that by your supplication we, and all who hold with us [the Christian faith], shall have great assistance from the supreme God.

56. Letter of Athanasius to Jovian[1] concerning the Faith.

1. A DESIRE to learn and a yearning for

heavenly things is suitable to a religious Emperor; for thus you will truly have 'your heart' also 'in the hand of God[2].' Since then your Piety desired[3] to learn from us the faith of the Catholic Church, giving thanks for these things to the Lord, we counselled above all things to remind your Piety of the faith confessed by the Fathers at Nicæa. For this certain set at nought, while plotting against us in many ways, because we would not comply with the Arian heresy, and they have become authors of heresy and schisms in the Catholic Church. For the true and pious faith in the Lord has become manifest to all, being both 'known and read[4]' from the Divine Scriptures. For in it both the saints were made perfect and suffered martyrdom, and now are departed in the Lord; and the faith would have abode inviolate always had not the wickedness of certain heretics presumed to tamper with it. For a certain Arius and those with him attempted to corrupt it, and to introduce impiety in its place, affirming that the Son of God was from nought, and a creature, and a thing made and changeable. But with these words they deceived many, so that even 'they that seemed to be somewhat were carried away[5],' with their blasphemy. And yet our holy Fathers, as we said before, came promptly together at the Synod at Nicæa, and anathematised them, and confessed in writing the faith of the Catholic Church, so that, this being everywhere preached, the heresy kindled by the heretics might be quenched. This faith then was everywhere in every Church sincerely known and preached. But since now certain who wish to renew the Arian heresy have presumed to set at nought this faith confessed at Nicæa by the Fathers, and while pretending to confess it, do in fact deny it, explaining away the 'Coessential[6],' and blaspheming of their own accord[7] against the Holy Spirit, in affirming that It is a creature, and came into being as a

secured the ear of the new Emperor before the Arian deputation from Alexandria could reach him. The letter before us (Migne xxvi. 813) was drawn up at Antioch, as it would seem in response to a request from Jovian on a doctrinal statement. The short letter of Jovian prefixed to the Epistle is a formal authorisation for the bishop's return to his see, with which, taught by his experience under Julian, he was careful to arm himself. The documents given as an appendix are notes made at Antioch, and carefully preserved, of the reception given by Jovian to the Arian deputation. They are probably the 'exemplaria' referred to in *Hist. Aceph.* § 14 (see note there). They are characteristic, and interesting in many ways; among others, as shewing how accurately Jovian had been primed by Athanasius with the leading facts of his case.

[2] Prov. xxi. 1. The letter as given by Theodoret adds, 'and you will peacefully enjoy a long reign :' probably the words were erased from our text on account of Jovian's premature death. If genuine, they stamp the prediction *supr.* p. 487, as, at least in part, a *vaticinium ex eventu*.

[3] Very probably orally, see Prolegg. *ubi supr.*

[4] 2 Cor. iii. 2.   [5] Gal. ii. 6, 13.

[6] This reference is explained above, Prolegg. ch. ii. § 9 *sub fin.*

[7] Ἀυτοί, i.e. adding this, as a feature of their own, to the Arianism they shared with their predecessors. Acacius seems to be specially referred to; he had just signed the Homousios with explanations; cf. Pseudo-Ath. *de Hypocr. Melet. et Euseb.*

---

[7] 'Do you, then, who confess all this, abstain, I pray, from condemning those who confess the same. But explain the words they use, nor, ignoring the latter, repel their authors. Nay, entreat and advise them, that they may be willing to come to one mind.' *ad Eus. Lucin.*, &c., *supr.* note 1.

[8] 1 Cor. i. 5.

[1] Cf. Prolegg. ch. ii. § 9, and ch. v. § 3, h. and *supr.* p. 487. Athanasius, on the first news of Julian's death, by a secret and rapid journey, succeeded in meeting Jovian, when still beyond the Euphrates on his return from the East. He thus

thing made by the Son, we hasten as of bounden duty, in view of the injury resulting to the people from such blasphemy, to hand to your Piety the faith confessed at Nicæa ; in order that thy religiousness may know what has been written with all accuracy, and how far wrong they are who teach contrary to it.

2. For know, most religious Augustus, that these things have been preached from time immemorial, and this faith the Fathers who met at Nicæa confessed ; and to it have assented all the Churches in every quarter, both those in Spain, and Britain, and the Gauls, and all Italy and Dalmatia, Dacia and Mœsia, Macedonia and all Greece, and in all Africa and Sardinia, and Cyprus and Crete, as well as Pamphylia, Lycia and Isauria, and those in Egypt and the Libyas, Pontus and Cappadocia, and those near at hand to us [8], and the Churches in the East, except a few who hold with Arius. For of all those above mentioned we have both learnt the opinion by experience, and we have letters. And you know, O most religious Augustus, that even if some few speak against this faith, they cannot create a demurrer [9], inasmuch as the whole world [10] holds the Apostolic faith. For they having long been infected by the Arian heresy, now the more obstinately oppose the truth. And that your Piety may know, although you know already, yet we hasten to append the faith confessed by the Bishops at Nicæa. The faith then confessed at Nicæa by the Fathers is as follows :—

3. We believe [11], &c., &c.

4. By this faith, Augustus, all must needs abide, as Divine and Apostolic, and none must unsettle it by plausibilities, and contentions about words, which is what the Arian madmen have done, saying that the Son of God is from nought, and that once there was when He was not, and that He is created, and made and changeable. For for this cause, as we said before, the Synod at Nicæa anathematised such heresy, but confessed the faith of the truth. For they have not merely said that the Son is like [12] the Father, lest He should be believed merely like God, instead of Very God from God ; but they wrote ' Coessential,' which was peculiar to a genuine and true Son, truly and naturally from the Father. Nor yet did they make the Holy Spirit alien from the

Father and the Son, but rather glorified Him together with the Father and the Son, in the one faith of the Holy Triad, because there is in the Holy Triad also one Godhead.

APPENDIX TO LETTER LVI.

Petition made at Antioch to Jovian the Emperor on the part of Lucius [1] and Bernicianus, and certain other Arians against Athanasius, Bishop of Alexandria.

First Petition which they made as the Emperor was departing to Camp, at the Roman Gate.

May it please your Might and your Majesty and your Piety to hear us. *The Emperor:* 'Who are you and where from?' *The Arians:* 'Christians, my Lord.' *Emperor:* 'Where from, and from what city?' *The Arians:* 'Alexandria.'—*Emperor:* 'What do you want?' *The Arians:* 'May it please your Might and your Majesty, give us a Bishop.' *Emperor:* 'I ordered the former one, whom you had before, Athanasius, to occupy the See.' *The Arians:* 'May it please your Might: he has been many years both in banishment, and under accusation.' Suddenly a soldier answered in indignation: 'May it please your Majesty, enquire of them who they are and where from, for these are the leavings and refuse of Cappadocia, the remains of that unholy George who desolated the city and the world.' The Emperor on hearing this set spurs to his horse, and departed to the Camp.

Second Petition of the Arians.

' We have accusations and clear proofs against Athanasius, in that ten and twenty years ago he was deprived by the ever memorable Constantine and Constantius, and incurred banishment under the most religious and philosophical and blessed Julian.' *Emperor:* 'Accusations ten, twenty, and thirty years old are now obsolete. Don't speak to me about Athanasius, for I know why he was accused, and how he was banished.'

Third Petition of the Arians.

'And now again, we have certain other accusations against Athanasius.' *Emperor:* 'The rights of the case will not appear by means of crowded numbers, and clamours, but choose two from yourselves, and from the party of the majority other two, for I cannot answer each one severally.' *Those from the majority:* 'These are the leavings from the unholy George, who desolated our province, and who would not allow a counsellor to dwell in the cities.' *The Arians:* 'May it please you, any one you will except Athanasius.' *Emperor:* 'I told you that the case of Athanasius was already settled,' (and then angrily) 'feri, feri [2] !' *The Arians:* 'May it please you, if you send Athanasius, our city is ruined, and no one assembles with him.' *Emperor:* 'Yet I took pains, and ascertained that he holds right opinions and is orthodox, and teaches aright.' *The Arians:* 'With his mouth he utters what is right, but in his soul he harbours guile.' *Emperor:* 'That will do, you have testified of him, that he utters what is right and teaches aright, but if he teaches and speaks aright with his tongue, but harbours evil thoughts in his soul, it concerns him before God. For we are men, and hear what is said ; but what is in the heart God knows.' *The Arians:* 'Authorise our holding communion together.' *Emperor:* 'Why, who prevents you?' *The Arians:* 'May it please you, he proclaims us as sectarians and dogmatisers.' *Emperor:* 'It is his duty, and that of those who teach aright.' *The Arians:* 'May it please your Might ; we cannot bear this man, and he has taken

---

[8] This points to Antioch as the place of composition, which is fairly certain on other grounds.

[9] πρόκριμα, a 'præjudicium' or *prima facie* objection in their favour.

[10] A pardonable exaggeration, but its very use is significant ; cf. *de Syn.* 33, and Bright's note, *Later Treatises,* p. 20.

[11] *Ut supr.* p. 75 ; the other authorities for the text of the creed in Hahn § 73, note. Cf. Hort, p. 54 *sqq.* The only important variant here not noticed by Hort is τὸν ἕνα κύριον.

[12] See above, pp. 83 and 84, note 4, also Prolegg. ii. § 8 (2) b.

[1] Originally Arian deacon (p. 70), and presently bishop of the Arians at Alexandria ; see *Hist. Aceph.* p. 499, and Prolegg. ch. ii. § 10.

[2] i.e. strike, strike ! probably a direction to the guard to silence the petitioners.

away the lands of the Churches.' *Emperor:* 'Oh then, it is on account of property you are come here, and not on account of the faith'—then he added—'go away, and keep the peace.' Once more he added to the Arians : 'Go away to the Church, to-morrow you have a Communion, and after the dismissal, there are Bishops here, and here is Nemesinus[3], each one of you shall sign as he believes : Athasasius is here too ; whoever does not know the word of faith, let him learn from Athanasius. You have to-morrow and the day after, for I am going out to Camp.' And a certain lawyer[4] belonging to the Cynics petitioned the Emperor : 'May it please your Majesty, on account of Bishop Athanasius, the Receiver-General[5] seized my houses.' *Emperor:* 'If the Receiver-General seized your houses what has that to do with Athanasius ?' Another lawyer, Patalas, said : 'I have a complaint against Athanasius.' *Emperor:* 'And what have you to do with Christians, being a heathen?' But certain of the majority of them of Antioch took Lucius and brought him to the Emperor, saying : 'May it please your Might and your Majesty, look whom they wanted to make a Bishop !' *Another petition made at the porch of the palace[6] on the part of Lucius:*—'May it please your Might, listen to me.' The Emperor stopped and said : 'I ask you, Lucius, how did you come here, by sea or by land ?' *Lucius:* 'May it please you, by sea.' *Emperor:* 'Well, Lucius, may the God of the world, and the radiant sun, and moon, be angry with those men that made the voyage with you, for not casting you into the sea ; and may that ship never again have fair winds, nor find a haven with her passengers when in a storm.' And through Euzoius[7] the unbelieving Arians asked Probatius and his fellows, the successors of Eusebius[8] and Bardio as eunuchs, that they might be granted an audience. The Emperor learned this, and tortured the eunuchs and said : 'If any one wants to make a petition against Christians let this be his fate.' And so the Emperor dismissed them.

LETTER LVII.
First Letter to Orsisius[1].

'AND having spent a few days there, he saith to the Abbat Theodorus : Since the Passover is nigh, visit the brethren after your manner ; and as the Lord shall dispose me, I will do. And he embraced him, and sent him away, having written a letter by him to the Abbat Orsisius and the brethren, to the following effect :'—

I have seen your fellow-worker and father of the brethren, Theodorus, and in him the master of our father Pachomius. And I rejoiced to see the sons of the Church, and they made me glad by their presence. But the Lord is their recompenser. And as Theodorus was about to leave me for you, he said to me : Remember me. And I said to him : If I

forget thee, O Jerusalem, let my right hand be forgotten, yea let my tongue cleave to my throat if I remember thee not[2].

LETTER LVIII.
Second Letter to Orsisius.

'BUT the most holy Archbishop Athanasius, when he heard about our father Theodorus, was grieved, and sent this letter to the Abbat Orsisius and the brethren to console them for his decease, as follows :'—

Athanasius to Orsisius, Abbat, father of monks, and to all with him who practise the solitary life, and are settled in faith in God, beloved brethren most longed for in the Lord, greeting.

I have heard about the decease of the blessed Theodorus[3], and the tidings caused me great anxiety, knowing as I did his value to you. Now if it had not been Theodorus, I should have used many words to you, with tears, considering what follows after death. But since it is Theodorus whom you and I have known, what need I say in my letter save 'Blessed is' Theodorus, 'who hath not walked in the council of the ungodly[4] ?' But if 'he is blessed that feareth the Lord[5],' we may now confidently call him blessed, having the firm assurance that he has reached as it were a haven, and has a life without care. Would that the same had also befallen each one of us ; would that each of us in his running might thus arrive ; would that each of us, on his voyage, might moor his own bark there in the stormless haven, so that, at rest with the fathers, he might say, 'here will I dwell, for I have a delight therein[6].' Wherefore, brethren beloved and most longed-for, weep not for Theodorus, for he 'is not dead, but sleepeth[7].'

---

[2] Ps. cxxxvii. 6, LXX.
[3] On Theodore see Amélineau, *S. Pakhôme*, &c., pp. xcv.—xcvii. The death of Theodore is fixed for April 27, 364, on the following grounds. He died (*Vit. Pachom.* 95) of a short and sudden illness, on Pachon 2 (April 27), and shortly after Easter. Moreover his death took place 18 years after that of Pachomius. But Ammon (as he tells us himself, *supr.* p. 487) became a Christian and a monk 'a year and more' after March 15, 351 (proclamation of Gallus as Cæsar), and six years after the death of Pachomius. (*Ep. Amm.* 4, 5.) This dates the latter event *a little less than five years before* March 15, 351. But Pachomius died, according to his *Life*, on Pachon 14 (May 9), of an epidemic which attacked the community after Easter. This double condition is satisfied by the year 346, in which Easter fell on Pharm. 4, forty days before the day of Pachomius' decease. If then Pachomius died in 346, Theodore died in 364. Against this result we have (1) the fact that in that year April 27 was twenty-three days after Easter ; but the Easter gathering of the monks would last over April 11 (Low Sunday), and the death of Theodore would come suddenly enough a fortnight later ; (2) the fragment (*supr.* p. 551) probably belonging to Letter 39, which a coptic life of Theodore makes him state that he received before his last Easter. But this cannot be correct ; for all known data forbid us to place the death of Theodore as late as 367. (Tillemont's tentative opinion, vii. 691, 761, is bound up with an obsolete chronology of the exiles of Athan.) On the other hand Theodore cannot have died as early as 363. Athanasius was with him (*supr.* p. 487) in the summer of that year, and when our present letter was written Ath. had clearly kept Easter at home, which suits 364, but excludes 363.   [4] Ps. i. 1.
[5] Ps cxii. 1.   [6] Ib. cxxxii. 14.   [7] Matt. ix 24.

---

[3] Possibly an imperial notary or registrar, see **D.C.B. iv. 15.**
[4] Σχολαστικός.   [5] καθολικός.
[6] In the New Town, on the island of the Orontes.
[7] Originally one of the Arian clergy of Alexandria (*supr.* **p. 70**), now Arian bishop of Antioch.   [8] *Hist. Ar.* 35, &c.
[1] Orsisius was chosen abbat of Tabenne in Upper Egypt, A.D. 347, in succession to Petronius. Presently, however, he resigned in favour of Theodorus, the favourite disciple of Pachomius. The two letters which follow are from the life of Pachomius, §§ 92, 96, *Acta SS.* for May, vol. iii. (Also in Migne xxvi. 977.) They belong, the first to the year 363 A.D., not long before the death of Julian (D.C.B. i. 199a), the second to the summer of the following year, 364 (*infr.* note 3). Both letters are characteristic ; the second a moving and simple consolation to mourners.

Let none weep when he remembers him, but imitate his life. For one must not grieve over one that is gone to the place where grief is not. This I write to you all in common ; but especially to you, beloved and most longed-for Orsisius, in order that, now that he is fallen asleep, you may take up the whole charge, and take his place among the brethren. For while he survived, you two were as one, and when one was away, the work of both was carried on : and when both were there you were as one, discoursing to the beloved ones what made for their good. Thus act, then, and so doing write and tell me of the safety of yourself and of the brotherhood. And I exhort you all to pray together that the Lord may grant further peace to the Churches. For we now kept festival with joy, both Easter and Pentecost, and we rejoice in the benefits of the Lord. I write to you all. Greet all who fear the Lord. Those with me greet you. I pray that you may be well in the Lord, beloved and much-longed-for brethren.

LETTER LIX.

To Epictetus.

To my Lord, beloved brother, and most-longed-for fellow-minister Epictetus[1], Athanasius greeting in the Lord. I thought that all vain talk of all heretics, many as they may be, had been stopped by the Synod which was held at Nicæa. For the Faith there confessed by the Fathers according to the divine Scriptures is enough by itself at once to overthrow all impiety, and to establish the religious belief in Christ. For this reason at the present time, at the assembling of diverse synods, both in Gaul and Spain, and great Rome[2], all who came together, as though moved by one spirit, unanimously anathematised those who still were secretly holding with Arius, namely Auxentius of Milan, Ursacius, Valens, and Gaius of Pannonia. And they wrote everywhere, that, whereas the above-said were devising the names of synods to cite on their side, no synod should be cited in the Catholic Church save only that which was held at Nicæa, which was a monument of victory over all heresy, but especially the Arian, which was the main reason of the synod assembling when it did. How then, after all this, are some attempting to raise doubts or questions ? If they belong to the Arians, this is not to be wondered at, that they find fault with what was drawn up against themselves, just as the Gentiles when they hear that ' the idols of the heathen are silver and gold, the work of men's hands[3],' think the doctrine of the divine Cross folly. But if those who desire to reopen everything by raising questions belong to those who think they believe aright, and love what the fathers have declared, they are simply doing what the prophet describes, giving their neighbour turbid confusion to drink[4], and fighting about words to no good purpose, save to the subversion of the simple.

2. I write this after reading the memoranda submitted by your piety, which I could wish had not been written at all, so that not even any record of these things should go down to posterity. For who ever yet heard the like? Who ever taught or learned it? For ' from Sion shall come forth the law of God, and the word of the Lord from Jerusalem[5] ;' but whence came forth this? What lower region has vomited the statement that the Body born of Mary is coessential with the Godhead of the Word? or that the Word has been changed into flesh, bones, hair, and the whole body, and altered from its own nature? Or who ever heard in a Church, or even from Christians, that the Lord wore a body putatively, not in nature ; or who ever went so far in impiety as to say and hold, that this Godhead, which is coessential with the Father, was circumcised and became imperfect instead of perfect ; and that what hung upon the tree was not the body, but the very creative Essence and Wisdom? Or who that hears that the Word transformed for Himself a passible body, not of Mary, but of His own Essence, could call him who said this a Christian? Or who devised this abominable impiety, for it to enter even his imagina-

---

[1] Of Epictetus, bishop of Corinth, nothing else is known. This letter reflects the uncertainty, which attended the victory of the Nicene Creed, as to the relation of the Historical Christ to the Eternal Son. The questions raised at Corinth were those which troubled the Eastern Church generally, and which came to a head in the system of Apollinarius, whose distinctive tenet, however, is not mentioned in this letter. Persons anxious to place the Nicene doctrine in intelligible connection with the matter of the Gospel Narrative had debated the question before Epictetus, and with deference to his ruling. Their tentative solutions (§ 2 *infr.*) fall into two classes, both of which, in attempting to solve the problem, proceed upon the assumption incidentally combated by Athan., that the Manhood of Christ was a Hypostasis or Person, which if invested with Divine attributes, would introduce a fourth hypostatic entity into the Trinity. To avoid this, one class identified the Logos and the Ἄνθρωπος, either by assuming that the Logos was changed into flesh, or that the flesh was itself non-natural and of the Divine Essence. The other class excluded the Man Jesus from the Trinity, explaining His relation to God on the lines of Photinus or the later Nestorians. Both alternatives are already glanced at (*supr.* p. 485) by the Council of 362. In the present case, both classes of suggestions seem to have been made tentatively and *bona fide* (§ 12). The letter must have been written before the two books against Apollinarianism, which (if genuine) fall about 372. Its more exact date depends on the identification of the Councils referred to in § 1 (νῦν γενομένων), and is therefore very doubtful. At any rate Apollinarianism proper is not alluded to, and Apollinarius is said to have expressed to Serapion of Thmuis his high opinion of our Letter (see *Letter* 54, note 1). It was much quoted in the Christological controversies of the next 80 years, e.g. by the Councils of Ephesus and Chalcedon, by Theodoret, Cyril, and Leo the Great (see Migne xxvi. 1050 ; Bright, *Later Treatises*, pp. 43 *sq.*, and D.C.B. s.v. EPICTETUS and APOLLINARIS the younger).

[2] Are these those referred to in the letter to Ruf., and held A.D. 362-3, or are they to be identified with one or other of those held under Damasus (see Introd. to *ad Afros.*)?   [3] Ps. cxv. 4.

[4] Hab. ii. 15, LXX.   [5] Isa. ii. 3 ; Mic. iv. 2.

tion, and for him to say that to pronounce the Lord's Body to be of Mary is to hold a Tetrad instead of a Triad in the Godhead? Those who think thus, saying that the Body of the Saviour which He put on from Mary, is of the Essence of the Triad. Or whence again have certain vomited an impiety as great as those already mentioned; saying namely, that the body is not newer than the Godhead of the Word, but was coeternal with it always, since it was compounded of the Essence of Wisdom. Or how did men called Christians venture even to doubt whether the Lord, Who proceeded from Mary, while Son of God by Essence and Nature, is of the seed of David according to the flesh [6], and of the flesh of the Holy Mary? Or who have been so venturesome as to say that Christ Who suffered in the flesh and was crucified is not Lord, Saviour, God, and Son of the Father [7]? Or how can they wish to be called Christians who say that the Word has descended upon a holy man as upon one of the prophets, and has not Himself become man, taking the body from Mary; but that Christ is one person, while the Word of God, Who before Mary and before the ages was Son of the Father, is another? Or how can they be Christians who say that the Son is one, and the Word of God another?

3. Such were the contents of the memoranda; diverse statements, but one in their sense and in their meaning; tending to impiety. It was for these things that men who make their boast in the confession of the fathers drawn up at Nicæa were disputing and quarrelling with one another. But I marvel that your piety suffered it, and that you did not stop those who said such things, and propound to them the right faith, so that upon hearing it they might hold their peace, or if they opposed it might be counted as heretics. For the statements are not fit for Christians to make or to hear, on the contrary they are in every way alien from the Apostolic teaching. For this reason, as I said above, I have caused what they say to be baldly inserted in my letter, so that one who merely hears may perceive the shame and impiety therein contained. And although it would be right to denounce and expose in full the folly of those who have had such ideas, yet it would be a good thing to close my letter here and write no more. For what is so manifestly shewn to be evil, it is not necessary to waste time in exposing further, lest contentious persons think the matter doubtful. It is enough merely to answer such things as follows: we are content

with the fact that this is not the teaching of the Catholic Church, nor did the fathers hold this. But lest the 'inventors of evil things [8]' make entire silence on our part a pretext for shamelessness, it will be well to mention a few points from Holy Scripture, in case they may even thus be put to shame, and cease from these foul devices.

4. Whence did it occur to you, sirs, to say that the Body is of one Essence with the Godhead of the Word? For it is well to begin at this point, in order that by shewing this opinion to be unsound, all the others too may be proved to be the same. Now from the divine Scriptures we discover nothing of the kind. For they say that God came in a human body. But the fathers who also assembled at Nicæa say that, not the body, but the Son Himself is coessential with the Father, and that while He is of the Essence of the Father, the body, as they admitted according to the Scriptures, is of Mary. Either then deny the Synod of Nicæa, and as heretics bring in your doctrine from the side; or, if you wish to be children of the fathers, do not hold the contrary of what they wrote. For here again you may see how monstrous it is: If the Word is coessential with the body which is of earthly nature, while the Word is, by your own confession, coessential with the Father, it will follow that even the Father Himself is coessential with the body produced from the earth. And why any longer blame the Arians for calling the Son a creature, when you go off to another form of impiety, saying that the Word was changed into flesh and bones and hair and muscles and all the body, and was altered from its own nature? For it is time for you to say openly that He was born of earth; for from earth is the nature of the bones and of all the body. What then is this great folly of yours, that you fight even with one another? For in saying that the Word is coessential with the Body, you distinguish the one from the other [9], while in saying that He has been changed into flesh, you imagine a change of the Word Himself. And who will tolerate you any longer if you so much as utter these opinions? For you have gone further in impiety than any heresy. For if the Word is coessential with the Body, the commemoration and the work of Mary are superfluous [10], inasmuch as the body could have existed before Mary, just as the Word also is eternal: if, that is, it is as you say coessential with the Body. Or what need was there even of the Word coming among us, to put on what was coessential with Himself,

6 Rom. i. 3.
7 This opinion seems to belong to that next to be mentioned, the two, however, are separate]y dealt with below, cc. 10 and 11.

8 Rom. i. 30.   9 ἕτερον πρὸς ἕτερον σημαίνετε.
10 Letter 61, § 3.

or to change His own nature and become a body? For the Deity does not take hold [11] of itself, so as to put on what is of its own Essence, any more than the Word sinned, in that it ransoms the sins of others, in order that changing into a body it should offer itself a sacrifice for itself, and ransom itself.

5. But this is not so, far be the thought. For he 'takes hold of the seed of Abraham [11],' as the apostle said; whence it behoved Him to be made like His brethren in all things, and to take a Body like us. This is why Mary is truly presupposed, in order that He may take it from her, and offer it for us as His own. And this Isaiah pointed to in his prophecy, in the words: 'Behold the Virgin [12],' while Gabriel is sent to her—not simply to a virgin, but 'to a virgin betrothed to a man [13],' in order that by means of the betrothed man he might shew that Mary was really a human being. And for this reason Scripture also mentions her bringing forth, and tells of her wrapping Him in swaddling clothes; and therefore, too, the paps which He sucked were called blessed [1]. And He was offered as a sacrifice, in that He Who was born had opened the womb [2]. Now all these things are proofs that the Virgin brought forth. And Gabriel preached the Gospel to her without uncertainty, saying not merely 'what is born in thee,' lest the body should be thought to be extraneously induced upon her, but 'of thee,' that what was born might be believed to be naturally from her, inasmuch as Nature clearly shews that it is impossible for a virgin to produce milk unless she has brought forth, and impossible for a body to be nourished with milk and wrapped in swaddling clothes unless it has previously been naturally brought forth. This is the meaning of His being circumcised on the eighth day: of Symeon taking Him in his arms, of His becoming a young child, and growing when He was twelve years old, and of His coming to His thirtieth year. For it was not, as some suppose, the very Essence of the Word that was changed, and was circumcised, because it is incapable of alteration or change. For the Saviour Himself says, 'Behold, behold, it is I, and I change not [3],' while Paul writes: 'Jesus Christ, the same yesterday, and to-day, and for ever [4].' But in the Body which was circumcised, and carried, and ate and drank, and was weary, and was nailed on the tree and suffered, there was the impassible and incorporeal Word of God. This Body it was that was laid in a grave, when the Word had left it, yet was not parted from it, to preach, as Peter says, also to the spirits in prison [5].

6. And this above all shews the foolishness of those who say that the Word was changed into bones and flesh. For if this had been so, there were no need of a tomb. For the Body would have gone by itself to preach to the spirits in Hades. But as it was, He Himself went to preach, while the Body Joseph wrapped in a linen cloth, and laid it away at Golgotha [6]. And so it is shewn to all that the Body was not the Word, but Body of the Word. And it was this that Thomas handled when it had risen from the dead, and saw in it the print of the nails, which the Word Himself had undergone, seeing them fixed in His own Body, and though able to prevent it, did not do so. On the contrary, the incorporeal Word made His own the properties of the Body, as being His own Body. Why, when the Body was struck by the attendant, as suffering Himself He asked, 'Why smitest thou Me [7]?' And being by nature intangible, the Word yet said, 'I gave My back to the stripes, and My cheeks to blows, and hid not My face from shame and spitting [8].' For what the human Body of the Word suffered, this the Word, dwelling in the body, ascribed to Himself, in order that we might be enabled to be partakers of the Godhead of the Word [9]. And verily it is strange that He it was Who suffered and yet suffered not. Suffered, because His own Body suffered, and He was in it, which thus suffered; suffered not, because the Word, being by Nature God, is impassible. And while He, the incorporeal, was in the passible Body, the Body had in it the impassible Word, which was destroying the infirmities inherent in the Body. But this He did, and so it was, in order that Himself taking what was ours and offering it as a sacrifice, He might do away with it, and conversely might invest us with what was His, and cause the Apostle to say: 'This corruptible must put on incorruption, and this mortal put on immortality [1].'

7. Now this did not come to pass putatively, as some have supposed: far be the thought: but the Saviour having in very truth become Man, the salvation of the whole man was brought about. For if the Word were in the Body putatively, as they say, and by putative is meant imaginary, it follows that both the salvation and the resurrection of man is apparent only, as the most impious Manichæus held. But truly our salvation is not merely apparent, nor does it extend to the body only, but the whole man, body and soul alike, has truly

<hr>

[11] Heb. ii. 16. [12] Isa. vii. 14. [13] Luke i. 27.
[1] Ib. xi. 27. [2] Ib. ii. 23. [3] Mal. iii. 6.
[4] Heb. xiii. 8.

[5] 1 Pet. iii. 19. [6] Mark xv. 46. [7] Joh. xviii. 23.
[8] Isa. l. 6. [9] 2 Pet. i. 4, above, p. 65, note 5. [1] 1 Cor. xv. 53.

obtained salvation in the Word Himself. That then which was born of Mary was according to the divine Scriptures human by nature, and the Body of the Lord was a true one; but it was this, because it was the same as our body, for Mary was our sister inasmuch as we all are from Adam. And no one can doubt of this when he remembers what Luke wrote. For after He had risen from the dead, when some thought that they did not see the Lord in the body derived from Mary, but were beholding a spirit instead, He said, 'See My hands and My feet, and the prints of the nails, that it is I Myself: handle Me and see; for a spirit hath not flesh and bones as ye see Me to have. And when He had said thus, He shewed them His hands and His feet [2].' Whence they can be refuted who have ventured to say that the Lord was transformed into flesh and bones. For He did not say, 'As ye see Me to be flesh and bone,' but 'as ye see Me to have,' in order that it might not be thought that the Word Himself was changed into these things, but that He might be believed to have them after His resurrection as well as before His death.

8. These things being thus demonstrated, it is superfluous to touch upon the other points, or to enter upon any discussion relating to them, since the body in which the Word was is not coessential with the Godhead, but was truly born of Mary, while the Word Himself was not changed into bones and flesh, but came in the flesh. For what John said, 'The Word was made flesh [3],' has this meaning, as we may see by a similar passage; for it is written in Paul: 'Christ has become a curse for us [4].' And just as He has not Himself become a curse, but is said to have done so because He took upon Him the curse on our behalf, so also He has become flesh not by being changed into flesh, but because He assumed on our behalf living flesh, and has become Man. For to say 'the Word became flesh,' is equivalent to saying 'the Word has become man;' according to what is said in Joel: 'I will pour forth of My Spirit upon all flesh [5];' for the promise did not extend to the irrational animals, but is for men, on whose account the Lord is become Man. As then this is the sense of the above text, they all will reasonably condemn themselves who have thought that the flesh derived from Mary existed before her, and that the Word, prior to her, had a human soul, and existed in it always even before His coming. And they too will cease who have said that the Flesh was not accessible to death, but belonged to the immortal Nature. For if it did not die, how

could Paul deliver to the Corinthians 'that Christ died for our sins, according to the Scriptures [6],' or how did He rise at all if He did not also die? Again, they will blush deeply who have even entertained the possibility of a Tetrad instead of a Triad resulting, if it were said that the Body was derived from Mary. For if (they argue) we say the Body is of one Essence with the Word, the Triad remains a Triad; for then the Word imports no foreign element into it; but if we admit that the Body derived from Mary is human, it follows, since the Body is foreign in Essence, and the Word is in it, that the addition of the Body causes a Tetrad instead of a Triad.

9. When they argue thus, they fail to perceive the contradiction in which they involve themselves. For even though they say that the Body is not from Mary, but is coessential with the Word, yet none the less (the very point they dissemble, to avoid being credited with their real opinion) this on their own premises can be proved to involve a Tetrad. For as the Son, according to the Fathers, is coessential with the Father, but is not the Father Himself, but is called coessential, as Son with Father, so the Body, which they call coessential with the Word, is not the Word Himself, but a distinct entity. But if so, on their own shewing, their Triad will be a Tetrad [7]. For the true, really perfect and indivisible Triad is not accessible to addition as is the Triad imagined by these persons. And how do these remain Christians who imagine another God in addition to the true one? For, once again, in their other fallacy one can see how great is their folly. For if they think because it is contained and stated in the Scriptures, that the Body of the Saviour is human and derived from Mary, that a Tetrad is substituted for a Triad, as though the Body created an addition, they go very far wrong, so much so as to make the creature equal to the Creator, and suppose that the Godhead can receive an addition. And they have failed to perceive that the Word is become Flesh, not by reason of an addition to the Godhead, but in order that the flesh may rise again. Nor did the Word proceed from Mary that He might be bettered, but that He might ransom the human race. How then can they think that the Body, ransomed and quickened by the Word, made an addition in respect of Godhead to the Word that had quickened it? For on the contrary, a great addition has accrued to the human Body itself from the fellowship and

---

[2] Luke xxiv. 39. [3] Joh. i. 14. [4] Gal. iii. 13.
[5] Joel ii. 28.

[6] 1 Cor. xv. 3.
[7] The argument rests on the principle that the Trinity is a trinity of Persons, not of Essences: the opponents implicitly tax the Nicene doctrine with the consequence that if truly man, Christ is a distinct *Personality* from the Son.

union of the Word with it. For instead of mortal it is become immortal ; and, though an animal [8] body, it is become spiritual, and though made from earth it entered the heavenly gates. The Triad, then, although the Word took a body from Mary, is a Triad, being inaccessible to addition or diminution ; but it is always perfect, and in the Triad one Godhead is recognised, and so in the Church one God is preached, the Father of the Word.

10. For this reason they also will henceforth keep silence, who once said that He who proceeded from Mary is not very Christ, or Lord, or God. For if He were not God in the Body, how came He, upon proceeding from Mary, straightway to be called ' Emmanuel, which is being interpreted God with us [9] ? ' Why again, if the Word was not in the flesh, did Paul write to the Romans ' of whom is Christ after the flesh, Who is above all God blessed for ever. Amen [1] ? ' Let them therefore confess, even they who previously denied that the Crucified was God, that they have erred ; for the divine Scriptures bid them, and especially Thomas, who, after seeing upon Him the print of the nails, cried out ' My Lord and my God [2] ! ' For the Son, being God, and Lord of glory [3], was in the Body which was ingloriously nailed and dishonoured ; but the Body, while it suffered, being pierced on the tree, and water and blood flowed from its side, yet because it was a temple of the Word was filled full of the Godhead. For this reason it was that the sun, seeing its creator suffering in His outraged body, withdrew its rays and darkened the earth. But the body itself being of mortal nature, beyond its own nature rose again by reason of the Word which was in it ; and it has ceased from natural corruption, and, having put on the Word which is above man, has become incorruptible.

11. But with regard to the imagination of some, who say that the Word came upon one particular man, the Son of Mary, just as it came upon each of the Prophets, it is superfluous to discuss it, since their madness carries its own condemnation manifestly with it. For if He came thus, why was that man born of a virgin, and not like others of a man and woman ? For in this way each of the saints also was begotten. Or why, if the Word came thus, is not the death of each one said to have taken place on our behalf, but only this man's death ? Or why, if the Word sojourned among us in the case of each one of the prophets, is it said only in the case of Him born of Mary that He sojourned here ' once at the consum-

mation of the ages [4] ? ' Or why, if He came as He had come in the saints of former times, did the Son of Mary alone,.while all the rest had died without rising as yet, rise again on the third day ? Or why, if the Word had come in like manner as He had done in the other cases, is the Son of Mary alone called Emmanuel, as though a Body filled full of the Godhead were born of her ? For Emmanuel is interpreted ' God with us.' Or why, if He came thus, is it not said that when each of the saints ate, drank, laboured, and died, that He (the Word) ate, drank, laboured, and died, but only in the case of the Son of Mary. For what that Body suffered is said to have been suffered by the Word. And while we are merely told of the others that they were born, and begotten, it is said in the case of the Son of Mary alone that ' The Word was made Flesh.'

12. This proves that while to all the others the Word came, in order that they might prophesy, from Mary the Word Himself took flesh, and proceeded forth as man ; being by nature and essence the Word of God, but after the flesh man of the seed of David, and made of the flesh of Mary, as Paul said [5]. Him the Father pointed out both in Jordan and on the Mount, saying, ' This is My beloved Son in whom I am well pleased [6].' Him the Arians denied, but we recognising worship, not dividing the Son and the Word, but knowing that the Son is the Word Himself, by Whom all things are made, and by Whom we were redeemed. And for this reason we wonder how any contention at all has arisen among you about things so clear. But thanks to the Lord, much as we were grieved at reading your memoranda, we were equally glad at their conclusion. For they departed with concord, and peacefully agreed in the confession of the pious and orthodox faith. This fact has induced me, after much previous consideration, to write these few words ; for I am anxious lest by my silence this matter should cause pain rather than joy to those whose concord occasions joy to ourselves. I therefore ask your piety in the first place, and secondly those who hear, to take my letter in good part, and if anything is lacking in it in respect of piety, to set that right, and inform me. But if it is written, as from one unpractised in speech, below the subject and imperfectly, let all allow for my feebleness in speaking. Greet all the brethren with you. All those with us greet you ; may you live in good health in the Lord, beloved and truly longed for.

---

[8] ψυχικόν. [9] Matt. i. 23. [1] Rom. ix. 5. [4] Heb. ix. 26. [5] Cf. Rom. i. 3 Gal. iv. 4. [6] Matt.
[2] John xx. 28 [3] 1 Cor. ii. 8. iii. 17, and xvii. 5.

LETTER LX.

To Adelphius[1], Bishop and Confessor: against the Arians.

WE have read what your piety has written to us, and genuinely approve your piety toward Christ. And above all we glorify God, Who has given you such grace as not only to have right opinions, but also, so far as that is possible, not to be ignorant of the devices[1a] of the devil. But we marvel at the perversity of the heretics, seeing that they have fallen into such a pit of impiety that they no longer retain even their senses, but have their understanding corrupted on all sides. But this attempt is a plot of the devil, and an imitation of the disobedient Jews. For as the latter, when refuted on all sides, kept devising excuses to their own hurt, if only they could deny the Lord and bring upon themselves what was prophesied against them, in like manner these men, seeing themselves proscribed on all hands, and perceiving that their heresy has become abominable to all, prove themselves 'inventors of evil things[2],' in order that, not ceasing their fightings against the truth, they may remain consistent and genuine adversaries of Christ. For whence has this new mischief of theirs sprung forth? How have they even ventured to utter this new blasphemy against the Saviour? But the impious man, it seems, is a worthless object, and truly 'reprobate concerning the Faith[3].' For formerly, while denying the Godhead of the only-begotten Son of God, they pretended at any rate to acknowledge His coming in the Flesh. But now, gradually going from bad to worse, they have fallen from this opinion of theirs, and become Godless on all hands, so as neither to acknowledge Him as God, nor to believe that He has become man. For if they believed this they would not have uttered such things as your piety has reported against them.

2. You, however, beloved and most truly longed-for, have done what befitted the tradition of the Church and your piety toward the Lord, in refuting, admonishing, and rebuking such men. But since, instigated by their father the devil, 'they knew not nor understood,' as it is written, 'but go on still in darkness[4],' let them learn from your piety that this error of theirs belongs to Valentinus and Marcion, and to Manichæus, of whom some substituted [the idea of] Appearance for Reality, while the others, dividing what is indivisible, denied the truth that 'the Word was made Flesh, and dwelt among us[5].' Why then, as they hold with those people, do they not also take up the heritage of their names? For it is reasonable, as they hold their error, to have their names as well, and for the future to be called Valentinians, Marcionists, and Manichæans. Perhaps even thus, being put to shame by the ill savour of the names, they may be enabled to perceive into what a depth of impiety they have fallen. And it would be within our rights not to answer them at all, according to the apostolic advice[6]: 'A man that is heretical, after a first and second admonition refuse, knowing that such an one is perverted, and sinneth, being self-condemned;' the more so, in that the Prophet says about such men: 'The fool shall utter foolishness, and his heart shall imagine vain things[7].' But since, like their leader, they too go about like lions seeking whom among the simple they shall devour[8], we are compelled to write in reply to your piety, that the brethren being once again instructed by your admonition may still further reprobate the vain teaching of those men.

3. We do not worship a creature. Far be the thought. For such an error belongs to heathens and Arians. But we worship the Lord of Creation, Incarnate, the Word of God. For if the flesh also is in itself a part of the created world, yet it has become God's body. And we neither divide the body, being such, from the Word, and worship it by itself[9], nor when we wish to worship the Word do we set Him far apart from the Flesh, but knowing, as we said above, that 'the Word was made flesh,' we recognise Him as God also, after having come in the flesh. Who, accordingly, is so senseless as to say to the Lord: 'Leave the Body that I may worship Thee,' or so impious as to join the senseless Jews in saying, on account of the Body, 'Why dost Thou, being a man, make Thyself God[10]?' But the leper was not one of this sort, for he worshipped God in the Body, and recognised that He was God, saying, 'Lord, if Thou wilt Thou canst make me clean[1].' Neither by reason of the Flesh did

---

1 Adelphius is named in the 'Tome' (above, p. 486), as bishop of Onuphis. Previously he had been exiled by the Arians to the Thebaid (above, pp. 297, &c.). Hence in the title of this letter he is styled 'Confessor.' The letter (Migne xxvi. 1072) is directed against the Arian Christology. Although Ath. treats it (§ 1) as a '*new* blasphemy,' it had been held by the Arians from the first; Epiph. *Anc.* 33, traces it back to Lucian: but doubtless it had by this time been brought more to the front in their teaching. We know that it occupied a prominent place in the Eunomian system. (References in Dorner III. i. 3.) After briefly refuting the doctrinal error, Athanasius turns to the Arian charge of creature-worship brought against the Nicene doctrine. Not forgetting to remind them that their own doctrine was really open to this charge, Ath. points out at greater length that the object of Catholic worship is not the human nature of Christ as such, but the Word Incarnate; and that the human Saviour is worshipped because He is the Word Himself. The date proposed by Montfaucon is adopted, though there is nothing to fix it absolutely. Its style closely resembles that of the writings of the 'third Exile.' (See also Bright, *Later Tr.*, p. 61.) 1a 2 Cor. ii. 11. 2 Rom. i. 30.
3 2 Tim. iii. 8.

4 Ps. lxxii. 5.   5 John i. 14.   6 Tit. iii. 10, 11.
7 Isa. xxxii. 6, LXX.   8 1 Pet. v. 8.
9 As some modern devotions at least tend to do.
10 John x. 33.   1 Matt. viii. 2.

he think the Word of God a creature : nor because the Word was the maker of all creation did he despise the Flesh which He had put on. But he worshipped the Creator of the universe as dwelling in a created temple, and was cleansed. So also the woman with an issue of blood, who believed, and only touched the hem of His garment, was healed[2], and the sea with its foaming waves heard the incarnate Word, and ceased its storm[3], while the man blind from birth was healed by the fleshly spitting of the Word[4]. And, what is greater and more startling (for perhaps this even offended those most impious men), even when the Lord was hanging upon the actual cross (for it was His Body, and the Word was in it), the sun was darkened and the earth shook, the rocks were rent, and the vail of the temple rent, and many bodies of the saints which slept arose.

4. These things then happened, and no one doubted, as the Arians now venture to doubt, whether one is to believe the incarnate Word ; but even from beholding the man, they recognised that He was their maker, and when they heard a human voice, they did not, because it was human, say that the Word was a creature. On the contrary, they trembled, and recognised nothing less than that it was being uttered from a holy Temple. How then can the impious fail to fear lest 'as they refused to have God in their knowledge, they may be given up to a reprobate mind, to do those things which are not fitting[5]?' For Creation does not worship a creature. Nor again did she on account of His Flesh refuse to worship her Lord. But she beheld her maker in the Body, and 'in the Name of Jesus every knee' bowed, yea and 'shall bow, of things in heaven and things on earth and things under the earth, and every tongue shall confess,' whether the Arians approve or no, 'that Jesus is Lord, to the Glory of God the Father[6].' For the Flesh did not diminish the glory of the Word ; far be the thought : on the contrary, it was glorified by Him. Nor, because the Son that was in the form of God took upon Him the form of a servant[7] was He deprived of His Godhead. On the contrary, He is thus become the Deliverer of all flesh and of all creation. And if God sent His Son brought forth from a woman, the fact causes us no shame but contrariwise glory and great grace. For He has become Man, that He might deify us in Himself, and He has been born of a woman, and begotten of a Virgin, in order to transfer to Himself our erring generation[8], and that we may become henceforth a

holy race, and 'partakers of the Divine Nature,' as blessed Peter wrote[9]. And 'what the law could not do in that it was weak through the flesh, God sending His own Son in the likeness of sinful flesh, and for sin, condemned sin in the flesh[1].'

5. Seeing then that Flesh was taken by the Word to deliver all men, raise all from the dead, and make redemption for sins, must not they appear ungrateful, and be worthy of all hatred, who make light of the Flesh, as well as those who on account of it charge the Son of God with being a thing created or made? For they as good as cry to God and say : 'Send not Thine Only-begotten Son in the Flesh, cause Him not to take flesh of a virgin, lest He redeem us from death and sin. We do not wish Him to come in the body, lest He should undergo death on our behalf : we do not desire the Word to be made flesh, lest in it He should become our Mediator to gain access to thee, and we so inhabit the heavenly mansions. Let the gates of the heavens be shut lest Thy Word consecrate for us the road thither through the veil, namely His Flesh[2].' These are their utterances, vented with diabolical daring, by the error they have devised. For they who do not wish to worship the Word made flesh, are ungrateful for His becoming man. And they who divide the Word from the Flesh do not hold that one redemption from sin has taken place, or one destruction of death. But where at all will these impious men find the Flesh which the Saviour took, apart from Him, that they should even venture to say 'we do not worship the Lord with the Flesh, but we separate the Body, and worship Him alone.' Why, the blessed Stephen saw in the heavens the Lord standing on [God's] right hand[3], while the Angels said to the disciples, 'He shall so come in like manner as ye beheld Him going into heaven[4] :' and the Lord Himself says, addressing the Father, 'I will that where I am, they also may be with Me[5].' And surely if the Flesh is inseparable from the Word, does it not follow that these men must either lay aside their error, and for the future worship the Father in the name of our Lord Jesus Christ, or, if they do not worship or serve the Word Who came in the Flesh, be cast out on all sides, and count no longer as Christians but either as heathens, or among the Jews.

6. Such then, as we have above described, is the madness and daring of those men. But our faith is right, and starts from the teaching

---

[2] Matt. ix 20.   [3] Ib. viii. 26.   [4] John ix. 6.
[5] Rom. i. 28   [6] Phil. ii. 10, 11.   [7] Ib. vv. 6, 7.
[8] πλανηθεῖσαν γέννησιν.

[9] 2 Pet. i. 4.   [1] Rom. viii. 3.   [2] Heb. x. 20.
[3] Acts vii. 55.   [4] Ib. i. 11.   [5] John xvii. 24.

of the Apostles and tradition of the fathers, being confirmed both by the New Testament and the Old. For the Prophets say: 'Send out Thy Word and Thy Truth[6],' and 'Behold the Virgin shall conceive and bear a son, and they shall call His name Emmanuel, which is being interpreted God with us[7].' But what does that mean, if not that God has come in the Flesh? While the Apostolic tradition teaches in the words of blessed Peter, 'Forasmuch then as Christ suffered for us in the Flesh;' and in what Paul writes, 'Looking for the blessed hope and appearing of our great God and Saviour Jesus Christ, Who gave Himself for us that He might redeem us from all iniquity, and purify unto Himself a people for His own possession, and zealous of good works[8].' How then has He given Himself, if He had not worn flesh? For flesh He offered, and gave Himself for us, in order that undergoing death in it, 'He might bring to nought him that had the power of death, that is, the devil[9].' Hence also we always give thanks in the name of Jesus Christ, and we do not set at nought the grace which came to us through Him. For the coming of the Saviour in the flesh has been the ransom and salvation of all creation. So then, beloved and most longed-for, let what I have said put in mind those who love the Lord, while as to those who have imitated the behaviour of Judas, and deserted the Lord to join Caiaphas, let them by these things be taught better, if maybe they are willing, if maybe they are ashamed. And let them know that in worshipping the Lord in the flesh we do not worship a creature, but, as we said above, the Creator Who has put on the created body.

7. But we should like your piety to ask them this. When Israel was ordered to go up to Jerusalem to worship at the temple of the Lord, where was the ark, 'and above it the Cherubim of glory overshadowing the Mercy-seat[1],' did they do well or the opposite? If they did ill, how came it that they who despised this law were liable to punishment? for it is written that if a man make light of it and go not up, he shall perish from among the people[2]. But if they did well, and in this proved well-pleasing to God, are not the Arians, abominable and most shameful of any heresy, many times worthy of destruction, in that while they approve the former People for the honour paid by them to the Temple, they will not worship the Lord Who is in the flesh as in a temple? And yet the former temple was constructed of stones and gold, as a shadow. But when the reality came, the type ceased from thenceforth, and there did not remain, according to the Lord's utterance, one stone upon another that was not broken down[3]. And they did not, when they saw the temple of stones, suppose that the Lord who spoke in the temple was a creature; nor did they set the Temple at nought and retire far off to worship. But they came to it according to the Law, and worshipped the God who uttered His oracles from the Temple. Since then this was so, how can it be other than right to worship the Body of the Lord, all-holy and all-reverend as it is, announced as it was by the archangel Gabriel, formed by the Holy Spirit, and made the Vesture of the Word? It was at any rate a bodily hand that the Word stretched out to raise her that was sick of a fever[4]: a human voice that He uttered to raise Lazarus from the dead[5]; and, once again, stretching out His hands upon the Cross, He overthrew the prince of the power of the air, that now works[6] in the sons of disobedience, and made the way clear for us into the heavens.

8. Therefore he that dishonours the Temple dishonours the Lord in the Temple; and he that separates the Word from the Body sets at nought the grace given to us in Him. And let not the most impious Arian madmen suppose that, since the Body is created, the Word also is a creature, nor let them, because the Word is not a creature, disparage His Body. For their error is matter for wonder, in that they at once confuse and disturb everything, and devise pretexts only in order to number the Creator among the creatures.

But let them listen. If the Word were a creature, He would not assume the created body to quicken it. For what help can creatures derive from a creature that itself needs salvation? But since the Word being Creator has Himself made the creatures, therefore also at the consummation of the ages[7] He put on the creature, that He as creator might once more consecrate it, and be able to recover it. But a creature could never be saved by a creature, any more than the creatures were created by a creature, if the Word was not creator. Accordingly let them not lie against the divine Scriptures nor give offence to simple brethren; but if they are willing let them change their mind in their turn, and no longer worship the creature instead of God, Who made all things. But if they wish to abide by their impieties, let them alone take their fill of them, and let them gnash their teeth like their

---

6 Ps. xliii. 3. 7 Matt. i. 23, and Isa. vii. 14. 8 Tit. ii. 13, 14. 9 Heb. ii. 14. 1 Heb. ix. 5. 2 Cf. Lev. xvii. 9; Num. ix. 13.

3 Matt. xxiv. 2. 4 Mark i. 31. 5 Joh. xi. 43. 6 Eph. ii. 2. Athan. here omits the τοῦ πνεύματος, thus increasing the difficulty of the gen. particp. 7 Heb. ix. 26.

father the devil, because the Faith of the Catholic Church knows that the Word of God is creator and maker of all things ; and we know that while 'in the beginning was the Word, and the Word was with God[8],' now that He has become also man for our salvation we worship Him, not as though He had come in the body equalising Himself with it, but as Master, assuming the form of the servant, and Maker and Creator coming in a creature in order that, in it delivering all things, He might bring the world nigh to the Father, and make all things to be at peace, things in heaven and things on the earth. For thus also we recognise His Godhead, even the Father's, and worship His Incarnate Presence, even if the Arian madmen burst themselves in sunder.

Greet all that love the Lord Jesus Christ. We pray that you may be well, and remember us to the Lord, beloved and truly most longed-for. If need be this is to be read to Hieracas[9] the presbyter.

LETTER LXI.

Letter to Maximus.

(Written about 371 A.D.)

To our beloved and most truly longed-for son, Maximus[1], philosopher, Athanasius greeting in the Lord.

Having read the letter now come from you, I approve your piety : but, marvelling at the rashness of those 'who understand neither what they say nor whereof they confidently affirm[2],' I had really decided to say nothing. For to reply upon matters which are so plain and which are clearer than light, is simply to give an excuse for shamelessness to such lawless men. And this we have learned from the Saviour. For when Pilate had washed his hands, and acquiesced in the false accusation of the Jews of that day, the Lord answered him no more, but rather warned his wife in a dream, so that He that was being judged might be believed to be God not in word, but in power. While after vouchsafing Caiaphas no reply to his folly, He Himself by his promise[3] brought all over to knowledge. Accordingly for some time I delayed, and have reluctantly

yielded to your zeal for the truth, in view of the argumentativeness of men without shame. And I have dictated nothing beyond what your letter contains, in order that the adversary may from henceforth be convinced on the points to which he has objected, and may 'keep his tongue from evil and his lips that they speak no guile[3a].' And would that they would no longer join the Jews who passed by of old in reproaching Him that hung upon the Tree : 'If thou be the Son of God save Thyself[4].' But if even after this they will not give in, yet do you remember the apostolic injunction, and 'a man that is heretical after a first and second admonition refuse, knowing that such an one is perverted and sinneth being self-condemned[5].' For if they are Gentiles, or of the Judaisers, who are thus daring, let them, as Jews, think the Cross of Christ a stumbling-block, or as Gentiles, foolishness[6]. But if they pretend to be Christians let them learn that the crucified Christ is at once Lord of Glory, and the Power of God and Wisdom of God[7].'

2. But if they are in doubt whether He is God at all, let them reverence Thomas, who handled the Crucified and pronounced Him Lord and God[8]. Or let them fear the Lord Himself, who said, after washing the feet of the disciples : 'Ye call Me Lord and Master[9], and ye say well, for so I am.' But in the same body in which He was when He washed their feet, He also carried up our sins to the Tree[1]. And He was witnessed to as Master of Creation, in that the Sun withdrew his beams and the earth trembled and the rocks were rent, and the executioners recognised that the Crucified was truly Son of God. For the Body they beheld was not that of some man, but of God, being in which, even when being crucified, He raised the dead. Accordingly it is no good venture of theirs to say that the Word of God came into a certain holy man ; for this was true of each of the prophets and of the other saints, and on that assumption He would clearly be born and die in the case of each one of them. But this is not so, far be the thought. But once for all 'at the consummation of the ages[2], to put away sin ' ' the Word was made flesh[3] ' and proceeded forth from Mary the Virgin, Man after our likeness, as also He said to the Jews, 'Wherefore seek ye to kill Me, a man that hath told you the truth[4] ?' And we are deified not by partaking of the body of some

---

[8] John i. 1.   [9] Perhaps the 'Hierax' of pp. 257, 297, 560, above.
[1] Maximus, probably the Cynic philosopher who plays so strange and grotesque a part in the history of S. Gregory Nazianzen's tenure of the see of Constantinople (the identification is questioned by Bright, p. 72, but without very cogent reasons), was the son of Alexandrian parents, persons of high social standing, who had suffered much for the Faith. He himself was an ardent opponent of Arianism and heathenism, and was banished under Valens (further particulars in *Dict. Gr. and Rom. Biogr.* s. v. Maximus Alexandrinus). The present letter compliments him on his success in refuting heretics, some of whom advocated the Arian Christology, others the doctrine of Paul of Samosata and Photinus. The Epistle has much in common with those to Epictetus and Adelphius ; Montfaucon's date for it is adopted. (See Migne xxvi. 1085 ; Bright, *Lat. Tr.*, p. 72.)
[2] 1 Tim. i. 7.   [3] Mark xv. 5 ; Matt. xxvi. 64 ; xxvii. 19.

[3a] Ps. xxxiv. 13.   [4] Matt. xxvii. 40 ; Luke xxviii. 37.
[5] Tit. iii. 10, 11.   [6] 1 Cor. i. 23.   [7] Cf. 1 Cor. i. 24, and ii. 8.
[8] John xx. 28.
[9] Ath. quotes John xiii. 13 in this, the order of several MSS. and later fathers, both here and elsewhere.   [1] 1 Pet. ii. 24.
[2] Heb. ix. 26.   [3] John i. 14.   [4] Ib. viii. 40.

man, but by receiving the Body of the Word Himself.

3. And at this also I am much surprised, how they have ventured to entertain such an idea as that the Word became man in consequence of His Nature. For if this were so, the commemoration of Mary would be superfluous.[5] For neither does Nature know of a Virgin bearing apart from a man. Whence by the good pleasure of the Father, being true God, and Word and Wisdom of the Father by nature, He became man in the body for our salvation, in order that having somewhat to offer[6] for us He might save us all, 'as many as through fear of death were all their life-time subject to bondage.[7]' For it was not some man that gave Himself up for us; since every man is under sentence of death, according to what was said to all in Adam, 'earth thou art and unto earth thou shalt return.[8]' Nor yet was it any other of the creatures, since every creature is liable to change. But the Word Himself offered His own Body on our behalf that our faith and hope might not be in man, but that we might have our faith in God the Word Himself. Why, even now that He is become man we behold His Glory, ' glory as of one only-begotten of His Father—full of grace and truth.[9]' For what He endured by means of the Body, He magnified as God. And while He hungered in the flesh, as God He fed the hungry. And if anyone is offended by reason of the bodily conditions, let him believe by reason of what God works. For humanly He enquires where Lazarus is laid, but raises him up divinely. Let none then laugh, calling Him a child, and citing His age, His growth, His eating, drinking and suffering, lest while denying what is proper for the body, he deny utterly also His sojourn among us. And just as He has not become Man in consequence of His nature, in like manner it was consistent that when He had taken a body He should exhibit what was proper to it, lest the imaginary theory of Manichæus should prevail. Again it was consistent that when He went about in the body, He should not hide what belonged to the Godhead, lest he of Samosata should find an excuse to call Him man, as distinct in person from God the Word.

4. Let then the unbelievers perceive this, and learn that while as a Babe He lay in a manger, He subjected the Magi and was worshipped by them; and while as a Child He came down to Egypt, He brought to

nought the hand-made objects of its idolatry[1]: and crucified in the flesh, He raised the dead long since turned to corruption. And it has been made plain to all that not for His own sake but for ours He underwent all things, that we by His sufferings might put on freedom from suffering and incorruption[2], and abide unto life eternal.

5. This then I have concisely dictated, following, as I said above, the lines of your own letter, without working out any point any further but only mentioning what relates to the Holy Cross, in order that the despisers may be taught better upon the points where they were offended, and may worship the Crucified. But do you thoroughly persuade the unbelievers; perhaps somehow they may come from ignorance to knowledge, and believe aright. And even though what your own letter contains is sufficient, yet it is as well to have added what I have for the sake of reminder in view of contentious persons; not so much in order that being refuted in their venturesome statements they may be put to shame, as that being reminded they may not forget the truth. For let what was confessed by the Fathers at Nicæa prevail. For it is correct, and enough to overthrow every heresy however impious, and especially that of the Arians which speaks against the Word of God, and as a logical consequence profanes His Holy Spirit. Greet all who hold aright. All that are with us greet you.

LETTER LXII.

To John and Antiochus.[1]

Athanasius to John and Antiochus, our beloved sons and fellow-presbyters in the Lord, greeting.

I was glad to receive your letter just now, the more so as you wrote from Jerusalem. I thank you for informing me about the brethren that there assembled, and about those who wish, on account of disputed points, to disturb the simple. But about these things let the Apostle charge them not to give heed to those who contend about words, and seek nothing else than to tell and hear some new thing[2]. But do you, having your foundation sure, even

---

5 Cf. *Ad Epict.* 5 (*supr.* p. 572.)   6 Cf. Heb. viii. 3.
7 Ib. ii. 15.   8 Gen. iii. 19, LXX.   9 John i. 14 b.

[1] Cf. *de Incarn.* 36. 4.   [2] Cf. 1 Cor. xv. 53.
[1] Of John and Antiochus nothing is known, unless the latter is the later bishop of Ptolemais and enemy of Chrysostom. Both men seem to belong to the class of well-meaning mischief-makers, given to retailing invidious stories. Hence the polite reserve of our little note (Migne xxvi. 115, and its laconic dismissal of the gossip about Basil, the new bishop of the Cappadocian Cæsarea (*supr.* p. 449). The main interest of this and the following letter, which seem to date from the winter 371—372, consists in the testimony of the high esteem of Athanasius for Basil, as well as his indifference to words where no essential principle was involved. The two recipients of this letter either lived or were visitors at Jerusalem. On Basil's difficulties at this time, see D.C.B. i. 288 a, 293, and on his relations with Athan., cf.Prolegg. ch. ii. § 10.
[2] 2 Tim. ii. 14; Acts xvii. 21.

Jesus Christ our Lord, and the confession of the fathers concerning the faith, avoid those who wish to say anything more or less than that, and rather aim at the profit of the brethren, that they may fear God and keep His commandments, in order that both by the teaching of the fathers, and by the keeping of the commandments, they may be able to appear well-pleasing to the Lord in the day of judgment. But I have been utterly astonished at the boldness of those who venture to speak against our beloved Basil the bishop, a true servant of God. For from such vain talk they can be convicted of not loving even the confession of the fathers.

Greet the brethren. They that are with me greet you. I pray that ye may be well in the Lord, beloved and much-desired sons.

LETTER LXIII.

Letter to the Presbyter Palladius [1].

To our beloved son Palladius, presbyter, Athanasius the Bishop greeting in the Lord.

I was glad to receive also the letter written by you alone, the more so that you breathe orthodoxy in it, as is your wont. And having learnt not for the first time, but long ago, the reason of your staying at present with our beloved Innocent [2], I am pleased with your piety. Since then you are acting as you are, write and let me know how are the brethren there, and what the enemies of the truth think about us. But whereas you have also told me of the monks at Cæsarea, and I have learned from our beloved Dianius [3] that they are vexed, and are opposing our beloved bishop Basil, I am glad you have informed me, and I have pointed out [4] to them what is fitting, namely that as children they should obey their father, and not oppose what he approves. For if he were suspected as touching the truth, they would do well to combat him. But if they are confident, as we all are, that he is a glory to the Church, contending rather on behalf of the truth and teaching those who require it, it is not right to combat such an one, but rather to accept with thanks his good conscience. For

from what the beloved Dianius has related, they appear to be vexed without cause. For he, as I am confident, to the weak becomes weak to gain the weak [5]. But let our beloved friends look at the scope of his truth, and at his special purpose [6], and glorify the Lord Who has given such a bishop to Cappadocia as any district must pray to have. And do you, beloved, be good enough to point out to them the duty of obeying, as I write. For this is at once calculated to render them well disposed toward their father, and will preserve peace to the churches. I pray that you may be well in the Lord, beloved son.

LETTER LXIV.

To Diodorus (fragment).

To my lord, son, and most beloved fellow-minister Diodorus [bishop of Tyre] [1], Athanasius greeting in the Lord.

I thank my Lord, Who is everywhere establishing His doctrine, and chiefly so by means of His own sons, such as actual fact shews you to be. For before your Reverence wrote, we knew how great grace has been brought to pass in Tyre by means of your perseverance. And we rejoice with you that by your means Tyre also has learned the right word of piety. And I indeed took an opportunity of writing to you, longed-for and beloved : but I marvel at your not having replied to my letter. Be not then slow to write at once, knowing that you give me refreshment, as a son to his father, and make me exceeding glad, as a herald of truth. And enter upon no controversy with the heretics, but overcome their argumentativeness with silence, their ill-will with courtesy. For thus your speech shall be 'with grace, seasoned with salt [2],' while they [will be judged] by the conscience of all. . . .

---

[1] On the general subject and date of this letter see note 1 to *Letter* 62. Of Palladius, who is clearly a resident at Cæsarea, nothing further is known. The tone of this letter is more confiding than that of the previous one. (Migne *ib.* 1167.)

[2] Perhaps a bishop in the neighbourhood of Cæsarea. See D.C.B. s.v. Innocentius (4).

[3] Namesake of a predecessor of Basil, otherwise unknown.

[4] The letter here referred to is lost. The monks in question had raised a cry against Basil on account of the reserve with which he spoke of the Divine Personality of the Holy Spirit. (See *supr.* p. 481.)

[5] 1 Cor. ix. 22.   [6] οἰκονομίαν.

[1] This fragment (Migne xxvi. 1261) is given by Facundus, *Def. Tr. Cap.* iv. 2, who claims it as addressed to Diodorus of Tarsus, the famous Antiochene confessor and master of Chrysostom and Theodore. Unfortunately this is impossible, as Diodore became bishop of Tarsus not before 378, i.e. after Athan. was dead. The letter itself decides for Diodorus *of Tyre*, whom Paulinus of Antioch had quite unwarrantably ordained to this see (cf. Rufin, *H.E.* ii. 21). Whether (as has been held on the authority of Rufinus) Diodorus, or (as Le Quien, *Or. Chr.* ii. 865 *sq.* holds) Zeno, the nominee of Meletius, was first in the field in the unseemly scramble, is doubtful. Zeno is already bishop in 365 (Soz. vi. 12) ; the date of the appointment of Diodorus, whose claim is at any rate no better than that of Paulinus himself, is quite uncertain (see also Prolegg. ch. ii. §§ 9, 10). Diodorus was the friend and correspondent of Epiphanius, and of Timothy, bishop of Alexandria, second from Athanasius. Facundus confuses him in these particulars also with his namesake of Tarsus, but the mistake is thoroughly sifted by Tillemont, *Mem.* viii. pp. 238, 712. The letter is important, along with *Letter* 56, and the correspondence of S. Basil, as illustrating the attitude of Athanasius with regard to the unhappy schism of Antioch.   [2] Col. iv. 6.

MEMORANDUM

On other Letters ascribed to Athanasius.

The above Collection of Letters is complete upon the principle stated in the Introduction (*supr.*, p. 495). But one or two fragments have been excluded which may be specified here.

(1.) Fragment of a letter 'to Eupsychius;' probably the Nicene Father referred to *Ep. Æg.* 8, (cf. D.C.B. ii. 299 (4)). The Greek is given by Montf. in Ath. *Opp.* 1. p. 1293 (Latin, *ib.* p. 1287). It was cited in *Conc. Nic.* II. Act vi., but although it has affinities with *Orat.* ii. 8 ('high-priestly *dress*'), it has the appearance of a polemical argument against Monophysitism. (Migne xxvi. 1245.)

(2.) 'To Epiphanius' (Migne xxvi. 1257). Against certain, who contentiously follow the Jews in celebrating Easter. (From '*Chron. Pasch.* pag. 4 postremæ editionis.')

(3.) Fragments of an 'Epistola ad Antiochenos' (not our 'Tomus,' *supr.*, p. 483): also a polemic against Monophysitism, and almost Nestorian in doctrine: 'Jesus Christus . . . non est Ipse' [i.e. ante sæcula et in sæcula, Heb. xiii. 8], and again 'duas personas' asserted of Christ. From Facundus, who says the letter was written against the Apollinarians, and who gives it on the authority of Peter, Ath.'s successor (Migne xxvi. 1259).

(4.) 'Ad Eusebium, Lucinianum, et socios.' (In Migne xxvi. 1325 *sq.*, from Mai, *Script. Vet.* 11. 583 *sq.*) A minute fragment. Cf. *supr.*, *Letter* 55, notes 1, 7.

(5.) Spurious letters (in Migne xxviii.) to Jovian, to Castor (2), to a 'bishop of the Persians,' and to and from popes Liberius, Marcus, Julius and Felix (made up out of late and spurious decretals, &c., &c.).

INDICES

INDEX OF SCRIPTURES CITED

II

GENERAL INDEX

N.B. An asterisk * denotes a bishop present at Sardica (see p. 147). A cross † denotes a bishop who signed the letter circulated by the Council (p. 127). In the latter case the name of his country is given *in italics*.

The identification of persons bearing the same name has nowhere been taken for granted without an attempt to weigh the evidence. Probably in a few cases names separated in the Index for lack of identifying evidence may yet in reality belong to one and the same person.